W9-BNU-469

Collins

SPANISH
DICTIONARY

HarperTorch
An Imprint of HarperCollins*Publishers*

ATTENTION: ORGANIZATIONS AND CORPORATIONS
Most HarperTorch paperbacks are available at special quantity discounts for bulk purchases for sales promotions, premiums, or fund raising. For information, please call or write:

Special Markets Department, HarperCollins Publishers, Inc., 10 East 53rd Street, New York, N.Y. 10022-5299. Telephone: (212) 207-7528. Fax: (212) 207-7222.

HARPERTORCH
An Imprint of HarperCollins*Publishers*
10 East 53rd Street
New York, New York 10022-5299

Third Edition 2006
© William Collins Sons & Co. Ltd. 1990
© HarperCollins Publishers 2000, 2006
ISBN-13: 978-0-06-113102-8
ISBN-10: 0-06-113102-4

All rights reserved. No part of this book may be used or reproduced in any manner whatsoever without written permission, except in the case of brief quotations embodied in critical articles and reviews. For information address HarperTorch, and Imprint of HarperCollins Publishers.

First HarperTorch paperback printing: June 2006

HarperCollins®, HarperTorch™, and ❦™ are trademarks of HarperCollins Publishers Inc.

Printed in the United States of America

Visit HarperTorch on the World Wide Web at www.harpercollins.com

20 19 18

If you purchased this book without a cover, you should be aware that this book is stolen property. It was reported as "unsold and destroyed" to the publisher, and neither the author nor the publisher has received any payment for this "stripped book."

ÍNDICE

CONTENTS

Marcas registradas
Las marcas que creemos que constituyen marcas registradas las denominamos como tales. Sin embargo, no debe considerarse que la presencia o la ausencia de esta designación tenga que ver con la situación legal de ninguna marca.

Note on trademarks
Words which we have reason to believe constitute trademarks have been designated as such. However, neither the presence nor the absence of such designation should be regarded as affecting the legal status of any trademark.

INTRODUCCIÓN

Estamos muy satisfechos de que hayas decidido comprar el Diccionario de Inglés Collins y esperamos que lo disfrutes y que te sirva de gran ayuda ya sea en el colegio, en el trabajo, en tus vacaciones o en casa.

Esta introducción pretende darte algunas indicaciones para ayurdarte a sacar el mayor provecho de este diccionario; no sólo de su extenso vocabulario, sino de toda la información que te proporciona cada entrada. Ésta te ayudará a leer y comprender – y también a comunicarte y a expresarte – en inglés moderno.

El Diccionario de Inglés Collins comienza con una lista de abreviaturas utilizadas en el texto y con una ilustración de los sonidos representados por los símbolos fonéticos. Además encontrarás una tabla de los verbos irregulares, y para terminar, una sección sobre el uso de los números y de las expresiones de tiempo.

EL MANEJO DE TU DICCIONARIO COLLINS

La amplia información que te ofrece este diccionario aparece presentada en distintas tipografías, con caracteres de diversos tamaños y con distintos símbolos, abreviaturas y paréntesis. Los apartados siguientes explican las reglas y símbolos utilizados.

Entradas

Las palabras que consultas en el diccionario – las "entradas" – aparecen ordenadas alfabéticamente y en **caracteres gruesos** para una identificación más rápida. Las dos palabras que ocupan el margen superior de cada página indican la primera y la última entrada de la página en cuestión.

La información sobre el uso o la forma de determinadas entradas aparece entre paréntesis, detrás de la transcripción fonética, y generalmente en forma abreviada y en cursiva (p. ej.: (*fam*), (*COM*)).

En algunos casos se ha considerado oportuno agrupar palabras de una misma familia (**nación, nacional; accept, acceptable**) bajo una misma entrada, en caracteres gruesos y precedidas por un símbolo cuadrado.

Las expresiones de uso corriente en las que aparece una entrada se dan en negrita (p. ej.: **hurry** [...] **to be in a ~**).

Símbolos fonéticos

La transcripción fonética de cada entrada inglesa (que indica su pronunciación) aparece entre corchetes, inmediatamente después de la entrada (p. ej. **knead** [niːd]). En la página xii encontrarás una lista de los símbolos fonéticos utilizados en este diccionario.

Traducciones

Las traducciones de las entradas aparecen en caracteres normales, y en los casos en los que existen significados o usos diferentes, éstos aparecen separados mediante en punto y coma. A menudo encontrarás también otras palabras en cursiva y entre paréntesis antes de las traducciones. Éstas sugieren contextos en los que la entrada podría aparecer (p. ej.: **admission** (*to college, club*) o proporcionan sinónimos (p. ej.: **admission** (*entry fee*) o (*confession*)).

Palabras clave

Particular relevancia reciben ciertas palabras inglesas y españolas que han sido consideradas palabras "clave" en cada lengua. Éstas pueden, por ejemplo, ser de utilización muy corriente o tener distintos usos (**de, haber; get, that**). La combinación de rombos ♦ y números te permitirá distinguir las diferentes categorías gramaticales y los diferentes significados. Las indicaciones en cursiva y entre paréntesis proporcionan además importante información adicional.

Información gramatical

Las categorías gramaticales aparecen en forma abreviada y en cursiva después de la transcripción fonética de cada entrada (*vt, adv, conj*).

También se indican la forma femenina y los plurales irregulares de los sustantivos del inglés (**child, -ren**).

INTRODUCTION

We are delighted that you have decided to buy the Collins Spanish Dictionary and hope you will enjoy and benefit from using it at school, at home, on vacation or at work.

This introduction gives you a few tips on how to get the most out of your dictionary – not simply from its comprehensive wordlist but also from the information provided in each entry. This will help you to read and understand modern Spanish, as well as communicate and express yourself in the language.

The Collins Spanish Dictionary begins by listing the abbreviations used in the text and illustrating the sounds shown by the phonetic symbols. In addition, you will find Spanish verb tables followed by a final section on numbers, time and date expressions.

USING YOUR COLLINS DICTIONARY

A wealth of information is presented in the dictionary, using various typefaces, sizes of type, symbols, abbreviations and brackets. The various conventions and symbols used are explained in the following sections.

Headwords

The words you look up in a dictionary – "headwords" – are listed alphabetically. They are printed in **bold type** for rapid identification. The two headwords appearing at the top of each page indicate the first and last word dealt with on that page.

Information about the usage or form of certain headwords is given in brackets after the phonetic spelling. This usually appears in abbreviated form and in italics (e.g. (*inf*), (*COMM*)).

Where appropriate, words related to headwords are grouped in the same entry (**nación, nacional**; **accept, acceptable**) in **bold type** and are preceded by a box symbol.

Common expressions in which the headword appears are shown in a different bold roman type (e.g. **calor** [...] **hacer ~**).

Phonetic spellings

The phonetic spelling of each English headword (indicating its pronunciation) is given in square brackets immediately after the headword (e.g. **knead** [niːd]). A list of these symbols is given on page xii.

Translations

Headword translations are given in ordinary type and, where more than one meaning or usage exists, these are separated by a semi-colon.

You will often find other words in italics in brackets before the translations. These offer suggested contexts in which the headword might appear (e.g. **grande** (*de tamaño*) or provide synonyms (e.g. **grande** (*alto*) o (*distinguido*)).

"Key" words

Special status is given to certain Spanish and English words which are considered as "key" words in each language. They may, for example, occur very frequently or have several types of usage (e.g. **de**, **haber**). A combination of lozenges ♦ and numbers helps you to distinguish different parts of speech and different meanings. Further helpful information is provided in brackets and italics.

Grammatical information

Parts of speech are given in abbreviated form in italics after the phonetic spellings of headwords (e.g. *vt*, *adv*, *conj*).

Genders of Spanish nouns are indicated as follows: *nm* for a masculine and *nf* for a feminine noun. Feminine and irregular plural forms of nouns are also shown (e.g. **irlandés, esa; luz** (*pl* **luces**)).

ABREVIATURAS

ABBREVIATIONS

abreviatura	**ab(b)r**	abbreviation
adjetivo	**adj**	adjective
administración	**ADMIN**	administration
adverbio	**adv**	adverb
aeronáutica	**AER**	aeronautics
agricultura	**AGR**	agriculture
alguien	**algn**	somebody, someone
anatomía	**ANAT**	anatomy
arquitectura	**ARQ, ARCH**	architecture
artículo	**art**	article
automóvil	**AUT(O)**	automobiles
auxiliar	**aux**	auxiliary
biología	**BIO(L)**	biology
botánica	**BOT**	botany
inglés británico	**BRIT**	British English
Centroamérica	**CAm**	Central America
química	**CHEM**	chemistry
comercio	**COM(M)**	commerce
informática	**COMPUT**	computing
conjunción	**conj**	conjunction
contracción	**cont**	contraction
compuesto	**cpd**	compound element
Cono Sur	**CS**	Southern Cone
culinario, cocina	**CULIN**	culinary, cooking
definido	**def**	definite
demostrativo	**demos**	demonstrative
economía	**ECON**	economy
electricidad, electrónica	**ELEC**	electricity, electronics
escolar	**ESCOL**	school
España	**ESP**	Spain
etcétera	**etc**	etcetera
excluyendo	**exc**	excluding
exclamación	**excl**	exclamation
femenino	**f**	feminine
lenguaje familiar (¡vulgar!)	**fam(!)**	informal language (offensive!)
ferrocarril	**FERRO**	railways
figurado	**fig**	figurative
fotografía	**FOTO**	photography
(verbo inglés) cuya partícula es inseparable	**fus**	(phrasal verb) where the particle is inseparable
generalmente	**gen**	generally
geografía, geología	**GEO**	geography, geology
geometría	**GEOM**	geometry
historia	**HIST**	history
impersonal	**impers**	impersonal
indefinido	**indef**	indefinite
lenguaje familiar (¡vulgar!)	**inf(!)**	informal language (offensive!)
infinitivo	**infin**	infinitive
informática	**INFORM**	computing
interrogativo	**interr**	interrogative
invariable	**inv**	invariable
irregular	**irreg**	irregular

jurídico	**JUR**	juridical, law
Latinoamérica	**LAm**	Latin America
lingüística, gramática	**LING**	linguistics, grammar
literalmente	**lit**	literally
masculino	**m**	masculine
matemáticas	**MAT(H)**	mathematics
medicina	**MED**	medicine
México	**MÉX, MEX**	Mexico
masculino y femenino	**mf**	masculine and feminine
masculino/femenino	**m/f**	masculine/feminine
militar, ejército	**MIL**	military, army
música	**MÚS, MUS**	music
nombre, sustantivo	**n**	noun
náutica	**NAÚT, NAUT**	nautical
sustantivo no empleado en el plural	**no pl**	collective (uncountable) noun, not used in plural
sustantivo numérico	**num**	numerical noun
(a) sí mismo	**o.s.**	oneself
peyorativo	**pey, pej**	pejorative
fotografía	**PHOT**	photography
plural	**pl**	plural
política	**POL**	politics
posesivo	**pos**	possessive
participio de pasado	**pp**	past participle
preposición	**prep**	preposition
pronombre	**pron**	pronoun
psicología	**PSICO, PSYCH**	psychology
química	**QUÍM**	chemistry
ferrocarril	**RAIL**	railways
religión	**REL**	religion
Río de la Plata	**RPl**	River Plate
alguien	**sb**	somebody
Cono Sur	**SC**	Southern Cone
escolar	**SCOL**	school
singular	**sg**	singular
España	**SP**	Spain
algo	**sth**	something
subjuntivo	**subjun**	subjunctive
sujeto	**suj**	subject
tauromaquia	**TAUR**	bullfighting
tecnología, técnico	**TEC(H)**	technology, technical
telecomunicaciones	**TEL**	telecommunications
tipografía	**TIP**	typography
televisión	**TV**	television
tipografía	**TYP**	typography
universidad	**UNIV**	university
inglés norteamericano	**US**	American English
verbo	**vb**	verb
verbo intransitivo	**vi**	intransitive verb
verbo pronominal	**vr**	reflexive verb
verbo transitivo	**vt**	transitive verb
zoología	**ZOOL**	zoology
marca registrada	**®**	registered trademark
equivalente cultural	**≈**	cultural equivalent

SPANISH PRONUNCIATION

○ Spanish Vowels

Spanish vowels are always clearly pronounced and not relaxed in unstressed syllables as happens in English.

a – Similar to **a** in **palm**
e – Similar to English **e** in **end**
i – Similar to English **i** in **machine**
o – Similar to English **o** in **for**
u – Similar to English **oo** in **pool**

○ Spanish Consonants

Note the pronunciation of the following letters.

b, v – These letters have the same value. At the start of a word, and after written **m** and **n**, the sound is similar to English **boy**
   – In all other positions the sound is softer, the lips do not touch
c – Before **a, o, u** or a consonant, like English **keep**
   – Before **e** or **i** it is pronounced like English **same**
ch – Like English **church**
d – At the start of the word and after **l** or **n**, it is pronounced similarly to English **deep**
   – Between vowels and after consonants (except **l** or **n**), it is pronounced very like English **though**
   – At the end of words it is often not pronounced
g – Before **e** or **i**, the sound is similar to English **house**
   – At the start of a word and after **n**, it is pronounced like English **get**
   – In other positions it is softer than in **get**
   – Note that in the group **gue, gui**, the **u** is silent, as in English **guitar** unless it is marked **güe, güi**, when it is pronounced like English **walk**
h – This is always silent
j – Like the sound in English lo**ch**
ll – Similar to English -**ll**- in mi**ll**ion, but often like English **yet**
ñ – As in English on**ion**
q – Always followed by silent letter **u**, and pronounced as in English **keep**, but softer
r – Single trill, in a way that does not exist in English
   – Pronounced like **rr** below at the start of a word and after **l, n** or **s**
rr – Strongly trilled, in a way that does not exist in English
s – Except where mentioned below, like English **sing**
   – When followed by **b, d, g, l, m, n** like English **rose**
w – Usually pronounced as English **v**, but sometimes kept as English **w**
y – Similar to English **yes**
z – Like English **send**

f, k, l, m, n, p, t, x are pronounced as in English.

LA PRONUNCIACIÓN INGLESA

O VOCALES

calm, part, rot	[ɑː]
hat	[æ]
egg, set, parent	[ɛ]
above	[ə]
earn, girl	[ɜː]
hit, give	[ɪ]
fairly, city	[i]
green, peace	[iː]
born	[ɔː]
hut	[ʌ]
full	[u]
pool	[uː]

O DIPTONGOS

buy, die, my	[aɪ]
house, now	[au]
pay, mate	[eɪ]
pair, mare	[ɛə]
no, boat	[ou]
here, near	[ɪə]
boy, coin	[ɔɪ]
tour, poor	[uə]

O CONSONANTES

ball	[b]
child	[tʃ]
field	[f]
good	[g]
hand	[h]
just	[dʒ]
kind, catch	[k]
left, little	[l]
mat	[m]
nest	[n]
long	[ŋ]
put	[p]
run	[r]
sit	[s]
shallow	[ʃ]
tag	[t]
thing	[θ]
this	[ð]
very	[v]
loch	[x]
ours, zipper	[z]
measure	[ʒ]

O SEMIVOCALES

yet, million	[j]
wet, why	[w]

O OTROS SÍMBOLOS

Acento	[']
Acento secundario	[ˌ]

Como guía para pronunciar el inglés correctamente, en la parte de inglés-español aparece la transcripción fonética tras el lema.

SPANISH VERB TABLES

1 Gerund 2 Imperative 3 Present 4 Preterite 5 Future 6 Present subjunctive 7 Imperfect subjunctive 8 Past participle 9 Imperfect. *Etc* indicates that the irregular root is used for all persons of the tense, *e.g.* oír: 6 oiga, oigas, oigamos, oigáis, oigan.

agradecer 3 agradezco 6 agradezca *etc*

aprobar 2 aprueba 3 apruebo, apruebas, aprueba, aprueban 6 apruebe, apruebes, apruebe, aprueben

atravesar 2 atraviesa 3 atravieso, atraviesas, atraviesa, atraviesan 6 atraviese, atravieses, atraviese, atraviesen

caber 3 quepo 4 cupe, cupiste, cupo, cupimos, cupisteis, cupieron 5 cabré *etc* 6 quepa *etc* 7 cupiera *etc*

caer 1 cayendo 3 caigo 4 cayó, cayeron 6 caiga *etc* 7 cayera *etc*

cerrar 2 cierra 3 cierro, cierras, cierra, cierran 6 cierre, cierres, cierre, cierren

COMER 1 comiendo 2 come, comed 3 como, comes, come, comemos, coméis, comen 4 comí, comiste, comió, comimos, comisteis, comieron 5 comeré, comerás, comerá, comeremos, comeréis, comerán 6 coma, comas, coma, comamos, comáis, coman 7 comiera, comieras, comiera, comiéramos, comierais, comieran 8 comido 9 comía, comías, comía, comíamos, comíais, comían

conocer 3 conozco 6 conozca *etc*

contar 2 cuenta 3 cuento, cuentas, cuenta, cuentan 6 cuente, cuentes, cuente, cuenten

dar 3 doy 4 di, diste, dio, dimos, disteis, dieron 7 diera *etc*

decir 2 di 3 digo 4 dije, dijiste, dijo, dijimos, dijisteis, dijeron 5 diré *etc* 6 diga *etc* 7 dijera *etc* 8 dicho

despertar 2 despierta 3 despierto, despiertas, despierta, despiertan 6 despierte, despiertes, despierte, despierten

divertir 1 divirtiendo 2 divierte 3 divierto, diviertes, divierte, divierten 4 divirtió, divirtieron 6 divierta, diviertas, divierta, divirtamos, divirtáis, diviertan 7 divirtiera *etc*

dormir 1 durmiendo 2 duerme 3 duermo, duermes, duerme, duermen 4 durmió, durmieron 6 duerma, duermas, duerma, durmamos, durmáis, duerman 7 durmiera *etc*

empezar 2 empieza 3 empiezo, empiezas, empieza, empiezan 4 empecé 6 empiece, empieces, empiece, empecemos, empecéis, empiecen

entender 2 entiende 3 entiendo, entiendes, entiende, entienden 6 entienda, entiendas, entienda, entiendan

ESTAR 2 está 3 estoy, estás, está, están 4 estuve, estuviste, estuvo, estuvimos, estuvisteis, estuvieron 6 esté, estés, esté, estén 7 estuviera *etc*

HABER 3 he, has, ha, hemos, han 4 hube, hubiste, hubo, hubimos, hubisteis, hubieron 5 habré *etc* 6 haya *etc* 7 hubiera *etc*

HABLAR 1 hablando 2 habla, hablad 3 hablo, hablas, habla, hablamos, habláis, hablan 4 hablé, hablaste, habló, hablamos, hablasteis, hablaron 5 hablaré, hablarás, hablará, hablaremos, hablaréis, hablarán 6 hable, hables, hable, hablemos, habléis, hablen 7 hablara, hablaras, hablara, habláramos, hablarais, hablaran 8 hablado 9 hablaba, hablabas, hablaba, hablábamos, hablabais, hablaban

hacer 2 haz 3 hago 4 hice, hiciste, hizo, hicimos, hicisteis, hicieron 5 haré *etc* 6 haga *etc* 7 hiciera *etc* 8 hecho

instruir 1 instruyendo 2 instruye 3 instruyo, instruyes, instruye, instruyen 4 instruyó, instruyeron 6 instruya *etc* 7 instruyera *etc*

ir 1 yendo 2 ve 3 voy, vas, va, vamos, vais, van 4 fui, fuiste, fue, fuimos, fuisteis, fueron 6 vaya, vayas, vaya, vayamos, vayáis, vayan 7 fuera *etc* 9 iba, ibas, iba, íbamos, ibais, iban

jugar 2 juega 3 juego, juegas, juega, juegan 4 jugué 6 juegue *etc*

leer 1 leyendo 4 leyó, leyeron 7 leyera *etc*

morir 1 muriendo 2 muere 3 muero,

xiii

mueres, muere, mueren 4 murió,
murieron 6 muera, mueras, muera,
muramos, muráis, mueran 7 muriera *etc*
8 muerto

mover 2 mueve 3 muevo, mueves,
mueve, mueven 6 mueva, muevas,
mueva, muevan

negar 2 niega 3 niego, niegas, niega,
niegan 4 negué 6 niegue, niegues,
niegue, neguemos, neguéis, nieguen

ofrecer 3 ofrezco 6 ofrezca *etc*

oír 1 oyendo 2 oye 3 oigo, oyes, oye,
oyen 4 oyó, oyeron 6 oiga *etc* 7 oyera
etc

oler 2 huele 3 huelo, hueles, huele,
huelen 6 huela, huelas, huela, huelan

parecer 3 parezco 6 parezca *etc*

pedir 1 pidiendo 2 pide 3 pido, pides,
pide, piden 4 pidió, pidieron 6 pida *etc*
7 pidiera *etc*

pensar 2 piensa 3 pienso, piensas,
piensa, piensan 6 piense, pienses, piense,
piensen

perder 2 pierde 3 pierdo, pierdes,
pierde, pierden 6 pierda, pierdas, pierda,
pierdan

poder 1 pudiendo 2 puede 3 puedo,
puedes, puede, pueden 4 pude, pudiste,
pudo, pudimos, pudisteis, pudieron
5 podré 6 pueda, puedas, pueda,
puedan 7 pudiera *etc*

poner 2 pon 3 pongo 4 puse, pusiste,
puso, pusimos, pusisteis, pusieron 5
pondré *etc* 6 ponga *etc* 7 pusiera *etc*
8 puesto

preferir 1 prefiriendo 2 prefiere
3 prefiero, prefieres, prefiere, prefieren
4 prefirió, prefirieron 6 prefiera,
prefieras, prefiera, prefiramos, prefiráis,
prefieran 7 prefiriera *etc*

querer 2 quiere 3 quiero, quieres,
quiere, quieren 4 quise, quisiste, quiso,
quisimos, quisisteis, quisieron 5 querré
etc 6 quiera, quieras, quiera, quieran
7 quisiera *etc*

reír 2 ríe 3 río, ríes, ríe, ríen 4 reí,
rieron 6 ría, rías, ría, riamos, riáis, rían
7 riera *etc*

repetir 1 repitiendo 2 repite 3 repito,
repites, repite, repiten 4 repitió,
repitieron 6 repita *etc* 7 repitiera *etc*

rogar 2 ruega 3 ruego, ruegas, ruega,
ruegan 4 rogué 6 ruegue, ruegues,

ruegue, roguemos, roguéis, rueguen

saber 3 sé 4 supe, supiste, supo,
supimos, supisteis, supieron 5 sabré *etc*
6 sepa *etc* 7 supiera *etc*

salir 2 sal 3 salgo 5 saldré *etc* 6 salga
etc

seguir 1 siguiendo 2 sigue 3 sigo,
sigues, sigue, siguen 4 siguió, siguieron
6 siga *etc* 7 siguiera *etc*

sentar 2 sienta 3 siento, sientas, sienta,
sientan 6 siente, sientes, siente, sienten

sentir 1 sintiendo 2 siente 3 siento,
sientes, siente, sienten 4 sintió, sintieron
6 sienta, sientas, sienta, sintamos, sintáis,
sientan 7 sintiera *etc*

SER 2 sé 3 soy, eres, es, somos, sois,
son 4 fui, fuiste, fue, fuimos, fuisteis,
fueron 6 sea *etc* 7 fuera *etc* 9 era, eras,
era, éramos, erais, eran

servir 1 sirviendo 2 sirve 3 sirvo,
sirves, sirve, sirven 4 sirvió, sirvieron
6 sirva *etc* 7 sirviera *etc*

soñar 2 sueña 3 sueño, sueñas, sueña,
sueñan 6 sueñe, sueñes, sueñe, sueñen

tener 2 ten 3 tengo, tienes, tiene,
tienen 4 tuve, tuviste, tuvo, tuvimos,
tuvisteis, tuvieron 5 tendré *etc* 6 tenga
etc 7 tuviera *etc*

traer 1 trayendo 3 traigo 4 traje,
trajiste, trajo, trajimos, trajisteis,
trajeron 6 traiga *etc* 7 trajera *etc*

valer 2 val 3 valgo 5 valdré *etc* 6 valga
etc

venir 2 ven 3 vengo, vienes, viene,
vienen 4 vine, viniste, vino, vinimos,
vinisteis, vinieron 5 vendré *etc* 6 venga
etc 7 viniera *etc*

ver 3 veo 6 vea *etc* 8 visto 9 veía *etc*

vestir 1 vistiendo 2 viste 3 visto, vistes,
viste, visten 4 vistió, vistieron 6 vista *etc*
7 vistiera *etc*

VIVIR 1 viviendo 2 vive, vivid 3 vivo,
vives, vive, vivimos, vivís, viven 4 viví,
viviste, vivió, vivimos, vivisteis, vivieron
5 viviré, vivirás, vivirá, viviremos, viviréis,
vivirán 6 viva, vivas, viva, vivamos, viváis,
vivan 7 viviera, vivieras, viviera,
viviéramos, vivierais, vivieran 8 vivido
9 vivía, vivías, vivía, vivíamos, vivías, vivían

volver 2 vuelve 3 vuelvo, vuelves,
vuelve, vuelven 6 vuelva, vuelvas, vuelva,
vuelvan 8 vuelto

VERBOS IRREGULARES EN INGLÉS

presente	pasado	participio de pasado	presente	pasado	participio de pasado
arise	arose	arisen	eat	ate	eaten
awake	awoke	awoken	fall	fell	fallen
be (am, is, are; being)	was, were	been	feed	fed	fed
			feel	felt	felt
			fight	fought	fought
bear	bore	born(e)	find	found	found
beat	beat	beaten	flee	fled	fled
become	became	become	fling	flung	flung
begin	began	begun	fly	flew	flown
bend	bent	bent	forbid	forbad(e)	forbidden
bet	bet, betted	bet, betted	forecast	forecast	forecast
			forget	forgot	forgotten
bid (at auction, cards)	bid	bid	forgive	forgave	forgiven
			forsake	forsook	forsaken
bid (say)	bade	bidden	freeze	froze	frozen
bind	bound	bound	get	got	got, (US) gotten
bite	bit	bitten			
bleed	bled	bled	give	gave	given
blow	blew	blown	go (goes)	went	gone
break	broke	broken	grind	ground	ground
breed	bred	bred	grow	grew	grown
bring	brought	brought	hang	hung	hung
build	built	built	hang (execute)	hanged	hanged
burn	burnt, burned	burnt, burned	have	had	had
burst	burst	burst	hear	heard	heard
buy	bought	bought	hide	hid	hidden
can	could	(be able)	hit	hit	hit
			hold	held	held
cast	cast	cast	hurt	hurt	hurt
catch	caught	caught	keep	kept	kept
choose	chose	chosen	kneel	knelt, kneeled	knelt, kneeled
cling	clung	clung			
come	came	come	know	knew	known
cost	cost	cost	lay	laid	laid
cost (work out price of)	costed	costed	lead	led	led
			lean	leant, leaned	leant, leaned
creep	crept	crept			
cut	cut	cut	leap	leapt, leaped	leapt, leaped
deal	dealt	dealt			
dig	dug	dug	learn	learnt, learned	learnt, learned
do (does)	did	done			
draw	drew	drawn	leave	left	left
dream	dreamed, dreamt	dreamed, dreamt	lend	lent	lent
			let	let	let
			lie (lying)	lay	lain
drink	drank	drunk	light	lit, lighted	lit, lighted
drive	drove	driven			
dwell	dwelt	dwelt			

xv

presente	pasado	participio de pasado	presente	pasado	participio de pasado
lose	lost	lost	**speed**	sped,	sped,
make	made	made		speeded	speeded
may	might	—	**spell**	spelt,	spelt,
mean	meant	meant		spelled	spelled
meet	met	met	**spend**	spent	spent
mistake	mistook	mistaken	**spill**	spilt,	spilt,
mow	mowed	mown,		spilled	spilled
		mowed	**spin**	spun	spun
must	(had to)	(had to)	**spit**	spat	spat
pay	paid	paid	**spoil**	spoiled,	spoiled,
put	put	put		spoilt	spoilt
quit	quit,	quit,	**spread**	spread	spread
	quitted	quitted	**spring**	sprang	sprung
read	read	read	**stand**	stood	stood
rid	rid	rid	**steal**	stole	stolen
ride	rode	ridden	**stick**	stuck	stuck
ring	rang	rung	**sting**	stung	stung
rise	rose	risen	**stink**	stank	stunk
run	ran	run	**stride**	strode	stridden
saw	sawed	sawed,	**strike**	struck	struck
		sawn	**strive**	strove	striven
say	said	said	**swear**	swore	sworn
see	saw	seen	**sweep**	swept	swept
seek	sought	sought	**swell**	swelled	swollen,
sell	sold	sold			swelled
send	sent	sent	**swim**	swam	swum
set	set	set	**swing**	swung	swung
sew	sewed	sewn	**take**	took	taken
shake	shook	shaken	**teach**	taught	taught
shear	sheared	shorn,	**tear**	tore	torn
		sheared	**tell**	told	told
shed	shed	shed	**think**	thought	thought
shine	shone	shone	**throw**	threw	thrown
shoot	shot	shot	**thrust**	thrust	thrust
show	showed	shown	**tread**	trod	trodden
shrink	shrank	shrunk	**wake**	woke,	woken,
shut	shut	shut		waked	waked
sing	sang	sung			
sink	sank	sunk	**wear**	wore	worn
sit	sat	sat	**weave**	wove	woven
slay	slew	slain	**weave**	weaved	weaved
sleep	slept	slept	*(wind)*		
slide	slid	slid	**wed**	wedded,	wedded,
sling	slung	slung		wed	wed
slit	slit	slit	**weep**	wept	wept
smell	smelt,	smelt,	**win**	won	won
	smelled	smelled	**wind**	wound	wound
sow	sowed	sown, sowed	**wring**	wrung	wrung
speak	spoke	spoken	**write**	wrote	written

NÚMEROS

NUMBERS

○ *los números cardinales*

0	zero, nought (Brit)	26	twenty-six
1	one	27	twenty-seven
2	two	28	twenty-eight
3	three	29	twenty-nine
4	four	30	thirty
5	five	40	forty
6	six	50	fifty
7	seven	60	sixty
8	eight	70	seventy
9	nine	80	eighty
10	ten	90	ninety
11	eleven	100	one hundred
12	twelve	101	one hundred and one
13	thirteen	200	two hundred
14	fourteen	500	five hundred
15	fifteen	1,000	one thousand
16	sixteen	1,001	one thousand and one
17	seventeen	1,500	one thousand five hundred
18	eighteen	2,000	two thousand
19	nineteen	5,000	five thousand
20	twenty	10,000	ten thousand
21	twenty-one	100,000	one hundred thousand
22	twenty-two	150,000	one hundred and fifty thousand
23	twenty-three		
24	twenty-four	1,000,000	one million
25	twenty-five	1,000,000,000	one billion

○ *los números ordinales*

1st	first	14th	fourteenth
2nd	second	15th	fifteenth
3rd	third	20th	twentieth
4th	fourth	21st	twenty-first
5th	fifth	22nd	twenty-second
6th	sixth	30th	thirtieth
7th	seventh	31st	thirty-first
8th	eighth	50th	fiftieth
9th	ninth	100th	hundredth
10th	tenth	101st	hundred and first
11th	eleventh	110th	hundred and tenth
12th	twelfth	1000th	thousandth
13th	thirteenth	2000th	two thousandth

cardinal numbers

0	cero	26	veintiséis
1	uno (un, una)	27	veintisiete
2	dos	28	veintiocho
3	tres	29	veintinueve
4	cuatro	30	treinta
5	cinco	40	cuarenta
6	seis	50	cincuenta
7	siete	60	sesenta
8	ocho	70	setenta
9	nueve	80	ochenta
10	diez	90	noventa
11	once	100	cien
12	doce	101	ciento uno (un, una)
13	trece	200	doscientos
14	catorce	500	quinientos
15	quince	1.000	mil
16	dieciséis	1.001	mil (y) uno (un, una)
17	diecisiete	1.500	mil quinientos
18	dieciocho	2.000	dos mil
19	diecinueve	5.000	cinco mil
20	veinte	10.000	diez mil
21	veintiuno (-ún, -una)	100.000	cien mil
22	veintidós	150.000	ciento cincuenta mil
23	veintitrés	1.000.000	un millón
24	veinticuatro	1.000.000.000	mil millones
25	veinticinco		

ordinal numbers

1º, 1ª/1º	primero (primer, primera)	15º/15º	decimoquinto/a
2º/2º	segundo/a	20º/20º	vigésimo/a
3º, 3ª/3º	tercero (tercer, tercera)	21º, 21ª/21º	vigésimo primero (primer, primera)
4º/4º	cuarto/a		
5º/5º	quinto/a	22º/22º	vigésimo segundo/a
6º/6º	sexto/a	30º/30º	trigésimo/a
7º/7º	séptimo/a	31º, 31ª/31º	trigésimo primero (primer, primera)
8º/8º	octavo/a		
9º/9º	noveno/a or nono/a	50º/50º	quincuagésimo/a
10º/10º	décimo/a	100º/100º	centésimo/a
11º/11º	undécimo/a	101º, 101ª/l	centésimo primero
12º/12º	duodécimo/a	101º	(primer, primera)
13º/13º	decimotercero/a or decimotercio/a	110º/110º	centésimo décimo/a
		1000º/1000º	milésimo/a
14º/14º	decimocuarto/a	2000º/2000º	dumilésimo/a

LA HORA

What time is it?

**It's one o'clock (in the morning/
in the afternoon)**
*Es la una (de la mañana/
de la tarde)*

It's ten to two
Son las dos menos diez

It's twenty to six
Son las seis menos veinte

It's nine o'clock
Son las nueve

THE TIME

¿Qué hora es?

It's quarter past one *o* **It's
one fifteen**
Es la una y cuarto

It's half past three
Son las tres y media

It's quarter to eight
Son las ocho menos cuarto

It's twelve noon
Son las doce del mediodía
———————
It's midnight
Son las doce de la noche

LA FECHA

DATES

○ *los días de la semana*

Monday
Tuesday
Wednesday
Thursday
Friday
Saturday
Sunday

○ *the days of the week*

lunes
martes
miércoles
jueves
viernes
sábado
domingo

○ *los meses*

January
February
March
April
May
June
July
August
September
October
November
December

○ *the months*

enero
febrero
marzo
abril
mayo
junio
julio
agosto
septiembre
octubre
noviembre
diciembre

○ *vocabulario útil*

What day is it today?
It's January 20th, 2003
on Saturday
on Saturdays
every Saturday
last Saturday
next Saturday
in February
January first *(US)*,
  the first of January *(BRIT)*
today
yesterday
tomorrow

○ *useful vocabulary*

¿Qué día es hoy?
Es el 20 de enero de 2003
el sábado
los sábados
todos los sábados
el sábado pasado
el sábado que viene
en febrero

el día 1 de enero
hoy
ayer
mañana

Collins
SPANISH
DICTIONARY

ESPAÑOL-INGLÉS
SPANISH-ENGLISH

Aa

a

PALABRA CLAVE

(*a* + *el* = *al*) *prep*

1 (*dirección*) to; **fueron a Acapulco/Chile** they went to Acapulco/Chile; **me voy a casa** I'm going home

2 (*distancia*): **está a 15 millas de aquí** it's 15 miles from here

3 (*posición*): **estar a la mesa** to be at table; **al lado de** next to, beside; *ver tb* **puerta**

4 (*tiempo*): **a las 10/a medianoche** at 10/ midnight; **a la mañana siguiente** the following morning; **a los pocos días** after a few days; **estamos a 9 de julio** it's July ninth; **a los 24 años** at the age of 24; **al año/a la semana** a year/week later

5 (*manera*): **a la francesa** the French way; **a caballo** on horseback; **a oscuras** in the dark

6 (*medio, instrumento*): **a lápiz** in pencil; **a mano** by hand; **estufa** (*MÉX*) o **cocina** (*LAm exc MÉX, ESP*) **a gas** gas stove

7 (*razón*): **a 30 pesos la libra** at 30 pesos a pound; **a más de 50 millas por hora** at more than 50 miles per hour

8 (*dativo*): **se lo di a él** I gave it to him; **vi al policía** I saw the policeman; **se lo compré a él** I bought it from him

9 (*tras ciertos verbos*): **voy a verlo** I'm going to see him; **empezó a trabajar** he started working o to work

10 (+ *infin*): **al verlo, lo reconocí inmediatamente** when I saw him I recognized him at once; **el camino a recorrer** the distance we *etc* have to travel; **¡a callar!** keep quiet!; **¡a comer!** let's eat!

abad, esa *nm/f* abbot (abbess) □ **abadía** *nf* abbey

abajo *adv* (*situación*) (down) below, underneath; (*en edificio*) downstairs; (*dirección*) down, downwards; **el** (*LAm*) **departamento de ~** the downstairs flat; **la parte de ~** the lower part; **¡~ el gobierno!** down with the government!; **cuesta/río ~** downhill/downstream; **de arriba ~** from top to bottom; **el ~ firmante** the undersigned; **más ~** lower o further down

abalanzarse *vr*: **~ sobre** o **contra** to throw o.s. at

abanderado, -a *nm/f* (*portaestandarte*) standard bearer; (*de un movimiento*) champion, leader; (*MÉX*: *linier*) linesman, assistant referee

abandonado, -a *adj* derelict; (*desatendido*) abandoned; (*desierto*) deserted; (*descuidado*) neglected

abandonar *vt* to leave; (*persona*) to abandon, desert; (*cosa*) to abandon, leave behind; (*descuidar*) to neglect; (*renunciar a*) to give up; (*INFORM*) to quit; **abandonarse** *vr*: **~se a** to abandon o.s. to □ **abandono** *nm* (*acto*) desertion, abandonment; (*estado*) abandon, neglect; (*renuncia*) withdrawal, retirement; **ganar por abandono** to win by default

abanicar *vt* to fan □ **abanico** *nm* fan; (*NÁUT*) derrick

abaratar *vt* to lower the price of; **abaratarse** *vr* to go o come down in price

abarcar *vt* to include, embrace; (*LAm*: *acaparar*) to monopolize

abarrotado, -a *adj* packed

abarrotar *vt* (*local, estadio, teatro*) to fill, pack

abarrotero, -a (*MÉX*) *nm/f* grocer □ **abarrotes** (*MÉX*) *nmpl* groceries; **tienda de abarrotes** (*MÉX, CAm*) grocery store

abastecer *vt*: **~ (de)** to supply (with) □ **abastecimiento** *nm* supply

abasto *nm* supply; **no dar ~ a** to be unable to cope with

abatido, -a *adj* dejected, downcast

abatimiento *nm* (*depresión*) dejection, depression

abatir *vt* (*muro*) to demolish; (*pájaro*) to shoot o bring down; (*fig*) to depress; **abatirse** *vr* to get depressed; **~se sobre** to swoop o pounce on

abdicación *nf* abdication

abdicar *vi* to abdicate

abdomen *nm* abdomen □ **abdominales** *nmpl* (*tb*: **ejercicios abdominales**) situps

abecedario *nm* alphabet

abedul *nm* birch

abeja *nf* bee

abejorro *nm* bumblebee

abertura *nf* = **apertura**

abeto *nm* fir

abierto, -a *pp de* **abrir** ♦ *adj* open

abigarrado, -a *adj* multi-colored (*US*), multi-coloured (*BRIT*)

abismal *adj* (*fig*) vast, enormous

abismar *vt* to humble, cast down;
  abismarse *vr* to sink; **~se en** (*fig*) to be
  plunged into
abismo *nm* abyss
abjurar *vi*: **~ de** to abjure, forswear
ablandar *vt* to soften; **ablandarse** *vr* to get
  softer
abnegación *nf* self-denial
abnegado, -a *adj* self-sacrificing
abocado, -a *adj*: **verse ~ al desastre** to be
  heading for disaster
abochornar *vt* to embarrass
abofetear *vt* to slap (in the face)
abogado, -a *nm/f* lawyer; (*en tribunal*)
  attorney (*US*), barrister (*BRIT*) ▶ **abogado
  defensor** defense attorney (*US*) o lawyer
abogar *vi*: **~ por** to plead for; (*fig*) to
  advocate
abolengo *nm* ancestry, lineage
abolición *nf* abolition
abolir *vt* to abolish; (*cancelar*) to cancel
abolladura *nf* dent
abollar *vt* to dent
abombarse (*LAm*) *vr* to go bad
abominable *adj* abominable
abonado, -a *adj* (*deuda*) paid(-up) ♦ *nm/f*
  subscriber
abonar *vt* (*deuda*) to settle; (*terreno*) to
  fertilize; (*idea*) to endorse; **abonarse** *vr* to
  subscribe ❑ **abono** *nm* (*pago*) payment;
  (*para plantas*) fertilizer; (*DEPORTE, FERRO*) season
  ticket; (*MÉx: pago parcial*) installment (*US*),
  instalment (*BRIT*)
abordar *vt* (*barco*) to board; (*asunto*) to
  broach
aborigen *nmf* aborigine
aborrecer *vt* to hate, loathe
abortar *vi* (*malparir*) to have a miscarriage;
  (*deliberadamente*) to have an abortion
  ❑ **aborto** *nm* miscarriage; abortion
abotonar *vt* to button (up), do up
abovedado, -a *adj* vaulted, domed
abrasar *vt* to burn (up); (*AGR*) to dry up, parch
abrazar *vt* to embrace, hug
abrazo *nm* embrace, hug; **un ~** (*en carta*) with
  best wishes
abrebotellas *nm inv* bottle opener
abrecartas *nm inv* letter opener
abrelatas *nm inv* can o tin (*BRIT*) opener
abreviar *vt* to abbreviate; (*texto*) to abridge;
  (*plazo*) to reduce ❑ **abreviatura** *nf*
  abbreviation
abridor *nm* bottle opener; (*de latas*) can o tin
  (*BRIT*) opener

abrigador, a (*MÉX*) *adj* warm
abrigar *vt* (*proteger*) to shelter; (*ropa*) to keep
  warm; (*fig*) to cherish
abrigo *nm* (*prenda*) coat, overcoat; (*lugar
  protegido*) shelter
abril *nm* April
abrillantar *vt* to polish
abrir *vt* to open (up) ♦ *vi* to open; **abrirse** *vr* to
  open (up); (*extenderse*) to open out; (*cielo*) to
  clear; **~se paso** to find o force a way through
abrochar *vt* (*con botones*) to button (up);
  (*zapato, con broche*) to do up
abrumar *vt* to overwhelm; (*sobrecargar*) to
  weigh down
abrupto, -a *adj* abrupt; (*empinado*) steep
absceso *nm* abscess
absentismo *nm* absenteeism
absolución *nf* (*REL*) absolution; (*JUR*)
  acquittal
absoluto, -a *adj* absolute; **en ~** *adv* not at all
absolver *vt* to absolve; (*JUR*) to
  pardon; (: *acusado*) to acquit
absorbente *adj* absorbent; (*interesante*)
  absorbing
absorber *vt* to absorb; (*embeber*) to soak up
absorción *nf* absorption; (*COM*) takeover
absorto, -a *pp de* **absorber** ♦ *adj*
  absorbed, engrossed
abstemio, -a *adj* teetotal
abstención *nf* abstention
abstenerse *vr*: **~ (de)** to abstain o refrain
  (from)
abstinencia *nf* abstinence; (*ayuno*) fasting
abstracción *nf* abstraction
abstracto, -a *adj* abstract
abstraer *vt* to abstract; **abstraerse** *vr* to be o
  become absorbed
abstraído, -a *adj* absent-minded
absuelto *pp de* **absolver**
absurdo, -a *adj* absurd
abuchear *vt* to boo
abuelo, -a *nm/f* grandfather(-mother); **~s**
  nmpl grandparents
abulia *nf* apathy
abultado, -a *adj* bulky
abultar *vi* to be bulky
abundancia *nf*: **una ~ de** plenty of
  ❑ **abundante** *adj* abundant, plentiful
abundar *vi* to abound, be plentiful
aburguesarse *vr* to become middle-class
aburrido, -a *adj* (*hastiado*) bored; (*que
  aburre*) boring ❑ **aburrimiento** *nm*
  boredom, tedium

aburrir vt to bore; **aburrirse** vr to be bored, get bored

abusado, -a (MÉX: fam) adj (astuto) sharp, cunning ♦ excl: ¡**abusado!** (inv) look out!, careful!

abusar vi to go too far; ~ **de** to abuse

abusivo, -a adj (precio) exorbitant

abuso nm abuse

abyecto, -a adj wretched, abject

acá adv (lugar) here; ¿**de cuándo ~?** since when?

acabado, -a adj finished, complete; (perfecto) perfect; (agotado) worn out; (fig) masterly ♦ nm finish

acabar vt (llevar a su fin) to finish, complete; (consumir) to use up; (rematar) to finish off ♦ vi to finish, end; **acabarse** vr to finish, stop; (terminarse) to be over; (agotarse) to run out; ~ **con** to put an end to; ~ **de llegar** to have just arrived; ~ **por hacer** to end (up) by doing; **¡se acabó!** it's all over!; (¡basta!) that's enough!

acabóse nm: **esto es el ~** this is the last straw

academia nf academy ⬜ **académico, -a** adj academic

acaecer vi to happen, occur

acallar vt (persona) to silence; (protestas, rumores) to suppress

acalorado, -a adj (discusión) heated

acalorarse vr (fig) to get heated

acampar vi to camp

acantilado nm cliff

acaparar vt to monopolize; (acumular) to hoard

acariciar vt to caress; (esperanza) to cherish

acarrear vt to transport; (fig) to cause, result in

acaso adv perhaps, maybe; (**por**) **si ~** (just) in case; ¿~ **tengo yo la culpa?** is it MY fault?

acatamiento nm respect; (ley) observance

acatar vt to respect; (ley) obey

acatarrarse vr to catch a cold

acaudalado, -a adj well-off

acaudillar vt to lead, command

acceder vi: ~ **a** (petición etc) to agree to; (tener acceso a) to have access to; (INFORM) to access

accesible adj accessible

acceso nm access, entry; (camino) access, approach; (MED) attack, fit

accesorio, -a adj, nm accessory

accidentado, -a adj uneven; (montañoso) hilly; (azaroso) eventful ♦ nm/f accident victim

accidental adj accidental ⬜ **accidentarse** vr to have an accident

accidente nm accident; **~s** nmpl (de terreno) unevenness sg

acción nf action; (acto) action, act; (COM) share; (JUR) action, lawsuit ⬜ **accionar** vt to work, operate; (INFORM) to drive

accionista nmf shareholder, stockholder

acebo nm holly; (árbol) holly tree

acechar vt to spy on; (aguardar) to lie in wait for ⬜ **acecho** nm: **estar al acecho (de)** to lie in wait (for)

aceitar vt to oil, lubricate

aceite nm oil ▶ **aceite de oliva** olive oil ⬜ **aceitera** nf oilcan ⬜ **aceitoso, -a** adj oily

aceituna nf olive

acelerador nm accelerator, gas pedal (US)

acelerar vt to accelerate

acelga nf chard, beet

acento nm accent; (acentuación) stress

acentuar vt to accent; to stress; (fig) to accentuate

acepción nf meaning

aceptable adj acceptable

aceptación nf acceptance; (aprobación) approval

aceptar vt to accept; (aprobar) to approve

acequia nf irrigation ditch

acera nf sidewalk (US), pavement (BRIT)

acerca: ~ **de** prep about, concerning

acercar vt to bring o move nearer; **acercarse** vr to approach, come near

acerico nm pincushion

acero nm steel

acérrimo, -a adj (partidario) staunch; (enemigo) bitter

acertado, -a adj correct; (apropiado) apt; (sensato) sensible

acertar vt (blanco) to hit; (solución) to get right; (adivinar) to guess ♦ vi to get it right, be right; ~ **a** to manage to; ~ **con** to happen o hit on

acertijo nm riddle, puzzle

achacar vt to attribute

achacoso, -a adj sickly

achantar (fam) vt to scare, frighten; **achantarse** vr to back down

achaque etc vb ver **achacar** ♦ nm ailment

achicar vt to reduce; (NÁUT) to bale out

achicharrar vt to scorch, burn

achichincle (MÉX: fam) nmf minion

achicoria nf chicory

achuras (RPI) nfpl offal sg

aciago, -a adj ill-fated, fateful

acicalar vt to polish; (*persona*) to dress up; **acicalarse** vr to get dressed up

acicate nm spur

acidez nf acidity

ácido, -a adj sour, acid ♦ nm acid

acierto etc vb ver **acertar** ♦ nm success; (*buen paso*) wise move; (*solución*) solution; (*habilidad*) skill, ability

acitronar (*MÉX: fam*) vt to brown

aclamación nf acclamation; (*aplausos*) applause

aclamar vt to acclaim; (*aplaudir*) to applaud

aclaración nf clarification, explanation

aclarar vt to clarify, explain; (*ropa*) to rinse ♦ vi to clear up; **aclararse** vr (*explicarse*) to understand; **~se la garganta** to clear one's throat

aclaratorio, -a adj explanatory

aclimatación nf acclimatization

aclimatar vt to acclimatize, acclimate (*US*); **aclimatarse** vr to become acclimatized

acné nm acne

acobardar vt to intimidate

acodarse vr: **~ en** to lean on

acogedor, a adj welcoming; (*hospitalario*) hospitable

acoger vt to welcome; (*abrigar*) to shelter; **acogerse** vr to take refuge

acogida nf reception; refuge

acomedido, -a (*MÉX*) adj helpful, obliging

acometer vt to attack; (*emprender*) to undertake ❏ **acometida** nf attack, assault

acomodado, -a adj (*persona*) well-to-do

acomodador, a nm/f usher(ette)

acomodar vt to adjust; (*alojar*) to accommodate; **acomodarse** vr to conform; (*instalarse*) to install o.s.; (*adaptarse*): **~se (a)** to adapt (to)

acompañar vt to accompany; (*documentos*) to enclose

acondicionar vt to arrange, prepare; (*pelo*) to condition

acongojar vt to distress, grieve

aconsejar vt to advise, counsel; **aconsejarse** vr: **~se con** to consult

acontecer vt to happen, occur ❏ **acontecimiento** nm event

acopio nm store, stock

acoplamiento nm coupling, joint ❏ **acoplar** vt to fit; (*ELEC*) to connect; (*vagones*) to couple

acorazado, -a adj armor-plated (*US*), armour-plated (*BRIT*) ♦ nm battleship

acordar vt (*resolver*) to agree, resolve; (*recordar*) to remind; **acordarse** vr to agree; **~se (de algo)** to remember (sth) ❏ **acorde** adj (*MÚS*) harmonious, in keeping with ♦ nm chord; **acorde a** o **con** (*ley*) in conformity o compliance with

acordeón nm accordion; (*MÉX: fam: en examen*) cheat-sheet

acordonado, -a adj (*calle*) cordoned-off

acorralar vt to round up, corral

acortar vt to shorten; (*duración*) to cut short; (*cantidad*) to reduce; **acortarse** vr to become shorter

acosar vt to pursue relentlessly; (*fig*) to hound, pester ❏ **acoso** nm harassment ▶ **acoso sexual** sexual harassment

acostar vt (*en cama*) to put to bed; (*en suelo*) to lay down; **acostarse** vr to go to bed; to lie down; **~se con algn** to sleep with sb

acostumbrado, -a adj usual; **~ a** used to

acostumbrar vt: **~ a algn a algo** to get sb used to sth ♦ vi: **~ (a) hacer** to be in the habit of doing; **acostumbrarse** vr: **~se a** to get used to

acotación nf marginal note; (*GEO*) elevation mark; (*de límite*) boundary mark; (*TEATRO*) stage direction

acotamiento (*MÉX*) nm shoulder (*US*), berm (*US*), hard shoulder (*BRIT*)

ácrata adj, nmf anarchist

acre adj (*olor*) acrid; (*fig*) biting ♦ nm acre

acrecentar vt to increase, augment

acreditar vt (*garantizar*) to vouch for, guarantee; (*autorizar*) to authorize; (*dar prueba de*) to prove; (*COM: abonar*) to credit; (*embajador*) to accredit; **acreditarse** vr to become famous

acreedor, a adj: **~ de** worthy of ♦ nm/f creditor

acribillar vt: **~ a balazos** to riddle with bullets

acróbata nmf acrobat

acta nf certificate; (*de comisión*) minutes pl, record ▶ **acta de nacimiento/ matrimonio** (*MÉX*) birth/marriage certificate ▶ **acta notarial** affidavit

actitud nf attitude; (*postura*) posture

activar vt to activate; (*acelerar*) to speed up

actividad nf activity

activo, -a adj active; (*vivo*) lively ♦ nm (*COM*) assets pl

acto nm act, action; (*ceremonia*) ceremony; (*TEATRO*) act; **en el ~** immediately

actor nm actor; (*JUR*) plaintiff ♦ adj: **parte ~a** prosecution

actriz *nf* actress

actuación *nf* action; (*comportamiento*) conduct, behavior (*US*), behaviour (*BRIT*); (*JUR*) proceedings *pl*; (*desempeño*) performance

actual *adj* present(-day), current □ **actualidad** *nf* present; **actualidades** *nfpl* (*noticias*) news *sg*; **en la actualidad** at present, presently (*US*); (*hoy día*) nowadays

⚠ No confundir **actual** con la palabra inglesa *actual*.

actualizar *vt* to update, modernize

actualmente *adv* at present; (*hoy día*) nowadays

⚠ No confundir **actualmente** con la palabra inglesa *actually*.

actuar *vi* (*obrar*) to work, operate; (*actor*) to act, perform ♦ *vt* to work, operate; **~ de** to act as

acuarela *nf* watercolor (*US*), watercolour (*BRIT*)

acuario *nm* aquarium; **A~** (*ASTROLOGÍA*) Aquarius

acuartelar *vt* (*MIL*) to confine to barracks

acuático, -a *adj* aquatic

acuchillar *vt* (*TEC*) to plane (down), smooth

acuciante *adj* urgent

acuciar *vt* to urge on

acudir *vi* (*asistir*) to attend; (*ir*) to go; **~ a** to turn to; **~ en ayuda de** to go to the aid of

acuerdo *etc vb ver* **acordar** ♦ *nm* agreement; **¡de ~!** agreed!; **de ~ con** (*persona*) in agreement with; (*acción, documento*) in accordance with; **estar de ~** to be agreed, agree

acumular *vt* to accumulate, collect

acuñar *vt* (*moneda*) to mint; (*frase*) to coin

acupuntura *nf* acupuncture

acurrucarse *vr* to crouch; (*ovillarse*) to curl up

acusación *nf* accusation

acusar *vt* to accuse; (*revelar*) to reveal; (*denunciar*) to denounce

acuse *nm*: **~ de recibo** acknowledgement of receipt

acústica *nf* acoustics *pl*

acústico, -a *adj* acoustic

adaptación *nf* adaptation

adaptador *nm* (*ELEC*) adapter ▶ **adaptador universal** universal adaptor

adaptar *vt* to adapt; (*acomodar*) to fit

a. de C. *abr* (= *antes de Cristo*) B.C.

adecuado, -a *adj* (*apto*) suitable; (*oportuno*) appropriate

adecuar *vt* to adapt; to make suitable

adelantado, -a *adj* advanced; (*reloj*) fast; **pagar por ~** to pay in advance

adelantamiento *nm* (*AUTO*) passing (*US*), overtaking (*BRIT*)

adelantar *vt* to move forward; (*avanzar*) to advance; (*acelerar*) to speed up; (*AUTO*) to pass (*US*), overtake (*BRIT*) ♦ *vi* to go forward, advance; **adelantarse** *vr* to go forward, advance

adelante *adv* forward(s), ahead ♦ *excl* come in!; **de hoy en ~** from now on; **más ~** later on; (*más allá*) further on

adelanto *nm* advance; (*mejora*) improvement; (*progreso*) progress

adelgazar *vt* to thin (down) ♦ *vi* to get thin; (*con régimen*) to slim down, lose weight

ademán *nm* gesture; **ademanes** *nmpl* manners; **en ~ de** as if to

además *adv* besides; (*por otra parte*) moreover; (*también*) also; **~ de** besides, in addition to

adentrarse *vr*: **~ en** to go into, get inside; (*penetrar*) to penetrate (into)

adentro *adv* inside, in; **mar ~** out at sea; **tierra ~** inland

adepto, -a *nm/f* supporter

aderezar *vt* (*ensalada*) to dress; (*comida*) to season □ **aderezo** *nm* dressing; seasoning

adeudar *vt* to owe; **adeudarse** *vr* to run into debt

adherirse *vr*: **~ a** to adhere to; (*partido*) to join

adhesión *nf* adhesion; (*fig*) adherence

adicción *nf* addiction

adición *nf* addition

adicto, -a *adj*: **~ a** addicted to; (*dedicado*) devoted to ♦ *nm/f* supporter, follower; (*toxicómano*) addict

adiestrar *vt* to train, teach; (*conducir*) to guide, lead; **adiestrarse** *vr* to practice; (*enseñarse*) to train o.s.

adinerado, -a *adj* wealthy

adiós *excl* (*para despedirse*) goodbye!, cheerio! (*BRIT*); (*al pasar*) hello!

aditivo *nm* additive

adivinanza *nf* riddle

adivinar *vt* to prophesy; (*conjeturar*) to guess □ **adivino, -a** *nm/f* fortune-teller

adj *abr* (= *adjunto*) encl

adjetivo *nm* adjective

adjudicación *nf* award; adjudication

adjudicar vt to award; **adjudicarse** vr: ~se **algo** to appropriate sth
adjuntar vt to attach, enclose
❏ **adjunto, -a** adj attached, enclosed ♦ nm/f assistant
administración nf administration; (dirección) management
❏ **administrador, a** nm/f administrator, manager(ess) ▶ **administrador de redes** system administrator
administrar vt to administer
❏ **administrativo, -a** adj administrative
admirable adj admirable
admiración nf admiration; (asombro) wonder; (LING) exclamation point (US) o mark (BRIT)
admirar vt to admire; (extrañar) to surprise; **admirarse** vr to be surprised
admisible adj admissible
admisión nf admission; (reconocimiento) acceptance
admitir vt to admit; (aceptar) to accept
admonición nf warning
adobar vt (CULIN) to season
adobe nm adobe, sun-dried brick
adoctrinar vt: ~ **en** to indoctrinate with
adolecer vi: ~ **de** to suffer from
adolescente nmf adolescent, teenager
adonde conj (to) where
adónde adv = **dónde**
adopción nf adoption
adoptar vt to adopt
adoptivo, -a (LAm exc MÉX) adj (padres) adoptive; (hijo) adopted
adoquín nm paving stone
adorar vt to adore
adormecer vt to put to sleep; **adormecerse** vr to become sleepy; (dormirse) to fall asleep
adornar vt to adorn
adorno nm ornament; (decoración) decoration
adosado, -a adj: **casa adosada** duplex (US), semi-detached house (BRIT)
adosar (MÉX) vt (adjuntar) to attach, enclose (with a letter)
adquiero etc vb ver **adquirir**
adquirir vt to acquire, obtain
adquisición nf acquisition
adrede adv on purpose
adscribir vt to appoint
adscrito pp de **adscribir**
ADSL nm (ADSL) broadband
aduana nf customs pl

aduanero, -a adj customs cpd ♦ nm/f customs officer
aducir vt to adduce; (dar como prueba) to offer as proof
adueñarse vr: ~ **de** to take possession of
adulación nf flattery
adular vt to flatter
adulterar vt to adulterate
adulterio nm adultery
adúltero, -a adj adulterous ♦ nm/f adulterer (adulteress)
adulto, -a adj, nm/f adult
adusto, -a adj stern; (austero) austere
advenedizo, -a nm/f upstart
advenimiento nm arrival; (al trono) accession
adverbio nm adverb
adversario, -a nm/f adversary
adversidad nf adversity; (contratiempo) setback
adverso, -a adj adverse
advertencia nf warning; (prefacio) preface, foreword
advertir vt to notice; (avisar): ~ **a algn de** to warn sb about o of
Adviento nm Advent
advierto etc vb ver **advertir**
adyacente adj adjacent
aéreo, -a adj aerial
aerobic (LAm exc MÉX, ESP) nm aerobics sg
❏ **aerobics** (MÉX) nmpl aerobics sg
aerodeslizador nm hovercraft
aeromozo, -a (LAm) nm/f air steward(ess)
aeronáutica nf aeronautics sg
aeronave nm spaceship
aeroplano nm airplane (US), aeroplane (BRIT)
aeropuerto nm airport
aerosol nm aerosol
afabilidad nf friendliness ❏ **afable** adj affable
afamado, -a adj famous
afán nm hard work; (deseo) desire
afanador, a (MÉX) nm/f (de limpieza) cleaner
afanar vt to harass; (fam) to pinch; **afanarse** vr: ~se **por hacer** to strive to do
afear vt to disfigure
afección nf (MED) disease
afectación nf affectation ❏ **afectado, -a** adj affected
afectar vt to affect
afectísimo, -a adj affectionate; **suyo** ~ yours truly

afectivo, -a *adj* (*problema etc*) emotional

afecto *nm* affection; **tenerle ~ a algn** to be fond of sb

afectuoso, -a *adj* affectionate

afeitar *vt* to shave; **afeitarse** *vr* to shave

afeminado, -a *adj* effeminate

Afganistán *nm* Afghanistan

afianzamiento *nm* strengthening; security

afianzar *vt* to strengthen; to secure; **afianzarse** *vr* to become established

afiche (*RPI*) *nm* poster

afición *nf* fondness, liking; **la ~** the fans *pl*; **pinto por ~** I paint as a hobby
□ **aficionado, -a** *adj* keen, enthusiastic; (*no profesional*) amateur ♦ *nm/f* enthusiast, fan; amateur; **ser aficionado a algo** to be very keen on *o* fond of sth

aficionar *vt*: **~ a algn a algo** to make sb like sth; **aficionarse** *vr*: **~se a algo** to grow fond of sth

afilado, -a *adj* sharp

afilar *vt* to sharpen

afiliarse *vr* to affiliate

afín *adj* (*parecido*) similar; (*conexo*) related

afinar *vt* (*TEC*) to refine; (*MÚS*) to tune ♦ *vi* (*tocar*) to play in tune; (*cantar*) to sing in tune

afincarse *vr* to settle

afinidad *nf* affinity; (*parentesco*) relationship; **por ~** by marriage

afirmación *nf* affirmation

afirmar *vt* to affirm, state
□ **afirmativo, -a** *adj* affirmative

aflicción *nf* affliction; (*dolor*) grief

afligir *vt* to afflict; (*apenar*) to distress; **afligirse** *vr* to grieve

aflojar *vt* to slacken; (*desatar*) to loosen, undo; (*relajar*) to relax; (*fam: dinero*) to fork out ♦ *vi* to drop; (*bajar*) to go down; **aflojarse** *vr* to relax

aflorar *vi* to come to the surface, emerge

afluente *adj* flowing ♦ *nm* tributary

afluir *vi* to flow

afmo, -a *abr* (= *afectísimo(a) suyo(a)*) Yours

afónico, -a *adj*: **estar ~** to have a sore throat; to have lost one's voice

aforo *nm* (*de teatro etc*) capacity

afortunado, -a *adj* fortunate, lucky

afrancesado, -a *adj* francophile; (*pey*) Frenchified

afrenta *nf* affront, insult; (*deshonra*) shame, dishonor (*US*), dishonour (*BRIT*)

África *nf* Africa □ **africano, -a** *adj*, *nm/f* African

afrontar *vt* to confront; (*poner cara a cara*) to bring face to face

afuera *adv* out, outside; **~s** *nfpl* outskirts

agachar *vt* to bend, bow; **agacharse** *vr* to stoop, bend; (*MÉX: fam: ceder*) to give in

agalla *nf* (*ZOOL*) gill; **tener ~s** (*fam*) to have guts

agarradera (*MÉX*) *nf* handle

agarrado, -a (*fam*) *adj* stingy, mean (*BRIT*)

agarrar *vt* to grasp, grab; (*LAm: tomar*) to take, catch; (*recoger*) to pick up ♦ *vi* (*planta*) to take root; **agarrarse** *vr* to hold on (tightly)

agarrotar *vt* (*persona*) to squeeze tightly; (*reo*) to garrotte; **agarrotarse** *vr* (*motor*) to seize up; (*MED*) to stiffen

agasajar *vt* to treat well, fête

agazaparse *vr* to crouch down

agencia *nf* agency ▶ **agencia de viajes** travel agency ▶ **agencia inmobiliaria** real estate (*US*) *o* estate (*BRIT*) agent's (office)

agenciarse *vr* to obtain, procure

agenda *nf* diary

⚠ No confundir **agenda** con la palabra inglesa **agenda**.

agente *nmf* agent ▶ **agente (de policía)** policeman(-woman) ▶ **agente de seguros** insurance agent ▶ **agente de tránsito** (*MÉX*) traffic cop ▶ **agente inmobiliario** Realtor® (*US*), estate agent (*BRIT*)

ágil *adj* agile, nimble □ **agilidad** *nf* agility, nimbleness

agilizar *vt* (*trámites*) to speed up

agiotista (*MÉX*) *nmf* (*usurero*) usurer

agitación *nf* (*de mano etc*) shaking, waving; (*de líquido etc*) stirring; (*fig*) agitation

agitado, -a *adj* hectic; (*viaje*) bumpy

agitar *vt* to wave, shake; (*líquido*) to stir; (*fig*) to stir up, excite; **agitarse** *vr* to get excited; (*inquietarse*) to get worried *o* upset

aglomeración *nf*: **~ de tráfico/gente** traffic jam/mass of people

aglomerar *vt* to crowd together; **aglomerarse** *vr* to crowd together

agnóstico, -a *adj*, *nm/f* agnostic

agobiar *vt* to weigh down; (*oprimir*) to oppress; (*cargar*) to burden

agolparse *vr* to crowd together

agonía *nf* death throes *pl*; (*fig*) agony, anguish

agonizante *adj* dying

agonizar *vi* to be dying

agosto *nm* August

agotado, -a *adj* (*persona*) exhausted; (*libros*) out of print; (*acabado*) finished; (*COM*) sold out

agotador, a *adj* exhausting

agotamiento *nm* exhaustion

agotar *vt* to exhaust; (*consumir*) to drain; (*recursos*) to use up, deplete; **agotarse** *vr* to be exhausted; (*acabarse*) to run out; (*libro*) to go out of print

agraciado, -a *adj* (*atractivo*) attractive; (*en sorteo etc*) lucky

agradable *adj* pleasant, nice

agradar *vt*: **él me agrada** I like him

agradecer *vt* to thank; (*favor etc*) to be grateful for ❏ **agradecido, -a** *adj* grateful; **¡muy agradecido!** thanks a lot! ❏ **agradecimiento** *nm* thanks *pl*; gratitude

agradezco *etc vb ver* **agradecer**

agrado *nm*: **ser de tu** *etc* **~** to be to your *etc* liking

agrandar *vt* to enlarge; (*fig*) to exaggerate; **agrandarse** *vr* to get bigger

agrario, -a *adj* agrarian, land *cpd*; (*política*) agricultural, farming

agravante *adj* aggravating ♦ *nm*: **con el ~ de que ...** with the further difficulty that ...

agravar *vt* (*pesar sobre*) to make heavier; (*irritar*) to aggravate; **agravarse** *vr* to worsen, get worse

agraviar *vt* to offend; (*ser injusto con*) to wrong; **agraviarse** *vr* to take offense (*US*) *o* offence (*BRIT*) ❏ **agravio** *nm* offense (*US*), offence (*BRIT*); wrong; (*JUR*) grievance

agredir *vt* to attack

agregado, -a *nm/f*: **A~** ≈ teacher (*who is not head of department*) ♦ *nm* aggregate; (*persona*) attaché

agregar *vt* to gather; (*añadir*) to add; (*persona*) to appoint

agresión *nf* aggression

agresivo, -a *adj* aggressive

agriar *vt* to (turn) sour; **agriarse** *vr* to turn sour

agrícola *adj* farming *cpd*, agricultural

agricultor, a *nm/f* farmer

agricultura *nf* agriculture, farming

agridulce *adj* bittersweet; (*CULIN*) sweet and sour

agrietarse *vr* to crack; (*piel*) to chap

agrimensor, a *nm/f* surveyor

agrio, -a *adj* bitter

agrupación *nf* group; (*acto*) grouping

agrupar *vt* to group

agua *nf* water; (*NÁUT*) wake; (*ARQ*) slope of a roof; **~s** *nfpl* (*de piedra*) water *sg*, sparkle *sg*; (*MED*) water *sg*, urine *sg*; (*NÁUT*) waters; **~s abajo/arriba** downstream/upstream ▶ **agua bendita/destilada/potable** holy/distilled/drinking water ▶ **agua caliente** hot water ▶ **agua corriente** running water ▶ **agua de colonia** eau de cologne ▶ **agua mineral (con/sin gas)** (carbonated/uncarbonated) mineral water ▶ **agua oxigenada** hydrogen peroxide ▶ **aguas jurisdiccionales** territorial waters

aguacate *nm* avocado (pear)

aguacero *nm* (heavy) shower, downpour

aguado, -a *adj* watery, watered down; (*MÉX, CAm*: *fam*: *aburrido*) boring

aguafiestas *nmf inv* spoilsport, killjoy

aguamiel (*MÉX*) *nf* fermented maguey *o* agave juice

aguanieve *nf* sleet

aguantar *vt* to bear, put up with; (*sostener*) to hold up ♦ *vi* to last; **aguantarse** *vr* to restrain o.s. ❏ **aguante** *nm* (*paciencia*) patience; (*resistencia*) endurance

aguar *vt* to water down

aguardar *vt* to wait for

aguardiente *nm* brandy, liquor

aguarrás *nm* turpentine

aguaviva (*RPl*) *nf* jellyfish

agudeza *nf* sharpness; (*ingenio*) wit

agudizar *vt* (*crisis*) to make worse; **agudizarse** *vr* to get worse

agudo, -a *adj* sharp; (*voz*) high-pitched, piercing; (*dolor, enfermedad*) acute

agüero *nm*: **buen/mal ~** good/bad omen

aguijón *nm* sting; (*fig*) spur

águila *nf* eagle; (*fig*) genius

aguileño, -a *adj* (*nariz*) aquiline; (*rostro*) sharp-featured

aguinaldo *nm* Christmas tip, Christmas box (*BRIT*)

aguja *nf* needle; (*de reloj*) hand; (*ARQ*) spire; (*TEC*) firing-pin; **~s** *nfpl* (*ZOOL*) ribs; (*FERRO*) points

agujerear *vt* to make holes in

agujero *nm* hole

agujetas *nfpl* stitch *sg*; (*rigidez*) stiffness *sg*; (*MÉX*: *cordones*) shoe laces

aguzar *vt* to sharpen; (*fig*) to incite

ahí *adv* there; **de ~ que** so that, with the result that; **~ llega** here he comes; **por ~** that way; (*allá*) over there; **200 o por ~** 200 or so

ahijado, -a *nm/f* godson/daughter

ahínco *nm* earnestness

ahogar vt to drown; (asfixiar) to suffocate, smother; (fuego) to put out; **ahogarse** vr (en el agua) to drown; (por asfixia) to suffocate

ahogo nm breathlessness; (fig) financial difficulty

ahondar vt to deepen, make deeper; (fig) to study thoroughly ♦ vi: ~ **en** to study thoroughly

ahora adv now; (hace poco) a moment ago, just now; (dentro de poco) in a moment; ~ **voy** I'm coming; ~ **mismo** right now; ~ **bien** now then; **por** ~ for the present

ahorcar vt to hang

ahorita (fam) adv (LAm: en este momento) right now; (MÉX: hace poco) just now; (: dentro de poco) in a minute

ahorrar vt (dinero) to save; (esfuerzos) to save, avoid □ **ahorro** nm (acto) saving; **ahorros** nmpl (dinero) savings

ahuecar vt to hollow (out); (voz) to deepen; **ahuecarse** vr to give o.s. airs

ahumar vt to smoke, cure; (llenar de humo) to fill with smoke ♦ vi to smoke; **ahumarse** vr to fill with smoke

ahuyentar vt to drive off, frighten off; (fig) to dispel

airado, -a adj angry

airar vt to anger; **airarse** vr to get angry

aire nm air; (viento) wind; (corriente) draft (US), draught (BRIT); (MÚS) tune; ~**s** nmpl: **darse** ~**s** to give o.s. airs; **al** ~ **libre** in the open air ▶ **aire acondicionado** air conditioning □ **airearse** vr (persona) to go out for a breath of fresh air □ **airoso, -a** adj windy; drafty (US), draughty (BRIT); (fig) graceful

aislado, -a adj isolated; (incomunicado) cut-off; (ELEC) insulated

aislar vt to isolate; (ELEC) to insulate

ajardinado, -a adj landscaped

ajedrez nm chess

ajeno, -a adj (que pertenece a otro) somebody else's; ~ **a** foreign to

ajetreado, -a adj busy

ajetreo nm bustle

ají (CS) nm chil(l)i, red pepper; (salsa) chil(l)i sauce

ajillo nm: **gambas al** ~ garlic prawns

ajo nm garlic

ajuar nm household furnishings pl; (de novia) trousseau; (de niño) layette

ajustado, -a adj (tornillo) tight; (cálculo) right; (ropa) tight(-fitting); (resultado) close

ajustar vt (adaptar) to adjust; (encajar) to fit; (TEC) to engage; (IMPRENTA) to make up; (apretar) to tighten; (concertar) to agree (on); (reconciliar) to reconcile; (cuentas, deudas) to settle ♦ vi to fit; **ajustarse** vr: ~**se a** (precio etc) to be in keeping with, fit in with; ~ **las cuentas a algn** to get even with sb

ajuste nm adjustment; (COSTURA) fitting; (acuerdo) compromise; (de cuenta) settlement

al cont (= **a** + **el**); ver **a**

ala nf wing; (de sombrero) brim; winger □ **ala delta** nf hang-glider

alabanza nf praise

alabar vt to praise

alacena nf kitchen closet (US), kitchen cupboard (BRIT)

alacrán nm scorpion

alambique nm still

alambrada nf wire fence; (red) wire netting

alambrado nm = **alambrada**

alambre nm wire; (MÉX CULIN) kebab ▶ **alambre de púas** barbed wire

alameda nf (plantío) poplar grove; (lugar de paseo) avenue, boulevard

álamo nm poplar ▶ **álamo temblón** aspen

alarde nm show, display; **hacer** ~ **de** to boast of

alargador nm (ELEC) extension lead

alargar vt to lengthen, extend; (paso) to hasten; (brazo) to stretch out; (cuerda) to pay out; (conversación) to spin out; **alargarse** vr to get longer

alarido nm shriek

alarma nf alarm ▶ **alarma social** public alarm □ **alarmante** adj alarming □ **alarmar** vt to alarm; **alarmarse** vr to get alarmed

alba nf dawn

albacea nmf executor/executrix

albahaca nf basil

Albania nf Albania

albañil nm bricklayer; (cantero) mason

albarán nm (COM) delivery note, invoice

albaricoque (ESP) nm apricot

albedrío nm: **libre** ~ free will

alberca nf reservoir; (MÉX: piscina) swimming pool

albergar vt to shelter

albergue etc vb ver **albergar** ♦ nm shelter, refuge ▶ **albergue juvenil** youth hostel

albóndiga nf meatball

albornoz nm (para el baño) bathrobe; (de los árabes) burnous

alborotar vi to make a row ♦ vt to agitate, stir up; **alborotarse** vr to get excited; (mar) · get rough □ **alboroto** nm row, uproa·

alborozar vt to gladden; **alborozarse** vr to rejoice

alborozo nm joy

álbum (pl ~s, ~es) nm album ▸ **álbum de recortes** scrapbook

albur (MÉX) nm (juego de palabras) pun; (doble sentido) double entendre

alcachofa nf artichoke

alcalde, -esa nm/f mayor(ess)

alcaldía nf mayoralty; (lugar) mayor's office

alcance etc vb ver **alcanzar** ♦ nm reach; (COM) adverse balance

alcancía (LAm) nf (para ahorrar) money box; (para colectas) collection box

alcantarilla nf (de aguas cloacales) sewer; (en la calle) gutter

alcanzar vt (algo: con la mano, el pie) to reach; (algn: en el camino etc) to catch up (with); (autobús) to catch; (bala) to hit, strike ♦ vi (ser suficiente) to be enough; **~ a hacer** to manage to do

alcaparra nf caper

alcayata nf hook

alcázar nm fortress; (NÁUT) quarter-deck

alcoba nf bedroom

alcohol nm alcohol ▸ **alcohol metílico** wood alcohol (US), methylated spirits pl (BRIT) ❑ **alcohólico, -a** adj, nm/f alcoholic

alcoholímetro nm Breathalyzer® (US), Breathalyser® (BRIT)

alcoholismo nm alcoholism

alcornoque nm cork tree; (fam) idiot

alcurnia nf lineage

aldaba nf (door) knocker

aldea nf village ❑ **aldeano, -a** adj village cpd ♦ nm/f villager

aleación nf alloy

aleatorio, -a adj random

aleccionar vt to instruct; (adiestrar) to train

alegación nf allegation

alegar vt to claim; (JUR) to plead ♦ vi (LAm: discutir) to argue

alegato nm (JUR) allegation; (LAm: discusión) argument

alegoría nf allegory

alegrar vt (causar alegría) to cheer (up); (fuego) to poke; (fiesta) to liven up; **alegrarse** vr (fam) to get merry o tight; **~se de** to be glad about

alegre adj happy, cheerful; (fam) merry, tight; (chiste) risqué, blue ❑ **alegría** nf happiness; merriment

alejamiento nm removal; (distancia) remoteness

alejar vt to remove; (fig) to estrange; **alejarse** vr to move away

alemán, -ana adj, nm/f German ♦ nm (LING) German

Alemania nf Germany

alentador, -a adj encouraging

alentar vt to encourage

alergia nf allergy

alero nm (de tejado) eaves pl; (guardabarros) fender (US), mudguard (BRIT)

alerta adj, nm alert

aleta nf (de pez) fin; (ala) wing; (de foca, DEPORTE) flipper; (AUTO) fender (US), mudguard (BRIT)

aletargar vt to make drowsy; (entumecer) to make numb; **aletargarse** vr to grow drowsy; to become numb

aletear vi to flutter

alevín nm fry, young fish

alevosía nf treachery

alfabeto nm alphabet

alfalfa nf alfalfa, lucerne

alfarería nf pottery; (tienda) pottery store (US) o shop (BRIT) ❑ **alfarero, -a** nm/f potter

alféizar nm window-sill

alférez nm (MIL) second lieutenant; (NÁUT) ensign

alfil nm (AJEDREZ) bishop

alfiler nm pin; (broche) clip

alfiletero nm needle case

alfombra nf carpet; (más pequeña) rug ❑ **alfombrar** vt to carpet ❑ **alfombrilla** nf rug, mat; (INFORM) mouse mat o pad

alforja nf saddlebag

algarabía (fam) nf gibberish; (griterío) hullabaloo

algas nfpl seaweed

álgebra nf algebra

álgido, -a adj (momento etc) crucial, decisive

algo pron something; anything ♦ adv somewhat, rather; **¿~ más?** anything else?; (en tienda) is that all?; **por ~ será** there must be some reason for it

algodón nm cotton; (planta) cotton plant ▸ **algodón de azúcar** cotton candy (US), candy floss (BRIT) ▸ **algodón hidrófilo** absorbent cotton (US), cotton wool (BRIT)

algodonero, -a adj cotton cpd ♦ nm/f cotton grower ♦ nm cotton plant

alguacil nm bailiff, constable (US); (TAUR) mounted official

alguien pron someone, somebody; (en frases interrogativas) anyone, anybody

alguno, -a adj (delante de nm: **algún**) some; (después de n): **no tiene talento ~** he has no talent, he doesn't have any talent ♦ pron (alguien) someone, somebody; **algún que otro libro** some book or other; **algún día iré** I'll go one o some day; **sin interés ~** without the slightest interest; **~ que otro** an occasional one; **~s piensan** some (people) think

alhaja nf jewel; (tesoro) precious object, treasure

alhelí nm wallflower, stock

aliado, -a adj allied

alianza nf alliance; (anillo) wedding ring

aliar vt to ally; **aliarse** vr to form an alliance

alias adv alias

alicatado (ESP) nm tiling

alicates nmpl pliers ▶ **alicates de uñas** nail clippers

aliciente nm incentive; (atracción) attraction

alienación nf alienation

aliento nm breath; (respiración) breathing; **sin ~** breathless

aligerar vt to lighten; (reducir) to shorten; (aliviar) to alleviate; (mitigar) to ease; (paso) to quicken

alijo nm consignment

alimaña nf pest

alimentación nf (comida) food; (acción) feeding; (tienda) grocery store (US), grocer's (shop) (BRIT) □ **alimentador** nm feeder ▶ **alimentador de papel** sheet-feeder

alimentar vt to feed; (nutrir) to nourish; **alimentarse** vr to feed

alimenticio, -a adj food cpd; (nutritivo) nourishing, nutritious

alimento nm food; (nutrición) nourishment

alineación nf alignment; (DEPORTE) line-up

alinear vt to align; **alinearse** vr (DEPORTE) to line up; **~se en** to fall in with

aliñar vt (CULIN) to season □ **aliño** nm (CULIN) dressing

alioli nm garlic mayonnaise

alisar vt to smooth

aliso nm alder

alistarse vr to enlist; (inscribirse) to enroll

aliviar vt (carga) to lighten; (persona) to relieve; (dolor) to relieve, alleviate; **aliviarse** vr (MÉX: fam: embarazada) to give birth

alivio nm alleviation, relief

aljibe nm cistern

allá adv (lugar) there; (por ahí) over there; (tiempo) then; **~ abajo** down there; **más ~**

further on; **más ~ de** beyond; **¡~ tú!** that's your problem!

allanamiento nm (LAm: de policía) raid ▶ **allanamiento de morada** (ESP) breaking and entering

allanar vt to flatten, level (out); (igualar) to smooth (out); (fig) to subdue; (JUR) to burgle, break into

allegado, -a adj near, close ♦ nm/f relation

allí adv there; **~ mismo** right there; **por ~** over there; (por ese camino) that way

alma nf soul; (persona) person

almacén nm (depósito) warehouse, store (US), shop (BRIT); (MIL) magazine; (CS: de comestibles) grocery (US), grocer's (shop) (BRIT); **grandes almacenes** department store sg □ **almacenaje** nm storage

almacenar vt to store, put in storage; (proveerse) to stock up with □ **almacenero** (CS) nm storekeeper (US), shopkeeper (BRIT)

almanaque nm almanac

almeja nf clam

almendra nf almond □ **almendro** nm almond tree

almíbar nm syrup

almidón nm starch □ **almidonar** vt to starch

almirante nm admiral

almirez nm mortar

almizcle nm musk

almohada nf pillow; (funda) pillowcase □ **almohadilla** nf cushion; (para alfileres) pincushion; (TEC) pad

almohadón nm large pillow; bolster

almorranas nfpl piles, hemorrhoids (US), haemorrhoids (BRIT)

almorzar vt: **~ una tortilla** to have an omelette for lunch ♦ vi to (have) lunch

almuerzo etc vb ver **almorzar** ♦ nm lunch

alocado, -a adj crazy

alojamiento nm lodging(s) pl; (viviendas) housing

alojar vt to lodge; **alojarse** vr to lodge, stay

alondra nf lark, skylark

alpargata nf rope-soled sandal, espadrille

Alpes nmpl: **los ~** the Alps

alpinismo nm mountaineering, climbing □ **alpinista** nmf mountaineer, climber

alpiste nm birdseed

alquilar vt (propietario: inmuebles) to let, rent out; (: carro) to rent (out), hire (out) (BRIT); (: TV) to rent (out); (alquilador: inmuebles, TV) to rent; (: carro) to rent, hire (BRIT); **"se alquila casa"** "house for rent (US) o to let (BRIT)"

alquiler nm renting; letting; (arriendo) rent; rental fee (US), hire charge (BRIT); ~ de automóviles car rental (US), car hire (BRIT); de ~ for rent, for hire (BRIT)

alquimia nf alchemy

alquitrán nm tar

alrededor adv around, about; ~ de around, about; **mirar a su** ~ to look (around) about one ❏ **alrededores** nmpl surroundings

alta nf (certificate of) discharge; **dar de** ~ to discharge

altanería nf haughtiness, arrogance ❏ **altanero, -a** adj arrogant, haughty

altar nm altar

altavoz nm loudspeaker; (amplificador) amplifier

alteración nf alteration; (alboroto) disturbance

alterar vt to alter; to disturb; **alterarse** vr (persona) to get upset

altercado nm argument

alternar vt to alternate ♦ vi to alternate; (turnar) to take turns; **alternarse** vr to alternate; to take turns; ~ **con** to mix with ❏ **alternativa** nf alternative; (elección) choice ❏ **alternativo, -a** adj alternative; (alterno) alternating ❏ **alterno, -a** adj alternate; (ELEC) alternating

Alteza nf (tratamiento) Highness

altibajos nmpl ups and downs

altiplanicie nf high plateau

altiplano nm = **altiplanicie**

altisonante adj high-flown, high-sounding

altitud nf height; (AVIAT, GEO) altitude

altivez nf haughtiness, arrogance ❏ **altivo, -a** adj haughty, arrogant

alto, -a adj high; (persona) tall; (sonido) high, sharp; (noble) high, lofty ♦ nm halt; (MÚS) alto; (GEO) hill ♦ adv (de sitio) high; (de sonido) loud, loudly ♦ excl halt!; **la pared tiene 2 metros de** ~ the wall is 2 meters high; **en alta mar** on the high seas; **en voz alta** in a loud voice; **las altas horas de la noche** the small o wee hours; **en lo** ~ **de** at the top of; **pasar por** ~ to overlook

altoparlante (LAm) nm loudspeaker

altruismo nm altruism

altura nf height; (NÁUT) depth; (GEO) latitude; **la pared tiene 1.80 de** ~ the wall is 1 meter 80cm high; **a estas** ~**s** at this stage; **a estas** ~**s del año** at this time of the year

alubia nf bean

alucinación nf hallucination

alucinar vi to hallucinate ♦ vt to deceive; (fascinar) to fascinate

alud nm avalanche; (fig) flood

aludir vi: ~ **a** to allude to; **darse por aludido** to take the hint

alumbrado nm lighting ❏ **alumbramiento** nm lighting; (MED) childbirth, delivery

alumbrar vt to light (up) ♦ vi (MED) to give birth

aluminio nm aluminum (US), aluminium (BRIT)

alumno, -a nm/f pupil, student

alunizar vi to land on the moon

alusión nf allusion

alusivo, -a adj allusive

aluvión nm alluvium; (fig) flood

alverja (LAm) nf pea

alza nf rise; (MIL) sight

alzada nf (de caballos) height; (JUR) appeal

alzamiento nm (rebelión) rising

alzar vt to lift (up); (precio, muro) to raise; (cuello de abrigo) to turn up; (AGR) to gather in; (IMPRENTA) to gather; **alzarse** vr to get up, rise; (rebelarse) to revolt; (COM) to go fraudulently bankrupt; (JUR) to appeal

ama nf lady of the house; (dueña) owner; (institutriz) governess; (madre adoptiva) foster mother ▶ **ama de casa** housewife ▶ **ama de llaves** housekeeper

amabilidad nf kindness; (simpatía) niceness ❏ **amable** adj kind; nice; **es usted muy amable** that's very kind of you

amaestrado, -a adj (animal: en circo etc) performing

amaestrar vt to train

amago nm threat; (gesto) threatening gesture; (MED) symptom

amainar vi (viento) to die down

amalgama nf amalgam ❏ **amalgamar** vt to amalgamate; (combinar) to combine, mix

amamantar vt to suckle, nurse

amanecer vi to dawn ♦ nm dawn; ~ **afiebrado** to wake up with a fever

amanerado, -a adj affected

amansar vt to tame; (persona) to subdue; **amansarse** vr (persona) to calm down

amante adj: ~ **de** fond of ♦ nmf lover

amapola nf poppy

amar vt to love

amargado, -a adj bitter

amargar vt to make bitter; (fig) to embitter; **amargarse** vr to become embittered

amargo, -a adj bitter □ **amargura** nf bitterness

amarillento, -a adj yellowish; (tez) sallow □ **amarillo, -a** adj, nm yellow

amarrado, -a (MÉX: fam) adj mean, stingy

amarrar vt to moor; (sujetar) to tie up

amarras nfpl: **soltar ~** to set sail

amasar vt (masa) to knead; (mezclar) to mix, prepare; (confeccionar) to concoct □ **amasijo** nm kneading; mixing; (fig) hodgepodge (US), hotchpotch (BRIT)

amateur nmf amateur

amazona nf horsewoman □ **Amazonas** nm: **el Amazonas** the Amazon

ambages nmpl: **sin ~** in plain language

ámbar nm amber

ambición nf ambition □ **ambicionar** vt to aspire to □ **ambicioso, -a** adj ambitious

ambidextro, -a adj ambidextrous

ambientación nf (CINE, TEATRO etc) setting; (RADIO) sound effects

ambiente nm atmosphere; (medio) environment

ambigüedad nf ambiguity □ **ambiguo, -a** adj ambiguous

ámbito nm (campo) field; (fig) scope

ambos, -as adj pl, pron pl both

ambulancia nf ambulance

ambulante adj itinerant, traveling cpd (US), travelling cpd (BRIT)

ambulatorio (ESP) nm out-patients department

amedrentar vt to scare

amén excl amen; **~ de** besides

amenaza nf threat

amenazar vt to threaten ♦ vi: **~ con hacer** to threaten to do

amenidad nf pleasantness

ameno, -a adj pleasant

América nf America ▶ **América Central/Latina** Central/Latin America ▶ **América del Norte/Sur** North/South America □ **americana** (ESP) nf coat, jacket; ver tb **americano** □ **americano, -a** adj, nm/f American

amerizar vi (nave) to land (on the sea)

ametralladora nf machine gun

amianto nm asbestos

amigable adj friendly

amígdala nf tonsil □ **amigdalitis** nf tonsillitis

amigo, -a adj friendly ♦ nm/f friend; (amante) lover; **ser ~ de algo** to be fond of sth; **ser muy ~s** to be close friends

amilanar vt to scare; **amilanarse** vr to get scared

aminorar vt to diminish; (reducir) to reduce; **~ la marcha** to slow down

amistad nf friendship; **~es** nfpl (amigos) friends □ **amistoso, -a** adj friendly

amnesia nf amnesia

amnistía nf amnesty

amo nm owner; (jefe) boss

amodorrarse vr to get sleepy

amolar (MÉX: fam) vt to ruin, damage

amoldar vt to mold; (adaptar) to adapt

amonestación nf warning; **amonestaciones** nfpl (REL) marriage banns

amonestar vt to warn; (REL) to publish the banns of

amontonar vt to collect, pile up; **amontonarse** vr to crowd together; (acumularse) to pile up

amor nm love; (amante) lover; **hacer el ~** to make love ▶ **amor propio** self-respect

amoratado, -a adj purple

amordazar vt to muzzle; (fig) to gag

amorfo, -a adj amorphous, shapeless

amoroso, -a adj affectionate, loving

amortajar vt to shroud

amortiguador nm shock absorber; (parachoques) bumper, fender (US); **~es** nmpl (AUTO) suspension sg

amortiguar vt to deaden; (ruido) to muffle; (color) to soften

amortización nf (de deuda) repayment; (de bono) redemption

amotinar vt to stir up, incite (to riot); **amotinarse** vr to mutiny

amparar vt to protect; **ampararse** vr to seek protection; (de la lluvia etc) to shelter □ **amparo** nm help, protection; **al amparo de** under the protection of

amperio nm ampere, amp

ampliación nf enlargement; (extensión) extension

ampliar vt to enlarge; to extend

amplificación nf enlargement □ **amplificador** nm amplifier

amplificar vt to amplify

amplio, -a adj spacious; (de falda etc) full; (extenso) extensive; (ancho) wide □ **amplitud** nf spaciousness; extent; (fig) amplitude

ampolla nf blister; (MED) ampoule

ampuloso, -a adj bombastic, pompous

amputar vt to cut off, amputate

amueblar vt to furnish

amurallar vt to wall up o in

anacronismo nm anachronism

anales nmpl annals

analfabetismo nm illiteracy ❑ **analfabeto, -a** adj, nm/f illiterate

analgésico nm painkiller, analgesic

análisis nm inv analysis

analista nmf (gen) analyst

analizar vt to analyze (US), analyse (BRIT)

analogía nf analogy

analógico, -a adj (INFORM) analog; (reloj) analogue, analog (US)

análogo, -a adj analogous, similar

ananá (RPl) nm pineapple

anaquel nm shelf

anarquía nf anarchy ❑ **anarquismo** nm anarchism ❑ **anarquista** nmf anarchist

anatomía nf anatomy

anca nf rump, haunch; **~s** nfpl (fam) behind sg

ancho, -a adj wide; (falda) full; (fig) liberal ♦ nm width; (FERRO) gauge; **ponerse ~** to get conceited; **estar a sus anchas** to be at one's ease

anchoa nf anchovy

anchura nf width; (extensión) wideness

anciano, -a adj old, aged ♦ nm/f old man (woman); elder

ancla nf anchor ❑ **ancladero** nm anchorage ❑ **anclar** vi to (drop) anchor

andadura nf gait; (de caballo) pace

Andalucía nf Andalusia ❑ **andaluz, a** adj, nm/f Andalusian

andamiaje nm = **andamio**

andamio nm scaffold(ing)

andar vt to go, cover, travel ♦ vi to go, walk, travel; (funcionar) to go, work; (estar) to be ♦ nm walk, gait, pace; **andarse** vr to go away; **~ a pie/a caballo/en bicicleta** to go on foot/ on horseback/by bicycle; **~ haciendo algo** to be doing sth; **¡anda!** (sorpresa) hey!; **anda por** o **en los 40** he's about 40; **¡ándale!** (MÉX: fam) come on!, hurry up!

andén nm (FERRO) platform; (NÁUT) quayside; (CAm: de la calle) sidewalk (US), pavement (BRIT)

Andes nmpl: **los ~** the Andes

andinismo (LAm) nm mountaineering, climbing

Andorra nf Andorra

andrajo nm rag ❑ **andrajoso, -a** adj ragged

anduve etc vb ver **andar**

anécdota nf anecdote, story

anegar vt to flood; (ahogar) to drown; **anegarse** vr to drown; (hundirse) to sink

anejo, -a adj, nm = **anexo**

anemia nf anemia (US), anaemia (BRIT)

anestesia nf (sustancia) anesthetic (US), anaesthetic (BRIT); (proceso) anesthesia (US), anaesthesia (BRIT)

anexar vt to annex; (documento) to attach ❑ **anexión** nf annexation ❑ **anexionamiento** nm annexation ❑ **anexo, -a** adj attached ♦ nm annex (US), annexe (BRIT)

anfibio, -a adj amphibious ♦ nm amphibian

anfiteatro nm amphitheater (US), amphitheatre (BRIT); (TEATRO) dress circle

anfitrión, -ona nm/f host(ess)

ánfora nf (cántaro) amphora; (MÉX POL) ballot box

ángel nm angel; **tener ~** to be charming ▶ **ángel de la guarda** guardian angel ❑ **angelical, angélico, a** adj angelic(al)

angina nf (MED) inflammation of the throat; **tener ~s** to have tonsillitis ▶ **angina de pecho** angina

anglicano, -a adj, nm/f Anglican

anglosajón, -ona adj Anglo-Saxon

angosto, -a adj narrow

anguila nf eel

angula nf elver, baby eel

ángulo nm angle; (esquina) corner; (curva) bend

angustia nf anguish ❑ **angustiar** vt to distress, grieve

anhelar vt to be eager for; (desear) to long for, desire ♦ vi to pant, gasp ❑ **anhelo** nm eagerness; desire

anidar vi to nest

anillo nm ring ▶ **anillo de boda** wedding ring

animación nf liveliness; (vitalidad) life; (actividad) activity; bustle

animado, -a adj lively; (vivaz) animated ❑ **animador, a** nm/f (TV) host(ess), compere (BRIT); (DEPORTE) cheerleader

animadversión nf ill-will, antagonism

animal adj animal; (fig) stupid ♦ nm animal; (fig) fool; (bestia) brute

animar vt (BIO) to animate, give life to; (fig) to liven up, brighten up, cheer up; (estimular) to stimulate; **animarse** vr to cheer up; to feel encouraged; (decidirse) to make up one's mind

ánimo nm (alma) soul; (mente) mind; (valentía) courage ♦ excl cheer up!

animoso, -a *adj* brave; (*vivo*) lively

aniquilar *vt* to annihilate, destroy

anís *nm* aniseed; (*licor*) anisette

aniversario *nm* anniversary

anoche *adv* last night; **antes de ~** the night before last

anochecer *vi* to get dark ♦ *nm* nightfall, dark; **al ~** at nightfall

anodino, -a *adj* dull, anodyne

anomalía *nf* anomaly

anonadado, -a *adj*: **estar/quedar/ sentirse ~** to be overwhelmed *o* amazed

anonimato *nm* anonymity

anónimo, -a *adj* anonymous; (*COM*) limited ♦ *nm* (*carta anónima*) anonymous letter; (: *maliciosa*) poison-pen letter

anormal *adj* abnormal

anotación *nf* note; annotation

anotar *vt* to note down; (*comentar*) to annotate

anquilosamiento *nm* (*fig*) paralysis; stagnation

anquilosarse *vr* (*fig*: *persona*) to get out of touch; (*método, costumbres*) to go out of date

ansia *nf* anxiety; (*añoranza*) yearning; **no comas ~s** (*MÉX*) don't worry ❏ **ansiar** *vt* to long for

ansiedad *nf* anxiety

ansioso, -a *adj* anxious; (*anhelante*) eager; **~ de** *o* **por algo** greedy for sth

antagónico, -a *adj* antagonistic; (*opuesto*) contrasting ❏ **antagonista** *nmf* antagonist

antaño *adv* long ago, formerly

Antártico *nm*: **el ~** the Antarctic

ante *prep* before, in the presence of; (*problema etc*) faced with ♦ *nm* (*piel*) suede; **~ todo** above all

anteanoche *adv* the night before last

anteayer *adv* the day before yesterday

antebrazo *nm* forearm

antecedente *adj* previous ♦ *nm* antecedent; **~s** *nmpl* (*historial*) record *sg* ▶ **antecedentes penales** criminal record

anteceder *vt* to precede, go before

antecesor, a *nm/f* predecessor

antedicho, -a *adj* aforementioned

antelación *nf*: **con ~** in advance

antemano: de ~ *adv* beforehand, in advance

antena *nf* antenna; (*de televisión etc*) aerial ▶ **antena parabólica** satellite dish, dish antenna (*US*)

antenoche (*LAm*) *adv* the night before last

anteojo *nm* eyeglass; **~s** *nmpl* (*LAm*: *gafas*) glasses, eyeglasses (*US*)

antepasados *nmpl* ancestors

anteponer *vt* to place in front; (*fig*) to prefer

anteproyecto *nm* preliminary sketch; (*fig*) blueprint

anterior *adj* preceding, previous ❏ **anterioridad** *nf*: **con anterioridad a** prior to, before

antes *adv* (*con prioridad*) before ♦ *prep*: **~ de** before ♦ *conj*: **~ de ir/de que te vayas** before going/before you go; **~ bien** (but) rather; **dos días ~** two days before *o* previously; **no quiso venir ~** she didn't want to come any earlier; **tomo el avión ~ que el barco** I take the plane rather than the boat; **~ que yo** before me; **lo ~ posible** as soon as possible; **cuanto ~ mejor** the sooner the better; **~ no** (*MÉX*) just as well, luckily

antiaéreo, -a *adj* anti-aircraft

antibalas *adj inv*: **chaleco ~** bullet-proof jacket

antibiótico *nm* antibiotic

anticipación *nf* anticipation; **con 10 minutos de ~** 10 minutes early

anticipado, -a *adj* (*pago*) advance; **por ~** in advance

anticipar *vt* to anticipate; (*adelantar*) to bring forward; (*COM*) to advance; **anticiparse** *vr*: **~se a su época** to be ahead of one's time

anticipo *nm* (*COM*) advance

anticonceptivo, -a *adj, nm* contraceptive

anticongelante *nm* antifreeze

anticuado, -a *adj* out-of-date, old-fashioned; (*desusado*) obsolete

anticuario *nm* antique dealer

anticuerpo *nm* (*MED*) antibody

antidepresivo *nm* antidepressant

antídoto *nm* antidote

antiestético, -a *adj* unsightly

antifaz *nm* mask; (*velo*) veil

antiglobalización *nf* anti-globalization ❏ **antiglobalizador, a** *adj* anti-globalization *cpd*

antigualla *nf* antique; (*reliquia*) relic

antiguamente *adv* formerly; (*hace mucho tiempo*) long ago

antigüedad *nf* antiquity; (*artículo*) antique; (*rango*) seniority

antiguo, -a *adj* old, ancient; (*que fue*) former

Antillas *nfpl*: **las ~** the West Indies

antílope *nm* antelope

antinatural *adj* unnatural

antipatía nf antipathy, dislike
❑ **antipático, -a** adj disagreeable, unpleasant

antirrobo adj inv (alarma etc) anti-theft

antisemita adj anti-Semitic ♦ nmf anti-Semite

antiséptico, -a adj antiseptic ♦ nm antiseptic

antítesis nf inv antithesis

antojadizo, -a adj capricious

antojarse vr (desear): **se me antoja comprarlo** I have a mind to buy it; (pensar): **se me antoja que** I have a feeling that

antojitos (MÉX) nmpl snacks, nibbles

antojo nm caprice, whim; (rosa) birthmark; (lunar) mole

antología nf anthology

antorcha nf flashlight, torch

antro nm cavern

antropófago, -a adj, nm/f cannibal

antropología nf anthropology

anual adj annual

anuario nm yearbook

anudar vt to knot, tie; (unir) to join; **anudarse** vr to get tied up

anulación nf annulment; (cancelación) cancellation

anular vt (contrato) to annul, cancel; (ley) to revoke, repeal; (suscripción) to cancel ♦ nm ring finger

Anunciación nf (REL) Annunciation

anunciante nmf (COM) advertiser

anunciar vt to announce; (proclamar) to proclaim; (COM) to advertise

anuncio nm announcement; (señal) sign; (COM) advertisement; (cartel) poster

anzuelo nm hook; (para pescar) fish hook

añadidura nf addition, extra; **por ~** besides, in addition

añadir vt to add

añejo, -a adj old; (vino) mellow

añicos nmpl: **hacer ~** to smash, shatter

añil nm (BOT: color) indigo

año nm year; **¡Feliz A~ Nuevo!** Happy New Year!; **tener 15 ~s** to be 15 (years old); **los ~s 90** the nineties; **el ~ que viene** next year ► **año bisiesto/escolar** leap/school year

añoranza nf nostalgia; (anhelo) longing

apa (MÉX) excl goodness me!, good gracious!

apabullar vt to crush, squash

apacentar vt to pasture, graze

apacible adj gentle, mild

apaciguar vt to pacify, calm (down)

apadrinar vt to sponsor, support; (REL) to be godfather to

apagado, -a adj (volcán) extinct; (color) dull; (voz) quiet; (sonido) muted, muffled; (persona: apático) listless; **estar ~** (fuego, luz) to be out; (RADIO, TV etc) to be off

apagar vt to put out; (ELEC, RADIO, TV) to switch off; (sonido) to silence, muffle; (sed) to quench

apagón nm power outage (US), power cut (BRIT)

apalabrar vt to agree to; (contratar) to engage

apalear vt to beat, thrash

apantallar (MÉX) vt to impress

apañar vt to pick up; (asir) to take hold of, grasp; (reparar) to mend, patch up; **apañarse** vr to manage, get along

apapachar (MÉX: fam) vt to cuddle, hug

aparador nm sideboard; (MÉX: escaparate) store (US) o shop (BRIT) window

aparato nm apparatus; (máquina) machine; (doméstico) appliance; (boato) ostentation ► **aparato de facsímil** facsimile (machine), fax ► **aparato digestivo** (ANAT) digestive system ❑ **aparatoso, -a** adj showy, ostentatious

aparcamiento (ESP) nm parking lot (US), car park (BRIT)

aparcar (ESP) vt, vi to park

aparear vt (objetos) to pair, match; (animales) to mate; **aparearse** vr to make a pair; to mate

aparecer vi to appear; **aparecerse** vr to appear

aparejado, -a adj fit, suitable; **llevar** o **traer ~ to** involve ❑ **aparejador, a** nm/f (ARQ) master builder

aparejo nm harness; rigging; (de poleas) block and tackle

aparentar vt (edad) to look; (fingir): **~ tristeza** to pretend to be sad

aparente adj apparent; (adecuado) suitable

aparezco etc vb ver **aparecer**

aparición nf appearance; (de libro) publication; (espectro) apparition

apariencia nf (outward) appearance; **en ~** outwardly, seemingly

apartado, -a adj separate; (lejano) remote ♦ nm (tipográfico) paragraph ► **apartado de correos** (ESP) post office box ► **apartado postal** (LAm) post office box

apartamento nm apartment, flat (BRIT)

apartamiento nm separation; (aislamiento) remoteness, isolation

apartar vt to separate; (quitar) to remove; **apartarse** vr to separate, part; (irse) to move away; to keep away

aparte adv (separadamente) separately; (además) besides ♦ nm aside; (tipográfico) new paragraph

aparthotel nm serviced apartments

apasionado, -a adj passionate

apasionar vt to excite; **apasionarse** vr to get excited; **le apasiona el tenis** she's crazy about tennis

apatía nf apathy

apático, -a adj apathetic

Apdo abr (= Apartado (de Correos)) PO Box

apeadero nm halt, stop, stopping place

apearse vr (jinete) to dismount; (bajarse) to get down o out; (AUTO, FERRO) to get off o out

apechugar vr: ~ **con algo** to face up to sth

apedrear vt to stone

apegarse vr: ~ **a** to become attached to ☐ **apego** nm attachment, devotion

apelación nf appeal

apelar vi to appeal; ~ **a** (fig) to resort to

apellidar vt to call, name; **apellidarse** vr: **se apellida Pérez** her surname o last name (US) is Perez

apellido nm surname, last name (US)

apelmazarse vr (masa, arroz) to go hard; (prenda de lana) to shrink

apenar vt to grieve, trouble; (LAm: avergonzar) to embarrass; **apenarse** vr to grieve; (LAm: avergonzarse) to be embarrassed

apenas adv scarcely, hardly ♦ conj as soon as, no sooner

apéndice nm appendix ☐ **apendicitis** nf appendicitis

aperitivo nm (bebida) aperitif; (comida) appetizer

apero nm (AGR) implement; ~**s** nmpl farm equipment sg

apertura nf opening; (POL) liberalization

apesadumbrar vt to grieve, sadden; **apesadumbrarse** vr to distress o.s.

apestar vt to infect ♦ vi: ~ **(a)** to stink (of)

apetecer (ESP) vt: **¿te apetece un café?** do you fancy a (cup of) coffee? ☐ **apetecible** adj desirable; (comida) appetizing

apetito nm appetite ☐ **apetitoso, -a** adj appetizing; (fig) tempting

apiadarse vr: ~ **de** to take pity on

ápice nm whit, iota

apilar vt to pile o heap up; **apilarse** vr to pile up

apiñarse vr to crowd o press together

apio nm celery

apisonadora nf steamroller

aplacar vt to placate; **aplacarse** vr to calm down

aplanar vt to smooth, level; (allanar) to roll flat, flatten

aplastante adj overwhelming; (lógica) compelling

aplastar vt to squash (flat); (fig) to crush

aplatanarse vr to get lethargic

aplaudir vt to applaud

aplauso nm applause; (fig) approval, acclaim

aplazamiento nm postponement

aplazar vt to postpone, defer

aplicación nf application; (esfuerzo) effort

aplicado, -a adj diligent, hard-working

aplicar vt (ejecutar) to apply; **aplicarse** vr to apply o.s.

aplique etc vb ver **aplicar** ♦ nm wall light

aplomo nm aplomb, self-assurance

apocado, -a adj timid

apodar vt to nickname

apoderado nm agent, representative

apoderarse vr: ~ **de** to take possession of

apodo nm nickname

apogeo nm peak, summit

apolillarse vr to get moth-eaten

apología nf eulogy; (defensa) defense (US), defence (BRIT)

⚠ No confundir **apología** con la palabra inglesa **apology**.

apoltronarse vr to get lazy

apoplejía nf apoplexy, stroke

apoquinar (fam) vt to fork out, cough up

aporrear vt to beat (up)

aportar vt to contribute ♦ vi to reach port; **aportarse** vr (LAm: llegar) to arrive, come

aposento nm lodging; (habitación) room

aposta adv deliberately, on purpose

apostar vt to bet, stake; (tropas etc) to station, post ♦ vi to bet

apóstol nm apostle

apóstrofo nm apostrophe

apoyar vt to lean, rest; (fig) to support, back; **apoyarse** vr: ~**se en** to lean on ☐ **apoyo** nm (gen) support; backing, help

apreciable adj considerable; (fig) esteemed

apreciar vt to evaluate, assess; (COM) to appreciate, value; (persona) to respect; (tamaño) to gauge, assess; (detalles) to notice

aprecio nm valuation, estimate; (fig) appreciation

aprehender vt to apprehend, detain

apremiante adj urgent, pressing

apremiar vt to compel, force ♦ vi to be urgent, press ◻ **apremio** nm urgency

aprender vt, vi to learn

aprendiz, a nm/f apprentice; (principiante) learner ▸ **aprendiz de conductor** learner driver ◻ **aprendizaje** nm apprenticeship

aprensión nm apprehension, fear ◻ **aprensivo, -a** adj apprehensive

apresar vt to seize; (capturar) to capture

aprestar vt to prepare, get ready; (TEC) to prime, size; **aprestarse** vr to get ready

apresurado, -a adj hurried, hasty ◻ **apresuramiento** nm hurry, haste

apresurar vt to hurry, accelerate; **apresurarse** vr to hurry, make haste

apretado, -a adj tight; (escritura) cramped

apretar vt to squeeze; (TEC) to tighten; (presionar) to press together, pack ♦ vi to be too tight

apretón nm squeeze ▸ **apretón de manos** handshake

aprieto nm squeeze; (dificultad) difficulty; **estar en un ~** to be in a fix

aprisa adv quickly, hurriedly

aprisionar vt to imprison

aprobación nf approval

aprobar vt to approve (of); (examen, materia) to pass ♦ vi to pass

apropiación nf appropriation

apropiado, -a adj suitable

apropiarse vr: ~ **de** to appropriate

aprovechado, -a adj industrious, hard-working; (económico) thrifty; (pey) unscrupulous ◻ **aprovechamiento** nm use; exploitation

aprovechar vt to use; (explotar) to exploit; (experiencia) to profit from; (oferta, oportunidad) to take advantage of ♦ vi to progress, improve; **aprovecharse** vr: ~**se de** to make use of; to take advantage of; ¡**que aproveche!** enjoy your meal!

aproximación nf approximation; (de lotería) consolation prize ◻ **aproximado, -a** adj approximate

aproximar vt to bring nearer; **aproximarse** vr to come near, approach

apruebo etc vb ver **aprobar**

aptitud nf aptitude

apto, -a adj suitable

apuesta nf bet, wager

apuesto, -a adj neat, elegant

apuntador nm prompter

apuntalar vt to prop up

apuntar vt (con arma) to aim at; (con dedo) to point at o to; (anotar) to note (down); (TEATRO) to prompt; **apuntarse** vr (DEPORTE: tanto, victoria) to score; (ESCOL) to enroll (US), enrol (BRIT)

⚠ No confundir **apuntar** con la palabra inglesa **appoint**.

apunte nm note

apuñalar vt to stab

apurado, -a adj needy; (difícil) difficult; (peligroso) dangerous; (LAm: con prisa) hurried, rushed

apurar vt (agotar) to drain; (recursos) to use up; (molestar) to annoy; **apurarse** vr (preocuparse) to worry; (LAm: darse prisa) to hurry

apuro nm (aprieto) fix, jam; (escasez) want, hardship; (vergüenza) embarrassment; (LAm: prisa) haste, urgency

aquejado, -a adj: ~ **de** (MED) afflicted by

aquel (f ~la, pl ~los, as) adj that; (pl) those

aquél (f ~la, pl ~los, as) pron that (one); (pl) those (ones)

aquello pron for that, that business

aquí adv (lugar) here; (tiempo) now; ~ **arriba** up here; ~ **mismo** right here; ~ **yace** here lies; **de ~ a siete días** a week from now

aquietar vt to calm (down), quiet (US) o quieten (BRIT) (down)

ara nf: **en ~s de** for the sake of

árabe adj, nmf Arab ♦ nm (LING) Arabic

Arabia nf Arabia ▸ **Arabia Saudí** o **Saudita** Saudi Arabia

arado nm plow

Aragón nm Aragon ◻ **aragonés, -esa** adj, nm/f Aragonese

arancel nm tariff, duty ▸ **arancel de aduanas** customs (duty)

arandela nf (TEC) washer

araña nf (ZOOL) spider; (lámpara) chandelier

arañar vt to scratch

arañazo nm scratch

arar vt to plow, till

arbitraje nm arbitration

arbitrar vt to arbitrate in; (DEPORTE) to referee ♦ vi to arbitrate

arbitrariedad nf arbitrariness; (acto) arbitrary act ◻ **arbitrario, -a** adj arbitrary

arbitrio nm free will; (JUR) adjudication, decision

árbitro nm arbitrator; (DEPORTE) referee; (TENIS) umpire

árbol nm (BOT) tree; (NÁUT) mast; (TEC) axle, shaft ❑ **arbolado, -a** adj wooded; (camino etc) tree-lined ♦ nm woodland

arboleda nf grove, plantation

arbusto nm bush, shrub

arca nf chest, box

arcada nf arcade; (de puente) arch, span; ~**s** nfpl (náuseas) retching sg

arcaico, -a adj archaic

arce nm maple tree

arcén nm (de autopista) berm (US), shoulder (US), hard shoulder (BRIT); (de carretera) verge

archipiélago nm archipelago

archivador nm filing cabinet

archivar vt to file (away) ❑ **archivo** nm file, archive(s) pl ▶ **archivo adjunto** (INFORM) attachment

arcilla nf clay

arco nm arch; (MAT) arc; (MIL, MÚS) bow ▶ **arco iris** rainbow

arder vi to burn; **estar que arde** (persona) to fume

ardid nm ploy, trick

ardiente adj burning, ardent

ardilla nf squirrel

ardor nm (calor) heat; (fig) ardor (US), ardour (BRIT) ▶ **ardor de estómago** heartburn

arduo, -a adj arduous

área nf area; (DEPORTE) penalty area

arena nf sand; (DEPORTE) arena ▶ **arenas movedizas** quicksand sg

arenal nm (arena movediza) quicksand

arengar vt to harangue

arenisca nf sandstone; (cascajo) grit

arenoso, -a adj sandy

arenque nm herring

arete (MÉX) nm earring

argamasa nf mortar, plaster

Argel n Algiers ❑ **Argelia** nf Algeria ❑ **argelino, -a** adj, nm/f Algerian

Argentina nf: (la) ~ Argentina

argentino, -a adj Argentinian; (de plata) silvery ♦ nm/f Argentinian

argolla nf (large) ring

argot (pl ~**s**) nm slang

argucia nf subtlety, sophistry

argüir vt to deduce; (discutir) to argue; (indicar) to indicate, imply; (censurar) to reproach ♦ vi to argue

argumentación nf (line of) argument

argumentar vt, vi to argue

argumento nm argument; (razonamiento) reasoning; (de novela etc) plot; (CINE, TV) storyline

aria nf aria

aridez nf aridity, dryness

árido, -a adj arid, dry ❑ **áridos** nmpl (COM) dry goods

Aries nm Aries

ario, -a adj Aryan

arisco, -a adj surly; (insociable) unsociable

aristócrata nmf aristocrat

aritmética nf arithmetic

arma nf arm; ~**s** nfpl arms ▶ **arma blanca** blade, knife ▶ **arma de fuego** firearm ▶ **armas cortas** small arms

armada nf armada; (flota) fleet

armadillo nm armadillo

armado, -a adj armed; (TEC) reinforced

armador nm (NÁUT) shipowner

armadura nf (MIL) armor (US), armour (BRIT); (TEC) framework; (ZOOL) skeleton; (FÍSICA) armature

armamento nm armament; (NÁUT) fitting-out

armar vt (soldado) to arm; (máquina) to assemble; (navío) to fit out; ~**la, ~ un lío** to start a row, kick up a fuss

armario nm (de ropa) closet (US), wardrobe; (de cocina, baño) closet (US), cupboard

armatoste nm (mueble) monstrosity; (máquina) contraption

armazón nm o f body, chassis; (de mueble etc) frame; (ARQ) skeleton

armería nf gunsmith's

armiño nm stoat; (piel) ermine

armisticio nm armistice

armonía nf harmony

armónica nf harmonica

armonioso, -a adj harmonious

armonizar vt to harmonize; (diferencias) to reconcile ♦ vi: ~ **con** (fig) to be in keeping with; (colores) to tone in with, blend

arnés nm armor (US), armour (BRIT); **arneses** nmpl (de caballo etc) harness sg

aro nm ring; (tejo) quoit; (CS: pendiente) earring

aroma nm aroma, scent

aromático, -a adj aromatic

arpa nf harp

arpía nf shrew

arpillera nf sacking, sackcloth

arpón nm harpoon

arquear vt to arch, bend; **arquearse** vr to arch, bend

arqueología nf archeology (US), archaeology (BRIT) ❑ **arqueólogo, -a** nm/f archeologist (US), archaeolgist (BRIT)

arquero nm archer, bowman

arquetipo nm archetype

arquitecto nm architect ❑ **arquitectura** nf architecture

arrabal nm poor suburb, slum; ~**es** nmpl (afueras) outskirts

arraigado, -a adj deep-rooted; (fig) established

arraigar vt to establish ♦ vi to take root; **arraigarse** vr to take root; (persona) to settle

arrancar vt (sacar) to extract, pull out; (arrebatar) to snatch (away); (INFORM) to boot; (fig) to extract ♦ vi (AUTO, máquina) to start; (ponerse en marcha) to get going; ~ **de** to stem from

arranque etc vb ver **arrancar** ♦ nm sudden start; (AUTO) start; (fig) fit, outburst

arrasar vt (aplanar) to level, flatten; (destruir) to demolish

arrastrado, -a adj poor, wretched; (RPl: servil) servile

arrastrar vt to drag (along); (fig) to drag down, degrade; (agua, viento) to carry away ♦ vi to drag, trail on the ground; **arrastrarse** vr to crawl; (fig) to grovel; **llevar algo arrastrado** to drag sth along

arrastre nm drag, dragging

arre excl gee up!

arrear vt to drive on, urge on ♦ vi to hurry along

arrebatado, -a adj rash, impetuous; (repentino) sudden, hasty

arrebatar vt to snatch (away), seize; (fig) to captivate; **arrebatarse** vr to get carried away, get excited

arrebato nm fit of rage, fury; (éxtasis) rapture

arrecife nm reef

arredrarse vr: ~ (ante algo) to be intimidated (by sth)

arreglado, -a adj (ordenado) neat, orderly; (moderado) moderate, reasonable

arreglar vt (poner orden) to tidy up; (algo roto) to fix, repair; (problema) to solve; **arreglarse** vr to reach an understanding; **arreglárselas** (fam) to get by, manage

arreglo nm settlement; (orden) order; (acuerdo) agreement; (MÚS) arrangement, setting

arrellanarse vr: ~ **en** to sit back in/on

arremangar vt to roll up, turn up; **arremangarse** vr to roll up one's sleeves

arremeter vi: ~ **contra** to attack, rush at

arrendamiento nm (de vivienda) renting; (de máquina) renting, hiring (BRIT) ❑ **arrendar** vt to let, lease; to rent ❑ **arrendatario, -a** nm/f tenant

arreos nmpl (de caballo) harness sg, trappings

arrepentimiento nm regret, repentance

arrepentirse vr to repent; ~ **de** to regret

arrestar vt to arrest; (encarcelar) to imprison ❑ **arresto** nm arrest; (MIL) detention; (audacia) boldness, daring ▶ **arresto domiciliario** house arrest

arriar vt (velas) to haul down; (bandera) to lower, strike; (cable) to pay out

---

arriba

PALABRA CLAVE

adv

1 (posición) above; **desde arriba** from above; **arriba de todo** at the very top, right on top; **Juan está arriba** Juan is upstairs; **lo arriba mencionado** the aforementioned

2 (dirección): **calle arriba** up the street

3: **de arriba abajo** from top to bottom; **mirar a algn de arriba abajo** to look sb up and down

4: **para arriba**: **de 5000 pesos para arriba** from 5000 pesos up(wards)

♦ adj: **de arriba**: **el piso de arriba** the upstairs apartment (US) o flat (BRIT); **la parte de arriba** the top o upper part

♦ prep: **arriba de** (LAm: por encima de) above; **arriba de 200 dólares** more than 200 dollars

♦ excl: **¡arriba!** up!; **¡manos arriba!** hands up!; **¡arriba México!** long live Mexico!

---

arribar vi to put into port; (llegar) to arrive

arribista nmf parvenu(e), upstart

arriendo etc vb ver **arrendar** ♦ nm = **arrendamiento**

arriero nm muleteer

arriesgado, -a adj (peligroso) risky; (audaz) bold, daring

arriesgar vt to risk; (poner en peligro) to endanger; **arriesgarse** vr to take a risk

arrimar vt (acercar) to bring close; (poner de lado) to set aside; **arrimarse** vr to come close o closer; ~**se a** to lean on

arrinconar vt (colocar) to put in a corner; (enemigo) to corner; (fig) to put on one side; (abandonar) to push aside

arrodillarse vr to kneel (down)

arrogancia nf arrogance ❑ **arrogante** adj arrogant

arrojar vt to throw, hurl; (humo) to emit, give out; (COM) to yield, produce; **arrojarse** vr to throw o hurl o.s.

arrojo nm daring

arrollador, a adj overwhelming

arrollar vt (AUTO etc) to run over, knock down; (DEPORTE) to crush

arropar vt to cover, wrap up; **arroparse** vr to wrap o.s. up

arroyo nm stream; (de la calle) gutter

arroz nm rice ▶ **arroz con leche** rice pudding

arruga nf (de cara) wrinkle; (de vestido) crease

arrugar vt to wrinkle; to crease; **arrugarse** vr to get creased

arruinar vt to ruin, wreck; **arruinarse** vr to be ruined, go bankrupt

arrullar vi to coo ♦ vt to lull to sleep

arsenal nm naval dockyard; (MIL) arsenal

arsénico nm arsenic

arte (gen m en sg y siempre f en pl) nm art; (maña) skill, guile; **~s** nfpl (bellas artes) arts

artefacto nm appliance

arteria nf artery

artesanía nf craftsmanship; (artículos) handicrafts pl □ **artesano, -a** nm/f artisan, craftsman(-woman)

ártico, -a adj Arctic ♦ nm: **el Á~** the Arctic

articulación nf articulation; (MED, TEC) joint □ **articulado, -a** adj articulated; jointed

articular vt to articulate; to join together

artículo nm article; (cosa) thing, article; **~s** nmpl (COM) goods

artífice nmf (fig) architect

artificial adj artificial

artificio nm art, skill; (astucia) cunning

artillería nf artillery

artillero nm artilleryman, gunner

artilugio nm gadget

artimaña nf trap, snare; (astucia) cunning

artista nmf (pintor) artist, painter; (TEATRO) artist, artiste ▶ **artista de cine** movie (US) o film (BRIT) actor (actress) □ **artístico, -a** adj artistic

artritis nf arthritis

arveja (LAm) nf pea

arzobispo nm archbishop

as nm ace

asa nf handle; (fig) lever

asado nm roast (meat); (LAm: barbacoa) barbecue

ASADO

Traditional Latin American barbecues, especially in the River Plate area, are celebrated in the open air around a large grill which is used to grill mainly beef and various kinds of spicy pork sausage. They are usually very common during the summer and can go on for several days. The head cook is nearly always a man.

---

asador nm spit

asadura (ESP) nf entrails pl, offal

asalariado, -a adj paid, salaried ♦ nm/f wage earner

asaltante nmf attacker

asaltar vt to attack, assault; (fig) to assail □ **asalto** nm attack, assault; (DEPORTE) round

asamblea nf assembly; (reunión) meeting

asar vt to roast

asbesto nm asbestos

ascendencia nf ancestry; (LAm: influencia) ascendancy; **de ~ francesa** of French origin

ascender vi (subir) to ascend, rise; (ser promovido) to gain promotion ♦ vt to promote; **~ a** to amount to □ **ascendiente** nm influence ♦ nmf ancestor

ascensión nf ascent; (REL): **la A~** the Ascension

ascenso nm ascent; (promoción) promotion

ascensor nm elevator (US), lift (BRIT)

ascético, -a adj ascetic

asco nm: **¡qué ~!** how revolting o disgusting!; **el ajo me da ~** I hate o loathe garlic; **estar hecho un ~** to be filthy; **poner a algn del ~** (MÉX: fam) to call sb all sorts of names

ascua nf ember; **estar en ~s** to be on tenterhooks

aseado, -a adj clean; (arreglado) tidy; (pulcro) smart

asear vt to clean, wash; to tidy (up)

asediar vt (MIL) to besiege, lay siege to; (fig) to chase, pester □ **asedio** nm siege; (COM) run

asegurado, -a adj insured

asegurador, a nm/f insurer

asegurar vt (consolidar) to secure, fasten; (dar garantía de) to guarantee; (preservar) to safeguard; (afirmar, dar por cierto) to assure, affirm; (tranquilizar) to reassure; (tomar un seguro) to insure; **asegurarse** vr to assure o.s., make sure

asemejarse vr to be alike; **~ a** to be like, resemble

asentado, -a adj established, settled

asentar vt (sentar) to seat, sit down; (poner) to place, establish; (alisar) to level, smooth down o out; (anotar) to note down ♦ vi to be suitable, suit

asentir vi to assent, agree; **~ con la cabeza** to nod (one's head)

aseo nm cleanliness

aséptico, -a adj germ-free, free from infection

asequible adj (precio) reasonable; (meta) attainable; (persona) approachable

aserradero nm sawmill ❑ **aserrar** vt to saw

asesinar vt to murder; (POL) to assassinate ❑ **asesinato** nm murder, homicide (US); (POL) assassination

asesino, -a nm/f murderer, killer; (POL) assassin

asesor, a nm/f adviser, consultant

asesorar vt (JUR) to advise, give legal advice to; (COM) to act as consultant to; **asesorarse** vr: **~se con** o **de** to take advice from, consult ❑ **asesoría** nf (cargo) consultancy; (oficina) consultant's office

asestar vt (golpe) to deal, strike

asfalto nm asphalt, blacktop (US)

asfixia nf asphyxia, suffocation

asfixiar vt to asphyxiate, suffocate; **asfixiarse** vr to be asphyxiated, suffocate

asgo etc vb ver **asir**

así adv (de esta manera) in this way, like this, thus; (aunque) although; (tan pronto como) as soon as; **~ que** so; **~ como** as well as; **~ y todo** even so; **¿no es ~?** isn't it?, didn't you? etc; **~ de grande** this big; **¡~ nomás!** (LAm: fam) anyhow, just like that

Asia nf Asia ❑ **asiático, -a** adj, nm/f Asian, Asiatic

asidero nm handle

asiduidad nf assiduousness ❑ **asiduo, -a** adj assiduous; (frecuente) frequent ♦ nm/f regular (customer)

asiento nm (mueble) seat, chair; (de carro, en tribunal etc) seat; (localidad) seat, place; (fundamento) site ▶ **asiento delantero/trasero** front/back seat

asignación nf (atribución) assignment; (reparto) allocation; (sueldo) salary ▶ **asignación (semanal)** allowance (US), pocket money (BRIT)

asignar vt to assign, allocate

asignatura nf subject; course

asilado, -a nm/f inmate; (POL) refugee

asilo nm (refugio) asylum, refuge; (establecimiento) home, institution ▶ **asilo político** political asylum

asimilación nf assimilation

asimilar vt to assimilate

asimismo adv in the same way, likewise

asir vt to seize, grasp

asistencia nf audience; (MED) attendance; (ayuda) assistance ❑ **asistente** nmf assistant; **los asistentes** those present ▶ **asistente social** social worker

asistido, -a adj: **~ por** (LAm) **computadora** computer-assisted

asistir vt to assist, help ♦ vi: **~ a** to attend, be present at

asma nf asthma

asno nm donkey; (fig) ass

asociación nf association; (COM) partnership ❑ **asociado, -a** adj associate ♦ nm/f associate; (COM) partner

asociar vt to associate

asolar vt to destroy

asomar vt to show, stick out ♦ vi to appear; **asomarse** vr to appear, show up; **~ la cabeza por la ventana** to put one's head out of the window

asombrar vt to amaze, astonish; **asombrarse** vr (sorprenderse) to be amazed; (asustarse) to get a fright ❑ **asombro** nm amazement, astonishment; (susto) fright ❑ **asombroso, -a** adj astonishing, amazing

asomo nm hint, sign

aspa nf (cruz) cross; (de molino) sail; **en ~** X-shaped

aspaviento nm exaggerated display of feeling; (fam) fuss

aspecto nm (apariencia) look, appearance; (fig) aspect

aspereza nf roughness; (agrura) sourness; (de carácter) surliness ❑ **áspero, -a** adj rough; bitter; sour; harsh

aspersión nf sprinkling

aspiración nf breath, inhalation; (MÚS) short pause; **aspiraciones** nfpl (ambiciones) aspirations

aspirador nm = **aspiradora**

aspiradora nf vacuum cleaner, Hoover®

aspirante nmf (candidato) candidate; (DEPORTE) contender

aspirar vt to breathe in ♦ vi: **~ a** to aspire to

aspirina nf aspirin

asquear vt to sicken ♦ vi to be sickening; **asquearse** vr to feel disgusted
❏ **asqueroso, -a** adj disgusting, sickening

asta nf lance; (arpón) spear; (mango) shaft, handle; (ZOOL) horn; **a media ~** at half mast

asterisco nm asterisk

astilla nf splinter; (pedacito) chip; **~s** nfpl (leña) firewood sg

astillero nm shipyard

astringente adj, nm astringent

astro nm star

astrología nf astrology ❏ **astrólogo, -a** nm/f astrologer

astronauta nmf astronaut

astronave nm spaceship

astronomía nf astronomy ❏ **astrónomo, -a** nm/f astronomer

astucia nf astuteness; (ardid) clever trick

asturiano, -a adj, nm/f Asturian

astuto, -a adj astute; (taimado) cunning

asumir vt to assume

asunción nf assumption; (REL): **A~** Assumption

asunto nm (tema) matter, subject; (negocio) business

asustar vt to frighten; **asustarse** vr to be (o become) frightened

atacar vt to attack

atadura nf bond, tie

atajar vt (enfermedad, mal) to stop ♦ vi (persona) to take a short cut

atajo nm short cut

atañer vi: **~ a** to concern

ataque etc vb ver **atacar** ♦ nm attack ► **ataque cardíaco** heart attack

atar vt to tie, tie up

atarantado, -a (MÉX) adj (aturdido) dazed

atardecer vi to get dark ♦ nm evening; (crepúsculo) dusk

atareado, -a adj busy

atascar vt to clog up; (obstruir) to jam; (fig) to hinder; **atascarse** vr to stall; (cañería) to get blocked up ❏ **atasco** nm obstruction; (AUTO) traffic jam

ataúd nm coffin, casket (US)

ataviar vt to deck, array; **ataviarse** vr to dress up

atavío nm attire, dress; **~s** nmpl finery sg

atemorizar vt to frighten, scare; **atemorizarse** vr to get scared

Atenas n Athens

atención nf attention; (bondad) kindness ♦ excl (be) careful!, look out!

atender vt to attend to, look after ♦ vi to pay attention

atenerse vr: **~ a** to abide by, adhere to

atentado nm crime, illegal act; (asalto) assault; **~ contra la vida de algn** attempt on sb's life

atentamente adv: **Le saluda ~** Sincerely yours (US), Yours sincerely (BRIT)

atentar vi: **~ a o contra** to commit an outrage against

atento, -a adj attentive, observant; (cortés) polite, thoughtful

atenuante adj extenuating

atenuar vt (disminuir) to lessen, minimize

ateo, -a adj atheistic ♦ nm/f atheist

aterciopelado, -a adj velvety

aterido, -a adj: **~ de frío** frozen stiff

aterrador, a adj frightening

aterrar vt to frighten; to terrify

aterrizaje nm landing

aterrizar vi to land

aterrorizar vt to terrify

atesorar vt to hoard

atestado, -a adj packed ♦ nm (JUR) affidavit

atestar vt to pack, stuff; (JUR) to attest, testify to

atestiguar vt to testify to, bear witness to

atiborrar vt to fill, stuff; **atiborrarse** vr to stuff o.s.

ático nm attic ► **ático de lujo** penthouse (apartment (US) o flat (BRIT))

atinado, -a adj (sensato) wise; (correcto) right, correct

atinar vi (al disparar): **~ al blanco** to hit the target; (fig) to be right

atisbar vt to spy on; (echar una ojeada) to peep at

atizar vt to poke; (horno etc) to stoke; (fig) to stir up, rouse

atlántico, -a adj Atlantic ♦ nm: **el (océano) A~** the Atlantic (Ocean)

atlas nm atlas

atleta nm athlete ❏ **atlético, -a** adj athletic ❏ **atletismo** nm athletics sg

atmósfera nf atmosphere

atolladero nm (fig) jam, fix

atolondramiento nm bewilderment; (insensatez) silliness

atómico, -a adj atomic

atomizador nm atomizer; (de perfume) spray

átomo nm atom

atónito, -a adj astonished, amazed

atontado, -a *adj* stunned; (*bobo*) stupid, dumb (*US*), daft (*BRIT*)

atontar *vt* to stun; **atontarse** *vr* to become confused

atormentar *vt* to torture; (*molestar*) to torment; (*acosar*) to plague, harass

atornillar *vt* to screw on *o* down

atosigar *vt* to harass, pester

atracador, a *nm/f* robber

atracar *vt* (*NÁUT*) to moor; (*robar*) to hold up, rob ♦ *vi* to moor; **atracarse** *vr*: **~se (de)** to stuff o.s. (with)

atracción *nf* attraction

atraco *nm* holdup, robbery

atracón *nm*: **darse** *o* **pegarse un ~ (de)** (*fam*) to stuff o.s. (with)

atractivo, -a *adj* attractive ♦ *nm* appeal

atraer *vt* to attract

atragantarse *vr*: **~ (con)** to choke (on); **se me ha atragantado el chico** I can't stand the boy

atrancar *vt* (*puerta*) to bar, bolt

atrapar *vt* to trap; (*resfriado etc*) to catch

atrás *adv* (*movimiento*) back(-wards); (*lugar*) behind; (*tiempo*) previously; **ir hacia ~** to go back(wards), go to the rear; **estar ~** to be behind *o* at the back

atrasado, -a *adj* slow; (*pago*) overdue, late; (*país*) backward

atrasar *vi* to be slow; **atrasarse** *vr* to remain behind; (*tren*) to be *o* run late ❑ **atraso** *nm* slowness; lateness, delay; (*de país*) backwardness; **atrasos** *nmpl* (*COM*) arrears

atravesar *vt* (*cruzar*) to cross (over); (*traspasar*) to pierce; to go through; (*poner al través*) to lay *o* put across; **atravesarse** *vr* to come in between; (*intervenir*) to interfere

atravieso *etc vb ver* **atravesar**

atrayente *adj* attractive

atreverse *vr* to dare; (*insolentarse*) to be insolent ❑ **atrevido, -a** *adj* daring; insolent ❑ **atrevimiento** *nm* daring; insolence

atribución *nf*: **atribuciones** (*POL*) powers; (*ADMIN*) responsibilities

atribuir *vt* to attribute; (*funciones*) to confer

atribular *vt* to afflict, distress

atributo *nm* attribute

atril *nm* (*para libro*) lectern; (*MÚS*) music stand

atrocidad *nf* atrocity, outrage

atropellar *vt* (*derribar*) to knock over *o* down; (*empujar*) to push (aside); (*AUTO*) to run over, run down; (*agraviar*) to insult; **atropellarse** *vr* to act hastily ❑ **atropello**

nm (*AUTO*) accident; (*empujón*) push; (*agravio*) wrong; (*atrocidad*) outrage

atroz *adj* atrocious, awful

ATS *nmf abr* (= *Ayudante Técnico Sanitario*) nurse

atto, -a *abr* = **atento**

atuendo *nm* attire

atún *nm* tuna

aturdir *vt* to stun; (*de ruido*) to deafen; (*fig*) to dumbfound, bewilder

atusar *vt* to smooth (down)

audacia *nf* boldness, audacity ❑ **audaz** *adj* bold, audacious

audible *adj* audible

audición *nf* hearing; (*TEATRO*) audition

audiencia *nf* audience; (*JUR*: *tribunal*) court

audífono *nm* (*para sordos*) hearing aid

auditor *nm* (*JUR*) judge advocate; (*COM*) auditor

auditorio *nm* audience; (*sala*) auditorium

auge *nm* boom; (*clímax*) climax

augurar *vt* to predict; (*presagiar*) to portend

augurio *nm* omen

aula *nf* classroom; (*en universidad etc*) lecture room

aullar *vi* to howl, yell

aullido *nm* howl, yell

aumentar *vt* to increase; (*precios*) to put up; (*producción*) to step up; (*con microscopio, anteojos*) to magnify ♦ *vi* to increase, be on the increase; **aumentarse** *vr* to increase, be on the increase ❑ **aumento** *nm* increase; rise

aun *adv* even; **~ así** even so; **~ más** even *o* yet more

aún *adv*: **~ está aquí** he's still here; **~ no lo sabemos** we don't know yet; **¿no ha venido ~?** hasn't she come yet?

aunque *conj* though, although, even though

aúpa *excl* (*para animar*) come on!

aureola *nf* halo

auricular *nm* (*TEL*) receiver; **~es** *nmpl* (*cascos*) headphones

aurora *nf* dawn

auscultar *vt* (*MED*: *pecho*) to listen to, sound

ausencia *nf* absence

ausentarse *vr* to go away; (*por poco tiempo*) to go out

ausente *adj* absent

auspicios *nmpl* auspices

austero, -a *adj* austere

austral *adj* southern ♦ *nm a former monetary unit of Argentina*

Australia nf Australia □ **australiano, -a** adj, nm/f Australian

Austria nf Austria □ **austríaco, -a** adj, nm/f Austrian

auténtico, -a adj authentic

autitos chocadores (RPl) nmpl bumper cars (US)

auto nm (JUR) edict, decree; (: orden) writ; (AUTO) car; **~s** nmpl (JUR) proceedings; (: acta) court record sg

autoadhesivo adj self-adhesive; (sobre) self-sealing

autobiografía nf autobiography

autobomba (RPl) nm firetruck (US), fire engine (BRIT)

autobronceador adj self-tanning

autobús nm bus

autocar (ESP) nm (passenger) bus (US), coach (BRIT)

autóctono, -a adj native, indigenous

autodefensa nf self-defense (US), self-defence (BRIT)

autodeterminación nf self-determination

autodidacta adj self-taught

autógrafo nm autograph

autómata nm automaton

automático, -a adj automatic ♦ nm snap (fastener) (US), press stud (BRIT)

automotor, -triz adj self-propelled ♦ nm diesel train

automóvil nm automobile (US), (motor) car (BRIT) □ **automovilismo** nm (actividad) motoring; (DEPORTE) motor racing □ **automovilista** nmf motorist, driver □ **automovilístico, -a** adj (industria) motor cpd

autonomía nf autonomy □ **autónomo, -a** (ESP) adj (POL) autonomous

autopista nf freeway (US), motorway (BRIT) ▶ **autopista de cuota** (MÉX) turnpike (US) o toll (BRIT) road ▶ **autopista de peaje** turnpike (US) o toll (BRIT) road

autopsia nf autopsy, postmortem

autor, a nm/f author

autoridad nf authority □ **autoritario, -a** adj authoritarian

autorización nf authorization □ **autorizado, -a** adj authorized; (aprobado) approved

autorizar vt to authorize; (aprobar) to approve

autorretrato nm self-portrait

autoservicio nm (tienda) self-service store (US) o shop (BRIT); (restaurante) self-service restaurant

autostop nm hitch-hiking; **hacer ~** to hitch-hike □ **autostopista** nmf hitch-hiker

autosuficiencia nf self-sufficiency

autovía nf ≈ state highway (US), ≈ A-road (BRIT), dual carriageway (BRIT)

auxiliar vt to help ♦ nmf assistant □ **auxilio** nm assistance, help; **primeros auxilios** first aid sg

Av abr (= Avenida) Av(e)

aval nm guarantee; (persona) guarantor

avalancha nf avalanche

avance nm advance; (pago) advance payment; (CINE) preview, trailer (BRIT)

avanzar vt, vi to advance

avaricia nf avarice, greed □ **avaricioso, -a** adj avaricious, greedy

avaro, -a adj miserly, stingy ♦ nm/f miser

avasallar vt to subdue, subjugate

Avda abr (= Avenida) Av(e)

AVE nm abr (= Alta Velocidad Española) ≈ bullet train

ave nf bird ▶ **ave de rapiña** bird of prey

avecinarse vr (tormenta: fig) to be on the way

avellana nf hazelnut □ **avellano** nm hazel tree

avemaría nm Hail Mary, Ave Maria

avena nf oats pl

avenida nf (calle) avenue

avenir vt to reconcile; **avenirse** vr to come to an agreement, reach a compromise

aventajado, -a adj outstanding

aventajar vt (sobrepasar) to surpass, outstrip

aventón (MÉX: fam) nm ride; **dar ~ a algn** to give sb a ride

aventura nf adventure □ **aventurado, -a** adj risky □ **aventurero, -a** adj adventurous

avergonzar vt to shame; (desconcertar) to embarrass; **avergonzarse** vr to be ashamed; to be embarrassed

avería nf (TEC) breakdown, fault

averiado, -a adj broken down; "**~**" "out of order"

averiguación nf investigation; (descubrimiento) ascertainment

averiguar vt to investigate; (descubrir) to find out, ascertain ♦ vr: **averiguárselas** (MÉX) to manage, get by

aversión nf aversion, dislike

avestruz nm ostrich

aviación nf aviation; (fuerzas aéreas) air force
aviador, a nm/f aviator, airman(-woman); (MÉX: fam) phantom employee
avicultura nf poultry farming
avidez nf avidity, eagerness ❏ **ávido, -a** adj avid, eager
avinagrado, -a adj sour, acid
avión nm airplane (US), aeroplane (BRIT); (ave) martin ▶ **avión de reacción** jet (plane)
avioneta nf light aircraft
avisar vt (advertir) to warn, notify; (informar) to tell; (aconsejar) to advise, counsel ❏ **aviso** nm warning; (noticia) notice
avispa nf wasp
avispado, -a adj sharp, clever
avispero nm wasp's nest
avispón nm hornet
avistar vt to sight, spot
avituallar vt to supply with food
avivar vt to strengthen, intensify; **avivarse** vr to revive, acquire new life
axila nf armpit
axioma nm axiom
ay excl (dolor) ow!, ouch!; (aflicción) oh!, oh dear!; **¡ay de mí!** poor me!
aya nf governess; (niñera) nursemaid (US), nanny (BRIT)
ayer adv, nm yesterday; **antes de ~** the day before yesterday
ayote (CAm) nm pumpkin
ayuda nf help, assistance ♦ nm page ❏ **ayudante, -a** nm/f assistant, helper; (ESCOL) assistant; (MIL) adjutant
ayudar vt to help, assist
ayunar vi to fast ❏ **ayunas** nfpl: **estar en ayunas** to be fasting ❏ **ayuno** nm fast; fasting
ayuntamiento nm (consejo) town (o city) council; (edificio) town (o city) hall
azabache nm jet
azada nf hoe
azafata (ESP) nf air stewardess
azafrán nm saffron
azahar nm orange/lemon blossom
azar nm (casualidad) chance, fate; (desgracia) misfortune, accident; **por ~** by chance; **al ~** at random
azoramiento nm alarm; (confusión) confusion
azorar vt to alarm; **azorarse** vr to get alarmed
Azores nfpl: **las ~** the Azores
azotar vt to whip, beat; (pegar) to spank ❏ **azote** nm (látigo) whip; (latigazo) lash,

stroke; (en las nalgas) spank; (calamidad) calamity
azotea nf (flat) roof
azteca adj, nmf Aztec
azúcar nm sugar ❏ **azucarado, -a** adj sugary, sweet
azucarero, -a adj sugar cpd ♦ nm sugar bowl
azucena nf white lily
azufre nm sulfur (US), sulphur (BRIT)
azul adj, nm blue ▶ **azul marino** navy blue
azulejo nm tile
azuzar vt to incite, egg on

Bb

B.A. abr (= Buenos Aires) B.A.
baba nf spittle, saliva ❏ **babear** vi to drool, slaver
babero nm bib
babor nm port (side)
babosada (MÉX, CAm: fam) nf drivel ❏ **baboso, -a** (LAm: fam) adj silly
baca nf (AUTO) luggage o roof rack
bacalao nm cod(fish)
bache nm pothole, rut; (fig) bad patch
bachillerato nm a two-year secondary school course leading to university
bacinica (LAm) nf potty
bacteria nf bacterium, germ
báculo nm stick, staff
bagaje nm baggage, luggage
Bahamas nfpl: **las (Islas) ~** the Bahamas
bahía nf bay
bailar vt, vi to dance ❏ **bailarín, -ina** nm/f (ballet) dancer ❏ **baile** nm dance; (formal) ball
baja nf drop, fall; (MIL) casualty; **dar de ~** (soldado) to discharge; (empleado) to dismiss
bajada nf descent; (camino) slope; (de aguas) ebb
bajar vi to go down, come down; (temperatura, precios) to drop, fall ♦ vt (cabeza) to bow; (escalera) to go down, come down; (precio, voz) to lower; (llevar abajo) to take down; **bajarse** vr (de carro) to get out; (de autobús, tren) to get off; **~ de** (carro) to get out of; (autobús, tren) to get off
bajeza nf baseness no pl; (una bajeza) vile deed
bajío (LAm) nm lowlands pl

bajo, -a adj (mueble, número, precio) low; (piso) ground; (de estatura) small, short; (color) pale; (sonido) faint, soft, low; (voz: en tono) deep; (metal) base; (humilde) low, humble ♦ adv (hablar) softly, quietly; (volar) low ♦ prep under, below, underneath ♦ nm (MÚS) bass; ~ **la lluvia** in the rain

bajón nm fall, drop

bala nf bullet

balacear (MÉX, CAm) vt to shoot

balance nm (COM) balance; (: libro) balance sheet; (: cuenta general) inventory (US), stocktaking (BRIT)

balancear vt to balance ♦ vi to swing (to and fro); (vacilar) to hesitate; **balancearse** vr to swing (to and fro), hesitate ❑ **balanceo** nm swinging

balanza nf scales pl, balance ▶ **balanza comercial** balance of trade ▶ **balanza de pagos** balance of payments

balar vi to bleat

balaustrada nf balustrade; (pasamanos) banisters pl

balazo nm (golpe) shot; (herida) bullet wound

balbucear vi, vt to stammer, stutter ❑ **balbuceo** nm stammering, stuttering

balbucir vi, vt to stammer, stutter

balcón nm balcony

balde nm (LAm) bucket, pail; **de ~** (for) free, for nothing; **en ~** in vain

baldío, -a adj uncultivated; (terreno) waste ♦ nm waste land

baldosa nf (azulejo) floor tile; (grande) flagstone ❑ **baldosín** nm (small) tile

Baleares nfpl: **las (islas) ~** the Balearic Islands

balero nm (LAm: juguete) cup-and-ball toy

balido nm bleat, bleating

baliza nf (AVIAT) beacon; (NÁUT) buoy

ballena nf whale

ballesta nf crossbow; (AUTO) spring

ballet (pl ~s) nm ballet

balneario nm spa; (CS: en la costa) seaside resort

balón nm ball

baloncesto nm basketball

balonmano nm handball

balonvolea nm volleyball

balsa nf raft; (BOT) balsa wood

bálsamo nm balsam, balm

baluarte nm bastion, bulwark

bambolear vi to swing, sway; (silla) to wobble; **bambolearse** vr to swing, sway; to

wobble ❑ **bamboleo** nm swinging, swaying; wobbling

bambú nm bamboo

banana (LAm) nf banana ❑ **banano** nm (LAm: árbol) banana tree; (CAm: fruta) banana

banca nf (COM) banking; (LAm: asiento) bench; (CS: escaño) seat

bancario, -a adj banking cpd, bank cpd

bancarrota nf bankruptcy; **hacer ~** to go bankrupt

banco nm bench; (ESCOL) desk; (COM) bank; (GEO) stratum ▶ **banco de arena** sandbank ▶ **banco de crédito/ahorros** credit/ savings bank ▶ **banco de datos** databank

banda nf band; (pandilla) gang; (NÁUT) side, edge ▶ **banda ancha** broadband ▶ **banda sonora** soundtrack ▶ **la Banda Oriental** Uruguay

bandada nf (de pájaros) flock; (de peces) shoal

bandazo nm: **dar ~s** to sway from side to side

bandeja nf tray

bandera nf flag

banderilla nf banderilla

banderín nm pennant, small flag

bandido nm bandit

bando nm (edicto) edict, proclamation; (facción) faction; **los ~s** (REL) the banns

bandolera nf: **llevar en ~** to wear across one's chest

bandolero nm bandit, brigand

banquero nm banker

banqueta nf stool; (MÉx: en calle) sidewalk (US), pavement (BRIT)

banquete nm banquet; (para convidados) formal dinner

banquillo nm (JUR) dock, prisoner's bench; (banco) bench; (para los pies) footstool

banquina (RPI) nf shoulder (US), berm (US), hard shoulder (BRIT)

bañadera (RPI) nf bathtub

bañador (ESP) nm bathing suit (US), swimming costume (BRIT)

bañar vt to bath, bathe; (objeto) to dip; (de barniz) to coat; **bañarse** vr (en el mar) to bathe, swim; (en la bañera) to take a bath

bañera (ESP) nf bath(tub)

bañero, -a (CS) nm/f lifeguard

bañista nmf bather

baño nm (en bañera) bath; (en río) dip, swim; (cuarto) bathroom; (bañera) bath(tub); (capa) coating

baqueta nf (MÚS) drumstick

bar nm bar

barahúnda nf uproar, hubbub

baraja nf pack (of cards) ❏ **barajar** vt (naipes) to shuffle; (fig) to jumble up

baranda nf = **barandilla**

barandilla nf rail, railing

barata (MÉX) nf (bargain) sale

baratija nf trinket

baratillo nm (tienda) junk shop; (subasta) bargain sale; (conjunto de cosas) secondhand goods pl

barato, -a adj cheap ♦ adv cheap, cheaply

baraúnda nf = **barahúnda**

barba nf (mentón) chin; (pelo) beard

barbacoa nf (parrilla) barbecue; (carne) barbecued meat

barbaridad nf barbarity; (acto) barbarism; (atrocidad) outrage; **una ~** (fam) loads; **¡qué ~!** (fam) how awful!

barbarie nf barbarism, savagery; (crueldad) barbarity

barbarismo nm = **barbarie**

bárbaro, -a adj barbarous, cruel; (grosero) rough, uncouth ♦ nm/f barbarian ♦ adv: **lo pasamos ~** (fam) we had a great time; **¡qué ~!** (fam) how marvelous (US) o marvellous (BRIT)!; **un éxito ~** (fam) a terrific success; **es un tipo ~** (fam) he's a great guy

barbecho nm fallow land

barbero, -a adj, nm/f (MÉX: fam) flatterer ♦ nm barber, hairdresser

barbilla nf chin, tip of the chin

barbo nm barbel ▶ **barbo de mar** red mullet, goatfish (US)

barbotear vt, vi to mutter, mumble

barbudo, -a adj bearded

barca nf (small) boat ▶ **barca de pasaje** ferry ▶ **barca pesquera** fishing boat ❏ **barcaza** nf barge ▶ **barcaza de desembarco** landing craft

Barcelona n Barcelona

barcelonés, -esa adj of o from Barcelona

barco nm boat; (grande) ship ▶ **barco de carga** cargo boat ▶ **barco de vela** sailboat (US), sailing boat (BRIT)

barda (MÉX) nf (de madera) fence

baremo nm (MAT: fig) scale

barítono nm baritone

barman nm bartender (US), barman (BRIT)

Barna n = **Barcelona**

barniz nm varnish; (en loza) glaze; (fig) veneer ❏ **barnizar** vt to varnish; (loza) to glaze

barómetro nm barometer

barquero nm boatman

barquillo nm cone, cornet

barra nf bar, rod; (de un bar, café) bar; (de pan) French stick; (palanca) lever ▶ **barra de carmín** o **labios** lipstick ▶ **barra libre** free bar

barraca nf hut, cabin

barranco nm ravine; (fig) difficulty

barrena nf drill ❏ **barrenar** vt to drill (through), bore ❏ **barreno** nm large drill

barrer vt to sweep; (quitar) to sweep away

barrera nf barrier

barriada nf quarter, district; (LAm: marginal) slum, shanty town

barricada nf barricade

barrida nf sweep, sweeping

barrido nm = **barrida**

barriga nf belly; (panza) paunch ❏ **barrigón, -ona** adj potbellied ❏ **barrigudo, -a** adj potbellied

barril nm barrel, cask

barrio nm (vecindad) area, neighborhood; (en afueras) suburb ▶ **barrio espontáneo** (CAm) shantytown

barro nm (lodo) mud; (objetos) earthenware; (MED) pimple

barroco, -a adj, nm baroque

barrote nm (de ventana) bar

barruntar vt (conjeturar) to guess; (presentir) to suspect ❏ **barrunto** nm guess; suspicion

bártola: **a la ~** adv: **tirarse a la ~** to take it easy, be lazy

bártulos nmpl things, belongings

barullo nm row, uproar

basar vt to base; **basarse** vr: **~se en** to be based on

báscula nf (platform) scales

base nf base; **a ~ de** on the basis of; (mediante) by means of ▶ **base de datos** (INFORM) database

básico, -a adj basic

basílica nf basilica

basquetbol (MÉX) (LAm **básquetbol**) nm basketball

bastante

PALABRA CLAVE

adj

1 (suficiente) enough; **bastante dinero** enough o sufficient money; **bastantes libros** enough books

2 (valor intensivo): **bastante gente** quite a lot of people; **tener bastante calor** to be rather hot

♦ adv: **bastante bueno/malo** quite good/ rather bad; **bastante rico** pretty rich; **(lo) bastante inteligente (como) para hacer algo** clever enough o sufficiently clever to do sth

bastar vi to be enough o sufficient; **bastarse** vr to be self-sufficient; ~ **para** to be enough to; **¡basta!** (that's) enough!

bastardilla nf italics

bastardo, -a adj, nm/f bastard

bastidor nm frame; (de carro) chassis; (TEATRO) wing; **entre ~es** (fig) behind the scenes

basto, -a adj coarse, rough

bastón nm stick, staff; (para pasear) walking stick

bastoncillo nm Q-tip® (US), cotton bud (BRIT)

bastos nmpl (NAIPES) ≈ clubs

basura nf garbage (US), rubbish (BRIT)

basurero nm (hombre) garbage man (US), dustman (BRIT); (lugar) dump; (MÉX: cubo) trash can (US), (rubbish) bin (BRIT)

bata nf (gen) dressing gown; (cubretodo) smock; (MED, TEC etc) lab(oratory) coat

batalla nf battle; **de ~** (fig) for everyday use

batallar vi to fight

batallón nm battalion

batata nf sweet potato

batería nf battery; (MÚS) drums ▶ **batería de cocina** kitchen utensils

batido, -a adj (camino) beaten, well-trodden ♦ nm (LAm: rebozo) batter; (ESP CULIN: de leche) milk shake

batidora nf beater, mixer ▶ **batidora eléctrica** food mixer, blender

batir vt to beat, strike; (vencer) to beat, defeat; (revolver) to beat, mix; **batirse** vr to fight; ~ **palmas** to applaud

batuta nf baton; **llevar la ~** (fig) to be the boss, be in charge

baúl nm trunk; (RPI AUTO) trunk (US), boot (BRIT)

bautismo nm baptism, christening

bautizar vt to baptize, christen; (fam: diluir) to water down □ **bautizo** nm baptism, christening

baya nf berry

bayeta nf floorcloth

baza nf trick; **meter ~** to butt in

bazar nm bazaar

bazofia nf trash

BCE nm abr (= Banco Central Europeo) ECB

be nf name of the letter B ▶ **be chica/grande** (MÉX) V/B ▶ **be larga** (LAm) B

beato, -a adj blessed; (piadoso) pious

bebé (pl ~s) nm baby

bebedero (MÉX, CS) nm drinking fountain

bebedor, a adj hard-drinking

beber vt, vi to drink

bebida nf drink □ **bebido, -a** adj drunk

beca nf grant, scholarship

becario, -a nm/f scholarship holder, grant holder

bedel nm (ESCOL) janitor; (UNIV) head custodian (US), head porter (BRIT)

beisbol (MÉX) (LAm exc MÉX, ESP **béisbol**) nm (DEPORTE) baseball

belén nm (de navidad) nativity scene, crib, crèche (US); **B~** Bethlehem

belga adj, nmf Belgian

Bélgica nf Belgium

bélico, -a adj (actitud) warlike □ **belicoso, -a** adj (guerrero) warlike; (agresivo) aggressive, bellicose

beligerante adj belligerent

belleza nf beauty

bello, -a adj beautiful, lovely; **Bellas Artes** Fine Art

bellota nf acorn

bemol nm (MÚS) flat; **esto tiene ~es** (fam) this is a tough one

bencina nf (QUÍM) benzine

bendecir vt to bless

bendición nf blessing

bendito, -a pp de **bendecir** ♦ adj holy; (afortunado) lucky; (feliz) happy; (sencillo) simple ♦ nm/f simple soul

beneficencia nf charity

beneficiar vt to benefit, be of benefit to; **beneficiarse** vr to benefit, profit □ **beneficiario, -a** nm/f beneficiary

beneficio nm (bien) benefit, advantage; (ganancia) profit, gain □ **beneficioso, -a** adj beneficial

benéfico, -a adj charitable

beneplácito nm approval, consent

benevolencia nf benevolence, kindness □ **benévolo, -a** adj benevolent, kind

benigno, -a adj kind; (suave) mild; (MED: tumor) benign, non-malignant

berberecho nm (ZOOL, CULIN) cockle

berenjena nf eggplant (US), aubergine (BRIT)

Berlín n Berlin □ **berlinés, -esa** adj of o from Berlin ♦ nm/f Berliner

berlinesa (RPl) nf doughnut, donut (US); ver tb **berlinés**

bermudas nfpl Bermuda shorts

berrear vi to bellow, low

berrido nm bellow(ing)

berrinche (fam) nm temper, tantrum

berro nm watercress

berza nf cabbage

besamel nf (CULIN) white sauce, bechamel sauce

besar vt to kiss; (fig: tocar) to graze; **besarse** vr to kiss (one another) ❑ **beso** nm kiss

bestia nf beast, animal; (fig) idiot ▶ **bestia de carga** beast of burden

bestial adj bestial; (fam) terrific ❑ **bestialidad** nf bestiality; (fam) stupidity

besugo nm sea bream; (fam) idiot

besuquear vt to cover with kisses; **besuquearse** vr to kiss and cuddle

betabel (MÉX) nm beet (US), beetroot (BRIT)

betún nm shoe polish; (QUÍM) bitumen

biberón nm feeding bottle

Biblia nf Bible

bibliografía nf bibliography

biblioteca nf library; (LAm: mueble) bookshelves ▶ **biblioteca de consulta** reference library ❑ **bibliotecario, -a** nm/f librarian

bicarbonato nm bicarbonate

bicho nm (animal) small animal; (sabandija) bug, insect; (TAUR) bull

bici (fam) nf bike

bicicleta nf bicycle, cycle; **ir en ~** to cycle

bidé (pl ~s) nm bidet

bidón nm (de aceite) drum; (de gasolina) can

---

bien

PALABRA CLAVE

nm

1 (bienestar) good; **te lo digo por tu bien** I'm telling you for your own good; **el bien y el mal** good and evil

2 (posesión): **bienes** goods ▶ **bienes de consumo** consumer goods ▶ **bienes inmuebles** o **raíces/bienes muebles** real estate sg /personal property sg

♦ adv

1 (de manera satisfactoria, correcta etc) well; **trabaja/come bien** she works/eats well; **contestó bien** he answered correctly; **me siento bien** I feel fine; **no me siento bien** I don't feel very well; **se está bien aquí** it's nice here

2 (frases): **hiciste bien en llamarme** you were right to call me

3 (valor intensivo) very; **un cuarto bien caliente** a nice warm room; **bien se ve que ...** it's quite clear that ...

4: **estar bien: estoy muy bien aquí** I feel very happy here; **está bien que vengan** it's all right for them to come; **¡está bien! lo haré** O.K.! o all right! I'll do it

5 (de buena gana): **yo bien que iría pero ...** I'd gladly go but ...

♦ excl: **¡bien!** (aprobación) O.K.!; **¡muy bien!** well done!

♦ adj inv (matiz despectivo): **niño bien** rich kid; **gente bien** posh people

♦ conj

1: **bien ... bien: bien en** (LAm) **carro bien en tren** either by car or by train

2: **no bien** (LAm): **no bien llegue te llamaré** as soon as I arrive I'll call you

3: **si bien** even though; ver tb **más**

---

bienal adj biennial

bienaventurado, -a adj (feliz) happy, fortunate

bienestar nm well-being, welfare

bienhechor, a adj beneficent ♦ nm/f benefactor (benefactress)

bienvenida nf welcome; **dar la ~ a algn** to welcome sb

bienvenido excl welcome!

bife (CS) nm steak

bifurcación nf fork

bifurcarse vr (camino, carretera, río) to fork

bigamia nf bigamy ❑ **bígamo, -a** adj bigamous ♦ nm/f bigamist

bigote nm mustache (US), moustache (BRIT) ❑ **bigotudo, -a** adj with a big mustache (US) o moustache (BRIT)

bikini nm o (RPl) f bikini

bilbaíno, a adj from o of Bilbao

bilingüe adj bilingual

billar nm billiards sg; (lugar) billiard hall; (minicasino) amusement arcade ▶ **billar americano** pool

billete nm (ESP) ticket; (de banco) bill (US), (bank)note (BRIT); (carta) note; **~ de 20 dólares** $20 bill (US) o note (BRIT) ▶ **billete de ida y vuelta** (ESP) round-trip (US) o return (BRIT) ticket ▶ **billete sencillo** o **de ida** (ESP) one-way (US) o single (BRIT) ticket

billetera nf wallet, billfold (US)

billetero nm = **billetera**

billón nm billion

bimensual *adj* twice monthly

bimotor *adj* twin-engined ♦ *nm* twin-engined plane

bingo *nm* bingo

biodegradable *adj* biodegradable

biografía *nf* biography □ **biógrafo, -a** *nm/f* biographer

biología *nf* biology □ **biológico, -a** *adj* biological; (*cultivo, producto*) organic □ **biólogo, -a** *nm/f* biologist

biombo *nm* (folding) screen

bioterrorismo *nm* bioterrorism

biquini *nm* o (*RPI*) *f* bikini

birlar (*fam*) *vt* to pinch

Birmania *nf* Burma

birome (*RPI*) *nf* ballpoint (pen)

birria *nf*: **ser una ~** (*película, libro*) to be trash (*US*) o garbage (*US*) o rubbish (*BRIT*)

bis *excl* encore! ♦ *adv*: **viven en el 27 ~** they live at 27a

bisabuelo, -a *nm/f* great-grandfather (-mother)

bisagra *nf* hinge

bisiesto *adj*: **año ~** leap year

bisnieto, -a *nm/f* great-grandson (-daughter)

bisonte *nm* bison

bisté *nm* = **bistec**

bistec *nm* steak

bisturí *nm* scalpel

bisutería *nf* costume jewelry (*US*) o jewellery (*BRIT*), imitation jewelry (*US*) o jewellery (*BRIT*)

bit *nm* (*INFORM*) bit

bizco, -a *adj* cross-eyed

bizcocho *nm* (*CULIN*) sponge cake

bizquear *vi* to squint

blanca *nf* (*MÚS*) minim; *ver tb* **blanco**

blanco, -a *adj* white ♦ *nm/f* white man (woman), white ♦ *nm* (*color*) white; (*en texto*) blank; (*MIL, fig*) target; **en ~** blank; **noche en ~** sleepless night

blancura *nf* whiteness

blandir *vt* to brandish

blando, -a *adj* soft; (*tierno*) tender, gentle; (*carácter*) mild; (*fam*) cowardly □ **blandura** *nf* softness; tenderness; mildness

blanqueador (*MÉX*) *nm* bleach

blanquear *vt* to whiten; (*fachada*) to whitewash; (*paño*) to bleach ♦ *vi* to turn white □ **blanquecino, -a** *adj* whitish

blanquillo (*MÉX, CAm*) *nm* egg

blasfemar *vi* to blaspheme, curse □ **blasfemia** *nf* blasphemy

blasón *nm* coat of arms

bledo *nm*: **me importa un ~** I couldn't care less

blindado, -a *adj* (*MIL*) armor-plated (*US*), armour-plated (*BRIT*); (*antibala*) bullet-proof; **carro** (*LAm*) o **coche** (*ESP*) **~** armored (*US*) o armoured (*BRIT*) car

blindaje *nm* armor-plating (*US*), armour-plating (*BRIT*)

bloc (*pl* **~s**) *nm* writing pad

blof (*MÉX*) *nm* bluff □ **blofear** (*MÉX*) (*CS* **blufear**) *vi* to bluff

blog *nm* blog

bloque *nm* block; (*POL*) bloc ▶ **bloque de cilindros** cylinder block

bloquear *vt* to blockade □ **bloqueo** *nm* blockade; (*COM*) freezing, blocking

blusa *nf* blouse

boato *nm* show, ostentation

bobada *nf* foolish action; foolish statement; **decir ~s** to talk nonsense

bobería *nf* = **bobada**

bobina *nf* (*TEC*) bobbin; (*FOTO*) spool; (*ELEC*) coil

bobo, -a *adj* (*tonto*) stupid, silly; (*cándido*) naïve ♦ *nm/f* fool, idiot ♦ *nm* (*TEATRO*) clown, funny man

boca *nf* mouth; (*de crustáceo*) pincer; (*de cañón*) muzzle; (*entrada*) mouth, entrance; **~s** *nfpl* (*de río*) mouth *sg*; **~ abajo/arriba** face down/up; **se me hace la ~ agua** my mouth is watering

bocacalle *nf* (entrance to a) street; **la primera ~** the first turning o street

bocadillo *nm* (*MÉX*: *aperitivo*) snack; (*ESP*: *sandwich*) sandwich

bocado *nm* mouthful, bite; (*de caballo*) bridle ▶ **bocado de Adán** Adam's apple

bocajarro: **a ~** *adv* (*disparar, preguntar*) point-blank

bocanada *nf* (*de vino*) mouthful, swallow; (*de aire*) gust, puff

bocata (*fam*) *nm* sandwich

bocazas (*fam*) *nm inv* bigmouth

boceto *nm* sketch, outline

bochorno *nm* (*vergüenza*) embarrassment; (*calor*): **hace ~** it's very muggy □ **bochornoso, -a** *adj* muggy; embarrassing

bocina *nf* (*MÚS*) trumpet; (*AUTO*) horn; (*para hablar*) megaphone; (*MÉX*: *de teléfono*) mouthpiece; (: *de equipo de música*) speaker

boda *nf* (*tb*: **~s**) wedding, marriage; (*fiesta*) wedding reception ▶ **bodas de plata/de oro** silver/golden wedding *sg*

bodega nf (de vino) (wine) cellar; (depósito) storeroom; (de barco) hold; (MÉX: almacén) warehouse; (CAm: de comestibles) grocery store (US), grocer's (shop) (BRIT)

bodegón nm (ARTE) still life

bofe nm (tb: ~s: de res) lights

bofetada nf slap (in the face)

bofetón nm = bofetada

boga nf: en ~ (fig) in vogue

bogar vi (remar) to row; (navegar) to sail

bogavante nm lobster

Bogotá n Bogotá

bohemio, -a adj, nm/f Bohemian

bohío (CAm) nm shack, hut

boicot (pl ~s) nm boycott ❏ **boicotear** vt to boycott ❏ **boicoteo** nm boycott

bóiler (MÉX) nm boiler

boina nf beret

bola nf ball; (canica) marble; (NAIPES) (grand) slam; (betún) shoe polish; (mentira) tale, story; ~s nfpl (LAm: caza) bolas sg ▶ **bola de billar** billiard ball ▶ **bola de nieve** snowball

bolchevique adj, nmf Bolshevik

boleadoras nfpl bolas sg; ver tb **gaucho**

bolear (MÉX) vt (zapatos) to polish, shine

bolera nf skittle o bowling alley

bolero, -a (MÉX) nm/f (limpiabotas) shoeshine boy (girl); ver tb **bolera**

boleta nf (LAm: de rifa) ticket; (CS: recibo) receipt ▶ **boleta de calificaciones** (MÉX) report card

boletería (LAm) nf ticket office

boletín nm bulletin; (periódico) journal, review ▶ **boletín de noticias** news bulletin

boleto nm (LAm) ticket ▶ **boleto de ida y vuelta** (LAm) round trip ticket ▶ **boleto redondo** (MÉX) round trip ticket

boli (fam) nm Biro®

bolígrafo nm ball-point pen, Biro®

bolilla (RPI) nf topic

bolillo (MÉX) nm (bread) roll

bolita (CS) nf marble

bolívar nm monetary unit of Venezuela

Bolivia nf Bolivia ❏ **boliviano, -a** adj, nm/f Bolivian

bollería nf cakes pl and pastries pl

bollo nm (pan) roll; (bulto) bump, lump; (abolladura) dent

bolo nm skittle; (píldora) (large) pill; (juego de) ~s nmpl skittles sg; (MÉX: de bautizo: dinero) coins thrown into the air by the godparents at a christening for people to catch

bolsa nf (para llevar algo) bag; (MÉX, CAm: bolsillo) pocket; (MÉX: de mujer) handbag; (ANAT) cavity, sac; (COM) stock exchange; (MINERÍA) pocket; **de ~** pocket cpd ▶ **bolsa de agua caliente** hot water bottle ▶ **bolsa de aire** air pocket; (LAm: airbag) airbag ▶ **bolsa de dormir** (MÉX, RPI) sleeping bag ▶ **bolsa de papel** paper bag ▶ **bolsa de plástico** plastic bag

bolsear (MÉX, CAm) vt: ~ a algn to pick sb's pocket

bolsillo nm pocket; (cartera) purse; **de ~** pocket(-size)

bolsista nmf stockbroker

bolso (ESP) nm (bolsa) bag; (de mujer) purse, handbag

bomba nf (MIL) bomb; (TEC) pump ♦ adj (fam): **noticia ~** bombshell ♦ adv (fam): **pasarlo ~** to have a great time ▶ **bomba atómica/de humo/de efecto retardado** atomic/ smoke/time bomb

bombacha (RPI) nf panties pl

bombardear vt to bombard; (MIL) to bomb ❏ **bombardeo** nm bombardment; bombing

bombardero nm bomber

bombazo nm (MÉX: explosión) explosion; (notición: fam) bombshell; (éxito: fam) smash hit

bombear vt (agua) to pump (out o up); **bombearse** vr to warp

bombero nm fireman

bombilla nf (light) bulb

bombín nm derby (US), bowler hat (BRIT)

bombita (RPI) nf (light) bulb

bombo nm (MÚS) bass drum; (TEC) drum

bombón nm chocolate; (MÉX: de caramelo) marshmallow

bonachón, -ona adj good-natured, easy-going

bonanza nf (NÁUT) fair weather; (fig) bonanza; (MINERÍA) rich pocket o vein

bondad nf goodness, kindness; **tenga la ~ de** (please) be good enough to ❏ **bondadoso, -a** adj good, kind

bonificación nf bonus

bonito, -a adj pretty; (agradable) nice ♦ nm (atún) tuna (fish)

bono nm voucher; (FINANZAS) bond

bonobús (ESP) nm bus pass

bonoloto (ESP) nf state-run weekly lottery

boquerón nm (pez) (kind of) anchovy; (agujero) large hole

boquete nm gap, hole

boquiabierto, -a adj: **quedar ~** to be amazed o flabbergasted

boquilla nf (para riego) nozzle; (de cigarro) cigarette holder; (MÚS) mouthpiece

borbotón nm: **salir a borbotones** to gush out

borda nf (NÁUT) (ship's) rail; **tirar algo/caerse por la ~** to throw sth/fall overboard

bordado nm embroidery

bordar vt to embroider

borde nm edge, border; (de camino etc) side; (en la costura) hem; **al ~ de** (fig) on the verge o brink of □ **bordear** vt to border

bordillo nm curb (US), kerb (BRIT)

bordo nm (NÁUT) side; **a ~** on board

borinqueño, -a adj, nm/f Puerto Rican

borla nf (adorno) tassel

borlote (MÉX) nm row, uproar

borrachera nf (ebriedad) drunkenness; (orgía) spree, binge

borracho, -a adj drunk ♦ nm/f (habitual) drunkard, drunk; (temporal) drunk, drunk man (woman)

borrador nm (escritura) first draft, rough sketch; (goma) eraser, rubber (BRIT)

borrar vt to erase, rub out

borrasca nf storm

borrego, -a nm/f (ZOOL: joven) (yearling) lamb; (adulto) sheep ♦ nm (MÉX: fam) false rumor (US) o rumour (BRIT)

borrico, -a nm/f donkey (she-donkey); (fig) stupid man (woman)

borrón nm (mancha) stain

borroso, -a adj vague, unclear; (escritura) illegible

bosque nm wood; (grande) forest

bosquejar vt to sketch □ **bosquejo** nm sketch

bostezar vi to yawn □ **bostezo** nm yawn

bota nf (calzado) boot; (para vino) leather wine bottle ▶ **botas de agua** o **goma** rubber boots (US), Wellingtons (BRIT)

botana (MÉX) nf snack, appetizer

botánica nf (ciencia) botany; ver tb **botánico**

botánico, -a adj botanical ♦ nm/f botanist

botar vt (pelota) to throw, hurl; (NÁUT) to launch; (LAm: echar) to throw out

bote nm (salto) bounce; (golpe) thrust; (embarcación) boat; (MÉX, CAm: pey: cárcel) jail; **de ~ en ~** packed, jammed full ▶ **bote de la basura** (MÉX) trash can (US), dustbin (BRIT) ▶ **bote salvavidas** lifeboat

botella nf bottle □ **botellín** nm small bottle

botica nf pharmacy, druggist's (US), chemist's (shop) (BRIT) □ **boticario, -a** nm/f pharmacist, druggist (US), chemist (BRIT)

botijo nm (earthenware) jug

botín nm (calzado) half boot; (polaina) spat; (MIL) booty

botiquín nm (armario) medicine cabinet; (portátil) first-aid kit

botón nm button; (BOT) bud ▶ **botón de oro** buttercup

botones nm inv bellhop (US), bellboy (BRIT)

bóveda nf (ARQ) vault

boxeador nm boxer

boxear vi to box

boxeo nm boxing

boya nf (NÁUT) buoy; (de caña) float

boyante adj prosperous

bozal nm (para caballos) halter; (de perro) muzzle

bracear vi (agitar los brazos) to wave one's arms

bracero nm laborer (US), labourer (BRIT); (en el campo) farmhand

bragas (ESP) nfpl (de mujer) panties, knickers (BRIT)

bragueta nf zipper (US), fly (BRIT), flies pl (BRIT)

braille nm braille

bramar vi to bellow, roar □ **bramido** nm bellow, roar

brasa nf live o hot coal

brasero nm brazier; (MÉX: chimenea) portable fireplace

brasier (MÉX) nm bra

Brasil nm: **(el) ~** Brazil □ **brasileño, -a** adj, nm/f Brazilian

brassier (MÉX) nm ver **brasier**

bravata nf boast

braveza nf (valor) bravery; (ferocidad) ferocity

bravío, -a adj wild; (feroz) fierce

bravo, -a adj (valiente) brave; (feroz) ferocious; (salvaje) wild; (mar etc) rough, stormy; (MÉX CULIN) hot, spicy ♦ excl bravo! □ **bravura** nf bravery; ferocity

braza nf fathom; **nadar a ~** to swim (the) breast-stroke

brazada nf stroke

brazado nm armful

brazalete nm (pulsera) bracelet; (banda) armband

brazo nm arm; (ZOOL) foreleg; (BOT) limb, branch; **luchar a ~ partido** to fight hand-to-hand; **ir cogidos del ~** to walk arm in arm

brea nf pitch, tar

brebaje nm potion

brecha nf (hoyo, vacío) gap, opening; (MIL: fig) breach

brega nf (lucha) struggle; (trabajo) hard work

breva nf early fig

breve adj short, brief ♦ nf (MÚS) breve ❑ **brevedad** nf brevity, shortness

brezo nm heather

bribón, -ona adj idle, lazy ♦ nm/f (pícaro) rascal, rogue

bricolaje nm do-it-yourself, DIY (BRIT)

brida nf bridle, rein; (TEC) clamp; **a toda ~** at top speed

bridge nm bridge

brigada nf (unidad) brigade; (de trabajadores) squad, gang ♦ nm ≈ staff-sergeant, sergeant-major

brillante adj brilliant ♦ nm diamond

brillar vi to shine; (joyas) to sparkle

brillo nm shine; (brillantez) brilliance; (fig) splendor (US), splendour (BRIT); **sacar ~ a** to polish

brincar vi to skip about, hop about, jump about; **está que brinca** he's hopping mad

brinco nm jump, leap

brindar vi: **~ a o por** to drink (a toast) to ♦ vt to offer, present

brindis nm inv toast

brío nm spirit, dash ❑ **brioso, -a** adj spirited, dashing

brisa nf breeze

británico, -a adj British ♦ nm/f Briton, British person

brizna nf (de hierba, paja) blade; (de tabaco) leaf

broca nf (TEC) drill, bit

brocal nm rim

brocha nf (large) paintbrush ▶ **brocha de afeitar** shaving brush

broche nm brooch

broma nf joke; **en ~** in fun, as a joke ▶ **broma pesada** practical joke ❑ **bromear** vi to joke

bromista adj fond of joking ♦ nmf joker, wag

bronca nf ruckus (US), row (BRIT); **echar una ~ a uno** to tick sb off

bronce nm bronze ❑ **bronceado, -a** adj bronze; (por el sol) tanned ♦ nm (sun)tan; (TEC) bronzing

bronceador nm suntan lotion

broncearse vr to get a suntan

bronco, -a adj (manera) rude, surly; (voz) harsh

bronquio nm (ANAT) bronchial tube

bronquitis nf inv bronchitis

brotar vi (BOT) to sprout; (aguas) to gush (forth); (MED) to break out

brote nm (BOT) shoot; (MED, fig) outbreak

bruces: de ~ adv: **caer o dar de ~** to fall headlong, fall flat

bruja nf witch ❑ **brujería** nf witchcraft

brujo nm wizard, magician

brújula nf compass

bruma nf mist ❑ **brumoso, -a** adj misty

bruñir vt to polish

brusco, -a adj (súbito) sudden; (áspero) brusque

Bruselas n Brussels

brutal adj brutal

brutalidad nf brutality

bruto, -a adj (idiota) stupid; (bestial) brutish; (peso) gross; **en ~** raw, unworked

Bs.As. abr (= Buenos Aires) B.A.

bucal adj oral; **por vía ~** orally

bucear vi to dive ♦ vt to explore ❑ **buceo** nm diving

bucle nm curl

budismo nm Buddhism

buen adj m ver **bueno**

buenamente adv (fácilmente) easily; (voluntariamente) willingly

buenaventura nf (suerte) good luck; (adivinación) fortune

buenmozo (MÉX) adj handsome

---

bueno, -a

PALABRA CLAVE

adj (antes de nmsg: **buen**)

1 (excelente etc) good; **es un libro bueno, es un buen libro** it's a good book; **hace bueno, hace buen tiempo** the weather is fine, it is fine; **el bueno de Paco** good old Paco; **fue muy bueno conmigo** he was very nice o kind to me

2 (apropiado): **ser bueno para** to be good for; **creo que vamos por buen camino** I think we're on the right track

3 (irónico): **le di un buen rapapolvo** I gave him a good telling off; **¡buen conductor estás hecho!** some o a fine driver you are!; **¡estaría bueno que ...!** a fine thing it would be if ...!

4 (atractivo, sabroso): **está bueno este bizcocho** this sponge cake is delicious; **Carmen está muy buena** Carmen is gorgeous

5 (*saludos*): **¡buen día!, ¡buenos días!** (good) morning!; **¡buenas (tardes)!** (good) afternoon!; (*más tarde*) (good) evening!; **¡buenas noches!** good night!

6 (*otras locuciones*): **estar de buenas** to be in a good mood; **por las buenas o por las malas** by hook or by crook; **de buenas a primeras** all of a sudden
♦ *excl*: **¡bueno!** all right!; **bueno, ¿y qué?** well, so what?

Buenos Aires *nm* Buenos Aires
buey *nm* ox
búfalo *nm* buffalo
bufanda *nf* scarf
bufar *vi* to snort
bufete *nm* (*despacho de abogado*) lawyer's office
buffer *nm* (*INFORM*) buffer
bufón *nm* clown
buhardilla *nf* attic
búho *nm* owl; (*fig*) hermit, recluse
buhonero *nm* pedlar
buitre *nm* vulture
bujía *nf* (*AUTO*) spark plug; (*vela*) candle; (*CAm: bombilla*) (light) bulb
bula *nf* (*papal*) bull
bulbo *nm* bulb
bulevar *nm* boulevard
Bulgaria *nf* Bulgaria ❑ **búlgaro, -a** *adj, nm/f* Bulgarian
bulla *nf* (*ruido*) uproar; (*de gente*) crowd
bullicio *nm* (*ruido*) uproar; (*movimiento*) bustle
bullir *vi* (*hervir*) to boil; (*burbujear*) to bubble
bulto *nm* (*paquete*) package; (*fardo*) bundle; (*tamaño*) size, bulkiness; (*MED*) swelling, lump; (*silueta*) vague shape
buñuelo *nm* ≈ doughnut, ≈ donut (*US*); (*fruta de sartén*) fritter
buque *nm* ship, vessel
burbuja *nf* bubble ❑ **burbujear** *vi* to bubble
burdel *nm* brothel
burdo, -a *adj* coarse, rough
burgués, -esa *adj* middle-class, bourgeois ❑ **burguesía** *nf* middle class, bourgeoisie
burla *nf* (*mofa*) gibe; (*broma*) joke; (*engaño*) trick
burladero *nm* (*bullfighter's*) refuge
burlar *vt* (*engañar*) to deceive ♦ *vi* to joke; **burlarse** *vr* to joke; **~se de** to make fun of
burlesco, -a *adj* burlesque
burlón, -ona *adj* mocking

buró (*MÉX*) *nm* bedside table
burocracia *nf* bureaucracy ▸ **burocracia pública** (*MÉX*) civil service
burócrata *nmf* (*MÉX: funcionario*) civil servant; (*pey*) bureaucrat
burrada *nf*: **decir/soltar ~s** to talk nonsense; **hacer ~s** to act stupid
burro, -a *nm/f* donkey/she-donkey; (*fig*) ass, idiot; (*MÉX: para planchar*) ironing board; (: *escalera*) stepladder
bursátil *adj* stock-exchange *cpd*
bus *nm* bus
busca *nf* search, hunt ♦ *nm* (*TEL*) bleeper; **en ~ de** in search of
buscar *vt* to look for, search for, seek ♦ *vi* to look, search, seek; **se busca secretaria** secretary wanted
busque *etc vb ver* **buscar**
búsqueda *nf* = **busca**
busto *nm* (*ANAT, ARTE*) bust
butaca *nf* armchair; (*de cine, teatro*) stall, seat
butano *nm* butane (gas)
buzo *nm* diver
buzón *nm* mailbox (*US*), letter box (*BRIT*)

Cc

C *abr* (= *centígrado*) C
c. *abr* (= *capítulo*) ch.
C/ *abr* (= *calle*) St
c.a. *abr* (= *corriente alterna*) AC
cabal *adj* (*exacto*) exact; (*correcto*) right, proper; (*acabado*) finished, complete
cábalas *nfpl*: **hacer ~** to guess
cabales *nmpl*: **no está en sus ~** he isn't in his right mind
cabalgar *vt, vi* to ride
cabalgata *nf* procession
caballa *nf* mackerel
caballeresco, -a *adj* noble, chivalrous
caballería *nf* mount; (*MIL*) cavalry
caballeriza *nf* stable ❑ **caballerizo** *nm* groom, stableman
caballero *nm* gentleman; (*de la orden de caballería*) knight; (*trato directo*) sir
caballerosidad *nf* chivalry
caballete *nm* (*ARTE*) easel; (*TEC*) trestle
caballito *nm* (*caballo pequeño*) small horse, pony; **~s** *nmpl* (*MÉX, ESP: en feria*) carousel, merry-go-round

caballo *nm* horse; *(AJEDREZ)* knight; *(NAIPES)* queen; **ir en ~** to ride ▶ **caballo de carreras** racehorse ▶ **caballo de vapor** *o* **fuerza** horsepower

cabaña *nf (casita)* hut, cabin

cabaré *(pl ~s) nm* cabaret

cabaret *(pl ~s) nm* cabaret

cabecear *vt, vi* to nod

cabecera *nf* head; *(IMPRENTA)* headline

cabecilla *nm* ringleader

cabellera *nf* (head of) hair; *(de cometa)* tail

cabello *nm (tb: ~s)* hair

caber *vi (entrar)* to fit, go; **caben 3 más** there's room for 3 more

cabestrillo *nm* sling

cabestro *nm* halter

cabeza *nf* head; *(POL)* chief, leader ▶ **cabeza rapada** skinhead ▢ **cabezada** *nf (golpe)* butt; *(ESP: sueñito)* nap; **dar cabezadas** to nod off ▢ **cabezón, -ona** *adj (vino)* heady; *(fam: persona)* pig-headed

cabida *nf* space

cabildo *nm (de iglesia)* chapter; *(POL)* town council

cabina *nf* cabin; *(de camión)* cab ▶ **cabina telefónica** telephone booth *o* box *(BRIT)*

cabizbajo, -a *adj* crestfallen, dejected

cable *nm* cable

cabo *nm (de objeto)* end, extremity; *(MIL)* corporal; *(NÁUT)* rope, cable; *(GEO)* cape; **al ~ de 3 días** after 3 days

cabra *nf* goat

cabré *etc vb ver* **caber**

cabrear *(fam) vt* to bug; **cabrearse** *vr (enfadarse)* to fly off the handle

cabrío, -a *adj* goatish; **macho ~** (he-)goat, billy goat

cabriola *nf* caper

cabritilla *nf* kid, kidskin

cabrito *nm* kid

cabrón *nm* cuckold; *(fam!)* bastard *(!)*

caca *(fam) nf* poop *(US)*, pooh *(BRIT)*

cacahuate *(MÉX) (ESP* **cacahuete***) nm* peanut

cacao *nm* cocoa; *(BOT)* cacao

cacarear *vi (persona)* to boast; *(gallina)* to crow

cacarizo, -a *(MÉX) adj* pockmarked

cacería *nf* hunt

cacerola *nf* pan, saucepan

cachalote *nm (ZOOL)* sperm whale

cacharro *nm* earthenware pot; **~s** *nmpl* pots and pans

cachear *vt* to search, frisk

cachemir *nm* cashmere

cacheo *nm* searching, frisking

cachetada *(LAm: fam) nf (bofetada)* slap

cachete *nm (ANAT)* cheek; *(ESP: bofetada)* slap (in the face)

cachiporra *(LAm) nf* (billy) club *(US)*, truncheon *(BRIT)*

cachivache *nm (trasto)* piece of junk; **~s** *nmpl* junk *sg*

cacho *nm (small)* bit; *(LAm: cuerno)* horn

cachondo, -a *adj (MÉX, ESP: fam: sexualmente)* horny, randy *(BRIT)*

cachorro, -a *nm/f (perro)* pup, puppy; *(león)* cub

cachucha *(MÉX: fam) nf* cap

cacique *nm* chief, local ruler; *(POL)* local party boss ▢ **caciquismo** *nm system of control by the local boss*

caco *nm* pickpocket

cacto *nm* cactus

cactus *nm inv* cactus

cada *adj inv* each; *(antes de número)* every; **~ día** each day, every day; **~ dos días** every other day; **~ uno/a** each one, every one; **~ vez más/menos** more and more/less and less; **uno de ~ diez** one out of every ten

cadalso *nm* scaffold

cadáver *nm (dead)* body, corpse

cadena *nf* chain; *(TV)* channel; **trabajo en ~** assembly line work ▶ **cadena perpetua** *(JUR)* life imprisonment

cadencia *nf* rhythm

cadera *nf* hip

cadete *nm* cadet

caducar *vi* to expire ▢ **caduco, -a** *adj* expired; *(persona)* very old

caer *vi* to fall (down); **caerse** *vr* to fall (down); **me cae bien/mal** I get on well with him/I can't stand him; **~ en la cuenta** to realize; **su cumpleaños cae en viernes** her birthday falls on a Friday

café *(pl ~s) nm (bebida, planta)* coffee; *(lugar)* café ♦ *adj (MÉX: color)* brown, tan ▶ **café con leche** coffee with cream *(US)*, white coffee *(BRIT)* ▶ **café negro** *(LAm)* black coffee ▶ **café solo** *(ESP)* black coffee

cafetera *nf* coffee pot

cafetería *nf (gen)* café

cafetero, -a *adj* coffee *cpd*; **ser muy ~** to be a coffee addict

cafishio *(CS) nm* pimp

caída nf fall; (declive) slope; (disminución) fall, drop

caído, -a adj drooping

caiga etc vb ver **caer**

caimán nm alligator

caja nf box; (para reloj) case; (de ascensor) shaft; (COM) cash box; (donde se hacen los pagos) cashier's desk (US), cash desk (BRIT); (: en supermercado) checkout ► **caja de ahorros** savings bank ► **caja de cambios** gearbox ► **caja fuerte** o **de caudales** safe, strongbox

cajero, -a nm/f cashier ► **cajero automático** cash dispenser, A.T.M. (US), automated teller machine (US)

cajetilla nf (de cigarrillos) pack (US), packet (BRIT)

cajón nm big box; (de mueble) drawer

cajuela (MÉX) nf (AUTO) trunk (US), boot (BRIT)

cal nf lime

cala nf (GEO) cove, inlet; (de barco) hold

calabacín nm (BOT) baby marrow; (: más pequeño) zucchini (US), courgette (BRIT)

calabacita (MÉX) nf zucchini (US), courgette (BRIT)

calabaza nf (BOT) pumpkin

calabozo nm (cárcel) prison; (celda) cell

calado, -a adj (prenda) lace cpd ♦ nm (NÁUT) draft (US), draught (BRIT)

calamar nm squid no pl

calambre nm (ESP ELEC) shock; (tb: ~s) cramp

calamidad nf calamity, disaster

calar vt to soak, drench; (penetrar) to pierce, penetrate; (comprender) to see through; (vela) to lower; **calarse** vr (AUTO) to stall; **~se las gafas** to stick one's glasses on

calavera nf skull

calcar vt (reproducir) to trace; (imitar) to copy

calcetín nm sock

calcinar vt to burn, blacken

calcio nm calcium

calcomanía nf transfer, decal (US)

calculador, a adj (persona) calculating

calculadora nf calculator

calcular vt (MAT) to calculate, compute; **~ que ...** to reckon that ... ❑ **cálculo** nm calculation

caldear vt to warm (up), heat (up)

caldera nf boiler

calderilla nf (moneda) small change

caldero nm small boiler

caldo nm stock; (consomé) consommé

calefacción nf heating ► **calefacción central** central heating

calefón (RPI) nm boiler

calendario nm calendar

calentador nm heater; (MÉX: cocina) stove ► **calentador de gas** (MÉX) gas fire

calentamiento nm (DEPORTE) warm-up ► **calentamiento global** global warming

calentar vt to heat (up); **calentarse** vr to heat up, warm up; (fig: discusión etc) to get heated

calentón (RPI: fam) adj (sexualmente) horny, randy (BRIT)

calentura (ESP) nf (MED) fever, (high) temperature

calesita (RPI) nf merry-go-round, carousel

calibrar vt to gauge, gage (US), measure ❑ **calibre** nm (de cañón) calibre, bore; (diámetro) diameter; (fig) calibre

calidad nf quality; **de ~** quality cpd; **en ~ de** in the capacity of, as

cálido, -a adj hot; (fig) warm

caliente etc vb ver **calentar** ♦ adj hot; (fig) fiery; (disputa) heated; (fam: cachondo) randy

calificación nf qualification; (de alumno) grade (US), mark (BRIT)

calificado, -a (LAm) adj (competente) qualified; (obrero) skilled

calificar vt to qualify; (alumno) to grade, mark; **~ de** to describe as

calima nf (cerca del mar) mist

cáliz nm chalice

caliza nf limestone

calizo, -a adj lime cpd

callado, -a adj quiet

callar vt (asunto delicado) to keep quiet about, say nothing about; (persona, opinión) to silence ♦ vi to keep quiet, be silent; **callarse** vr to keep quiet, be silent; **¡cállate!** be quiet!, shut up!

calle nf street; (DEPORTE) lane; **~ arriba/abajo** up/down the street ► **calle de sentido único** one-way street ► **calle mayor** (ESP) main (US) o high (BRIT) street ► **calle principal** (LAm) main (US) o high (BRIT) street

calleja nf alley, narrow street ❑ **callejear** vi to wander (about) the streets ❑ **callejero, -a** adj street cpd ♦ nm street map ❑ **callejón** nm (ESP: calleja) alley, passage ► **callejón sin salida** cul-de-sac ❑ **callejuela** nf side-street, alley

callista nmf podiatrist (US), chiropodist (BRIT)

callo nm callus; (en el pie) corn; **~s** nmpl (ESP CULIN) tripe sg

calma nf calm

calmante nm sedative, tranquillizer

calmar vt to calm, calm down ♦ vi (tempestad) to abate; (mente etc) to become calm

calmoso, -a adj calm, quiet

calor nm heat; (agradable) warmth; **hace ~** it's hot; **tener ~** to be hot

caloría nf calorie

calumnia nf calumny, slander
❑ **calumnioso, -a** adj slanderous

caluroso, -a adj hot; (sin exceso) warm; (fig) enthusiastic

calva nf bald patch; (en bosque) clearing

calvario nm stations pl of the cross

calvicie nf baldness

calvo, -a adj bald; (terreno) bare, barren; (tejido) threadbare

calza nf wedge, chock

calzada nf roadway, highway

calzado, -a adj shod ♦ nm footwear

calzador nm shoehorn

calzar vt (zapatos etc) to wear; (mueble) to put a wedge under; **calzarse** vr: ~**se los zapatos** to put on one's shoes; **¿qué (número) calza?** what size do you take?

calzón nm (ESP: pantalón corto) shorts; (LAm: ropa interior: de hombre) underpants, shorts (US), pants (BRIT); (: de mujer) panties, knickers (BRIT)

calzoncillos nmpl underpants, shorts (US), pants (BRIT)

cama nf bed ▶ **cama individual/de matrimonio** single/double bed

camafeo nm cameo

camaleón nm chameleon

cámara nf chamber; (habitación) room; (sala) hall; (CINE) cine camera; (fotográfica) camera ♦ nmf (ESP) cameraman(-woman) ▶ **cámara de comercio** chamber of commerce ▶ **cámara digital** digital camera ▶ **cámara frigorífica** cold-storage room

camarada nm comrade, companion; (MÉX: amigo) buddy (US)

camarera (ESP) nf (en restaurante) waitress; (en casa, hotel) maid

camarero (ESP) nm waiter

camarilla nf clique

camarógrafo, -a (LAm) nm/f cameraman (-woman)

camarón (LAm) nm prawn, shrimp

camarote nm cabin

cambiable adj (variable) changeable, variable; (intercambiable) interchangeable

cambiante adj variable

cambiar vt to change; (dinero) to exchange ♦ vi to change; **cambiarse** vr (mudarse) to move; (de ropa) to change; ~ **de idea** to change one's mind; ~ **de ropa** to change (one's clothes)

cambio nm change; (trueque) exchange; (COM) rate of exchange; (oficina) bureau de change; (dinero menudo) small change; **en ~** on the other hand; (en lugar de) instead ▶ **cambio climático** climate change ▶ **cambio de divisas** foreign exchange ▶ **cambio de marchas** o **velocidades** gear shift (US), gear stick (BRIT)

camelar vt to sweet-talk

camello nm camel; (fam: traficante) pusher

camerino nm dressing room

camilla nf (MED) stretcher

caminante nmf traveler (US), traveller (BRIT)

caminar vi (marchar) to walk, go ♦ vt (recorrer) to cover, travel

caminata nf long walk; (por el campo) hike

camino nm way, road; (sendero) track; **a medio ~** halfway (there); **en el ~** on the way, en route; ~ **de** on the way to ▶ **camino particular** private road

camión nm truck (US), lorry (BRIT); (MÉX: autobús) bus ▶ **camión cisterna** tanker ❑ **camionero, -a** nm/f truck (US) o lorry (BRIT) driver; (MÉX: en autobús) bus driver

camioneta nf van, light truck; (LAm: carro) station wagon (US), estate car (BRIT)

camisa nf shirt; (BOT) skin ▶ **camisa de fuerza** straitjacket ❑ **camisería** nf haberdasher's (US), outfitter's (shop) (BRIT)

camiseta nf (prenda) tee-shirt; (: ropa interior) undershirt (US), vest (BRIT); (de deportista) top

camisón nm nightgown (US), nightdress (BRIT)

camorra nf: **buscar ~** to look for trouble

camote nm (MÉX, CS: batata) sweet potato, yam; (MÉX: bulbo) tuber, bulb; (CS: fam: enamoramiento) crush

campamento nm camp

campana nf bell ▶ **campana de cristal** bell jar ❑ **campanada** nf peal ❑ **campanario** nm belfry

campanilla nf small bell

campaña nf (MIL, POL) campaign

campechano, -a adj (franco) open

campeón, -ona nm/f champion ❑ **campeonato** nm championship

cámper (LAm) nm o f trailer (US), caravan (BRIT)

campera (RPl) nf anorak

campesino, -a *adj* country *cpd*, rural; (*gente*) peasant *cpd* ♦ *nm/f* countryman (-woman); (*agricultor*) farmer

campestre *adj* country *cpd*, rural

camping (*pl* **~s**) *nm* camping; (*lugar*) campsite, campground (*US*); **ir de** *o* **hacer ~** to go camping

campo *nm* (*fuera de la ciudad*) country, countryside; (*AGR, ELEC*) field; (*cancha*) field, pitch (*BRIT*); (*de golf*) course; (*MIL*) camp ▶ **campo de batalla** battlefield ▶ **campo de deportes** sports ground, playing field

camposanto *nm* cemetery

camuflaje *nm* camouflage

cana *nf* white *o* gray (*US*) *o* grey (*BRIT*) hair; **tener ~s** to be going gray (*US*) *o* grey (*BRIT*)

Canadá *nm* Canada ❑ **canadiense** *adj, nmf* Canadian ♦ *nf* fur-lined jacket

canal *nm* canal; (*GEO*) channel, strait; (*de televisión*) channel; (*de tejado*) gutter ▶ **canal de Panamá** Panama Canal

canaleta (*LAm exc MÉX*) *nf* (*de tejado*) gutter

canalizar *vt* to channel

canalla *nf* rabble, mob ♦ *nm* swine

canalón *nm* (*conducto vertical*) drainpipe

canapé (*pl* **~s**) *nm* sofa, settee; (*CULIN*) canapé

Canarias *nfpl*: **las Islas ~** the Canary Islands, the Canaries

canario, -a *adj, nm/f* (native) of the Canary Isles ♦ *nm* (*ZOOL*) canary

canasta *nf* (round) basket ❑ **canastilla** *nf* small basket; (*de niño*) layette

canasto *nm* large basket

cancela *nf* gate

cancelación *nf* cancellation

cancelar *vt* to cancel; (*una deuda*) to write off

cáncer *nm* (*MED*) cancer; **C~** (*ASTROLOGÍA*) Cancer

cancha *nf* (*de baloncesto*) court; (*LAm: campo*) field, pitch (*BRIT*) ▶ **cancha de tenis** (*LAm*) tennis court

canciller *nm* chancellor

canción *nf* song ▶ **canción de cuna** lullaby ❑ **cancionero** *nm* song book

candado *nm* padlock

candente *adj* red-hot; (*fig: tema*) burning

candidato, -a *nm/f* candidate

candidez *nf* (*sencillez*) simplicity; (*simpleza*) naiveté ❑ **cándido, -a** *adj* simple; naive

⚠ No confundir **cándido** con la palabra inglesa **candid**.

candil *nm* oil lamp ❑ **candilejas** *nfpl* (*TEATRO*) footlights

candor *nm* (*sinceridad*) frankness; (*inocencia*) innocence

canela *nf* cinnamon

canelones *nmpl* cannelloni

cangrejo *nm* crab

canguro *nm* kangaroo; **hacer de ~** (*ESP*) to babysit

caníbal *adj, nmf* cannibal

canica *nf* marble

canijo, -a *adj* frail, sickly

canilla (*RPl*) *nf* faucet (*US*), tap (*BRIT*)

canino, -a *adj* canine ♦ *nm* canine (tooth)

canjear *vt* to exchange

cano, -a *adj* white-haired, gray-haired (*US*), grey-haired (*BRIT*)

canoa *nf* canoe

canon *nm* canon; (*pensión*) rent; (*COM*) tax

canónigo *nm* canon

canonizar *vt* to canonize

canoso, -a *adj* gray-haired (*US*), grey-haired (*BRIT*)

cansado, -a *adj* tired, weary; (*tedioso*) tedious, boring

cansancio *nm* tiredness, fatigue

cansar *vt* (*fatigar*) to tire, tire out; (*aburrir*) to bore; (*fastidiar*) to bother; **cansarse** *vr* to tire, get tired; (*aburrirse*) to get bored

cantábrico, -a *adj* Cantabrian; **mar C~** Bay of Biscay

cantante *adj* singing ♦ *nmf* singer

cantar *vt* to sing ♦ *vi* to sing; (*insecto*) to chirp ♦ *nm* (*acción*) singing; (*canción*) song; (*poema*) poem

cántara *nf* large pitcher

cántaro *nm* pitcher, jug; **llover a ~s** to rain cats and dogs

cante *nm* (*MÚS*) Andalusian folk song ▶ **cante jondo** flamenco singing

cantera *nf* quarry

cantero (*RPl*) *nm* (*arriate*) border

cantidad *nf* quantity, amount

cantimplora *nf* (*frasco*) water bottle, canteen

cantina *nf* canteen; (*de estación*) buffet; (*LAm: bar*) bar

cantinero, -a (*MÉX*) *nm/f* bartender (*US*)

canto *nm* singing; (*canción*) song; (*borde*) edge, rim; (*de cuchillo*) back ▶ **canto rodado** boulder

cantor, a *nm/f* singer

canturrear *vi* to sing softly

canuto *nm* (*tubo*) small tube

caña nf (BOT: tallo) stem, stalk; (carrizo) reed; (ESP: vaso) tumbler; (: de cerveza) glass of beer; (ANAT) shinbone ▶ **caña de azúcar** sugar cane ▶ **caña de pescar** fishing rod

cañada nf (entre dos montañas) gully, ravine; (camino) cattle track

cáñamo nm hemp

cañería nf (tubo) pipe

caño nm (tubo) tube, pipe; (de albañal) sewer; (MÚS) pipe; (de fuente) jet

cañón nm (MIL) cannon; (de fusil) barrel; (GEO) canyon, gorge

caoba nf mahogany

caos nm chaos

cap. abr (= capítulo) ch.

capa nf cloak, cape; (GEO) layer, stratum; **so ~ de** under the pretext of ▶ **capa de ozono** ozone layer

capacidad nf (medida) capacity; (aptitud) capacity, ability

capacitar vt: ~ **a algn para (hacer)** to enable sb to (do)

capar vt to castrate, geld

caparazón nm shell

capataz nm foreman

capaz adj able, capable; (amplio) capacious, roomy

capcioso, -a adj wily, deceitful

capellán nm chaplain; (sacerdote) priest

caperuza nf hood

capicúa adj inv (número, fecha) reversible

capilla nf chapel

capital adj capital ♦ nm (COM) capital ♦ nf (ciudad) capital ▶ **capital social** share o authorized capital

capitalismo nm capitalism ❑ **capitalista** adj, nmf capitalist

capitán nm captain ▶ **capitán de meseros** (MÉX) head waiter

capitanear vt to captain

capitulación nf (rendición) capitulation, surrender; (acuerdo) agreement, pact; **capitulaciones (matrimoniales)** nfpl marriage contract sg

capitular vi to make an agreement

capítulo nm chapter

capó (LAm exc MÉX, ESP) nm (AUTO) hood (US), bonnet (BRIT)

capón nm (gallo) capon

capota nf (de mujer) bonnet; (AUTO) top (US), hood (BRIT)

capote nm (abrigo: de militar) greatcoat; (de torero) cloak

capricho nm whim, caprice ❑ **caprichoso, -a** adj capricious

Capricornio nm Capricorn

cápsula nf capsule

captar vt (comprender) to understand; (RADIO) to pick up; (atención, apoyo) to attract

captura nf capture; (JUR) arrest ❑ **capturar** vt to capture; to arrest

capucha nf hood, cowl

capullo nm (BOT) bud; (ZOOL) cocoon

caqui nm khaki

cara nf (ANAT: de moneda) face; (de disco) side; (LAm: de reloj, dial) face; (descaro) boldness; ~ **a** facing; **de ~** opposite, facing; **dar la ~** to face the consequences; **¿~ o cruz?** (LAm exc MÉX, ESP) heads or tails?; **¡qué ~ (más dura)!** what a nerve!

carabina nf carbine, rifle

Caracas n Caracas

caracol nm (ZOOL) snail; (concha) (sea) shell

carácter (pl caracteres) nm character; **tener buen/mal ~** to be good natured/bad tempered

característica nf characteristic

característico, -a adj characteristic

caracterizar vt to characterize, typify

caradura nmf: **es un ~** he's got a nerve

carajillo nm coffee with a dash of brandy

caramba excl good gracious!

carámbano nm icicle

caramelo nm (dulce) piece of candy (US), sweet (BRIT); (azúcar fundida) caramel

caravana nf (ESP: remolque) trailer (US), caravan (BRIT); (fig) group; (AUTO) line of traffic (US), tailback (BRIT)

carbón nm coal; **papel ~** carbon paper ❑ **carboncillo** nm (ARTE) charcoal ❑ **carbonero, -a** nm/f coal merchant ❑ **carbonilla** nf coal dust

carbonizar vt to carbonize; (quemar) to char

carbono nm carbon

carburador nm carburetor (US), carburettor (BRIT)

carburante nm (para motor) fuel

carcajada nf (loud) laugh, guffaw

cárcel nf prison, jail; (TEC) clamp ❑ **carcelero, -a** adj prison cpd ♦ nm/f jailer

carcoma nf woodworm

carcomer vt to bore into, eat into; (fig) to undermine; **carcomerse** vr to become worm-eaten; (fig) to decay

cardar vt (pelo) to backcomb

cardenal nm (REL) cardinal; (ESP MED) bruise

cardíaco, -a adj cardiac, heart cpd
cardinal adj cardinal
cardo nm thistle
carearse vr to come face to face
carecer vi: ~ **de** to lack, be in need of
carencia nf lack; (escasez) shortage; (MED)
deficiency
carente adj: ~ **de** lacking in, devoid of
carestía nf (escasez) scarcity, shortage; (COM)
high cost
careta nf mask
carga nf (peso, ELEC) load; (de barco) cargo,
freight; (MIL) charge; (responsabilidad) duty,
obligation
cargado, -a adj loaded; (ELEC) live; (café, té)
strong; (cielo) overcast
cargamento nm (acción) loading;
(mercancías) load, cargo
cargar vt (barco, arma) to load; (ELEC) to
charge; (COM: algo en cuenta) to charge;
(INFORM) to load ♦ vi (MIL) to charge; (AUTO) to
load (up); **cargarse** vr (fam: estropear) to
break; (: matar) to bump off; ~ **con** to pick up,
carry away; (: peso: fig) to shoulder, bear
cargo nm (puesto) post, office;
(responsabilidad) duty, obligation; (JUR)
charge; **hacerse ~ de** to take charge of o
responsibility for
carguero nm freighter, cargo boat; (avión)
freight plane
Caribe nm: **el ~** the Caribbean; **del ~**
Caribbean
caribeño, -a adj Caribbean
caricatura nf caricature
caricia nf caress
caridad nf charity
caries nf inv tooth decay
cariño nm affection, love; (caricia) caress; (en
carta) love ...; **tener ~ a** to be fond of
❑ **cariñoso, -a** adj affectionate
carisma nm charisma
caritativo, -a adj charitable
cariz nm: **tener** o **tomar buen/mal ~** to look
good/bad
carmesí adj, nm crimson
carmín nm lipstick
carnal adj carnal; **primo ~** first cousin
carnaval nm carnival

CARNAVAL

Carnaval is a popular festival celebrated in
many Latin American countries, especially
those in the Caribbean, during the three days
before Ash Wednesday and the beginning of
Lent. The parades of dancers and musicians
in costume are accompanied by lively music,
such as Brazilian samba. The celebrations
draw to a close on Mardi Gras (Shrove
Tuesday, which is known as "Carnival
Tuesday").

carne nf flesh; (CULIN) meat ► **carne de
cerdo/cordero/ternera/vaca** pork/lamb/
veal/beef ► **carne de gallina** (fig)
gooseflesh; **se me pone la ~ de gallina sólo
verlo** I get the creeps just seeing it ► **carne
molida** (LAm) ground meat (US), mince (BRIT)
► **carne picada** (RPI, ESP) ground meat (US),
mince (BRIT)
carné (ESP) (pl ~s) nm card ► **carné de
conducir** driver's license (US), driving
licence (BRIT) ► **carné de identidad**
identity card
carnero nm sheep, ram; (carne) mutton; (RPI:
rompehuelgas) strikebreaker, scab
carnet (ESP) (pl ~s) nm = **carné**
carnicería nf butcher's; (fig: matanza)
carnage, slaughter
carnicero, -a adj carnivorous ♦ nm/f
butcher; (carnívoro) carnivore
carnívoro, -a adj carnivorous
carnoso, -a adj beefy, fat
caro, -a adj dear; (COM) dear, expensive ♦ adv
dear, dearly
carpa nf (pez) carp; (de circo) big top; (LAm:
tienda de campaña) tent
carpeta nf folder, file
carpintería nf carpentry, joinery (BRIT)
❑ **carpintero** nm carpenter
carraspear vi to clear one's throat
carraspera nf hoarseness
carrera nf (acción) run(ning); (espacio
recorrido) run; (competición) race; (trayecto)
course; (profesión) career; (ESCOL) course
carreta nf wagon, cart
carrete nm reel, spool; (TEC) coil
carretera nf (main) road, highway
► **carretera de circunvalación** (LAm exc
MÉX, ESP) beltway (US), ring road (BRIT)
► **carretera nacional** ≈ state highway
(US), ≈ A road (BRIT)
carretilla nf trolley; (AGR) (wheel)barrow
carril nm furrow; (de autopista) lane; (FERRO)
rail
carrillo nm (ANAT) cheek; (TEC) pulley
carrito nm (de compras) cart (US), trolley (BRIT)
carro nm (LAm: coche) car; (carreta) cart,
wagon; (MIL) tank ► **carro blindado** (LAm)
armored (US) o armoured (BRIT) car ► **carro**

de bomberos (*LAm*) firetruck (*US*), fire engine (*BRIT*) ▶ **carro de carreras** (*LAm*) race car (*US*), racing car (*BRIT*) ▶ **carro patrulla** (*LAm*) patrol o panda (*BRIT*) car ▶ **carros chocones** (*MÉX*) bumper cars (*US*), dodgems (*BRIT*) ▶ **carros locos** (*LAm exc MÉX*) bumper cars (*US*), dodgems (*BRIT*)

carrocería *nf* bodywork, coachwork

carroña *nf* carrion *no pl*

carroza *nf* (*carruaje*) coach

carrusel (*LAm*) *nm* merry-go-round, carousel

carta *nf* letter; (*CULIN*) menu; (*naipe*) card; (*mapa*) map; (*JUR*) document ▶ **carta certificada** registered letter ▶ **carta de ajuste** (*TV*) test card ▶ **carta de crédito** credit card ▶ **carta marítima** chart ▶ **carta verde** (*AUTO*) green card

cartabón *nm* set square, triangle (*US*)

cartel *nm* (*anuncio*) poster, placard; (*ESCOL*) wall chart; (*COM*) cartel ❏ **cartelera** *nf* billboard, hoarding (*BRIT*); (*en periódico etc*) entertainments guide; **"en cartelera"** "showing"

cartera *nf* (*de bolsillo*) wallet, billfold (*US*); (*ESP: de colegial, cobrador*) satchel; (*LAm exc MÉX: de señora*) handbag, purse (*US*); (*ESP: para documentos*) briefcase; (*COM*) portfolio; **ocupa la ~ de Agricultura** she is Minister of Agriculture

carterista *nmf* pickpocket

cartero *nm* mailman (*US*), postman (*BRIT*)

cartilla *nf* primer, first reading book ▶ **cartilla de ahorros** savings book

cartón *nm* cardboard ▶ **cartón piedra** papier-mâché

cartucho *nm* (*MIL*) cartridge

cartulina *nf* card

casa *nf* house; (*hogar*) home; (*COM*) firm, company; **en ~** at home ▶ **casa consistorial** town hall ▶ **casa de huéspedes** boarding house ▶ **casa de socorro** first aid post ▶ **casa rodante** (*CS*) trailer (*US*), caravan (*BRIT*)

casado, -a *adj* married ♦ *nm/f* married man (woman)

casamiento *nm* marriage, wedding

casar *vt* to marry; (*JUR*) to quash, annul; **casarse** *vr* to marry, get married

cascabel *nm* (small) bell

cascada *nf* waterfall

cascanueces *nm inv* nutcrackers *pl*

cascar *vt* to crack, split, break (open); **cascarse** *vr* to crack, split, break (open)

cáscara *nf* (*de huevo, fruta seca*) shell; (*de fruta*) skin; (*de limón*) peel

casco *nm* (*de bombero, soldado*) helmet; (*NÁUT: de barco*) hull; (*ZOOL: de caballo*) hoof; (*botella*) empty bottle; (*de ciudad*): **el ~ antiguo** the old part; **el ~ urbano** the town center (*US*) o (*BRIT*) centre; **los ~s azules** the UN peace-keeping force, the blue helmets ▶ **casco de la estancia** (*RPl*) farmhouse

cascote *nm* rubble

casero, -a *adj* (*pan etc*) home-made ♦ *nm/f* (*propietario*) landlord(-lady); **ser muy ~** to be home-loving; **"comida casera"** "home cooking"

caseta *nf* hut; (*para bañista*) cubicle; (*de feria*) stall

casete *nf* (*cinta*) cassette ♦ *nm* (*ESP*) cassette player

casi *adv* almost, nearly; **~ nada** hardly anything; **~ nunca** hardly ever, almost never; **~ te caes** you almost fell

casilla *nf* (*casita*) hut, cabin; (*AJEDREZ*) square; (*para cartas*) pigeonhole ▶ **casilla de correo** (*CS*) Post Office Box ❏ **casillero** *nm* (*para cartas*) pigeonholes *pl*

casino *nm* club; (*de juego*) casino

caso *nm* case; **en ~ de ...** in case of ...; **en ~ de que ...** in case ...; **el ~ es que** the fact is that; **en ese ~** in that case; **hacer ~ a** to pay attention to; **hacer** o **venir al ~** to be relevant

caspa *nf* dandruff

cassette *nm* o *f* = **casete**

casta *nf* caste; (*raza*) breed; (*linaje*) lineage

castaña *nf* chestnut

castañetear *vi* (*dientes*) to chatter

castaño, -a *adj* brown, chestnut(-colored) (*US*), chestnut(-coloured) (*BRIT*) ♦ *nm* chestnut tree

castañuelas *nfpl* castanets

castellano, -a *adj, nm/f* Castilian ♦ *nm* (*LING*) Castilian, Spanish

castidad *nf* chastity, purity

castigar *vt* to punish; (*DEPORTE*) to penalize ❏ **castigo** *nm* punishment; (*DEPORTE*) penalty

Castilla *nf* Castile

castillo *nm* castle

castizo, -a *adj* (*LING*) pure

casto, -a *adj* chaste, pure

castor *nm* beaver

castrar *vt* to castrate

castrense *adj* (*disciplina, vida*) military

casual *adj* chance, accidental ❏ **casualidad** *nf* chance, accident;

(*combinación de circunstancias*) coincidence; **¡qué casualidad!** what a coincidence!

> ⚠ No confundir **casual** con la palabra inglesa *casual*.

cataclismo *nm* cataclysm

catador, a *nm/f* wine taster

catalán, -ana *adj, nm/f* Catalan ♦ *nm* (*LING*) Catalan

catalizador *nm* catalyst; (*AUTO*) catalytic convertor

catalogar *vt* to catalogue, catalog (*US*); **~ a algn (de)** (*fig*) to categorize sb (as)

catálogo *nm* catalogue, catalog (*US*)

Cataluña *nf* Catalonia

catar *vt* to taste, sample

catarata *nf* (*GEO*) waterfall; (*MED*) cataract

catarro *nm* catarrh; (*constipado*) cold

catástrofe *nf* catastrophe

catear (*MÉX*) *vt* (*vivienda*) to search

cátedra *nf* (*UNIV*) chair, professorship

catedral *nf* cathedral

catedrático, -a *nm/f* professor

categoría *nf* category; (*rango*) rank, standing; (*calidad*) quality; **de ~** (*hotel*) top-class

categórico, -a *adj* categorical

catolicismo *nm* Catholicism

católico, -a *adj, nm/f* Catholic

catorce *num* fourteen

cauce *nm* (*de río*) riverbed; (*fig*) channel

caución *nf* bail ◻ **caucionar** *vt* (*JUR*) to bail, go bail for

caudal *nm* (*de río*) volume, flow; (*fortuna*) wealth; (*abundancia*) abundance ◻ **caudaloso, -a** *adj* (*río*) large

caudillo *nm* leader, chief

causa *nf* cause; (*razón*) reason; (*JUR*) lawsuit, case; **a ~ de** because of

causar *vt* to cause

cautela *nf* caution, cautiousness ◻ **cauteloso, -a** *adj* cautious, wary

cautivar *vt* to capture; (*atraer*) to captivate

cautiverio *nm* captivity

cautividad *nf* = **cautiverio**

cautivo, -a *adj, nm/f* captive

cauto, -a *adj* cautious, careful

cava *nm* champagne-type wine

cavar *vt* to dig

caverna *nf* cave, cavern

cavidad *nf* cavity

cavilar *vt* to ponder

cayado *nm* (*de pastor*) crook; (*de obispo*) crozier

cayendo *etc vb ver* **caer**

caza *nf* (*acción: gen*) hunting; (: *con fusil*) shooting; (*una caza*) hunt, chase; (*de animales*) game ♦ *nm* (*AVIAT*) fighter

cazador, a *nm/f* hunter ◻ **cazadora** *nf* jacket

cazar *vt* to hunt; (*perseguir*) to chase; (*prender*) to catch

cazo *nm* saucepan

cazuela *nf* (*vasija*) pan; (*guisado*) casserole

CD *nm abr* (= *compact disc*) CD

CD-ROM *nm abr* CD-ROM

CE *nf abr* (= *Comunidad Europea*) EC

cebada *nf* barley

cebar *vt* (*animal*) to fatten (up); (*anzuelo*) to bait; (*MIL, TEC*) to prime

cebo *nm* (*para animales*) feed, food; (*para peces, fig*) bait; (*de arma*) charge

cebolla *nf* onion ◻ **cebolleta** *nf* green onion (*US*), spring onion (*BRIT*)

cebra *nf* zebra

cecear *vi* to lisp ◻ **ceceo** *nm* lisp

ceder *vt* to hand over, give up, part with ♦ *vi* (*renunciar*) to give in, yield; (*disminuir*) to diminish, decline; (*romperse*) to give way

cedro *nm* cedar

cédula *nf* certificate, document ▶ **cédula de identidad** (*LAm*) identity card ▶ **cédula electoral** (*LAm*) ballot

cegar *vt* to blind; (*tubería etc*) to block up, stop up ♦ *vi* to go blind; **cegarse** *vr*: **~se (de)** to be blinded (by)

ceguera *nf* blindness

CEI *nf abr* (= *Confederación de Estados Independientes*) CIS

ceja *nf* eyebrow

cejar *vi* (*fig*) to back down

celador, a *nm/f* (*de edificio*) watchman; (*de museo etc*) attendant

celda *nf* cell

celebración *nf* celebration

celebrar *vt* to celebrate; (*alabar*) to praise ♦ *vi* to be glad; **celebrarse** *vr* to occur, take place

célebre *adj* famous

celebridad *nf* fame; (*persona*) celebrity

celeste *adj* (*azul*) sky-blue

celestial *adj* celestial, heavenly

celibato *nm* celibacy

célibe *adj, nmf* celibate

celo¹ nm zeal; (REL) fervor (US), fervour (BRIT); (ZOOL): **en ~** on heat; **~s** nmpl jealousy sg; **tener ~s** to be jealous

celo² (ESP) nm Scotch tape® (US), Sellotape® (BRIT)

celofán nm cellophane

celoso, -a adj jealous; (trabajador) zealous

celta adj Celtic ♦ nmf Celt

célula nf cell ▶ **célula solar** solar cell

celular nm cellphone ▶ **celular con cámara** camera phone

celulitis nf cellulite

cementerio nm cemetery, graveyard

cemento nm cement; (hormigón) concrete; (LAm: cola) glue

cena nf evening meal, dinner

cenagal nm bog, quagmire

cenar vt to have for dinner ♦ vi to have dinner

cenicero nm ashtray

cenit nm zenith

ceniza nf ash, ashes pl

censo nm census ▶ **censo electoral** list of registered voters (US), electoral roll (BRIT)

censura nf (POL) censorship

censurar vt (idea) to censure; (cortar: película) to censor

centella nf spark

centellear vi (metal) to gleam; (estrella) to twinkle; (fig) to sparkle

centenar nm hundred

centenario, -a adj centennial ♦ nm centennial (US), centenary (BRIT)

centeno nm (BOT) rye

centésimo, -a adj hundredth

centígrado adj centigrade

centímetro nm centimeter (US), centimetre (BRIT)

céntimo nm cent

centinela nm sentry, guard

centollo nm spider crab

central adj central ♦ nf head office; (TEC) plant; (TEL) exchange ▶ **central eléctrica** power station ▶ **central nuclear** nuclear power station ▶ **central telefónica** telephone central office (US), telephone exchange (BRIT)

centralita (ESP) nf switchboard

centralizar vt to centralize

centrar vt to center (US), centre (BRIT)

céntrico, -a adj central

centrifugar vt to spin-dry

centrista adj center cpd (US), centre cpd (BRIT)

centro nm center (US), centre (BRIT) ▶ **centro comercial** shopping mall: **~ de atención al cliente** call center (US) o centre (BRIT) ▶ **centro juvenil** youth club

centroamericano, -a adj, nm/f Central American

ceñido, -a adj (chaqueta, pantalón) tight(-fitting)

ceñir vt (rodear) to encircle, surround; (ajustar) to fit (tightly)

ceño nm frown, scowl; **fruncir el ~** to frown, knit one's brow

cepillar vt to brush; (madera) to plane (down)

cepillo nm brush; (para madera) plane ▶ **cepillo de dientes** toothbrush

cera nf wax

cerámica nf pottery; (arte) ceramics

cerca nf fence ♦ adv near, nearby, close; **~ de** near, close to

cercanías nfpl (afueras) outskirts, suburbs

cercano, -a adj close, near

cercar vt to fence in; (rodear) to surround

cerciorar vt (asegurar) to assure; **cerciorarse** vr (asegurarse) to make sure

cerco nm (AGR) enclosure; (LAm: valla) fence; (MIL) siege

cerdo, -a nm/f pig/sow, hog (US)

cereal nm cereal; **~es** nmpl cereals, grain sg

cerebro nm brain; (fig) brains pl

ceremonia nf ceremony ❑ **ceremonial** adj, nm ceremonial ❑ **ceremonioso, -a** adj ceremonious

cereza nf cherry

cerilla (ESP) nf (fósforo) match

cerillo (MÉX) nm match

cernerse vr to hover

cero nm nothing, zero

cerquillo (CAm, RPl) nm bangs pl (US), fringe (BRIT)

cerrado, -a adj closed, shut; (con llave) locked; (tiempo) cloudy, overcast; (curva) sharp; (acento) thick, broad

cerradura nf (acción) closing; (mecanismo) lock

cerrajero nm locksmith

cerrar vt to close, shut; (paso, carretera) to close; (grifo) to turn off; (cuenta, negocio) to close ♦ vi to close, shut; (noche) to come down; **cerrarse** vr to close, shut; **~ con llave** to lock; **~ un trato** to strike a bargain

cerro nm hill

cerrojo nm (herramienta) bolt; (de puerta) latch

certamen nm competition, contest

certero, -a adj (gen) accurate

certeza nf certainty

certidumbre nf = **certeza**

certificado nm certificate

certificar vt (asegurar, atestar) to certify

cervatillo nm fawn

cervecería nf (fábrica) brewery; (bar) beer hall (US), public house (BRIT), pub (BRIT)

cerveza nf beer

cesante adj laid-off, redundant (BRIT)

cesar vi to cease, stop ♦ vt (funcionario) to remove from office

cesárea nf (MED) Caesarean operation o section

cese nm (de trabajo) dismissal; (de pago) suspension

césped (ESP) nm grass, lawn

cesta nf basket

cesto nm (large) basket, hamper

cetro nm scepter (US), sceptre (BRIT)

cfr abr (= confróntese) cf.

chabacano, -a adj vulgar, coarse ♦ nm (MÉX: durazno) apricot

chacal nm jackal

chacha (fam) nf maid

cháchara nf chatter; **estar de ~** to chatter away

chacra (CS) nf smallholding

chafa (MÉX: fam) adj useless, dud

chafar vt (aplastar) to crush; (plan etc) to ruin

chal nm shawl

chalado, -a (fam) adj crazy

chalé (pl ~s) nm villa, ≈ detached house (BRIT)

chaleco nm vest, waistcoat (BRIT)
  ► **chaleco salvavidas** life preserver (US) o jacket (BRIT)

chalet (pl ~s) nm = **chalé**

chamaco, -a (MÉX) nm/f (niño) kid

chambear (MÉX: fam) vi to earn one's living

champán nm champagne

champaña nm = **champán**

champiñón nm mushroom

champú (pl ~es, ~s) nm shampoo

chamuscar vt to scorch, sear, singe

chance (LAm) nm chance

chancho, -a (LAm exc MÉX) nm/f pig, hog (US)

chanchullo (fam) nm fiddle

chándal (ESP) nm sweat suit (US), tracksuit (BRIT)

chantaje nm blackmail

chapa nf (de metal) plate, sheet; (de madera) board, panel; (RPI AUTO) license (US) o number (BRIT) plate ❑ **chapado, -a** adj: **chapado en oro** gold-plated

chaparrón nm downpour, cloudburst

chaperón (MÉX) nm: **hacer de ~** to play gooseberry ❑ **chaperona** (LAm) nf: **hacer de chaperona** to play gooseberry

chapopote (MÉX) nm tar

chapotear vi to splash about

chapulín (MÉX, CAm) nm grasshopper

chapurrear vt (idioma) to speak badly

chapuza nf botched job

chapuzón nm: **darse un ~** to go for a dip

chaqueta nf jacket

chaquetón nm long jacket

charca nf pond, pool

charco nm pool, puddle

charcutería nf (tienda) store selling chiefly pork meat products; (productos) cooked pork meats pl

charla nf talk, chat; (conferencia) lecture

charlar vi to talk, chat

charlatán, -ana nm/f (hablador) chatterbox; (estafador) trickster

charol nm varnish; (cuero) patent leather

charola (MÉX) nf tray

charro (MÉX) nm typical Mexican

chascarrillo (fam) nm funny story

chasco nm (desengaño) disappointment

chasis nm inv chassis

chasquear vt (látigo) to crack; (lengua) to click ❑ **chasquido** nm crack; click

chatarra nf scrap (metal)

chato, -a adj flat; (nariz) snub

chaucha (RPI) nf pole (US) o runner (BRIT) bean

chaval, a (ESP) nm/f kid, lad/lass

chavo, -a (MÉX: fam) nm/f guy (girl)

checar (MÉX) vt: **~ tarjeta** (al entrar) to clock in o on; (: al salir) to clock off o out

checo, -a adj, nm/f Czech ♦ nm (LING) Czech

checoslovaco, -a adj, nm/f (HIST) Czech, Czechoslovak

Checoslovaquia nf (HIST) Czechoslovakia

cheque nm check (US), cheque (BRIT)
  ► **cheque de viaje** traveler's check (US), traveller's cheque (BRIT)

chequeo nm (MED) check-up; (AUTO) service

chequera (LAm) nf checkbook (US), chequebook (BRIT)

chévere (LAm: fam) adj great

chicano, -a adj, nm/f chicano

chícharo (MÉX, CAm) nm pea ► **chícharo de olor** sweet pea

chichón nm bump, lump

chicle nm chewing gum

chico, -a adj small, little ♦ nm/f (niño) child; (muchacho) boy (girl)

chiflado, -a adj crazy

chiflar vt to hiss, boo

chilango, -a (MÉX) adj of/from Mexico City

Chile nm Chile

chile nm chilli pepper

chileno, -a adj, nm/f Chilean

chillar vi (persona) to yell, scream; (animal salvaje) to howl; (cerdo) to squeal

chillido nm (de persona) yell, scream; (de animal) howl

chillón, -ona adj (niño) noisy; (color) loud, gaudy

chimenea nf chimney; (hogar) fireplace

China nf: (la) ~ China

chinche nf (insecto) (bed)bug; (LAm TEC) thumbtack (US), drawing pin (BRIT) ♦ nmf nuisance, pest

chincheta (ESP) nf thumbtack (US), drawing pin (BRIT)

chingada (MÉX: fam!) nf: hijo de la ~ bastard

chino, -a adj, nm/f Chinese ♦ nm (LING) Chinese; (MÉX: rizo) curl

chipirón nm (ZOOL, CULIN) squid

Chipre nf Cyprus ❏ **chipriota** adj, nmf Cypriot

chiquillo, -a nm/f (fam) kid

chirimoya nf custard apple, cherimoya (US)

chiringuito (ESP) nm small open-air bar

chiripa nf fluke

chirriar vi to creak, squeak

chirrido nm creak(ing), squeak(ing)

chis excl sh!

chisme nm (habladurías) piece of gossip; (fam: objeto) thingummyjig

chismoso, -a adj gossiping ♦ nm/f gossip

chispa nf spark; (fig) sparkle; (ingenio) wit; (fam) drunkenness

chispear vi (lloviznar) to drizzle

chisporrotear vi (fuego) to throw out sparks; (leña) to crackle; (aceite) to hiss, splutter

chiste nm joke, funny story

chistoso, -a adj funny, amusing

chivo, -a nm/f (billy-/nanny-)goat ▶ **chivo expiatorio** scapegoat

chocante adj startling; (extraño) odd; (ofensivo) shocking

chocar vi (vehículos etc) to collide, crash ♦ vt to shock; (sorprender) to startle; ~ **con** to collide with; (fig) to run into, run up against; ¡chócala! (fam) put it there!

chochear vi to be senile

chocho, -a adj doddering, senile; (fig) soft, doting

choclo (CS) nm (grano) sweet corn; (mazorca) corn on the cob

chocolate adj, nm chocolate ❏ **chocolatina** nf chocolate

chofer (LAm) (ESP **chófer**) nm chauffeur; (LAm: conductor) driver

choque etc vb ver **chocar** ♦ nm (impacto) impact; (golpe) jolt; (AUTO) crash; (fig) conflict ▶ **choque frontal** head-on collision

chorizo nm hard pork sausage, (type of) salami

chorrear vi to gush (out), spout (out); (gotear) to drip, trickle

chorro nm jet; (fig) stream

choza nf hut, shack

chubasco nm squall

chubasquero nm cagoule

chuchería nf trinket

chuleta nf chop, cutlet

chulo, -a adj (MÉX, CAm, ESP: fam): ¡qué vestido más ~! what a pretty dress!

chupaleta (MÉX) nf lollipop

chupar vt to suck; (absorber) to absorb; **chuparse** vr to grow thin

chupete (CS, ESP) nm pacifier (US), dummy (BRIT)

chupetín (RPl) nf lollipop

chupito (fam) nm shot

chupón (LAm) nm pacifier (US), dummy (BRIT)

churro nm (type of) fritter; (CAm: fam: porro) joint

chusma nf rabble, mob

chutar vi to shoot (at goal)

Cía. abr (= compañía) Co.

cianuro nm cyanide

cibercafé nm cybercafé

ciberterrorista nmf cyberterrorist

cicatriz nf scar ❏ **cicatrizarse** vr to heal (up), form a scar

ciclismo nm cycling

ciclista adj cycle cpd ♦ nmf cyclist

ciclo nm cycle

ciclón nm cyclone

cicloturismo nm: **hacer** ~ to go on a cycling vacation (US) or holiday (BRIT)

ciego, -a adj blind ♦ nm/f blind man (woman)

cielo nm sky; (REL) heaven; ¡~s! good heavens!

ciempiés nm inv centipede

cien num ver **ciento**

ciénaga nf marsh, swamp

ciencia nf science; **~s** nfpl (ESCOL) science sg
❏ **ciencia-ficción** nf science fiction

cieno nm mud, mire

científico, -a adj scientific ♦ nm/f scientist

ciento (tb: **cien**) num hundred; **pagar al 10 por ~** to pay at 10 percent

cierre etc vb ver **cerrar** ♦ nm closing, shutting; (con llave) locking; (LAm: cremallera) zipper (US), zip (fastener) (BRIT)

cierro etc vb ver **cerrar**

cierto, -a adj sure, certain; (un tal) a certain; (correcto) right, correct; **~ hombre** a certain man; **ciertas personas** certain o some people; **sí, es ~** yes, that's correct

ciervo nm deer; (macho) stag

cierzo nm north wind

cifra nf number; (secreta) code

cifrar vt to code, write in code

cigala nf Dublin Bay Shrimp

cigarra nf cicada

cigarrillo nm cigarette

cigarro nm cigarette; (puro) cigar

cigüeña nf stork

cilíndrico, -a adj cylindrical

cilindro nm cylinder

cima nf (de montaña) top, peak; (de árbol) top; (fig) height

cimbrearse vr to sway

cimentar vt to lay the foundations of; (fig: fundar) to found

cimiento nm foundation

cinc nm zinc

cincel nm chisel ❏ **cincelar** vt to chisel

cinco num five

cincuenta num fifty

cine nm cinema

cineasta nmf moviemaker (US), film maker (BRIT)

cinematográfico, -a adj cine-, film cpd

cínico, -a adj cynical ♦ nm/f cynic

cinismo nm cynicism

cinta nf band, strip; (de tela) ribbon; (película) reel; (de máquina de escribir) ribbon; (MÉX: cordón) lace ▶ **cinta adhesiva** adhesive tape ▶ **cinta de video** (LAm) video tape ▶ **cinta de vídeo** (ESP) video tape ▶ **cinta magnetofónica** tape ▶ **cinta métrica** tape measure

cintura nf waist

cinturón nm belt ▶ **cinturón de seguridad** safety belt

ciprés nm cypress (tree)

circo nm circus

circuito nm circuit

circulación nf circulation; (AUTO) traffic

circular adj, nf circular ♦ vi, vt to circulate ♦ vi (AUTO) to drive; **"circule por la derecha"** "keep (to the) right"

círculo nm circle ▶ **círculo vicioso** vicious circle

circuncidar vt to circumcise

circundar vt to surround

circunferencia nf circumference

circunscribir vt to circumscribe; **circunscribirse** vr to be limited

circunscripción nf (POL) constituency

circunspecto, -a adj circumspect, cautious

circunstancia nf circumstance

cirio nm (wax) candle

ciruela nf plum ▶ **ciruela pasa** prune

cirugía nf surgery ▶ **cirugía estética** o **plástica** plastic surgery

cirujano nm surgeon

cisne nm swan

cisterna nf tank, cistern

cita nf appointment, meeting; (de novios) date; (referencia) quotation

citación nf (JUR) summons sg

citar vt (gen) to make an appointment with; (JUR) to summons; (un autor, texto) to quote; **citarse** vr: **se ~on en el cine** they arranged to meet at the movies (US) o cinema (BRIT)

citología (ESP) nf pap smear (US), smear test (BRIT)

cítricos nmpl citrus fruit(s)

ciudad nf town; (más grande) city
❏ **ciudadanía** nf citizenship
❏ **ciudadano, -a** nm/f citizen

cívico, -a adj civic

civil adj civil ♦ nm (guardia) policeman

civilización nf civilization

civilizar vt to civilize

civismo nm public spirit

cizaña nf (fig) discord

cl. abr (= centilitro) cl.

clamar vt to cry out for, clamor (US) o clamour (BRIT) for ♦ vi to cry out, clamor (US), clamour (BRIT)

clamor nm protest, clamor (US), clamour (BRIT)

clandestino, -a adj clandestine; (POL) underground

claqué (LAm exc MÉX) nm tap dancing

clara nf (de huevo) egg white

claraboya nf skylight

clarear vi (el día) to dawn; (el cielo) to clear up, brighten up; **clarearse** vr to be transparent

clarete nm rosé (wine)

claridad nf (de día) brightness; (de estilo) clarity

clarificar vt to clarify

clarinete nm clarinet

clarividencia nf clairvoyance; (fig) far-sightedness

claro, -a adj clear; (luminoso) bright; (color) light; (evidente) clear, evident; (poco espeso) thin ♦ nm (en bosque) clearing ♦ adv clearly ♦ excl: ¡~ que sí! of course!

clase nf class ▶ **clase alta/media/obrera** upper/middle/working class ▶ **clases particulares** private lessons o tuition sg

clásico, -a adj classical

clasificación nf classification; (DEPORTE) league (table)

clasificar vt to classify

claudicar vi to give in

claustro nm cloister

cláusula nf clause

clausura nf closing, closure ❑ **clausurar** (congreso etc) to bring to a close

clavar vt (clavo) to hammer in; (cuchillo) to stick, thrust

clave nf key; (MÚS) clef ▶ **clave de acceso** password ▶ **clave lada** (MÉX) area (US) o dialling (BRIT) code

clavel nm carnation

clavícula nf collar bone

clavija nf peg, dowel, pin; (ELEC) plug

clavo nm (de metal) nail; (BOT) clove

claxon (pl ~s) nm horn

clemencia nf mercy, clemency

cleptómano, -a nm/f kleptomaniac

clérigo nm priest

clero nm clergy

cliché nm cliché; (FOTO) negative

cliente, -a nm/f client, customer

clientela nf clientele, customers pl

clima nm climate

climatizado, -a adj air-conditioned

clímax nm inv climax

clínica nf clinic; (particular) private hospital

clip (pl ~s) nm paper clip

clítoris nm inv (ANAT) clitoris

cloaca nf sewer; (MÉX: de tejado) gutter

cloro nm chlorine; (MÉX, CAM: lejía) (household) bleach

clóset (MÉX) nm cupboard, closet (US)

club (pl ~s o ~es) nm club ▶ **club nocturno** night club

cm abr (= centímetro, centímetros) cm

coacción nf coercion, compulsion ❑ **coaccionar** vt to coerce

coagular vt (leche, sangre) to clot; **coagularse** vr to clot ❑ **coágulo** nm clot

coalición nf coalition

coartada nf alibi

coartar vt to limit, restrict

coba (MÉX, ESP) nf: **dar ~ a algn** to soft-soap sb

cobarde adj cowardly ♦ nm coward ❑ **cobardía** nf cowardice

cobaya nf guinea pig

cobertizo nm shelter

cobertura nf cover

cobija (LAm) nf blanket

cobijar vt (cubrir) to cover; (proteger) to shelter ❑ **cobijo** nm shelter

cobra nf cobra

cobrador, a nm/f (de autobús) conductor (conductress); (de impuestos, gas) collector

cobrar vt (cheque) to cash; (sueldo) to collect, draw; (objeto) to recover; (precio) to charge; (deuda) to collect ♦ vi to be paid; **cóbrese al entregar** cash on delivery

cobre nm copper; ~s nmpl (MÚS) brass instruments

cobro nm (de cheque) cashing; **presentar al ~** to cash

cocaína nf cocaine

cocción nf (CULIN) cooking; (en agua) boiling

cocear vi to kick

cocer vt, vi to cook; (en agua) to boil; (en horno) to bake

coche nm (ESP AUTO) automobile (US), car (BRIT); (de tren, de caballos) coach, carriage; (para niños) baby carriage (US), pram (BRIT); **ir en ~** (ESP) to drive ▶ **coche celular** (ESP) police van, patrol wagon (US) ▶ **coche de bomberos** (ESP) firetruck (US), fire engine (BRIT) ▶ **coche dormitorio** (CS) sleeping car ▶ **coche fúnebre** hearse ❑ **coche-cama** (pl coches-cama) nm (FERRO) sleeping car, Pullman (US), sleeper (BRIT)

cochera nf (MÉX, ESP: de carros) garage; (de autobuses, trenes) depot

coche restaurante (pl coches restaurante) nm (FERRO) dining car, diner

cochinillo nm (CULIN) suckling pig, sucking pig

cochino, -a adj filthy, dirty ♦ nm/f pig

cocido nm stew

cocina nf kitchen; (LAm exc MÉX, ESP: aparato) stove, cooker (BRIT); (acto) cookery ► **cocina eléctrica/de gas** (LAm exc MÉX, ESP) electric/gas stove o cooker (BRIT) ► **cocina francesa** French cuisine ❏ **cocinar** vt, vi to cook

cocinero, -a nm/f cook

coco nm coconut

cocodrilo nm crocodile

cocotero nm coconut palm

cóctel nm cocktail

codazo nm: **dar un ~ a algn** to nudge sb

codicia nf greed ❏ **codiciar** vt to covet ❏ **codicioso, -a** adj covetous

código nm code ► **código civil** common law ► **código de barras** bar code ► **código de (la) circulación** highway code ► **código de la zona** (LAm) area (US) o dialling (BRIT) code ► **código postal** zip code (US), postcode (BRIT)

codillo nm (ZOOL) knee; (TEC) elbow (joint)

codo nm (ANAT, de tubo) elbow; (ZOOL) knee

codorniz nf quail

coerción nf coercion

coetáneo, -a adj, nm/f contemporary

coexistir vi to coexist

cofradía nf brotherhood, fraternity

cofre nm (de joyas) case; (de dinero) chest; (MÉX AUTO) hood (US), bonnet (BRIT)

coger vt (ESP: tomar) to take (hold of); (ESP: objeto caído) to pick up; (ESP: frutas) to pick, harvest; (ESP: resfriado, ladrón, pelota) to catch **cogerse** vr (dedo) to catch; **~ por: cogió por esta calle** he went down this street; **~se a algo/algn** to hold on to sth/sb

cogollo nm (de lechuga) heart

cogote nm back o nape of the neck

cohabitar vi to live together, cohabit

cohecho nm (acción) bribery; (soborno) bribe

coherente adj coherent

cohesión nm cohesion

cohete nm rocket

cohibido, -a adj (PSICO) inhibited; (tímido) shy

cohibir vt to restrain, restrict

coincidencia nf coincidence

coincidir vi (en idea) to coincide, agree; (en lugar) to coincide

coito nm intercourse, coitus

coja etc vb ver **coger**

cojear vi (persona) to limp, hobble; (mueble) to wobble, rock

cojera nf limp

cojín nm cushion ❏ **cojinete** nm (TEC) ball bearing

cojo, -a etc vb ver **coger** ♦ adj (que no puede andar) lame, crippled; (mueble) wobbly ♦ nm/f lame person, cripple

cojonudo, -a (fam) adj great, fantastic

col nf (ESP) cabbage ► **coles de Bruselas** Brussels sprouts

cola nf tail; (de gente) line (US), queue (BRIT); (lugar) end, last place; (para pegar) glue, gum; **hacer ~** to line (up) (US), queue (up) (BRIT)

colaborador, a nm/f collaborator

colaborar vi to collaborate

colador nm (para líquidos) strainer; (para verduras etc) colander

colapso nm collapse; **~ nervioso** nervous breakdown

colar vt (líquido) to strain off; (metal) to cast ♦ vi to ooze, seep (through); **colarse** vr to cut in line (US), jump the queue (BRIT); **~se en** to get into without paying; (fiesta) to gatecrash

colcha nf bedspread

colchón nm mattress ► **colchón inflable** o **neumático** air bed o mattress

colchoneta nf (en gimnasio) mat; (de playa) air bed

colección nf collection ❏ **coleccionar** vt to collect ❏ **coleccionista** nmf collector

colecta nf collection

colectivo, -a adj collective, joint

colega nmf colleague

colegial, a nm/f schoolboy(-girl)

colegio nm college; (escuela) school; (de abogados etc) association ► **colegio electoral** polling place (US), polling station (BRIT)

colegir vt to infer, conclude

cólera nf (ira) anger; (MED) cholera ❏ **colérico, -a** adj irascible, bad-tempered

colesterol nm cholesterol

coleta nf pigtail

colgante adj hanging ♦ nm (joya) pendant

colgar vt to hang (up); (ropa) to hang out ♦ vi to hang; (TEL) to hang up

cólico nm colic

coliflor nf cauliflower

colilla nf cigarette end, butt

colina nf hill

colisión nf collision ► **colisión frontal** head-on crash

collar nm necklace; (de perro) collar

colmar vt to fill to the brim; (fig) to realize, fulfill (US), fulfil (BRIT)

colmena nf beehive

colmillo nm (diente) eye tooth; (de elefante) tusk; (de perro) fang

colmo nm: **¡es el ~!** it's the limit!

colocación nf (acto) placing; (empleo) job, position

colocar vt to place, put, position; (dinero) to invest; (poner en empleo) to find a job for; **colocarse** vr to get a job

Colombia nf Colombia ❑ **colombiano, -a** adj, nm/f Colombian

colonia nf colony; (de casas) residential area; (agua de colonia) cologne ▶ **colonia proletaria** (MÉX) shantytown

colonización nf colonization ❑ **colonizador, a** adj colonizing ♦ nm/f colonist, settler

colonizar vt to colonize

coloquio nm conversation; (congreso) conference

color nm color (US), colour (BRIT)

colorado, -a adj (rojo) red; (MÉX: chiste) smutty, rude

colorante nm coloring (US), colouring (BRIT)

colorear vt to color (US), colour (BRIT)

colorete nm blusher

colorido nm coloring (US), colouring (BRIT)

columna nf column; (pilar) pillar; (apoyo) support

columpiar vt to swing; **columpiarse** vr to swing ❑ **columpio** nm swing

coma nf comma ♦ nm (MED) coma

comadre nf (madrina) godmother; (chismosa) gossip ❑ **comadrona** nf midwife

comal (MÉX, CAm) nm griddle

comandancia nf command

comandante nm commandant

comarca nf region

combar vt to bend, curve

combate nm fight ❑ **combatiente** nm combatant

combatir vt to fight, combat

combinación nf combination; (QUÍM) compound; (prenda) slip

combinar vt to combine

combustible nm fuel

combustión nf combustion

comedia nf comedy; (TEATRO) play, drama

comediante nmf (comic) actor (actress)

comedido, -a adj moderate

comedor, a nm (habitación) dining room; (cantina) canteen

comensal nmf fellow guest (o diner)

comentar vt to comment on

comentario nm comment, remark; (literario) commentary; **~s** nmpl (chismes) gossip sg

comentarista nmf commentator

comenzar vt, vi to begin, start; **~ a hacer algo** to begin o start doing sth

comer vt to eat; (DAMAS, AJEDREZ) to take, capture ♦ vi to eat; (MÉX: almorzar) to have lunch; **comerse** vr to eat up

comercial adj commercial; (relativo al negocio) business cpd ♦ nm (LAm TV, RADIO) commercial ❑ **comercializar** vt (producto) to market; (pey) to commercialize

comerciante nmf trader, merchant

comerciar vi to trade, do business

comercio nm commerce, trade; (negocio) business; (fig) dealings pl ▶ **comercio electrónico** e-commerce

comestible adj eatable, edible ❑ **comestibles** nmpl food sg, foodstuffs

cometa nm comet ♦ nf kite

cometer vt to commit

cometido nm task, assignment

comezón nf itch, itching

cómic nm (LAm: para niños) comic (BRIT); (para adultos) comic book (US), comic (BRIT)

comicios nmpl elections

cómico, -a adj comic(al) ♦ nm/f comedian

comida nf (alimento) food; (almuerzo, cena) meal; (MÉX: de mediodía) lunch ▶ **comida basura** (LAm exc MÉX, ESP) junk food ▶ **comida chatarra** (MÉX) junk food

comidilla nf: **ser la ~ de la ciudad** to be the talk of the town

comienzo etc vb ver **comenzar** ♦ nm beginning, start

comillas nfpl quotation marks, quotes (US)

comilona (fam) nf blow-out

comino nm: **(no) me importa un ~** I don't give a damn

comisaría nf (de policía) police station; (MIL) commissariat

comisario nm (MIL etc) commissary; (POL) commissar

comisión nf commission

comité (pl ~s) nm committee

comitiva nf retinue

como adv as; (tal): **~ like**; (aproximadamente) about, approximately ♦ conj (ya que, puesto que) as, since; **~ si** as if; **es tan alto ~ ancho** it is as high as it is wide

cómo *adv* how?, why? ♦ *excl* what?, I beg your pardon? ♦ *nm*: **el ~ y el porqué** the whys and wherefores; **¡~ no!** of course!

cómoda *nf* chest of drawers

comodidad *nf* comfort; **venga a su ~** come at your convenience

comodín *nm* joker

cómodo, -a *adj* comfortable; (*práctico, de fácil uso*) convenient

compact disc *nm* compact disk player

compacto, -a *adj* compact

compadecer *vt* to pity, be sorry for; **compadecerse** *vr*: **~se de** to pity, be o feel sorry for

compadre *nm* (*padrino*) godfather; (*amigo*) friend, pal

compañero, -a *nm/f* companion; (*novio*) boy/girlfriend ▶ **compañero de clase** classmate

compañía *nf* company

comparación *nf* comparison; **en ~ con** in comparison with

comparar *vt* to compare

comparecer *vi* to appear (in court)

comparsa *nmf* (*TEATRO*) extra

compartimiento *nm* (*FERRO*) compartment

compartir *vt* to share; (*dinero, comida etc*) to divide (up), share (out)

compás *nm* (*MÚS*) beat, rhythm; (*MAT*) compasses *pl*; (*NÁUT etc*) compass

compasión *nf* compassion, pity

compasivo, -a *adj* compassionate

compatibilidad *nf* compatibility

compatible *adj* compatible

compatriota *nmf* compatriot, fellow countryman(-woman)

compendiar *vt* to summarize ❑ **compendio** *nm* summary

compenetrarse *vr* to be in tune

compensación *nf* compensation

compensar *vt* to compensate

competencia *nf* (*incumbencia*) domain, field; (*JUR, habilidad*) competence; (*rivalidad*) competition

competente *adj* competent

competición *nf* competition

competir *vi* to compete

compilar *vt* to compile

compinche (*LAm*) *nmf* buddy (*US*), pal (*BRIT*)

complacencia *nf* (*placer*) pleasure; (*tolerancia excesiva*) complacency

complacer *vt* to please; **complacerse** *vr* to be pleased

complaciente *adj* kind, obliging, helpful

complejo, -a *adj, nm* complex ▶ **complejo habitacional** (*LAm*) housing development

complementario, -a *adj* complementary

completar *vt* to complete

completo, -a *adj* complete; (*perfecto*) perfect; (*lleno*) full ♦ *nm* full complement

complicado, -a *adj* complicated; **estar ~ en** to be mixed up in

cómplice *nmf* accomplice

complot (*pl* **~s**) *nm* plot

componer *vt* (*MÚS, LITERATURA, IMPRENTA*) to compose; (*algo roto*) to mend, repair; (*arreglar*) to arrange; **componerse** *vr*: **~se de** to consist of; **componérselas para hacer algo** to manage to do sth

comportamiento *nm* conduct, behavior (*US*), behaviour (*BRIT*)

comportarse *vr* to behave

composición *nf* composition

compositor, a *nm/f* composer

compostura *nf* (*actitud*) composure

compra *nf* purchase; **ir de ~s** to go shopping ❑ **comprador, a** *nm/f* buyer, purchaser

comprar *vt* to buy, purchase

comprender *vt* to understand; (*incluir*) to comprise, include

comprensión *nf* understanding ❑ **comprensivo, -a** *adj* (*actitud*) understanding

compresa (*ESP*) *nf* (*para mujer*) sanitary napkin (*US*) o towel (*BRIT*)

comprimido, -a *adj* compressed ♦ *nm* (*MED*) pill, tablet

comprimir *vt* to compress

comprobante *nm* proof; (*COM*) voucher ▶ **comprobante de compra** proof of purchase

comprobar *vt* to check; (*probar*) to prove; (*TEC*) to check, test

comprometer *vt* to compromise; (*poner en peligro*) to endanger; **comprometerse** *vr* (*involucrarse*) to get involved

compromiso *nm* (*obligación*) obligation; (*cometido*) commitment; (*convenio*) agreement; (*apuro*) awkward situation

compuesto, -a *adj*: **~ de** composed of, made up of ♦ *nm* compound

computador (*LAm*) *nm* = **computadora**

computadora (*LAm*) *nf* computer ▶ **computadora central** mainframe (computer) ▶ **computadora personal** personal computer

cómputo *nm* calculation

comulgar vi to receive communion

común adj common ♦ nm: **el ~** the community

comunicación nf communication; (informe) report

comunicado nm announcement ▶ **comunicado de prensa** press release

comunicar vt, vi to communicate; **comunicarse** vr to communicate; **está comunicando** (TEL) the line's busy (US) o engaged (BRIT) ❑ **comunicativo, -a** adj communicative

comunidad nf community ▶ **comunidad autónoma** (ESP POL) autonomous region ▶ **Comunidad (Económica) Europea** European (Economic) Community

comunión nf communion

comunismo nm communism ❑ **comunista** adj, nmf communist

---

con

PALABRA CLAVE

prep

1 (medio, compañía) with; **comer con cuchara** to eat with a spoon; **pasear con algn** to go for a walk with sb

2 (a pesar de): **con todo, merece nuestros respetos** all the same, he deserves our respect

3 (para con): **es muy bueno para con los niños** he's very good with (the) children

4 (+ infin): **con llegar tan tarde se quedó sin comer** by arriving so late he missed out on eating

♦ conj: **con que: será suficiente con que le escribas** it will be sufficient if you write to her

---

conato nm attempt ▶ **conato de robo** attempted robbery

concebir vt, vi to conceive

conceder vt to concede

concejal, a nm/f councilman(-woman), councilor (US), councillor (BRIT)

concentración nf concentration

concentrar vt to concentrate; **concentrarse** vr to concentrate

concepción nf conception

concepto nm concept

concernir vi to concern; **en lo que concierne a ...** as far as ... is concerned; **en lo que a mí concierne** as far as I'm concerned

concertar vt (MÚS) to harmonize; (acordar: precio) to agree; (: tratado) to conclude; (trato) to arrange, fix up; (combinar: esfuerzos) to coordinate ♦ vi to harmonize, be in tune

concesión nf concession

concesionario nm (licensed) dealer, agent

concha nf shell

conciencia nf conscience; **tener/tomar ~ de** to be/become aware of; **tener la ~ limpia/tranquila** to have a clear conscience

concienciar vt to make aware; **concienciarse** vr to become aware

concienzudo, -a adj conscientious

concierto etc vb ver **concertar** ♦ nm concert; (obra) concerto

conciliar vt to reconcile

concilio nm council

conciso, -a adj concise

concluir vt, vi to conclude; **concluirse** vr to conclude

conclusión nf conclusion

concluyente adj (prueba, información) conclusive

concordar vt to reconcile ♦ vi to agree, tally

concordia nf harmony

concretar vt to make concrete, make more specific; **concretarse** vr to become more definite

concreto, -a adj, nm (LAm: hormigón) concrete; **en ~** (en resumen) to sum up; (específicamente) specifically; **no hay nada en ~** there's nothing definite

concurrencia nf turnout

concurrido, -a adj (calle) busy; (local, reunión) crowded

concurrir vi (juntarse: ríos) to meet, come together; (: personas) to gather, meet

concursante nmf competitor

concurso nm (de público) crowd; (ESCOL, DEPORTE, competencia) competition; (ayuda) help, cooperation

condal adj: **la Ciudad C~** Barcelona

conde nm count

condecoración nf (MIL) medal

condecorar vt (MIL) to decorate

condena nf sentence

condenación nf condemnation; (REL) damnation

condenar vt to condemn; (JUR) to convict; **condenarse** vr (REL) to be damned

condensar vt to condense

condesa nf countess

condición nf condition ❑ **condicional** adj conditional

condicionar vt (acondicionar) to condition; **~ algo a** to make sth conditional on

condimento nm seasoning

condolerse *vr* to sympathize

condominio (*LAm*) *nm* condominium (*US*), block of flats (*BRIT*)

condón *nm* condom

conducir *vt* to take, convey; (*ESP AUTO*) to drive ♦ *vi* (*ESP AUTO*) to drive; (*fig*) to lead; **conducirse** *vr* to behave

conducta *nf* conduct, behavior (*US*), behaviour (*BRIT*)

conducto *nm* pipe, tube; (*fig*) channel

conductor, a *adj* leading, guiding ♦ *nm* (*FÍSICA*) conductor ♦ *nm/f* (*ESP: de vehículo*) driver

conduje *etc vb ver* **conducir**

conduzco *etc vb ver* **conducir**

conectado, -a *adj* (*INFORM*) on-line

conectar *vt* to connect (up); (*enchufar*) plug in

conejillo *nm* (*ZOOL*): **~ de Indias** guinea pig

conejo *nm* rabbit

conexión *nf* connection

confección *nf* preparation; (*industria*) clothing industry

confeccionar *vt* to make (up)

confederación *nf* confederation

conferencia *nf* conference; (*lección*) lecture; (*ESP TEL*) call

conferenciante (*ESP*) (*LAm* **conferencista**) *nmf* lecturer

conferir *vt* to award

confesar *vt* to confess, admit

confesión *nf* confession

confesionario *nm* confessional

confeti *nm* confetti

confiado, -a *adj* (*crédulo*) trusting; (*seguro*) confident

confianza *nf* trust; (*seguridad*) confidence; (*familiaridad*) intimacy, familiarity

confiar *vt* to entrust ♦ *vi* to trust

confidencia *nf* confidence

confidencial *adj* confidential

confidente *nmf* confidant/e; (*policial*) informer

configurar *vt* to shape, form

confín *nm* limit; **confines** *nmpl* confines, limits

confinar *vi* to confine; (*desterrar*) to banish

confirmar *vt* to confirm

confiscar *vt* to confiscate

confite *nm* candy (*US*), sweet (*BRIT*)

confitería (*ESP*) *nf* (*tienda*) confectioner's, candy store (*US*)

confitura *nf* preserve, jelly (*US*), jam (*BRIT*)

conflictivo, -a *adj* (*asunto, propuesta*) controversial; (*país, situación*) troubled

conflicto *nm* conflict; (*fig*) clash

confluir *vi* (*ríos*) to meet; (*gente*) to gather

conformar *vt* to shape, fashion ♦ *vi* to agree; **conformarse** *vr* to conform; (*resignarse*) to resign o.s.

conforme *adj* (*correspondiente*): **~ con** in line with; (*de acuerdo*): **estar ~s (con algo)** to be in agreement (with sth) ♦ *adv* as ♦ *excl* agreed! ♦ *prep*: **~ a** in accordance with; **quedarse ~ (con algo)** to be satisfied (with sth)

conformidad *nf* (*semejanza*) similarity; (*acuerdo*) agreement □ **conformista** *adj*, *nmf* conformist

confortable *adj* comfortable

confortar *vt* to comfort

confrontar *vt* to confront; (*dos personas*) to bring face to face; (*cotejar*) to compare

confundir *vt* (*equivocar*) to mistake, confuse; (*turbar*) to confuse; **confundirse** *vr* (*turbarse*) to get confused; (*equivocarse*) to make a mistake; (*mezclarse*) to mix

confusión *nf* confusion

confuso, -a *adj* confused

congelado, -a *adj* frozen □ **congelador** *nm* (*aparato*) freezer, deep freeze □ **congelados** *nmpl* frozen food(s)

congelar *vt* to freeze; **congelarse** *vr* (*sangre, grasa*) to congeal

congeniar *vi* to get along (*US*) *o* on (*BRIT*) well

congestión *nf* congestion

congestionar *vt* to congest

congoja *nf* distress, grief

congraciarse *vr* to ingratiate o.s.

congratular *vt* to congratulate

congregación *nf* congregation

congregar *vt* to gather together; **congregarse** *vr* to gather together

congresista *nmf* delegate, congressman (-woman)

congreso *nm* congress

congrio *nm* conger eel

conjetura *nf* guess □ **conjeturar** *vt* to guess

conjugar *vt* to combine, fit together; (*LING*) to conjugate

conjunción *nf* conjunction

conjunto, -a *adj* joint, united ♦ *nm* whole; (*MÚS*) band; **en ~** as a whole

conjurar *vt* (*REL*) to exorcise; (*fig*) to ward off ♦ *vi* to plot

conmemoración *nf* commemoration

conmemorar vt to commemorate

conmigo pron with me

conmoción nf shock; (fig) upheaval
▶ **conmoción cerebral** (MED) concussion

conmovedor, a adj touching, moving;
(emocionante) exciting

conmover vt to shake, disturb; (fig) to move

conmutador nm switch; (LAm: centralita)
switchboard; (: central) telephone central
office (US), telephone exchange (BRIT)

cono nm cone ▶ **Cono Sur** Southern Cone

conocedor, a adj expert, knowledgeable
♦ nm/f expert

conocer vt to know; (por primera vez) to
meet, get to know; (entender) to know about;
(reconocer) to recognize; **conocerse** vr (una
persona) to know o.s.; (dos personas) to (get to)
know each other

conocido, -a adj (well-)known ♦ nm/f
acquaintance

conocimiento nm knowledge; (MED)
consciousness; **~s** nmpl (saber) knowledge sg

conozco etc vb ver **conocer**

conque conj and so, so then

conquista nf conquest
❑ **conquistador, a** adj conquering ♦ nm
conqueror

conquistar vt to conquer

consagrar vt (REL) to consecrate; (fig) to
devote

consciente adj conscious

consecución nf acquisition; (de fin)
attainment

consecuencia nf consequence, outcome;
(coherencia) consistency

consecuente adj consistent

consecutivo, -a adj consecutive

conseguir vt to get, obtain; (objetivo) to
attain

consejero, -a nm/f adviser, consultant; (POL)
councilor (US), councillor (BRIT)

consejo nm advice; (POL) council ▶ **consejo
de administración** (COM) board of
directors ▶ **consejo de guerra** court
martial ▶ **consejo de ministros** cabinet
meeting

consenso nm consensus

consentimiento nm consent

consentir vt (permitir, tolerar) to consent to;
(mimar) to pamper, spoil; (aguantar) to put up
with ♦ vi to agree, consent; **~ que algn haga
algo** to allow sb to do sth

conserje nm (de colegio) janitor; (de facultad)
head custodian (US), head porter (BRIT); (de
hotel) doorman, hall porter (BRIT); (de edificio
oficial, museo) janitor, caretaker (Brit)

conservación nf conservation; (de
alimentos, vida) preservation

conservador, a adj (POL) conservative
♦ nm/f conservative

conservante nm preservative

conservar vt to conserve, keep; (alimentos,
vida) to preserve; **conservarse** vr to survive

conservas nfpl canned food(s) pl

conservatorio nm (MÚS) conservatoire,
conservatory

considerable adj considerable

consideración nf consideration;
(estimación) respect

considerado, -a adj (atento) considerate;
(respetado) respected

considerar vt to consider

consigna nf (orden) order, instruction; (para
equipajes) checkroom (US), left-luggage office
(BRIT)

consigo etc vb ver **conseguir** ♦ pron (m)
with him; (f) with her; (Vd) with you; (reflexivo)
with o.s.

consiguiendo etc vb ver **conseguir**

consiguiente adj consequent; **por ~** and
so, therefore, consequently

consistente adj consistent; (sólido) solid,
firm; (válido) sound

consistir vi: **~ en** (componerse de) to consist
of

consola nf (mueble) console table; (de
videojuegos) console

consolación nf consolation

consolar vt to console

consolidar vt to consolidate

consomé (pl ~s) nm consommé, clear soup

consonante adj consonant, harmonious
♦ nf consonant

consorcio nm consortium

conspiración nf conspiracy

conspirador, a nm/f conspirator

conspirar vi to conspire

constancia nf constancy; **dejar ~ de** to put
on record

constante adj, nf constant

constar vi (evidenciarse) to be clear o evident;
~ de to consist of

constatar vt to verify

consternación nf consternation

constipado, -a *adj*: **estar ~** to have a cold ♦ *nm* cold

⚠ No confundir **constipado** con la palabra inglesa *constipated*.

constitución *nf* constitution
❏ **constitucional** *adj* constitutional

constituir *vt* (*formar, componer*) to constitute, make up; (*fundar, erigir, ordenar*) to constitute, establish

constituyente *adj* constituent

constreñir *vt* (*restringir*) to restrict

construcción *nf* construction, building

constructor, a *nm/f* builder

construir *vt* to build, construct

construyendo *etc vb ver* **construir**

consuelo *nm* consolation, solace

cónsul *nm* consul ❏ **consulado** *nm* consulate

consulta *nf* consultation; (*MED*): **horas de ~** office hours (*US*), surgery hours (*BRIT*)

consultar *vt* to consult

consultorio *nm* (*MED*) doctor's office (*US*), surgery (*BRIT*)

consumar *vt* to complete, carry out; (*crimen*) to commit; (*sentencia*) to carry out

consumición *nf* consumption; (*bebida*) drink; (*comida*) food ▶ **consumición mínima** cover charge

consumidor, a *nm/f* consumer

consumir *vt* to consume; **consumirse** *vr* to be consumed; (*persona*) to waste away

consumismo *nm* consumerism

consumo *nm* consumption

contabilidad *nf* accounting, book-keeping; (*profesión*) accountancy ❏ **contable** (*ESP*) *nmf* accountant

contacto *nm* contact; (*ESP AUTO*) ignition

contado, -a *adj*: **~s** (*escasos*) numbered, scarce, few ♦ *nm*: **pagar al ~** to pay (in) cash

contador, a *nm* (*ESP: aparato*) meter ♦ *nm/f* (*LAm COM*) accountant

contagiar *vt* (*enfermedad*) to pass on, transmit; (*persona*) to infect; **contagiarse** *vr* to become infected

contagio *nm* infection ❏ **contagioso, -a** *adj* infectious; (*fig*) catching

contaminación *nf* contamination; (*polución*) pollution

contaminar *vt* to contaminate; (*aire, agua*) to pollute

contante *adj*: **dinero ~ (y sonante)** cash

contar *vt* (*páginas, dinero*) to count; (*anécdota, chiste etc*) to tell ♦ *vi* to count; **~ con** to rely on, count on

contemplación *nf* contemplation

contemplar *vt* to contemplate; (*mirar*) to look at

contemporáneo, -a *adj, nm/f* contemporary

contendiente *nmf* contestant

contenedor *nm* container

contener *vt* to contain, hold; (*retener*) to hold back, contain; **contenerse** *vr* to control *o* restrain o.s.

contenido, -a *adj* (*moderado*) restrained; (*risa etc*) suppressed ♦ *nm* contents *pl*, content

contentar *vt* (*satisfacer*) to satisfy; (*complacer*) to please; **contentarse** *vr* to be satisfied

contento, -a *adj* (*alegre*) pleased; (*feliz*) happy

contestación *nf* answer, reply

contestador *nm* (*tb*: **~ automático**) answering machine

contestar *vt* to answer, reply; (*JUR*) to corroborate, confirm

⚠ No confundir **contestar** con la palabra inglesa *contest*.

contexto *nm* context

contienda *nf* contest

contigo *pron* with you

contiguo, -a *adj* adjacent, adjoining

continente *adj, nm* continent

contingencia *nf* contingency; (*riesgo*) risk ❏ **contingente** *adj, nm* contingent

continuación *nf* continuation; **a ~** then, next

continuar *vt* to continue, go on with ♦ *vi* to continue, go on; **~ hablando** to continue talking *o* to talk

continuidad *nf* continuity

continuo, -a *adj* (*sin interrupción*) continuous; (*acción perseverante*) continual

contorno *nm* outline; (*GEO*) contour; **~s** *nmpl* neighborhood *sg*, surrounding area *sg*

contorsión *nf* contortion

contra *prep, adv* against ♦ *nm inv* con ♦ *nf*: **la C~** (*de Nicaragua*) the Contras *pl*

contraataque *nm* counter-attack

contrabajo *nm* double bass

contrabandista *nmf* smuggler

contrabando *nm* (*acción*) smuggling; (*mercancías*) contraband

contracción nf contraction

contracorriente: (a) ~ adv against the current

contradecir vt to contradict

contradicción nf contradiction

contradictorio, -a adj contradictory

contraer vt to contract; (limitar) to restrict; **contraerse** vr to contract; (limitarse) to limit o.s.

contraluz nf: **a** ~ against the light

contrapartida nf: **como** ~ (**de**) in return (for)

contrapelo: **a** ~ adv the wrong way

contrapesar vt to counterbalance; (fig) to offset □ **contrapeso** nm counterweight

contraportada nf (de revista) back cover

contraproducente adj counterproductive

contrariar vt (oponerse) to oppose; (poner obstáculo) to impede; (enfadar) to vex

contrariedad nf (obstáculo) obstacle, setback; (disgusto) vexation, annoyance

contrario, -a adj contrary; (persona) opposed; (sentido, lado) opposite ♦ nm/f enemy, adversary; (DEPORTE) opponent; **al/por el** ~ on the contrary; **de lo** ~ otherwise

contrarreloj nf (tb: **prueba** ~) time trial

contrarrestar vt to counteract

contrasentido nm: **es un** ~ **que él ...** it doesn't make sense for him to ...

contraseña nf (INFORM) password

contrastar vt, vi to contrast

contraste nm contrast

contratar vt (firmar un acuerdo para) to contract for; (empleados, obreros) to hire, engage; **contratarse** vr to sign on

contratiempo nm setback

contratista nmf contractor

contrato nm contract

contravenir vi: ~ **a** to contravene, violate

contraventana nf shutter

contribución nf (municipal etc) tax; (ayuda) contribution

contribuir vt, vi to contribute; (COM) to pay (in taxes)

contribuyente nmf (COM) taxpayer; (que ayuda) contributor

contrincante nm opponent

control nm control; (inspección) inspection, check □ **controlador, a** nm/f controller ▶ **controlador aéreo** air-traffic controller

controlar vt to control; (inspeccionar) to inspect, check

controversia nf controversy

contundente adj (instrumento) blunt; (argumento, derrota) overwhelming

contusión nf bruise

convalecencia nf convalescence

convalecer vi to convalesce, get better

convaleciente adj, nmf convalescent

convalidar vt (título) to recognize

convencer vt to convince

convencimiento nm (certidumbre) conviction

convención nf convention

conveniencia nf suitability; (conformidad) agreement; (utilidad, provecho) usefulness; ~**s** nfpl (convenciones) conventions; (COM) property sg

conveniente adj suitable; (útil) useful

convenio nm agreement, treaty

convenir vi (estar de acuerdo) to agree; (venir bien) to suit, be suitable

⚠ No confundir **convenir** con la palabra inglesa **convene**.

convento nm convent

convenza etc vb ver **convencer**

converger vi to converge

convergir vi = **converger**

conversación nf conversation

conversar vi to talk, converse

conversión nf conversion

convertir vt to convert

convicción nf conviction

convicto, -a adj convicted

convidado, -a nm/f guest

convidar vt to invite

convincente adj convincing

convite nm invitation; (banquete) banquet

convivencia nf coexistence, living together

convivir vi to live together

convocar vt to summon, call (together)

convocatoria nf (de oposiciones, elecciones) notice; (de huelga) call

convulsión nf convulsion

conyugal adj conjugal □ **cónyuge** nmf spouse

coñac (pl ~**s**) nm cognac, brandy

cooperación nf cooperation

cooperar vi to cooperate

cooperativa nf cooperative

coordinadora nf (comité) coordinating committee

coordinar vt to coordinate

copa nf cup; (vaso) glass; (bebida): **tomar una ~** (to have a) drink; (de árbol) top; (de sombrero) crown; **~s** nfpl (NAIPES) ≈ hearts

copia nf copy ▶ **copia de respaldo** o **seguridad** (INFORM) back-up copy ❑ **copiar** vt to copy

copioso, -a adj copious, plentiful

copla nf verse; (canción) (popular) song

copo nm (de nieve) flake ▶ **copo de nieve** snowflake ▶ **copos de maíz** cornflakes

coqueta adj flirtatious, coquettish ❑ **coquetear** vi to flirt

coraje nm courage; (ánimo) spirit; (ira) anger

coral adj choral ♦ nf (MÚS) choir ♦ nm (ZOOL) coral

coraza nf (armadura) armor (US), armour (BRIT); (blindaje) armor-plating

corazón nm heart

corazonada nf impulse; (presentimiento) hunch

corbata nf tie, necktie (US)

corchete nm catch, clasp

corcho nm cork; (PESCA) float

cordel nm cord, line

cordero nm lamb

cordial adj cordial ❑ **cordialidad** nf warmth, cordiality

cordillera nf range (of mountains)

Córdoba n Cordova

cordón nm (cuerda) cord, string; (de zapatos) lace; (MIL etc) cordon ▶ **cordón de la banqueta** (MÉX) curb (US), kerb (BRIT) ▶ **cordón de la vereda** (RPI) curb (US), kerb (BRIT)

cordura nf: **con ~** (obrar, hablar) sensibly

corneta nf bugle

cornisa nf (ARQ) cornice

coro nm chorus; (conjunto de cantores) choir

corona nf crown; (de flores) garland ❑ **coronación** nf coronation ❑ **coronar** vt to crown

coronel nm colonel

coronilla nf (ANAT) crown (of the head)

corporación nf corporation

corporal adj corporal, bodily

corpulento, -a adj (persona) heavily-built

corral nm farmyard; (LAm: parque) playpen

correa nf strap; (cinturón) belt; (de perro) lead, leash

corrección nf correction; (reprensión) rebuke ❑ **correccional** nf (LAm) o m (ESP) reformatory

correcto, -a adj correct; (persona) well-mannered

corredizo, -a adj (puerta etc) sliding

corredor, a nm (pasillo) corridor; (balcón corrido) gallery; (COM) agent, broker ♦ nm/f (DEPORTE) runner

corregir vt (error) to correct; **corregirse** vr to reform

correo nm mail (US), post (BRIT); (persona) courier; (LAm: edificio) post office; **C~s** nmpl (ESP) post office sg ▶ **correo aéreo** airmail ▶ **correo basura** (INFORM) spam, junk email ▶ **correo electrónico** email, electronic mail

correr vt to run; (cortinas) to draw; (cerrojo) to shoot ♦ vi to run; (líquido) to run, flow; **correrse** vr to slide, move; (colores) to run

correspondencia nf correspondence; (FERRO) connection

corresponder vi to correspond; (convenir) to be suitable; (pertenecer) to belong; (concernir) to concern; **corresponderse** vr (por escrito) to correspond; (amarse) to love one another

correspondiente adj corresponding

corresponsal nmf correspondent

corrida nf (de toros) bullfight

corrido, -a nm (MÉX) ballad ♦ adj: **3 noches corridas** 3 nights running; **un kilo ~** a good kilo

corriente adj (agua) running; (dinero etc) current; (común) ordinary, normal ♦ nf current ♦ nm current month ▶ **corriente eléctrica** electric current

corrija etc vb ver **corregir**

corrillo nm ring, circle (of people); (fig) clique

corro nm ring, circle (of people)

corroborar vt to corroborate

corroer vt to corrode; (GEO) to erode

corromper vt (madera) to rot; (fig) to corrupt

corrosivo, -a adj corrosive

corrupción nf rot, decay; (fig) corruption

corsé nm corset

cortacésped (ESP) nm (lawn)mower

cortado, -a adj (gen) cut; (leche) sour; (tímido) shy; (avergonzado) embarrassed ♦ nm coffee (with a little milk)

cortar vt to cut; (suministro) to cut off; (un pasaje) to cut out ♦ vi to cut; **cortarse** vr (avergonzarse) to become embarrassed; (leche) to turn, curdle; **~se el pelo** to have one's hair cut

cortauñas nm inv nail clippers pl

corte nm cut, cutting; (de tela) piece, length ♦ nf: **las C~s** (ESP) the Spanish Parliament ▶ **corte de luz** power outage (US) o cut

(BRIT) ▶ **corte y confección** dressmaking
▶ **Corte Suprema** (LAm) Supreme Court

cortejar vt to court

cortejo nm entourage ▶ **cortejo fúnebre** funeral procession

cortés adj courteous, polite

cortesía nf courtesy

corteza nf (de árbol) bark; (de pan) crust

cortina nf curtain, drape (US)

corto, -a adj (breve) short; (tímido) bashful; ~ **de luces** not very bright; ~ **de vista** near-sighted (US), shortsighted (BRIT); **estar ~ de fondos** to be short of funds
❏ **cortocircuito** nm short circuit
❏ **cortometraje** nm (CINE) short

cosa nf thing; ~ **de** about; **eso es ~ mía** that's my business

coscorrón nm bump on the head

cosecha nf (AGR) harvest; (de vino) vintage

cosechar vt to harvest, gather (in)

coser vt to sew

cosmético, -a adj, nm cosmetic

cosquillas nfpl: **hacer ~** to tickle; **tener ~** to be ticklish

costa nf (GEO) coast; **a toda ~** at all costs
▶ **Costa Brava** Costa Brava ▶ **Costa Cantábrica** Cantabrian Coast ▶ **Costa del Sol** Costa del Sol

costado nm side

costanera (CS) nf promenade, sea front

costar vt (valer) to cost; **me cuesta hablarle** I find it hard to talk to him

Costa Rica nf Costa Rica ❏ **costarricense** adj, nmf Costa Rican ❏ **costarriqueño, -a** adj, nm/f Costa Rican

coste nm = **costo**

costear vt to pay for

costero, -a adj (pueblecito, camino) coastal

costilla nf rib; (CULIN) cutlet

costo nm cost, price ▶ **costo de (la) vida** cost of living ❏ **costoso, -a** adj costly, expensive

costra nf (corteza) crust; (MED) scab

costumbre nf custom, habit

costura nf sewing, needlework; (zurcido) seam

costurera nf dressmaker

costurero nm sewing box o case

cotejar vt to compare

cotidiano, -a adj daily, day to day

cotización nf (COM) quotation, price; (de club) dues pl

cotizar vt (COM) to quote, price; **cotizarse** vr: ~**se a** to sell at, fetch; (BOLSA) to stand at, be quoted at

coto nm (terreno cercado) enclosure; (de caza) reserve

cotorra nf parrot

COU (ESP) nm abr (= Curso de Orientación Universitaria) 1 year course leading to final school-leaving certificate and university entrance examinations

coyote nm coyote, prairie wolf; (MÉX, CAm: fam: intermediario) fixer

coyuntura nf juncture, occasion

coz nf kick

crack nm (droga) crack

cráneo nm skull, cranium

cráter nm crater

crayón (MÉX, RPl) nm crayon, chalk

creación nf creation

creador, a adj creative ♦ nm/f creator

crear vt to create, make

crecer vi to grow; (precio) to rise

creces: **con ~** adv amply, fully

crecido, -a adj (persona, planta) full-grown; (cantidad) large

creciente adj growing; (cantidad) increasing; (luna) crescent ♦ nm crescent

crecimiento nm growth; (aumento) increase

credencial nf (LAm: tarjeta) card; ~**es** nfpl credentials ▶ **credencial de socio** (LAm) membership card

crédito nm credit

credo nm creed

crédulo, -a adj credulous

creencia nf belief

creer vt, vi to think, believe; **creerse** vr to believe o.s. (to be); ~ **en** to believe in; **¡ya lo creo!** I should think so!

creíble adj credible, believable

creído, -a adj (engreído) conceited

crema nf cream ▶ **crema batida** (LAm) whipped cream ▶ **crema de rasurar** (MÉX) shaving cream ▶ **crema pastelera** (confectioner's) custard

cremallera (ESP) nf zipper (US), zip (fastener) (BRIT)

crematorio nm (tb: **horno ~**) crematorium

crepitar vi to crackle

crepúsculo nm twilight, dusk

cresta nf (GEO, ZOOL) crest

creyendo etc vb ver **creer**

creyente nmf believer

creyó etc vb ver **creer**

crezco etc vb ver **crecer**

cría etc vb ver **criar** ♦ nf (de animales) rearing, breeding; (animal) young; ver tb **crío**

criadero nm (ZOOL) breeding place

criado, -a nm servant ♦ nf servant, maid

criador nm breeder

crianza nf rearing, breeding; (fig) breeding

criar vt (educar) to bring up; (producir) to grow, produce; (animales) to breed

criatura nf creature; (niño) baby, (small) child

criba nf sieve ❏ **cribar** vt to sieve

crimen nm crime

criminal adj, nmf criminal

crin nf (tb: ~es) mane

crío, -a (fam) nm/f (niño) kid

crisis nf inv crisis ► **crisis nerviosa** nervous breakdown

crispar vt (nervios) to set on edge

cristal nm crystal; (de ventana) glass, pane; (lente) lens ❏ **cristalino, -a** adj crystalline; (fig) clear ♦ nm lens (of the eye) ❏ **cristalizar** vt, vi to crystallize

cristiandad nf Christendom

cristianismo nm Christianity

cristiano, -a adj, nm/f Christian

Cristo nm Christ; (crucifijo) crucifix

criterio nm criterion; (juicio) judgement

crítica nf criticism; ver tb **crítico**

criticar vt to criticize

crítico, -a adj critical ♦ nm/f critic

Croacia nf Croatia

croar vi to croak

cromo nm chrome

crónica nf chronicle, account

crónico, -a adj chronic

cronómetro nm stopwatch

croqueta nf croquette

cruce etc vb ver **cruzar** ♦ nm crosswalk (US), crossing (BRIT); (de carreteras) crossroads

crucero nm (viaje) cruise ► **crucero de ferrocarril** (MÉX) railroad crossing (US), level crossing (BRIT)

crucificar vt to crucify

crucifijo nm crucifix

crucigrama nm crossword (puzzle)

cruda (MÉX, CAm: fam) nf hangover

crudo, -a adj raw; (no maduro) unripe; (petróleo) crude; (rudo, cruel) cruel ♦ nm crude (oil)

cruel adj cruel ❏ **crueldad** nf cruelty

crujido nm (de madera etc) creak

crujiente adj (galleta etc) crunchy

crujir vi (madera etc) to creak; (dedos) to crack; (dientes) to grind; (nieve, arena) to crunch

cruz nf cross; (de moneda) tails sg ► **cruz gamada** swastika

cruzada nf crusade

cruzado, -a adj crossed ♦ nm crusader

cruzar vt to cross; **cruzarse** vr (líneas etc) to cross; (personas) to pass each other

Cruz Roja nf Red Cross

cuaderno nm notebook; (de escuela) workbook (US), exercise book (BRIT); (NÁUT) logbook

cuadra nf (caballeriza) stable; (LAm: entre calles) block

cuadrado, -a adj square ♦ nm (MAT) square

cuadrar vt to square ♦ vi: ~ **con** to square with, tally with; **cuadrarse** vr (soldado) to stand to attention

cuadrilátero nm (DEPORTE) boxing ring; (GEOM) quadrilateral

cuadrilla nf party, group

cuadro nm square; (ARTE) painting; (TEATRO) scene; (diagrama) chart; (DEPORTE, MED) team; **tela a** ~**s** checkered (US) o chequered (BRIT) material

cuádruple adj quadruple

cuajar vt (leche) to curdle; (sangre) to congeal; (CULIN) to set; **cuajarse** vr to curdle; to congeal; to set; (llenarse) to fill up

cuajo nm: **de** ~ (arrancar) by the roots; (cortar) completely

cual adv like, as ♦ pron: **el** ~ etc which; (persona sujeto) who; (: objeto) whom ♦ adj such as; **cada** ~ each one; **déjalo tal** ~ leave it just as it is

cuál pron interr which (one)

cualesquier, a pl de **cualquier(a)**

cualidad nf quality

cualquier adj ver **cualquiera**

cualquiera (pl **cualesquiera**) adj (delante de nm y f: **cualquier**) any ♦ pron anybody; **un** (LAm) carro ~ **servirá** any car will do; **no es un hombre** ~ he isn't just anybody; **cualquier día/libro** any day/book; **eso** ~ **lo sabe hacer** anybody can do that; **es un** ~ he's a nobody

cuando adv when; (aún sí) if, even if ♦ conj (puesto que) since ♦ prep: **yo,** ~ **niño ...** when I was a child ...; ~ **no sea así** even if it is not so; ~ **más** at (the) most; ~ **menos** at least; ~ **no** if not, otherwise; **de** ~ **en** ~ from time to time

cuándo adv when; **¿desde** ~**?, ¿de** ~ **acá?** since when?

cuantía nf (importe: de pérdidas, deuda, daños) extent

cuantioso, -a *adj* substantial

---

cuanto, -a

PALABRA CLAVE

adj

1 (*todo*): **tiene todo cuanto desea** he's got everything he wants; **le daremos cuantos ejemplares necesite** we'll give him as many copies as *o* all the copies he needs; **cuantos hombres la ven** all the men who see her

2: **unos cuantos: había unos cuantos periodistas** there were a few journalists

3 (+ *más*): **cuanto más vino bebes peor te sentirás** the more wine you drink the worse you'll feel

♦ *pron*: **tiene cuanto desea** he has everything he wants; **tome cuanto/cuantos quiera** take as much/many as you want

♦ *adv*: **en cuanto: en cuanto profesor** as a teacher; **en cuanto a mí** as for me; *ver tb* **antes**

♦ *conj*

1: **cuanto más gana menos gasta** the more he earns the less he spends; **cuanto más joven más confiado** the younger you are the more trusting you are

2: **en cuanto: en cuanto llegue/llegué** as soon as I arrive/arrived

---

cuánto, -a *adj* (*exclamación*) what a lot of; (*interr: sg*) how much?; (: *pl*) how many?
♦ *pron, adv* how; (: *interr: sg*) how much?; (: *pl*) how many?; **¡cuánta gente!** what a lot of people!; **¿~ cuesta?** how much does it cost?; **¿a ~s estamos?** what's the date?; **Señor no sé ~s** Mr. So-and-So

cuarenta *num* forty

cuarentena *nf* quarantine

cuaresma *nf* Lent

cuarta *nf* (*MAT*) quarter, fourth; (*palmo*) span

cuartel *nm* (*MIL*) barracks *pl* ▶ **cuartel de bomberos** (*RPI*) fire station ▶ **cuartel general** headquarters *pl*

cuarteto *nm* quartet

cuarto, -a *adj* fourth ♦ *nm* (*MAT*) quarter, fourth; (*habitación*) room ▶ **cuarto de baño** bathroom ▶ **cuarto de estar** living room ▶ **cuarto de hora** quarter (of an) hour ▶ **cuarto de kilo** quarter kilo ▶ **cuarto de triques** (*MÉX*) utility room

cuatro *num* four

Cuba *nf* Cuba

cuba *nf* cask, barrel

cubano, -a *adj, nm/f* Cuban

cubata *nm* (*fam*) large drink (*of rum and coke etc*)

cubeta (*MÉX, ESP*) *nf* (*balde*) bucket, tub

cúbico, -a *adj* cubic

cubierta *nf* cover, covering; (*neumático*) tire (*US*), tyre (*BRIT*); (*NÁUT*) deck

cubierto, -a *pp de* **cubrir** ♦ *adj* covered ♦ *nm* cover; (*lugar en la mesa*) place; **~s** *nmpl* flatware *sg* (*US*), cutlery *sg* (*BRIT*); **a ~** under cover

cubil *nm* den ❑ **cubilete** *nm* (*en juegos*) cup

cubito *nm* (*tb:* **~ de hielo**) ice-cube

cubo *nm* (*MAT*) cube; (*ESP: balde*) bucket, tub; (*TEC*) drum

cubrecama *nm* bedspread

cubrir *vt* to cover; **cubrirse** *vr* (*cielo*) to become overcast

cucaracha *nf* cockroach

cuchara *nf* spoon; (*TEC*) scoop ❑ **cucharada** *nf* spoonful ❑ **cucharadita** *nf* teaspoonful

cucharilla *nf* teaspoon

cucharón *nm* ladle

cuchichear *vi* to whisper

cuchilla *nf* (*large*) knife; (*de arma blanca*) blade ▶ **cuchilla de afeitar** (*ESP*) razor blade

cuchillo *nm* knife

cuchitril *nm* hovel

cuclillas *nfpl*: **en ~** squatting

cuco, -a *adj* pretty; (*astuto*) sharp ♦ *nm* cuckoo

cucurucho *nm* cornet

cueca *nf* Chilean national dance

CUECA

The **cueca** is the national dance of Chile. It is a complex dance, which came into practice in Chile in the mid-nineteenth century, although its exact origin is the subject of considerable debate. The band accompanying the dance may consist of several singers, a guitar, a harp, a drum, and sometimes a piano or accordion and other instruments.

---

cuello *nm* (*ANAT*) neck; (*de vestido, camisa*) collar

cuenca *nf* (*ANAT*) eye socket; (*GEO*) bowl, deep valley

cuenco *nm* bowl

cuenta *etc vb ver* **contar** ♦ *nf* (*cálculo*) count, counting; (*en café, restaurante*) bill (*BRIT*); (*COM*) account; (*de collar*) bead; **a fin de ~s** in the end; **caer en la ~** to catch on; **darse ~ de** to realize; **tener en ~** to bear in mind; **echar ~s** to take stock ▶ **cuenta atrás** countdown ▶ **cuenta corriente/de**

ahorros checking (US) o current (BRIT)/ savings account ► **cuenta de correo** (INFORM) email account
❏ **cuentakilómetros** nm inv ≈ milometer, ≈ mileometer (BRIT); (de velocidad) speedometer

cuento etc vb ver **contar** ♦ nm story

cuerda nf rope; (fina) string; (de reloj) spring; **dar ~ a un reloj** to wind up a clock ► **cuerda de saltar** (LAm) jump (US) o skipping (BRIT) rope ► **cuerda floja** tightrope

cuerdo, -a adj sane; (prudente) wise, sensible

cuerno nm horn

cuero nm leather; **en ~s** stark naked ► **cuero cabelludo** scalp

cuerpo nm body

cuervo nm crow

cuesta etc vb ver **costar** ♦ nf slope; (en camino etc) hill; **~ arriba/abajo** uphill/ downhill; **a ~s** on one's back

cueste etc vb ver **costar**

cuestión nf matter, question, issue

cuete adj (MÉX: fam) drunk ♦ nm (LAm: cohete) rocket; (MÉX, RPl: fam: embriaguez) drunkenness; (MÉX CULIN) steak

cueva nf cave

cuidado nm care, carefulness; (preocupación) care, worry ♦ excl careful!, look out!

cuidadoso, -a adj careful; (preocupado) anxious

cuidar vt (MED) to care for; (ocuparse de) to take care of, look after ♦ vi: **~ de** to take care of, look after; **cuidarse** vr to look after o.s.; **~se de hacer algo** to take care to do sth

culata nf (de fusil) butt

culebra nf snake

culebrón (fam) nm (TV) soap(-opera)

culinario, -a adj culinary, cooking cpd

culminación nf culmination

culo nm bottom, backside; (de vaso, botella) bottom

culpa nf fault; (JUR) guilt; **por ~ de** because of; **tener la ~ (de)** to be to blame (for)
❏ **culpabilidad** nf guilt ❏ **culpable** adj guilty ♦ nmf culprit

culpar vt to blame; (acusar) to accuse

cultivar vt to cultivate

cultivo nm (acto) cultivation; (plantas) crop

culto, -a adj (que tiene cultura) cultured, educated ♦ nm (homenaje) worship; (religión) cult

cultura nf culture

culturismo nm body-building

cumbia nf popular Colombian dance

CUMBIA

The **cumbia** is a Colombian dance which comes from those communities on the Atlantic coast of Colombia which are African in origin; historically, it originates from the "Cumbe" music of Guinea in Africa. It is characterised by its rhythmic energy and blend of Spanish melodies, native American harmonies and African rhythms.

cumbre nf summit, top

cumpleaños nm inv birthday

cumplido, -a adj (abundante) plentiful; (cortés) courteous ♦ nm compliment; **visita de ~** courtesy call

cumplidor, a adj reliable

cumplimentar vt to congratulate

cumplimiento nm (de un deber) fulfillment (US), fulfilment (BRIT); (acabamiento) completion

cumplir vt (orden) to carry out, obey; (promesa) to carry out, fulfill (US), fulfil (BRIT); (condena) to serve ♦ vi: **~ con** (deber) to carry out, fulfill (US), fulfil (BRIT); **cumplirse** vr (plazo) to expire; **hoy cumple dieciocho años** he is eighteen today

cúmulo nm heap

cuna nf cradle, crib (US), cot (BRIT)

cundir vi (noticia, rumor, pánico) to spread; (rendir) to go a long way

cuneta nf ditch

cuña nf wedge

cuñado, -a nm/f brother-/sister-in-law

cuota nf (parte proporcional) share; (cotización) fee, dues pl; (MÉX: peaje) toll

cupe etc vb ver **caber**

cupiera etc vb ver **caber**

cupo vb ver **caber** ♦ nm quota

cupón nm coupon

cúpula nf dome

cura nf (curación) cure; (método curativo) treatment ♦ nm priest

curación nf cure; (acción) curing

curandero, -a nm/f quack

curar vt (MED: herida) to treat, dress; (: enfermo) to cure; (CULIN) to cure, salt; (cuero) to tan; **curarse** vr to get well, recover

curiosear vt to glance at, look over ♦ vi to look round, wander round; (explorar) to poke about

curiosidad nf curiosity

curioso, -a adj curious ♦ nm/f bystander, onlooker

curita (*LAm*) *nf* Bandaid® (*US*), (sticking) plaster (*BRIT*)

currículo *nm* = **curriculum**

curriculum *nm* résumé (*US*), curriculum vitae (*BRIT*)

cursi (*fam*) *adj* affected

cursillo *nm* short course

cursiva *nf* italics *pl*

curso *nm* course; **en ~** (*año*) current; (*proceso*) going on, under way

cursor *nm* (*INFORM*) cursor

curtido, -a *adj* (*cara etc*) weather-beaten; (*fig: persona*) experienced

curtir *vt* (*cuero etc*) to tan

curul (*MÉX*) *nm* (*escaño*) seat

curva *nf* curve, bend

cúspide *nf* (*GEO*) peak; (*fig*) top

custodia *nf* safekeeping; custody
❏ **custodiar** *vt* (*conservar*) to take care of; (*vigilar*) to guard

cutis *nm inv* skin, complexion

cuyo, -a *pron* (*de quien*) whose; (*de que*) whose, of which; **en ~ caso** in which case

C.V. *abr* (= *caballos de vapor*) H.P.

Dd

D. *abr* (= *Don*) Mr, Esq. (*BRIT*)

Da. *abr* = **Doña**

dádiva *nf* (*donación*) donation; (*regalo*) gift
❏ **dadivoso, -a** *adj* generous

dado, -a *pp de* **dar** ♦ *nm* die; **~s** *nmpl* dice; **~ que** given that

daltónico, -a *adj* color-blind (*US*), colour-blind (*BRIT*)

dama *nf* (*gen*) lady; (*AJEDREZ*) queen; **~s** *nfpl* (*juego*) checkers (*US*), draughts *sg* (*BRIT*)

damasco (*RPL*) *nm* apricot

damnificar *vt* to harm; (*persona*) to injure

danés, -esa *adj* Danish ♦ *nm/f* Dane

danzar *vt, vi* to dance

dañar *vt* (*objeto*) to damage; (*persona*) to hurt; **dañarse** *vr* (*objeto*) to get damaged

dañino, -a *adj* harmful

daño *nm* (*objeto*) damage; (*persona*) harm, injury; **~s y perjuicios** (*JUR*) damages; **hacer ~ a** to damage; (*persona*) to hurt, injure; **hacerse ~** to hurt o.s.

dar
PALABRA CLAVE

vt

1 (*gen*) to give; (*obra de teatro*) to put on; (*película*) to show; (*fiesta*) to hold; **dar algo a algn** to give sb sth o sth to sb; **dar de beber a algn** to give sb a drink

2 (*producir: intereses*) to yield; (*fruta*) to produce

3 (*locuciones + n*): **da gusto escucharla** it's a pleasure to listen to her; *ver tb* **paseo** *y otros sustantivos*

4 (*+ n: = perífrasis de verbo*): **me da asco** it sickens me

5 (*considerar*): **dar algo por descontado/ entendido** to take sth for granted/as read; **dar algo por concluido** to consider sth finished

6 (*hora*): **el reloj dio las 6** the clock struck 6 (o'clock)

7 **me da lo mismo** it's all the same to me; *ver tb* **igual**, **más**

♦ *vi*

1 **dar con**: **dimos con él dos horas más tarde** we came across him two hours later; **al final di con la solución** I eventually came up with the answer

2 **dar en** (*blanco, suelo*) to hit; **el sol me da en la cara** the sun is shining (right) on my face

3 **dar de sí** (*zapatos etc*) to stretch, give;

♦ *darse vr*

1 **darse por vencido** to give up

2 (*ocurrir*): **se han dado muchos casos** there have been a lot of cases

3 **darse a**: **se ha dado a la bebida** he's taken to drinking

4 **se me dan bien/mal las ciencias** I'm good/bad at science

5 **dárselas de: se las da de experto** he makes himself out to be an expert

dardo *nm* dart

datar *vi*: **~ de** to date from

dátil *nm* date

dato *nm* fact, piece of information ▶ **datos personales** personal details

dcha. *abr* (= *derecha*) r.h.

d. de C. *abr* (= *después de Cristo*) A.D.

de
PALABRA CLAVE

prep (*de + el = del*)

1 (*posesión*) of; **la casa de Isabel/mis padres** Isabel's/my parents' house; **es de ellos** it's theirs

2 (*origen, distancia, con números*) from; **soy de Oaxaca** I'm from Oaxaca; **de 8 a 20** from 8 to 20; **salir del cine** to go out of o leave the movie theater (*US*) o cinema (*BRIT*); **de 2 en 2** 2 by 2, 2 at a time

3 (*valor descriptivo*): **una copa de vino** a glass of wine; **la mesa de la cocina** the kitchen table; **un billete de 100 pesos** a 100-peso note; **un niño de tres años** a three-year-old (child); **una máquina de coser** a sewing machine; **ir vestido de gris** to be dressed in gray (*US*) o grey (*BRIT*); **la niña del vestido azul** the girl in the blue dress; **trabaja de profesora** she works as a teacher; **de lado** sideways; **de atrás/delante** rear/front

4 (*hora, tiempo*): **a las 8 de la mañana** at 8 o'clock in the morning; **de día/noche** by day/ night; **de hoy en ocho días** a week from now; **de niño era gordo** as a child he was fat

5 (*comparaciones*): **más/menos de cien personas** more/less than a hundred people; **el más caro de la tienda** the most expensive in the store (*US*) o shop (*BRIT*); **menos/más de lo pensado** less/more than expected

6 (*causa*): **del calor** from the heat; **de puro tonto** out of sheer stupidity

7 (*tema*) about; **clases de inglés** English classes; **¿sabes algo de él?** do you know anything about him?; **un libro de física** a physics book

8 (*adj + de + infin*): **fácil de entender** easy to understand

9 (*oraciones pasivas*): **fue respetado de todos** he was loved by all

10 (*condicional + infin*) if; **de ser posible** if possible; **de no terminarlo hoy** if I *etc* don't finish it today

dé *vb ver* **dar**

deambular *vi* to wander

debajo *adv* underneath; **~ de** below, under; **por ~ de** beneath

debate *nm* debate ❏ **debatir** *vt* to debate

deber *nm* duty ♦ *vt* to owe ♦ *vi*: **debe (de)** it must, it should; **~es** *nmpl* (*ESCOL*) homework; **deberse** *vr*: **~se a** to be owing o due to; **debo hacerlo** I must do it; **debe de ir** he should go

debido, -a *adj* proper, just; **~ a** due to, because of

débil *adj* (*persona, carácter*) weak; (*luz*) dim ❏ **debilidad** *nf* weakness; dimness

debilitar *vt* to weaken; **debilitarse** *vr* to grow weak

débito *nm* debit ▶ **débito bancario** (*LAm*) direct billing (*US*) o debit (*BRIT*)

debutar *vi* to make one's debut

década *nf* decade

decadencia *nf* (*estado*) decadence; (*proceso*) decline, decay

decaer *vi* (*declinar*) to decline; (*debilitarse*) to weaken

decaído, -a *adj*: **estar ~** (*abatido*) to be down

decaimiento *nm* (*declinación*) decline; (*desaliento*) discouragement; (*MED: estado débil*) weakness

decano, -a *nm/f* (*de universidad etc*) dean

decapitar *vt* to behead

decena *nf*: **una ~** ten (or so)

decencia *nf* decency

decente *adj* decent

decepción *nf* disappointment

⚠ No confundir **decepción** con la palabra inglesa *deception*.

decepcionar *vt* to disappoint

decidir *vt, vi* to decide; **decidirse** *vr*: **~se a** to make up one's mind to

décimo, -a *adj* tenth ♦ *nm* tenth

decir *vt* to say; (*contar*) to tell; (*hablar*) to speak ♦ *nm* saying; **decirse** *vr*: **se dice que** it is said that; **~ para** o **entre sí** to say to o.s.; **querer ~** to mean; **¡díga(me)!** (*ESP TEL*) hello!; (: *en tienda*) can I help you?

decisión *nf* (*resolución*) decision; (*firmeza*) decisiveness

decisivo, -a *adj* decisive

declaración *nf* (*manifestación*) statement; (*de amor*) declaration ▶ **declaración fiscal** o **de la renta** income-tax return

declarar *vt* to declare; (*JUR*) to testify; **declararse** *vr* to propose

declinar *vt* (*gen*) to decline; (*JUR*) to reject ♦ *vi* (*el día*) to draw to a close

declive *nm* (*cuesta*) slope; (*fig*) decline

decodificador *nm* decoder

decolorarse *vr* to become discolored (*US*) o discoloured (*BRIT*)

decoración *nf* decoration

decorado *nm* (*CINE, TEATRO*) scenery, set

decorar *vt* to decorate ❏ **decorativo, -a** *adj* ornamental, decorative

decoro *nm* (*respeto*) respect; (*dignidad*) decency; (*recato*) propriety ❏ **decoroso, -a** *adj* (*decente*) decent; (*modesto*) modest; (*digno*) proper

decrecer *vi* to decrease, diminish

decrépito, -a *adj* decrepit

decretar *vt* to decree ❏ **decreto** *nm* decree

dedal nm thimble

dedicación nf dedication

dedicar vt (libro) to dedicate; (tiempo, dinero) to devote; (palabras: decir, consagrar) to dedicate, devote □ **dedicatoria** nf (de libro) dedication

dedo nm finger; **hacer ~** (CS: fam) to hitch (a ride) ▶ **dedo anular** ring finger ▶ **dedo corazón** middle finger ▶ **dedo (del pie)** toe ▶ **dedo índice** index finger ▶ **dedo meñique** little finger ▶ **dedo pulgar** thumb

deducción nf deduction

deducir vt (concluir) to deduce, infer; (COM) to deduct

defecto nm defect, flaw □ **defectuoso, -a** adj defective, faulty

defender vt to defend

defensa nf defense (US), defence (BRIT); (MÉX AUTO) bumper ♦ nm (DEPORTE) defender, back □ **defensivo, -a** adj defensive; **a la defensiva** on the defensive

defensor, a adj defending ♦ nm/f (abogado defensor) defending counsel; (protector) protector

deficiencia nf deficiency

deficiente adj (defectuoso) defective; **~ en** lacking o deficient in; **ser un ~ mental** to be mentally handicapped

déficit (pl ~s) nm deficit

definición nf definition

definir vt (determinar) to determine, establish; (decidir) to define; (aclarar) to clarify □ **definitivo, -a** adj definitive; **en definitiva** definitively; (en resumen) in short

deformación nf (alteración) deformation; (RADIO etc) distortion

deformar vt (gen) to deform; **deformarse** vr to become deformed □ **deforme** adj (informe) deformed; (feo) ugly; (malhecho) misshapen

defraudar vt (decepcionar) to disappoint; (estafar) to defraud

defunción nf death, demise

degeneración nf (de las células) degeneration; (moral) degeneracy

degenerar vi to degenerate

degollar vt to behead; (fig) to slaughter

degradar vt to debase, degrade; **degradarse** vr to demean o.s.

degustación nf sampling, tasting

deificar vt to deify

dejadez nf (negligencia) neglect; (descuido) untidiness, carelessness

dejar vt to leave; (permitir) to allow, let; (abandonar) to abandon, forsake; (beneficios) to produce, yield ♦ vi: **~ de** (parar) to stop; (no hacer) to fail to; **no dejes de comprar un** (LAm) **boleto** make sure you buy a ticket; **~ a un lado** to leave o set aside

dejo nm (LING) accent

del cont = **de + el**; ver **de**

delantal nm apron

delante adv in front; (enfrente) opposite; (adelante) ahead; **~ de** in front of, before

delantera nf (de vestido, casa etc) front part; (DEPORTE) forward line; **llevar la ~ (a algn)** to be ahead (of sb)

delantero, -a adj front ♦ nm (DEPORTE) forward, striker

delatar vt to inform on o against, betray □ **delator, a** nm/f informer

delegación nf (acción, delegados) delegation ▶ **delegación de policía** (MÉX) police station

delegado, -a nm/f delegate; (COM) agent

delegar vt to delegate

deletrear vt to spell (out)

deleznable adj brittle; (excusa, idea) feeble

delfín nm dolphin

delgadez nf thinness, slimness

delgado, -a adj thin; (persona) slim, thin; (tela etc) light, delicate

deliberación nf deliberation

deliberar vt to debate, discuss

delicadeza nf (gen) delicacy; (refinamiento, sutileza) refinement

delicado, -a adj (gen) delicate; (sensible) sensitive; (quisquilloso) touchy

delicia nf delight

delicioso, -a adj (gracioso) delightful; (exquisito) delicious

delimitar vt (función, responsabilidades) to define

delincuencia nf delinquency □ **delincuente** nmf delinquent; (criminal) criminal

delineante nmf draftsman(-woman) (US), draughtsman(-woman) (BRIT)

delinear vt (dibujo) to draw; (fig, contornos) to outline

delinquir vi to commit an offense (US) o offence (BRIT)

delirante adj delirious

delirar vi to be delirious, rave

delirio nm (MED) delirium; (palabras insensatas) ravings pl

delito nm (gen) crime; (infracción) offense (US), offence (BRIT)

delta nm delta

demacrado, -a adj: **estar ~** to look pale and drawn, be wasted away

demagogo, -a nm/f demagogue, demagog (US)

demanda nf (pedido, COM) demand; (petición) request; (JUR) action, lawsuit

demandante nmf claimant

demandar vt (gen) to demand; (JUR) to sue, file a lawsuit against

demarcación nf (de terreno) demarcation

demás adj: **los ~ niños** the other children, the remaining children ♦ pron: **los/las ~** the others, the rest (of them); **lo ~** the rest (of it)

demasía nf (exceso) excess, surplus; **comer en ~** to eat to excess

demasiado, -a adj: **~ vino** too much wine ♦ adv (antes de adj, adv) too; **~s libros** too many books; **¡esto es ~!** that's the limit!; **hace ~ calor** it's too hot; **~ despacio** too slowly; **~s** too many

demencia nf (locura) madness ☐ **demente** nmf lunatic ♦ adj mad, insane

democracia nf democracy

demócrata nmf democrat ☐ **democrático, -a** adj democratic

demoler vt to demolish ☐ **demolición** nf demolition

demonio nm devil, demon; **¡~s!** hell!, damn!; **¿cómo ~s?** how the hell?

demora nf delay ☐ **demorar** vt (retardar) to delay, hold back; (detener) to hold up ♦ vi to linger, stay on; **demorarse** vr to be delayed

demos vb ver **dar**

demostración nf (MAT) proof; (de afecto) show, display

demostrar vt (probar) to prove; (mostrar) to show; (manifestar) to demonstrate

demudado, -a adj (rostro) pale

den vb ver **dar**

denegar vt (rechazar) to refuse; (JUR) to reject

denigrar vt (desacreditar, infamar) to denigrate; (injuriar) to insult

denotar vt to denote

densidad nf density; (fig) thickness

denso, -a adj dense; (espeso, pastoso) thick; (fig) heavy

dentadura nf (set of) teeth pl ▶ **dentadura postiza** false teeth pl

dentera nf (sensación desagradable) the shivers pl

dentífrico, -a adj dental ♦ nm toothpaste

dentista nmf dentist

dentro adv inside ♦ prep: **~ de** in, inside, within; **por ~** (on the) inside; **mirar por ~** to look inside; **~ de tres meses** within three months

denuncia nf (delación) denunciation; (acusación) accusation; (de accidente) report ☐ **denunciar** vt to report; (delatar) to inform on o against

departamento nm (sección administrativa) department, section; (LAm: apartamento) apartment (US), flat (BRIT)

dependencia nf dependence; (POL) dependency; (COM) office, section

depender vi: **~ de** to depend on

dependienta nf sales clerk (US), sales assistant (BRIT)

dependiente adj dependent ♦ nm salesclerk (US), sales assistant (BRIT)

depilar vt (con cera) to wax; (cejas) to pluck ☐ **depilatorio** nm hair remover

deplorable adj deplorable

deplorar vt to deplore

deponer vt to lay down ♦ vi (JUR) to give evidence; (declarar) to make a statement

deportar vt to deport

deporte nm sport; **hacer ~** to play sports ☐ **deportista** adj sports cpd ♦ nmf sportsman(-woman) ☐ **deportivo, -a** adj (club, periódico) sports cpd ♦ nm sports car

depositar vt (dinero) to deposit; (mercancías) to put away, store; **depositarse** vr to settle ☐ **depositario, -a** nm/f trustee

depósito nm (gen) deposit; (almacén) warehouse, store; (de agua, gasolina etc) tank ▶ **depósito de cadáveres** mortuary

depreciar vt to depreciate, reduce the value of; **depreciarse** vr to depreciate, lose value

depredador, a adj predatory ♦ nm predator

depresión nf depression

deprimido, -a adj depressed

deprimir vt to depress; **deprimirse** vr (persona) to become depressed

deprisa adv quickly, hurriedly

depuración nf purification; (POL) purge

depurar vt to purify; (purgar) to purge

derecha nf right(-hand) side; (POL) right; **a la ~** (estar) on the right; (torcer etc) (to the) right

derecho, -a adj right, right-hand ♦ nm (privilegio) right; (lado) right(-hand) side; (leyes) law ♦ adv straight, directly; **~s** nmpl (de aduana) duty sg; (de autor) royalties; **tener ~ a** to have a right to

deriva *nf*: **ir** *o* **estar a la ~** to drift, be adrift

derivado *nm* (*COM*) by-product

derivar *vt* to derive; (*desviar*) to direct ♦ *vi* to derive, be derived; (*NÁUT*) to drift; **derivarse** *vr* to derive, be derived; to drift

derramamiento *nm* (*dispersión*) spilling ▶ **derramamiento de sangre** bloodshed

derramar *vt* to spill; (*verter*) to pour out; (*esparcir*) to scatter; **derramarse** *vr* to pour out; **~ lágrimas** to weep

derrame *nm* (*de líquido*) spilling; (*de sangre*) shedding; (*de tubo etc*) overflow; (*pérdida*) leakage; (*MED*) discharge

derredor *adv*: **al** *o* **en ~ de** around, about

derretido, -a *adj* melted; (*metal*) molten

derretir *vt* (*gen*) to melt; (*nieve*) to thaw; **derretirse** *vr* to melt

derribar *vt* to knock down; (*construcción*) to demolish; (*persona, gobierno, político*) to bring down

derrocar *vt* (*gobierno*) to bring down, overthrow

derrochar *vt* to squander ❑ **derroche** *nm* (*despilfarro*) waste, squandering

derrota *nf* (*NÁUT*) course; (*MIL, DEPORTE etc*) defeat, rout ❑ **derrotar** *vt* (*gen*) to defeat ❑ **derrotero** *nm* (*rumbo*) course

derruir *vt* (*edificio*) to demolish

derrumbar *vt* (*edificio*) to knock down; **derrumbarse** *vr* to collapse

derruyendo *etc vb ver* **derruir**

des *etc vb ver* **dar**

desabotonar *vt* to unbutton, undo; **desabotonarse** *vr* to come undone

desabrido, -a *adj* (*comida*) insipid, tasteless; (*persona*) rude, surly; (*respuesta*) sharp; (*tiempo*) unpleasant

desabrochar *vt* (*botones, broches*) to undo, unfasten; **desabrocharse** *vr* (*ropa etc*) to come undone

desacato *nm* (*falta de respeto*) disrespect; (*JUR*) contempt

desacertado, -a *adj* (*equivocado*) mistaken; (*inoportuno*) unwise

desacierto *nm* mistake, error

desaconsejado, -a *adj* ill-advised

desaconsejar *vt* to advise against

desacreditar *vt* (*desprestigiar*) to discredit, bring into disrepute; (*denigrar*) to run down

desacuerdo *nm* disagreement, discord

desafiar *vt* (*retar*) to challenge; (*enfrentarse a*) to defy

desafilado, -a *adj* blunt

desafinado, -a *adj*: **estar ~** to be out of tune

desafinar *vi* (*al cantar*) to be *o* go out of tune

desafío *etc vb ver* **desafiar** ♦ *nm* (*reto*) challenge; (*combate*) duel; (*resistencia*) defiance

desaforado, -a *adj* (*grito*) ear-splitting; (*comportamiento*) outrageous

desafortunadamente *adv* unfortunately

desafortunado, -a *adj* (*desgraciado*) unfortunate, unlucky

desagradable *adj* (*fastidioso, enojoso*) unpleasant; (*irritante*) disagreeable

desagradar *vi* (*disgustar*) to displease; (*molestar*) to bother

desagradecido, -a *adj* ungrateful

desagrado *nm* (*disgusto*) displeasure; (*contrariedad*) dissatisfaction

desagraviar *vt* to make amends to

desagüe *nm* (*de un líquido*) drainage; (*cañería*) drainpipe; (*salida*) outlet, drain

desaguisado *nm* outrage

desahogado, -a *adj* (*holgado*) comfortable; (*espacioso*) roomy, large

desahogar *vt* (*aliviar*) to ease, relieve; (*ira*) to vent; **desahogarse** *vr* (*relajarse*) to relax; (*desfogarse*) to let off steam

desahogo *nm* (*alivio*) relief; (*comodidad*) comfort, ease

desahuciar *vt* (*enfermo*) to give up hope for; (*inquilino*) to evict ❑ **desahucio** *nm* eviction

desairar *vt* (*menospreciar*) to slight, snub

desaire *nm* (*menosprecio*) slight; (*falta de garbo*) unattractiveness

desajustar *vt* (*desarreglar*) to disarrange; (*desconcertar*) to throw off balance; **desajustarse** *vr* to get out of order; (*aflojarse*) to loosen

desajuste *nm* (*de máquina*) disorder; (*situación*) imbalance

desalentador, a *adj* discouraging

desalentar *vt* (*desanimar*) to discourage

desaliento *etc vb ver* **desalentar** ♦ *nm* discouragement

desaliño *nm* slovenliness

desalmado, -a *adj* (*cruel*) cruel, heartless

desalojar *vt* (*expulsar, echar*) to eject; (*abandonar*) to move out of ♦ *vi* to move out

desamor *nm* (*frialdad*) indifference; (*odio*) dislike

desamparado, -a *adj* (*persona*) helpless; (*lugar: expuesto*) exposed; (*desierto*) deserted

desamparar vt (*abandonar*) to desert, abandon; (*JUR*) to leave defenceless (*US*) o defenceless (*BRIT*); (*barco*) to abandon

desandar vt: ~ **lo andado** o **el camino** to retrace one's steps

desangrar vt to bleed; (*fig: persona*) to bleed dry; **desangrarse** vr to lose a lot of blood

desanimado, -a adj (*persona*) downhearted; (*espectáculo, fiesta*) dull

desanimar vt (*desalentar*) to discourage; (*deprimir*) to depress; **desanimarse** vr to lose heart

desapacible adj (*gen*) unpleasant

desaparecer vi (*gen*) to disappear; (*el sol, el luz*) to vanish □ **desaparecido, -a** adj missing □ **desaparición** nf disappearance

desapasionado, -a adj dispassionate, impartial

desapego nm (*frialdad*) coolness; (*distancia*) detachment

desapercibido, -a adj (*desprevenido*) unprepared; **pasar ~** to go unnoticed

desaprensivo, -a adj unscrupulous

desaprobar vt (*reprobar*) to disapprove of; (*condenar*) to condemn; (*no consentir*) to reject

desaprovechado, -a adj (*oportunidad, tiempo*) wasted; (*estudiante*) slack

desaprovechar vt to waste

desarmador (*MÉX*) nm screwdriver

desarmar vt (*MIL, fig*) to disarm; (*TEC*) to take apart, dismantle □ **desarme** nm disarmament

desarraigar vt to uproot □ **desarraigo** nm uprooting

desarreglar vt (*desordenar*) to disarrange; (*trastocar*) to upset, disturb

desarreglo nm (*de casa, persona*) untidiness; (*desorden*) disorder

desarrollar vt (*gen*) to develop; **desarrollarse** vr to develop; (*ocurrir*) to take place; (*FOTO*) to develop □ **desarrollo** nm development

desarticular vt (*hueso*) to dislocate; (*objeto*) to take apart; (*fig*) to break up

desasir vt to loosen

desasosegar vt (*inquietar*) to disturb, make uneasy; **desasosegarse** vr to become uneasy

desasosiego etc vb ver **desasosegar** ♦ nm (*intranquilidad*) uneasiness, restlessness; (*ansiedad*) anxiety

desastrado, -a adj (*desaliñado*) shabby; (*sucio*) dirty

desastre nm disaster □ **desastroso, -a** adj disastrous

desatado, -a adj (*desligado*) untied; (*violento*) violent, wild

desatar vt (*nudo*) to untie; (*paquete*) to undo; (*separar*) to detach; **desatarse** vr (*zapatos*) to come untied; (*tormenta*) to break

desatascar vt (*cañería*) to unblock, clear

desatender vt (*no prestar atención a*) to disregard; (*abandonar*) to neglect

desatento, -a adj (*distraído*) inattentive; (*descortés*) discourteous

desatinado, -a adj foolish, silly □ **desatino** nm (*idiotez*) foolishness, folly; (*error*) blunder

desatornillar vt to unscrew

desatrancar vt (*puerta*) to unbolt; (*cañería*) to clear, unblock

desautorizado, -a adj unauthorized

desautorizar vt (*oficial*) to deprive of authority; (*informe*) to deny

desavenencia nf (*desacuerdo*) disagreement; (*discrepancia*) quarrel

desayunar vi to have breakfast ♦ vt to have for breakfast □ **desayuno** nm breakfast

desazón nf anxiety

desazonarse vr to worry, be anxious

desbandarse vr (*MIL*) to disband; (*fig*) to flee in disorder

desbarajuste nm confusion, disorder

desbaratar vt (*deshacer, destruir*) to ruin

desbloquear vt (*negociaciones, tráfico*) to get going again; (*COM: cuenta*) to unfreeze

desbocado, -a adj (*caballo*) runaway

desbordar vt (*sobrepasar*) to go beyond; (*exceder*) to exceed; **desbordarse** vr (*río*) to overflow; (*entusiasmo*) to erupt

descabalgar vi to dismount

descabellado, -a adj (*disparatado*) wild, crazy

descafeinado, -a adj decaffeinated ♦ nm decaffeinated coffee

descalabro nm blow; (*desgracia*) misfortune

descalificar vt to disqualify; (*desacreditar*) to discredit

descalzar vt (*zapato*) to take off □ **descalzo, -a** adj barefoot(ed)

descambiar vt to exchange

descaminado, -a adj (*equivocado*) on the wrong road; (*fig*) misguided

descampado nm open space

descansado, -a adj (*gen*) rested; (*que tranquiliza*) restful

descansar vt (gen) to rest ♦ vi to rest, have a rest; (echarse) to lie down

descansillo nm (de escalera) landing

descanso nm (reposo) rest; (alivio) relief; (pausa) break; (DEPORTE) interval, half time

descapotable nm (tb: carro ~) convertible

descarado, -a adj shameless; (insolente) sassy (US), cheeky (BRIT)

descarga nf (ARQ, ELEC, MIL) discharge; (NÁUT) unloading

descargar vt to unload; (golpe) to let fly; **descargarse** vr to unburden o.s. ❏ **descargo** nm (COM) receipt; (JUR) evidence

descaro nm nerve

descarriar vt (descaminar) to misdirect; (fig) to lead astray; **descarriarse** vr (perderse) to lose one's way; (separarse) to stray; (pervertirse) to err, go astray

descarrilamiento nm (de tren) derailment

descarrilar vi to be derailed

descartar vt (rechazar) to reject; (eliminar) to rule out; **descartarse** vr (NAIPES) to discard; **~se de** to shirk

descascarillado, -a adj (paredes) peeling

descendencia nf (origen) origin, descent; (hijos) offspring

descender vt (bajar: escalera) to go down ♦ vi to descend; (temperatura, nivel) to fall, drop; **~ de** to be descended from

descendiente nmf descendant

descenso nm descent; (de temperatura) drop

descifrar vt to decipher; (mensaje) to decode

descolgar vt (bajar) to take down; (teléfono) to pick up; **descolgarse** vr to let o.s. down

descolorido, -a adj faded; (pálido) pale

descompasado, -a adj (sin proporción) out of all proportion; (excesivo) excessive

descomponer vt (desordenar) to disarrange, disturb; (TEC) to put out of order; (dividir) to break down (into parts); (fig) to provoke; **descomponerse** vr (corromperse) to rot, decompose; (LAm TEC) to break down

descomposición nf (de un objeto) breakdown; (de fruta etc) decomposition

descompostura nf (MÉX: avería) breakdown, fault; (LAm: diarrea) diarrhea (US), diarrhoea (BRIT)

descompuesto, -a adj (corrompido) decomposed; (LAm: roto) broken

descomunal adj (enorme) huge

desconcertado, -a adj disconcerted, bewildered

desconcertar vt (confundir) to baffle; (incomodar) to upset, put out; **desconcertarse** vr (turbarse) to be upset

desconchado, -a adj (pintura) peeling

desconcierto etc vb ver **desconcertar** ♦ nm (gen) disorder; (desorientación) uncertainty; (inquietud) uneasiness

desconectar vt to disconnect

desconfianza nf distrust

desconfiar vi to be distrustful; **~ de** to distrust, suspect

descongelar vt to defrost; (COM, POL) to unfreeze

descongestionar vt (cabeza, tráfico) to clear

desconocer vt (ignorar) not to know, be ignorant of

desconocido, -a adj unknown ♦ nm/f stranger

desconocimiento nm (falta de conocimientos) ignorance

desconsiderado, -a adj inconsiderate; (insensible) thoughtless

desconsolar vt to distress; **desconsolarse** vr to despair

desconsuelo etc vb ver **desconsolar** ♦ nm (tristeza) distress; (desesperación) despair

descontado, -a adj: **dar por ~ (que)** to take (it) for granted (that)

descontar vt (deducir) to take away, deduct; (rebajar) to discount

descontento, -a adj dissatisfied ♦ nm dissatisfaction, discontent

descorazonar vt to discourage, dishearten

descorchar vt to uncork

descorrer vt (cortinas, cerrojo) to draw back

descortés adj (mal educado) discourteous; (grosero) rude

descoser vt to unstitch; **descoserse** vr to come apart (at the seams)

descosido, -a adj (COSTURA) unstitched

descrédito nm discredit

descreído, -a adj (incrédulo) incredulous; (falto de fe) unbelieving

descremado, -a adj (LAm) low-fat

descremar (LAm) vt (leche) to skim

describir vt to describe ❏ **descripción** nf description

descrito pp de **describir**

descuartizar vt (animal) to cut up

descubierto, -a pp de **descubrir** ♦ adj uncovered, bare; (persona) bareheaded ♦ nm (bancario) overdraft; **al ~** in the open

descubrimiento nm (hallazgo) discovery; (revelación) revelation

descubrir vt to discover, find; (inaugurar) to unveil; (vislumbrar) to detect; (revelar) to reveal, show; (destapar) to uncover; **descubrirse** vr to reveal o.s.; (quitarse sombrero) to take off one's hat; (confesar) to confess

descuento etc vb ver **descontar ♦** nm discount

descuidado, -a adj (sin cuidado) careless; (desordenado) untidy; (olvidadizo) forgetful; (dejado) neglected; (desprevenido) unprepared

descuidar vt (dejar) to neglect; (olvidar) to overlook; **descuidarse** vr (distraerse) to be careless; (abandonarse) to let o.s. go; (desprevenirse) to drop one's guard; **¡descuida!** don't worry! ❑ **descuido** nm (dejadez) carelessness; (olvido) negligence

---

desde

PALABRA CLAVE

prep

1 (lugar) from; **desde Cancún hasta mi casa hay 30 millas** it's 30 miles from Cancún to my house

2 (posición): **hablaba desde el balcón** she was speaking from the balcony

3 (tiempo: + adv, n): **desde ahora** from now on; **desde la boda** since the wedding; **desde niño** since I etc was a child; **desde 3 años atrás** since 3 years ago

4 (tiempo: + vb, fecha) since; for; **nos conocemos desde 1992/desde hace 20 años** we've known each other since 1992/for 20 years; **no le veo desde 1997/desde hace 5 años** I haven't seen him since 1997/for 5 years

5 (gama): **desde los más lujosos hasta los más económicos** from the most luxurious to the most reasonably priced

6: **desde luego (que no)** of course (not)

♦ conj: **desde que: desde que recuerdo** for as long as I can remember; **desde que llegó no ha salido** he hasn't been out since he arrived

desdecirse vr to retract; **~ de** to go back on

desdén nm scorn

desdeñar vt (despreciar) to scorn

desdicha nf (desgracia) misfortune; (infelicidad) unhappiness ❑ **desdichado, -a** adj (sin suerte) unlucky; (infeliz) unhappy

desdoblar vt (extender) to spread out; (desplegar) to unfold

desear vt to want, desire, wish for

desecar vt to dry up; **desecarse** vr to dry up

desechar vt (basura) to throw out o away; (ideas) to reject, discard ❑ **desechos** nmpl garbage sg (US), rubbish sg (BRIT)

desembalar vt to unpack

desembarazar vt (desocupar) to clear; (desenredar) to free; **desembarazarse** vr: **~se de** to free o.s. of, get rid of

desembarcar vt (mercancías etc) to unload **♦** vi to disembark; **desembarcarse** vr to disembark

desembocadura nf (de río) mouth; (de calle) opening

desembocar vi (río) to flow into; (fig) to result in

desembolso nm payment

desembragar vi to declutch

desembrollar vt (madeja) to unravel; (asunto, malentendido) to sort out

desemejanza nf dissimilarity

desempaquetar vt (regalo) to unwrap; (mercancía) to unpack

desempatar vi to replay, hold a play-off ❑ **desempate** nm (FÚTBOL) replay, play-off; (TENIS) tie-break(er)

desempeñar vt (cargo) to hold; (papel) to perform; (lo empeñado) to redeem; **~ un papel** (fig) to play (a role)

desempeño nm redeeming; (de cargo) occupation

desempleado, -a nm/f unemployed person ❑ **desempleo** nm unemployment

desempolvar vt (muebles etc) to dust; (lo olvidado) to revive

desencadenar vt to unchain; (ira) to unleash; **desencadenarse** vr to break loose; (tormenta) to burst; (guerra) to break out

desencajar vt (hueso) to dislocate; (mecanismo, pieza) to disconnect, disengage

desencanto nm disillusionment

desenchufar vt to unplug

desenfadado, -a adj (desenvuelto) uninhibited; (descarado) forward ❑ **desenfado** nm (libertad) freedom; (comportamiento) free and easy manner; (descaro) forwardness

desenfocado, -a adj (FOTO) out of focus

desenfrenado, -a adj (descontrolado) uncontrolled; (inmoderado) unbridled ❑ **desenfreno** nm wildness; (de las pasiones) lack of self-control

desenganchar vt (gen) to unhook; (FERRO) to uncouple

desengañar vt to disillusion; **desengañarse** vr to become disillusioned ❑ **desengaño** nm disillusionment; (decepción) disappointment

desenlace nm outcome

desenmarañar vt (fig) to unravel

desenmascarar vt to unmask

desenredar vt (pelo) to untangle; (problema) to sort out

desenroscar vt to unscrew

desentenderse vr: ~ **de** to pretend not to know about; (apartarse) to have nothing to do with

desenterrar vt to exhume; (tesoro, fig) to unearth, dig up

desentonar vi (MÚS) to sing (o play) out of tune; (color) to clash

desentrañar vt (misterio) to unravel

desentumecer vt (pierna etc) to stretch

desenvoltura nf ease

desenvolver vt (paquete) to unwrap; (fig) to develop; **desenvolverse** vr (desarrollarse) to unfold, develop; (arreglárselas) to cope

deseo nm desire, wish ❑ **deseoso, -a** adj: **estar deseoso de** to be anxious to

desequilibrado, -a adj unbalanced

desertar vi to desert

desértico, -a adj desert cpd

desesperación nf (impaciencia) desperation, despair; (irritación) fury

desesperar vt to drive to despair; (exasperar) to drive to distraction ♦ vi: ~ **de** to despair of; **desesperarse** vr to despair, lose hope

desestabilizar vt to destabilize

desestimar vt (menospreciar) to have a low opinion of; (rechazar) to reject

desfachatez nf (insolencia) impudence; (descaro) rudeness

desfalco nm embezzlement

desfallecer vi (perder las fuerzas) to become weak; (desvanecerse) to faint

desfasado, -a adj (anticuado) old-fashioned ❑ **desfase** nm (diferencia) gap

desfavorable adj unfavorable (US), unfavourable (BRIT)

desfigurar vt (cara) to disfigure; (cuerpo) to deform

desfiladero nm gorge

desfilar vi to parade ❑ **desfile** nm procession

desfogarse vr (fig) to let off steam

desgajar vt (arrancar) to tear off; (romper) to break off; **desgajarse** vr to come off

desgana nf (falta de apetito) loss of appetite; (apatía) unwillingness ❑ **desganado, -a** adj: **estar desganado** (sin apetito) to have no appetite; (sin entusiasmo) to have lost interest

desgarrador, a adj (fig) heartrending

desgarrar vt to tear (up); (fig) to shatter ❑ **desgarro** nm (en tela) tear; (aflicción) grief

desgastar vt (deteriorar) to wear away o down; (estropear) to spoil; **desgastarse** vr to get worn out ❑ **desgaste** nm wear (and tear)

desglosar vt (factura) to break down

desgracia nf misfortune; (accidente) accident; (vergüenza) disgrace; (contratiempo) setback; **por ~** unfortunately

desgraciado, -a adj (sin suerte) unlucky, unfortunate; (miserable) wretched; (infeliz) miserable

desgravación nf (COM: tb: ~ **fiscal**) tax relief

desgravar vt (impuestos) to reduce the tax o duty on

desguace (ESP) nm junkyard

deshabitado, -a adj uninhabited

deshacer vt (casa) to break up; (TEC) to take apart; (enemigo) to defeat; (diluir) to melt; (contrato) to break; (intriga) to solve; **deshacerse** vr (disolverse) to melt; (despedazarse) to come apart o undone; ~**se de** to get rid of; ~**se en lágrimas** to burst into tears

desharrapado, -a adj (persona) shabby

deshecho, -a adj undone; (roto) smashed; (persona) **estar ~** to be pooped (US) o shattered (BRIT)

desheredar vt to disinherit

deshidratar vt to dehydrate

deshielo nm thaw

deshonesto, -a adj indecent

deshonra nf (deshonor) dishonor (US), dishonour (BRIT); (vergüenza) shame

deshora: **a ~** adv at the wrong time

deshuesadero (MÉX) nm junkyard

deshuesar vt (carne) to bone; (fruta) to stone

desierto, -a adj (casa, calle, negocio) deserted ♦ nm desert

designar vt (nombrar) to designate; (indicar) to fix

designio nm plan

desigual adj (terreno) uneven; (lucha etc) unequal

desilusión nf disillusionment; (decepción) disappointment ❑ **desilusionar** vt to disillusion; to disappoint; **desilusionarse** vr to become disillusioned

desinfectar vt to disinfect

desinflar vt to deflate

desintegración nf disintegration

desinterés nm (desgana) lack of interest; (altruismo) unselfishness

desintoxicarse vr (drogadicto) to undergo detoxification

desistir vi (renunciar) to stop, desist

desleal adj (infiel) disloyal; (COM: competencia) unfair ❑ **deslealtad** nf disloyalty

desleír vt (líquido) to dilute; (sólido) to dissolve

deslenguado, -a adj (grosero) foul-mouthed

desligar vt (desatar) to untie, undo; (separar) to separate; **desligarse** vr (de un compromiso) to extricate o.s.

desliz nm (fig) lapse ❑ **deslizar** vt to slip, slide

deslucido, -a adj dull; (torpe) awkward, graceless; (deslustrado) tarnished

deslumbrar vt to dazzle

desmadrarse (fam) vr (descontrolarse) to run wild; (divertirse) to let one's hair down ❑ **desmadre** (fam) nm (desorganización) chaos; (jaleo) commotion

desmán nm (exceso) outrage; (abuso de poder) abuse

desmandarse vr (portarse mal) to behave badly; (excederse) to get out of hand; (caballo) to bolt

desmantelar vt (deshacer) to dismantle; (casa) to strip

desmaquillador nm make-up remover

desmayar vi to lose heart; **desmayarse** vr (MED) to faint ❑ **desmayo** nm (MED: acto) faint; (: estado) unconsciousness

desmedido, -a adj excessive

desmejorar vt (dañar) to impair, spoil; (MED) to weaken

desmembrar vt (MED) to dismember; (fig) to separate

desmemoriado, -a adj forgetful

desmentir vt (contradecir) to contradict; (refutar) to deny

desmenuzar vt (deshacer) to crumble; (carne) to chop; (examinar) to examine closely

desmerecer vt to be unworthy of ♦ vi (deteriorarse) to deteriorate

desmesurado, -a adj disproportionate

desmontable adj (que se quita: pieza) detachable; (plegable) collapsible, folding

desmontar vt (deshacer) to dismantle; (tierra) to level ♦ vi to dismount

desmoralizar vt to demoralize

desmoronar vt to wear away, erode; **desmoronarse** vr (edificio, dique) to collapse; (economía) to decline

desnatado, -a (ESP) adj low-fat

desnivel nm (de terreno) unevenness

desnudar vt (desvestir) to undress; (despojar) to strip; **desnudarse** vr (desvestirse) to get undressed ❑ **desnudo, -a** adj naked ♦ nm/f nude; **desnudo de** devoid o bereft of

desnutrición nf malnutrition ❑ **desnutrido, -a** adj undernourished

desobedecer vt, vi to disobey ❑ **desobediencia** nf disobedience

desocupado, -a adj at leisure; (desempleado) unemployed; (deshabitado) empty, vacant

desocupar vt to vacate

desodorante nm deodorant

desolación nf (de lugar) desolation; (fig) grief

desolar vt to ruin, lay waste

desorbitado, -a adj (excesivo: ambición) boundless; (deseos) excessive; (: precio) exorbitant

desorden nm confusion; (político) disorder, unrest

desorganización nf (de persona) disorganization; (en empresa, oficina) disorder, chaos

desorganizar vt (desordenar) to disorganize

desorientar vt (extraviar) to mislead; (confundir, desconcertar) to confuse; **desorientarse** vr (perderse) to lose one's way

despabilado, -a adj (despierto) wide-awake; (fig) alert, sharp

despabilar vt (el ingenio) to sharpen ♦ vi to wake up; (fig) to get a move on; **despabilarse** vr to wake up; to get a move on

despachar vt (negocio) to do, complete; (enviar) to send, dispatch; (vender) to sell, deal in; (billete) to issue; (mandar ir) to send away

despacho nm (oficina) office; (de paquetes) dispatch; (venta) sale; (comunicación) message

despacio adv slowly

desparpajo nm self-confidence; (pey) nerve

desparramar vt (esparcir) to scatter; (líquido) to spill

despavorido, -a adj terrified

despecho nm spite; **a ~ de** in spite of

despectivo, -a adj (despreciativo) derogatory; (LING) pejorative

despedazar vt to tear to pieces

despedida nf (adiós) farewell; (de obrero) sacking

despedir vt (visita) to see off, show out; (empleado) to dismiss; (inquilino) to evict; (objeto) to hurl; (olor etc) to give out o off; **despedirse** vr: ~**se de** to say goodbye to

despegar vt to unstick ♦ vi (avión) to take off; **despegarse** vr to come loose, come unstuck □ **despego** nm detachment

despegue etc vb ver **despegar** ♦ nm takeoff

despeinado, -a adj unkempt, disheveled (US), dishevelled (BRIT)

despejado, -a adj (lugar) clear, free; (cielo) clear; (persona) wide-awake, bright

despejar vt (gen) to clear; (misterio) to clear up ♦ vi (el tiempo) to clear; **despejarse** vr (tiempo, cielo) to clear (up); (misterio) to become clearer; (cabeza) to clear

despellejar vt (animal) to skin

despensa nf larder

despeñadero nm (GEO) cliff, precipice

despeñarse vr to hurl o.s. down; (vehículo) to tumble over

desperdicio nm (despilfarro) squandering; ~s nmpl (basura) garbage sg (US), rubbish sg (BRIT); (residuos) waste sg

desperdigarse vr (rebaño, familia) to scatter, spread out; (granos de arroz, semillas) to scatter

desperezarse vr to stretch

desperfecto nm (deterioro) slight damage; (defecto) flaw, imperfection

despertador nm alarm clock

despertar nm awakening ♦ vt (persona) to wake up; (recuerdos) to revive; (sentimiento) to arouse ♦ vi to awaken, wake up; **despertarse** vr to awaken, wake up

despiadado, -a adj (ataque) merciless; (persona) heartless

despido etc vb ver **despedir** ♦ nm dismissal, sacking

despierto, -a etc vb ver **despertar** ♦ adj awake; (fig) sharp, alert

despilfarro nm (derroche) squandering; (lujo desmedido) extravagance

despistar vt to throw off the track o scent; (confundir) to mislead, confuse; **despistarse** vr to take the wrong road; (confundirse) to become confused

despiste nm absent-mindedness; **un ~** a mistake, a slip

desplazamiento nm displacement

desplazar vt to move; (NÁUT) to displace; (INFORM) to scroll; (fig) to oust; **desplazarse** vr (persona) to travel

desplegar vt (tela, papel) to unfold, open out; (bandera) to unfurl □ **despliegue** etc vb ver **desplegar** ♦ nm display

desplomarse vr (edificio, gobierno, persona) to collapse

desplumar vt (ave) to pluck; (fam: estafar) to fleece

despoblado, -a adj (sin habitantes) uninhabited

despojar vt (algn: de sus bienes) to divest of, deprive of; (casa) to strip, leave bare; (algn: de su cargo) to strip of

despojo nm (acto) plundering; (objetos) plunder, loot; ~s nmpl (de ave, res) offal sg

desposado, -a adj, nm/f newly-wed

desposar vt to marry; **desposarse** vr to get married

desposeer vt: ~ **a algn de** (puesto, autoridad) to strip sb of

déspota nmf despot

despreciar vt (desdeñar) to despise, scorn; (afrentar) to slight □ **desprecio** nm scorn, contempt; slight

desprender vt (broche) to unfasten; (olor) to give off; **desprenderse** vr (botón: caerse) to fall off; (broche) to come unfastened; (olor, perfume) to be given off; ~**se de algo que ...** to draw from sth that ...

desprendimiento nm (gen) loosening; (generosidad) disinterestedness; (de tierra, rocas) landslide

despreocupado, -a adj (sin preocupación) unworried, nonchalant; (negligente) careless

despreocuparse vr not to worry; ~ **de** to have no interest in

desprestigiar vt (criticar) to run down; (desacreditar) to discredit

desprevenido, -a adj (no preparado) unprepared, unready

desproporcionado, -a adj disproportionate, out of proportion

desprovisto, -a adj: ~ **de** to be devoid of

después adv afterward, later; (próximo paso) next; ~ **de comer** after lunch; **un año** ~ a year later; ~ **se debatió el tema** next the matter was discussed; ~ **de corregido el texto** after the text had been corrected; ~ **de todo** after all

desquiciado, -a adj deranged

desquite nm (satisfacción) satisfaction; (venganza) revenge

destacar vt to emphasize, point up; (MIL) to detach, detail ♦ vi (resaltarse) to stand out; (persona) to be outstanding o exceptional; **destacarse** vr to stand out; to be outstanding o exceptional

destajo nm: **trabajar a ~** to do piecework

destapar vt (botella) to open; (cacerola) to take the lid off; (descubrir) to uncover; **destaparse** vr (revelarse) to reveal one's true character

destartalado, -a adj (desordenado) untidy; (ruinoso) tumbledown

destello nm (de estrella) twinkle; (de faro) signal light

destemplado, -a adj (MÚS) out of tune; (voz) harsh; (MED) out of sorts; (tiempo) unpleasant, nasty

desteñir vt to fade ♦ vi to fade; **desteñirse** vr to fade; **esta tela no destiñe** this fabric will not run

desternillarse vr: **~ de risa** to split one's sides laughing

desterrar vt (exiliar) to exile; (fig) to banish, dismiss

destiempo: a ~ adv out of turn

destierro etc vb ver **desterrar** ♦ nm exile

destilar vt to distill ❑ **destilería** nf distillery

destinar vt (funcionario) to appoint, assign; (fondos): **~ (a)** to set aside (for)

destinatario, -a nm/f addressee

destino nm (suerte) destiny; (de avión, viajero) destination

destituir vt to dismiss

destornillador nm screwdriver

destornillar vt (tornillo) to unscrew; **destornillarse** vr to unscrew

destreza nf (habilidad) skill; (maña) dexterity

destrozar vt (romper) to smash, break (up); (estropear) to ruin; (nervios) to shatter

destrozo nm (acción) destruction; (desastre) smashing; **~s** nmpl (pedazos) pieces; (daños) havoc sg

destrucción nf destruction

destruir vt to destroy

desuso nm disuse; **caer en ~** to become obsolete

desvalido, -a adj (desprotegido) destitute; (sin fuerzas) helpless

desvalijar vt (persona) to rob; (casa, tienda) to ransack; (vehículo) to break into

desván nm attic

desvanecer vt (disipar) to dispel; (borrar) to blur; **desvanecerse** vr (humo etc) to vanish, disappear; (color) to fade; (recuerdo, sonido) to fade away; (MED) to pass out; (duda) to be dispelled

desvanecimiento nm (desaparición) disappearance; (de colores) fading; (evaporación) evaporation; (MED) fainting spell (US), fainting fit (BRIT)

desvariar vi (enfermo) to be delirious ❑ **desvarío** nm delirium

desvelar vt to keep awake; **desvelarse** vr (no poder dormir) to stay awake; (preocuparse) to be vigilant o watchful

desvelos nmpl worrying sg

desvencijado, -a adj (silla) rickety; (máquina) broken-down

desventaja nf disadvantage

desventura nf misfortune

desvergonzado, -a adj shameless

desvergüenza nf (descaro) shamelessness; (insolencia) impudence; (mala conducta) effrontery

desvestir vt to undress; **desvestirse** vr to undress

desviación nf deviation; (AUTO) detour, diversion (BRIT)

desviar vt to turn aside; (río) to alter the course of; (navío) to divert, re-route; (conversación) to sidetrack; **desviarse** vr (apartarse del camino) to turn aside; (: barco) to go off course

desvío etc vb ver **desviar** ♦ nm (desviación) detour, diversion (BRIT); (fig) indifference

desvirtuar vt to distort

desvivirse vr: **~ por** (anhelar) to long for, crave for; (hacer lo posible por) to do one's utmost for

detallar vt to detail

detalle nm detail; (gesto) gesture, token; **al ~** in detail; (COM) retail

detallista nmf (COM) retailer

detective nmf detective

detener vt (gen) to stop; (JUR) to arrest; (objeto) to keep; **detenerse** vr to stop; (demorarse): **~se en** to delay over, linger over

detenidamente adv (minuciosamente) carefully; (extensamente) at great length

detenido, -a adj (arrestado) under arrest ♦ nm/f person under arrest, prisoner

detenimiento nm: **con ~** thoroughly; (observar, considerar) carefully

detergente nm detergent

deteriorar vt to spoil, damage; **deteriorarse** vr to deteriorate ❑ **deterioro** nm deterioration

determinación nf (empeño) determination; (decisión) decision ☐ **determinado, -a** adj specific

determinar vt (plazo) to fix; (precio) to settle; **determinarse** vr to decide

detestar vt to detest

detractor, a nm/f slanderer, libeller

detrás adv behind; (atrás) at the back; **~ de** behind

detrimento nm: **en ~ de** to the detriment of

deuda nf debt

devaluación nf devaluation

devastar vt (destruir) to devastate

deveras (MÉX) nf inv: **un amigo de (a) ~** a true o real friend

devoción nf devotion

devolución nf (reenvío) return, sending back; (reembolso) repayment; (JUR) devolution

devolver vt to return; (lo extraviado, lo prestado) to give back; (carta al correo) to send back; (COM) to repay, refund ♦ vi (vomitar) to throw up

devorar vt to devour

devoto, -a adj devout ♦ nm/f admirer

devuelto pp de **devolver**

devuelva etc vb ver **devolver**

di etc vb ver **dar**; **decir**

día nm day; **¿qué ~ es?** what's the date?; **estar/poner al ~** to be/keep up to date; **el ~ de hoy/de mañana** today/tomorrow; **al ~ siguiente** (on) the following day; **vivir al ~** to live from hand to mouth; **de ~** by day, in daylight; **en pleno ~** in full daylight ► **día feriado** (LAm) holiday ► **día festivo** (ESP) holiday ► **día libre** day off

diabetes nf diabetes

diablo nm devil ☐ **diablura** nf prank

diadema nf tiara

diafragma nm diaphragm

diagnosis nf inv diagnosis

diagnóstico nm = **diagnosis**

diagonal adj diagonal

diagrama nm diagram ► **diagrama de flujo** flowchart

dial nm dial

dialecto nm dialect

dialogar vi: **~ con** (POL) to hold talks with

diálogo nm dialogue, dialog (US)

diamante nm diamond

diana nf (MIL) reveille; (de blanco) center, bull's-eye

diapositiva nf (FOTO) slide, transparency

diario, -a adj daily ♦ nm newspaper; **a ~** daily; **de ~** everyday

diarrea nf diarrhea (US), diarrhoea (BRIT)

dibujar vt to draw, sketch ☐ **dibujo** nm drawing ► **dibujos animados** cartoons

diccionario nm dictionary

dice etc vb ver **decir**

dicho, -a pp de **decir** ♦ adj: **en ~s países** in the aforementioned countries ♦ nm saying

dichoso, -a adj happy

diciembre nm December

dictado nm dictation

dictador nm dictator ☐ **dictadura** nf dictatorship

dictamen nm (opinión) opinion; (juicio) judgment; (informe) report

dictar vt (carta) to dictate; (JUR: sentencia) to pronounce; (decreto) to issue; (LAm: clase) to give

didáctico, -a adj educational

diecinueve num nineteen

dieciocho num eighteen

dieciséis num sixteen

diecisiete num seventeen

diente nm (ANAT, TEC) tooth; (ZOOL) fang; (: de elefante) tusk; (de ajo) clove; **hablar entre ~s** to mutter, mumble

diera etc vb ver **dar**

diesel adj: **motor ~** diesel engine

diestro, -a adj (derecho) right; (hábil) skillful (US), skilful (BRIT)

dieta nf diet ☐ **dietética** nf dietetics sg ☐ **dietético, -a** adj diet; (atr) dietary

diez num ten

diezmar vt (población) to decimate

difamar vt (JUR: hablando) to slander; (: por escrito) to libel

diferencia nf difference ☐ **diferenciar** vt to differentiate between ♦ vi to differ; **diferenciarse** vr to differ, be different; (distinguirse) to distinguish o.s.

diferente adj different

diferido nm: **en ~** (TV etc) recorded

difícil adj difficult

dificultad nf difficulty; (problema) trouble

dificultar vt (complicar) to complicate, make difficult; (estorbar) to obstruct

difteria nf diphtheria

difundir vt (calor, luz) to diffuse; (RADIO, TV) to broadcast; **difundirse** vr to spread (out); **~ una noticia** to spread a piece of news

difunto, -a adj dead, deceased ♦ nm/f deceased (person)

difusión nf (RADIO, TV) broadcasting

diga etc vb ver **decir**

digerir vt to digest; (fig) to absorb
□ **digestión** nf digestion □ **digestivo, -a** adj digestive

digital adj digital

dignarse vr to deign to

dignatario, -a nm/f dignitary

dignidad nf dignity

digno, -a adj worthy

digo etc vb ver **decir**

dije etc vb ver **decir**

dilapidar vt (dinero, herencia) to squander, waste

dilatar vt (cuerpo) to dilate; (prolongar) to prolong

dilema nm dilemma

diligencia nf diligence; (ocupación) errand, job; ~s nfpl (JUR) formalities □ **diligente** adj diligent

diluir vt to dilute

diluvio nm deluge, flood

dimensión nf dimension

diminuto, -a adj tiny, diminutive

dimitir vi to resign

dimos vb ver **dar**

Dinamarca nf Denmark

dinámico, -a adj dynamic

dinamita nf dynamite

dínamo nm (LAm) o f (ESP) dynamo

dineral nm large sum of money, fortune

dinero nm money ▶ **dinero contante** o **efectivo** (ready) cash ▶ **dinero suelto** (loose) change

dio vb ver **dar**

dios nm god; ¡D~ mío! (oh), my God!

diosa nf goddess

diploma nm diploma

diplomacia nf diplomacy; (fig) tact

diplomado, -a adj qualified

diplomático, -a adj diplomatic ♦ nm/f diplomat

diputación nf (tb: ~ provincial) ≈ county commission (US); ≈ county council (BRIT)

diputado, -a nm/f delegate; (POL) ≈ representative (US), ≈ member of parliament (BRIT)

dique nm dike (US), dyke (BRIT)

diré etc vb ver **decir**

dirección nf direction; (señas) address; (AUTO) steering; (gerencia) management; (POL) leadership ▶ **dirección única/prohibida** one-way street/no entry

direccional (MÉX) nf (AUTO) turn signal (US), indicator (BRIT)

directa nf (AUTO) top gear

directiva nf (tb: **junta** ~) board of directors

directo, -a adj direct; (RADIO, TV) live; **transmitir en** ~ to broadcast live

director, a adj leading ♦ nm/f director; (ESCOL) principal (US), head(teacher) (BRIT); (gerente) manager(-ess); (PRENSA) editor ▶ **director de cine** movie (US) o film (BRIT) director ▶ **director general** managing director

directorio (MÉX) nm (telefónico) phone book

dirigente nmf (POL) leader

dirigir vt to direct; (carta) to address; (obra de teatro, película) to direct; (MÚS) to conduct; (negocio) to manage; **dirigirse** vr: ~**se a** to go towards, make one's way towards; (hablar con) to speak to

dirija etc vb ver **dirigir**

discernir vt to discern

disciplina nf discipline

discípulo, -a nm/f disciple

disco nm disc; (DEPORTE) discus; (TEL) dial; (AUTO: semáforo) light; (MÚS) record ▶ **disco compacto/de larga duración** compact disc/long-playing record ▶ **disco de freno** brake disc ▶ **disco flexible/duro** o **rígido** (INFORM) floppy/hard disk

disconforme adj differing; **estar** ~ **(con)** to be in disagreement (with)

discordia nf discord

discoteca nf disco(theque)

discreción nf discretion; (reserva) prudence; **comer a** ~ to eat as much as one wishes □ **discrecional** adj (facultativo) discretionary

discrepancia nf (diferencia) discrepancy; (desacuerdo) disagreement

discreto, -a adj discreet

discriminación nf discrimination

disculpa nf excuse; (pedir perdón) apology; **pedir** ~**s a/por** to apologize to/for □ **disculpar** vt to excuse, pardon; **disculparse** vr to excuse o.s.; to apologize

discurrir vi (pensar, reflexionar) to think, meditate; (el tiempo) to pass, go by

discurso nm speech

discusión nf (diálogo) discussion; (riña) argument

discutir vt (debatir) to discuss; (pelear) to argue about; (contradecir) to argue against ♦ vi (debatir) to discuss; (pelearse) to argue

disecar vt (conservar: animal) to stuff; (: planta) to dry

diseminar vt to disseminate, spread

diseñar vt, vi to design

diseño nm design

disfraz nm (máscara) disguise; (excusa) pretext □ **disfrazar** vt to disguise; **disfrazarse** vr to dress (o.s) up; **disfrazarse de** to disguise o.s. as

disfrutar vt to enjoy ♦ vi to enjoy o.s.; ~ **de** to enjoy, possess

disgregarse vr (muchedumbre) to disperse

disgustar vt (no gustar) to displease; (contrariar, enojar) to annoy, upset; **disgustarse** vr (enfadarse) to get upset; (dos personas) to fall out

⚠ No confundir **disgustar** con la palabra inglesa *disgust*.

disgusto nm (contrariedad) annoyance; (tristeza) grief; (riña) quarrel

disidente nm dissident

disimular vt (ocultar) to hide, conceal ♦ vi to dissemble

disipar vt to dispel; (fortuna) to squander; **disiparse** vr (nubes) to vanish; (indisciplinarse) to dissipate

dislocarse vr (articulación) to sprain, dislocate

disminución nf decrease, reduction

disminuido, -a nm/f handicapped person ▶ **disminuido mental/físico** mentally/physically handicapped person

disminuir vt to decrease, diminish

disociarse vr: ~ **(de)** to dissociate o.s. (from)

disolver vt (gen) to dissolve; **disolverse** vr to dissolve; (COM) to go into liquidation

dispar adj different

disparar vt, vi to shoot, fire

disparate nm (tontería) foolish remark; (error) blunder; **decir ~s** to talk nonsense

disparo nm shot

dispensar vt to dispense; (disculpar) to excuse

dispersar vt to disperse; **dispersarse** vr to scatter

disponer vt (arreglar) to arrange; (ordenar) to put in order; (preparar) to prepare, get ready ♦ vi: ~ **de** to have, own; **disponerse** vr: ~**se a** o **para hacer** to prepare to do

disponible adj available

disposición nf arrangement, disposition; (INFORM) layout; **a la ~ de** at the disposal of ▶ **disposición de ánimo** state of mind

dispositivo nm device, mechanism

dispuesto, -a pp de **disponer** ♦ adj (arreglado) arranged; (preparado) disposed

disputar vt (carrera) to compete in

disquete nm floppy disk, diskette

distancia nf distance

distanciar vt to space out; **distanciarse** vr to become estranged

distante adj distant

distar vi: **dista 5km de aquí** it is 5km from here

diste vb ver **dar**

disteis vb ver **dar**

distensión nf (en las relaciones) relaxation; (POL) détente; (muscular) strain

distinción nf distinction; (elegancia) elegance; (honor) honor (US), honour (BRIT)

distinguido, -a adj distinguished

distinguir vt to distinguish; (escoger) to single out; **distinguirse** vr to be distinguished

distintivo nm badge; (fig) characteristic

distinto, -a adj different; (claro) clear

distracción nf distraction; (pasatiempo) hobby, pastime; (olvido) absent-mindedness, distraction

distraer vt (atención) to distract; (divertir) to amuse; (fondos) to embezzle; **distraerse** vr (entretenerse) to amuse o.s.; (perder la concentración) to allow one's attention to wander

distraído, -a adj (gen) absent-minded; (entretenido) amusing

distribuidor, a nm/f distributor □ **distribuidora** nf (COM) dealer, agent; (CINE) distributor

distribuir vt to distribute

distrito nm (sector, territorio) region; (barrio) district ▶ **Distrito Federal** (MÉX) Federal District

disturbio nm disturbance; (desorden) riot

disuadir vt to dissuade

disuelto pp de **disolver**

disyuntiva nf dilemma

DIU nm abr (= dispositivo intrauterino) IUD

diurno, -a adj day cpd

divagar vi (desviarse) to digress

diván nm divan

divergencia nf divergence

diversidad nf diversity, variety

diversificar vt to diversify

diversión nf (gen) entertainment; (actividad) hobby, pastime

diverso, -a adj diverse; **~s libros** several books □ **diversos** nmpl sundries

divertido, -a adj (chiste) amusing; (fiesta etc) enjoyable

divertir vt (entretener, recrear) to amuse; **divertirse** vr (pasarlo bien) to have a good time; (distraerse) to amuse o.s.

dividendos nmpl (COM) dividends

dividir vt (gen) to divide; (distribuir) to distribute, share out

divierta etc vb ver **divertir**

divino, -a adj divine

divirtiendo etc vb ver **divertir**

divisa nf (emblema) emblem, badge; **~s** nfpl foreign exchange sg

divisar vt to make out, distinguish

división nf (gen) division; (de partido) split; (de país) partition

divorciar vt to divorce; **divorciarse** vr to get divorced □ **divorcio** nm divorce

divulgar vt (ideas) to spread; (secreto) to divulge

DNI (ESP) nm abr (= Documento Nacional de Identidad) national identity card

Dña. abr (= doña) Mrs

do nm (MÚS) do, C

dobladillo nm (de vestido) hem; (de pantalón: vuelta) cuff (US), turn-up (BRIT)

doblar vt to double; (papel) to fold; (caño) to bend; (la esquina) to turn, go round; (película) to dub ♦ vi to turn; (campana) to toll; **doblarse** vr (plegarse) to fold (up), crease; (encorvarse) to bend

doble adj double; (de dos aspectos) dual; (fig) two-faced ♦ nm double ♦ nmf (TEATRO) double, stand-in; **~s** nmpl (DEPORTE) doubles sg; **con ~ sentido** with a double meaning

doblegar vt to fold, crease; **doblegarse** vr to yield

doblez nm fold, hem ♦ nf insincerity, duplicity

doce num twelve □ **docena** nf dozen

docente adj: **centro/personal ~** teaching establishment/staff

dócil adj (pasivo) docile; (obediente) obedient

docto, -a adj: **~ en** instructed in

doctor, a nm/f doctor

doctorado nm doctorate

doctrina nf doctrine, teaching

documentación nf documentation, papers pl

documental adj, nm documentary

documento nm (certificado) document ▶ **documento adjunto** (INFORM)

attachment ▶ **documento nacional de identidad** (ESP) identity card

dólar nm dollar

doler vt, vi to hurt; (fig) to grieve; **dolerse** vr (de su situación) to grieve, feel sorry; (de las desgracias ajenas) to sympathize; **me duele el brazo** my arm hurts

dolor nm pain; (fig) grief, sorrow ▶ **dolor de cabeza** headache ▶ **dolor de estómago** stomachache

domar vt to tame

domesticar vt = **domar**

doméstico, -a adj (vida, servicio) home; (tareas) household; (animal) tame, pet

domicilio nm home; **sin ~ fijo** of no fixed abode ▶ **domicilio particular** private residence ▶ **domicilio social** (COM) head office

dominante adj dominant; (persona) domineering

dominar vt (gen) to dominate; (idiomas) to be fluent in ♦ vi to dominate, prevail; **dominarse** vr to control o.s.

domingo nm Sunday; (MÉX: paga) allowance (US), pocket money (BRIT)

dominio nm (tierras) domain; (autoridad) power, authority; (de las pasiones) grip, hold; (de idiomas) command

don nm (talento) gift; **~ Juan Gómez** Mr Juan Gómez, Juan Gómez Esq. (BRIT)

dona (MÉX) nf doughnut, donut (US)

donaire nm charm

donar vt to donate

donativo nm donation

doncella nf (criada) maid

donde adv where ♦ prep: **la moto está allí ~ el farol** the motorbike is over there by the lamppost o where the lamppost is; **en ~** where, in which

dónde adv interr where?; **¿a ~ vas?** where are you going (to)?; **¿de ~ vienes?** where have you been?; **¿por ~?** where?, whereabouts?

dondequiera adv anywhere ♦ conj: **~ que** wherever; **por ~** everywhere, all over the place

donut® (ESP) nm doughnut, donut (US)

doña nf: **~ Alicia** Alicia; **~ Victoria Benito** Mrs Victoria Benito

dorado, -a adj (color) golden; (TEC) gilt

dormir vt: **~ la siesta** to have an afternoon nap ♦ vi to sleep; **dormirse** vr to fall asleep

dormitar vi to doze

dormitorio nm bedroom ▶ **dormitorio común** dormitory

dorsal *nm* (*DEPORTE*) number

dorso *nm* (*de mano*) back; (*de hoja*) other side

dos *num* two

dosis *nf inv* dose, dosage

dotado, -a *adj* gifted, exceptional (*US*); ~ **de** endowed with

dotar *vt* to endow □ **dote** *nf* dowry; **dotes** *nfpl* (*talentos*) gifts

doy *vb ver* **dar**

dragar *vt* (*río*) to dredge; (*minas*) to sweep

drama *nm* drama

dramaturgo, -a *nm/f* dramatist, playwright

drástico, -a *adj* drastic

drenaje *nm* drainage

droga *nf* drug

drogadicto, -a *nm/f* drug addict

droguería (*ESP*) *nf* hardware store (*US*) o shop (*BRIT*)

ducha *nf* (*baño*) shower; (*MED*) douche; **ducharse** *vr* to take a shower

duda *nf* doubt □ **dudar** *vt, vi* to doubt □ **dudoso, -a** *adj* (*incierto*) hesitant; (*sospechoso*) doubtful

duela *etc vb ver* **doler**

duelo *vb ver* **doler** ♦ *nm* (*combate*) duel; (*luto*) mourning

duende *nm* imp, goblin

dueño, -a *nm/f* (*propietario*) owner; (*de pensión, taberna*) landlord(-lady); (*empresario*) employer

duermo *etc vb ver* **dormir**

dulce *adj* sweet ♦ *adv* gently, softly ♦ *nm* candy (*US*), sweet (*BRIT*)

dulcería (*LAm*) *nf* candy store (*US*), sweet shop (*BRIT*)

dulzura *nf* sweetness; (*ternura*) gentleness

duna *nf* (*GEO*) dune

dúo *nm* duet

duplicar *vt* (*hacer el doble de*) to duplicate; **duplicarse** *vr* to double

duque *nm* duke □ **duquesa** *nf* duchess

duración *nf* (*de película, disco etc*) length; (*de pila etc*) life; (*curso: de acontecimientos etc*) duration

duradero, -a *adj* (*tela etc*) hard-wearing; (*fe, paz*) lasting

durante *prep* during

durar *vi* to last; (*recuerdo*) to remain

durazno (*LAm*) *nm* (*fruta*) peach; (*árbol*) peach tree

durex® (*MÉX*) *nm* (*tira adhesiva*) Scotch tape® (*US*), Sellotape® (*BRIT*)

dureza *nf* (*calidad*) hardness

duro, -a *adj* hard; (*carácter*) tough ♦ *adv* hard ♦ *nm* (*moneda*) five-peseta coin o piece

DVD *nm abr* (= *disco de vídeo digital*) DVD

Ee

E *abr* (= *este*) E

e *conj* and

ebanista *nmf* cabinetmaker

ébano *nm* ebony

ebrio, -a *adj* drunk

ebullición *nf* boiling

eccema *nf* (*MED*) eczema

echar *vt* to throw; (*agua, vino*) to pour (out); (*empleado: despedir*) to fire, sack; (*hojas*) to sprout; (*cartas*) to mail (*US*), post (*BRIT*); (*humo*) to emit, give out ♦ *vi*: ~ **a correr/llorar** to run off/burst into tears; **echarse** *vr* to lie down; ~ **llave a** to lock (up); ~ **abajo** (*gobierno*) to overthrow; (*edificio*) to demolish; ~ **mano a** to lay hands on; ~ **una mano a algn** (*ayudar*) to give sb a hand; ~ **de menos** to miss

eclesiástico, -a *adj* ecclesiastical

eco *nm* echo; **tener** ~ to catch on

ecología *nf* ecology □ **ecológico, -a** *adj* (*producto, método*) environmentally-friendly; (*agricultura*) organic □ **ecologista** *adj* ecological, environmental ♦ *nmf* environmentalist

economato *nm* cooperative store

economía *nf* (*sistema*) economy; (*carrera*) economics

económico, -a *adj* (*barato*) cheap, economical; (*ahorrativo*) thrifty; (*COM: año etc*) financial; (*: situación*) economic

economista *nmf* economist

ECU *nm* ECU

ecuador *nm* equator; (**el**) **E~** Ecuador

ecuánime *adj* (*carácter*) level-headed; (*estado*) calm

ecuatoriano, -a *adj, nm/f* Ecuadorian

ecuestre *adj* equestrian

eczema *nm* = **eccema**

edad *nf* age; **¿qué** ~ **tienes?** how old are you?; **tiene ocho años de** ~ he is eight (years old); **de** ~ **mediana/avanzada** middle-aged/ advanced in years; **la E~ Media** the Middle Ages

edición *nf* (*acto*) publication; (*ejemplar*) edition

edificar vt, vi to build

edificio nm building; (fig) edifice, structure

Edimburgo nm Edinburgh

editar vt (publicar) to publish; (preparar textos) to edit

editor, a nm/f (que publica) publisher; (redactor) editor ♦ adj: **casa ~a** publishing house, publisher ❑ **editorial** adj editorial ♦ nm editorial, leading article (BRIT); **casa editorial** publisher

edredón nm comforter (US), duvet (BRIT)

educación nf education; (crianza) upbringing; (modales) (good) manners pl

educado, -a adj: **bien/mal ~** well/badly behaved

educar vt to educate; (criar) to bring up; (voz) to train

EE.UU. nmpl abr (= Estados Unidos) US(A)

efectista adj sensationalist

efectivamente adv (como respuesta) exactly, precisely; (verdaderamente) really; (de hecho) in fact

efectivo, -a adj effective; (real) actual, real ♦ nm: **pagar en ~** to pay (in) cash; **hacer ~ un cheque** to cash a check (US) o cheque (BRIT)

efecto nm effect, result; **~s** nmpl (efectos personales) effects; (bienes) goods; (COM) assets; **en ~** in fact; (respuesta) exactly, indeed; **~ 2000** millennium bug ▶ **efecto invernadero** greenhouse effect

efectuar vt to carry out; (viaje) to make

eficacia nf (de persona) efficiency; (de medicamento etc) effectiveness

eficaz adj (persona) efficient; (acción) effective

eficiente adj efficient

efusivo, -a adj effusive; **mis más efusivas gracias** my warmest thanks

egipcio, -a adj, nm/f Egyptian

Egipto nm Egypt

egoísmo nm egoism

egoísta adj egoistical, selfish ♦ nmf egoist

egregio, -a adj eminent, distinguished

Eire nm Eire

ej. abr (= ejemplo) eg

eje nm (GEO, MAT) axis; (de rueda) axle; (de máquina) shaft, spindle

ejecución nf execution; (cumplimiento) fulfillment (US), fulfilment (BRIT); (MÚS) performance; (JUR: embargo de deudor) attachment

ejecutar vt to execute, carry out; (matar) to execute; (cumplir) to fulfill (US), fulfil (BRIT);

(MÚS) to perform; (JUR: embargar) to attach, distrain (on)

ejecutivo, -a adj executive; **el (poder) ~** the executive (power)

ejemplar adj exemplary ♦ nm example; (ZOOL) specimen; (de libro) copy; (de periódico) number, issue

ejemplo nm example; **por ~** for example

ejercer vt to exercise; (influencia) to exert; (un oficio) to practice (US), practise (BRIT) ♦ vi (practicar): **~ (de)** to practice (US) o practise (BRIT) (as)

ejercicio nm exercise; (período) tenure ▶ **ejercicio comercial** financial year

ejército nm army; **entrar en el ~** to join the army, join up

ejote (MÉX) nm green bean

el

PALABRA CLAVE

(f **la**, pl **los, las**, neutro **lo**) art def

1 the; **el libro/la mesa/los estudiantes** the book/table/students

2 (con n abstracto: no se traduce): **el amor/la juventud** love/youth

3 (posesión: se traduce a menudo por adj posesivo): **romperse el brazo** to break one's arm; **levantó la mano** he put his hand up; **se puso el sombrero** she put her hat on

4 (valor descriptivo): **tener la boca grande/los ojos azules** to have a big mouth/blue eyes

5 (con días) on; **me iré el viernes** I'll leave on Friday; **los domingos suelo ir a nadar** on Sundays I generally go swimming

6 (lo + adj): **lo difícil/caro** what is difficult/ expensive; (= cuán): **no se da cuenta de lo pesado que es** he doesn't realise how boring he is

♦ pron demos

1: **mi libro y el de usted** my book and yours; **las de Pepe son mejores** Pepe's are better; **no la(s) blanca(s) sino la(s) roja(s)** not the white one(s) but the red one(s)

2: **lo de: lo de ayer** what happened yesterday; **lo de las facturas** that business about the invoices

♦ pron relativo: **el que** etc

1 (indef): **el (los) que quiera(n) que se vaya(n)** anyone who wants to can leave; **llévese el que más le guste** take the one you like best

2 (def): **el que compré ayer** the one I bought yesterday; **los que se van** those who leave

3: **lo que: lo que pienso yo/más me gusta** what I think/like most

♦ conj: **el que: el que lo diga** the fact that he says so; **el que sea tan vago me molesta** his being so lazy bothers me

♦ excl: **¡el susto que me diste!** what a fright you gave me!

♦ pron personal

1 (persona: m) him; (: f) her; (: pl) them; **lo/las veo** I can see him/them

2 (animal, cosa: sg) it; (: pl) them; **lo** (o **la**) **veo** I can see it; **los** (o **las**) **veo** I can see them

3: **lo** (como sustituto de frase): **no lo sabía** I didn't know; **ya lo entiendo** I understand now

él pron (persona) he; (cosa) it; (después de prep: persona) him; (: cosa) it; **de él** his

elaborar vt (producto) to make, manufacture; (preparar) to prepare; (madera, metal etc) to work; (proyecto etc) to work on o out

elasticidad nf elasticity

elástico, -a adj elastic; (flexible) flexible ♦ nm elastic; (un elástico) rubber band, elastic band (BRIT)

elección nf election; (selección) choice, selection

electorado nm electorate, voters pl

electricidad nf electricity

electricista nmf electrician

eléctrico, -a adj electric

electro... prefijo electro...

❏ **electrocardiograma** nm electrocardiogram ❏ **electrocutar** vt to electrocute ❏ **electrodo** nm electrode ❏ **electrodomésticos** nmpl (electrical) household appliances ❏ **electromagnético, -a** adj electromagnetic

electrónica nf electronics sg

electrónico, -a adj electronic

elefante nm elephant

elegancia nf elegance, grace; (estilo) stylishness

elegante adj elegant, graceful; (estiloso) stylish, fashionable

elegir vt (escoger) to choose, select; (optar) to opt for; (presidente) to elect

elemental adj (claro, obvio) elementary; (fundamental) elemental, fundamental

elemento nm element; (fig) ingredient; **~s** nmpl elements, rudiments

elepé (pl **~s**) nm L.P.

elevación nf elevation; (acto) raising, lifting; (de precios) rise; (GEO etc) height, altitude

elevar vt to raise, lift (up); (precio) to put up; **elevarse** vr (edificio) to rise; (precios) to go up

eligiendo etc vb ver **elegir**

elija etc vb ver **elegir**

eliminar vt to eliminate, remove

eliminatoria nf heat, preliminary (round)

élite, elite nf elite

ella pron (persona) she; (cosa) it; (después de prep: persona) her; (: cosa) it; **de ~** hers

ellas pron (personas y cosas) they; (después de prep) them; **de ~** theirs

ello pron it

ellos pron they; (después de prep) them; **de ~** theirs

elocuencia nf eloquence

elogiar vt to praise ❏ **elogio** nm praise

elote (MÉX) nm corn on the cob

eludir vt to avoid

email nm email; (dirección) email address; **mandar un ~ a algn** to email sb, send sb an email

emanar vi: **~ de** to emanate from, come from; (derivar de) to originate in

emancipar vt to emancipate; **emanciparse** vr to become emancipated, free o.s.

embadurnar vt to smear

embajada nf embassy

embajador, a nm/f ambassador (ambassadress)

embalaje nm packing

embalar vt to parcel, wrap (up); **embalarse** vr to go fast

embalsamar vt to embalm

embalse nm (presa) dam; (lago) reservoir

embarazada adj pregnant ♦ nf pregnant woman

⚠ No confundir **embarazada** con la palabra inglesa **embarrassed**.

embarazo nm (de mujer) pregnancy; (impedimento) obstacle, obstruction; (timidez) embarrassment ❏ **embarazoso, -a** adj awkward, embarrassing

embarcación nf (barco) boat, craft; (acto) embarkation, boarding

embarcadero nm pier, landing stage

embarcar vt (cargamento) to ship, stow; (persona) to embark, put on board; **embarcarse** vr to embark, go on board

embargar vt (JUR) to seize, impound

embargo nm (JUR) seizure; (COM, POL) embargo

embargue etc vb ver **embargar**

embarque etc vb ver **embarcar** ♦ nm shipment, loading

embaucar vt to trick, fool

embeber vt (absorber) to absorb, soak up; (empapar) to saturate ♦ vi to shrink; **embeberse** vr: ~**se en un libro** to be engrossed o absorbed in a book

embellecer vt to embellish, beautify

embestida nf attack, onslaught; (carga) charge

embestir vt to attack, assault; to charge, attack ♦ vi to attack

emblema nm emblem

embobado, -a adj (atontado) stunned, bewildered

embolia nf (MED) clot

émbolo nm (AUTO) piston

embolsar vt to pocket, put in one's pocket

emborrachar vt to make drunk, intoxicate; **emborracharse** vr to get drunk

emboscada nf ambush

embotar vt to blunt, dull; **embotarse** vr (adormecerse) to go numb

embotellamiento nm (AUTO) traffic jam

embotellar vt to bottle

embrague nm (tb: **pedal de ~**) clutch

embriagar vt (emborrachar) to make drunk; **embriagarse** vr (emborracharse) to get drunk

embrión nm embryo

embrollar vt (el asunto) to confuse, complicate; (implicar) to involve, embroil; **embrollarse** vr (confundirse) to get into a muddle o mess

embrollo nm (enredo) muddle, confusion; (aprieto) fix, jam

embrujado, -a adj bewitched; **casa embrujada** haunted house

embrutecer vt (atontar) to stupefy; **embrutecerse** vr to be stupefied

embudo nm funnel

embuste nm (mentira) lie ❏ **embustero, -a** adj lying, deceitful ♦ nm/f (mentiroso) liar

embutido nm (CULIN) sausage; (TEC) inlay

emergencia nf emergency; (surgimiento) emergence

emerger vi to emerge, appear

emigración nf emigration; (de pájaros) migration

emigrar vi (personas) to emigrate; (pájaros) to migrate

eminencia nf eminence ❏ **eminente** adj eminent, distinguished; (elevado) high

emisario nm emissary

emisión nf (acto) emission; (COM etc) issue; (RADIO, TV: acto) broadcasting; (: programa) broadcast, program (US), programme (BRIT)

emisora nf radio o broadcasting station

emitir vt (olor etc) to emit, give off; (moneda etc) to issue; (opinión) to express; (RADIO) to broadcast

emoción nf emotion; (excitación) excitement; (sentimiento) feeling

emocionante adj (excitante) exciting, thrilling

emocionar vt (excitar) to excite, thrill; (conmover) to move, touch; (impresionar) to impress

emoticón, emoticono nm smiley

emotivo, -a adj emotional

empacar vt (gen) to pack; (en caja) to bale, crate

empacho nm (MED) indigestion; (fig) embarrassment

empadronarse vr (POL: como elector) to register

empalagoso, -a adj cloying; (fig) tiresome

empalmar vt to join, connect ♦ vi (dos caminos) to meet, join ❏ **empalme** nm joint, connection; (de vías, carreteras) intersection (US), junction (BRIT); (de trenes) connection

empanada nf pie, pasty

empantanarse vr to get swamped; (fig) to get bogged down

empañarse vr (cristales etc) to steam up

empapar vt (mojar) to soak, saturate; (absorber) to soak up, absorb; **empaparse** vr: ~**se de** to soak up

empapelar (LAm exc MÉX, ESP) vt (paredes) to paper

empaquetar vt to pack, parcel up

empastar vt (embadurnar) to paste; (diente) to fill

empaste nm (de diente) filling

empatar vi to tie, draw (BRIT) ❏ **empate** nm tie, draw (BRIT)

empecé etc vb ver **empezar**

empedernido, -a adj hard, heartless; (fumador) inveterate

empedrado, -a adj paved ♦ nm paving

empeine nm (de pie, zapato) instep

empellón nm push, shove

empeñado, -a adj (persona) determined; (objeto) pawned

empeñar vt (objeto) to pawn, pledge; (persona) to compel; **empeñarse** vr *(endeudarse)* to get into debt; **~se en** to be set on, be determined to

empeño *nm (determinación, insistencia)* determination, insistence; **casa de ~s** pawnshop

empeorar *vt* to make worse, worsen ♦ *vi* to get worse, deteriorate

empequeñecer *vt* to dwarf; *(minusvalorar)* to belittle

emperador *nm* emperor □ **emperatriz** *nf* empress

empezar *vt, vi* to begin, start

empiece *etc vb ver* **empezar**

empiezo *etc vb ver* **empezar**

empinar *vt* to raise; **empinarse** *vr (persona)* to stand on tiptoe; *(animal)* to rear up; *(camino)* to climb, steeply

empírico, -a *adj* empirical

emplasto *nm (MED)* plaster

emplazamiento *nm* site, location; *(JUR)* summons *sg*

emplazar *vt (ubicar)* to site, place, locate; *(JUR)* to summons; *(convocar)* to summon

empleado, -a *nm/f (gen)* employee; *(de banco etc)* clerk

emplear *vt (usar)* to use, employ; *(dar trabajo a)* to employ; **emplearse** *vr (conseguir trabajo)* to be employed; *(ocuparse)* to occupy o.s.

empleo *nm (puesto)* job; *(puestos: colectivamente)* employment; *(uso)* use, employment

empobrecer *vt* to impoverish; **empobrecerse** *vr* to become poor *o* impoverished

emporio *nm (LAm: gran almacén)* department store

empotrado, -a *adj (armario etc)* built-in

emprender *vt (empezar)* to begin, embark on; *(acometer)* to tackle, take on

empresa *nf (de espíritu etc)* enterprise; *(COM)* company, firm □ **empresario, -a** *nm/f (COM)* businessman(-woman)

empréstito *nm (public)* loan

empujar *vt* to push, shove

empujón *nm* push, shove

empuñar *vt (asir)* to grasp, take (firm) hold of

emular *vt* to emulate; *(rivalizar)* to rival

---

en

PALABRA CLAVE

prep

1 *(posición)* in; *(: sobre)* on; **está en el cajón** it's in the drawer; **en Argentina/La Paz** in Argentina/La Paz; **en la oficina/el colegio** at the office/school; **está en el suelo/quinto piso** it's on the floor/the fifth floor

2 *(dirección)* into; **entró en el aula** she went into the classroom; **meter algo en la bolsa** to put sth into one's bag

3 *(tiempo)* in; on; **en 1605/3 semanas/invierno** in 1605/3 weeks/winter; **en (el mes de) enero** in (the month of) January; **en aquella ocasión/época** on that occasion/at that time; **en la tarde** *(LAm)* in the afternoon

4 *(precio)* for; **lo vendió en 20 dólares** he sold it for 20 dollars

5 *(diferencia)* by; **reducir/aumentar en una tercera parte/un 20 por ciento** to reduce/increase by a third/20 per cent

6 *(manera)*: **en avión/autobús** by plane/bus; **escrito en inglés** written in English

7 *(después de vb que indica gastar etc)* on; **han cobrado demasiado en dietas** they've charged too much to expenses; **se le va la mitad del sueldo en comida** he spends half his salary on food

8 *(tema, ocupación)*: **experto en la materia** expert on the subject; **trabaja en la construcción** he works in the building industry

9 *(adj + en + infin)*: **lento en reaccionar** slow to react

---

enaguas *nfpl* petticoat *sg*, underskirt *sg*

enajenación *nf (PSICO: tb: ~ mental)* mental derangement

enajenar *vt (volver loco)* to drive mad

enamorado, -a *adj* in love ♦ *nm/f* lover

enamorar *vt* to win the love of; **enamorarse** *vr*: **~se de algn** to fall in love with sb

enano, -a *adj* tiny ♦ *nm/f* dwarf

enardecer *vt (pasión)* to fire, inflame; *(persona)* to fill with enthusiasm; **enardecerse** *vr*: **~se por** to get excited about; *(entusiasmarse)* to get enthusiastic about

encabezamiento *nm (de carta)* heading; *(de periódico)* headline

encabezar *vt (movimiento, revolución)* to lead, head; *(lista)* to head, be at the top of; *(carta)* to put a heading to

encadenar *vt* to chain (together); *(poner grilletes a)* to shackle

encajar *vt (ajustar)*: **~ (en)** to fit (into); *(fam: golpe)* to take ♦ *vi* to fit (well); *(fig: corresponder a)* to match; **encajarse** *vr*: **~se en un sillón** to squeeze into a chair

encaje *nm (labor)* lace

encalar *vt (pared)* to whitewash

encallar vi (NÁUT) to run aground

encaminar vt to direct, send; **encaminarse** vr: ~se a to set out for

encantado, -a adj (hechizado) bewitched; (muy contento) delighted; ¡~! how do you do!, pleased to meet you!

encantador, a adj charming, lovely ♦ nm/f magician, enchanter (enchantress)

encantar vt (agradar) to charm, delight; (hechizar) to bewitch, cast a spell on; **me encanta eso** I love that ❑ **encanto** nm (hechizo) spell, charm; (fig) charm, delight

encarcelar vt to imprison, jail

encarecer vt to put up the price of; **encarecerse** vr to get dearer

encarecimiento nm price increase

encargado, -a adj in charge ♦ nm/f agent, representative; (responsable) person in charge

encargar vt to entrust; (recomendar) to urge, recommend; **encargarse** vr: ~se de to look after, take charge of

encargo nm (tarea) assignment, job; (responsabilidad) responsibility; (COM) order

encariñarse vr: ~ con to grow fond of, get attached to

encarnación nf incarnation, embodiment

encarnizado, -a adj (lucha) bloody, fierce

encarrilar vt (tren) to put back on the rails; (fig) to correct, put on the right track

encasillar vt (fig) to pigeonhole; (actor) to typecast

encauzar vt to channel

encendedor nm lighter

encender vt (con fuego) to light; (luz, radio) to put on, switch on; (avivar: pasión) to inflame; **encenderse** vr to catch fire; (excitarse) to get excited; (de cólera) to flare up; (el rostro) to blush

encendido nm (AUTO) ignition

encerado nm (ESCOL) blackboard, chalkboard (US)

encerar vt (suelo) to wax, polish

encerrar vt (confinar) to shut in, shut up; (comprender, incluir) to include, contain

encharcado, -a adj (terreno) flooded

encharcarse vr to get flooded

enchufado, -a (fam) nm/f well-connected person

enchufar vt (ELEC) to plug in; (TEC) to connect, fit together ❑ **enchufe** nm (ELEC: clavija) plug; (: toma) socket, outlet (US); (de dos tubos) joint, connection; (fam: influencia) contact, connection; (: puesto) cushy job

encía nf gum

encienda etc vb ver **encender**

encierro etc vb ver **encerrar** ♦ nm shutting in, shutting up; (calabozo) prison

encima adv (sobre) above, over; (además) besides; ~ **de** (en) on, on top of; (sobre) above, over; (además de) besides, on top of; **por ~ de** over; ¿**llevas dinero ~?** have you (got) any money on you?; **se me vino ~** it took me by surprise

encina nf holm oak

encinta adj pregnant

enclenque adj weak, sickly

encoger vt to shrink, contract; **encogerse** vr to shrink, contract; (fig) to cringe; ~**se de hombros** to shrug one's shoulders

encolar vt (engomar) to glue, paste; (pegar) to stick down

encolerizar vt to anger, provoke; **encolerizarse** vr to get angry

encomendar vt to entrust, commend; **encomendarse** vr: ~**se a** to put one's trust in

encomiar vt to praise, pay tribute to

encomienda etc vb ver **encomendar** ♦ nf (encargo) charge, commission; (elogio) tribute ▶ **encomienda postal** (LAm) package, parcel (BRIT)

encontrado, -a adj (contrario) contrary, conflicting

encontrar vt (hallar) to find; (inesperadamente) to meet, run into; **encontrarse** vr to meet (each other); (situarse) to be (situated); ~**se con** to meet; ~**se bien (de salud)** to feel well

encrespar vt (cabellos) to curl; (fig) to anger, irritate; **encresparse** vr (el mar) to get rough; (fig) to get cross, get irritated

encrucijada nf crossroads sg

encuadernación nf binding

encuadernador, a nm/f bookbinder

encuadrar vt (retrato) to frame; (ajustar) to fit, insert; (contener) to contain

encubrir vt (ocultar) to hide, conceal; (criminal) to shelter, harbor (US), harbour (BRIT)

encuentro etc vb ver **encontrar** ♦ nm (de personas) meeting; (AUTO etc) collision, crash; (DEPORTE) game, match; (MIL) encounter

encuerado, -a (MÉX) adj nude, naked

encuesta nf inquiry, investigation; (sondeo) (public) opinion poll ▶ **encuesta judicial** post mortem

encumbrar vt (persona) to exalt

endeble adj (persona) weak; (argumento, excusa, persona) weak

endémico, -a adj (MED) endemic; (fig) rife, chronic

endemoniado, -a adj possessed (of the devil); (travieso) devilish

enderezar vt (poner derecho) to straighten (out); (: verticalmente) to set upright; (situación) to straighten o sort out; (dirigir) to direct; **enderezarse** vr (persona sentada) to straighten up

endeudarse vr to get into debt

endiablado, -a adj devilish, diabolical; (travieso) mischievous

endilgar (fam) vt: **~le algo a algn** to lumber sb with sth; **~le un sermón a algn** to lecture sb

endosar vt (cheque etc) to endorse

endulzar vt to sweeten; (suavizar) to soften

endurecer vt to harden; **endurecerse** vr to harden, grow hard

enema nm (MED) enema

enemigo, -a adj enemy, hostile ♦ nm/f enemy

enemistad nf enmity

enemistar vt to make enemies of, cause a rift between; **enemistarse** vr to become enemies; (amigos) to fall out

energía nf (vigor) energy, drive; (empuje) push; (TEC, ELEC) energy, power ▶ **energía eólica** wind power ▶ **energía solar** solar energy/power

enérgico, -a adj (gen) energetic; (voz, modales) forceful

energúmeno, -a (fam) nm/f (fig) madman(-woman)

enero nm January

enfadado, -a (ESP) adj angry, annoyed

enfadar (ESP) vt to anger, annoy; **enfadarse** vr to get angry o annoyed

enfado nm (enojo) anger, annoyance; (disgusto) trouble, bother

énfasis nm emphasis, stress

enfático, -a adj emphatic

enfermar vt to make ill ♦ vi to fall ill, be taken ill

enfermedad nf illness ▶ **enfermedad venérea** venereal disease

enfermera nf nurse

enfermería nf infirmary; (de colegio etc) sick bay

enfermero nm (male) nurse

enfermizo, -a adj (persona) sickly, unhealthy; (fig) unhealthy

enfermo, -a adj ill, sick ♦ nm/f invalid, sick person; (en hospital) patient

enflaquecer vt (adelgazar) to make thin; (debilitar) to weaken

enfocar vt (foto etc) to focus; (problema etc) to approach

enfoque etc vb ver **enfocar** ♦ nm focus

enfrascarse vr: **~ en algo** to bury o.s. in sth

enfrentar vt (peligro) to face (up to), confront; (oponer) to bring face to face; **enfrentarse** vr (dos personas) to face o confront each other; (DEPORTE: dos equipos) to meet; **~se a o con** to face up to, confront

enfrente adv opposite; **la casa de ~** the house opposite, the house across the street; **~ de** opposite, facing

enfriamiento nm chilling, refrigeration; (MED) cold, chill

enfriar vt (alimentos) to cool, chill; (algo caliente) to cool down; **enfriarse** vr to cool down; (MED) to catch a chill; (amistad) to cool

enfurecer vt to enrage, madden; **enfurecerse** vr to become furious, fly into a rage; (mar) to get rough

engalanar vt (adornar) to adorn; (ciudad) to decorate; **engalanarse** vr to get dressed up

enganchar vt to hook; (dos vagones) to hitch up; (TEC) to couple, connect; (MIL) to recruit; **engancharse** vr (MIL) to enlist, join up

enganche nm hook; (acto) hooking (up); (MIL) recruitment, enlistment; (MÉX: depósito) deposit

engañar vt to deceive; (estafar) to cheat, swindle; **engañarse** vr (equivocarse) to be wrong; (disimular la verdad) to deceive o.s.

engaño nm deceit; (estafa) trick, swindle; (error) mistake, misunderstanding; (ilusión) delusion ❑ **engañoso, -a** adj (tramposo) crooked; (mentiroso) dishonest, deceitful; (aspecto) deceptive; (consejo) misleading

engarzar vt (joya) to set, mount; (fig) to link, connect

engatusar (fam) vt to coax

engendrar vt to breed; (procrear) to beget; (causar) to cause, produce ❑ **engendro** nm (BIO) fetus (US), foetus (BRIT); (fig) monstrosity

englobar vt to include, comprise

engordar vt to fatten ♦ vi to get fat, put on weight

engorroso, -a adj bothersome, trying

engranaje nm (AUTO) gear

engrandecer vt to enlarge, magnify; (alabar) to praise, speak highly of; (exagerar) to exaggerate

engrasar vt (TEC: poner grasa) to grease; (: lubricar) to lubricate, oil; (manchar) to make greasy

engreído, -a adj vain, conceited

engrosar vt (ensanchar) to enlarge; (aumentar) to increase; (hinchar) to swell

enhebrar vt to thread

enhorabuena excl: ¡~! congratulations! ♦ nf: dar la ~ a to congratulate

enigma nm enigma; (problema) puzzle; (misterio) mystery

enjabonar vt to soap; (fam: adular) to soft-soap

enjambre nm swarm

enjaular vt to (put in a) cage; (fam) to jail, lock up

enjuagar vt (ropa) to rinse (out)

enjuague etc vb ver **enjuagar** ♦ nm (MED) mouthwash; (de ropa) rinse, rinsing; (LAm: para el pelo) conditioner

enjugar vt to wipe (off); (lágrimas) to dry; (déficit) to wipe out

enjuiciar vt (JUR: procesar) to prosecute, try; (fig) to judge

enjuto, -a adj (flaco) lean, skinny

enlace nm link, connection; (relación) relationship; (tb: ~ matrimonial) marriage; (de carretera, trenes) connection ▶ **enlace sindical** union representative, shop steward (BRIT)

enlatado, -a adj (alimentos, productos) canned, tinned (BRIT)

enlazar vt (unir con lazos) to bind together; (atar) to tie; (conectar) to link, connect; (LAm: caballo) to lasso

enlodar vt to cover in mud; (fig: manchar) to stain; (: rabajar) to debase

enloquecer vt to drive mad ♦ vi to go mad; **enloquecerse** vr to go mad

enlutado, -a adj (persona) in mourning

enmarañar vt (enredar) to tangle (up), entangle; (complicar) to complicate; (confundir) to confuse; **enmarañarse** vr (enredarse) to become entangled; (confundirse) to get confused

enmarcar vt (cuadro) to frame

enmascarar vt to mask; **enmascararse** vr to put on a mask

enmendar vt to emend, correct; (constitución etc) to amend; (comportamiento) to reform; **enmendarse** vr to reform, mend one's ways ❑ **enmienda** nf correction; amendment; reform

enmohecerse vr (metal) to rust, go rusty; (muro, plantas) to get moldy (US) o mouldy (BRIT)

enmudecer vi (perder el habla) to fall silent; (guardar silencio) to remain silent

ennegrecer vt (poner negro) to blacken; (oscurecer) to darken; **ennegrecerse** vr to turn black; (oscurecerse) to get dark, darken

ennoblecer vt to ennoble

enojado, -a (LAm) adj angry

enojar (LAm) vt (encolerizar) to anger; (disgustar) to annoy, upset; **enojarse** vr to get angry; to get annoyed

enojo nm (cólera) anger; (irritación) annoyance ❑ **enojoso, -a** adj annoying

enorgullecerse vr to be proud; ~ **de** to pride o.s. on, be proud of

enorme adj enormous, huge; (fig) monstrous ❑ **enormidad** nf hugeness, immensity

enrarecido, -a adj (atmósfera, aire) rarefied

enredadera nf (BOT) creeper, climbing plant

enredar vt (cables, hilos etc) to tangle (up), entangle; (situación) to complicate, confuse; (meter cizaña) to sow discord among o between; (implicar) to embroil, implicate; **enredarse** vr to get entangled, get tangled (up); (situación) to get complicated; (persona) to get embroiled; (LAm: fam) to meddle

enredo nm (maraña) tangle; (confusión) mix-up, confusion; (intriga) intrigue

enrejado nm fence, railings pl

enrevesado, -a adj (asunto) complicated, involved

enriquecer vt to make rich, enrich; **enriquecerse** vr to get rich

enrojecer vt to redden ♦ vi (persona) to blush; **enrojecerse** vr to blush

enrolar vt (MIL) to enlist; (reclutar) to recruit; **enrolarse** vr (MIL) to join up; (afiliarse) to enroll (US), enrol (BRIT)

enrollar vt to roll (up), wind (up)

enroscar vt (torcer, doblar) to coil (round), wind; (tornillo, rosca) to screw in; **enroscarse** vr to coil, wind

ensalada nf salad ▶ **ensalada de frutas** (LAm) fruit salad ❑ **ensaladilla (rusa)** (ESP) nf Russian salad

ensalzar vt (alabar) to praise, extol; (exaltar) to exalt

ensamblaje nm assembly; (TEC) joint

ensanchar vt (hacer más ancho) to widen; (agrandar) to enlarge, expand; (COSTURA) to let out; **ensancharse** vr to get wider, expand ❑ **ensanche** nm (de calle) widening

ensangrentar *vt* to stain with blood

ensañar *vt* to enrage; **ensañarse** *vr:* **~se con** to treat brutally

ensartar *vt* (*cuentas, perlas etc*) to string (together)

ensayar *vt* to test, try (out); (*TEATRO*) to rehearse

ensayo *nm* test, trial; (*QUÍM*) experiment; (*TEATRO*) rehearsal; (*DEPORTE*) try; (*ESCOL, LITERATURA*) essay

enseguida *adv* at once, right away

ensenada *nf* inlet, cove

enseñanza *nf* (*educación*) education; (*acción*) teaching; (*doctrina*) teaching, doctrine

enseñar *vt* (*educar*) to teach; (*mostrar, señalar*) to show

enseres *nmpl* belongings

ensillar *vt* to saddle (up)

ensimismarse *vr* (*abstraerse*) to become lost in thought; (*LAm: envanecerse*) to become conceited

ensombrecer *vt* to darken, cast a shadow over; (*fig*) to overshadow, put in the shade

ensordecer *vt* to deafen ♦ *vi* to go deaf

ensortijado, -a *adj* (*pelo*) curly

ensuciar *vt* (*manchar*) to dirty, soil; (*fig*) to defile; **ensuciarse** *vr* to get dirty; (*bebé*) to dirty one's diaper (*US*) o nappy (*BRIT*)

ensueño *nm* (*sueño*) dream, fantasy; (*ilusión*) illusion; **de ~** dream-like

entablar *vt* (*recubrir*) to board (up); (*AJEDREZ, DAMAS*) to set up; (*conversación*) to strike up; (*JUR*) to file ♦ *vi* to draw

entablillar *vt* (*MED*) to (put in a) splint

entallar *vt* (*traje*) to tailor ♦ *vi*: **el traje entalla bien** the suit fits well

ente *nm* (*organización*) body, organization; (*fam: persona*) odd character

entender *vt* (*comprender*) to understand; (*darse cuenta*) to realize ♦ *vi* to understand; (*creer*) to think, believe; **entenderse** *vr* (*comprenderse*) to be understood; (*llevarse bien*) to get on with sb; (*ponerse de acuerdo*) to agree, reach an agreement; **~ de** to know all about; **~ algo de** to know a little about; **~ en** to deal with, have to do with; **llevarse mal** to get on badly

entendido, -a *adj* (*comprendido*) understood; (*hábil*) skilled; (*inteligente*) knowledgeable ♦ *nm/f* (*experto*) expert ♦ *excl* agreed! ❑ **entendimiento** *nm* (*comprensión*) understanding; (*inteligencia*) mind, intellect; (*juicio*) judgement

enterado, -a *adj* well-informed; **estar ~ de** to know about, be aware of

enteramente *adv* entirely, completely

enterar *vt* (*informar*) to inform, tell; **enterarse** *vr* to find out, get to know

entereza *nf* (*totalidad*) entirety; (*fig: de carácter*) strength of mind; (: *honradez*) integrity

enterito (*RPI*) *nm* overalls (*US*), boiler suit (*BRIT*)

enternecer *vt* (*ablandar*) to soften; (*apiadar*) to touch, move; **enternecerse** *vr* to be touched, be moved

entero, -a *adj* (*total*) whole, entire; (*fig: honesto*) honest; (: *firme*) firm, resolute ♦ *nm* (*COM: punto*) point

enterrador *nm* gravedigger

enterrar *vt* to bury

entibiar *vt* (*enfriar*) to cool; (*calentar*) to warm; **entibiarse** *vr* (*fig*) to cool

entidad *nf* (*empresa*) firm, company; (*organismo*) body; (*sociedad*) society; (*FILOSOFÍA*) entity

entiendo *etc vb ver* **entender**

entierro *nm* (*acción*) burial; (*funeral*) funeral

entonación *nf* (*LING*) intonation

entonar *vt* (*canción*) to intone; (*colores*) to tone; (*MED*) to tone up ♦ *vi* to be in tune

entonces *adv* then, at that time; **desde ~** since then; **en aquel ~** at that time; **(pues) ~** and so

entornar *vt* (*puerta, ventana*) to half-close, leave ajar; (*los ojos*) to screw up

entorpecer *vt* (*entendimiento*) to dull; (*impedir*) to obstruct, hinder; (: *tránsito*) to slow down, delay

entrada *nf* (*acción*) entry, access; (*sitio*) entrance, way in; (*INFORM*) input; (*COM*) receipts *pl*, takings *pl*; (*LAm CULIN*) appetizer, starter (*BRIT*); (*DEPORTE*) innings *sg*; (*TEATRO*) house, audience; (*billete*) ticket; **~s y salidas** (*COM*) income and expenditure; **de ~** from the outset ▸ **entrada de aire** (*TEC*) air intake o inlet

entrado, -a *adj*: **~ en años** elderly; **una vez ~ el verano** in the summer(time), when summer comes

entramparse *vr* to get into debt

entrante *adj* next, coming ♦ *nm* (*ESP CULIN*) appetizer, starter (*BRIT*); **mes/año ~** next month/year

entraña *nf* (*fig: centro*) heart, core; (*raíz*) root; **~s** *nfpl* (*ANAT*) entrails; (*fig*) heart *sg*; **sin ~s** (*fig*) heartless ❑ **entrañable** *adj* close, intimate ❑ **entrañar** *vt* to entail

entrar vt (introducir) to bring in; (INFORM) to input ♦ vi (meterse) to go in, come in, enter; (comenzar): ~ **diciendo** to begin by saying; **hacer** ~ to show in; **no me entra** I can't get the hang of it

entre prep (dos) between; (más de dos) among(st)

entreabrir vt to half-open, open halfway

entrecejo nm: **fruncir el** ~ to frown

entrecortado, -a adj (respiración) difficult; (habla) faltering

entredicho nm (JUR) injunction; **poner en** ~ to cast doubt on; **estar en** ~ to be in doubt

entrega nf (de mercancías) delivery; (de novela etc) installment (US), instalment (BRIT)

entregar vt (dar) to hand (over), deliver; **entregarse** vr (rendirse) to surrender, give in, submit; (dedicarse) to devote o.s.

entrelazar vt to entwine

entremeses nmpl hors d'œuvres

entremeter vt to insert, put in; **entremeterse** vr to meddle, interfere ❑ **entremetido, -a** adj meddling, interfering

entremezclar vt to intermingle; **entremezclarse** vr to intermingle

entrenador, a nm/f trainer, coach

entrenarse vr to train

entrepierna nf crotch

entresacar vt to pick out, select

entresuelo nm mezzanine

entretanto adv meanwhile, meantime

entretecho (CS) nm attic

entretejer vt to interweave

entretener vt (divertir) to entertain, amuse; (detener) to hold up, delay; **entretenerse** vr (divertirse) to amuse o.s.; (retrasarse) to delay, linger ❑ **entretenido, -a** adj entertaining, amusing ❑ **entretenimiento** nm entertainment, amusement

entrever vt to glimpse, catch a glimpse of

entrevista nf interview ❑ **entrevistar** vt to interview; **entrevistarse** vr to have an interview

entristecer vt to sadden, grieve; **entristecerse** vr to grow sad

entrometerse vr: ~ **(en)** to interfere (in o with)

entroncar vi to be connected o related

entumecer vt to numb, benumb; **entumecerse** vr (por el frío) to go o become numb ❑ **entumecido, -a** adj numb, stiff

enturbiar vt (el agua) to make cloudy; (fig) to confuse; **enturbiarse** vr (oscurecerse) to become cloudy; (fig) to get confused, become obscure

entusiasmar vt to excite, fill with enthusiasm; (gustar mucho) to delight; **entusiasmarse** vr: ~**se con** o **por** to get enthusiastic o excited about

entusiasmo nm enthusiasm; (excitación) excitement

entusiasta adj enthusiastic ♦ nmf enthusiast

enumerar vt to enumerate

enunciación nf enunciation

enunciado nm enunciation

envainar vt to sheathe

envalentonar vt to give courage to; **envalentonarse** vr (pey: jactarse) to boast, brag

envanecer vt to make conceited; **envanecerse** vr to grow conceited

envasar vt (empaquetar) to pack, wrap; (enfrascar) to bottle; (enlatar) to can; (embolsar) to pocket

envase nm (en paquete) packing, wrapping; (en botella) bottling; (en lata) canning; (recipiente) container; (paquete) package; (botella) bottle; (lata) can, tin (BRIT)

envejecer vt to make old, age ♦ vi (volverse viejo) to grow old; (parecer viejo) to age; **envejecerse** vr to grow old; to age

envenenar vt to poison; (fig) to embitter

envergadura nf (fig) scope, compass

envés nm (de tela) back, wrong side

enviar vt to send

enviciarse vr: ~ **(con)** to get addicted (to)

envidia nf envy; **tener** ~ **a** to envy, be jealous of ❑ **envidiar** vt to envy

envío nm (acción) sending; (de mercancías) consignment; (de dinero) remittance

enviudar vi to be widowed

envoltorio nm package

envoltura nf (cobertura) cover; (embalaje) wrapper, wrapping

envolver vt to wrap (up); (cubrir) to cover; (enemigo) to surround; (implicar) to involve, implicate

envuelto pp de **envolver**

enyesar vt (pared) to plaster; (MED) to put in plaster

enzarzarse vr: ~ **en** (pelea) to get mixed up in; (disputa) to get involved in

épica nf epic

épico, -a adj epic

epidemia nf epidemic

epilepsia nf epilepsy

epílogo nm epilog

episodio nm episode

epístola nf epistle

época nf period, time; (HIST) age, epoch; **hacer ~** to be epoch-making

equilibrar vt to balance ☐ **equilibrio** nm balance, equilibrium ☐ **equilibrista** nmf (funámbulo) tightrope walker; (acróbata) acrobat

equipaje nm luggage, baggage ▶ **equipaje de mano** hand luggage

equipar vt (proveer) to equip

equipararse vr: ~ **con** to be on a level with

equipo nm (conjunto de cosas) equipment; (DEPORTE) team; (de obreros) shift

equis nf inv (the letter) X

equitación nf horse riding

equitativo, -a adj equitable, fair

equivalente adj, nm equivalent

equivaler vi to be equivalent o equal

equivocación nf mistake, error

equivocado, -a adj wrong, mistaken

equivocarse vr to be wrong, make a mistake; ~ **de camino** to take the wrong road

equívoco, -a adj (dudoso) suspect; (ambiguo) ambiguous ♦ nm ambiguity; (malentendido) misunderstanding

era vb ver **ser** ♦ nf era, age

erais vb ver **ser**

éramos vb ver **ser**

eran vb ver **ser**

erario nm treasury, exchequer (BRIT)

eras vb ver **ser**

erección nf erection

eres vb ver **ser**

erguir vt to raise, lift; (poner derecho) to straighten; **erguirse** vr to straighten up

erigir vt to erect, build; **erigirse** vr: ~**se en** to set o.s. up as

erizarse vr (pelo: de perro) to bristle; (: de persona) to stand on end

erizo nm (ZOOL) hedgehog ▶ **erizo de mar** sea-urchin

ermita nf hermitage

ermitaño, -a nm/f hermit

erosión nf erosion

erosionar vt to erode

erótico, -a adj erotic ☐ **erotismo** nm eroticism

erradicar vt to eradicate

errante adj wandering, errant

errar vi (vagar) to wander, roam; (equivocarse) to be mistaken ♦ vt: ~ **el camino** to take the wrong road; ~ **el tiro** to miss

erróneo, -a adj (equivocado) wrong, mistaken

error nm error, mistake; (INFORM) bug ▶ **error de imprenta** misprint

eructar vt to belch, burp

erudito, -a adj erudite, learned

erupción nf eruption; (MED) rash

es vb ver **ser**

esa (pl ~**s**) adj demos ver **ese**

ésa (pl ~**s**) pron demos ver **ése**

esbelto, -a adj slim, slender

esbozo nm sketch, outline

escabeche nm brine; (de aceitunas etc) pickle; **en ~** pickled

escabroso, -a adj (accidentado) rough, uneven; (fig) tough, difficult; (: atrevido) risqué

escabullirse vr to slip away, clear out

escafandra nf (buzo) diving suit; (escafandra espacial) space suit

escala nf (proporción, MÚS) scale; (de mano) ladder; (AVIAT) stopover; **hacer ~ en** to stop o call in at

escalafón nm (escala de salarios) salary scale, wage scale

escalar vt to climb, scale

escalera nf stairs pl, staircase; (escala) ladder; (NAIPES) run ▶ **escalera de caracol** spiral staircase ▶ **escalera mecánica** escalator

escalfar vt (huevos) to poach

escalinata nf staircase

escalofriante adj chilling

escalofrío nm (MED) chill; ~**s** nmpl (fig) shivers

escalón nm step, stair; (de escalera) rung

escalope nm (CULIN) cutlet (US), escalope (BRIT)

escama nf (de pez, serpiente) scale; (de jabón) flake; (fig) resentment

escamar vt (fig) to make wary o suspicious

escamotear vt (robar) to lift, swipe; (hacer desaparecer) to make disappear

escampar vb impers to stop raining

escandalizar vt to scandalize, shock; **escandalizarse** vr to be shocked; (ofenderse) to be offended

escándalo nm scandal; (alboroto, tumulto) row, uproar ☐ **escandaloso, -a** adj scandalous, shocking

escandinavo, -a adj, nm/f Scandinavian

escaño nm bench; (POL) seat

escapar vi (gen) to escape, run away; (DEPORTE) to break away; **escaparse** vr to escape, get away; (agua, gas) to leak (out)

escaparate nm store (US) o shop (BRIT) window

escape nm (de agua, gas) leak; (de motor) exhaust

escarabajo nm beetle

escaramuza nf skirmish

escarbar vt (tierra) to scratch

escarceos nmpl (fig): **en mis ~ con la política ...** in my dealings with politics ...
▶ **escarceos amorosos** love affairs

escarcha nf frost

escarchado, -a adj (CULIN: fruta) crystallized

escarlata adj inv scarlet □ **escarlatina** nf scarlet fever

escarmentar vt to punish severely ♦ vi to learn one's lesson

escarmiento etc vb ver **escarmentar** ♦ nm (ejemplo) lesson; (castigo) punishment

escarnio nm mockery; (injuria) insult

escarola nf curly, escarole (US)

escarpado, -a adj (pendiente) sheer, steep; (rocas) craggy

escasear vi to be scarce

escasez nf (falta) shortage, scarcity; (pobreza) poverty

escaso, -a adj (poco) scarce; (raro) rare; (ralo) thin, sparse; (limitado) limited

escatimar vt to skimp (on), be sparing with

escayola (ESP) nf plaster

escena nf scene

escenario nm (TEATRO) stage; (CINE) set; (fig) scene □ **escenografía** nf set design

⚠ No confundir **escenario** con la palabra inglesa **scenery**.

escepticismo nm skepticism (US), scepticism (BRIT) □ **escéptico, -a** adj skeptical (US), sceptical (BRIT) ♦ nm/f skeptic (US), sceptic (BRIT)

escisión nf (de partido, secta) split

esclarecer vt (misterio, problema) to shed light on

esclavitud nf slavery

esclavizar vt to enslave

esclavo, -a nm/f slave

esclusa nf (de canal) lock; (compuerta) floodgate

escoba nf broom □ **escobilla** nf brush

escocer vi to burn, sting; **escocerse** vr to chafe, get chafed

escocés, -esa adj Scottish ♦ nm/f Scotsman(-woman), Scot

Escocia nf Scotland

escoger vt to choose, pick, select □ **escogido, -a** adj chosen, selected

escolar adj school cpd ♦ nmf schoolboy(-girl), pupil

escollo nm (obstáculo) pitfall

escolta nf escort □ **escoltar** vt to escort

escombros nmpl (basura) garbage sg (US), rubbish sg (BRIT); (restos) debris sg

esconder vt to hide, conceal; **esconderse** vr to hide □ **escondidas** (LAm) nfpl: **a escondidas** secretly □ **escondite** nm hiding place □ **escondrijo** nm hiding place, hideout

escopeta nf shotgun

escoria nf (de alto horno) slag; (fig) scum, dregs pl

Escorpio nm Scorpio

escorpión nm scorpion

escotado, -a adj low-cut

escote nm (de vestido) low neck; **pagar a ~** to share the expenses

escotilla nf (NÁUT) hatch(way)

escozor nm (dolor) sting(ing)

escribible adj writable

escribir vt, vi to write; **~ a máquina** to type; **¿cómo se escribe?** how do you spell it?

escrito, -a pp de **escribir** ♦ nm (documento) document; (manuscrito) text, manuscript; **por ~** in writing

escritor, a nm/f writer

escritorio nm desk

escritura nf (acción) writing; (caligrafía) (hand)writing; (JUR: documento) deed

escrúpulo nm scruple; (minuciosidad) scrupulousness □ **escrupuloso, -a** adj scrupulous

escrutar vt to scrutinize, examine; (votos) to count

escrutinio nm (examen atento) scrutiny; (POL: recuento de votos) count(ing)

escuadra nf (MIL etc) squad; (NÁUT) squadron; (flota: de vehículos) fleet □ **escuadrilla** nf (de aviones) squadron; (LAm: de obreros) gang

escuadrón nm squadron

escuálido, -a adj skinny, scraggy; (sucio) squalid

escuchar vt to listen to ♦ vi to listen

escudilla nf bowl, basin

escudo nm shield

escudriñar vt (examinar) to investigate, scrutinize; (mirar de lejos) to scan

escuela *nf* school ► **escuela de choferes** (*LAm*) driving school ► **escuela de manejo** (*MÉX*) driving school ► **escuela normal** teacher training college

escueto, -a *adj* plain; (*estilo*) simple

escuincle, -a (*MÉX: fam*) *nm/f* kid

esculpir *vt* to sculpt; (*grabar*) to engrave; (*tallar*) to carve ☐ **escultor, a** *nm/f* sculptor(-tress) ☐ **escultura** *nf* sculpture

escupidera *nf* spittoon, cuspidor (*US*)

escupir *vt*, *vi* to spit (out)

escurreplatos (*ESP*) *nm inv* drainboard (*US*), draining board (*BRIT*)

escurridero (*LAm*) *nm* drainboard (*US*), draining board (*BRIT*)

escurridizo, -a *adj* slippery

escurridor *nm* colander

escurrir *vt* (*ropa*) to wring out; (*verduras, platos*) to drain ♦ *vi* (*líquidos*) to drip; **escurrirse** *vr* (*secarse*) to drain; (*resbalarse*) to slip, slide; (*escaparse*) to slip away

ese (*f* **esa**, *pl* **esos, esas**) *adj demos* that; (*pl*) those

ése (*f* **ésa**, *pl* **ésos, ésas**) *pron* (*sg*) that (one); (*pl*) those (ones); **~ ... éste ...** the former ... the latter ...; **no me vengas con ésas** don't give me any more of that nonsense

esencia *nf* essence ☐ **esencial** *adj* essential

esfera *nf* sphere ☐ **esférico, -a** *adj* spherical

esforzarse *vr* to exert o.s., make an effort

esfuerzo *etc vb ver* **esforzar** ♦ *nm* effort

esfumarse *vr* (*apoyo, esperanzas*) to fade away

esgrima *nf* fencing

esgrimir *vt* (*arma*) to brandish; (*argumento*) to use

esguince *nm* (*MED*) sprain

eslabón *nm* link

eslip *nm* briefs *pl*, pants *pl* (*BRIT*)

eslovaco, -a *adj*, *nm/f* Slovak, Slovakian ♦ *nm* (*LING*) Slovak, Slovakian

Eslovaquia *nf* Slovakia

esmaltar *vt* to enamel ☐ **esmalte** *nm* enamel ► **esmalte de uñas** nail polish *o* varnish (*BRIT*)

esmerado, -a *adj* careful, neat

esmeralda *nf* emerald

esmerarse *vr* (*aplicarse*) to take great pains, exercise great care; (*afanarse*) to work hard

esmero *nm* (great) care

esnob (*pl* **~s**) *adj* (*persona*) snobbish ♦ *nmf* snob ☐ **esnobismo** *nm* snobbery

eso *pron* that, that thing *o* matter; **~ de su moto** that business about his motorbike; **~ de ir al cine** all that about going to the movies (*US*) *o* cinema (*BRIT*); **a ~ de las cinco** at about five o'clock; **en ~** thereupon, at that point; **~ es** that's it; **¡~ sí que es vida!** now that is really living!; **por ~ te lo dije** that's why I told you; **y ~ que llovía** in spite of the fact it was raining

esos *adj demos ver* **ese**

ésos *pron ver* **ése**

espabilar *vt*, *vi* = **despabilar**

espacial *adj* (*del espacio*) space *cpd*

espaciar *vt* to space (out)

espacio *nm* space; (*MÚS*) interval; (*RADIO, TV*) program (*US*), programme (*BRIT*); **el ~** space ☐ **espacioso, -a** *adj* spacious, roomy

espada *nf* sword; **~s** *nfpl* (*NAIPES*) spades

espaguetis *nmpl* spaghetti *sg*

espalda *nf* (*gen*) back; **~s** *nfpl* (*hombros*) shoulders; **a ~s de algn** behind sb's back; **tenderse de ~s** to lie (down) on one's back; **volver la ~ a algn** to cold-shoulder sb

espantajo *nm* = **espantapájaros**

espantapájaros *nm inv* scarecrow

espantar *vt* (*asustar*) to frighten, scare; (*ahuyentar*) to frighten off; (*asombrar*) to horrify, appall (*US*), appal (*BRIT*); **espantarse** *vr* to get frightened *o* scared; to be appalled

espanto *nm* (*susto*) fright; (*terror*) terror; (*asombro*) astonishment ☐ **espantoso, -a** *adj* frightening; terrifying; astonishing

España *nf* Spain ☐ **español, a** *adj* Spanish ♦ *nm/f* Spaniard ♦ *nm* (*LING*) Spanish

esparadrapo *nm* Bandaid® (*US*), (sticking) plaster (*BRIT*)

esparcimiento *nm* (*dispersión*) spreading; (*diseminación*) scattering; (*fig*) cheerfulness

esparcir *vt* to spread; (*diseminar*) to scatter; **esparcirse** *vr* to spread (out), scatter; (*divertirse*) to enjoy o.s.

espárrago *nm* asparagus

esparto *nm* esparto (grass)

espasmo *nm* spasm

espátula *nf* spatula

especia *nf* spice

especial *adj* special ☐ **especialidad** *nf* specialty (*US*), speciality (*BRIT*)

especie *nf* (*BIO*) species; (*clase*) kind, sort; **en ~** in kind

especificar *vt* to specify ☐ **específico, -a** *adj* specific

espécimen (*pl* **especímenes**) *nm* specimen

espectáculo nm (gen) spectacle; (TEATRO etc) show

espectador, a nm/f spectator

espectro nm ghost; (fig) specter (US), spectre (BRIT)

especular vt, vi to speculate

espejismo nm mirage

espejo nm mirror ▶ **(espejo) retrovisor** rear-view mirror

espeluznante adj horrifying, hair-raising

espera nf (pausa, intervalo) wait; (JUR: plazo) respite; **en ~ de** waiting for; (con expectativa) expecting

esperanza nf (confianza) hope; (expectativa) expectation; **hay pocas ~s de que venga** there is little prospect of his coming

esperar vt (aguardar) to wait for; (tener expectativa de) to expect; (desear) to hope for ♦ vi to wait; to expect; to hope

esperma nf sperm

espesar vt to thicken; **espesarse** vr to thicken, get thicker

espeso, -a adj thick □ **espesor** nm thickness

espía nmf spy □ **espiar** vt (observar) to spy on

espiga nf (BOT: de trigo etc) ear

espigón nm (BOT) ear; (NÁUT) breakwater

espina nf thorn; (de pez) bone ▶ **espina dorsal** (ANAT) spine

espinaca nf spinach

espinazo nm spine, backbone

espinilla nf (ANAT: tibia) shin(bone); (grano) blackhead

espinoso, -a adj (planta) thorny, prickly; (asunto) difficult

espionaje nm spying, espionage

espiral adj, nf spiral

espirar vt to breathe out, exhale

espiritista adj, nmf spiritualist

espíritu nm spirit □ **espiritual** adj spiritual

espita nf spigot (US), tap (BRIT)

espléndido, -a adj (magnífico) magnificent, splendid; (generoso) generous

esplendor nm splendor (US), splendour (BRIT)

espolear vt to spur on

espoleta nf (de bomba) fuse, fuze (US)

espolón nm sea wall

espolvorear vt to dust, sprinkle

esponja nf sponge; (fig) sponger □ **esponjoso, -a** adj spongy

espontaneidad nf spontaneity □ **espontáneo, -a** adj spontaneous

esposar vt to handcuff □ **esposas** nfpl handcuffs

esposo, -a nm/f husband/wife

espray nm spray

espuela nf spur

espuma nf foam; (de cerveza) froth, head; (de jabón) lather ▶ **espuma de afeitar** shaving foam ▶ **espuma de rasurar** (MÉX) shaving foam

espumadera nf (utensilio) skimmer

espumoso, -a adj frothy, foamy; (vino) sparkling

esqueleto nm skeleton

esquema nm (diagrama) diagram; (dibujo) plan; (FILOSOFÍA) schema

esquí (pl ~s) nm (objeto) ski; (DEPORTE) skiing ▶ **esquí acuático** water-skiing □ **esquiar** vi to ski

esquilar vt to shear

esquimal adj, nmf Eskimo

esquina nf corner

esquinazo nm: **dar ~ a algn** to give sb the slip

esquivar vt to avoid

esquivo, -a adj evasive; (tímido) reserved; (huraño) unsociable

esta adj demos ver **este²**

ésta pron ver **éste**

está vb ver **estar**

estabilidad nf stability □ **estable** adj stable

establecer vt to establish; **establecerse** vr to establish o.s.; (echar raíces) to settle (down) □ **establecimiento** nm establishment

establo nm (AGR) stable

estaca nf stake, post; (de tienda de campaña) peg

estacada nf (cerca) fence, fencing; (palenque) stockade

estación nf station; (del año) season; (LAm RADIO) station ▶ **estación balnearia** seaside resort ▶ **estación de autobuses** bus station ▶ **estación de servicio** service o (US) gas station

estacionamiento nm (LAm AUTO) parking lot (US), car park (BRIT); (MIL) stationing

estacionar vt (AUTO) to park; (MIL) to station □ **estacionario, -a** adj stationary; (COM: mercado) slack

estadía (LAm exc MÉX) nf stay

estadio nm (fase) stage, phase; (DEPORTE) stadium

estadista nm (POL) statesman; (ESTADÍSTICA) statistician

estadística nf figure, statistic; (ciencia) statistics sg

estado nm (POL: condición) state; **estar en ~** to be pregnant; **(los) E~s Unidos** nmpl the United States (of America) sg ▸ **estado civil** marital status ▸ **estado de ánimo** state of mind ▸ **estado de cuenta** bank statement ▸ **estado de sitio** state of siege ▸ **estado mayor** staff

estadounidense adj United States cpd, American ♦ nmf American

estafa nf swindle, trick ❑ **estafar** vt to swindle, defraud

estafeta nf (oficina de correos) post office ▸ **estafeta diplomática** diplomatic bag

estáis vb ver **estar**

estallar vi to burst; (bomba) to explode, go off; (epidemia, guerra, rebelión) to break out; **~ en llanto** to burst into tears ❑ **estallido** nm explosion; (fig) outbreak

estampa nf print, engraving

estampado, -a adj printed ♦ nm (impresión: acción) printing; (: efecto) print; (marca) stamping

estampar vt (imprimir) to print; (marcar) to stamp; (metal) to engrave; (poner sello en) to stamp; (fig) to stamp, imprint

estampida nf stampede

estampido nm bang, report

estampilla (LAm) nf (postage) stamp

están vb ver **estar**

estancado, -a adj stagnant

estancar vt (aguas) to hold up, hold back; (COM) to monopolize; (fig) to block, hold up; **estancarse** vr to stagnate

estancia nf (MÉX, ESP: permanencia) stay; (sala) room; (RPl: de ganado) farm, ranch ❑ **estanciero** (RPl) nm farmer, rancher

estanco, -a adj watertight ♦ nm (ESP) smoke shop (US), tobacconist's (shop) (BRIT)

estándar adj, nm standard ❑ **estandarizar** vt to standardize

estandarte nm banner, standard

estanque nm (lago) pool, pond; (AGR) reservoir

estanquero, -a nm/f tobacco dealer (US), tobacconist (BRIT)

estante nm (armario) rack, stand; (biblioteca) bookcase; (anaquel) shelf ❑ **estantería** nf shelving, shelves pl

estaño nm tin

---

estar

PALABRA CLAVE

vi

1 (posición) to be; **está en la plaza** it's in the square; **¿está Juan?** is Juan in?; **estamos a 30 millas de Jalapa** we're 30 miles from Jalapa

2 (+ adj: estado) to be; **está enfermo** to be sick; **está muy elegante** he's looking very smart; **¿cómo estás?** how are you keeping?

3 (+ gerundio) to be; **estoy leyendo** I'm reading

4 (uso pasivo): **está condenado a muerte** he's been condemned to death; **está envasado en ...** it's packed in ...

5 (con fechas): **¿a cuántos estamos?** what's the date today?; **estamos a 5 de mayo** it's May 5th

6 (locuciones): **¿estamos?** (¿de acuerdo?) okay?; (¿listo?) ready?; **¡ya está bien!** that's enough!

7: **estar de**: **estar de vacaciones/viaje** to be on vacation (US) o on holiday (BRIT) o on a trip; **está de camarero** he's working as a waiter

8: **estar para**: **está para salir** he's about to leave; **no estoy para bromas** I'm not in the mood for jokes

9: **estar por** (propuesta etc) to be in favor (US) o favour (BRIT) of; (persona etc) to support, side with; **está por limpiar** it still has to be cleaned

10: **estar sin**: **estar sin dinero** to have no money; **está sin terminar** it isn't finished yet;

♦ **estarse** vr: **se estuvo en la cama toda la tarde** he stayed in bed all afternoon

---

estas adj demos ver **este²**

éstas pron ver **éste**

estatal adj state cpd

estático, -a adj static

estatua nf statue

estatura nf stature, height

estatuto nm (JUR) statute; (de ciudad) bye-law; (de comité) rule

este¹ nm east

este² (f esta, pl estos, estas) adj demos (sg) this; (pl) these

esté etc vb ver **estar**

éste (f ésta, pl éstos, éstas) pron (sg) this (one); (pl) these (ones); **ése ... ~ ...** the former ... the latter ...

estelar adj (ASTRONOMÍA) stellar; (actuación, reparto) star atr

estén etc vb ver **estar**

estepa nf (GEO) steppe

estera nf mat(ting)

estéreo adj inv, nm stereo ❑ **estereotipo** nm stereotype

estéril adj sterile, barren; (fig) vain, futile ❑ **esterilizar** vt to sterilize

esterlina adj: **libra ~** pound sterling

estés etc vb ver **estar**

estética nf esthetics sg (US), aesthetics sg (BRIT)

estético, -a adj esthetic (US), aesthetic (BRIT)

estibador nm stevedore, longshoreman (US), docker (BRIT)

estiércol nm dung, manure

estigma nm stigma

estilarse vr to be in fashion

estilo nm style; (TEC) stylus; (NATACIÓN) stroke; **algo por el ~** something along those lines

estima nf esteem, respect

estimación nf (evaluación) estimation; (aprecio, afecto) esteem, regard

estimar vt (evaluar) to estimate; (valorar) to value, appraise; (apreciar) to esteem, respect; (pensar, considerar) to think, reckon

estimulante adj stimulating ♦ nm stimulant

estimular vt to stimulate; (excitar) to excite

estímulo nm stimulus; (ánimo) encouragement

estipulación nf stipulation, condition

estipular vt to stipulate

estirado, -a adj (tenso) (stretched o drawn) tight; (fig: persona) stiff, pompous

estirar vt to stretch; (dinero, suma etc) to stretch out; **estirarse** vr to stretch

estira y afloja (MÉX: fig) nm tug-of-war

estirón nm pull, tug; (crecimiento) spurt, sudden growth; **dar un ~** (niño) to shoot up

estirpe nf stock, lineage

estival adj summer cpd

esto pron this, this thing o matter; **~ de la boda** this business about the wedding

Estocolmo nm Stockholm

estofado nm stew

estofar vt to stew

estómago nm stomach; **tener ~** to be thick-skinned

estorbar vt to hinder, obstruct; (molestar) to bother, disturb ♦ vi to be in the way ❑ **estorbo** nm (molestia) bother, nuisance; (obstáculo) hindrance, obstacle

estornudar vi to sneeze

estos adj demos ver **este²**

éstos pron ver **éste**

estoy vb ver **estar**

estrado nm platform

estrafalario, -a adj odd, eccentric

estrago nm ruin, destruction; **hacer ~s en** to wreak havoc among

estragón nm tarragon

estrambótico, -a adj (persona) eccentric; (peinado, ropa) outlandish

estrangulador, a nm/f strangler ♦ nm (TEC) throttle; (AUTO) choke

estrangular vt (persona) to strangle; (MED) to strangulate

estratagema nf (MIL) stratagem; (astucia) cunning

estrategia nf strategy ❑ **estratégico, -a** adj strategic

estrato nm stratum, layer

estrechamente adv (íntimamente) closely, intimately; (pobremente: vivir) poorly

estrechar vt (reducir) to narrow; (COSTURA) to take in; (abrazar) to hug, embrace; **estrecharse** vr (reducirse) to narrow, grow narrow; (abrazarse) to embrace; **~ la mano** to shake hands

estrechez nf narrowness; (de ropa) tightness; **estrecheces** nfpl (dificultades económicas) financial difficulties

estrecho, -a adj narrow; (apretado) tight; (íntimo) close, intimate; (miserable) mean ♦ nm strait; **~ de miras** narrow-minded

estrella nf star ▶ **estrella de mar** (ZOOL) starfish ▶ **estrella fugaz** shooting star ❑ **estrellado, -a** adj (forma) star-shaped; (cielo) starry

estrellar vt (hacer añicos) to smash (to pieces); (huevos) to fry; **estrellarse** vr to smash; (chocarse) to crash; (fracasar) to fail

estremecer vt to shake; **estremecerse** vr to shake, tremble ❑ **estremecimiento** nm (temblor) trembling, shaking

estrenar vt (vestido) to wear for the first time; (casa) to move into; (película, obra de teatro) to première; **estrenarse** vr (persona) to make one's debut ❑ **estreno** nm (CINE etc) première

estreñido, -a adj constipated

estreñimiento nm constipation

estrépito nm noise, racket; (fig) fuss ❑ **estrepitoso, -a** adj noisy; (fiesta) rowdy

estría nf groove

estribación nf (GEO) spur, foothill

estribar vi: **~ en** to lie on

estribillo nm (LITERATURA) refrain; (MÚS) chorus

estribo nm (de jinete) stirrup; (de vehículo) step; (de puente) support; (GEO) spur; **perder los ~s** to fly off the handle

estribor nm (NÁUT) starboard

estricto, -a adj (riguroso) strict; (severo) severe

estridente adj (color) loud; (voz) raucous

estropajo nm scourer

estropear vt to spoil; (dañar) to damage; **estropearse** vr (objeto) to get damaged; (persona, piel) to be ruined

estructura nf structure

estruendo nm (ruido) racket, din; (fig: alboroto) uproar, turmoil

estrujar vt (apretar) to squeeze; (aplastar) to crush; (fig) to drain, bleed

estuario nm estuary

estuche nm box, case

estudiante nmf student □ **estudiantil** adj student cpd

estudiar vt to study

estudio nm study; (CINE, ARTE, RADIO) studio; **~s** nmpl studies; (erudición) learning sg □ **estudioso, -a** adj studious

estufa nf (LAm exc MÉX, ESP) heater; (MÉX: cocina) stove, cooker (BRIT) ▶ **estufa de gas** (MÉX) gas stove o cooker (BRIT)

estupefaciente nm drug, narcotic

estupefacto, -a adj speechless, thunderstruck

estupendo, -a adj wonderful, terrific; (fam) great; **¡~!** that's great!, fantastic!

estupidez nf (torpeza) stupidity; (acto) stupid thing (to do)

estúpido, -a adj stupid, silly

estupor nm stupor; (fig) astonishment, amazement

estuve etc vb ver **estar**

esvástica nf swastika

ETA (ESP) nf abr (= Euskadi ta Askatasuna) ETA

etapa nf (de viaje) stage; (DEPORTE) leg; (parada) stopping place; (fase) stage, phase

etarra nmf member of ETA

etc. abr (= etcétera) etc

etcétera adv etcetera

eternidad nf eternity □ **eterno, -a** adj eternal, everlasting

ética nf ethics pl

ético, -a adj ethical

etiqueta nf (modales) etiquette; (rótulo) label, tag

Eucaristía nf Eucharist

eufemismo nm euphemism

euforia nf euphoria

euro nm (moneda) euro

eurodiputado, -a nm/f Euro MP, MEP

Europa nf Europe □ **europeo, -a** adj, nm/f European

Euskadi nm the Basque Country o Provinces pl

euskera nm (LING) Basque

evacuación nf evacuation

evacuar vt to evacuate

evadir vt to evade, avoid; **evadirse** vr to escape

evaluar vt to evaluate

evangelio nm gospel

evaporar vt to evaporate; **evaporarse** vr to vanish

evasión nf escape, flight; (fig) evasion ▶ **evasión de capitales** flight of capital

evasiva nf (pretexto) excuse

evasivo, -a adj evasive, non-committal

evento nm event

eventual adj possible, conditional (upon circumstances)

⚠ No confundir **eventual** con la palabra inglesa **eventual**.

evidencia nf evidence, proof □ **evidenciar** vt (hacer patente) to make evident; (probar) to prove, show; **evidenciarse** vr to be evident

evidente adj obvious, clear, evident

evitar vt (evadir) to avoid; (impedir) to prevent

evocar vt to evoke, call forth

evolución nf (desarrollo) evolution, development; (cambio) change; (MIL) maneuver (US), manoeuvre (BRIT) □ **evolucionar** vi to evolve; to maneuver (US), manoeuvre (BRIT)

ex adj ex-; **el ex ministro** the former minister, the ex-minister

exacerbar vt to irritate, annoy

exactamente adv exactly

exactitud nf exactness; (precisión) accuracy; (puntualidad) punctuality □ **exacto, -a** adj exact; accurate; punctual; **¡exacto!** exactly!

exageración nf exaggeration

exagerar vt, vi to exaggerate

exaltado, -a adj (apasionado) over-excited, worked-up; (POL) extreme

exaltar vt to exalt, glorify; **exaltarse** vr (excitarse) to get excited o worked up

examen nm examination

examinar vt to examine; **examinarse** vr to be examined, take an examination

exasperar vt to exasperate; **exasperarse** vr to get exasperated, lose patience

Exca. abr = **Excelencia**

excavadora nf excavator

excavar vt to excavate

excedencia nf: **estar en ~** to be on leave; **pedir** o **solicitar la ~** to ask for leave

excedente adj, nm excess, surplus

exceder vt to exceed, surpass; **excederse** vr (extralimitarse) to go too far

excelencia nf excellence; **E~** Excellency ❏ **excelente** adj excellent

excentricidad nf eccentricity ❏ **excéntrico, -a** adj, nm/f eccentric

excepción nf exception ❏ **excepcional** adj exceptional

excepto adv excepting, except (for)

exceptuar vt to except, exclude

excesivo, -a adj excessive

exceso nm (gen) excess; (COM) surplus ▶ **exceso de equipaje/peso** excess baggage/weight

excitación nf (sensación) excitement; (acción) excitation

excitado, -a adj excited; (emociones) aroused

excitar vt to excite; (incitar) to urge; **excitarse** vr to get excited

exclamación nf exclamation

exclamar vi to exclaim

excluir vt to exclude; (dejar fuera) to shut out; (descartar) to reject ❏ **exclusión** nf exclusion

exclusiva nf (PRENSA) exclusive, scoop; (COM) sole right

exclusivo, -a adj exclusive; **derecho ~** sole o exclusive right

Excmo. abr = **excelentísimo**

excomulgar vt (REL) to excommunicate

excomunión nf excommunication

excursión nf excursion, outing ❏ **excursionista** nmf (turista) sightseer

excusa nf excuse; (disculpa) apology

excusar vt to excuse; **excusarse** vr (disculparse) to apologize

exhalar vt to exhale, breathe out; (olor etc) to give off; (suspiro) to breathe, heave

exhaustivo, -a adj (análisis) thorough; (estudio) exhaustive

exhausto, -a adj exhausted

exhibición nf exhibition, display, show

exhibir vt to exhibit, display, show

exhortar vt: **~ a** to exhort to

exigencia nf demand, requirement ❏ **exigente** adj demanding

exigir vt (gen) to demand, require; **~ el pago** to demand payment

exiliado, -a adj exiled ♦ nm/f exile

exilio nm exile

eximir vt to exempt

existencia nf existence; **~s** nfpl stock(s) pl

existir vi to exist, be

éxito nm (triunfo) success; (MÚS etc) hit; **tener ~** to be successful

⚠ No confundir **éxito** con la palabra inglesa **exit**.

exonerar vt to exonerate; **~ de una obligación** to free from an obligation

exorbitante adj (precio) exorbitant; (cantidad) excessive

exorcizar vt to exorcize

exótico, -a adj exotic

expandir vt to expand

expansión nf expansion

expansivo, -a adj: **onda expansiva** shock wave

expatriarse vr to emigrate; (POL) to go into exile

expectativa nf (espera) expectation; (perspectiva) prospect

expedición nf (excursión) expedition

expediente nm expedient; (JUR: procedimiento) action, proceedings pl; (: papeles) dossier, file, record

expedir vt (despachar) to send, forward; (pasaporte) to issue

expendedor, a nm/f (vendedor) dealer

expensas nfpl: **a ~ de** at the expense of

experiencia nf experience

experimentado, -a adj experienced

experimentar vt (en laboratorio) to experiment with; (probar) to test, try out; (notar, observar) to experience; (deterioro, pérdida) to suffer ❏ **experimento** nm experiment

experto, -a adj expert, skilled ♦ nm/f expert

expiar vt to atone for

expirar vi to expire

explanada nf (llano) plain

explayarse vr (en discurso) to speak at length; **~ con algn** to confide in sb

explicación nf explanation

explicar vt to explain; **explicarse** vr to explain (o.s.)

explícito, -a adj explicit

explique etc vb ver **explicar**

explorador, a nm/f (pionero) explorer; (MIL) scout ♦ nm (MED) probe; (TEC) (radar) scanner

explorar vt to explore; (MED) to probe; (radar) to scan

explosión nf explosion □ **explosivo, -a** adj explosive

explotación nf exploitation; (de planta etc) running

explotar vt to exploit to run, operate ♦ vi to explode

exponer vt to expose; (cuadro) to display; (vida) to risk; (idea) to explain; **exponerse** vr: **~se a (hacer) algo** to run the risk of (doing) sth

exportación nf (acción) export; (mercancías) exports pl

exportar vt to export

exposición nf (gen) exposure; (de arte) show, exhibition; (explicación) explanation; (declaración) account, statement

expresamente adv (decir) clearly; (a propósito) expressly

expresar vt to express □ **expresión** nf expression

expresivo, -a adj (persona, gesto, palabras) expressive; (cariñoso) affectionate

expreso, -a pp de **expresar** ♦ adj (explícito) express; (claro) specific, clear; (tren) fast ♦ adv: **mandar ~** to send by express (delivery)

express (LAm) adv: **enviar algo ~** to send sth special delivery

exprimidor nm squeezer

exprimir vt (fruta) to squeeze; (zumo) to squeeze out

expropiar vt to expropriate

expuesto, -a pp de **exponer** ♦ adj exposed; (cuadro etc) on show, on display

expulsar vt (echar) to eject, throw out; (alumno) to expel; (despedir) to fire, sack; (DEPORTE) to eject (US), send off (BRIT) □ **expulsión** nf expulsion; sending-off

exquisito, -a adj exquisite; (comida) delicious

éxtasis nm ecstasy

extender vt to extend; (los brazos) to stretch out, hold out; (mapa, tela) to spread (out), open (out); (mantequilla) to spread; (certificado) to issue; (cheque, recibo) to make out; (documento) to draw up; **extenderse** vr (gen) to extend; (persona: en el suelo) to stretch out; (epidemia) to spread □ **extendido, -a** adj (abierto) spread out, open; (brazos) outstretched; (costumbre) widespread

extensión nf (de terreno, mar) expanse, stretch; (de tiempo) length, duration; (TEL) extension; **en toda la ~ de la palabra** in every sense of the word

extenso, -a adj extensive

extenuar vt (debilitar) to weaken

exterior adj (de fuera) external; (afuera) outside, exterior; (apariencia) outward; (deuda, relaciones) foreign ♦ nm (gen) exterior, outside; (aspecto) outward appearance; (DEPORTE) wing(er); (países extranjeros) abroad; **en el ~** abroad; **al ~** outwardly, on the surface

exterminar vt to exterminate □ **exterminio** nm extermination

externo, -a adj (exterior) external, outside; (superficial) outward ♦ nm/f day pupil

extinguir vt (fuego) to extinguish, put out; (raza, población) to wipe out; **extinguirse** vr (fuego) to go out; (BIO) to die out, become extinct

extinto, -a adj extinct

extintor nm (fire) extinguisher

extirpar vt (MED) to remove (surgically)

extorsión nf extortion

extra adj inv (tiempo) extra; (chocolate, vino) good-quality ♦ nmf extra ♦ nm extra; (bono) bonus

extracción nf extraction; (en lotería) draw

extracto nm extract

extradición nf extradition

extraer vt to extract, take out

extraescolar adj: **actividad ~** extracurricular activity

extralimitarse vr to go too far

extranjero, -a adj foreign ♦ nm/f foreigner ♦ nm foreign countries pl; **en el ~** abroad

⚠ No confundir **extranjero** con la palabra inglesa **stranger**.

extrañar vt (sorprender) to find strange o odd; (LAm: echar de menos) to miss; **extrañarse** vr (sorprenderse) to be amazed, be surprised

extrañeza nf (rareza) strangeness, oddness; (asombro) amazement, surprise

extraño, -a adj (extranjero) foreign; (raro, sorprendente) strange, odd

extraordinario, -a adj extraordinary; (edición, número) special ♦ nm (de periódico) special edition; **horas extraordinarias** overtime sg

extrarradio nm suburbs

extravagancia nf oddness; outlandishness □ **extravagante** adj (excéntrico) eccentric; (estrafalario) outlandish

extraviado, -a *adj* lost, missing
extraviar *vt* (*persona: desorientar*) to mislead, misdirect; (*perder*) to lose, misplace; **extraviarse** *vr* to lose one's way, get lost □ **extravío** *nm* loss; (*fig*) deviation
extremar *vt* to carry to extremes; **extremarse** *vr* to do one's utmost, make every effort
extremaunción *nf* extreme unction
extremidad *nf* (*punta*) extremity; **~es** *nfpl* (ANAT) extremities
extremo, -a *adj* extreme; (*último*) last ♦ *nm* end; (*límite, grado sumo*) extreme; **en último ~** as a last resort
extrovertido, -a *adj, nm/f* extrovert
exuberancia *nf* exuberance □ **exuberante** *adj* exuberant; (*fig*) luxuriant, lush
eyacular *vt, vi* to ejaculate

Ff

f.a.b. *abr* (= franco a bordo) f.o.b.
fabada *nf* bean and sausage stew
fábrica *nf* factory; **marca de ~** trademark; **precio de ~** factory price

⚠ No confundir **fábrica** con la palabra inglesa **fabric**.

fabricación *nf* (*manufactura*) manufacture; (*producción*) production; **de ~ casera** home-made; **~ en serie** mass production
fabricante *nmf* manufacturer
fabricar *vt* (*manufacturar*) to manufacture, make; (*construir*) to build; (*cuento*) to fabricate, devise
fábula *nf* (*cuento*) fable; (*chisme*) rumor (US), rumour (BRIT); (*mentira*) fib
fabuloso, -a *adj* (*oportunidad, tiempo*) fabulous, great
facción *nf* (POL) faction; **facciones** *nfpl* (*de rostro*) features
faceta *nf* facet
facha (*fam*) *nf* (*aspecto*) look; (*cara*) face
fachada *nf* (ARQ) façade, front
fácil *adj* (*simple*) easy; (*probable*) likely
facilidad *nf* (*capacidad*) ease; (*sencillez*) simplicity; (*de palabra*) fluency; **~es** *nfpl* facilities
facilitar *vt* (*hacer fácil*) to make easy; (*proporcionar*) to provide
fácilmente *adv* easily

facsímil *nm* facsimile, fax
factible *adj* feasible
factor *nm* factor
factura *nf* (*cuenta*) check (US), bill (BRIT) □ **facturación** *nf* (*de equipaje*) check-in □ **facturar** *vt* (COM) to invoice, charge for; (ESP: equipaje) to check in
facultad *nf* (*aptitud, ESCOL etc*) faculty; (*poder*) power
faena *nf* (*trabajo*) work; (*quehacer*) task, job
faisán *nm* pheasant
faja *nf* (*para la cintura*) sash; (*de mujer*) corset; (*de tierra*) strip
fajo *nm* (*de papeles*) bundle; (*de billetes*) wad
falacia *nf* fallacy
falda *nf* (*prenda de vestir*) skirt
falla *nf* (*defecto*) fault, flaw
fallar *vt* (JUR) to pronounce sentence on ♦ *vi* (*memoria*) to fail; (*motor*) to miss
fallecer *vi* to pass away, die □ **fallecimiento** *nm* decease, demise
fallido, -a *adj* (*gen*) frustrated, unsuccessful
fallo *nm* (JUR) verdict, ruling; (*fracaso*) failure ▶ **fallo cardíaco** heart failure
falsedad *nf* falseness; (*hipocresía*) hypocrisy; (*mentira*) falsehood
falsificar *vt* (*firma etc*) to forge; (*moneda*) to counterfeit
falso, -a *adj* false; (*documento, moneda etc*) fake; **en ~** falsely
falta *nf* (*defecto*) fault, flaw; (*privación*) lack, want; (*ausencia*) absence; (*carencia*) shortage; (*equivocación*) mistake; (DEPORTE) foul; **echar en ~** to miss; **hacer ~ hacer algo** to be necessary to do sth; **me hace ~ una pluma** I need a pen ▶ **falta de educación** bad manners *pl*
faltar *vi* (*escasear*) to be lacking, be wanting; (*ausentarse*) to be absent, be missing; **faltan 2 horas para llegar** there are 2 hours to go till arrival; **~ al respeto a algn** to be disrespectful to sb; **¡no faltaba más!** (*no hay de qué*) don't mention it
fama *nf* (*renombre*) fame; (*reputación*) reputation
famélico, -a *adj* starving
familia *nf* family ▶ **familia política** in-laws *pl*
familiar *adj relativo a la familia*, family *cpd*; (*conocido, informal*) familiar ♦ *nm* relative, relation □ **familiaridad** *nf* (*gen*) familiarity; (*informalidad*) homeliness □ **familiarizarse** *vr*: **familiarizarse con** to familiarize o.s. with

famoso, -a *adj* (*renombrado*) famous

fanático, -a *adj* fanatical ♦ *nm/f* fanatic; (*CINE, DEPORTE*) fan ❑ **fanatismo** *nm* fanaticism

fanfarrón, -ona *adj* boastful

fango *nm* mud ❑ **fangoso, -a** *adj* muddy

fantasía *nf* fantasy, imagination; **joyas de ~** imitation jewelry *sg* (*US*) o jewellery *sg* (*BRIT*)

fantasma *nm* (*espectro*) ghost, apparition; (*fanfarrón*) show-off

fantástico, -a *adj* fantastic

farmacéutico, -a *adj* pharmaceutical ♦ *nm/f* druggist (*US*), chemist (*BRIT*)

farmacia *nf* drugstore (*US*), chemist's (shop) (*BRIT*) ▶ **farmacia de guardia** all-night chemist ▶ **farmacia de turno** duty chemist

fármaco *nm* drug

faro *nm* (*NÁUT: torre*) lighthouse; (*AUTO*) headlamp ▶ **faros antiniebla** fog lamps ▶ **faros delanteros/traseros** headlights/ rear lights

farol *nm* lantern, lamp; (*LAm: farola*) street light, lamppost

farola (*ESP*) *nf* street light, lamppost

farra (*LAm: fam*) *nf* party; **ir de ~** to go on a binge

farsa *nf* (*gen*) farce

farsante *nmf* fraud, fake

fascículo *nm* (*de revista*) part, installment (*US*), instalment (*BRIT*)

fascinar *vt* (*gen*) to fascinate

fascismo *nm* fascism ❑ **fascista** *adj, nmf* fascist

fase *nf* phase

fastidiar *vt* (*molestar*) to annoy, bother; (*estropear*) to spoil; **fastidiarse** *vr*: **¡que se fastidie!** (*fam*) he'll just have to put up with it!

fastidio *nm* (*molestia*) annoyance ❑ **fastidioso, -a** *adj* (*molesto*) annoying

fastuoso, -a *adj* (*banquete, boda*) lavish; (*acto*) pompous

fatal *adj* (*gen*) fatal; (*desgraciado*) ill-fated; (*fam: malo, pésimo*) awful ❑ **fatalidad** *nf* (*destino*) fate; (*mala suerte*) misfortune

fatiga *nf* (*cansancio*) fatigue, weariness

fatigar *vt* to tire, weary; **fatigarse** *vr* to get tired

fatigoso, -a *adj* (*cansador*) tiring

fatuo, -a *adj* (*vano*) fatuous; (*presuntuoso*) conceited

favor *nm* favor (*US*), favour (*BRIT*); **estar a ~ de** to be in favor (*US*) o favour (*BRIT*) of; **haga el ~ de...** would you be so good as to..., kindly...;

por ~ please ❑ **favorable** *adj* favorable (*US*), favourable (*BRIT*)

favorecer *vt* to favor (*US*), favour (*BRIT*); (*vestido etc*) to become, flatter; **este peinado le favorece** this hairstyle suits him

favorito, -a *adj, nm/f* favorite (*US*), favourite (*BRIT*)

fax *nm inv* fax; **mandar por ~** to fax

faz *nf* face; **la ~ de la tierra** the face of the earth

fe *nf* (*REL*) faith; (*documento*) certificate; **prestar fe a** to believe, credit; **actuar con buena/mala fe** to act in good/bad faith; **dar fe de** to bear witness to

fealdad *nf* ugliness

febrero *nm* February

febril *adj* (*fig: actividad*) hectic; (*mente, mirada*) feverish

fecha *nf* date; **con ~ adelantada** postdated; **en ~ próxima** soon; **hasta la ~** to date, so far; **poner ~** to date ▶ **fecha de caducidad** (*de producto alimenticio*) sell-by date; (*de contrato etc*) expiry date ❑ **fechar** *vt* to date

fecundar *vt* (*generar*) to fertilize, make fertile ❑ **fecundo, -a** *adj* (*fértil*) fertile; (*fig*) prolific; (*productivo*) productive

federación *nf* federation

felicidad *nf* happiness; **~es** *nfpl* (*felicitaciones*) best wishes, congratulations

felicitación *nf*: **¡felicitaciones!** congratulations!

felicitar *vt* to congratulate

feligrés, -esa *nm/f* parishioner

feliz *adj* happy

felpudo *nm* doormat

femenino, -a *adj, nm* feminine

feminista *adj, nmf* feminist

fenomenal *adj* = **fenómeno**

fenómeno *nm* phenomenon; (*fig*) freak, accident ♦ *adj* great ♦ *excl* great!, fantastic!

feo, -a *adj* (*gen*) ugly; (*desagradable*) bad, nasty

féretro *nm* (*ataúd*) coffin, casket (*US*); (*sarcófago*) bier

feria *nf* (*gen*) fair; (*descanso*) holiday, rest day; (*MÉX: cambio*) small o loose (*BRIT*) change; (*CS: mercado*) village market

feriado (*LAm*) *nm* holiday

fermentar *vi* to ferment

ferocidad *nf* fierceness, ferocity

feroz *adj* (*cruel*) cruel; (*salvaje*) fierce

férreo, -a *adj* iron

ferretería *nf* (*tienda*) hardware store, ironmonger's (shop) (*BRIT*)

ferrocarril *nm* railroad (*US*), railway (*BRIT*)

ferroviario, -a *adj* rail *cpd*

fértil *adj* (*productivo*) fertile; (*rico*) rich ❑ **fertilidad** *nf* (*gen*) fertility; (*productividad*) fruitfulness

ferviente *adj* fervent

fervor *nm* fervor (*US*), fervour (*BRIT*) ❑ **fervoroso, -a** *adj* fervent

festejar *vt* (*celebrar*) to celebrate

festejo *nm* celebration; **~s** *nmpl* (*fiestas*) festivals

festín *nm* feast, banquet

festival *nm* festival ▶ **Festival Internacional Cervantino** (*MÉX*) International Cervantes Festival

---

FESTIVAL INTERNACIONAL CERVANTINO

The **Festival Internacional Cervantino** of Guanajuato is a cultural homage to Miguel de Cervantes, author of "Don Quijote de la Mancha", which has become one of the most important cultural festivals in Latin America since it began in 1972. Around 150,000 people visit Guanajuato during the month of October to see exhibitions, concerts, ballet, opera, plays and contemporary dance which are held all over the city.

---

festividad *nf* festivity

festivo, -a *adj* (*de fiesta*) festive; (*CINE, LITERATURA*) humorous; **día ~** holiday

fétido, -a *adj* foul-smelling

feto *nm* fetus (*US*), foetus (*BRIT*)

fiable *adj* (*persona*) trustworthy; (*máquina*) reliable

fiador, a *nm/f* (*JUR*) guarantor, bondsman (*US*); (*COM*) backer; **salir ~ por algn** to stand bail for sb

fiambre *nm* cold meat

fianza *nf* surety; (*JUR*): **libertad bajo ~** release on bail

fiar *vt* (*salir garante de*) to guarantee; (*vender a crédito*) to sell on credit; (*secreto*): **~ a** to confide (to) ♦ *vi* to trust; **fiarse** *vr* to trust (in), rely on; **~se de algn** to rely on sb

fibra *nf* fiber ▶ **fibra óptica** optical fiber (*US*) *o* fibre (*BRIT*)

ficción *nf* fiction

ficha *nf* (*TEL*) token; (*en juegos*) counter, marker; (*tarjeta*) (index) card ❑ **fichar** *vt* (*archivar*) to file, index; (*DEPORTE*) to sign; **estar fichado** to have a record ❑ **fichero** *nm* box file; (*INFORM*) file

ficticio, -a *adj* (*imaginario*) fictitious; (*falso*) fabricated

fidelidad *nf* (*lealtad*) fidelity, loyalty; **alta ~** high fidelity, hi-fi

fidelización *nf* (*COM*) loyalty

fideos *nmpl* noodles

fiebre *nf* (*MED*) fever; (*fig*) fever, excitement; **tener ~** to have a temperature ▶ **fiebre amarilla/del heno** yellow/hay fever ▶ **fiebre palúdica** malaria

fiel *adj* (*leal*) faithful, loyal; (*fiable*) reliable; (*exacto*) accurate, faithful ♦ *nm*: **los ~es** the faithful

fieltro *nm* felt

fiera *nf* (*animal feroz*) wild animal *o* beast; (*fig*) dragon; *ver tb* **fiero**

fiero, -a *adj* (*cruel*) cruel; (*feroz*) fierce; (*duro*) harsh

fiesta *nf* party; (*de pueblo*) festival; (*vacaciones: tb*: **~s**) holiday *sg* ▶ **fiesta de guardar** (*REL*) day of obligation

figura *nf* (*gen*) figure; (*forma, imagen*) shape, form; (*NAIPES*) face card

figurar *vt* (*representar*) to represent; (*fingir*) to figure ♦ *vi* to figure; **figurarse** *vr* (*imaginarse*) to imagine; (*suponer*) to suppose

fijador *nm* (*FOTO etc*) fixative; (*de pelo*) gel

fijar *vt* (*gen*) to fix; (*estampilla*) to affix, stick (on); **fijarse** *vr*: **~se en** to notice

fijo, -a *adj* (*gen*) fixed; (*firme*) firm; (*permanente*) permanent ♦ *adv*: **mirar ~** to stare

fila *nf* row; (*MIL*) rank; **ponerse en ~** to line up, get into line

filántropo, -a *nm/f* philanthropist

filatelia *nf* philately, stamp collecting

filete *nm* (*de carne*) fillet *o* filet (*US*) steak; (*de pescado*) fillet, filet (*US*)

filiación *nf* (*POL*) affiliation

filial *adj* filial ♦ *nf* subsidiary

Filipinas *nfpl*: **las ~** the Philippines ❑ **filipino, -a** *adj, nm/f* Philippine

filmar *vt* to film, shoot

filo *nm* (*gen*) edge; **sacar ~ a** to sharpen; **al ~ del mediodía** at about midday; **de doble ~** double-edged

filón *nm* (*MINERÍA*) vein, lode; (*fig*) goldmine

filosofía *nf* philosophy ❑ **filósofo, -a** *nm/f* philosopher

filtrar *vt, vi* to filter, strain; **filtrarse** *vr* to filter ❑ **filtro** *nm* (*TEC, utensilio*) filter

fin *nm* end; (*objetivo*) aim, purpose; **al ~ y al cabo** when all's said and done; **a ~ de** in order to; **por ~** finally; **en ~** in short ▶ **fin de semana** weekend

final adj final ♦ nm end, conclusion ♦ nf final ❏ **finalidad** nf (propósito) purpose, intention ❏ **finalista** nmf finalist ❏ **finalizar** vt to end, finish; (INFORM) to log out o off ♦ vi to end, come to an end

financiar vt to finance ❏ **financiero, -a** adj financial ♦ nm/f financier

finca nf (casa de campo) country house; (ESP: bien inmueble) property, land; (LAm: granja) farm

fingir vt (simular) to simulate, feign ♦ vi (aparentar) to pretend

finlandés, -esa adj Finnish ♦ nm/f Finn ♦ nm (LING) Finnish

Finlandia nf Finland

fino, -a adj fine; (delgado) slender; (de buenas maneras) polite, refined; (jerez) fino, dry

firma nf signature; (COM) firm, company

firmamento nm firmament

firmar vt to sign

firme adj firm; (estable) stable; (sólido) solid; (constante) steady; (decidido) resolute ♦ nm road (surface) ❏ **firmemente** adv firmly ❏ **firmeza** nf firmness; (constancia) steadiness; (solidez) solidity

fiscal adj fiscal ♦ nmf public prosecutor, district attorney (US); **año ~** tax o fiscal year

fisco nm (hacienda) treasury, exchequer (BRIT)

fisgar vt to pry into

fisgonear vt to poke one's nose into ♦ vi to pry, spy

física nf physics sg; ver tb **físico**

físico, -a adj physical ♦ nm physique ♦ nm/f physicist

fisura nf crack; (MED) fracture

flác(c)ido, -a adj flabby

flaco, -a adj (muy delgado) skinny, thin; (débil) weak, feeble

flagrante adj flagrant

flama (MÉX) nf flame

flamable (MÉX) adj flammable

flamante (fam) adj brilliant; (nuevo) brand-new

flamenco, -a adj (de Flandes) Flemish; (baile, música) flamenco ♦ nm (baile, música) flamenco; (LAm exc MÉX, ESP ZOOL) flamingo

flamingo (MÉX) nm flamingo

flan nm creme caramel

⚠ No confundir **flan** con la palabra inglesa **flan**.

flaqueza nf (delgadez) thinness, leanness; (fig) weakness

flash (pl ~ o ~es) nm (FOTO) flash

flauta nf (MÚS) flute

flecha nf arrow

flechazo nm love at first sight

fleco (MÉX) nm bangs pl (US), fringe (BRIT)

flema nm phlegm

flequillo nm (pelo) bangs pl (US), fringe (BRIT)

flexible adj flexible

flexión nf push-up (US), press-up (BRIT)

flexo nm adjustable table-lamp

flojera (LAm: fam) nf: **me da ~** I can't be bothered

flojo, -a adj (gen) loose; (sin fuerzas) limp; (débil) weak; (persona) lazy

flor nf flower; **a ~ de** on the surface of ❏ **florecer** vi (BOT) to flower, bloom; (fig) to flourish ❏ **floreciente** adj (BOT) in flower, flowering; (fig) thriving ❏ **florería** (LAm) nf flower store (US), florist's (shop) (BRIT) ❏ **florero** nm vase ❏ **floristería** nf flower store (US), florist's (shop) (BRIT)

flota nf fleet

flotador nm (gen) float; (para nadar) life preserver (US), rubber ring (BRIT)

flotar vi (gen) to float ❏ **flote** nm: **a flote** afloat; **salir a flote** (fig) to get back on one's feet

fluctuar vi (oscilar) to fluctuate

fluidez nf fluidity; (fig) fluency

fluido, -a adj, nm fluid

fluir vi to flow

flujo nm flow ▶ **flujo y reflujo** ebb and flow

flúor nm fluoride

fluvial adj (navegación, cuenca) fluvial, river cpd

foca nf seal

foco nm focus; (ELEC) floodlight; (MÉX: bombilla) (light) bulb

fofo, -a adj soft, spongy; (carnes) flabby, pudgy (US)

fogata nf bonfire

fogón nm (de cocina) ring, burner

fogoso, -a adj spirited

folio nm folio, page

follaje nm foliage

folletín nm newspaper serial

folleto nm (POL) pamphlet

fomentar vt (MED) to foment ❏ **fomento** nm (promoción) promotion

fonda nf inn

fondo nm (de mar) bottom; (de vehículo, sala) back; (ARTE etc) background; (reserva) fund; (MÉX: combinación) slip; **~s** nmpl (COM) funds, resources; **una investigación a ~** a thorough investigation; **en el ~** at bottom, deep down

fonobuzón *nm* voice mail

fontanería (*CAm, ESP*) *nf* plumbing
❑ **fontanero, -a** *nm/f* plumber

footing (*ESP*) *nm* jogging; **hacer ~** to jog, go jogging

forastero, -a *nm/f* stranger

forcejear *vi* (*luchar*) to struggle

forense *nmf* pathologist

forjar *vt* to forge

forma *nf* (*figura*) form, shape; (*MED*) fitness; (*método*) way, means; **las ~s** the conventions; **estar en ~** to be fit

formación *nf* (*gen*) formation; (*educación*) education ▶ **formación profesional** vocational training

formal *adj* (*gen*) formal; (*fig: serio*) serious; (*: de fiar*) reliable ❑ **formalidad** *nf* formality; seriousness ❑ **formalizar** *vt* (*JUR*) to formalize; (*situación*) to put in order, regularize; **formalizarse** *vr* (*situación*) to be put in order, be regularized

formar *vt* (*componer*) to form, shape; (*constituir*) to make up, constitute; (*ESCOL*) to train, educate; **formarse** *vr* (*ESCOL*) to be trained, educated; (*cobrar forma*) to form, take form; (*desarrollarse*) to develop

formatear *vt* to format

formativo, -a *adj* (*lecturas, años*) formative

formato *nm* format

formidable *adj* (*temible*) formidable; (*estupendo*) tremendous

fórmula *nf* formula

formular *vt* (*queja*) to make, lodge; (*petición*) to draw up; (*pregunta*) to pose

formulario *nm* form

fornido, -a *adj* well-built

foro *nm* (*POL, INFORM, HIST*) forum

forrar *vt* (*abrigo*) to line; (*libro*) to cover ❑ **forro** *nm* (*de cuaderno*) cover; (*COSTURA*) lining; (*de sillón*) upholstery

fortalecer *vt* to strengthen

fortaleza *nf* (*MIL*) fortress, stronghold; (*fuerza*) strength; (*determinación*) resolution

fortuito, -a *adj* accidental

fortuna *nf* (*suerte*) fortune, (good) luck; (*riqueza*) fortune, wealth

forzar *vt* (*puerta*) to force (open); (*compeler*) to compel

forzoso, -a *adj* necessary

fosa *nf* (*sepultura*) grave; (*en tierra*) pit ▶ **fosas nasales** nostrils

fósforo *nm* (*QUÍM*) phosphorus; (*cerilla*) match

foso *nm* ditch; (*TEATRO*) pit; (*AUTO*) inspection pit

foto *nf* photo, snap(shot); **sacar una ~** to take a photo *o* picture

fotocopia *nf* photocopy
❑ **fotocopiadora** *nf* photocopier
❑ **fotocopiar** *vt* to photocopy

fotografía *nf* (*ARTE*) photography; (*una fotografía*) photograph ❑ **fotografiar** *vt* to photograph

fotógrafo, -a *nm/f* photographer

fracasar *vi* (*gen*) to fail

fracaso *nm* failure

fracción *nf* fraction ❑ **fraccionamiento** (*MÉX*) *nm* housing development (*US*) *o* estate (*BRIT*)

fractura *nf* fracture, break

fragancia *nf* (*olor*) fragrance, perfume

frágil *adj* (*débil*) fragile; (*COM*) breakable

fragmento *nm* (*pedazo*) fragment

fragua *nf* forge ❑ **fraguar** *vt* to forge; (*fig*) to concoct ♦ *vi* to harden

fraile *nm* (*REL*) friar; (*: monje*) monk

frambuesa *nf* raspberry

francamente *adv* (*hablar, decir*) frankly; (*realmente*) really

francés, -esa *adj* French ♦ *nm/f* Frenchman(-woman) ♦ *nm* (*LING*) French

Francia *nf* France

franco, -a *adj* (*cándido*) frank, open; (*COM: exento*) free ♦ *nm* (*moneda*) franc

francotirador, a *nm/f* sniper

franela *nf* flannel

franja *nf* (*banda*) strip; (*borde*) border

franquear *vt* (*camino*) to clear; (*carta, paquete postal*) to frank, stamp; (*obstáculo*) to overcome

franqueo *nm* postage

franqueza *nf* (*candor*) frankness

frasco *nm* bottle, flask; **~ al vacío** (vacuum) flask

frase *nf* sentence ▶ **frase hecha** set phrase; (*pey*) stock phrase

fraterno, -a *adj* brotherly, fraternal

fraude *nm* (*cualidad*) dishonesty; (*acto*) fraud ❑ **fraudulento, -a** *adj* fraudulent

frazada (*LAm*) *nf* blanket

frecuencia *nf* frequency; **con ~** frequently, often

frecuentar *vt* to frequent

fregadero *nm* (kitchen) sink

fregar vt (*frotar*) to scrub; (*platos*) to wash, wash (up) (*BRIT*); (*LAm: fam: fastidiar*) to annoy; (: *malograr*) to screw up

fregona (*ESP*) nf mop

freír vt to fry

frenar vt to brake; (*fig*) to check

frenazo nm: **dar un ~** to brake sharply

frenesí nm frenzy ❑ **frenético, -a** adj frantic

freno nm (*TEC, AUTO*) brake; (*de cabalgadura*) bit; (*fig*) check

frente nm (*ARQ, POL*) front; (*de objeto*) front part ♦ nf forehead, brow; **~ a** in front of; (*en situación opuesta de*) opposite; **al ~ de** (*fig*) at the head of; **chocar de ~** to crash head-on; **hacer ~ a** to face up to

fresa nf strawberry

fresco, -a adj (*nuevo*) fresh; (*frío*) cool; (*descarado*) sassy (*US*), cheeky (*BRIT*) ♦ nm (*aire*) fresh air; (*ARTE*) fresco; (*LAm: jugo*) fruit drink ♦ nm/f (*fam*): **ser un ~** to have a nerve; **tomar el ~** to get some fresh air ❑ **frescura** nf freshness; (*descaro*) cheek, nerve

frialdad nf (*gen*) coldness; (*indiferencia*) indifference

fricción nf (*gen*) friction; (*acto*) rub(bing); (*MED*) massage

frigidez nf frigidity

frigorífico (*ESP*) nm refrigerator, icebox (*US*)

frijol (*LAm*) nm kidney bean

frío, -a etc vb ver **freír** ♦ adj cold; (*indiferente*) indifferent ♦ nm cold; indifference; **hace ~** it's cold; **tener ~** to be cold

frito, -a adj fried; **me trae ~ ese hombre** I'm sick and tired of that man ❑ **fritos** nmpl fried food

frívolo, -a adj frivolous

frontal adj frontal; **choque ~** head-on collision

frontera nf frontier ❑ **fronterizo, -a** adj frontier cpd; (*contiguo*) bordering

frontón nm (*DEPORTE: cancha*) pelota court; (: *juego*) pelota

frotar vt to rub; **frotarse** vr: **~se las manos** to rub one's hands

fructífero, -a adj fruitful

fruncir vt to pucker; (*COSTURA*) to pleat; **~ el ceño** to knit one's brow

frustrar vt to frustrate

fruta nf fruit ❑ **frutería** nf fruit store (*US*) o shop (*BRIT*) ❑ **frutero, -a** adj fruit cpd ♦ nm/f fruiterer ♦ nm fruit bowl

frutilla (*CS*) nf strawberry

fruto nm fruit; (*fig: resultado*) result; (: *beneficio*) benefit ► **frutos secos** nuts and dried fruit pl

fue vb ver **ser; ir**

fuego nm (*gen*) fire; (*LAm: calentura*) cold sore; **a ~ lento** on a low heat; **¿tienes ~?** have you (got) a light? ► **fuegos artificiales** fireworks

fuente nf fountain; (*manantial: fig*) spring; (*origen*) source; (*plato*) large dish

fuera etc vb ver **ser; ir** ♦ adv out(side); (*en otra parte*) away; (*excepto, salvo*) except, save ♦ prep: **~ de** outside; (*fig*) besides; **~ de sí** beside o.s.; **por ~** (on the) outside

fuera-borda nm speedboat

fuerte adj strong; (*golpe*) hard; (*ruido*) loud; (*comida*) rich; (*lluvia*) heavy; (*dolor*) intense ♦ adv strongly; hard; loud(ly)

fuerza etc vb ver **forzar** ♦ nf (*fortaleza*) strength; (*TEC, ELEC*) power; (*coacción*) force; (*MIL*): **~s** forces pl; **a ~ de** by dint of; **cobrar ~s** to recover one's strength; **tener ~s para** to have the strength to; **a la ~** forcibly, by force; **por ~** of necessity ► **fuerza de voluntad** willpower

fuga nf (*huida*) flight, escape; (*de gas etc*) leak

fugarse vr to flee, escape

fugaz adj fleeting

fugitivo, -a adj, nm/f fugitive

fui vb ver **ser; ir**

fulano, -a nm/f so-and-so, what's-his-name/ what's-her-name

fulminante adj (*fig: mirada*) fierce; (*MED: enfermedad, ataque*) sudden; (*fam: éxito, golpe*) sudden

fumador, a nm/f smoker

fumar vt, vi to smoke; **~ en pipa** to smoke a pipe

función nf function; (*en trabajo*) duties pl; (*espectáculo*) show; **entrar en funciones** to take up one's duties

funcionar vi (*gen*) to function; (*máquina*) to work; **"no funciona"** "out of order"

funcionario, -a nm/f civil servant

funda nf (*gen*) cover; (*de almohada*) pillowcase

fundación nf foundation

fundamental adj fundamental, basic

fundamentar vt (*poner base*) to lay the foundations of; (*establecer*) to found; (*fig*) to base ❑ **fundamento** nm (*base*) foundation

fundar vt to found; **fundarse** vr: **~se en** to be founded on

fundición nf fusing; (*fábrica*) foundry

fundir vt (gen) to fuse; (metal) to smelt, melt down; (nieve etc) to melt; (COM) to merge; (estatua) to cast; **fundirse** vr (colores etc) to merge, blend; (unirse) to fuse together; (ELEC: fusible, lámpara etc) to fuse, blow; (nieve etc) to melt

fúnebre adj funeral cpd, funereal

funeral nm funeral □ **funeraria** nf undertaker's

funesto, -a adj (día) ill-fated; (decisión) fatal

furgón nm wagon □ **furgoneta** nf (AUTO, COM) pick-up (truck) (US), (transit) van (BRIT)

furia nf (ira) fury; (violencia) violence □ **furibundo, -a** adj furious □ **furioso, -a** adj (iracundo) furious; (violento) violent □ **furor** nm (cólera) rage

furtivo, -a adj furtive ♦ nm poacher

fusible nm fuse, fuze (US)

fusil nm rifle □ **fusilar** vt to shoot

fusión nf (gen) melting; (unión) fusion; (COM) merger

futbol (MÉX) (LAm exc MÉX, ESP **fútbol**) nm soccer (US), football (BRIT) ▶ **futbol** o **fútbol americano** football (US), American football (BRIT) □ **futbolín** nm Foosball® (US), table football (BRIT) □ **futbolista** nmf soccer (US) o football (BRIT) player

futuro, -a adj, nm future

Gg

gabardina nf raincoat, gabardine

gabinete nm (estudio) study; (de abogados etc) office; (POL) cabinet

gaceta nf gazette

gachas nfpl porridge sg

gafas (ESP) nfpl glasses, eyeglasses (US) ▶ **gafas de sol** sunglasses

gaita nf bagpipes pl

gajes nmpl: ~ **del oficio** occupational hazards

gajo nm (de naranja) segment

gala nf (traje de etiqueta) full dress; ~**s** nfpl (ropa) finery sg; **estar de ~** to be in one's best clothes; **hacer ~ de** to display

galante adj gallant □ **galantería** nf (caballerosidad) gallantry; (cumplido) politeness; (comentario) compliment

galápago nm (ZOOL) turtle

galardón nm award, prize

galaxia nf galaxy

galera nf (nave) galley; (carro) wagon; (IMPRENTA) galley

galería nf (gen) gallery; (balcón) veranda(h); (pasillo) corridor

Gales nm (tb: **País de ~**) Wales □ **galés, -esa** adj Welsh ♦ nm/f Welshman(-woman) ♦ nm (LING) Welsh

galgo, -a nm/f greyhound

galimatías nmpl (lenguaje) gibberish sg, nonsense sg

gallardía nf (valor) bravery

gallego, -a adj, nm/f Galician

galleta nf cookie (US), biscuit (BRIT)

gallina nf hen ♦ nmf (fam: cobarde) chicken □ **gallinero** nm henhouse; (TEATRO) top gallery

gallo nm rooster, cock

galón nm (MIL) stripe; (COSTURA) braid; (medida) gallon

galopar vi to gallop

gama nf (fig) range

gamba (ESP) nf shrimp (US), prawn (BRIT)

gamuza nf chamois

gana nf (deseo) desire, wish; (apetito) appetite; (voluntad) will; (añoranza) longing; **de buena ~** willingly; **de mala ~** reluctantly; **me da ~s de** I feel like, I want to; **no me da la ~** I don't feel like it; **tener ~s de** to feel like

ganadería nf (ganado) livestock; (ganado vacuno) cattle pl; (cría, comercio) cattle raising

ganadero, -a (ESP) nm/f (hacendado) rancher

ganado nm livestock ▶ **ganado lanar** sheep pl ▶ **ganado mayor** cattle pl ▶ **ganado porcino** pigs pl

ganador, a adj winning ♦ nm/f winner

ganancia nf (lo ganado) gain; (aumento) increase; (beneficio) profit; ~**s** nfpl (ingresos) earnings; (beneficios) profit sg, winnings

ganar vt (obtener) to get, obtain; (sacar ventaja) to gain; (salario etc) to earn; (DEPORTE, premio) to win; (derrotar a) to beat; (alcanzar) to reach ♦ vi (DEPORTE) to win; **ganarse** vr: ~**se la vida** to earn one's living

ganchillo nm crochet

gancho nm (gen) hook; (LAm: colgador) hanger

gandul, a adj, nm/f good-for-nothing, layabout

ganga nf bargain

gangrena nf gangrene

ganso, -a nm/f (ZOOL) goose; (fam) idiot

ganzúa nf skeleton key

garabatear vi, vt (al escribir) to scribble, scrawl

garabato nm (escritura) scrawl, scribble

garaje nm garage

garante adj responsible ♦ nmf guarantor

garantía nf guarantee

garantizar vt to guarantee

garbanzo nm chickpea, garbanzo (US)

garbo nm grace, elegance

garfio nm grappling iron

garganta nf (ANAT) throat; (de botella) neck
❏ **gargantilla** nf necklace

gárgaras nfpl: **hacer ~** to gargle

gargarear (LAm) vi to gargle

garita nf cabin, hut; (MIL) sentry box

garra nf (de gato, TEC) claw; (de ave) talon;
(fam: mano) hand, paw

garrafa nf carafe, decanter; (RPI: de gas)
cylinder

garrapata nf tick

garronero, -a (RPI: fam) nm/f scrounger

garrote nm (palo) stick; (porra) cudgel;
(suplicio) garrotte

garza nf heron

gas nm gas

gasa nf gauze

gaseosa nf lemonade

gaseoso, -a adj sparkling, carbonated

gasoil nm diesel (oil)

gasóleo nm = **gasoil**

gasolina nf gas(oline) (US), petrol (BRIT)
❏ **gasolinera** nf gas (US) o petrol (BRIT)
station

gastado, -a adj (dinero) spent; (ropa) worn
out; (usado: frase etc) trite

gastar vt (dinero, tiempo) to spend; (fuerzas)
to use up; (desperdiciar) to waste; (llevar) to
wear; **gastarse** vr to wear out; (estropearse) to
waste; **~ en** to spend on; **~ bromas** to crack
jokes; **¿qué número gastas?** what size (shoe)
do you take?

gasto nm (desembolso) expenditure,
spending; (consumo, uso) use; **~s** nmpl
(desembolsos) expenses; (cargos) charges,
costs

gastronomía nf gastronomy

gatear vi (andar a gatas) to go on all fours

gatillo nm (de arma de fuego) trigger; (de
dentista) forceps

gato, -a nm/f cat ♦ nm (TEC) jack; **andar a
gatas** to go on all fours

gaucho nm gaucho

GAUCHO

Gauchos are the herdsmen or riders of the
Southern Cone plains. Although popularly
associated with Argentine folklore, **gauchos**
belong equally to the cattle-raising areas of
Southern Brazil and Uruguay. **Gauchos'**
traditions and clothing reflect their mixed
ancestry and cultural roots. Their baggy
trousers are Arabic in origin, while the horse
and guitar are inherited from the Spanish
conquistadors; the poncho, maté and
boleadoras (strips of leather weighted at
either end with stones) form part of the
Indian tradition.

gaviota nf seagull

gay adj inv, nm gay, homosexual

gazpacho nm gazpacho

gel nm gel ▶ **gel de baño/ducha** bath/
shower gel

gelatina nf Jell-O® (US), jelly (BRIT); (polvos
etc) gelatine

gema nf gem

gemelo, -a adj, nm/f twin; **~s** nmpl (de
camisa) cufflinks; (prismáticos) field glasses,
binoculars

gemido nm (quejido) moan, groan; (aullido)
howl

Géminis nm Gemini

gemir vi (quejarse) to moan, groan; (aullar) to
howl

generación nf generation

general adj general ♦ nm general; **por lo ~,
en ~** in general

la Generalitat nf Catalan parliament

generalizar vt to generalize; **generalizarse**
vr to become generalized, spread

generalmente adv generally

generar vt to generate

género nm (clase) kind, sort; (tipo) type; (BIO)
genus; (LING) gender; (COM) material
▶ **género humano** human race

generosidad nf generosity
❏ **generoso, -a** adj generous

genial adj inspired; (idea) great; (estupendo)
wonderful

genio nm (carácter) nature, disposition;
(humor) temper; (facultad creadora) genius;
de mal ~ bad-tempered

genital adj genital ❏ **genitales** nmpl
genitals

gente nf (personas) people pl; (parientes)
relatives pl

gentil adj (elegante) graceful; (encantador) charming ❑ **gentileza** nf grace; charm; (cortesía) courtesy

⚠ No confundir **gentil** con la palabra inglesa *gentle*.

gentío nm crowd, throng
genuino, -a adj genuine
geografía nf geography
geología nf geology
geometría nf geometry
gerencia nf management ❑ **gerente** nmf (supervisor) manager; (jefe) director
geriatría nf (MED) geriatrics sg
germen nm germ
germinar vi to germinate
gesticulación nf gesticulation; (mueca) grimace ❑ **gesticular** vi to gesticulate; (hacer muecas) to grimace
gestión nf management; (diligencia, acción) negotiation ❑ **gestionar** vt (lograr) to try to arrange; (dirigir) to manage
gesto nm (mueca) grimace; (ademán) gesture
Gibraltar nm Gibraltar
❑ **gibraltareño, -a** adj, nm/f Gibraltarian
gigante adj, nmf giant ❑ **gigantesco, -a** adj gigantic
gilipollas (fam) adj inv stupid ♦ nmf inv dork (US), wally (BRIT)
gimnasia nf gymnastics pl ❑ **gimnasio** nm gymnasium ❑ **gimnasta** nmf gymnast
gimotear vi to whine, whimper
ginebra nf gin
ginecólogo, -a nm/f gynecologist (US), gynaecologist (BRIT)
gira nf tour, trip
girar vt (dar la vuelta) to turn (around); (: rápidamente) to spin; (COM: giro postal) to draw; (: letra de cambio) to issue ♦ vi to turn (round); (rápido) to spin
girasol nm sunflower
giratorio, -a adj revolving
giro nm (movimiento) turn, revolution; (LING) expression; (COM) draft ▶ **giro bancario/ postal** bank draft/money order
gis (MÉX) nm chalk
gitano, -a adj, nm/f gypsy
glacial adj icy, freezing
glaciar nm glacier
glándula nf gland
global adj global
globalización nf globalization
globo nm (esfera) globe, sphere; (aerostato, juguete) balloon

glóbulo nm globule; (ANAT) corpuscle
gloria nf glory
glorieta nf (de jardín) bower, arbor (US), arbour (BRIT); (plazoleta) traffic circle (US), roundabout (BRIT)
glorificar vt (enaltecer) to glorify, praise
glorioso, -a adj glorious
glotón, -ona adj gluttonous, greedy ♦ nm/f glutton
glucosa nf glucose
gobernador, a adj governing ♦ nm/f governor ❑ **gobernante** adj governing
gobernar vt (dirigir) to guide, direct; (POL) to rule, govern ♦ vi to govern; (NÁUT) to steer
gobierno etc vb ver **gobernar** ♦ nm (POL) government; (dirección) guidance, direction; (NÁUT) steering
goce etc vb ver **gozar** ♦ nm enjoyment
gol nm goal
golf nm golf
golfa (fam!) nf (mujer) slut, whore
golfo, -a nm (GEO) gulf ♦ nm/f (fam: niño) urchin; (gamberro) lout
golondrina nf swallow
golosina nf (dulce) candy (US), sweet (BRIT) ❑ **goloso, -a** adj sweet-toothed
golpe nm blow; (de puño) punch; (de mano) smack; (de remo) stroke; (fig: choque) clash; **no dar ~** to be bone idle; **de un ~** with one blow; **de ~** suddenly ▶ **golpe (de estado)** coup (d'état) ❑ **golpear** vt, vi to strike, knock; (asestar) to beat; (de puño) to punch; (golpetear) to tap
goma nf (caucho) rubber; (elástico) elastic; (una goma) rubber o elastic (BRIT) band ▶ **goma de borrar** eraser, rubber (BRIT) ▶ **goma de pegar** gum, glue ▶ **goma espuma** foam rubber
gomina nf hair gel
gomita (RPI) nf rubber o elastic (BRIT) band
googlear vi, vt to Google®
gordo, -a adj (gen) fat; (fam) enormous; **el (premio) ~** (en lotería) first prize ❑ **gordura** nf fat; (corpulencia) fatness, stoutness
gorila nm gorilla
gorjear vi to twitter, chirp
gorra nf cap; (de bebé) bonnet; (militar) bearskin; **entrar de ~** (fam) to gatecrash; **ir de ~** to sponge ▶ **gorra de baño** (LAm) swimming cap
gorrión nm sparrow
gorro nm (gen) cap; (de bebé, mujer) bonnet
gorrón, -ona nm/f scrounger ❑ **gorronear** (fam) vi to scrounge

gota nf (gen) drop; (de sudor) bead; (MED) gout
❑ **gotear** vi to drip; (lloviznar) to drizzle
❑ **gotera** nf leak

gozar vi to enjoy o.s.; ~ **de** (disfrutar) to enjoy; (poseer) to possess

gozne nm hinge

gozo nm (alegría) joy; (placer) pleasure

gr. abr (= gramo, gramos) g

grabación nf recording

grabado nm print, engraving

grabadora nf tape-recorder

grabar vt to engrave; (discos, cintas) to record

gracia nf (encanto) grace, gracefulness; (humor) humor (US), humour (BRIT), wit; **¡(muchas) ~s!** thanks (very much)!; **~s a** thanks to; **tener ~** (chiste etc) to be funny; **no me hace ~** I am not keen ❑ **gracioso, -a** adj (divertido) funny, amusing; (cómico) comical ♦ nm/f (TEATRO) comic character

grada nf (de escalera) step; (de anfiteatro) tier, row; **~s** nfpl (DEPORTE: de estadio) terraces

gradería nf (gradas) (flight of) steps pl; (de anfiteatro) tiers pl, rows pl; (DEPORTE: de estadio) terraces pl ▶ **gradería cubierta** covered stand

grado nm degree; (de aceite, vino) grade; (grada) step; (MIL) rank; **de buen ~** willingly

graduación nf (del alcohol) proof, strength; (ESCOL) graduation; (MIL) rank

gradual adj gradual

graduar vt (gen) to graduate; (MIL) to commission; **graduarse** vr to graduate; **~se la vista** to have one's eyes tested

gráfica nf graph

gráfico, -a adj graphic ♦ nm diagram; **~s** nmpl (INFORM) graphics

grajo nm rook

Gral abr (= General) Gen

gramática nf grammar

gramo nm gram (US), gramme (BRIT)

gran adj ver **grande**

grana nf (color, tela) scarlet

granada nf pomegranate; (MIL) grenade

granate adj deep red

Gran Bretaña nf Great Britain

grande (antes de nmsg: **gran**) adj (de tamaño) big, large; (alto) tall; (distinguido) great; (impresionante) grand ♦ nm grandee ❑ **grandeza** nf greatness

grandioso, -a adj magnificent, grand

granel: a ~ adv (COM) in bulk

granero nm granary, barn

granito nm (AGR) small grain; (roca) granite

granizado nm iced drink

granizar vi to hail ❑ **granizo** nm hail

granja nf (gen) farm ❑ **granjear** vt to win, gain ❑ **granjearse** vr to win, gain ❑ **granjero, -a** nm/f farmer

grano nm grain; (semilla) seed; (de café) bean; (MED) pimple, spot

granuja nmf rogue; (golfillo) urchin

grapa nf staple; (TEC) clamp ❑ **grapadora** nf stapler

grasa nf (gen) grease; (de cocinar) fat, lard; (sebo) suet; (mugre) filth ❑ **grasiento, -a** adj greasy; (de aceite) oily ❑ **graso, -a** adj (leche, queso, carne) fatty; (pelo, piel) greasy

gratificación nf (bono) bonus; (recompensa) reward

gratificar vt to reward

gratinar vt to cook au gratin

gratis adv free

gratitud nf gratitude

grato, -a adj (agradable) pleasant, agreeable

gratuito, -a adj (gratis) free; (sin razón) gratuitous

gravamen nm (impuesto) tax

gravar vt to tax

grave adj heavy; (serio) grave, serious ❑ **gravedad** nf gravity

gravilla nf gravel

gravitar vi to gravitate; ~ **sobre** to rest on

graznar vi (cuervo) to squawk; (pato) to quack; (hablar ronco) to croak

Grecia nf Greece

gremio nm trade, industry

greña nf (cabellos) shock of hair

gresca nf uproar

griego, -a adj, nm/f Greek

grieta nf crack

grifo (ESP) nm faucet (US), tap (BRIT)

grilletes nmpl fetters

grillo nm (ZOOL) cricket

gripa (MÉX), **gripe** nf flu, influenza

gris adj (color) gray (US), grey (BRIT)

gritar vt, vi to shout, yell ❑ **grito** nm shout, yell; (de horror) scream

grosella nf (red)currant ▶ **grosella negra** blackcurrant

grosería nf (actitud) rudeness; (comentario) vulgar comment ❑ **grosero, -a** adj (poco cortés) rude, bad-mannered; (ordinario) vulgar, crude

grosor nm thickness

grotesco, -a adj grotesque

grúa nf (TEC) crane; (de petróleo) derrick

grueso, -a adj thick; (persona) stout ♦ nm bulk; **el ~ de** the bulk of

grulla nf crane

grumo nm clot, lump

gruñido nm grunt; (de persona) grumble

gruñir vi (animal) to growl; (persona) to grumble

grupa nf (ZOOL) rump

grupo nm group; (TEC) unit, set

gruta nf grotto

guacho, -a nm/f (CS) homeless child

guadaña nf scythe

guajolote (MÉX) nm turkey

guante nm glove ❑ **guantera** nf glove compartment

guapo, -a adj good-looking, attractive; (elegante) smart

guarda nmf (persona) guard, keeper ♦ nf (acto) guarding; (custodia) custody ❑ **guardabarros** (LAm exc MÉX, ESP) nm inv fender (US), mudguard (BRIT) ❑ **guardabosques** nmf inv gamekeeper ❑ **guardacostas** nm inv coastguard vessel ♦ nmf guardian, protector ❑ **guardaespaldas** nmf inv bodyguard ❑ **guardameta** nmf goalkeeper ❑ **guardar** vt (gen) to keep; (vigilar) to guard, watch over; (dinero: ahorrar) to save; **guardarse** vr (preservarse) to protect o.s.; (evitar) to avoid; **guardar cama** to stay in bed ❑ **guardarropa** nm (armario) wardrobe; (en establecimiento público) checkroom (US), cloakroom (BRIT)

guardería nf nursery, daycare center (US)

guardia nf (MIL) guard; (cuidado) care, custody ♦ nmf guard; (policía) policeman(-woman); **estar de ~** to be on guard; **montar ~** to mount guard ▶ **Guardia Civil** Civil Guard ▶ **Guardia Nacional** National Guard

guardián, -ana nm/f (gen) guardian, keeper

guarecer vt (proteger) to protect; (abrigar) to shelter; **guarecerse** vr to take refuge

guarida nf (de animal) den, lair; (refugio) refuge

guarnecer vt (equipar) to provide; (adornar) to adorn; (TEC) to reinforce ❑ **guarnición** nf (de vestimenta) trimming; (de piedra) mount; (CULIN) garnish; (arneses) harness; (MIL) garrison

guarro, -a nm/f pig, hog (US)

guasa nf joke ❑ **guasón, -ona** adj (bromista) joking ♦ nm/f wit; joker

Guatemala nf Guatemala

guay (fam) adj super, great

gubernativo, -a adj governmental

güero, -a (MÉX) adj blond(e)

guerra nf war; **dar ~** to annoy ▶ **guerra civil** civil war ▶ **guerra fría** cold war ❑ **guerrear** vi to wage war ❑ **guerrero, -a** adj fighting; (carácter) warlike ♦ nm/f warrior

guerrilla nf guerrilla warfare; (tropas) guerrilla band o group

guía etc vb ver **guiar** ♦ nmf (persona) guide; (nf: libro) guidebook ▶ **guía de ferrocarriles** railroad (US) o railway (BRIT) timetable ▶ **guía telefónica** (LAm exc MÉX, ESP) telephone directory, phone book

guiar vt to guide, direct; (AUTO) to steer; **guiarse** vr: **~se por** to be guided by

guijarro nm pebble

guillotina nf guillotine

guinda nf morello cherry, sour cherry (US)

guindilla nf chil(l)i pepper

guiñapo nm (harapo) rag; (persona) reprobate, rogue

guiñar vt to wink

guión nm (LING) hyphen, dash; (CINE) script ❑ **guionista** nmf scriptwriter

guirnalda nf garland

guisado nm stew

guisante nm pea

guisar vt to cook ❑ **guiso** nm cooked dish

guitarra nf guitar

gula nf gluttony, greed

gusano nm worm; (lombriz) earthworm

gustar vt to taste, sample ♦ vi to please, be pleasing; **~ de algo** to like o enjoy sth; **me gustan las uvas** I like grapes; **le gusta nadar** she likes o enjoys swimming

gusto nm (sentido, sabor) taste; (placer) pleasure; **tiene ~ a menta** it tastes of mint; **tener buen ~** to have good taste; **sentirse a ~** to feel at ease; **mucho ~ (en conocerle)** pleased to meet you; **el ~ es mío** the pleasure is mine; **con ~** willingly, gladly ❑ **gustoso, -a** adj (sabroso) tasty; (agradable) pleasant

Hh

ha vb ver **haber**

haba nf bean

Habana nf: **la ~** Havana

habano nm Havana cigar

habéis vb ver **haber**

---
haber

PALABRA CLAVE

vb aux

1 (tiempos compuestos) to have; **había comido** I had eaten; **antes/después de haberlo visto** before seeing/after seeing o having seen it

2 ¡**haberlo dicho antes!** you should have said so before!

3 **haber de:** **he de hacerlo** I have to do it; **ha de llegar mañana** it should arrive tomorrow

♦ vb impers

1 (existencia: sg) there is; (: pl) there are; **hay un hermano/dos hermanos** there is one brother/there are two brothers; **¿cuánto hay de aquí a Acapulco?** how far is it from here to Acapulco?

2 (obligación): **hay que hacer algo** something must be done; **hay que apuntarlo para acordarse** you have to write it down to remember

3 ¡**hay que ver!** well I never!

4 ¡**no hay de** o (LAm) **por qué!** don't mention it, not at all!

5 **¿qué hay?** (¿qué pasa?) what's up?, what's the matter?; (¿qué tal?) how's it going?; **¿qué hubo?** (MÉX fam) how are things?

♦ **haberse** vr: **habérselas con algn** to have it out with sb

♦ vt: **he aquí unas sugerencias** here are some suggestions; **no hay cintas blancas pero sí las hay rojas** there aren't any white ribbons but there are some red ones

♦ nm (en cuenta) credit side; **haberes** nmpl assets; **¿cuánto tengo en el haber?** how much do I have in my account?; **tiene varias novelas en su haber** he has several novels to his credit

habichuela nf kidney bean

hábil adj (listo) clever, smart; (capaz) fit, capable; (experto) expert; **día ~** working day ❑ **habilidad** nf skill, ability

habilitar vt (capacitar) to enable; (dar instrumentos) to equip; (financiar) to finance

hábilmente adv expertly, skillfully (US), skilfully (BRIT)

habitación nf (cuarto) room; (BIO: morada) habitat ▸ **habitación doble** o **de matrimonio** double room ▸ **habitación individual** o **sencilla** single room

habitante nmf inhabitant

habitar vt (residir en) to inhabit; (ocupar) to occupy ♦ vi to live

hábito nm habit

habitual adj usual

habituar vt to accustom; **habituarse** vr: **~se a** to get used to

habla nf (capacidad de hablar) speech; (idioma) language; (dialecto) dialect; **perder el ~** to become speechless; **de ~ francesa** French-speaking; **estar al ~** to be in contact; (TEL) to be on the line; ¡**González al ~!** (TEL) González speaking!

hablador, a adj talkative; (MÉX: mentiroso) lying ♦ nm/f chatterbox

habladuría nf rumor (US), rumour (BRIT); **~s** nfpl gossip sg

hablante adj speaking ♦ nmf speaker

hablar vt to speak, talk; (MÉX TEL) to phone ♦ vi to speak; **hablarse** vr to speak to each other; **~ con** to speak to; **~ de** to speak of o about; **"se habla inglés"** "English spoken here"; ¡**ni ~!** it's out of the question!

habré etc vb ver **haber**

hacendado (LAm) nm rancher, farmer

hacendoso, -a adj industrious

---
hacer

PALABRA CLAVE

vt

1 (fabricar, producir) to make; (construir) to build; **hacer una película/un ruido** to make a movie (US) o film (BRIT)/noise ; **el guisado lo hice yo** I made o cooked the stew

2 (ejecutar trabajo etc) to do; **hacer la colada** to do the washing; **hacer la comida** to do the cooking; **¿qué haces?** what are you doing?; **hacer el malo** o **el papel del malo** (TEATRO) to play the villain

3 (estudios, algunos deportes) to do; **hacer español/económicas** to do o study Spanish/economics; **hacer yoga/gimnasia** to do yoga/go to gym

4 (transformar, incidir en): **esto lo hará más difícil** this will make it more difficult; **salir te hará sentir mejor** going out will make you feel better

5 (cálculo): **2 y 2 hacen 4** 2 and 2 make 4; **éste hace 100** this one makes 100

6 (+ subjun): **esto hará que ganemos** this will make us win; **harás que no quiera venir** you'll stop him wanting to come

7 (como sustituto de vb) to do; **él bebió y yo hice lo mismo** he drank and I did likewise

8: **no hace más que criticar** all he does is criticize

♦ *vb semi-aux*: **hacer** + *infin*

1 (*directo*): **les hice venir** I made *o* had them come; **hacer trabajar a los demás** to get others to work

2 (*por intermedio de otros*): **hacer reparar algo** to get sth repaired

♦ *vi*

1: **haz como que no lo sabes** act as if you don't know

2 (*ser apropiado*): **si os hace** if it's alright with you

3: **hacer de: hacer de madre para algn** to be like a mother to sb; (*TEATRO*): **hacer de Otelo** to play Othello

♦ *vb impers*

1: **hace calor/frío** it's hot/cold; *ver tb* **bueno, sol, tiempo**

2 (*tiempo*): **hace 3 años** 3 years ago; **hace un mes que voy/no voy** I've been going/I haven't been for a month

3: **¿cómo has hecho para llegar tan rápido?** how did you manage to get here so quickly?

♦ **hacerse** *vr*

1 (*volverse*) to become; **se hicieron amigos** they became friends

2 (*acostumbrarse*): **hacerse a** to get used to

3: **se hace con huevos y leche** it's made out of eggs and milk; **eso no se hace** that's not done

4 (*obtener*): **hacerse de** *o* **con algo** to get hold of sth

5 (*fingirse*): **hacerse el sueco** to turn a deaf ear

hacha *nf* ax (*US*), axe (*BRIT*); (*antorcha*) torch

hachís *nm* hashish

hacia *prep* (*en dirección de*) towards; (*cerca de*) near; (*actitud*) towards; **~ arriba/abajo** up(wards)/down(wards); **~ mediodía** about noon

hacienda *nf* (*propiedad*) property; (*finca*) farm; (*LAm: rancho*) ranch; (**Ministerio de) H~** Treasury Department (*US*), Exchequer (*BRIT*) ▶ **hacienda pública** public finance

hada *nf* fairy

hágalo usted mismo (*MÉX*) *nm* do-it-yourself

hago *etc vb ver* **hacer**

Haití *nm* Haiti

halagar *vt* to flatter

halago *nm* flattery ❑ **halagüeño, -a** *adj* flattering

halcón *nm* falcon, hawk

hallar *vt* (*gen*) to find; (*descubrir*) to discover; (*toparse con*) to run into; **hallarse** *vr* to be (*situated*) ❑ **hallazgo** *nm* discovery; (*cosa*) find

halterofilia *nf* weightlifting

hamaca *nf* hammock; (*RPl: columpio*) swing

hambre *nf* hunger; (*plaga*) famine; (*deseo*) longing; **tener ~** to be hungry ❑ **hambriento, -a** *adj* hungry, starving

hamburguesa *nf* hamburger ❑ **hamburguesería** *nf* burger bar

han *vb ver* **haber**

harapiento, -a *adj* tattered, in rags

harapos *nmpl* rags

haré *vb ver* **hacer**

harina *nf* flour

hartar *vt* to satiate, glut; (*fig*) to tire, sicken; **hartarse** *vr* (*de comida*) to fill o.s., gorge o.s.; (*cansarse*): **~se (de)** to get fed up (with) ❑ **hartazgo** *nm* surfeit, glut ❑ **harto, -a** *adj* (*lleno*) full; (*cansado*) fed up ♦ *adv* (*bastante*) enough; (*muy*) very; **estar harto de** to be fed up with

has *vb ver* **haber**

hasta *adv* even ♦ *prep* (*alcanzando a*) as far as; up to; down to; (*de tiempo: a tal hora*) till, until; (*antes de*) before ♦ *conj*: **~ que** until; **~ luego/ el sábado** see you soon/on Saturday

hastiar *vt* (*gen*) to weary; (*aburrir*) to bore; **hastiarse** *vr*: **~se de** to get fed up with ❑ **hastío** *nm* weariness; boredom

hatillo *nm* belongings *pl*, kit; (*montón*) bundle, heap

hay *vb ver* **haber**

Haya *nf*: **la ~** The Hague

haya *etc vb ver* **haber** ♦ *nf* beech tree

haz *vb ver* **hacer** ♦ *nm* (*de luz*) beam

hazaña *nf* feat, exploit

hazmerreír *nm inv* laughing stock

he *vb ver* **haber**

hebilla *nf* buckle, clasp

hebra *nf* thread; (*BOT: fibra*) grain, fiber (*US*), fibre (*BRIT*)

hebreo, -a *adj, nm/f* Hebrew ♦ *nm* (*LING*) Hebrew

hechizar *vt* to cast a spell on, bewitch

hechizo *nm* witchcraft, magic; (*acto de magia*) spell, charm

hecho, -a *pp de* **hacer** ♦ *adj* (*ESP: carne*) done; (*COSTURA*) ready-to-wear ♦ *nm* deed, act; (*dato*) fact; (*cuestión*) matter; (*suceso*) event ♦ *excl* agreed!, done!; **¡bien ~!** (*ESP*) well done!; **de ~** in fact, as a matter of fact

hechura nf (forma) form, shape; (de persona) build

hectárea nf hectare

heder vi to stink, smell

hediondo, -a adj stinking

hedor nm stench

helada nf frost

heladera (LAm) nf (refrigerador) refrigerator, icebox (US)

helado, -a adj frozen; (glacial) icy; (fig) chilly, cold ♦ nm ice cream ► **helado de agua** (CS) Popsicle® (US), ice lolly (BRIT)

helar vt to freeze, ice (up); (dejar atónito) to amaze; (desalentar) to discourage ♦ vi to freeze; **helarse** vr to freeze

helecho nm fern

hélice nf (TEC) propeller

helicóptero nm helicopter

hembra nf (BOT, ZOOL) female; (mujer) woman; (TEC) nut

hemorragia nf hemorrhage (US), haemorrhage (BRIT)

hemorroides nfpl piles, hemorrhoids (US), haemorrhoids (BRIT)

hemos vb ver **haber**

hendidura nf crack, split

heno nm hay

herbicida nm weedkiller

heredad nf landed property; (granja) farm

heredar vt to inherit ❏ **heredero, -a** nm/f heir(ess)

hereje nmf heretic

herencia nf inheritance

herida nf wound, injury; ver tb **herido**

herido, -a adj injured, wounded ♦ nm/f casualty

herir vt to wound, injure; (fig) to offend

hermanastro, -a nm/f stepbrother (-sister)

hermandad nf brotherhood

hermano, -a nm/f brother (sister) ► **hermano(-a) gemelo(-a)** twin brother (sister) ► **hermano(-a) político(-a)** brother-in-law (sister-in-law)

hermético, -a adj hermetic; (fig) watertight

hermoso, -a adj beautiful, lovely; (estupendo) splendid; (guapo) handsome ❏ **hermosura** nf beauty

hernia nf hernia

héroe nm hero

heroína nf (mujer) heroine; (droga) heroin

heroísmo nm heroism

herradura nf horseshoe

herramienta nf tool

herrero nm blacksmith

herrumbre nf rust

hervidero nm (fig) swarm; (POL etc) hotbed

hervir vi to boil; (burbujear) to bubble; (fig): ~ **de** to teem with; ~ **a fuego lento** to simmer ❏ **hervor** nm boiling; (fig) ardor (US), ardour (BRIT), fervor (US), fervour (BRIT)

heterosexual adj heterosexual

hice etc vb ver **hacer**

hidratante adj: **crema** ~ moisturizing cream, moisturizer ❏ **hidratar** vt (piel) to moisturize

hidrato nm hydrate ► **hidratos de carbono** carbohydrates

hidráulica nf hydraulics sg

hidráulico, -a adj hydraulic

hidro... prefijo hydro..., water-... ❏ **hidroeléctrico, -a** adj hydroelectric ❏ **hidrofobia** nf hydrophobia, rabies ❏ **hidrógeno** nm hydrogen

hiedra nf ivy

hiel nf gall, bile; (fig) bitterness

hiela etc vb ver **helar**

hielo nm (gen) ice; (escarcha) frost; (fig) coldness, reserve

hiena nf hyena

hierba nf (pasto) grass; (CULIN, MED: planta) herb; (LAm exc MÉX, ESP: fam: droga) pot; **mala** ~ (ESP) weed ❏ **hierbabuena** nf mint

hierro nm (metal) iron; (objeto) iron object

hígado nm liver

higiene nf hygiene ❏ **higiénico, -a** adj hygienic

higo nm fig ❏ **higuera** nf fig tree

hijastro, -a nm/f stepson(-daughter)

hijo, -a nm/f son (daughter), child; ~s nmpl children, sons and daughters ► **hijo de papá/mamá** daddy's/mummy's boy

hilar vt to spin; ~ **fino** to split hairs

hilera nf row, file

hilo nm thread; (BOT) fiber (US), fibre (BRIT); (metal) wire; (de agua) trickle, thin stream

hilvanar vt (COSTURA) to baste (US), tack (BRIT); (fig) to do hurriedly

himno nm hymn ► **himno nacional** national anthem

hincapié nm: hacer ~ **en** to emphasize

hincar vt to drive (in), thrust (in); **hincarse** vr: ~**se de rodillas** to kneel down

hincha (fam) nmf fan

hinchado, -a adj (gen) swollen; (persona) pompous

hinchar vt (gen) to swell; (inflar) to blow up, inflate; (fig) to exaggerate; **hincharse** vr (inflarse) to swell up; (fam: de comer) to stuff o.s. ◻ **hinchazón** nf (MED) swelling; (altivez) arrogance

hinojo nm fennel

hipermercado (ESP) nm superstore, hypermarket (BRIT)

hípico, -a adj horse cpd

hipnotismo nm hypnotism ◻ **hipnotizar** vt to hypnotize

hipo nm hiccups pl

hipocresía nf hypocrisy ◻ **hipócrita** adj hypocritical ◆ nmf hypocrite

hipódromo nm racecourse

hipopótamo nm hippopotamus

hipoteca nf mortgage

hipótesis nf inv hypothesis

hiriente adj offensive, wounding

hispánico, -a adj Hispanic

hispano, -a adj Hispanic, Spanish, Hispano-◆ nm/f Spaniard ◻ **Hispanoamérica** nf Latin America ◻ **hispanoamericano, -a** adj, nm/f Latin American

histeria nf hysteria

historia nf history; (cuento) story, tale; ~s nfpl (chismes) gossip sg; **dejarse de ~s** to come to the point; **pasar a la ~** to go down in history ◻ **historiador, a** nm/f historian ◻ **historial** nm (profesional) résumé (US), curriculum vitae (BRIT), C.V. (BRIT); (MED) case history ◻ **histórico, -a** adj historical; (memorable) historic

historieta nf tale, anecdote; (dibujos) comic strip

hito nm (fig) landmark

hizo vb ver **hacer**

Hnos abr (= Hermanos) Bros

hocico nm snout

hockey nm field hockey (US), hockey (BRIT) ▶ **hockey sobre hielo** hockey (US), ice hockey (BRIT)

hogar nm fireplace, hearth; (casa) home; (vida familiar) home life ◻ **hogareño, -a** adj home cpd; (persona) home-loving

hoguera nf (gen) bonfire

hoja nf (gen) leaf; (de flor) petal; (de papel) sheet; (página) page ▶ **hoja de afeitar** (LAm) razor blade ▶ **hoja de rasurar** (MÉX) razor blade ▶ **hoja electrónica o de cálculo** spreadsheet

hojalata nf tin(plate)

hojaldre nm (CULIN) puff pastry

hojear vt to leaf through, turn the pages of

hojuela (MÉX) nf flake ▶ **hojuelas de avena** porridge

hola excl hello!

holá (RPI) excl hello?

Holanda nf Holland ◻ **holandés, -esa** adj Dutch ◆ nm/f Dutchman(-woman) ◆ nm (LING) Dutch

holgado, -a adj (ropa) loose, baggy; (rico) comfortable

holgar vi (descansar) to rest; (sobrar) to be superfluous; **huelga decir que** it goes without saying that

holgazán, -ana adj idle, lazy ◆ nm/f loafer

holgura nf looseness, bagginess; (TEC) play, free movement; (vida) comfortable living

hollín nm soot

hombre nm (gen) man; (raza humana): **el ~** man(kind) ◆ excl: **¡sí ~! (claro)** of course!; (para énfasis) man, old boy ▶ **hombre de negocios** businessman ▶ **hombre de pro** honest man ▶ **hombre-rana** frogman

hombrera nf shoulder strap

hombro nm shoulder

hombruno, -a adj mannish

homenaje nm (gen) homage; (tributo) tribute

homicida adj homicidal ◆ nmf murderer ◻ **homicidio** nm murder, homicide

homologar vt (COM: productos, tamaños) to standardize ◻ **homólogo, -a** nm/f: **su** etc **homólogo** his etc counterpart o opposite number

homosexual adj, nmf homosexual

honda (CS) nf slingshot (US), catapult (BRIT); ver tb **hondo**

hondo, -a adj deep; **lo ~** the depth(s) pl, the bottom ◻ **hondonada** nf hollow, depression; (cañón) ravine

Honduras nf Honduras

hondureño, -a adj, nm/f Honduran

honestidad nf purity, chastity; (decencia) decency ◻ **honesto, -a** adj chaste; decent; honest; (justo) just

hongo nm (BOT: gen) fungus; (LAm: comestible) mushroom; (: venenoso) toadstool

honor nm (gen) honor (US), honour (BRIT); **en ~ a la verdad** to be fair ◻ **honorable** adj honorable (US), honourable (BRIT)

honorario, -a adj honorary ◻ **honorarios** nmpl fees

honra nf (gen) honor (US), honour (BRIT); (renombre) good name ◻ **honradez** nf honesty; (de persona) integrity ◻ **honrado, -a** adj honest, upright

honrar vt to honor (US), honour (BRIT); **honrarse** vr: ~**se con algo/de hacer algo** to be honored (US) o honoured (BRIT) by sth/to do sth

honroso, -a adj (honrado) honorable (US), honourable (BRIT); (respetado) respectable

hora nf (una hora) hour; (tiempo) time; **¿qué ~ es?** what time is it?; **¿a qué ~?** at what time?; **media ~** half an hour; **a la ~ de recreo** at playtime o (US) recess; **a primera ~** first thing (in the morning); **a última ~** at the last moment; **a altas ~s** in the small hours; **¡a buena ~!** about time too!; **dar la ~** to strike the hour ▶ **horas de oficina/de trabajo** office/working hours ▶ **horas de visita** visiting times ▶ **horas extras** o **extraordinarias** overtime sg ▶ **horas pico** (LAm) rush o peak hours ▶ **horas punta** (ESP) rush o peak hours

horadar vt to drill, bore

horario, -a adj hourly, hour cpd ♦ nm timetable ▶ **horario comercial** business hours pl

horca nf gallows sg

horcajadas: a ~ adv astride

horchata nf cold drink made from tiger nuts and water, tiger nut milk

horizontal adj horizontal

horizonte nm horizon

horma nf mold (US), mould (BRIT)

hormiga nf ant; **~s** nfpl (MED) pins and needles

hormigón nm concrete ▶ **hormigón armado/pretensado** reinforced/prestressed concrete

hormigonera nf cement mixer

hormigueo nm (comezón) itch

hormona nf hormone

hornada nf batch (of loaves etc)

hornillo nm (cocina) portable stove

horno nm (CULIN) oven; (TEC) furnace; **alto ~** blast furnace

horóscopo nm horoscope

horquilla nf hairpin; (AGR) pitchfork; (MÉX: de ropa) clothes pin (US) o peg (BRIT)

horrendo, -a adj horrendous, frightful

horrible adj horrible, dreadful

horripilante adj hair-raising, horrifying

horror nm horror, dread; (atrocidad) atrocity; **¡qué ~!** (fam) how awful! ☐ **horrorizar** vt to horrify, frighten; **horrorizarse** vr to be horrified ☐ **horroroso, -a** adj horrifying, ghastly

hortaliza nf vegetable

hortelano, -a nm/f truck farmer (US), (market) gardener (BRIT)

hortera (ESP: fam) adj tacky

hosco, -a adj sullen, gloomy

hospedar vt to put up; **hospedarse** vr to stay, lodge

hospital nm hospital

hospitalario, -a adj (acogedor) hospitable ☐ **hospitalidad** nf hospitality

hostal nm small hotel

hostelería nf hotel business o trade

hostia nf (REL) host, consecrated wafer; (fam!: golpe) whack, punch ♦ excl (fam!): **¡~(s)!** damn!

hostigar vt to whip; (fig) to harass, pester

hostil adj hostile ☐ **hostilidad** nf hostility

hotdog (LAm) nm hot dog

hotel nm hotel ☐ **hotelero, -a** adj hotel cpd ♦ nm/f hotelier

hoy adv (este día) today; (la actualidad) now(adays) ♦ nm present time; **~ (en) día** now(adays)

hoyo nm hole, pit ☐ **hoyuelo** nm dimple

hoz nf sickle

hube etc vb ver **haber**

hucha (ESP) nf money box

hueco, -a adj (vacío) hollow, empty; (resonante) booming ♦ nm hollow, cavity; (LAm: vacío) gap

huelga etc vb ver **holgar** ♦ nf strike; **declararse en ~** to go on strike, come out on strike ▶ **huelga de hambre** hunger strike

huelguista nmf striker

huella nf (pisada) tread; (marca del paso) footprint, footstep; (: de animal, máquina) track ▶ **huella digital** fingerprint

huelo etc vb ver **oler**

huérfano, -a adj orphan(ed) ♦ nm/f orphan

huerta nf truck farm (US), market garden (BRIT); (en Murcia y Valencia) irrigated region

huerto nm kitchen garden; (de árboles frutales) orchard

hueso nm (ANAT) bone; (de fruta) pit (US), stone (BRIT)

huésped, -a nm/f guest

huesudo, -a adj bony, big-boned

hueva nf roe

huevera nf eggcup

huevo nm egg ▶ **huevo a la copa** (CS) soft-boiled egg ▶ **huevo duro/escalfado** hard-boiled/poached egg ▶ **huevo estrellado** (LAm) fried egg ▶ **huevo frito** (ESP) fried egg ▶ **huevo pasado por agua** (LAm exc MÉX, ESP) soft-boiled egg ▶ **huevo tibio** (MÉX) soft-boiled egg ▶ **huevos revueltos** scrambled eggs

huida *nf* escape, flight

huidizo, -a *adj* shy

huir *vi* (*escapar*) to flee, escape; (*evitar*) to avoid; **huirse** *vr* (*MÉX: escaparse*) to escape

hule *nm* oilskin; (*MÉX: goma*) rubber

hulera (*MÉX*) *nf* slingshot (*US*), catapult (*BRIT*)

humanidad *nf* (*género humano*) man(kind); (*cualidad*) humanity

humanitario, -a *adj* humanitarian

humano, -a *adj* (*gen*) human; (*humanitario*) humane ♦ *nm* human; **ser ~** human being

humareda *nf* cloud of smoke

humedad *nf* (*de clima*) humidity; (*de pared etc*) dampness; **a prueba de ~** damp-proof ❑ **humedecer** *vt* to moisten, wet; **humedecerse** *vr* to get wet

húmedo, -a *adj* (*mojado*) damp, wet; (*tiempo etc*) humid

humildad *nf* humility, humbleness ❑ **humilde** *adj* humble, modest

humillación *nf* humiliation ❑ **humillante** *adj* humiliating

humillar *vt* to humiliate; **humillarse** *vr* to humble o.s., grovel

humo *nm* (*de fuego*) smoke; (*gas nocivo*) fumes *pl*; (*vapor*) vapor (*US*), vapour (*BRIT*); **~s** *nmpl* (*fig*) conceit *sg*

humor *nm* (*disposición*) mood, temper; (*lo que divierte*) humor (*US*), humour (*BRIT*); **de buen/mal ~** in a good/bad mood ❑ **humorista** *nmf* comic ❑ **humorístico, -a** *adj* funny, humorous

hundimiento *nm* (*gen*) sinking; (*colapso*) collapse

hundir *vt* to sink; (*edificio, plan*) to ruin, destroy; **hundirse** *vr* to sink, collapse

húngaro, -a *adj, nm/f* Hungarian

Hungría *nf* Hungary

huracán *nm* hurricane

huraño, -a *adj* (*antisocial*) unsociable

hurgar *vt* to poke, jab; (*remover*) to stir (up); **hurgarse** *vr*: **~se (las narices)** to pick one's nose

hurón, -ona *nm* (*ZOOL*) ferret

hurtadillas: a ~ *adv* stealthily, on the sly

hurtar *vt* to steal ❑ **hurto** *nm* theft, stealing

husmear *vt* (*oler*) to sniff out, scent; (*fam*) to pry into

huyo *etc vb ver* **huir**

Ii

iba *etc vb ver* **ir**

ibérico, -a *adj* Iberian

iberoamericano, -a *adj, nm/f* Latin American

Ibiza *nf* Ibiza

iceberg *nm* iceberg

icono *nm* ikon, icon

iconoclasta *adj* iconoclastic ♦ *nmf* iconoclast

ictericia *nf* jaundice

I + D *abr* (= *Investigación y Desarrollo*) R & D

ida *nf* going, departure; **~ y vuelta** round trip (*US*), return (*BRIT*)

idea *nf* idea; **no tengo la menor ~** I haven't a clue

ideal *adj, nm* ideal ❑ **idealista** *nmf* idealist ❑ **idealizar** *vt* to idealize

idear *vt* to think up; (*aparato*) to invent; (*viaje*) to plan

ídem *pron* ditto

idéntico, -a *adj* identical

identidad *nf* identity

identificación *nf* identification

identificar *vt* to identify; **identificarse** *vr*: **~se con** to identify with

ideología *nf* ideology

idilio *nm* love-affair

idioma *nm* (*gen*) language

⚠ No confundir **idioma** con la palabra inglesa *idiom*.

idiota *adj* idiotic ♦ *nmf* idiot ❑ **idiotez** *nf* idiocy

ídolo *nm* (*tb: fig*) idol

idóneo, -a *adj* suitable

iglesia *nf* church

ignorancia *nf* ignorance ❑ **ignorante** *adj* ignorant, uninformed ♦ *nmf* ignoramus

ignorar *vt* not to know, be ignorant of; (*no hacer caso a*) to ignore

igual *adj* (*gen*) equal; (*similar*) like, similar; (*mismo*) (the) same; (*constante*) constant; (*temperatura*) even ♦ *nmf* equal; **~ que** like, the same as; **me da o es ~** I don't care; **son ~es** they're the same; **al ~ que** (*prep, conj*) like, just like

igualada *nf* equaliser

igualar *vt* (*gen*) to equalize, make equal; (*allanar, nivelar*) to level (off), even (out); **igualarse** *vr* (*platos de balanza*) to balance out

igualdad nf equality; (similitud) sameness; (uniformidad) uniformity

igualmente adv equally; (también) also, likewise ♦ excl the same to you!

ikurriña nf Basque flag

ilegal adj illegal

ilegítimo, -a adj illegitimate

ileso, -a adj unhurt

ilícito, -a adj illicit

ilimitado, -a adj unlimited

ilógico, -a adj illogical

iluminación nf illumination; (alumbrado) lighting

iluminar vt to illuminate, light (up); (fig) to enlighten

ilusión nf illusion; (quimera) delusion; (esperanza) hope; **hacerse ilusiones** to build up one's hopes ❑ **ilusionado, -a** adj excited ❑ **ilusionar** vi: **le ilusiona ir de vacaciones** he's looking forward to going on vacation (US) o holiday (BRIT); **ilusionarse** vr: **ilusionarse (con)** to get excited (about)

ilusionista nmf conjurer

iluso, -a adj easily deceived ♦ nm/f dreamer

ilusorio, -a adj (de ilusión) illusory, deceptive; (esperanza) vain

ilustración nf illustration; (saber) learning, erudition; **la l~** the Enlightenment ❑ **ilustrado, -a** adj illustrated; learned

ilustrar vt to illustrate; (instruir) to instruct; (explicar) to explain, make clear; **ilustrarse** vr to acquire knowledge

ilustre adj famous, illustrious

imagen nf (gen) image; (dibujo) picture

imaginación nf imagination

imaginar vt (gen) to imagine; (idear) to think up; (suponer) to suppose; **imaginarse** vr to imagine ❑ **imaginario, -a** adj imaginary ❑ **imaginativo, -a** adj imaginative

imán nm magnet

imbécil nmf imbecile, idiot

imitación nf imitation

imitar vt to imitate; (parodiar, remedar) to mimic, ape

impaciencia nf impatience ❑ **impaciente** adj impatient; (nervioso) anxious

impacto nm impact

impalpable (RPI) adj: **azúcar ~** confectioner's sugar (US)

impar adj odd

imparcial adj impartial, fair

impartir vt to impart, give

impasible adj impassive

impecable adj impeccable

impedimento nm impediment, obstacle

impedir vt (obstruir) to impede, obstruct; (estorbar) to prevent

impenetrable adj impenetrable; (fig) incomprehensible

imperar vi (reinar) to rule, reign; (fig) to prevail, reign; (precio) to be current

imperativo, -a adj (urgente, LING) imperative

imperceptible adj imperceptible

imperdible (LAm exc MÉX, ESP) nm safety pin

imperdonable adj unforgivable, inexcusable

imperfección nf imperfection

imperfecto, -a adj imperfect

imperial adj imperial ❑ **imperialismo** nm imperialism

imperio nm empire; (autoridad) rule, authority; (fig) pride, haughtiness ❑ **imperioso, -a** adj imperious; (urgente) urgent; (imperativo) imperative

impermeable adj waterproof ♦ nm raincoat, mac (BRIT)

impersonal adj impersonal

impertinencia nf impertinence ❑ **impertinente** adj impertinent

imperturbable adj imperturbable

ímpetu nm (impulso) impetus, impulse; (impetuosidad) impetuosity; (violencia) violence

impetuoso, -a adj impetuous; (río) rushing; (acto) hasty

impío, -a adj impious, ungodly

implacable adj implacable

implantar vt to introduce

implemento (LAm) nm tool, implement

implicar vt to involve; (entrañar) to imply

implícito, -a adj (tácito) implicit; (sobreentendido) implied

implorar vt to beg, implore

imponente adj (impresionante) impressive, imposing; (solemne) grand

imponer vt (gen) to impose; (exigir) to exact; **imponerse** vr to assert o.s.; (prevalecer) to prevail ❑ **imponible** adj (COM) taxable

impopular adj unpopular

importación nf (acto) importing; (mercancías) imports pl

importancia nf importance; (valor) value, significance; (extensión) size, magnitude ❑ **importante** adj important; valuable, significant

importar vt (del extranjero) to import; (costar) to amount to ♦ vi to be important, matter; **me importa un rábano** I couldn't care less; **no importa** it doesn't matter; **¿le importa que fume?** do you mind if I smoke?

importe nm (total) amount; (valor) value

importunar vt to bother, pester

imposibilidad nf impossibility ❑ **imposibilitar** vt to make impossible, prevent

imposible adj (gen) impossible; (insoportable) unbearable, intolerable

imposición nf imposition; (COM: impuesto) tax; (: inversión) deposit

impostor, a nm/f impostor

impotencia nf impotence ❑ **impotente** adj impotent

impracticable adj (irrealizable) impracticable; (intransitable) impassable

impreciso, -a adj imprecise, vague

impregnar vt to impregnate; **impregnarse** vr to become impregnated

imprenta nf (acto) printing; (aparato) press; (casa) printer's; (letra) print

imprescindible adj essential, vital

impresión nf (gen) impression; (IMPRENTA) printing; (edición) edition; (FOTO) print; (marca) imprint ▶ **impresión digital** fingerprint

impresionable adj (sensible) impressionable

impresionante adj impressive; (tremendo) tremendous; (maravilloso) great, marvelous (US), marvellous (BRIT)

impresionar vt (conmover) to move; (afectar) to impress, strike; (película fotográfica) to expose; **impresionarse** vr to be impressed; (conmoverse) to be moved

impreso, -a pp de **imprimir** ♦ adj printed ♦ nm (ESP: formulario) form ❑ **impresora** nf printer ❑ **impresos** nmpl printed matter

imprevisto, -a adj (gen) unforeseen; (inesperado) unexpected

imprimir vt to imprint, impress, stamp; (textos) to print; (INFORM) to output, print out

improbable adj improbable; (inverosímil) unlikely

improcedente adj inappropriate

improductivo, -a adj unproductive

improperio nm insult

impropio, -a adj improper

improvisado, -a adj improvised

improvisar vt to improvise

improviso, -a adj: **de ~** unexpectedly, suddenly

imprudencia nf imprudence; (indiscreción) indiscretion; (descuido) carelessness ❑ **imprudente** adj unwise, imprudent; (indiscreto) indiscreet

impúdico, -a adj shameless; (lujurioso) lecherous

impuesto, -a adj imposed ♦ nm tax ▶ **impuesto al valor agregado** o **añadido** (LAm) ≈ sales tax (US), value added tax (BRIT) ▶ **impuesto sobre el valor añadido** (ESP) ≈ sales tax (US), value added tax (BRIT)

impugnar vt to oppose, contest; (refutar) to refute, impugn

impulsar vt to drive; (promover) to promote, stimulate

impulsivo, -a adj impulsive ❑ **impulso** nm impulse; (fuerza, empuje) thrust, drive; (fig: sentimiento) urge, impulse

impune adj unpunished

impureza nf impurity ❑ **impuro, -a** adj impure

imputar vt to attribute

inacabable adj (infinito) endless; (interminable) interminable

inaccesible adj inaccessible

inacción nf inactivity

inaceptable adj unacceptable

inactividad nf inactivity; (COM) dullness ❑ **inactivo, -a** adj inactive

inadecuado, -a adj (insuficiente) inadequate; (inapto) unsuitable

inadmisible adj inadmissible

inadvertido, -a adj (no visto) unnoticed

inagotable adj inexhaustible

inaguantable adj unbearable

inalterable adj immutable, unchangeable

inanición nf starvation

inanimado, -a adj inanimate

inapreciable adj (cantidad, diferencia) imperceptible; (ayuda, servicio) invaluable

inaudito, -a adj unheard-of

inauguración nf inauguration; opening

inaugurar vt to inaugurate; (exposición) to open

inca nmf Inca

incalculable adj incalculable

incandescente adj incandescent

incansable adj tireless, untiring

incapacidad nf incapacity; (incompetencia) incompetence ▶ **incapacidad física/ mental** physical/mental disability

incapacitar vt (inhabilitar) to incapacitate, render unfit; (descalificar) to disqualify

incapaz adj incapable

incautación nf confiscation

incautarse vr: ~ **de** to seize, confiscate

incauto, -a adj (imprudente) incautious, unwary

incendiar vt to set fire to; (fig) to inflame; **incendiarse** vr to catch fire
❏ **incendiario, -a** adj incendiary

incendio nm fire

incentivo nm incentive

incertidumbre nf (inseguridad) uncertainty; (duda) doubt

incesante adj incessant

incesto nm incest

incidencia nf (MAT) incidence

incidente nm incident

incidir vi (influir) to influence; (afectar) to affect; ~ **en un error** to fall into error

incienso nm incense

incierto, -a adj uncertain

incineración nf incineration; (de cadáveres) cremation

incinerar vt to burn; (cadáveres) to cremate

incipiente adj incipient

incisión nf incision

incisivo, -a adj sharp, cutting; (fig) incisive

incitar vt to incite, rouse

inclemencia nf (severidad) harshness, severity; (del tiempo) inclemency

inclinación nf (gen) inclination; (de tierras) slope, incline; (de cabeza) nod, bow; (fig) leaning, bent

inclinar vt to incline; (cabeza) to nod, bow ♦ vi to lean, slope; **inclinarse** vr to bow; (encorvarse) to stoop; ~**se a** (parecerse a) to take after, resemble; ~**se ante** to bow down to; **me inclino a pensar que** I'm inclined to think that

incluir vt to include; (incorporar) to incorporate; (meter) to enclose

inclusive adv inclusive ♦ prep including

incluso adv even

incógnita nf (MAT) unknown quantity

incógnito nm: **de ~** incognito

incoherente adj incoherent

incoloro, -a adj colorless (US), colourless (BRIT)

incólume adj unhurt, unharmed

incomodar vt to inconvenience; (molestar) to bother, trouble; (fastidiar) to annoy; **incomodarse** vr to put o.s. out; (fastidiarse) to get annoyed

incomodidad nf inconvenience; (fastidio, enojo) annoyance; (de vivienda) discomfort

incómodo, -a adj (silla, situación) uncomfortable; (molesto) annoying; (inconveniente) inconvenient

incomparable adj incomparable

incompatible adj incompatible

incompetencia nf incompetence
❏ **incompetente** adj incompetent

incompleto, -a adj incomplete, unfinished

incomprensible adj incomprehensible

incomunicado, -a adj (aislado) cut off, isolated; (confinado) in solitary confinement

inconcebible adj inconceivable

incondicional adj unconditional; (apoyo) wholehearted; (partidario) staunch

inconexo, -a adj (gen) unconnected; (desunido) disconnected

inconfundible adj unmistakable

incongruente adj incongruous

inconsciencia nf unconsciousness; (fig) thoughtlessness ❏ **inconsciente** adj unconscious; thoughtless

inconsecuente adj inconsistent

inconsiderado, -a adj inconsiderate

inconsistente adj weak; (tela) flimsy

inconstancia nf inconstancy; (inestabilidad) unsteadiness ❏ **inconstante** adj inconstant

incontable adj countless, innumerable

incontestable adj unanswerable; (innegable) undeniable

incontinencia nf incontinence

inconveniencia nf unsuitability, inappropriateness; (descortesía) impoliteness ❏ **inconveniente** adj unsuitable; impolite ♦ nm obstacle; (desventaja) disadvantage; **el inconveniente es que ...** the trouble is that ...

incordiar (fam) vt to bug, annoy

incorporación nf incorporation

incorporar vt to incorporate; **incorporarse** vr to sit up

incorrección nf (gen) incorrectness, inaccuracy; (descortesía) bad-mannered behavior (US) o behaviour (BRIT)
❏ **incorrecto, -a** adj (gen) incorrect, wrong; (comportamiento) bad-mannered

incorregible adj incorrigible

incredulidad nf incredulity; (escepticismo) skepticism (US), scepticism (BRIT)
❏ **incrédulo, -a** adj incredulous, unbelieving; skeptical (US), sceptical (BRIT)

increíble adj incredible

incremento nm increment; (aumento) rise, increase

increpar vt to reprimand

incruento, -a adj bloodless

incrustar *vt* to incrust; *(piedras: en joya)* to inlay

incubar *vt* to incubate

inculcar *vt* to inculcate

inculpar *vt (acusar)* to accuse; *(achacar, atribuir)* to charge, blame

inculto, -a *adj (persona)* uneducated; *(grosero)* uncouth ♦ *nm/f* ignoramus

incumplimiento *nm* non-fulfillment *(US)*, non-fulfilment *(BRIT)*; **~ de contrato** breach of contract

incurrir *vi*: **~ en** to incur; *(crimen)* to commit; **~ en un error** to make a mistake

indagación *nf* investigation; *(búsqueda)* search; *(JUR)* inquest

indagar *vt* to investigate; to search; *(averiguar)* to ascertain

indecente *adj* indecent, improper; *(lascivo)* obscene

indecible *adj* unspeakable; *(indescriptible)* indescribable

indeciso, -a *adj (por decidir)* undecided; *(vacilante)* hesitant

indefenso, -a *adj* defenseless *(US)*, defenceless *(BRIT)*

indefinido, -a *adj* indefinite; *(vago)* vague, undefined

indeleble *adj* indelible

indemne *adj (objeto)* undamaged; *(persona)* unharmed, unhurt

indemnizar *vt* to indemnify; *(compensar)* to compensate

independencia *nf* independence ▶ **Día de la Independencia** Independence Day

DÍA DE LA INDEPENDENCIA

Every Latin American country celebrates its Independence Day according to the continent's colonial history. In Mexico, these celebrations are known as **El Grito** ("The Cry"), in commemoration of the 16th September 1810, when Father Hidalgo rang the bell of his church to summon the Mexican people to fight for their independence. The celebrations begin in the afternoon of September 15th, with food, Mariachi music, fireworks and dancing, and culminate in the main square at midnight, when the town mayor rings the bell and gives "The Cry".

independiente *adj (libre)* independent; *(autónomo)* self-sufficient

indeterminado, -a *adj* indefinite; *(desconocido)* indeterminate

India *nf*: **la ~** India

indicación *nf* indication; *(señal)* sign; *(sugerencia)* suggestion, hint

indicado, -a *adj (momento, método)* right; *(tratamiento)* appropriate; *(solución)* likely

indicador *nm* indicator; *(TEC)* meter, gauge, gage *(US)*

indicar *vt (mostrar)* to indicate, show; *(termómetro etc)* to read, register; *(señalar)* to point to

índice *nm* index; *(catálogo)* catalogue, catalog *(US)*; *(ANAT)* index finger, forefinger

indicio *nm* indication, sign; *(en pesquisa etc)* clue

indiferencia *nf* indifference; *(apatía)* apathy ❑ **indiferente** *adj* indifferent

indígena *adj* indigenous, native ♦ *nmf* native

indigencia *nf* poverty, need

indigestión *nf* indigestion

indigesto, -a *adj (alimento)* indigestible; *(fig)* turgid

indignación *nf* indignation

indignar *vt* to anger, make indignant; **indignarse** *vr*: **~se por** to get indignant about

indigno, -a *adj (despreciable)* low, contemptible; *(inmerecido)* unworthy

indio, -a *adj, nm/f* Indian

indirecta *nf* insinuation, innuendo; *(sugerencia)* hint

indirecto, -a *adj* indirect

indiscreción *nf (imprudencia)* indiscretion; *(irreflexión)* tactlessness; *(acto)* gaffe, faux pas

indiscreto, -a *adj* indiscreet

indiscriminado, -a *adj* indiscriminate

indiscutible *adj* indisputable, unquestionable

indispensable *adj* indispensable, essential

indisponer *vt* to spoil, upset; *(salud)* to make ill; **indisponerse** *vr* to fall ill; **~se con algn** to fall out with sb

indisposición *nf* indisposition

indispuesto, -a *adj (enfermo)* unwell, indisposed

indistinto, -a *adj* indistinct; *(vago)* vague

individual *adj* individual; *(habitación)* single ♦ *nm (DEPORTE)* singles *sg*

individuo, -a *adj, nm* individual

índole *nf (naturaleza)* nature; *(clase)* sort, kind

indómito, -a *adj* indomitable

inducir *vt* to induce; *(inferir)* to infer; *(persuadir)* to persuade

indudable *adj* undoubted; *(incuestionable)* unquestionable

indulgencia *nf* indulgence
indultar *vt* (*perdonar*) to pardon, reprieve; (*librar de pago*) to exempt ❏ **indulto** *nm* pardon; exemption
industria *nf* industry; (*habilidad*) skill ❏ **industrial** *adj* industrial ♦ *nm* industrialist
inédito, -a *adj* (*texto*) unpublished; (*nuevo*) new
inefable *adj* ineffable, indescribable
ineficaz *adj* (*inútil*) ineffective; (*ineficiente*) inefficient
ineludible *adj* inescapable, unavoidable
ineptitud *nf* ineptitude, incompetence ❏ **inepto, -a** *adj* inept, incompetent
inequívoco, -a *adj* unequivocal; (*inconfundible*) unmistakable
inercia *nf* inertia; (*pasividad*) passivity
inerme *adj* (*sin armas*) unarmed; (*indefenso*) defenseless (*US*), defenceless (*BRIT*)
inerte *adj* inert; (*inmóvil*) motionless
inesperado, -a *adj* unexpected, unforeseen
inestable *adj* unstable
inevitable *adj* inevitable
inexactitud *nf* inaccuracy ❏ **inexacto, -a** *adj* inaccurate; (*falso*) untrue
inexperto, -a *adj* (*novato*) inexperienced
infalible *adj* infallible; (*plan*) foolproof
infame *adj* infamous; (*horrible*) dreadful ❏ **infamia** *nf* infamy; (*deshonra*) disgrace
infancia *nf* infancy, childhood
infantería *nf* infantry
infantil *adj* (*pueril, aniñado*) infantile; (*cándido*) childlike; (*literatura, ropa etc*) children's
infarto *nm* (*tb: ~ de miocardio*) heart attack
infatigable *adj* tireless, untiring
infección *nf* infection ❏ **infeccioso, -a** *adj* infectious
infectar *vt* to infect; **infectarse** *vr* to become infected
infeliz *adj* unhappy, wretched ♦ *nmf* wretch
inferior *adj* inferior; (*situación*) lower ♦ *nmf* inferior, subordinate
inferir *vt* (*deducir*) to infer, deduce; (*causar*) to cause
infestar *vt* to infest
infidelidad *nf* (*gen*) infidelity, unfaithfulness
infiel *adj* unfaithful, disloyal; (*erróneo*) inaccurate ♦ *nmf* infidel, unbeliever
infierno *nm* hell
infiltrarse *vr*: ~ **en** to infiltrate in(to); (*persona*) to work one's way in(to)

ínfimo, -a *adj* (*más bajo*) lowest; (*despreciable*) vile, mean
infinidad *nf* infinity; (*abundancia*) great quantity
infinito, -a *adj, nm* infinite
inflación *nf* (*hinchazón*) swelling; (*monetaria*) inflation; (*fig*) conceit ❏ **inflacionario, -a** *adj* inflationary
inflamable *adj* flammable
inflamar *vt* (*MED: fig*) to inflame; **inflamarse** *vr* to catch fire; to become inflamed
inflar *vt* (*hinchar*) to inflate, blow up; (*fig*) to exaggerate; **inflarse** *vr* to swell (up); (*fig*) to get conceited
inflexible *adj* inflexible; (*fig*) unbending
infligir *vt* to inflict
influencia *nf* influence ❏ **influenciar** *vt* to influence
influir *vt* to influence
influjo *nm* influence
influya *etc vb ver* **influir**
influyente *adj* influential
información *nf* information; (*noticias*) news *sg*; (*JUR*) inquiry; **I~** (*oficina*) Information Office; (*mostrador*) Information Desk; (*TEL*) directory assistance (*US*), directory enquiries (*BRIT*)
informal *adj* (*gen*) informal
informar *vt* (*gen*) to inform; (*revelar*) to reveal, make known ♦ *vi* (*JUR*) to plead; (*denunciar*) to inform; (*dar cuenta de*) to report on; **informarse** *vr* to find out; **~se de** to inquire into
informática *nf* computer science, information technology
informe *adj* shapeless ♦ *nm* report
infortunio *nm* misfortune
infracción *nf* infraction, infringement
infranqueable *adj* impassable; (*fig*) insurmountable
infravalorar *vt* to undervalue, underestimate
infringir *vt* to infringe, contravene
infructuoso, -a *adj* fruitless, unsuccessful
infundado, -a *adj* groundless, unfounded
infundir *vt* to infuse, instil (*US*), instil (*BRIT*)
infusión *nf* infusion ▶ **infusión de manzanilla** camomile tea
ingeniar *vt* to think up, devise; **ingeniarse** *vr*: **~se para** to manage to
ingeniería *nf* engineering ▶ **ingeniería genética** genetic engineering ❏ **ingeniero, -a** *nm/f* engineer ▶ **ingeniero civil/de sonido** civil engineer/sound engineer

ingenio nm (talento) talent; (agudeza) wit; (habilidad) ingenuity, inventiveness
▶ **ingenio azucarero** (LAm) sugar refinery

ingenioso, -a adj ingenious, clever; (divertido) witty

ingenuidad nf ingenuousness; (sencillez) simplicity ❏ **ingenuo, -a** adj ingenuous

ingerir vt to ingest; (tragar) to swallow; (consumir) to consume

Inglaterra nf England

ingle nf groin

inglés, -esa adj English ♦ nm/f Englishman(-woman) ♦ nm (LING) English

ingratitud nf ingratitude ❏ **ingrato, -a** adj (gen) ungrateful

ingrediente nm ingredient

ingresar vt (dinero) to deposit ♦ vi to come in; ~ **en un club** to join a club; ~ **en el hospital** to go to the hospital

ingreso nm (entrada) entry; (en hospital etc) admission; ~**s** nmpl (dinero) income sg; (COM) takings pl

inhabitable adj uninhabitable

inhalar vt to inhale

inherente adj inherent

inhibir vt to inhibit

inhóspito, -a adj (región, paisaje) inhospitable

inhumano, -a adj inhuman

inicial adj, nf initial

iniciar vt (persona) to initiate; (empezar) to begin, commence; (conversación) to start up

iniciativa nf initiative ▶ **iniciativa privada** private enterprise

ininterrumpido, -a adj uninterrupted

injerencia nf interference

injertar vt to graft ❏ **injerto** nm graft

injuria nf (agravio, ofensa) offense (US), offence (BRIT); (insulto) insult ❏ **injuriar** vt to insult ❏ **injurioso, -a** adj offensive; insulting

⚠ No confundir **injuria** con la palabra inglesa *injury*.

injusticia nf injustice

injusto, -a adj unjust, unfair

inmadurez nf immaturity

inmediaciones nfpl environs, neighborhood sg (US), neighbourhood sg (BRIT)

inmediato, -a adj immediate; (contiguo) adjoining; (rápido) prompt; (próximo) next, neighboring (US), neighbouring (BRIT); **de ~** immediately

inmejorable adj unsurpassable; (precio) unbeatable

inmenso, -a adj immense, huge

inmerecido, -a adj undeserved

inmigración nf immigration

inmiscuirse vr to interfere, meddle

inmobiliaria nf real estate agency (US), estate agency (BRIT)

inmobiliario, -a adj real-estate cpd, property cpd

inmolar vt to immolate, sacrifice

inmoral adj immoral

inmortal adj immortal ❏ **inmortalizar** vt to immortalize

inmóvil adj immobile

inmueble adj: **bienes ~s** real estate, landed property ♦ nm property

inmundicia nf filth ❏ **inmundo, -a** adj filthy

inmune adj: ~ **(a)** (MED) immune (to)

inmunidad nf immunity

inmutarse vr to turn pale; **no se inmutó** he didn't turn a hair

innato, -a adj innate

innecesario, -a adj unnecessary

innoble adj ignoble

innovación nf innovation

innovar vt to introduce

inocencia nf innocence

inocentada nf practical joke

inocente adj (ingenuo) naïve, innocent; (inculpable) innocent; (sin malicia) harmless ♦ nmf simpleton

inodoro nm toilet, lavatory (BRIT)

inofensivo, -a adj inoffensive, harmless

inolvidable adj unforgettable

inopinado, -a adj unexpected

inoportuno, -a adj untimely; (molesto) inconvenient

inoxidable adj: **acero** ~ stainless steel

inquebrantable adj unbreakable

inquietar vt to worry, trouble; **inquietarse** vr to worry, get upset ❏ **inquieto, -a** adj anxious, worried ❏ **inquietud** nf anxiety, worry

inquilino, -a nm/f tenant

inquirir vt to enquire into, investigate

insaciable adj insatiable

insalubre adj unhealthy

inscribir vt to inscribe; ~ **a algn en** (lista) to put sb on; (: censo) to register sb on

inscripción *nf* inscription; (*ESCOL etc*) enrollment (*US*), enrolment (*BRIT*); (*en censo*) registration

insecticida *nm* insecticide

insecto *nm* insect

inseguridad *nf* insecurity

inseguro, -a *adj* insecure; (*inconstante*) unsteady; (*incierto*) uncertain

insensato, -a *adj* foolish, stupid

insensibilidad *nf* (*gen*) insensitivity; (*dureza de corazón*) callousness

insensible *adj* (*gen*) insensitive; (*movimiento*) imperceptible; (*sin sentido*) numb

insertar *vt* to insert

inservible *adj* useless

insidioso, -a *adj* insidious

insignia *nf* (*señal distintiva*) badge; (*estandarte*) flag

insignificante *adj* insignificant

insinuar *vt* to insinuate, imply

insípido, -a *adj* insipid

insistencia *nf* insistence

insistir *vi* to insist; **~ en algo** to insist on sth; (*enfatizar*) to stress sth

insolación *nf* (*MED*) sunstroke

insolencia *nf* insolence ❑ **insolente** *adj* insolent

insólito, -a *adj* unusual

insoluble *adj* insoluble

insolvencia *nf* insolvency

insomnio *nm* insomnia

insondable *adj* bottomless; (*fig*) impenetrable

insonorizado, -a *adj* (*cuarto etc*) soundproof

insoportable *adj* unbearable

insospechado, -a *adj* (*inesperado*) unexpected

inspección *nf* inspection, check ❑ **inspeccionar** *vt* (*examinar*) to inspect, examine; (*controlar*) to check

inspector, a *nm/f* inspector

inspiración *nf* inspiration

inspirar *vt* to inspire; (*MED*) to inhale; **inspirarse** *vr*: **~se en** to be inspired by

instalación *nf* (*equipo*) fittings *pl*, equipment ▸ **instalación eléctrica** wiring

instalar *vt* (*establecer*) to install (*US*), instal (*BRIT*); (*erguir*) to set up, erect; **instalarse** *vr* to establish o.s.; (*en una vivienda*) to move into

instancia *nf* (*JUR*) petition; (*ruego*) request; **en última ~** as a last resort

instantánea *nf* snap(shot)

instantáneo, -a *adj* instantaneous; **café ~** instant coffee

instante *nm* instant, moment

instar *vt* to press, urge

instaurar *vt* (*costumbre*) to establish; (*normas, sistema*) to bring in, introduce; (*gobierno*) to install (*US*), instal (*BRIT*)

instigar *vt* to instigate

instinto *nm* instinct; **por ~** instinctively

institución *nf* institution, establishment

instituir *vt* to establish; (*fundar*) to found ❑ **instituto** *nm* (*gen*) institute; (*ESP ESCOL*) ≈ high (*US*) o comprehensive (*BRIT*) school

institutriz *nf* governess

instrucción *nf* instruction

instructivo, -a *adj* instructive

instruir *vt* (*gen*) to instruct; (*enseñar*) to teach, educate

instrumento *nm* (*gen*) instrument; (*ESP: herramienta*) tool, implement

insubordinarse *vr* to rebel

insuficiencia *nf* (*carencia*) lack; (*inadecuación*) inadequacy ❑ **insuficiente** *adj* (*gen*) insufficient; (*ESCOL: calificación*) unsatisfactory

insufrible *adj* insufferable

insular *adj* insular

insultar *vt* to insult ❑ **insulto** *nm* insult

insumiso, -a *nm/f* (*POL*) person who refuses to do military service or its substitute, community service

insuperable *adj* (*excelente*) unsurpassable; (*problema etc*) insurmountable

insurgente *adj, nmf* insurgent

insurrección *nf* insurrection, rebellion

intachable *adj* irreproachable

intacto, -a *adj* intact

integral *adj* integral; (*completo*) complete; **pan ~** wholewheat (*US*) o wholemeal (*BRIT*) bread

integrar *vt* to make up, compose; (*MAT: fig*) to integrate

integridad *nf* wholeness; (*carácter*) integrity ❑ **íntegro, -a** *adj* whole, entire; (*honrado*) honest

intelectual *adj, nmf* intellectual

inteligencia *nf* intelligence; (*ingenio*) ability ❑ **inteligente** *adj* intelligent

inteligible *adj* intelligible

intemperie *nf*: **a la ~** out in the open, exposed to the elements

intempestivo, -a *adj* untimely

intención *nf* (*gen*) intention, purpose; **con segundas intenciones** maliciously; **con ~** deliberately

intencionado, -a *adj* deliberate; **bien ~** well-meaning; **mal ~** ill-disposed, hostile

intensidad *nf* (*gen*) intensity; (*ELEC, TEC*) strength; **llover con ~** to rain hard

intenso, -a *adj* intense; (*sentimiento*) profound, deep

intentar *vt* (*tratar*) to try, attempt ❏ **intento** *nm* attempt

interactivo, -a *adj* (*INFORM*) interactive

intercalar *vt* to insert

intercambio *nm* exchange, swap

interceder *vi* to intercede

interceptar *vt* to intercept

intercesión *nf* intercession

interés *nm* (*gen*) interest; (*parte*) share, part; (*pey*) self-interest ▶ **intereses creados** vested interests

interesado, -a *adj* interested; (*prejuiciado*) prejudiced; (*pey*) mercenary, self-seeking

interesante *adj* interesting

interesar *vt, vi* to interest, be of interest to; **interesarse** *vr*: **~se en** o **por** to take an interest in

interferir *vt* to interfere with; (*TEL*) to jam ♦ *vi* to interfere

interfón (*MÉX*) *nm* entry phone

interfono *nm* intercom

interino, -a *adj* temporary ♦ *nm/f* temporary holder of a post; (*MED*) locum; (*ESCOL*) substitute teacher (*US*), supply teacher (*BRIT*)

interior *adj* inner, inside; (*COM*) domestic, internal ♦ *nm* interior, inside; (*fig*) soul, mind; **Ministerio del I~** ≈ Department of the Interior (*US*), ≈ Home Office (*BRIT*)

interiorista (*ESP*) *nmf* interior designer

interjección *nf* interjection

interlocutor, a *nm/f* speaker

intermedio, -a *adj* intermediate ♦ *nm* intermission, interval

interminable *adj* endless

intermitente *adj* intermittent ♦ *nm* (*LAm exc MÉX, ESP AUTO*) turn signal (*US*), indicator (*BRIT*)

internacional *adj* international

internado *nm* boarding school

internar *vt* to intern; (*en un manicomio*) to commit; **internarse** *vr* (*penetrar*) to penetrate

Internet *nm* o *f*: **el** o **la ~** the Internet

interno, -a *adj* internal, interior; (*POL etc*) domestic ♦ *nm/f* (*alumno*) boarder

interponer *vt* to interpose, put in; **interponerse** *vr* to intervene

interpretación *nf* interpretation

interpretar *vt* to interpret; (*TEATRO, MÚS*) to perform, play ❏ **intérprete** *nmf* (*LING*) interpreter; (*MÚS, TEATRO*) performer, artist(e)

interrogación *nf* interrogation; (*LING: tb*: **signo de ~**) question mark

interrogar *vt* to interrogate, question

interrumpir *vt* to interrupt

interrupción *nf* interruption

interruptor *nm* (*ELEC*) switch

intersección *nf* intersection

interurbano, -a *adj*: **llamada interurbana** long-distance call

intervalo *nm* interval; (*descanso*) break; **a ~s** at intervals, every now and then

intervenir *vt* (*controlar*) to control, supervise; (*MED*) to operate on ♦ *vi* (*participar*) to take part, participate; (*mediar*) to intervene

interventor, a *nm/f* inspector; (*COM*) auditor

intestino *nm* (*MED*) intestine

intimar *vi* to become friendly

intimidad *nf* intimacy; (*familiaridad*) familiarity; (*vida privada*) private life; (*JUR*) privacy

íntimo, -a *adj* intimate

intolerable *adj* intolerable, unbearable

intoxicación *nf* poisoning

intranet *nf* intranet

intranquilizarse *vr* to get worried o anxious ❏ **intranquilo, -a** *adj* worried

intransitable *adj* impassable

intrépido, -a *adj* intrepid

intriga *nf* intrigue; (*plan*) plot ❏ **intrigar** *vt, vi* to intrigue

intrincado, -a *adj* intricate

intrínseco, -a *adj* intrinsic

introducción *nf* introduction

introducir *vt* (*gen*) to introduce; (*moneda etc*) to insert; (*INFORM*) to input, enter

intromisión *nf* interference, meddling

introvertido, -a *adj, nm/f* introvert

intruso, -a *adj* intrusive ♦ *nm/f* intruder

intuición *nf* intuition

inundación *nf* flood(ing) ❏ **inundar** *vt* to flood; (*fig*) to swamp, inundate

inusitado, -a *adj* unusual, rare

inútil *adj* useless; (*esfuerzo*) vain, fruitless ❏ **inutilidad** *nf* uselessness

inutilizar *vt* to make o render useless; **inutilizarse** *vr* to become useless

invadir *vt* to invade

inválido, -a *adj* invalid ♦ *nm/f* invalid

invariable *adj* invariable

invasión *nf* invasion

invasor, a *adj* invading ♦ *nm/f* invader

invención *nf* invention

inventar *vt* to invent

inventario *nm* inventory

inventiva *nf* inventiveness

invento *nm* invention

inventor, a *nm/f* inventor

invernadero *nm* greenhouse

inverosímil *adj* implausible

inversión *nf* (COM) investment

inverso, -a *adj* inverse, opposite; **en el orden ~** in reverse order; **a la inversa** inversely, the other way round

inversor, a *nm/f* (COM) investor

invertir *vt* (COM) to invest; (*volcar*) to turn upside down; (*tiempo etc*) to spend

investigación *nf* investigation; (ESCOL) research ► **investigación y desarrollo** research and development

investigar *vt* to investigate; (ESCOL) to do research into

invierno *nm* winter

invisible *adj* invisible

invitado, -a *nm/f* guest

invitar *vt* to invite; (*incitar*) to entice; (*pagar*) to buy, pay for

invocar *vt* to invoke, call on

involucrar *vt*: **~ en** to involve in; **involucrarse** *vr* (*persona*): **~ en** to get mixed up in

involuntario, -a *adj* (*movimiento, gesto*) involuntary; (*error*) unintentional

inyección *nf* injection

inyectar *vt* to inject

---

ir

PALABRA CLAVE

vi

1 to go; (*a pie*) to walk; (*viajar*) to travel; **ir caminando** to walk; **fui en tren** I went *o* traveled (US) *o* travelled (BRIT) by train; **¡(ahora) voy!** (I'm just) coming!

2: **ir (a) por**: **ir (a) por el médico** to fetch the doctor

3 (*progresar: persona, cosa*) to go; **el trabajo va muy bien** work is going very well; **¿cómo te va?** how are things going?; **me va muy bien** I'm getting on very well; **le fue fatal** (ESP) it went awfully badly for him

4 (*funcionar*): **el** (*LAm*) **carro no va muy bien** the car isn't running very well

5: **esa camisa te va estupendamente** that shirt suits you fantastically well

6 (*locuciones*): **¿vino? -- ¡qué va!** did he come? -- of course not!; **vamos, no llores** come on, don't cry; **¡vaya** (*LAm*) **carro!** what a car!, that's some car!

7: **no vaya a ser: tienes que correr, no vaya a ser que pierdas el tren** you'll have to run so as not to miss the train

8 (+ *pp*): **iba vestido muy bien** he was very well dressed

9: **no me** *etc* **va ni me viene** I *etc* don't care

♦ *vb aux*

1: **ir a: voy/iba a hacerlo hoy** I am/was going to do it today

2 (+ *gerundio*): **iba anocheciendo** it was getting dark; **todo se me iba aclarando** everything was gradually becoming clearer to me

3 (+ *pp = pasivo*): **van vendidos 300 ejemplares** 300 copies have been sold so far

♦ **irse** *vr*

1: **¿por dónde se va al zoológico?** which is the way to the zoo?

2 (*marcharse*) to leave; **ya se habrán ido** they must already have left *o* gone

---

ira *nf* anger, rage

Irak *nm* = **Iraq**

Irán *nm* Iran □ **iraní** *adj, nmf* Iranian

Iraq *nm* Iraq □ **iraquí** *adj, nmf* Iraqi

iris *nm inv* (ANAT) iris; **arco ~** rainbow

Irlanda *nf* Ireland □ **irlandés, -esa** *adj* Irish ♦ *nm/f* Irishman(-woman); **los irlandeses** the Irish

ironía *nf* irony □ **irónico, -a** *adj* ironic(al)

IRPF *n abr* (= *Impuesto sobre la Renta de las Personas Físicas*) (personal) income tax

irreal *adj* unreal

irrecuperable *adj* irrecoverable, irretrievable

irreflexión *nf* thoughtlessness

irregular *adj* (*gen*) irregular; (*situación*) abnormal

irremediable *adj* irremediable; (*vicio*) incurable

irreparable *adj* (*daños*) irreparable; (*pérdida*) irrecoverable

irresoluto, -a *adj* irresolute, hesitant

irrespetuoso, -a *adj* disrespectful

irresponsable *adj* irresponsible

irreversible *adj* irreversible

irrigar vt to irrigate

irrisorio, -a adj derisory, ridiculous

irritar vt to irritate, annoy

irrupción nf irruption; (*invasión*) invasion

isla nf island

islandés, -esa adj Icelandic ♦ nm/f Icelander

Islandia nf Iceland

isleño, -a adj island cpd ♦ nm/f islander

Israel nm Israel ❏ **israelí** adj, nmf Israeli

istmo nm isthmus

Italia nf Italy ❏ **italiano, -a** adj, nm/f Italian

itinerario nm itinerary, route

ITV (*ESP*) nf abr (= *inspección técnica de vehículos*) roadworthiness test, ≈ MOT (*BRIT*)

IVA (*ESP*) nm abr (= *impuesto sobre el valor añadido*) VAT (*BRIT*)

izar vt to hoist

izdo, -a abr (= *izquierdo, a*) l

izquierda nf left; (*POL*) left (wing); **a la ~** (*estar*) on the left; (*torcer etc*) (to the) left

izquierdista nmf left-winger, leftist

izquierdo, -a adj left

Jj

jabalí nm wild boar

jabalina nf javelin

jabón nm soap ❏ **jabonar** vt to soap

jaca nf pony

jacal (*MÉX*) nm shack

jacinto nm hyacinth

jactarse vr to boast, brag

jadear vi to pant, gasp for breath ❏ **jadeo** nm panting, gasping

jaguar nm jaguar

jaiba (*LAm*) nf crab

jalar (*LAm*) vt to pull

jalea (*ESP*) nf Jell-O® (*US*), jelly (*BRIT*)

jaleo (*ESP*) nm racket, uproar; **armar un ~** to kick up a racket

jalón (*LAm*) nm tug

jamás adv never

jamón nm ham ► **jamón dulce** o **de York** cooked ham ► **jamón serrano** (*ESP*) cured ham

Japón nm: **el ~** Japan ❏ **japonés, -esa** adj, nm/f Japanese ♦ nm (*LING*) Japanese

jaque nm (*AJEDREZ*) check ► **jaque mate** checkmate

jaqueca nf (very bad) headache, migraine

jarabe nm syrup

jarcia nf (*NÁUT*) ropes pl, rigging

jardín nm garden ► **jardín de infantes** (*RPl*) nursery school, kindergarten ► **jardín de niños** (*MÉX*) nursery school, kindergarten ► **jardín infantil** (*LAm exc MÉX*) nursery school, kindergarten ❏ **jardinería** nf gardening ❏ **jardinero, -a** nm/f gardener

jarra nf jar; (*jarro*) jug, pitcher (*US*)

jarro nm jug, pitcher (*US*)

jarrón nm vase

jaula nf cage

jauría nf pack of hounds

jazmín nm jasmine

J.C. abr (= *Jesucristo*) J.C.

jeans (*LAm exc MÉX*) nmpl jeans, denims; **unos ~** a pair of jeans

jefa nf ver **jefe**

jefatura nf: **~ de policía** police headquarters sg

jefe, -a nm/f (*gen*) chief, head; (*patrón*) boss ► **jefe de cocina** chef ► **jefe de estación** stationmaster ► **jefe de estado** head of state

jengibre nm ginger

jeque nm sheik

jerarquía nf (*orden*) hierarchy; (*rango*) rank ❏ **jerárquico, -a** adj hierarchic(al)

jerez nm sherry

jerga nf jargon

jeringa nf syringe; (*LAm: molestia*) annoyance, bother ► **jeringa de engrase** grease gun ❏ **jeringar** (*LAm: fam*) vt to annoy, bother ❏ **jeringuilla** nf syringe

jeroglífico nm hieroglyphic

jersey (*ESP*) (pl **~s**) nm jersey, pullover

Jerusalén n Jerusalem

Jesucristo nm Jesus Christ

jesuita adj, nm Jesuit

Jesús nm Jesus; **¡~!** good heavens!; (*ESP: al estornudar*) bless you!

jinete nmf horseman(-woman), rider

jipijapa (*LAm*) nm straw hat

jirafa nf giraffe

jirón nm rag, shred

jitomate (*MÉX*) nm tomato

jocoso, -a adj humorous, jocular

jofaina nf washbowl (*US*), washbasin (*BRIT*)

jogging (*RPl*) nm sweat suit (*US*), tracksuit (*BRIT*)

jornada nf (viaje de un día) day's journey; (camino o viaje entero) journey; (día de trabajo) working day

jornal nm (day's) wage □ **jornalero, -a** nm/f (day) laborer (US) o labourer (BRIT)

joroba nf hump, hunched back □ **jorobado, -a** adj hunchbacked ♦ nm/f hunchback

jota nf (the letter) J; (danza) Aragonese dance; **no saber ni ~** to have no idea

joven (pl **jóvenes**) adj young ♦ nm young man, youth ♦ nf young woman, girl

jovial adj cheerful, jolly

joya nf jewel, gem; (fig: persona) gem □ **joyería** nf (joyas) jewelry (US), jewellery (BRIT); (tienda) jewelry store (US), jeweller's (shop) (BRIT) □ **joyero, -a** nm/f (persona) jeweler (US), jeweller (BRIT) ♦ nm (caja) jewel case

juanete nm (del pie) bunion

jubilación nf (retiro) retirement

jubilado, -a adj retired ♦ nm/f senior citizen, pensioner (BRIT)

jubilar vt to pension off, retire; (fam) to discard; **jubilarse** vr to retire

júbilo nm joy, rejoicing □ **jubiloso, -a** adj jubilant

judía (ESP) nf (CULIN) bean ▶ **judía verde** pole (US) o French (BRIT) bean; ver tb **judío**

judicial adj judicial

judío, -a adj Jewish ♦ nm/f Jew(ess)

judo nm judo

juego etc vb ver **jugar** ♦ nm (gen) play; (pasatiempo, partido) game; (en casino) gambling; (conjunto) set; **fuera de ~** (DEPORTE: persona) offside; (: pelota) out of play ▶ **juego de computadora** (LAm) computer game ▶ **Juegos Olímpicos** Olympic Games

jueves nm inv Thursday

juez nmf judge ▶ **juez de línea** linesman ▶ **juez de salida** starter

jugada nf play; **buena ~** good move/shot/ stroke etc

jugador, a nm/f player; (en casino) gambler

jugar vt, vi to play; (en casino) to gamble; (apostar) to bet; **~ a algo** to play sth

juglar nm minstrel

jugo nm (BOT) juice; (fig) essence, substance ▶ **jugo de naranja** (LAm) orange juice □ **jugoso, -a** adj juicy; (fig) substantial, important

juguete nm toy □ **juguetear** vi to play □ **juguetería** nf toystore (US), toyshop (BRIT)

juguetón, -ona adj playful

juicio nm judgement; (razón) sanity, reason; (opinión) opinion □ **juicioso, -a** adj wise, sensible

julio nm July

jumper (LAm) nm jumper (US), pinafore dress (BRIT)

junco nm rush, reed

jungla nf jungle

junio nm June

junta nf (asamblea) meeting, assembly; (comité, consejo) council, committee; (COM, FINANZAS) board; (TEC) joint

juntar vt to join, unite; (maquinaria) to assemble, put together; (dinero) to collect; **juntarse** vr to join, meet; (reunirse: personas) to meet, assemble; (arrimarse) to approach, draw closer; **~se con algn** to join sb

junto, -a adj joined; (unido) united; (anexo) near, close; (contiguo, próximo) next, adjacent ♦ adv: **todo ~** all at once; **~s** together; **~ a** near (to), next to

jurado nm (JUR: individuo) juror; (: grupo) jury; (de concurso: grupo) panel (of judges); (: individuo) member of a panel

juramento nm oath; (maldición) oath, curse; **prestar ~** to take the oath; **tomar ~ a** to swear in, administer the oath to

jurar vt, vi to swear; **~ en falso** to commit perjury; **tenérsela jurada a algn** (fam) to have it in for sb

jurídico, -a adj legal

jurisdicción nf (poder, autoridad) jurisdiction; (territorio) district

jurisprudencia nf jurisprudence

jurista nmf jurist

justamente adv justly, fairly; (precisamente) just, exactly

justicia nf justice; (equidad) fairness, justice □ **justiciero, -a** adj just, righteous

justificación nf justification □ **justificar** vt to justify

justo, -a adj (equitativo) just, fair, right; (preciso) exact, correct; (ajustado) tight ♦ adv (precisamente) exactly, precisely; (LAm: apenas a tiempo) just in time

juvenil adj youthful

juventud nf (adolescencia) youth; (jóvenes) young people pl

juzgado nm tribunal; (JUR) court

juzgar vt to judge; **a ~ por ...** to judge by ..., judging by ...

Kk

karate (*LAm*) (*ESP* **kárate**) *nm* karate

kg *abr* (= *kilogramo*) kg

kilo *nm* kilo □ **kilogramo** *nm* kilogram (*US*), kilogramme (*BRIT*) □ **kilometraje** *nm* distance in kilometers (*US*) o kilometres (*BRIT*), ≈ mileage □ **kilómetro** *nm* kilometer (*US*), kilometre (*BRIT*) □ **kilovatio** *nm* kilowatt

kiosco *nm* = **quiosco**

kleenex® *nm* paper handkerchief, tissue

km *abr* (= *kilómetro*) km

Kosovo *nm* Kosovo

kv *abr* (= *kilovatio*) kw

Ll

l *abr* (= *litro*) l

la *art def* the ♦ *pron* her; (*Ud.*) you; (*cosa*) it ♦ *nm* (*MÚS*) la; **la del sombrero rojo** the girl in the red hat; *ver tb* **el**

laberinto *nm* labyrinth

labia *nf* fluency; (*pey*) glib tongue

labio *nm* lip

labor *nf* labor (*US*), labour (*BRIT*); (*AGR*) farm work; (*tarea*) job, task; (*COSTURA*) needlework □ **laborable** *adj* (*AGR*) workable; **día laborable** working day □ **laboral** *adj* (*accidente*) at work; (*jornada*) working

laboratorio *nm* laboratory

laborioso, -a *adj* (*persona*) hard-working; (*trabajo*) tough

laborista *adj*: **Partido L~** Labour Party (*BRIT*)

labrado, -a *adj* worked; (*madera*) carved; (*metal*) wrought

labrador, a *adj* farming *cpd* ♦ *nm/f* farmer

labranza *nf* (*AGR*) cultivation

labrar *vt* (*gen*) to work; (*madera etc*) to carve; (*fig*) to cause, bring about

labriego, -a *nm/f* peasant

laca *nf* lacquer

lacayo *nm* lackey

lacio, -a *adj* (*pelo*) straight

lacón *nm* shoulder of pork

lacónico, -a *adj* laconic

lacra *nf* (*fig*) blot □ **lacrar** *vt* (*cerrar*) to seal (with sealing wax) □ **lacre** *nm* sealing wax

lactancia *nf* lactation

lactar *vt*, *vi* to suckle

lácteo, -a *adj*: **productos ~s** dairy products

ladear *vt* to tip, tilt ♦ *vi* to tilt; **ladearse** *vr* to lean

ladera *nf* slope

lado *nm* (*gen*) side; (*fig*) protection; (*MIL*) flank; **al ~ de** beside; **poner de ~** to put on its side; **poner a un ~** to put aside; **por todos ~s** on all sides, all round (*BRIT*)

ladrar *vi* to bark □ **ladrido** *nm* bark, barking

ladrillo *nm* (*gen*) brick; (*azulejo*) tile

ladrón, -ona *nm/f* thief

lagartija *nf* (*ZOOL*) (small) lizard

lagarto *nm* (*ZOOL*) lizard

lago *nm* lake

lágrima *nf* tear

laguna *nf* (*lago*) lagoon; (*hueco*) gap

laico, -a *adj* lay

lamentable *adj* lamentable, regrettable; (*miserable*) pitiful

lamentar *vt* (*sentir*) to regret; (*deplorar*) to lament; **lamentarse** *vr* to lament; **lo lamento mucho** I'm very sorry □ **lamento** *nm* lament

lamer *vt* to lick

lámina *nf* (*plancha delgada*) sheet; (*para estampar, estampa*) plate

lámpara *nf* lamp ► **lámpara de alcohol/gas** spirit/gas lamp ► **lámpara de pie** standard lamp

lamparón *nm* grease spot

lana *nf* wool

lancha *nf* launch ► **lancha de pesca** fishing boat ► **lancha salvavidas/torpedera** lifeboat/torpedo boat

langosta *nf* (*crustáceo*) lobster; (: *de río*) crawfish (*US*), crayfish (*BRIT*) □ **langostino** *nm* king-size shrimp (*US*), king prawn (*BRIT*)

languidecer *vi* to languish □ **languidez** *nf* languor □ **lánguido, -a** *adj* (*gen*) languid; (*sin energía*) listless

lanilla *nf* nap

lanza *nf* (*arma*) lance, spear

lanzamiento *nm* (*gen*) throwing; (*NÁUT, COM*) launch, launching ► **lanzamiento de peso** putting the shot

lanzar *vt* (*gen*) to throw; (*DEPORTE: pelota*) to bowl; (*NÁUT, COM*) to launch; (*JUR*) to evict; **lanzarse** *vr* to throw o.s.

lapa *nf* limpet

lapicero (*CAm*) *nm* (*bolígrafo*) ballpoint pen, Biro® (*BRIT*)

lápida *nf* stone ► **lápida conmemorativa** memorial stone ► **lápida mortuoria** headstone □ **lapidario, -a** *adj*, *nm* lapidary

lápiz nm pencil ► **lápiz de color** colored (US) o coloured (BRIT) pencil ► **lápiz de labios** lipstick ► **lápiz labial** (LAm) lipstick

lapón, -ona nm/f Laplander, Lapp

lapso nm (de tiempo) interval; (error) error

lapsus nm inv error, mistake

largar vt (soltar) to release; (aflojar) to loosen; (fam) to let fly; (velas) to unfurl; (LAm: lanzar) to throw; **largarse** vr (fam: irse) to beat it; **~se a** (CS: empezar) to start to

largo, -a adj (longitud) long; (tiempo) lengthy; (fig) generous ♦ nm length; (MÚS) largo; **dos años ~s** two long years; **tiene 9 metros de ~** it is 9 meters long; **a lo ~ de** along; (tiempo) all through, throughout □ **largometraje** nm feature movie (US) o film (BRIT)

⚠ No confundir **largo** con la palabra inglesa **large**.

laringe nf larynx □ **laringitis** nf laryngitis

larva nf larva

las art def the ♦ pron them; **~ que cantan** the ones/women/girls who sing; ver tb **el**

lascivo, -a adj lewd

láser nm laser

lástima nf (pena) pity; **dar ~** to be pitiful; **es una ~ que** it's a pity that; **¡qué ~!** what a pity!; **ella está hecha una ~** she looks pitiful

lastimar vt (herir) to wound; (ofender) to offend; **lastimarse** vr to hurt o.s. □ **lastimero, -a** adj pitiful, pathetic

lastre nm (TEC, NÁUT) ballast; (fig) dead weight

lata nf (metal) tin; (caja) can, tin (BRIT); (fam) nuisance; **en ~** canned, tinned (BRIT); **dar (la) ~** to be a nuisance

latente adj latent

lateral adj side cpd, lateral ♦ nm (TEATRO) wings

latido nm (de corazón) beat

latifundio nm large estate □ **latifundista** nmf owner of a large estate

latigazo nm (golpe) lash; (sonido) crack

látigo nm whip

latín nm Latin

latino, -a adj Latin □ **latinoamericano, -a** adj, nm/f Latin-American

latir vi (corazón, pulso) to beat

latitud nf (GEO) latitude

latón nm brass

latoso, -a adj (molesto) annoying; (aburrido) boring

laúd nm lute

laurel nm (BOT) laurel; (CULIN) bay

lava nf lava

lavabo nm (pila) sink, washbasin (BRIT); (tb: ~s) bathroom (US), washroom (US), toilet (BRIT)

lavado nm washing; (de ropa) laundry; (ARTE) wash ► **lavado de cerebro** brainwashing ► **lavado en seco** dry-cleaning

lavadora nf washing machine

lavanda nf lavender

lavandería nf laundry; (automática) Laundromat® (US), Launderette® (BRIT)

lavaplatos nm inv dishwasher; (MÉX: fregadero) (kitchen) sink

lavar vt to wash; (borrar) to wipe away; **lavarse** vr to wash o.s.; **~se las manos** to wash one's hands; **~se los dientes** to brush one's teeth; **~ y marcar** (pelo) to shampoo and set; **~ en seco** to dry-clean; **~ los platos** to wash the dishes

lavarropas (RPl) nm inv washing machine

lavavajillas nm inv dishwasher

laxante nm laxative

lazada nf bow

lazarillo nm: **perro ~** guide dog

lazo nm knot; (lazada) bow; (para animales) lasso; (trampa) snare; (vínculo) tie

le pron (directo) him (o her); (: usted) you; (indirecto) to him (o her o it); (: usted) to you

leal adj loyal □ **lealtad** nf loyalty

lección nf lesson

leche nf milk ► **leche condensada** condensed milk ► **leche descremada** (LAm) skim (US) o skimmed (BRIT) milk ► **leche desnatada** (ESP) skim (US) o skimmed (BRIT) milk ► **leche malteada** (LAm) milkshake □ **lechera** nf (vendedora) milkmaid; (recipiente) (milk) churn; (MÉX, RPL: vaca) cow □ **lechero, -a** adj dairy

lecho nm (cama: de río) bed; (GEO) layer

lechón nm suckling (US) o sucking (BRIT) pig

lechoso, -a adj milky

lechuga nf lettuce

lechuza nf owl

lector, a nm/f reader ♦ nm: **~ de discos compactos** CD player

lectura nf reading

leer vt to read

legado nm (don) bequest; (herencia) legacy; (enviado) legate

legajo nm file

legal adj (gen) legal; (persona) trustworthy □ **legalidad** nf legality

legalizar vt to legalize; (documento) to authenticate

legaña nf sleep (in eyes)

legar vt to bequeath, leave

legendario, -a adj legendary

legión nf legion □ **legionario, -a** adj legionary ♦ nm legionnaire

legislación nf legislation

legislar vi to legislate

legislatura nf (POL) period of office

legitimar vt to legitimize □ **legítimo, -a** adj (genuino) authentic; (legal) legitimate

lego, -a adj (REL) secular; (ignorante) ignorant ♦ nm layman

legua nf league

legumbres nfpl pulses

leído, -a adj well-read

lejanía nf distance □ **lejano, -a** adj far-off; (en el tiempo) distant; (fig) remote

lejía (LAm exc MÉX, ESP) nf (household) bleach

lejos adv far, far away; **a lo ~** in the distance; **de** o **desde ~** from afar; **~ de** far from

lelo, -a adj silly ♦ nm/f idiot

lema nm motto; (POL) slogan

lencería nf linen, drapery

lengua nf tongue; (LING) language; **morderse la ~** to hold one's tongue

lenguado nm sole

lenguaje nm language

lengüeta nf (ANAT) epiglottis; (zapatos) tongue; (MÚS) reed

lente nf lens; (lupa) magnifying glass; **~s** nfpl lenses nmpl (LAm: gafas) glasses ▶ **lentes bifocales/de sol** (LAm) bifocals/sunglasses ▶ **lentes de contacto** contact lenses

lenteja nf lentil □ **lentejuela** nf sequin

lentilla (ESP) nf contact lens

lentitud nf slowness; **con ~** slowly

lento, -a adj slow

leña nf firewood □ **leñador, a** nm/f woodcutter

leño nm (trozo de árbol) log; (madero) timber; (fig) blockhead

Leo nm Leo

león nm lion ▶ **león marino** sea lion

leopardo nm leopard

leotardos nmpl woolen pantyhose (US), woollen tights (BRIT)

lepra nf leprosy □ **leproso, -a** nm/f leper

lerdo, -a adj (lento) slow; (patoso) clumsy

les pron (directo) them; (: ustedes) you; (indirecto) to them; (: ustedes) to you

lesbiana adj, nf lesbian

lesión nf wound, lesion; (DEPORTE) injury □ **lesionado, -a** adj injured ♦ nm/f injured person

letal adj lethal

letanía nf litany

letargo nm lethargy

letra nf letter; (escritura) handwriting; (MÚS) lyrics pl ▶ **letra de cambio** bill of exchange ▶ **letra de imprenta** print □ **letrado, -a** adj learned ♦ nm/f lawyer, attorney (US) □ **letrero** nm (cartel) sign; (etiqueta) label

letrina nf latrine

leucemia nf leukemia (US), leukaemia (BRIT)

levadizo adj: **puente ~** drawbridge

levadura nf (para el pan) yeast; (de cerveza) brewer's yeast

levantamiento nm raising, lifting; (rebelión) revolt, uprising ▶ **levantamiento de pesos** weight-lifting

levantar vt (gen) to raise; (del suelo) to pick up; (hacia arriba) to lift (up); (plan) to make, draw up; (mesa) to clear; (campamento) to strike; (fig) to cheer up, hearten; **levantarse** vr to get up; (enderezarse) to straighten up; (rebelarse) to rebel; **~ el ánimo** to cheer up

levante nm east coast; **el L~** region of Spain extending from Castellón to Murcia

levar vt to weigh

leve adj light; (fig) trivial □ **levedad** nf lightness

levita nf frock coat

léxico nm (vocabulario) vocabulary

ley nf (gen) law; (metal) standard

leyenda nf legend

leyó etc vb ver **leer**

liar vt to tie (up); (unir) to bind; (envolver) to wrap (up); (enredar) to confuse; (cigarrillo) to roll; **liarse** vr (fam) to get involved; **~se a palos** to get involved in a fight

Líbano nm: **el ~** (the) Lebanon

libelo nm satire, lampoon

libélula nf dragonfly

liberación nf liberation; (de la cárcel) release

liberal adj, nmf liberal □ **liberalidad** nf liberality, generosity

liberar vt to liberate

libertad nf liberty, freedom ▶ **libertad bajo fianza** bail ▶ **libertad bajo palabra** parole ▶ **libertad condicional** probation ▶ **libertad de culto/de prensa/de comercio** freedom of worship/of the press/ of trade

libertar vt (preso) to set free; (de una obligación) to release; (eximir) to exempt

libertino, -a adj permissive ♦ nm/f permissive person

libra nf pound; **L~** (ASTROLOGÍA) Libra ► **libra esterlina** pound sterling

libramiento (MÉX) nm beltway (US), ring road (BRIT)

librar vt (de peligro) to save; (batalla) to wage, fight; (de impuestos) to exempt; (cheque) to make out; (JUR) to exempt; **librarse** vr: **~se de** to escape from, free o.s. from

libre adj free; (lugar) unoccupied; (asiento) vacant; (de deudas) free of debts; **~ de impuestos** free of tax; **tiro ~** free kick; **los 100 metros ~** the 100 meters free-style (race); **al aire ~** in the open air

librería nf (tienda) book store (US), bookshop (BRIT) ❏ **librero, -a** nm/f bookseller ♦ nm (MÉX: mueble) bookcase

⚠ No confundir **librería** con la palabra inglesa **library**.

libreta nf notebook ► **libreta de ahorros** savings book ► **libreta de calificaciones** (LAm) report card (US), (school) report (BRIT)

libro nm book ► **libro de bolsillo** paperback ► **libro de caja** cashbook ► **libro de cheques** checkbook (US), chequebook (BRIT) ► **libro de texto** textbook ► **libro electrónico** e-book

Lic. abr = **licenciado, a**

licencia nf (gen) license (US), licence (BRIT); (permiso) permission ► **licencia de caza** game license (US) o licence (BRIT) ► **licencia de manejo** (LAm) driver's license (US), driving licence (BRIT) ► **licencia por enfermedad** (MÉX, RPI) sick leave ❏ **licenciado, -a** adj licensed ♦ nm/f graduate ❏ **licenciar** vt (empleado) to dismiss; (permitir) to permit, allow; (soldado) to discharge; (estudiante) to confer a degree upon; **licenciarse** vr: **licenciarse en letras** to graduate in arts

licencioso, -a adj licentious

licitar vt to bid for; (LAm: subastar) to sell by auction

lícito, -a adj (legal) lawful; (justo) fair, just; (permisible) permissible

licor nm liquor (US), spirits pl (BRIT); (de frutas etc) liqueur

licuadora nf blender

licuar vt to liquidize

líder nmf leader ❏ **liderato** nm leadership ❏ **liderazgo** nm leadership

lidia nf bullfighting; (una lidia) bullfight; **toros de ~** fighting bulls ❏ **lidiar** vt, vi to fight

liebre nf hare

lienzo nm linen; (ARTE) canvas; (ARQ) wall

liga nf (de medias) garter (US), suspender (BRIT); (LAm: goma) rubber o elastic (US) band; (confederación) league

ligadura nf bond, tie; (MED, MÚS) ligature

ligamento nm ligament

ligar vt (atar) to tie; (unir) to join; (MED) to bind up; (MÚS) to slur ♦ vi to mix, blend; **ligarse** vr to commit o.s.; **(él) liga mucho** (fam) he pulls a lot of women

ligereza nf lightness; (rapidez) swiftness; (agilidad) agility; (superficialidad) flippancy

ligero, -a adj (de peso) light; (tela) thin; (rápido) swift, quick; (ágil) agile, nimble; (de importancia) slight; (de carácter) flippant, superficial ♦ adv: **a la ligera** superficially

liguero nm garter (US) o suspender (BRIT) belt

lija nf (ZOOL) dogfish; (tb: **papel de ~**) sandpaper

lila nf lilac

lima nf file; (LAm exc MÉX, ESP BOT) lime ► **lima de uñas** nailfile ❏ **limar** vt to file

limitación nf limitation, limit ► **limitación de velocidad** speed limit

limitar vt to limit; (reducir) to reduce, cut down ♦ vi: **~ con** to border on; **limitarse** vr: **~se a** to limit o.s. to

límite nm (gen) limit; (fin) end; (frontera) border ► **límite de velocidad** speed limit

limítrofe adj neighboring (US), neighbouring (BRIT)

limón nm lemon ♦ adj: **amarillo ~** lemon-yellow ► **limón verde** (MÉX) lime ❏ **limonada** nf lemonade

limosna nf alms pl; **vivir de ~** to live on charity

limpiador (MÉX) nm windshield (US) o windscreen (BRIT) wiper

limpiaparabrisas nm inv windshield (US) o windscreen (BRIT) wiper

limpiar vt to clean; (con trapo) to wipe; (quitar) to wipe away; (zapatos) to shine, polish; (fig) to clean up

limpieza nf (estado) cleanliness; (acto) cleaning; (: de las calles) cleansing; (: de zapatos) polishing; (habilidad) skill; (fig: POLICÍA) clean-up; (pureza) purity ► **limpieza en seco** dry cleaning ► **limpieza étnica** ethnic cleansing

limpio, -a adj clean; (moralmente) pure; (COM) clear, net; (fam) honest ♦ adv: **jugar ~** to play fair; **pasar a** (ESP) o **en** (LAm) **~** to make a clean copy of

linaje nm lineage, family

lince nm lynx

linchar vt to lynch

lindar vi to adjoin; ~ **con** to border on ◻ **linde** nm o f boundary ◻ **lindero, -a** adj adjoining ♦ nm boundary

lindo, -a adj pretty, nice ♦ adv: **nos divertimos de lo** ~ we had a great time; **canta muy** ~ (LAm) he sings beautifully

línea nf (gen) line; **en** ~ (INFORM) on line ▶ **línea aérea** airline ▶ **línea de meta** goal line; (en carrera) finishing line ▶ **línea recta** straight line

lingote nm ingot

lingüista nmf linguist ◻ **lingüística** nf linguistics sg

lino nm linen; (BOT) flax

linóleo nm linoleum, lino (BRIT)

linterna nf flashlight (US), torch (BRIT)

lío nm bundle; (fam) fuss; (desorden) muddle, mess; **armar un** ~ to make a fuss

liquen nm lichen

liquidación nf liquidation; **venta de** ~ clearance sale

liquidar vt (mercancías) to liquidate; (deudas) to pay off; (empresa) to wind up

líquido, -a adj liquid; (ganancia) net ♦ nm liquid ▶ **líquido imponible** net taxable income

lira nf (MÚS) lyre; (moneda) lira

lírico, -a adj lyrical

lirio nm (BOT) iris

lirón nm (ZOOL) dormouse; (fig) sleepyhead

Lisboa n Lisbon

lisiado, -a adj injured ♦ nm/f cripple

lisiar vt to maim; **lisiarse** vr to injure o.s.

liso, -a adj (terreno) flat; (cabello) straight; (superficie) even; (tela) plain

lisonja nf flattery

lista nf list; (de alumnos) register, school list (US); (de libros) catalogue, catalog (US); (de platos) menu; (de precios) price list; **pasar** ~ to call the roll; **tela de** ~**s** striped material ▶ **lista de correos** general delivery (US), poste restante (BRIT) ▶ **lista de espera** waiting list ◻ **listín** (ESP) nm: **listín telefónico** o **de teléfonos** telephone directory

listo, -a adj (perspicaz) smart, clever; (preparado) ready

listón nm (de madera, metal) strip

litera nf (en barco, tren) berth; (en dormitorio) bunk, bunk bed

literal adj literal

literario, -a adj literary

literato, -a adj literary ♦ nm/f writer

literatura nf literature

litigar vt to fight ♦ vi (JUR) to go to law; (fig) to dispute, argue

litigio nm (JUR) lawsuit; (fig): **en** ~ **con** in dispute with

litografía nf lithography; (una litografía) lithograph

litoral adj coastal ♦ nm coast, seaboard

litro nm liter (US), litre (BRIT)

liviano, -a adj (cosa, objeto) trivial

lívido, -a adj livid

llaga nf wound

llama nf flame; (ZOOL) llama

llamada nf call ▶ **llamada al orden** call to order ▶ **llamada de atención** warning ▶ **llamada a cobro revertido** (LAm exc MÉX, ESP) collect (US) o reverse-charge (BRIT) call ▶ **llamada local** (LAm) local call ▶ **llamada por cobrar** (MÉX) collect (US) o reverse-charge (BRIT) call

llamamiento nm call

llamar vt to call; (atención) to attract ♦ vi (por teléfono) to telephone; (a la puerta) to knock (o ring); (por señas) to beckon; (MIL) to call up; **llamarse** vr to be called, be named; **¿cómo se llama usted?** what's your name?

llamarada nf (llamas) blaze; (rubor) flush

llamativo, -a adj showy; (color) loud

llano, -a adj (superficie) flat; (persona) straightforward; (estilo) clear ♦ nm plain, flat ground

llanta nf (ESP) (wheel) rim ▶ **llanta (de goma)** (LAm: neumático) tire (US), tyre (BRIT); (: cámara) inner (tube) ▶ **llanta de refacción** (MÉX) spare tire ▶ **llanta de repuesto** (LAm) spare tire

llanto nm weeping

llanura nf plain

llave nf key; (del agua) faucet (US), tap (BRIT); (MECÁNICA) wrench (US), spanner (BRIT); (de la luz) switch; (MÚS) key; **echar la** ~ **a** to lock up ▶ **llave de encendido** (LAm AUTO) ignition key ▶ **llave de paso** stopcock ▶ **llave inglesa** monkey wrench ▶ **llave maestra** master key ◻ **llavero** nm keyring

llegada nf arrival

llegar vi to arrive; (alcanzar) to reach; (bastar) to be enough; **llegarse** vr: ~**se a** to approach; ~ **a** to manage to, succeed in; ~ **a saber** to find out; ~ **a ser** to become; ~ **a las manos de** to come into the hands of

llenar vt to fill; (espacio) to cover; (formulario) to fill out (US) o (BRIT) in; (fig) to heap

lleno, -a adj full, filled; (repleto) full up ♦ nm (TEATRO) full house; **dar de ~ contra un muro** to hit a wall head-on

llevadero, -a adj bearable, tolerable

llevar vt to take; (ropa) to wear; (cargar) to carry; (quitar) to take away; (en vehículo) to drive; (transportar) to transport; (traer: dinero) to carry; (conducir) to lead; (MAT) to carry ♦ vi (suj: camino etc): ~ **a** to lead to; **llevarse** vr to carry off, take away; **llevamos dos días aquí** we have been here for two days; **él me lleva 2 años** he's 2 years older than me; **~ las cuentas** (COM) to keep the books; **~se bien** to get on well (together)

llorar vt, vi to cry, weep; **~ de risa** to cry with laughter

lloriquear vi to snivel, whimper

lloro nm crying, weeping □ **llorón, -ona** adj tearful ♦ nm/f cry-baby □ **lloroso, -a** adj (gen) weeping, tearful; (triste) sad, sorrowful

llover vi to rain

llovizna nf drizzle □ **lloviznar** vi to drizzle

llueve etc vb ver **llover**

lluvia nf rain ▶ **lluvia radioactiva** (radioactive) fallout □ **lluvioso, -a** adj rainy

lo art def: **lo bello** the beautiful, what is beautiful, that which is beautiful ♦ pron (persona) him; (cosa) it; ver tb **el**

loable adj praiseworthy □ **loar** vt to praise

lobo nm wolf ▶ **lobo de mar** (fig) sea dog ▶ **lobo marino** seal

lóbrego, -a adj dark; (fig) gloomy

lóbulo nm lobe

local adj local ♦ nm place, site; (oficinas) premises pl □ **localidad** nf (barrio) locality; (lugar) location; (TEATRO) seat, ticket □ **localizar** vt (ubicar) to locate, find; (restringir) to localize; (situar) to place

loción nf lotion ▶ **loción para después de afeitarse** (LAm) after-shave (lotion) ▶ **loción para después de rasurarse** (MÉX) after-shave (lotion)

loco, -a adj mad ♦ nm/f lunatic, mad person

locomotora nf engine, locomotive

locuaz adj loquacious

locución nf expression

locura nf madness; (acto) crazy act

locutor, a nm/f (RADIO) announcer; (comentarista) commentator; (TV) newscaster, newsreader (BRIT)

locutorio nm (en telefónica) phone booth (US), telephone box (BRIT)

lodo nm mud

lógica nf logic

lógico, -a adj logical

login nm login

logística nf logistics sg

logotipo nm logo

logrado, -a adj (interpretación, reproducción) polished, excellent

lograr vt to achieve; (obtener) to get, obtain; **~ hacer** to manage to do; **~ que algn venga** to manage to get sb to come

logro nm achievement, success

lóker (LAm) nm locker

loma nf small hill, hillock (BRIT)

lombriz nf worm

lomo nm (de animal) back; (CULIN: de cerdo) pork loin; (: de vaca) rib steak; (de libro) spine

lona nf canvas

loncha nf = **lonja**

lonchería (LAm) nf snack bar, diner (US)

Londres n London

longaniza nf pork sausage

longitud nf length; (GEO) longitude; **tener 3 metros de ~** to be 3 meters long ▶ **longitud de onda** wavelength

lonja nf slice

loro nm parrot

los art def the ♦ pron them; (ustedes) you; **mis libros y ~ tuyos** my books and yours; ver tb **el**

losa nf stone ▶ **losa sepulcral** gravestone

lote nm portion; (COM) lot

lotería nf lottery; (juego) lotto

loza nf crockery

lubina nf sea bass

lubricante nm lubricant

lubricar vt to lubricate

lucha nf fight, struggle ▶ **lucha de clases** class struggle ▶ **lucha libre** wrestling □ **luchar** vi to fight

lucidez nf lucidity

lúcido, -a adj (persona) lucid; (mente) logical; (idea) crystal-clear

luciérnaga nf glow-worm

lucir vt to illuminate, light (up); (ostentar) to show off ♦ vi (brillar) to shine; **lucirse** vr (irónico) to make a fool of o.s.

lucro nm profit, gain

lúdico, -a adj (aspecto, actividad) play cpd

luego adv (después) next; (más tarde) later, afterward

lugar nm place; (sitio) spot; **en ~ de** instead of; **hacer ~** to make room; **fuera de ~** out of place; **tener ~** to take place ▶ **lugar común** commonplace

lugareño, -a adj village cpd ♦ nm/f villager

lugarteniente nm deputy

lúgubre adj mournful

lujo nm luxury; (fig) profusion, abundance ❏ **lujoso, -a** adj luxurious

lujuria nf lust

lumbre nf fire; (para cigarrillo) light

lumbrera nf luminary

luminoso, -a adj luminous, shining

luna nf moon; (de un espejo) glass; (de gafas) lens; (fig) crescent; **estar en la ~** to have one's head in the clouds ▶ **luna de miel** honeymoon ▶ **luna llena/nueva** full/new moon

lunar adj lunar ♦ nm (ANAT) mole; **tela de ~es** spotted material

lunes nm inv Monday

lupa nf magnifying glass

lustrar vt (mueble) to polish; (LAm exc MÉX: zapatos) to shine ❏ **lustre** nm polish; (fig) luster (US), lustre (BRIT); **dar lustre a** to polish ❏ **lustroso, -a** adj shining

luto nm mourning; **llevar el o vestirse de ~** to be in mourning

Luxemburgo nm Luxembourg

luz (pl **luces**) nf light; **dar a ~ un niño** to give birth to a child; **sacar a la ~** to bring to light; **prender** (LAm) **o dar o encender** (ESP)/**apagar la ~** to switch the light on/off; **a todas luces** by any reckoning; **tener pocas luces** to be dim o stupid; **traje de luces** bullfighter's costume ▶ **luz roja/verde** red/green light ▶ **luz de freno** brake light ▶ **luz solar** sunlight

Mm

m abr (= metro) m; (= minuto) m

macana (MÉX) nf billy club (US), truncheon (BRIT)

macarrones nmpl macaroni sg

macedonia (ESP) nf (tb: ~ **de frutas**) fruit salad

macerar vt to macerate

maceta nf (de flores) pot of flowers; (para plantas) flowerpot

machacar vt to crush, pound ♦ vi (insistir) to go on, keep on

machete nm machete, (large) knife

machetear (MÉX) vt to grind away (US), swot (BRIT)

machismo nm male chauvinism ❏ **machista** adj, nm sexist

macho adj male; (fig) virile ♦ nm male; (fig) he-man

macizo, -a adj (grande) massive; (fuerte, sólido) solid ♦ nm mass, chunk

madeja nf (de lana) skein, hank; (de pelo) mass, mop

madera nf wood; (fig) nature, character; **una ~ a piece of wood**

madero nm beam

madrastra nf stepmother

madre adj mother cpd ♦ nf mother; (de vino etc) dregs pl ▶ **madre política/soltera** mother-in-law/unmarried mother

Madrid n Madrid

madriguera nf burrow

madrileño, -a adj of o from Madrid ♦ nm/f native of Madrid

madrina nf godmother; (ARQ) prop, shore; (TEC) brace; (de boda) bridesmaid

madrugada nf early morning; (alba) dawn, daybreak

madrugador, a adj early-rising

madrugar vi to get up early; (fig) to get ahead

madurar vt, vi (fruta) to ripen; (fig) to mature ❏ **madurez** nf ripeness; maturity ❏ **maduro, -a** adj ripe; mature

maestra nf ver maestro

maestría nf mastery; (habilidad) skill, expertise; ~ **en Letras/Ciencias** (LAm) Master of Arts/Science

maestro, -a adj masterly; (principal) main ♦ nm/f master (mistress); (profesor) teacher ♦ nm (autoridad) authority; (MÚS) maestro; (experto) master ▶ **maestro albañil** master mason

magdalena nf fairy cake

magia nf magic ❏ **mágico, -a** adj magic(al) ♦ nm/f magician

magisterio nm (enseñanza) teaching; (profesión) teaching profession; (maestros) teachers pl

magistrado nm magistrate

magistral adj magisterial; (fig) masterly

magnánimo, -a adj magnanimous

magnate nm magnate, tycoon

magnético, -a adj magnetic ❏ **magnetizar** vt to magnetize

magnetofón nm tape recorder ❏ **magnetofónico, -a** adj: **cinta magnetofónica** recording tape

magnetófono nm = **magnetofón**

magnífico, -a adj splendid, magnificent

magnitud nf magnitude

mago, -a nm/f magician; **los Reyes M~s** the Magi, the Three Wise Men

magro, -a adj (carne) lean

maguey nm maguey; ver tb **pulque**

magullar vt (amoratar) to bruise; (dañar) to damage

mahometano, -a adj Mohammedan

mahonesa nf mayonnaise

maître (LAm exc MÉX, ESP) nm head waiter

maíz nm corn (US), maize (BRIT); sweet corn

majadero, -a adj silly, stupid

majestad nf majesty ◻ **majestuoso, -a** adj majestic

majo, -a adj nice; (guapo) attractive, good-looking; (elegante) smart

mal adv badly; (equivocadamente) wrongly ◆ adj = **malo** ◆ nm evil; (desgracia) misfortune; (daño) harm, damage; (MED) illness; **~ que bien** rightly or wrongly; **ir de ~ en peor** to get worse and worse

malabarismo nm juggling ◻ **malabarista** nmf juggler

malaria nf malaria

malcriado, -a adj spoiled

maldad nf evil, wickedness

maldecir vt to curse ◆ vi: **~ de** to speak ill of

maldición nf curse

maldito, -a adj (condenado) damned; (perverso) wicked; **¡~ sea!** damn it!

maleante nmf criminal, crook

malecón (LAm) nm sea front, promenade

maledicencia nf slander, scandal

maleducado, -a adj bad-mannered, rude

malentendido nm misunderstanding

malestar nm (gen) discomfort; (fig: inquietud) uneasiness; (POL) unrest

maleta nf case, suitcase; **hacer las ~s** to pack ◻ **maletero** nm (LAm exc MÉX, ESP AUTO) trunk (US), boot (BRIT); (persona) porter ◻ **maletín** nm small case, bag

malévolo, -a adj malicious, spiteful

maleza nf (LAm: malas hierbas) weeds pl; (arbustos) thicket

malgastar vt (tiempo, dinero) to waste; (salud) to ruin

malhechor, a nm/f delinquent

malhumorado, -a adj bad-tempered

malicia nf (maldad) wickedness; (astucia) slyness, guile; (mala intención) malice, spite; (carácter travieso) mischievousness ◻ **malicioso, -a** adj wicked, evil; sly, crafty; malicious, spiteful; mischievous

maligno, -a adj evil; (malévolo) malicious; (MED) malignant

malla nf mesh; (RPl: de baño) bathing suit (US); (de ballet, gimnasia) leotard; **~s** nfpl tights ▸ **malla de alambre** wire mesh

Mallorca nf Majorca

malo, -a adj bad, false ◆ nm/f villain; **estar ~** to be ill

malograr vt to spoil; (plan) to upset; (ocasión) to waste; **malograrse** vr (plan etc) to fail, come to grief; (persona) to die before one's time

malparado, -a adj: **salir ~** to come off badly

malpensado, -a adj nasty

malsano, -a adj unhealthy

malteada (LAm) nf milkshake

maltratar vt to ill-treat, mistreat

maltrecho, -a adj battered, damaged

malvado, -a adj evil, villainous

malversar vt to embezzle, misappropriate

Malvinas: Islas ~ nfpl Falkland Islands

malvivir vi to live poorly

mama nf (de animal) teat; (de mujer) breast ▸ **Mama Negra** Ecuadorean festival

MAMA NEGRA

The festival of the **Mama Negra** ("Black Mama") is celebrated in Latacunga in Ecuador. It is a pagan celebration which dates back to the period of the Spanish empire. According to tradition, the black native servants refused to work until the Spanish governor of the town agreed to dress as a black woman on the Day of the Virgin. Nowadays, the men join in the parades and dancing dressed as women.

mamá (pl **~s**) nf (fam) mom(my) (US), mum(my) (BRIT)

mamar vt, vi to suck

mamarracho nm sight, mess

mameluco (RPl) nm overalls pl (US), dungarees pl (BRIT)

mamífero nm mammal

mampara nf (entre habitaciones) partition; (biombo) screen

mampostería nf masonry

manada nf (ZOOL) herd; (: de leones) pride; (: de lobos) pack

manantial nm spring

manar vi to run, flow

mancha nf stain, mark; (ZOOL) patch ◻ **manchar** vt (gen) to stain, mark; (ensuciar) to soil, dirty

manchego, -a adj of o from La Mancha

manco, -a adj (de un brazo) one-armed; (de una mano) one-handed; (fig) defective, faulty

mancomunar vt to unite, bring together; (recursos) to pool; (JUR) to make jointly responsible ▫ **mancomunidad** nf union, association; (comunidad) community; (JUR) joint responsibility

mancuernas (MÉX) nfpl cufflinks

mandado (LAm) nm errand

mandamiento nm (orden) order, command; (REL) commandment
▶ **mandamiento judicial** warrant

mandar vt (ordenar) to order; (dirigir) to lead, command; (enviar) to send; (pedir) to order, ask for ♦ vi to be in charge; (pey) to be bossy; ¿**mande**? (MÉX: ¿cómo dice?) pardon?, excuse me?; ~ **hacer un traje** to have a suit made

mandarina (ESP) nf tangerine, mandarin (orange)

mandato nm (orden) order; (POL: periodo) term of office; (: territorio) mandate
▶ **mandato judicial** (search) warrant

mandíbula nf jaw

mandil nm apron

mando nm (MIL) command; (de país) rule; (el primer lugar) lead; (POL) term of office; (TEC) control; ~ **a la izquierda** left-hand drive

mandón, -ona adj bossy, domineering

manejable adj manageable

manejar vt to manage; (máquina) to work, operate; (caballo etc) to handle; (casa) to run, manage; (LAm AUTO) to drive; **manejarse** vr (comportarse) to act, behave; (arreglárselas) to manage ▫ **manejo** nm (de bicicleta) handling; (de negocio) management, running; (LAm AUTO) driving; (facilidad de trato) ease, confidence; **manejos** nmpl (intrigas) intrigues

manera nf way, manner, fashion; ~**s** nfpl (modales) manners; **su** ~ **de ser** the way he is; (aire) his manner; **de ninguna** ~ no way, by no means; **de otra** ~ otherwise; **de todas** ~**s** at any rate; **no hay** ~ **de persuadirle** there's no way of convincing him

manga nf (de camisa) sleeve; (de riego) hose

mangar (fam) vt to pinch, nick

mango nm handle; (BOT) mango

mangonear vi (meterse) to meddle, interfere; (ser mandón) to boss people about

manguera nf hose

maní (LAm exc MÉX) nm peanut

manía nf (MED) mania; (fig: moda) rage, craze; (disgusto) dislike; (malicia) spite ▫ **maníaco, -a** adj maniac(al) ♦ nm/f maniac

maniatar vt to tie the hands of

maniático, -a adj maniac(al) ♦ nm/f maniac

manicomio nm insane asylum (US), mental hospital (BRIT)

manifestación nf (declaración) statement, declaration; (de emoción) show, display; (POL: desfile) demonstration; (: concentración) mass meeting

manifestar vt to show, manifest; (declarar) to state, declare ▫ **manifiesto, -a** adj clear, manifest ♦ nm manifesto

manillar nm handlebars pl

maniobra nf maneuver (US), manoeuvre (BRIT); ~**s** nfpl (MIL) maneuvers (US), manoeuvres (BRIT) ▫ **maniobrar** vt to maneuver (US), manoeuvre (BRIT)

manipulación nf manipulation

manipular vt to manipulate; (manejar) to handle

maniquí nm dummy ♦ nmf model

manirroto, -a adj lavish, extravagant ♦ nm/f spendthrift

manivela nf crank

manjar nm (tasty) dish

mano nf hand; (ZOOL) foot, paw; (de pintura) coat; (serie) lot, series; **a** ~ by hand; **a** ~ **derecha/izquierda** on the right(-hand side)/left(-hand side); **de primera** ~ (at) first hand; **de segunda** ~ (at) second hand; **robo a** ~ **armada** armed robbery; **estrechar la** ~ **a algn** to shake sb's hand ▶ **mano de obra** labor (US), labour (BRIT)

manojo nm handful, bunch; ~ **de llaves** bunch of keys

manopla nf mitten

manoseado, -a adj well-worn

manosear vt (tocar) to handle, touch; (desordenar) to mess up, rumple; (insistir en) to overwork; (LAm: acariciar) to caress, fondle

manotazo nm slap, smack

mansalva: a ~ adv indiscriminately

mansedumbre nf gentleness, meekness

mansión nf mansion

manso, -a adj gentle, mild; (animal) tame

manta (ESP) nf blanket

manteca nf fat; (CS: mantequilla) butter
▶ **manteca de cerdo** lard

mantel nm tablecloth

mantendré etc vb ver **mantener**

mantener vt to support, maintain; (alimentar) to sustain; (conservar) to keep; (TEC) to maintain, service; **mantenerse** vr (seguir de pie) to be still standing; (no ceder) to hold one's ground; (subsistir) to sustain o.s., keep going ▫ **mantenimiento** nm maintenance; sustenance; (sustento) support

mantequilla nf butter ▶ **mantequilla de cacahuate** (MÉX) peanut butter ▶ **mantequilla de maní** (LAm exc MÉX) peanut butter

mantilla nf mantilla; ~s nfpl (de bebé) baby clothes

manto nm (capa) cloak; (de ceremonia) robe, gown

mantuve etc vb ver **mantener**

manual adj manual ♦ nm manual, handbook

manufactura nf manufacture; (fábrica) factory ❑ **manufacturado, -a** adj (producto) manufactured

manuscrito, -a adj handwritten ♦ nm manuscript

manutención nf maintenance; (sustento) support

manzana nf apple

manzanilla nf (planta) camomile; (infusión) camomile tea

manzano nm apple tree

maña nf (gen) skill, dexterity; (pey) guile; (destreza) trick, knack

mañana adv tomorrow ♦ nm future ♦ nf morning; **de o por la ~** in the morning; **¡hasta ~!** see you tomorrow!; ~ **por la** ~ tomorrow morning

mañoso, -a adj (hábil) skillful (US), skilful (BRIT); (astuto) smart, clever

mapa nm map

maple (LAm) nm maple

maqueta nf (scale) model

maquiladora (MÉX) nf (COM) bonded assembly plant

MAQUILADORA

These are assembly plants belonging to the United States, but situated in Mexico, near to the border with the United States. Multinational companies build them in Mexico because salaries and corporate taxes are much lower there. Apart from this, Mexican workers generally have fewer rights and are obliged to work longer hours than their US counterparts.

maquillaje nm make-up; (acto) making up

maquillar vt to make up; **maquillarse** vr to put on (some) make-up

máquina nf machine; (de tren) locomotive, engine; (FOTO) camera; (fig) machinery; **escrito a ~** typewritten ▶ **máquina de afeitar** (LAm) razor ▶ **máquina de coser** sewing machine ▶ **máquina de discos** (RPl, ESP) jukebox ▶ **máquina de escribir** typewriter ▶ **máquina tragamonedas** (LAm) slot machine

maquinación nf machination, plot

maquinal adj (fig) mechanical, automatic

maquinaria nf (máquinas) machinery; (mecanismo) mechanism, works pl

maquinilla (ESP) nf (tb: ~ **de afeitar**) razor

maquinista nmf (de tren) railroad engineer (US), engine driver (BRIT); (TEC) operator; (NÁUT) engineer

mar nm o f sea; ~ **adentro** o **afuera** out at sea; **en alta ~** on the high seas; **la ~ de** (fam) lots of; **el M~ Negro/Báltico** the Black/Baltic Sea

maraña nf (maleza) thicket; (confusión) tangle

maravilla nf marvel, wonder; (BOT) marigold ❑ **maravillar** vt to astonish, amaze; **maravillarse** vr to be astonished, be amazed ❑ **maravilloso, -a** adj wonderful, marvelous (US), marvellous (BRIT)

marca nf (gen) mark; (sello) stamp; (COM) make, brand; **de ~** excellent, outstanding ▶ **marca de fábrica** trademark ▶ **marca registrada** registered trademark

marcado, -a adj marked, strong

marcador nm (DEPORTE) scoreboard; (: persona) scorer

marcapasos nm inv pacemaker

marcar vt (gen) to mark; (número de teléfono) to dial; (gol) to score; (números) to record, keep a tally of; (pelo) to set ♦ vi (DEPORTE) to score; (TEL) to dial; ~ **tarjeta** (LAm: al entrar) to clock in o on; (: al salir) to clock off o out

marcha nf march; (TEC) running, working; (AUTO) gear; (velocidad) speed; (fig) progress; (dirección) course; **poner en** ~ to put into gear; (fig) to set in motion, get going; **dar** ~ **atrás** (LAm exc MÉX, ESP) to reverse, put into reverse; **estar en** ~ to be under way, be in motion

marchar vi (ir) to go; (funcionar) to work, go; **marcharse** vr to go (away), leave

marchitar vt to wither, dry up; **marchitarse** vr (BOT) to wither; (fig) to fade away ❑ **marchito, -a** adj withered, faded; (fig) in decline

marcial adj martial, military

marciano, -a adj, nm/f Martian

marco nm frame; (moneda) mark; (fig) framework

marea nf tide

marear vt (fig) to annoy, upset; (MED): ~ **a algn** to make sb feel sick; **marearse** vr (tener náuseas) to feel sick; (desvanecerse) to feel faint; (*aturdirse*) to feel dizzy; (*fam: emborracharse*) to get tipsy

maremoto *nm* tidal wave

mareo *nm* (*náusea*) sick feeling; (*en viaje*) travel sickness; (*aturdimiento*) dizziness; (*fam: lata*) nuisance

marfil *nm* ivory

margarina *nf* margarine

margarita *nf* (*BOT*) daisy ▶ **(rueda) margarita** daisywheel

margen *nm* (*borde*) edge, border; (*fig*) margin, space ♦ *nf* (*de río etc*) bank; **dar ~ para** to give an opportunity for; **mantenerse al ~** to keep out (of things)

marginar *vt* (*socialmente*) to marginalize, ostracize

mariachi *nm* (*persona*) mariachi musician; (*grupo*) mariachi band

---

MARIACHI

Mariachi music is the musical style most characteristic of Mexico. From the state of Jalisco in the 19th century, this music spread rapidly throughout the country, until each region had its own particular style of the **Mariachi** "sound". A **Mariachi** band can be made up of several singers, up to eight violins, two trumpets, guitars, a "vihuela" (an old form of guitar), and a harp. The dance associated with this music is called the "zapateado".

---

marica (*fam*) *nm* sissy

maricón (*fam*) *nm* queer

marido *nm* husband

mariguana (*LAm*) (*ESP* **marihuana**) *nf* marijuana, cannabis

marina *nf* navy ▶ **marina mercante** merchant marine (*US*) o navy (*BRIT*)

marinero, -a *adj* sea *cpd* ♦ *nm* sailor, seaman

marino, -a *adj* sea *cpd*, marine ♦ *nm* sailor

marioneta *nf* puppet

mariposa *nf* butterfly

mariquita *nf* ladybug (*US*), ladybird (*BRIT*)

marisco (*ESP*) *nm* shellfish *inv*, seafood ❑ **mariscos** (*LAm*) *nmpl* shellfish *inv*, seafood

marítimo, -a *adj* sea *cpd*, maritime

mármol *nm* marble

marqués, -esa *nm/f* marquis (marchioness)

marrón *adj* brown

marroquí *adj, nmf* Moroccan ♦ *nm* Morocco (leather)

Marruecos *nm* Morocco

martes *nm inv* Tuesday

martillo *nm* hammer ▶ **martillo neumático** jackhammer, pneumatic drill (*BRIT*)

mártir *nmf* martyr ❑ **martirio** *nm* martyrdom; (*fig*) torture, torment

marxismo *nm* Marxism ❑ **marxista** *adj, nmf* Marxist

marzo *nm* March

---

más

PALABRA CLAVE

adj, adv

1: **más (que/de)** (*compar*) more (than), ... + *er* (than); **más grande/inteligente** bigger/more intelligent; **trabaja más (que yo)** he works more (than me); *ver tb* **cada**

2 (*superl*): **el más** the most, ... + *est*; **el más grande/inteligente (de)** the biggest/most intelligent (in)

3 (*negativo*): **no tengo más dinero** I haven't got any more money; **no viene más por aquí** he doesn't come round here any more

4 (*adicional*): **no le veo más solución que ...** I see no other solution than to ...; **¿quién más?** anybody else?

5 (+ *adj: valor intensivo*): **¡qué perro más sucio!** what a filthy dog!; **¡es más tonto!** he's so stupid!

6 (*locuciones*): **más o menos** more or less; **los más** most people; **es más** furthermore; **más bien** rather; **¡qué más da!** what does it matter!; *ver tb* **no**

7: **por más: por más que te esfuerces** no matter how hard you try; **por más que quisiera ...** much as I should like to ...

8: **de más: veo que aquí estoy de más** I can see I'm not needed here; **tenemos uno de más** we've got one extra

♦ *prep*: **2 más 2 son 4** 2 and o plus 2 are 4

♦ *nm inv*: **este trabajo tiene sus más y sus menos** this job's got its good points and its bad points

---

mas *conj* but

masa *nf* (*mezcla*) dough; (*volumen*) volume, mass; (*FÍSICA*) mass; **en ~** en masse; **las ~s** (*POL*) the masses

masacre *nf* massacre

masaje *nm* massage

máscara *nf* mask ❑ **mascarilla** *nf* (*de belleza, MED*) mask

masculino, -a *adj* masculine; (*BIO*) male

masía *nf* farmhouse

masificación *nf* overcrowding

masivo, -a *adj* mass *cpd*

masón *nm* (free)mason

masoquista *nmf* masochist

masticar *vt* to chew

mástil *nm* (*de navío*) mast; (*de guitarra*) neck

mastín *nm* mastiff

masturbación *nf* masturbation

masturbarse *vr* to masturbate

mata *nf* (*arbusto*) bush, shrub; (*de hierba*) tuft

matadero (*LAm exc MÉX*) *nm* slaughterhouse, abattoir (*BRIT*)

matador, a *adj* killing ♦ *nm/f* killer ♦ *nm* (*TAUR*) matador, bullfighter

matamoscas *nm inv* (*pala*) fly swat

matanza *nf* slaughter

matar *vt*, *vi* to kill; **matarse** *vr* (*suicidarse*) to kill o.s., commit suicide; (*morir*) to be o get killed; **~ el hambre** to stave off hunger

matasellos *nm inv* postage stamp, postmark

mate *adj* matt ♦ *nm* (*en ajedrez*) (check)mate; (*LAm: hierba*) maté; (: *vasija*) gourd

matemáticas *nfpl* mathematics ❏ **matemático, -a** *adj* mathematical ♦ *nm/f* mathematician, math specialist (*US*)

materia *nf* (*gen*) matter; (*TEC*) material; (*ESCOL*) subject; **en ~ de** on the subject of ▶ **materia prima** raw material ❏ **material** *adj* material ♦ *nm* material; (*TEC*) equipment ❏ **materialismo** *nm* materialism ❏ **materialista** *adj* materialist(ic) ❏ **materialmente** *adv* materially; (*fig*) absolutely

maternal *adj* motherly, maternal

maternidad *nf* motherhood, maternity ❏ **materno, -a** *adj* maternal; (*lengua*) mother *cpd*

matinal *adj* morning *cpd*

matiz *nm* shade ❏ **matizar** *vt* (*variar*) to vary; (*ARTE*) to blend; **matizar de** to tinge with

matón *nm* bully

matorral *nm* thicket

matraca *nf* rattle

matrícula *nf* (*registro*) register; (*AUTO*) license number (*US*), registration number (*BRIT*); (*placa*) license plate (*US*), number plate (*BRIT*) ❏ **matricular** *vt* to register, enroll (*US*), enrol (*BRIT*)

matrimonial *adj* matrimonial

matrimonio *nm* (*pareja*) (married) couple; (*unión*) marriage

matriz *nf* (*ANAT*) womb; (*TEC*) mold (*US*), mould (*BRIT*); **casa ~** (*COM*) head office

matrona *nf* (*persona de edad*) matron; (*comadrona*) midwife

matufia (*RPl: fam*) *nf* put-up job

maullar *vi* to mew, miaow

maxilar *nm* jaw(bone)

máxima *nf* maxim

máxime *adv* especially

máximo, -a *adj* maximum; (*más alto*) highest; (*más grande*) greatest ♦ *nm* maximum

mayo *nm* May

mayonesa *nf* mayonnaise

mayor *adj* main, chief; (*adulto*) adult; (*de edad avanzada*) elderly; (*MÚS*) major; (*compar: de tamaño*) bigger; (: *de edad*) older; (*superl: de tamaño*) biggest; (: *de edad*) oldest ♦ *nmf* (*adulto*) adult; (*LAm MIL*) major; **~es** *nmpl* (*antepasados*) ancestors; **al por ~** wholesale ▶ **mayor de edad** adult

mayoral *nm* foreman

mayordomo *nm* butler

mayoría *nf* majority, greater part

mayorista *nmf* wholesaler

mayoritario, -a *adj* majority *cpd*

mayúscula *nf* capital letter

mayúsculo, -a *adj* (*fig*) big, tremendous

mazapán *nm* marzipan

mazo *nm* (*martillo*) mallet; (*de flores*) bunch; (*DEPORTE*) bat

me *pron* (*directo*) me; (*indirecto*) (to) me; (*reflexivo*) (to) myself; **¡dámelo!** give it to me!

mear (*fam*) *vi* to pee, piss (*!*)

mecánica *nf* (*ESCOL*) mechanics *sg*; (*mecanismo*) mechanism; *ver tb* **mecánico**

mecánico, -a *adj* mechanical ♦ *nm/f* mechanic

mecanismo *nm* mechanism; (*marcha*) gear

mecanografía *nf* typewriting ❏ **mecanógrafo, -a** *nm/f* typist

mecate (*MÉX, CAm*) *nm* rope

mecedora *nf* rocking chair

mecer *vt* (*cuna*) to rock; **mecerse** *vr* to rock; (*rama*) to sway

mecha *nf* (*de vela*) wick; (*de bomba*) fuse, fuze (*US*)

mechero (*ESP*) *nm* (cigarette) lighter

mechón *nm* (*gen*) tuft; (*de pelo*) lock

medalla *nf* medal

media *nf* stocking; (*LAm*) sock; (*promedio*) average

mediado, -a *adj* half-full; (*trabajo*) half-completed; **a ~s de** in the middle of, halfway through

mediano, -a *adj* (*regular*) medium, average; (*mediocre*) mediocre

medianoche nf midnight

mediante adv by (means of), through

mediar vi (interceder) to mediate, intervene

medicación nf medication, treatment

medicamento nm medicine, drug

medicina nf medicine

medición nf measurement

médico, -a adj medical ♦ nm/f doctor

medida nf measure; (medición) measurement; (prudencia) moderation, prudence; **en cierta/gran ~** up to a point/to a great extent; **un traje a la ~** a made-to-measure suit; **~ de cuello** collar size; **a ~ de** in proportion to; (de acuerdo con) in keeping with; **a ~ que** (conforme) as ❑ **medidor** (LAm) nm meter ▶ **medidor de gas** gas meter

medio, -a adj half (a); (punto) mid, middle; (promedio) average ♦ adv half ♦ nm (centro) middle, center (US), centre (BRIT); (promedio) average; (método) means, way; (ambiente) environment; **~s** nmpl means, resources; **~ litro** half a liter (US) o litre (BRIT); **las tres y media** half past three; **a ~ terminar** half finished; **pagar a medias** to share the cost ▶ **medio ambiente** environment ▶ **Medio Oriente** Middle East ❑ **medioambiental** adj (política, efectos) environmental

mediocre adj mediocre

mediodía nm midday, noon

medir vt, vi (gen) to measure

meditar vt to ponder, think over, meditate on; (planear) to think out

mediterráneo, -a adj Mediterranean ♦ nm: **el M~** the Mediterranean (Sea)

médula nf (ANAT) marrow ▶ **médula espinal** spinal cord

medusa (ESP) nf jellyfish

megafonía nf public address system, PA system ❑ **megáfono** nm megaphone

megalómano, -a nm/f megalomaniac

mejicano, -a (ESP) adj, nm/f Mexican

Méjico (ESP) nm Mexico

mejilla nf cheek

mejillón nm mussel

mejor adj, adv (compar) better; (superl) best; **a lo ~** probably; (quizá) maybe; **~ dicho** rather; **tanto ~** so much the better

mejora nf improvement ❑ **mejorar** vt to improve, make better ♦ vi to improve, get better; **mejorarse** vr to improve, get better

melancólico, -a adj (triste) sad, melancholy; (soñador) dreamy

melena nf (de persona) long hair; (ZOOL) mane

mellizo, -a adj, nm/f twin

melocotón (ESP) nm peach

melodía nf melody, tune

melodrama nm melodrama ❑ **melodramático, -a** adj melodramatic

melón nm melon

membrete nm letterhead

membrillo nm quince; **carne de ~** quince jelly

memorable adj memorable

memoria nf (gen) memory; **~s** nfpl (de autor) memoirs ❑ **memorizar** vt to memorize

menaje nm (tb: **artículos de ~**) household items

mencionar vt to mention

mendigar vt to beg (for)

mendigo, -a nm/f beggar

mendrugo nm crust

menear vt to move; **menearse** vr to shake; (balancearse) to sway; (moverse) to move; (fig) to get a move on

menestra nf (tb: **~ de verduras**) vegetable stew

menguante adj decreasing, diminishing

menguar vt to lessen, diminish ♦ vi to diminish, decrease

menopausia nf menopause

menor adj (más pequeño: compar) smaller; (: superl) smallest; (más joven: compar) younger; (: superl) youngest; (MÚS) minor ♦ nmf (joven) young person, juvenile; **no tengo la ~ idea** I haven't the faintest idea; **al por ~** retail ▶ **menor de edad** person under age

Menorca nf Minorca

---

menos

PALABRA CLAVE

adj

1: **menos (que/de)** (compar: cantidad) less (than); (: número) fewer (than); **con menos entusiasmo** with less enthusiasm; **menos gente** fewer people; ver tb **cada**

2 (superl): **es el que menos culpa tiene** he is the least to blame

♦ adv

1 (compar): **menos (que/de)** less (than); **me gusta menos que el otro** I like it less than the other one

2 (superl): **es el menos listo (de su clase)** he's the least bright in his class; **de todas ellas es la que menos me agrada** out of all of them she's the one I like least; **(por) lo menos** at (the very) least

3 (locuciones): **no quiero verla y menos visitarla** I don't want to see her, let alone visit her; **tenemos 7 de menos** we're seven short ♦ prep except; (cifras) minus; **todos menos él** everyone except (for) him; **5 menos 2** 5 minus 2

♦ conj: **a menos que: a menos que venga mañana** unless he comes tomorrow

menospreciar vt to underrate, undervalue; (despreciar) to scorn, despise

mensaje nm message ▶ **mensaje de texto** text message; **enviar un ~ de texto a algn** to text sb ☐ **mensajero, -a** nm/f messenger

menso, -a (MÉX: fam) adj stupid

menstruación nf menstruation

menstruar vi to menstruate

mensual adj monthly; **5000 pesos ~es** 5000 pesos a month ☐ **mensualidad** nf (salario) monthly salary; (COM) monthly payment, monthly installment (US) o instalment (BRIT)

menta nf mint

mental adj mental ☐ **mentalidad** nf mentality ☐ **mentalizar** vt (sensibilizar) to make aware; (convencer) to convince; (padres) to prepare (mentally); **mentalizarse** vr (concienciarse) to become aware; **mentalizarse (de)** to get used to the idea (of); **mentalizarse de que ...** (convencerse) to get it into one's head that ...

mentar vt to mention, name

mente nf mind

mentir vi to lie

mentira nf (una mentira) lie; (acto) lying; (invención) fiction; **parece ~ que ...** it seems incredible that ..., I can't believe that ...

mentiroso, -a adj lying ♦ nm/f liar

menú (pl ~s) nm menu ▶ **menú del día** set menu

menudencias (LAm) nfpl giblets

menudo, -a adj (pequeño) small, tiny; (sin importancia) petty, insignificant; **¡~ negocio!** (fam) some deal!; **a ~** often, frequently

meñique nm little finger

meollo nm (fig) core

mercado nm market ▶ **mercado de chácharas** (MÉX) flea market ▶ **mercado de pulgas** (LAm) flea market

mercancía nf commodity; **~s** nfpl goods, merchandise sg

mercantil adj mercantile, commercial

mercenario, -a adj, nm mercenary

mercería nf notions pl (US), haberdashery (BRIT); (tienda) notions store (US), haberdasher's (BRIT)

mercurio nm mercury

merecer vt to deserve, merit ♦ vi to be deserving, be worthy; **merece la pena** it's worthwhile ☐ **merecido, -a** adj (well) deserved; **llevar su merecido** to get one's deserts

merendar vt to have for tea ♦ vi to have tea; (en el campo) to have a picnic ☐ **merendero** nm open-air cafe

merengue nm meringue

meridiano nm (GEO) meridian

merienda nf (light) tea, afternoon snack; (de campo) picnic

mérito nm merit; (valor) worth, value

merluza nf hake

merma nf decrease; (pérdida) wastage ☐ **mermar** vt to reduce, lessen ♦ vi to decrease, dwindle

mermelada nf (de fresa, ciruela etc) jelly (US), jam (BRIT); (de naranja) marmalade

mero, -a adj mere; (MÉX, CAm: fam) very

merodear vi: **~ por** to prowl about

mes nm month

mesa nf table; (de trabajo) desk; (GEO) plateau; **poner/quitar la ~** to lay/clear the table ▶ **mesa de juntas** conference table ▶ **mesa redonda** (reunión) round table ☐ **mesero, -a** (LAm) nm/f waiter (waitress)

meseta nf (GEO) plateau, tableland

mesilla nf (tb: **~ de noche**) bedside table

mesón nm inn

mestizo, -a adj of mixed race, half-caste (BRIT) ♦ nm/f person of mixed race, half-caste (BRIT)

mesura nf moderation, restraint

meta nf goal; (de carrera) finish

metabolismo nm metabolism

metáfora nf metaphor

metal nm (materia) metal; (MÚS) brass ☐ **metálico, -a** adj metallic; (de metal) metal ♦ nm (dinero contante) cash

metalurgia nf metallurgy

meteoro nm meteor ☐ **meteorología** nf meteorology

meter vt (colocar) to put, place; (introducir) to put in, insert; (involucrar) to involve; (causar) to make, cause; **meterse** vr: **~se en** to go into, enter; (fig) to interfere in, meddle in; **~se a** to start; **~se a escritor** to become a writer; **~se con algn** to provoke sb, pick a quarrel with sb

meticuloso, -a adj meticulous, thorough

metódico, -a adj methodical
método nm method
metralleta nf sub-machine-gun
métrico, -a adj metric
metro nm meter (US), metre (BRIT); (tren) subway (US), underground (BRIT)
México (LAm) nm Mexico; **Ciudad de ~** Mexico City
mezcla nf mixture ❏ **mezcladora** (MÉX) nf (tb: **mezcladora de cemento**) cement mixer ❏ **mezclar** vt to mix (up); **mezclarse** vr to mix, mingle; **mezclarse en** to get mixed up in, get involved in
mezquino, -a adj stingy, mean (BRIT)
mezquita nf mosque
mg. abr (= miligramo) mg
mi adj pos my ♦ nm (MÚS) E
mí pron me; myself
mía pron ver **mío**
miaja nf crumb
michelín (fam) nm (de grasa) spare tire (US) o tyre (BRIT)
microbio nm microbe
micrófono nm microphone
microondas nm inv (tb: **horno ~**) microwave (oven)
microscopio nm microscope
miedo nm fear; (nerviosismo) apprehension, nervousness; **tener ~** to be afraid; **de ~** wonderful, great; **hace un frío de ~** (fam) it's terribly cold ❏ **miedoso, -a** adj fearful, timid
miel nf honey
miembro nm limb; (socio) member ▶ **miembro viril** penis
mientras conj while; (duración) as long as ♦ adv meanwhile; **~ tanto** meanwhile; **más tiene, más quiere** the more he has, the more he wants
miércoles nm inv Wednesday
miga nf crumb; (fig: meollo) essence; **hacer buenas ~s** (fam) to get on well
mil num thousand; **cinco ~ dólares** five thousand dollars
milagro nm miracle ❏ **milagroso, -a** adj miraculous
milésima nf (de segundo) thousandth
milicia nf militia; (servicio militar) military service
milímetro nm millimeter (US), millimetre (BRIT)
militante adj militant
militar adj military ♦ nmf soldier ♦ vi (MIL) to serve; (en un partido) to be a member

milla nf mile
millar nm thousand
millón num million ❏ **millonario, -a** nm/f millionaire
milusos (MÉX) nm inv odd-job man
mimar vt to spoil, pamper
mimbre nm wicker
mímica nf (para comunicarse) sign language; (imitación) mimicry
mimo nm (caricia) caress; (de niño) spoiling; (TEATRO) mime; (: actor) mime artist
mina nf mine ❏ **minar** vt to mine; (fig) to undermine
mineral adj mineral ♦ nm (GEO) mineral; (mena) ore
minero, -a adj mining cpd ♦ nm/f miner
miniatura adj inv, nf miniature
minidisco nm MiniDisc®
minifalda nf miniskirt
mínimo, -a adj, nm minimum
minino, -a (fam) nm/f puss, pussy
ministerio nm (LAm exc MÉX, ESP) Ministry ▶ **Ministerio de Hacienda** Treasury, Treasury Department (US) ▶ **Ministerio de Relaciones Exteriores** (LAm exc MÉX) State Department (US), Foreign Office (BRIT)
ministro, -a nm/f secretary (US), minister (BRIT)
minoría nf minority
minucioso, -a adj thorough, meticulous; (prolijo) very detailed
minúscula nf small letter
minúsculo, -a adj tiny, minute
minusválido, -a adj (physically) handicapped ♦ nm/f (physically) handicapped person
minuta nf (de comida) menu
minutero nm minute hand
minuto nm minute
mío, -a pron: **el ~/la mía** mine; **un amigo ~** a friend of mine; **lo ~** what is mine
miope adj near-sighted (US), shortsighted (BRIT)
mira nf (de arma) sight(s) (pl); (fig) aim, intention
mirada nf look, glance; (expresión) look, expression; **clavar la ~ en** to stare at; **echar una ~ a** to glance at
mirado, -a adj (sensato) sensible; (considerado) considerate; **bien/mal ~** well/not well thought of; **bien ~** all things considered

mirador nm viewpoint, vantage point

mirar vt to look at; (observar) to watch; (considerar) to consider, think over; (vigilar, cuidar) to watch, look after ♦ vi to look; (ARQ) to face; **mirarse** vr (dos personas) to look at each other; ~ **bien/mal** to think highly of/ have a poor opinion of; ~**se al espejo** to look at o.s. in the mirror

mirilla nf spyhole, peephole

mirlo nm blackbird

misa nf mass

miserable adj (avaro) stingy, mean (BRIT); (nimio) miserable, paltry; (lugar) squalid; (fam) vile, despicable ♦ nmf (malvado) rogue

miseria nf (pobreza) poverty; (tacañería) stinginess, meanness (BRIT); (condiciones) squalor; **una** ~ a pittance

misericordia nf (compasión) compassion, pity; (piedad) mercy

misil nm missile

misión nf mission ❑ **misionero, -a** nm/f missionary

mismo, -a adj (semejante) same; (después de pron) -self; (para énfasis) very ♦ adv: **aquí/hoy** ~ right here/this very day ♦ conj: **lo** ~ **que** just like, just as; **el** ~ **traje** the same suit; **en ese** ~ **momento** at that very moment; **vino el** ~ **Ministro** the minister himself came; **yo** ~ **lo vi** I saw it myself; **ahora** ~ right now; **lo** ~ the same (thing); **da lo** ~ it's all the same; **quedamos en las mismas** we're no further forward; **por lo** ~ for the same reason

misterio nm mystery ❑ **misterioso, -a** adj mysterious

mitad nf (medio) half; (centro) middle; **a** ~ **de precio** (at) half-price; **en** o **a** ~ **del camino** halfway along the road; **cortar por la** ~ to cut through the middle

mitigar vt to mitigate; (dolor) to ease; (sed) to quench

mitin (pl **mítines**) nm meeting

mito nm myth

mixto, -a adj mixed

ml. abr (= mililitro) ml

mm. abr (= milímetro) mm

mobiliario nm furniture

mochila nf backpack, rucksack (BRIT)

moción nf motion

moco nm mucus; ~**s** nmpl (fam) snot; **limpiarse los** ~**s de la nariz** (fam) to wipe one's nose

moda nf fashion; (estilo) style; **a la** o **de** ~ in fashion, fashionable; **pasado de** ~ out of fashion

modales nmpl manners

modalidad nf kind, variety

modelar vt to model

modelo adj inv, nmf model

módem nm (INFORM) modem

moderado, -a adj moderate

moderar vt to moderate; (violencia) to restrain, control; (velocidad) to reduce; **moderarse** vr to restrain o.s., control o.s.

modernizar vt to modernize

moderno, -a adj modern; (actual) present-day

modestia nf modesty ❑ **modesto, -a** adj modest

módico, -a adj moderate, reasonable

modificar vt to modify

modisto, -a nm/f (diseñador) couturier, designer; (que confecciona) dressmaker

modo nm way, manner; (MÚS) mode; ~**s** nmpl manners; **de ningún** ~ in no way; **de todos** ~**s** at any rate ▶ **modo de empleo** directions pl (for use)

modorra nf drowsiness

mofa nf: hacer ~ **de** to mock ❑ **mofarse** vr: **mofarse de** to mock, scoff at

mofle (MÉX, CAm) nm muffler (US), silencer (BRIT)

moho nm mold (US), mould (BRIT), mildew; (en metal) rust ❑ **mohoso, -a** adj moldy (US), mouldy (BRIT); rusty

mojar vt to wet; (humedecer) to damp(en), moisten; (calar) to soak; **mojarse** vr to get wet

mojón nm boundary stone

molcajete (MÉX) nm mortar

molde nm mold (US), mould (BRIT); (COSTURA) pattern; (fig) model ❑ **moldeado** nm light perm ❑ **moldear** vt to mold (US), mould (BRIT)

mole nf mass, bulk; (edificio) pile

moler vt to grind, crush

molestar vt to bother; (fastidiar) to annoy; (incomodar) to inconvenience, put out ♦ vi to be a nuisance; **molestarse** vr to bother; (incomodarse) to go to trouble; (ofenderse) to take offense (US) o offence (BRIT); **¿(no) te molesta si ...?** do you mind if ...?

⚠ No confundir **molestar** con la palabra inglesa **molest**.

molestia nf bother, trouble; (incomodidad) inconvenience; (MED) discomfort; **es una** ~ it's a nuisance ❑ **molesto, -a** adj (que fastidia) annoying; (incómodo) inconvenient; (inquieto) uncomfortable, ill at ease; (enfadado) annoyed

molido, -a adj: **estar ~** (fig) to be exhausted o dead beat

molinillo nm hand mill ▶ **molinillo de café** coffee grinder

molino nm (edificio) mill; (máquina) grinder

momentáneo, -a adj momentary

momento nm moment; **de ~** at the moment, for the moment

momia nf mummy

monarca nmf monarch, ruler
❑ **monarquía** nf monarchy
❑ **monárquico, -a** nm/f royalist, monarchist

monasterio nm monastery

mondar vt to peel

mondongo (LAm exc MÉX) nm tripe

moneda nf (tipo de dinero) currency, money; (pieza) coin; **una ~ de 10 pesos** a 10-peso piece ❑ **monedero** nm coin purse (US), purse (BRIT) ❑ **monetario, -a** adj monetary, financial

monitor, a nm/f instructor, coach ♦ nm (TV) set; (INFORM) monitor

monja nf nun

monje nm monk

mono, -a adj (bonito) pretty, attractive; (gracioso) nice, charming ♦ nm/f monkey, ape ♦ nm (ESP: overol) coveralls pl (US), overalls pl (BRIT); (: con peto) dungarees pl, overalls pl (US)

monopatín nm skateboard; (CS: moto) scooter

monopolio nm monopoly
❑ **monopolizar** vt to monopolize

monotonía nf (sonido) monotone; (fig) monotony

monótono, -a adj monotonous

monstruo nm monster ♦ adj inv fantastic
❑ **monstruoso, -a** adj monstrous

montaje nm assembly; (TEATRO) décor; (CINE) montage

montaña nf (monte) mountain; (sierra) mountains pl, mountainous area
▶ **montaña rusa** roller coaster
❑ **montañero, -a** nm/f mountaineer
❑ **montañés, -esa** nm/f highlander
❑ **montañismo** nm mountaineering

montar vt (subir a) to mount, get on; (TEC) to assemble, put together; (negocio) to set up; (arma) to cock; (colocar) to lift on to; (CULIN) to beat ♦ vi to mount, get on; (sobresalir) to overlap; **~ en cólera** to get angry; **~ a caballo** to ride, go horseriding

monte nm (montaña) mountain; (bosque) woodland; (área sin cultivar) wild area, wild country ▶ **monte de piedad** pawnshop

montón nm heap, pile; (fig): **un ~ de** heaps of, lots of

monumento nm monument

monzón nm monsoon

moño nm bun

moqueta (ESP) nf fitted carpet

mora nf blackberry; ver tb **moro**

morada nf (casa) dwelling, abode

morado, -a adj purple, violet ♦ nm bruise

moral adj moral ♦ nf (ética) ethics pl; (moralidad) morals pl, morality; (ánimo) morale

moraleja nf moral

moralidad nf morals pl, morality

morboso, -a adj morbid

morcilla nf blood sausage, ≈ black pudding (BRIT)

mordaz adj (crítica) biting, scathing

mordaza nf (para la boca) gag; (TEC) clamp

morder vt to bite; (fig: consumir) to eat away, eat into ❑ **mordisco** nm bite

moreno, -a adj (color) (dark) brown; (de tez) dark; (de pelo moreno) dark-haired; (negro) black

morfina nf morphine

moribundo, -a adj dying

morir vi to die; (fuego) to die down; (luz) to go out; **morirse** vr to die; (fig) to be dying; **murió en un accidente** he was killed in an accident; **~se por algo** to be dying for sth

moro, -a adj Moorish ♦ nm/f Moor

moroso, -a nm/f bad debtor, defaulter

morral nm backpack, rucksack (BRIT)

morraña (MÉX) nf (cambio) small o loose (BRIT) change

morro nm (ZOOL) snout, nose; (AUTO, AVIAT) nose

morsa nf walrus

mortadela nf mortadella

mortaja nf shroud

mortal adj mortal; (golpe) deadly
❑ **mortalidad** nf mortality

mortero nm mortar

mortífero, -a adj deadly, lethal

mortificar vt to mortify

mosca nf fly

Moscú n Moscow

mosquearse (fam) vr (enojarse) to get cross; (ofenderse) to take offense (US) o offence (BRIT)

mosquitero nm mosquito net

mosquito nm mosquito

mostaza nf mustard

mosto nm (unfermented) grape juice

mostrador nm (de tienda) counter; (de café) bar

mostrar vt to show; (exhibir) to display, exhibit; (explicar) to explain; **mostrarse** vr: ~**se amable** to be kind; to prove to be kind; **no se muestra muy inteligente** he doesn't seem (to be) very intelligent

mota nf speck, tiny piece; (en diseño) dot; (MÉX: fam) pot

mote nm nickname

motín nm (del pueblo) revolt, rising; (del ejército) mutiny

motivar vt (causar) to cause, motivate; (explicar) to explain, justify ❏ **motivo** nm motive, reason

moto (fam) nf = **motocicleta**

motocicleta nf motorcycle, motorbike (BRIT)

motoneta (CS) nf scooter

motor nm motor, engine ▶ **motor a chorro** o **de reacción/de explosión** jet engine/internal combustion engine

motora nf motorboat

movedizo, -a adj ver **arena**

mover vt to move; (cabeza) to shake; (accionar) to drive; (fig) to cause, provoke; **moverse** vr to move; (fig) to get a move on

móvil nm motive ♦ adj mobile; (pieza de máquina) moving; (mueble) movable; **teléfono ~** (ESP) mobile phone ❏ **movilidad** nf mobility ❏ **movilizar** vt to mobilize

movimiento nm movement; (TEC) motion; (actividad) activity

mozo, -a adj (joven) young ♦ nm/f youth, young man (girl); (CS: mesero) waiter (waitress)

mucama (RPI) nf maid

muchacho, -a nm/f (niño) boy (girl)

muchedumbre nf crowd

---

mucho, -a

PALABRA CLAVE

adj

1 (cantidad) a lot of, much; (número) lots of, a lot of, many; **mucho dinero** a lot of money; **hace mucho calor** it's very hot; **muchas amigas** lots o a lot of friends

2 (sg: grande); **ésta es mucha casa para él** this house is much too big for him

♦ pron: **tengo mucho que hacer** I've got a lot to do; **muchos dicen que ...** a lot of people say that ...; ver tb **tener**

♦ adv

1: **me gusta mucho** I like it a lot; **lo siento mucho** I'm very sorry; **come mucho** he eats a lot; **¿te vas a quedar mucho?** are you going to be staying long?

2 (respuesta) very; **¿estás cansado?** -- **¡mucho!** are you tired? -- very!

3 (locuciones): **como mucho** at (the) most; **con mucho: el mejor con mucho** by far the best; **ni mucho menos: no es rico ni mucho menos** he's far from being rich

4: **por mucho que: por mucho que le creas** no matter how o however much you believe her

---

muda nf change of clothes

mudanza nf (de casa) move

mudar vt to change; (ZOOL) to shed ♦ vi to change; **mudarse** vr (ropa) to change; ~**se de casa** to move house

mudo, -a adj dumb; (callado, CINE) silent

mueble nm piece of furniture; ~**s** nmpl furniture sg

mueca nf face, grimace; **hacer** ~**s a** to make faces at

muela nf back tooth

muelle nm spring; (NÁUT) wharf; (malecón) pier

muero etc vb ver **morir**

muerte nf death; (homicidio) murder; **dar** ~ **a** to kill

muerto, -a pp de **morir** ♦ adj dead ♦ nm/f dead man (woman); (difunto) deceased; (cadáver) corpse; **estar** ~ **de cansancio** to be dead tired ▶ **Día de los Muertos** (MÉX) All Soul's Day

DÍA DE LOS MUERTOS

Día de los Muertos (or "Day of the Dead") in Mexico coincides with All Saints' Day, which is celebrated in the Catholic countries of Latin America on November 1st and 2nd. **Día de los Muertos** is actually a celebration which begins in the evening of October 31st and continues until November 2nd. It is a combination of the Catholic tradition of honoring the Christian saints and martyrs, and the ancient Mexican or Aztec traditions, in which death was not something sinister. For this reason all the dead are honored by bringing offerings of food, flowers and candles to the cemetery.

muestra nf (señal) indication, sign; (demostración) demonstration; (prueba) proof; (estadística) sample; (modelo) model, pattern; (testimonio) token

muestreo nm sample, sampling
muestro etc vb ver **mostrar**
muevo etc vb ver **mover**
mugir vi (vaca) to moo
mugre nf dirt, filth □ **mugriento, -a** adj dirty, filthy
mujer nf woman; (esposa) wife □ **mujeriego** nm womanizer
mula nf mule
muleta nf (para andar) crutch; (TAUR) stick with red cape attached
mullido, -a adj (cama) soft; (hierba) soft, springy
multa nf fine; **poner una ~ a** to fine □ **multar** vt to fine
multicines nmpl multiscreen movie theater sg (US) o cinema sg (BRIT)
multinacional nf multinational
múltiple adj multiple; (pl) many, numerous
multiplicar vt (MAT) to multiply; (fig) to increase; **multiplicarse** vr (BIO) to multiply; (fig) to be everywhere at once
multitud nf (muchedumbre) crowd; **~ de** lots of
mundano, -a adj worldly
mundial adj world-wide, universal; (guerra, récord) world cpd
mundo nm world; **todo el ~** everybody; **tener ~** to be experienced, know one's way around
munición nf ammunition
municipal adj municipal, local
municipio nm (ayuntamiento) town council, corporation; (territorio administrativo) town, municipality
muñeca nf (ANAT) wrist; (juguete) doll
muñeco nm (figura) figure; (marioneta) puppet; (fig) puppet, pawn
mural adj mural, wall cpd ♦ nm mural
muralismo nm muralism

MURALISMO

Muralismo, or mural painting, is an artistic movement which began in Mexico in the 1920s. It was a new popular culture with roots in the pre-Columbian Indian culture and traditions of Mexico. Diego Rivera, José Clemente Orozco, and David Alfaro Siqueiros are some of Mexico's most famous muralists.

---

muralla nf (city) wall(s) (pl)
murciélago nm bat
murmullo nm murmur(ing); (cuchicheo) whispering

murmuración nf gossip □ **murmurar** vi to murmur, whisper; (cotillear) to gossip
muro nm wall
muscular adj muscular
músculo nm muscle
museo nm museum ▶ **museo de arte** art gallery
musgo nm moss
música nf music; ver tb **músico**
músico, -a adj musical ♦ nm/f musician
muslo nm thigh
mustio, -a adj (persona) depressed, gloomy; (planta) faded, withered
musulmán, -ana nm/f Moslem
mutación nf (BIO) mutation; (cambio) (sudden) change
mutilar vt to mutilate; (a una persona) to maim
mutismo nm (de persona) uncommunicativeness; (de autoridades) silence
mutuamente adv mutually
mutuo, -a adj mutual
muy adv very; (demasiado) too; **M~ Señor mío** Dear Sir; **~ de noche** very late at night; **eso es ~ de él** that's just like him

Nn

N abr (= norte) N
nabo nm turnip
nácar nm mother-of-pearl
nacer vi to be born; (de huevo) to hatch; (vegetal) to sprout; (río) to rise; **nací en Monterrey** I was born in Monterrey; **nació una sospecha en su mente** a suspicion formed in her mind □ **nacido, -a** adj born; **recién nacido** newborn □ **naciente** adj new, emerging; (sol) rising □ **nacimiento** nm birth; (de Navidad) Nativity; (de río) source
nación nf nation □ **nacional** adj national □ **nacionalismo** nm nationalism □ **nacionalista** nmf nationalist □ **nacionalizar** vt to nationalize; **nacionalizarse** vr (persona) to become naturalized
nada pron nothing ♦ adv not at all, in no way; **no decir ~** to say nothing, not to say anything; **~ más** nothing else; **de ~** don't mention it
nadador, a nm/f swimmer
nadar vi to swim

nadie *pron* nobody, no-one; **~ habló** nobody spoke; **no había ~** there was nobody there, there wasn't anybody there

nado: **a ~** *adv*: **pasar a ~** to swim across

nafta (*RPI*) *nf* gas (*US*), petrol (*BRIT*)

naipe *nm* (playing) card; **~s** *nmpl* cards

nalgas *nfpl* buttocks

nalguear (*MÉX, CAm*) *vt* to spank

naranja *adj inv, nf* orange; **media ~** (*fam*) better half ❏ **naranjada** *nf* orangeade ❏ **naranjo** *nm* orange tree

narciso *nm* narcissus

narcótico, -a *adj, nm* narcotic ❏ **narcotizar** *vt* to drug ❏ **narcotráfico** *nm* drug trafficking *o* running

nardo *nm* lily

narigudo, -a *adj* big-nosed

nariz *nf* nose

narración *nf* narration ❏ **narrador, a** *nm/f* narrator

narrar *vt* to narrate, recount ❏ **narrativa** *nf* narrative

nata (*ESP*) *nf* cream ▸ **nata montada** whipped cream

natación *nf* swimming

natal *adj*: **ciudad ~** home town ❏ **natalidad** *nf* birth rate

natillas *nfpl* custard *sg*

nativo, -a *adj, nm/f* native

nato, -a *adj* born; **un músico ~** a born musician

natural *adj* natural; (*fruta etc*) fresh ♦ *nmf* native ♦ *nm* (*disposición*) nature

naturaleza *nf* nature; (*género*) nature, kind ▸ **naturaleza muerta** still life

naturalidad *nf* naturalness

naturalmente *adv* (*de modo natural*) in a natural way; **¡~!** of course!

naufragar *vi* to sink ❏ **naufragio** *nm* shipwreck ❏ **náufrago, -a** *nm/f* castaway, shipwrecked person

nauseabundo, -a *adj* nauseating, sickening

náuseas *nfpl* nausea *sg*; **me da ~** it makes me feel sick

náutico, -a *adj* nautical

navaja *nf* knife; (*de barbero, peluquero*) razor

naval *adj* naval

Navarra *n* Navarre

nave *nf* (*barco*) ship, vessel; (*ARQ*) nave ▸ **nave espacial** spaceship

navegación *nf* navigation; (*viaje*) sea journey ▸ **navegación aérea** air traffic ▸ **navegación costera** coastal shipping

❏ **navegador** *nm* (*INFORM*) browser

❏ **navegante** *nmf* navigator ❏ **navegar** *vi* (*barco*) to sail; (*avión*) to fly

Navidad *nf* Christmas; **~es** *nfpl* Christmas time; **¡Feliz ~!** Merry Christmas! ❏ **navideño, -a** *adj* Christmas *cpd*

navío *nm* ship

nazca *etc vb ver* **nacer**

nazi *adj, nmf* Nazi

NE *abr* (= *nor(d)este*) NE

neblina *nf* mist

nebulosa *nf* nebula

necesario, -a *adj* necessary

neceser *nm* travel kit (*US*), toilet bag (*BRIT*); (*bolsa grande*) carryall (*US*), holdall (*BRIT*)

necesidad *nf* need; (*lo inevitable*) necessity; (*miseria*) poverty; **en caso de ~** in case of need *o* emergency; **hacer sus ~es** to relieve o.s.

necesitado, -a *adj* needy, poor; **~ de** in need of

necesitar *vt* to need, require

necio, -a *adj* foolish

necrópolis *nf inv* cemetery

nectarina *nf* nectarine

nefasto, -a *adj* ill-fated, unlucky

negación *nf* negation; (*rechazo*) refusal, denial

negar *vt* (*renegar, rechazar*) to refuse; (*prohibir*) to refuse, deny; (*desmentir*) to deny; **negarse** *vr*: **~se a** to refuse to

negativa *nf* negative; (*rechazo*) refusal, denial

negativo, -a *adj, nm* negative

negligencia *nf* negligence ❏ **negligente** *adj* negligent

negociado *nm* department, section

negociante *nmf* businessman(-woman)

negociar *vt, vi* to negotiate; **~ en** to deal in, trade in

negocio *nm* (*COM*) business; (*asunto*) affair, business; (*operación comercial*) deal, transaction; (*lugar*) place of business; **los ~s** business *sg*; **hacer ~** to do business

negra *nf* (*MÚS*) quarter note (*US*), crotchet (*BRIT*); *ver tb* **negro**

negro, -a *adj* black; (*suerte*) awful ♦ *nm* black ♦ *nm/f* black man (woman)

nene, -a *nm/f* baby, small child

nenúfar *nm* water lily

neologismo *nm* neologism

neón *nm*: **luces/lámpara de ~** neon lights/lamp

neoyorquino, -a *adj* (of) New York

nervio nm nerve □ **nerviosismo** nm nervousness, nerves pl □ **nervioso, -a** adj nervous

neto, -a adj net

neumático, -a adj pneumatic ♦ nm tire (US), tyre (BRIT) ► **neumático de recambio** spare tire

neurasténico, a adj (fig) hysterical

neurólogo, -a nm/f neurologist

neurona nf nerve cell

neutral adj neutral □ **neutralizar** vt to neutralize; (contrarrestar) to counteract

neutro, -a adj (BIO, LING) neuter

neutrón nm neutron

nevada nf snowstorm; (caída de nieve) snowfall

nevar vi to snow

nevera (ESP) nf refrigerator, icebox (US)

nevería (MÉX) nf ice-cream parlor (US) o parlour (BRIT)

nexo nm link, connection

ni conj nor, neither; (tb: **ni siquiera**) not ... even; **ni aunque que** not even if; **ni blanco ni negro** neither white nor black

Nicaragua nf Nicaragua □ **nicaragüense** adj, nmf Nicaraguan

nicho nm niche

nicotina nf nicotine

nido nm nest

niebla nf fog; (neblina) mist

niego etc vb ver **negar**

nieto, -a nm/f grandson/daughter; **~s** nmpl grandchildren

nieve etc vb ver **nevar** ♦ nf snow; (MÉX: helado) sorbet

NIF nm abr (= Número de Identificación Fiscal) ID number used for financial and tax purposes

nimiedad nf triviality

nimio, -a adj trivial, insignificant

ninfa nf nymph

ningún adj ver **ninguno**

ninguno, -a (delante de nm: **ningún**) adj no ♦ pron (nadie) nobody; (ni uno) none, not one; (ni uno ni otro) neither; **de ninguna manera** by no means, not at all

niña nf (ANAT) pupil; ver tb **niño**

niñera nf nursemaid (US), child's nurse (US), nanny (BRIT) □ **niñería** nf childish act

niñez nf childhood; (infancia) infancy

niño, -a adj (joven) young; (inmaduro) immature ♦ nm/f child, boy (girl)

nipón, -ona adj, nm/f Japanese

níquel nm nickel □ **niquelar** vt (TEC) to nickel-plate

níspero nm medlar

nitidez nf (claridad) clarity; (: de imagen) sharpness □ **nítido, -a** adj clear; sharp

nitrato nm nitrate

nitrógeno nm nitrogen

nivel nm (GEO) level; (norma) level, standard; (altura) height ► **nivel de aceite** oil level ► **nivel de aire** spirit level ► **nivel de vida** standard of living □ **nivelar** vt to level out; (fig) to even up; (COM) to balance

NN.UU. nfpl abr (= Naciones Unidas) UN sg

no adv no; not; (con verbo) not ♦ excl no!; **no tengo nada** I don't have anything, I have nothing; **no es el mío** it's not mine; **ahora no** not now; **¿no lo sabes?** don't you know?; **no mucho** not much; **no bien termine, lo entregaré** as soon as I finish, I'll hand it over; **no más, ayer no más** just yesterday; **¡pase no más!** come in!; **¡a que no lo sabes!** I bet you don't know!; **¡cómo no!** of course!; **los países no alineados** the non-aligned countries; **la no intervención** non-intervention

noble adj, nmf noble □ **nobleza** nf nobility

noche nf night; night-time; (la tarde) evening; **de ~, por la ~** at night; **es de ~** it's dark

Nochebuena nf Christmas Eve

Nochevieja (ESP) nf New Year's Eve

noción nf notion

nocivo, -a adj harmful

noctámbulo, -a nm/f sleepwalker

nocturno, -a adj (de la noche) nocturnal, night cpd; (de la tarde) evening cpd ♦ nm nocturne

nodriza nf wet nurse; **buque** o **nave ~** supply ship

nogal nm walnut tree

nómada adj nomadic ♦ nmf nomad

nombramiento nm naming; (a un empleo) appointment

nombrar vt (designar) to name; (mencionar) to mention; (dar puesto a) to appoint

nombre nm name; (sustantivo) noun; **~ y apellidos** name in full; **poner ~ a** to call, name ► **nombre común/propio** common/proper noun ► **nombre de pila/soltera** Christian/maiden name

nómina nf (lista) payroll; (hoja) wage statement (US), pay slip (BRIT)

nominal adj nominal

nominar vt to nominate

nominativo, -a adj (COM): **cheque ~ a X** check (US) o cheque (BRIT) made out to X

nono, -a adj ninth

nordeste adj north-east, north-eastern, north-easterly ♦ nm north-east

nórdico, -a adj Nordic

noreste adj, nm = **nordeste**

noria nf (AGR) waterwheel; (ESP: de carnaval) Ferris (US) o big (BRIT) wheel

norma nf rule (of thumb)

normal adj (corriente) normal; (habitual) usual, natural ❑ **normalidad** nf normality, normalcy (US); **restablecer la normalidad** to restore order ❑ **normalizar** vt (reglamentar) to normalize; (TEC) to standardize ❑ **normalizarse** vr to return to normal ❑ **normalmente** adv normally

normando, -a adj, nm/f Norman

normativa nf (set of) rules pl, regulations pl

noroeste adj north-west, north-western, north-westerly ♦ nm north-west

norte adj north, northern, northerly ♦ nm north; (fig) guide

norteamericano, -a adj, nm/f (North) American

Noruega nf Norway

noruego, -a adj, nm/f Norwegian

nos pron (directo) us; (indirecto) us; to us; for us; from us; (reflexivo) (to) ourselves; (recíproco) (to) each other; **~ levantamos a las 7** we get up at 7

nosotros, -as pron (suj) we; (después de prep) us

nostalgia nf nostalgia

nota nf note; (ESCOL) grade (US), mark (BRIT)

notable adj notable; (ESCOL) outstanding

notar vt to notice, note; **notarse** vr to be obvious; **se nota que ...** one observes that ...

notarial adj: **acta ~** affidavit

notario nm notary

noticia nf (información) piece of news; **las ~s** the news sg; **tener ~s de algn** to hear from sb

⚠ No confundir **noticia** con la palabra inglesa **notice**.

noticiero (LAm) nm news bulletin

notificación nf notification ❑ **notificar** vt to notify, inform

notoriedad nf fame, renown ❑ **notorio, -a** adj (público) well-known; (evidente) obvious

novato, -a adj inexperienced ♦ nm/f beginner, novice

novecientos, -as num nine hundred

novedad nf (calidad de nuevo) newness; (noticia) piece of news; (cambio) change, (new) development

novel adj new; (inexperto) inexperienced ♦ nmf beginner

novela nf novel

noveno, -a adj ninth

noventa num ninety

novia nf ver **novio**

noviazgo nm engagement

novicio, -a nm/f novice

noviembre nm November

novillada nf (TAUR) bullfight with young bulls ❑ **novillero** nm novice bullfighter ❑ **novillo** nm young bull, bullock; **hacer novillos** (fam) to play truant

novio, -a nm/f boyfriend (girlfriend); (prometido) fiancé (fiancée); (recién casado) bridegroom (bride); **los ~s** the newly-weds

nubarrón nm storm cloud

nube nf cloud

nublado, -a adj cloudy; **nublarse** vr to grow dark

nubosidad nf cloudiness; **había mucha ~** it was very cloudy

nuca nf nape of the neck

nuclear adj nuclear

núcleo nm (centro) core; (FÍSICA) nucleus

nudillo nm knuckle

nudista adj nudist

nudo nm knot ❑ **nudoso, -a** adj knotty

nuera nf daughter-in-law

nuestro, -a adj pos or ♦ pron ours; **~ padre** our father; **un amigo ~** a friend of ours; **es el ~** it's ours

nueva nf piece of news

nuevamente adv (otra vez) again; (de nuevo) anew

Nueva York n New York

Nueva Zelanda nf New Zealand

nueve num nine

nuevo, -a adj (gen) new; **de ~** again

nuez nf walnut; (ANAT) Adam's apple ▶ **nuez de la India** (MÉX) cashew (nut) ▶ **nuez moscada** nutmeg

nulidad nf (incapacidad) incompetence; (abolición) nullity

nulo, -a adj (inepto, torpe) useless; (inválido) (null and) void; (DEPORTE) drawn, tied

núm. abr (= número) no.

numeración nf (cifras) numbers pl; (arábiga, romana etc) numerals pl

numeral nm numeral

numerar *vt* to number

número *nm* (*gen*) number; (*tamaño: de zapato*) size; (*ejemplar: de diario*) number, issue; **sin ~** numberless, unnumbered
▶ **número atrasado** back number
▶ **número de matrícula/teléfono** registration/telephone number

numeroso, -a *adj* numerous

nunca *adv* (*jamás*) never; **~ lo pensé** I never thought it; **no viene ~** he never comes; **~ más** never again; **más que ~** more than ever

nupcias *nfpl* wedding *sg*, nuptials

nutria *nf* otter

nutrición *nf* nutrition

nutrido, -a *adj* (*alimentado*) nourished; (*fig: grande*) large; (*abundante*) abundant

nutrir *vt* (*alimentar*) to nourish; (*dar de comer*) to feed; (*fig*) to strengthen ◻ **nutritivo, -a** *adj* nourishing, nutritious

nylon *nm* nylon

Ññ

ñango, -a (*MÉX*) *adj* puny

ñapa (*LAm*) *nf* extra

ñata (*LAm: fam*) *nf* nose; *ver tb* **ñato**

ñato, -a (*LAm*) *adj* snub-nosed

ñoñería *nf* insipidity

ñoño, -a *adj* (*fam: tonto*) silly, stupid; (*soso*) insipid; (*persona*) spineless; (*ESP: película, novela*) sentimental

Oo

O *abr* (= *oeste*) W

o *conj* or

o/ *abr* (= *orden*) o

oasis *nm inv* oasis

obcecarse *vr* to get o become stubborn

obedecer *vt* to obey ◻ **obediencia** *nf* obedience ◻ **obediente** *adj* obedient

obertura *nf* overture

obesidad *nf* obesity ◻ **obeso, -a** *adj* obese

obispo *nm* bishop

obituario (*LAm*) *nm* obituary

objeción *nf* objection; **poner objeciones to** raise objections

objetar *vt, vi* to object

objetivo, -a *adj, nm* objective

objeto *nm* (*cosa*) object; (*fin*) aim

objetor, a *nm/f* objector

oblicuo, -a *adj* oblique; (*mirada*) sidelong

obligación *nf* obligation; (*COM*) bond

obligar *vt* to force; **obligarse** *vr* to bind o.s. ◻ **obligatorio, -a** *adj* compulsory, obligatory

oboe *nm* oboe

obra *nf* work; (*ARQ*) construction, building; (*TEATRO*) play; **por ~ de** thanks to (the efforts of) ▶ **obra maestra** masterpiece ▶ **obras públicas** public works ◻ **obrar** *vt* to work; (*tener efecto*) to have an effect on ♦ *vi* to act, behave; (*tener efecto*) to have an effect; **la carta obra en su poder** the letter is in his/her possession

obrero, -a *adj* (*clase*) working; (*movimiento*) labor *cpd* (*US*), labour *cpd* (*BRIT*) ♦ *nm/f* (*gen*) worker; (*sin oficio*) laborer (*US*), labourer (*BRIT*)

obscenidad *nf* obscenity ◻ **obsceno, -a** *adj* obscene

obsequiar *vt* (*ofrecer*) to present with; (*agasajar*) to make a fuss of, lavish attention on ◻ **obsequio** *nm* (*regalo*) gift; (*cortesía*) courtesy, attention

observación *nf* observation; (*reflexión*) remark

observador, a *nm/f* observer

observar *vt* to observe; (*anotar*) to notice; **observarse** *vr* to keep to, observe

obsesión *nf* obsession ◻ **obsesivo, -a** *adj* obsessive

obsoleto, -a *adj* obsolete

obstáculo *nm* obstacle; (*impedimento*) hindrance, drawback

obstante: no ~ *adv* nevertheless

obstinado, -a *adj* obstinate, stubborn

obstinarse *vr* to be obstinate; **~ en** to persist in

obstrucción *nf* obstruction ◻ **obstruir** *vt* to obstruct

obtener *vt* (*gen*) to obtain; (*premio*) to win

obturador *nm* (*FOTO*) shutter

obvio, -a *adj* obvious

oca *nf* (*animal*) goose; (*juego*) ≈ snakes and ladders

ocasión *nf* (*oportunidad*) opportunity, chance; (*momento*) occasion, time; (*causa*) cause; **de ~** secondhand ◻ **ocasionar** *vt* to cause

ocaso *nm* (*fig*) decline

occidente *nm* west

OCDE nf abr (= Organización de Cooperación y Desarrollo Económico) OECD

océano nm ocean; **el ~ Índico** the Indian Ocean

ochenta num eighty

ocho num eight; **~ días** a week

ocio nm (tiempo) leisure; (pey) idleness ❏ **ocioso, -a** adj (inactivo) idle; (inútil) useless

octavilla nf leaflet, pamphlet

octavo, -a adj eighth

octubre nm October

ocular adj ocular, eye cpd; **testigo ~** eyewitness

oculista nmf oculist

ocultar vt (esconder) to hide; (callar) to conceal ❏ **oculto, -a** adj hidden; (fig) secret

ocupación nf occupation

ocupado, -a adj (persona) busy; (plaza) occupied, taken; (teléfono) busy, engaged (BRIT) ❏ **ocupar** vt (gen) to occupy; **ocuparse** vr: **ocuparse de** o **en** (gen) to concern o.s. with; (cuidar) to look after

ocurrencia nf (idea) bright idea

ocurrir vi to happen; **ocurrirse** vr: **se me ocurrió que ...** it occurred to me that ...

odiar vt to hate ❏ **odio** nm hate, hatred ❏ **odioso, -a** adj (gen) hateful; (malo) nasty

odontólogo, -a nm/f dentist, dental surgeon

OEA nf abr (= Organización de Estados Americanos) OAS

oeste nm west; **una película del ~** a western

ofender vt (agraviar) to offend; (insultar) to insult; **ofenderse** vr to take offense (US) o offence (BRIT) ❏ **ofensa** nf offense (US), offence (BRIT) ❏ **ofensiva** nf offensive ❏ **ofensivo, -a** adj offensive

oferta nf offer; (propuesta) proposal; **la ~ y la demanda** supply and demand; **artículos en ~** goods on offer

oficial adj official ♦ nm (MIL) officer

oficina nf office ► **oficina de correos** post office ► **oficina de turismo** tourist office ❏ **oficinista** nmf clerk

oficio nm (profesión) profession; (puesto) post; (REL) service; **ser del ~** to be an old hand; **tener mucho ~** to have a lot of experience ► **oficio de difuntos** funeral service

oficioso, -a adj (pey) officious; (no oficial) unofficial, informal

ofimática nf office automation

ofrecer vt (dar) to offer; (proponer) to propose; **ofrecerse** vr (persona) to offer o.s., volunteer; (situación) to present itself; **¿qué**

se le ofrece?, ¿se le ofrece algo? what can I do for you?, can I get you anything?

ofrecimiento nm offer

oftalmólogo, -a nm/f ophthalmologist

ofuscar vt (por pasión) to blind; (por luz) to dazzle

oída nf: **de ~s** by hearsay

oído nm (ANAT) ear; (sentido) hearing

oigo etc vb ver **oír**

oír vt (gen) to hear; (atender a) to listen to; **¡oiga!** listen!; **~ misa** to attend mass

OIT nf abr (= Organización Internacional del Trabajo) ILO

ojal nm buttonhole

ojalá excl if only (it were so)!, some hope! ♦ conj if only ...!, would that ...!; **~ (que) venga hoy** I hope he comes today

ojeada nf glance

ojera nf: **tener ~s** to have bags under one's eyes

ojeriza nf ill-will

ojeroso, -a adj haggard

ojo nm eye; (de puente) span; (de cerradura) keyhole ♦ excl careful!; **tener ~ para** to have an eye for ► **ojo de buey** porthole

okey (LAm) excl O.K.

ola nf wave

olé excl bravo!, olé!

oleada nf big wave, swell; (fig) wave

oleaje nm swell

óleo nm oil ❏ **oleoducto** nm (oil) pipeline

oler vt (gen) to smell; (inquirir) to pry into; (fig: sospechar) to sniff out ♦ vi to smell; **~ a** to smell of

olfatear vt to smell; (inquirir) to pry into ❏ **olfato** nm sense of smell

oligarquía nf oligarchy

olimpiada nf: **las O~s** the Olympics ❏ **olímpico, -a** adj Olympic

oliva nf (aceituna) olive; **aceite de ~** olive oil ❏ **olivo** nm olive tree

olla nf pan; (comida) stew ► **olla de presión** (LAm) pressure cooker ► **olla podrida** type of Spanish stew

olmo nm elm (tree)

olor nm smell ❏ **oloroso, -a** adj scented

olvidar vt to forget; (omitir) to omit; **olvidarse** vr (fig) to forget o.s.; **se me olvidó** I forgot

olvido nm oblivion; (despiste) forgetfulness

ombligo nm navel

omelette (LAm) nf omelet(te)

omisión nf (abstención) omission; (descuido) neglect

omiso, -a adj: **hacer caso ~ de** to ignore, pass over

omitir vt to omit

omnipotente adj omnipotent

omóplato nm shoulder blade

OMS nf abr (= Organización Mundial de la Salud) WHO

once num eleven ❑ **onces** (CS) nfpl tea break sg

onda nf wave ▶ **onda corta/larga/media** short/long/medium wave ❑ **ondear** vt, vi to wave; (tener ondas) to be wavy; (agua) to ripple; **ondearse** vr to swing, sway

ondulación nf undulation ❑ **ondulado, -a** adj wavy

ondular vt (el pelo) to wave ♦ vi to undulate; **ondularse** vr to undulate

ONG nf abr (= organización no gubernamental) NGO

ONU nf abr (= Organización de las Naciones Unidas) UNO

opaco, -a adj opaque

opción nf (gen) option; (derecho) right, option

OPEP nf abr (= Organización de Países Exportadores de Petróleo) OPEC

ópera nf opera ▶ **ópera bufa** o **cómica** comic opera

operación nf (gen) operation; (COM) transaction, deal

operador, a nm/f operator; (CINE: de proyección) projectionist; (: de rodaje) cameraman

operar vt (producir) to produce, bring about; (MED) to operate on ♦ vi (COM) to operate, deal; **operarse** vr to occur; (MED) to have an operation

opereta nf operetta

opinar vt to think ♦ vi to give one's opinion ❑ **opinión** nf (creencia) belief; (criterio) opinion

opio nm opium

oponente nmf opponent

oponer vt (resistencia) to put up, offer; **oponerse** vr (objetar) to object; (estar frente a frente) to be opposed; (dos personas) to oppose each other; **~ A a B** to set A against B; **me opongo a pensar que ...** I refuse to believe o think that ...

oportunidad nf (ocasión) opportunity; (posibilidad) chance

oportuno, -a adj (en su tiempo) opportune, timely; (respuesta) suitable; **en el momento ~** at the right moment

oposición nf opposition; **oposiciones** nfpl (ESCOL) public examinations

opositor, a nm/f (adversario) opponent; (candidato): **~ (a)** candidate (for)

opresión nf oppression ❑ **opresivo, -a** adj oppressive ❑ **opresor, a** nm/f oppressor

oprimir vt to squeeze; (fig) to oppress

optar vi (elegir) to choose; **~ por** to opt for ❑ **optativo, -a** adj optional

óptica nf optician's; **desde esta ~** from this point of view

óptico, -a adj optic(al) ♦ nm/f optician

optimismo nm optimism ❑ **optimista** nmf optimist

óptimo, -a adj (el mejor) very best

opuesto, -a adj (contrario) opposite; (antagónico) opposing

opulencia nf opulence ❑ **opulento, -a** adj opulent

oración nf (REL) prayer; (LING) sentence

orador, a nm/f (conferenciante) speaker, orator

oral adj oral

orangután nm orangutan

orar vi to pray

oratoria nf oratory

órbita nf orbit

orden nm (gen) order ♦ nf (gen) order; (INFORM) command; **de primer ~** first-rate; **en ~ de prioridad** in order of priority ▶ **orden del día** agenda

ordenado, -a adj (metódico) methodical; (arreglado) orderly

ordenador (ESP) nm computer ▶ **ordenador central** mainframe (computer)

ordenanza nf ordinance

ordenar vt (mandar) to order; (poner orden) to put in order, arrange; **ordenarse** vr (REL) to be ordained

ordeñar vt to milk

ordinario, -a adj (común) ordinary, usual; (vulgar) vulgar, common

orégano nm oregano

oreja nf ear; (MECÁNICA) lug, flange

orfanato nm orphanage

orfandad nf orphanhood

orfebrería nf gold/silver work

orgánico, -a adj organic

organigrama nm flow chart

organismo nm (BIO) organism; (POL) organization

organización nf organization ❑ **organizar** vt to organize

órgano nm organ

orgasmo nm orgasm

orgía nf orgy

orgullo nm pride ❑ **orgulloso, -a** adj (gen) proud; (altanero) haughty

orientación nf (posición) position; (dirección) direction

oriental adj eastern; (del Lejano Oriente) oriental

orientar vt (situar) to orientate; (señalar) to point; (dirigir) to direct; (guiar) to guide; **orientarse** vr to get one's bearings

oriente nm east; **el O~ Medio** the Middle East; **el Próximo/Extremo O~** the Near/Far East

origen nm origin

original adj (nuevo) original; (extraño) odd, strange ❑ **originalidad** nf originality

originar vt to start, cause; **originarse** vr to originate ❑ **originario, -a** adj original; **originario de** native of

orilla nf (borde) border; (de río) bank; (de bosque, tela) edge; (de mar) shore

orina nf urine ❑ **orinal** nm (chamber) pot ❑ **orinar** vi to urinate; **orinarse** vr to wet o.s. ❑ **orines** nmpl urine sg

oriundo, -a adj: **~ de** native of

ornitología nf ornithology, bird-watching

oro nm gold; **~s** nmpl (NAIPES) hearts

oropel (LAm) nm tinsel

orquesta nf orchestra; **~ sinfónica/de cámara** symphony/chamber orchestra

orquídea nf orchid

ortiga nf nettle

ortodoxo, -a adj orthodox

ortografía nf spelling

ortopedia nf orthopedics sg (US), orthopaedics sg (BRIT) ❑ **ortopédico, -a** adj orthopedic (US), orthopaedic (BRIT)

oruga nf caterpillar

orzuelo nm stye

os (ESP) pron (gen) you; (a vosotros) to you

osa nf (she-)bear ▶ **Osa Mayor/Menor** Great/Little Bear

osadía nf daring

osar vi to dare

oscilación nf (movimiento) oscillation; (fluctuación) fluctuation

oscilar vi to oscillate; (cambiar) to fluctuate between

oscurecer vt to darken ♦ vi to grow dark; **oscurecerse** vr to grow o get dark

oscuridad nf obscurity; (tinieblas) darkness

oscuro, -a adj dark; (fig) obscure; **a oscuras** in the dark

óseo, -a adj bone cpd

oso nm bear ▶ **oso de peluche** teddy bear ▶ **oso hormiguero** anteater

ostentación nf (gen) ostentation; (acto) display

ostentar vt (gen) to show; (pey) to flaunt, show off; (poseer) to have, possess

ostión (MÉX) nm oyster

ostra (LAm exc MÉX, ESP) nf oyster

OTAN nf abr (= Organización del Tratado del Atlántico Norte) NATO

otear vt to observe; (fig) to look into

otitis nf earache

otoñal adj autumnal

otoño nm fall (US), autumn (BRIT)

otorgar vt (conceder) to concede; (dar) to grant

otorrino, -a, otorrinolaringólogo, a nm/f ear, nose and throat specialist

---

otro, -a

PALABRA CLAVE

adj

1 (distinto: sg) another; (: pl) other; **con otros amigos** with other o different friends

2 (adicional): **tráigame otro café (más), por favor** can I have another coffee, please; **otros 10 días más** another ten days

♦ pron

1: **el otro** the other one; **(los) otros** (the) others; **de otro** somebody else's; **que lo haga otro** let somebody else do it

2 (recíproco): **se odian (la) una a (la) otra** they hate one another o each other

3: **otro tanto: comer otro tanto** to eat the same o as much again; **recibió una decena de telegramas y otras tantas llamadas** he got about ten telegrams and as many calls

---

ovación nf ovation

oval adj oval ❑ **ovalado, -a** adj oval ❑ **óvalo** nm oval

ovario nm ovary

oveja nf sheep

overol (LAm) nm coveralls pl (US), overalls pl (BRIT); (con peto) dungarees pl, overalls pl (US)

ovillo nm (de lana) ball of wool; **hacerse un ~** to curl up

OVNI nm abr (= objeto volante no identificado) UFO

ovulación nf ovulation □ **óvulo** nm ovum

oxidación nf rusting

oxidar vt to rust; **oxidarse** vr to go rusty

óxido nm oxide

oxigenado, -a adj (QUÍM) oxygenated; (pelo) bleached

oxígeno nm oxygen

oyente nmf (RADIO) listener

oyes etc vb ver **oír**

ozono nm ozone

Pp

P abr (= padre) Fr.

pabellón nm bell tent; (ARQ) pavilion; (de hospital etc) block, section; (bandera) flag

pacer vi to graze

paciencia nf patience

paciente adj, nmf patient

pacificación nf pacification

pacificar vt to pacify; (tranquilizar) to calm

pacífico, -a adj (persona) peaceable; (existencia) peaceful; **el (océano) P~** the Pacific (Ocean)

pacifismo nm pacifism □ **pacifista** nmf pacifist

pacotilla nf: **de ~** (actor, escritor) third-rate; (mueble etc) cheap

pactar vt to agree to o on ♦ vi to come to an agreement

pacto nm (tratado) pact; (acuerdo) agreement

padecer vt (sufrir) to suffer; (soportar) to endure, put up with □ **padecimiento** nm suffering

padrastro nm stepfather

padre nm father ♦ adj (fam): **un éxito ~** a tremendous success; **~s** nmpl parents

padrino nm (REL) godfather; (tb: ~ **de boda**) best man; (fig) sponsor, patron; **~s** nmpl godparents

padrón nm (censo) census, roll

padrote (MÉX: fam) nm pimp

paella nf paella, dish of rice with meat, shellfish etc

paga nf (pago) payment; (sueldo) pay, wages pl

pagano, -a adj, nm/f pagan, heathen

pagar vt to pay; (las compras, crimen) to pay for; (fig: favor) to repay ♦ vi to pay; **~ al contado/a plazos** to pay (in) cash/in installments

pagaré nm I.O.U.

página nf page ▶ **página de inicio** (INFORM) home page

pago nm (dinero) payment; **~ anticipado/a cuenta/contra reembolso/en especie** advance payment/payment on account/cash on delivery/payment in kind; **en ~ de** in return for

pág(s). abr (= página(s)) p(p).

pague etc vb ver **pagar**

país nm (gen) country; (región) land; **los P~es Bajos** the Low Countries; **el P~ Vasco** the Basque Country

paisaje nm landscape, scenery

paisano, -a adj of the same country ♦ nm/f (compatriota) fellow countryman(-woman); **vestir de ~** (soldado) to be in civvies; (guardia) to be in plain clothes

paja nf straw; (fig) trash (US), rubbish (BRIT)

pajarita nf (corbata) bow tie

pájaro nm bird ▶ **pájaro carpintero** woodpecker

pajita nf (drinking) straw

pala nf spade, shovel; (raqueta etc) bat; (: de tenis) racquet; (CULIN) slice ▶ **pala mecánica** power shovel

palabra nf word; (facultad) (power of) speech; (derecho de hablar) right to speak; **tomar la ~** (en mitin) to take the floor

palabrota nf swearword

palacio nm palace; (mansión) mansion, large house ▶ **palacio de justicia** courthouse ▶ **palacio municipal** town o city hall

paladar nm palate □ **paladear** vt to taste

palanca nf lever; (fig) pull, influence

palangana nf washbowl (US), washbasin (BRIT)

palco nm box

Palestina nf Palestine □ **palestino, -a** nm/f Palestinian

paleta nf (de pintor) palette; (de albañil) trowel; (de ping-pong) bat; (MÉX, CAm: helado) Popsicle® (US), ice lolly (BRIT)

paleto, -a (fam, pey) nm/f yokel, hick (US)

paliar vt (mitigar) to mitigate, alleviate □ **paliativo** nm palliative

palidecer vi to turn pale □ **palidez** nf paleness □ **pálido, -a** adj pale

palillo nm (mondadientes) toothpick; (para comer) chopstick

palito (RPI) nm (helado) Popsicle® (US), ice lolly (BRIT)

paliza nf beating, thrashing

palma nf (ANAT) palm; (árbol) palm tree; **batir
o dar ~s** to clap, applaud □ **palmada** nf
slap; **palmadas** nfpl clapping sg, applause sg

palmar (MÉX, ESP: fam) vi (tb: **~la**) to die, kick
the bucket

palmear vi to clap

palmera nf (BOT) palm tree

palmo nm (medida) span; (fig) small amount;
~ a ~ inch by inch

palo nm stick; (poste) post; (mango) handle,
shaft; (golpe) blow, hit; (de golf) club; (de
béisbol) bat; (LAm: de carpa) tent pole; (NÁUT)
mast; (NAIPES) suit

paloma nf dove, pigeon

palomita (MÉX) nf tick, check mark (US)

palomitas nfpl popcorn sg

palpar vt to touch, feel

palpitación nf palpitation

palpitante adj palpitating; (fig) burning

palpitar vi to palpitate; (latir) to beat

palta (CS) nf avocado

paludismo nm malaria

pamela nf picture hat, sun hat

pampa nf pampas, prairie

pan nm bread; (una barra) loaf ▶ **pan
integral** wholewheat (US) o wholemeal
(BRIT) bread ▶ **pan rallado** breadcrumbs pl
▶ **pan tostado** (MÉX: tostada) toast

pana nf corduroy

panadería nf baker's □ **panadero, -a** nm/
f baker

Panamá nm Panama □ **panameño, -a** adj
Panamanian

Panamericana nf: **la ~** the Pan-American
highway

PANAMERICANA

The Pan-American highway is a system of
highways stretching almost without
interruption from Alaska to Patagonia.

---

pancarta nf placard, banner

panceta (RPI, ESP) nf bacon

pancho (RPI) nm hot dog

pancito (LAm exc MÉX) nm (bread) roll

panda nm (ZOOL) panda

pandereta nf tambourine

pandilla nf set, group; (de criminales) gang;
(pey: camarilla) clique

panel nm panel ▶ **panel solar** solar panel

panfleto nm pamphlet

pánico nm panic

panorama nm panorama; (vista) view

panqué (MÉX) nm pancake

panqueque (LAm) nm pancake

pantalla nf (de cine) screen; (de lámpara)
lampshade

pantalón nm (US), trousers (BRIT);
pantalones nmpl pants (US), trousers (BRIT)
▶ **pantalones de mezclilla** (MÉX) jeans,
denims

pantano nm (ciénaga) marsh, swamp;
(depósito: de agua) reservoir; (fig) jam,
difficulty

panteón nm (monumento) pantheon
▶ **panteón familiar** family vault

pantera nf panther

pantimedias (MÉX) nfpl pantyhose (US),
tights (BRIT)

pantis nmpl pantyhose (US), tights (BRIT)

pantomima nf mime

pantorrilla nf calf (of the leg)

pants (MÉX) nmpl sweat suit (US), tracksuit
(BRIT)

pantufla nf slipper

panty(s) nm(pl) pantyhose (US), tights (BRIT)

panza nf belly, paunch; (MÉX CULIN) tripe

pañal nm diaper (US), nappy (BRIT); **~es** nmpl
(fig) early stages, infancy sg

paño nm (tela) cloth; (pedazo de tela) (piece of)
cloth; (trapo) dustcloth, rag ▶ **paño
higiénico** sanitary towel ▶ **paños
menores** underclothes

pañuelo nm handkerchief, hanky; (fam: para
la cabeza) (head)scarf

papa nf: **el P~** the Pope ♦ nf (LAm: patata)
potato ▶ **papas fritas** French fries, chips
(BRIT); (de bolsa) potato chips (US), crisps (BRIT)

papá (pl **~s** (fam)) nm pop, dad(dy), pop (US)

papada nf double chin

papagayo nm parrot

papalote (MÉX, CAm) nm kite

papanatas (fam) nm inv simpleton

Papanicolau (LAm) nm pap smear (US),
smear test (BRIT)

paparrucha nf piece of nonsense

papaya nf papaya

papear (fam) vt, vi to scoff

papel nm paper; (hoja de papel) sheet of
paper; (TEATRO: fig) role ▶ **papel de
aluminio** aluminum (US) o aluminium (BRIT)
foil ▶ **papel de arroz/envolver/fumar**
rice/wrapping/cigarette paper ▶ **papel de
estaño** o **plata** tinfoil ▶ **papel de lija**
sandpaper ▶ **papel higiénico** toilet paper
▶ **papel moneda** paper money ▶ **papel
secante** blotting paper

papeleo nm red tape

papelera nf wastepaper basket; (en la calle) trash can (US), litter bin (BRIT) ▶ **papelera (de reciclaje)** (INFORM) wastebasket

papelería nf stationery store (US), stationer's (shop) (BRIT)

paperas nfpl mumps sg

papilla nf (de bebé) baby food

paquete nm (CORREOS etc) package, parcel; (de cigarrillos etc) pack (US), packet (BRIT); **darse ~** (MÉX: fam) to give o.s. airs ▶ **paquete turístico** package tour

par adj (igual) like, equal; (MAT) even ♦ nm equal; (de guantes) pair; (de veces) couple; (POL) peer; (GOLF, COM) par; **abrir de ~ en ~** to open wide

para prep for; **no es ~ comer** it's not for eating; **decir ~ sí** to say to o.s.; **¿~ qué lo quieres?** what do you want it for?; **se casaron ~ separarse otra vez** they married only to separate again; **lo tendré ~ mañana** I'll have it (for) tomorrow; **ir ~ casa** to go home, head for home; **~ profesor es muy estúpido** he's very stupid for a teacher; **¿quién es usted ~ gritar así?** who are you to shout like that?; **tengo bastante ~ vivir** I have enough to live on; ver tb **con**

parabién nm congratulations pl

parábola nf parable; (MAT) parabola ❑ **parabólica** nf (tb: **antena parabólica**) satellite dish

parabrisas nm inv windshield (US), windscreen (BRIT)

paracaídas nm inv parachute ❑ **paracaidista** nmf parachutist; (MIL) paratrooper; (MÉX: ocupante) squatter

parachoques (LAm exc MÉX) nm inv (AUTO) bumper, fender (US); (MECÁNICA etc) shock absorber

parada nf stop; (acto) stopping; (de industria) shutdown, stoppage; (lugar) stopping place ▶ **parada de autobús** bus stop

paradero nm stopping-place; (situación) whereabouts

parado, -a adj (persona) motionless, standing still; (fábrica) closed, at a standstill; (vehículo) stopped; (LAm: de pie) standing (up)

paradoja nf paradox

parador nm (state-run) tourist hotel

paráfrasis nf inv paraphrase

paragolpes (RPI) nm inv (AUTO) bumper, fender (US)

paraguas nm inv umbrella

Paraguay nm: **el ~** Paraguay ❑ **paraguayo, -a** adj, nm/f Paraguayan

paraíso nm paradise, heaven

paraje nm place, spot

paralelo, -a adj parallel

parálisis nf inv paralysis ❑ **paralítico, -a** adj, nm/f paralytic

paralizar vt to paralyze (US), paralyse (BRIT); **paralizarse** vr to become paralyzed; (fig) to come to a standstill

paramilitar adj paramilitary

páramo nm bleak plateau

parangón nm: **sin ~** incomparable

paranoico, -a nm/f paranoiac

parapente nm (deporte) paragliding; (aparato) paraglider

parapléjico, -a adj, nm/f paraplegic

parar vt to stop; (golpe) to ward off ♦ vi to stop; **pararse** vr to stop; (LAm: ponerse de pie) to stand up; **ha parado de llover** it has stopped raining; **van a ir a ~ a comisaria** they're going to end up in the police station; **~se en** to pay attention to

pararrayos nm inv lightning rod (US), lightning conductor (BRIT)

parásito, -a nm/f parasite

parcela nf plot, piece of ground

parche nm (gen) patch

parchís nm ludo

parcial adj (pago) part-; (eclipse) partial; (JUR) prejudiced, biased; (POL) partisan ❑ **parcialidad** nf prejudice, bias

pardillo, -a (pey) adj yokel

parecer nm (opinión) opinion, view; (aspecto) looks pl ♦ vi (tener apariencia) to seem, look; (asemejarse) to look o seem like; (aparecer, llegar) to appear; **parecerse** vr to look alike, resemble each other; **~se a** to look like, resemble; **según parece** evidently, apparently; **me parece que** I think (that), it seems to me that

parecido, -a adj similar ♦ nm similarity, likeness, resemblance; **bien ~** good-looking, nice-looking

pared nf wall

pareja nf (par) pair; (dos personas) couple; (otro: de un par) other one (of a pair); (persona) partner

parentela nf relations pl

parentesco nm relationship

paréntesis nm inv parenthesis; (en escrito) bracket

parezco etc vb ver **parecer**

pariente, -a nm/f relative, relation

⚠ No confundir **pariente** con la palabra inglesa **parent**.

parir vt to give birth to ♦ vi (mujer) to give birth, have a baby

París n Paris

parka (LAm) nf anorak

parking nm parking lot (US), car park (BRIT)

parlamentar vi to parley

parlamentario, -a adj parliamentary ♦ nm/f member of parliament

parlamento nm parliament

parlanchín, -ina adj indiscreet ♦ nm/f chatterbox

parlar vi to chatter (away)

paro nm (huelga) stoppage (of work), strike; (ESP: desempleo) unemployment

parodia nf parody □ **parodiar** vt to parody

parpadear vi (ojos) to blink; (luz) to flicker

párpado nm eyelid

parque nm (lugar verde) park; (MÉX: munición) ammunition ▶ **parque de atracciones** fairground ▶ **parque de bomberos** (ESP) fire station ▶ **parque infantil/zoológico** playground/zoo

parqué nm parquet (flooring)

parquímetro nm parking meter

parra nf (grape)vine

párrafo nm paragraph; **echar un ~** (fam) to have a chat

parranda (fam) nf spree, binge

parrilla nf (CULIN) broiler (US), grill (BRIT); (AUTO) grille; **(carne a la) ~** barbecue □ **parrillada** nf barbecue

párroco nm parish priest

parroquia nf parish; (iglesia) parish church; (COM) clientele, customers pl □ **parroquiano, -a** nm/f (REL) parishioner; (COM) client, customer

parsimonia nf calmness, level-headedness

parte nm message; (informe) report ♦ nf part; (lado, cara) side; (de reparto) share; (JUR) party; **en alguna ~ de Europa** somewhere in Europe; **en/por todas ~s** everywhere; **en gran ~** to a large extent; **la mayor ~ de los españoles** most Spaniards; **de un tiempo a esta ~** for some time past; **de ~ de algn** on sb's behalf; **¿de ~ de quién?** (TEL) who is speaking?; **por ~ de** on the part of; **yo por mi ~** I for my part; **por otra ~** on the other hand; **dar ~** to inform; **tomar ~** to take part

partición nf division, sharing-out; (POL) partition

participación nf (acto) participation, taking part; (parte, COM) share; (de lotería) shared prize; (aviso) notice, notification

participante nmf participant

participar vt to notify, inform ♦ vi to take part, participate

partícipe nmf participant

particular adj (especial) particular, special; (individual, personal) private, personal ♦ nm (punto, asunto) particular, point; (individuo) individual; **tiene** (LAm) **carro ~** he has a car of his own

partida nf (salida) departure; (COM) entry, item; (juego) game; (grupo de personas) band, group; **mala ~** dirty trick

partidario, -a adj partisan ♦ nm/f supporter, follower

partido nm (POL) party; (DEPORTE) game; **sacar ~ de** to profit o benefit from; **tomar ~** to take sides

partir vt (dividir) to split, divide; (compartir, distribuir) to share (out), distribute; (romper) to break open, split open; (rebanada) to cut (off) ♦ vi (ponerse en camino) to set off o out; (comenzar) to start (off o out); **partirse** vr to crack o split o break (in two etc); **a ~ de** (starting) from

partitura nf (MÚS) score

parto nm birth; (fig) product, creation; **estar de ~** to be in labor (US) o labour (BRIT)

parvulario (ESP) nm nursery school, kindergarten

pasa nf raisin ▶ **pasa de Corinto/Esmirna** currant/sultana

pasacintas (LAm) nm cassette player

pasada nf passing, passage; **de ~** in passing, incidentally; **una mala ~** a dirty trick

pasadizo nm (pasillo) passage, corridor; (callejuela) alley

pasado, -a adj past; (malo: comida, fruta) bad; (muy cocido) overdone; (anticuado) out of date ♦ nm past; **~ mañana** the day after tomorrow; **el mes ~** last month

pasador nm (cerrojo) bolt; (de pelo) barrette (US), hair slide (BRIT); (horquilla) hairpin

pasaje nm passage; (pago de viaje) fare; (los pasajeros) passengers pl; (pasillo) passageway

pasajero, -a adj passing; (situación, estado) temporary; (amor, enfermedad) brief ♦ nm/f passenger

pasamontañas nm inv balaclava helmet

pasaporte nm passport

pasar vt to pass; (tiempo) to spend; (desgracias) to suffer, endure; (noticia) to give, pass on; (río) to cross; (barrera) to pass through; (falta) to overlook, tolerate; (contrincante) to surpass, do better than; (vehículo) to pass, overtake (BRIT); (CINE) to show; (enfermedad) to give, infect with ♦ vi *(gen)* to pass; *(terminarse)* to be over; *(ocurrir)* to happen; **pasarse** *vr (flores)* to fade; *(comida)* to go bad o off; *(fig)* to overdo it, go too far; **~se un alto** *(MÉX, CAm)* o **una luz roja** *(LAm)* to go through a red light; **~ de** to go beyond, exceed; **~ por** *(LAm)* to fetch; **~lo bien/mal** to have a good/bad time; **¡pase!** come in!; **hacer ~** to show in; **~se al enemigo** to go over to the enemy; **se me pasó** I forgot; **no se le pasa nada** he misses nothing; **pase lo que pase** come what may; **¿qué pasa?** what's going on?, what's up?; **¿qué te pasa?** what's wrong?

pasarela *nf* footbridge; *(en barco)* gangway

pasatiempo *nm* pastime, hobby

Pascua *nf (en Semana Santa)* Easter; **~s** *nfpl* Christmas (time); **¡felices ~s!** Merry Christmas!

pase *(ESP) nm* pass; *(CINE)* performance, showing

pasear *vt* to take for a walk; *(exhibir)* to parade, show off ♦ *vi* to walk, go for a walk; **pasearse** *vr* to walk, go for a walk; **~ en** *(LAm)* **carro** to go for a drive ❏ **paseo** *nm (avenida)* avenue; *(distancia corta)* walk, stroll; **dar un** o **ir de paseo** to go for a walk ▶ **paseo marítimo** *(ESP)* promenade

pasillo *nm* passage, corridor

pasión *nf* passion

pasivo, -a *adj* passive; *(inactivo)* inactive ♦ *nm (COM)* liabilities *pl*, debts *pl*

pasmar *vt (asombrar)* to amaze, astonish ❏ **pasmo** *nm* amazement, astonishment; *(resfriado)* chill; *(fig)* wonder, marvel ❏ **pasmoso, -a** *adj* amazing, astonishing

paso, -a *adj* dried ♦ *nm* step; *(modo de andar)* walk; *(huella)* footprint; *(rapidez)* speed, pace, rate; *(camino accesible)* way through, passage; *(cruce)* crossing; *(pasaje)* passing, passage; *(GEO)* pass; *(estrecho)* strait; **a ese ~** *(fig)* at that rate; **salir al ~ de** o **a** to waylay; **estar de ~** to be passing through; **prohibido el ~** no entry; **ceda el ~** yield *(US)*, give way *(BRIT)* ▶ **paso a nivel** *(LAm exc MÉX, ESP FERRO)* grade *(US)* o level *(BRIT)* crossing ▶ **paso de peatones** crosswalk *(US)*, pedestrian crossing *(BRIT)* ▶ **paso elevado** overpass *(US)*, flyover *(BRIT)*

pasta *nf* paste; *(CULIN: masa)* dough; (: *de bizcochos etc)* pastry; *(fam)* dough; **~s** *nfpl (bizcochos)* pastries, small cakes; *(fideos, espaguetis etc)* pasta ▶ **pasta dentífrica** o **de dientes** toothpaste

pastar *vt, vi* to graze

pastel *nm (dulce)* cake; *(ARTE)* pastel ▶ **pastel de carne** meat pie ❏ **pastelería** *nf* baker's, cake shop *(BRIT)*

pasteurizado, -a *adj* pasteurized

pastilla *nf (de jabón, chocolate)* bar; *(píldora)* tablet, pill

pasto *nm (LAm: hierba)* grass, lawn; *(lugar)* pasture, field

pastor, a *nm/f* shepherd(ess) ♦ *nm (REL)* clergyman, pastor ▶ **pastor alemán** German shepherd

pata *nf (pierna)* leg; *(pie)* foot; *(de muebles)* leg; **~s arriba** upside down; **metedura de ~** *(fam)* gaffe; **meter la ~** *(fam)* to put one's foot in it; **tener buena/mala ~** to be lucky/unlucky ▶ **pata de cabra** *(TEC)* crowbar ❏ **patada** *nf* kick; *(en el suelo)* stamp

patalear *vi (en el suelo)* to stamp one's feet

patata *(ESP) nf* potato ▶ **patatas fritas** French fries, chips *(BRIT)*; *(de bolsa)* potato chips *(US)*, crisps *(BRIT)*

paté *nm* pâté

patear *vt (pisar)* to stamp on, trample (on); *(pegar con el pie)* to kick ♦ *vi* to stamp (with rage), stamp one's feet

patentar *vt* to patent

patente *adj* obvious, evident; *(COM)* patent ♦ *nf* patent

paternal *adj* fatherly, paternal ❏ **paterno, -a** *adj* paternal

patético, -a *adj* pathetic, moving

patilla *nf (de gafas)* side(piece), temple *(US)*; **~s** *nfpl* sideburns

patín *nm* skate; *(de trineo)* runner ❏ **patinaje** *nm* skating ❏ **patinar** *vi* to skate; *(resbalarse)* to skid, slip; *(fam)* to slip up, blunder

patineta *nf (MÉX: patinete)* scooter; *(CS: monopatín)* skateboard

patinete *(LAm exc MÉX, ESP) nm* scooter

patio *nm (de casa)* patio, courtyard ▶ **patio de recreo** playground

pato, -a *adj (CS: fam: sin dinero)* broke ♦ *nm* duck; **pagar el ~** *(fam)* to take the blame, carry the can

patológico, -a *adj* pathological

patoso, -a *(fam) adj* clumsy

patotero *(CS) nm* hooligan, lout

patraña *nf* story, fib

patria *nf* native land, mother country

patrimonio *nm* inheritance; *(fig)* heritage

patriota *nmf* patriot ❏ **patriotismo** *nm* patriotism

patrocinar *vt* to sponsor ❏ **patrocinio** *nm* sponsorship

patrón, -ona nm/f (jefe) boss, chief, master (mistress); (propietario) landlord(-lady); (REL) patron saint ♦ nm (TEC, COSTURA) pattern

patronal adj: **la clase ~** management

patronato nm sponsorship; (acto) patronage; (fundación benéfica) trust, foundation

patrulla nf patrol

pausa nf pause, break

pausado, -a adj slow, deliberate

pauta nf line, guide line

pava (RPI) nf tea kettle (US), kettle

pavimento nm (de losa) pavement, paving

pavo nm turkey ▶ **pavo real** peacock

pavor nm dread, terror

payaso, -a nm/f clown

payo, -a nm/f non-gipsy

paz nf peace; (tranquilidad) peacefulness, tranquillity; **hacer las paces** to make peace; (fig) to make up

pazo nm country house

P.D. abr (= posdata) P.S., p.s.

peaje nm toll

peatón nm pedestrian

peca nf freckle

pecado nm sin ❑ **pecador, a** adj sinful ♦ nm/f sinner

pecaminoso, -a adj sinful

pecar vi (REL) to sin; **peca de generoso** he is generous to a fault

pecera nf fish tank; (redonda) goldfish bowl

pecho nm (ANAT) chest; (de mujer) breast; **dar el ~ a** to breast-feed; **tomar algo a ~** to take sth to heart

pechuga nf breast

peculiar adj special, peculiar; (característico) typical, characteristic ❑ **peculiaridad** nf peculiarity; special feature, characteristic

pedal nm pedal ❑ **pedalear** vi to pedal

pedante adj pedantic ♦ nmf pedant ❑ **pedantería** nf pedantry

pedazo nm piece, bit; **hacerse ~s** to smash, shatter

pedernal nm flint

pediatra nmf pediatrician (US), paediatrician (BRIT)

pedido nm (COM) order; (petición) request

pedir vt to ask for, request; (comida, COM, mandar) to order; (necesitar) to need, demand, require ♦ vi to ask; **me pidió que cerrara la puerta** he asked me to shut the door; **¿cuánto piden por la moto?** how much are they asking for the motorbike?

pedo (fam!) nm fart

pega nf snag; **poner ~s (a)** to complain (about)

pegadizo, -a adj (MÚS) catchy

pegajoso, -a adj sticky, adhesive

pegamento nm gum, glue

pegar vt (papel, sellos) to stick (on); (cartel) to stick up; (coser) to sew (on); (unir: partes) to join, fix together; (MED) to give, infect with; (dar: golpe) to give, deal; (INFORM) to paste ♦ vi (adherirse) to stick, adhere; (ir juntos: colores) to match, go together; (golpear) to hit; (quemar: el sol) to strike hot, burn; **pegarse** vr (gen) to stick; (dos personas) to hit each other, fight; (fam): **~ un grito** to let out a yell; **~ un salto** to jump (with fright); **~ en** to touch; **~se un tiro** to shoot o.s.

pegatina (ESP) nf sticker

pegote (fam) nm eyesore, sight

peinado nm hairstyle

peinar vt to comb; (hacer estilo) to style; **peinarse** vr to comb one's hair

peine nm comb ❑ **peineta** nf ornamental comb

p.ej. abr (= por ejemplo) e.g.

Pekín n Pekin(g)

pelado, -a adj (fruta, patata etc) peeled; (cabeza) shorn; (campo, fig) bare; (fam: sin dinero) broke

pelaje nm (ZOOL) fur, coat; (fig) appearance

pelapapas (LAm) (ESP **pelapatatas**) nm inv potato peeler

pelar vt (fruta, patatas etc) to peel; (cortar el pelo a) to cut the hair of; (quitar la piel: animal) to skin; **pelarse** vr (la piel) to peel off; **voy a ~me** I'm going to get my hair cut

peldaño nm step

pelea nf (lucha) fight; (discusión) quarrel, row

peleado, -a adj: **estar ~ (con algn)** to have fallen out (with sb)

pelear vi to fight; **pelearse** vr to fight; (reñirse) to fall out, quarrel

pelela (CS) nf potty

peletería nf furrier's, fur store

pelícano nm pelican

película nf movie (US), film (BRIT); (cobertura ligera) thin covering; (FOTO: rollo) roll o reel of film

peligro nm danger; (riesgo) risk; **correr ~ de** to run the risk of ❑ **peligroso, -a** adj dangerous; risky

pelirrojo, -a adj red-haired, red-headed ♦ nm/f redhead

pellejo nm (de animal) skin, hide

pellizcar vt to pinch, nip

pelmazo (fam) nm pain (in the neck)

pelo nm (cabellos) hair; (de barba, bigote) whisker; (de animal: pellejo) hair, fur, coat; **al ~** just right; **venir al ~** to be exactly what one needs; **un hombre de ~ en pecho** a brave man; **por los ~s** by the skin of one's teeth; **no tener ~s en la lengua** to be outspoken, not mince words; **tomar el ~ a algn** to pull sb's leg

pelota nf ball; **en ~** stark naked ▶ **pelota vasca** pelota

pelotari nm pelota player

pelotón nm (MIL) squad, detachment

peluca nf wig

peluche nm: **oso/muñeco de ~** teddy bear/ soft toy

peludo, -a adj hairy, shaggy

peluquería nf hairdresser's □ **peluquero, -a** nm/f hairdresser

pelusa nf (BOT) down; (en tela) fluff

pena nf (congoja) grief, sadness; (remordimiento) regret; (dificultad) trouble; (dolor) pain; (JUR) sentence; **merecer** o **valer la ~** to be worthwhile; **a duras ~s** with great difficulty; **¡qué ~!** what a shame! ▶ **pena capital** capital punishment ▶ **pena de muerte** death penalty

penal adj penal ♦ nm (cárcel) prison

penalidad nf (problema, dificultad) trouble, hardship; (JUR) penalty, punishment; **~es** nfpl trouble sg, hardship sg

penalti (pl ~s) nm penalty (kick)

penalty (pl ~s o **penalties**) nm ver **penalti**

pendiente adj pending, unsettled ♦ nm earring ♦ nf hill, slope

pene nm penis

penetración nf (acto) penetration; (agudeza) sharpness, insight

penetrante adj (herida) deep; (persona, arma) sharp; (sonido) penetrating, piercing; (mirada) searching; (viento, ironía) biting

penetrar vt to penetrate, pierce; (entender) to grasp ♦ vi to penetrate, go in; (entrar) to enter, go in; (líquido) to soak in; (fig) to pierce

penicilina nf penicillin

península nf peninsula □ **peninsular** adj peninsular

penique nm penny

penitencia nf penance

penoso, -a adj (lamentable) distressing; (difícil) arduous, difficult

pensador, a nm/f thinker

pensamiento nm thought; (mente) mind; (idea) idea

pensar vt to think; (considerar) to think over, think out; (proponerse) to intend, plan; (imaginarse) to think up, invent ♦ vi to think; **~ en** to aim at, aspire to □ **pensativo, -a** adj thoughtful, pensive

pensión nf (casa) boarding o guest house; (dinero) pension; (cama y comida) board and lodging; **~ completa** full board; **media ~** half-board □ **pensionista** nmf (jubilado) (old-age) pensioner; (huésped) lodger

penúltimo, -a adj penultimate, last but one

penumbra nf half-light

penuria nf shortage, want

peña nf (roca) rock; (cuesta) cliff, crag; (grupo) group, circle; (LAm: club) folk club

peñasco nm large rock, boulder

peñón nm wall of rock; **el P~** the Rock (of Gibraltar)

peón nm laborer (US), labourer (BRIT); (LAm AGR) farm laborer (US) o labourer (BRIT), farmhand; (AJEDREZ) pawn

peonza nf spinning top

peor adj (comparativo) worse; (superlativo) worst ♦ adv worse; worst; **de mal en ~** from bad to worse

pepinillo nm gherkin

pepino nm cucumber; **me importa un ~** (fam) I don't care one bit

pepita nf (BOT) pip; (MINERÍA) nugget

pequeñez nf smallness, littleness; (trivialidad) trifle, triviality

pequeño, -a adj small, little

pera nf pear □ **peral** nm pear tree

percance nm setback, misfortune

percatarse vr: **~ de** to notice, take note of

percebe nm barnacle

percepción nf (vista) perception; (idea) notion, idea

percha nf (ESP: para ropa) (coat)hanger; (: ganchos) coat hooks pl; (de ave) perch

percibir vt to perceive, notice; (COM) to earn, get

percusión nf percussion

perdedor, a adj losing ♦ nm/f loser

perder vt to lose; (tiempo, palabras) to waste; (oportunidad) to lose, miss; (tren) to miss ♦ vi to lose; **perderse** vr (extraviarse) to get lost; (desaparecer) to disappear, be lost to view; (arruinarse) to be ruined; **echar a ~** (comida) to spoil, ruin; (oportunidad) to waste

perdición nf perdition, ruin

pérdida nf loss; (de tiempo) waste; **~s** nfpl (COM) losses

perdido, -a *adj* lost

perdiz *nf* partridge

perdón *nm* (*disculpa*) pardon, forgiveness; (*clemencia*) mercy; ¡~! sorry!, I beg your pardon! □ **perdonar** *vt* to pardon, forgive; (*la vida*) to spare; (*excusar*) to exempt, excuse; ¡**perdone (usted)!** sorry!, I beg your pardon!

perdurar *vi* (*resistir*) to last, endure; (*seguir existiendo*) to stand, still exist

perecedero, -a *adj* perishable

perecer *vi* to perish, die

peregrinación *nf* (*REL*) pilgrimage

peregrino, -a *adj* (*idea*) strange, absurd ♦ *nm/f* pilgrim

perejil *nm* parsley

perenne *adj* everlasting, perennial

pereza *nf* laziness, idleness □ **perezoso, -a** *adj* lazy, idle

perfección *nf* perfection □ **perfeccionar** *vt* to perfect; (*mejorar*) to improve; (*acabar*) to complete, finish

perfectamente *adv* perfectly

perfecto, -a *adj* perfect; (*total*) complete

perfil *nm* profile; (*contorno*) silhouette, outline; (*ARQ*) (cross) section; **~es** *nmpl* features □ **perfilar** *vt* (*trazar*) to outline; (*fig*) to shape, give character to

perforación *nf* perforation; (*con taladro*) drilling □ **perforadora** *nf* punch

perforar *vt* to perforate; (*agujero*) to drill, bore; (*papel*) to punch a hole in ♦ *vi* to drill, bore

perfume *nm* perfume, scent (*BRIT*)

pericia *nf* skill, expertise

periferia *nf* periphery; (*de ciudad*) outskirts *pl*

periférico (*LAm*) *nm* beltway (*US*), ring road (*BRIT*)

perilla (*LAm*) *nf* (*de puerta*) knob of door, door handle

perímetro *nm* perimeter

periódico, -a *adj* periodic(al) ♦ *nm* newspaper

periodismo *nm* journalism □ **periodista** *nmf* journalist

periodo *nm* period

período *nm* = periodo

periquito *nm* budgerigar, budgie

perito, -a *adj* (*experto*) expert; (*diestro*) skilled, skillful (*US*), skilful (*BRIT*) ♦ *nm/f* expert; skilled worker; (*técnico*) technician

perjudicar *vt* (*gen*) to damage, harm □ **perjudicial** *adj* damaging, harmful; (*en detrimento*) detrimental □ **perjuicio** *nm* damage, harm

perjurar *vi* to commit perjury

perla *nf* pearl; **me viene de ~s** it suits me fine

permanecer *vi* (*quedarse*) to stay, remain; (*seguir*) to continue to be

permanencia *nf* permanence; (*estancia*) stay

permanente *adj* permanent, constant ♦ *nf* permanent (*US*), perm (*BRIT*)

permiso *nm* permission; (*licencia*) permit, license (*US*), licence (*BRIT*); **con ~** excuse me; **estar de ~** (*MIL*) to be on leave ▶ **permiso de conducir** driver's license (*US*), driving licence (*BRIT*) ▶ **permiso de excedencia** (*LAm*) leave of absence ▶ **permiso por enfermedad** (*LAm*) sick leave

permitir *vt* to permit, allow

pernera *nf* pant (*US*) o trouser (*BRIT*) leg

pernicioso, -a *adj* pernicious

pero *conj* but; (*aún*) yet ♦ *nm* (*defecto*) flaw, defect; (*reparo*) objection

perpendicular *adj* perpendicular

perpetrar *vt* to perpetrate

perpetuar *vt* to perpetuate □ **perpetuo, -a** *adj* perpetual

perplejo, -a *adj* perplexed, bewildered

perra *nf* (*ZOOL*) bitch

perrera *nf* kennel

perrito *nm* (*CULIN*: *tb*: ~ **caliente**) hot dog

perro *nm* dog

persa *adj*, *nmf* Persian

persecución *nf* pursuit, chase; (*REL, POL*) persecution

perseguir *vt* to pursue, hunt; (*cortejar*) to chase after; (*molestar*) to pester, annoy; (*REL, POL*) to persecute

perseverante *adj* persevering, persistent

perseverar *vi* to persevere, persist

persiana *nf* (Venetian) blind

persignarse *vr* to cross o.s.

persistente *adj* persistent

persistir *vi* to persist

persona *nf* person ▶ **persona mayor** elderly person

personaje *nm* important person, celebrity; (*TEATRO etc*) character

personal *adj* (*particular*) personal; (*para una persona*) single, for one person ♦ *nm* personnel, staff □ **personalidad** *nf* personality

personarse *vr* to appear in person

personificar *vt* to personify

perspectiva nf perspective; (vista, panorama) view, panorama; (posibilidad futura) outlook, prospect

perspicacia nf discernment, perspicacity

perspicaz adj shrewd

persuadir vt (gen) to persuade; (convencer) to convince; **persuadirse** vr to become convinced ❑ **persuasión** nf persuasion ❑ **persuasivo, -a** adj persuasive; convincing

pertenecer vi to belong; (fig) to concern ❑ **perteneciente** adj: **perteneciente a** belonging to ❑ **pertenencia** nf ownership; **pertenencias** nfpl (bienes) possessions, property sg

pertenezca etc vb ver **pertenecer**

pértiga (ESP) nf: **salto con ~** pole vault

pertinente adj relevant, pertinent; (apropiado) appropriate; **~ a** concerning, relevant to

perturbación nf (POL) disturbance; (MED) upset, disturbance

perturbado, a adj mentally unbalanced

perturbar vt (el orden) to disturb; (MED) to upset, disturb; (mentalmente) to perturb

Perú nm: **el ~** Peru ❑ **peruano, -a** adj, nm/f Peruvian

perversión nf perversion ❑ **perverso, -a** adj perverse; (depravado) depraved

pervertido, -a adj perverted ♦ nm/f pervert

pervertir vt to pervert, corrupt

pesa nf weight; (DEPORTE) shot

pesadez nf (peso) heaviness; (lentitud) slowness; (aburrimiento) tediousness

pesadilla nf nightmare, bad dream

pesado, -a adj heavy; (lento) slow; (difícil, duro) tough, hard; (aburrido) boring, tedious; (tiempo) sultry

pésame nm expression of condolence, message of sympathy; **dar el ~** to express one's condolences

pesar vt to weigh ♦ vi to weigh; (ser pesado) to weigh a lot, be heavy; (fig: opinión) to carry weight ♦ nm (arrepentimiento) regret; (pena) grief, sorrow; **a ~ de o pese a (que)** in spite of, despite; **no pesa mucho** it is not very heavy

pesca nf (acto) fishing; (lo pescado) catch; **ir de ~** to go fishing

pescadería nf fish store/shop, fishmonger's (BRIT)

pescadilla nf whiting

pescado nm fish

pescador, a nm/f fisherman(-woman)

pescar vt (tomar) to catch; (intentar tomar) to fish for; (conseguir: trabajo) to manage to get ♦ vi to fish, go fishing

pescuezo nm neck

pesebre nm manger

peseta nf peseta

pesimista adj pessimistic ♦ nmf pessimist

pésimo, -a adj awful, dreadful; (LAm: enfermo) lousy

peso nm weight; (balanza) scales pl; (moneda) peso; **vender al ~** to sell by weight ▸ **peso bruto/neto** gross/net weight

pesquero, -a adj fishing cpd

pesquisa nf inquiry, investigation

pestaña nf (ANAT) eyelash; (borde) rim ❑ **pestañear** vi to blink

peste nf plague; (mal olor) stink, stench

pesticida nm pesticide

pestillo nm (cerrojo) bolt; (picaporte) door handle

petaca nf (de cigarros) cigarette case; (de pipa) tobacco pouch; (MÉX: maleta) suitcase

pétalo nm petal

petardo nm firework, firecracker

petición nf (pedido) request, plea; (memorial) petition; (JUR) plea

peto (ESP) nm dungarees pl, overalls pl (US)

petrificar vt to petrify

petróleo nm oil, petroleum ❑ **petrolero, -a** adj petroleum cpd ♦ nm (oil) tanker

peyorativo, -a adj pejorative

pez nm fish ▸ **pez de colores** goldfish ▸ **pez dorado** (MÉX) goldfish

pezón nm teat, nipple

pezuña nf hoof

piadoso, -a adj (devoto) pious, devout; (misericordioso) kind, merciful

pianista nmf pianist

piano nm piano

piar vi to cheep

pibe, -a (RPI) nm/f boy (girl)

picadero nm riding school

picadillo nm ground meat (US), mince (BRIT)

picado, -a adj pricked, punctured; (CULIN: ajo, cebolla etc) chopped; (carne) ground (US), minced (BRIT); (mar) choppy; (diente) bad; (tabaco) cut; (enfadado) cross

picador nm (TAUR) picador; (minero) faceworker

picadura nf (pinchazo) puncture; (de abeja) sting; (de mosquito) bite; (tabaco picado) cut tobacco

picante *adj* hot; (*comentario*) racy, spicy

picaporte *nm* (*manija*) door handle; (*pestillo*) latch

picar *vt* (*agujerear, perforar*) to prick, puncture; (*abeja*) to sting; (*mosquito, serpiente*) to bite; (*CULIN: ajo, cebolla etc*) to chop; (*carne*) to grind (*US*), mince (*BRIT*); (*incitar*) to incite, goad; (*dañar, irritar*) to annoy, bother; (*quemar: lengua*) to burn, sting ♦ *vi* (*pez*) to bite, take the bait; (*sol*) to burn, scorch; (*abeja, MED*) to sting; (*mosquito*) to bite; **picarse** *vr* (*agriarse*) to turn sour, go off; (*ofenderse*) to take offense (*US*) *o* offence (*BRIT*)

picardía *nf* villainy; (*astucia*) slyness, craftiness; (*una picardía*) dirty trick; (*palabra*) rude/bad word *o* expression

pícaro, -a *adj* (*malicioso*) villainous; (*travieso*) mischievous ♦ *nm* (*astuto*) crafty sort; (*sinvergüenza*) rascal, scoundrel

pichi (*ESP*) *nm* jumper (*US*), pinafore dress (*BRIT*)

pichón *nm* young pigeon

pico *nm* (*de ave*) beak; (*punta*) sharp point; (*TEC*) pick, pickax (*US*), pickaxe (*BRIT*); (*GEO*) peak, summit; **y ~** and a bit; **horas ~** (*LAm: de electricidad, teléfono*) peak hours; (*: del tráfico*) rush hours; **¿~ o mona?** (*MÉX*) heads or tails?

picor *nm* itch

picoso, -a (*MÉX*) *adj* (*comida*) hot

picotear *vt* to peck ♦ *vi* to nibble, pick

picudo, -a *adj* pointed, with a point

pidió *etc vb ver* **pedir**

pido *etc vb ver* **pedir**

pie (*pl ~s*) *nm* foot; (*fig: motivo*) motive, basis; (*: fundamento*) foothold; **ir a ~** to go on foot, walk; **estar de ~** to be standing (up); **ponerse de ~** to stand up; **de ~s a cabeza** from top to bottom; **al ~ de la letra** (*citar*) literally, verbatim; (*copiar*) exactly, word for word; **en ~ de guerra** on a war footing; **dar ~ a** to give cause for; **hacer ~** (*en el agua*) to touch (the) bottom

piedad *nf* (*lástima*) pity, compassion; (*clemencia*) mercy; (*devoción*) piety, devotion

piedra *nf* stone; (*roca*) rock; (*de mechero*) flint; (*METEOROLOGÍA*) hailstone

piel *nf* (*ANAT*) skin; (*ZOOL*) skin, hide, fur; (*cuero*) leather; (*BOT*) skin, peel

pienso *etc vb ver* **pensar**

pierdo *etc vb ver* **perder**

pierna *nf* leg

pieza *nf* piece; (*CS: habitación*) room ▶ **pieza de recambio** *o* **repuesto** spare (part)

pigmeo, -a *adj, nm/f* pigmy

pijama (*ESP*) *nm* pajamas *pl* (*US*), pyjamas *pl* (*BRIT*)

pila *nf* (*ELEC*) battery; (*montón*) heap, pile; (*lavabo*) sink

píldora *nf* pill; **la ~ (anticonceptiva)** the (contraceptive) pill

pileta (*RPl*) *nf* (*fregadero*) (kitchen) sink; (*piscina*) (swimming) pool

pillaje *nm* pillage, plunder

pillar *vt* (*saquear*) to pillage, plunder; (*fam: coger*) to catch; (*: agarrar*) to grasp, seize; (*: entender*) to grasp, catch on to; **pillarse** *vr*: **~se un dedo con la puerta** to catch one's finger in the door

pillo, -a *adj* villainous; (*astuto*) sly, crafty ♦ *nm/f* rascal, rogue, scoundrel

piloto *nm* pilot; (*de aparato*) (pilot) light; (*AUTO: luz*) tail *o* rear light; (*: conductor*) driver

pimentón *nm* paprika

pimienta *nf* pepper

pimiento *nm* pepper, pimiento

pin (*pl ~s*) *nm* badge

pinacoteca *nf* art gallery

pinar *nm* pine grove (*US*), pine forest (*BRIT*)

pincel *nm* paintbrush

pinchar *vt* (*perforar*) to prick, pierce; (*neumático*) to puncture; (*fig*) to prod

pinchazo *nm* (*perforación*) prick; (*de neumático*) blow-out, puncture (*BRIT*); (*fig*) prod

pincho (*ESP*) *nm* savory (*US*) *o* savoury (*BRIT*) (snack) ▶ **pincho de tortilla** small slice of omelette ▶ **pincho moruno** shish kebab

ping-pong *nm* table tennis

pingüino *nm* penguin

pino *nm* pine (tree)

pinta *nf* spot; (*de líquidos*) spot, drop; (*ESP: aspecto*) appearance, look(s) (*pl*); **irse de ~** (*MÉX: fam*) to play hooky (*US*) *o* truant (*BRIT*) ❏ **pintado, -a** *adj* spotted; (*de colores*) colorful (*US*), colourful (*BRIT*); **pintadas** *nfpl* graffiti *sg*

pintar *vt* to paint ♦ *vi* to paint; (*fam*) to count, be important; **pintarse** *vr* to put on make-up

pintor, a *nm/f* painter

pintoresco, -a *adj* picturesque

pintura *nf* painting ▶ **pintura a la acuarela** watercolor (*US*), watercolour (*BRIT*) ▶ **pintura al óleo** oil painting

pinza *nf* (*ZOOL*) claw; (*para colgar ropa*) clothes pin (*US*), clothes peg (*BRIT*); (*TEC*) pincers *pl*; **~s** *nfpl* (*para depilar etc*) tweezers *pl*

piña *nf* (*de pino*) pine cone; (*fruta*) pineapple; (*fig*) group

piñata *nf* container hung up at parties to be beaten with sticks until sweets or presents fall out

PIÑATA

Piñata is a very popular party game in Mexico. The **piñata** itself is a hollow figure made of papier maché, or, traditionally, from adobe, in the shape of an object, a star, a person, or an animal. It is filled with either candy and toys, or, traditionally, fruit and yam beans. The game consists of hanging the **piñata** from the ceiling, and beating it with a stick, blindfolded, until it breaks and the presents fall out.

piñón *nm* (*fruto*) pine nut; (*TEC*) pinion

pío, -a *adj* (*devoto*) pious, devout; (*misericordioso*) merciful

piojo *nm* louse

pionero, -a *adj* pioneering ♦ *nm/f* pioneer

pipa *nf* pipe; **~s** *nfpl* (*BOT*) (edible) sunflower seeds

pipí (*fam*) *nm*: **hacer ~** to have to go (wee-wee) (*US*), have a wee(-wee) (*BRIT*)

pique *nm* (*resentimiento*) pique, resentment; (*rivalidad*) rivalry, competition; **irse a ~** to sink; (*esperanza, familia*) to be ruined

piqueta *nf* pick, pickax (*US*), pickaxe (*BRIT*)

piquete *nm* (*MIL*) squad, party; (*de obreros*) picket; (*MÉX: de insecto*) bite ❏ **piquetear** (*LAm*) *vt* to picket

pirado, -a (*fam*) *adj* round the bend ♦ *nm/f* nutter

piragua *nf* canoe ❏ **piragüismo** *nm* canoeing

pirámide *nf* pyramid

pirata *adj* pirate ♦ *nmf* pirate ▶ **pirata informático/a** hacker

Pirineo(s) *nm(pl)* Pyrenees *pl*

pirómano, -a *nm/f* (*MED, JUR*) arsonist

piropo *nm* compliment, (piece of) flattery

pirueta *nf* pirouette

pis (*fam*) *nm* pee, piss; **hacer ~** to have a pee; (*para niños*) to wee-wee

pisada *nf* (*paso*) footstep; (*huella*) footprint

pisar *vt* (*caminar sobre*) to walk on, tread on; (*apretar con el pie*) to press; (*fig*) to trample on, walk all over ♦ *vi* to tread, step, walk

piscina (*LAm exc MÉX, ESP*) *nf* (swimming) pool

Piscis *nm* Pisces

piso *nm* (*suelo, planta*) floor; (*ESP: apartamento*) apartment (*US*), flat (*BRIT*); **primer ~** (*LAm: a nivel del suelo*) first floor (*US*), ground floor (*BRIT*); (*ESP: un piso más arriba*) second floor (*US*), first floor (*BRIT*)

pisotear *vt* to trample (on *o* underfoot)

pista *nf* track, trail; (*indicio*) clue ▶ **pista de aterrizaje** runway ▶ **pista de baile** dance floor ▶ **pista de hielo** ice rink

pistola *nf* pistol; (*TEC*) spray-gun ❏ **pistolero, -a** *nm/f* gunman(-woman), gangster

pistón *nm* (*TEC*) piston; (*MÚS*) key

pitar *vt* (*silbato*) to blow; (*rechiflar*) to whistle at, boo ♦ *vi* to whistle; (*AUTO*) to sound *o* toot one's horn; (*LAm: fumar*) to smoke

pitillo *nm* cigarette

pito *nm* whistle; (*de vehículo*) horn

pitón *nm* (*ZOOL*) python

pitonisa *nf* fortune-teller

pitorreo *nm* joke; **estar de ~** to be joking

piyama (*LAm*) *nm* pajamas *pl* (*US*), pyjamas *pl* (*BRIT*)

pizarra *nf* (*piedra*) slate; (*ESP: encerado*) blackboard, chalkboard (*US*)

pizarrón (*LAm*) *nm* blackboard, chalkboard (*US*)

pizca *nf* pinch, spot; (*fig*) spot, speck; **ni ~** not a bit

placa *nf* plate; (*distintivo*) badge, insignia ▶ **placa de matrícula** (*LAm*) license (*US*) *o* number (*BRIT*) plate

placard (*RPl*) *nm* cupboard, closet (*US*)

placentero, -a *adj* pleasant, agreeable

placer *nm* pleasure ♦ *vt* to please

plácido, -a *adj* placid

plaga *nf* pest; (*MED*) plague; (*abundancia*) abundance ❏ **plagar** *vt* to infest, plague; (*llenar*) to fill

plagio *nm* plagiarism

plan *nm* (*esquema, proyecto*) plan; (*idea, intento*) idea, intention; **tener ~** (*fam*) to have a date; **tener un ~** (*fam*) to have an affair; **en ~ económico** (*fam*) on the cheap; **vamos en ~ de turismo** we're going as tourists; **si te pones en ese ~ ...** if that's your attitude ...

plana *nf* sheet (of paper), page; (*TEC*) trowel; **en primera ~** on the front page ▶ **plana mayor** staff

plancha *nf* (*para planchar*) iron; (*rótulo*) plate, sheet; (*NÁUT*) gangway; **a la ~** (*CULIN*) grilled ❏ **planchado** *nm* ironing ❏ **planchar** *vt* to iron ♦ *vi* to do the ironing

planeador *nm* glider

planear *vt* to plan ♦ *vi* to glide

planeta *nm* planet

planicie *nf* plain

planificación *nf* planning ▶ **planificación familiar** family planning

plano, -a adj flat, level, even ♦ nm (MAT, TEC) plane; (FOTO) shot; (ARQ) plan; (GEO) map; (de ciudad) map, street plan; **primer ~** close-up; **caer de ~** to fall flat

planta nf (BOT, TEC) plant; (ANAT) sole of the foot, foot; (piso) floor; (LAm: personal) staff ▶ **planta baja** first (US) o ground (BRIT) floor

plantación nf (AGR) plantation; (acto) planting

plantar vt (BOT) to plant; (levantar) to erect, set up; **plantarse** vr to stand firm; **~ a algn en la calle** to throw sb out; **dejar plantado a algn** (fam) to stand sb up

plantear vt (problema) to pose; (dificultad) to raise

plantilla nf (de zapato) insole; (ESP: personal) personnel

plantón nm (MIL) guard, sentry; (fam) long wait; **dar (un) ~ a algn** to stand sb up

plasmar vt (dar forma) to shape, mold (US), mould (BRIT); (representar) to represent; **plasmarse** vr: **~se en** to take the form of

plástico, -a adj plastic ♦ nm plastic

Plastilina® nf Plasticine®

plata nf (metal) silver; (cosas hechas de plata) silverware; (CS: dinero) cash, dough; **hablar en ~** to speak bluntly o frankly

plataforma nf platform ▶ **plataforma de lanzamiento/perforación** launch(ing) pad/drilling rig

plátano nm (fruta) banana; (árbol) plane tree; banana tree

platea nf (TEATRO) orchestra (section) (US), stalls pl (BRIT)

plateado, -a adj silver; (TEC) silver-plated

plática (MÉX, CAm) nf talk, chat □ **platicar** (MÉX, CAm) vi to talk, chat

platillo nm saucer; **~s** nmpl (MÚS) cymbals ▶ **platillo volante** flying saucer

platino nm platinum; **~s** nmpl (AUTO) contact points

plato nm plate, dish; (parte de comida) course; (comida) dish; **primer ~** first course ▶ **plato combinado** set main course (served on one plate) ▶ **plato fuerte** main course

playa nf beach; (costa) seaside ▶ **playa de estacionamiento** (CS) parking lot (US), car park (BRIT)

playera nf (MÉX: camiseta) T-shirt; **~s** nfpl (zapatos) canvas shoes

plaza nf square; (mercado) market(place); (sitio) room, space; (de vehículo) seat, place; (colocación) post, job ▶ **plaza de toros** bullring

plazo nm (lapso de tiempo) time, period; (fecha de vencimiento) expiry date; (pago parcial) installment (US), instalment (BRIT); **a corto/largo ~** short-/long-term; **comprar algo a ~s** to buy sth on time (US) o on hire purchase (BRIT)

plazoleta nf small square

pleamar nf high tide

plebe nf: **la ~** the common people pl, the masses pl □ **plebeyo, -a** adj plebeian; (pey) coarse, common

plebiscito nm plebiscite

plegable adj collapsible; (silla) folding

plegar vt (doblar) to fold, bend; (COSTURA) to pleat; **plegarse** vr to yield, submit

pleito nm (JUR) lawsuit, case; (fig) dispute, feud

plenilunio nm full moon

plenitud nf plenitude, fullness; (abundancia) abundance

pleno, -a adj full; (completo) complete ♦ nm plenum; **en ~ día** in broad daylight; **en ~ verano** at the height of summer; **en plena cara** full in the face

pliego etc vb ver **plegar** ♦ nm (hoja) sheet (of paper); (carta) sealed letter/document ▶ **pliego de condiciones** details pl, specifications pl

pliegue etc vb ver **plegar** ♦ nm fold, crease; (de vestido) pleat

plomería (LAm) nf plumbing □ **plomero** (LAm) nm plumber

plomo nm (metal) lead; (ELEC) fuse, fuze (US); **sin ~** unleaded

pluma nf feather ▶ **pluma (estilográfica)** ink pen ▶ **pluma fuente** (LAm) fountain pen

plumero nm (para el polvo) feather duster

plumón nm (de ave) down

plural adj plural □ **pluralidad** nf plurality

pluriempleo nm having more than one job

plus nm bonus □ **plusvalía** nf (COM) appreciation

población nf population; (pueblo, ciudad) town, city

poblado, -a adj inhabited ♦ nm (aldea) village; (pueblo) (small) town; **densamente ~** densely populated

poblador, a nm/f settler, colonist

poblar vt (colonizar) to colonize; (fundar) to found; (habitar) to inhabit

pobre adj poor □ nmf poor person □ **pobreza** nf poverty

pocilga nf pigpen (US), pigsty (BRIT)

pócima nf potion

poco, -a

PALABRA CLAVE

adj

1 (*sg*) little, not much; **poco tiempo** little o not much time; **de poco interés** of little interest, not very interesting; **poca cosa** not much

2 (*pl*) few, not many; **unos pocos** a few, some; **pocos niños comen lo que les conviene** few children eat what they should

♦ *adv*

1 little, not much; **cuesta poco** it doesn't cost much

2 (+ *adj: negativo, antónimo*): **poco amable/inteligente** not very nice/intelligent

3: **por poco me caigo** I almost fell

4: **a poco: a poco de haberse casado** shortly after getting married

5: **poco a poco** little by little

♦ *nm* a little, a bit; **un poco triste/de dinero** a little sad/money

podar *vt* to prune

poder

PALABRA CLAVE

vi

1 (*tener capacidad*) can, be able to; **no puedo hacerlo** I can't do it, I'm unable to do it

2 (*tener permiso*) can, may, be allowed to; **¿se puede?** may I (o we)?; **puedes irte ahora** you may go now; **no se puede fumar en este hospital** smoking is not allowed in this hospital

3 (*tener posibilidad*) may, might, could; **puede llegar mañana** he may o might arrive tomorrow; **pudiste haberte hecho daño** you might o could have hurt yourself; **¡podías habérmelo dicho antes!** you might have told me before!

4: **puede ser: puede ser** perhaps; **puede ser que lo sepa Tomás** Tomás may o might know

5: **¡no puedo más!** I've had enough!; **no pude menos que dejarlo** I couldn't help but leave it; **es tonto a más no poder** he's as stupid as they come

6: **poder con: no puedo con este crío** this kid's too much for me

♦ *nm* power; **detentar** o **ocupar** o **estar en el poder** to be in power ▶ **poder adquisitivo** purchasing power

poderoso, -a *adj* (*político, país*) powerful

podio *nm* (*DEPORTE*) podium

podium *nm* = **podio**

podrido, -a *adj* rotten, bad; (*fig*) rotten, corrupt

podrir *vt* = **pudrir**

poema *nm* poem

poesía *nf* poetry

poeta *nmf* poet ❑ **poético, -a** *adj* poetic(al)

poetisa *nf* (woman) poet

póker *nm* poker

polaco, -a *adj* Polish ♦ *nm/f* Pole

polar *adj* polar ❑ **polaridad** *nf* polarity ❑ **polarizarse** *vr* to polarize

polea *nf* pulley

polémica *nf* polemics *sg*; (*una polémica*) controversy, polemic

polen *nm* pollen

policía *nmf* policeman(-woman) ♦ *nf* police ❑ **policíaco, -a** *adj* police *cpd*; **novela policíaca** detective story ❑ **policial** *adj* police *cpd*

polideportivo *nm* sports center (*US*) o centre (*BRIT*)

poligamia *nf* polygamy

polígono *nm* (*MAT*) polygon

polilla *nf* moth

polio *nf* polio

política *nf* politics *sg*; (*económica, agraria etc*) policy; *ver tb* **político**

político, -a *adj* political; (*discreto*) tactful; (*de familia*) -in-law ♦ *nm/f* politician; **padre ~** father-in-law

póliza *nf* certificate, voucher; (*impuesto*) tax stamp ▶ **póliza de seguro(s)** insurance policy

polizón *nm* stowaway

pollera (*CS*) *nf* skirt

pollería *nf* poulterer's (shop)

pollo *nm* chicken

polo *nm* (*GEO, ELEC*) pole; (*ESP: helado*) Popsicle® (*US*), ice lolly (*BRIT*); (*DEPORTE*) polo; (*suéter*) turtleneck ▶ **polo Norte/Sur** North/South Pole

Polonia *nf* Poland

poltrona *nf* easy chair

polución *nf* pollution

polvera *nf* powder compact

polvo *nm* dust; (*QUÍM, CULIN, MED*) powder; **~s** *nmpl* (*maquillaje*) powder *sg*; **quitar el ~** to dust; **~ de talco** talcum powder; **estar hecho ~** (*fam*) to be worn out o exhausted

pólvora *nf* gunpowder; (*fuegos artificiales*) fireworks *pl*

polvoriento, -a *adj* (*superficie*) dusty; (*sustancia*) powdery

pomada *nf* cream, ointment; (*RPI*: *betún*) (shoe) polish

pomelo (*CS*, *ESP*) *nm* grapefruit, pomelo (*US*)

pómez *nf*: **piedra** ~ pumice stone

pomo *nm* doorknob

pompa *nf* (*burbuja*) bubble; (*bomba*) pump; (*esplendor*) pomp, splendor (*US*), splendour (*BRIT*) ❑ **pomposo, -a** *adj* splendid, magnificent; (*pey*) pompous

pómulo *nm* cheekbone

pon *vb ver* **poner**

ponchadura (*MÉX*) *nf* flat (*US*), puncture (*BRIT*) ❑ **ponchar** (*MÉX*) *vt* (*llanta*) to puncture

ponche *nm* punch

poncho *nm* poncho

ponderar *vt* (*considerar*) to weigh up, consider; (*elogiar*) to praise highly, speak in praise of

pondré *etc vb ver* **poner**

poner

PALABRA CLAVE

vt

1 (*colocar*) to put; (*telegrama*) to send; (*obra de teatro*) to put on; (*película*) to show; **ponlo más fuerte** turn it up; **¿qué ponen en el Excelsior?** what's on at the Excelsior?

2 (*tienda*) to open; (*instalar: gas etc*) to put in; (*radio, TV*) to switch o turn on

3 (*suponer*): **pongamos que ...** let's suppose that ...

4 (*contribuir*): **el gobierno ha puesto otro millón** the government has contributed another million

5 (*ESP TEL*): **póngame con el Sr. López** can you put me through to Mr. López?

6: **poner de: le han puesto de director general** they've appointed him general manager

7 (+ *adj*) to make; **me estás poniendo nerviosa** you're making me nervous

8 (*dar nombre*): **al hijo le pusieron Diego** they called their son Diego

♦ *vi* (*gallina*) to lay

♦ **ponerse** *vr*

1 (*colocarse*): **se puso a mi lado** he came and stood beside me; **tú ponte en esa silla** you go and sit on that chair

2 (*vestido, cosméticos*) to put on; **¿por qué no te pones el vestido nuevo?** why don't you put on o wear your new dress?

3 (+ *adj*) to turn; to get, become; **se puso muy serio** he got very serious; **después de**

lavarla la tela se puso azul after washing it the material turned blue

4: **ponerse a: se puso a llorar** he started to cry; **tienes que ponerte a estudiar** you must get down to studying

5: **ponerse a bien con algn** to make it up with sb; **ponerse a mal con algn** to get on the wrong side of sb

pongo *etc vb ver* **poner**

poniente *nm* (*occidente*) west; (*viento*) west wind

pontífice *nm* pope, pontiff

popa *nf* stern

popote (*MÉX*) *nm* straw

popular *adj* popular; (*cultura*) of the people, folk *cpd* ❑ **popularidad** *nf* popularity ❑ **popularizarse** *vr* to become popular

por

PALABRA CLAVE

prep

1 (*objetivo*) for; **luchar por la patria** to fight for one's country

2 (+ *infin*): **por no llegar tarde** so as not to arrive late; **por citar unos ejemplos** to give a few examples

3 (*causa*) out of, because of; **por escasez de fondos** through o for lack of funds

4 (*ESP tiempo*): **por la mañana/noche** in the morning/at night; **se queda por una semana** she's staying (for) a week

5 (*lugar*): **pasar por Monterrey** to pass through Monterrey; **ir a Guayaquil por Quito** to go to Guayaquil via Quito; **caminar por la calle** to walk along the street; *ver tb* **todo**

6 (*cambio, precio*): **te doy uno nuevo por el que tienes** I'll give you a new one (in return) for the one you've got

7 (*valor distributivo*): **100 pesos por hora/cabeza** 100 pesos an o per hour/a o per head

8 (*modo, medio*) by; **por correo/avión** by mail (*US*) o post (*BRIT*)/air; **día por día** day by day; **entrar por la entrada principal** to go in through the main entrance

9: **10 por 10 son 100** 10 times 10 is 100

10 (*en lugar de*): **vino él por su jefe** he came instead of his boss

11: **por mí que revienten** as far as I'm concerned they can drop dead

12: **¿por qué?** why?; **¿por qué no?** why not?

porcelana *nf* porcelain; (*china*) china

porcentaje *nm* percentage

porción nf (parte) portion, share; (cantidad) quantity, amount

pordiosero, -a nm/f beggar

porfiar vi to persist, insist; (disputar) to argue stubbornly

pormenor nm detail, particular

pornografía nf pornography

poro nm pore; (MÉX: puerro) leek

pororó (RPI) nm popcorn

poroso, -a adj porous

poroto (CS) nm bean

porque conj (a causa de) because; (ya que) since; (con el fin de) so that, in order that

porqué nm reason, cause

porquería nf (suciedad) filth, dirt; (acción) dirty trick; (objeto) small thing, trifle; (fig) garbage (US), rubbish (BRIT)

porrazo nm blow, bump

porro (LAm exc MÉX, ESP: fam) nm (droga) joint (fam)

porrón nm glass wine jar with a long spout

portaaviones nm inv aircraft carrier

portada nf (de revista) cover

portador, a nm/f carrier, bearer; (COM) bearer, payee

portaequipajes nm inv (AUTO: maletero) trunk (US), boot (BRIT); (: baca) luggage rack

portafolio (LAm) nm briefcase

portal nm (entrada) vestibule, hall; (portada) porch, doorway; (puerta de entrada) main door; **~es** nmpl (LAm) arcade sg

portamaletas (LAm exc MÉX, ESP) nm inv (AUTO: maletero) trunk (US), boot (BRIT); (: baca) roof rack

portarse vr to behave, conduct o.s.

portátil adj portable

portavoz nmf spokesman(-woman)

portazo nm: **dar un ~** to slam the door

porte nm (COM) transport; (precio) transport charges pl

portento nm marvel, wonder □ **portentoso, -a** adj extraordinary, marvelous (US), marvellous (BRIT)

porteño, -a adj of o from Buenos Aires

portería nf (oficina) janitor's office, caretaker's office (BRIT); (DEPORTE) goal

portero, -a nm/f (de edificio) janitor, caretaker (BRIT); (ujier) doorman, porter (BRIT); (DEPORTE) goalkeeper ▸ **portero eléctrico** (LAm: ESP) entry phone

pórtico nm (patio) portico, porch; (fig) gateway; (arcada) arcade

portorriqueño, -a adj Puerto Rican

Portugal nm Portugal □ **portugués, -esa** adj, nm/f Portuguese ♦ nm (LING) Portuguese

porvenir nm future

pos prep: **en ~ de** after, in pursuit of

posada nf (refugio) shelter, lodging; (mesón) guest house; (MÉX: fiesta) Christmas celebration; **dar ~ a** to give shelter to, take in

---

POSADA

Posadas are celebrations which mark the beginning of the Christmas vacations in Mexico; there are nine days of processions, parades, and parties, between December 16th and 25th. Every afternoon, the children take part in Christmas plays and parade through the streets asking for **posada** (shelter and food). After the procession, there are parties, where the children can destroy **piñatas** and pick up the candy and presents.

---

posaderas nfpl backside sg, buttocks

posar vt (en el suelo) to lay down, put down; (la mano) to place, put gently ♦ vi (modelo) to sit, pose; **posarse** vr to settle; (pájaro) to perch; (avión) to land, come down

posavasos nm inv coaster; (para cerveza) beermat

posdata nf postscript

pose nf pose

poseedor, a nm/f owner, possessor; (de récord, puesto) holder

poseer vt to possess, own; (ventaja) to enjoy; (récord, puesto) to hold

posesión nf possession □ **posesionarse** vr: **posesionarse de** to take possession of, take over

posesivo, -a adj possessive

posgrado nm: **curso de ~** postgraduate course

posibilidad nf possibility; (oportunidad) chance □ **posibilitar** vt to make possible; (hacer realizable) to make feasible

posible adj possible; (realizable) feasible; **de ser ~ if** possible; **en lo ~** as far as possible

posición nf position; (rango social) status

positivo, -a adj positive

poso nm sediment; (heces) dregs pl

posponer vt (relegar) to put behind/below; (aplazar) to postpone

posta nf: **a ~** deliberately, on purpose

postal adj postal ♦ nf postcard

poste nm (de telégrafos etc) post, pole; (columna) pillar

póster (pl **~es**, **~s**) nm poster

postergar vt to postpone, delay
posteridad nf posterity
posterior adj back, rear; (siguiente) following, subsequent; (más tarde) later ❑ **posterioridad** nf: **con posterioridad** later, subsequently
postgrado nm = **posgrado**
postizo, -a adj false, artificial ♦ nm hairpiece
postor, a nm/f bidder
postre nm dessert
postrero, -a (delante de nmsg **postrer**) adj (último) last; (que viene detrás) rear
postulado nm postulate
póstumo, -a adj posthumous
postura nf (del cuerpo) posture, position; (fig) attitude, position
potable adj drinkable; **agua ~** drinking water
potaje nm thick vegetable soup
pote nm pot, jar
potencia nf power ❑ **potencial** adj, nm potential ❑ **potenciar** vt to boost
potente adj powerful
potro, -a nm/f (ZOOL) colt/filly ♦ nm (de gimnasia) vaulting horse
pozo nm well; (de río) deep pool; (de mina) shaft
P.P. abr (= porte pagado) CP
práctica nf practice; (método) method; (arte, capacidad) skill; **en la ~** in practice
practicable adj practicable; (camino) passable
practicante nmf (MED: ayudante de doctor) medical assistant; (: enfermero) nurse; (quien practica algo) practitioner ♦ adj practicing (US), practising (BRIT)
practicar vt to practice (US), practise (BRIT); (DEPORTE) to play; (realizar) to carry out, perform
práctico, -a adj practical; (instruido: persona) skilled, expert
practique etc vb ver **practicar**
pradera nf meadow; (de EE.UU., Canadá) prairie
prado nm (campo) meadow, field; (pastizal) pasture
Praga n Prague
pragmático, -a adj pragmatic
preámbulo nm preamble, introduction
precario, -a adj precarious
precaución nf (medida preventiva) preventive measure, precaution; (prudencia) caution, wariness

precaver vt to guard against; (impedir) to forestall; **precaverse** vr: **~se de** o **contra algo** to (be on one's) guard against sth ❑ **precavido, -a** adj cautious, wary
precedente adj preceding; (anterior) former ♦ nm precedent
preceder vt, vi to precede, go before, come before
precepto nm precept
preciado, -a adj (estimado) esteemed, valuable
preciarse vr to boast; **~ de** to pride o.s. on, boast of being
precinto nm (tb: **~ de garantía**) seal
precio nm price; (costo) cost; (valor) value, worth; (de viaje) fare ▶ **precio al contado/ de costo/de compra** cash/cost/purchase price ▶ **precio al por menor** retail price ▶ **precio tope** top price
preciosidad nf (valor) (high) value, (great) worth; (encanto) charm; (cosa bonita) beautiful thing; **es una ~** it's really beautiful, it's lovely
precioso, -a adj precious; (de mucho valor) valuable; (fam) beautiful, lovely
precipicio nm cliff, precipice; (fig) abyss
precipitación nf haste; (lluvia) rainfall
precipitado, -a adj (conducta) hasty, rash; (salida) hasty, sudden
precipitar vt (arrojar) to hurl down, throw; (apresurar) to hasten; (acelerar) to speed up, accelerate; **precipitarse** vr to throw o.s.; (apresurarse) to rush; (actuar sin pensar) to act rashly
precisamente adv precisely; (exactamente) precisely, exactly
precisar vt (necesitar) to need, require; (fijar) to determine exactly, fix; (especificar) to specify
precisión nf (exactitud) precision
preciso, -a adj (exacto) precise; (necesario) necessary, essential
preconcebido, -a adj preconceived
precoz adj (persona) precocious; (calvicie etc) premature
precursor, a nm/f predecessor, forerunner
predecir vt to predict, forecast
predestinado, -a adj predestined
predicar vt, vi to preach
predicción nf prediction
predilecto, -a adj favorite (US), favourite (BRIT)

predisponer vt to predispose; (pey) to prejudice ❑ **predisposición** nf inclination; prejudice, bias

predominante adj predominant

predominar vt to dominate ♦ vi to predominate; (prevalecer) to prevail ❑ **predominio** nm predominance; prevalence

preescolar adj preschool

prefabricado, -a adj prefabricated

prefacio nm preface

preferencia nf preference; **de ~** preferably, for preference

preferible adj preferable

preferir vt to prefer

prefiero etc vb ver **preferir**

prefijo (ESP) nm (TEL) area code (US), dialling code (BRIT)

pregonar vt to proclaim, announce

pregunta nf question; **hacer una ~** to ask a question ▶ **preguntas frecuentes** FAQs, frequently asked questions

preguntar vt to ask; (cuestionar) to question ♦ vi to ask; **preguntarse** vr to wonder; **~ por algn** to ask for sb

preguntón, -ona adj inquisitive

prehistórico, -a adj prehistoric

prejuicio nm (acto) prejudgement; (idea preconcebida) preconception; (parcialidad) prejudice, bias

preliminar adj preliminary

preludio nm prelude

prematuro, -a adj premature

premeditación nf premeditation

premeditar vt to premeditate

premiar vt to reward; (en un concurso) to give a prize to

premio nm reward; prize; (COM) premium

premonición nf premonition

prenatal adj antenatal, prenatal

prenda nf (ropa) garment, article of clothing; (garantía) pledge; **~s** nfpl (talentos) talents, gifts

prendedor nm brooch

prender vt (captar) to catch, capture; (detener) to arrest; (COSTURA) to pin, attach; (sujetar) to fasten; (LAm: luz etc) to turn o switch on ♦ vi to catch; (arraigar) to take root; **prenderse** vr (encenderse) to catch fire

prendido, -a (LAm) adj (luz etc) on

prensa nf press; **la ~** the press ❑ **prensar** vt to press

preñado, -a adj pregnant; **~ de** pregnant with, full of

preocupación nf worry, concern; (ansiedad) anxiety

preocupado, -a adj worried, concerned; (ansioso) anxious

preocupar vt to worry; **preocuparse** vr to worry; **~se de algo** (hacerse cargo) to take care of sth

preparación nf (acto) preparation; (estado) readiness; (entrenamiento) training

preparado, -a adj (dispuesto) prepared; (CULIN) ready (to serve) ♦ nm preparation

preparar vt (disponer) to prepare, get ready; (TEC: tratar) to prepare, process; (entrenar) to teach, train; **prepararse** vr: **~se o para** to prepare to o for, get ready to o for ❑ **preparativo, -a** adj preparatory, preliminary ❑ **preparativos** nmpl preparations ❑ **preparatoria** (MÉX) nf senior high school (US), sixth-form college (BRIT)

prerrogativa nf prerogative, privilege

presa nf (cosa apresada) catch; (víctima) victim; (de animal) prey; (de agua) dam

presagiar vt to presage, forebode ❑ **presagio** nm omen

prescindir vi: **~ de** (privarse de) to do without, go without; (descartar) to dispense with

prescribir vt to prescribe ❑ **prescripción** nf prescription

presencia nf presence ❑ **presencial** adj: **testigo presencial** eyewitness ❑ **presenciar** vt to be present at; (asistir a) to attend; (ver) to see, witness

presentación nf presentation; (introducción) introduction

presentador, a nm/f host(ess), compere (BRIT)

presentar vt to present; (ofrecer) to offer; (mostrar) to show, display; (a una persona) to introduce; **presentarse** vr (llegar inesperadamente) to appear, turn up; (ofrecerse: como candidato) to run, stand; (aparecer) to show, appear; (solicitar empleo) to apply

presente adj present ♦ nm present; **hacer ~** to state, declare; **tener ~** to remember, bear in mind

presentimiento nm premonition, presentiment

presentir vt to have a premonition of

preservación nf protection, preservation

preservar vt to protect, preserve ❑ **preservativo** nm sheath, condom

presidencia *nf* presidency; *(de comité)* chairmanship

presidente *nmf* president; *(de comité)* chairman(-woman)

presidiario *nm* convict

presidio *nm* prison, penitentiary

presidir *vt (dirigir)* to preside at, preside over; *(: comité)* to take the chair at; *(dominar)* to dominate, rule ♦ *vi* to preside; to take the chair

presión *nf* pressure □ **presionar** *vt* to press; *(fig)* to press, put pressure on ♦ *vi*: **presionar para** to press for

preso, -a *nm/f* prisoner; **tomar** *o* **llevar ~ a algn** to arrest sb, take sb prisoner

prestación *nf* service; *(subsidio)* benefit □ **prestaciones** *nfpl (TEC, AUTO)* performance features

prestado, -a *adj* on loan; **pedir ~** to borrow

prestamista *nmf* moneylender

préstamo *nm* loan ▶ **préstamo hipotecario** mortgage

prestar *vt* to lend, loan; *(atención)* to pay; *(ayuda)* to give

presteza *nf* speed, promptness

prestigio *nm* prestige □ **prestigioso, -a** *adj (honorable)* prestigious; *(famoso, renombrado)* renowned, famous

presumido, -a *adj (persona)* vain

presumir *vt* to presume ♦ *vi (tener aires)* to be conceited; **según cabe ~** as may be presumed, presumably □ **presunción** *nf* presumption □ **presunto, -a** *adj (supuesto)* supposed, presumed; *(así llamado)* so-called □ **presuntuoso, -a** *adj* conceited, presumptuous

presuponer *vt* to presuppose

presupuesto *pp de* **presuponer** ♦ *nm (FINANZAS)* budget; *(estimación: de costo)* estimate

pretencioso, -a *adj* pretentious

pretender *vt (intentar)* to try to, seek to; *(reivindicar)* to claim; *(buscar)* to seek, try for; *(cortejar)* to woo, court; **~ que** to expect that □ **pretendiente** *nmf (amante)* suitor; *(al trono)* pretender □ **pretensión** *nf (aspiración)* aspiration; *(reivindicación)* claim; *(orgullo)* pretension

⚠ No confundir **pretender** con la palabra inglesa *pretend*.

pretexto *nm* pretext; *(excusa)* excuse

prevalecer *vi* to prevail

prevención *nf* prevention; *(precaución)* precaution

prevenido, -a *adj* prepared, ready; *(cauteloso)* cautious

prevenir *vt (impedir)* to prevent; *(predisponer)* to prejudice, bias; *(avisar)* to warn; *(preparar)* to prepare, get ready; **prevenirse** *vr* to get ready, prepare; **~se contra** to take precautions against □ **preventivo, -a** *adj* preventive, precautionary

prever *vt* to foresee

previo, -a *adj (anterior)* previous; *(preliminar)* preliminary ♦ *prep*: **~ acuerdo de los otros** subject to the agreement of the others

previsión *nf (perspicacia)* foresight; *(predicción)* forecast □ **previsto, -a** *adj* anticipated, forecast

PRI *(MÉX) nm abr =* **Partido Revolucionario Institucional**

prima *nf (COM)* bonus; *(de seguro)* premium; *ver tb* **primo**

primacía *nf* primacy

primario, -a *adj* primary

primavera *nf* spring(-time)

primera *nf (AUTO)* first gear; *(FERRO: tb:* **~ clase**) first class; **de ~** *(fam)* first-class, first-rate

primero, -a *(delante de nmsg:* **primer**) *adj* first; *(principal)* prime ♦ *adv* first; *(más bien)* sooner, rather; **primera plana** front page

primicia *nf (tb:* **~ informativa**) scoop

primitivo, -a *adj* primitive; *(original)* original

primo, -a *adj* prime ♦ *nm/f* cousin; **materias primas** raw materials ▶ **primo hermano** first cousin

primogénito, -a *adj* first-born

primordial *adj* basic, fundamental

primoroso, -a *adj* exquisite, delicate

princesa *nf* princess

principal *adj* principal, main ♦ *nm (jefe)* chief, principal

príncipe *nm* prince

principiante *nmf* beginner

principio *nm (comienzo)* beginning, start; *(origen)* origin; *(primera etapa)* rudiment, basic idea; *(moral)* principle; **a ~s de** at the beginning of

pringoso, -a *adj (grasiento)* greasy; *(pegajoso)* sticky

pringue *nm (grasa)* grease, fat, dripping

prioridad *nf* priority

prisa *nf (apresuramiento)* hurry, haste; *(rapidez)* speed; *(urgencia)* (sense of) urgency; **a** *o* **de ~** quickly; **correr ~** to be urgent; **darse**

~ to hurry up; **estar de** o **tener** ~ to be in a
hurry

prisión *nf (cárcel)* prison; *(período de cárcel)*
imprisonment ❑ **prisionero, -a** *nm/f*
prisoner

prismáticos *nmpl* binoculars

privación *nf* deprivation; *(falta)* want,
privation

privado, -a *adj* private

privar *vt* to deprive ❑ **privativo, -a** *adj*
exclusive

privilegiado, -a *adj* privileged; *(memoria)*
very good

privilegiar *vt* to grant a privilege to;
(favorecer) to favor *(US)*, favour *(BRIT)*

privilegio *nm* privilege; *(concesión)*
concession

pro *nm o f* profit, advantage ♦ *prep*:
asociación ~ ciegos association for the blind
♦ *prefijo*: ~ **soviético/americano** pro-Soviet/
American; **en ~ de** on behalf of, for; **los ~s y
los contras** the pros and cons

proa *nf* bow, prow; **de ~** bow *cpd*, fore

probabilidad *nf* probability, likelihood;
(oportunidad, posibilidad) chance, prospect
❑ **probable** *adj* probable, likely

probador *nm (en tienda)* fitting room

probar *vt (demostrar)* to prove; *(someter a
prueba)* to test, try out; *(ropa)* to try on;
(comida) to taste ♦ *vi* to try; **~se un traje** to try
on a suit

probeta *nf* test tube

problema *nm* problem

procedente *adj (razonable)* reasonable;
(conforme a derecho) proper, fitting; **~ de**
coming from, originating in

proceder *vi (avanzar)* to proceed; *(actuar)* to
act; *(ser correcto)* to be right (and proper), be
fitting ♦ *nm (comportamiento)* conduct,
behavior *(US)*, behaviour *(BRIT)*; **~ de** to come
from, originate in ❑ **procedimiento** *nm*
procedure; *(proceso)* process; *(método)* means
pl, method

procesado, -a *nm/f* accused

procesador *nm* processor ▶ **procesador
de textos** word processor

procesar *vt* to try, put on trial

procesión *nf* procession

proceso *nm* process; *(JUR)* trial

proclamar *vt* to proclaim

procreación *nf* procreation

procrear *vt, vi* to procreate

procurador, a *nm/f* attorney

procurar *vt (intentar)* to try, endeavor *(US)*,
endeavour *(BRIT)*; *(conseguir)* to get, obtain;
(asegurar) to secure; *(producir)* to produce

prodigio *nm* prodigy; *(milagro)* wonder,
marvel ❑ **prodigioso, -a** *adj* prodigious,
marvelous *(US)*, marvellous *(BRIT)*

pródigo, -a *adj*: **hijo ~** prodigal son

producción *nf (gen)* production; *(producto)*
output ▶ **producción en serie** mass
production

producir *vt* to produce; *(causar)* to cause,
bring about; **producirse** *vr (cambio)* to come
about; *(accidente)* to take place; *(problema etc)*
to arise; *(hacerse)* to be produced, be made;
(estallar) to break out

productividad *nf* productivity
❑ **productivo, -a** *adj* productive;
(provechoso) profitable

producto *nm* product

productor, a *adj* productive, producing
♦ *nm/f* producer

proeza *nf* exploit, feat

profanar *vt* to desecrate, profane
❑ **profano, -a** *adj* profane ♦ *nm/f*
layman(-woman)

profecía *nf* prophecy

proferir *vt (palabra, sonido)* to utter; *(injuria)*
to hurl, let fly

profesión *nf* profession ❑ **profesional**
adj professional

profesor, a *nm/f* teacher ❑ **profesorado**
nm teaching staff, faculty *(US)*

profeta *nmf* prophet ❑ **profetizar** *vt, vi* to
prophesy

prófugo, -a *nm/f* fugitive; *(MIL: desertor)*
deserter

profundidad *nf* depth ❑ **profundizar** *vi*:
profundizar en to go deeply into
❑ **profundo, -a** *adj* deep; *(misterio,
pensador)* profound

progenitor *nm* ancestor; **~es** *nmpl (padres)*
parents

programa *nm* program *(US)*, programme
(BRIT) ❑ **programación** *nf* programing *(US)*,
programming *(BRIT)* ❑ **programador, a**
nm/f programer *(US)*, programmer *(BRIT)*
❑ **programar** *vt* to program

progresar *vi* to progress, make progress
❑ **progresista** *adj, nmf* progressive
❑ **progresivo, -a** *adj* progressive; *(gradual)*
gradual; *(continuo)* continuous ❑ **progreso**
nm progress

prohibición *nf* prohibition, ban

prohibir vt to prohibit, ban, forbid; **se prohibe fumar, prohibido fumar** no smoking; **"prohibido el paso"** "no entry"

prójimo, -a nm/f fellow man; (vecino) neighbor (US), neighbour (BRIT)

proletariado nm proletariat

proletario, -a adj, nm/f proletarian

proliferación nf proliferation

proliferar vi to proliferate □ **prolífico, -a** adj prolific

prólogo nm prologue, prolog (US)

prolongación nf extension □ **prolongado, -a** adj (largo) long; (alargado) lengthy

prolongar vt to extend; (reunión etc) to prolong; (calle, tubo) to extend

promedio nm average; (de distancia) middle, mid-point

promesa nf promise

prometer vt to promise ♦ vi to show promise; **prometerse** vr (novios) to get engaged □ **prometido, -a** adj promised; engaged ♦ nm/f fiancé (fiancée)

prominente adj prominent

promiscuo, -a adj promiscuous

promoción nf promotion

promotor nm promoter; (instigador) instigator

promover vt to promote; (causar) to cause; (instigar) to instigate, stir up

promulgar vt to promulgate; (anunciar) to proclaim

pronombre nm pronoun

pronosticar vt to predict, foretell, forecast □ **pronóstico** nm prediction, forecast ▶ **pronóstico del tiempo** weather forecast

pronto, -a adj (rápido) prompt, quick; (preparado) ready ♦ adv quickly, promptly; (en seguida) at once, right away; (dentro de poco) soon; (temprano) early ♦ nm: **tener ~s de enojo** to be quick-tempered; **de ~** suddenly; **por lo ~** meanwhile, for the present

pronunciación nf pronunciation

pronunciar vt to pronounce; (discurso) to make, deliver; **pronunciarse** vr to revolt, rebel; (declararse) to declare o.s.

propagación nf propagation

propaganda nf (POL) propaganda; (COM) advertising

propagar vt to propagate

propensión nf inclination, propensity □ **propenso, -a** adj inclined to; **ser**

propenso a to be inclined to, have a tendency to

propicio, -a adj favorable (US), favourable (BRIT)

propiedad nf property; (posesión) possession, ownership ▶ **propiedad particular** private property

propietario, -a nm/f owner, proprietor

propina nf tip

propio, -a adj own, of one's own; (característico) characteristic, typical; (debido) proper; (mismo) selfsame, very; **el ~ ministro** the minister himself; **¿tienes casa propia?** have you a house of your own?

proponer vt to propose, put forward; (problema) to pose; **proponerse** vr to propose, intend

proporción nf proportion; (MAT) ratio; **proporciones** nfpl (dimensiones) dimensions; (fig) size sg □ **proporcionado, -a** adj proportionate; (regular) medium, middling; (justo) just right □ **proporcionar** vt (dar) to give, supply, provide

proposición nf proposition; (propuesta) proposal

propósito nm purpose; (intento) aim, intention ♦ adv: **a ~** by the way, incidentally; (a posta) on purpose, deliberately; **a ~ de** about, with regard to

propuesta vb ver **proponer** ♦ nf proposal

propulsar vt to drive, propel; (fig) to promote, encourage □ **propulsión** nf propulsion ▶ **propulsión a chorro** o **por reacción** jet propulsion

prórroga nf extension; (JUR) stay; (COM) deferment; (DEPORTE) overtime (US), extra time (BRIT) □ **prorrogar** vt (período) to extend; (decisión) to defer, postpone

prorrumpir vi to burst forth, break out

prosa nf prose

proscrito, -a adj banned

proseguir vt to continue, carry on ♦ vi to continue, go on

prospección nf exploration; (del oro) prospecting

prospecto nm prospectus

prosperar vi to prosper, thrive, flourish □ **prosperidad** nf prosperity; (éxito) success □ **próspero, -a** adj prosperous, flourishing; (que tiene éxito) successful

prostíbulo nm brothel, house of prostitution (US)

prostitución nf prostitution

prostituir vt to prostitute; **prostituirse** vr to prostitute o.s., become a prostitute

prostituta *nf* prostitute

protagonista *nmf* protagonist

protagonizar *vt* to take the chief role in

protección *nf* protection

protector, a *adj* protective, protecting ♦ *nm/f* protector

proteger *vt* to protect □ **protegido, -a** *nm/f* protégé/protégée

proteína *nf* protein

protesta *nf* protest; (*declaración*) protestation

protestante *adj* Protestant

protestar *vt* to protest, declare ♦ *vi* to protest

protocolo *nm* protocol

prototipo *nm* prototype

prov. *abr* (= *provincia*) prov

provecho *nm* advantage, benefit; (*FINANZAS*) profit; **¡buen ~!** bon appétit!; **en ~ de** to the benefit of; **sacar ~ de** to benefit from, profit by

proveer *vt* to provide, supply ♦ *vi:* **~ a** to provide for

provenir *vi:* **~ de** to come from, stem from

proverbio *nm* proverb

providencia *nf* providence

provincia *nf* province □ **provinciano, -a** *adj* provincial; (*del campo*) country *cpd*

provisión *nf* provision; (*abastecimiento*) provision, supply; (*medida*) measure, step

provisional *adj* provisional

provocación *nf* provocation

provocar *vt* to provoke; (*alentar*) to tempt, invite; (*causar*) to bring about, lead to; (*promover*) to promote; (*estimular*) to rouse, stimulate; **¿te provoca un café?** (*CAm*) would you like a coffee? □ **provocativo, -a** *adj* provocative

proxeneta *nm* pimp

próximamente *adv* shortly, soon

proximidad *nf* closeness, proximity □ **próximo, -a** *adj* near, close; (*vecino*) neighboring (*US*), neighbouring (*BRIT*); (*siguiente*) next

proyectar *vt* (*objeto*) to hurl, throw; (*luz*) to cast, shed; (*CINE*) to screen, show; (*planear*) to plan

proyectil *nm* projectile, missile

proyecto *nm* plan; (*estimación de costo*) detailed estimate

proyector *nm* (*CINE*) projector

prudencia *nf* (*sabiduría*) wisdom; (*cuidado*) care □ **prudente** *adj* sensible, wise; (*conductor*) careful

prueba *etc vb ver* **probar** ♦ *nf* proof; (*ensayo*) test, trial; (*degustación*) tasting, sampling; (*de ropa*) fitting; **a ~** on trial; **a ~ de** proof against; **a ~ de agua/fuego** waterproof/fireproof; **someter a ~** to put to the test

prurito *nm* itch; (*de bebé*) diaper (*US*) o nappy (*BRIT*) rash

psico... *prefijo* psycho... □ **psicoanálisis** *nm inv* psychoanalysis □ **psicología** *nf* psychology □ **psicológico, -a** *adj* psychological □ **psicólogo, -a** *nm/f* psychologist □ **psicópata** *nmf* psychopath □ **psicosis** *nf inv* psychosis

psiquiatra *nmf* psychiatrist □ **psiquiátrico, -a** *adj* psychiatric

psíquico, -a *adj* psychic(al)

pta(s) *abr* = **peseta(s)**

pts *abr* = **pesetas**

púa *nf* (*BOT, ZOOL*) prickle, spine; (*para guitarra*) pick (*US*), plectrum (*BRIT*); **alambre de ~** barbed wire

pubertad *nf* puberty

publicación *nf* publication

publicar *vt* (*editar*) to publish; (*hacer público*) to publicize; (*divulgar*) to make public, divulge

publicidad *nf* publicity; (*COM: propaganda*) advertising □ **publicitario, -a** *adj* publicity *cpd*; advertising *cpd*

público, -a *adj* public ♦ *nm* public; (*TEATRO etc*) audience

puchero *nm* (*CULIN: guiso*) stew; (*: olla*) cooking pot; **hacer ~s** to pout

pucho (*CS: fam*) *nm* cigarette, fag (*BRIT*)

pude *etc vb ver* **poder**

púdico, -a *adj* modest

pudiente *adj* (*rico*) wealthy, well-to-do

pudiera *etc vb ver* **poder**

pudor *nm* modesty

pudrir *vt* to rot; **pudrirse** *vr* to rot, decay

pueblo *nm* people; (*nación*) nation; (*aldea*) village

puedo *etc vb ver* **poder**

puente *nm* bridge; **hacer ~** (*fam*) *to take extra days off work between 2 public holidays; to take a long weekend* ▶ **puente aéreo** shuttle service ▶ **puente colgante** suspension bridge

puerco, -a *nm/f* pig/sow ♦ *adj* (*sucio*) dirty, filthy; (*obsceno*) disgusting ▶ **puerco espín** porcupine

pueril *adj* childish

puerro *nm* leek

puerta nf door; (de jardín) gate; (portal) doorway; (fig) gateway; (portería) goal; **a la ~** at the door; **a ~ cerrada** behind closed doors ▶ **puerta giratoria** revolving door

puerto nm port; (paso) pass; (fig) haven, refuge ▶ **puerto deportivo** marina

Puerto Rico nm Puerto Rico ❑ **puertorriqueño, -a** adj, nm/f Puerto Rican

pues adv (entonces) then; (bueno) well, well then; (así que) so ♦ conj (ya que) since; **¡~ sí!** yes!, certainly!

puesta nf (apuesta) bet, stake ▶ **puesta en marcha** starting ▶ **puesta de sol** sunset

puesto, -a pp de **poner** ♦ adj: **tener algo ~** to have sth on, be wearing sth ♦ nm (lugar, posición) place; (trabajo) post, job; (COM) stall ♦ conj: **~ que** since, as

púgil nm boxer

pugna nf battle, conflict ❑ **pugnar** vi (luchar) to struggle, fight; (pelear) to fight

pujar vi (en subasta) to bid; (esforzarse) to struggle, strain

pulcro, -a adj neat, tidy

pulga nf flea; **mercado de ~s** (LAm) flea market

pulgada nf inch

pulgar nm thumb

pulir vt to polish; (alisar) to smooth; (fig) to polish up, touch up

pulla nf cutting remark

pulmón nm lung ❑ **pulmonía** nf pneumonia

pulpa nf pulp; (de fruta) flesh, soft part

pulpería (LAm) nf (tienda) small grocery store

púlpito nm pulpit

pulpo nm octopus

pulque nm pulque

PULQUE

Pulque is a thick, white, alcoholic drink which is very popular in Mexico. In ancient times it was considered sacred by the Aztecs. It is produced by fermenting the juice of the **maguey**, a Mexican cactus similar to the agave. It can be drunk by itself or mixed with fruit or vegetable juice.

---

pulsación nf beat; **pulsaciones** pulse rate

pulsar vt (tecla) to touch, tap; (MÚS) to play; (botón) to press, push

pulsera nf bracelet

pulso nm (ANAT) pulse; (fuerza) strength; (firmeza) steadiness, steady hand

pulverizador nm spray, spray gun

pulverizar vt to pulverize; (líquido) to spray

puna (CAm) nf mountain sickness

punitivo, -a adj punitive

punta nf point, tip; (extremo) end; (fig) touch, trace; **horas ~s** (ESP: de electricidad, teléfono) peak hours; (: del tráfico) rush hours; **sacar ~ a** to sharpen

puntada nf (COSTURA) stitch

puntal nm prop, support

puntapié nm kick

puntear vt to tick, mark

puntería nf (de arma) aim, aiming; (destreza) marksmanship

puntero, -a adj leading ♦ nm (palo) pointer

puntiagudo, -a adj sharp, pointed

puntilla nf (encaje) lace edging o trim; **(andar) de ~s** (to walk) on tiptoe

punto nm (gen) point; (señal diminuta) spot, dot; (MED) stitch; (lugar) spot, place; (momento) point, moment; **a ~** ready; **estar a ~ de** to be on the point of o about to; **en ~** on the dot ▶ **punto de interrogación** question mark ▶ **punto de vista** point of view, viewpoint ▶ **punto final** period (US), full stop (BRIT) ▶ **punto muerto** dead center; (AUTO) neutral (gear) ▶ **punto y coma** semicolon

puntocom, punto.com adj inv, nf inv dotcom, dot.com

puntuación nf punctuation; (puntos: en examen) grade (US), mark(s) (pl) (BRIT); (DEPORTE) score

puntual adj (a tiempo) punctual; (exacto) exact, accurate ❑ **puntualidad** nf punctuality; exactness, accuracy ❑ **puntualizar** vt to fix, specify

puntuar vi (DEPORTE) to score, count

punzada nf (dolor) twinge

punzante adj (dolor) shooting, sharp; (herramienta) sharp ❑ **punzar** vt to prick, pierce ♦ vi to shoot, stab

puñado nm handful

puñal nm dagger ❑ **puñalada** nf stab

puñetazo nm punch

puño nm (ANAT) fist; (cantidad) fistful, handful; (COSTURA) cuff; (de herramienta) handle

pupila nf pupil

pupitre nm desk

puré nm purée; (sopa) (thick) soup ▶ **puré de papas** (LAm) mashed potatoes ▶ **puré de patatas** (ESP) mashed potatoes

pureza nf purity

purga nf purge ❑ **purgante** adj, nm purgative ❑ **purgar** vt to purge

purgatorio *nm* purgatory

purificar *vt* to purify; (*refinar*) to refine

puritano, -a *adj* (*actitud*) puritanical; (*iglesia, tradición*) puritan ♦ *nm/f* puritan

puro, -a *adj* pure; (*verdad*) simple, plain ♦ *adv*: **de ~ cansado** out of sheer tiredness ♦ *nm* cigar

púrpura *nf* purple ☐ **purpúreo, -a** *adj* purple

pus *nm* pus

puse *etc vb ver* **poder**

pusiera *etc vb ver* **poder**

pústula *nf* pimple, sore

puta (*fam!*) *nf* whore, prostitute

putrefacción *nf* rotting, putrefaction

PVP (*ESP*) *nm abr* (= *precio venta al público*) RRP

pyme, PYME *nf abr* (= *Pequeña y Mediana Empresa*) SME

Qq

que
PALABRA CLAVE

conj

1 (*con oración subordinada: muchas veces no se traduce*) that; **dijo que vendría** he said (that) he would come; **espero que lo encuentres** I hope (that) you find it; *ver tb* **el**

2 (*en oración independiente*): **¡que entre!** send him in!; **¡que se mejore tu padre!** I hope your father gets better

3 (*enfático*): **¿me quieres? -- ¡que sí!** do you love me? -- of course!

4 (*consecutivo: muchas veces no se traduce*) that; **es tan grande que no lo puedo levantar** it's so big (that) I can't lift it

5 (*comparaciones*) than; **yo que tú/él** if I were you/him; *ver tb* **más; menos; mismo**

6 (*valor disyuntivo*): **que le guste o no** whether he likes it or not; **que venga o que no venga** whether he comes or not

7 (*porque*): **no puedo, que tengo que quedarme en casa** I can't, I've got to stay in house ♦ *pron*

1 (*cosa*) that, which; (+ *prep*) which; **el sombrero que te compraste** the hat (that *o* which) you bought; **la cama en que dormí** the bed (that *o* which) I slept in

2 (*persona: suj*) that, who; (: *objeto*) that, whom; **el amigo que me acompañó al museo** the friend that *o* who went to the museum with me; **la chica que invité** the girl (that *o* whom) I invited

qué *adj* what?, which? ♦ *pron* what?; **¡~ divertido!** how funny!; **¿~ edad tienes?** how old are you?; **¿de ~ me hablas?** what are you saying to me?; **¿~ tal?** how are you?, how are things?; **¿~ hay (de nuevo)?** what's new?

quebradizo, -a *adj* fragile; (*persona*) frail

quebrado, -a *adj* (*roto*) broken ♦ *nm/f* bankrupt ♦ *nm* (*MAT*) fraction

quebrantar *vt* (*infringir*) to violate, transgress; **quebrantarse** *vr* (*persona*) to fail in health

quebranto *nm* damage, harm; (*dolor*) grief, pain

quebrar *vt* to break, smash ♦ *vi* to go bankrupt; **quebrarse** *vr* (*LAm: romperse*) to break, get broken; (*MED*) to be ruptured

quedar *vi* to stay, remain; (*encontrarse: sitio*) to be; (*haber aún*) to remain, be left; **quedarse** *vr* to remain, stay (behind); **~se (con) algo** to keep sth; **~ en** (*acordar*) to agree on/to; **~ en nada** to come to nothing; **~ por hacer** to be still to be done; **~se ciego/mudo** to be left blind/dumb; **no te queda bien ese vestido** that dress doesn't suit you; **eso queda muy lejos** that's a long way (away); **quedamos a las seis** we agreed to meet at six

quedo, -a *adj* still ♦ *adv* softly, gently

quehacer *nm* task, job; **~es (domésticos)** *nmpl* household chores

queja *nf* complaint ☐ **quejarse** *vr* (*enfermo*) to moan, groan; (*protestar*) to complain; **quejarse de que** to complain (about the fact) that ☐ **quejido** *nm* moan

quemado, -a *adj* burnt

quemadura *nf* burn, scald

quemar *vt* to burn; (*fig: malgastar*) to burn up, squander ♦ *vi* to be burning hot; **quemarse** *vr* (*consumirse*) to burn (up); (*del sol*) to get sunburnt

quemarropa: a ~ *adv* point-blank

quepo *etc vb ver* **caber**

querella *nf* (*JUR*) charge; (*disputa*) dispute ☐ **querellarse** *vr* (*JUR*) to file a complaint

querer
PALABRA CLAVE

vt

1 (*desear*) to want; **quiero más dinero** I want more money; **quisiera** *o* **querría un té** I'd like a tea; **sin querer** unintentionally; **quiero ayudar/que vayas** I want to help/you to go

2 *(preguntas: para pedir algo):* **¿quiere abrir la ventana?** could you open the window?; **¿quieres echarme una mano?** can you give me a hand?

3 *(amar)* to love; *(tener cariño a)* to be fond of; **quiere mucho a sus hijos** he's very fond of his children

4 *(requerir):* **esta planta quiere más luz** this plant needs more light

5: le pedí que me dejara ir pero no quiso I asked him to let me go but he refused

querido, -a *adj* dear ♦ *nm/f* darling; *(amante)* lover

queso *nm* cheese ▶ **queso crema** *(LAm)* cream cheese

quicio *nm* hinge; **sacar a algn de ~** to get on sb's nerves

quiebra *nf* break, split; *(COM)* bankruptcy; *(ECON)* slump

quiebro *nm (del cuerpo)* swerve

quien *pron* who; **hay ~ piensa que** there are those who think that; **no hay ~ lo haga** no-one will do it

quién *pron* who, whom; **¿~ es?** who's there?

quienquiera *(pl* **quienesquiera)** *pron* whoever

quiero *etc vb ver* **querer**

quieto, -a *adj* still; *(carácter)* placid ❏ **quietud** *nf* stillness

⚠ No confundir **quieto** con la palabra inglesa *quiet*.

quilate *nm* carat

quilla *nf* keel

quimera *nf* chimera ❏ **quimérico, -a** *adj* fantastic

químico, -a *adj* chemical ♦ *nm/f* chemist ♦ *nf* chemistry

quincalla *nf* hardware, ironmongery *(BRIT)*

quince *num* fifteen; **~ días** two weeks, a fortnight *(BRIT)* ❏ **quinceañero, -a** *nm/f* teenager ❏ **quincena** *nf* two weeks, fortnight *(BRIT)*; *(pago)* bimonthly pay *(US)*, fortnightly pay *(BRIT)* ❏ **quincenal** *adj* bimonthly *(US)*, fortnightly *(BRIT)*

quiniela *(ESP) nf* sports lottery *(US)*, football pools *pl (BRIT)*; **~s** *nfpl (impreso)* sports lottery ticket *sg (US)*, pools coupon *sg (BRIT)*

quinientos, -as *adj, num* five hundred

quinina *nf* quinine

quinto, -a *adj* fifth ♦ *nf* country house ♦ *nm (MÉX: moneda)* nickel; **estar sin un ~** *(MÉX: fam)* to be broke

quiosco *nm (de música)* bandstand; *(de periódicos)* news stand

quirófano *nm* operating room *(US)* o theatre *(BRIT)*

quirúrgico, -a *adj* surgical

quise *etc vb ver* **querer**

quisiera *etc vb ver* **querer**

quisquilloso, -a *adj (susceptible)* touchy; *(meticuloso)* persnickety *(US)*, pernickety *(BRIT)*

quiste *nm* cyst

quitaesmalte *nm* nail-polish remover

quitamanchas *nm inv* stain remover

quitanieves *nm inv* snowplow *(US)*, snowplough *(BRIT)*

quitar *vt* to remove, take away; *(ropa)* to take off; *(dolor)* to relieve; **quitarse** *vr* to withdraw; *(ropa)* to take off; **se quitó el sombrero** he took off his hat

quite *nm (esgrima)* parry; *(evasión)* dodge

Quito *n* Quito

quizá(s) *adv* perhaps, maybe

Rr

rábano *nm* radish; **me importa un ~** I don't give a damn

rabia *nf (MED)* rabies *sg*; *(ira)* fury, rage ❏ **rabiar** *vi* to have rabies; to rage, be furious; **rabiar por algo** to long for sth

rabieta *nf* tantrum, fit of temper

rabino *nm* rabbi

rabioso, -a *adj* rabid; *(fig)* furious

rabo *nm* tail

racha *nf* gust of wind; **buena/mala ~** spell of good/bad luck

racial *adj* racial, race *cpd*

racimo *nm* bunch

raciocinio *nm* reason

ración *(ESP) nf* portion; **raciones** *nfpl* rations

racional *adj (razonable)* reasonable; *(lógico)* rational ❏ **racionalizar** *vt* to rationalize

racionar *vt* to ration (out)

racismo *nm* racism ❏ **racista** *adj, nm* racist

radar *nm* radar

radiactivo, -a *adj* = **radioactivo**

radiador *nm* radiator

radiante *adj* radiant

radical *adj, nmf* radical

radicar vi: ~ **en** (dificultad, problema) to lie in; (solución) to consist in; **radicarse** vr to establish o.s., put down (one's) roots

radio nm (LAm) o f (CS, ESP) radio; (aparato) radio (set) ♦ nm (MAT) radius; (QUÍM) radium ❑ **radioactividad** nf radioactivity ❑ **radioactivo, -a** adj radioactive ❑ **radiodifusión** nf broadcasting ❑ **radioemisora** nf transmitter, radio station ❑ **radioescucha** nmf listener ❑ **radiografía** nf X-ray ❑ **radiografiar** vt to X-ray ❑ **radioterapia** nf radiotherapy ❑ **radioyente** nmf listener

ráfaga nf gust; (de luz) flash; (de tiros) burst

raído, -a adj (ropa) threadbare

raigambre nf (BOT) roots pl; (fig) tradition

raíz nf root; **a ~ de** as a result of ▸ **raíz cuadrada** square root

raja nf (de melón etc) slice; (grieta) crack ❑ **rajar** vt to split; (fam) to slash; **rajarse** vr to split, crack; **rajarse de** to back out of

rajatabla: a ~ adv (estrictamente) strictly, to the letter

rallador nm grater

rallar vt to grate

rama nf branch ❑ **ramaje** nm branches pl, foliage ❑ **ramal** nm (de cuerda) strand; (FERRO) branch line; (AUTO) branch (road)

rambla nf (avenida) avenue

ramificación nf ramification

ramificarse vr to branch out

ramillete nm bouquet

ramo nm branch; (sección) department, section

rampa nf ramp

ramplón, -ona adj uncouth, coarse

rana nf frog; **salto de ~** leapfrog

ranchero (MÉX) nm (hacendado) rancher; smallholder

rancho nm (MÉX: grande) ranch; (pequeño) small farm; (LAm: choza) shack

rancio, -a adj (comestibles) rancid; (vino) aged, mellow; (fig) ancient

rango nm rank, standing

ranura nf groove; (de teléfono etc) slot

rapar vt to shave; (pelo) to crop

rapaz (nf~a) nm/f young boy (girl) ♦ adj (ZOOL) predatory

rape nm (pez) monkfish; **al ~** cropped

rapé nm snuff

rapidez nf speed, rapidity ❑ **rápido, -a** adj fast, quick ♦ adv quickly ♦ nm (FERRO) express ❑ **rápidos** nmpl rapids

rapiña nm robbery; **ave de ~** bird of prey

raptar vt to kidnap ❑ **rapto** nm kidnapping, kidnaping (US); (impulso) sudden impulse; (éxtasis) ecstasy, rapture

raqueta nf racquet

raquítico, -a adj stunted; (fig) poor, inadequate ❑ **raquitismo** nm rickets sg

rareza nf rarity; (fig) eccentricity

raro, -a adj (poco común) rare; (extraño) odd, strange; (excepcional) remarkable

ras nm: **a ~ de** level with; **a ~ de tierra** at ground level

rasar vt (igualar) to level

rascacielos nm inv skyscraper

rascar vt (con las uñas etc) to scratch; (raspar) to scrape; **rascarse** vr to scratch (o.s.)

rasgar vt to tear, rip (up)

rasgo nm (con pluma) stroke; **~s** nmpl (facciones) features, characteristics; **a grandes ~s** in outline, broadly

rasguñar vt to scratch ❑ **rasguño** nm scratch

raso, -a adj (liso) flat, level; (a baja altura) very low ♦ nm satin; **cielo ~** clear sky

raspadura nf (acto) scrape, scraping; (marca) scratch; **~s** nfpl (de papel etc) scrapings

raspar vt to scrape; (arañar) to scratch; (limar) to file

rastra nf (AGR) rake; **a ~s** by dragging; (fig) unwillingly

rastreador nm tracker ▸ **rastreador de minas** minesweeper

rastrear vt (seguir) to track

rastrero, -a adj (BOT, ZOOL) creeping; (fig) despicable, mean

rastrillo nm rake

rastro nm (AGR) rake; (pista) track, trail; (vestigio) trace; (MÉX: matadero) slaughterhouse, abattoir (BRIT)

rastrojo nm stubble

rasurado (MÉX) nm shaving ❑ **rasuradora** (MÉX) nf electric shaver ❑ **rasurar** (MÉX) vt to shave; **rasurarse** vr to shave

rata nf rat

ratear vt (robar) to steal

ratero, -a adj light-fingered ♦ nm/f (carterista) pickpocket; (ladrón) petty thief

ratificar vt to ratify

rato nm while, short time; **a ~s** from time to time; **hay para ~** there's still a long way to go; **al poco ~** soon afterward; **pasar el ~** to kill time; **pasar un buen/mal ~** to have a good/ rough time; **en mis ~s libres** in my spare time

ratón nm mouse ❑ **ratonera** nf mousetrap

raudal nm torrent; **a ~es** in abundance

raya nf line; (marca) scratch; (en tela) stripe; (de pelo) part (US), parting (BRIT); (límite) boundary; (pez) ray; (puntuación) dash; **a ~s** striped; **pasarse de la ~** to go too far; **tener a ~** to keep in check □ **rayar** vt to line; to scratch; (subrayar) to underline ♦ vi: **rayar en** o **con** to border on

rayo nm (del sol) ray, beam; (de luz) shaft; (en una tormenta) (flash of) lightning ▶ **rayos X** X-rays

raza nf race ▶ **raza humana** human race

razón nf reason; (justicia) right, justice; (razonamiento) reasoning; (motivo) reason, motive; (MAT) ratio; **a ~ de 10 cada día** at the rate of 10 a day; **"~: ..."** "inquiries to ..."; **en ~ de** with regard to; **dar la ~ a algn** to agree that sb is right; **tener ~** to be right ▶ **razón de ser** raison d'être ▶ **razón directa/inversa** direct/inverse proportion □ **razonable** adj reasonable; (justo, moderado) fair □ **razonamiento** nm (juicio) judg(e)ment; (argumento) reasoning □ **razonar** vt, vi to reason, argue

reacción nf reaction; **avión a ~** jet plane ▶ **reacción en cadena** chain reaction □ **reaccionar** vi to react □ **reaccionario, -a** adj reactionary

reacio, -a adj stubborn

reactivar vt to revitalize

reactor nm reactor

readaptación nf readjustment ▶ **readaptación profesional** industrial retraining

reajuste nm readjustment

real adj real; (del rey, fig) royal

realce nm (lustre, fig) splendor (US), splendour (BRIT); **poner de ~** to emphasize

realidad nf reality, fact; (verdad) truth

realista nmf realist

realización nf fulfillment (US), fulfilment (BRIT)

realizador, a nm/f (CINE, TV) producer

realizar vt (objetivo) to achieve; (plan) to carry out; (viaje) to make, undertake; **realizarse** vr to come about, come true

realmente adv really, actually

realquilar vt to sublet

realzar vt to enhance; (acentuar) to highlight

reanimar vt to revive; (alentar) to encourage; **reanimarse** vr to revive

reanudar vt (renovar) to renew; (historia, viaje) to resume

reaparición nf reappearance

rearme nm rearmament

rebaja nf (COM) reduction; (: descuento) discount; **~s** nfpl (COM) sale □ **rebajar** vt (bajar) to lower; (reducir) to reduce; (disminuir) to lessen; (humillar) to humble

rebanada nf slice

rebañar vt (comida) to scrape up; (plato) to scrape clean

rebaño nm herd; (de ovejas) flock

rebasar vt (tb: ~ **de**) to exceed; (MÉX: adelantar) to overtake, pass

rebatir vt to refute

rebeca (ESP) nf cardigan

rebelarse vr to rebel, revolt

rebelde adj rebellious; (niño) unruly ♦ nmf rebel □ **rebeldía** nf rebelliousness; (desobediencia) disobedience

rebelión nf rebellion

reblandecer vt to soften

rebobinar vt (cinta, película de video) to rewind

rebosante adj overflowing

rebosar vi (líquido, recipiente) to overflow; (abundar) to abound, be plentiful

rebotar vt to bounce; (rechazar) to repel ♦ vi (pelota) to bounce; (bala) to ricochet □ **rebote** nm rebound; **de rebote** on the rebound

rebozado, -a adj fried in batter o breadcrumbs

rebozar vt to wrap up; (CULIN) to fry in batter o breadcrumbs

rebuscado, -a adj (amanerado) affected; (palabra) recherché; (idea) far-fetched

rebuscar vi: ~ **(en/por)** to search carefully (in/for)

rebuznar vi to bray

recado nm (mensaje) message; (ESP: encargo) errand; **tomar un ~** (TEL) to take a message

recaer vi to relapse; ~ **en** to fall to o on; (criminal etc) to fall back into, relapse into □ **recaída** nf relapse

recalcar vt (fig) to stress, emphasize

recalcitrante adj recalcitrant

recalentar vt (volver a calentar) to reheat; (calentar demasiado) to overheat

recámara (MÉX) nf bedroom

recambio nm spare; (de pluma) refill

recapacitar vi to reflect

recargado, -a adj overloaded

recargar vt to overload; (batería) to recharge □ **recargo** nm surcharge; (aumento) increase

recatado, -a adj (modesto) modest, demure; (prudente) cautious

recato nm (*modestia*) modesty, demureness; (*cautela*) caution

recaudación nf (*acción*) collection; (*cantidad*) takings pl; (*en deporte*) gate ❑ **recaudador, a** nm/f tax collector

recelar vt: ~ **que** (*sospechar*) to suspect that; (*temer*) to fear that ♦ vi: ~ **de** to distrust ❑ **recelo** nm distrust, suspicion ❑ **receloso, -a** adj distrustful, suspicious

recepción nf reception ❑ **recepcionista** nmf receptionist

receptáculo nm receptacle

receptivo, -a adj receptive

receptor, a nm/f recipient ♦ nm (*TEL*) receiver

recesión nf (*COM*) recession

receta nf (*CULIN*) recipe; (*MED*) prescription

⚠ No confundir **receta** con la palabra inglesa **receipt**.

rechazar vt to reject; (*oferta*) to turn down; (*ataque*) to repel

rechazo nm rejection

rechifla nf hissing, booing; (*fig*) derision

rechinar vi to creak; (*dientes*) to grind

rechistar vi: **sin ~** without a murmur

rechoncho, -a (*fam*) adj heavy-set, thickset

rechupete: **de ~** adj (*comida*) delicious, scrumptious

recibidor nm entrance hall

recibimiento nm reception, welcome

recibir vt to receive; (*dar la bienvenida*) to welcome ♦ vi to entertain; **recibirse** vr (*LAm UNIV*) to graduate; **~se de** (*LAm*) to qualify as ❑ **recibo** nm receipt

reciclar vt to recycle

recién adv recently, newly; **los ~ casados** the newly-weds; **el ~ llegado** the newcomer; **el ~ nacido** the newborn child

reciente adj recent; (*fresco*) fresh ❑ **recientemente** adv recently

recinto nm enclosure; (*área*) area, place

recio, -a adj strong, tough; (*voz*) loud ♦ adv hard, loud(ly)

recipiente nm receptacle

reciprocidad nf reciprocity ❑ **recíproco, -a** adj reciprocal

recital nm (*MÚS*) recital; (*LITERATURA*) reading

recitar vt to recite

reclamación nf claim, demand; (*queja*) complaint

reclamar vt to claim, demand ♦ vi: ~ **contra** to complain about; ~ **a algn en justicia** to take sb to court ❑ **reclamo** nm (*anuncio*) advertisement; (*tentación*) attraction

reclinar vt to recline, lean; **reclinarse** vr to lean back

recluir vt to intern, confine

reclusión nf (*prisión*) prison; (*refugio*) seclusion ▶ **reclusión perpetua** life imprisonment

recluta nmf recruit ♦ nf recruitment ❑ **reclutamiento** nm recruitment ❑ **reclutar** vt (*datos*) to collect; (*dinero*) to collect up

recobrar vt (*salud*) to recover; (*rescatar*) to get back; **recobrarse** vr to recover

recodo nm (*de río, camino*) bend

recogedor nm dustpan

recoger vt to collect; (*AGR*) to harvest; (*levantar*) to pick up; (*juntar*) to gather; (*pasar a buscar*) to come for, get; (*dar asilo*) to give shelter to; (*faldas*) to gather up; (*pelo*) to put up; **recogerse** vr (*retirarse*) to retire ❑ **recogido, -a** adj (*lugar*) quiet, secluded; (*pequeño*) small ♦ nf (*CORREOS*) collection; (*AGR*) harvest

recolección nf (*AGR*) harvesting; (*colecta*) collection

recomendación nf (*sugerencia*) suggestion, recommendation; (*referencia*) reference

recomendar vt to suggest, recommend; (*confiar*) to entrust

recompensa nf reward, recompense ❑ **recompensar** vt to reward, recompense

recomponer vt to mend

reconciliación nf reconciliation

reconciliar vt to reconcile; **reconciliarse** vr to become reconciled

recóndito, -a adj (*lugar*) hidden, secret

reconfortar vt to comfort

reconocer vt to recognize; (*registrar*) to search; (*MED*) to examine ❑ **reconocido, -a** adj recognized; (*agradecido*) grateful ❑ **reconocimiento** nm recognition; search; examination; gratitude; (*confesión*) admission

reconquista nf reconquest; **la R~** the Reconquest (of Spain)

reconstituyente nm tonic

reconstruir vt to reconstruct

reconversión nf (*reestructuración*) restructuring ▶ **reconversión industrial** industrial rationalization

recopilación nf (*resumen*) summary; (*compilación*) compilation ❑ **recopilar** vt to compile

récord (*pl* ~**s**) adj inv, nm record

recordar vt (acordarse de) to remember; (acordar a otro) to remind ♦ vi to remember

⚠ No confundir **recordar** con la palabra inglesa **record**.

recorrer vt (país) to cross, travel through; (distancia) to cover; (registrar) to search; (repasar) to look over ❏ **recorrido** nm run, journey; **tren de largo recorrido** main-line train

recortado, -a adj uneven, irregular

recortar vt to cut out ❏ **recorte** nm (acción, de prensa) clipping, cutting (BRIT); (de telas, chapas) ▶ **recorte presupuestario** budget cut

recostado, -a adj leaning; **estar ~** to be lying down

recostar vt to lean; **recostarse** vr to lie down

recoveco nm (de camino, río etc) bend; (en casa) cubby hole

recreación nf recreation

recrear vt (entretener) to entertain; (volver a crear) to recreate ❏ **recreativo, -a** adj recreational ❏ **recreo** nm recreation; (ESCOL) recess (US), break (BRIT)

recriminar vt to reproach ♦ vi to recriminate; **recriminarse** vr to reproach each other

recrudecer vt, vi to worsen; **recrudecerse** vr to worsen

recrudecimiento nm upsurge

recta nf straight line

rectángulo, -a adj rectangular ♦ nm rectangle

rectificar vt to rectify; (volverse recto) to straighten ♦ vi to correct o.s.

rectitud nf straightness

recto, -a adj straight; (persona) honest, upright ♦ nm rectum

rector, a adj governing

recuadro nm box; (TIP) inset

recubrir vt: ~ **(con)** (pintura, crema) to cover (with)

recuento nm inventory; **hacer el ~ de** to count o reckon up

recuerdo nm souvenir; **~s** nmpl (memorias) memories; **¡~s a tu madre!** give my regards to your mother!

recular vi to back down

recuperable adj recoverable

recuperación nf recovery

recuperar vt to recover; (tiempo) to make up; **recuperarse** vr to recuperate

recurrir vi (JUR) to appeal; ~ **a** to resort to; (persona) to turn to ❏ **recurso** nm resort; (medios) means pl; (JUR) appeal

recusar vt to reject, refuse

red nf net, mesh; (FERRO etc) network; (trampa) trap; **la R~** (Internet) the Net

redacción nf (acción) editing; (personal) editorial staff; (ESCOL) essay, composition

redactar vt to draw up, draft; (periódico) to edit

redactor, a nm/f editor

redada nf (de la policía) raid, round-up

redención nf redemption

redicho, -a adj affected

redil nm sheepfold

redimir vt to redeem

rédito nm interest, yield

redoblar vt to redouble ♦ vi (tambor) to roll

redomado, -a adj (astuto) sly, crafty; (perfecto) utter

redonda nf: **a la ~** around, round about

redondear vt to round, round off

redondel nm (círculo) circle; (TAUR) bullring, arena

redondo, -a adj (circular) round; (completo) complete

reducción nf reduction

reducido, -a adj reduced; (limitado) limited; (pequeño) small

reducir vt to reduce; to limit; **reducirse** vr to diminish

redundancia nf redundancy

reembolsar vt (persona) to reimburse; (dinero) to repay, pay back; (depósito) to refund ❏ **reembolso** nm reimbursement; refund

reemplazar vt to replace ❏ **reemplazo** nm replacement; **de reemplazo** (MIL) reserve

reencuentro nm reunion

refacción (MÉX) nf spare (part)

referencia nf reference; **con ~ a** with reference to

referéndum (pl ~s) nm referendum

referente adj: ~ **a** concerning, relating to

réferi (LAm) nmf referee

referir vt (contar) to tell, recount; (relacionar) to refer, relate; **referirse** vr: ~**se a** to refer to

refilón: de ~ adv obliquely

refinado, -a adj refined

refinamiento nm refinement

refinar vt to refine ❏ **refinería** nf refinery

reflejar vt to reflect □ **reflejo, -a** adj reflected; (movimiento) reflex ♦ nm reflection; (ANAT) reflex

reflexión nf reflection □ **reflexionar** vt to reflect on ♦ vi to reflect; (detenerse) to pause (to think)

reflexivo, -a adj thoughtful; (LING) reflexive

reflujo nm ebb

reforma nf reform; (ARQ etc) repair
▶ **reforma agraria** agrarian reform

reformar vt to reform; (modificar) to change, alter; (ARQ) to repair; **reformarse** vr to mend one's ways

reformatorio nm reformatory

reforzar vt to strengthen; (ARQ) to reinforce; (fig) to encourage

refractario, -a adj (TEC) heat-resistant

refrán nm proverb, saying

refregar vt to scrub

refrenar vt to check, restrain

refrendar vt (firma) to endorse, countersign; (ley) to approve

refrescante adj refreshing, cooling

refrescar vt to refresh ♦ vi to cool down; **refrescarse** vr to get cooler; (tomar aire fresco) to go out for a breath of fresh air; (beber) to have a drink

refresco nm soft drink, cool drink; **"~s"** "refreshments"

refriega nf scuffle, brawl

refrigeración nf refrigeration; (de sala) air-conditioning

refrigerador (LAm) nm refrigerator, icebox (US)

refrigerar vt to refrigerate; (sala) to air-condition

refuerzo nm reinforcement; (TEC) support

refugiado, -a nm/f refugee

refugiarse vr to take refuge, shelter

refugio nm refuge; (protección) shelter

refunfuñar vi to grunt, growl; (quejarse) to grumble

refutar vt to refute

regadera nf watering can; (MÉX: ducha) shower

regadío nm irrigated land

regalado, -a adj comfortable, luxurious; (gratis) free, for nothing

regalar vt (dar) to give (as a present); (entregar) to give away; (mimar) to pamper, make a fuss of

regaliz nm licorice (US), liquorice (BRIT)

regalo nm (obsequio) gift, present; (gusto) pleasure

regañadientes: a ~ adv reluctantly

regañar vt to scold ♦ vi to grumble □ **regañón, -ona** adj nagging

regar vt to water, irrigate; (fig) to scatter, sprinkle

regatear vt (COM) to bargain over; (escatimar) to be sparing with ♦ vi to bargain, haggle; (DEPORTE) to dribble □ **regateo** nm bargaining; dribbling; (del cuerpo) swerve, dodge

regazo nm lap

regeneración nf regeneration

regenerar vt to regenerate

regentar vt to direct, manage □ **regente** nm (COM) manager; (POL) regent

régimen (pl **regímenes**) nm regime; (MED) diet

regimiento nm regiment

regio, -a adj royal, regal; (fig: suntuoso) splendid; (CS: fam) great, terrific

región nf region

regir vt to govern, rule; (dirigir) to manage, run ♦ vi to apply, be in force

registrar vt (buscar) to search; (: en cajón) to look through; (inspeccionar) to inspect; (anotar) to register, record; (INFORM) to log; **registrarse** vr to register; (ocurrir) to happen

registro nm (acto) registration; (MÚS, libro) register; (inspección) inspection, search
▶ **registro civil** county clerk's office (US), registry office (BRIT)

regla nf (ley) rule, regulation; (de medir) ruler, rule; (MED: período) period

reglamentación nf (acto) regulation; (lista) rules pl

reglamentar vt to regulate
□ **reglamentario, -a** adj statutory
□ **reglamento** nm rules pl, regulations pl

regocijarse vr: ~ **de** to rejoice at, be happy about □ **regocijo** nm joy, happiness

regodearse vr to be glad, be delighted
□ **regodeo** nm delight

regresar vi to come back, go back, return □ **regresivo, -a** adj backward; (fig) regressive □ **regreso** nm return

reguero nm (de sangre etc) trickle; (de humo) trail

regulador nm regulator; (de radio etc) knob, control

regular adj regular; (normal) normal, usual; (común) ordinary; (organizado) regular, orderly; (mediano) average; (fam) not bad, so-so ♦ adv so-so, alright ♦ vt (controlar) to control, regulate; (TEC) to adjust; **por lo ~** as a

rule ❑ **regularidad** *nf* regularity
❑ **regularizar** *vt* to regularize

regusto *nm* aftertaste

rehabilitación *nf* rehabilitation; (*ARQ*) restoration

rehabilitar *vt* to rehabilitate; (*ARQ*) to restore; (*reintegrar*) to reinstate

rehacer *vt* (*reparar*) to mend, repair; (*volver a hacer*) to redo, repeat; **rehacerse** *vr* (*MED*) to recover

rehén *nm* hostage

rehuir *vt* to avoid, shun

rehusar *vt, vi* to refuse

reina *nf* queen ❑ **reinado** *nm* reign

reinante *adj* (*fig*) prevailing

reinar *vi* to reign

reincidir *vi* to relapse

reincorporarse *vr:* ~ **a** to rejoin

reino *nm* kingdom; **el R~ Unido** the United Kingdom

reintegrar *vt* (*reconstituir*) to reconstruct; (*persona*) to reinstate; (*dinero*) to refund, pay back; **reintegrarse** *vr:* ~**se a** to return to

reír *vi* to laugh; **reírse** *vr* to laugh; ~**se de** to laugh at

reiterar *vt* to reiterate

reivindicación *nf* (*demanda*) claim, demand; (*justificación*) vindication

reivindicar *vt* to claim

reja *nf* (*de ventana*) grille, bars *pl*; (*en la calle*) grating

rejilla *nf* grating, grille; (*muebles*) wickerwork; (*de ventilación*) vent; (*de vehículo*) luggage rack

rejoneador *nm* mounted bullfighter

rejuvenecer *vt, vi* to rejuvenate

relación *nf* relation, relationship; (*MAT*) ratio; (*narración*) report; **con ~ a, en ~ con** in relation to ▶ **relaciones públicas** public relations ❑ **relacionar** *vt* to relate, connect; **relacionarse** *vr* to be connected, be linked

relajación *nf* relaxation

relajado, -a *adj* (*disoluto*) loose; (*cómodo*) relaxed; (*MED*) ruptured

relajar *vt* to relax; **relajarse** *vr* to relax

relamerse *vr* to lick one's lips

relamido, -a *adj* (*pulcro*) overdressed; (*afectado*) affected

relámpago *nm* flash of lightning; **visita/ huelga ~** lightning visit/strike ❑ **relampaguear** *vi* to flash

relatar *vt* to tell, relate

relativo, -a *adj* relative; **en lo ~ a** concerning

relato *nm* (*narración*) story, tale

relegar *vt* to relegate

relevante *adj* eminent, outstanding

relevar *vt* (*sustituir*) to relieve; **relevarse** *vr* to relay; ~ **a algn de un cargo** to relieve sb of his post

relevo *nm* relief; **carrera de ~s** relay race

relieve *nm* (*ARTE, TEC*) relief; (*fig*) prominence, importance; **bajo ~** bas-relief

religión *nf* religion ❑ **religioso, -a** *adj* religious ♦ *nm/f* monk/nun

relinchar *vi* to neigh ❑ **relincho** *nm* neigh; (*acto*) neighing

reliquia *nf* relic ▶ **reliquia de familia** heirloom

rellano *nm* (*ARQ*) landing

rellenar *vt* (*llenar*) to fill up; (*CULIN*) to stuff; (*COSTURA*) to pad ❑ **relleno, -a** *adj* full up; stuffed ♦ *nm* stuffing; (*de tapicería*) padding

reloj *nm* clock; **poner el ~** to set one's watch (*o* the clock) ▶ **reloj (de pulsera)** wristwatch ▶ **reloj despertador** alarm (clock) ❑ **relojero, -a** *nm/f* clockmaker; watchmaker

reluciente *adj* brilliant, shining

relucir *vi* to shine; (*fig*) to excel

relumbrar *vi* to dazzle, shine brilliantly

remachar *vt* to rivet; (*fig*) to hammer home, drive home ❑ **remache** *nm* rivet

remanente *nm* remainder; (*COM*) balance; (*de producto*) surplus

remangar *vt* to roll up

remanso *nm* pool

remar *vi* to row

rematado, -a *adj* complete, utter

rematar *vt* to finish off; (*COM*) to sell off cheap ♦ *vi* to end, finish off; (*DEPORTE*) to shoot

remate *nm* end, finish; (*punta*) tip; (*DEPORTE*) shot; (*ARQ*) top; (*LAm: subasta*) auction; **para ~** to top *o* crown (*BRIT*) it all

remedar *vt* to imitate

remediar *vt* to remedy; (*subsanar*) to make good, repair; (*evitar*) to avoid

remedio *nm* remedy; (*alivio*) relief, help; (*JUR*) recourse, remedy; (*LAm: medicamento*) medicine; **poner ~ a** to correct, stop; **no tener más ~** to have no alternative; **¡qué ~!** there's no choice!; **sin ~** hopeless

remedo *nm* imitation; (*pey*) parody

remendar *vt* to repair; (*con parche*) to patch

remesa *nf* remittance; (*COM*) shipment

remiendo *nm* mend; (*con parche*) patch; (*cosido*) darn

remilgado, -a *adj* prim; (*afectado*) affected

remilgo *nm* primness; (*afectación*) affectation

reminiscencia *nf* reminiscence

remiso, -a *adj* slack, slow

remite *nm* (*en sobre*) name and address of sender

remitente *nmf* sender

remitir *vt* to remit, send ♦ *vi* to slacken; (*en carta*): **remite: X** sender: X

remo *nm* (*de barco*) oar; (*DEPORTE*) rowing

remojar *vt* to steep, soak; (*galleta etc*) to dip, dunk

remojo *nm*: **dejar la ropa en ~** to leave clothes to soak

remolacha (*LAm exc MÉX, ESP*) *nf* beet (*US*), beetroot (*BRIT*)

remolcador *nm* (*NÁUT*) tug; (*AUTO*) tow truck (*US*), breakdown van (*BRIT*)

remolcar *vt* to tow

remolino *nm* eddy; (*de agua*) whirlpool; (*de viento*) whirlwind; (*de gente*) crowd

remolque *nm* tow, towing; (*cuerda*) towrope; **llevar a ~** to tow

remontar *vt* to mend; **remontarse** *vr* to soar; **~se a** (*COM*) to amount to; **~ el vuelo** to soar

remorder *vt* to distress, disturb; **no me remuerde la conciencia** I don't have any qualms about it ❑ **remordimiento** *nm* remorse

remoto, -a *adj* remote

remover *vt* to stir; (*tierra*) to turn over; (*objetos*) to move round

remozar *vt* (*ARQ*) to refurbish

remuneración *nf* remuneration

remunerar *vt* to remunerate; (*premiar*) to reward

renacer *vi* to be reborn; (*fig*) to revive ❑ **renacimiento** *nm* rebirth; **el Renacimiento** the Renaissance

renacuajo *nm* (*ZOOL*) tadpole

renal *adj* renal, kidney *cpd*

rencilla *nf* quarrel

rencor *nm* rancor (*US*), rancour (*BRIT*), bitterness ❑ **rencoroso, -a** *adj* spiteful

rendición *nf* surrender

rendido, -a *adj* (*sumiso*) submissive; (*cansado*) worn-out, exhausted

rendija *nf* (*hendedura*) crack, cleft

rendimiento *nm* (*producción*) output; (*TEC, COM*) efficiency

rendir *vt* (*vencer*) to defeat; (*producir*) to produce; (*dar beneficio*) to yield; (*agotar*) to exhaust ♦ *vi* to pay; **rendirse** *vr* (*someterse*) to surrender; (*cansarse*) to wear o.s. out; **~ homenaje** *o* **culto a** to pay homage to

renegar *vi* (*renunciar*) to renounce; (*blasfemar*) to blaspheme; (*quejarse*) to complain

renglón *nm* (*línea*) line; (*COM*) item, article; **a ~ seguido** immediately after

renombrado, -a *adj* renowned

renombre *nm* renown

renovación *nf* (*de contrato*) renewal; (*ARQ*) renovation

renovar *vt* to renew; (*ARQ*) to renovate

renta *nf* (*ingresos*) income; (*beneficio*) profit; (*MÉX: alquiler*) rent ▸ **renta vitalicia** annuity ❑ **rentable** *adj* profitable ❑ **rentar** *vt* to produce, yield; (*MÉX: alquilar*) to rent

renuncia *nf* resignation

renunciar *vt* to renounce; (*tabaco, alcohol etc*): **~ a** to give up; (*oferta, oportunidad*) to turn down; (*puesto*) to resign ♦ *vi* to resign

reñido, -a *adj* (*batalla*) bitter, hard-fought; **estar ~ con algn** to be on bad terms with sb

reñir *vt* (*regañar*) to scold ♦ *vi* (*estar peleado*) to quarrel, fall out; (*combatir*) to fight

reo *nmf* culprit, offender; (*acusado*) accused, defendant

reojo: de ~ *adv* out of the corner of one's eye

reparación *nf* (*acto*) mending, repairing; (*TEC*) repair; (*fig*) amends *pl*, reparation

reparar *vt* to repair; (*fig*) to make amends for; (*observar*) to observe ♦ *vi*: **~ en** (*darse cuenta de*) to notice; (*prestar atención a*) to pay attention to

reparo *nm* (*advertencia*) observation; (*duda*) doubt; (*dificultad*) difficulty; **poner ~s (a)** to raise objections (to)

repartición *nf* distribution; (*división*) division ❑ **repartidor, a** *nm/f* distributor

repartir *vt* to distribute, share out; (*CORREOS*) to deliver ❑ **reparto** *nm* distribution; delivery; (*TEATRO, CINE*) cast; (*CAm: urbanización*) real estate development (*US*), housing estate (*BRIT*)

repasador (*RPl*) *nm* dishtowel (*US*)

repasar *vt* (*ESCOL*) to review (*US*), revise (*BRIT*); (*MECÁNICA*) to check, overhaul; (*COSTURA*) to mend ❑ **repaso** *nm* (*ESCOL*) reviewing (*US*), revision (*BRIT*); (*inspección*) overhaul, checkup; (*COSTURA*) mending

repatriar *vt* to repatriate

repecho *nm* steep incline

repelente *adj* repellent, repulsive

repeler *vt* to repel

repensar *vt* to reconsider

repente nm: **de ~** suddenly ▶ **repente de ira** fit of anger

repentino, -a adj sudden

repercusión nf repercussion

repercutir vi (objeto) to rebound; (sonido) to echo; **~ en** (fig) to have repercussions on

repertorio nm list; (TEATRO) repertoire

repetición nf repetition

repetir vt to repeat; (plato) to have a second helping of ♦ vi to repeat; (sabor) to come back; **repetirse** vr (volver sobre un tema) to repeat o.s.

repetitivo, -a adj repetitive, repetitious

repicar vt (campanas) to ring

repique nm pealing, ringing ❑ **repiqueteo** nm pealing; (de tambor) drumming

repisa nf ledge, shelf; (de ventana) windowsill; **la ~ de la chimenea** the mantelpiece

repito etc vb ver **repetir**

replantearse vr: **~ un problema** to reconsider a problem

replegarse vr to fall back, retreat

repleto, -a adj replete, full up

réplica nf answer; (ARTE) replica

replicar vi to answer; (objetar) to argue, answer back

repliegue nm (MIL) withdrawal

repoblación nf repopulation; (de río) restocking ▶ **repoblación forestal** reafforestation

repoblar vt to repopulate; (con árboles) to reafforest

repollito (CS) nm: **~s de Bruselas** (Brussels) sprouts

repollo nm cabbage

reponer vt to replace, put back; (TEATRO) to revive; **reponerse** vr to recover; **~ que** to reply that

reportaje nm report, article

reportero, -a nm/f reporter

reposacabezas nm inv headrest

reposado, -a adj (descansado) restful; (tranquilo) calm

reposar vi to rest, repose

reposera (RPI) nf deck chair

reposición nf replacement; (CINE) remake

reposo nm rest

repostar vt to replenish; (AUTO) to fill up (with gas (US) o petrol (BRIT))

repostería nf cakes and pastries pl ❑ **repostero, -a** nm/f confectioner

reprender vt to reprimand

represa nf dam; (lago artificial) lake, pool

represalia nf reprisal

representación nf representation; (TEATRO) performance ❑ **representante** nmf representative; performer

representar vt to represent; (TEATRO) to perform; (edad) to look; **representarse** vr to imagine ❑ **representativo, -a** adj representative

represión nf repression

reprimenda nf reprimand, rebuke

reprimir vt to repress

reprobar vt to censure, reprove; (LAm: alumno) to fail

reprochar vt to reproach ❑ **reproche** nm reproach

reproducción nf reproduction

reproducir vt to reproduce; **reproducirse** vr to breed; (situación) to recur

reproductor, a adj reproductive

reptil nm reptile

república nf republic ▶ **República Dominicana** Dominican Republic ❑ **republicano, -a** adj, nm republican

repudiar vt to repudiate; (fe) to renounce

repuesto nm (pieza de recambio) spare (part); (abastecimiento) supply; **rueda de ~** spare tire (US), spare wheel (BRIT)

repugnancia nf repugnance ❑ **repugnante** adj repugnant, repulsive

repugnar vt to disgust

repulsa nf rebuff

repulsión nf repulsion, aversion ❑ **repulsivo, -a** adj repulsive

reputación nf reputation

requemado, -a adj (quemado) scorched; (bronceado) tanned

requerimiento nm request; (JUR) summons

requerir vt (pedir) to ask, request; (exigir) to require; (llamar) to send for, summon

requesón nm cottage cheese

requete... prefijo extremely

réquiem (pl **~s**) nm requiem

requisito nm requirement, requisite

res nf beast, animal

resaca nf (de mar) undertow, undercurrent; (fam) hangover

resaltar vi to project, stick out; (fig) to stand out

resarcir vt to compensate; **resarcirse** vr to make up for

resbaladero (MÉX) nm slide

resbaladizo, -a adj slippery

resbalar vi to slip, slide; (fig) to slip (up); **resbalarse** vr to slip, slide; to slip (up) ❑ **resbalón** nm (acción) slip

rescatar vt (salvar) to save, rescue; (objeto) to get back, recover; (cautivos) to ransom

rescate nm rescue; (de objeto) recovery; **pagar un ~** to pay a ransom

rescindir vt to rescind

rescisión nf cancellation

rescoldo nm embers pl

resecar vt to dry thoroughly; (MED) to cut out, remove; **resecarse** vr to dry up

reseco, -a adj very dry; (fig) skinny

resentido, -a adj resentful

resentimiento nm resentment, bitterness

resentirse vr (debilitarse: persona) to suffer; **~ de** (consecuencias) to feel the effects of; **~ de** (o por) **algo** to resent sth, be bitter about sth

reseña nf (cuenta) account; (informe) report; (LITERATURA) review

reseñar vt to describe; (LITERATURA) to review

reserva nf reserve; (reservación) reservation; **a ~ de que ...** unless ...; **con toda ~** in strictest confidence

reservado, -a adj reserved; (retraído) cold, distant ♦ nm private room

reservar vt (guardar) to keep; (habitación, entrada) to reserve; **reservarse** vr to save o.s.; (callar) to keep to o.s.

resfriado nm cold ❑ **resfriarse** vr to cool; (MED) to catch a cold

resguardar vt to protect, shield; **resguardarse** vr: **~se de** to guard against ❑ **resguardo** nm defense (US), defence (BRIT); (vale) voucher; (recibo) receipt, slip

residencia nf residence ❑ **residencial** adj residential

residente adj, nmf resident

residir vi to reside, live; **~ en** to reside in, lie in

residuo nm residue

resignación nf resignation ❑ **resignarse** vr: **resignarse a** o **con** to resign o.s. to, be resigned to

resina nf resin

resistencia nf (dureza) endurance, strength; (oposición, ELEC) resistance ❑ **resistente** adj strong, hardy; resistant

resistir vt (soportar) to bear; (oponerse a) to resist, oppose; (aguantar) to put up with ♦ vi to resist; (aguantar) to last, endure; **resistirse** vr: **~se a** to refuse to, resist

resolución nf resolution; (decisión) decision ❑ **resoluto, -a** adj resolute

resolver vt to resolve; (solucionar) to solve, resolve; (decidir) to decide, settle; **resolverse** vr to make up one's mind

resonancia nf (del sonido) resonance; (repercusión) repercussion

resonar vi to ring, echo

resoplar vi to snort ❑ **resoplido** nm heavy breathing

resorte nm spring; (fig) lever

resortera (MÉX) nf slingshot (US), catapult (BRIT)

respaldar vt to back (up), support; **respaldarse** vr to lean back; **~se con** o **en** (fig) to take one's stand on ❑ **respaldo** nm (de sillón) back; (fig) support, backing

respectivo, -a adj respective; **en lo ~ a** with regard to

respecto nm: **al ~** on this matter; **con ~ a**, **~ de** with regard to, in relation to

respetable adj respectable

respetar vt to respect ❑ **respeto** nm respect; (acatamiento) deference; **respetos** nmpl respects ❑ **respetuoso, -a** adj respectful

respingo nm start, jump

respiración nf breathing; (MED) respiration; (ventilación) ventilation

respirar vi to breathe ❑ **respiratorio, -a** adj respiratory ❑ **respiro** nm breathing; (fig: descanso) respite

resplandecer vi to shine ❑ **resplandeciente** adj resplendent, shining ❑ **resplandor** nm brilliance, brightness; (de luz, fuego) blaze

responder vt to answer ♦ vi to answer; (fig) to respond; (pey) to answer back; **~ de** o **por** to answer for ❑ **respondón, -ona** adj cheeky

responsabilidad nf responsibility

responsabilizarse vr to make o.s. responsible, take charge

responsable adj responsible

respuesta nf answer, reply

resquebrajar vt to crack, split; **resquebrajarse** vr to crack, split

resquemor nm resentment

resquicio nm chink; (hendedura) crack

restablecer vt to re-establish, restore; **restablecerse** vr to recover

restallar vi to crack

restante adj remaining; **lo ~** the remainder

restar vt (MAT) to subtract; (fig) to take away ♦ vi to remain, be left

restauración nf restoration

restaurante nm restaurant

restaurar vt to restore

restitución nf return, restitution

restituir vt (devolver) to return, give back; (rehabilitar) to restore

resto nm (residuo) rest, remainder; (apuesta) stake; **~s** nmpl remains

restregar vt to scrub, rub

restricción nf restriction

restrictivo, -a adj restrictive

restringir vt to restrict, limit

resucitar vt, vi to resuscitate, revive

resuello nm (aliento) breath; **estar sin ~** to be breathless

resuelto, -a pp de **resolver** ♦ adj resolute, determined

resultado nm result; (conclusión) outcome □ **resultante** adj resulting, resultant

resultar vi (ser) to be; (llegar a ser) to turn out to be; (salir bien) to turn out well; (COM) to amount to; **~ de** to stem from; **me resulta difícil hacerlo** it's difficult for me to do it

resumen (pl resúmenes) nm summary, résumé; **en ~** in short

resumir vt to sum up; (cortar) to abridge, cut down; (condensar) to summarize

⚠ No confundir **resumir** con la palabra inglesa **resume**.

resurgir vi (reaparecer) to reappear

resurrección nf resurrection

retablo nm altarpiece

retaguardia nf rearguard

retahíla nf series, string

retal nm remnant

retar vt to challenge; (desafiar) to defy, dare

retardar vt (demorar) to delay; (hacer más lento) to slow down; (retener) to hold back

retazo nm fragment, snippet (BRIT)

retener vt (intereses) to withhold

reticente adj (tono) insinuating; (postura) reluctant; **ser ~ a hacer algo** to be reluctant o unwilling to do sth

retina nf retina

retintín nm jangle, jingle

retirada nf (MIL, refugio) retreat; (de dinero) withdrawal; (de embajador) recall □ **retirado, -a** adj (lugar) remote; (vida) quiet; (jubilado) retired

retirar vt to withdraw; (quitar) to remove; (jubilar) to retire, pension off; **retirarse** vr to retreat, withdraw; to retire; (acostarse) to retire, go to bed □ **retiro** nm retreat; retirement; (pago) pension

reto nm dare, challenge

retocar vt (fotografía) to touch up, retouch

retoño nm sprout, shoot; (fig) offspring, child

retoque nm retouching

retorcer vt to twist; (manos, lavado) to wring; **retorcerse** vr to become twisted; (mover el cuerpo) to writhe

retorcido, -a adj (persona) devious

retorcijón (LAm) nm (tb: ~ de tripas) stomach cramp

retórica nf rhetoric; (pey) affectedness □ **retórico, -a** adj rhetorical

retornar vt to return, give back ♦ vi to return, go/come back □ **retorno** nm return

retozar vi (juguetear) to frolic, romp; (saltar) to gambol □ **retozón, -ona** adj playful

retracción nf retraction

retractarse vr to retract; **me retracto** I take that back

retraerse vr to retreat, withdraw □ **retraído, -a** adj shy, retiring □ **retraimiento** nm retirement; (timidez) shyness

retransmisión nf repeat (broadcast)

retransmitir vt (mensaje) to relay; (TV etc) to repeat, retransmit; (: en vivo) to broadcast live

retrasado, -a adj late; (MED) mentally retarded; (país etc) backward, underdeveloped

retrasar vt (demorar) to postpone, put off; (retardar) to slow down ♦ vi (atrasarse) to be late; (reloj) to be slow; (producción) to fall (off); (quedarse atrás) to lag behind; **retrasarse** vr to be late; to be slow; to fall (off); to lag behind

retraso nm (demora) delay; (lentitud) slowness; (tardanza) lateness; (atraso) backwardness; **~s** nmpl (FINANZAS) arrears; **llegar con ~** to arrive late; **~ mental** mental deficiency

retratar vt (ARTE) to paint the portrait of; (fotografiar) to photograph; (fig) to depict, describe; **retratarse** vr to have one's portrait painted; to have one's photograph taken □ **retrato** nm portrait; (fig) likeness ▶ **retrato hablado** (LAm) Identikit®

retreta nf retreat

retrete nm toilet

retribución nf (recompensa) reward; (pago) pay, payment

retribuir vt (recompensar) to reward; (pagar) to pay

retro... prefijo retro...

retroactivo, -a adj retroactive, retrospective

retroceder vi (echarse atrás) to move back(wards); (fig) to back down

retroceso nm backward movement; (MED) relapse; (fig) backing down

retrógrado, -a adj retrograde, retrogressive; (POL) reactionary

retrospectivo, -a adj retrospective

retrovisor nm (tb: espejo ~) rear-view mirror

retumbar vi to echo, resound

reúma, reuma nm rheumatism

reumatismo nm = **reúma**

reunificar vt to reunify

reunión nf (asamblea) meeting; (fiesta) party

reunir vt (juntar) to reunite, join (together); (recoger) to gather (together); (personas) to get together; (cualidades) to combine; **reunirse** vr (personas: en asamblea) to meet, gather

revalidar vt (ratificar) to confirm, ratify

revalorizar vt to revalue, reassess

revancha nf revenge

revelación nf revelation

revelado nm developing

revelar vt to reveal; (FOTO) to develop

reventa nf resale; (de entradas: para concierto) scalping (US), touting (BRIT)

reventar vt to burst, explode

reventón (LAm exc MÉX, ESP) nm (AUTO) flat, blow-out

reverencia nf reverence ❏ **reverenciar** vt to revere

reverendo, -a adj reverend

reverente adj reverent

reversa (MÉX, CAm) nf (reverse) gear

reversible adj (prenda) reversible

reverso nm back, other side; (de moneda) reverse

revertir vi to revert

revés nm back, wrong side; (fig) reverse, setback; (DEPORTE) backhand; **al ~** the wrong way round; (de arriba abajo) upside down; (ropa) inside out; **volver algo del ~** to turn sth round; (ropa) to turn sth inside out

revestir vt (cubrir) to cover, coat

revisar vt (examinar) to check; (texto etc) to revise; (ESP AUTO) to service ❏ **revisión** nf revision

revisor, a (ESP) nm/f (FERRO) ticket collector

revista nf magazine, review; (TEATRO) revue; (inspección) inspection; **pasar ~ a** to review, inspect

revivir vi to revive

revocación nf repeal

revocar vt to revoke

revolcarse vr to roll about

revolotear vi to flutter

revoltijo nm mess, jumble

revoltoso, -a adj (travieso) naughty, unruly

revolución nf revolution ❏ **revolucionar** vt to revolutionize ❏ **revolucionario, -a** adj, nm/f revolutionary

revolver vt (desordenar) to disturb, mess up; (mover) to move about ♦ vi: **~ en** to go through, rummage (about) in; **revolverse** vr (volver contra) to turn on o against

revólver nm revolver

revuelo nm fluttering; (fig) commotion

revuelta nf (motín) revolt; (agitación) commotion

revuelto, -a pp de **revolver** ♦ adj (mezclado) mixed-up, in disorder

rey nm king ▶ **Día de (los) Reyes (Magos)** Epiphany

DÍA DE LOS REYES MAGOS

The **Día de los Reyes Magos** is celebrated in many Catholic countries on January 6th. Celebrations include parties, food and gifts for the children. In Mexico it is also traditional to eat **Rosca de Reyes**, a ring-shaped cake with small baby shapes inside. According to tradition, anybody who gets a piece of cake with a baby inside has to throw a party before February 2nd, when the Christmas vacations finally come to an end in Mexico.

reyerta nf quarrel, brawl

rezagado, -a nm/f straggler

rezagar vt (dejar atrás) to leave behind; (retrasar) to delay, postpone

rezar vi to pray; **~ con** (fam) to concern, have to do with ❏ **rezo** nm prayer

rezongar vi to grumble

rezumar vt to ooze

ría nf estuary

riada nf flood

ribera nf (de río) bank; (: área) riverside

ribete nm (de vestido) border; (fig) addition ❏ **ribetear** vt to edge, border

ricino nm: **aceite de ~** castor oil

rico, -a adj rich; (adinerado) wealthy, rich; (lujoso) luxurious; (comida) delicious; (niño) cute, lovely ♦ nm/f rich person

rictus nm (mueca) sneer, grin

ridiculez nf absurdity

ridiculizar vt to ridicule

ridículo, -a *adj* ridiculous; **hacer el ~** to make a fool of o.s.; **poner a algn en ~** to make a fool of sb

riego *nm* (*aspersión*) watering; (*irrigación*) irrigation

riel *nm* rail

rienda *nf* (*lotería*) rein; **dar ~ suelta a** to give free rein to

riesgo *nm* risk; **correr el ~ de** to run the risk of

rifa *nf* (*lotería*) raffle ❏ **rifar** *vt* to raffle

rifle *nm* rifle

rigidez *nf* rigidity, stiffness; (*fig*) strictness ❏ **rígido, -a** *adj* rigid, stiff; strict, inflexible

rigor *nm* strictness, rigor (*US*), rigour (*BRIT*); (*inclemencia*) harshness; **de ~** de rigueur, essential ❏ **riguroso, -a** *adj* rigorous; harsh; (*severo*) severe

rimar *vi* to rhyme

rimbombante *adj* pompous

rímel *nm* mascara

rímmel *nm* = **rímel**

rin (*MÉX*) *nm* (*wheel*) rim

rincón *nm* corner (*inside*)

rinoceronte *nm* rhinoceros

riña *nf* (*disputa*) argument; (*pelea*) brawl

riñón *nm* kidney

río *etc vb ver* **reír** ♦ *nm* river; (*fig*) torrent, stream; **~ abajo/arriba** downstream/upstream ▶ **Río de la Plata** River Plate, Plata River (*US*)

rioja *nm* (*vino*) rioja (wine)

rioplatense *adj* of o from the River Plate region

riqueza *nf* wealth, riches *pl*; (*cualidad*) richness

risa *nf* laughter; (*una risa*) laugh; **¡qué ~!** what a laugh!

risco *nm* crag, cliff

risible *adj* ludicrous, laughable

risotada *nf* guffaw, loud laugh

ristra *nf* string

risueño, -a *adj* (*sonriente*) smiling; (*contento*) cheerful

ritmo *nm* rhythm; **a ~ lento** slowly; **trabajar a ~ lento** to go slow

rito *nm* rite

ritual *adj, nm* ritual

rival *adj, nmf* rival ❏ **rivalidad** *nf* rivalry ❏ **rivalizar** *vi*: **rivalizar con** to rival, vie with

rizado, -a *adj* curly ♦ *nm* curls *pl*

rizar *vt* to curl; **rizarse** *vr* (*pelo*) to curl; (*agua*) to ripple ❏ **rizo** *nm* curl; ripple

RNE *nf abr* = **Radio Nacional de España**

robar *vt* to rob; (*objeto*) to steal; (*casa etc*) to break into; (*NAIPES*) to draw

roble *nm* oak ❏ **robledal** *nm* oakwood

robo *nm* robbery, theft

robot *nm* robot

robustecer *vt* to strengthen

robusto, -a *adj* robust, strong

roca *nf* rock

roce *nm* (*caricia*) brush; (*TEC*) friction; (*en la piel*) graze; **tener ~ con** to be in close contact with

rociar *vt* to spray

rocín *nm* nag, hack

rocío *nm* dew

rocola (*LAm*) *nf* jukebox

rocoso, -a *adj* rocky

rodaballo *nm* turbot

rodado, -a *adj* (*con ruedas*) wheeled

rodaja *nf* slice

rodaje *nm* (*CINE*) shooting, filming; (*AUTO*): **en ~** breaking in (*US*), running in (*BRIT*)

rodar *vt* (*vehículo*) to wheel (along); (*escalera*) to roll down; (*viajar por*) to travel (over) ♦ *vi* to roll; (*vehículo*) to go, run; (*CINE*) to shoot, film

rodear *vt* to surround ♦ *vi* to go round; **rodearse** *vr*: **~se de amigos** to surround o.s. with friends

rodeo *nm* (*ruta indirecta*) detour; (*evasión*) evasion; (*DEPORTE*) rodeo; **hablar sin ~s** to come to the point, speak plainly

rodilla *nf* knee; **de ~s** kneeling; **ponerse de ~s** to kneel (down)

rodillo *nm* roller; (*CULIN*) rolling-pin

roedor, a *adj* gnawing ♦ *nm* rodent

roer *vt* (*masticar*) to gnaw; (*corroer, fig*) to corrode

rogar *vt, vi* (*pedir*) to ask for; (*suplicar*) to beg, plead; **se ruega no fumar** please do not smoke

rojizo, -a *adj* reddish

rojo, -a *adj, nm* red; **al ~ vivo** red-hot

rol *nm* list, roll; (*papel*) role

rollito *nm* (*tb*: **~ de primavera**) spring roll

rollizo, -a *adj* (*objeto*) cylindrical; (*persona*) plump

rollo *nm* roll; (*de cuerda*) coil; (*madera*) log

Roma *n* Rome

romance *nm* (*amoroso*) romance; (*LITERATURA*) ballad

romano, -a *adj, nm/f* Roman; **a la romana** in batter

romanticismo *nm* romanticism

romántico, -a *adj* romantic

rombo nm (GEOM) rhombus

romería nf (REL) pilgrimage; (excursión) trip, outing

romero, -a nm/f pilgrim ♦ nm rosemary

romo, -a adj blunt; (fig) dull

rompecabezas nm inv riddle, puzzle; (juego) jigsaw (puzzle)

rompehuelgas (LAm) nm inv strikebreaker, scab

rompeolas nm inv breakwater

romper vt to break; (hacer pedazos) to smash; (papel, tela etc) to tear, rip ♦ vi (olas) to break; (sol, diente) to break through; **~ un contrato** to break a contract; **~ a** (empezar a) to start (suddenly) to; **~ a llorar** to burst into tears; **~ con algn** to fall out with sb

ron nm rum

roncar vi to snore

ronco, -a adj (afónico) hoarse; (áspero) raucous

ronda nf (gen) round; (patrulla) patrol □ **rondar** vt to patrol ♦ vi to patrol; (fig) to prowl round

ronquido nm snore, snoring

ronronear vi to purr □ **ronroneo** nm purr

roña nf (VETERINARIA) mange; (mugre) dirt, grime; (óxido) rust

roñoso, -a adj (mugriento) filthy; (tacaño) stingy, mean (BRIT)

ropa nf clothes pl, clothing ▶ **ropa blanca** linen ▶ **ropa de cama** bed linen ▶ **ropa interior** underwear ▶ **ropa sucia** dirty washing □ **ropaje** nm gown, robes pl

ropero nm linen closet (US), linen cupboard (BRIT); (guardarropa) wardrobe

rosa adj pink ♦ nf rose; **~ de los vientos** the compass

rosado, -a adj pink ♦ nm rosé

rosal nm rosebush

rosario nm (REL) rosary; **rezar el ~** to say the rosary

rosca nf (de tornillo) thread; (de humo) coil, spiral; (pan, postre) ring-shaped roll/pastry

rosetón nm rosette; (ARQ) rose window

rosquilla nf donut-shaped fritter

rostro nm (cara) face

rotación nf rotation; **~ de cultivos** crop rotation

rotativo, -a adj rotary

roto, -a pp de **romper** ♦ adj broken

rotonda nf traffic circle (US), roundabout (BRIT)

rótula nf kneecap; (TEC) ball-and-socket joint

rotulador nm felt-tip pen

rotular vt (carta, documento) to head, entitle; (objeto) to label □ **rótulo** nm heading, title; label; (letrero) sign

rotundamente adv (negar) flatly; (responder, afirmar) emphatically □ **rotundo, -a** adj round; (enfático) emphatic

rotura nf (acto) breaking; (MED) fracture

roturar vt to plow (US), plough (BRIT)

rozadura nf abrasion, graze

rozar vt (frotar) to rub; (arañar) to scratch; (tocar ligeramente) to shave, touch lightly; **rozarse** vr to rub (together); **~se con** (fam) to rub shoulders with

rte. abr (= remite, remitente) sender

RTVE (ESP) nf abr = **Radiotelevisión Española**

rubí nm ruby; (de reloj) jewel

rubio, -a adj fair-haired, blond(e) ♦ nm/f blond/blonde; **tabaco ~** Virginia tobacco

rubor nm (sonrojo) blush; (timidez) bashfulness □ **ruborizarse** vr to blush

rúbrica nf (de la firma) flourish □ **rubricar** vt (firmar) to sign with a flourish; (concluir) to sign and seal

rudimentario, -a adj rudimentary □ **rudimento** nm rudiment

rudo, -a adj (sin pulir) unpolished; (grosero) coarse; (violento) violent; (sencillo) simple

rueda nf wheel; (círculo) ring, circle; (rodaja) slice, round ▶ **rueda de auxilio** (RPl) spare tire (US) o tyre (BRIT) ▶ **rueda de la fortuna** (MÉX) Ferris (US) o big (BRIT) wheel ▶ **rueda delantera/trasera** front/back wheel ▶ **rueda de prensa** press conference ▶ **rueda de repuesto** spare tire (US) o tyre (BRIT) ▶ **rueda gigante** (LAm) Ferris (US) o big (BRIT) wheel

ruedo nm (círculo) circle; (TAUR) arena, bullring

ruego etc vb ver **rogar** ♦ nm request

rufián nm scoundrel

rugby nm rugby

rugido nm roar

rugir vi to roar

rugoso, -a adj (arrugado) wrinkled; (áspero) rough; (desigual) ridged

ruido nm noise; (sonido) sound; (alboroto) racket, row; (escándalo) commotion, rumpus □ **ruidoso, -a** adj noisy, loud; (fig) sensational

ruin adj contemptible, mean

ruina nf ruin; (colapso) collapse; (de persona) ruin, downfall

ruindad nf lowness, meanness; (acto) low o mean act

ruinoso, -a *adj* ruinous; (*destartalado*) dilapidated, tumbledown; (*COM*) disastrous

ruiseñor *nm* nightingale

rulero (*RPl*) *nm* roller

ruleta *nf* roulette

rulo *nm* (*para el pelo*) curler

Rumanía *nf* Rumania

rumba *nf* rumba

rumbo *nm* (*ruta*) route, direction; (*ángulo de dirección*) course, bearing; (*fig*) course of events; **ir con ~ a** to be heading for

rumboso, -a *adj* generous

rumiante *nm* ruminant

rumiar *vt* to chew; (*fig*) to chew over ♦ *vi* to chew the cud

rumor *nm* (*ruido sordo*) low sound; (*murmuración*) murmur, buzz

rumorearse *vr*: **se rumorea que** it is rumored (*US*) o rumoured (*BRIT*) that

runrún *nm* (*de voces*) murmur, sound of voices; (*fig*) rumor (*US*), rumour (*BRIT*)

rupestre *adj* rock *cpd*

ruptura *nf* rupture

rural *adj* rural ♦ *nf* (*RPl*: *camioneta*) station wagon (*US*), estate car (*BRIT*)

Rusia *nf* Russia ❑ **ruso, -a** *adj*, *nm/f* Russian

rústica *nf*: **libro en ~** paperback (book); *ver tb* **rústico**

rústico, -a *adj* rustic; (*ordinario*) coarse, uncouth ♦ *nm/f* yokel, hillbilly (*US*)

ruta *nf* route ▶ **Ruta Maya** Maya Road

RUTA MAYA

The **Ruta Maya** is the informal name given to a geographical, tourist and archeological area which extends from the state of Yucatán in Mexico to Honduras. The archeological sites in this area are among the most spectacular and majestic in the world, with their breathtaking Mayan ruins, temples, and pyramids.

---

rutina *nf* routine ❑ **rutinario, -a** *adj* routine

Ss

S *abr* (= *santo, a*) St; (= *sur*) S

s. *abr* (= *siglo*) C.; (= *siguiente*) foll

S.A. *abr* (= *Sociedad Anónima*) Inc. (*US*), Ltd. (*BRIT*)

sábado *nm* Saturday

sábana *nf* sheet

sabandija *nf* bug, insect

sabañón *nm* chilblain

saber *vt* to know; (*llegar a conocer*) to find out, learn; (*tener capacidad de*) to know how to ♦ *vi*: **~ a** to taste of, taste like ♦ *nm* knowledge, learning; **a ~** namely; **¿sabes conducir/ nadar?** can you drive/swim?; **¿sabes francés?** do you speak French?; **~ de memoria** to know by heart; **hacer ~ algo a algn** to inform sb of sth, let sb know sth

sabiduría *nf* (*conocimientos*) wisdom; (*instrucción*) learning

sabiendas: **a ~** *adv* knowingly

sabio, -a *adj* (*docto*) learned; (*prudente*) wise, sensible

sabor *nm* taste, flavor (*US*), flavour (*BRIT*) ❑ **saborear** *vt* to taste, savor (*US*), savour (*BRIT*); (*fig*) to relish

sabotaje *nm* sabotage

saboteador, a *nm/f* saboteur

sabotear *vt* to sabotage

sabré *etc vb ver* **saber**

sabroso, -a *adj* tasty; (*fig*: *fam*) racy, salty

sacacorchos *nm inv* corkscrew

sacapuntas *nm inv* pencil sharpener

sacar *vt* to take out; (*fig*: *extraer*) to get (out); (*quitar*) to remove, get out; (*hacer salir*) to bring out; (*conclusión*) to draw; (*novela etc*) to publish, bring out; (*ropa*) to take off; (*obra*) to make; (*premio*) to receive; (*entradas*) to get; (*TENIS*) to serve; **~ adelante** (*niño*) to bring up; (*negocio*) to carry on, go on with; **~ a algn a bailar** to get sb up to dance; **~ una foto** to take a photo; **~ la lengua** to stick out one's tongue; **~ buenas/malas notas** to get good/ bad marks

sacarina *nf* saccharin(e)

sacerdote *nm* priest

saciar *vt* (*hambre, sed*) to satisfy; **saciarse** *vr* (*de comida*) to get full up; **comer hasta ~se** to eat one's fill

saco *nm* bag; (*grande*) sack; (*su contenido*) bagful; (*LAm*: *chaqueta*) jacket ▶ **saco de dormir** (*LAm exc MÉX, ESP*) sleeping bag

sacramento *nm* sacrament

sacrificar *vt* to sacrifice ❑ **sacrificio** *nm* sacrifice

sacrilegio *nm* sacrilege ❑ **sacrílego, -a** *adj* sacrilegious

sacristía *nf* sacristy

sacro, -a *adj* sacred

sacudida nf (agitación) shake, shaking; (sacudimiento) jolt, bump ▶ **sacudida eléctrica** electric shock

sacudir vt to shake; (golpear) to hit; (MÉX: desempolvar) to dust

sádico, -a adj sadistic ♦ nm/f sadist □ **sadismo** nm sadism

saeta nf (flecha) arrow

sagacidad nf shrewdness, cleverness □ **sagaz** adj shrewd, clever

sagitario nm Sagittarius

sagrado, -a adj sacred, holy

Sáhara nm: el ~ the Sahara (desert)

sal vb ver **salir** ♦ nf salt

sala nf room; (tb: ~ **de estar**) living room; (TEATRO) house, auditorium; (de hospital) ward ▶ **sala de apelación** court ▶ **sala de espera** waiting room ▶ **sala de estar** living room ▶ **sala de fiestas** dance hall

salado, -a adj salty; (fig) witty, amusing; **agua salada** salt water

salar vt to salt, add salt to

salarial adj (aumento, revisión) wage cpd, salary cpd

salario nm wage, pay

salchicha nf (pork) sausage □ **salchichón** nm (salami-type) sausage

saldar vt to pay; (vender) to sell off; (fig) to settle, resolve □ **saldo** nm (pago) settlement; (de una cuenta) balance; (lo restante) remnant(s) (pl), remainder; **saldos** nmpl (en tienda) sale

saldré etc vb ver **salir**

salero nm salt shaker (US), salt cellar (BRIT)

salgo etc vb ver **salir**

salida nf (puerta etc) exit, way out; (acto) leaving, going out; (de tren, AVIAT) departure; (TEC) output, production; (fig) way out; (COM) opening; (GEO, válvula) outlet; (de gas) leak; **calle sin ~** cul-de-sac ▶ **salida de baño** (RPI) bathrobe ▶ **salida de incendios** fire escape

saliente adj (ARQ) projecting; (sol) rising; (fig) outstanding

salir
PALABRA CLAVE
vi

1 (partir: tb: **salir de**) to leave; **Juan ha salido** Juan is out; **salió de la cocina** he came out of the kitchen

2 (aparecer) to appear; (disco, libro) to come out; **anoche salió en la tele** she appeared o was on TV last night; **salió en todos los periódicos** it was in all the papers

3 (resultar): **la muchacha nos salió muy trabajadora** the girl turned out to be a very hard worker; **la comida te ha salido exquisita** the food was delicious; **sale muy caro** it's very expensive

4: **salirle a algn algo: la entrevista que hice me salió bien/mal** the interview I did went o turned out well/badly

5: **salir adelante: no sé como haré para salir adelante** I don't know how I'll get by ♦ **salirse** vr (líquido) to spill; (animal) to escape

saliva nf saliva

salmo nm psalm

salmón nm salmon

salmonete nm red mullet

salmuera nf pickle, brine

salón nm (de casa) living room, lounge; (muebles) lounge suite ▶ **salón de baile** dance hall ▶ **salón de belleza** beauty parlor (US) o parlour (BRIT)

salpicadera (MÉX) nf fender (US), mudguard (BRIT)

salpicadero (ESP) nm (AUTO) dashboard

salpicar vt (rociar) to sprinkle, spatter; (esparcir) to scatter

salpicón nm (tb: ~ **de marisco**) seafood salad

salsa nf sauce; (con carne asada) gravy; (fig) spice

saltamontes nm inv grasshopper

saltar vt to jump (over), leap (over); (dejar de lado) to skip, miss out ♦ vi to jump, leap; (pelota) to bounce; (al aire) to fly up; (quebrarse) to break; (al agua) to dive; (fig) to explode, blow up

salto nm jump, leap; (al agua) dive ▶ **salto de agua** waterfall ▶ **salto de altura** high jump

saltón, -ona adj (ojos) bulging, popping; (dientes) protruding

salud nf health; **¡a su ~!** cheers!, good health!; **¡~!** (LAm: al estornudar) bless you! □ **saludable** adj (de buena salud) healthy; (provechoso) good, beneficial

saludar vt to greet; (MIL) to salute □ **saludo** nm greeting; **"saludos"** (en carta) "best wishes", "regards"

salva nf (de aplausos) storm

salvación nf salvation; (rescate) rescue

salvado nm bran

salvaguardar vt to safeguard

salvajada nf atrocity

salvaje adj wild; (tribu) savage □ **salvajismo** nm savagery

salvamento nm rescue

salvapantallas nm inv screen saver

salvar vt (rescatar) to save, rescue; (resolver) to overcome, resolve; (cubrir distancias) to cover, travel; (hacer excepción) to except, exclude; (barco) to salvage

salvavidas adj inv: **bote ~** lifeboat; **chaleco ~** life jacket; **cinturón ~** life preserver (US), lifebelt (BRIT)

salvo, -a adj safe ♦ adv except (for), save; **a ~** out of danger; **~ que** unless □ **salvoconducto** nm safe-conduct

san adj saint; **S~ Juan** St John

sanar vt (herida) to heal; (persona) to cure ♦ vi (persona) to get well, recover; (herida) to heal

sanatorio nm sanitarium (US), sanatorium (BRIT)

sanción nf sanction □ **sancionar** vt to sanction

sancochado, -a (MÉX) adj (CULIN) underdone, rear

sandalia nf sandal

sandez nf foolishness

sandía nf watermelon

sandwich (pl ~s, ~es) nm sandwich

saneamiento nm sanitation

sanear vt to clean up; (terreno) to drain

sangrar vt, vi to bleed □ **sangre** nf blood

sangría nf sangria, sweetened drink of red wine with fruit

sangriento, -a adj bloody

sanguijuela nf (ZOOL, fig) leech

sanguinario, -a adj bloodthirsty

sanguíneo, -a adj blood cpd

sanidad nf (tb: **~ pública**) public health

sanitario, -a adj health cpd □ **sanitarios** (LAm) nmpl washroom (US), toilets (BRIT)

sano, -a adj healthy; (sin daños) sound; (comida) wholesome; (entero) whole, intact; **~ y salvo** safe and sound

⚠ No confundir **sano** con la palabra inglesa **sane**.

Santiago nm: **~ (de Chile)** Santiago

santiamén nm: **en un ~** in no time at all

santidad nf holiness, sanctity

santiguarse vr to make the sign of the cross

santo, -a adj holy; (fig) wonderful, miraculous ♦ nm/f saint ♦ nm saint's day; **~ y seña** password

santuario nm sanctuary, shrine

saña nf rage, fury

sapo nm toad

saque nm (TENIS) service, serve; (FÚTBOL) throw-in ▶ **saque de esquina** corner (kick)

saquear vt (MIL) to sack; (robar) to loot, plunder; (fig) to ransack □ **saqueo** nm sacking; looting, plundering; ransacking

sarampión nm measles sg

sarcasmo nm sarcasm □ **sarcástico, -a** adj sarcastic

sardina nf sardine

sargento nm sergeant

sarmiento nm (BOT) vine shoot

sarna nf itch; (MED) scabies

sarpullido nm (MED) rash

sarro nm (en dientes) tartar, plaque

sartén nf frying pan

sastre nm tailor □ **sastrería** nf (arte) tailoring; (tienda) tailor's (shop)

Satanás nm Satan

satélite nm satellite

sátira nf satire

satisfacción nf satisfaction

satisfacer vt to satisfy; (gastos) to meet; (pérdida) to make good; **satisfacerse** vr to satisfy o.s., be satisfied; (vengarse) to take revenge □ **satisfecho, -a** adj satisfied; (contento) content(ed), happy; (tb: **satisfecho de sí mismo**) self-satisfied, smug

saturar vt to saturate; **saturarse** vr (mercado, aeropuerto) to reach saturation point

sauce nm willow ▶ **sauce llorón** weeping willow

sauna nf sauna

savia nf sap

saxofón nm saxophone

sazonar vt to ripen; (CULIN) to season, flavor (US), flavour (BRIT)

scone (MÉX, CS) nm biscuit (US)

scooter (ESP) nf scooter

Scotch® (LAm) nm Scotch tape® (US), Sellotape® (BRIT)

SE abr (= sudeste) SE

---

se

PALABRA CLAVE

pron

1 (reflexivo: sg: m) himself; (: f) herself; (: pl) themselves; (: cosa) itself; (: de Vd) yourself; (: de Vds) yourselves; **se está preparando** she's preparing herself; para usos léxicos del pron ver el vb en cuestión, p.ej. **arrepentirse**

2 (con complemento indirecto) to him; to her; to them; to it; to you; **a usted se lo dije ayer** I told you yesterday; **se compró un sombrero** he bought himself a hat; **se rompió la pierna** he broke his leg

3 (*uso recíproco*) each other, one another; **se miraron (el uno al otro)** they looked at each other o one another

4 (*en oraciones pasivas*): **se han vendido muchos libros** a lot of books have been sold

5 (*impers*): **se dice que** people say that, it is said that; **allí se come muy bien** the food there is very good, you can eat very well there

sé *etc vb ver* **saber**; **ser**

sea *etc vb ver* **ser**

sebo *nm* fat, grease

secador *nm* dryer ▶ **secador de pelo** hair dryer ❑ **secadora** *nf* dryer, tumble dryer (*BRIT*) ▶ **secadora de pelo** (*MÉX*) hair dryer

secar *vt* to dry; **secarse** *vr* to dry (off); (*río, planta*) to dry up

sección *nf* section

seco, -a *adj* dry; (*carácter*) cold; (*respuesta*) sharp, curt; **habrá pan a secas** there will be just bread; **decir algo a secas** to say sth curtly; **parar en ~** to stop dead

secretaría *nf* secretariat; (*MÉX: ministerio*) department, ministry (*BRIT*) ▶ **Secretaría de Estado** (*MÉX*) State Department (*US*), Foreign Office (*BRIT*) ▶ **Secretaría de Gobernación** (*MÉX*) Ministry of the Interior

secretario, -a *nm/f* secretary ▶ **Secretario de Relaciones Exteriores** (*MÉX*) Secretary of State (*US*), Foreign Secretary (*BRIT*)

secreto, -a *adj* secret; (*persona*) secretive ♦ *nm* secret; (*calidad*) secrecy

secta *nf* sect ❑ **sectario, -a** *adj* sectarian

sector *nm* sector

secuela *nf* consequence

secuencia *nf* sequence

secuestrar *vt* to kidnap; (*bienes*) to seize, confiscate ❑ **secuestro** *nm* kidnapping, kidnaping (*US*); seizure, confiscation

secular *adj* secular

secundar *vt* to second, support

secundario, -a *adj* secondary

sed *nf* thirst; **tener ~** to be thirsty

seda *nf* silk

sedal *nm* fishing line

sedán (*LAm*) *nm* sedan (*US*), saloon (*BRIT*)

sedante *nm* sedative

sede *nf* (*de gobierno*) seat; (*de compañía*) headquarters *pl* ▶ **Santa S~** Holy See

sedentario, -a *adj* sedentary

sediento, -a *adj* thirsty

sedimento *nm* sediment

sedoso, a *adj* silky, silken

seducción *nf* seduction

seducir *vt* to seduce; (*cautivar*) to charm, fascinate; (*atraer*) to attract ❑ **seductor, a** *adj* seductive; charming, fascinating; attractive ♦ *nm/f* seducer

segar *vt* (*mies*) to reap, cut; (*hierba*) to mow, cut

seglar *adj* secular, lay

segregación *nf* segregation ▶ **segregación racial** racial segregation

segregar *vt* to segregate, separate

seguida *nf*: **en ~** at once, right away

seguido, -a *adj* (*continuo*) continuous, unbroken; (*recto*) straight ♦ *adv* (*directo*) straight (on); (*después*) after; (*LAm: a menudo*) often; **~s** consecutive, successive; **5 días ~s** 5 days running, 5 days in a row

seguimiento *nm* chase, pursuit; (*continuación*) continuation

seguir *vt* to follow; (*venir después*) to follow on, come after; (*proseguir*) to continue; (*perseguir*) to chase, pursue ♦ *vi* (*gen*) to follow; (*continuar*) to continue, carry o go on; **seguirse** *vr* to follow; **sigo sin comprender** I still don't understand; **sigue lloviendo** it's still raining

según *prep* according to ♦ *adv*: **¿irás? -- ~** are you going? -- it all depends ♦ *conj* as; **~ caminamos** while we walk

segundo, -a *adj* second ♦ *nm* second ♦ *adv* second meaning; **de segunda mano** second-hand; **segunda (clase)** second class; **segunda (marcha)** (*AUTO*) second (gear)

seguramente *adv* surely; (*con certeza*) for sure, with certainty

seguridad *nf* safety; (*del estado, de casa etc*) security; (*certidumbre*) certainty; (*confianza*) confidence; (*estabilidad*) stability ▶ **seguridad social** welfare (*US*), social security (*BRIT*)

seguro, -a *adj* (*cierto*) sure, certain; (*fiel*) trustworthy; (*libre de peligro*) safe; (*bien defendido, firme*) secure ♦ *adv* for sure, certainly ♦ *nm* (*COM*) insurance; (*MÉX: imperdible*) safety pin ▶ **seguro contra terceros/a todo riesgo** third party/comprehensive insurance ▶ **seguros sociales** welfare *sg* (*US*), social security *sg* (*BRIT*)

seis *num* six

seísmo *nm* tremor, earthquake

selección *nf* selection ❑ **seleccionar** *vt* to pick, choose, select

selecto, -a *adj* select, choice; (*escogido*) selected

sellar vt (documento oficial) to seal; (pasaporte, visado) to stamp

sello nm (ESP CORREOS) stamp; (precinto) seal

selva nf (bosque) forest, woods pl; (jungla) jungle

semáforo nm (AUTO) traffic lights pl; (FERRO) signal

semana nf week; **entre ~** during the week ▶ **Semana Santa** Holy Week ❑ **semanal** adj weekly ❑ **semanario** nm weekly magazine

semblante nm face; (fig) look

sembrar vt to sow; (objetos) to sprinkle, scatter about; (noticias etc) to spread

semejante adj (parecido) similar ♦ nm fellow man, fellow creature; **~s** alike, similar; **nunca hizo cosa ~** he never did any such thing ❑ **semejanza** nf similarity, resemblance

semejar vi to seem like, resemble; **semejarse** vr to look alike, be similar

semen nm semen

semestral adj six-monthly, semi-annual (US), half-yearly (BRIT)

semicalificado, -a (LAm) adj semiskilled

semicírculo nm semicircle

semidescremado, -a (LAm) adj semi-skimmed

semidesnatado, -a (ESP) adj semi-skimmed

semifinal nf semifinal

semilla nf seed

seminario nm (REL) seminary; (ESCOL) seminar

sémola nf semolina

Sena nm: **el ~** the (river) Seine

senado nm senate ❑ **senador, a** nm/f senator

sencillez nf simplicity; (de persona) naturalness ❑ **sencillo, -a** adj simple; natural, unaffected ♦ nm (LAm: vuelto) small o loose (BRIT) change

senda nf path, track

senderismo nm hiking

sendero nm path, track

sendos, -as adj pl: **les dio ~ golpes** he hit both of them

senil adj senile

seno nm (ANAT) bosom, bust; (fig) bosom; **~s** breasts

sensación nf sensation; (sentido) sense; (sentimiento) feeling ❑ **sensacional** adj sensational

sensato, -a adj sensible

sensible adj sensitive; (apreciable) perceptible, appreciable; (pérdida) considerable ❑ **sensiblero, -a** adj sentimental

⚠ No confundir **sensible** con la palabra inglesa **sensible**.

sensitivo, -a adj sense cpd

sensorial adj sensory

sensual adj sensual

sentada nf sitting; (protesta) sit-in

sentado, -a adj: **estar ~** to sit, be sitting (down); **dar por ~** to take for granted, assume

sentar vt to sit, seat; (fig) to establish ♦ vi (vestido) to suit; (alimento): **~ bien/mal a** to agree/disagree with; **sentarse** vr (persona) to sit, sit down; (los depósitos) to settle

sentencia nf (máxima) maxim, saying; (JUR) sentence ❑ **sentenciar** vt to sentence

sentido, -a adj (pérdida) regrettable; (carácter) sensitive ♦ nm sense; (sentimiento) feeling; (significado) sense, meaning; (dirección) direction; **mi más ~ pésame** my deepest sympathy; **tener ~** to make sense ▶ **sentido del humor** sense of humor (US) o humour (BRIT) ▶ **sentido único** one-way (street)

sentimental adj sentimental; **vida ~** love life

sentimiento nm feeling

sentir vt to feel; (LAm: percibir) to perceive, sense; (lamentar) to regret, be sorry for ♦ vi (tener la sensación) to feel; (lamentarse) to feel sorry ♦ nm opinion, judgement; **~se bien/ mal** to feel well/ill; **lo siento** I'm sorry

seña nf sign; (MIL) password; **~s** nfpl (dirección) address sg ▶ **señas personales** personal description sg

señal nf sign; (síntoma) symptom; (FERRO, TEL) signal; (marca) mark; **en ~ de** as a token o sign of ❑ **señalar** vt to mark; (indicar) to point out, indicate

señor nm (hombre) man; (caballero) gentleman; (dueño) owner, master; (trato: antes de nombre propio) Mr; (: hablando directamente) sir; **muy ~ mío** Dear Sir; **el ~ alcalde/presidente** the mayor/president

señora nf (dama) lady; (trato: antes de nombre propio) Mrs; (: hablando directamente) madam; (esposa) wife; **Nuestra S~** Our Lady

señorita nf (con nombre y/o apellido) Miss; (mujer joven) young lady

señorito nm young gentleman; (pey) rich kid

señuelo nm decoy

sepa etc vb ver **saber**

separación nf separation; (división) division; (hueco) gap

separar vt to separate; (dividir) to divide; **separarse** vr (parte) to come away; (partes) to come apart; (persona) to leave, go away; (matrimonio) to separate ☐ **separatismo** nm separatism

sepia nf cuttlefish

septentrional adj northern

septiembre nm September

séptimo, -a adj, nm seventh

sepulcral adj (fig: silencio, atmósfera) deadly ☐ **sepulcro** nm tomb, grave

sepultar vt to bury ☐ **sepultura** nf (acto) burial; (tumba) grave, tomb

sequedad nf dryness; (fig) brusqueness, curtness

sequía nf drought

séquito nm (de rey etc) retinue; (seguidores) followers pl

---

ser
PALABRA CLAVE
vi

1 (descripción) to be; **es médica/muy alta** she's a doctor/very tall; **la familia es de Cuzco** his (o her etc) family is from Cuzco; **soy Ana** (ESP TEL) Ana speaking o here

2 (propiedad): **es de Joaquín** it's Joaquín's, it belongs to Joaquín

3 (horas, fechas, números): **es la una** it's one o'clock; **son las seis y media** it's half-past six; **es el 1 de junio** it's June first (US), it's the first of June (BRIT); **somos/son seis** there are six of us/them

4 (en oraciones pasivas): **ha sido descubierto ya** it's already been discovered

5: **es de esperar que ...** it is to be hoped o I etc hope that ...

6 (locuciones con subj): **o sea** that is to say; **sea él sea su hermana** either him or his sister

7: **a no ser por él ...** but for him ...

8: **a no ser que: a no ser que tenga uno ya** unless he's got one already

♦ nm being; **ser humano** human being

serenarse vr to calm down

sereno, -a adj (persona) calm, unruffled; (el tiempo) fine, settled; (ambiente) calm, peaceful ♦ nm night watchman

serial (LAm) nm serial

serie nf series; (cadena) sequence, succession; (ESP TV) serial; **fuera de ~** out of order; (fig) special, out of the ordinary; **fabricación en ~** mass production

seriedad nf seriousness; (formalidad) reliability

serigrafía nf silk-screen printing

serio, -a adj serious; (fiable) reliable, dependable; (severo) grave, serious; **en ~** adv seriously

sermón nm (REL) sermon

seropositivo, -a adj HIV positive

serpentear vi to wriggle; (camino, río) to wind, snake

serpentina nf streamer

serpiente nf snake ▶ **serpiente de cascabel** rattlesnake, rattler (US)

serranía nf mountainous area

serrar vt = **aserrar**

serrín nm = **aserrín**

serrucho nm saw

service (RPI) nm (AUTO) service

servicio nm service; (LAm AUTO) service; **~s** nmpl (ESP) rest room sg (US), toilet(s) (BRIT); **~ incluido** service charge included ▶ **servicio militar** military service

---

SERVICIO MILITAR

In many Latin American countries military service is a civic obligation for every male citizen over the age of 18. This generally lasts for one year and consists of military training. Recently, community service has been introduced in some countries for conscientious objectors.

---

servidumbre nf (sujeción) servitude; (criados) servants pl, staff

servil adj servile

servilleta nf napkin, serviette (BRIT)

servir vt to serve ♦ vi to serve; (tener utilidad) to be of use, be useful; **servirse** vr to serve o help o.s.; **~se de algo** to make use of sth, use sth; **sírvase pasar** please come in

sesenta num sixty

sesgo nm slant; (fig) slant, twist

sesión nf (POL) session, sitting; (CINE) showing

seso nm brain ☐ **sesudo, -a** adj sensible, wise

seta nf mushroom

setecientos, -as adj, num seven hundred

setenta num seventy

seto nm hedge

seudónimo nm pseudonym

severidad nf severity ☐ **severo, -a** adj severe

Sevilla n Seville ☐ **sevillano, -a** adj of o from Seville ♦ nm/f native o inhabitant of Seville

sexo nm sex

sexto, -a adj, nm sixth

sexual adj sexual; **vida ~** sex life

si conj if; **me pregunto si ...** I wonder if o whether ...

sí adv yes ♦ nm consent ♦ pron (uso impersonal) oneself; (sg: m) himself; (: f) herself; (: de cosa) itself; (de usted) yourself; (pl) themselves; (de ustedes) yourselves; (recíproco) each other; **él no quiere pero yo sí** he doesn't want to but I do; **ella sí vendrá** she will certainly come, she is sure to come; **claro que sí** of course; **creo que sí** I think so

siamés, -esa adj, nm/f Siamese

SIDA nm abr (= Síndrome de Inmunodeficiencia Adquirida) AIDS

siderúrgico, -a adj iron and steel cpd

sidra nf cider, hard cider (US)

siembra nf sowing

siempre adv always; (todo el tiempo) all the time; **~ que** (cada vez) whenever; (dado que) provided that; **como ~** as usual; **para ~** for ever

sien nf temple

siento etc vb ver **sentar; sentir**

sierra nf (TEC) saw; (cadena de montañas) mountain range

siervo, -a nm/f slave

siesta nf siesta, nap; **echar la ~** to have an afternoon nap o a siesta

siete num seven

sífilis nf syphilis

sifón nm syphon; **whisky con ~** whiskey and soda

sigla nf abbreviation; acronym

siglo nm century; (fig) age

significación nf significance

significado nm (de palabra etc) meaning

significar vt to mean, signify; (notificar) to make known, express □ **significativo, -a** adj significant

signo nm sign ▶ **signo de admiración** o **exclamación** exclamation point (US) o mark (BRIT) ▶ **signo de interrogación** question mark

sigo etc vb ver **seguir**

siguiente adj next, following

siguió etc vb ver **seguir**

sílaba nf syllable

silbar vt, vi to whistle □ **silbato** nm whistle □ **silbido** nm whistle, whistling

silenciador nm (AUTO) muffler (US), silencer (BRIT)

silenciar vt (persona) to silence; (escándalo) to hush up □ **silencio** nm silence, quiet □ **silencioso, -a** adj silent, quiet

silla nf (asiento) chair; (tb: **~ de montar**) saddle ▶ **silla de playa** (LAm) deck chair ▶ **silla de ruedas** wheelchair

sillón nm armchair, easy chair

silueta nf silhouette; (de edificio) outline; (figura) figure

silvestre adj wild

simbólico, -a adj symbolic(al)

simbolizar vt to symbolize

símbolo nm symbol

simetría nf symmetry

simiente nf seed

similar adj similar

simio nm ape

simpatía nf liking; (afecto) affection; (amabilidad) kindness □ **simpático, -a** adj nice, pleasant; kind

⚠ No confundir **simpático** con la palabra inglesa **sympathetic**.

simpatizante nmf sympathizer

simpatizar vi: **~ con** to get on well with

simple adj simple; (elemental) simple, easy; (mero) mere; (puro) pure, sheer ♦ nmf simpleton □ **simpleza** nf simpleness; (necedad) silly thing □ **simplificar** vt to simplify

simposio nm symposium

simular vt to simulate

simultáneo, -a adj simultaneous

sin prep without; **la ropa está ~ lavar** the clothes are unwashed; **~ que** without; **~ embargo** however, still

sinagoga nf synagogue

sinceridad nf sincerity □ **sincero, -a** adj sincere

sincronizar vt to synchronize

sindical adj labor union cpd (US), trade union cpd (BRIT) □ **sindicalista** adj, nmf union member, trade unionist (BRIT)

sindicato nm (de trabajadores) labor union (US), trade union (BRIT); (de negociantes) syndicate

síndrome nm (MED) syndrome ▶ **síndrome de abstinencia** (MED) withdrawal symptoms

sinfín nm: **un ~ de** a great many, no end of

sinfonía nf symphony

singular adj singular; (fig) outstanding, exceptional; (raro) peculiar, odd □ **singularidad** nf singularity, peculiarity

❑ **singularizarse** vr to distinguish o.s., stand out

siniestro, -a adj sinister ♦ nm (accidente) accident

sinnúmero nm = **sinfín**

sino nm fate, destiny ♦ conj (pero) but; (salvo) except, save

sinónimo, -a adj synonymous ♦ nm synonym

síntesis nf synthesis ❑ **sintético, -a** adj synthetic

sintetizar vt to synthesize

sintió vb ver **sentir**

síntoma nm symptom

sintonía nf (RADIO, MÚS: de programa) tuning ❑ **sintonizar** vt (RADIO: emisora) to tune (in)

sinvergüenza nmf rogue, scoundrel; **¡es un ~!** he's got a nerve!

siquiera conj even if, even though ♦ adv at least; **ni ~** not even

Siria nf Syria

sirviente, -a nm/f servant

sirvo etc vb ver **servir**

sisear vt, vi to hiss

sistema nm system; (método) method ❑ **sistemático, -a** adj systematic

sitiar vt to besiege, lay siege to

sitio nm (lugar) place; (espacio) room, space; (MIL) siege ▶ **sitio de taxis** (MÉX: parada) taxi stand (US) o rank (BRIT) ▶ **sitio Web** (INFORM) website

situación nf situation, position; (estatus) position, standing

situado, -a adj situated, placed

situar vt to place, put; (edificio) to locate, situate

slip nm underpants pl, shorts pl (US), pants pl (BRIT)

smoking (pl ~s) nm tuxedo (US), dinner jacket (BRIT)

⚠ No confundir **smoking** con la palabra inglesa **smoking**.

snob adj, nmf = **esnob**

SO abr (= suroeste) SW

sobaco nm armpit

sobar vt (ropa) to rumple; (comida) to play around with

soberanía nf sovereignty ❑ **soberano, -a** adj sovereign; (fig) supreme ♦ nm/f sovereign

soberbia nf pride; haughtiness, arrogance; magnificence

soberbio, -a adj (orgulloso) proud; (altivo) arrogant; (estupendo) magnificent, superb

sobornar vt to bribe ❑ **soborno** nm bribe

sobra nf excess, surplus; **~s** nfpl left-overs, scraps; **de ~** surplus, extra; **tengo de ~** I've more than enough ❑ **sobrado, -a** adj (más que suficiente) more than enough; (superfluo) excessive ❑ **sobrante** adj remaining, extra ♦ nm surplus, remainder

sobrar vt to exceed, surpass ♦ vi (tener de más) to be more than enough; (quedar) to remain, be left (over)

sobrasada nf pork sausage spread

sobre prep (gen) on; (encima) on (top of); (por encima de, arriba de) over, above; (más que) more than; (además) in addition to, besides; (alrededor de) about ♦ nm envelope; **~ todo** above all

sobrecama nf bedspread

sobrecargar vt (camión) to overload; (COM) to surcharge

sobredosis nf inv overdose

sobreentender vt to deduce, infer; **sobreentenderse** vr: **se sobreentiende que ...** it is implied that ...

sobrehumano, -a adj superhuman

sobrellevar vt to bear, endure

sobremesa nf: **programa de ~** (TV) afternoon program (US) o programme (BRIT)

sobrenatural adj supernatural

sobrenombre nm nickname

sobrepasar vt to exceed, surpass

sobreponerse vr: **~ a** to overcome

sobresaliente adj outstanding, excellent

sobresalir vi to project, jut out; (fig) to stand out, excel

sobresaltar vt (asustar) to scare, frighten; (sobrecoger) to startle ❑ **sobresalto** nm (movimiento) start; (susto) scare; (turbación) sudden shock

sobretodo nm overcoat

sobrevenir vi (ocurrir) to happen (unexpectedly); (resultar) to follow, ensue

sobreviviente adj surviving ♦ nmf survivor

sobrevivir vi to survive

sobrevolar vt to fly over

sobriedad nf sobriety, soberness; (moderación) moderation, restraint

sobrino, -a nm/f nephew/niece

sobrio, -a adj sober; (moderado) moderate, restrained

socarrón, -ona adj (sarcástico) sarcastic, ironic(al)

socavar vt to undermine

socavón nm (hoyo) hole

sociable adj (persona) sociable, friendly; (animal) social

social adj social; (COM) company cpd

socialdemócrata nmf social democrat

socialista adj, nm socialist

socializar vt to socialize

sociedad nf society; (COM) company ▶ **sociedad anónima** corporation (US), limited liability company (BRIT) ▶ **sociedad de consumo** consumer society

socio, -a nm/f (miembro) member; (COM) partner

sociología nf sociology □ **sociólogo, -a** nm/f sociologist

socorrer vt to help □ **socorrista** nmf first aider; (en piscina, playa) lifeguard □ **socorro** nm (ayuda) help, aid; (MIL) relief; ¡**socorro**! help!

soda nf (sosa) soda; (bebida) soda (water)

sofá (pl ~s) nm sofa, settee □ **sofá-cama** nm studio couch; sofa bed

sofisticación nf sophistication

sofocar vt to suffocate; (apagar) to smother, put out; **sofocarse** vr to suffocate; (fig) to blush, feel embarrassed □ **sofoco** nm suffocation; embarrassment

sofreír vt (CULIN) to fry lightly

soga nf rope

sois etc (ESP) vb ver **ser**

soja (ESP) nf soy (US), soya (BRIT)

sol nm sun; (luz) sunshine, sunlight; **hace** ~ **it** is sunny

solamente adv only, just

solapa nf (de chaqueta) lapel; (de libro) jacket

solapado, -a adj (intenciones) underhand; (gestos, movimiento) sly

solar adj solar, sun cpd

solaz nm recreation, relaxation □ **solazar** vt (divertir) to amuse

soldado nm soldier ▶ **soldado raso** private

soldador nm soldering iron; (persona) welder

soldar vt to solder, weld

soleado, -a adj sunny

soledad nf solitude; (estado infeliz) loneliness

solemne adj solemn □ **solemnidad** nf solemnity

soler vi to be in the habit of, be accustomed to; **suele salir a las ocho** she usually goes out at 8 o'clock

solfeo nm (MÚS) sol-fa

solicitar vt (permiso) to ask for, seek; (puesto) to apply for; (votos) to canvass for; (atención) to attract

solícito, -a adj (diligente) diligent; (cuidadoso) careful □ **solicitud** nf (calidad) great care; (petición) request; (a un puesto) application

solidaridad nf solidarity □ **solidario, -a** adj (participación) joint, common; (compromiso) mutually binding

solidez nf solidity □ **sólido, -a** adj solid

soliloquio nm soliloquy

solista nmf soloist

solitario, -a adj (persona) lonely, solitary; (lugar) lonely, desolate ♦ nm/f (recluso) recluse; (en la sociedad) loner ♦ nm solitaire

sollozar vi to sob □ **sollozo** nm sob

solo, -a adj (único) single, sole; (sin compañía) alone; (solitario) lonely; **hay una sola dificultad** there is just one difficulty; **a solas** alone, by oneself

sólo adv only, just

solomillo nm sirloin

soltar vt (dejar ir) to let go of; (desprender) to unfasten, loosen; (librar) to release, set free; (risa etc) to let out

soltero, -a adj single, unmarried ♦ nm/f bachelor (single woman) □ **solterón, -ona** nm/f old bachelor (spinster)

soltura nf looseness, slackness; (de los miembros) agility, ease of movement; (en el hablar) fluency, ease

soluble adj (QUÍM) soluble; (problema) solvable; ~ **en agua** soluble in water

solución nf solution □ **solucionar** vt (problema) to solve; (asunto) to settle, resolve

solventar vt (pagar) to settle, pay; (resolver) to resolve □ **solvente** adj (ECON: empresa, persona) solvent

sombra nf shadow; (como protección) shade; ~**s** nfpl (oscuridad) darkness sg, shadows; **tener buena/mala** ~ to be lucky/unlucky

sombrero nm hat

sombrilla nf parasol, sunshade

sombrío, -a adj (oscuro) dark; (triste) sad, somber (US), sombre (BRIT); (persona) gloomy

somero, -a adj superficial

someter vt (país) to conquer; (persona) to subject to one's will; (informe) to present, submit; **someterse** vr to give in, yield, submit; ~ **a** to subject to

somier (pl ~s) n spring mattress

somnífero nm sleeping pill

somnolencia nf sleepiness, drowsiness

somos vb ver **ser**

son vb ver **ser** ♦ nm sound; **en ~ de broma** as a joke

sonaja (MÉX) nf (baby's) rattle

sonajero nm (baby's) rattle

sonambulismo nm sleepwalking ❑ **sonámbulo, -a** nm/f sleepwalker

sonar vt to ring ♦ vi to sound; (hacer ruido) to make a noise; (pronunciarse) to be sounded, be pronounced; (ser conocido) to sound familiar; (campana) to ring; (reloj) to strike, chime; **sonarse** vr: **~se (las narices)** to blow one's nose; **me suena ese nombre** that name rings a bell

sonda nf (NÁUT) sounding; (TEC) bore, drill; (MED) probe

sondear vt to sound; to bore (into), drill; to probe, sound; (fig) to sound out ❑ **sondeo** nm sounding; boring, drilling; (fig) poll, enquiry

sonido nm sound

sonoro, -a adj sonorous; (resonante) loud, resonant

sonreír vi to smile; **sonreírse** vr to smile ❑ **sonriente** adj smiling ❑ **sonrisa** nf smile

sonrojarse vr to blush, go red ❑ **sonrojo** nm blush

soñador, a nm/f dreamer

soñar vt, vi to dream; **~ con** to dream about o of

soñoliento, -a adj sleepy, drowsy

sopa nf soup

sopesar vt to consider, weigh up

soplar vt (polvo) to blow away, blow off; (inflar) to blow up; (vela) to blow out ♦ vi to blow ❑ **soplo** nm blow, puff; (de viento) puff, gust

soplón, -ona (fam) nm/f (niño) telltale; (de policía) fink (US), grass (BRIT)

sopor nm drowsiness

soporífero nm sleeping pill

soportable adj bearable

soportar vt to bear, carry; (fig) to bear, put up with

⚠ No confundir **soportar** con la palabra inglesa **support**.

soporte nm support; (fig) pillar, support

soprano nf soprano

sorber vt (chupar) to sip; (absorber) to soak up, absorb

sorbete nm sherbert (US), sorbet (BRIT)

sorbo nm (trago: grande) gulp, swallow; (: pequeño) sip

sordera nf deafness

sórdido, -a adj dirty, squalid

sordo, -a adj (persona) deaf ♦ nm/f deaf person ❑ **sordomudo, -a** adj deaf and dumb

sorna nf sarcastic tone

soroche (CAm) nm mountain sickness

sorprendente adj surprising

sorprender vt to surprise ❑ **sorpresa** nf surprise

sortear vt to draw lots for; (rifar) to raffle; (dificultad) to avoid ❑ **sorteo** nm (en lotería) draw; (rifa) raffle

sortija nf ring; (rizo) ringlet, curl

sosegado, -a adj quiet, calm

sosegar vt to quieten, calm; (el ánimo) to reassure ♦ vi to rest ❑ **sosiego** nm quiet(ness), calm(ness)

soslayo: **de ~** adv obliquely, sideways

soso, -a adj (CULIN) tasteless; (aburrido) dull, uninteresting

sospecha nf suspicion ❑ **sospechar** vt to suspect ❑ **sospechoso, -a** adj suspicious; (testimonio, opinión) suspect ♦ nm/f suspect

sostén nm (apoyo) support; (LAm exc MÉX, ESP: sujetador) bra; (alimentación) sustenance, food

sostener vt to support; (mantener) to keep up, maintain; (alimentar) to sustain, keep going; **sostenerse** vr to support o.s.; (seguir) to continue, remain ❑ **sostenido, -a** adj continuous, sustained; (prolongado) prolonged

sotana nf (REL) cassock

sótano nm basement

soviético, -a adj (HIST) Soviet; **los ~s** the Soviets

soy vb ver **ser**

soya (LAm) nf soy (US), soya (BRIT)

Sr. abr (= Señor) Mr.

Sra. abr (= Señora) Mrs.

S.R.C. abr (= se ruega contestación) R.S.V.P.

Sres. abr (= Señores) Messrs

Srta. abr (= Señorita) Miss

Sta. abr (= Santa) St.

status nm inv status

Sto. abr (= Santo) St.

su pron (de él) his; (de ella) her; (de una cosa) its; (de ellos, ellas) their; (de usted, ustedes) your

suave adj gentle; (superficie) smooth; (trabajo) easy; (música, voz) soft, sweet ❑ **suavidad** nf gentleness; smoothness; softness, sweetness ❑ **suavizante** nm (de ropa) softener; (ESP: del pelo) conditioner

❑ **suavizar** vt to soften; (quitar la aspereza) to smooth (out)

subalimentado, -a adj undernourished

subasta nf auction ❑ **subastar** vt to auction (off)

subcampeón, -ona nm/f runner-up

subconsciente adj, nm subconscious

subdesarrollado, -a adj underdeveloped

subdesarrollo nm underdevelopment

subdirector, a nm/f assistant director

súbdito, -a nm/f subject

subestimar vt to underestimate, underrate

subida nf (de montaña etc) ascent, climb; (de precio) rise, increase; (pendiente) slope, hill

subir vt (objeto) to raise, lift up; (cuesta, calle) to go up; (colina, montaña) to climb; (precio) to raise, put up ♦ vi to go up, come up; (a un carro) to get in; (a un autobús, tren o avión) to get on, board; (precio) to rise, go up; (río, marea) to rise; **subirse** vr to get up, climb

súbito, -a adj (repentino) sudden; (imprevisto) unexpected

subjetivo, -a adj subjective

sublevación nf revolt, rising

sublevar vt to rouse to revolt; **sublevarse** vr to revolt, rise

sublime adj sublime

submarinismo nm scuba diving

submarino, -a adj underwater ♦ nm submarine

subnormal adj subnormal ♦ nmf subnormal person

subordinado, -a adj, nm/f subordinate

subrayar vt to underline

subsanar vt to rectify

subscribir vt = **suscribir**

subsidio nm (ayuda) aid, financial help; (subvención) subsidy, grant; (de enfermedad, paro etc) benefit, allowance

subsistencia nf subsistence

subsistir vi to subsist; (sobrevivir) to survive, endure

subte (RPI) nm subway (US), underground (BRIT)

subterráneo, -a adj underground, subterranean ♦ nm (túnel) underground passage; (metro) subway (US), underground (BRIT)

subtítulo nm (CINE) subtitle

suburbano, -a adj suburban

suburbio nm (barrio) slum quarter

subvención nf (ECON) subsidy, grant ❑ **subvencionar** vt to subsidize

subversión nf subversion ❑ **subversivo, -a** adj subversive

subyugar vt (país) to subjugate, subdue; (enemigo) to overpower; (voluntad) to dominate

sucedáneo, -a adj substitute ♦ nm substitute (food)

suceder vt, vi to happen; (seguir) to succeed, follow; **lo que sucede es que ...** the fact is that ... ❑ **sucesión** nf succession; (serie) sequence, series

sucesivamente adv: **y así ~** and so on

sucesivo, -a adj successive, following; **en lo ~** in future, from now on

suceso nm (hecho) event, happening; (incidente) incident

⚠ No confundir **suceso** con la palabra inglesa *success*.

suciedad nf (estado) dirtiness; (mugre) dirt, filth

sucinto, -a adj (conciso) succinct, concise

sucio, -a adj dirty

suculento, -a adj succulent

sucumbir vi to succumb

sucursal nf branch (office)

sudadera nf sweatshirt

Sudáfrica nf South Africa

Sudamérica nf South America ❑ **sudamericano, -a** adj, nm/f South American

sudar vt, vi to sweat

sudeste nm south-east

sudoeste nm south-west

sudor nm sweat ❑ **sudoroso, -a** adj sweaty, sweating

Suecia nf Sweden ❑ **sueco, -a** adj Swedish ♦ nm/f Swede

suegro, -a nm/f father-/mother-in-law

suela nf sole

sueldo nm pay, wage(s) (pl)

suele etc vb ver **soler**

suelo nm (tierra) ground; (de casa) floor

suelto, -a adj loose; (libre) free; (separado) detached; (ágil) quick, agile

sueñito (LAm) nm nap

sueño etc vb ver **soñar** ♦ nm sleep; (somnolencia) sleepiness, drowsiness; (lo soñado, fig) dream; **tener ~** to be sleepy

suero nm (MED) serum; (de leche) whey

suerte nf (fortuna) luck; (azar) chance; (destino) fate, destiny; (especie) sort, kind; **tener ~** to be lucky; **de otra ~** otherwise, if not; **de ~ que** so that, in such a way that

suéter (*LAm*) *nm* sweater

suficiente *adj* enough, sufficient ♦ *nm* (*ESCOL*) passing grade (*US*), pass mark (*BRIT*)

sufragio *nm* (*voto*) vote; (*derecho de voto*) suffrage

sufrido, -a *adj* (*persona*) tough; (*paciente*) long-suffering, patient

sufrimiento *nm* (*dolor*) suffering

sufrir *vt* (*padecer*) to suffer; (*soportar*) to bear, put up with; (*apoyar*) to hold up, support ♦ *vi* to suffer

sugerencia *nf* suggestion

sugerir *vt* to suggest; (*sutilmente*) to hint

sugestión *nf* suggestion; (*sutil*) hint □ **sugestionar** *vt* to influence

sugestivo, -a *adj* stimulating; (*fascinante*) fascinating

suicida *adj* suicidal ♦ *nmf* suicidal person; (*muerto*) suicide, person who has committed suicide □ **suicidarse** *vr* to commit suicide, kill o.s. □ **suicidio** *nm* suicide

Suiza *nf* Switzerland □ **suizo, -a** *adj, nm/f* Swiss

sujeción *nf* subjection

sujetador (*ESP*) *nm* (*sostén*) bra

sujetar *vt* (*fijar*) to fasten; (*detener*) to hold down; **sujetarse** *vr* to subject o.s. □ **sujeto, -a** *adj* fastened, secure ♦ *nm* subject; (*individuo*) individual; **sujeto a** subject to

suma *nf* (*cantidad*) total, sum; (*de dinero*) sum; (*acto*) adding (up), addition; **en ~** in short

sumamente *adv* extremely, exceedingly

sumar *vt* to add (up) ♦ *vi* to add up

sumario, -a *adj* brief, concise ♦ *nm* summary

sumergir *vt* to submerge; (*hundir*) to sink

suministrar *vt* to supply, provide □ **suministro** *nm* supply; (*acto*) supplying, providing

sumir *vt* to sink, submerge; (*fig*) to plunge

sumisión *nf* (*acto*) submission; (*calidad*) submissiveness, docility □ **sumiso, -a** *adj* submissive, docile

sumo, -a *adj* great, extreme; (*autoridad*) highest, supreme

suntuoso, -a *adj* sumptuous, magnificent

supe *etc vb ver* **saber**

supeditar *vt*: **~ algo a algo** to subordinate sth to sth

super... *prefijo* super..., over...

súper *nm* supermarket

superar *vt* (*sobreponerse a*) to overcome; (*rebasar*) to surpass, do better than; (*pasar*) to go beyond; **superarse** *vr* to excel o.s.

superávit *nm inv* surplus

superbueno *adj* great, fantastic

superficial *adj* superficial; (*medida*) surface *cpd*, of the surface

superficie *nf* surface; (*área*) area

superfluo, -a *adj* superfluous

superior *adj* (*piso, clase*) upper; (*temperatura, número, nivel*) higher; (*mejor: calidad, producto*) superior, better ♦ *nmf* superior □ **superioridad** *nf* superiority

supermercado *nm* supermarket

superponer *vt* to superimpose

supersónico, -a *adj* supersonic

superstición *nf* superstition □ **supersticioso, -a** *adj* superstitious

supervisar *vt* to supervise

supervivencia *nf* survival

superviviente *adj* surviving

supiera *etc vb ver* **saber**

suplantar *vt* to supplant

suplemento *nm* supplement

suplente *adj, nm* substitute

supletorio, -a *adj* supplementary ♦ *nm* supplement; **teléfono ~** extension

súplica *nf* request; (*JUR*) petition

suplicar *vt* (*cosa*) to beg (for), plead for; (*persona*) to beg, plead with

suplicio *nm* torture

suplir *vt* (*compensar*) to make good, make up for; (*reemplazar*) to replace, substitute ♦ *vi*: **~ a** to take the place of, substitute for

supo *etc vb ver* **saber**

suponer *vt* to suppose □ **suposición** *nf* supposition

supremacía *nf* supremacy

supremo, -a *adj* supreme

supresión *nf* suppression; (*de derecho*) abolition; (*de palabra etc*) deletion; (*de restricción*) cancellation, lifting

suprimir *vt* to suppress; (*derecho, costumbre*) to abolish; (*palabra etc*) to delete; (*restricción*) to cancel, lift

supuesto, -a *pp de* **suponer** ♦ *adj* (*hipotético*) supposed ♦ *nm* assumption, hypothesis; **~ que** since; **por ~** of course

sur *nm* south

surcar *vt* to plow (*US*), plough (*BRIT*) □ **surco** *nm* (*en metal, disco*) groove; (*AGR*) furrow

surgir *vi* to arise, emerge; (*dificultad*) to come up, crop up

Tt

suroeste nm south-west

surtido, -a adj mixed, assorted ♦ nm (selección) selection, assortment; (abastecimiento) supply, stock ❏ **surtidor** nm (tb: **surtidor de gasolina**) gas pump (US), petrol pump (BRIT)

surtir vt to supply, provide ♦ vi to spout, spurt

susceptible adj susceptible; (sensible) sensitive; ~ **de** capable of

suscitar vt to cause, provoke; (interés, sospechas) to arouse

suscribir vt (firmar) to sign; (respaldar) to subscribe to, endorse; **suscribirse** vr to subscribe ❏ **suscripción** nf subscription

susodicho, -a adj above-mentioned

suspender vt (objeto) to hang (up), suspend; (trabajo) to stop, suspend; (ESCOL) to fail; (interrumpir) to adjourn; (atrasar) to postpone

suspense (ESP) nm suspense; **película/ novela de ~** thriller

suspensión nf suspension; (fig) stoppage, suspension

suspenso, -a adj hanging, suspended; (ESP ESCOL) failed ♦ nm (ESP ESCOL) fail; (LAm: misterio) suspense; **quedar** o **estar en ~** to be pending; **película/novela de ~** (LAm) thriller

suspicacia nf suspicion, mistrust ❏ **suspicaz** adj suspicious, distrustful

suspirar vi to sigh ❏ **suspiro** nm sigh

sustancia nf substance

sustentar vt (alimentar) to sustain, nourish; (objeto) to hold up, support; (idea, teoría) to maintain, uphold; (fig) to sustain, keep going ❏ **sustento** nm support; (alimento) sustenance, food

sustituir vt to substitute, replace ❏ **sustituto, -a** nm/f substitute, replacement

susto nm fright, scare

sustraer vt to remove, take away; (MAT) to subtract

susurrar vi to whisper ❏ **susurro** nm whisper

sutil adj (aroma, diferencia) subtle; (tenue) thin; (inteligencia, persona) sharp ❏ **sutileza** nf subtlety; thinness

suyo, -a (con artículo o después del verbo **ser**) adj (de él) his; (de ella) hers; (de ellos, ellas) theirs; (de Ud, Uds) yours; **un amigo ~** a friend of his (o hers o theirs o yours)

tabacalera nf: **T~** Spanish state tobacco monopoly

tabaco nm tobacco; (ESP: fam) cigarettes pl

tabaquería (LAm) nf smoke shop (US), tobacconist's (shop) (BRIT) ❏ **tabaquero, -a** (LAm) nm/f tobacconist

taberna nf bar, pub (BRIT)

tabique nm partition (wall)

tabla nf (de madera) plank; (estante) shelf; (de vestido) pleat; (ARTE) panel; ~**s** nfpl: **estar** o **quedar en** ~**s** to draw ❏ **tablado** nm (plataforma) platform; (TEATRO) stage

tablao nm (tb: ~ **flamenco**) flamenco show

tablero nm (de madera) plank, board; (de ajedrez, damas) board ► **tablero de mandos** (LAm AUTO) dashboard

tableta nf (MED) tablet; (de chocolate) bar

tablón nm (de suelo) plank; (de techo) beam ► **tablón de anuncios** (ESP) bulletin (US) o notice (BRIT) board

tabú nm taboo

tabular vt to tabulate

taburete nm stool

tacaño, -a adj stingy, mean (BRIT)

tacha nf flaw; (TEC) stud ❏ **tachar** vt (borrar) to cross out; **tachar de** to accuse of

tacho (CS) nm (balde) bucket ► **tacho de la basura** trash can (US), rubbish bin (BRIT)

tácito, -a adj tacit

taciturno, -a adj silent

taco nm (BILLAR) cue; (CS: de zapato) heel; (tarugo) peg

tacón nm heel; **de ~ alto** high-heeled ❏ **taconeo** nm (heel) stamping

táctica nf tactics pl

táctico, -a adj tactical

tacto nm touch; (fig) tact

taimado, -a adj (astuto) sly

tajada nf slice

tajante adj sharp

tajo nm (corte) cut; (GEO) cleft

tal adj such ♦ pron (persona) someone, such a one; (cosa) something, such a thing ♦ adv: ~ **como** (igual) just as ♦ conj: **con ~ de que** provided that; ~ **vez** perhaps; ~ **como** such as; ~ **para cual** (dos iguales) two of a kind; ~ **cual** (como es) just as it is; **¿qué ~?** how are things?; **¿qué ~ te gusta?** how do you like it?

taladrar vt to drill ❏ **taladro** nm drill

talante nm (humor) mood; (voluntad) will, willingness

talar vt to fell, cut down; (devastar) to devastate

talco nm (polvos) talcum powder

talego nm sack

talento nm talent; (capacidad) ability

talismán nm talisman

talla nf (estatura, fig, MED) height, stature; (palo) measuring rod; (ARTE) carving; (medida) size

tallado, -a adj carved ♦ nm carving

tallar vt (madera) to carve; (metal etc) to engrave; (medir) to measure

tallarines nmpl noodles

talle nm (ANAT) waist; (fig) appearance; (RPI: talla) size

taller nm (TEC) workshop; (de artista) studio

tallo nm (de planta) stem; (de hierba) blade; (brote) shoot

talón nm (ANAT) heel; (COM) counterfoil; (ESP: cheque) check (US), cheque (BRIT)

talonario nm (de cheques) checkbook (US), chequebook (BRIT); (de recibos) receipt book

tamaño, -a adj (tan grande) such a big; (tan pequeño) such a small ♦ nm size; **de ~ natural** full-size

tamarindo nm tamarind

tambalearse vr (persona) to stagger; (vehículo) to sway

también adv (igualmente) also, too, as well; (además) besides

tambor nm drum; (ANAT) eardrum ▶ **tambor del freno** brake drum

tamiz nm sieve ❏ **tamizar** vt to sieve

tampoco adv nor, neither; **yo ~ lo compré** I didn't buy it either

tampón nm tampon

tan adv so; **~ es así que ...** so much so that ...

tanda nf (gen) series; (turno) shift

tangente nf tangent

Tánger n Tangier(s)

tangerina (LAm) nf tangerine

tangible adj tangible

tanque nm (cisterna, MIL) tank; (AUTO) tanker; (LAm: bombona) cylinder

tantear vt (calcular) to reckon (up); (medir) to take the measure of; (probar) to test, try out; (tomar la medida: persona) to take the measurements of; (situación) to weigh up; (persona: opinión) to sound out ♦ vi (DEPORTE) to score ❏ **tanteo** nm (cálculo) (rough) calculation; (prueba) test, trial; (DEPORTE) scoring

tanto, -a adj (cantidad) so much, as much ♦ adv (cantidad) so much, as much; (tiempo) so long, as long ♦ nm (suma) certain amount; (proporción) so much; (punto) point; (gol) goal ♦ conj: **en ~ que** while ♦ pron: **cada uno paga ~** each one pays so much; **~ tú como yo** both you and I; **20 y ~s** 20-odd; **hasta ~ (que)** until such time as; **un ~ perezoso** somewhat lazy; **~s** so many, as many; **~ como eso** as much as that; **~ más ... cuanto que** all the more ... because; **~ mejor/peor** so much the better/the worse; **~ si viene como si va** whether he comes or whether he goes; **~ es así que** so much so that; **por o por lo ~** therefore; **me he vuelto ronco de o con ~ hablar** I have become hoarse with so much talking; **a ~s de agosto** on such and such a day in August

tap (MÉX) nm tap dancing

tapa nf (de caja, olla) lid; (CS: de botella) top; (de libro) cover; (ESP: comida) snack

tapadera nf lid, cover

tapar vt (cubrir) to cover; (envolver) to wrap o cover up; (vista) to obstruct; (persona, falta) to conceal; (MÉX, CAm: diente) to fill; **taparse** vr to wrap o.s. up

taparrabo nm loincloth

tapete nm table cover; (MÉX: alfombra) rug

tapia nf (garden) wall ❏ **tapiar** vt to wall in

tapicería nf tapestry; (para muebles) upholstery; (tienda) upholsterer's (shop)

tapiz nm (alfombra) carpet; (tela tejida) tapestry ❏ **tapizar** vt (muebles) to upholster; (MÉX: empapelar) to paper

tapón nm (de botella) top; (de lavabo) plug ▶ **tapón de rosca** screw-top

taquigrafía nf shorthand, stenography (US) ❏ **taquígrafo, -a** nm/f shorthand writer, stenographer (US)

taquilla nf (ESP: donde se compra) ticket o booking (BRIT) office; (suma recogida) take (US), takings pl (BRIT) ❏ **taquillero, -a** adj: **función taquillera** box office success ♦ nm/f ticket clerk

tara nf (defecto) defect; (COM) tare

tarántula nf tarantula

tararear vi to hum

tardar vi (tomar tiempo) to take a long time; (llegar tarde) to be late; (demorar) to delay; **¿tarda mucho el tren?** does the train take (very) long?; **a más ~** at the latest; **no tardes en venir** come soon

tarde adv late ♦ nf (de día) afternoon; (al anochecer) evening; **de ~ en ~** from time to time; **¡buenas ~s!** good afternoon!; **a o por la ~** in the afternoon; in the evening

tardío, -a *adj* (*retrasado*) late; (*lento*) slow (to arrive)

tarea *nf* task; (*faena*) chore; (*ESCOL*) homework

tarifa *nf* (*lista de precios*) price list; (*precio*) tariff

tarima *nf* (*plataforma*) platform

tarjeta *nf* card ▶ **tarjeta postal/de crédito/de Navidad** postcard/credit card/ Christmas card

tarro *nm* jar, pot; (*MÉX: taza*) mug

tarta *nf* (*ESP: pastel*) cake; (*de base dura*) tart

tartamudear *vi* to stammer
□ **tartamudo, -a** *adj* stammering ♦ *nm/f* stammerer

tártaro, -a *adj*: **salsa tártara** tartar(e) sauce

tasa *nf* (*precio*) (fixed) price, rate; (*valoración*) valuation, appraisal; (*medida, norma*) measure, standard ▶ **tasa de cambio/ interés** exchange/interest rate ▶ **tasas de aeropuerto** airport tax ▶ **tasas universitarias** university fees □ **tasación** *nf* valuation, appraisal (*US*) □ **tasador, a** *nm/f* appraiser (*US*), valuer (*BRIT*)

tasar *vt* (*arreglar el precio*) to fix a price for; (*valorar*) to value, assess

tasca (*fam*) *nf* bar, pub (*BRIT*)

tatarabuelo, -a *nm/f* great-great-grandfather(-mother)

tatuaje *nm* (*dibujo*) tattoo; (*acto*) tattooing

tatuar *vt* to tattoo

taurino, -a *adj* bullfighting *cpd*

Tauro *nm* Taurus

tauromaquia *nf* tauromachy, (art of) bullfighting

taxi *nm* taxi

taxista *nmf* taxi *o* cab (*US*) driver

taza *nf* cup; (*de retrete*) bowl; **~ para café** coffee cup ▶ **taza de café** cup of coffee □ **tazón** *nm* (*taza grande*) mug, large cup; (*de fuente*) basin

te *pron* (*complemento de objeto*) you; (*complemento indirecto*) (to) you; (*reflexivo*) (to) yourself; **¿te duele mucho el brazo?** does your arm hurt a lot?; **te equivocas** you're wrong; **¡cálmate!** calm down!

té *nm* tea

tea *nf* torch

teatral *adj* theater *cpd* (*US*), theatre *cpd* (*BRIT*); (*fig*) theatrical

teatro *nm* theater (*US*), theatre (*BRIT*); (*LITERATURA*) plays *pl*, drama

tebeo (*ESP*) *nm* comic book (*US*), (children's) comic (*BRIT*)

techo *nm* (*externo*) roof; (*interno*) ceiling

▶ **techo corredizo** sunroof

tecla *nf* key □ **teclado** *nm* keyboard □ **teclear** *vi* (*MÚS*) to strum; (*con los dedos*) to tap ♦ *vt* (*INFORM*) to key in

técnica *nf* technique; (*tecnología*) technology; *ver tb* **técnico**

técnico, -a *adj* technical ♦ *nm/f* technician; (*experto*) expert

tecnología *nf* technology ▶ **tecnología inalámbrica** wireless technology □ **tecnológico, -a** *adj* technological

tecolote (*MÉX*) *nm* owl

tedio *nm* boredom, tedium □ **tedioso, -a** *adj* boring, tedious

teja *nf* tile; (*BOT*) lime (tree) □ **tejado** *nm* (tiled) roof

tejemaneje *nm* (*lío*) fuss; (*intriga*) intrigue

tejer *vt* to weave; (*hacer punto*) to knit; (*fig*) to fabricate □ **tejido** *nm* (*tela*) material, fabric; (*telaraña*) web; (*ANAT*) tissue

tel *abr* (= *teléfono*) tel

tela *nf* (*tejido*) material; (*telaraña*) web; (*en líquido*) skin □ **telar** *nm* (*máquina*) loom

telaraña *nf* cobweb

tele (*fam*) *nf* tube (*US*), telly (*BRIT*)

tele... *prefijo* tele... □ **telecomunicación** *nf* telecommunication □ **telecontrol** *nm* remote control □ **telediario** *nm* television news □ **teledifusión** *nf* (television) broadcast □ **teledirigido, -a** *adj* remote-controlled

teléf *abr* (= *teléfono*) tel

teleférico *nm* (*de esquí*) ski-lift

telefonear *vi* to telephone

telefónico, -a *adj* telephone *cpd*

telefonillo *nm* (*de puerta*) intercom

telefonista *nmf* telephonist

teléfono *nm* (tele)phone; **estar hablando al ~** to be on the phone; **llamar a algn por ~** to phone *o* ring (*BRIT*) sb (up) ▶ **teléfono con cámara** camera phone ▶ **teléfono celular** (*LAm*) cellphone ▶ **teléfono inalámbrico** cordless phone ▶ **teléfono móvil** (*ESP*) cellphone

telegrafía *nf* telegraphy

telégrafo *nm* telegraph

telegrama *nm* telegram

tele: □ **teleimpresor** *nm* teletypewriter (*US*), teleprinter (*BRIT*) □ **telenovela** *nf* soap (opera) □ **teleobjetivo** *nm* telephoto lens □ **telepatía** *nf* telepathy □ **telepático, -a** *adj* telepathic □ **telescópico, -a** *adj* telescopic □ **telescopio** *nm* telescope □ **telesilla** *nm* chairlift

❏ **telespectador, a** nm/f viewer
❏ **telesquí** nm ski-lift ❏ **teletarjeta** nf phonecard ❏ **teletipo** nm teletype
❏ **teletrabajador, a** nm/f teleworker
❏ **teletrabajo** nm teleworking
❏ **televentas** nfpl telesales
televidente nmf viewer
televisar vt to televise
televisión nf television ▸ **televisión digital** digital television
televisor nm television set
télex nm inv telex
telón nm curtain ▸ **telón de acero** (POL) iron curtain ▸ **telón de fondo** backcloth, background
tema nm (asunto) subject, topic; (MÚS) theme ❏ **temática** nf (social, histórica, artística) range of topics ❏ **temático, -a** adj thematic
temblar vi to shake, tremble; (por frío) to shiver ❏ **temblón, -ona** adj shaking ❏ **temblor** nm trembling; (de tierra) earthquake ❏ **tembloroso, -a** adj trembling
temer vt to fear ♦ vi to be afraid; **temo que llegue tarde** I am afraid he may be late
temerario, -a adj (descuidado) reckless; (irreflexivo) hasty ❏ **temeridad** nf (imprudencia) rashness; (audacia) boldness
temeroso, -a adj (miedoso) fearful; (que inspira temor) frightful
temible adj fearsome
temor nm (miedo) fear; (duda) suspicion
témpano nm (tb: ~ de hielo) ice-floe
temperamento nm temperament
temperatura nf temperature
tempestad nf storm ❏ **tempestuoso, -a** adj stormy
templado, -a adj (moderado) moderate; (frugal) frugal; (agua) lukewarm; (clima) mild; (MÚS) well-tuned ❏ **templanza** nf moderation; mildness
templar vt (moderar) to moderate; (furia) to restrain; (calor) to reduce; (afinar) to tune (up); (acero) to temper; (tuerca) to tighten up ❏ **temple** nm (ajuste) tempering; (afinación) tuning; (pintura) tempera
templo nm (iglesia) church; (pagano etc) temple
temporada nf time, period; (estación) season
temporal adj (no permanente) temporary ♦ nm storm
tempranero, -a adj (BOT) early; (persona) early-rising

temprano, -a adj early; (demasiado pronto) too soon, too early
ten vb ver **tener**
tenaces adj pl ver **tenaz**
tenacidad nf tenacity; (dureza) toughness; (terquedad) stubbornness
tenacillas nfpl tongs; (para el pelo) curling irons (US), curling tongs (BRIT); (MED) forceps
tenaz adj (material) tough; (persona) tenacious; (creencia, resistencia) stubborn
tenaza(s) nf(pl) (MED) forceps; (TEC) pliers; (ZOOL) pincers
tendedero nm (para ropa) drying place; (cuerda) clothes line
tendencia nf tendency; **tener ~ a** to tend to, have a tendency to ❏ **tendencioso, -a** adj tendentious
tender vt (extender) to spread out; (colgar) to hang out; (vía férrea, cable) to lay; (estirar) to stretch ♦ vi: **~ a** to tend to, have a tendency towards; **tenderse** vr to lie down; **~ la cama/mesa** (LAm) to make the bed/set (US) o lay (BRIT) the table
tenderete nm (puesto) stall; (exposición) display of goods
tendero, -a nm/f storekeeper (US), shopkeeper (BRIT)
tendido, -a adj (acostado) lying down, flat; (colgado) hanging ♦ nm (TAUR) front rows of seats; **a galope ~** flat out
tendón nm tendon
tendré etc vb ver **tener**
tenebroso, -a adj (oscuro) dark; (fig) gloomy
tenedor nm (CULIN) fork ▸ **tenedor de libros** book-keeper
tenencia nf (de casa) tenancy; (de oficio) tenure; (de propiedad) possession

---

tener

PALABRA CLAVE

vt

1 (poseer, gen) to have; (en la mano) to hold; **¿tienes un boli?** have you got a pen?; **va a tener un niño** she's going to have a baby; **¡ten** (o **tenga**)!, **¡aquí tienes** (o **tiene**)!** here you are!

2 (edad, medidas) to be; **tiene 7 años** she's 7 (years old); **tiene 15 cm de largo** it's 15 cm long; ver **calor, hambre** etc

3 (considerar): **lo tengo por inteligente** I consider him to be intelligent; **tener en mucho a algn** to think very highly of sb

4 (+ pp: = pretérito): **tengo terminada ya la mitad del trabajo** I've done half the work already

5: **tener que hacer algo** to have to do sth; **tengo que acabar este trabajo hoy** I have to finish this job today

6: **¿qué tienes, estás enfermo?** what's the matter with you, are you sick?

♦ **tenerse** vr

1: **tenerse en pie** to stand up

2: **tenerse por** to think o.s.; **se tiene por muy listo** he thinks himself very clever

tengo etc vb ver **tener**

tenia nf tapeworm

teniente nm (rango) lieutenant; (ayudante) deputy

tenis nm tennis ▶ **tenis de mesa** table tennis ❑ **tenista** nmf tennis player

tenor nm (sentido) meaning; (MÚS) tenor; **a ~ de** on the lines of

tensar vt to tighten; (arco) to draw

tensión nf tension; (TEC) stress; **tener la ~ alta** to have high blood pressure ▶ **tensión arterial** blood pressure

tenso, -a adj tense

tentación nf temptation

tentáculo nm tentacle

tentador, a adj tempting

tentar vt (seducir) to tempt; (atraer) to attract ❑ **tentativa** nf attempt ▶ **tentativa de asesinato** attempted murder

tentempié nm snack

tenue adj (delgado) thin, slender; (neblina) light; (lazo, vínculo) slight

teñir vt to dye; (fig) to tinge; **teñirse** vr to dye; **~se el pelo** to dye one's hair

teología nf theology

teoría nf theory; **en ~** in theory ❑ **teóricamente** adv theoretically ❑ **teórico, -a** adj theoretic(al) ♦ nm/f theoretician, theorist ❑ **teorizar** vi to theorize

Teotihuacán nm Teotihuacán

TEOTIHUACÁN

The city of **Teotihuacán**, located towards the northeast of Mexico City, was the largest city in all the Americas in pre-Columbian times. It is not known when the city was built, but it is thought to be over 2,000 years old.

terapéutico, -a adj therapeutic

terapia nf therapy

tercer adj ver **tercero**

tercermundista adj Third World cpd

tercero, -a adj (tercer: delante de nmsg) third ♦ nm (JUR) third party

terceto nm trio

terciar vi (participar) to take part; (hacer de árbitro) to mediate; **terciarse** vr to come up ❑ **terciario, -a** adj tertiary

tercio nm third

terciopelo nm velvet

terco, -a adj obstinate

tergal® nm type of polyester

tergiversar vt to distort

termal adj thermal

termas nfpl hot springs

térmico, -a adj thermal

terminación nf (final) end; (conclusión) conclusion, ending

terminal adj, nf (MÉX) o m (LAm exc MÉX, ESP) terminal

terminante adj (final) final, definitive; (tajante) categorical ❑ **terminantemente** adv: **terminantemente prohibido** strictly forbidden

terminar vt (completar) to complete, finish; (concluir) to end ♦ vi (llegar a su fin) to end; (parar) to stop; (acabar) to finish; **terminarse** vr to come to an end; **~ por hacer algo** to end up (by) doing sth

término nm end, conclusion; (parada) terminus; (límite) boundary; **en último ~** (a fin de cuentas) in the last analysis; (como último recurso) as a last resort ▶ **término medio** average; (fig) middle way

terminología nf terminology

termodinámico, -a adj thermodynamic

termómetro nm thermometer

termonuclear adj thermonuclear

termo(s)® nm Thermos®

termostato nm thermostat

ternero, -a nm/f (animal) calf ♦ nf (carne) veal

ternura nf (trato) tenderness; (palabra) endearment; (cariño) fondness

terquedad nf obstinacy

terrado nm terrace

terraplén nm embankment

terrateniente nmf landowner

terraza nf (balcón) balcony; (tejado) (flat) roof; (AGR) terrace

terremoto nm earthquake

terrenal adj earthly

terreno nm (tierra) land; (parcela) plot; (suelo) soil; (fig) field; **un ~** a piece of land

terrestre adj terrestrial; (ruta) land cpd

terrible *adj* terrible, awful

territorio *nm* territory

terrón *nm (de azúcar)* lump; *(de tierra)* clod, lump

terror *nm* terror ❑ **terrorífico, -a** *adj* terrifying ❑ **terrorista** *adj, nmf* terrorist ▶ **terrorista suicida** suicide bomber

terso, -a *adj (liso)* smooth; *(pulido)* polished ❑ **tersura** *nf* smoothness

tertulia *nf (reunión informal)* social gathering; *(grupo)* group, circle

tesis *nf inv* thesis

tesón *nm (firmeza)* firmness; *(tenacidad)* tenacity

tesorero, -a *nm/f* treasurer

tesoro *nm* treasure; *(COM, POL)* treasury

testaferro *nm* figurehead

testamentario, -a *adj* testamentary ♦ *nm/f* executor/executrix

testamento *nm* will

testar *vi* to make a will

testarudo, -a *adj* stubborn

testículo *nm* testicle

testificar *vt* to testify; *(fig)* to attest ♦ *vi* to give evidence

testigo *nmf* witness ▶ **testigo de cargo/descargo** witness for the prosecution/defense *(US) o* defence *(BRIT)* ▶ **testigo ocular** eye witness

testimoniar *vt* to testify to; *(fig)* to show ❑ **testimonio** *nm* testimony

teta *nf (de biberón)* nipple *(US)*, teat *(BRIT)*; *(ANAT: fam)* breast

tétanos *nm* tetanus

tetera *nf* teapot

tétrico, -a *adj* gloomy, dismal

textil *adj* textile

texto *nm* text ❑ **textual** *adj* textual

textura *nf (de tejido)* texture

tez *nf (cutis)* complexion

ti *pron* you; *(reflexivo)* yourself

tía *nf (pariente)* aunt

tibieza *nf (temperatura)* tepidness; *(actitud)* coolness ❑ **tibio, -a** *adj* lukewarm

tiburón *nm* shark

tic *nm (ruido)* click; *(de reloj)* tick ▶ **tic nervioso** nervous tic

tictac *nm (de reloj)* ticktock

tiempo *nm* time; *(época, período)* age, period; *(METEOROLOGÍA)* weather; *(LING)* tense; *(DEPORTE)* half; **a ~** in time; **a un o al mismo ~** at the same time; **al poco ~** very soon (after); **se quedó poco ~** he didn't stay very long; **hace poco ~** not long ago; **mucho ~** a long time;

de ~ en ~ from time to time; **hace buen/mal ~** the weather is fine/bad; **estar a ~** to be in time; **hace ~** some time ago; **hacer ~** to while away the time; **motor de 2 ~s** two-stroke engine; **primer ~** first half

tienda *nf* store *(US)*, shop *(BRIT)* ▶ **tienda de abarrotes** *(MÉX, CAm)* grocery store *(US)*, grocer's *(BRIT)* ▶ **tienda de alimentación o comestibles** grocery store *(US)*, grocer's *(BRIT)* ▶ **tienda de campaña** *(ESP)* tent

tienes *etc vb ver* **tener**

tienta *etc vb ver* **tentar** ♦ *nf:* **andar a ~s** to grope one's way along

tiento *etc vb ver* **tentar** ♦ *nm (tacto)* touch; *(precaución)* wariness

tierno, -a *adj (blando)* tender; *(fresco)* fresh; *(amable)* sweet

tierra *nf* earth; *(suelo)* soil; *(mundo)* earth, world; *(país)* country, land; **~ adentro** inland

tieso, -a *adj (rígido)* rigid; *(duro)* stiff; *(fam: orgulloso)* conceited

tiesto *nm* flowerpot

tifoidea *nf* typhoid

tifón *nm* typhoon

tifus *nm* typhus

tigre *nm* tiger

tijera *nf* scissors *pl*; *(ZOOL)* claw; **~s** *nfpl* scissors; *(para plantas)* shears

tijeretear *vt* to snip

tila *nf* lime blossom tea

tildar *vt:* **~ de** to brand as

tilde *nf (TIP)* tilde

tilín *nm* tinkle

tilo *nm* lime tree

timar *vt (estafar)* to swindle

timbal *nm* small drum

timbrar *vt* to stamp

timbre *nm (MÉX: sello)* stamp; *(campanilla)* bell; *(tono)* timbre; *(COM)* revenue stamp *(US)*, stamp duty *(BRIT)*

timidez *nf* shyness ❑ **tímido, -a** *adj* shy

timo *nm* swindle

timón *nm* helm, rudder ❑ **timonel** *nm* helmsman

tímpano *nm (ANAT)* eardrum; *(MÚS)* small drum

tina *nf* tub; *(LAm: baño)* bath(tub) ❑ **tinaja** *nf* large jar

tinglado *nm (cobertizo)* shed; *(fig: truco)* trick; *(intriga)* intrigue

tinieblas *nfpl* darkness *sg*; *(sombras)* shadows

tino *nm (habilidad)* skill; *(juicio)* insight

tinta *nf* ink; *(TEC)* dye; *(ARTE)* color *(US)*, colour *(BRIT)*

tinte nm dye

tintero nm inkwell, ink bottle (US)

tintinear vt to tinkle

tinto nm red wine

tintorería nf dry cleaner's

tintura nf (QUÍM) dye; (farmacéutico) tincture

tío nm (pariente) uncle

tiovivo (ESP) nm carousel, merry-go-round

típico, -a adj typical

tipo nm (clase) type, kind; (hombre) guy, bloke (BRIT); (ANAT: de hombre) build; (: de mujer) figure; (IMPRENTA) type ▶ **tipo bancario/de descuento/de interés/de cambio** bank/ discount/interest/exchange rate

tipografía nf printing cpd
❑ **tipográfico, -a** adj printing cpd

tíquet (pl ~s) nm ticket; (en tienda) receipt, cash slip

tiquismiquis nm inv fussy person ♦ nmpl (querellas) squabbling sg; (escrúpulos) silly scruples

tira nf strip; (fig) abundance ♦ nmf (MÉX: fam) cop; **~ y afloja** (LAm exc MÉX, ESP) give and take

tirabuzón nm (rizo) curl

tirachinas (LAm exc MÉX, ESP) nm inv slingshot (US), catapult (BRIT)

tirada nf (acto) cast, throw; (serie) series; (TIP) printing, edition; **de una ~** at one go

tirado, -a adj (barato) dirt-cheap; (fam: fácil) very easy

tirador nm (mango) handle; ~es nmpl (RPl: tirantes) suspenders (US), braces (BRIT)

tiranía nf tyranny ❑ **tirano, -a** adj tyrannical ♦ nm/f tyrant

tirante adj (cuerda etc) tight, taut; (relaciones) strained ♦ nm (ARQ) brace; (TEC) stay; ~s nmpl (de pantalón) suspenders (US), braces (BRIT) ❑ **tirantez** nf tightness; (fig) tension

tirar vt to throw; (dejar caer) to drop; (volcar) to upset; (derribar) to knock down o over; (desechar) to throw out o away; (dinero) to squander; (imprimir) to print ♦ vi (disparar) to shoot; (CS, ESP: de la puerta etc) to pull; (fam: andar) to go; (tender a, buscar realizar) to tend to; (DEPORTE) to shoot; **tirarse** vr to throw o.s.; **~ abajo** to bring down, destroy; **tira más a su padre** he takes more after his father; **ir tirando** to manage; **a todo ~** at the most

tirita (ESP) nf Bandaid® (US), (sticking) plaster (BRIT)

tiritar vi to shiver

tiro nm (lanzamiento) throw; (disparo) shot; (DEPORTE) shot; (GOLF, TENIS) drive; (alcance) range; **~ al blanco** target practice; **caballo de ~** cart-horse; **andar de ~s largos** to be all dressed up

tirón nm (CS, ESP: sacudida) pull, tug; **de un ~** in one go, all at once

tiroteo nm exchange of shots, shooting

tísico, -a adj consumptive

tisis nf inv consumption, tuberculosis

títere nm puppet

titiritero, -a nm/f puppeteer

titubeante adj (al andar) shaky, tottering; (al hablar) stammering; (dudoso) hesitant

titubear vi to stagger; to stammer; (fig) to hesitate ❑ **titubeo** nm staggering; stammering; hesitation

titulado, -a adj (libro) entitled; (persona) titled

titular adj titular ♦ nmf holder ♦ nm headline ♦ vt to title; **titularse** vr to be entitled ❑ **título** nm title; (de diario) headline; (certificado) professional qualification; (universitario) (university) degree; **a título de** in the capacity of

tiza nf chalk

tiznar vt to blacken

tizón nm brand

toalla nf towel ▶ **toalla higiénica** (LAm) sanitary napkin (US) o towel (BRIT)

tobillo nm ankle

tobogán nm (en parque) slide; (en piscina) chute, slide

tocadiscos nm inv record player

tocado, -a adj (fam) touched ♦ nm headdress

tocador nm (mueble) dressing table; (cuarto) boudoir; (fam) ladies' room o toilet (BRIT)

tocante: **~ a** prep with regard to

tocar vt to touch; (MÚS) to play; (referirse a) to allude to; (timbre) to ring ♦ vi (a la puerta) to knock (on o at the door); (ser de turno) to fall to, be the turn of; (ser hora) to be due; **tocarse** vr (cubrirse la cabeza) to cover one's head; (tener contacto) to touch (each other); **por lo que a mí me toca** as far as I am concerned; **te toca a ti** it's your turn

tocayo, -a nm/f namesake

tocino (LAm) nm bacon

todavía adv (aun) even; (aún) still, yet; **~ más** yet more; **~ no** not yet

---

todo, -a

PALABRA CLAVE

adj

1 (con artículo sg) all; **toda la carne** all the meat; **toda la noche** all night, the whole night; **todo el libro** the whole book; **toda una botella** a whole bottle; **todo lo contrario** quite the opposite; **está toda sucia** she's all dirty; **por todo el país** throughout the whole country

2 (*con artículo pl*) all; every; **todos los libros** all the books; **todas las noches** every night; **todos los que quieran salir** all those who want to leave

♦ *pron*

1 everything, all; **todos** everyone, everybody; **lo sabemos todo** we know everything; **todos querían más tiempo** everybody o everyone wanted more time; **nos marchamos todos** all of us left

2: **con todo: con todo él me sigue gustando** even so I still like him

♦ *adv* all; **vaya todo seguido** keep straight on o ahead

♦ *nm*: **como un todo** as a whole; **del todo: no me agrada del todo** I don't entirely like it

todopoderoso, -a *adj* all powerful; (*REL*) almighty

Todos Santos Cuchumatán *nm* Todos Santos Cuchumatán

TODOS SANTOS CUCHUMATÁN

The people of **Todos Santos Cuchumatán**, situated in the mountains of Guatemala, celebrate All Saints' Day with a famous horse race. On November 1st, the men of the town, who prepare for the race by drinking huge quantities of beer and brandy the previous night, pay to run in the race which begins at eight o'clock in the morning and finishes without any winners at dusk.

todoterreno *nm inv* SUV, four-wheel drive

toga *nf* toga; (*ESCOL*) gown

Tokio *n* Tokyo

toldo *nm* (*en tienda, balcón*) awning; (*para el sol*) parasol, sunshade; (*para fiesta*) garden tent (*US*), marquee (*BRIT*)

tolerancia *nf* tolerance ◻ **tolerante** *adj* (*sociedad*) liberal; (*persona*) open-minded

tolerar *vt* to tolerate; (*resistir*) to endure

toma *nf* (*acto*) taking; (*MED*) dose ▶ **toma de corriente** socket ◻ **tomacorriente** (*LAm*) *nm* socket

tomar *vt* to take; (*aspecto*) to take on; (*beber*) to drink ♦ *vi* to take; (*LAm: beber*) to drink; **tomarse** *vr* to take; **~se por** to consider o.s. to be; **~ a bien/a mal** to take well/badly; **~ en serio** to take seriously; **~ el pelo a algn** to pull sb's leg; **~la con algn** to pick a quarrel with sb; **¡tome!** here you are!; **~ el sol** to sunbathe

tomate *nm* tomato

tomillo *nm* thyme

tomo *nm* (*libro*) volume

ton *abr* = **tonelada** ♦ *nm*: **sin ~ ni son** without rhyme or reason

tonada *nf* tune

tonalidad *nf* tone

tonel *nm* barrel

tonelada *nf* ton ◻ **tonelaje** *nm* tonnage

tónica *nf* (*MÚS*) tonic; (*fig*) keynote

tónico, -a *adj* tonic ♦ *nm* (*MED*) tonic

tonificar *vt* to tone up

tono *nm* tone; **fuera de ~** inappropriate; **darse ~** to put on airs

tontería *nf* (*estupidez*) foolishness; (*cosa*) stupid thing; (*acto*) foolish act; **~s** *nfpl* (*disparates*) nonsense *sg*, garbage *sg* (*US*), rubbish *sg* (*BRIT*)

tonto, -a *adj* stupid, silly ♦ *nm/f* fool

topar *vi*: **~ contra** o **en** to run into; **~ con** to run up against

tope *adj* maximum ♦ *nm* (*fin*) end; (*límite*) limit; (*FERRO*) buffer; (*AUTO*) fender (*US*), bumper (*BRIT*); **al ~** end to end

tópico, -a *adj* topical ♦ *nm* platitude

topo *nm* (*ZOOL*) mole; (*fig*) blunderer

topografía *nf* topography ◻ **topógrafo, -a** *nm/f* topographer

toque *etc vb ver* **tocar** ♦ *nm* touch; (*MÚS*) beat; (*de campana*) peal; (*MÉX ELEC*) shock; (: *fam*: *porro*) joint; **dar un ~ a** to warn ▶ **toque de queda** curfew

toqué *etc vb ver* **tocar**

toquetear *vt* to finger

toquilla *nf* (*pañuelo*) headscarf; (*chal*) shawl

tórax *nm* thorax

torbellino *nm* whirlwind; (*fig*) whirl

torcedura *nf* twist; (*MED*) sprain

torcer *vt* to twist; (*la esquina*) to turn; (*MED*) to sprain ♦ *vi* (*desviar*) to turn off; **torcerse** *vr* (*ladearse*) to bend; (*desviarse*) to go astray; (*fracasar*) to go wrong ◻ **torcido, -a** *adj* twisted; (*fig*) crooked ♦ *nm* curl

tordo, -a *adj* dappled ♦ *nm* thrush

torear *vt* (*fig: evadir*) to avoid; (*jugar con*) to tease ♦ *vi* to fight bulls ◻ **toreo** *nm* bullfighting ◻ **torero, -a** *nm/f* bullfighter

tormenta *nf* storm; (*fig: confusión*) turmoil

tormento *nm* torture; (*fig*) anguish

tornar *vt* (*devolver*) to return, give back; (*transformar*) to transform ♦ *vi* to go back; **tornarse** *vr* (*ponerse*) to become

tornasolado, -a *adj* (*brillante*) iridescent; (*reluciente*) shimmering

torneo *nm* tournament

tornillo nm screw

torniquete nm (MED) tourniquet

torno nm (TEC) winch; (tambor) drum; **en ~ (a)** round, about

toro nm bull; (fam) he-man; **los ~s** bullfighting

toronja (LAm) nf grapefruit, pomelo (US)

torpe adj (poco hábil) clumsy, awkward; (necio) dim; (lento) slow

torpedo nm torpedo

torpeza nf (falta de agilidad) clumsiness; (lentitud) slowness; (error) mistake

torre nf tower; (de petróleo) derrick

torrefacto, -a adj roasted

torrente nm torrent

tórrido, -a adj torrid

torrija nf French toast

torsión nf twisting

torso nm torso

torta nf (LAm: pastel) pie; (MÉX: de pan) filled roll

tortícolis nm inv stiff neck

tortilla nf omelette; (LAm: de maíz) maize pancake ▶ **tortilla de papas** (LAm) potato omelette ▶ **tortilla de patatas** (ESP) potato omelette ▶ **tortilla francesa** (ESP) plain omelette

tórtola nf turtledove

tortuga nf tortoise

tortuoso, -a adj winding

tortura nf torture ▢ **torturar** vt to torture

tos nf cough ▶ **tos ferina** whooping cough

tosco, -a adj coarse

toser vi to cough

tostada (LAm exc MÉX, ESP) nf piece of toast ▢ **tostado, -a** adj toasted; (por el sol) dark brown; (piel) tanned

tostador (ESP) nm toaster ▢ **tostadora** (LAm) nf toaster

tostar vt to toast; (café) to roast; (persona) to tan; **tostarse** vr to get brown

total adj total ♦ adv in short; (al fin y al cabo) when all is said and done ♦ nm total; **~ que** to make (US) o cut (BRIT) a long story short

totalidad nf whole

totalitario, -a adj totalitarian

tóxico, -a adj toxic ♦ nm poison ▢ **toxicómano, -a** nm/f drug addict

toxina nf toxin

tozudo, -a adj obstinate

traba nf bond, tie; (cadena) shackle

trabajador, a adj hard-working ♦ nm/f worker

trabajar vt to work; (AGR) to till; (empeñarse en) to work at; (convencer) to persuade ♦ vi to work; (esforzarse) to strive ▢ **trabajo** nm work; (tarea) task; (POL) labor (US), labour (BRIT); (fig) effort; **tomarse el trabajo de** to take the trouble to; **trabajo por turno/a destajo** shift work/piecework ▢ **trabajoso, -a** adj hard

trabalenguas nm inv tongue twister

trabar vt (juntar) to join, unite; (atar) to tie down, fetter; (agarrar) to seize; (amistad) to strike up; **trabarse** vr to become entangled; **se le traba la lengua** he gets tongue-tied

tracción nf traction ▶ **tracción delantera/ trasera** front-wheel/rear-wheel drive

tractor nm tractor

tradición nf tradition ▢ **tradicional** adj traditional

traducción nf translation

traducir vt to translate ▢ **traductor, a** nm/f translator

traer vt to bring; (llevar) to carry; (llevar puesto) to wear; (incluir) to carry; (causar) to cause; **traerse** vr: **~se algo** to be up to sth

traficar vi to trade

tráfico nm (COM) trade; (AUTO) traffic

tragaluz nm skylight

tragamonedas (LAm) nm inv slot machine

tragar vt to swallow; (devorar) to devour, bolt down; (RPl: fam: estudiar) to grind away (US), swot (BRIT); **tragarse** vr to swallow

tragedia nf tragedy ▢ **trágico, -a** adj tragic

trago nm (líquido) drink; (bocado) gulp; (fam: de bebida) swig; (desgracia) blow

traición nf treachery; (JUR) treason; (una traición) act of treachery ▢ **traicionar** vt to betray

traicionero, -a adj treacherous

traidor, a adj treacherous ♦ nm/f traitor

traigo etc vb ver **traer**

trailero, -a (MÉX) nm/f truck (US) o lorry (BRIT) driver

traje vb ver **traer** ♦ nm (de hombre) suit; (de mujer) dress; (vestido típico) costume ▶ **traje de baño** swimsuit ▶ **traje de luces** bullfighter's costume

trajera etc vb ver **traer**

trajín nm (fam: movimiento) bustle ▢ **trajinar** vi (moverse) to bustle about

trama nf (intriga) plot; (de tejido) weft ▢ **tramar** vt to plot; (TEC) to weave

tramitar vt (asunto) to transact; (negociar) to negotiate

trámite nm (paso) step; (JUR) transaction; **~s** nmpl (burocracia) procedure sg; (JUR) proceedings

tramo nm (de tierra) plot; (de escalera) flight; (de vía) section

tramoya nf (TEATRO) piece of stage machinery ☐ **tramoyista** nmf scene shifter; (fig) trickster

trampa nf trap; (en el suelo) trapdoor; (truco) trick; (engaño) fiddle ☐ **trampear** vt, vi to cheat

trampolín nm (de piscina etc) diving board

tramposo, -a adj crooked, cheating ♦ nm/f crook, shyster (US)

tranca nf (palo) stick; (de puerta, ventana) bar ☐ **trancar** vt to bar

trance nm (momento difícil) difficult moment o juncture; (estado hipnotizado) trance

tranquilidad nf (calma) calmness, stillness; (paz) peacefulness

tranquilizar vt (calmar) to calm (down); (asegurar) to reassure; **tranquilizarse** vr to calm down ☐ **tranquilo, -a** adj (calmado) calm; (apacible) peaceful; (mar) calm; (mente) untroubled

transacción nf transaction

transbordador nm ferry

transbordar vt to transfer ☐ **transbordo** nm transfer; **hacer transbordo** to change (trains etc)

transcurrir vi (tiempo) to pass; (hecho) to take place

transcurso nm: **~ del tiempo** lapse (of time)

transeúnte nmf passer-by

transferencia nf transference; (COM) transfer

transferir vt to transfer

transformador nm (ELEC) transformer

transformar vt to transform; (convertir) to convert

tránsfuga nmf (MIL) deserter; (POL) turncoat

transfusión nf transfusion

transgénico, -a adj genetically modified, GM

transición nf transition

transigir vi to compromise, make concessions

transitar vi to go (from place to place) ☐ **tránsito** nm transit; (AUTO) traffic ☐ **transitorio, -a** adj transitory

transmisión nf (TEC) transmission; (transferencia) transfer ▶ **transmisión exterior/en directo** outside/live broadcast

transmitir vt to transmit; (RADIO, TV) to broadcast

transparencia nf transparency; (claridad) clearness, clarity; (foto) slide

transparentar vt to reveal ♦ vi to be transparent ☐ **transparente** adj transparent; (claro) clear

transpirar vi to perspire

transportar vt to transport; (llevar) to carry ☐ **transporte** nm transportation (US), transport (BRIT); (COM) haulage

transversal adj transverse, cross

tranvía nm streetcar (US), tram (BRIT)

trapeador (LAm) nm mop ☐ **trapear** (LAm) vt to mop

trapecio nm trapeze ☐ **trapecista** nmf trapeze artist

trapero, -a nm/f ragman

trapicheo (fam) nm scheme, fiddle

trapo nm (tela) rag; (de cocina) cloth

tráquea nf windpipe

traqueteo nm rattling

tras prep (detrás) behind; (después) after

trasatlántico nm (barco) (cabin) cruiser

trascendencia nf (importancia) importance; (FILOSOFÍA) transcendence

trascendental adj important; (FILOSOFÍA) transcendental

trascender vi (noticias) to come out; (suceso) to have a wide effect

trasero, -a adj back, rear ♦ nm (ANAT) bottom

trasfondo nm background

trasgredir vt to contravene

trashumante adj (animales) migrating

trasladar vt to move; (persona) to transfer; (postergar) to postpone; (copiar) to copy; **trasladarse** vr (mudarse) to move ☐ **traslado** nm move; (mudanza) move, removal

traslucir vt to show; **traslucirse** vr to be translucent; (fig) to be revealed

trasluz nm reflected light; **al ~** against o up to the light

trasnochador, a nm/f night owl

trasnochar vi (acostarse tarde) to stay up late

traspapelar vt (documento, carta) to mislay, misplace

traspasar vt (suj: bala etc) to pierce, go through; (propiedad) to sell, transfer; (calle) to cross over; (límites) to go beyond; (ley) to break ☐ **traspaso** nm (venta) transfer, sale

traspatio (LAm) nm backyard

traspié nm (tropezón) trip; (error) blunder

trasplantar *vt* to transplant

traste *nm* (*MÚS*) fret; **~s** *nmpl* (*MÉX, CAm: de cocina*) pots and pans; **dar al ~ con algo** to ruin sth

trastero *nm* storage room

trastienda *nf* back of store (*US*) *o* shop (*BRIT*)

trasto (*pey*) *nm* (*cosa*) piece of junk; (*persona*) dead loss

trastornado, -a *adj* (*loco*) mad, crazy

trastornar *vt* (*fig: planes*) to disrupt; (*: nervios*) to shatter; (*: persona*) to drive crazy; **trastornarse** *vr* (*volverse loco*) to go mad *o* crazy ◻ **trastorno** *nm* (*acto*) overturning; (*confusión*) confusion

tratable *adj* friendly

tratado *nm* (*POL*) treaty; (*COM*) agreement

tratamiento *nm* treatment ▸ **tratamiento de textos** (*INFORM*) word processing *cpd*

tratar *vt* (*ocuparse de*) to treat; (*manejar, TEC*) to handle; (*MED*) to treat; (*dirigirse a: persona*) to address ♦ *vi*: **~ de** (*hablar sobre*) to deal with, be about; (*intentar*) to try to; **tratarse** *vr* to treat each other; **~ con** (*COM*) to trade in; (*negociar*) to negotiate with; (*tener contactos*) to have dealings with; **¿de qué se trata?** what's it about? ◻ **trato** *nm* dealings *pl*; (*relaciones*) relationship; (*comportamiento*) manner; (*COM*) agreement

trauma *nm* trauma

través *nm* (*fig*) reverse; **al ~** across, crossways; **a ~ de** across; (*sobre*) over; (*por*) through

travesaño *nm* (*ARQ*) crossbeam; (*DEPORTE*) crossbar

travesía *nf* (*calle*) cross-street; (*NÁUT*) crossing

travesura *nf* (*broma*) prank; (*ingenio*) wit

traviesa *nf* (*ARQ*) crossbeam

travieso, -a *adj* (*niño*) naughty

trayecto *nm* (*ruta*) road, way; (*viaje*) journey; (*tramo*) stretch ◻ **trayectoria** *nf* trajectory; (*fig*) path

traza *nf* (*aspecto*) looks *pl*; (*señal*) sign ◻ **trazado, -a** *adj*: **bien trazado** shapely, well-formed ♦ *nm* (*ARQ*) plan, design; (*fig*) outline

trazar *vt* (*ARQ*) to plan; (*ARTE*) to sketch; (*fig*) to trace; (*plan*) to draw up ◻ **trazo** *nm* (*línea*) line; (*bosquejo*) sketch

trébol *nm* (*BOT*) clover

trece *num* thirteen

trecho *nm* (*distancia*) distance; (*tiempo*) while; **de ~ en ~** at intervals

tregua *nf* (*MIL*) truce; (*fig*) respite

treinta *num* thirty

tremendo, -a *adj* (*terrible*) terrible; (*imponente: cosa*) imposing; (*fam: fabuloso*) tremendous

trémulo, -a *adj* quivering

tren *nm* train ▸ **tren de aterrizaje** undercarriage

trenca *nf* duffel coat

trenza *nf* (*de pelo*) braid (*US*), plait (*BRIT*) ◻ **trenzar** *vt* (*pelo*) to braid; **trenzarse** *vr* (*LAm: enzarzarse*) to become involved

trepadora *nf* (*BOT*) climber

trepar *vt, vi* to climb

trepidante *adj* (*acción*) fast; (*ritmo*) hectic

tres *num* three

tresillo *nm* (*ESP*) three-piece set (*US*) *o* suite (*BRIT*); (*MÚS*) triplet

treta *nf* trick

triángulo *nm* triangle

tribu *nf* tribe

tribuna *nf* (*plataforma*) platform; (*DEPORTE*) (grand)stand

tribunal *nm* (*JUR*) court; (*comisión, fig*) tribunal

tributar *vt* (*gen*) to pay ◻ **tributo** *nm* (*COM*) tax

tricotar *vi* to knit

trigal *nm* wheat field

trigo *nm* wheat

trigueño, -a *adj* (*pelo*) corn-colored (*US*), corn-coloured (*BRIT*)

trillado, -a *adj* threshed; (*asunto*) trite, hackneyed ◻ **trilladora** *nf* threshing machine

trillar *vt* (*AGR*) to thresh

trimestral *adj* quarterly; (*ESCOL*) termly

trimestre *nm* (*ESCOL*) term

trinar *vi* (*pájaros*) to sing; (*rabiar*) to fume, be angry

trinchar *vt* to carve

trinchera *nf* (*fosa*) trench

trineo *nm* sled

trinidad *nf* trio; (*REL*): **la T~** the Trinity

trino *nm* trill

tripa *nf* (*ANAT*) intestine; (*fam: tb: ~s*) insides *pl*

triple *adj* triple

triplicado, -a *adj*: **por ~** in triplicate

tripulación *nf* crew

tripulante *nmf* crewman(-woman)

tripular *vt* (*barco*) to man; (*AUTO*) to drive

triquiñuela *nf* trick

tris *nm inv* crack; **en un ~** in an instant

triste adj sad; (lamentable) sorry, miserable □ **tristeza** nf (aflicción) sadness; (melancolía) melancholy

triturar vt (moler) to grind; (mascar) to chew

triunfar vi (tener éxito) to triumph; (ganar) to win □ **triunfo** nm triumph

trivial adj trivial □ **trivializar** vt to minimize, play down

triza nf: **hacer ~s** to smash to bits; (papel) to tear to shreds

trocar vt to exchange

trocear vt (carne, manzana) to cut up, cut into pieces

trocha nf short cut

troche: a ~ y moche adv helter-skelter, pell-mell

trofeo nm (premio) trophy; (éxito) success

tromba nf downpour

trombón nm trombone

trombosis nf inv thrombosis

trompa nf horn; (trompo) humming top; (hocico) snout; (fam): **cogerse una ~** to get tight

trompazo nm bump, bang

trompeta nf trumpet; (clarín) bugle

trompicón nm trip, stumble; **a trompicones** in fits and starts

trompo nm spinning top

trompón nm bump

tronar vt (MÉX, CAM: fusilar) to shoot; (MÉX: examen) to flunk ♦ vi to thunder; (fig) to rage

tronchar vt (árbol) to chop down; (fig: vida) to cut short; (: esperanza) to shatter; (persona) to tire out; **troncharse** vr to fall down

tronco nm (de árbol, ANAT) trunk

trono nm throne

tropa nf (MIL) troop; (soldados) soldiers pl

tropel nm (muchedumbre) crowd

tropezar vi to trip, stumble; (errar) to slip up; **~ con** to run into; (topar con) to bump into □ **tropezón** nm trip; (fig) blunder

tropical adj tropical

trópico nm tropic

tropiezo vb ver **tropezar** ♦ nm (error) slip, blunder; (desgracia) misfortune; (obstáculo) snag

trotamundos nm inv globetrotter

trotar vi to trot □ **trote** nm trot; (fam) traveling (US), travelling (BRIT); **de mucho trote** tough, hard-wearing (BRIT)

trozar (LAm) vt to cut up, cut into pieces

trozo nm bit, piece

trucha nf trout

truco nm (habilidad) knack; (engaño) trick

trueno nm thunder; (estampido) bang

trueque etc vb ver **trocar** ♦ nm exchange; (COM) barter

trufa nf (BOT) truffle

truhán, -ana nm/f rogue, shyster (US)

truncar vt (cortar) to truncate; (fig: la vida etc) to cut short; (: el desarrollo) to stunt

tu adj your

tú pron you

tubérculo nm (BOT) tuber

tuberculosis nf inv tuberculosis

tubería nf pipes pl; (conducto) pipeline

tubo nm tube, pipe; (MÉX: para el pelo) roller ▶ **tubo de ensayo** test tube ▶ **tubo de escape** exhaust (pipe)

tuerca nf nut

tuerto, -a adj blind in one eye ♦ nm/f one-eyed person

tuerza etc vb ver **torcer**

tuétano nm squash (US), marrow (BRIT); (BOT) pith

tufo nm (hedor) stench

tul nm tulle

tulipán nm tulip

tullido, -a adj crippled

tumba nf (sepultura) tomb

tumbar vt to knock down; **tumbarse** vr (echarse) to lie down; (extenderse) to stretch out

tumbo nm: **dar ~s** to stagger

tumbona nf (butaca) easy chair; (ESP: de playa) beach o deck chair

tumor nm tumor (US), tumour (BRIT)

tumulto nm turmoil

tuna nf (MÚS) student music group; ver tb **tuno**

tunante nmf rascal

tunda nf (golpeo) beating

túnel nm tunnel

Túnez nm Tunisia; (ciudad) Tunis

tuno, -a nm/f (fam) rogue ♦ nm member of student music group

tupido, -a adj (denso) dense; (tela) close-woven

turba nf crowd

turbante nm turban

turbar vt (molestar) to disturb; (incomodar) to upset; **turbarse** vr to be disturbed

turbina nf turbine

turbio, -a adj cloudy; (tema etc) confused

turbulencia nf turbulence; (fig) restlessness □ **turbulento, -a** adj turbulent; (fig: intranquilo) restless; (: ruidoso) noisy

turco, -a adj Turkish ♦ nm/f Turk

turismo nm tourism; (ESP AUTO) sedan (US), saloon (BRIT) □ **turista** nmf tourist □ **turístico, -a** adj tourist cpd

turnar vi to take (it in) turns; **turnarse** vr to take (it in) turns □ **turno** nm (de trabajo) shift; (en juegos etc) turn

turquesa nf turquoise

Turquía nf Turkey

turrón nm (dulce) nougat

tutear vt to address as familiar "tú"; **tutearse** vr to be on familiar terms

tutela nf (legal) guardianship □ **tutelar** adj tutelary ♦ vt to protect

tutor, a nm/f (legal) guardian; (ESCOL) tutor

tuve etc vb ver **tener**

tuviera etc vb ver **tener**

tuyo, -a adj yours, of yours ♦ pron yours; **un amigo** ~ a friend of yours; **los ~s** (fam) your relations, your family

TV nf abr (= televisión) TV

TVE nf abr = **Televisión Española**

Uu

u conj or

ubicar vt to place, situate; (LAm: encontrar) to find; **ubicarse** vr (LAm: encontrarse) to lie, be located

ubre nf udder

UCI nf abr (= Unidad de Cuidados Intensivos) ICU

Ud(s) abr = **usted(es)**

UE nf abr (= Unión Europea) EU

ufanarse vr to boast; ~ **de** to pride o.s. on □ **ufano, -a** adj (arrogante) arrogant; (presumido) conceited

ujier nm usher; (portero) doorman

úlcera nf ulcer

ulcerar vt to make sore; **ulcerarse** vr to ulcerate

ulterior adj (más allá) farther, further; (subsecuente, siguiente) subsequent

últimamente adv (recientemente) lately, recently

ultimar vt to finish; (finalizar) to finalize; (LAm: matar) to kill

ultimátum (pl ~s) nm ultimatum

último, -a adj last; (más reciente) latest, most recent; (más bajo) bottom; (más alto) top; **en las últimas** on one's last legs; **por** ~ finally

ultra adj ultra ♦ nmf extreme right-winger

ultrajar vt (ofender) to outrage; (insultar) to insult, abuse □ **ultraje** nm outrage; insult

ultramar nm: **de** o **en** ~ abroad, overseas

ultramarinos nmpl groceries; **tienda de** ~ grocery store (US), grocer's (shop) (BRIT)

ultranza: a ~ adv (a todo trance) at all costs; (completo) outright

ultratumba nf: **la vida de** ~ the next life

umbral nm (gen) threshold

umbrío, -a adj shady

un, una
PALABRA CLAVE

art indef
a; (antes de vocal) an; **una mujer/naranja** a woman/an orange
♦ adj: **unos** (o **unas**): **hay unos regalos para ti** there are some presents for you; **hay unas cervezas en la nevera** there are some beers in the icebox

unánime adj unanimous □ **unanimidad** nf unanimity

undécimo, -a adj eleventh

ungir vt to anoint

ungüento nm ointment

únicamente adv solely, only

único, -a adj only, sole; (sin par) unique

unidad nf unity; (COM, TEC etc) unit

unido, -a adj joined, linked; (fig) united

unificar vt to unite, unify

uniformar vt to make uniform, level up; (persona) to put into uniform

uniforme adj uniform, equal; (superficie) even ♦ nm uniform □ **uniformidad** nf uniformity; (de terreno) levelness, evenness

unilateral adj unilateral

unión nf union; (acto) uniting, joining; (unidad) unity; (TEC) joint ▶ **Unión Europea** European Union

unir vt (juntar) to join, unite; (atar) to tie, fasten; (combinar) to combine; **unirse** vr to join together, unite; (empresas) to merge

unísono nm: **al** ~ in unison

universal adj universal; (mundial) world cpd

universidad nf university

universitario, -a adj university cpd ♦ nm/f (profesor) lecturer; (estudiante) (university) student; (graduado) graduate

universo nm universe

uno, -a
PALABRA CLAVE

adj
one; **es todo uno** it's all one and the same; **unos pocos** a few; **unos cien** about a hundred

♦ *pron*

1 one; **quiero sólo uno** I only want one; **uno de ellos** one of them

2 *(alguien)* somebody, someone; **conozco a uno que se te parece** I know somebody o someone who looks like you; **uno mismo** oneself; **unos querían quedarse** some (people) wanted to stay

3: **(los) unos ... (los) otros ...** some ... others; **una y otra son muy agradables** they're both very nice

♦ *nf* one; **es la una** it's one o'clock
♦ *nm* (number) one

untar *vt (mantequilla)* to spread; *(engrasar)* to grease, oil

uña *nf (ANAT)* nail; *(garra)* claw; *(casco)* hoof; *(arranca clavos)* claw

uranio *nm* uranium

urbanidad *nf* courtesy, politeness

urbanismo *nm* town planning

urbanización *(ESP) nf (barrio)* housing development *(US)* o estate *(BRIT)*

urbanizar *vt (zona)* to develop, urbanize

urbano, -a *adj (de ciudad)* urban; *(cortés)* courteous, polite

urbe *nf* large city

urdimbre *nf (de tejido)* warp; *(intriga)* intrigue

urdir *vt* to warp; *(complot)* to plot, contrive

urgencia *nf* urgency; *(prisa)* haste, rush; *(emergencia)* emergency; **servicios de ~** emergency services; **"U~s"** "emergency room" *(US)*, "accident & emergency" *(BRIT)* ❑ **urgente** *adj* urgent

urgir *vi* to be urgent; **me urge** I'm in a hurry for it

urinario, -a *adj* urinary ♦ *nm* urinal

urna *nf* urn; *(POL)* ballot box

urraca *nf* magpie

URSS *nf (HIST)*: **la ~** the USSR

Uruguay *nm*: **el ~** Uruguay ❑ **uruguayo, -a** *adj, nm/f* Uruguayan

usado, -a *adj* used; *(de segunda mano)* secondhand

usar *vt* to use; *(ropa)* to wear; *(tener costumbre)* to be in the habit of; **usarse** *vr* to be used ❑ **uso** *nm* use; wear; *(costumbre)* usage, custom; *(moda)* fashion; **al uso** in keeping with custom; **al uso de** in the style of

usted *pron (sg)* you *sg*; *(pl)*: **~es** you *pl*

usual *adj* usual

usuario, -a *nm/f* user

usura *nf* usury ❑ **usurero, -a** *nm/f* usurer

usurpar *vt* to usurp

utensilio *nm* tool; *(CULIN)* utensil

útero *nm* uterus, womb

útil *adj* useful ♦ *nm* tool ❑ **utilidad** *nf* usefulness; *(COM)* profit ❑ **utilizar** *vt* to use, utilize

utopía *nf* Utopia ❑ **utópico, -a** *adj* Utopian

uva *nf* grape

Vv

v *abr (= voltio)* v

va *vb ver* **ir**

vaca *nf (animal)* cow; **carne de ~** beef

vacaciones *nfpl* vacation *sg (US)*, holidays *(BRIT)*

vacante *adj* vacant, empty ♦ *nf* vacancy

vaciar *vt* to empty out; *(ahuecar)* to hollow out; *(moldear)* to cast; **vaciarse** *vr* to empty

vacilante *adj* unsteady; *(habla)* faltering; *(dudoso)* hesitant

vacilar *vi* to be unsteady; *(al hablar)* to falter; *(dudar)* to hesitate, waver; *(memoria)* to fail

vacío, -a *adj* empty; *(puesto)* vacant; *(desocupado)* idle; *(vano)* vain ♦ *nm* emptiness; *(FÍSICA)* vacuum; *(un vacío)* (empty) space

vacuna *nf* vaccine ❑ **vacunar** *vt* to vaccinate

vacuno, -a *adj* cow *cpd*; **ganado ~** cattle

vacuo, -a *adj* empty

vadear *vt (río)* to ford ❑ **vado** *nm* ford

vagabundo, -a *adj* wandering ♦ *nm* tramp, bum *(US)*

vagamente *adv* vaguely

vagancia *nf (pereza)* idleness, laziness

vagar *vi* to wander; *(no hacer nada)* to idle

vagina *nf* vagina

vago, -a *adj* vague; *(perezoso)* lazy ♦ *nm/f* *(vagabundo)* tramp; *(flojo)* lazybones *sg*, idler

vagón *nm (FERRO: de pasajeros)* passenger car *(US)*, carriage *(BRIT)*; *(: de mercancías)* wagon

vaguedad *nf* vagueness

vaho *nm (vapor)* steam, vapor *(US)*, vapour *(BRIT)*; *(respiración)* breath

vaina *nf* sheath

vainilla *nf* vanilla

vais *vb ver* **ir**

vaivén *nm* to-and-fro movement; (*de tránsito*) coming and going; **vaivenes** *nmpl* (*fig*) ups and downs

vajilla *nf* dishes *pl*, crockery (*BRIT*); (*juego*) service, set

valdré *etc vb ver* **valer**

vale *nm* voucher; (*recibo*) receipt; (*pagaré*) IOU

valedero, -a *adj* valid

valentía *nf* courage, bravery

valer *vt* to be worth; (*MAT*) to equal; (*costar*) to cost ♦ *vi* (*ESP*: *ser útil*) to be useful; (*ser válido*) to be valid; **valerse** *vr* to take care of oneself; **~se de** to make use of, take advantage of; **~ la pena** to be worthwhile; **¿vale?** (*ESP*) OK?; **¡eso a mí no me vale!** (*MÉX*: *fam*: *no importar*) I couldn't care less about that!

valeroso, -a *adj* brave, valiant

valgo *etc vb ver* **valer**

valía *nf* worth, value

validar *vt* to validate ❑ **validez** *nf* validity ❑ **válido, -a** *adj* valid

valiente *adj* brave, valiant ♦ *nm* hero

valija (*CS*) *nf* (suit)case

valioso, -a *adj* valuable

valla *nf* fence; (*DEPORTE*) hurdle ▶ **valla publicitaria** billboard (*US*), hoarding (*BRIT*) ❑ **vallar** *vt* to fence in

valle *nm* valley

valor *nm* value, worth; (*precio*) price; (*valentía*) valor (*US*), valour (*BRIT*), courage; (*importancia*) importance; **~es** *nmpl* (*COM*) securities ❑ **valorar** *vt* to value

vals *nm inv* waltz

válvula *nf* valve

vamos *vb ver* **ir**

vampiro, -resa *nm/f* vampire

van *vb ver* **ir**

vanagloriarse *vr* to boast

vandalismo *nm* vandalism ❑ **vándalo, -a** *nm/f* vandal

vanguardia *nf* vanguard; (*ARTE etc*) avant-garde

vanidad *nf* vanity ❑ **vanidoso, -a** *adj* vain, conceited

vano, -a *adj* vain

vapor *nm* vapor (*US*), vapour (*BRIT*); (*vaho*) steam; **al ~** (*CULIN*) steamed ❑ **vaporizador** *nm* atomizer ❑ **vaporizar** *vt* to vaporize ❑ **vaporoso, -a** *adj* vaporous

vapulear *vt* to beat, thrash

vaquero, -a *adj* cattle *cpd* ♦ *nm* cowboy; **~s** *nmpl* (*ESP*: *pantalones*) jeans

vaquilla *nf* (*ZOOL*) heifer

vara *nf* stick; (*TEC*) rod

variable *adj, nf* variable

variación *nf* variation

variar *vt* to vary; (*modificar*) to modify; (*cambiar de posición*) to switch around ♦ *vi* to vary

varicela *nf* chickenpox

varices (*LAm* **várices**) *nfpl* varicose veins

variedad *nf* variety

varilla *nf* stick; (*BOT*) twig; (*TEC*) rod; (*de rueda*) spoke

vario, -a *adj* varied; **~s** various, several

varita *nf* (*tb*: **~ mágica**) magic wand

varón *nm* male, man ❑ **varonil** *adj* manly, virile

Varsovia *n* Warsaw

vas *vb ver* **ir**

vasco, -a *adj, nm/f* Basque

vaselina (*ESP*) *nf* Vaseline®

vasija *nf* container, vessel

vaso *nm* glass, tumbler; (*ANAT*) vessel

⚠ No confundir **vaso** con la palabra inglesa *vase*.

vástago *nm* (*BOT*) shoot; (*TEC*) rod; (*fig*) offspring

vasto, -a *adj* vast, huge

Vaticano *nm*: **el ~** the Vatican

vatio *nm* (*ELEC*) watt

vaya *etc vb ver* **ir**

Vd(s) *abr* = **usted(es)**

ve *vb ver* **ir**; **ver**

vecindad *nf* neighborhood (*US*), neighbourhood (*BRIT*); (*habitantes*) residents *pl*

vecindario *nm* neighborhood (*US*), neighbourhood (*BRIT*); (*habitantes*) residents *pl*

vecino, -a *adj* neighboring (*US*), neighbouring (*BRIT*) ♦ *nm/f* neighbor (*US*), neighbour (*BRIT*); (*residente*) resident

veda *nf* prohibition

vedar *vt* (*prohibir*) to ban, prohibit; (*impedir*) to stop, prevent

vegetación *nf* vegetation

vegetal *adj, nm* vegetable

vegetariano, -a *adj, nm/f* vegetarian

vehemencia *nf* vehemence ❑ **vehemente** *adj* vehement

vehículo *nm* vehicle; (*MED*) carrier

veía *etc vb ver* **ver**

veinte *num* twenty

vejación nf vexation; (humillación) humiliation

vejar vt (irritar) to annoy, vex; (humillar) to humiliate

vejez nf old age

vejiga nf (ANAT) bladder

vela nf (de cera) candle; (NÁUT) sail; (insomnio) sleeplessness; (vigilia) vigil; (MIL) sentry duty; **estar a dos ~s** (fam: sin dinero) to be broke

velado, -a adj veiled; (sonido) muffled; (FOTO) blurred ♦ nf soiree

velar vt (vigilar) to keep watch over ♦ vi to stay awake; **~ por** to watch over, look after

velatorio nm (funeral) wake

veleidad nf (ligereza) fickleness; (capricho) whim

velero nm (NÁUT) sailing ship; (AVIAT) glider

veleta nf weather vane

veliz (MÉX) nm (suit)case

vello nm down, fuzz

velo nm veil

velocidad nf speed; (TEC, AUTO) gear

velocímetro nm speedometer

velorio (LAm) nm (funeral) wake

veloz adj fast

ven vb ver **venir**

vena nf vein

venado nm deer

vencedor, a adj victorious ♦ nm/f victor, winner

vencer vt (dominar) to defeat, beat; (derrotar) to vanquish; (superar, controlar) to overcome, master ♦ vi (triunfar) to win (through), triumph; (plazo) to expire □ **vencido, -a** adj (derrotado) defeated, beaten; (COM) due ♦ adv: **pagar vencido** to pay in arrears □ **vencimiento** nm (COM) maturity

venda nf bandage □ **vendaje** nm bandage, dressing □ **vendar** vt to bandage; **vendar los ojos** to blindfold

vendaval nm (viento) gale

vendedor, a nm/f seller

vender vt to sell; **~ al contado/al por mayor/al por menor** to sell for cash/ wholesale/retail

vendimia nf grape harvest

vendré etc vb ver **venir**

veneno nm poison; (de serpiente) venom □ **venenoso, -a** adj poisonous; venomous

venerable adj venerable □ **venerar** vt (respetar) to revere; (adorar) to worship

venéreo, -a adj: **enfermedad venérea** venereal disease

venezolano, -a adj Venezuelan

Venezuela nf Venezuela

venganza nf vengeance, revenge □ **vengar** vt to avenge; **vengarse** vr to take revenge □ **vengativo, -a** adj (persona) vindictive

vengo etc vb ver **venir**

venia nf (perdón) pardon; (permiso) consent

venial adj venial

venida nf (llegada) arrival; (regreso) return

venidero, -a adj coming, future

venir vi to come; (llegar) to arrive; (ocurrir) to happen; (fig): **~ de** to stem from; **bien/mal** to be suitable/unsuitable; **el año que viene** next year; **~se abajo** to collapse

venta nf (COM) sale; **"en ~"** "for sale" ▶ **venta a domicilio** door-to-door selling ▶ **venta a plazos** installment plan (US), hire purchase (BRIT) ▶ **venta al contado/al por mayor/ al por menor** o **al detalle** cash sale/ wholesale/retail

ventaja nf advantage □ **ventajoso, -a** adj advantageous

ventana nf window □ **ventanilla** nf (de taquilla) window (of ticket office etc)

ventilación nf ventilation; (corriente) draft (US), draught (BRIT)

ventilador nm fan

ventilar vt to ventilate; (para secar) to put out to dry; (asunto) to air, discuss

ventisca nf blizzard

ventrílocuo, -a nm/f ventriloquist

ventura nf (felicidad) happiness; (buena suerte) luck; (destino) fortune; **a la (buena) ~** at random □ **venturoso, -a** adj happy; (afortunado) lucky, fortunate

veo etc vb ver **ver**

ver vt to see; (mirar) to look at, watch; (entender) to understand; (investigar) to look into ♦ vi to see; to understand; **verse** vr (encontrarse) to meet; (dejarse ver) to be seen; (hallarse: en un apuro) to find o.s., be; **a ~** let's see; **no tener nada que ~ con** to have nothing to do with; **a mi modo de ~** as I see it

vera nf edge, verge; (de río) bank

veracidad nf truthfulness

veranear vi to spend the summer □ **veraneo** nm summer vacation (US), summer holiday (BRIT) □ **veraniego, -a** adj summer cpd

verano nm summer

veras nfpl truth sg; **de ~** really, truly

veraz adj truthful

verbal adj verbal

verbena nf (baile) open-air dance

verbo *nm* verb ❑ **verboso, -a** *adj* verbose

verdad *nf* truth; *(fiabilidad)* reliability; **de ~** real, proper; **a decir ~** to tell the truth ❑ **verdadero, -a** *adj (veraz)* true, truthful; *(fiable)* reliable; *(fig)* real

verde *adj* green; *(LAm exc MÉX, ESP: chiste)* dirty, blue ♦ *nm* green; **viejo ~** dirty old man ❑ **verdear** *vi* to turn green ❑ **verdor** *nm* greenness

verdugo *nm* executioner

verdulero, -a *nm/f* vegetable merchant *(US)*, greengrocer *(BRIT)*

verduras *nfpl (CULIN)* greens

vereda *nf* path; *(CS: acera)* sidewalk *(US)*, pavement *(BRIT)*

veredicto *nm* verdict

vergonzoso, -a *adj* shameful; *(tímido)* timid, bashful

vergüenza *nf* shame, sense of shame; *(timidez)* bashfulness; *(pudor)* modesty; **me da ~** I'm ashamed

verídico, -a *adj* true, truthful

verificar *vt* to check; *(corroborar)* to verify; *(llevar a cabo)* to carry out; **verificarse** *vr* *(predicción)* to prove to be true

verja *nf (cancela)* iron gate; *(valla)* iron railings *pl; (de ventana)* grille

vermut *(pl ~s) nm* vermouth

verosímil *adj* likely, probable; *(relato)* credible

verruga *nf* wart

versado, -a *adj:* **~ en** versed in

versátil *adj* versatile

versión *nf* version

verso *nm* verse; **un ~** a line of poetry

vértebra *nf* vertebra

verter *vt (líquido: adrede)* to empty, pour (out); *(: sin querer)* to spill; *(basura)* to dump ♦ *vi* to flow

vertical *adj* vertical

vértice *nm* vertex, apex

vertidos *nmpl* waste *sg*

vertiente *nf* slope; *(fig)* aspect

vertiginoso, -a *adj* giddy, dizzy

vértigo *nm* vertigo; *(mareo)* dizziness

vesícula *nf* blister

vespino® *nm* moped

vestíbulo *nm* hall; *(de teatro)* foyer

vestido *nm (ropa)* clothes *pl*, clothing; *(de mujer)* dress, frock ♦ *pp de* **vestir**; **~ de azul/marinero** dressed in blue/as a sailor

vestidor *(MÉX) nm (DEPORTE)* locker *(US)* o changing *(BRIT)* room

vestigio *nm (huella)* trace; **~s** *nmpl (restos)* remains

vestimenta *nf* clothing

vestir *vt (poner: ropa)* to put on; *(llevar: ropa)* to wear; *(proveer de ropa a)* to clothe; *(sastre)* to make clothes for ♦ *vi* to dress; *(verse bien)* to look good; **vestirse** *vr* to get dressed, dress o.s.

vestuario *nm* clothes *pl*, wardrobe; *(TEATRO: cuarto)* dressing room; *(DEPORTE)* changing room

veta *nf (vena)* vein, seam; *(en carne)* streak; *(de madera)* grain

vetar *vt* to veto

veterano, -a *adj, nm* veteran

veterinaria *nf* veterinary science; *ver tb* **veterinario**

veterinario, -a *nm/f* veterinarian *(US)*, veterinary surgeon *(BRIT)*

veto *nm* veto

vez *nf* time; *(turno)* turn; **a la ~ que** at the same time as; **a su ~** in its turn; **otra ~** again; **una ~** once; **de una ~** in one shot *(US)* o go *(BRIT)*; **de una ~ para siempre** once and for all; **en ~ de** instead of; **a** o **algunas veces** sometimes; **una y otra ~** repeatedly; **de ~ en cuando** from time to time; **7 veces 9** 7 times 9; **hacer las veces de** to stand in for; **tal ~** perhaps

vía *nf* track, route; *(FERRO)* line; *(fig)* way; *(ANAT)* passage, tube ♦ *prep* via, by way of; **por ~ judicial** by legal means; **por ~ oficial** through official channels; **en ~s de** in the process of ▶ **vía aérea** airway ▶ **Vía Láctea** Milky Way ▶ **vía pública** public road o thoroughfare

viable *adj (solución, plan, alternativa)* feasible

viaducto *nm* viaduct

viajante *nm* traveling salesman *(US)*, commercial traveller *(BRIT)*

viajar *vi* to travel ❑ **viaje** *nm* journey; *(gira)* tour; *(NÁUT)* voyage; **estar de viaje** to be on a trip ▶ **viaje de ida y vuelta** round trip ▶ **viaje de novios** honeymoon ❑ **viajero, -a** *adj* traveling *(US)*, travelling *(BRIT)*; *(ZOOL)* migratory ♦ *nm/f (quien viaja)* traveler *(US)*, traveller *(BRIT)*; *(pasajero)* passenger

vial *adj* road *cpd*, traffic *cpd*

víbora *nf (ZOOL)* viper; *(MÉX: venenoso)* poisonous snake

vibración *nf* vibration

vibrar *vt, vi* to vibrate

vicario *nm* curate

vicepresidente *nmf* vice-president

viceversa *adv* vice versa

viciado, -a adj (corrompido) corrupt; (contaminado) foul, contaminated □ **viciar** vt (pervertir) to pervert; (JUR) to nullify; (estropear) to spoil; **viciarse** vr to become corrupted

vicio nm vice; (mala costumbre) bad habit □ **vicioso, -a** adj (muy malo) vicious; (corrompido) depraved ♦ nm/f depraved person

vicisitud nf vicissitude

víctima nf victim

victoria nf victory □ **victorioso, -a** adj victorious

vid nf vine

vida nf (gen) life; (duración) lifetime; **de por ~** for life; **en la/mi ~** never; **estar con ~** to be still alive; **ganarse la ~** to earn one's living

video (LAm) (ESP **vídeo**) nm video ♦ adj inv: **película de** (LAm) **~** video movie (US) o film (BRIT) □ **videocámara** nf camcorder □ **videocasete** nm video cassette, videotape □ **videoclub** nm video store □ **videojuego** nm video game

vidriero, -a nm/f glazier ♦ nf (ventana) stained-glass window; (LAm: de tienda) store (US) o shop (BRIT) window; (puerta) glass door

vidrio nm glass

vieira nf scallop

viejo, -a adj old ♦ nm/f old man (woman); **hacerse ~** to get old

Viena n Vienna

vienes etc vb ver **venir**

vienés, -esa adj Viennese

viento nm wind; **hacer ~** to be windy

vientre nm belly; (matriz) womb

viernes nm inv Friday ▶ **Viernes Santo** Good Friday

Vietnam nm: **el ~** Vietnam □ **vietnamita** adj Vietnamese

viga nf beam, rafter; (de metal) girder

vigencia nf validity; **estar en ~** to be in force □ **vigente** adj valid, in force; (imperante) prevailing

vigésimo, -a adj twentieth

vigía nm look-out

vigilancia nf: **tener a algn bajo ~** to keep watch on sb

vigilar vt to watch over ♦ vi (gen) to be vigilant; (hacer guardia) to keep watch; **~ por** to take care of

vigilia nf wakefulness, being awake; (REL) fast

vigor nm vigor (US), vigour (BRIT), vitality; **en ~** in force; **entrar/poner en ~** to come/put into effect □ **vigoroso, -a** adj vigorous

VIH nm abr (= virus de la inmunodeficiencia humana) HIV ▶ **VIH positivo/negativo** HIV-positive/-negative

vil adj vile, low □ **vileza** nf vileness; (acto) base deed

vilipendiar vt to vilify, revile

villa nf (casa) villa; (pueblo) small town; (municipalidad) municipality

villancico nm (Christmas) carol

villorrio nm shantytown

vilo: en ~ adv in the air, suspended; (fig) on tenterhooks, in suspense

vinagre nm vinegar

vinagreta nf vinaigrette, French dressing

vinculación nf (lazo) link, bond; (acción) linking

vincular vt to link, bind □ **vínculo** nm link, bond

vine etc vb ver **venir**

vinicultura nf wine growing

viniera etc vb ver **venir**

vino vb ver **venir** ♦ nm wine ▶ **vino blanco/ tinto** white/red wine

viña nf vineyard □ **viñedo** nm vineyard

viola nf viola

violación nf violation; (sexual) rape

violar vt to violate; (sexualmente) to rape

violencia nf violence, force; (incomodidad) embarrassment; (acto injusto) unjust act □ **violentar** vt to force; (casa) to break into; (agredir) to assault; (violar) to violate □ **violento, -a** adj violent; (furioso) furious; (situación) embarrassing; (acto) forced, unnatural

violeta nf violet

violín nm violin

violón nm double bass

viraje nm turn; (de vehículo) swerve; (fig) change of direction □ **virar** vi to change direction

virgen adj, nf virgin

Virgo nm Virgo

viril adj virile □ **virilidad** nf virility

virtud nf virtue; **en ~ de** by virtue of □ **virtuoso, -a** adj virtuous ♦ nm/f virtuoso

viruela nf smallpox

virulento, -a adj virulent

virus nm inv virus

visa (LAm) nf visa

visado (ESP) nm visa

víscera nf (ANAT, ZOOL) gut, bowel; **~s** nfpl entrails

visceral adj (odio) intense; **reacción ~** gut reaction

viscoso, -a adj viscous

visera nf visor

visibilidad nf visibility □ **visible** adj visible; (fig) obvious

visillos nmpl net curtains

visión nf (ANAT) vision, (eye)sight; (fantasía) vision, fantasy

visita nf call, visit; (persona) visitor; **hacer una ~** to pay a visit

visitar vt to visit, call on

vislumbrar vt to glimpse, catch a glimpse of

viso nm (del metal) glint, gleam; (de tela) sheen; (aspecto) appearance; (RPI: combinación) slip

visón nm mink

visor nm (FOTO) viewfinder

víspera nf: **la ~ de ...** the day before ...

vista nf sight, vision; (capacidad de ver) (eye)sight; (mirada) look(s) (pl); **a primera ~** at first glance; **hacer la ~ gorda** to turn a blind eye; **volver la ~** to look back; **está a ~ que** it's obvious that; **en ~ de** in view of; **en ~ de que** in view of the fact that; **¡hasta la ~!** so long!, see you!; **con ~s a** with a view to □ **vistazo** nm glance; **dar o echar un vistazo a** to glance at

visto, -a pp de **ver** ♦ vb ver tb **vestir** ♦ adj seen; (considerado) considered ♦ nm: **~ bueno** approval; **"~ bueno"** "approved"; **por lo ~** apparently; **está ~ que** it's clear that; **está bien/mal ~** it's acceptable/unacceptable; **~ que** since, considering that

vistoso, -a adj colorful (US), colourful (BRIT)

visual adj visual

vital adj life cpd, living cpd; (fig) vital; (persona) lively, vivacious □ **vitalicio, -a** adj for life □ **vitalidad** nf (de persona, negocio) energy; (de ciudad) liveliness

vitamina nf vitamin

viticultor, a nm/f wine grower □ **viticultura** nf wine growing

vitorear vt to cheer, acclaim

vitrina nf show case; (LAm: escaparate) store (US) o shop (BRIT) window

viudez nf widowhood

viudo, -a nm/f widower/widow

viva excl hurrah!; **¡~ el rey!** long live the king!

vivacidad nf (vigor) vigor (US), vigour (BRIT); (vida) liveliness

vivaracho, -a adj jaunty, lively; (ojos) bright, twinkling

vivaz adj lively

víveres nmpl provisions

vivero nm (para plantas) nursery; (para peces) fish farm; (fig) hotbed

viveza nf liveliness; (agudeza: mental) sharpness

vivienda nf housing; (una vivienda) house; (piso) apartment (US), flat (BRIT)

viviente adj living

vivir vt, vi to live ♦ nm life, living

vivo, -a adj living, alive; (fig: descripción) vivid; (persona: astuto) smart, clever; **en ~** (transmisión etc) live

vocablo nm (palabra) word; (término) term

vocabulario nm vocabulary

vocación nf vocation □ **vocacional** (LAm) nf ≈ technical college

vocal adj vocal ♦ nf vowel □ **vocalizar** vt to vocalize

vocear vt (para vender) to cry; (aclamar) to acclaim; (fig) to proclaim ♦ vi to yell □ **vocerío** nm shouting

vocero nmf spokesman/woman

voces pl de **voz**

vociferar vt to shout ♦ vi to yell

vodka nm vodka

vol abr = **volumen**

volado, -a (MÉX) adv in a rush, hastily

volador, a adj flying ♦ nm (pez) flying fish ▶ **Voladores de Papantla** popular Mexican dance

VOLADORES DE PAPANTLA

The **Voladores de Papantla** tradition derives from an ancient agricultural fertility rite in Mexico. Four or six men are tied to a platform held up by a log. They dance on the platform before coming slowly down to the ground, going around the log, while the rope fastened to them uncoils.

volandas: en ~ adv in the air

volante adj flying ♦ nm (de vehículo) steering wheel; (de reloj) balance

volar vt (edificio) to blow up ♦ vi to fly

volátil adj volatile

volcán nm volcano □ **volcánico, -a** adj volcanic

volcar vt to upset, overturn; (tumbar, derribar) to knock over; (vaciar) to empty out ♦ vi to overturn; **volcarse** vr to tip over

voleibol nm volleyball

volqué etc vb ver **volcar**

voltaje nm voltage

voltear vt to turn over; (volcar) to turn upside down

voltereta nf somersault

voltio nm volt

voluble adj fickle

volumen (pl volúmenes) nm volume ❏ **voluminoso, -a** adj voluminous; (enorme) massive

voluntad nf will; (resolución) willpower; (deseo) desire, wish

voluntario, -a adj voluntary ♦ nm/f volunteer

voluntarioso, -a adj headstrong

voluptuoso, -a adj voluptuous

volver vt (gen) to turn; (dar vuelta a) to turn (over); (voltear) to turn round, turn upside down; (poner al revés) to turn inside out; (devolver) to return ♦ vi to return, go back, come back; **volverse** vr to turn round; **~ la espalda** to turn one's back; **~ triste** etc a algn to make sb sad etc; **~ a hacer** to do again; **~ en sí** to come to; **~se insoportable/muy caro** to get o become unbearable/very expensive; **~se loco** to go mad

vomitar vt, vi to vomit ❏ **vómito** nm vomit

voraz adj voracious

vos (LAm) pron you

vosotros, -as (ESP) pron you; (reflexivo): **entre/para ~** among/for yourselves

votación nf (acto) voting; (voto) vote

votar vi to vote ❏ **voto** nm vote; (promesa) vow; **votos** (good) wishes

voy vb ver **ir**

voz nf voice; (grito) shout; (rumor) rumor (US), rumour (BRIT); (LING) word; **dar voces** to shout, yell; **a media ~** in a low voice; **a ~ en cuello** o **grito** at the top of one's voice; **de viva ~** verbally; **en ~ alta** aloud; **~ de mando** command

vuelco vb ver **volcar** ♦ nm spill, overturning

vuelo vb ver **volar** ♦ nm flight; (encaje) lace, frill; **coger al ~** to catch in flight ▶ **vuelo chárter/regular** charter/scheduled flight ▶ **vuelo libre** (DEPORTE) hang-gliding

vuelque etc vb ver **volcar**

vuelta nf (gen) turn; (curva) bend, curve; (regreso) return; (revolución) revolution; (de circuito) lap; (de papel, tela) reverse; (cambio) change; **a la ~** on one's return; **a ~ de correo** by return of mail (US) o post (BRIT); **dar ~s** (cabeza) to spin; **dar ~s a una idea** to turn over an idea (in one's head); **estar de ~** to be back; **dar una ~** to go for a walk; (en vehículo) to go for a drive ▶ **vuelta ciclista** (DEPORTE) (cycle) tour

vuelto pp de **volver** ♦ nm (LAm: sencillo) small o loose (BRIT) change

vuelvo etc vb ver **volver**

vuestro, -a (ESP) adj your ♦ pron: **el ~/la vuestra, los ~s/las vuestras** yours; **un amigo ~** a friend of yours

vulgar adj (ordinario) vulgar; (común) common ❏ **vulgaridad** nf commonness; (acto) vulgarity; (expresión) coarse expression ❏ **vulgarizar** vt to popularize

vulgo nm common people

vulnerable adj vulnerable

vulnerar vt (ley, acuerdo) to violate, breach; (derechos, intimidad) to violate; (reputación) to damage

walkie-talkie (pl ~s) nm walkie-talkie

Walkman® nm Walkman®

wáter nm (taza) toilet; (LAm: lugar) rest room (US), toilet (BRIT)

web nm o f (página) website; (red) (World Wide) Web ▶ **web site** website

webcam nf webcam

webmaster nmf webmaster

western (pl ~s) nm western

whisky nm whiskey (US, IRELAND), whisky (BRIT)

windsurf nm windsurfing; **hacer ~** to go windsurfing

xenofobia nf xenophobia

xilófono nm xylophone

xocoyote, -a (MÉX) nm/f baby of the family, youngest child

y conj and

ya adv (gen) already; (ahora) now; (en seguida) at once; (pronto) soon ♦ excl all right! ♦ conj (ahora que) now that; **ya lo sé** I know; **ya que** since

yacaré (CS) nm cayman
yacer vi to lie
yacimiento nm (de mineral) deposit; (arqueológico) site
yanqui (fam) adj, nmf Yankee
yate nm yacht
yazco etc vb ver **yacer**
yedra nf ivy
yegua nf mare
yema nf (del huevo) yolk; (BOT) leaf bud; (fig) best part ▶ **yema del dedo** fingertip
yergo etc vb ver **erguir**
yermo, -a adj (estéril, fig) barren ♦ nm wasteland
yerno nm son-in-law
yerro etc vb ver **errar**
yeso nm plaster
yo pron I; **soy yo** it's me, it is I
yodo nm iodine
yoga nm yoga
yogur(t) nm yoghurt
yuca nf (alimento) cassava, manioc root
yugo nm yoke
Yugoslavia nf (HIST) Yugoslavia
yugular adj jugular
yunque nm anvil
yunta nf yoke
yuxtaponer vt to juxtapose
❏ **yuxtaposición** nf juxtaposition
yuyo (RPI) nm (mala hierba) weed

Zz

zafar vt (soltar) to untie; (superficie) to clear; **zafarse** vr (escaparse) to escape; (TEC) to slip off
zafio, -a adj coarse
zafiro nm sapphire
zaga nf: **a la ~** behind, in the rear
zaguán nm hallway
zaherir vt (criticar) to criticize
zaino, -a adj (caballo) chestnut
zalamería nf flattery ❏ **zalamero, -a** adj flattering; (cobista) suave
zamarra nf (chaqueta) sheepskin jacket
zambullirse vr to dive
zampar vt to gobble down
zanahoria nf carrot
zancada nf stride
zancadilla nf trip

zanco nm stilt
zancudo, -a adj long-legged ♦ nm (LAm ZOOL) mosquito
zángano nm drone
zanja nf ditch ❏ **zanjar** vt (resolver) to resolve
zapata nf (MECÁNICA) shoe
zapatear vi to tap with one's feet
zapatería nf (oficio) shoemaking; (tienda) shoe store (US), shoe shop (BRIT); (fábrica) shoe factory ❏ **zapatero, -a** nm/f shoemaker
zapatilla nf slipper ▶ **zapatilla de deporte** sneaker, training shoe
zapatista adj, nmf Zapatista

ZAPATISTAS

The Indian movement called the **Zapatistas** (officially, the National Liberation Zapatista Army) is a revolutionary group founded in Chiapas in 1994 with the aim of securing some basic rights for Mexican Indians. Unlike other revolutionary groups, it does not aspire to power.

zapato nm shoe ▶ **zapatos de piso** (MÉX) flat shoes
zapping nm channel-surfing; **hacer ~** to flick through the channels
zar nm czar, tsar
zarandear (fam) vt to shake vigorously
zarpa nf (garra) claw
zarpar vi to weigh anchor
zarza nf (BOT) bramble ❏ **zarzal** nm (matorral) bramble patch
zarzamora nf blackberry
zarzuela nf Spanish light opera
zigzag nm zigzag ❏ **zigzaguear** vi to zigzag
zinc nm zinc
zíper (MÉX, CAm) nm zipper (US), zip (fastener) (BRIT)
zócalo nm (ARQ) plinth, base; (LAm exc MÉX, ESP: de pared) baseboard (US), skirting board (BRIT); (MÉX: plaza) main o public square
zoclo (MÉX) nm baseboard (US), skirting board (BRIT)
zodíaco nm (ASTROLOGÍA) zodiac
zona nf zone ▶ **zona fronteriza** border area ▶ **zona industrial** (LAm) industrial park (US) ▶ **zona roja** (LAm) red-light district
zonzo, -a (LAm: fam) adj silly ♦ nm/f fool
zoo nm zoo
zoología nf zoology ❏ **zoológico, -a** adj zoological ♦ nm (tb: **parque zoológico**) zoo ❏ **zoólogo, -a** nm/f zoologist

zoom *nm* zoom lens

zopilote (*MÉX, CAm*) *nm* buzzard

zoquete *nm* (*fam*) blockhead

zorro, -a *adj* crafty ♦ *nm/f* fox/vixen

zozobra *nf* (*fig*) anxiety ❏ **zozobrar** *vi*
(*hundirse*) to capsize; (*fig*) to fail

zueco *nm* clog

zumbar *vt* (*golpear*) to hit ♦ *vi* to buzz
❏ **zumbido** *nm* buzzing

zumo (*ESP*) *nm* juice ▶ **zumo de naranja**
orange juice

zurcir *vt* (*coser*) to darn

zurdo, -a *adj* (*persona*) left-handed

zurrar (*fam*) *vt* to wallop

ENGLISH-SPANISH
INGLÉS-ESPAÑOL

Aa

A [eɪ] *n* (*MUS*) la *m*

a

KEYWORD

[eɪ, ə] *indef art* (*before vowel or silent h: an*)

1 un(a); **a book** un libro; **an apple** una manzana; **she's a doctor** (ella) es médica

2 (*instead of the number "one"*) un(a); **a year ago** hace un año; **a hundred/thousand** *etc* **dollars** cien/mil *etc* dólares

3 (*in expressing ratios, prices etc*): **3 a day/week** 3 al día/a la semana; **10 miles an hour** 10 millas por hora; **$20 a person** $20 por persona; **50 cents a pound** 50 centavos la libra

A.A. *n abbr* (= *Alcoholics Anonymous*) Alcohólicos Anónimos; (*BRIT*: = *Automobile Association*) asociación automovilística británica

A.A.A. (*US*) *n abbr* (= *American Automobile Association*) asociación automovilística estadounidense

aback [əˈbæk] *adv*: **to be taken ~** quedar desconcertado

abandon [əˈbændən] *vt* abandonar; (*give up*) renunciar a

abate [əˈbeɪt] *vi* (*storm*) amainar; (*anger*) aplacarse; (*terror*) disminuir

abattoir [ˈæbətwɑːr] (*BRIT*) *n* rastro (*MEX*), matadero (*LAm exc MEX*)

abbey [ˈæbi] *n* abadía

abbot [ˈæbət] *n* abad *m*

abbreviation [əbriːviˈeɪʃən] *n* (*short form*) abreviatura

ABC (*US*) *n abbr* = **American Broadcasting Company**

abdicate [ˈæbdɪkeɪt] *vt* renunciar a ♦ *vi* abdicar

abdomen [ˈæbdəmən] *n* abdomen *m*

abduct [æbˈdʌkt] *vt* raptar, secuestrar

abeyance [əˈbeɪəns] *n*: **in ~** (*law*) en desuso; (*matter*) en suspenso

abide [əˈbaɪd] *vt*: **I can't ~ it/him** no le/lo puedo ver ▸ **abide by** *vt fus* atenerse a

ability [əˈbɪləti] *n* habilidad *f*, capacidad *f*; (*talent*) talento

abject [ˈæbdʒekt] *adj* (*poverty*) miserable; (*apology*) rastrero

ablaze [əˈbleɪz] *adj* en llamas, ardiendo

able [ˈeɪbəl] *adj* capaz; (*skilled*) hábil; **to be ~ to do sth** poder hacer algo ❑ **able-bodied** *adj* sano ❑ **ably** *adv* hábilmente

abnormal [æbˈnɔːrməl] *adj* anormal

aboard [əˈbɔːrd] *adv* a bordo ♦ *prep* a bordo de

abode [əˈboud] *n*: **of no fixed ~** sin domicilio fijo

abolish [əˈbɑːlɪʃ] *vt* suprimir, abolir

aborigine [æbəˈrɪdʒəni] *n* aborigen *mf*

abort [əˈbɔːrt] *vt*, *vi* abortar ❑ **abortion** *n* aborto; **to have an abortion** abortar, hacerse abortar ❑ **abortive** *adj* malogrado

about

KEYWORD

[əˈbaut] *adv*

1 (*approximately*) más o menos, aproximadamente; **about a hundred/thousand** *etc* unos (unas) cien/mil *etc*; **it takes about 10 hours** se tarda unas *or* más o menos 10 horas; **at about 2 o'clock** sobre las dos; **I've just about finished** casi he terminado

2 (*referring to place*) por todas partes; **to leave things lying about** dejar las cosas (tiradas) por ahí; **to run about** correr por todas partes; **to walk about** pasearse, ir y venir

3: **to be about to do sth** estar a punto de hacer algo

♦ *prep*

1 (*relating to*) de, sobre, acerca de; **a book about Boston** un libro sobre *or* acerca de Boston; **what is it about?** ¿de qué se trata?; **we talked about it** hablamos de eso *or* ello; **what** *or* **how about doing this?** ¿qué tal si hacemos esto?

2 (*referring to place*) por; **to walk about the town** caminar por la ciudad

above [əˈbʌv] *adv* encima, por encima, arriba ♦ *prep* encima de; (*greater than: in number*) más de; (: *in rank*) superior a; **mentioned ~** susodicho; **~ all** sobre todo ❑ **above board** *adj* legítimo

abrasive [əˈbreɪsɪv] *adj* abrasivo; (*manner*) brusco

abreast [əˈbrest] *adv* de frente; **to keep ~ of** (*fig*) mantenerse al corriente de

abroad [əˈbrɔːd] *adv* (*to be*) en el extranjero; (*to go*) al extranjero

abrupt [ə'brʌpt] *adj* (*sudden*) brusco; (*curt*) áspero

abruptly [ə'brʌptli] *adv* (*leave*) repentinamente; (*speak*) bruscamente

abscess ['æbses] *n* absceso

abscond [əb'skɒnd] *vi* (*thief*): **to ~ with** fugarse con; (*prisoner*): **to ~ (from)** escaparse (de)

absence ['æbsəns] *n* ausencia

absent ['æbsənt] *adj* ausente ❑ **absentee** [æbsən'tiː] *n* ausente *mf* ❑ **absent-minded** *adj* distraído

absolute ['æbsəluːt] *adj* absoluto ❑ **absolutely** [æbsə'luːtli] *adv* (*totally*) totalmente; (*certainly!*) ¡por supuesto (que sí)!

absolve [əb'zɒlv] *vt*: **to ~ sb (from)** absolver a algn (de)

absorb [əb'zɔːrb] *vt* absorber; **to be ~ed in a book** estar absorto en un libro ❑ **absorbent** *adj* absorbente ❑ **absorbent cotton** (*US*) *n* algodón *m* (hidrófilo) ❑ **absorbing** *adj* absorbente

absorption [əb'zɔːrpʃən] *n* absorción *f*

abstain [əb'steɪn] *vi*: **to ~ (from)** abstenerse (de)

abstinence ['æbstɪnəns] *n* abstinencia

abstract ['æbstrækt] *adj* abstracto

absurd [əb'sɜːrd] *adj* absurdo

abundance [ə'bʌndəns] *n* abundancia

abuse [*n* ə'bjuːs, *vb* ə'bjuːz] *n* (*insults*) insultos *mpl*, injurias *fpl*; (*mistreatment*) malos tratos *mpl*; (*misuse*) abuso ♦ *vt* insultar; maltratar; abusar de ❑ **abusive** *adj* ofensivo

abysmal [ə'bɪzməl] *adj* pésimo; (*failure*) garrafal; (*ignorance*) supino

abyss [ə'bɪs] *n* abismo

AC *abbr* (= *alternating current*) corriente *f* alterna; (*US*: *air conditioning*) aire *m* acondicionado

academic [ækə'dæmɪk] *adj* académico, universitario; (*pej*: *issue*) puramente teórico ♦ *n* estudioso(-a), profesor(a) *m/f* universitario(-a)

academy [ə'kædəmi] *n* (*learned body*) academia; (*school*) instituto, colegio; **~ of music** conservatorio

accelerate [æk'seləreɪt] *vt*, *vi* acelerar ❑ **accelerator** *n* acelerador *m*

accent ['æksent] *n* acento; (*fig*) énfasis *m*

accept [æk'sept] *vt* aceptar; (*responsibility*, *blame*) admitir ❑ **acceptable** *adj* aceptable ❑ **acceptance** *n* aceptación *f*

access ['ækses] *n* acceso; **to have ~ to** tener libre acceso a ❑ **accessible** [æk'sesəbəl] *adj*

(*place*, *person*) accesible; (*knowledge etc*) asequible

accessory [æk'sesəri] *n* accesorio; (*LAW*): **~ to** cómplice de

accident ['æksɪdənt] *n* accidente *m*; (*chance event*) casualidad *f*; **by ~** (*unintentionally*) sin querer; (*by chance*) por casualidad ❑ **accidental** [æksɪ'dentl] *adj* accidental, fortuito ❑ **accidentally** [æksɪ'dentli] *adv* sin querer; por casualidad ❑ **accident insurance** *n* seguro contra accidentes ❑ **accident-prone** *adj* propenso a los accidentes

acclaim [ə'kleɪm] *vt* aclamar, aplaudir ♦ *n* aclamación *f*, aplausos *mpl*

acclimate ['æklɪmeɪt] (*US*), **acclimatize** *vt*: **to become ~d** aclimatarse

accommodate [ə'kɒmədeɪt] *vt* (*person*) alojar, hospedar; (*car*, *hotel etc*) tener cabida para; (*oblige*, *help*) complacer ❑ **accommodating** *adj* servicial, complaciente

accommodation [əkɒmə'deɪʃən] (*BRIT*) *n* = **accommodations**

accommodations [əkɒmə'deɪʃənz] (*US*) *npl* alojamiento

accompany [ə'kʌmpəni] *vt* acompañar

accomplice [ə'kʌmplɪs] *n* cómplice *mf*

accomplish [ə'kʌmplɪʃ] *vt* (*finish*) concluir; (*achieve*) lograr ❑ **accomplished** *adj* experto, hábil ❑ **accomplishment** *n* (*skill*: *gen pl*) talento; (*completion*) realización *f*

accord [ə'kɔːrd] *n* acuerdo ♦ *vt* conceder; **of his own ~** espontáneamente ❑ **accordance** *n*: **in accordance with** de acuerdo con ❑ **according**: **according to** *prep* según; (*in accordance with*) conforme a ❑ **accordingly** *adv* (*appropriately*) de acuerdo con esto; (*as a result*) en consecuencia

accordion [ə'kɔːrdiən] *n* acordeón *m*

accost [ə'kɒst] *vt* abordar, dirigirse a

account [ə'kaunt] *n* (*COMM*) cuenta; (*report*) informe *m*; **~s** *npl* (*COMM*) cuentas *fpl*; **of no ~** de ninguna importancia; **on ~** a cuenta; **on no ~** bajo ningún concepto; **on ~ of** a causa de, por motivo de; **to take into ~**, **take ~ of** tener en cuenta ▶ **account for** *vt fus* (*explain*) explicar; (*represent*) representar ❑ **accountable** *adj*: **accountable (to)** responsable (ante) ❑ **accountancy** *n* contabilidad *f* ❑ **accountant** *n* contador(a) *m/f* (*LAm*), contable *mf* (*SP*) ❑ **account number** *n* (*at bank etc*) número de cuenta

accredited [ə'kredɪtɪd] *adj* autorizado

accrued interest [əˈkruːdˈɪntrɪst] n interés m acumulado

accumulate [əˈkjuːmjəleɪt] vt acumular ♦ vi acumularse

accuracy [ˈækjurəsi] n (of total) exactitud f; (of description etc) precisión f

accurate [ˈækjurɪt] adj (total) exacto; (description) preciso; (person) cuidadoso; (device) de precisión □ **accurately** adv con precisión

accusation [ækjuˈzeɪʃən] n acusación f

accuse [əˈkjuːz] vt: **to ~ sb (of sth)** acusar a algn (de algo) □ **accused** n (LAW) acusado(-a)

accustom [əˈkʌstəm] vt acostumbrar □ **accustomed** adj: **accustomed to** acostumbrado a

ace [eɪs] n as m

ache [eɪk] n dolor m ♦ vi doler; **my head ~s** me duele la cabeza

achieve [əˈtʃiːv] vt (aim, result) alcanzar; (success) lograr, conseguir □ **achievement** n (completion) realización f; (success) éxito

acid [ˈæsɪd] adj ácido; (taste) agrio ♦ n ácido □ **acid rain** n lluvia ácida

acknowledge [əkˈnɒlɪdʒ] vt (letter: also: ~ receipt of) acusar recibo de; (fact, situation, person) reconocer □ **acknowledgement** n acuse m de recibo

acne [ˈækni] n acné m

acorn [ˈeɪkɔːrn] n bellota

acoustic [əˈkuːstɪk] adj acústico □ **acoustics** n(pl) acústica sg

acquaint [əˈkweɪnt] vt: **to ~ sb with sth** (inform) poner a algn al corriente de algo; **to be ~ed with** conocer □ **acquaintance** n (person) conocido(-a); (with person, subject) conocimiento

acquire [əˈkwaɪər] vt adquirir □ **acquisition** [ækwɪˈzɪʃən] n adquisición f

acquit [əˈkwɪt] vt absolver, exculpar; **to ~ o.s. well** salir con éxito

acre [ˈeɪkər] n acre m

acrid [ˈækrɪd] adj acre

acrobat [ˈækrəbæt] n acróbata mf

across [əˈkrɔːs] prep (on the other side) al or del otro lado de; (crosswise) a través de ♦ adv de un lado a otro, de una parte a otra; a través, al través; (measurement): **the road is 10m ~** la carretera tiene 10m de ancho; **to run/swim ~** atravesar corriendo/nadando; **~ from** enfrente de

acrylic [əˈkrɪlɪk] adj, n acrílico

ACT n abbr (= American College Test) prueba de aptitud estándar que por lo general hacen los estudiantes que quieren entrar a la universidad por primera vez

act [ækt] n acto, acción f; (of play) acto; (in theater etc) número; (LAW) decreto, ley f ♦ vi (behave) comportarse; (have effect: drug, chemical) hacer efecto; (THEATER) actuar; (pretend) fingir; (take action) obrar ♦ vt (part) hacer el papel de; **in the ~ of: to catch sb in the ~ of ...** atrapar a algn en el momento en que ...; **to ~ as** actuar or hacer de □ **acting** adj suplente ♦ n (activity) actuación f; (profession) profesión f de actor

action [ˈækʃən] n acción f, acto; (MIL) acción f, batalla; (LAW) proceso, demanda; **out of ~** (person) fuera de combate; (thing) descompuesto (LAm), estropeado (SP); **to take ~** tomar medidas □ **action replay** (BRIT) n (TV) repetición f

activate [ˈæktɪveɪt] vt activar

active [ˈæktɪv] adj activo, enérgico; (volcano) en actividad □ **actively** adv (participate) activamente; (discourage, dislike) enérgicamente □ **activity** [ækˈtɪvəti] n actividad f □ **activity holiday** n vacaciones fpl con actividades organizadas

actor [ˈæktər] n actor m

actress [ˈæktrɪs] n actriz f

actual [ˈæktʃuəl] adj verdadero, real; (emphatic use) propiamente dicho □ **actually** adv realmente, en realidad; (even) incluso

⚠ Be careful not to translate **actual** by the Spanish word **actual**.

⚠ Be careful not to translate **actually** by the Spanish word **actualmente**.

acumen [ˈækjumən] n perspicacia

acupuncture [ˈækjupʌŋktʃər] n acupuntura

acute [əˈkjuːt] adj agudo

ad [æd] n abbr = **advertisement**

A.D. adv abbr (= anno Domini) d. de C.

adamant [ˈædəmənt] adj firme, inflexible

adapt [əˈdæpt] vt adaptar ♦ vi: **to ~ (to)** adaptarse (a), ajustarse (a) □ **adaptable** adj adaptable □ **adapter, adaptor** n (ELEC) adaptador m

add [æd] vt añadir, agregar; (figures: also: ~ up) sumar ♦ vi: **to ~ to** (increase) aumentar, acrecentar; **it doesn't ~ up** (fig) no tiene sentido

adder [ˈædər] n víbora

addict [ˈædɪkt] n adicto(-a); (enthusiast) entusiasta mf □ **addicted** [əˈdɪktɪd] adj: **to be addicted to** ser adicto a, ser fanático de □ **addiction** [əˈdɪkʃən] n (to drugs etc) adicción f ♦ **addictive** [ə'dıktıv] *adj* que causa adicción

addition [ə'dıʃən] *n* (*adding up*) adición f; (*thing added*) añadidura, añadido; **in ~** además, por añadidura; **in ~ to** además de ◻ **additional** *adj* adicional

additive ['ædıtıv] *n* aditivo

address [ə'dres] *n* dirección f, señas fpl; (*speech*) discurso ♦ *vt* (*letter*) dirigir; (*speak to*) dirigirse a, dirigir la palabra a; (*problem*) tratar

adept [ə'dept] *adj*: **~ at** experto *or* hábil en

adequate ['ædıkwıt] *adj* (*satisfactory*) adecuado; (*enough*) suficiente

adhere [æd'hıər] *vi*: **to ~ to** (*stick to*) pegarse a; (*fig: abide by*) observar; (: *belief etc*) ser partidario de

adhesive [æd'hi:sıv] *n* adhesivo ◻ **adhesive tape** *n* cinta adhesiva

ad hoc [æd'hɑ:k] *adj* ad hoc

adjacent [ə'dʒeısənt] *adj*: **~ to** contiguo *or* inmediato a

adjective ['ædʒıktıv] *n* adjetivo

adjoining [ə'dʒɔınıŋ] *adj* contiguo, vecino

adjourn [ə'dʒɜ:rn] *vt* aplazar ♦ *vi* aplazarse

adjudicate [ə'dʒu:dıkeıt] *vi* sentenciar

adjust [ə'dʒʌst] *vt* (*change*) modificar; (*clothing*) arreglar; (*machine*) ajustar ♦ *vi*: **to ~ (to)** adaptarse (a) ◻ **adjustable** *adj* ajustable ◻ **adjustment** *n* adaptación f; (*to machine, prices*) ajuste m

ad-lib ['æd'lıb] *vt, vi* improvisar ◻ **ad lib** *adv* de forma improvisada

administer [æd'mınıstər] *vt* administrar ◻ **administration** [ædmınıstreıʃən] *n* (*management*) administración f; (*government*) gobierno ◻ **administrative** [æd'mınıstreıtıv] *adj* administrativo

admiral ['ædmərəl] *n* almirante m ◻ **Admiralty** (*BRIT*) *n* Secretaría de Marina, Almirantazgo

admiration [ædmə'reıʃən] *n* admiración f

admire [æd'maıər] *vt* admirar ◻ **admirer** *n* (*fan*) admirador(a) *m/f*

admission [æd'mıʃən] *n* (*to college, club*) ingreso; (*entry fee*) entrada; (*confession*) confesión f

admit [æd'mıt] *vt* (*confess*) confesar; (*permit to enter*) dejar entrar, dar entrada a; (*to club, organization*) admitir; (*accept: defeat*) reconocer; **to be ~ted to hospital** ingresar en el hospital ▶ **admit to** *vt fus* confesarse culpable de ◻ **admittance** *n* entrada ◻ **admittedly** *adv* es cierto *or* verdad que

admonish [əd'mɑ:nıʃ] *vt* amonestar

ad nauseam [æd'nɔ:ziəm] *adv* hasta el cansancio

ado [ə'du:] *n*: **without (any) more ~** sin más (ni más)

adolescent [ædl'esənt] *adj, n* adolescente mf

adopt [ə'dɑ:pt] *vt* adoptar ◻ **adopted** *adj* adoptado (*MEX, SP*), adoptivo (*LAm exc MEX*) ◻ **adoption** *n* adopción f

adore [ə'dɔ:r] *vt* adorar

Adriatic [eıdri'ætık] *n*: **the ~ (Sea)** el (Mar) Adriático

adrift [ə'drıft] *adv* a la deriva

adult [ə'dʌlt] *n* adulto(-a) ♦ *adj* (*grown-up*) adulto; (*for adults*) para adultos

adultery [ə'dʌltəri] *n* adulterio

advance [æd'væns] *n* (*progress*) adelanto, progreso; (*money*) anticipo, préstamo; (*MIL*) avance m ♦ *vt* (*money*) anticipar; (*theory, idea*) proponer (para la discusión) ♦ *vi* avanzar, adelantarse ♦ *adj*: **~ booking** venta anticipada; **~ notice, ~ warning** previo aviso; **to make ~s (to sb)** hacer proposiciones (a algn); **in ~** por adelantado ◻ **advanced** *adj* avanzado; (*SCOL: studies*) adelantado

advantage [æd'væntıdʒ] *n* (*also TENNIS*) ventaja; **to take ~ of** (*person*) aprovecharse de; (*opportunity*) aprovechar

Advent ['ædvent] *n* (*REL*) Adviento

adventure [æd'ventʃər] *n* aventura ◻ **adventurous** *adj* atrevido; aventurero

adverb ['ædvɜ:rb] *n* adverbio

adverse [æd'vɜ:rs] *adj* adverso, contrario

adversity [æd'vɜ:rsıti] *n* infortunio

advert ['ædvərt] (*BRIT*) *n abbr* = **advertisement**

advertise ['ædvərtaız] *vi* (*in newspaper etc*) anunciar, hacer publicidad ♦ *vt* anunciar; **to ~ for** (*staff, accommodations etc*) buscar por medio de anuncios ◻ **advertisement** [ædvər'taızmənt] *n* (*COMM*) anuncio ◻ **advertiser** *n* anunciante mf ◻ **advertising** *n* publicidad f, anuncios mpl; (*industry*) industria publicitaria

advice [æd'vaıs] *n* consejo, consejos mpl; (*notification*) aviso; **a piece of ~** un consejo; **to get legal ~** consultar con un abogado

advisable [əd'vaızəbəl] *adj* aconsejable, conveniente

advise [əd'vaız] *vt* aconsejar; (*inform*): **to ~ sb of sth** informar a algn de algo; **to ~ sb against sth/doing sth** desaconsejar algo a algn/aconsejar a algn que no haga algo ◻ **advisedly** [əd'vaızıdli] *adv* (*deliberately*) deliberadamente ◻ **adviser** *n* = **advisor**

❏ **advisor** n consejero(-a); (consultant) asesor(a) m/f ❏ **advisory** adj consultivo

advocate [vb 'ædvəkɪt, n 'ædvəkeɪt] vt abogar por ♦ n (lawyer) abogado(-a); (supporter): ~ **of** defensor(a) m/f de

Aegean [ɪ'dʒiːən] n: **the ~ (Sea)** el (Mar) Egeo

aerial ['ɛərɪəl] n antena ♦ adj aéreo

aerobics [ɛə'rəʊbɪks] n aerobics mpl (MEX), aerobic m (LAm exc MEX, SP)

aeroplane ['ɛərəpleɪn] (BRIT) n avión m

aerosol ['ɛərəsɒl] n aerosol m

aesthetic [es'θetɪk] (BRIT) adj = **esthetic**

afar [ə'fɑːr] adv: **from ~** desde lejos

affair [ə'fɛər] n asunto; (also: **love ~**) aventura (amorosa)

affect [ə'fekt] vt (influence) afectar, influir en; (afflict, concern) afectar; (move) conmover ❏ **affected** adj afectado

affection [ə'fekʃən] n afecto, cariño ❏ **affectionate** adj afectuoso, cariñoso

affidavit [æfɪ'deɪvɪt] n declaración f jurada

affinity [ə'fɪnɪtɪ] n (bond, rapport): **to feel an ~ with** sentirse identificado con; (resemblance) afinidad f

affirm [ə'fɜːrm] vt afirmar

afflict [ə'flɪkt] vt afligir

affluence ['æfluəns] n opulencia, riqueza

affluent ['æfluənt] adj (wealthy) acomodado; **the ~ society** la sociedad opulenta

afford [ə'fɔːrd] vt (provide) proporcionar; **can we ~ (to buy) it?** ¿tenemos bastante dinero para comprarlo?

Afghanistan [æf'gænɪstæn] n Afganistán m

afield [ə'fiːld] adv: **far ~** muy lejos

afloat [ə'fləʊt] adv (floating) a flote

afoot [ə'fʊt] adv: **there is something ~** algo se está tramando

afraid [ə'freɪd] adj: **to be ~ of** (person) tener miedo a; (thing) tener miedo de; **to be ~ to** tener miedo de, temer; **I am ~ that** me temo que; **I am ~ not/so** me temo que no/sí

afresh [ə'freʃ] adv de nuevo, otra vez

Africa ['æfrɪkə] n África ❏ **African** adj, n africano(-a) ❏ **African-American** adj, n afroamericano(-a)

after ['æftər] prep (time) después de; (place, order) detrás de, tras ♦ adv después ♦ conj después (de) que; **what/who are you ~?** ¿qué/a quién busca usted?; **~ having done/he left** después de haber hecho/de que se marchó; **to name sb ~ sb** llamar a algn por algn; **it's twenty ~ eight** (US) son las ocho y veinte; **to ask ~ sb** preguntar por algn; **~ all** después de todo, al fin y al cabo; **~ you!** ¡pase usted! ❏ **aftercare** n asistencia postoperatoria ❏ **after-effects** npl consecuencias fpl, efectos mpl ❏ **aftermath** n consecuencias fpl, resultados mpl ❏ **afternoon** n tarde f ❏ **afters** (BRIT: inf) npl (dessert) postre m ❏ **after-sales service** (BRIT) n servicio post-venta ❏ **after-shave (lotion)** n loción f para después de rasurarse (MEX) or afeitarse (LAm), aftershave m (SP) ❏ **after-sun (lotion/cream)** n loción f/ crema para después del sol, aftersun m ❏ **aftertaste** n (lit, fig) regusto ❏ **afterthought** n ocurrencia (tardía) ❏ **afterward** (US) (BRIT **afterwards**) adv después, más tarde

again [ə'gen] adv otra vez, de nuevo; **to do sth ~** volver a hacer algo; **~ and ~** una y otra vez

against [ə'genst] prep (in opposition to) en contra de; (leaning on, touching) contra, junto a

age [eɪdʒ] n edad f; (period) época ♦ vi envejecer(se) ♦ vt envejecer; **to come of ~** llegar a la mayoría de edad; **it's been ~s since I saw you** hace siglos que no te veo ❏ **aged** [adj eɪdʒd, npl 'eɪdʒɪd] adj: **aged 10** de 10 años de edad ♦ npl: **the aged** los ancianos ❏ **age group** n: **to be in the same age group** tener la misma edad ❏ **age limit** n edad f mínima (or máxima)

agency ['eɪdʒənsɪ] n agencia

agenda [ə'dʒendə] n orden m del día

⚠ Be careful not to translate **agenda** by the Spanish word **agenda**.

agent ['eɪdʒənt] n agente mf; (COMM: holding concession) representante mf, delegado(-a); (CHEM, fig) agente m

aggravate ['ægrəveɪt] vt (situation) agravar; (person) irritar

aggregate ['ægrɪgɪt] n conjunto

aggressive [ə'gresɪv] adj (belligerent) agresivo; (assertive) enérgico

aggrieved [ə'griːvd] adj ofendido, agraviado

aghast [ə'gæst] adj horrorizado

agile ['ædʒəl] adj ágil

agitate ['ædʒɪteɪt] vt (trouble) inquietar ♦ vi: **to ~ for/against** hacer campaña pro or en favor de/en contra de

AGM (BRIT) n abbr (= annual general meeting) asamblea anual

ago [ə'gəʊ] adv: **2 days ~** hace 2 días; **not long ~** hace poco; **how long ~?** ¿hace cuánto tiempo?

agog [əˈgɒɡ] adj (eager) ansioso; (excited) emocionado

agonizing [ˈæɡənaɪzɪŋ] adj (pain) atroz; (decision, wait) angustioso

agony [ˈæɡənɪ] n (pain) dolor m agudo; (distress) angustia; **to be in ~** retorcerse de dolor

agree [əˈɡriː] vt (price, date) acordar, quedar en ♦ vi (have same opinion): **to ~ (with/that)** estar de acuerdo (con/que); (correspond) coincidir, concordar; (consent) acceder; **to ~ with** (person) estar or ponerse de acuerdo con; (food) sentar bien a; (LING) concordar con; **to ~ to sth/to do sth** consentir en algo/ aceptar hacer algo; **to ~ that** (admit) estar de acuerdo en que ❑ **agreeable** adj (sensation) agradable; (person) simpático; (willing) de acuerdo, conforme ❑ **agreed** adj (time, place) convenido ❑ **agreement** n acuerdo; (contract) contrato; **in agreement** de acuerdo, conforme

agricultural [æɡrɪˈkʌltʃərəl] adj agrícola

agriculture [ˈæɡrɪkʌltʃər] n agricultura

aground [əˈɡraund] adv: **to run ~** (NAUT) encallar, embarrancar

ahead [əˈhɛd] adv (in front) delante; (into the future): **she had no time to think ~** no tenía tiempo de hacer planes para el futuro; **~ of** delante de; (in advance of) antes de; **~ of time** antes de la hora; **go right** or **straight ~** (direction) siga adelante; (permission) hazlo (or hágalo)

aid [eɪd] n ayuda, auxilio; (device) aparato ♦ vt ayudar, auxiliar; **in ~ of** a beneficio de

aide [eɪd] n (person, also MIL) ayudante mf

AIDS [eɪdz] n abbr (= acquired immune deficiency syndrome) SIDA m

ailment [ˈeɪlmənt] n enfermedad f, achaque m

aim [eɪm] vt (gun, camera) apuntar; (missile, remark) dirigir; (blow) asestar ♦ vi (also: **take ~**) apuntar ♦ n (in shooting: skill) puntería; (objective) propósito, meta; **to ~ at** (with weapon) apuntar a; (objective) aspirar a, pretender; **to ~ to do** tener la intención de hacer ❑ **aimless** adj sin propósito or objeto

ain't [eɪnt] (inf) cont = **am not**; **aren't**; **isn't**

air [eər] n aire m; (appearance) aspecto ♦ vt (room) ventilar; (clothes, ideas) airear ♦ cpd aéreo; **to throw sth into the ~** (ball etc) lanzar algo al aire; **by ~** (travel) en avión; **to be on the ~** (RADIO, TV) estar en el aire, estar al aire (MEX) ❑ **air bag** n airbag m, bolsa de aire (LAm) ❑ **air bed** (BRIT) n colchón m inflable ❑ **air-conditioned** adj climatizado ❑ **air conditioning** n aire m acondicionado

❑ **aircraft** n inv avión m ❑ **aircraft carrier** n porta(a)viones m inv ❑ **airfield** n campo de aviación ❑ **Air Force** n fuerzas fpl aéreas, aviación f ❑ **air freshener** n aromatizante m (ambiental) (MEX), ambientador m (LAm exc MEX, SP), desodorante m ambiental (SC) ❑ **air gun** n escopeta de aire comprimido ❑ **air hostess** (BRIT) n aeromoza (LAm), azafata (SP) ❑ **air letter** (BRIT) n carta aérea ❑ **airlift** n puente m aéreo ❑ **airline** n línea aérea ❑ **airliner** n avión m de pasajeros ❑ **airmail** n: **by airmail** por avión ❑ **air mattress** n colchón m neumático ❑ **airplane** (US) n avión m ❑ **airport** n aeropuerto ❑ **air raid** n ataque m aéreo ❑ **airsick** adj: **to be airsick** marearse (en avión) ❑ **airspace** n espacio aéreo ❑ **airtight** adj hermético ❑ **air-traffic controller** n controlador(a) m/f aéreo(-a) ❑ **airy** adj (room) bien ventilado; (fig: manner) desenfadado

aisle [aɪl] n (of church) nave f; (of theater, supermarket) pasillo ❑ **aisle seat** n (on plane) asiento de pasillo

ajar [əˈdʒɑːr] adj entreabierto

alarm [əˈlɑːrm] n (anxiety) inquietud f; (in store, bank) alarma ♦ vt asustar, inquietar ❑ **alarm clock** n despertador m

alas [əˈlæs] adv desgraciadamente

albeit [ɔːlˈbiːɪt] conj aunque

album [ˈælbəm] n álbum m; (L.P.) elepé m

alcohol [ˈælkəhɒl] n alcohol m ❑ **alcoholic** [ælkəˈhɒlɪk] adj, n alcohólico(-a)

ale [eɪl] n cerveza

alert [əˈlɜːrt] adj (attentive) atento; (to danger, opportunity) alerta ♦ n alerta, alarma ♦ vt poner sobre aviso; **to be on the ~** (also MIL) estar alerta or sobre aviso

algebra [ˈældʒɪbrə] n álgebra

Algeria [ælˈdʒɪərɪə] n Argelia

alias [ˈeɪlɪəs] adv alias, conocido por ♦ n (of criminal) apodo; (of writer) seudónimo

alibi [ˈælɪbaɪ] n coartada

alien [ˈeɪlɪən] n (foreigner) extranjero(-a); (extraterrestrial) extraterrestre mf ♦ adj: **~ to** ajeno a ❑ **alienate** vt enajenar, alejar

alight [əˈlaɪt] adj ardiendo; (eyes) brillante ♦ vi (person) apearse, bajarse; (bird) posarse

align [əˈlaɪn] vt alinear

alike [əˈlaɪk] adj semejantes, iguales ♦ adv igualmente, del mismo modo; **to look ~** parecerse

alimony [ˈælɪmouni] n manutención f

alive [əˈlaɪv] adj vivo; (lively) alegre

all

KEYWORD

[ɔːl] *adj* (*sg*) todo(-a); (*pl*) todos(-as); **all day** todo el día; **all night** toda la noche; **all men** todos los hombres; **all five came** vinieron los cinco; **all the books** todos los libros; **all his life** toda su vida

♦ *pron*

1 todo; **I ate it all, I ate all of it** me lo comí todo; **all of us went** fuimos todos; **all the boys went** fueron todos los chicos; **is that all?** ¿eso es todo?, ¿algo más?; (*in store*) ¿algo más?, ¿alguna cosa más?

2 (*in phrases*): **above all** sobre todo; por encima de todo; **after all** después de todo; **at all: not at all** (*in answer to question*) en absoluto; (*in answer to thanks*) ¡de nada!, ¡no hay de qué!; **I'm not at all tired** no estoy nada cansado(-a); **anything at all will do** cualquier cosa viene bien; **all in all** a fin de cuentas

♦ *adv*: **all alone** completamente solo(-a); **it's not as hard as all that** no es tan difícil como lo pintas; **all the more/the better** tanto más/ mejor; **all but** casi; **the score is 2 all** están empatados a 2

all clear *n* (*after attack etc*) fin *m* de la alerta; (*fig*) luz *f* verde

allege [əˈlɛdʒ] *vt* pretender ❑ **allegedly** [əˈlɛdʒɪdlɪ] *adv* supuestamente, según se afirma

allegiance [əˈliːdʒəns] *n* lealtad *f*

allergy [ˈælədʒɪ] *n* alergia

alleviate [əˈliːvɪeɪt] *vt* aliviar

alley [ˈælɪ] *n* calle estrecha (*LAm*), callejón *m* (*SP*)

alliance [əˈlaɪəns] *n* alianza

allied [ˈælaɪd] *adj* aliado

alligator [ˈælɪgeɪtər] *n* (*ZOOL*) caimán *m*

all-in (*BRIT*) *adj, adv* (*charge*) todo incluido

all-inclusive [ˈɔːlɪnˈkluːsɪv] *adj* (*price*) con todo incluido

all-night *adj* (*café, store*) abierto toda la noche; (*party*) que dura toda la noche

allocate [ˈæləkeɪt] *vt* (*money etc*) asignar

allot [əˈlɒt] *vt* asignar ❑ **allotment** *n* ración *f*; (*garden*) parcela

all-out *adj* (*effort etc*) supremo ❑ **all out** *adv* con todas las fuerzas

allow [əˈlaʊ] *vt* permitir, dejar; (*a claim*) admitir; (*sum, time etc*) dar, conceder; (*concede*): **to ~ that** reconocer que; **to ~ sb to do** permitir a algn hacer; **he is ~ed to ...** se le permite ... ▶ **allow for** *vt fus* tener en cuenta

allowance *n* subvención *f*; (*welfare payment*) subsidio, prestación *f*; (*US: spending money*) domingo (*MEX*), dinero de bolsillo (*LAm exc MEX, SP*); (*tax allowance*) desgravación *f*; **to make allowances for** (*person*) disculpar a; (*thing*) tener en cuenta

alloy [ˈælɔɪ] *n* mezcla

all: ❑ **all right** *adv* bien; (*as answer*) ¡conforme!, ¡está bien! ❑ **all-rounder** (*BRIT*) *n*: **he's a good all-rounder** se le da bien todo ❑ **all-time** *adj* (*record*) de todos los tiempos

alluring [əˈlʊrɪŋ] *adj* atractivo, tentador(a)

ally [ˈælaɪ] *n* aliado(-a) ♦ *vt*: **to ~ o.s. with** aliarse con

almighty [ɔːlˈmaɪtɪ] *adj* todopoderoso; (*uproar etc*) imponente

almond [ˈɑːmənd] *n* almendra

almost [ˈɔːlmoʊst] *adv* casi

alone [əˈloʊn] *adj, adv* solo; **to leave sb ~** dejar a algn en paz; **to leave sth ~** no tocar algo, dejar algo sin tocar; **let ~ ...** y mucho menos ...

along [əˈlɔːŋ] *prep* a lo largo de, por ♦ *adv*: **is he coming ~ with us?** ¿viene con nosotros?; **he was limping ~** iba cojeando; **~ with** junto con; **all ~** (*all the time*) desde el principio ❑ **alongside** *prep* al lado de ♦ *adv* al lado

aloof [əˈluːf] *adj* reservado ♦ *adv*: **to stand ~** mantenerse apartado

aloud [əˈlaʊd] *adv* en voz alta

alphabet [ˈælfəbɛt] *n* alfabeto

Alps [ælps] *npl*: **the ~** los Alpes

already [ɔːlˈrɛdɪ] *adv* ya

alright [ɔːlˈraɪt] (*BRIT*) *adv* = **all right**

Alsatian [ælˈseɪʃən] *n* (*dog*) pastor *m* alemán

also [ˈɔːlsoʊ] *adv* también, además

altar [ˈɔːltər] *n* altar *m*

alter [ˈɔːltər] *vt* cambiar, modificar ♦ *vi* cambiar ❑ **alteration** [ɔːltəˈreɪʃən] *n* cambio; (*to clothes*) arreglo; (*to building*) arreglos *mpl*

alternate [*adj* ˈɔːltərnɪt, *vb* ˈɔːltərneɪt] *adj* (*actions etc*) alternativo; (*events*) alterno; (*US*) = **alternative** ♦ *vi*: **to ~ (with)** alternar (con); **on ~ days** un día sí y otro no ❑ **alternating current** *n* corriente *f* alterna

alternative [ɔːlˈtɜːrnətɪv] *adj* alternativo ♦ *n* alternativa; **~ medicine** medicina alternativa ❑ **alternatively** *adv*: **alternatively one could ...** por otra parte se podría ...

although [ɔːlˈðoʊ] *conj* aunque

altitude [ˈæltɪtuːd] *n* altitud *f*

alto [ˈæltoʊ] *n* (*female*) contralto *f*; (*male*) alto

altogether [ɔːltə'geðər] *adv* completamente, del todo; (*on the whole*) en total, en conjunto

aluminum (*US*) [ə'luːmɪnəm] (*BRIT* **aluminium** [æljuˈmɪnɪəm]) *n* aluminio

alumnus [ə'lʌmnəs] (*pl* **alumni**) *n* graduado(-a)

always ['ɔːlweɪz] *adv* siempre

Alzheimer's (disease) ['ɑːltshaɪmərz (dɪ'ziːz)] *n* enfermedad *f* de Alzheimer

AM *n abbr* (= *Assembly Member*) diputado(-a)

am [æm] *vb see* **be**

a.m. *adv abbr* (= *ante meridiem*) de la mañana

amalgamate [ə'mælgəmeɪt] *vi* amalgamarse ♦ *vt* amalgamar, unir

amateur ['æmətər] *n* aficionado(-a), amateur *mf* ❑ **amateurish** *adj* inexperto

amaze [ə'meɪz] *vt* asombrar, pasmar; **to be ~d (at)** quedar pasmado (de) ❑ **amazement** *n* asombro, sorpresa ❑ **amazing** *adj* extraordinario; (*fantastic*) increíble

Amazon ['æməzɔːn] *n*: **the ~s** el Amazonas

ambassador [æm'bæsədər] *n* embajador(a) *m/f*

amber ['æmbər] *n* ámbar *m*; **at ~** (*BRIT AUT*) en ámbar

ambience ['æmbɪəns] *n* ambiente *m*

ambiguous [æm'bɪgjuəs] *adj* ambiguo

ambition [æm'bɪʃən] *n* ambición *f* ❑ **ambitious** *adj* ambicioso

ambulance ['æmbjuləns] *n* ambulancia

ambush ['æmbuʃ] *n* emboscada ♦ *vt* tender una emboscada a

amenable [ə'miːnəbəl] *adj*: **to be ~ to** dejarse influir por

amend [ə'mɛnd] *vt* enmendar; **to make ~s** dar cumplida satisfacción

amenities [ə'mɛnɪtiz] *npl* comodidades *fpl*

America [ə'mɛrɪkə] *n* (*USA*) Estados *mpl* Unidos ❑ **American** *adj*, *n* norteamericano(-a); estadounidense *mf*

amiable ['eɪmɪəbəl] *adj* amable, simpático

amicable ['æmɪkəbəl] *adj* amistoso, amigable

amid(st) [ə'mɪd(st)] *prep* entre, en medio de

amiss [ə'mɪs] *adv*: **to take sth ~** tomar algo a mal; **there's something ~** pasa algo

ammonia [ə'məunjə] *n* amoníaco

ammunition [æmju'nɪʃən] *n* munición *f*, parque *m* (*MEX*)

amnesty ['æmnɪsti] *n* amnistía

amok [ə'mʌk] *adv*: **to run ~** enloquecerse, desbocarse

among(st) [ə'mʌŋ(st)] *prep* entre, en medio de

amorous ['æmərəs] *adj* amoroso

amount [ə'maunt] *n* (*gen*) cantidad *f*; (*of bill etc*) suma, importe *m* ♦ *vi*: **to ~ to** sumar; (*be same as*) equivaler a, significar

amp(ère) ['æmp(ɪər)] *n* amperio

ample ['æmpəl] *adj* (*large*) grande; (*abundant*) abundante; (*enough*) bastante, suficiente

amplifier ['æmplɪfaɪər] *n* amplificador *m*

amuse [ə'mjuːz] *vt* divertir; (*distract*) distraer, entretener ❑ **amusement** *n* diversión *f*; (*pastime*) pasatiempo; (*laughter*) risa ❑ **amusement arcade** *n* sala de juegos ❑ **amusement park** *n* parque *m* de atracciones

an [æn] *indef art see* **a**

anaemic [ə'niːmɪk] (*BRIT*) *adj* = **anemic**

anaesthetic [ænɪs'θɛtɪk] (*BRIT*) *n* = **anesthetic**

analogue ['ænəlɔːg] (*US: also:* **analog**) *adj* (*computer, watch*) analógico

analyse ['ænəlaɪz] (*BRIT*) *vt* = **analyze** ❑ **analysis** [ə'næləsɪs] (*pl* **analyses**) *n* análisis *m inv* ❑ **analyst** ['ænəlɪst] *n* (*political analyst, psychoanalyst*) analista *mf*

analyze (*US*) ['ænəlaɪz] (*BRIT* **analyse**) *vt* analizar

anarchist ['ænərkɪst] *n* anarquista *mf*

anatomy [ə'nætəmi] *n* anatomía

ancestor ['ænsestər] *n* antepasado

anchor ['æŋkər] *n* ancla, áncora; (*TV, RADIO*) presentador(a) *m/f* ♦ *vi* (*also:* **to drop ~**) anclar ♦ *vt* anclar; **to weigh ~** levar anclas

anchovy ['æntʃouvi] *n* anchoa

ancient ['eɪnʃənt] *adj* antiguo

ancillary ['ænsɪleri] *adj* auxiliar

and [ænd] *conj* y; (*before i-, hi- + consonant*) e; **men ~ women** hombres y mujeres; **father ~ son** padre e hijo; **trees ~ grass** árboles y hierba; **~ so on** etcétera, y así sucesivamente; **try ~ come** procura venir; **he talked ~ talked** habló sin parar; **better ~ better** cada vez mejor

Andes ['ændiːz] *npl*: **the ~** los Andes

anemic (*US*) [ə'niːmɪk] (*BRIT* **anaemic**) *adj* anémico(-a); (*fig*) soso, insípido

anesthetic (*US*) [ænɪs'θɛtɪk] (*BRIT* **anaesthetic**) *n* anestesia

anew [ə'nuː] *adv* de nuevo, otra vez

angel ['eɪndʒəl] *n* ángel *m*

anger ['æŋgər] *n* cólera

angina [æn'dʒaɪnə] *n* angina (del pecho)

angle ['æŋgəl] n ángulo; **from their ~** desde su punto de vista

angler ['æŋglər] n pescador(a) m/f (de caña)

Anglican ['æŋglɪkən] adj, n anglicano(-a)

angling ['æŋglɪŋ] n pesca con caña

Anglo... ['æŋglou] prefix anglo...

angrily ['æŋgrəlɪ] adv con ira, airadamente

angry ['æŋgrɪ] adj enojado (LAm), enfadado (SP); (wound) inflamado; **to be ~ with sb/at sth** estar enojado (LAm) or enfadado (SP) con algn/por algo; **to get ~** enojarse (LAm), enfadarse (SP)

anguish ['æŋgwɪʃ] n (physical) tormentos mpl; (mental) angustia

animal ['ænɪməl] n animal m; (pej: person) bestia ♦ adj animal

animate ['ænɪmɪt] adj vivo ◻ **animated** ['ænɪmeɪtɪd] adj animado

aniseed ['ænɪsiːd] n anís m

ankle ['æŋkəl] n tobillo m ◻ **anklet** n calcetín m corto

annex (US) [n 'æneks, vb æ'neks] n (BRIT: also: **~e**: building) edificio anexo ♦ vt (territory) anexionar

annihilate [ə'naɪəleɪt] vt aniquilar

anniversary [ænɪ'vɜːrsərɪ] n aniversario

announce [ə'nauns] vt anunciar ◻ **announcement** n anuncio; (official) declaración f ◻ **announcer** n (RADIO) locutor(a) m/f; (TV) presentador(a) m/f

annoy [ə'nɔɪ] vt molestar, fastidiar; **don't get ~ed!** ¡no te enojes! ◻ **annoyance** n enojo ◻ **annoying** adj molesto, fastidioso; (person) pesado

annual ['ænjuəl] adj anual ♦ n (BOT) anual m; (book) anuario ◻ **annually** adv anualmente, cada año

annul [ə'nʌl] vt anular

annum ['ænəm] n see **per**

anonymous [ə'nɒnɪməs] adj anónimo

anorak ['ænəræk] n anorak m, chamarra (rompevientos) (MEX), parka (LAm), campera (RPI)

anorexia [ænə'reksɪə] n (MED: also: **~ nervosa**) anorexia

another [ə'nʌðər] adj (one more, a different one) otro ♦ pron otro; see **one**

answer ['ænsər] n contestación f, respuesta; (to problem) solución f ♦ vi contestar, responder ♦ vt (reply to) contestar a, responder a; (problem) resolver; (prayer) escuchar; **in ~ to your letter** contestando or en contestación a su carta; **to ~ the phone** contestar el teléfono; **to ~ the door** acudir a la puerta ▶ **answer back** vi replicar, ser

respondón(-ona) m/f ▶ **answer for** vt fus responder de or por ▶ **answer to** vt fus (description) corresponder a ◻ **answerable** adj: **answerable to sb for sth** responsable ante algn de algo ◻ **answering machine** n contestador m automático

ant [ænt] n hormiga

antagonism [æn'tægənɪzəm] n antagonismo, hostilidad f

antagonize [æn'tægənaɪz] vt provocar la enemistad de

Antarctic [ænt'ɑːrktɪk] n: **the ~** el Antártico

antelope ['æntəloup] n antílope m

antenatal ['æntɪ'neɪtl] adj antenatal, prenatal ◻ **antenatal clinic** n clínica prenatal

antenna [æn'tenə] n (TV, RADIO) antena

anthem ['ænθəm] n: **national ~** himno nacional

anthropology [ænθrə'pɑːlədʒɪ] n antropología

anti... [ænti] prefix anti... ◻ **anti-aircraft** adj antiaéreo ◻ **antibiotic** [æntibaɪ'ɑːtɪk] n antibiótico ◻ **antibody** n anticuerpo

anticipate [æn'tɪsɪpeɪt] vt prever; (expect) esperar, contar con; (look forward to) esperar con ilusión; (do first) anticiparse a, adelantarse a ◻ **anticipation** [æntɪsɪ'peɪʃən] n (expectation) previsión f; (eagerness) ilusión f, expectación f

anticlimax [ænti'klaɪmæks] n decepción f

anticlockwise [ænti'klɒ:kwaɪz] (BRIT) adv en dirección contraria a la de las agujas del reloj

antics ['æntɪks] npl gracias fpl

anticyclone [ænti'saɪkloun] n anticiclón m

antidepressant [æntɪdɪ'presənt] n antidepresivo

antidote ['æntɪdout] n antídoto

antifreeze ['æntifriːz] n anticongelante m

anti-globalization ['æntɪgloubəlɪ'zeɪʃən] n antiglobalización f; **~ protestors** manifestantes mfpl antiglobalización

antihistamine [ænti'hɪstəmɪn] n antihistamínico

antiperspirant [ænti'pɜːrspərənt] n antitranspirante m

antiquated ['æntɪkweɪtɪd] adj anticuado

antique [æn'tiːk] n antigüedad f ♦ adj antiguo ◻ **antique dealer** n anticuario(-a) ◻ **antique store** (US) (BRIT **antique shop**) n tienda de antigüedades

antiquity [æn'tɪkwɪtɪ] n antigüedad f

antiseptic [ænti'septɪk] adj, n antiséptico

antlers ['æntlərz] npl cuernos fpl, cornamenta sg

anus ['eɪnəs] n ano

anvil ['ænvɪl] n yunque m

anxiety [æŋ'zaɪətɪ] n inquietud f; (MED) ansiedad f; **~ to do** deseo de hacer

anxious ['æŋkʃəs] adj inquieto, preocupado; (worrying) preocupante; (keen): **to be ~ to do** tener muchas ganas de hacer

any
KEYWORD

['enɪ] adj

1 (in questions etc) algún (alguna); **do you have any butter/children?** ¿tienes mantequilla/hijos?; **if there are any tickets left** si quedan boletos, si queda algún boleto

2 (with negative): **I don't have any money/books** no tengo dinero/libros

3 (no matter which) cualquier; **any excuse will do** valdrá or servirá cualquier excusa; **choose any book you like** escoge el libro que quieras; **any teacher you ask will tell you** cualquier profesor al que preguntes te lo dirá

4 (in phrases): **in any case** de todas formas, en cualquier caso; **any day now** cualquier día (de estos); **at any moment** en cualquier momento, de un momento a otro; **at any rate** en todo caso; **any time: come (at) any time** ven cuando quieras; **he might come (at) any time** podría llegar de un momento a otro

♦ pron

1 (in questions etc): **have you got any?** ¿tienes alguno(s)/a(s)?; **can any of you sing?** ¿sabe cantar alguno de vosotros/ustedes?

2 (with negative): **I don't have any (of them)** no tengo ninguno

3 (no matter which one(s)): **take any of those books (you like)** toma el libro que quieras de ésos

♦ adv

1 (in questions etc): **do you want any more soup/sandwiches?** ¿quieres más sopa/sándwiches?; **are you feeling any better?** ¿te sientes algo mejor?

2 (with negative): **I can't hear him any more** ya no lo oigo; **don't wait any longer** no esperes más

anybody ['enɪbɑːdɪ] pron cualquiera; (in interrogative sentences) alguien; (in negative sentences): **I don't see ~** no veo a nadie; **if ~ should call ...** si llama alguien ...

anyhow ['enɪhaʊ] adv (at any rate) de todos modos, de todas formas; (haphazard): **she leaves things just ~** deja las cosas como quiera or de cualquier modo; **I shall go ~** de todos modos iré

anyone ['enɪwʌn] pron = **anybody**

anyplace ['enɪpleɪs] (US) adv = **anywhere**

anything ['enɪθɪŋ] pron (in questions etc) algo, alguna cosa; (with negative) nada; **can you see ~?** ¿ves algo?; **if ~ happens to me ...** si algo me ocurre ...; **you can say ~ you like** puedes decir lo que quieras; **~ will do** vale todo or cualquier cosa; **he'll eat ~** come de todo or lo que sea

anyway ['enɪweɪ] adv (at any rate) de todos modos, de todas formas; **I shall go ~** iré de todos modos; **~, I couldn't come even if I wanted to** además, no podría venir aunque quisiera; **why are you calling, ~?** ¿entonces, por qué llamas?, ¿por qué llamas, pues?

anyways ['enɪweɪz] (US: inf) adv = **anyway**

anywhere
KEYWORD

['enɪwɛər] adv

1 (in questions etc): **can you see him anywhere?** ¿le ves por algún lado?; **are you going anywhere?** ¿vas a algún sitio?

2 (with negative): **I can't see him anywhere** no le veo por ninguna parte

3 (no matter where): **anywhere in the world** en cualquier parte (del mundo); **put the books down anywhere** deja los libros donde quieras

apart [ə'pɑːrt] adv (aside) aparte; (situation): **~ (from)** separado (de); (movement): **to pull ~** separar; **10 miles ~** separados por 10 millas; **to take ~** desmontar; **~ from** prep aparte de

apartheid [ə'pɑːrteɪt] n apartheid m

apartment [ə'pɑːrtmənt] n (US) departamento (LAm), piso (SP); (room) cuarto ❑ **apartment building** (US) n edificio de departamentos

apathetic [æpə'θetɪk] adj apático, indiferente

ape [eɪp] n simio ♦ vt imitar, remedar

aperitif [əperɪ'tiːf] n aperitivo

aperture ['æpərtʃuər] n rendija, resquicio; (PHOT) abertura

APEX ['eɪpeks] n abbr (= Advanced Purchase Excursion) tarifa APEX

apex n ápice m; (fig) cumbre f

apiece [ə'piːs] adv cada uno

aplomb [ə'plɑːm] n aplomo

apologetic [əpɒləˈdʒɛtɪk] adj de disculpa; (person) arrepentido

apologize [əˈpɒlədʒaɪz] vi: **to ~ (for sth to sb)** disculparse (con algn de algo)

apology [əˈpɒlədʒɪ] n disculpa, excusa

⚠ Be careful not to translate **apology** by the Spanish word *apología*.

apostrophe [əˈpɒstrəfɪ] n apóstrofo

appall (US) [əˈpɔːl] (BRIT **appal**) vt horrorizar, espantar □ **appalling** adj espantoso; (awful) pésimo

apparatus [æpəˈrætəs] n (equipment) equipo; (organization) aparato; (in gymnasium) aparatos mpl

apparel [əˈpærəl] (US) n ropa

apparent [əˈpærənt] adj aparente; (obvious) evidente □ **apparently** adv por lo visto, al parecer

appeal [əˈpiːl] vi (LAW) apelar ♦ n (LAW) apelación f; (request) llamamiento; (plea) petición f; (charm) atractivo; **to ~ for** reclamar; **to ~ to** (be attractive to) atraer; **it doesn't ~ to me** no me atrae, no me llama la atención □ **appealing** adj (attractive) atractivo

appear [əˈpɪər] vi aparecer, presentarse; (LAW) comparecer; (publication) salir (a la luz), publicarse; (seem) parecer; **to ~ on TV/in "Hamlet"** salir por la tele/hacer un papel en "Hamlet"; **it would ~ that** parecería que □ **appearance** n aparición f; (look) apariencia, aspecto

appease [əˈpiːz] vt (pacify) apaciguar; (satisfy) satisfacer

appendices [əˈpɛndɪsiːz] npl of **appendix**

appendicitis [əpɛndɪˈsaɪtɪs] n apendicitis f

appendix [əˈpɛndɪks] (pl **appendices**) n apéndice m

appetite [ˈæpɪtaɪt] n apetito; (fig) deseo, anhelo

appetizer [ˈæpɪtaɪzər] n (drink) aperitivo; (food) aperitivo, botana (MEX)

applaud [əˈplɔːd] vt, vi aplaudir

applause [əˈplɔːz] n aplausos mpl

apple [ˈæpəl] n manzana □ **apple tree** n manzano

appliance [əˈplaɪəns] n aparato

applicable [ˈæplɪkəbəl] adj (relevant): **to be ~ (to)** referirse (a)

applicant [ˈæplɪkənt] n candidato(-a); solicitante mf

application [æplɪˈkeɪʃən] n aplicación f; (for a job etc) solicitud f, petición f □ **application form** n solicitud f

applied [əˈplaɪd] adj aplicado

apply [əˈplaɪ] vt (paint etc) poner; (law etc: put into practice) poner en vigor ♦ vi: **to ~ to** (ask) dirigirse a; (be applicable) ser aplicable a; **to ~ for** (permit, grant, job) solicitar; **to ~ o.s. to** aplicarse a, dedicarse a

appoint [əˈpɔɪnt] vt (to post) nombrar □ **appointed** adj: **at the appointed time** a la hora señalada □ **appointment** n (with client) cita; (act) nombramiento; (post) puesto; (at hairdresser etc): **to have an appointment** tener una cita, tener hora; **to make an appointment (with sb)** concertar una cita (con algn)

⚠ Be careful not to translate **appoint** by the Spanish word *apuntar*.

appraisal [əˈpreɪzəl] n valoración f

appraise [əˈpreɪz] vt valorar, tasar

appreciate [əˈpriːʃɪeɪt] vt apreciar, tener en mucho; (be grateful for) agradecer; (be aware) comprender ♦ vi (COMM) aumentar(se) en valor □ **appreciation** [əpriːʃɪˈeɪʃən] n apreciación f; (gratitude) reconocimiento, agradecimiento; (COMM) aumento en valor

appreciative [əˈpriːʃɪətɪv] adj apreciativo; (comment) agradecido

apprehensive [æprɪˈhɛnsɪv] adj aprensivo

apprentice [əˈprɛntɪs] n aprendiz(a) m/f □ **apprenticeship** n aprendizaje m

approach [əˈprəʊtʃ] vi acercarse ♦ vt acercarse a; (ask, apply to) dirigirse a; (situation, problem) abordar ♦ n acercamiento; (access) acceso; (to problem, situation): **~ (to)** actitud f (ante) □ **approachable** adj (person, place) accesible

appropriate [adj əˈprəʊprɪɪt, vb əˈprəʊprɪeɪt] adj apropiado, conveniente ♦ vt (take) apropiarse de

approval [əˈpruːvəl] n aprobación f, visto bueno; (permission) consentimiento; **on ~** (COMM) a prueba

approve [əˈpruːv] vt aprobar ▶ **approve of** vt fus (thing) aprobar; (person): **they don't approve of her** (ella) no les parece bien

approximate [əˈprɒksɪmɪt] adj aproximado □ **approximately** adv aproximadamente, más o menos

apricot [ˈeɪprɪkɒt] n albaricoque m, chabacano (MEX), damasco (RPl)

April [ˈeɪprəl] n abril m □ **April Fools' Day** n el primero de abril, ≈ día m de los Inocentes (28 December)

apron [ˈeɪprən] n delantal m; mandil m

apt [æpt] adj acertado, apropiado; (likely): **~ to do** propenso a hacer

aquarium [əˈkweəriəm] n acuario

Aquarius [əˈkweəriəs] n Acuario

Arab [ˈærəb] adj, n árabe mf

Arabian [əˈreibiən] adj árabe

Arabic [ˈærəbik] adj árabe; (numerals) arábigo
♦ n árabe m

arable [ˈærəbəl] adj cultivable

Aragon [ˈærəgɔːn] n Aragón m

arbitrary [ˈɑːbitreri] adj arbitrario

arbitration [ɑːbiˈtreiʃən] n arbitraje m

arbor (US) [ˈɑːbər] (BRIT **arbour**) n cenador m

arcade [ɑːˈkeid] n (around a square) arcos mpl
(MEX), portales mpl (LAm); (shopping mall)
galería comercial

arch [ɑːtʃ] n arco; (of foot) puente m ♦ vt
arquear

archaeology etc [ɑːkiˈɔlədʒi] (BRIT)
= **archeology** etc

archbishop [ɑːtʃˈbiʃəp] n arzobispo

archeologist (US) [ɑːkiˈɔlədʒist] (BRIT
archaeologist) n arqueólogo(-a)

archeology (US) [ɑːkiˈɔlədʒi] (BRIT
archaeology) n arqueología

archery [ˈɑːtʃəri] n tiro al arco

architect [ˈɑːkitekt] n arquitecto(-a)
❑ **architecture** n arquitectura

archives [ˈɑːkaivz] npl archivo

Arctic [ˈɑːktik] adj ártico ♦ n: **the ~** el Ártico

ardent [ˈɑːdnt] adj ardiente, apasionado

ardor (US) [ˈɑːdər] (BRIT **ardour**) n ardor m,
pasión f

arduous [ˈɑːdjuəs] adj (task) arduo; (journey)
agotador(a)

are [ɑː] vb see **be**

area [ˈeəriə] n área, región f; (part of place)
zona; (MATH etc) área, superficie f; (in room: e.g.
dining area) parte f; (of knowledge, experience)
campo ❑ **area code** (US) n clave f lada (MEX),
código de la zona (LAm), prefijo (SP)

arena [əˈriːnə] n estadio; (of circus) pista

aren't [ɑːrənt] cont = **are not**

Argentina [ɑːdʒənˈtiːnə] n Argentina
❑ **Argentinian** [ɑːdʒənˈtiniən] adj, n
argentino(-a)

arguably [ˈɑːgjuəbli] adv posiblemente

argue [ˈɑːgjuː] vi (quarrel) discutir, pelearse;
(reason) razonar, argumentar; **to ~ that**
sostener que

argument [ˈɑːgjəmənt] n discusión f, pelea;
(reasons) argumento ❑ **argumentative**
[ɑːgjuˈmentətiv] adj discutidor(a)

Aries [ˈeəriz] n Aries m

arise [əˈraiz] (pt arose, pp arisen) vi surgir,
presentarse

arisen [əˈrizən] pp of **arise**

aristocrat [əˈristəkræt] n aristócrata mf

arithmetic [əˈriθmətik] n aritmética

ark [ɑːk] n: Noah's A~ el Arca de Noé

arm [ɑːm] n brazo ♦ vt armar; **~s** npl armas fpl;
~ in ~ cogidos del brazo

armaments [ˈɑːməmənts] npl armamento

armchair [ˈɑːmˌtʃeər] n sillón m, butaca

armed [ɑːmd] adj armado; **the ~ forces** las
fuerzas armadas ❑ **armed robbery** n robo
a mano armada

armor (US) [ˈɑːmər] (BRIT **armour**) n
armadura; (MIL: tanks) blindaje m ❑ **armored
car** (US) (BRIT **armoured car**) n carro (LAm) or
coche m (SP) blindado

armour [ˈɑːmər] (BRIT) n = **armor**

armpit [ˈɑːmpit] n sobaco, axila

armrest [ˈɑːmˌrest] n apoyabrazos m inv

army [ˈɑːmi] n ejército; (fig) multitud f

aroma [əˈroumə] n aroma m, fragancia
❑ **aromatherapy** n aromaterapia

arose [əˈrouz] pt of **arise**

around [əˈraund] adv alrededor; (in the area):
there is no one else ~ no hay nadie más por
aquí ♦ prep alrededor de; (surrounding): **~ his
neck/the table** en su cuello/alrededor de la
mesa; (in a circular movement): **to move ~ the
room/sail ~ the world** dar una vuelta a la
habitación/navigar por el mundo; (in various
directions): **to move ~ a room/house**
moverse por toda la habitación/casa;
(approximately) alrededor de ♦ adv: **all ~** por
todos lados; **the long way ~** por el camino
menos directo; **all the year ~** durante todo el
año; **it's just ~ the corner** (fig) está a la vuelta
de la esquina; **to go ~ to sb's (house)** ir a casa
de algn; **to go ~ the back** pasar por atrás;
enough to go ~ bastante (para todos)

arouse [əˈrauz] vt despertar; (anger) provocar

arrange [əˈreindʒ] vt arreglar, ordenar;
(organize) organizar; **to ~ to do sth** quedar en
hacer algo ❑ **arrangement** n arreglo;
(agreement) acuerdo; **arrangements** npl
(preparations) preparativos mpl

array [əˈrei] n: **~ of** (things) serie f de; (people)
conjunto de

arrears [əˈriərz] npl atrasos mpl; **to be in ~
with one's rent** estar atrasado en el pago de
la renta

arrest [əˈrest] vt detener; (sb's attention) llamar
♦ n detención f; **under ~** detenido

arrival [əˈraivəl] n llegada; **new ~** recién
llegado(-a); (baby) recién nacido(-a)

arrive [əˈraiv] vi llegar; (baby) nacer

arrogant [ˈærəgənt] adj arrogante

arrow ['ærou] n flecha

arse [ɑːrs] (BRIT: infl) n culo, trasero

arson ['ɑːrsən] n incendio premeditado

art [ɑːrt] n arte m; (skill) destreza; **A~s** npl (SCOL) Letras fpl

artery ['ɑːrtəri] n arteria

art gallery n pinacoteca; (saleroom) galería de arte

arthritis [ɑːrˈθraɪtɪs] n artritis f

artichoke ['ɑːrtɪtʃouk] n alcachofa, alcaucil m (RPl); **Jerusalem ~** aguaturma, pataca

article ['ɑːrtɪkəl] n artículo; **~s** npl (BRIT LAW training) contrato de aprendizaje; **~ of clothing** prenda de vestir

articulate [adj ɑːrˈtɪkjulɪt, vb ɑːrˈtɪkjuleɪt] adj claro, bien expresado ♦ vt expresar □ **articulated lorry** (BRIT) n trailer m

artificial [ɑːrtɪˈfɪʃəl] adj artificial; (affected) afectado

artillery [ɑːrˈtɪləri] n artillería

artisan ['ɑːrtɪzən] n artesano

artist ['ɑːrtɪst] n artista mf; (MUS) intérprete mf □ **artistic** [ɑːrˈtɪstɪk] adj artístico □ **artistry** n arte m, habilidad f (artística)

art school n escuela de bellas artes

as

KEYWORD

[æz] conj

1 (referring to time) cuando, mientras; a medida que; **the years went by** con el paso de los años; **he came in as I was leaving** entró cuando me iba; **as from tomorrow** desde or a partir de mañana

2 (in comparisons): **as big as** tan grande como; **twice as big as** el doble de grande que; **as much money/many books as** tanto dinero/tantos libros como; **as soon as** en cuanto

3 (since, because) como, ya que; **he left early as he had to be home by 10** se fue temprano ya que tenía que estar en casa a las 10

4 (referring to manner, way): **do as you wish** haz lo que quieras; **as she said** como dijo; **he gave it to me as a present** me lo dio de regalo

5 (in the capacity of): **he works as a bricklayer** trabaja de albañil; **as chairman of the company, he ...** como presidente de la compañía ...

6 (concerning): **as for** or **to that** por or en lo que respecta a eso

7: **as if** or **though** como si; **he looked as if he was sick** parecía como si estuviera enfermo, tenía aspecto de enfermo; see also **long; such; well**

a.s.a.p. abbr (= as soon as possible) cuanto antes

asbestos [æsˈbestəs] n asbesto, amianto

ascend [əˈsend] vt subir; (throne) ascender or subir a

ascent [əˈsent] n subida; (slope) cuesta, pendiente f

ascertain [æsərˈteɪn] vt averiguar

ash [æʃ] n ceniza; (tree) fresno

ashamed [əˈʃeɪmd] adj avergonzado, apenado (LAm); **to be ~ of** avergonzarse or estar avergonzado de

ashore [əˈʃɔːr] adv en tierra; (swim etc) a tierra

ashtray ['æʃtreɪ] n cenicero

Ash Wednesday n miércoles m de Ceniza

Asia ['eɪʒə] n Asia □ **Asian** adj, n asiático(-a)

aside [əˈsaɪd] adv a un lado ♦ n aparte m

ask [æsk] vt (question) preguntar; (invite) invitar; **to ~ sb sth/to do sth** preguntar algo a algn/pedir a algn que haga algo; **to ~ sb about sth** preguntar algo a algn; **to ~ (sb) a question** hacer una pregunta (a algn); **to ~ sb out to dinner** invitar a cenar a algn ▶ **ask after** vt fus preguntar por ▶ **ask for** vt fus pedir; (trouble) buscar

asking price n precio inicial

asleep [əˈsliːp] adj dormido; **to fall ~** dormirse, quedarse dormido

asparagus [əˈspærəgəs] n (plant) espárrago; (food) espárragos mpl

aspect ['æspekt] n aspecto, apariencia; (direction in which a building etc faces) orientación f

aspersions [əˈspɜːrʒənz] npl: **to cast ~ on** difamar or calumniar a

asphyxiation [æsfɪksiˈeɪʃən] n asfixia

aspire [əˈspaɪər] vi: **to ~ to** aspirar a, ambicionar

aspirin ['æsprɪn] n aspirina

ass [æs] n asno, burro; (inf: idiot) imbécil mf; (US: infl) culo, trasero

assailant [əˈseɪlənt] n asaltante mf, agresor(a) m/f

assassinate [əˈsæsɪneɪt] vt asesinar

assassination [əsæsɪˈneɪʃən] n asesinato

assault [əˈsɔːlt] n asalto; (LAW) agresión f ♦ vt asaltar, atacar; (sexually) violar

assemble [ə'sembəl] vt reunir, juntar; (TECH) montar ♦ vi reunirse, juntarse

assembly [ə'sembli] n reunión f, asamblea; (parliament) parlamento; (construction) montaje m ❑ **assembly line** n cadena de montaje

assent [ə'sent] n asentimiento, aprobación f

assert [ə'sɜːrt] vt afirmar; (authority) hacer valer ❑ **assertion** n afirmación f

assess [ə'ses] vt valorar, calcular; (tax, damages) fijar; (for tax) gravar ❑ **assessment** n valoración f; (for tax) gravamen m ❑ **assessor** n asesor(a) m/f

asset ['æset] n ventaja; ~s npl (COMM) activo; (property, funds) fondos mpl

assign [ə'saɪn] vt: to ~ (to) (date) fijar (para); (task) asignar (a); (resources) destinar (a) ❑ **assignment** n tarea

assist [ə'sɪst] vt ayudar ❑ **assistance** n ayuda, auxilio ❑ **assistant** n ayudante mf; (BRIT: also: **shop assistant**) dependiente(-a) m/f

associate [adj, n ə'səusɪɪt, vb ə'səusɪeɪt] adj asociado ♦ n (at work) colega mf ♦ vt asociar; (ideas) relacionar ♦ vi: to ~ with sb tratar con algn

association [əsəusi'eɪʃən] n asociación f

assorted [ə'sɔːtɪd] adj surtido, variado

assortment [ə'sɔːrtmənt] n (of shapes, colors) surtido; (of books) colección f; (of people) mezcla

assume [ə'suːm] vt suponer; (responsibilities) asumir; (attitude) adoptar, tomar

assumption [ə'sʌmpʃən] n suposición f, presunción f; (of power etc) toma

assurance [ə'ʃurəns] n garantía, promesa; (confidence) confianza, aplomo; (BRIT: insurance) seguro

assure [ə'ʃuər] vt asegurar

asthma ['æzmə] n asma

astonish [ə'stɒnɪʃ] vt asombrar, pasmar ❑ **astonishment** n asombro, sorpresa

astound [ə'staund] vt asombrar, pasmar

astray [ə'streɪ] adv: to go ~ extraviarse; to lead ~ (morally) llevar por mal camino

astride [ə'straɪd] prep a caballo or horcajadas sobre

astrology [ə'strɒlədʒɪ] n astrología

astronaut ['æstrənɔːt] n astronauta mf

astronomy [ə'strɒnəmɪ] n astronomía

asylum [ə'saɪləm] n (refuge) asilo; (mental hospital) manicomio

---

at

KEYWORD

[æt] prep

1 (referring to position) en; (direction) a; **at the top** en lo alto; **at home/school** en casa/la escuela; **to look at sth/sb** mirar algo/a algn

2 (referring to time): **at 4 o'clock** a las 4; **at night** por la noche; **at Christmas** en Navidad; **at times** a veces

3 (referring to rates, speed etc): **at $2 a pound** a dos dólares la libra; **two at a time** de dos en dos; **at 50 miles an hour** a 50 millas por hora

4 (referring to manner): **at a stroke** de un golpe; **at peace** en paz

5 (referring to activity): **to be at work** estar trabajando; (in the office etc) estar en el trabajo; **to play cowboys** jugar a los vaqueros; **to be good at sth** ser bueno en algo

6 (referring to cause): **shocked/surprised/annoyed at sth** asombrado/sorprendido/fastidiado por algo; **I went at his suggestion** fui a instancias suyas

---

ate [eɪt] pt of **eat**

atheist ['eɪθiɪst] n ateo(-a)

Athens ['æθɪnz] n Atenas

athlete ['æθliːt] n atleta mf

athletic [æθ'letɪk] adj atlético ❑ **athletics** n (US) deportes mpl; (BRIT) atletismo

Atlantic [ət'læntɪk] adj atlántico ♦ n: **the ~ (Ocean)** el (Océano) Atlántico

atlas ['ætləs] n atlas m inv

A.T.M. n abbr (= automated telling machine) cajero automático

atmosphere ['ætməsfɪər] n atmósfera; (of place) ambiente m

atom ['ætəm] n átomo ❑ **atomic** [ə'tɒːmɪk] adj atómico ❑ **atom(ic) bomb** n bomba atómica ❑ **atomizer** n atomizador m

atone [ə'təun] vi: to ~ for expiar

atrocious [ə'trəuʃəs] adj atroz

attach [ə'tætʃ] vt (fasten) atar; (join) unir, sujetar; (document, letter) adjuntar; (importance etc) dar, conceder; **to be ~ed to sb/sth** (to like) tener cariño a algn/algo

attaché [ætə'ʃeɪ] n agregado(-a) ❑ **attaché case** n maletín m

attachment [ə'tætʃmənt] n (tool) accesorio; (love): ~ **(to)** apego (a); (COMPUT) anexo (MEX), archivo adjunto (LAm exc MEX, SP)

attack [ə'tæk] vt (MIL) atacar; (criminal) agredir, asaltar; (criticize) criticar; (task) emprender ♦ n ataque m, asalto; (on sb's life) atentado; (fig:

criticism) crítica; (*of illness*) ataque *m*; **heart ~** infarto (de miocardio) ❑ **attacker** *n* asaltante *mf*, agresor(a) *m/f*

attain [əˈteɪn] *vt* (*also:* **~ to**) alcanzar; (*achieve*) lograr, conseguir

attempt [əˈtɛmpt] *n* tentativa, intento; (*attack*) atentado ♦ *vt* intentar ❑ **attempted** *adj:* **attempted burglary/ murder/suicide** tentativa or intento de robo/ asesinato/suicidio

attend [əˈtɛnd] *vt* asistir a; (*patient*) atender ▶ **attend to** *vt fus* ocuparse de; (*customer, patient*) atender a ❑ **attendance** *n* asistencia, presencia; (*people present*) concurrencia ❑ **attendant** *n* ayudante *mf*; (*in garage etc*) encargado(-a) ♦ *adj* (*dangers*) concomitante

attention [əˈtɛnʃən] *n* atención *f*; (*care*) atenciones *fpl* ♦ *excl* (*MIL*) ¡firme(s)!; **for the ~ of ...** (*ADMIN*) atención ...

attentive [əˈtɛntɪv] *adj* atento

attic [ˈætɪk] *n* desván *m*, altillo, entretecho (*SC*)

attitude [ˈætɪtuːd] *n* actitud *f*; (*disposition*) disposición *f*

attorney [əˈtɜːrni] (*US*) *n* (*lawyer*) abogado(-a) ❑ **Attorney General** *n* (*US*) ≈ Procurador(a) *m/f* General de Justicia; (*BRIT*) ≈ Fiscal *mf* General del Estado

attract [əˈtrækt] *vt* atraer; (*sb's attention*) llamar ❑ **attraction** *n* encanto; (*gen pl: amusements*) diversiones *fpl*; (*PHYSICS*) atracción *f*; (*fig: towards sb, sth*) atractivo ❑ **attractive** *adj* guapo; (*interesting*) atrayente

attribute [*n* ˈætrɪbjuːt, *vb* əˈtrɪbjuːt] *n* atributo ♦ *vt:* **to ~ sth to** atribuir algo a

attrition [əˈtrɪʃən] *n:* **war of ~** guerra de agotamiento

aubergine [ˈoʊbərʒiːn] (*BRIT*) *n* berenjena; (*color*) morado

auburn [ˈɔːbərn] *adj* color castaño rojizo

auction [ˈɔːkʃən] *n* (*also:* **sale by ~**) subasta ♦ *vt* subastar ❑ **auctioneer** [ˌɔːkʃəˈnɪər] *n* subastador(a) *m/f*

audible [ˈɔːdɪbəl] *adj* audible, que se puede oír

audience [ˈɔːdɪəns] *n* público; (*RADIO*) radioescuchas *mpl*; (*TV*) telespectadores *mpl*; (*interview*) audiencia

audio-visual [ˈɔːdɪoʊˈvɪʒuəl] *adj* audiovisual ❑ **audio-visual aid** *n* ayuda audiovisual

audit [ˈɔːdɪt] *vt* revisar, intervenir

audition [ɔːˈdɪʃən] *n* audición *f*

auditor [ˈɔːdɪtər] *n* auditor(a) *m/f* (de cuentas)

augment [ɔːgˈmɛnt] *vt* aumentar

augur [ˈɔːgər] *vi:* **it ~s well** es un buen augurio

August [ˈɔːgəst] *n* agosto

aunt [ænt] *n* tía ❑ **auntie** *n diminutive of* **aunt** ❑ **aunty** *n diminutive of* **aunt**

au pair [ˈoʊˈpɛər] *n* (*also:* **~ girl**) (chica) au pair *f*

auspicious [ɔːˈspɪʃəs] *adj* propicio, de buen augurio

Australia [ɔːˈstreɪljə] *n* Australia ❑ **Australian** *adj, n* australiano(-a)

Austria [ˈɔːstrɪə] *n* Austria ❑ **Austrian** *adj, n* austríaco(-a)

authentic [ɔːˈθɛntɪk] *adj* auténtico

author [ˈɔːθər] *n* autor(a) *m/f*

authoritarian [əθɔːrɪˈtɛərɪən] *adj* autoritario

authoritative [əˈθɔːrɪteɪtɪv] *adj* autorizado; (*manner*) autoritario

authority [əˈθɔːrɪti] *n* autoridad *f*; (*official permission*) autorización *f*; **the authorities** *npl* las autoridades

authorize [ˈɔːθəraɪz] *vt* autorizar

auto [ˈɔːtoʊ] (*US*) *n* carro (*LAm*), coche *m* (*SP*)

auto: ❑ **autobiography** [ˌɔːtəbaɪˈɑːgrəfi] *n* autobiografía ❑ **autograph** [ˈɔːtəgræf] *n* autógrafo ♦ *vt* (*photo etc*) dedicar; (*program*) firmar ❑ **automated** [ˈɔːtəmeɪtɪd] *adj* automatizado ❑ **automatic** [ɔːtəˈmætɪk] *adj* automático ♦ *n* (*gun*) pistola automática; (*car*) carro (*LAm*) or coche *m* (*SP*) automático ❑ **automatically** *adv* automáticamente ❑ **automation** [ˌɔːtəˈmeɪʃən] *n* reconversión *f* ❑ **automobile** [ˌɔːtəməˈbiːl] (*US*) *n* carro (*LAm*), coche *m* (*SP*) ❑ **autonomy** [ɔːˈtɑːnəmi] *n* autonomía

autumn [ˈɔːtəm] (*BRIT*) *n* otoño

auxiliary [ɔːgˈzɪljəri] *adj, n* auxiliar *mf*

avail [əˈveɪl] *vt:* **to ~ o.s. of** aprovechar(se) de ♦ *n:* **to no ~** en vano, sin resultado

available [əˈveɪləbəl] *adj* disponible; (*unoccupied*) libre; (*person: unattached*) soltero y sin compromiso

avalanche [ˈævəlæntʃ] *n* alud *m*, avalancha

avant-garde [ˈævãŋˈgɑːrd] *adj* de vanguardia

Ave. *abbr* = **avenue**

avenge [əˈvɛndʒ] *vt* vengar

avenue [ˈævənjuː] *n* avenida; (*fig*) camino

average ['ævərɪdʒ] n promedio, término medio ♦ adj medio, de término medio; (ordinary) regular, corriente ♦ vt sacar un promedio de; **on ~** por regla general
▶ **average out** vi: **to average out at** salir en un promedio de

averse [ə'vɜːrs] adj: **to be ~ to sth/doing** sentir aversión or antipatía por algo/por hacer

avert [ə'vɜːrt] vt prevenir; (blow) desviar; (one's eyes) apartar

aviary ['eɪvɪeri] n pajarera, avería

avocado [ævə'kɑːdəʊ] n (also: BRIT: also: **~ pear**) aguacate m, palta (SC)

avoid [ə'vɔɪd] vt evitar, eludir

await [ə'weɪt] vt esperar, aguardar

awake [ə'weɪk] (pt **awoke** or **~d**) adj despierto ♦ vt despertar ♦ vi despertarse; **to be ~** estar despierto ❑ **awakening** n el despertar

award [ə'wɔːrd] n premio; (LAW: damages) indemnización f ♦ vt otorgar, conceder; (LAW: damages) adjudicar

aware [ə'weər] adj: **~ (of)** consciente (de); **to become ~ of/that** (realize) darse cuenta de/de que; (learn) enterarse de/de que ❑ **awareness** n conciencia; (knowledge) conocimiento

away [ə'weɪ] adv fuera; (movement): **she went ~** se marchó; **far ~** lejos; **two miles ~** a dos millas de distancia; **two hours ~ by bus** a dos horas en autobús; **the vacation was two weeks ~** faltaban dos semanas para las vacaciones; **he's ~ for a week** estará ausente una semana; **to take ~ (from)** quitar (a); (subtract) substraer (de); **to work/pedal ~** seguir trabajando/pedaleando; **to fade ~** (color) desvanecerse; (sound) apagarse ❑ **away game** n (SPORT) partido como visitante

awe [ɔː] n admiración f respetuosa ❑ **awe-inspiring** adj imponente

awesome ['ɔːsəm] (US) adj (excellent) formidable

awful ['ɔːfəl] adj horroroso; (quantity): **an ~ lot (of)** cantidad (de) ❑ **awfully** adv (very) terriblemente

awkward ['ɔːkwərd] adj desmañado, torpe; (shape) incómodo; (embarrassing) delicado, difícil

awning ['ɔːnɪŋ] n (of tent, store) toldo

awoke [ə'wəʊk] pt of **awake**

awoken [ə'wəʊkən] pp of **awake**

awry [ə'raɪ] adv: **to be ~** estar descolocado or mal puesto

ax (US) [æks] (BRIT **axe**) n hacha ♦ vt (project) cortar; (jobs) reducir

axes ['æksiːz] npl of **axis**

axis ['æksɪs] (pl **axes**) n eje m

axle ['æksəl] n eje m, árbol m

ay(e) [aɪ] excl sí

Bb

B [biː] n (MUS) si m

B.A. abbr = **Bachelor of Arts**

baby ['beɪbɪ] n bebé mf; (US: inf: darling) mi amor ❑ **baby carriage** (US) n cochecito ❑ **baby-sit** vi cuidar niños ❑ **baby-sitter** n baby sitter mf (LAm), canguro mf (SP) ❑ **baby wipe** n toallita húmeda (para bebés)

baccalaureate [bækə'lɔːrɪɪt] (US) n licenciatura

bachelor ['bætʃələr] n soltero; **B~ of Arts/ Science** licenciado(-a) en Filosofía y Letras/ Ciencias

back [bæk] n (of person) espalda; (of animal) lomo; (of hand) dorso; (as opposed to front) parte f de atrás; (of chair) respaldo; (of page) reverso; (of book) final m; (SPORT) defensa m; (of crowd): **the ones at the ~** los del fondo ♦ vt (candidate: also: **~ up**) respaldar, apoyar; (horse: at races) apostar a; (car) dar marcha atrás a or con ♦ vi (car etc) ir (or salir or entrar) marcha atrás ♦ adj (payment, rent) atrasado; (seats, wheels) de atrás ♦ adv (not forward) (hacia) atrás; **he's ~** (returned) está de vuelta, ha vuelto; **he ran ~** volvió corriendo; **throw the ball ~** devuelve la pelota; **can I have it ~?** ¿me lo devuelve?; **to call sb ~** (TEL: call again) volver a llamar a algn; (: return call) devolver la llamada a ▶ **back down** vi echarse atrás
▶ **back out** vi (of promise) volverse atrás
▶ **back up** vt (person) apoyar, respaldar; (theory) defender; (COMPUT) hacer una copia de seguridad de ❑ **backbencher** (BRIT) n miembro del parlamento sin cargo relevante ❑ **backbone** n columna vertebral ❑ **backdate** vt (pay rise) dar efecto retroactivo a; (letter) poner fecha atrasada a ❑ **backdrop** n telón m de fondo ❑ **backfire** vi (AUT) petardear, producir explosiones; (plans) fallar, salir mal ❑ **background** n fondo; (of events) antecedentes mpl; (basic knowledge) bases fpl; (experience) conocimientos mpl, educación f; **family background** origen m, antecedentes mpl ❑ **backhand** n (TENNIS: also: **backhand stroke**) revés m ❑ **backhander** (BRIT) n (bribe)

soborno ❑ **backing** n (fig) apoyo, respaldo ❑ **backlash** n reacción f ❑ **backlog** n: **backlog of work** trabajo atrasado ❑ **back number** n (of magazine etc) número atrasado ❑ **backpack** n mochila ❑ **backpacker** n mochilero(-a) ❑ **back pay** n pago atrasado ❑ **backside** (inf) n trasero, culo ❑ **backstage** adv entre bastidores ❑ **backstroke** n espalda ❑ **backup** adj suplementario; (COMPUT) de reserva ♦ n (support) apoyo; (also: **back-up file**) copia preventiva or de reserva ❑ **backward** adj (person, country) atrasado ❑ **backwards** adv hacia atrás; (read a list) al revés; (fall) de espaldas ❑ **backyard** n patio trasero, traspatio (LAm)

bacon ['beɪkən] n tocino (LAm), panceta (RPl, SP)

bacteria [bæk'tɪərɪə] npl bacterias fpl

bad [bæd] adj malo; (mistake, accident) grave; (food) podrido, pasado; **his ~ leg** su pierna lisiada; **to go ~** (food) pasarse

bad(e) [bæd] pt of **bid**

badge [bædʒ] n insignia; (policeman's) placa, insignia

badger ['bædʒər] n tejón m

badly ['bædlɪ] adv mal; **to reflect ~ on sb** influir negativamente en la reputación de algn; **~ wounded** gravemente herido; **he needs it ~** le hace gran falta

badminton ['bædˌmɪntən] n bádminton m

bad-tempered adj de mal genio or carácter; (temporarily) de mal humor

bag [bæg] n (paper, plastic) bolsa; (handbag) bolsa (MEX), bolso (LAm exc MEX, SP); (satchel) mochila; (case) petaca (MEX), maleta (LAm exc MEX, SP), valija (SC); **~s of** (BRIT: inf) un montón de ❑ **baggage** n equipaje m ❑ **baggage allowance** n límite m de equipaje ❑ **baggage (re)claim** n recogida de equipajes ❑ **baggy** adj amplio ❑ **bag lunch** (US) n almuerzo frío ❑ **bagpipes** npl gaita

Bahamas [bə'hɑːməz] npl: **the ~** las (Islas) Bahamas

bail [beɪl] n fianza ♦ vt (prisoner: gen: grant bail to) poner en libertad bajo fianza; (boat: also: **~ out**) achicar; **on ~** (prisoner) bajo fianza; **to ~ sb out** obtener la libertad de algn bajo fianza; see also **bale**

bailiff ['beɪlɪf] n alguacil m

bait [beɪt] n cebo ♦ vt poner cebo en; (tease) tomar el pelo a

bake [beɪk] vt cocer (al horno) ♦ vi cocerse ❑ **baked beans** npl frijoles mpl (LAm) or porotos mpl (SC) or judías fpl (SP) en salsa de tomate con tocino ❑ **baked potato** n papa

(LAm) or patata (SP) al horno ❑ **baker** n panadero ❑ **bakery** n panadería; (for cakes) pastelería ❑ **baking** n (act) amasar m; (batch) hornada ❑ **baking powder** n levadura (en polvo)

balance ['bæləns] n equilibrio; (COMM: sum) balance m; (remainder) resto; (scales) balanza ♦ vt equilibrar; (budget) nivelar; (account) saldar; (make equal) equilibrar; **~ of trade/ payments** balanza de comercio/pagos ❑ **balanced** adj (personality, diet) equilibrado; (report) objetivo ❑ **balance sheet** n balance m

balcony ['bælkənɪ] n (open) balcón m; (closed) galería; (in theater) anfiteatro

bald [bɔːld] adj calvo; (tire) liso

bale [beɪl] n (AGR) paca, fardo; (of papers etc) fajo ▶ **bale out** vi lanzarse en paracaídas

Balearics [bælɪ'ærɪks] npl: **the ~** las Baleares

ball [bɔːl] n pelota; (football) balón m; (of wool, string) ovillo; (dance) baile m; **to play ~** (fig) cooperar

ballast ['bæləst] n lastre m

ball bearings npl cojinetes mpl de bolas

ballerina [bælə'riːnə] n bailarina

ballet ['bæleɪ] n ballet m ❑ **ballet dancer** n bailarín(-ina) m/f

balloon [bə'luːn] n globo

ballot ['bælət] n (voting) votación f; (paper) cédula (LAm) or papeleta (SP) (electoral)

ballpoint (pen) ['bɔːlpɔɪnt('pɛn)] n bolígrafo, birome f (RPl)

ballroom ['bɔːlruːm] n salón m de baile

baloney [bə'lounɪ] n (US: inf) tonterías fpl

Baltic ['bɔːltɪk] n: **the ~ (Sea)** el (Mar) Báltico

ban [bæn] n prohibición f, proscripción f ♦ vt prohibir, proscribir

banal [bə'næl] adj banal, vulgar

banana [bə'nænə] n plátano, banana (LAm), banano (CAm)

band [bænd] n grupo; (strip) faja, tira; (stripe) lista; (MUS: jazz) orquesta; (: rock) grupo; (MIL) banda ▶ **band together** vi juntarse, asociarse

bandage ['bændɪdʒ] n venda, vendaje m ♦ vt vendar

Bandaid® ['bændeɪd] (US) n curita (LAm), tirita (SP)

bandit ['bændɪt] n bandido

bandy-legged ['bændɪ'lɛgd] adj patizambo, estevado

bang [bæŋ] n (of gun, exhaust) estallido, detonación f; (of door) portazo; (blow) golpe m

♦ vt (door) cerrar de golpe; (one's head) golpear ♦ vi estallar; (door) cerrar de golpe

Bangladesh [bæŋglə'deʃ] n Bangladesh m

bangs [bæŋz] (US) npl flequillo, fleco (MEX), cerquillo (CAm, RPl)

banish ['bænɪʃ] vt desterrar

banister(s) ['bænɪstər(z)] n(pl) barandilla, pasamanos m inv

bank [bæŋk] n (COMM) banco; (of river, lake) ribera, orilla; (of earth) terraplén m ♦ vi (AVIAT) ladearse ▶ **bank on** vt fus contar con □ **bank account** n cuenta bancaria □ **bank card** n tarjeta bancaria □ **banker** n banquero □ **banker's card** (BRIT) n = **bank card** □ **Bank holiday** (BRIT) n día m festivo □ **banking** n banca □ **bank note** n billete m de banco □ **bank rate** n tipo de interés bancario

bankrupt ['bæŋkrʌpt] adj quebrado, insolvente; **to go ~** quebrar, ir a la quiebra or bancarrota; **to be ~** estar en quiebra or bancarrota □ **bankruptcy** n quiebra, bancarrota

bank statement n balance m or detalle m de cuenta

banned substance [bænd–] n (SPORT) substancia prohibida

banner ['bænər] n pancarta

bannister(s) ['bænɪstər(z)] n(pl) = **banister(s)**

baptism ['bæptɪzəm] n bautismo; (act) bautizo

bar [bɑːr] n (pub) bar m; (counter) mostrador m; (rod) barra; (of window, cage) reja; (of soap) pastilla; (of chocolate) tableta; (fig: hindrance) obstáculo; (prohibition) proscripción f; (MUS) barra ♦ vt (road) obstruir; (person) excluir; (activity) prohibir; **the B~** (LAW) la abogacía; **behind ~s** tras las rejas (MEX), entre rejas (LAm exc MEX, SP); **~ none** sin excepción

barbaric [bɑːr'bærɪk] adj bárbaro

barbecue ['bɑːrbɪkjuː] n barbacoa

barbed wire ['bɑːrbd'waɪər] n alambre m de púas

barber ['bɑːrbər] n peluquero, barbero □ **barber shop** (US) n (BRIT: also: **barber's (shop)**) peluquería f

bar code n código de barras

bare [bɛər] adj desnudo; (trees) sin hojas; (necessities etc) básico ♦ vt desnudar; (teeth) enseñar □ **bareback** adv a pelo, sin silla □ **barefaced** adj descarado □ **barefoot** adj, adv descalzo □ **barely** adv apenas

barf [bɑːrf] (US: inf) vi arrojar (inf)

bargain ['bɑːrgɪn] n pacto, negocio; (good buy) ganga ♦ vi negociar; (haggle) regatear;

into the ~ además, por añadidura ▶ **bargain for** vt fus: **he got more than he bargained for** le resultó peor de lo que esperaba

barge [bɑːrdʒ] n barcaza ▶ **barge in** vi irrumpir; (interrupt: conversation) interrumpir

bark [bɑːrk] n (of tree) corteza; (of dog) ladrido ♦ vi ladrar

barley ['bɑːrli] n cebada

barmaid ['bɑːrmeɪd] (BRIT) n barman f, cantinera (MEX)

barman ['bɑːrmən] (BRIT) n barman m, cantinero (MEX)

barn [bɑːrn] n granero

barometer [bə'rɑːmɪtər] n barómetro

baron ['bærən] n barón m; (press baron etc) magnate m □ **baroness** n baronesa

barracks ['bærəks] npl cuartel m

barrage [bɑː'rɑːʒ] n (MIL) descarga, bombardeo; (dam) presa; (of criticism) lluvia, aluvión m

barrel ['bærəl] n barril m; (of gun) cañón m

barren ['bærən] adj estéril

barrette [bə'ret] (US) n pasador m, broche m (MEX)

barricade ['bærɪkeɪd] n barricada

barrier ['bæriər] n barrera

barring ['bɑːrɪŋ] prep excepto, salvo

barrister ['bærɪstər] (BRIT) n abogado(-a)

barrow ['bærou] n (cart) carretilla (de mano)

bartender ['bɑːrtendər] (US) n barman mf, cantinero(-a) (MEX)

barter ['bɑːrtər] vt: **to ~ sth for sth** trocar algo por algo

base [beɪs] n base f ♦ vt: **to ~ sth on** basar or fundar algo en ♦ adj bajo, infame

baseball ['beɪsbɔːl] n beisbol m (MEX), béisbol m (LAm exc MEX, SP)

BASEBALL

Al beisbol se le conoce en Estados Unidos como el "pasatiempo nacional" y goza de una enorme popularidad. De ahí que muchas expresiones hayan pasado al lenguaje coloquial de los americanos. Por ejemplo **to hit a home run** (literalmente hacer un jonrón) significa tener éxito, **to go to bat** (lit. ir a batear) significa salir en apoyo de alguien.

---

baseboard ['beɪsbɔːrd] (US) n zoclo (MEX), zócalo (LAm exc MEX, SP)

basement ['beɪsmənt] n sótano

bases¹ ['beɪsiz] npl of **basis**

bases² ['beɪsiz] npl of **base**

bash [bæʃ] (inf) vt golpear

bashful ['bæʃfəl] adj tímido, vergonzoso

basic ['beɪsɪk] *adj* básico ❑ **basically** *adv*
fundamentalmente, en el fondo; *(simply)*
sencillamente ❑ **basics** *npl*: **the basics** los
fundamentos

basil ['beɪzəl] *n* albahaca

basin ['beɪsɪn] *n* cuenco, tazón *m*; *(GEO)*
cuenca; *(also:* **wash~)** lavabo

basis ['beɪsɪs] *(pl* **bases)** *n* base *f*; **on a part-
time/trial ~** a tiempo parcial/a prueba

bask [bæsk] *vi*: **to ~ in the sun** tomar el sol

basket ['bæskɪt] *n* cesta, cesto; canasta
❑ **basketball** *n* baloncesto

Basque [bæsk] *adj, n* vasco(-a) ❑ **Basque
Country** *n* Euskadi *m*, País *m* Vasco

bass [beɪs] *n (MUS: instrument)* bajo; *(: double
bass)* contrabajo; *(: singer)* bajo

bassoon [bə'suːn] *n* fagot *m*

bastard ['bæstərd] *n (illegitimate child)*
bastardo(-a); *(inf!)* hijo(-a) de puta *(!)* or *(MEX!)*
de la chingada

baste [beɪst] *(US) vt (stitch)* hilvanar

bat [bæt] *n (ZOOL)* murciélago; *(for ball games)*
palo; *(BRIT: for table tennis)* pala ♦ *vt*: **he didn't
~ an eye** ni pestañeó

batch [bætʃ] *n (of bread)* hornada; *(of letters
etc)* lote *m*

bated ['beɪtɪd] *adj*: **with ~ breath** sin respirar

bath [bɑːθ, *pl* bɑːðz] *n (action)* baño; *(bathtub)*
tina *(LAm)*, bañadera *(RPl)*, bañera *(SP)* ♦ *vt*
bañar; **to take a ~** bañarse, tomar un baño;
see also **baths**

bathe [beɪð] *vi* bañarse ♦ *vt (wound)* lavar
❑ **bather** *(BRIT)* *n* bañista *mf*

bathing ['beɪðɪŋ] *n* el bañarse ❑ **bathing
cap** *n* gorro de baño ❑ **bathing suit** *(US)*
(BRIT **bathing costume)** *n* traje *m* de baño

bath: ❑ **bathrobe** *n* bata de baño, albornoz
m, salida de baño *(RPl)* ❑ **bathroom** *n*
cuarto de baño ❑ **baths** *npl (also:* **swimming
baths)** alberca *(MEX)*, piscina *(LAm exc MEX, SP)*,
pileta *(RPl)* ❑ **bath towel** *n* toalla de baño

bathtub ['bɑːθˌtʌb] *(US)* *n* tina *(LAm)*,
bañadera *(RPl)*, bañera *(SP)*

baton [bə'tɑːn] *n (MUS)* batuta; *(ATHLETICS)*
testigo; *(weapon)* macana *(MEX)*, cachiporra
(LAm), porra *(SP)*

batter ['bætər] *vt* maltratar; *(rain etc)* azotar
♦ *n* masa (para rebozar) ❑ **battered** *adj (hat,
pan)* estropeado

battery ['bætəri] *n (AUT)* batería; *(of torch)* pila

battle ['bætl] *n* batalla; *(fig)* lucha ♦ *vi* luchar
❑ **battleship** *n* acorazado

bawl [bɔːl] *vi* chillar, gritar; *(child)* berrear

bay [beɪ] *n (GEO)* bahía; **B~ of Biscay** ≈ mar
Cantábrico; **to hold sb at ~** mantener a algn

a raya ❑ **bay leaf** *n* hoja de laurel ❑ **bay
window** *n* ventana salediza

bazaar [bə'zɑːr] *n* bazar *m*; *(fete)* venta con fines
benéficos

B. & B. *n abbr (= bed and breakfast) (place)*
pensión *f*; *(terms)* cama y desayuno

BBC *(BRIT) n abbr (= British Broadcasting
Corporation)* cadena de radio y televisión estatal
británica

B.C. *adv abbr (= before Christ)* a. de C.

---

be

KEYWORD

[biː] *(pt* **was, were,** *pp* **been)** *aux vb*

1 *(with present participle: forming continuous
tenses)*: **what are you doing?** ¿qué estás
haciendo?, ¿qué haces?; **they're coming
tomorrow** vienen mañana; **I've been
waiting for you for hours** llevo horas
esperándote

2 *(with pp: forming passives)* ser *(but often
replaced by active or reflective constructions)*; **to
be murdered** ser asesinado; **the box had
been opened** habían abierto la caja; **the
thief was nowhere to be seen** no se veía al
ladrón por ninguna parte

3 *(in tag questions)*: **it was fun, wasn't it?** fue
divertido, ¿no? or ¿verdad?; **he's good-
looking, isn't he?** es guapo, ¿no te parece?;
she's back again, is she? entonces, ¿ha
vuelto?

4 *(+ to + infin)*: **the house is to be sold**
(necessity) hay que vender la casa; *(future)* van
a vender la casa; **he's not to open it** no tiene
que abrirlo

♦ *vb + complement*

1 *(with n or num complement, but see also* **3, 4, 5**
and impers vb) ser; **he's a doctor** es médico; **2
and 2 are 4** 2 y 2 son 4

2 *(with adj complement: expressing permanent
or inherent quality)* ser; *(: expressing state seen as
temporary or reversible)* estar; **I'm American**
soy americano(-a); **she's tall/pretty** es alta/
bonita; **he's young** es joven; **be careful/
good/quiet** ten cuidado/pórtate bien/
cállate; **I'm tired** estoy cansado(-a); **it's dirty**
está sucio(-a)

3 *(of health)* estar; **how are you?** ¿cómo
estás?; **he's very sick** está muy enfermo; **I'm
better now** ya estoy mejor

4 *(of age)* tener; **how old are you?** ¿cuántos
años tienes?; **I'm sixteen (years old)** tengo
dieciséis años

5 *(cost)* costar; ser; **how much was the
meal?** ¿cuánto fue *or* costó la comida?; **that'll**

be $5.75, please son $5.75, por favor; **this shirt is $35** esta camisa cuesta $35
♦ *vi*

1 (*exist, occur etc*) existir, haber; **the best singer that ever was** el mejor cantante que existió jamás; **is there a God?** ¿hay un Dios?, ¿existe Dios?; **be that as it may** sea como sea; **so be it** así sea

2 (*referring to place*) estar; **I won't be here tomorrow** no estaré aquí mañana

3 (*referring to movement*): **where have you been?** ¿dónde has estado?
♦ *impers vb*

1 (*referring to time*): **it's 5 o'clock** son las 5; **it's April 28th** estamos a 28 de abril

2 (*referring to distance*): **it's 10 miles to the village** el pueblo está a 10 millas

3 (*referring to the weather*): **it's too hot/cold** hace demasiado calor/frío; **it's windy today** hace viento hoy

4 (*emphatic*): **it's me** soy yo; **it was Maria who paid the check** fue María la que pagó la cuenta

beach [biːtʃ] *n* playa ♦ *vt* varar

beacon ['biːkən] *n* (*lighthouse*) faro; (*marker*) guía

bead [biːd] *n* cuenta; (*of sweat etc*) gota

beak [biːk] *n* pico

beaker ['biːkər] *n* (*US: glass*) vaso; (*BRIT: plastic*) vaso (de plástico duro); (*CHEM*) vaso de precipitación

beam [biːm] *n* (*ARCH*) viga, travesaño; (*of light*) rayo, haz *m* de luz ♦ *vi* brillar; (*smile*) sonreír

bean [biːn] *n* frijol *m* (*LAm*), poroto (*SC*), judía (*SP*); **kidney/lima ~** frijol *m* (*LAm*), poroto (*SC*) or judía (*SP*)/frijol *m* (*LAm*) or poroto (*SC*) blanco or judía blanca (*SP*); **coffee ~** grano de café □ **bean sprouts** *npl* brotes *mpl* de soja

bear [beər] *n* (*pt* **bore**, *pp* **borne**) *n* oso ♦ *vt* (*weight etc*) llevar; (*cost*) pagar; (*responsibility*) tener; (*endure*) soportar, aguantar; (*children*) parir, tener; (*fruit*) dar ♦ *vi*: **to ~ right/left** torcer a la derecha/izquierda ▶ **bear out** *vt* (*suspicions*) corroborar, confirmar; (*person*) dar la razón a ▶ **bear up** *vi* (*remain cheerful*) mantenerse animado

beard [bɪərd] *n* barba □ **bearded** *adj* con barba, barbudo

bearer ['beərər] *n* portador(a) *m/f*

bearing ['beərɪŋ] *n* porte *m*, comportamiento; (*connection*) relación *f*; **~s** *npl* (*also:* **ball ~s**) cojinetes *mpl* a bolas; **to take a ~** tomar marcaciones; **to find one's ~s** orientarse

beast [biːst] *n* bestia; (*inf*) bruto, salvaje *m* □ **beastly** (*inf*) *adj* horrible

beat [biːt] (*pt ~*, *pp ~***en**) *n* (*of heart*) latido; (*MUS*) ritmo, compás *m*; (*of policeman*) ronda ♦ *vt* pegar, golpear; (*eggs*) batir; (*defeat: opponent*) vencer, derrotar; (: *record*) sobrepasar ♦ *vi* (*heart*) latir; (*drum*) redoblar; (*rain, wind*) azotar; **to ~ it** (*inf*) largarse ▶ **beat off** *vt* rechazar ▶ **beat up** *vt* (*attack*) dar una paliza a □ **beating** *n* paliza

beautiful ['bjuːtɪful] *adj* precioso, hermoso, bello □ **beautifully** *adv* maravillosamente

beauty ['bjuːti] *n* belleza □ **beauty salon** *n* salón *m* de belleza □ **beauty spot** *n* (*TOURISM*) lugar *m* pintoresco

beaver ['biːvər] *n* castor *m*

became [bɪˈkeɪm] *pt* of **become**

because [bɪˈkɒz] *conj* porque; **~ of** debido a, a causa de

beckon ['bekən] *vt* (*also:* **~ to**) llamar con señas

become [bɪˈkʌm] *irreg vt* (*suit*) favorecer, sentar bien a ♦ *vi* (+ *n*) hacerse, llegar a ser; (+ *adj*) ponerse, volverse; **to ~ fat** engordar

becoming [bɪˈkʌmɪŋ] *adj* (*behavior*) decoroso; (*clothes*) favorecedor(a)

bed [bed] *n* cama; (*of flowers*) macizo; (*of coal, clay*) capa; (*of river*) lecho; (*of sea*) fondo; **to go to ~** acostarse □ **bed and breakfast** *n* (*place*) pensión *f*; (*terms*) cama y desayuno □ **bedclothes** *npl* ropa de cama □ **bedding** *n* ropa de cama

bedraggled [bɪˈdrægəld] *adj* (*untidy: person*) desastrado; (*clothes, hair*) desordenado

bed: □ **bedridden** *adj* postrado (en cama) □ **bedroom** *n* dormitorio, recámara (*MEX*), pieza (*SC*) □ **bedside** *n*: **at the bedside of** a la cabecera de □ **bedsit(ter)** (*BRIT*) *n* cuarto de alquiler □ **bedspread** *n* cubrecama *m*, colcha □ **bedtime** *n* hora de acostarse

bee [biː] *n* abeja

beech [biːtʃ] *n* haya

beef [biːf] *n* carne *f* de vaca; **roast ~** rosbif *m* □ **beefburger** *n* hamburguesa □ **Beefeater** (*BRIT*) *n* alabardero de la Torre de Londres

beehive ['biːhaɪv] *n* colmena

beeline ['biːlaɪn] *n*: **to make a ~ for** ir derecho a

been [bɪn] *pp* of **be**

beep ['biːp] *n* pitido; (*on answering machine*) señal *f* ♦ *vi* sonar

beeper ['biːpər] *n* bíper *m* (*LAm*), busca *m* (*SP*)

beer [bɪər] *n* cerveza

beet [bi:t] (US) n (also: **red ~**) betabel m (MEX), remolacha (LAm exc MEX, SP)

beetle ['bi:tl] n escarabajo

beetroot ['bi:tru:t] (BRIT) n betabel m (MEX), remolacha (LAm exc MEX, SP)

before [bɪ'fɔ:r] prep (of time) antes de; (of space) delante de ♦ conj antes (de) que ♦ adv antes, anteriormente; delante, adelante; ~ going antes de marcharse; ~ she goes antes de que se vaya; **the week ~** la semana anterior; **I've never seen it ~** no lo he visto nunca ❑ **beforehand** adv de antemano, con anticipación

beg [beg] vi pedir limosna ♦ vt pedir, rogar; (entreat) suplicar; **to ~ sb to do sth** rogar a algn que haga algo; see also **pardon**

began [bɪ'gæn] pt of **begin**

beggar ['begər] n mendigo(-a)

begin [bɪ'gɪn] (pt **began**, pp **begun**) vt, vi empezar, comenzar; **to ~ doing** or **to do sth** empezar a hacer algo ❑ **beginner** n principiante mf ❑ **beginning** n principio, comienzo

begun [bɪ'gʌn] pp of **begin**

behalf [bɪ'hæf] n: **on ~ of** en nombre de, por; (for benefit of) en beneficio de; **on my/his ~** por mí/él

behave [bɪ'heɪv] vi (person) portarse, comportarse; (well: also: ~ o.s.) portarse bien ❑ **behavior** (US) (BRIT **behaviour**) n comportamiento, conducta

behind [bɪ'haɪnd] prep detrás de; (supporting): **to be ~ sb** apoyar a algn ♦ adv detrás, por detrás, atrás ♦ n trasero; **to be ~ (schedule)** ir retrasado; **~ the scenes** (fig) entre bastidores

behold [bɪ'hould] irreg vt contemplar

beige [beɪʒ] adj color beige

Beijing ['beɪ'dʒɪŋ] n Pekín m

being ['bi:ɪŋ] n ser m; (existence): **in ~** existente; **to come into ~** aparecer

Beirut [beɪ'ru:t] n Beirut m

Belarus [belə'ru:s] n Bielorrusia

belated [bɪ'leɪtɪd] adj atrasado, tardío

belch [beltʃ] vi eructar ♦ vt (gen: belch out: smoke etc) arrojar

Belgian ['beldʒən] adj, n belga mf

Belgium ['beldʒəm] n Bélgica

belief [bɪ'li:f] n opinión f; (faith) fe f

believe [bɪ'li:v] vt, vi creer; **to ~ in** creer en ❑ **believer** n partidario(-a); (REL) creyente mf, fiel mf

belittle [bɪ'lɪtl] vt quitar importancia a

bell [bel] n campana; (small) campanilla; (on door) timbre m

bellhop ['bel,hɑ:p] (US) n botones m inv

belligerent [bɪ'lɪdʒərənt] adj agresivo

bellow ['belou] vi bramar; (person) rugir

belly ['beli] n barriga, panza

belong [bɪ'lɔ:ŋ] vi: **to ~ to** pertenecer a; (club etc) ser socio de; **this book ~s here** este libro va aquí ❑ **belongings** npl pertenencias fpl

beloved [bɪ'lʌvɪd] adj querido

below [bɪ'lou] prep bajo, debajo de; (less than) inferior a ♦ adv abajo, (por) debajo; **see ~** véase más abajo

belt [belt] n cinturón m; (TECH) correa, cinta ♦ vt (thrash) pegar con correa ❑ **beltway** (US) n (AUT) libramiento (MEX), carretera de circunvalación (LAm exc MEX, SP)

bench [bentʃ] n banco; **the B~** (LAW: judges) magistratura; **the Government/Opposition ~es** (BRIT POL) (los asientos de) los miembros del Gobierno/de la Oposición

bend [bend] (pt, pp **bent**) vt doblar ♦ vi inclinarse ♦ n (in road, river) curva; (in pipe) codo ► **bend down** vi inclinarse, doblarse ► **bend over** vi inclinarse

beneath [bɪ'ni:θ] prep bajo, debajo de; (unworthy) indigno de ♦ adv abajo, (por) debajo

benefactor ['benɪfæktər] n bienhechor m

beneficial [benɪ'fɪʃəl] adj beneficioso

benefit ['benɪfɪt] n beneficio; (allowance of money) subsidio ♦ vt beneficiar ♦ vi: **he'll ~ from it** le sacará provecho

benevolent [bɪ'nevələnt] adj (person) benévolo

benign [bɪ'naɪn] adj benigno; (smile) afable

bent [bent] pt, pp of **bend** ♦ n inclinación f ♦ adj: **to be ~ on** estar empeñado en

bequest [bɪ'kwest] n legado

bereaved [bɪ'ri:vd] npl: **the ~** los íntimos de una persona afligidos por su muerte

beret [bə'reɪ] n boina

Berlin [bər'lɪn] n Berlín

berm [bɜ:rm] (US) n (AUT) arcén m, acotamiento (MEX), banquina (RPl)

Bermuda [bər'mju:də] n las Bermudas

berry ['beri] n baya

berserk [bər'sɜ:rk] adj: **to go ~** perder los estribos

berth [bɜ:rθ] n (bed) litera; (cabin) camarote m; (for ship) amarradero ♦ vi atracar, amarrar

beseech [bɪ'si:tʃ] (pt, pp **besought**) vt suplicar

beset [br'sɛt] (*pt, pp* ~) *vt* (*person*) acosar

beside [br'saɪd] *prep* junto a, al lado de; **to be ~ o.s. with anger** estar fuera de sí ❑ **besides** *adv* además ♦ *prep* además de; **that's besides the point** eso no tiene nada que ver

besiege [br'siːdʒ] *vt* sitiar; (*fig*) asediar

besought [br'sɔːt] *pp, pt of* **beseech**

best [bɛst] *adj* (el/la) mejor ♦ *adv* (lo) mejor; **the ~ part of** (*quantity*) la mayor parte de; **at ~** en el mejor de los casos; **to make the ~ of sth** sacar el mejor partido de algo; **to do one's ~** hacer todo lo posible; **to the ~ of my knowledge** que yo sepa; **to the ~ of my ability** como mejor puedo ❑ **best-before date** *n* fecha de consumo preferente ❑ **best man** *n* padrino de boda

bestow [br'stou] *vt* (*title*) otorgar

bestseller ['bɛst'sɛlər] *n* éxito de librería, bestseller *m*

bet [bɛt] (*pt, pp* ~ *or* ~**ted**) *n* apuesta ♦ *vi* apostar ♦ *vt*: **to ~ money on** apostar dinero por; **to ~ sb sth** apostar algo a algn

betray [br'treɪ] *vt* traicionar; (*trust*) faltar a ❑ **betrayal** *n* traición *f*

better ['bɛtər] *adj, adv* mejor ♦ *vt* superar ♦ *vi*: **to get the ~ of sb** quedar por encima de algn; **you had ~ do it** más vale que lo hagas; **he thought ~ of it** cambió de parecer; **to get ~** (*MED*) mejorar(se) ❑ **better off** *adj* mejor; (*wealthier*) más acomodado

betting ['bɛtɪŋ] *n* juego, el apostar ❑ **betting shop** (*BRIT*) *n* agencia de apuestas

between [br'twiːn] *prep* entre ♦ *adv* (*time*) mientras tanto; (*place*) en medio

beverage ['bɛvərɪdʒ] *n* bebida

beware [br'wɛər] *vi*: **to ~ (of)** tener cuidado (con); **"~ of the dog"** "cuidado con el perro"

bewildered [br'wɪldərd] *adj* aturdido, perplejo

beyond [br'ɑːnd] *prep* más allá de; (*past: understanding*) fuera de; (*after: date*) después de, más allá de; (*above*) superior a ♦ *adv* (*in space*) más allá; (*in time*) posteriormente; **~ doubt** fuera de toda duda; **~ repair** irreparable

bias ['baɪəs] *n* (*prejudice*) prejuicio, pasión *f*; (*preference*) predisposición *f* ❑ **bias(s)ed** *adj* parcial

bib [bɪb] *n* babero

Bible ['baɪbəl] *n* Biblia

Bible Belt (*US*) *n*: **the ~** *los estados ultraprotestantes de EE.UU.*

BIBLE BELT

El cinturón bíblico o **Bible Belt** corresponde a una división geográfica y cultural de EE.UU. y es un término creado en el siglo XX por el conocido polemista antirreligioso H. L. Mencken para referirse a los fundamentalistas religiosos del mediooeste rural y que incluía también a casi todas las ciudades del sur del país. Cuando se acuñó, el término pareció ofensivo a los habitantes del sur de Estados Unidos, pero más tarde lo adoptaron como seña de identidad de su propio sentimiento religioso.

---

bicarbonate of soda [baɪˈkɑːrbənətəvˈsoudə] (*BRIT*) *n* bicarbonato sódico

bicker ['bɪkər] *vi* pelearse

bicycle ['baɪsɪkəl] *n* bicicleta ❑ **bicycle lane** *n* carril-bici *m* ❑ **bicycle path** *n* carril-bici *m*

bid [bɪd] (*pt* **bade** *or* **bid**, *pp* **bidden** *or* **bid**) *n* oferta, postura; (*in tender*) licitación *f*; (*attempt*) tentativa, conato ♦ *vi* hacer una oferta ♦ *vt* (*offer*) ofrecer; **to ~ sb good day** dar a algn los buenos días ❑ **bidder** *n*: **the highest bidder** el mejor postor ❑ **bidding** *n* (*at auction*) ofertas *fpl*

bide [baɪd] *vt*: **to ~ one's time** esperar el momento adecuado

bifocals ['baɪ,foukəlz] *npl* lentes *mpl* (*LAm*) *or* anteojos *mpl* (*LAm*) *or* gafas *fpl* (*SP*) bifocales

big [bɪg] *adj* grande; (*brother, sister*) mayor

bigheaded ['bɪg'hɛdɪd] *adj* engreído

bigot ['bɪgət] *n* fanático(-a), intolerante *mf* ❑ **bigoted** *adj* fanático, intolerante ❑ **bigotry** *n* fanatismo, intolerancia

big top *n* (*at circus*) carpa

bike [baɪk] *n* bici *f* ❑ **bike lane** *n* carril *m* de bicicleta, carril *m* bici ❑ **bikeway** (*US*) *n* ruta para ciclistas

bikini [br'kiːni] *n* bikini *m*

bilingual [baɪ'lɪŋgwəl] *adj* bilingüe

bill [bɪl] *n* (*invoice*) factura; (*POL*) proyecto de ley; (*US: banknote*) billete *m*; (*of bird*) pico; (*of show*) programa *m*; (*BRIT: restaurant*) cuenta; **"post no ~s"** "prohibido fijar carteles"; **to fit** *or* **fill the ~** (*fig*) cumplir con los requisitos ❑ **billboard** (*US*) *n* cartelera

billet ['bɪlɪt] *n* alojamiento

billfold ['bɪl,fould] (*US*) *n* cartera

billiards ['bɪljərdz] *n* billar *m*

billion ['bɪljən] *n* (*US*) mil millones *mpl*; (*BRIT*) billón *m* (*millón de millones*)

Bill of Rights n conjunto de las diez enmiendas originales a la Constitución de EE.UU.

BILL OF RIGHTS

El **Bill of Rights** es un apéndice añadido en 1791 a la Constitución de EE.UU. que incluye una serie de enmiendas para garantizar algunos de los derechos individuales de todos los ciudadanos estadounidenses. La primera enmienda se refiere a la libre elección de la religión, a la libertad de palabra, de prensa, y al derecho de reunión, y la segunda enmienda protege el derecho de los ciudadanos a llevar armas.

billy ['bɪlɪ] (US) n (also: ~ **club**) porra

bimbo ['bɪmbou] (inf) n muchacha guapa pero tonta

bimonthly ['baɪ'mʌnθlɪ] (US) adj de cada quince días, quincenal ♦ adv cada quince días, quincenalmente

bin [bɪn] n (container) recipiente m; (BRIT: for garbage) cubo o bote m (MEX) or tacho (SC) de la basura

bind [baɪnd] (pt, pp bound) vt atar; (book) encuadernar; (oblige) obligar ♦ n (inf: nuisance) lata ◻ **binding** adj (contract) obligatorio

binge [bɪndʒ] (inf) n: **to go on a ~** ir de farra (LAm) or juerga (SP)

bingo ['bɪŋgou] n bingo m

binoculars [bəˈnɑːkjələrz] npl binoculares mpl, prismáticos mpl

bio... [baɪou] prefix: ◻ **biochemistry** n bioquímica ◻ **biodegradable** [ˌbaɪoudrˈgreɪdəbəl] adj biodegradable ◻ **biography** [baɪˈɑːɡrəfɪ] n biografía ◻ **biological** adj biológico ◻ **biology** [baɪˈɑːlədʒɪ] n biología ◻ **bioterrorism** n bioterrismo

birch [bɜːrtʃ] n (tree) abedul m

bird [bɜːrd] n ave f, pájaro; (BRIT: inf: girl) chica ◻ **bird flu** n gripa or gripe f aviar ◻ **bird's eye view** n (aerial view) vista aérea or a vuelo de pájaro; (overview) visión f de conjunto ◻ **bird watcher** n ornitólogo(-a)

Biro® ['baɪrou] (BRIT) n bolígrafo, birome f (RPI)

birth [bɜːrθ] n nacimiento; **to give ~ to** parir, dar a luz ◻ **birth certificate** n acta (MEX) or certificado (LAm exc MEX) de nacimiento ◻ **birth control** n (policy) control m de natalidad; (methods) métodos mpl anticonceptivos ◻ **birthday** n cumpleaños m inv ♦ cpd (cake, card etc) de cumpleaños ◻ **birthplace** n lugar m de nacimiento ◻ **birth rate** n (tasa de) natalidad f

biscuit ['bɪskɪt] n (US: cake) bollo, scone m (MEX, SC); (BRIT: cookie) galleta

bisect [baɪˈsekt] vt bisecar

bishop ['bɪʃəp] n obispo; (CHESS) alfil m

bit [bɪt] pt of **bite** ♦ n trozo, pedazo, pedacito; (COMPUT) bit m, bitio; (for horse) freno, bocado; **a ~ of** un poco de; **a ~ mad** un poco loco; **~ by ~** poco a poco

bitch [bɪtʃ] n (female dog) perra

bite [baɪt] (pt **bit**, pp **bitten**) vt, vi morder; (insect etc) picar ♦ n (insect bite) picadura, piquete m (MEX); (mouthful) bocado; **to ~ one's nails** comerse las uñas; **let's have a ~ (to eat)** (inf) vamos a comer algo

bitter ['bɪtər] adj amargo; (wind) cortante, penetrante; (battle) encarnizado ♦ n (BRIT: beer) cerveza típica británica a base de lúpulos ◻ **bitterness** n lo amargo, amargura; (anger) rencor m

bizarre [bɪˈzɑːr] adj raro, extraño

black [blæk] adj negro; (tea, coffee) solo ♦ n color m negro; (person): B~ negro(-a) ♦ vt (BRIT INDUSTRY) boicotear; **to give sb a ~ eye** ponerle a algn el ojo morado; **~ and blue** (bruised) amoratado; **to be in the ~** (bank account) estar en números negros ◻ **blackberry** n zarzamora ◻ **blackbird** n mirlo ◻ **blackboard** n pizarrón m (LAm), pizarra (SP) ◻ **black coffee** n café m negro (LAm) or solo (SP) ◻ **blackcurrant** n grosella negra ◻ **blacken** vt (fig) desacreditar ◻ **black ice** n hielo invisible en la carretera ◻ **blackleg** (BRIT) n rompehuelgas m inv (LAm), carnero (RPI) ◻ **blacklist** n lista negra ◻ **blackmail** n chantaje m ♦ vt chantajear ◻ **black market** n mercado negro ◻ **blackout** n (MIL) oscurecimiento; (power cut) apagón m; (TV, RADIO) interrupción f de programas; (fainting) desvanecimiento ◻ **Black Sea** n: **the Black Sea** el Mar Negro ◻ **black sheep** n (fig) oveja negra ◻ **blacksmith** n herrero ◻ **black spot** n (BRIT AUT) lugar m peligroso; (for unemployment etc) punto negro

blacktop ['blæk,tɑːp] (US) n asfalto m

bladder ['blædər] n vejiga

blade [bleɪd] n hoja; (of propeller) paleta; **a ~ of grass** una brizna de hierba

blame [bleɪm] n culpa ♦ vt: **to ~ sb for sth** echar a algn la culpa de algo; **to be to ~ (for)** tener la culpa (de)

bland [blænd] adj (music, taste) soso

blank [blæŋk] adj en blanco; (look) sin expresión ♦ n (of memory): **my mind is a ~** no puedo recordar nada; (on form) blanco, espacio en blanco; (cartridge) cartucho sin bala or de fogueo ❑ **blank check** n cheque m en blanco

blanket ['blæŋkɪt] n cobija (*LAm*), manta (*SP*); (*of snow*) capa; (*of fog*) manto

blare [bleər] vi sonar estrepitosamente

blasé [blɑ:'zeɪ] adj hastiado

blast [blæst] n (*of wind*) ráfaga, soplo; (*of explosive*) explosión f ♦ vt (*blow up*) volar ❑ **blast-off** n (*SPACE*) lanzamiento

blatant ['bleɪtnt] adj descarado

blaze [bleɪz] n (*fire*) fuego; (*fig: of color*) despliegue m; (: *of glory*) esplendor m ♦ vi arder en llamas; (*fig*) brillar ♦ vt: **to ~ a trail** (*fig*) abrir (un) camino; **in a ~ of publicity** con gran publicidad

blazer ['bleɪzər] n chaqueta de uniforme de colegial o de socio de club

bleach [bli:tʃ] n (*also*: **household ~**) cloro (*MEX, CAm*), lejía (*LAm exc MEX, SP*) ♦ vt blanquear ❑ **bleached** adj (*hair*) teñido (de rubio) ❑ **bleachers** (*US*) npl (*SPORT*) gradas fpl al sol

bleak [bli:k] adj (*countryside*) desierto; (*prospect*) poco prometedor(a); (*weather*) crudo; (*smile*) triste

bleat [bli:t] vi balar

bleed [bli:d] (*pt, pp* **bled**) vt, vi sangrar; **my nose is ~ing** me está sangrando la nariz

bleeper ['bli:pər] n bíper m (*LAm*), busca m (*SP*)

blemish ['blemɪʃ] n marca, mancha; (*on reputation*) tacha

blend [blend] n mezcla ♦ vt mezclar; (*colors etc*) combinar, mezclar ♦ vi (*colors etc: also*: **~ in**) combinarse, mezclarse

blender ['blendər] n (*CULIN*) licuadora

bless [bles] (*pt, pp* **~ed** or **blest**) vt bendecir; **~ you!** (*after sneeze*) ¡salud! (*LAm*), ¡Jesús! (*SP*) ❑ **blessing** n (*approval*) aprobación f; (*godsend*) don m del cielo, bendición f; (*advantage*) beneficio, ventaja

blew [blu:] pt of **blow**

blind [blaɪnd] adj ciego; (*fig*): **~ (to)** ciego (a) ♦ n (*for window*) persiana ♦ vt cegar; (*dazzle*) deslumbrar; (*deceive*): **to ~ sb to ...** cegar a algn a ... ♦ npl: **the ~** los ciegos ❑ **blind alley** n callejón m sin salida ❑ **blind corner** (*BRIT*) n esquina escondida ❑ **blindfold** n venda ♦ adv con los ojos vendados ♦ vt vendar los ojos a ❑ **blindly** adv a ciegas, ciegamente ❑ **blindness** n ceguera ❑ **blind spot** n (*AUT*) ángulo ciego

blink [blɪŋk] vi parpadear, pestañear; (*light*) oscilar ❑ **blinkers** (*US*) npl direccional f (*MEX*), intermitente m (*LAm exc MEX, SP*)

bliss [blɪs] n felicidad f

blister ['blɪstər] n ampolla ♦ vi (*paint*) ampollarse

blizzard ['blɪzərd] n ventisca

bloated ['bloʊtɪd] adj hinchado; (*person: full*) ahíto

blob [blɑ:b] n (*drop*) gota; (*indistinct object*) bulto

bloc [blɑ:k] n (*POL*) bloque m

block [blɑ:k] n bloque m; (*in pipes*) obstáculo; (*of buildings*) cuadra (*LAm*), manzana (*SP*) ♦ vt obstruir, cerrar; (*progress*) estorbar; **~ of flats** (*BRIT*) bloque m de departamentos (*LAm*) or pisos (*SP*); **mental ~** bloqueo mental ❑ **blockade** [blɑ:'keɪd] n bloqueo ♦ vt bloquear ❑ **blockage** n estorbo, obstrucción f ❑ **blockbuster** n (*book*) bestseller m; (*movie*) éxito de público ❑ **block letters** npl letras fpl de molde ❑ **block party** (*US*) n fiesta de barrio

BLOCK PARTY

Un **block** designa, en EE.UU., el área comprendida entre varias calles de una ciudad o de una zona residencial. De ahí que un **block party** sea una especie de fiesta de barrio realizada colectivamente por todos los habitantes de una zona. Este tipo de fiestas callejeras se suelen celebrar durante el día en los meses de verano y suelen incluir la degustación de diversos platos sencillos colocados a lo largo de una mesa grande.

blog [blɑ:g] n blog m

bloke [bloʊk] (*BRIT: inf*) n tipo

blond(e) [blɑ:nd] adj, n rubio(-a)

blood [blʌd] n sangre f ❑ **blood donor** n donante mf de sangre ❑ **blood group** n grupo sanguíneo ❑ **bloodhound** n sabueso ❑ **blood poisoning** n septicemia, envenenamiento de la sangre ❑ **blood pressure** n presión f sanguínea ❑ **bloodshed** n derramamiento de sangre ❑ **bloodshot** adj inyectado en sangre ❑ **bloodstream** n corriente f sanguínea ❑ **blood test** n análisis m inv de sangre ❑ **bloodthirsty** adj sanguinario ❑ **blood vessel** n vaso sanguíneo ❑ **bloody** adj sangriento; (*nose etc*) lleno de sangre; (*BRIT: infl*): **this bloody...** este condenado o puñetero ... (*!*) ♦ adv: **bloody strong/good** (*BRIT: infl*) terriblemente fuerte/bueno ❑ **bloody-minded** (*BRIT: inf*) adj (*stubborn*) terco, empecinado; (*awkward*) atravesado, difícil

bloom [blu:m] n flor f ♦ vi florecer

blossom ['blɑ:səm] n flor f ♦ vi florecer

blot [blɑ:t] n borrón m; (fig) mancha ♦ vt (stain) manchar ► **blot out** vt (view) tapar

blotchy ['blɑ:tʃɪ] adj (complexion) lleno de manchas

blotting paper ['blɑ:tɪŋˌpeɪpər] n papel m secante

blouse [blaus] n blusa

blow [bləu] (pt **blew**, pp **blown**) n golpe m; (with sword) espadazo ♦ vi soplar; (dust, sand etc) volar; (fuse) fundirse ♦ vt (wind) llevarse; (fuse) quemar; (instrument) tocar; **to ~ one's nose** sonarse ► **blow away** vt llevarse, arrancar ► **blow down** vt derribar ► **blow off** vt arrebatar ► **blow out** vi apagarse ► **blow over** vi amainar ► **blow up** vi estallar ♦ vt volar; (tire) inflar; (PHOT) ampliar ❑ **blow-dry** n moldeado (con secador) ❑ **blowlamp** (BRIT) n = **blowtorch** ❑ **blow-out** n (of tire) ponchadura (MEX), reventón m (LAm exc MEX, SP); (inf) comilona (inf); fiestón m (inf) ❑ **blowtorch** n soplete m, lámpara de soldar

blue [blu:] adj azul; (depressed) deprimido; ~ **movie/joke** película/chiste m verde; **out of the ~** (fig) de repente ❑ **bluebell** n campanilla, campánula azul ❑ **bluebottle** n moscarda, mosca azul ❑ **blueprint** n (fig) anteproyecto

bluff [blʌf] vi blofear (MEX), hacer un bluff (LAm exc MEX), blufear (SC) ♦ n blof m (MEX), bluff m (LAm exc MEX); **to call sb's ~** quitar (LAm) or coger (SP) a algn la palabra

blunder ['blʌndər] n patinazo, metedura de pata ♦ vi cometer un error, meter la pata

blunt [blʌnt] adj (pencil) despuntado; (knife) desafilado, romo; (person) franco, directo

blur [blɜ:r] n (shape): **to become a ~** hacerse borroso ♦ vt (vision) enturbiar; (distinction) borrar

blush [blʌʃ] vi ruborizarse, ponerse colorado ♦ n rubor m

blustery ['blʌstərɪ] adj (weather) tempestuoso, tormentoso

boar [bɔ:r] n cerdo (macho)

board [bɔ:rd] n (cardboard) cartón m; (wooden) tabla, tablero; (on wall) tablón m; (for chess etc) tablero; (committee) junta, consejo; (in firm) mesa or junta directiva; (NAUT, AVIAT): **on ~** a bordo ♦ vt (ship) embarcarse en; (train) subir a; **full ~** pensión completa; **half ~** media pensión; **to go by the ~** (fig) ser abandonado or olvidado ► **board up** vt (door) tapiar ❑ **board and lodging** n casa y comida ❑ **boarder** (BRIT) n (SCOL) interno(-a) ❑ **boarding card** (BRIT) n = **boarding pass** ❑ **boarding house** n casa de

huéspedes ❑ **boarding pass** (US) n tarjeta de embarque ❑ **boarding school** n internado ❑ **boardroom** n sala de juntas ❑ **boardwalk** (US) n paseo marítimo entablado

boast [bəust] vi: **to ~ (about or of)** alardear (de)

boat [bəut] n barco, buque m; (small) barca, bote m

boatswain ['bəusən] n contramaestre m

bob [bɑ:b] vi (also: ~ **up and down**) menearse, balancearse ► **bob up** vi (re)aparecer de repente

bobby ['bɑ:bɪ] (BRIT: inf) n poli m

bobby pin (US) n horquilla

bobsled (US) ['bɑ:bsled] (BRIT **bobsleigh**) n bob m

bode [bəud] vi: **to ~ well/ill (for)** ser prometedor/poco prometedor (para)

bodily ['bɑ:dɪlɪ] adj corporal ♦ adv (move: person) en peso

body ['bɑ:dɪ] n cuerpo; (corpse) cadáver m; (of car) caja, carrocería; (fig: group) grupo; (: organization) organismo ❑ **body-building** n culturismo ❑ **bodyguard** n guardaespaldas m inv ❑ **bodywork** n carrocería

bog [bɑ:g] n pantano, ciénaga ♦ vt: **to get ~ged down** (fig) empantanarse, atascarse

bogus ['bəugəs] adj falso, fraudulento

boil [bɔɪl] vt (water) hervir; (eggs) pasar por agua, cocer ♦ vi hervir; (fig: with anger) estar furioso; (: with heat) asfixiarse ♦ n (MED) furúnculo, divieso; **to come to a** (US) **or the** (BRIT) **~** comenzar a hervir; **to ~ down to** (fig) reducirse a ► **boil over** vi salirse, rebosar; (anger etc) llegar al colmo ❑ **boiled egg** n (soft) huevo tibio (MEX) or pasado por agua (LAm exc MEX, SP) or a la copa (SC); (hard) huevo duro ❑ **boiled potatoes** npl papas fpl (LAm) or patatas fpl (SP) cocidas or hervidas ❑ **boiler** n caldera, bóiler m (MEX), calefón m (RPl) ❑ **boiler suit** (BRIT) n overol m (LAm) or mono (SP) (de trabajo) ❑ **boiling point** n punto de ebullición

boisterous ['bɔɪstərəs] adj (noisy) bullicioso; (excitable) exuberante; (crowd) tumultuoso

bold [bəuld] adj valiente, audaz; (pej) descarado; (color) llamativo

Bolivia [bə'lɪvɪə] n Bolivia ❑ **Bolivian** adj, n boliviano(-a)

bollard ['bɑ:lərd] (BRIT) n (AUT) poste m

bolt [bəult] n (lock) cerrojo; (with nut) perno, tornillo ♦ adv: **~ upright** rígido, erguido ♦ vt (door) echar el cerrojo a; (also: ~ **together**)

sujetar con tornillos; (*food*) engullir ♦ *vi*
fugarse; (*horse*) desbocarse

bomb [bɑːm] *n* bomba ♦ *vt* bombardear
❏ **bomb disposal** *n* desmontaje *m* de
explosivos ❏ **bomber** *n* (*AVIAT*) bombardero
❏ **bombshell** *n* (*fig*) bomba

bond [bɑːnd] *n* (*promise*) fianza; (*FINANCE*)
bono; (*link*) vínculo, lazo; (*COMM*): **in ~** en
depósito bajo fianza

bondage ['bɑːndɪdʒ] *n* esclavitud *f*

bone [boun] *n* hueso; (*of fish*) espina ♦ *vt*
deshuesar; quitar las espinas a ❏ **bone idle**
adj gandul ❏ **bone marrow** *n* médula

bonfire ['bɑːn,faɪər] *n* hoguera, fogata

bonnet ['bɑːnɪt] *n* gorra; (*BRIT: of car*) capó *m*

bonus ['bounəs] *n* (*payment*) paga
extraordinaria, plus *m*; (*fig*) bendición *f*

bony ['bouni] *adj* (*arm, face*) huesudo; (*MED:
tissue*) óseo; (*meat*) lleno de huesos; (*fish*)
lleno de espinas

boo [buː] *excl* ¡uh! ♦ *vt* abuchear, rechiflar

booby trap ['buːbi,træp] *n* trampa explosiva

book [buk] *n* libro; (*of tickets*) talonario; (*of
stamps etc*) librito ♦ *vt* (*ticket*) sacar; (*seat,
room*) reservar; **~s** *npl* (*COMM*) cuentas *fpl*,
contabilidad *f* ❏ **bookcase** *n* librero (*MEX*),
biblioteca (*LAm*), librería (*SP*) ❏ **bookie** *n*
= **bookmaker** ❏ **booking office** *n* (*BRIT
RAIL*) mostrador *m* de boletos (*LAm*) or billetes
(*SP*); (*THEATER*) boletería (*LAm*), taquilla (*SP*)
❏ **book-keeping** *n* contabilidad *f*
❏ **booklet** *n* folleto ❏ **bookmaker** *n*
corredor *m* de apuestas ❏ **bookseller** *n*
librero ❏ **bookshelf** *n* estante *m* para libros
❏ **book store** (*US*) (*BRIT* **bookshop**) *n*
librería

boom [buːm] *n* (*noise*) trueno, estampido; (*in
prices etc*) alza rápida; (*ECON, in population*)
boom *m* ♦ *vi* (*cannon*) hacer gran estruendo,
retumbar; (*ECON*) estar en alza ❏ **boom box**
(*US*) *n* radiocasete *m* portátil

boon [buːn] *n* favor *m*, beneficio

boost [buːst] *n* estímulo, empuje *m* ♦ *vt*
estimular, empujar ❏ **booster** *n* (*MED*)
reinyección *f*

boot [buːt] *n* bota; (*BRIT: of car*) cajuela (*MEX*),
maletero (*LAm exc MEX, SP*), baúl (*RPl*) ♦ *vt*
(*COMPUT*) arrancar, iniciar; **to ~** (*in addition*)
además, por añadidura

booth [buːθ] *n* (*telephone booth, voting booth*)
cabina

booze [buːz] (*inf*) *n* bebida

border ['bɔːrdər] *n* borde *m*, margen *m*; (*of a
country*) frontera; (*for flowers*) arriate *m*,
cantero (*RPl*) ♦ *vt* (*road*) bordear; (*another

country: also:* **~ on**) lindar con ▶ **border on** *vt
fus* (*insanity etc*) rayar en ❏ **borderline** *n*: **on
the borderline** en el límite ❏ **borderline
case** *n* caso dudoso

bore [bɔːr] *pt of* **bear** ♦ *vt* (*hole*) hacer un
agujero en; (*well*) perforar; (*person*) aburrir ♦ *n*
(*person*) aburrido(-a); (*of gun*) calibre *m*; **to be
~d** estar aburrido ❏ **boredom** *n*
aburrimiento

boring ['bɔːrɪŋ] *adj* aburrido

born [bɔːrn] *adj*: **to be ~** nacer; **I was ~ in
1960** nací en 1960

borne [bɔːrn] *pp of* **bear**

borough ['bʌrou] *n* municipio

borrow ['bɔːrou] *vt*: **to ~ sth (from sb)** tomar
algo prestado (a algn)

Bosnia(-Herzegovina) ['bɑːsniə-
(hɜːrtsəgouˈviːnə)] *n* Bosnia(-Herzegovina)

bosom ['buzəm] *n* pecho

boss [bɔːs] *n* jefe *m* ♦ *vt* (*also: ~* **around**)
mangonear ❏ **bossy** *adj* mandón(-ona)

bosun ['bousən] *n* = **boatswain**

botany ['bɑːtni] *n* botánica

botch [bɑːtʃ] *vt* (*also: ~* **up**) arruinar, estropear

both [bouθ] *adj, pron* ambos(-as), los (las) dos
♦ *adv*: **~ A and B** tanto A como B; **~ of us
went, we ~ went** fuimos los dos, ambos
fuimos

bother ['bɑːðər] *vt* (*worry*) preocupar;
(*disturb*) molestar, fastidiar ♦ *vi* (*also: ~* **o.s.**)
molestarse ♦ *n* (*trouble*) dificultad *f*; (*nuisance*)
molestia, lata; **to ~ doing** tomarse la molestia
de hacer

bottle ['bɑːtl] *n* botella; (*small*) frasco; (*baby's*)
biberón *m* ♦ *vt* embotellar ▶ **bottle up** *vt*
suprimir ❏ **bottle bank** *n* contenedor *m* de
vidrio ❏ **bottleneck** *n* (*AUT*)
embotellamiento; (*in supply*) obstáculo
❏ **bottle-opener** *n* abridor *m* (*MEX*),
destapador *m* (*LAm*), abrebotellas *m inv* (*SP*)

bottom ['bɑːtəm] *n* (*of box, sea*) fondo;
(*buttocks*) trasero, culo; (*of page*) pie *m*; (*of list*)
final *m*; (*of class*) último(-a) ♦ *adj* (*lowest*) más
bajo; (*last*) último

bough [bau] *n* rama

bought [bɔːt] *pt, pp of* **buy**

bouillon cube [bulˈjɑːn,kjuːb] (*US*) *n* cubito
de caldo

boulder ['bouldər] *n* canto rodado

boulevard ['buːləvɑːrd] *n* bulevar *m*, zócalo
(*MEX*)

bounce [bauns] *vi* (*ball*) (re)botar; (*check*) ser
rechazado ♦ *vt* hacer (re)botar ♦ *n* (*rebound*)
(re)bote *m* ❏ **bouncer** *n* (*inf*) gorila *m*

bound [baund] *pt, pp of* **bind** ♦ *n* (*leap*) salto; (*gen pl: limit*) límite *m* ♦ *vi* (*leap*) saltar ♦ *vt* (*border*) rodear ♦ *adj*: **~ by** rodeado de; **to be ~ to do sth** (*obliged*) tener el deber de hacer algo; **he's ~ to come** es seguro que vendrá; **out of ~s** prohibido el paso; **~ for** con destino a

boundary [baundri] *n* límite *m*

bouquet [bou'kei] *n* (*of flowers*) ramo

bourgeois [burʒwaː] *adj* burgués(-esa)

bout [baut] *n* (*of malaria etc*) ataque *m*; (*of activity*) período; (*BOXING etc*) combate *m*, encuentro

boutique [buːˈtiːk] *n* boutique *f*

bow¹ [bou] *n* (*knot*) lazo; (*weapon, MUS*) arco

bow² [bau] *n* (*of the head*) reverencia; (*NAUT: also:* **~s**) proa ♦ *vi* inclinarse, hacer una reverencia; (*yield*): **to ~ to** *or* **before** ceder ante, someterse a

bowels [bauəlz] *npl* intestinos *mpl*, vientre *m*; (*fig*) entrañas *fpl*

bowl [boul] *n* tazón *m*, cuenco; (*ball*) bola ♦ *vi* (*CRICKET*) arrojar la pelota; *see also* **bowls**

bow-legged [bou'legid] *adj* patizambo, estevado

bowler [boulər] *n* (*US SPORT*) jugador(a) *m/f* de bolos; (*BRIT CRICKET*) lanzador *m* (de la pelota); (*BRIT: also:* **~ hat**) hongo, bombín *m*

bowling [boulɪŋ] *n* (*game*) bochas *fpl*; boliche *m* (*MEX*), (juego de) bolos *mpl* (*LAm exc MEX, SP*) ❑ **bowling alley** *n* boliche *m* (*MEX*), bolera (*LAm exc MEX, SP*) ❑ **bowling green** *n* pista para bochas

bowls [boulz] *n* (*tenpin bowling*) bolos *mpl*; (*BRIT: on green*) bochas *fpl*, bolos *mpl*

bow tie [bou,tai] *n* corbata de lazo, pajarita

box [baːks] *n* (*also:* **cardboard ~**) caja, cajón *m*; (*THEATER*) palco ♦ *vt* encajonar ♦ *vi* (*SPORT*) boxear ❑ **box car** (*US*) *n* (*RAIL*) vagón *m or* furgón *m* (de mercancías) ❑ **boxer** *n* (*person*) boxeador *m* ❑ **boxing** *n* (*SPORT*) boxeo ❑ **Boxing Day** (*BRIT*) *n* día en que se dan los aguinaldos, 26 de diciembre ❑ **boxing gloves** *npl* guantes *mpl* de boxeo ❑ **boxing ring** *n* ring *m*, cuadrilátero ❑ **box office** *n* boletería (*LAm*), taquilla (*SP*) ❑ **boxroom** (*BRIT*) *n* trastero

boy [bɔi] *n* (*young*) niño; (*older*) muchacho, chico; (*son*) hijo

boycott [bɔikət] *n* boicot *m* ♦ *vt* boicotear

boyfriend [bɔi,frend] *n* novio

boyish [bɔiiʃ] *adj* juvenil; (*girl*) con aspecto de muchacho

bra [braː] *n* brasier *m* (*MEX*), sostén *m* (*LAm exc MEX, SP*)

brace [breis] *n* (*also:* **~s: on teeth**) frenos *mpl* (*LAm*), aparato(s) *m(pl)* (*SP*); (*tool*) berbiquí *m* ♦ *vt* (*knees, shoulders*) tensionar; **~s** *npl* (*BRIT*) tirantes *mpl*, tiradores *mpl* (*RPl*); **to ~ o.s.** (*fig*) prepararse

bracelet [breislit] *n* pulsera, brazalete *m*

bracing [breisɪŋ] *adj* vigorizante, tónico

bracket [brækit] *n* (*TECH*) soporte *m*, puntal *m*; (*group*) clase *f*, categoría; (*BRIT: also:* **round ~**) paréntesis *m inv*; (*BRIT: also:* **square ~**) corchete *m* ♦ *vt* (*word etc*) poner entre paréntesis

brag [bræg] *vi* jactarse

braid [breid] *n* (*trimming*) galón *m*; (*US: of hair*) trenza

brain [brein] *n* cerebro; **~s** *npl* sesos *mpl*; **she's got ~s** es muy lista ❑ **brainstorm** (*US*) *n* (*good idea*) idea luminosa ❑ **brainwash** *vt* lavar el cerebro a ❑ **brainwave** (*BRIT*) *n* = **brainstorm** ❑ **brainy** *adj* muy inteligente

braise [breiz] *vt* cocer a fuego lento

brake [breik] *n* (*on vehicle*) freno ♦ *vi* frenar ❑ **brake light** *n* luz *f* de frenado

bran [bræn] *n* salvado

branch [bræntʃ] *n* rama; (*COMM*) sucursal *f* ▶ **branch out** *vi* (*fig*) extenderse

brand [brænd] *n* marca; (*fig: type*) tipo ♦ *vt* (*cattle*) marcar con hierro candente ❑ **brand-new** *adj* flamante, completamente nuevo

brandy [brændi] *n* coñac *m*

brash [bræʃ] *adj* (*forward*) descarado

brass [bræs] *n* latón *m*; **the ~** (*MUS*) los metales *or* bronces *mpl* ❑ **brass band** *n* banda de metal

brat [bræt] (*pej*) *n* mocoso(-a)

brave [breiv] *adj* valiente, valeroso ♦ *vt* (*face up to*) desafiar ❑ **bravery** [breivəri] *n* valor *m*, valentía

brawl [brɔːl] *n* pelea, reyerta

brazen [breizən] *adj* descarado ♦ *vt*: **to ~ it out** echarle cara

Brazil [brəˈzil] *n* Brasil *m* ❑ **Brazilian** *adj, n* brasileño(-a)

breach [briːtʃ] *vt* abrir brecha en ♦ *n* (*gap*) brecha; (*breaking*): **~ of contract** infracción *f* de contrato; **~ of the peace** perturbación *f* del orden público

bread [bred] *n* pan *m* ❑ **bread and butter** *n* pan con mantequilla; (*fig*) pan (de cada día) ❑ **breadbox** *n* panera ❑ **breadcrumbs** *npl* migajas *fpl*; (*CULIN*) pan rallado ❑ **breadline** *n*: **on the breadline** en la miseria

breadth [bredθ] *n* anchura; (*fig*) amplitud *f*

breadwinner [bred,winər] *n* sustento *m* de la familia

break [breɪk] (*pt* **broke**, *pp* **broken**) *vt*
romper; (*promise*) faltar a; (*law*) violar,
infringir; (*record*) batir ♦ *vi* romperse,
quebrarse; (*storm*) estallar; (*weather*) cambiar;
(*dawn*) despuntar; (*news etc*) darse a conocer
♦ *n* (*gap*) abertura; (*fracture*) fractura; (*time*)
intervalo; (*at school*) (período de) recreo;
(*chance*) oportunidad *f*; **to ~ the news to sb**
comunicar la noticia a algn ► **break down**
vt (*figures, data*) analizar, descomponer ♦ *vi*
(*machine*) estropearse; (*AUT*) descomponerse
(*LAm*), averiarse (*SP*); (*person*) romper a llorar;
(*talks*) fracasar ► **break even** *vi* cubrir los
gastos ► **break free** *or* **loose** *vi* escaparse
► **break in** *vt* (*horse etc*) domar ♦ *vi* (*burglar*)
forzar una entrada; (*interrupt*) interrumpir
► **break into** *vt fus* (*house*) forzar ► **break
off** *vi* (*speaker*) pararse, detenerse; (*branch*)
partir ► **break open** *vt* (*door etc*) abrir por la
fuerza, forzar ► **break out** *vi* estallar;
(*prisoner*) escaparse; **he broke out in a rash** le
salió un sarpullido ► **break up** *vi* (*ship*)
hacerse pedazos; (*crowd, meeting*) disolverse;
(*marriage*) deshacerse; (*couple*) separarse;
(*SCOL*) terminar (el curso) ♦ *vt* (*rocks etc*) partir;
(*journey*) partir; (*fight etc*) acabar con
❑ **breakage** *n* rotura ❑ **breakdown** *n*
(*AUT*) descompostura (*MEX*), avería (*LAm exc
MEX, SP*); (*in communications*) interrupción *f*;
(*MED: also*: **nervous breakdown**) colapso,
crisis *f* nerviosa; (*of marriage, talks*) fracaso; (*of
statistics*) análisis *m inv* ❑ **breakdown van**
(*BRIT*) *n* (camión *m*) grúa ❑ **breaker** *n* (ola)
rompiente *f*

breakfast ['brɛkfəst] *n* desayuno

break: ❑ **break-in** *n* robo con allanamiento
de morada ❑ **breaking and entering** *n*
(*LAW*) violación *f* de domicilio, allanamiento
de morada ❑ **breakthrough** *n* (*also fig*)
avance *m* ❑ **breakwater** *n* rompeolas *m inv*

breast [brɛst] *n* (*of woman*) pecho, seno;
(*chest*) pecho; (*of bird*) pechuga ❑ **breast-
feed** *irreg vt* amamantar ♦ *vi* dar el pecho, dar
de mamar ❑ **breast-stroke** *n* braza (de
pecho)

breath [brɛθ] *n* aliento, respiración *f*; **to take
a deep ~** respirar hondo; **out of ~** sin aliento,
sofocado

Breathalyzer® (*US*) ['brɛθə,laɪzər] (*BRIT*
Breathalyser®) *n* alcoholímetro *m*

breathe [bri:ð] *vt*, *vi* respirar ► **breathe in**
vt, *vi* aspirar ► **breathe out** *vt*, *vi* espirar
❑ **breather** *n* respiro ❑ **breathing** *n*
respiración *f*

breath: ❑ **breathless** *adj* sin aliento,
jadeante ❑ **breathtaking** *adj* imponente,
pasmoso

breed [bri:d] (*pt*, *pp* **bred**) *vt* criar ♦ *vi*
reproducirse, procrear ♦ *n* (*ZOOL*) raza, casta;
(*type*) tipo ❑ **breeding** *n* (*of person*)
educación *f*

breeze [bri:z] *n* brisa

breezy ['bri:zi] *adj* de mucho viento, ventoso;
(*person*) despreocupado

brevity ['brɛvɪti] *n* brevedad *f*

brew [bru:] *vt* (*tea*) hacer; (*beer*) elaborar ♦ *vi*
(*fig*: *trouble*) prepararse; (*storm*) amenazar
❑ **brewery** *n* fábrica de cerveza, cervecería

bribe [braɪb] *n* soborno ♦ *vt* sobornar,
cohechar ❑ **bribery** *n* soborno, cohecho

bric-a-brac ['brɪkəbræk] *n inv* baratijas *fpl*

brick [brɪk] *n* ladrillo ❑ **bricklayer** *n* albañil
m

bridal ['braɪdl] *adj* nupcial

bride [braɪd] *n* novia ❑ **bridegroom** *n*
novio ❑ **bridesmaid** *n* dama de honor

bridge [brɪdʒ] *n* puente *m*; (*NAUT*) puente *m*
de mando; (*of nose*) caballete *m*; (*CARDS*)
bridge *m* ♦ *vt* (*fig*): **to ~ a gap** llenar un vacío

bridle ['braɪdl] *n* brida, freno ❑ **bridle path**
n camino de herradura

brief [bri:f] *adj* breve, corto ♦ *n* (*LAW*) escrito;
(*task*) cometido, encargo ♦ *vt* informar; **~s** *npl*
(*for men*) calzoncillos *mpl*; (*for women*)
calzones *mpl* (*LAm*), bombachas *fpl* (*RPl*),
bragas *fpl* (*SP*) ❑ **briefcase** *n* portafolio
(*LAm*), cartera (*SP*) ❑ **briefing** *n* (*PRESS*)
informe *m* ❑ **briefly** *adv* (*glance*)
fugazmente; (*say*) en pocas palabras

brigadier [brɪgə'dɪər] *n* general *m* de brigada

bright [braɪt] *adj* brillante; (*room*) luminoso;
(*day*) de sol; (*person: clever*) listo, inteligente;
(*: lively*) alegre; (*color*) vivo; (*future*)
prometedor(a) ❑ **brighten** (*also*: **brighten
up**) *vt* (*room*) hacer más alegre; (*event*)
alegrar ♦ *vi* (*weather*) despejarse; (*person*)
animarse, alegrarse; (*prospects*) mejorar

brilliance ['brɪljəns] *n* brillo, brillantez *f*; (*of
talent etc*) brillantez

brilliant ['brɪljənt] *adj* brillante; (*BRIT: inf*)
fenomenal

brim [brɪm] *n* borde *m*; (*of hat*) ala

brine [braɪn] *n* (*CULIN*) salmuera

bring [brɪŋ] (*pt*, *pp* **brought**) *vt* (*thing, person:
with you*) traer; (*: to sb*) llevar, conducir;
(*trouble, satisfaction*) causar ► **bring about**
vt ocasionar, producir ► **bring around** *vt*
(*BRIT: also*: **bring round**: *unconscious person*)
hacer volver en sí; (*persuade*) convencer

▶ **bring back** vt volver a traer; (return) devolver ▶ **bring down** vt (government, plane) derribar; (price) rebajar ▶ **bring forward** vt adelantar ▶ **bring off** vt (task, plan) lograr, conseguir ▶ **bring out** vt sacar; (book etc) publicar; (meaning) subrayar ▶ **bring up** vt subir; (person) educar, criar; (question) sacar a colación; (food: vomit) devolver, vomitar

brink [brɪŋk] n borde m

brisk [brɪsk] adj (abrupt: tone) brusco; (person) enérgico, vigoroso; (pace) rápido; (trade) activo

bristle ['brɪsəl] n cerda ♦ vi: **to ~ in anger** temblar de rabia

Britain ['brɪtn] n (also: **Great ~**) Gran Bretaña

British ['brɪtɪʃ] adj británico ♦ npl: **the ~** los británicos □ **British Isles** npl: **the British Isles** las Islas Británicas

Briton ['brɪtn] n británico(-a)

brittle ['brɪtl] adj quebradizo, frágil

broach [broutʃ] vt (subject) abordar

broad [brɔːd] adj ancho; (range) amplio; (smile) abierto; (general: outlines etc) general; (accent) cerrado; **in ~ daylight** en pleno día □ **broadband** n banda ancha □ **broadcast** irreg n emisión f ♦ vt (RADIO) emitir; (TV) transmitir ♦ vi emitir; transmitir □ **broadcaster** n (TV) presentador(a) m/f; (RADIO) locutor(a) m/f □ **broaden** vt ampliar ♦ vi ensancharse; **to broaden sb's horizon** ampliar los horizontes de algn □ **broadly** adv en general □ **broad-minded** adj tolerante, liberal

Broadway ['brɔːdweɪ] n Broadway m

BROADWAY

Broadway es una amplia avenida diagonal que recorre la isla de Manhattan y que atraviesa el centro del famoso distrito teatral de Nueva York. Además, el término **Broadway** ya ha pasado a designar algo más que la propia calle, y se refiere a toda la zona teatral de Nueva York. También es frecuente su uso como parte de la descripción de un tipo determinado de espectáculos.

broccoli ['brɒkəli] n brócoli m

brochure [brou'ʃuər] n folleto m

broil [brɔɪl] (US) vt (CULIN) asar a la parrilla □ **broiler** (US) n parrilla

broke [brouk] pt of **break** ♦ adj (inf: without money) pelado, sin un centavo (MEX), pato (SC)

broken ['broukən] pp of **break** ♦ adj roto; (machine: also: **~ down**) descompuesto (LAm),

averiado (SP); **~ leg** pierna rota; **in ~ English** en un inglés imperfecto □ **broken-hearted** adj con el corazón partido

broker ['broukər] n agente mf, bolsista mf; (insurance broker) agente de seguros

brolly ['brɒli] (BRIT: inf) n paraguas m inv

bronchitis [brɒŋ'kaɪtɪs] n bronquitis f

bronze [brɒnz] n bronce m

brooch [broutʃ] n prendedor m, broche m

brood [bruːd] n camada, cría ♦ vi (person) dejarse obsesionar

broom [bruːm] n escoba; (BOT) retama

Bros. abbr (= Brothers) Hnos

broth [brɒθ] n caldo

brothel ['brɒθəl] n burdel m

brother ['brʌðər] n hermano □ **brother-in-law** n cuñado

brought [brɔːt] pt, pp of **bring**

brow [brau] n (forehead) frente m; (eyebrow) ceja; (of hill) cumbre f

brown [braun] adj (color) café (MEX), marrón (LAm exc MEX, SP); (hair) castaño; (tanned) bronceado, moreno ♦ n (color) color m marrón or pardo ♦ vt (CULIN) dorar □ **brown bread** n pan m integral

Brownie ['brauni] (US) n niña exploradora □ **brownie** n (US: cookie) pastel de chocolate con nueces

brown paper n papel m de estraza

brown sugar n azúcar m moreno or morena

browse [brauz] vi (through book) hojear; (in store) mirar; (Internet) navegar por Internet □ **browser** n (COMPUT) navegador m

bruise [bruːz] n moretón m ♦ vt magullar

brunch [brʌntʃ] n desayuno-almuerzo

brunette [bruː'nɛt] n morena

brunt [brʌnt] n: **to bear the ~ of** llevar el peso de

brush [brʌʃ] n cepillo; (for painting, shaving etc) brocha; (artist's) pincel m; (with police etc) roce m ♦ vt (sweep) barrer; (groom) cepillar; (also: **~ against**) rozar al pasar ▶ **brush aside** vt rechazar, no hacer caso a ▶ **brush up** vt (knowledge) repasar, refrescar □ **brushwood** n (sticks) leña

Brussels ['brʌsəlz] n Bruselas □ **Brussels sprout** n col f de Bruselas

brute [bruːt] n bruto; (person) bestia ♦ adj: **by ~ force** a fuerza bruta

B.Sc. abbr (= Bachelor of Science) licenciado en Ciencias

BSE n abbr (= bovine spongiform encephalopathy) encefalopatía espongiforme bovina

BTW abbr (= by the way) por cierto

bubble ['bʌbəl] n burbuja ♦ vi burbujear, borbotar ❑ **bubble bath** n espuma para el baño ❑ **bubble gum** n chicle m de globo

buck [bʌk] n (rabbit) conejo macho; (deer) ciervo macho; (US: inf) dólar m ♦ vi corcovear; **to pass the ~ (to sb)** echar (a algn) el muerto ▸ **buck up** vi (cheer up) animarse, cobrar ánimo

bucket ['bʌkɪt] n cubeta (MEX, SP), balde m (LAm)

buckle ['bʌkəl] n hebilla ♦ vt abrochar con hebilla ♦ vi combarse

bud [bʌd] n (of plant) brote m, yema; (of flower) capullo ♦ vi brotar, echar brotes

Buddhism ['buːdɪzəm] n Budismo

budding ['bʌdɪŋ] adj en ciernes

buddy ['bʌdi] n (US) camarada mf (MEX), compinche mf (LAm), colega mf (SP)

budge [bʌdʒ] vt mover; (fig) hacer ceder ♦ vi moverse, ceder

budgerigar ['bʌdʒərɪgɑːr] n periquito

budget ['bʌdʒɪt] n presupuesto ♦ vi: **to ~ for sth** presupuestar algo

budgie ['bʌdʒi] n = **budgerigar**

buff [bʌf] adj (color) color de ante ♦ n (inf: enthusiast) entusiasta mf

buffalo ['bʌfələu] n (pl ~ or ~es) n búfalo m; (US: bison) bisonte m

buffer ['bʌfər] n (COMPUT) memoria intermedia; (BRIT RAIL) tope m

buffet¹ ['bʌfɪt] vt golpear

buffet² [bə'feɪ] n cafetería; (food) buffet m; (BRIT: in station) bar m ❑ **buffet car** n (RAIL) coche-comedor m

bug [bʌg] n (US: insect) bicho, sabandija; (COMPUT) error m; (germ) microbio, bacilo; (spy device) micrófono oculto ♦ vt (inf: annoy) fastidiar; (room) poner micrófono oculto en

buggy ['bʌgi] n cochecito de niño

bugle ['bjuːgəl] n corneta, clarín m

build [bɪld] (pt, pp built) n (of person) tipo ♦ vt construir, edificar ▸ **build up** vt (morale, forces, production) acrecentar; (stocks) acumular ❑ **builder** n (contractor) contratista mf ❑ **building** n construcción f; (structure) edificio ❑ **building society** (BRIT) n sociedad f inmobiliaria

built [bɪlt] pt, pp of **build** ♦ adj: **~-in** (wardrobe etc) empotrado ❑ **built-up area** n zona urbanizada

bulb [bʌlb] n (BOT) bulbo; (ELEC) foco (MEX), bombilla (LAm exc MEX, SP), bujía (CAm), bombita (RPI)

Bulgaria [bʌl'geəriə] n Bulgaria ❑ **Bulgarian** adj, n búlgaro(-a)

bulge [bʌldʒ] n bulto, protuberancia ♦ vi bombearse, pandearse; (pocket etc): **to ~ (with)** rebosar (de)

bulk [bʌlk] n masa, mole f; **in ~** (COMM) a granel; **the ~ of** la mayor parte de ❑ **bulky** adj voluminoso, abultado

bull [bul] n toro; (male elephant, whale) macho ❑ **bulldog** n bul(l)dog m

bulldoze ['buldəuz] vt (site) nivelar (con motoniveladora); (building) arrasar (con motoniveladora); (fig: opposition) arrollar ❑ **bulldozer** n bulldozer m

bullet ['bulɪt] n bala

bulletin ['bulɪtn] n (US) anuncio, parte m; (journal) boletín m ❑ **bulletin board** n (US) tablón m de anuncios; (COMPUT) tablero de noticias

bulletproof ['bulɪt.pruːf] adj a prueba de balas

bullfight ['bulfaɪt] n corrida de toros ❑ **bullfighter** n torero ❑ **bullfighting** n los toros, el toreo

bullhorn (US) ['bul.hɔːrn] n megáfono

bullion ['buljən] n oro (or plata) en barras

bullock ['bulək] n novillo

bullring ['bulrɪŋ] n plaza de toros

bull's-eye n centro del blanco

bully ['buli] n valentón m, matón m ♦ vt intimidar, tiranizar

bum [bʌm] n (US: tramp) vagabundo(-a); (BRIT: inf: backside) culo

bumblebee ['bʌmbəlbiː] n abejorro

bump [bʌmp] n (blow) tope m, choque m; (jolt) sacudida; (on road etc) bache m; (on head etc) chichón m ♦ vt (strike) chocar contra ▸ **bump into** vt fus chocar contra, tropezar con; (person) topar con ❑ **bumper** n (AUT) defensa (MEX), parachoques m inv (LAm exc MEX, SP), paragolpes m inv (RPI) ♦ adj: **bumper crop or harvest** cosecha abundante ❑ **bumper cars** (US) npl carros mpl chocones (MEX) or locos (LAm exc MEX), autitos mpl chocadores (RPI) ❑ **bumpy** adj (road) lleno de baches

bun [bʌn] n (US: bread) bollo; (BRIT: cake) pastel m; (of hair) moño

bunch [bʌntʃ] n (of flowers) ramo; (of keys) manojo; (of bananas) piña; (of people) grupo; (pej) pandilla; **~es** npl (in hair) coletas fpl

bundle ['bʌndl] n bulto, fardo; (of sticks) haz m; (of papers) legajo ♦ vt (also: ~ up) atar, envolver; **to ~ sth/sb into** meter algo/a algn precipitadamente en

bungalow ['bʌŋgəlou] n bungalow m, chalé m

bungle ['bʌŋgəl] vt hacer mal

bunion ['bʌnjən] n juanete m

bunk [bʌŋk] n litera ❑ **bunk beds** npl literas fpl

bunker ['bʌŋkər] n (MIL) refugio; (coal store) carbonera; (GOLF) búnker m

bunny ['bʌni] n (inf: also: ~ **rabbit**) conejito

buoy ['buːi:] n boya ❑ **buoyant** adj (ship) capaz de flotar; (economy) boyante; (person) optimista

burden ['bɜːrdn] n carga ♦ vt cargar

bureau ['bjuərou] (pl ~x) n (agency) oficina, agencia; (US: government department) departamento m; (US: chest of drawers) cómoda; (BRIT: writing desk) escritorio, buró m

bureaucracy [bju'rɑːkrəsi] n burocracia

burger ['bɜːrgər] n hamburguesa

burglar ['bɜːrglər] n ladrón(-ona) m/f ❑ **burglar alarm** n alarma f antirrobo ❑ **burglarize** ['bɜːrgləraiz] (US) vt robar en, desvalijar ❑ **burglary** n robo con allanamiento, robo de una casa

burial ['beriəl] n entierro

burly ['bɜːrli] adj fornido, membrudo

Burma ['bɜːrmə] n Birmania

burn [bɜːrn] (pt, pp ~**ed**, (BRIT) pt, pp ~**ed** or ~**t**) vt quemar; (house) incendiar ♦ vi quemarse, arder; incendiarse; (sting) escocer ♦ n quemadura ▸ **burn down** vt incendiar ❑ **burner** n (on stove etc) quemador m ❑ **burning** adj (building etc) en llamas; (hot: sand etc) abrasador(a); (ambition) ardiente

burp [bɜːp] (inf) n eructo ♦ vi eructar

burqa ['bɜːka] n burka m, burqa m

burrow ['bʌrou] n madriguera ♦ vi hacer una madriguera; (rummage) hurgar

bursar ['bɜːrsər] n (UNIV) tesorero(-a)

bursary ['bɜːrsəri] (BRIT) n beca

burst [bɜːrst] (pt, pp ~) vt reventar; (river: banks etc) romper ♦ vi reventarse ♦ n (of gunfire) ráfaga; (also: ~ **pipe**) reventón m; **a ~ of energy/speed/enthusiasm** una explosión de energía/un ímpetu de velocidad/un arranque de entusiasmo; **to ~ into flames** estallar en llamas; **to ~ into tears** deshacerse en lágrimas; **to ~ out laughing** soltar la carcajada; **to ~ open** abrirse de golpe; **to be ~ing with** (container) estar lleno a rebosar de;

(person) reventar por or de ▸ **burst into** vt fus (room etc) irrumpir en

bury ['beri] vt enterrar; (body) enterrar, sepultar

bus [bʌs] (pl ~**es**) n autobús m ❑ **bus boy** (US) n ayudante m de mesero (MEX) or camarero (LAm exc MEX, SP) or mozo (SC)

bush [buʃ] n arbusto; (scrub land) monte m; **to beat about the ~** andar(se) con rodeos

bushy ['buʃi] adj (thick) espeso, poblado

busily ['bizili] adv afanosamente

business ['biznis] n (matter) asunto; (trading) comercio, negocios mpl; (firm) empresa, casa; (occupation) oficio; **to be away on ~** estar en viaje de negocios; **it's my ~ to ...** me toca or corresponde ...; **it's none of my ~** yo no tengo nada que ver; **he means ~** habla en serio ❑ **business college** n escuela or colegio de ciencias empresariales ❑ **businesslike** adj eficiente ❑ **businessman** n hombre m de negocios ❑ **business trip** n viaje m de negocios ❑ **businesswoman** n mujer f de negocios

busing ['bʌsiŋ] (US) n transporte m escolar

busker ['bʌskər] (BRIT) n músico(-a) ambulante

bus: ❑ **bus shelter** n parada cubierta ❑ **bus station** n estación f de autobuses ❑ **bus-stop** n parada de autobús

bust [bʌst] n (ANAT) pecho; (sculpture) busto ♦ adj (inf: broken) roto, estropeado; **to go ~** quebrar

bustle ['bʌsəl] n bullicio, movimiento ♦ vi menearse, apresurarse ❑ **bustling** adj (town) animado, bullicioso

busy ['bizi] adj ocupado, atareado; (store, street) concurrido, animado; (TEL: line) comunicando ♦ vt: **to ~ o.s. with** ocuparse en ❑ **busybody** n entrometido(-a) ❑ **busy signal** (US) n (TEL) señal f de comunicando

---

but

KEYWORD

[bʌt] conj

1 pero; **he's not very bright, but he's hard-working** no es muy inteligente, pero es trabajador

2 (in direct contradiction) sino; **he's not American but Canadian** no es americano sino canadiense; **he didn't sing but shouted** no cantó sino que gritó

3 (showing disagreement, surprise etc): **but that's far too expensive!** ¡pero eso es carísimo!; **but it does work!** ¡(pero) sí que funciona!

♦ prep (apart from, except) menos, salvo; **we've had nothing but trouble** no hemos tenido más que problemas; **no-one but him can do it** nadie más que él puede hacerlo; **who but a lunatic would do such a thing?** ¡sólo un loco haría una cosa así!; **but for you/your help** si no fuera por ti/tu ayuda; **anything but that** cualquier cosa menos eso

♦ adv (just, only): **she's but a child** no es más que una niña; **had I but known** si lo hubiera sabido; **I can but try** al menos lo puedo intentar; **it's all but finished** está casi acabado

butcher ['butʃər] n carnicero ♦ vt hacer una carnicería con; (cattle etc) matar ❑ **butcher's (store)** (US) (BRIT **butcher's (shop)**) n carnicería

butler ['bʌtlər] n mayordomo

butt [bʌt] n (barrel) tonel m; (of gun) culata; (US: of cigarette) colilla; (US: inf: bottom) trasero; (BRIT: fig: target) blanco ♦ vt dar cabezadas contra, top(et)ar ► **butt in** vi (interrupt) interrumpir

butter ['bʌtər] n mantequilla, manteca (RPI) ♦ vt untar con mantequilla or (RPI) manteca ❑ **buttercup** n botón m de oro

butterfly ['bʌtərflaɪ] n mariposa; (SWIMMING: also: ~ stroke) braza de mariposa

buttocks ['bʌtəks] npl nalgas fpl

button ['bʌtn] n botón m; (US) placa, chapa ♦ vt (also: ~ up) abotonar, abrochar ♦ vi abrocharse

buttress ['bʌtrɪs] n contrafuerte m

buy [baɪ] (pt, pp bought) vt comprar ♦ n compra; **to ~ sb sth/sth from sb** comprarle algo a algn; **to ~ sb a drink** invitar a algn a tomar algo ❑ **buyer** n comprador(a) m/f

buzz [bʌz] n zumbido; (inf: phone call) llamada (por teléfono) ♦ vi zumbar ❑ **buzzer** n timbre m ❑ **buzz word** n palabra que está de moda

by
KEYWORD
[baɪ] prep

1 (referring to cause, agent) por; de; **killed by lightning** muerto por un relámpago; **a painting by Picasso** un cuadro de Picasso

2 (referring to method, manner, means): **by bus/car/train** en autobús/carro/tren; **to pay by check** pagar con un cheque; **by moonlight/candlelight** a la luz de la luna/una vela; **by saving hard he ...** ahorrando ...

3 (via, through) por; **we came by Cleveland** vinimos por Cleveland

4 (close to, past): **the house by the river** la casa junto al río; **she rushed by me** pasó a mi lado como una exhalación; **I go by the post office every day** paso por delante de Correos todos los días

5 (time: not later than) para; (: during): **by daylight** de día; **by 4 o'clock** para las cuatro; **by this time tomorrow** mañana a estas horas; **by the time I got here it was too late** cuando llegué ya era demasiado tarde

6 (amount): **by the meter/pound** por metro/libra; **paid by the hour** pagado por hora

7 (MATH, measure): **to divide/multiply by 3** dividir/multiplicar por 3; **a room 10 feet by 15** una habitación de 10 pies por 15; **it's broader by a foot** es un pie más ancho

8 (according to) según, de acuerdo con; **it's 3 o'clock by my watch** según mi reloj, son las tres; **it's all right by me** por mí, está bien

9: **(all) by oneself** etc todo solo; **he did it (all) by himself** lo hizo él solo; **he was standing (all) by himself in a corner** estaba de pie solo en un rincón

10: **by the way** a propósito, por cierto; **this wasn't my idea, by the way** pues, no fue idea mía

♦ adv

1 see go; pass etc

2: **by and by** finalmente; **they'll come back by and by** acabarán volviendo; **by and large** en líneas generales, en general

bye(-bye) ['baɪ('baɪ)] excl adiós, hasta luego

by(e)-law n ordenanza municipal

by: ❑ **by-election** (BRIT) n elección f parcial ❑ **bygone** adj pasado, del pasado ♦ n: **let bygones be bygones** lo pasado, pasado está ❑ **bypass** n libramiento (MEX), carretera de circunvalación (LAm exc MEX, SP); (MED) (operación f de) by-pass m ♦ vt evitar ❑ **by-product** n subproducto, derivado; (of situation) consecuencia ❑ **bystander** n espectador(a) m/f

byte [baɪt] n (COMPUT) byte m, octeto

byword ['baɪˌwɜːrd] n: **to be a ~ for** ser sinónimo de

Cc

C [siː] n (MUS) do m

C. abbr (= centigrade) C.

C.A. (BRIT) abbr = **chartered accountant**

cab [kæb] n taxi m; (of truck) cabina

cabbage ['kæbɪdʒ] n repollo

cab driver n taxista mf

cabin ['kæbɪn] n cabaña; (on ship) camarote m; (on plane) cabina □ **cabin crew** n tripulación f de cabina □ **cabin cruiser** n yate m de motor

cabinet ['kæbɪnɪt] n (POL) gabinete m (ministerial), consejo de ministros; (furniture) armario; (also: display ~) vitrina

cable ['keɪbəl] n cable m ♦ vt cablegrafiar □ **cable-car** n teleférico □ **cable television** n televisión f por cable

cache [kæʃ] n (of arms, drugs etc) alijo

cackle ['kækəl] vi lanzar risotadas; (hen) cacarear

cactus ['kæktəs] (pl **cacti**) n cacto

cadet [kə'dɛt] n cadete m

cadge [kædʒ] (BRIT: inf) vt gorronear

Caesarean [sɪ'zɛərɪən] adj: ~ (**section**) cesárea

café [kæ'feɪ] n café m

cafeteria [kæfɪ'tɪərɪə] n cafetería

caffeine ['kæfiːn] n cafeína

cage [keɪdʒ] n jaula

cagey ['keɪdʒɪ] (inf) adj cauteloso, reservado

cagoule [kə'guːl] n chubasquero

cajole [kə'dʒəʊl] vt engatusar

Cajun ['keɪdʒən] adj cajún ♦ n (person) cajún mf; (LING) cajún m; see also **Creole**

CAJUN/CREOLE

El pueblo cajún está formado por los nativos de Louisiana, descendientes de los francocanadienses mientras que los criollos son los descendientes de los primeros colonizadores franceses de Louisiana. El término criollo también se usa como referencia a la gente de ascendencia mixta africano europea y a la lengua del mismo origen. Algunos platos típicos de su cocina, como el gumbo y la jambalaya, son muy populares entre los americanos, sobre todo en el sur.

---

cake [keɪk] n (CULIN: large) pastel m (LAm), tarta (SP); (: small) pastel m; (of soap) pastilla □ **caked** adj: **caked with** cubierto de

calculate ['kælkjʊleɪt] vt calcular □ **calculation** [kælkjʊ'leɪʃən] n cálculo, cómputo □ **calculator** n calculadora

calendar ['kæləndər] n calendario □ **calendar month/year** n mes m/año natural

calf [kɑːf] (pl **calves**) n (of cow) ternero, becerro; (of other animals) cría; (also: ~**skin**) piel f de becerro; (ANAT) pantorrilla

caliber (US) ['kælɪbər] (BRIT **calibre**) n calibre m

call [kɔːl] vt llamar; (meeting) convocar ♦ vi (shout) llamar; (TEL) llamar (por teléfono); (visit: also: ~ **in**, ~ **around**) hacer una visita ♦ n llamada; (of bird) canto; **to be ~ed** llamarse; **on ~** (on duty) de guardia ▶ **call back** vi (return) volver; (TEL) volver a llamar ▶ **call for** vt fus (demand) requerir, exigir; (fetch) pasar a recoger ▶ **call off** vt (cancel: meeting, race) suspender; (: deal) anular; (: strike) desconvocar ▶ **call on** vt fus (visit) visitar; (turn to) acudir a ▶ **call out** vi gritar ▶ **call up** vt (MIL) llamar a filas; (TEL) llamar □ **call box** (BRIT) n cabina telefónica □ **call center** n centro de atención al cliente □ **caller** n visita; (TEL) usuario(-a) □ **call girl** n prostituta (que concierta citas por teléfono) □ **call-in** (US) n programa m coloquio (por teléfono) □ **calling** n vocación f; (occupation) profesión f □ **calling card** (US) n tarjeta de visita

callous ['kæləs] adj insensible, cruel

calm [kɑːm] adj tranquilo; (sea) liso, en calma ♦ n calma, tranquilidad f ♦ vt calmar, tranquilizar ▶ **calm down** vi calmarse, tranquilizarse ♦ vt calmar, tranquilizar

Calor gas® ['kælər,gæs] (BRIT) n butano

calorie ['kælərɪ] n caloría

calves [kævz] npl of **calf**

Cambodia [kæm'bəʊdɪə] n Camboya

camcorder ['kæm,kɔːrdər] n videocámara

came [keɪm] pt of **come**

camel ['kæməl] n camello

camera ['kæmərə] n cámara (fotográfica); (CINEMA, TV) cámara; **in ~** (LAW) a puerta cerrada □ **cameraman** n camarógrafo(-a) (LAm), cámara mf (SP) □ **camera phone** n teléfono con cámara

camouflage ['kæməflɑːʒ] n camuflaje m ♦ vt camuflar

camp [kæmp] n campamento; (MIL) campamento; (for prisoners) campo; (fig: faction) bando ♦ vi acampar ♦ adj afectado, afeminado

campaign [kæm'peɪn] n (MIL, POL etc) campaña ♦ vi hacer campaña

camp: ❏ **camp bed** (*BRIT*) *n* cama de campaña ❏ **camper** *n* campista *mf*; (*vehicle*) cámper *m or f* (*LAm*), casa rodante (*SC*), caravana (*SP*) ❏ **campground** (*US*) *n* camping *m*, campamento ❏ **camping** *n* camping *m*, campamento; **to go camping** ir de camping *or* campamento ❏ **campsite** *n* camping *m*, campamento

campus ['kæmpəs] *n* campus *m* (universitario)

can¹ [kæn] *n* (*of oil, water*) bidón *m*; (*of food, drink*) lata ♦ *vt* enlatar

---

can²

KEYWORD

[kæn] (*negative* **cannot, can't**; *conditional and pt* **could**) *aux vb*

1 (*be able to*) poder; **you can do it if you try** puedes hacerlo si lo intentas; **I can't see you** no te veo

2 (*know how to*) saber; **I can swim/play tennis/drive** sé nadar/jugar al tenis/ conducir; **can you speak French?** ¿hablas *or* sabes hablar francés?

3 (*may*) poder; **can I use your phone?** ¿me dejas *or* puedo usar tu teléfono?

4 (*expressing disbelief, puzzlement etc*): **it can't be true!** ¡no puede ser (verdad)!; **what CAN he want?** ¿qué querrá?

5 (*expressing possibility, suggestion etc*): **he could be in the library** podría estar en la biblioteca; **she could have been delayed** pudo haberse retrasado

---

Canada ['kænədə] *n* (el) Canadá ❏ **Canadian** [kə'neɪdɪən] *adj, n* canadiense *mf*

canal [kə'næl] *n* canal *m*

canary [kə'neərɪ] *n* canario ❏ **the Canary Islands** *npl* las (Islas) Canarias

cancel ['kænsəl] *vt* cancelar; (*train*) suprimir; (*cross out*) tachar, borrar ❏ **cancellation** [kænsə'leɪʃən] *n* cancelación *f*; supresión *f*

cancer ['kænsər] *n* cáncer *m*; **C~** (*ASTROLOGY*) Cáncer *m*

candid ['kændɪd] *adj* franco, abierto

⚠ Be careful not to translate **candid** by the Spanish word *cándido*.

candidate ['kændɪdeɪt] *n* candidato(-a)

candle ['kændl] *n* vela; (*in church*) cirio ❏ **candle holder** *n* candelero ❏ **candlelight** *n*: **by candlelight** a la luz de una vela ❏ **candlestick** *n* (*single*) candelero; (*low*) palmatoria; (*bigger, ornate*) candelabro

candor (*US*) ['kændər] (*BRIT* **candour**) *n* franqueza

candy ['kændɪ] (*US*) *n* dulce *m* ❏ **candy bar** (*US*) *n* barrita (*dulce*) ❏ **candy floss** (*BRIT*) *n* algodón *m* (azucarado) ❏ **candy store** (*US*) *n* dulcería (*LAm*), confitería (*SP*)

cane [keɪn] *n* (*BOT*) caña; (*stick*) vara, palmeta; (*for furniture*) mimbre *f* ♦ *vt* (*BRIT SCOL*) castigar (con vara)

canister ['kænɪstər] *n* lata, bote *m*; (*of gas*) bombona

canker sore ['kæŋkər,sɔːr] (*US*) *n* llaga en la boca

cannabis ['kænəbɪs] *n* cannabis *m*, hachís *m*

canned [kænd] *adj* en o de lata, enlatado

cannon ['kænən] (*pl* ~ *or* ~**s**) *n* cañón *m*

cannot ['kænɒt] *cont* = **can not**

canoe [kə'nuː] *n* canoa; (*SPORT*) piragua ❏ **canoeing** *n* piragüismo

canon ['kænən] *n* (*clergyman*) canónigo; (*standard*) canon *m*

can-opener *n* abrelatas *m inv*

canopy ['kænəpɪ] *n* dosel *m*, toldo

can't [kænt] *cont* = **can not**

canteen [kæn'tiːn] *n* (*eating place*) cantina, comedor *m*; (*bottle*) cantimplora; (*BRIT: of cutlery*) juego

canter ['kæntər] *vi* ir a medio galope

canvas ['kænvəs] *n* (*material*) lona; (*painting*) lienzo; (*NAUT*) velas *fpl*

canvass ['kænvəs] *vi* (*POL*): **to ~ for** solicitar votos por ♦ *vt* (*COMM*) sondear

canyon ['kænjən] *n* cañón *m*

cap [kæp] *n* (*hat*) gorra; (*of pen*) tapa (*LAm*), capuchón *m* (*SP*); (*of bottle*) tapón *m*, tapa (*SC*); (*contraceptive*) diafragma *m*; (*for toy gun*) cápsula ♦ *vt* (*outdo*) superar; (*limit*) recortar

capability [keɪpə'bɪlɪtɪ] *n* capacidad *f*

capable ['keɪpəbəl] *adj* capaz

capacity [kə'pæsɪtɪ] *n* capacidad *f*; (*position*) calidad *f*

cape [keɪp] *n* capa; (*GEO*) cabo

caper ['keɪpər] *n* (*CULIN: gen pl*: **capers**) alcaparra; (*prank*) broma

capital ['kæpɪtl] *n* (*also*: ~ **city**) capital *f*; (*money*) capital *m*; (*also*: ~ **letter**) mayúscula ❏ **capital gains tax** *n* impuesto sobre la(s) plusvalía(s) ❏ **capitalism** *n* capitalismo ❏ **capitalist** *adj, n* capitalista *mf* ▶ **capitalize on** *vt fus* aprovechar ❏ **capital punishment** *n* pena de muerte

Capitol ['kæpɪtl] (*US*) *n* Capitolio

> **CAPITOL**
>
> El Capitolio es el edificio del Congreso
> (**Congress**) de los Estados Unidos, situado en
> la ciudad de Washington. Por extensión,
> también se suele llamar así al edificio en el
> que tienen lugar las sesiones parlamentarias
> de la cámara de representantes de muchos
> de los estados.

Capricorn ['kæprɪkɔːrn] *n* Capricornio

capsize ['kæpsaɪz] *vt* volcar, hacer zozobrar
♦ *vi* volcarse, zozobrar

capsule ['kæpsəl] *n* cápsula

captain ['kæptɪn] *n* capitán

caption ['kæpʃən] *n* (*heading*) título; (*to picture*) pie *m* de foto

captive ['kæptɪv] *adj, n* cautivo(-a)

capture ['kæptʃər] *vt* prender, apresar; (*animal*, COMPUT) capturar; (*place*) tomar; (*attention*) captar, llamar ♦ *n* apresamiento; captura; toma; (*data capture*) formulación *f* de datos

car [kɑːr] *n* carro (*LAm*), coche *m* (*SP*); (*US RAIL*) vagón *m*

carafe [kəˈræf] *n* jarra

carat ['kærət] *n* quilate *m*

caravan ['kærəvæn] *n* caravana; (*BRIT*) cámper *m* or *f* (*LAm*), casa rodante (*SC*), caravana (*SP*) ☐ **caravanning** (*BRIT*) *n*: **to go caravanning** viajar en cámper (*LAm*) or caravana (*SP*) ☐ **caravan site** (*BRIT*) *n* camping *m* para cámpers (*LAm*) or caravanas (*SP*)

carbohydrate [kɑːrbouˈhaɪdreɪt] *n* hidrato de carbono; (*food*) fécula

carbon ['kɑːrbən] *n* carbono ☐ **carbonated** *adj* (*water*) con gas ☐ **carbon paper** *n* papel *m* carbón

car boot sale (*BRIT*) *n* venta de objetos usados (*en un mercadillo*)

carburetor (*US*) [kɑːrbəˈreɪtər] (*BRIT* **carburettor**) *n* carburador *m*

card [kɑːrd] *n* (*material*) cartulina; (*index card etc*) ficha; (*playing card*) carta, naipe *m*; (*visiting card, greetings card etc*) tarjeta ☐ **cardboard** *n* cartón *m*

cardiac ['kɑːrdiæk] *adj* cardíaco

cardigan ['kɑːrdɪgən] *n* chaqueta de punto (*LAm*), rebeca (*SP*)

cardinal ['kɑːrdɪnl] *adj* cardinal; (*importance, principal*) esencial ♦ *n* cardenal *m*

card index *n* fichero

care [kɛər] *n* cuidado; (*worry*) inquietud *f*; (*charge*) cargo, custodia ♦ *vi*: **to ~ about** (*person, animal*) tener cariño a; (*thing, idea*) preocuparse por; **~ of** en casa de, al cuidado de; **in sb's ~** a cargo de algn; **to take ~ to** cuidarse de, tener cuidado de; **to take ~ of** cuidar; (*problem etc*) ocuparse de; **I don't ~** no me importa; **I couldn't ~ less** eso me trae sin cuidado ▶ **care for** *vt fus* cuidar a; (*like*) querer

careen [kəˈriːn] *vt* carenar

career [kəˈrɪər] *n* profesión *f*; (*in work, school*) carrera ♦ *vi* (*also*: **~ along**) correr a toda velocidad ☐ **career woman** *n* mujer *f* de carrera

care: ☐ **carefree** *adj* despreocupado ☐ **careful** *adj* cuidadoso; (*cautious*) cauteloso; (**be) careful!** ¡tenga cuidado! ☐ **carefully** *adv* con cuidado, cuidadosamente; con cautela ☐ **caregiver** (*US*) *n* cuidador(a) *m/f* (*de atención domiciliaria*) ☐ **careless** *adj* descuidado; (*heedless*) poco atento ☐ **carelessness** *n* descuido, falta de atención ☐ **carer** (*BRIT*) *n* (*professional*) enfermero(-a); (*unpaid*) persona que cuida a un pariente o vecino

caress [kəˈrɛs] *n* caricia ♦ *vt* acariciar

caretaker ['kɛərˌteɪkər] *n* (*US*: *caregiver*) cuidador(a) *m/f* (*de atención domiciliaria*); (*BRIT*: *of school, residence*) conserje *mf*

cargo ['kɑːrgou] (*pl* **~es**) *n* cargamento, carga

car hire *n* alquiler *m* de carros (*LAm*) or coches (*SP*)

Caribbean [kærəˈbiːən] *n*: **the ~ (Sea)** el (Mar) Caribe

caring ['kɛərɪŋ] *adj* humanitario; (*behavior*) afectuoso

carnation [kɑːrˈneɪʃən] *n* clavel *m*

carnival ['kɑːrnɪvəl] *n* carnaval *m*; (*US*: *funfair*) parque *m* de atracciones

carol ['kærəl] *n*: (**Christmas**) **~** villancico

carp [kɑːrp] *n* (*fish*) carpa

car park (*BRIT*) *n* estacionamiento (*LAm*), aparcamiento (*SP*)

carpenter ['kɑːrpɪntər] *n* carpintero(-a)

carpet ['kɑːrpɪt] *n* alfombra, tapete *m* (*MEX*); (*fitted*) alfombra (*LAm*), moqueta (*SP*) ♦ *vt* alfombrar

car phone *n* teléfono celular (*LAm*) or móvil (*SP*) (de automóvil)

car rental (*US*) *n* alquiler *m* de carros (*LAm*) or coches (*SP*)

carriage ['kærɪdʒ] *n* (*horse-drawn*) carruaje *m*; (*of goods*) transporte *m*; (: *cost*) porte *m*, flete *m*; (*BRIT RAIL*) vagón *m* ☐ **carriageway** (*BRIT*) *n* (*part of road*) calzada

carrier ['kæriər] *n* (*transport company*) transportista, empresa de transportes; (*MED*) portador(a) *m/f* ❑ **carrier bag** (*BRIT*) *n* bolsa (de papel *or* plástico)

carrot ['kærət] *n* zanahoria

carry ['kæri] *vt* (*person*) llevar; (*transport*) transportar; (*involve: responsibilities etc*) entrañar, implicar; (*MED*) ser portador de ♦ *vi* (*sound*) oírse; **to get carried away** (*fig*) entusiasmarse ▶ **carry on** *vi* (*continue*) seguir (adelante), continuar ▶ *vt* proseguir, continuar ▶ **carry out** *vt* (*orders*) cumplir; (*investigation*) llevar a cabo, realizar ❑ **carryall** (*US*) *n* bolsa de viaje ❑ **carry cot** (*BRIT*) *n* capazo, cuna portátil ❑ **carry-on** (*inf*) *n* (*fuss*) lío

cart [kɑːrt] *n* carro, carreta; (*US: for shopping*) carrito; (*US: motorized*) cochecito ♦ *vt* (*inf: transport*) acarrear

carton ['kɑːrtn] *n* (*box*) caja (de cartón); (*of milk etc*) cartón *m*; (*of yogurt*) tarrina

cartoon [kɑːrˈtuːn] *n* (*PRESS*) caricatura; (*comic strip*) tira cómica; (*movie*) dibujos *mpl* animados

cartridge ['kɑːrtrɪdʒ] *n* cartucho; (*of pen*) recambio; (*of tape player*) cápsula

carve [kɑːrv] *vt* (*meat*) trinchar; (*wood, stone*) cincelar, esculpir; (*initials etc*) grabar ▶ **carve up** *vt* dividir, repartir ❑ **carving** *n* (*object*) escultura; (*design*) talla; (*art*) tallado ❑ **carving knife** *n* trinchante *m*

car wash *n* lavado de coches

case [keɪs] *n* (*container*) caja; (*MED*) caso; (*for jewels etc*) estuche *m*; (*LAW*) causa, proceso; (*also: suit~*) maleta, valija (*RPl*); **in ~ of** en caso de; **in any ~** en todo caso; **just in ~** por si acaso

cash [kæʃ] *n* dinero en efectivo, dinero contante ♦ *vt* cobrar, hacer efectivo; **to pay (in) ~** pagar al contado; **~ on delivery** cóbrese al entregar ❑ **cashbook** *n* libro de caja ❑ **cash card** *n* tarjeta (del cajero automático) ❑ **cash desk** (*BRIT*) *n* caja ❑ **cash dispenser** *n* cajero automático ❑ **cash point** *n* cajero automático

cashew ['kæʃuː] *n* (*also: ~ nut*) nuez *f* de la India (*MEX*), anacardo (*LAm exc MEX, SP*)

cash flow *n* flujo de caja, cash-flow *m*

cashier [kæˈʃɪər] *n* cajero(-a) ❑ **cashier's check** (*US*) *n* cheque *m* bancario ❑ **cashier's desk** (*US*) *n* caja

cashmere ['kæʒmɪr] *n* cachemira

cash register *n* caja

casing ['keɪsɪŋ] *n* revestimiento

casino [kəˈsiːnou] *n* casino

casket ['kæskɪt] *n* cofre *m*, estuche *m*; (*US: coffin*) ataúd *m*

casserole ['kæsəroul] *n* (*food, pot*) cazuela

cassette [kəˈset] *n* casete *f*, cinta ❑ **cassette player** *n* pasacintas *m inv* (*LAm*), casete *m* (*SP*) ❑ **cassette recorder** *n* grabadora (de casetes) (*LAm*), casete *m* (*SP*)

cast [kæst] (*pt, pp ~*) *vt* (*throw*) echar, arrojar, lanzar; (*glance, eyes*) dirigir; (*THEATER*): **to ~ sb as Othello** dar a algn el papel de Otelo ♦ *vi* (*FISHING*) lanzar ♦ *n* (*THEATER*) reparto; (*also: plaster ~*) vaciado; **to ~ one's vote** votar; **to ~ doubt on** suscitar dudas acerca de ▶ **cast off** *vi* (*NAUT*) desamarrar; (*KNITTING*) cerrar (los puntos) ▶ **cast on** *vi* (*KNITTING*) poner los puntos

castanets [kæstəˈnets] *npl* castañuelas *fpl*

castaway ['kæstəˌweɪ] *n* náufrago(-a)

caster sugar ['kæstərˌʃugər] (*BRIT*) *n* azúcar *m* extrafino

Castile [kæˈstiːl] *n* Castilla ❑ **Castilian** *adj*, *n* castellano(-a)

casting vote ['kæstɪŋˌvout] *n* voto decisivo

cast iron *n* hierro fundido

castle ['kæsəl] *n* castillo; (*CHESS*) torre *f*

castor oil ['kæstərˌɔɪl] *n* aceite *m* de ricino

casual ['kæʒuəl] *adj* fortuito; (*irregular: work etc*) eventual, temporero; (*unconcerned*) despreocupado; (*clothes*) informal ❑ **casually** *adv* de manera despreocupada; (*dress*) de informal

⚠ Be careful not to translate **casual** by the Spanish word **casual**.

casualty ['kæʒuəlti] *n* víctima, herido; (*dead*) muerto; (*BRIT MED department*) urgencias *fpl*

cat [kæt] *n* gato; (*big cat*) felino

Catalan ['kætələn] *adj*, *n* catalán-(ana) *m/f*

catalogue ['kætəlɔːg] (*US* **catalog**) *n* catálogo ♦ *vt* catalogar

Catalonia [kætəˈlouniə] *n* Cataluña

catalyst ['kætəlɪst] *n* catalizador *m*

catalytic convertor [kætəˈlɪtɪkkənˈvɜːrtər] *n* catalizador *m*

catamaran [ˌkætəməˈræn] *n* catamarán *m*

catapult ['kætəpʌlt] *n* (*AER, MIL*) catapulta; (*BRIT: slingshot*) hulera (*MEX*), resortera (*MEX*), tirachinas *m inv* (*LAm exc MEX, SP*), honda (*SC*)

catarrh [kəˈtɑːr] *n* catarro

catastrophe [kəˈtæstrəfi] *n* catástrofe *f*

catch [kætʃ] (*pt, pp* **caught**) *vt* agarrar (*LAm*), coger (*SP*); (*arrest*) detener; (*grasp*) asir; (*breath*) contener; (*surprise: person*) sorprender; (*attract: attention*) captar; (*hear*) oír; (*MED*) contagiarse de, coger; (*also: ~ up*) alcanzar ♦ *vi* (*fire*) encenderse; (*in branches etc*) enredarse ♦ *n* (*fish etc*) pesca; (*act of* _catching_ cogida; (_hidden problem_) dificultad f; (_game_) pilla-pilla; (_of lock_) pestillo, cerradura; **to ~ fire** encenderse; **to ~ sight of** divisar ▶ **catch on** vi (_understand_) caer en la cuenta; (_grow popular_) hacerse popular ▶ **catch up** vi (_fig_) ponerse al día ❑ **catching** adj (_MED_) contagioso ❑ **catchment area** n zona de captación ❑ **catch phrase** n latiguillo; eslogan m ❑ **catchy** adj (_tune_) pegadizo

category ['kætɪɡəːri] n categoría, clase f

cater ['keɪtər] vi (_needs_) atender a; (_COMM: parties etc_) proveer comida a; **to ~ to** (_US_) or **for** (_BRIT_) atender a ❑ **caterer** n proveedor(a) m/f (de hostelería) ❑ **catering** n (_trade_) hostelería

caterpillar ['kætərpɪlər] n oruga, gusano

cathedral [kə'θiːdrəl] n catedral f

catholic ['kæθəlɪk] adj (_tastes etc_) amplio ❑ **Catholic** adj, n (_REL_) católico(-a)

CAT scan ['kæt.skæn] n TAC f, tomografía

Catseye® ['kæts'aɪ] (_BRIT_) n (_AUT_) catafaro

catsup ['kætsəp] (_US_) n salsa de tomate, catsup m

cattle ['kætl] npl ganado

catty ['kætɪ] adj malicioso, rencoroso

caucus ['kɔːkəs] n (_POL_) camarilla política; (: _US: to elect candidates_) comité m electoral

caught [kɔːt] pt, pp of **catch**

cauliflower ['kɑːlɪflauər] n coliflor f

cause [kɔːz] n causa, motivo, razón f; (_principle, also POL_) causa ♦ vt causar

causeway ['kɔːzweɪ] n calzada or carretera elevada

caution ['kɔːʃən] n cautela, prudencia; (_warning_) advertencia, amonestación f ♦ vt amonestar ❑ **cautious** adj cauteloso, prudente, precavido

cavalry ['kævəlrɪ] n caballería

cave [keɪv] n cueva, caverna ▶ **cave in** vi (_roof etc_) derrumbarse, hundirse

caviar(e) ['kævɪɑːr] n caviar m

cayenne [kaɪ'en] n (_also:_ **~ pepper**) pimentón m

CB n abbr (= _Citizens' Band (Radio)_) banda ciudadana

CBI n abbr (= _Confederation of British Industry_) organización empresarial británica

CBS (_US_) n abbr = **Columbia Broadcasting System**

cc abbr = **carbon copy; cubic centimeters**

CCTV n abbr (= _closed-circuit television_) circuito cerrado de televisión

CD n abbr (= _compact disc_) CD m; (_player_) (reproductor m de) CD m ❑ **CD player** n

reproductor m de CD ❑ **CD-ROM** [siːdiːˈrɑːm] n abbr CD-ROM m

cease [siːs] vt, vi cesar ❑ **ceasefire** n alto m el fuego ❑ **ceaseless** adj incesante

cedar ['siːdər] n cedro

ceiling ['siːlɪŋ] n techo; (_fig_) límite m

celebrate ['seləbreɪt] vt celebrar ♦ vi divertirse ❑ **celebrated** adj célebre ❑ **celebration** [selɪ'breɪʃən] n fiesta, celebración f

celebrity [sə'lebrɪtɪ] n (_fame, person_) celebridad f

celery ['selərɪ] n apio

cell [sel] n celda; (_BIOL_) célula; (_ELEC_) elemento

cellar ['selər] n sótano; (_for wine_) bodega

cello ['tʃeləu] n violoncelo

Cellophane® ['seləfeɪn] n celofán m

cellphone ['sel.fəun] n teléfono celular

Celt [kelt, selt] adj, n celta mf ❑ **Celtic** adj celta

cement [sə'ment] n cemento ❑ **cement mixer** n hormigonera, mezcladora de cemento (_MEX_)

cemetery ['semɪterɪ] n cementerio

censor ['sensər] n censor m ♦ vt (_cut_) censurar ❑ **censorship** n censura

censure ['senʃər] vt censurar

census ['sensəs] n censo

cent [sent] n (_unit of dollar_) centavo; (_unit of euro_) céntimo; _see also_ **per**

centenary [sen'tenərɪ] (_BRIT_) n centenario

centennial [sen'tenɪəl] (_US_) n centenario

center (_US_) ['sentər] (_BRIT_ **centre**) n centro; (_fig_) núcleo ♦ vt centrar ❑ **center-forward** n (_SPORT_) delantero centro ❑ **center-half** n (_SPORT_) medio centro

centi... ['sentɪ] prefix: ❑ **centigrade** adj centígrado ❑ **centiliter** (_US_) (_BRIT_ **centilitre**) n centilitro ❑ **centimeter** (_US_) (_BRIT_ **centimetre**) n centímetro

centipede ['sentɪpiːd] n ciempiés m inv

central ['sentrəl] adj central; (_of house etc_) céntrico ❑ **Central America** n Centroamérica ❑ **central heating** n calefacción f central ❑ **centralize** vt centralizar

centre ['sentər] (_BRIT_) n, vt = **center**

century ['sentʃərɪ] n siglo; **20th ~** siglo veinte

CEO (_US_) n abbr = **Chief Executive Officer**

ceramic [sə'ræmɪk] adj cerámico ❑ **ceramics** n cerámica

cereal ['sɪərɪəl] n cereal m

ceremony ['serɪmounɪ] n ceremonia; **to stand on ~** hacer ceremonias, estar de cumplido

certain ['sɜːtn] adj seguro; (person): **a ~ Mr Smith** un tal Sr Smith; (particular, some) cierto; **for ~** a ciencia cierta ❑ **certainly** adv (undoubtedly) ciertamente; (of course) desde luego, por supuesto ❑ **certainty** n certeza, certidumbre f, seguridad f; (inevitability) certeza

certificate [sər'tɪfɪkɪt] n certificado

certified ['sɜːrtɪfaɪd] adj (check) certificado ❑ **certified mail** (US) n correo certificado ❑ **certified public accountant** (US) n contador(a) m/f público(-a) (LAm)

certify ['sɜːrtɪfaɪ] vt certificar; (award diploma to) conceder un diploma a; (declare insane) declarar loco

cervical ['sɜːrvɪkəl] adj cervical

cervix ['sɜːrvɪks] n cuello del útero

cf. abbr (= compare) cfr

CFC n abbr (= chlorofluorocarbon) CFC m

ch. abbr (= chapter) cap

chain [tʃeɪn] n cadena; (of mountains) cordillera; (of events) sucesión f ♦ vt (also: ~ up) encadenar ❑ **chain reaction** n reacción f en cadena ❑ **chain-smoke** vi fumar un cigarrillo tras otro ❑ **chain store** n tienda (de una cadena)

chair [tʃeər] n silla; (armchair) sillón m, butaca; (of university) cátedra; (of meeting etc) presidencia ♦ vt (meeting) presidir ❑ **chairlift** n telesilla ❑ **chairman** n presidente m ❑ **chairwoman** n presidenta

chalk [tʃɔːk] n (GEO) creta; (for writing) tiza, gis m (MEX) ❑ **chalkboard** (US) n pizarrón (LAm), pizarra (SP)

challenge ['tʃælɪndʒ] n desafío, reto ♦ vt desafiar, retar; (statement, right) poner en duda; **to ~ sb to do sth** retar a algn a que haga algo ❑ **challenging** adj exigente; (tone) de desafío

chamber ['tʃeɪmbər] n cámara, sala; (POL) cámara; (BRIT LAW gen pl) despacho; **~s** npl despacho; **~ of commerce** cámara de comercio ❑ **chambermaid** n camarera

chamois ['ʃæmɪ] n gamuza

champagne [ʃæm'peɪn] n champán m

champion ['tʃæmpɪən] n campeón(-ona) m/f; (of cause) defensor(a) m/f ❑ **championship** n campeonato

chance [tʃɑːns] n (opportunity) ocasión f, oportunidad f; (likelihood) posibilidad f; (risk) riesgo ♦ vt arriesgar, probar ♦ adj fortuito, casual; **to ~ it** arriesgarse, intentarlo; **to take a ~** arriesgarse; **by ~** por casualidad

chancellor ['tʃænsələr] (BRIT) n canciller m ❑ **Chancellor of the Exchequer** (BRIT) n ≈ Ministro de Hacienda

chandelier [ʃændə'lɪər] n araña (de luces)

change [tʃeɪndʒ] vt cambiar; (replace) cambiar, reemplazar; (clothes, job) cambiar de; (transform) transformar ♦ vi cambiar(se); (change trains) hacer transbordo; (traffic lights) cambiar de color; (be transformed): **to ~ into** transformarse en ♦ n cambio; (alteration) modificación f; (transformation) transformación f; (of clothes) muda; (coins) feria (MEX), morralla (MEX), sencillo (LAm exc MEX), suelto (SP); (money returned) cambio; **to ~ one's mind** cambiar de opinión or idea; **for a ~** para variar; **to ~ gear** (BRIT AUT) cambiar de marcha ❑ **changeable** adj (weather) cambiable ❑ **change machine** n máquina de cambio ❑ **changeover** n (to new system) cambio ❑ **changing** adj cambiante ❑ **changing room** (BRIT) n vestuario

channel ['tʃænəl] n (TV) canal m; (of river) cauce m; (groove) conducto; (fig: medium) medio ♦ vt (river etc) encauzar; **the (English) C~** el Canal (de la Mancha); **the C~ Islands** las Islas Normandas; **the C~ Tunnel** el túnel del Canal de la Mancha, el Eurotúnel ❑ **channel-hopping**, **channel-surfing** n (TV) zapping m

chant [tʃɑːnt] n (of crowd) gritos mpl; (REL) canto ♦ vt (slogan, word) repetir a gritos

chaos ['keɪɑːs] n caos m

chap [tʃæp] (BRIT: inf) n (man) tipo

chapel ['tʃæpəl] n capilla

chaperone ['ʃæpəroun] n carabina

chaplain ['tʃæplɪn] n capellán m

chapped [tʃæpt] adj agrietado

chapter ['tʃæptər] n capítulo

char [tʃɑːr] vt (burn) carbonizar, chamuscar

character ['kærɪktər] n carácter m, naturaleza, índole f; (moral strength, personality) carácter; (in novel, movie) personaje m ❑ **characteristic** [kærɪktə'rɪstɪk] adj característico ♦ n característica

charcoal ['tʃɑːrkoul] n carbón m vegetal; (ART) carboncillo

charge [tʃɑːrdʒ] n (LAW) cargo, acusación f; (cost) precio, coste m; (responsibility) cargo ♦ vt (LAW): **to ~ (with)** acusar (de); (battery) cargar; (price) pedir; (customer) cobrar ♦ vi precipitarse; (MIL) cargar, atacar; **~s** npl tarifa f; **to reverse the ~s** (TEL) revertir el cobro; **to**

take ~ of hacerse cargo de, encargarse de; **to be in ~ of** estar encargado de; (*business*) mandar; **how much do you ~?** ¿cuánto cobra usted?; **to ~ an expense (up) to sb's account** cargar algo a cuenta de algn ❑ **charge card** *n* tarjeta de crédito

charity ['tʃærɪtɪ] *n* caridad *f*; (*organization*) sociedad *f* benéfica; (*money, gifts*) limosnas *fpl*

charm [tʃɑːrm] *n* encanto, atractivo; (*talisman*) hechizo; (*on bracelet*) dije *m* ♦ *vt* encantar ❑ **charming** *adj* encantador(a)

chart [tʃɑːrt] *n* (*diagram*) cuadro; (*graph*) gráfico; (*map*) carta de navegación ♦ *vt* (*course*) trazar; (*progress*) seguir; **the ~s** *npl* (*Top 40*) ≈ la lista de éxitos

charter ['tʃɑːrtər] *vt* (*plane*) alquilar; (*ship*) fletar ♦ *n* (*document*) carta; (*of university, company*) estatutos *mpl* ❑ **chartered accountant** (*BRIT*) *n* contador(a) *m/f* público(-a) (*LAm*) ❑ **chartered public accountant** (*US*) *n* contador(a) *m/f* público(-a) (*LAm*) ❑ **charter flight** *n* vuelo chárter

chase [tʃeɪs] *vt* (*pursue*) perseguir; (*also: ~ away*) ahuyentar ♦ *n* persecución *f*

chasm ['kæzəm] *n* sima

chassis ['ʃæsɪ] *n* chasis *m*

chat [tʃæt] *vi* (*also:* **have a ~**) charlar, platicar (*MEX, CAm*) ♦ *n* charla, plática (*MEX, CAm*) ❑ **chat room** *n* (*INTERNET*) chat *m*, canal *m* de charla ❑ **chat show** (*BRIT*) *n* programa *m* de entrevistas

chatter ['tʃætər] *vi* (*person*) charlar; (*teeth*) castañetear ♦ *n* (*of birds*) parloteo; (*of people*) cháchara ❑ **chatterbox** (*inf*) *n* parlanchín(-ina) *m/f*

chatty ['tʃætɪ] *adj* (*style*) informal; (*person*) hablador(a)

chauffeur ['ʃoʊfər] *n* chofer *m* (*LAm*), chófer *m* (*SP*)

chauvinist ['ʃoʊvɪnɪst] *n* (*male chauvinist*) machista *m*; (*nationalist*) chovinista *mf*, patriotista *mf*

cheap [tʃiːp] *adj* barato; (*joke*) de mal gusto; (*poor quality*) de mala calidad ♦ *adv* barato ❑ **cheap day return** (*BRIT*) *n* boleto (*LAm*) or billete *m* (*SP*) de ida y vuelta (en un día) ❑ **cheaper** *adj* más barato ❑ **cheaply** *adv* barato, a bajo precio

cheat [tʃiːt] *vi* hacer trampa ♦ *vt*: **to ~ sb (out of sth)** estafar (algo) a algn ♦ *n* (*person*) tramposo(-a)

check [tʃɛk] *vt* (*examine*) controlar; (*facts*) comprobar; (*halt*) parar, detener; (*restrain*) refrenar, restringir; (*US: mark*) marcar ♦ *n*

(*inspection*) control *m*, inspección *f*; (*curb*) freno; (*US*) cheque *m*; (*US: in restaurant etc*) nota, cuenta; (*pattern: gen pl*) cuadro ♦ *adj* (*also:* **~ed**: *pattern, cloth*) a cuadros ▶ **check in** *vi* (*at hotel*) firmar el registro; (*at airport*) facturar *or* (*MEX*) registrar el equipaje ♦ *vt* (*luggage*) facturar ▶ **check out** *vi* (*of hotel*) (pagar e) irse ▶ **check up** *vi*: **to check up on sth** comprobar algo; **to check up on sb** investigar a algn ❑ **checkbook** (*US*) (*BRIT* **chequebook**) *n* chequera (*LAm*), talonario de cheques (*SP*) ❑ **check card** (*US*) *n* tarjeta de cheque ❑ **checkered** (*US*) (*BRIT* **chequered**) *adj* (*pattern, cloth*) a cuadros; (*fig*) accidentado ❑ **checkers** (*US*) *n* juego de damas ❑ **check-in (desk)** *n* mostrador *m* de facturación *or* (*MEX*) registro ❑ **checking account** (*US*) *n* cuenta corriente ❑ **check mark** (*US*) *n* visto (bueno), palomita (*MEX*) ❑ **checkmate** *n* jaque *m* mate ❑ **checkout** *n* (*also:* **checkout counter**) caja ❑ **checkpoint** *n* control *m* ❑ **checkroom** (*US*) *n* consigna ❑ **checkup** *n* (*MED*) reconocimiento general

cheek [tʃiːk] *n* mejilla; (*impudence*) descaro; **what a ~!** (*BRIT*) ¡qué cara! ❑ **cheekbone** *n* pómulo ❑ **cheeky** (*BRIT*) *adj* fresco, descarado

cheep [tʃiːp] *vi* piar

cheer [tʃɪər] *vt* vitorear, aplaudir; (*gladden*) alegrar, animar ♦ *vi* dar vivas ♦ *n* viva *m*; **~s** *npl* aplausos *mpl*; **~s!** ¡salud! ▶ **cheer up** *vi* animarse ♦ *vt* alegrar, animar ❑ **cheerful** *adj* alegre

cheerio [tʃɪrɪ'oʊ] (*BRIT*) *excl* ¡hasta luego!

cheerleader ['tʃɪrˌliːdər] (*US*) *n* animador(a) *m/f*

cheese [tʃiːz] *n* queso ❑ **cheeseboard** *n* tabla de quesos

cheetah ['tʃiːtə] *n* guepardo

chef [ʃɛf] *n* chef *mf*

chemical ['kɛmɪkəl] *adj* químico ♦ *n* producto químico

chemist ['kɛmɪst] *n* (*scientist*) químico(-a); (*BRIT: pharmacist*) farmacéutico(-a) ❑ **chemistry** *n* química ❑ **chemist's (shop)** (*BRIT*) *n* farmacia

cheque [tʃɛk] (*BRIT*) *n* cheque *m* ❑ **chequebook** (*BRIT*) *n* = **checkbook**

chequered ['tʃɛkərd] (*BRIT*) *adj* = **checkered**

cherish ['tʃɛrɪʃ] *vt* (*love*) querer, apreciar; (*protect*) cuidar; (*hope etc*) abrigar

cherry ['tʃɛrɪ] *n* cereza; (*also:* **~ tree**) cerezo

chess [tʃɛs] *n* ajedrez *m* ❑ **chessboard** *n* tablero (de ajedrez)

chest [tʃest] n (ANAT) pecho; (box) cofre m, cajón m ❏ **chest of drawers** n cómoda

chestnut ['tʃes,nʌt] n castaña; (also: ~ tree) castaño

chew [tʃuː] vt mascar, masticar ❏ **chewing gum** n chicle m

chic [ʃiːk] adj elegante

chick [tʃik] n pollito, polluelo; (inf: girl) chica

chicken ['tʃikin] n gallina, pollo; (food) pollo; (inf: coward) gallina mf ▶ **chicken out** (inf) vi rajarse ❏ **chickenpox** n varicela

chickpea ['tʃikpiː] n garbanzo

chicory ['tʃikəri] n (for coffee) achicoria; (salad) escarola

chief [tʃiːf] n jefe(-a) m/f ♦ adj principal ❏ **chief executive** n director(a) m/f general ❏ **chiefly** adv principalmente

chilblain ['tʃilbleɪn] n sabañón m

child [tʃaɪld] (pl ~ren) n niño(-a); (offspring) hijo(-a) ❏ **childbirth** n parto ❏ **child-care** n cuidado de los niños ❏ **childhood** n niñez f, infancia ❏ **childish** adj pueril, aniñado ❏ **childlike** adj de niño ❏ **child minder** (BRIT) n baby sitter mf (LAm), canguro mf (SP) ❏ **children** ['tʃildrən] npl of child

Chile ['tʃili] n Chile m ❏ **Chilean** adj, n chileno(-a)

chill [tʃil] n frío; (MED) resfriado ♦ vt enfriar; (CULIN) congelar ▶ **chill out** (inf) vi relajarse; **chill out, man!** (inf) ¡relax!, ¡tranqui tronco!

chil(l)i ['tʃili] n chile m, ají m (SC)

chilly ['tʃili] adj frío

chime [tʃaɪm] n repique m; (of clock) campanada ♦ vi repicar; sonar

chimney ['tʃimni] n chimenea ❏ **chimney sweep** n deshollinador m

chimpanzee [tʃimpæn'ziː] n chimpancé m

chin [tʃin] n mentón m, barbilla

china ['tʃaɪnə] n porcelana; (crockery) loza

China ['tʃaɪnə] n China ❏ **Chinese** [tʃaɪ'niːz] adj chino ♦ n inv chino(-a); (LING) chino

chink [tʃiŋk] n (opening) grieta, hendedura; (noise) tintineo

chip [tʃip] n (US: also: potato ~) papa (LAm) or patata (SP) frita; (gen pl: BRIT: CULIN) papas fpl or patatas fpl fritas; (of wood) astilla; (of glass, stone) lasca; (at poker) ficha; (COMPUT) chip m ♦ vt (cup, plate) desconchar

chiropodist [kɪ'rɒpədɪst] (BRIT) n pedicuro(-a), podólogo(-a)

chiropractor ['kaɪrə,præktər] n quiropráctico(-a)

chirp [tʃɜːrp] vi (bird) gorjear, piar

chisel ['tʃizəl] n (for wood) escoplo; (for stone) cincel m

chit [tʃit] n nota

chitchat ['tʃit,tʃæt] n chismes mpl, habladurías fpl

chivalry ['ʃivəlri] n caballerosidad f

chives [tʃaɪvz] npl cebollinos mpl, cebolletas fpl

chlorine ['klɔːriːn] n cloro

chock-a-block ['tʃɒkə,blɒk] adj atestado

chock-full ['tʃɒk'ful] adj atestado

chocolate ['tʃɒk(ə)lɪt] n chocolate m; (candy) bombón m

choice [tʃɔɪs] n elección f, selección f; (option) opción f; (preference) preferencia ♦ adj escogido

choir ['kwaɪər] n coro ❏ **choirboy** n niño de coro

choke [tʃouk] vi ahogarse; (on food) atragantarse ♦ vt estrangular, ahogar; (block): **to be ~d with** estar atascado de ♦ n (AUT) estárter m

cholesterol [kə'lestərɒl] n colesterol m

choose [tʃuːz] (pt chose, pp chosen) vt escoger, elegir; (team) seleccionar; **to ~ to do sth** optar por hacer algo

choosy ['tʃuːzi] adj delicado

chop [tʃɒp] vt (wood) cortar, tajar; (CULIN: also: ~ up) picar ♦ n (CULIN) chuleta; ~s npl (mouth) boca, labios mpl

chopper ['tʃɒpər] n (helicopter) helicóptero

choppy ['tʃɒpi] adj (sea) picado, agitado

chopsticks ['tʃɒp,stɪks] npl palillos mpl (chinos)

chord [kɔːrd] n (MUS) acorde m

chore [tʃɔːr] n faena, tarea; (routine task) trabajo rutinario

chorus ['kɔːrəs] n coro; (repeated part of song) estribillo

chose [tʃouz] pt of choose

chosen ['tʃouzən] pp of choose

chowder ['tʃaudər] n (US) sopa de pescado

Christ [kraɪst] n Cristo

christen ['krɪsən] vt bautizar

Christian ['krɪstʃən] adj, n cristiano(-a) ❏ **Christianity** [krɪstʃi'ænɪti] n cristianismo ❏ **Christian name** n nombre m de pila

Christmas ['krɪsməs] n Navidad f; **Merry ~!** ¡Feliz Navidad! ❏ **Christmas card** n tarjeta de Navidad ❏ **Christmas Day** n día m de Navidad ❏ **Christmas Eve** n Nochebuena ❏ **Christmas tree** n árbol m de Navidad

chrome [kroum] n cromo

chronic ['krɒnɪk] adj crónico

chronological [krɑːnəˈlɑdːʒɪkəl] *adj*
cronológico

chubby ['tʃʌbi] *adj* regordete

chuck [tʃʌk] *(inf) vt* lanzar, arrojar; *(BRIT: also:* ~
up) abandonar ▸ **chuck out** *vt* (*person*)
echar (fuera); (*garbage etc*) tirar

chuckle ['tʃʌkl] *vi* reírse entre dientes

chug [tʃʌɡ] *vi* resoplar; (*car, boat: also:* ~ **along**)
avanzar traqueteando

chum [tʃʌm] *n* amigo(-a), compañero(-a)

chunk [tʃʌŋk] *n* pedazo, trozo

church [tʃɜːrtʃ] *n* iglesia ❑ **churchyard** *n*
cementerio

churn [tʃɜːrn] *n* (*for butter*) mantequera; (*for
milk*) lechera ▸ **churn out** *vt* producir en
serie

chute [ʃuːt] *n* (*also:* **garbage** ~) vertedero; (*for
coal etc*) rampa de caída

chutney ['tʃʌtni] *n salsa picante de frutas y
especias*

CIA (*US*) *n abbr* (= *Central Intelligence Agency*)
CIA *f*

CID (*BRIT*) *n abbr* (= *Criminal Investigation
Department*) policía judicial británica

cider ['saɪdər] *n* sidra

cigar [sɪˈɡɑːr] *n* puro

cigarette [sɪɡəˈret] *n* cigarrillo ❑ **cigarette
butt** *n* colilla ❑ **cigarette case** *n* cigarrera,
pitillera

Cinderella [sɪndəˈrelə] *n* Cenicienta

cinders ['sɪndərz] *npl* cenizas *fpl*

cine camera ['sɪnɪˌkæmərə] (*BRIT*) *n* cámara
cinematográfica

cinema ['sɪnəmə] (*BRIT*) *n* cine *m*

cinnamon ['sɪnəmən] *n* canela

circle ['sɜːrkəl] *n* círculo; (*in theater*) anfiteatro
♦ *vi* dar vueltas ♦ *vt* (*surround*) rodear, cercar;
(*move around*) dar la vuelta a

circuit ['sɜːrkɪt] *n* circuito; (*tour*) gira; (*track*)
pista; (*lap*) vuelta ❑ **circuitous** [sərˈkjuːɪtəs]
adj indirecto

circular ['sɜːrkjələr] *adj* circular ♦ *n* circular *f*

circulate ['sɜːrkjuleɪt] *vi* circular; (*person: at
party etc*) hablar con los invitados ♦ *vt* poner
en circulación ❑ **circulation** *n* circulación *f*;
(*of newspaper*) tirada

circumstances ['sɜːrkəmstænsɪz] *npl*
circunstancias *fpl*; (*financial condition*)
situación *f* económica

circus ['sɜːrkəs] *n* circo

CIS *n abbr* (= *Commonwealth of Independent
States*) CEI *f*

cistern ['sɪstərn] *n* cisterna, tanque *m*; (*toilet
cistern*) cisterna

citizen ['sɪtɪzən] *n* (*POL*) ciudadano(-a); (*of city*)
habitante *mf* ❑ **citizenship** *n* ciudadanía

citrus fruits ['sɪtrəsˌfruːts] *npl* cítricos *mpl*

city ['sɪti] *n* ciudad *f*; **the C~** (*BRIT*) centro
financiero de Londres

civic ['sɪvɪk] *adj* cívico; (*authorities*) municipal
❑ **civic centre** (*BRIT*) *n* centro público

civil ['sɪvɪl] *adj* civil; (*polite*) atento, cortés
❑ **civil engineer** *n* ingeniero(-a) civil
❑ **civilian** [sɪˈvɪliən] *adj* civil ♦ *n* civil *mf*,
paisano(-a)

civilization [sɪvɪlɪˈzeɪʃən] *n* civilización *f*

civilized ['sɪvɪlaɪzd] *adj* civilizado

civil: ❑ **civil law** *n* derecho civil ❑ **civil
liberties** *n* libertades *fpl* civiles ❑ **civil
rights** *n* derechos *mpl* civiles ❑ **civil
servant** *n* funcionario(-a) (del Estado),
burócrata *mf* (*MEX*) ❑ **civil service** *n*
administración *f or* (*MEX*) burocracia pública
❑ **civil war** *n* guerra civil

CIVIL RIGHTS

En Estados Unidos, el término **civil rights**
hace referencia a los derechos garantizados a
todos los ciudadanos por las enmiendas 13,
14, 15 y 19 de la Constitución. Entre estos
derechos están el derecho al voto y a un
tratamiento de igualdad por parte de la ley.
El movimiento moderno de derechos civiles
(**Modern Civil Rights Movement**) logró la
aprobación de la ley de derechos civiles en
1964, que prohibía la segregación y la
discriminación pública por motivos racistas.

claim [kleɪm] *vt* exigir, reclamar; (*rights etc*)
reivindicar; (*assert*) pretender ♦ *vi* (*for
insurance*) reclamar ♦ *n* reclamación *f*;
pretensión *f* ❑ **claimant** *n* (*in court*)
demandante *mf*

clairvoyant [klɛərˈvɔɪənt] *n* clarividente *mf*

clam [klæm] *n* almeja

clamber ['klæmbər] *vi* trepar

clammy ['klæmi] *adj* (frío y) húmedo

clamor (*US*) ['klæmər] (*BRIT* **clamour**) *vi*: **to ~
for** clamar por, pedir a voces

clamp [klæmp] *n* abrazadera, grapa ♦ *vt* (2
things together) cerrar fuertemente; (*one thing
on another*) afianzar (con abrazadera); (*AUT:
wheel*) poner un cepo a ▸ **clamp down on**
vt fus (*government, police*) tomar medidas
drásticas contra

clang [klæŋ] *vi* sonar, hacer estruendo

clap [klæp] *vi* aplaudir ❑ **clapping** *n*
aplausos *mpl*

claret ['klærət] *n* burdeos *m inv*

clarify ['klærɪfaɪ] *vt* aclarar

clarinet [klɛrɪ'net] n clarinete m

clash [klæʃ] n enfrentamiento; choque m; desacuerdo; estruendo ♦ vi (fight) enfrentarse; (beliefs) chocar; (disagree) estar en desacuerdo; (colors) desentonar; (two events) coincidir

clasp [klæsp] n (hold) apretón m; (of necklace, bag) cierre m ♦ vt apretar; abrazar

class [klæs] n clase f ♦ vt clasificar

classic ['klæsɪk] adj, n clásico ❑ **classical** adj clásico

classified ['klæsɪfaɪd] adj (information) confidencial, secreto ❑ **classified advertisement** n anuncio clasificado (LAm)

classmate ['klæsmeɪt] n compañero(-a) de clase

classroom ['klæsruːm] n clase f, aula

clatter ['klætər] n estrépito ♦ vi hacer ruido or estrépito

clause [klɔːz] n cláusula; (LING) oración f

claw [klɔː] n (of cat) uña; (of bird of prey) garra; (of lobster) pinza

clay [kleɪ] n arcilla

clean [kliːn] adj limpio; (record, reputation) bueno, intachable; (joke) decente ♦ vt limpiar; (hands etc) lavar ► **clean out** vt limpiar ► **clean up** vt limpiar, asear ❑ **clean-cut** (person) bien parecido ❑ **cleaner** n (person) limpiador(a) m/f; (substance) producto de limpieza ❑ **cleaner's** n tintorería ❑ **cleaning** n limpieza ❑ **cleanliness** ['klɛnlɪnɪs] n limpieza

cleanse [klɛnz] vt limpiar ❑ **cleanser** n producto de limpieza; (for face) crema or loción f limpiadora

clean-shaven adj (bien) afeitado or (MEX) rasurado

cleansing department (BRIT) n servicio de limpieza

clear [klɪər] adj claro; (road, way) libre; (conscience) limpio, tranquilo; (skin) terso; (sky) despejado ♦ vt (space) despejar, limpiar; (LAW: suspect) absolver; (obstacle) salvar, saltar por encima de; (check) aceptar ♦ vi (fog etc) despejarse ♦ adv: ~ of a distancia de; to ~ the table recoger la mesa ► **clear up** vt limpiar; (mystery) aclarar, resolver ❑ **clearance** n (removal) despeje m; (permission) acreditación f ❑ **clear-cut** adj bien definido, nítido ❑ **clearing** n (in wood) claro ❑ **clearing bank** (BRIT) n banco central or de compensación ❑ **clearing house** n (FINANCE) cámara de compensación ❑ **clearly** adv claramente; (evidently) sin

duda ❑ **clearway** (BRIT) n tramo de carretera donde no se puede parar

cleat [kliːt] (US) n (on sport shoe) taco

clef [klɛf] n (MUS) clave f

cleft [klɛft] n (in rock) grieta, hendidura

clench [klɛntʃ] vt apretar, cerrar

clergy ['klɜːrdʒi] n clero ❑ **clergyman** n clérigo

clerical ['klɛrɪkəl] adj de oficina; (REL) clerical

clerk [klɜːrk] n (in office) oficinista mf; (in bank) empleado(-a); (in hotel) recepcionista mf; (US: in store) dependiente(-a) m/f

clever ['klɛvər] adj (intelligent) inteligente, listo; (skillful) hábil; (device, arrangement) ingenioso

cliché [kliː'ʃeɪ] n cliché m

click [klɪk] vt (tongue) chasquear; (heels) taconear ♦ vi (COMPUT) hacer clic; to ~ on an icon hacer clic en un icono

client ['klaɪənt] n cliente(-a) m/f

cliff [klɪf] n acantilado

climate ['klaɪmɪt] n clima m ❑ **climate change** cambio climático

climax ['klaɪmæks] n (of battle, career) apogeo; (of movie, book) punto culminante; (sexual) orgasmo

climb [klaɪm] vi subir; (plant) trepar; (move with effort): to ~ over a wall/into a car trepar a una tapia/subir a un coche ♦ vt (stairs) subir; (tree) trepar a; (mountain) escalar ♦ n subida ❑ **climb-down** n vuelta atrás ❑ **climber** n (rock climber) escalador(a) m/f; (mountaineer) alpinista mf (MEX, SP), andinista mf (LAm) ❑ **climbing** n alpinismo (MEX, SP), andinismo (LAm)

clinch [klɪntʃ] vt (deal) cerrar; (argument) remachar

cling [klɪŋ] (pt, pp clung) vi: to ~ to agarrarse a; (clothes) pegarse a

clinic ['klɪnɪk] n clínica ❑ **clinical** adj clínico; (fig) frío

clink [klɪŋk] vi tintinar

clip [klɪp] n (for hair) pasador m, broche m (MEX); (also: **paper ~**) clip m, sujetapapeles m inv; (TV, CINEMA) fragmento ♦ vt (cut) cortar; (also: ~ **together**) unir ❑ **clippers** npl (for nails) cortaúñas m inv; (for gardening) tijeras fpl ❑ **clipping** n (newspaper) recorte m

cloak [kloʊk] n capa, manto ♦ vt (fig) encubrir, disimular ❑ **cloakroom** n guardarropa; (BRIT: WC) baño (LAm), lavabo (SP)

clock [klɑːk] n reloj m ► **clock in** or **on** vi checar (MEX) or marcar (LAm) tarjeta (al entrar) ► **clock off** or **out** vi checar (MEX) or marcar (LAm) tarjeta (al salir) ❑ **clockwise** adv en el sentido de las agujas del reloj ❑ **clockwork** n mecanismo de relojería ♦ adj (toy) de cuerda

clod [klɑːd] n (of earth) terrón m; (idiot) imbécil mf

clog [klɑːg] n zueco, chanclo ♦ vt atascar ♦ vi (also: ~ **up**) atascarse

cloister ['klɔɪstər] n claustro

clone [kloʊn] n clon m ♦ vt clonar

close¹ [kloʊs] adj (near): ~ (**to**) cerca (de); (friend) íntimo; (connection) estrecho; (examination) detallado, minucioso; (weather) bochornoso ♦ adv cerca; ~ **by**, ~ **at hand** muy cerca; **to have a ~ shave** (fig) escaparse por los pelos ▶ **close to** prep cerca de

close² [kloʊz] vt (shut) cerrar; (end) concluir, terminar ♦ vi (store etc) cerrarse; (end) concluirse, terminarse ♦ n (end) fin m, final m, conclusión f ▶ **close down** vi cerrarse definitivamente ❑ **closed** adj (store etc) cerrado ❑ **closed shop** n empresa con todo el personal afiliado a un solo sindicato

close-knit ['kloʊs'nɪt] adj (fig) muy unido

closely ['kloʊsli] adv (study) con detalle; (watch) de cerca; (resemble) estrechamente

closet ['klɑːzɪt] n (us) armario, clóset m (MEX), placard m (RPI)

close-up ['kloʊsʌp] n primer plano

closure ['kloʊʒər] n cierre m

clot [klɑːt] n (gen) coágulo ♦ vi (blood) coagularse

cloth [klɑːθ] n (material) tela, paño; (rag) trapo

clothe [kloʊð] vt vestir ❑ **clothes** npl ropa ❑ **clothes brush** n cepillo (para la ropa) ❑ **clothes line** n cuerda de tender ❑ **clothes pin** (us) (BRIT **clothes peg**) n pinza or (MEX) horquilla (de la ropa)

clothing ['kloʊðɪŋ] n = **clothes**

cloud [klaʊd] n nube f ❑ **cloudburst** n aguacero ❑ **cloudy** adj nublado, nubloso; (liquid) turbio

clout [klaʊt] vt dar un tortazo a

clove [kloʊv] n clavo; ~ **of garlic** diente m de ajo

clover ['kloʊvər] n trébol m

clown [klaʊn] n payaso ♦ vi (also: ~ **around**) hacer el payaso

cloying ['klɔɪɪŋ] adj empalagoso

club [klʌb] n (society) club m; (weapon) macana (MEX), cachiporra (LAm), porra (SP); (also: **golf ~**) palo ♦ vt aporrear ♦ vi: **to ~ together** (BRIT: for gift) comprar entre todos; **~s** npl (CARDS) tréboles mpl ❑ **clubbing** n: **to go clubbing** ir a la discoteca ❑ **club class** n (AVIAT) clase f preferente ❑ **clubhouse** n sede f (de un club)

cluck [klʌk] vi cacarear

clue [kluː] n pista; (in crosswords) indicación f; **I haven't a ~** no tengo ni idea

clump [klʌmp] n (of trees) grupo

clumsy ['klʌmzi] adj (person) torpe, desmañado; (tool) difícil de manejar; (movement) desgarbado

clung [klʌŋ] pt, pp of **cling**

cluster ['klʌstər] n grupo ♦ vi agruparse, apiñarse

clutch [klʌtʃ] n (AUT) embrague m; (grasp): **~es** garras fpl ♦ vt asir; agarrar

clutter ['klʌtər] vt atestar

cm abbr (= centimeter) cm

CND n abbr (= Campaign for Nuclear Disarmament) plataforma pro desarme nuclear

Co. abbr = **county**; **company**

c/o abbr (= care of) c/a, a/c

coach [koʊtʃ] n autobús m; (horse-drawn) coche m, carruaje m; (of train) vagón m, coche m; (SPORT) entrenador(a) m/f, instructor(a) m/f; (tutor) profesor(a) m/f particular ♦ vt (SPORT) entrenar; (student) preparar, enseñar ❑ **coach trip** n excursión f en autobús

coal [koʊl] n carbón m ❑ **coalface** n frente m de carbón ❑ **coalfield** n yacimiento de carbón

coalition [koʊə'lɪʃən] n coalición f

coal mine n mina de carbón

coal miner n minero(-a) (del carbón)

coarse [kɔːrs] adj basto, burdo; (vulgar) grosero, ordinario

coast [koʊst] n costa, litoral m ♦ vi (AUT) ir en punto muerto ❑ **coastal** adj costero, costanero ❑ **Coast Guard** n servicio de guardacostas ❑ **coastline** n litoral m

coat [koʊt] n abrigo; (of animal) pelaje m; (of paint) mano f, capa ♦ vt cubrir, revestir ❑ **coat hanger** n gancho (LAm), percha (SP) ❑ **coating** n capa, baño ❑ **coat of arms** n escudo de armas

coax [koʊks] vt engatusar

cobbler ['kɑːblər] n zapatero (remendón)

cobbles ['kɑːbəlz], **cobblestones** npl adoquines mpl

cobweb ['kɑːbwɛb] n telaraña

cocaine [koʊ'keɪn] n cocaína

cock [kɑːk] n (male bird) macho; (rooster) gallo ♦ vt (gun) amartillar ❑ **cockerel** n gallito

cockle ['kɑːkəl] n berberecho

cockney ['kɑːkni] (BRIT) n persona nacida en el este de Londres y especialmente de clase obrera

cockpit ['kɑːkpɪt] n cabina

cockroach ['kɑːkroʊtʃ] n cucaracha

cocktail ['kɒk,teɪl] n cóctel m, combinado ❑ **cocktail cabinet** n mueble-bar m ❑ **cocktail party** n cóctel m

cocoa ['koukou] n cacao; (drink) chocolate m

coconut ['koukənʌt] n coco

cod [kɒd] n bacalao

C.O.D. abbr (= cash on delivery) pago contra reembolso

code [koud] n código; (cipher) clave f; (area code) clave f lada (MEX), código de la zona (LAm), prefijo (SP); (zip code) código postal

cod-liver oil ['kɒd'lɪvər,ɔɪl] n aceite m de hígado de bacalao

co-ed ['kou,ɛd] adj mixto ♦ n (US: female student) alumna de un colegio mixto

coercion [kou'ɜːrʃən] n coacción f

coffee ['kɒfɪ] n café m ❑ **coffee bar** (BRIT) n cafetería ❑ **coffee bean** n grano de café ❑ **coffee break** n descanso (para el café) ❑ **coffee house** n café m ❑ **coffeepot** n cafetera ❑ **coffee shop** n café m ❑ **coffee table** n mesa de centro

coffin ['kɒfɪn] n ataúd m

cog [kɒg] n (wheel) rueda dentada; (tooth) diente m

cogent ['koudʒənt] adj convincente

cognac ['kounjæk] n coñac m

coil [kɔɪl] n rollo; (ELEC) bobina, carrete m; (contraceptive) DIU m, dispositivo intrauterino ♦ vt enrollar

coin [kɔɪn] n moneda ♦ vt (word) inventar, idear ❑ **coinage** n moneda ❑ **coin-box** (BRIT) n cabina telefónica

coincide [koum'saɪd] vi coincidir; (agree) estar de acuerdo ❑ **coincidence** [kou'ɪnsɪdəns] n casualidad f

Coke® [kouk] n Coca-Cola®

coke [kouk] n (coal) coque m

colander ['kɒləndər] n colador m, escurridor m

cold [kould] adj frío ♦ n frío; (MED) resfriado; **it's ~** hace frío; **to be ~** (person) tener frío; **to catch ~** enfriarse; **to catch a ~** resfriarse, acatarrarse; **in ~ blood** a sangre fría ❑ **cold-shoulder** vt dar o volver la espalda a ❑ **cold sore** n fuego (LAm), calentura (SP)

coleslaw ['koulslɔː] n ensalada de repollo, zanahoria, cebolla y mayonesa

colic ['kɒlɪk] n cólico

collapse [kə'læps] vi hundirse, derrumbarse; (MED) sufrir un colapso ♦ n hundimiento, derrumbamiento; (MED) colapso ❑ **collapsible** adj plegable

collar ['kɒlər] n (of coat, shirt) cuello; (of dog etc) collar ❑ **collarbone** n clavícula

collateral [kə'lætərəl] n garantía colateral

colleague ['kɒliːg] n colega mf; (at work) compañero(-a)

collect [kə'lekt] vt (litter, mail etc) recoger; (as a hobby) coleccionar, recoger; (debts, subscriptions etc) recaudar; (BRIT: call and pick up) recoger ♦ vi reunirse; (dust) acumularse; **to call ~** (US TEL) llamar por cobrar (MEX) o a cobro revertido (LAm exc MEX, SP) ❑ **collect call** (US) n llamada por cobrar (MEX) o a cobro revertido (LAm exc MEX, SP) ❑ **collection** n colección f; (of mail, for charity) recogida ❑ **collector** n coleccionista mf

college ['kɒlɪdʒ] n (part of university) colegio universitario; (of agriculture, technology) escuela universitaria; (US: of Law, Arts etc) ≈ facultad m

collide [kə'laɪd] vi chocar

colliery ['kɒljərɪ] (BRIT) n mina de carbón

collision [kə'lɪʒən] n choque m

colloquial [kə'loukwɪəl] adj familiar, coloquial

cologne [kə'loun] n (also: **eau de ~**) agua de colonia, colonia

Colombia [kə'lʌmbɪə] n Colombia ❑ **Colombian** adj, n colombiano(-a)

colon ['koulən] n (sign) dos puntos; (MED) colon m

colonel ['kɜːrnl] n coronel m

colonial [kə'lounɪəl] adj colonial

colony ['kɒlənɪ] n colonia

color (US) ['kʌlər] (BRIT **colour**) n color m ♦ vt color(e)ar; (dye) teñir; (fig: account) adornar; (: judgement) distorsionar ♦ vi (blush) sonrojarse; **~s** npl (of party, club) colores mpl; **in ~** en color ▶ **color in** vt colorear ❑ **color bar** n segregación f racial ❑ **color-blind** (US) (BRIT **colour-blind**) adj daltónico ❑ **colored** (US) (BRIT **coloured**) adj de color; (photo) en color ❑ **color film** n película en color ❑ **colorful** (US) (BRIT **colourful**) adj lleno de color; (story) fantástico; (person) excéntrico ❑ **coloring** (US) (BRIT **colouring**) n (complexion) tez f; (in food) colorante m ❑ **color scheme** n combinación f de colores ❑ **color television** n televisión f en color

colt [koult] n potro

column ['kɒləm] n columna ❑ **columnist** ['kɒləmnɪst] n columnista mf

coma ['koumə] n coma m

comb [koum] n peine m; (ornamental) peineta ♦ vt (hair) peinar; (area) registrar a fondo

combat ['kɒmbæt] n combate m ♦ vt combatir

combination [kɑːmbɪˈneɪʃən] n
combinación f

combine [vb kəmˈbaɪn, n ˈkɑːmbaɪn] vt
combinar; (qualities) reunir ♦ vi combinarse
♦ n (ECON) grupo empresarial ❑ **combine
(harvester)** n cosechadora

---

come

KEYWORD

[kʌm] (pt **came**, pp **come**) vi

1 (movement towards) venir; **to come
running** venir corriendo

2 (arrive) llegar; **he's come here to work** ha
venido aquí para trabajar; **to come home**
volver a casa

3 (reach): **to come to** llegar a; **the check
came to $90** la cuenta ascendía a noventa
dólares

4 (occur): **an idea came to me** se me ocurrió
una idea

5 (be, become): **to come loose/undone** etc
aflojarse/desabrocharse/desatarse etc; **I've
come to like him** por fin ha llegado a caerme
bien or gustarme

▶ **come about** vi suceder, ocurrir

▶ **come across** vt fus (person) topar con;
(thing) dar con

▶ **come around** (US) (BRIT **come round**) vi
(after faint, operation) volver en sí

▶ **come away** vi (leave) marcharse; (become
detached) desprenderse

▶ **come back** vi (return) volver

▶ **come by** vt fus (acquire) conseguir

▶ **come down** vi (price) bajar; (tree, building)
ser derribado

▶ **come forward** vi presentarse

▶ **come from** vt fus (place, source) ser de

▶ **come in** vi (visitor) entrar; (train, report)
llegar; (fashion) ponerse de moda; (on deal etc)
entrar

▶ **come in for** vt fus (criticism etc) recibir

▶ **come into** vt fus (money) heredar; (be
involved) tener que ver con; **to come into
fashion** ponerse de moda

▶ **come off** vi (button) soltarse,
desprenderse; (attempt) salir bien

▶ **come on** vi (pupil) progresar; (work, project)
desarrollarse; (lights) encenderse; (electricity)
volver; **come on!** ¡vamos!

▶ **come out** vi (fact) salir a la luz; (book, sun)
salir; (stain) quitarse

▶ **come to** vi (wake) volver en sí

▶ **come up** vi (sun) salir; (problem) surgir;
(event) aproximarse; (in conversation)
mencionarse

▶ **come up against** vt fus (resistance etc)
tropezar con

▶ **come up with** vt fus (idea) sugerir; (money)
conseguir

▶ **come upon** vt fus (find) dar con

comeback [ˈkʌmbæk] n (US: response)
réplica, (: witty) respuesta aguda; **to make a ~**
(on stage) volver a las tablas

comedian [kəˈmiːdiən] n humorista mf,
cómico(-a) ❑ **comedienne** [kəmiːdiˈɛn] n
cómica

comedy [ˈkɑːmɪdi] n comedia; (humor)
comicidad f

comet [ˈkɑːmɪt] n cometa m

comeuppance [kʌmˈʌpəns] n: **to get one's
~** llevarse su merecido

comfort [ˈkʌmfərt] n bienestar m; (relief)
alivio ♦ vt consolar; **~s** npl (of home etc)
comodidades fpl ❑ **comfortable** adj
cómodo; (financially) acomodado; (easy) fácil
❑ **comfortably** adv (sit) cómodamente;
(live) holgadamente ❑ **comforter** (US) n
edredón m ❑ **comfort station** (US) n baño
(LAm), servicios (SP)

comic [ˈkɑːmɪk] adj (also: **~al**) cómico ♦ n
(comedian) cómico; (BRIT: for children) cómic m
(LAm), tebeo (SP); (BRIT: for adults) cómic m
❑ **comic book** (US) n cómic m ❑ **comic
strip** n tira cómica

coming [ˈkʌmɪŋ] n venida, llegada ♦ adj que
viene; **~s and goings** npl idas fpl y venidas,
ajetreo

comma [ˈkɑːmə] n coma

command [kəˈmænd] n orden f, mandato;
(MIL: authority) mando; (mastery) dominio ♦ vt
(troops) mandar; (give orders to): **to ~ sb to do**
mandar or ordenar a algn hacer
❑ **commandeer** [kɑːmənˈdɪər] vt requisar
❑ **commander** n (MIL) comandante mf,
jefe(-a) m/f

commemorate [kəˈmɛməreɪt] vt
conmemorar

commence [kəˈmɛns] vt, vi comenzar,
empezar

commencement [kəˈmɛnsmənt] (US) n
(UNIV) (ceremonia de) graduación f

commend [kəˈmɛnd] vt elogiar, alabar;
(recommend) recomendar

commensurate [kəˈmɛnsərɪt] adj: **~ with**
en proporción a, que corresponde a

comment [ˈkɑːmɛnt] n comentario ♦ vi: **to ~
on** hacer comentarios sobre; **"no ~"** (written)
"sin comentarios"; (spoken) "no tengo nada

que decir" ❑ **commentary** n comentario
❑ **commentator** n comentarista mf

commerce ['kɑ:mərs] n comercio

commercial [kə'mɜ:rʃəl] adj comercial ♦ n
(TV, RADIO) comercial m (LAm), anuncio
(publicitario) (SP)

commiserate [kə'mɪzəreɪt] vi: **to ~ with**
compadecerse de, condolerse de

commission [kə'mɪʃən] n (committee, fee)
comisión f ♦ vt (work of art) encargar; **out of ~**
fuera de servicio ❑ **commissionaire**
[kəmɪʃə'neər] (BRIT) n portero
❑ **commissioner** n (POLICE) comisario de
policía

commit [kə'mɪt] vt (act) cometer; (resources)
dedicar; (to sb's care) entregar; **to ~ o.s. (to
do)** comprometerse (a hacer); **to ~ suicide**
suicidarse ❑ **commitment** n compromiso;
(to ideology etc) entrega

committee [kə'mɪti] n comité m

commodity [kə'mɑ:dɪti] n mercancía

common ['kɑ:mən] adj común; (pej)
ordinario ♦ n campo común; **the C~s** npl (BRIT)
(la Cámara de) los Comunes mpl; **in ~** en
común ❑ **commoner** (BRIT) n plebeyo
❑ **common law** n derecho
consuetudinario ❑ **commonly** adv
comúnmente ❑ **commonplace** adj de lo
más común ❑ **commonroom** (BRIT) n sala
común ❑ **common sense** n sentido
común ❑ **the Commonwealth** (BRIT) n
(HIST) la Commonwealth

commotion [kə'mouʃən] n tumulto,
confusión f

commune [n 'kɑ:mju:n, vb kə'mju:n] n
(group) comuna ♦ vi: **to ~ with** comulgar or
conversar con

communicate [kə'mju:nɪkeɪt] vt comunicar
♦ vi: **to ~ (with)** comunicarse (con); (in writing)
estar en contacto (con)

communication [kəmju:nɪ'keɪʃən] n
comunicación f ❑ **communication cord**
(BRIT) n alarma (en tren)

communion [kə'mju:njən] n (also: **Holy C~**)
comunión f

communiqué [kəmju:nɪ'keɪ] n
comunicado, parte f

communism ['kɑ:mjənɪzəm] n comunismo
❑ **communist** adj, n comunista mf

community [kə'mju:nɪti] n comunidad f;
(large group) colectividad f ❑ **community
center** n centro social ❑ **community
chest** (US) n arca comunitaria, fondo común

❑ **community college** (US) n
establecimiento docente de educación terciaria

COMMUNITY COLLEGE

En los Estados Unidos, el **community
college** es un establecimiento docente de
educación terciaria donde se realizan cursos
de dos años.

commutation ticket [kɑ:mju'teɪʃən,tɪkɪt]
(US) n abono

commute [kə'mju:t] vi viajar a diario (de la casa
al trabajo) ♦ vt conmutar ❑ **commuter** n
persona (que viaja ...); see vi

compact [adj kəm'pækt, n 'kɑ:mpækt] adj
compacto ♦ n (also: **powder ~**) polvera
❑ **compact disc** n compact m (disc)
❑ **compact disc player** n (reproductor m
de) compact m (disc)

companion [kəm'pænjən] n compañero(-a)
❑ **companionship** n compañerismo

company ['kʌmpəni] n compañía; (COMM)
sociedad f, compañía; **to keep sb ~**
acompañar a algn ❑ **company secretary**
(BRIT) n jefe(-a) m/f de administración

comparative [kəm'perətɪv] adj relativo;
(study) comparativo ❑ **comparatively** adv
(relatively) relativamente

compare [kəm'peər] vt: **to ~ sth/sb with/to**
comparar algo/a algn con ♦ vi: **to ~ (with)**
compararse (con) ❑ **comparison**
[kəm'perɪsən] n comparación f

compartment [kəm'pɑ:rtmənt] n (also: RAIL)
compartimento

compass ['kʌmpəs] n brújula; **~es** npl (MATH)
compás m

compassion [kəm'pæʃən] n compasión f
❑ **compassionate** adj compasivo

compatible [kəm'pætɪbəl] adj compatible

compel [kəm'pel] vt obligar

compensate ['kɑ:mpənseɪt] vt compensar
♦ vi: **to ~ for** compensar ❑ **compensation**
[kɑ:mpən'seɪʃən] n (for loss) indemnización f

compere ['kɑ:mpeər] (BRIT) n presentador(a)
m/f

compete [kəm'pi:t] vi (take part) tomar parte,
concurrir; (vie with): **to ~ with** competir con,
hacer competencia a

competent ['kɑ:mpɪtənt] adj competente,
capaz

competition [kɑ:mpɪ'tɪʃən] n (contest)
concurso; (rivalry) competencia

competitive [kəm'petɪtɪv] adj (ECON, SPORT)
competitivo

competitor [kəmˈpɛtɪtər] n (rival) competidor(a) m/f; (participant) concursante mf

complacency [kəmˈpleɪsənsi] n autosatisfacción f

complacent [kəmˈpleɪsənt] adj autocomplaciente

complain [kəmˈpleɪn] vi quejarse; (COMM) reclamar □ **complaint** n queja; reclamación f; (MED) enfermedad f

complement [n ˈkɑːmplɪmənt, vb ˈkɑːmplɪment] n complemento; (esp of ship's crew) dotación f ♦ vt (enhance) complementar □ **complementary** [kɑːmplɪˈmentəri] adj complementario

complete [kəmˈpliːt] adj (full) completo; (finished) acabado ♦ vt (fulfill) completar; (finish) acabar; (a form) llenar □ **completely** adv completamente □ **completion** n terminación f; (of contract) realización f

complex [ˈkɑːmplɛks] adj, n complejo

complexion [kəmˈplɛkʃən] n (of face) cutis m, tez f

compliance [kəmˈplaɪəns] n (submission) sumisión f; (agreement) conformidad f; **in ~ with** de acuerdo con

complicate [ˈkɑːmplɪkeɪt] vt complicar □ **complicated** adj complicado □ **complication** [kɑːmplɪˈkeɪʃən] n complicación f

compliment [n ˈkɑːmplɪmənt, vb ˈkɑːmplɪment] n (formal) cumplido ♦ vt felicitar; **~s** npl (regards) saludos mpl; **to pay sb a ~** hacer cumplidos a algn □ **complimentary** [kɑːmplɪˈmentəri] adj elogioso; (free) de regalo

comply [kəmˈplaɪ] vi: **to ~ with** cumplir con

component [kəmˈpounənt] adj componente ♦ n (TECH) pieza

compose [kəmˈpouz] vt: **to be ~d of** componerse de; (music etc) componer; **to ~ o.s.** tranquilizarse □ **composed** adj sosegado ♦ **composer** n (MUS) compositor(a) m/f □ **composition** [kɑːmpəˈzɪʃən] n composición f

compost [ˈkɑːmpoust] n abono (vegetal)

composure [kəmˈpouʒər] n serenidad f, calma

compound [ˈkɑːmpaʊnd] n (CHEM) compuesto; (LING) palabra compuesta; (enclosure) recinto ♦ adj compuesto; (fracture) complicado

comprehend [kɑːmprɪˈhend] vt comprender □ **comprehension** n comprensión f

comprehensive [kɑːmprɪˈhensɪv] adj exhaustivo; (INSURANCE) contra todo riesgo □ **comprehensive (school)** (BRIT) n centro estatal de enseñanza secundaria

compress [vb kəmˈpres, n ˈkɑːmpres] vt comprimir; (information) condensar ♦ n (MED) compresa

comprise [kəmˈpraɪz] vt (also: **be ~d of**) comprender, constar de; (constitute) constituir

compromise [ˈkɑːmprəmaɪz] n (agreement) arreglo ♦ vt comprometer ♦ vi transigir

compulsion [kəmˈpʌlʃən] n compulsión f; (force) obligación f

compulsive [kəmˈpʌlsɪv] adj compulsivo; (viewing, reading) obligado

compulsory [kəmˈpʌlsəri] adj obligatorio

computer [kəmˈpjuːtər] n computadora (LAm), ordenador m (SP) □ **computer game** n juego de computadora (LAm) or ordenador (SP) □ **computer-generated** adj realizado por computadora (LAm) or ordenador (SP) □ **computerize** vt (data) computarizar, computerizar; (system) informatizar □ **computer programmer** n programador(a) m/f □ **computer programming** n programación f □ **computer science** n informática □ **computing** n (activity, science) informática

comrade [ˈkɑːmræd] n (POL, MIL) camarada; (friend) compañero(-a) □ **comradeship** n camaradería, compañerismo

con [kɑːn] vt (deceive) engañar; (cheat) estafar ♦ n estafa

conceal [kənˈsiːl] vt ocultar

conceit [kənˈsiːt] n presunción f □ **conceited** adj presumido

conceive [kənˈsiːv] vt, vi concebir

concentrate [ˈkɑːnsəntreɪt] vi concentrarse ♦ vt concentrar

concentration [kɑːnsənˈtreɪʃən] n concentración f

concept [ˈkɑːnsept] n concepto

concern [kənˈsɜːrn] n (matter) asunto; (COMM) empresa; (anxiety) preocupación f ♦ vt (worry) preocupar; (involve) afectar; (relate to) tener que ver con; **to be ~ed (about)** interesarse (por), preocuparse (por) □ **concerning** prep sobre, acerca de

concert [ˈkɑːnsert] n concierto □ **concerted** [kənˈsɜːrtɪd] adj (efforts etc) concertado □ **concert hall** n sala de conciertos

concerto [kənˈtʃeərtou] n concierto

concession [kən'sɛʃən] n concesión f; **tax ~** exención fiscal or tributaria

concierge [kɔ'sjɛrʒ] n conserje m

conclude [kən'klu:d] vt concluir; (treaty etc) firmar; (agreement) llegar a; (decide) llegar a la conclusión de ◻ **conclusion** n conclusión f; firma ◻ **conclusive** adj decisivo, concluyente

concoct [kən'kɑ:kt] vt confeccionar; (plot) tramar ◻ **concoction** n mezcla

concourse ['kɑ:nkɔ:rs] n vestíbulo

concrete ['kɑ:ŋkri:t] n hormigón m, concreto (LAm) ◆ adj de concreto or hormigón; (fig) concreto

concur [kən'kɜ:r] vi estar de acuerdo, asentir

concurrently [kən'kɜ:rəntli] adv al mismo tiempo

concussion [kən'kʌʃən] n conmoción f cerebral

condemn [kən'dɛm] vt condenar; (building) declarar en ruina

condense [kən'dɛns] vi condensarse ◆ vt condensar, abreviar ◻ **condensed milk** n leche f condensada

condiment ['kɑ:ndimənt] n condimento

condition [kən'dɪʃən] n condición f, estado; (requirement) condición f ◆ vt condicionar; **on ~ that** a condición (de) que ◻ **conditioner** n enjuague m (LAm), suavizante m (SP)

condo ['kɑ:ndou] (US) n = **condominium**

condolences [kən'doulənsɪz] npl pésame m

condom ['kɑ:ndəm] n condón m

condominium [kɑ:ndə'mɪniəm] (US) n condominio (LAm), bloque m de pisos (SP)

condone [kən'doun] vt condonar

conducive [kən'du:sɪv] adj: **~ to** conducente a

conduct [n 'kɑ:ndʌkt, vb kən'dʌkt] n conducta, comportamiento ◆ vt (lead) conducir; (manage) llevar a cabo, dirigir; (MUS) dirigir; **to ~ o.s.** comportarse ◻ **conducted tour** (BRIT) n visita guiada ◻ **conductor** n (of orchestra) director(a) m/f; (US: on train) revisor(a) m/f; (on bus) cobrador(a) m/f; (ELEC) conductor m ◻ **conductress** (BRIT) n (on bus) cobradora

cone [koun] n cono; (pine cone) piña; (on road) cono, pivote m; (for ice-cream) cucurucho

confectioner [kən'fekʃənər] n repostero(-a) ◻ **confectioner's (shop)** (BRIT) n confitería ◻ **confectioner's sugar** (US) n azúcar f glas or (RPI) impalpable ◻ **confectionery** n dulces mpl

confer [kən'fɜ:r] vt: **to ~ sth on** otorgar algo a ◆ vi conferenciar

conference ['kɑ:nfərəns] n (meeting) reunión f; (convention) congreso

confess [kən'fes] vt confesar ◆ vi admitir ◻ **confession** n confesión f

confetti [kən'feti] n confeti m

confide [kən'faɪd] vi: **to ~ in** confiar en

confidence ['kɑ:nfɪdəns] n (also: **self-~**) confianza; (secret) confidencia; **in ~** (speak, write) en confianza ◻ **confidence game** n timo ◻ **confident** adj seguro de sí mismo; (certain) seguro ◻ **confidential** [kɑ:nfɪ'denʃəl] adj confidencial

confine [kən'faɪn] vt (limit) limitar; (shut up) encerrar ◻ **confined** adj (space) reducido ◻ **confinement** n (prison) prisión f ◻ **confines** ['kɑ:nfaɪnz] npl confines mpl

confirm [kən'fɜ:rm] vt confirmar ◻ **confirmation** [kɑ:nfər'meɪʃən] n confirmación f ◻ **confirmed** adj empedernido

confiscate ['kɑ:nfɪskeɪt] vt confiscar

conflict [n 'kɑ:nflɪkt, vb kən'flɪkt] n conflicto ◆ vi (opinions) chocar ◻ **conflicting** adj contradictorio

conform [kən'fɔ:rm] vi conformarse; **to ~ to** ajustarse a

confound [kən'faund] vt confundir

confront [kən'frʌnt] vt (problems) hacer frente a; (enemy, danger) enfrentarse con ◻ **confrontation** [kɑ:nfrən'teɪʃən] n enfrentamiento

confuse [kən'fju:z] vt (perplex) aturdir, desconcertar; (mix up) confundir; (complicate) complicar ◻ **confused** adj confuso; (person) perplejo ◻ **confusing** adj confuso ◻ **confusion** n confusión f

congeal [kən'dʒi:l] vi (blood) coagularse; (sauce etc) cuajarse

congested [kən'dʒestɪd] adj congestionado ◻ **congestion** n congestión f

congratulate [kən'grætʃəleɪt] vt: **to ~ sb (on)** felicitar a algn (por) ◻ **congratulations** [kəngrætʃə'leɪʃənz] npl felicitaciones fpl; **congratulations!** ¡enhorabuena!

congregate ['kɑ:ŋgrɪgeɪt] vi congregarse ◻ **congregation** [kɑ:ŋgrɪ'geɪʃən] n (of a church) feligreses mpl

congress ['kɑ:ŋgrɪs] n congreso; **C~** (US) Congreso ◻ **congressional** [kəŋ'greʃənəl] adj del congreso ◻ **Congressman** (US) n miembro del Congreso

conifer ['kɑ:nɪfər] n conífera

conjunctivitis [kəndʒʌŋktɪ'vaɪtɪs] n conjuntivitis f

conjure ['kʌndʒər] vi hacer juegos de manos ▶ **conjure up** vt (ghost, spirit) hacer aparecer; (memories) evocar ❑ **conjurer** n prestidigitador(a) m/f, ilusionista mf

con man ['kɔːn,mæn] n estafador m

connect [kə'nekt] vt juntar, unir; (ELEC) conectar; (TEL: subscriber) poner; (: caller) poner al habla; (fig) relacionar, asociar ♦ vi: to ~ **with** (train) enlazar con; **to be ~ed with** (associated) estar relacionado con ❑ **connection** n juntura, unión f; (ELEC) conexión f; (RAIL) enlace m; (TEL) comunicación f; (fig) relación f

connive [kə'naɪv] vi: to ~ **at** hacer la vista gorda a

connoisseur [kɔnɪ'sɜːr] n experto(-a), entendido(-a)

conquer ['kɔŋkər] vt (territory) conquistar; (enemy, feelings) vencer ❑ **conqueror** n conquistador m

conquest ['kɔŋkwest] n conquista

cons [kɔnz] npl see **convenience**; **pro**

conscience ['kɔnʃəns] n conciencia

conscientious [kɔnʃɪ'enʃəs] adj concienzudo; (objection) de conciencia

conscious ['kɔnʃəs] adj (deliberate) deliberado; (awake, aware) consciente ❑ **consciousness** n conciencia; (MED) conocimiento

conscript ['kɔnskrɪpt] n recluta m ❑ **conscription** [kən'skrɪpʃən] n servicio militar obligatorio

consensus [kən'sensəs] n consenso

consent [kən'sent] n consentimiento ♦ vi: to ~ **(to)** consentir (en)

consequence ['kɔnsɪkwəns] n consecuencia; (significance) importancia

consequently ['kɔnsɪkwentli] adv por consiguiente

conservation [kɔnsər'veɪʃən] n conservación f

conservative [kən'sɜːrvətɪv] adj conservador(a); (estimate etc) cauteloso ❑ **Conservative** (BRIT) adj, n (POL) conservador(a) m/f

conservatory [kən'sɜːrvətɔːri] n invernadero; (MUS) conservatorio

conserve [kən'sɜːrv] vt conservar ♦ n conserva

consider [kən'sɪdər] vt considerar; (take into account) tener en cuenta; (study) estudiar, examinar; **to ~ doing sth** pensar en (la posibilidad de) hacer algo ❑ **considerable** adj considerable ❑ **considerably** adv notablemente ❑ **considerate** adj

considerado ❑ **consideration** [kənsɪdə'reɪʃən] n consideración f; (factor) factor m; **to give sth further consideration** estudiar algo más a fondo ❑ **considering** prep teniendo en cuenta

consign [kən'saɪn] vt: to ~ **to** (sth unwanted) relegar a; (person) destinar a ❑ **consignment** n envío

consist [kən'sɪst] vi: to ~ **of** consistir en

consistency [kən'sɪstənsi] n (of argument etc) coherencia; consecuencia; (thickness) consistencia

consistent [kən'sɪstənt] adj (person) consecuente; (argument etc) coherente

consolation [kɔnsə'leɪʃən] n consuelo

console¹ [kən'soul] vt consolar

console² ['kɔnsoul] n consola

consonant ['kɔnsənənt] n consonante f

consortium [kən'sɔːrtiəm] n consorcio

conspicuous [kən'spɪkjuəs] adj (visible) visible

conspiracy [kən'spɪrəsi] n conjura, complot m

constable ['kɔnstəbəl] (BRIT) n policía mf; **chief ~** ≈ jefe(-a) m/f de policía

constabulary [kən'stæbjuleri] (BRIT) n ≈ policía

constant ['kɔnstənt] adj constante ❑ **constantly** adv constantemente

constipated ['kɔnstɪpeɪtɪd] adj estreñido ❑ **constipation** n estreñimiento

⚠ Be careful not to translate **constipated** by the Spanish word **constipado**.

constituency [kən'stɪtʃjuənsi] n (POL: area) distrito electoral; (: electors) electorado ❑ **constituent** n (POL) elector(a) m/f; (part) componente m

constitution [kɔnstɪ'tuːʃən] n constitución f ❑ **constitutional** adj constitucional

CONSTITUTION

Una constitución es un documento en el que se establecen las leyes fundamentales y los principios de un estado. La primera constitución norteamericana, conocida como **the Articles of Confederation**, se adoptó en 1781 y fue reemplazada en 1789 por la constitución vigente en la actualidad y que constituye la base del estado norteamericano. El **Bill of Rights**, que atañe a los derechos individuales, se añadió a la constitución como una primera serie de enmiendas en 1791.

constraint [kən'streɪnt] n obligación f; (limit) restricción f

construct [kən'strʌkt] vt construir ❑ **construction** n construcción f ❑ **construction worker** n (builder) obrero(-a) de la construcción; (contractor) contratista mf ❑ **constructive** adj constructivo

consul ['kɒnsəl] n cónsul mf ❑ **consulate** n consulado

consult [kən'sʌlt] vt consultar ❑ **consultant** n (MED) especialista mf; (other specialist) asesor(a) m/f ❑ **consultation** [kɒnsəl'teɪʃən] n consulta ❑ **consulting room** (BRIT) n consultorio

consume [kən'su:m] vt (eat) comerse; (drink) beberse; (fire etc, COMM) consumir ❑ **consumer** n consumidor(a) m/f ❑ **consumer goods** npl bienes mpl de consumo

consummate ['kɒnsəmeɪt] vt consumar

consumption [kən'sʌmpʃən] n consumo

cont. abbr (= continued) sigue

contact ['kɒntækt] n contacto; (person) contacto; (: pej) enchufe m ♦ vt ponerse en contacto con ❑ **contact lenses** npl lentes mpl (LAm) or fpl (SP) de contacto

contagious [kən'teɪdʒəs] adj contagioso

contain [kən'teɪn] vt contener; **to ~ o.s.** contenerse ❑ **container** n recipiente m; (for shipping etc) contenedor m

contaminate [kən'tæmɪneɪt] vt contaminar

cont'd abbr (= continued) sigue

contemplate ['kɒntəmpleɪt] vt contemplar; (reflect upon) considerar

contemporary [kən'tempərəri] adj, n contemporáneo(-a)

contempt [kən'tempt] n desprecio; **~ of court** (LAW) desacato (al tribunal) ❑ **contemptible** adj despreciable ❑ **contemptuous** adj desdeñoso

contend [kən'tend] vt (argue) afirmar ♦ vi: **to ~ with/for** luchar contra/por ❑ **contender** n (SPORT) contendiente mf

content [adj, vb kən'tent, n 'kɒntent] adj (happy) contento; (satisfied) satisfecho ♦ vt contentar; satisfacer ♦ n contenido; **~s** npl contenido; **(table of) ~s** índice m de materias ❑ **contented** adj contento; satisfecho

contention [kən'tenʃən] n (assertion) aseveración f; (disagreement) discusión f

contest [n 'kɒntest, vb kən'test] n lucha; (competition) concurso ♦ vt (dispute) impugnar; (BRIT POL) presentarse como

candidato(-a) en ❑ **contestant** [kən'testənt] n concursante mf; (in fight) contendiente mf

⚠ Be careful not to translate **contest** by the Spanish word *contestar*.

context ['kɒntekst] n contexto

continent ['kɒntɪnənt] n continente m; **the C~** (BRIT) el continente europeo ❑ **continental** [kɒntɪ'nentl] adj continental ❑ **continental breakfast** n desayuno continental ❑ **continental quilt** (BRIT) n edredón m

contingency [kən'tɪndʒənsi] n contingencia

continual [kən'tɪnjuəl] adj continuo ❑ **continually** adv constantemente

continuation [kəntɪnju'eɪʃən] n prolongación f; (after interruption) reanudación f

continue [kən'tɪnju] vi, vt seguir, continuar

continuing education n cursos de enseñanza para adultos

continuous [kən'tɪnjuəs] adj continuo

contort [kən'tɔ:rt] vt retorcer

contour ['kɒntuər] n contorno; (also: ~ line) curva de nivel

contraband ['kɒntrəbænd] n contrabando

contraceptive [kɒntrə'septɪv] adj, n anticonceptivo

contract [n 'kɒntrækt, vb kən'trækt] n contrato ♦ vi (COMM): **to ~ to do sth** firmar un contrato para hacer algo; (become smaller) contraerse, encogerse ♦ vt contraer ❑ **contraction** [kən'trækʃən] n contracción f ❑ **contractor** n contratista mf

contradict [kɒntrə'dɪkt] vt contradecir ❑ **contradiction** n contradicción f

contraption [kən'træpʃən] (pej) n artilugio m

contrary[1] ['kɒntrəri] adj contrario ♦ n lo contrario; **on the ~** al contrario; **unless you hear to the ~** a no ser que le digan lo contrario

contrary[2] [kən'treri] adj (perverse) terco

contrast [n 'kɒntræst, vt kən'træst] n contraste m ♦ vt comparar; **in ~ to** en contraste con

contravene [kɒntrə'vi:n] vt infringir

contribute [kən'trɪbju:t] vi contribuir ♦ vt: **to ~ $20/an article to** contribuir con 20 dólares/un artículo a; **to ~ to** (charity) donar a; (newspaper) escribir para; (discussion) intervenir en ❑ **contribution** [kɒntrɪ'bju:ʃən] n (donation) donativo; (to debate) intervención f; (to journal) colaboración f; (BRIT: for social security) cotización f ❑ **contributor** n contribuyente mf; (to newspaper) colaborador(a) m/f

contrive [kən'traɪv] vt (invent) idear ♦ vi: **to ~ to do** lograr hacer

control [kən'trəʊl] vt controlar; (process etc) dirigir; (machinery) manejar; (temper) dominar; (disease) contener ♦ n control m; **~s** npl (of vehicle) mandos mpl; (of radio) botones mpl (de control); (governmental) medidas fpl de control; **under ~** bajo control; **to be in ~ of** tener el mando de; **to be out of ~** estar fuera de control ❑ **controlled substance** n sustancia controlada ❑ **control panel** n tablero de mandos ❑ **control room** n sala de mando ❑ **control tower** n (AVIAT) torre f de control

controversial [ˌkɒntrə'vɜːʃəl] adj polémico

controversy ['kɒntrəvɜːsi] n polémica

convalesce [ˌkɒnvə'les] vi convalecer

convector [kən'vektər] n calentador m de aire

convene [kən'viːn] vt convocar ♦ vi reunirse

⚠ Be careful not to translate **convene** by the Spanish word **convenir**.

convenience [kən'viːnjəns] n (easiness) comodidad f; (suitability) idoneidad f; (advantage) ventaja; **at your ~** cuando le sea conveniente; **all modern ~s, all mod cons** (BRIT) todo confort ❑ **convenience store** n ≈ (tienda) 24 m horas

CONVENIENCE STORE

En EE.UU., un **convenience store** es un establecimiento que permanece abierto desde primeras horas de la mañana hasta última hora de la noche, y en algunos casos, incluso durante las 24 horas del día. En este tipo de tiendas se pueden adquirir normalmente cosas para el aperitivo, periódicos, revistas, tabaco, productos básicos para la casa, y a veces combustible. Suelen estar ubicados en las carreteras de mayor tráfico o en los cruces.

convenient [kən'viːnjənt] adj (useful) útil; (place, time) conveniente

convent ['kɒnvənt] n convento

convention [kən'venʃən] n convención f; (meeting) asamblea; (agreement) convenio ❑ **conventional** adj convencional

converge [kən'vɜːdʒ] vi convergir; (people): **to ~ on** dirigirse todos a

conversant [kən'vɜːsənt] adj: **to be ~ with** estar al tanto de

conversation [ˌkɒnvər'seɪʃən] n conversación f ❑ **conversational** adj familiar; **conversational skill** facilidad f de palabra

converse [n 'kɒnvɜːs, vb kən'vɜːs] n inversa ♦ vi conversar ❑ **conversely** [kən'vɜːsli] adv a la inversa

conversion [kən'vɜːrʒən] n conversión f

convert [vb kən'vɜːrt, n 'kɒnvɜːrt] vt (REL, COMM) convertir; (alter): **to ~ sth into/to** transformar algo en/convertir algo a en; converso(-a) ❑ **convertible** adj convertible ♦ n descapotable m

convey [kən'veɪ] vt llevar; (thanks) comunicar; (idea) expresar ❑ **conveyor belt** n cinta transportadora

convict [vb kən'vɪkt, n 'kɒnvɪkt] vt (find guilty) declarar culpable a ♦ n presidiario(-a) ❑ **conviction** [kən'vɪkʃən] n condena; (belief, certainty) convicción f

convince [kən'vɪns] vt convencer ❑ **convinced** adj: **convinced of/that** convencido de/de que ❑ **convincing** adj convincente

convoluted ['kɒnvəluːtɪd] adj (argument etc) enrevesado

convoy ['kɒnvɔɪ] n convoy m

convulse [kən'vʌls] vt: **to be ~d with laughter** desternillarse de risa ❑ **convulsion** n convulsión f

cook [kʊk] vt (stew etc) guisar; (meal) preparar ♦ vi cocer; (person) cocinar ♦ n cocinero(-a) ❑ **cookbook** n libro de cocina ❑ **cooker** (BRIT) n cocina ❑ **cookery** n cocina ❑ **cookery book** (BRIT) n = **cookbook** ❑ **cookie** (US) n galleta ❑ **cooking** n cocina

cool [kuːl] adj fresco; (not afraid) tranquilo; (unfriendly) frío; (calm) sereno ♦ vt enfriar ♦ vi enfriarse ❑ **coolness** n frescura; tranquilidad f; (indifference) falta de entusiasmo

coop [kuːp] n gallinero ♦ vt: **to ~ up** (fig) encerrar

cooperate [kəʊ'ɒpəreɪt] vi cooperar, colaborar ❑ **cooperation** [kəʊˌɒpə'reɪʃən] n cooperación f, colaboración f ❑ **cooperative** adj (business) cooperativo; (person) servicial ♦ n cooperativa

coordinate [vb kəʊ'ɔːrdneɪt, n kəʊ'ɔːrdnɪt] vt coordinar ♦ n (MATH) coordenada; **~s** npl (clothes) prendas fpl para combinar ❑ **coordination** [kəʊˌɔːrd'neɪʃən] n coordinación f

co-ownership [kəʊ'əʊnərʃɪp] n co-propiedad f

cop [kɑːp] n (inf) poli mf, tira mf (MEX)

cope [koup] vi: **to ~ with** (problem) hacer frente a

copper ['kɑːpər] n (metal) cobre m; (BRIT: inf) poli mf, tira mf (MEX); **~s** npl (BRIT: money) feria (MEX), morralla (MEX), sencillo (LAm exc MEX), suelto (SP)

copulate ['kɑːpjuleɪt] vi copularse

copy ['kɑːpi] n copia; (of book etc) ejemplar m ♦ vt copiar ❑ **copyright** n derechos mpl de autor

coral ['kɔːrəl] n coral m

cord [kɔːrd] n cuerda; (ELEC) cable m; (fabric) pana

cordial ['kɔːrdʒəl] adj cordial ♦ n cordial m

cordon ['kɔːrdn] n cordón m ▶ **cordon off** vt acordonar

corduroy ['kɔːrdərɔɪ] n pana

core [kɔːr] n centro, núcleo; (of fruit) corazón m; (of problem) meollo ♦ vt quitar el corazón de

coriander [kɔːri'ændər] n cilantro, culantro

cork [kɔːrk] n corcho; (tree) alcornoque m ❑ **corkscrew** n sacacorchos m inv

corn [kɔːrn] n (US: maize) maíz m, elote m (MEX); (BRIT: cereal crop) trigo; (on foot) callo; **~ on the cob** (CULIN) mazorca, elote m (MEX), choclo (SC)

corned beef ['kɔːrnd,biːf] n carne f acecinada (en lata)

corner ['kɔːrnər] n (outside) esquina; (inside) rincón m; (in road) curva; (FOOTBALL) saque m de esquina, córner m; (BOXING) esquina ♦ vt (trap) arrinconar; (COMM) acaparar ♦ vi (in car) girar ❑ **cornerstone** n (also fig) piedra angular

cornet [kɔːr'net] n (MUS) corneta; (BRIT: of ice-cream) cucurucho

cornflakes ['kɔːrn,fleɪks] npl copos mpl de maíz, cornflakes mpl

cornflour ['kɔːrn,flaʊər] (BRIT) n = **cornstarch**

cornmeal ['kɔːrn,miːl] (US) n harina de maíz

cornstarch ['kɔːrn,stɑːrtʃ] (US) n harina de maíz, maizena®

Cornwall ['kɔːrnwɔːl] n Cornualles m

corny ['kɔːrni] (inf) adj cursi

coronary ['kɔːrəneri] n (also: ~ **thrombosis**) infarto

coronation [kɔːrə'neɪʃən] n coronación f

coroner ['kɔːrənər] n = juez mf de instrucción

corporal ['kɔːrpərəl] n cabo ♦ adj: **~ punishment** castigo corporal

corporate ['kɔːrpərɪt] adj (action, ownership) colectivo; (finance, image) corporativo

corporation [kɔːrpə'reɪʃən] n (of city) ayuntamiento; (US: limited company) sociedad f anónima; (BRIT COMM) corporación f

corps [kɔːr, pl kɔːrz] n inv cuerpo; **diplomatic ~** cuerpo diplomático; **press ~** gabinete m de prensa

corpse [kɔːrps] n cadáver m

correct [kə'rekt] adj justo, exacto; (proper) correcto ♦ vt corregir; (exam) corregir, calificar ❑ **correction** n (act) corrección f; (instance) rectificación f

correspond [kɔːri'spɑːnd] vi (write): **to ~ (with)** escribirse (con); (be equivalent to): **to ~ (to)** corresponder (a); (be in accordance): **to ~ (with)** corresponder (con) ❑ **correspondence** n correspondencia ❑ **correspondence course** n curso por correspondencia ❑ **correspondent** n corresponsal mf

corridor ['kɔːrɪdər] n pasillo

corrode [kə'roud] vt corroer ♦ vi corroerse

corrugated ['kɔːrəgeɪtɪd] adj ondulado ❑ **corrugated iron** n chapa ondulada

corrupt [kə'rʌpt] adj (person) corrupto; (COMPUT) corrompido ♦ vt corromper; (COMPUT) degradar

corruption [kə'rʌpʃən] n corrupción f

Corsica ['kɔːrsɪkə] n Córcega

cosmetic [kɑːz'metɪk] adj, n cosmético; **~s** npl cosméticos mpl

cosmopolitan [kɑːzmə'pɑːlɪtn] adj cosmopolita

cost [kɔːst] (pt, pp ~) n (price) precio; (LAW) costas fpl ♦ vi costar, valer ♦ vt preparar el presupuesto de; **~s** npl (COMM) costos mpl (LAm), costes mpl (SP); **how much does it ~?** ¿cuánto cuesta?; **at the ~ of his life/health** a costa de su vida/salud; **it ~ him his life** le costó la vida; **at all ~s** cueste lo que cueste

co-star ['kou,stɑːr] n coprotagonista mf

Costa Rica ['kɔːstə'riːkə] n Costa Rica ❑ **Costa Rican** adj, n costarricense mf

cost-effective ['kɔːstɪ,fektɪv] adj rentable

costly ['kɔːstli] adj costoso

cost-of-living [kɔːstəv'lɪvɪŋ] adj: **~ allowance** plus m de carestía de vida; **~ index** índice m del costo de vida

cost price (BRIT) n precio de coste

costume ['kɑːstuːm] n traje m; (BRIT: also: **swimming ~**) traje de baño ❑ **costume jewelry** n bisutería

cosy ['kouzi] (BRIT) adj = **cozy**

cot [kɒt] n (US: camp bed) cama de campaña; (BRIT: child's) cuna

cottage ['kɒtɪdʒ] n casita de campo, chalet m □ **cottage cheese** n requesón m

cotton ['kɒtn] n algodón m; (thread) hilo
▶ **cotton on to** (inf) vt fus caer en la cuenta de □ **cotton candy** (US) n algodón m (de azúcar) □ **cotton wool** (BRIT) n algodón m (hidrófilo)

couch [kautʃ] n sofá m; (doctor's etc) diván m

couchette [kuːˈʃet] (BRIT) n litera

cough [kɒːf] vi toser ♦ n tos f □ **cough drop** n pastilla para la tos

could [kud] pt of **can²** □ **couldn't** cont = **could not**

council ['kaunsəl] n consejo; **city** or **town ~** ayuntamiento □ **council estate** (BRIT) n urbanización de viviendas municipales de alquiler □ **council house** (BRIT) n vivienda municipal de alquiler □ **councilor** (US) (BRIT **councillor**) n concejal(a) m/f

counsel ['kaunsəl] n (advice) consejo; (lawyer) abogado(-a) ♦ vt aconsejar □ **counsellor** (BRIT) n abogado(-a) □ **counselor** (US) n (PSYCH) consejero(-a); (adviser) asesor(a) m/f; (lawyer) abogado(-a)

count [kaunt] vt contar; (include) incluir ♦ vi contar ♦ n cuenta; (of votes) escrutinio; (level) nivel m; (nobleman) conde m ▶ **count on** vt fus contar con □ **countdown** n cuenta atrás

countenance ['kauntɪnəns] n semblante m, rostro ♦ vt (tolerate) aprobar, tolerar

counter ['kauntər] n (in store) mostrador m; (in bank) ventanilla; (in games) ficha ♦ vt contrarrestar ♦ adv: **to run ~** ser contrario a, ir en contra de □ **counteract** vt contrarrestar

counterclockwise ['kauntərˈklɒːkwaɪz] (US) adv en sentido contrario al de las agujas del reloj

counterfeit ['kauntərfɪt] n falsificación f, simulación f ♦ vt falsificar ♦ adj falso, falsificado

counterfoil ['kauntərfɔɪl] n talón m

counterpart ['kauntərpɑːrt] n homólogo(-a)

counter-productive ['kauntərprəˈdʌktɪv] adj contraproducente

countersign ['kauntərˌsaɪn] vt refrendar

countess ['kauntɪs] n condesa

countless ['kauntlɪs] adj innumerable

country ['kʌntrɪ] n país m; (native land) patria; (as opposed to town) campo; (region) región f, tierra □ **country and western (music)** n (música) country m □ **country dancing** (BRIT) n baile m regional □ **country house** (BRIT) n casa de campo □ **countryman** n (compatriot) compatriota m; (rural) campesino, paisano □ **countryside** n campo

county ['kauntɪ] n condado

coup [kuː] (pl ~s) n (also: ~ **d'état**) golpe m (de estado); (achievement) éxito

couple ['kʌpəl] n (of things) par m; (of people) pareja; (married couple) matrimonio; **a ~ of** un par de

coupon ['kuːpɑːn] n cupón m; (voucher) vale m

courage ['kʌrɪdʒ] n valor m, valentía □ **courageous** [kəˈreɪdʒəs] adj valiente

courgette [kuərˈʒet] (BRIT) n calabacín m, calabacita (MEX)

courier ['kuriər] n mensajero(-a); (for tourists) guía mf

course [kɔːrs] n (direction) dirección f; (of river, SCOL) curso; (process) transcurso; (MED): **~ of treatment** tratamiento; (of ship) rumbo; (part of meal) plato; (GOLF) campo; **of ~** desde luego, naturalmente; **of ~!** ¡claro!

court [kɔːrt] n (LAW) tribunal m, juzgado; (TENNIS) cancha (LAm), pista (SP); (royal) corte f ♦ vt (woman) cortejar a; **to take to ~** demandar

courteous ['kɜːtiəs] adj cortés

courtesy ['kɜːrtəsi] n cortesía; **(by) ~ of** por cortesía de □ **courtesy bus**, **courtesy coach** n autobús m gratuito

courthouse ['kɔːrtˌhaus] (US) n palacio de justicia

courtier ['kɔːrtiər] n cortesano

court-martial (pl **courts-martial**) n consejo de guerra

courtroom ['kɔːrtˌruːm] n sala de justicia

courtyard ['kɔːrtˌjɑːrd] n patio

cousin ['kʌzən] n primo(-a); **first ~** primo(-a) hermano(-a) or carnal

cove [kouv] n cala, ensenada

covenant ['kʌvənənt] n pacto

cover ['kʌvər] vt cubrir; (feelings, mistake) ocultar; (with lid) tapar; (book etc) forrar; (distance) recorrer; (include) abarcar; (protect: also: INSURANCE) cubrir; (PRESS) investigar; (discuss) tratar ♦ n cubierta; (lid) tapa; (for chair etc) funda; (envelope) sobre m; (for book) forro; (of magazine) portada; (shelter) abrigo; (INSURANCE) cobertura; (of spy) cobertura; **~s** npl (on bed) sábanas; mantas; **to take ~** (shelter) protegerse, resguardarse; **under ~** (indoors) bajo techo; **under ~ of darkness** al amparo de la oscuridad; **under separate ~** (COMM) por separado ▶ **cover up** vi: **to cover up for sb** encubrir a algn ❑ **coverage** n (TV, PRESS) cobertura ❑ **coveralls** (US) npl overol m (LAm) or mono (SP) (de trabajo) ❑ **cover charge** n (precio del) cubierto ❑ **covering** n capa ❑ **cover letter** (US) (BRIT **covering letter**) n carta adjunta ❑ **cover note** n (INSURANCE) póliza provisional

covert ['kʌvərt] adj secreto, encubierto

cover-up n encubrimiento

cow [kau] n vaca; (BRIT: infl: woman) bruja ♦ vt intimidar

coward ['kauərd] n cobarde mf ❑ **cowardice** n cobardía ❑ **cowardly** adj cobarde

cowboy ['kau.bɔɪ] n vaquero

cower ['kauər] vi encogerse (de miedo)

coy [kɔɪ] adj tímido

cozy (US) ['kouzi] (BRIT **cosy**) adj (person) cómodo; (room) acogedor(a)

C.P.A. (US) n abbr = **certified public accountant**

crab [kræb] n cangrejo ❑ **crab apple** n manzana silvestre

crack [kræk] n grieta; (noise) crujido; (drug) crack m ♦ vt agrietar, romper; (nut) cascar; (solve: problem) resolver; (: code) descifrar; (whip etc) chasquear; (knuckles) crujir; (joke) contar ♦ adj (expert) de primera ▶ **crack down on** vt fus adoptar fuertes medidas contra ▶ **crack up** vi (MED) sufrir una crisis nerviosa ❑ **cracker** n (biscuit) galleta salada, crácker f; (BRIT: Christmas cracker) petardo (sorpresa)

crackle ['krækəl] vi crepitar

cradle ['kreɪdl] n cuna

craft [kræft] n (skill) arte m; (trade) oficio; (cunning) astucia; (boat: pl inv) barco; (plane: pl inv) avión m

craftsman ['kræftsmən] n artesano ❑ **craftsmanship** n (quality) destreza

crafty ['kræfti] adj astuto

crag [kræg] n peñasco

cram [kræm] vt (fill): **to ~ sth with** llenar algo (a reventar) de; (put): **to ~ sth into** meter algo a la fuerza en ♦ vi (for exams) matarse (estudiando), machetear (MEX), tragar (RPI)

cramp [kræmp] n (MED) calambre m ❑ **cramped** adj apretado, estrecho

cranberry ['krænberi] n arándano agrio

crane [kreɪn] n (TECH) grúa; (bird) grulla

crank [kræŋk] n manivela; (person) chiflado(-a)

cranny ['kræni] n see **nook**

crash [kræʃ] n (noise) estrépito; (of cars etc) accidente m; (COMM) quiebra ♦ vt (car, plane) estrellar ♦ vi (car, plane) estrellarse; (two cars) chocar; (COMM) quebrar ❑ **crash course** n curso acelerado ❑ **crash helmet** n casco (protector) ❑ **crash landing** n aterrizaje m forzado

crass [kræs] adj grosero, maleducado

crate [kreɪt] n cajón m de embalaje; (for bottles) caja

cravat(e) [krə'væt] n pañuelo

crave [kreɪv] vt, vi: **to ~ (for)** ansiar, anhelar

crawfish ['krɔː.fɪʃ] (US) n inv (freshwater) cangrejo de río; (saltwater) cigala

crawl [krɔːl] vi (drag o.s.) arrastrarse; (child) andar a gatas, gatear; (vehicle) avanzar (lentamente) ♦ n (SWIMMING) crol m

crayfish ['kreɪfɪʃ] (BRIT) n = **crawfish**

crayon ['kreɪɑːn] n lápiz m de color

craze [kreɪz] n (fashion) moda

crazy ['kreɪzi] adj (person) loco; (idea) disparatado; (inf: keen): **~ about sb/sth** loco por algn/algo

creak [kriːk] vi (floorboard) crujir; (hinge etc) chirriar, rechinar

cream [kriːm] n (of milk) crema (de leche); (lotion) crema; (fig) flor f y nata ♦ adj (color) crema ❑ **cream cake** (BRIT) n pastel m con crema or (SP) nata ❑ **cream cheese** n queso crema (LAm) or (blanco) para untar (SP) ❑ **creamy** adj cremoso; (color) color crema

crease [kriːs] n (fold) pliegue m; (in pants) raya; (wrinkle) arruga ♦ vt (wrinkle) arrugar ♦ vi (wrinkle up) arrugarse

create [kriː'eɪt] vt crear ❑ **creation** n creación f ❑ **creative** adj creativo ❑ **creator** n creador(a) m/f

creature ['kriːtʃər] n (animal) animal m, bicho; (person) criatura

crèche [kreʃ] n nacimiento; (BRIT) guardería (infantil)

credence ['kriːdns] n: **to lend** or **give ~ to** creer en, dar crédito a

credentials [krɪ'denʃlz] npl (references) referencias fpl; (identity papers) documentos mpl de identidad

credible ['kredɪbəl] adj creíble; (trustworthy) digno de confianza

credit ['kredɪt] n crédito; (merit) honor m, mérito ♦ vt (COMM) abonar; (believe: also: **give ~ to**) creer, prestar fe a ♦ adj crediticio; **~s** npl (FILM) fichas fpl técnicas; **to be in ~** (person) tener saldo a favor; **to ~ sb with** (fig) reconocer a algn el mérito de ❑ **credit card**

n tarjeta de crédito ❑ **creditor** *n* acreedor(a) *m/f*

creed [kriːd] *n* credo

creek [kriːk] *n* (*US*) riachuelo; (*BRIT*) cala, ensenada

creep [kriːp] (*pt, pp* **crept**) *vi* arrastrarse ❑ **creeper** *n* enredadera ❑ **creepy** *adj* (*frightening*) horripilante

cremate ['krɪːmeɪt] *vt* incinerar

crematorium [krɪːmə'tɔːrɪəm] (*pl* **crematoria**) *n* crematorio

Creole *adj* criollo ♦ *n* (*person*) criollo(-a); (*LING*) lengua criolla; *see also* **Cajun**

crêpe [kreɪp] *n* (*fabric*) crespón *m*; (*also: ~* **rubber**) crepé *m* ❑ **crêpe bandage** (*BRIT*) *n* venda de crepé

crept [krept] *pt, pp of* **creep**

crescent ['krɛsənt] *n* media luna; (*BRIT: street*) calle *f* (*en forma de media luna*)

cress [krɛs] *n* berro

crest [krɛst] *n* (*of bird*) cresta; (*of hill*) cima, cumbre *f*; (*of coat of arms*) blasón *m* ❑ **crestfallen** *adj* alicaído

crevice ['krɛvɪs] *n* grieta

crew [kruː] *n* (*of ship etc*) tripulación *f*; (*TV, CINEMA*) equipo ❑ **crew cut** *n* pelado al rape ❑ **crew neck** *n* cuello a la caja

crib [krɪb] *n* (*US: for toddler*) cuna; (*BRIT: for infant*) pesebre *m* ♦ *vt* (*inf*) plagiar

crick [krɪk] *n* (*in neck*) tortícolis *f*

cricket ['krɪkɪt] *n* (*insect*) grillo; (*BRIT: game*) críquet *m*

crime [kraɪm] *n* (*no pl: illegal activities*) crimen *m*; (*illegal action*) delito ❑ **criminal** ['krɪmɪnəl] *n* criminal *mf*, delincuente *mf* ♦ *adj* criminal; (*illegal*) delictivo; (*law*) penal

crimson ['krɪmzən] *adj* carmesí

cringe [krɪndʒ] *vi* agacharse, encogerse

crinkle ['krɪŋkəl] *vt* arrugar

cripple ['krɪpəl] *n* lisiado(-a), cojo(-a) ♦ *vt* lisiar, mutilar

crisis ['kraɪsɪs] (*pl* **crises**) *n* crisis *f inv*

crisp [krɪsp] *adj* fresco; (*vegetables etc*) crujiente; (*manner*) seco ❑ **crisps** (*BRIT*) *npl* papas *fpl* (*LAm*) or patatas *fpl* (*SP*) fritas

crisscross ['krɪskrɔːs] *adj* entrelazado

criterion [kraɪ'tɪrɪən] (*pl* **criteria**) *n* criterio

critic ['krɪtɪk] *n* crítico(-a) ❑ **critical** *adj* crítico; (*illness*) grave ❑ **critically** *adv* (*speak etc*) en tono crítico; (*ill*) gravemente ❑ **criticism** ['krɪtɪsɪzəm] *n* crítica ❑ **criticize** ['krɪtɪsaɪz] *vt* criticar

croak [krəuk] *vi* (*frog*) croar; (*raven*) graznar; (*person*) gruñir

Croatia [krəu'eɪʃə] *n* Croacia

crochet [krəu'ʃeɪ] *n* ganchillo

crockery ['krɒkərɪ] (*BRIT*) *n* vajilla, loza

crocodile ['krɒkədaɪl] *n* cocodrilo

crocus ['krəukəs] *n* azafrán *m*

croft [krɒft] (*BRIT*) *n* granja pequeña

crony ['krəunɪ] (*inf. pej*) *n* compinche *mf*

crook [kruk] *n* ladrón(-ona) *m/f*; (*of shepherd*) cayado ❑ **crooked** ['krukɪd] *adj* torcido; (*dishonest*) nada honrado

crop [krɒp] *n* (*produce*) cultivo; (*amount produced*) cosecha; (*riding crop*) fusta ♦ *vt* cortar, recortar ▶ **crop up** *vi* surgir, presentarse

cross [krɔːs] *n* cruz *f*; (*hybrid*) cruce *m* ♦ *vt* (*street etc*) cruzar, atravesar ♦ *adj* de mal humor, enojado ▶ **cross out** *vt* tachar ▶ **cross over** *vi* cruzar ❑ **crossbar** *n* travesaño ❑ **cross-country (race)** *n* cross *m* ❑ **cross-examine** *vt* interrogar ❑ **cross-eyed** *adj* bizco ❑ **crossfire** *n* fuego cruzado ❑ **crossing** *n* (*sea passage*) travesía; (*BRIT: also:* **pedestrian crossing**) paso de peatones ❑ **crossing guard** (*US*) *n* persona encargada de ayudar a los niños a cruzar la calle ❑ **cross purposes** *npl*: **we were talking at cross purposes** hablábamos de cosas distintas ❑ **cross-reference** *n* referencia, llamada ❑ **crossroads** *n* cruce *m*, encrucijada ❑ **cross section** *n* corte *m* transversal; (*of population*) muestra (representativa) ❑ **crosswalk** (*US*) *n* paso de peatones ❑ **crosswind** *n* viento de costado ❑ **crossword** *n* crucigrama *m*

crotch [krɒtʃ] *n* (*ANAT, of garment*) entrepierna

crotchet ['krɒtʃɪt] (*BRIT*) *n* (*MUS*) negra

crouch [krautʃ] *vi* agacharse, acurrucarse

crow [krəu] *n* (*bird*) cuervo; (*of cock*) canto, cacareo ♦ *vi* (*cock*) cantar

crowbar ['krəubɑːr] *n* palanca

crowd [kraud] *n* muchedumbre *f*, multitud *f* ♦ *vt* (*fill*) llenar ♦ *vi* (*gather*): **to ~ around** reunirse en torno a; (*cram*): **to ~ in** entrar en tropel ❑ **crowded** *adj* (*full*) abarrotado, atestado; (*densely populated*) superpoblado

crown [kraun] *n* corona; (*of head*) coronilla; (*for tooth*) funda; (*of hill*) cumbre *f* ♦ *vt* coronar; (*fig*) completar, rematar ❑ **crown jewels** *npl* joyas *fpl* reales ❑ **crown prince** *n* príncipe *m* heredero

crow's feet *npl* patas *fpl* de gallo

crucial ['kruːʃəl] *adj* decisivo

crucifix ['kruːsɪfɪks] *n* crucifijo ❑ **crucifixion** [kruːsɪ'fɪkʃən] *n* crucifixión *f*

crude [kru:d] *adj* (*materials*) bruto; (*fig: basic*) tosco; (: *vulgar*) ordinario, vulgar ❑ **crude (oil)** *n* (petróleo) crudo

cruel ['kru:əl] *adj* cruel ❑ **cruelty** *n* crueldad *f*

cruise [kru:z] *n* crucero ♦ *vi* (*ship*) hacer un crucero; (*car*) ir a velocidad de crucero ❑ **cruiser** *n* (*motorboat*) yate *m* de motor; (*warship*) crucero

crumb [krʌm] *n* miga, migaja

crumble ['krʌmbəl] *vt* desmenuzar ♦ *vi* (*building, also fig*) desmoronarse ❑ **crumbly** *adj* que se desmigaja fácilmente

crumpet ['krʌmpɪt] (*BRIT*) *n* ≈ bollo para tostar

crumple ['krʌmpəl] *vt* (*paper*) estrujar; (*material*) arrugar

crunch [krʌntʃ] *vt* (*with teeth*) mascar; (*underfoot*) hacer crujir ♦ *n* (*fig*) hora *or* momento de la verdad ❑ **crunchy** *adj* crujiente

crusade [kru:'seɪd] *n* cruzada

crush [krʌʃ] *n* (*crowd*) aglomeración *f*; (*infatuation*): **to have a ~ on sb** estar loco por algn; (*BRIT: drink*): **lemon ~** limonada ♦ *vt* aplastar; (*paper*) estrujar; (*cloth*) arrugar; (*fruit*) exprimir; (*opposition*) aplastar; (*hopes*) destruir

crust [krʌst] *n* corteza; (*of snow, ice*) costra

crutch [krʌtʃ] *n* muleta

crux [krʌks] *n*: **the ~ of** lo esencial de, el quid de

cry [kraɪ] *vi* llorar; (*shout: also: ~ out*) gritar ♦ *n* (*shriek*) chillido; (*shout*) grito ▶ **cry off** *vi* echarse atrás

cryptic ['krɪptɪk] *adj* enigmático, secreto

crystal ['krɪstl] *n* cristal *m* ❑ **crystal-clear** *adj* claro como el agua

cub [kʌb] *n* cachorro; (*also: ~ scout*) niño explorador

Cuba ['kju:bə] *n* Cuba ❑ **Cuban** *adj, n* cubano(-a)

cube [kju:b] *n* cubo; (*of sugar*) terrón *m*; (*of cheese*) dado ♦ *vt* (*MATH*) cubicar ❑ **cubic** *adj* cúbico

cubicle ['kju:bɪkəl] *n* (*at pool*) caseta; (*for bed*) cubículo

cuckoo ['kuku:] *n* cuco ❑ **cuckoo clock** *n* reloj *m* de cuco

cucumber ['kju:kʌmbər] *n* pepino

cuddle ['kʌdl] *vt* abrazar ♦ *vi* abrazarse

cue [kju:] *n* (*snooker cue*) taco; (*THEATER etc*) señal *f*

cuff [kʌf] *n* (*of sleeve*) puño; (*US: of pants*) vuelta; (*blow*) bofetada; **off the ~** *adv* de improviso ❑ **cufflinks** *npl* gemelos *mpl*, mancuernas *fpl* (*MEX*)

cuisine [kwɪ'zi:n] *n* cocina

cul-de-sac ['kʌldəˌsæk] *n* callejón *m* sin salida

cull [kʌl] *vt* (*idea*) sacar ♦ *n* (*of animals*) matanza selectiva

culminate ['kʌlmɪneɪt] *vi*: **to ~ in** terminar en ❑ **culmination** [kʌlmɪ'neɪʃən] *n* culminación *f*, colmo

culottes ['ku:lɒts] *npl* falda pantalón

culprit ['kʌlprɪt] *n* culpable *mf*

cult [kʌlt] *n* culto

cultivate ['kʌltɪveɪt] *vt* cultivar ❑ **cultivated** *adj* culto ❑ **cultivation** [kʌltɪ'veɪʃən] *n* cultivo

cultural ['kʌltʃərəl] *adj* cultural

culture ['kʌltʃər] *n* (*also fig*) cultura; (*BIOL*) cultivo ❑ **cultured** *adj* culto

cumbersome ['kʌmbərsəm] *adj* de mucho bulto, voluminoso; (*process*) enrevesado

cunning ['kʌnɪŋ] *n* astucia ♦ *adj* astuto

cup [kʌp] *n* taza; (*as prize*) copa

cupboard ['kʌbərd] *n* armario, clóset *m* (*MEX*), placard *m* (*RPl*); (*in kitchen*) alacena

cup tie *n* (*SPORT*) eliminatoria de copa

curate ['kjuərɪt] *n* cura *m*

curator [kjuə'reɪtər] *n* director(a) *m/f*

curb [kɜ:rb] *vt* refrenar; (*person*) reprimir ♦ *n* freno; (*US: at edge of road*) bordillo, cordón *m* de la banqueta (*MEX*) *or* vereda (*RPl*)

curdle ['kɜ:rdl] *vi* cuajarse

cure [kjuər] *vt* curar ♦ *n* cura, curación *f*; (*fig: solution*) remedio

curfew ['kɜ:rfju:] *n* toque *m* de queda

curiosity [kjuri'ɒsɪti] *n* curiosidad *f*

curious ['kjuriəs] *adj* curioso; (*person: interested*): **to be ~** sentir curiosidad

curl [kɜ:rl] *n* rizo, chino (*MEX*) ♦ *vt* (*hair*) rizar ♦ *vi* rizarse ▶ **curl up** *vi* (*person*) hacerse un ovillo ❑ **curler** *n* rulo ❑ **curly** *adj* rizado

currant ['kʌrənt] *n* pasa (de Corinto); (*blackcurrant*) grosella

currency ['kʌrənsi] *n* moneda; **to gain ~** (*fig*) difundirse

current ['kʌrənt] *n* corriente *f* ♦ *adj* (*accepted*) corriente; (*present*) actual ❑ **current account** (*BRIT*) *n* cuenta corriente ❑ **current affairs** *npl* (*temas fpl de*) actualidad *f* ❑ **currently** *adv* actualmente

curriculum [kə'rɪkjuləm] (*pl* ~**s** *or* **curricula**) *n* plan *m* de estudios ❑ **curriculum vitae** (*BRIT*) *n* currículum *m*

curry ['kʌri] n curry m ♦ vt: **to ~ favour with** buscar favores con ❏ **curry powder** n curry m en polvo

curse [kɜːrs] vi insultar ♦ vt maldecir ♦ n maldición f; (swearword) palabrota, taco

cursor ['kɜːrsər] n (COMPUT) cursor m

cursory ['kɜːrsəri] adj rápido, superficial

curt [kɜːrt] adj corto, seco

curtail [kərˈteɪl] vt (visit etc) acortar; (freedom) restringir; (expenses etc) reducir

curtain ['kɜːrtn] n cortina; (THEATER) telón m

curts(e)y ['kɜːrtsɪ] vi hacer una reverencia

curve [kɜːrv] n curva ♦ vi (road) hacer una curva; (line etc) curvarse

cushion ['kʊʃən] n cojín m; (of air) colchón m ♦ vt (shock) amortiguar

custard ['kʌstərd] n natillas fpl

custody ['kʌstədi] n custodia; **to take into ~** detener

custom ['kʌstəm] n costumbre f; (BRIT COMM) clientela ❏ **customary** adj acostumbrado

customer ['kʌstəmər] n cliente(-a) m/f

customized ['kʌstəmaɪzd] adj (car etc) hecho a encargo

custom-made adj hecho a la medida

customs ['kʌstəmz] npl aduana ❏ **customs officer** n oficial mf de aduanas

cut [kʌt] (pt, pp ~) vt cortar; (price) rebajar; (text, program) acortar; (reduce) reducir ♦ vi cortar ♦ n (of garment) corte m; (in skin) cortadura; (in salary etc) rebaja; (in spending) reducción f, recorte m; (slice of meat) tajada; **to ~ a tooth** echar un diente; **to ~ and paste** (COMPUT) cortar y pegar; **to ~ to the chase** (US) ir al grano ▶ **cut down** vt (tree) derribar; (reduce) reducir ▶ **cut off** vt cortar; (person, place) aislar; (TEL) desconectar ▶ **cut out** vt (shape) recortar; (stop: activity etc) dejar; (remove) quitar ▶ **cut up** vt cortar (en pedazos) ❏ **cutback** n reducción f

cute [kjuːt] adj mono

cuticle ['kjuːtɪkəl] n cutícula

cutlery ['kʌtləri] n cubiertos mpl

cutlet ['kʌtlɪt] n chuleta; (nut etc cutlet) plato vegetariano hecho con nueces y verdura en forma de chuleta

cut: ❏ **cutout** n (switch) cortacircuitos m inv, disyuntor m; (cardboard cutout) recortable m ❏ **cut-price** (BRIT) adj = **cut-rate** ❏ **cut-rate** (US) adj a precio reducido ❏ **cutthroat** n asesino(-a) ♦ adj feroz

cutting ['kʌtɪŋ] adj (remark) mordaz ♦ n (BRIT: from newspaper) recorte m; (from plant) esqueje m

CV (BRIT) n abbr = **curriculum vitae**

cwt abbr = **hundredweight(s)**

cyanide ['saɪənaɪd] n cianuro

cybercafé ['saɪbərkæˌfeɪ] n cibercafé m

cycle ['saɪkəl] (BRIT) n ciclo; (bicycle) bicicleta ♦ vi ir en bicicleta ❏ **cycle path** (BRIT) n carril-bici m ❏ **cycling** n ciclismo ❏ **cyclist** n ciclista mf

cyclone ['saɪkloun] n ciclón m

cygnet ['sɪgnɪt] n pollo de cisne

cylinder ['sɪlɪndər] n cilindro; (of gas) tanque m (LAm), garrafa (RPl), bombona (SP) ❏ **cylinder-head gasket** n junta de culata

cymbals ['sɪmbəlz] npl platillos mpl

cynic ['sɪnɪk] n cínico(-a) ❏ **cynical** adj cínico ❏ **cynicism** ['sɪnɪsɪzəm] n cinismo

Cyprus ['saɪprəs] n Chipre f

cyst [sɪst] n quiste m ❏ **cystitis** [sɪsˈtaɪtɪs] n cistitis f

czar [zɑːr] n zar m

Czech [tʃek] adj, n checo(-a) ❏ **Czech Republic** n: **the Czech Republic** la República Checa

Dd

D [diː] n (MUS) re m

dab [dæb] vt (eyes, wound) tocar (ligeramente); (paint, cream) poner un poco de

dabble ['dæbəl] vi: **to ~ in** ser algo aficionado a

dad [dæd] n = **daddy**

daddy ['dædi] n papá m

daffodil ['dæfədɪl] n narciso

daft [dæft] (BRIT) adj tonto

dagger ['dægər] n puñal m, daga

daily ['deɪli] adj diario, cotidiano ♦ adv todos los días, cada día

dainty ['deɪnti] adj delicado

dairy ['deəri] n (store) lechería; (on farm) vaquería ❏ **dairy farm** n granja ❏ **dairy products** npl productos mpl lácteos ❏ **dairy store** (US) n lechería

daisy ['deɪzi] n margarita

dale [deɪl] n valle m

dam [dæm] n presa ♦ vt construir una presa sobre, represar

damage ['dæmɪdʒ] n lesión f; daño; (dents etc) desperfectos mpl; (fig) perjuicio ♦ vt dañar, perjudicar; (spoil, break) estropear; **~s** npl (LAW) daños mpl y perjuicios

damn [dæm] vt condenar; (curse) maldecir ♦ n (inf): **I don't give a ~** me importa un pito ♦ adj (inf: also: **~ed**) maldito; **~ (it)!** ¡maldito sea! ❑ **damning** adj (evidence) irrecusable

damp [dæmp] adj húmedo, mojado ♦ n humedad f ♦ vt (also: **~en**: cloth, rag) mojar; (: enthusiasm) enfriar

damson ['dæmzən] n ciruela damascena

dance [dɑːns] n baile m ♦ vi bailar ❑ **dance hall** n salón m de baile ❑ **dancer** n bailador(a) m/f; (professional) bailarín(-ina) m/f ❑ **dancing** n baile m

dandelion ['dændɪlaɪən] n diente m de león

dandruff ['dændrəf] n caspa

Dane [deɪn] n danés(-esa) m/f

danger ['deɪndʒər] n peligro; (risk) riesgo; **~!** (on sign) ¡peligro de muerte!; **to be in ~ of** correr riesgo de ❑ **dangerous** adj peligroso ❑ **dangerously** adv peligrosamente

dangle ['dæŋgəl] vt colgar ♦ vi pender, colgar

Danish ['deɪnɪʃ] adj danés(-esa) ♦ n (LING) danés m

dare [dɛər] vt: **to ~ sb to do** desafiar a algn a hacer ♦ vi: **to ~ (to) do sth** atreverse a hacer algo; **I ~ say** (I suppose) puede ser (que) ❑ **daring** adj atrevido, osado ♦ n atrevimiento, osadía

dark [dɑːrk] adj oscuro; (hair, complexion) moreno ♦ n: **in the ~** a oscuras; **to be in the ~ about** (fig) no saber nada de; **after ~** después del anochecer ❑ **darken** vt (color) hacer más oscuro ♦ vi oscurecerse ❑ **dark glasses** (BRIT) npl anteojos mpl oscuros (LAm), gafas fpl oscuras (SP) ❑ **darkness** n oscuridad f ❑ **darkroom** n cuarto oscuro

darling ['dɑːrlɪŋ] adj, n querido(-a)

darn [dɑːrn] vt zurcir

dart [dɑːrt] n dardo; (in sewing) sisa ♦ vi precipitarse ► **dart away/along** vi salir/ marchar disparado ❑ **dartboard** n diana ❑ **darts** n dardos mpl

dash [dæʃ] n (small quantity: of liquid) gota, chorrito; (: of solid) pizca; (sign) raya ♦ vt (throw) tirar; (hopes) defraudar ♦ vi precipitarse, ir de prisa ► **dash away** or **off** vi marcharse apresuradamente

dashboard ['dæʃbɔːrd] n (AUT) tablero de mandos (LAm), salpicadero (SP)

dashing ['dæʃɪŋ] adj gallardo

data ['deɪtə] npl datos mpl ❑ **database** n base f de datos ❑ **data processing** n proceso de datos

date [deɪt] n (day) fecha; (with friend) cita; (fruit) dátil m ♦ vt fechar; (person) salir con; **~ of birth** fecha de nacimiento; **to ~** adv hasta la fecha ❑ **dated** adj anticuado ❑ **date rape** n violación ocurrida durante una cita con un conocido

daub [dɔːb] vt embadurnar

daughter ['dɔːtər] n hija ❑ **daughter-in-law** n nuera, hija política

daunting ['dɔːntɪŋ] adj desalentador(a)

dawdle ['dɔːdl] vi (go slowly) andar muy despacio

dawn [dɔːn] n alba, amanecer m; (fig) nacimiento ♦ vi (day) amanecer; (fig): **it ~ed on him that ...** cayó en la cuenta de que ...

day [deɪ] n día m; (working day) jornada; (heyday) tiempos mpl, días mpl; **the ~ before/after** el día anterior/siguiente; **the ~ after tomorrow** pasado mañana; **the ~ before yesterday** anteayer; **the following ~** el día siguiente; **by ~** de día ❑ **daybreak** n amanecer m ❑ **daycare center** (US) n guardería ❑ **daydream** vi soñar despierto ❑ **daylight** n luz f (del día) ❑ **day return** (BRIT) n boleto (LAm) or billete m (SP) de ida y vuelta (en un día) ❑ **daytime** n día m ❑ **day-to-day** adj cotidiano

daze [deɪz] vt (stun) aturdir ♦ n: **in a ~** aturdido

dazzle ['dæzəl] vt deslumbrar

DC abbr (= direct current) corriente f continua

D.C. (US) abbr = **District of Columbia**

dead [dɛd] adj muerto; (limb) dormido; (telephone) cortado; (battery) agotado ♦ adv (completely) totalmente; (exactly) exactamente ♦ npl: **the ~** los muertos; **to shoot sb ~** matar a algn a tiros; **~ tired** muerto (de cansancio); **to stop ~** parar en seco; **to be a ~ loss** (inf: person) ser un inútil ❑ **deaden** vt (blow, sound) amortiguar; (pain etc) aliviar ❑ **dead end** n callejón m sin salida ❑ **dead heat** n (SPORT) empate m ❑ **deadline** n fecha (or hora) tope ❑ **deadlock** n: **to reach deadlock** llegar a un punto muerto ❑ **deadly** adj mortal, fatal ❑ **deadpan** adj sin expresión ❑ **the Dead Sea** n el Mar Muerto

deaf [dɛf] adj sordo ❑ **deafen** vt ensordecer ❑ **deafness** n sordera

deal [diːl] (pt, pp **~t**) n (agreement) pacto, convenio; (business deal) trato ♦ vt dar; (card) repartir; **a great ~ (of)** bastante, mucho ► **deal in** vt fus tratar en, comerciar en ► **deal with** vt fus (people) tratar con; (problem) ocuparse de; (subject) tratar de ❑ **dealings** npl (COMM) transacciones fpl; (relations) relaciones fpl

dealt [dɛlt] pt, pp of **deal**

dean [di:n] n (REL) deán m; (US) decano, rector m; (BRIT SCOL) decano

dear [dɪər] adj querido; (BRIT: expensive) caro ♦ n: **my ~** mi querido(-a) ♦ excl: **~ me!** ¡Dios mío!; **D~ Sir/Madam** (in letter) Muy Señor Mío, Estimado Señor/Estimada Señora; **D~ Mr./Mrs. X** Estimado(-a) Señor(a) X ❑ **dearly** adv (love) mucho; (pay) caro

death [deθ] n muerte f ❑ **death certificate** n partida de defunción ❑ **deathly** adj (white) como un muerto; (silence) sepulcral ❑ **death penalty** n pena de muerte ❑ **death rate** n mortalidad f ❑ **death toll** n número de víctimas

debacle [dɪ'bɑ:kəl] n desastre m

debase [dɪ'beɪs] vt degradar

debatable [dɪ'beɪtəbəl] adj discutible

debate [dɪ'beɪt] n debate m ♦ vt discutir

debit ['debɪt] n debe m ♦ vt: **to ~ a sum to sb** or **to sb's account** cargar una suma en la cuenta de algn

debris [də'bri:] n escombros mpl

debt [det] n deuda; **to be in ~** tener deudas ❑ **debtor** n deudor(a) m/f

debut ['deɪbju:] n presentación f

decade ['dekeɪd] n decenio, década

decadence ['dekədəns] n decadencia

decaf ['di:kæf] (inf) n descafeinado

decaffeinated [dɪ'kæfɪneɪtɪd] adj descafeinado

decal ['di:kæl] (US) n calcomanía

decanter [dɪ'kæntər] n licorera

decay [dɪ'keɪ] n (of building) desmoronamiento; (of tooth) caries f inv ♦ vi (rot) pudrirse

deceased [dɪ'si:st] n: **the ~** el (la) difunto(-a)

deceit [dɪ'si:t] n engaño ❑ **deceitful** adj engañoso ❑ **deceive** vt engañar

December [dɪ'sembər] n diciembre m

decent ['di:sənt] adj (proper) decente; (person: kind) amable, bueno

deception [dɪ'sepʃən] n engaño

⚠ Be careful not to translate **deception** by the Spanish word **decepción**.

deceptive [dɪ'septɪv] adj engañoso

decibel ['desɪbəl] n decibel(io) m

decide [dɪ'saɪd] vt (person) decidir; (question, argument) resolver ♦ vi decidir; **to ~ to do/ that** decidir hacer/que; **to ~ on sth** decidirse por algo ❑ **decided** adj (resolute) decidido; (clear, definite) indudable ❑ **decidedly** [dɪ'saɪdɪdlɪ] adv decididamente; (emphatically) con resolución

deciduous [dɪ'sɪdʒuəs] adj de hoja caduca

decimal ['desəməl] adj decimal ♦ n decimal m ❑ **decimal point** n coma or punto decimal

decipher [dɪ'saɪfər] vt descifrar

decision [dɪ'sɪʒən] n decisión f

decisive [dɪ'saɪsɪv] adj decisivo; (person) decidido

deck [dek] n (NAUT) cubierta; (of vehicle) piso; (record deck) platina; (of cards) baraja ❑ **deck chair** n silla de playa (LAm), reposera (RPl), tumbona (SP)

declaration [deklə'reɪʃən] n declaración f ❑ **the Declaration of Independence** (US) n la Declaración de Independencia (de EE.UU.); see also **Independence Day**

DECLARATION OF INDEPENDENCE

Thomas Jefferson redactó la Declaración de Independencia en 1776 con el fin de acabar formalmente con los lazos que mantenían las colonias americanas con el Reino Unido y favorecer la formación de un nuevo estado norteamericano independiente. El nuevo Congreso de los EE.UU. adoptó el documento de Jefferson el 4 de julio de 1776, que se convertiría en la fecha del nacimiento oficial de la nación norteamericana.

declare [dɪ'kleər] vt declarar

decline [dɪ'klaɪn] n disminución f, descenso ♦ vt rehusar ♦ vi (person, business) decaer; (strength) disminuir

decoder [di:'koʊdər] n (TV) decodificador m

décor [deɪ'kɔ:r] n decoración f; (THEATER) decorado

decorate ['dekəreɪt] vt (adorn): **to ~ (with)** adornar (de), decorar (de); (paint) pintar; (paper) empapelar ❑ **decoration** [dekə'reɪʃən] n adorno; (act) decoración f; (medal) condecoración f ❑ **decorator** n decorador(a) m/f

decorum [dɪ'kɔ:rəm] n decoro

decoy ['di:kɔɪ] n señuelo

decrease [n 'di:kri:s, vb dɪ'kri:s] n: **~ (in)** disminución f (de) ♦ vt disminuir, reducir ♦ vi reducirse

decree [dɪ'kri:] n decreto ❑ **decree nisi** n sentencia provisional de divorcio

dedicate ['dedɪkeɪt] vt dedicar ❑ **dedication** [dedɪ'keɪʃən] n (devotion) dedicación f; (in book) dedicatoria

deduce [dɪ'du:s] vt deducir

deduct [dɪ'dʌkt] vt restar; descontar ❑ **deduction** n (amount deducted) descuento; (conclusion) deducción f, conclusión f

deed [di:d] *n* hecho, acto; (*feat*) hazaña; (*LAW*) escritura

deep [di:p] *adj* profundo; (*expressing measurements*) de profundidad; (*voice*) bajo; (*breath*) profundo; (*color*) intenso ♦ *adv*: **the spectators stood 20 ~** los espectadores se formaron de 20 en fondo; **to be 4 feet ~** tener 4 pies de profundidad ❏ **deepen** *vt* ahondar, profundizar ♦ *vi* aumentar, crecer ❏ **deep-freeze** *n* congelador *m* ❏ **deep-fry** *vt* freír en aceite abundante ❏ **deeply** *adv* (*breathe*) a pleno pulmón; (*interested, moved, grateful*) profundamente, hondamente ❏ **deep-sea diving** *n* buceo de altura ❏ **deep-seated** *adj* (*beliefs*) (profundamente) arraigado

deer [dɪər] *n inv* ciervo

deface [dɪˈfeɪs] *vt* (*wall, surface*) estropear, pintarrajear

default [dɪˈfɔːlt] *n*: **by ~** (*win*) por incomparecencia ♦ *adj* (*COMPUT*) por defecto

defeat [dɪˈfiːt] *n* derrota ♦ *vt* derrotar, vencer ❏ **defeatist** *adj*, *n* derrotista *mf*

defect [*n* ˈdiːfekt, *vb* dɪˈfekt] *n* defecto ♦ *vi*: **to ~ to the enemy** pasarse al enemigo ❏ **defective** [dɪˈfektɪv] *adj* defectuoso

defence [dɪˈfens] (*BRIT*) *n* = **defense**

defend [dɪˈfend] *vt* defender ❏ **defendant** *n* acusado(-a); (*in civil case*) demandado(-a) ❏ **defender** *n* defensor(a) *m/f*; (*SPORT*) defensa *mf*

defense (*US*) [dɪˈfens] (*BRIT* **defence**) *n* defensa ❏ **defenseless** (*US*) (*BRIT* **defenceless**) *adj* indefenso

defensive [dɪˈfensɪv] *adj* defensivo ♦ *n*: **on the ~** a la defensiva

defer [dɪˈfɜːr] *vt* aplazar

defiance [dɪˈfaɪəns] *n* desafío; **in ~ of** en contra de ❏ **defiant** *adj* (*challenging*) desafiante, retador(a)

deficiency [dɪˈfɪʃənsɪ] *n* (*lack*) falta; (*defect*) defecto ❏ **deficient** *adj* deficiente

deficit [ˈdefɪsɪt] *n* déficit *m*

define [dɪˈfaɪn] *vt* (*word etc*) definir; (*limits etc*) determinar

definite [ˈdefɪnɪt] *adj* (*fixed*) determinado; (*obvious*) claro; (*certain*) indudable; **he was ~ about it** no dejó lugar a dudas (sobre ello) ❏ **definitely** *adv* desde luego, por supuesto

definition [defəˈnɪʃən] *n* definición *f*; (*clearness*) nitidez *f*

deflate [diːˈfleɪt] *vt* desinflar

deflect [dɪˈflekt] *vt* desviar

defogger [diːˈfɒgər] (*US*) *n* (*AUT*) luneta térmica, dispositivo antivaho

defraud [dɪˈfrɔːd] *vt*: **to ~ sb of sth** estafar algo a algn

defrost [diːˈfrɒst] *vt* descongelar ❏ **defroster** (*US*) *n* (*defogger*) luneta térmica, dispositivo antivaho; (*BRIT*: *of refrigerator*) descongelación *f*

deft [deft] *adj* diestro, hábil

defunct [dɪˈfʌŋkt] *adj* difunto; (*organization etc*) ya que no existe

defuse [diːˈfjuːz] *vt* desactivar; (*situation*) calmar

defy [dɪˈfaɪ] *vt* (*resist*) oponerse a; (*challenge*) desafiar; (*fig*): **it defies description** resulta imposible describirlo

degenerate [*vb* dɪˈdʒenəreɪt, *adj* dɪˈdʒenərɪt] *vi* degenerar ♦ *adj* degenerado

degree [dɪˈgriː] *n* grado; (*SCOL*) título; **to have a ~ in English** tener una licenciatura en filología inglesa; **by ~s** (*gradually*) poco a poco, por etapas; **to some ~** hasta cierto punto

dehydrated [diːhaɪˈdreɪtɪd] *adj* deshidratado; (*milk*) en polvo

de-ice [diːˈaɪs] *vt* descongelar

deign [deɪn] *vi*: **to ~ to do** dignarse hacer

dejected [dɪˈdʒektɪd] *adj* abatido, desanimado

delay [dɪˈleɪ] *vt* demorar, aplazar; (*person*) entretener; (*train*) retrasar ♦ *vi* tardar ♦ *n* demora, retraso; **to be ~ed** retrasarse; **without ~** en seguida, sin tardar

delectable [dɪˈlektəbəl] *adj* (*person*) encantador(a); (*food*) delicioso

delegate [*n* ˈdelɪgɪt, *vb* ˈdelɪgeɪt] *n* delegado(-a) ♦ *vt* (*person*) delegar en; (*task*) delegar

delete [dɪˈliːt] *vt* suprimir, tachar

deli [ˈdelɪ] *n* = **delicatessen**

deliberate [*adj* dɪˈlɪbərɪt, *vb* dɪˈlɪbəreɪt] *adj* (*intentional*) intencionado; (*slow*) pausado, lento ♦ *vi* deliberar ❏ **deliberately** *adv* (*on purpose*) a propósito

delicacy [ˈdelɪkəsɪ] *n* delicadeza; (*choice food*) manjar *m*

delicate [ˈdelɪkɪt] *adj* delicado; (*fragile*) frágil

delicatessen [delɪkəˈtesən] *n* ultramarinos *mpl* finos

delicious [dɪˈlɪʃəs] *adj* delicioso

delight [dɪˈlaɪt] *n* (*feeling*) placer *m*, deleite *m*; (*person, experience etc*) encanto, delicia ♦ *vt* encantar, deleitar; **to take ~ in** deleitarse en ❏ **delighted** *adj*: **delighted (at** *or* **with/to do)** encantado (con/de hacer) ❏ **delightful** *adj* encantador(a), delicioso

delinquent [dɪ'lɪŋkwənt] *adj, n* delincuente *mf*

delirious [dɪ'lɪriəs] *adj*: **to be ~** delirar, desvariar; **to be ~ with** estar loco de

deliver [dɪ'lɪvər] *vt* (*distribute*) repartir; (*hand over*) entregar; (*message*) comunicar; (*speech*) pronunciar; (*MED*) asistir al parto de ❑ **delivery** *n* reparto; entrega; (*of speaker*) modo de expresarse; (*MED*) parto, alumbramiento; **to take delivery of** recibir ❑ **delivery man** *n* repartidor *m*

delude [dɪ'lu:d] *vt* engañar

deluge ['dɛlju:dʒ] *n* diluvio

delusion [dɪ'lu:ʒən] *n* ilusión *f*, engaño

de luxe [də'lʌks] *adj* de lujo

demand [dɪ'mænd] *vt* (*gen*) exigir; (*rights*) reclamar ♦ *n* exigencia; (*claim*) reclamación *f*; (*ECON*) demanda; **to be in ~** ser muy solicitado; **on ~** a solicitud ❑ **demanding** *adj* (*boss*) exigente; (*work*) absorbente

demean [dɪ'mi:n] *vt*: **to ~ o.s.** rebajarse

demeanor (*US*) [dɪ'mi:nər] (*BRIT* **demeanour**) *n* porte *m*, conducta

demented [dɪ'mɛntɪd] *adj* demente

demise [dɪ'maɪz] *n* (*death*) fallecimiento

demister [di:'mɪstər] (*BRIT*) *n* (*AUT*) = **defogger**

demo ['dɛmou] (*BRIT: inf*) *n abbr* (= **demonstration**) manifestación *f*

democracy [dɪ'mɑ:krəsi] *n* democracia ❑ **democrat** ['dɛməkræt] *n* demócrata *mf*; (*US*): **Democrat** demócrata *mf*; ❑ **democratic** [dɛmə'krætɪk] *adj* democrático; **Democratic** (*US*) demócrata; **the Democratic Party** (*US*) el Partido Demócrata

demolish [dɪ'mɑ:lɪʃ] *vt* derribar, demoler; (*fig: argument*) destruir

demon ['di:mən] *n* (*evil spirit*) demonio

demonstrate ['dɛmənstreɪt] *vt* demostrar; (*skill, appliance*) mostrar ♦ *vi* manifestarse ❑ **demonstration** [dɛmən'streɪʃən] *n* (*POL*) manifestación *f*; (*proof, exhibition*) demostración *f* ❑ **demonstrator** *n* (*POL*) manifestante *mf*; (*COMM*) demostrador(a) *m/f*; vendedor(a) *m/f*

demote [dɪ'mout] *vt* degradar

demure [dɪ'mjuər] *adj* recatado

den [dɛn] *n* (*of animal*) guarida; (*room*) habitación *f*

denial [dɪ'naɪəl] *n* (*refusal*) negativa; (*of report etc*) negación *f*

denim ['dɛnɪm] *n* tela de mezclilla (*MEX*), tela de jeans (*LAm exc MEX*), tela vaquera (*SP*); **~s** *npl* pantalones *mpl* de mezclilla (*MEX*), jeans *mpl* (*LAm exc MEX*), vaqueros *mpl* (*SP*)

Denmark ['dɛnmɑ:rk] *n* Dinamarca

denomination [dɪnɑ:mɪ'neɪʃən] *n* valor *m*; (*REL*) confesión *f*

denounce [dɪ'nauns] *vt* denunciar

dense [dɛns] *adj* (*crowd*) denso; (*thick*) espeso; (: *foliage etc*) tupido; (*inf: stupid*) torpe ❑ **densely** *adv*: **densely populated** con una alta densidad de población

density ['dɛnsɪti] *n* densidad *f*; **single/double~ disk** *n* (*COMPUT*) disco de densidad sencilla/de doble densidad

dent [dɛnt] *n* abolladura ♦ *vt* (*also*: **make a ~ in**) abollar

dental ['dɛntl] *adj* dental ❑ **dental floss** *n* hilo *or* seda dental ❑ **dental surgeon** *n* odontólogo(-a)

dentist ['dɛntɪst] *n* dentista *mf*

dentures ['dɛntʃərz] *npl* dentadura (postiza)

deny [dɪ'naɪ] *vt* negar; (*charge*) rechazar

deodorant [di:'oudərənt] *n* desodorante *m*

depart [dɪ'pɑ:rt] *vi* irse, marcharse; (*train*) salir; **to ~ from** (*fig: differ from*) apartarse de

department [dɪ'pɑ:rtmənt] *n* (*COMM*) sección *f*; (*SCOL*) departamento; (*POL*) ministerio ❑ **department store** *n* gran almacén *m*

departure [dɪ'pɑ:rtʃər] *n* partida, ida; (*of train*) salida; (*of employee*) marcha; **a new ~** un nuevo rumbo ❑ **departure lounge** *n* (*at airport*) sala de embarque

depend [dɪ'pɛnd] *vi*: **to ~ on** depender de; (*rely on*) contar con; **it ~s** depende, según; **~ing on the result** según el resultado ❑ **dependable** *adj* (*person*) formal, serio; (*watch*) exacto; (*car*) seguro ❑ **dependant** *n* dependiente *mf* ❑ **dependent** *adj*: **to be dependent on** depender de ♦ *n* = **dependant**

depict [dɪ'pɪkt] *vt* (*in picture*) pintar; (*describe*) representar

depleted [dɪ'pli:tɪd] *adj* reducido

deploy [dɪ'plɔɪ] *vt* desplegar

deport [dɪ'pɔ:rt] *vt* deportar

deposit [dɪ'pɑ:zɪt] *n* depósito; (*CHEM*) sedimento; (*of ore, oil*) yacimiento ♦ *vt* (*gen*) depositar ❑ **deposit account** (*BRIT*) *n* cuenta de ahorros

depot ['di:pou] *n* (*storehouse*) depósito; (*for vehicles*) parque *m*; (*US: of buses, trains*) estación *f*

depreciate [dɪ'pri:ʃieɪt] *vi* depreciarse, perder valor

depress [dɪ'pres] vt deprimir; (wages etc) hacer bajar; (press down) apretar
❑ **depressed** adj deprimido
❑ **depressing** adj deprimente
❑ **depression** n depresión f

deprivation [deprɪ'veɪʃən] n privación f

deprive [dɪ'praɪv] vt: **to ~ sb of** privar a algn de ❑ **deprived** adj necesitado

depth [depθ] n profundidad f; (of cupboard) fondo; **to be in the ~s of despair** sentir la mayor desesperación; **to be out of one's ~** (in water) no hacer pie; (fig) sentirse totalmente perdido

deputize ['depjətaɪz] vi: **to ~ for sb** suplir a algn

deputy ['depjətɪ] n sustituto(-a), suplente mf; (US POL) diputado(-a); (US: also: ~ **sheriff**) ayudante mf del sheriff ♦ adj (BRIT: also: ~ **head**) subdirector(a) m/f

derail [dɪ'reɪl] vt: **to be ~ed** descarrilarse

deranged [dɪ'reɪndʒd] adj trastornado

derby ['dɑːrbɪ] (US) n (SPORT): **local ~** derbi m; (hat) hongo

derelict ['derɪlɪkt] adj abandonado

derisory [dɪ'raɪzərɪ] adj (sum) irrisorio

derive [dɪ'raɪv] vt (benefit etc) obtener ♦ vi: **to ~ from** derivarse de

derogatory [dɪ'rɑːgətərɪ] adj despectivo

descend [dɪ'send] vt, vi descender, bajar; **to ~ from** descender de; **to ~ to** rebajarse a ❑ **descendant** n descendiente mf

descent [dɪ'sent] n descenso; (origin) descendencia

describe [dɪ'skraɪb] vt describir ❑ **description** [dɪ'skrɪpʃən] n descripción f; (sort) clase f, género

desecrate ['desɪkreɪt] vt profanar

desert [n 'dezərt, vb dɪ'zɜːrt] n desierto ♦ vt abandonar ♦ vi (MIL) desertar ❑ **deserter** [dɪ'zɜːrtər] n desertor(a) m/f ❑ **desertion** [dɪ'zɜːrʃən] n deserción f; (LAW) abandono ❑ **desert island** n isla desierta ❑ **deserts** [dɪ'zɜːrts] npl: **to get one's just deserts** llevar su merecido

deserve [dɪ'zɜːrv] vt merecer, ser digno de ❑ **deserving** adj (person) digno; (action, cause) meritorio

design [dɪ'zaɪn] n (sketch) bosquejo; (layout, shape) diseño; (pattern) dibujo; (intention) intención f ♦ vt diseñar

designate [vb 'dezɪgneɪt, adj 'dezɪgnɪt] vt (appoint) nombrar; (destine) designar ♦ adj designado

designer [dɪ'zaɪnər] n diseñador(a) m/f; (fashion designer) modisto(-a), diseñador(a) m/f de moda

desirable [dɪ'zaɪərəbəl] adj (proper) deseable; (attractive) atractivo

desire [dɪ'zaɪər] n deseo ♦ vt desear

desk [desk] n (in office) escritorio; (for pupil) pupitre m; (in hotel, at airport) recepción f; (BRIT: in shop, restaurant) caja

desk-top publishing n autoedición f

desolate ['desəlɪt] adj (place) desierto; (person) afligido

despair [dɪ'speər] n desesperación f ♦ vi: **to ~ of** perder la esperanza de

despatch [dɪ'spætʃ] n, vt = **dispatch**

desperate ['despərɪt] adj desesperado; (fugitive) peligroso; **to be ~ for sth/to do** necesitar urgentemente algo/hacer ❑ **desperately** adv desesperadamente; (very) terriblemente, gravemente

desperation [despə'reɪʃən] n desesperación f; **in (sheer) ~** (absolutamente) desesperado

despicable [dɪ'spɪkəbəl] adj vil, despreciable

despise [dɪ'spaɪz] vt despreciar

despite [dɪ'spaɪt] prep a pesar de, pese a

despondent [dɪs'pɑːndənt] adj deprimido, abatido

dessert [dɪ'zɜːrt] n postre m ❑ **dessertspoon** n cuchara (de postre)

destination [destɪ'neɪʃən] n destino

destiny ['destɪnɪ] n destino

destitute ['destɪtuːt] adj desamparado, indigente

destroy [dɪ'strɔɪ] vt destruir; (animal) sacrificar ❑ **destroyer** n (NAUT) destructor m

destruction [dɪ'strʌkʃən] n destrucción f

detach [dɪ'tætʃ] vt separar; (unstick) despegar ❑ **detached** adj (attitude) objetivo, imparcial ❑ **detached house** (BRIT) n ≈ chalé m, ≈ chalet m ❑ **detachment** n (aloofness) frialdad f; (MIL) destacamento

detail ['diːteɪl] n detalle m; (no pl: in picture etc) detalles mpl; (trifle) pequeñez f ♦ vt detallar; (MIL) destacar; **in ~** detalladamente ❑ **detailed** adj detallado

detain [dɪ'teɪn] vt retener; (in captivity) detener

detect [dɪ'tekt] vt descubrir; (MED, POLICE) identificar; (MIL, RADAR, TECH) detectar ❑ **detection** n descubrimiento; identificación f ❑ **detective** n detective mf ❑ **detective story** n novela policíaca ❑ **detector** n detector m

detention [dɪ'tenʃən] n detención f, arresto; (SCOL) castigo

deter [dɪ'tɜ:r] vt (dissuade) disuadir

detergent [dɪ'tɜ:rdʒənt] n detergente m

deteriorate [dɪ'tɪəriəreɪt] vi deteriorarse
□ **deterioration** [dɪtɪəriə'reɪʃən] n deterioro

determination [dɪtɜ:rmɪ'neɪʃən] n
resolución f

determine [dɪ'tɜ:rmɪn] vt determinar
□ **determined** adj (person) resuelto,
decidido; **determined to do** resuelto a hacer

deterrent [dɪ'tɜ:rənt] n (MIL) fuerza de
disuasión

detest [dɪ'test] vt aborrecer

detonate ['detneɪt] vi estallar ♦ vt hacer
detonar

detour ['di:tur] n (gen, AUT) desviación f ♦ vt
(US) desviar

detract [dɪ'trækt] vt: **to ~ from** quitar mérito
a, desvirtuar

detriment ['detrɪmənt] n: **to the ~ of** en
perjuicio de □ **detrimental** [detrɪ'mentl]
adj: **detrimental (to)** perjudicial (a)

devaluation [dɪvælju'eɪʃən] n devaluación f

devalue [di:'vælju:] vt (currency) devaluar;
(fig) quitar mérito a

devastate ['devəsteɪt] vt devastar; (fig): **to be
~d by** quedar destrozado por
□ **devastating** adj devastador(a); (fig)
arrollador(a)

develop [dɪ'veləp] vt desarrollar; (PHOT)
revelar; (disease) coger; (habit) adquirir; (fault)
empezar a tener ♦ vi desarrollarse; (advance)
progresar; (facts, symptoms) aparecer
□ **developer** n promotor m
□ **developing country** n país m en (vías
de) desarrollo □ **development** n
desarrollo; (advance) progreso; (of affair, case)
desenvolvimiento; (of land) urbanización f

deviation [di:vi'eɪʃən] n desviación f

device [dɪ'vaɪs] n (apparatus) aparato,
mecanismo

devil ['devəl] n diablo, demonio

devious ['di:viəs] adj taimado

devise [dɪ'vaɪz] vt idear, inventar

devoid [dɪ'vɔɪd] adj: **~ of** desprovisto de

devolution [di:və'lu:ʃən] n (POL)
descentralización f

devote [dɪ'vəut] vt: **to ~ sth to** dedicar algo a
□ **devoted** adj (loyal) leal, fiel; **to be
devoted to sb** querer con devoción a algn;
the book is devoted to politics el libro trata
de política □ **devotee** [devə'ti:] n entusiasta
mf; (REL) devoto(-a) □ **devotion** n
dedicación f; (REL) devoción f

devour [dɪ'vauər] vt devorar

devout [dɪ'vaut] adj devoto

dew [du:] n rocío

diabetes [daɪə'bi:tɪs] n diabetes f
□ **diabetic** [daɪə'betɪk] adj, n diabético(-a)

diabolic [daɪə'bɑ:lɪk] adj (weather, behavior)
pésimo □ **diabolical** (inf) adj = **diabolic**

diagnosis [daɪəg'nəusɪs] (pl **-ses**) n
diagnóstico

diagonal [daɪ'ægənəl] adj, n diagonal f

diagram ['daɪəgræm] n diagrama m,
esquema m

dial ['daɪəl] n cara (LAm), esfera (SP); (on radio
etc) dial m; (of phone) disco ♦ vt (number)
marcar

dialect ['daɪəlekt] n dialecto

dial tone (US) n señal f or tono de marcar

dialling code (BRIT) n clave f lada (MEX),
código de la zona (LAm), prefijo (SP)

dialogue ['daɪəlɑ:g] (US **dialog**) n diálogo

dialysis [daɪ'ælɪsɪs] n diálisis f inv

diameter [daɪ'æmɪtər] n diámetro

diamond ['daɪmənd] n diamante m; (shape)
rombo; **~s** npl (CARDS) diamantes mpl

diaper ['daɪpər] (US) n pañal m; **~ rash** prurito

diaphragm ['daɪəfræm] n diafragma m

diarrhea (US) [daɪə'ri:ə] (BRIT **diarrhoea**) n
diarrea

diary ['daɪəri] n (daily account) diario; (book)
agenda

dice [daɪs] n inv dados mpl ♦ vt (CULIN) cortar en
cuadritos

Dictaphone® ['dɪktəfəun] n dictáfono®

dictate ['dɪkteɪt] vt dictar; (conditions)
imponer □ **dictation** [dɪk'teɪʃən] n dictado;
(giving of orders) órdenes fpl

dictator ['dɪkteɪtər] n dictador m
□ **dictatorship** n dictadura

dictionary ['dɪkʃəneri] n diccionario

did [dɪd] pt of **do**

didn't ['dɪdnt] cont = **did not**

die [daɪ] vi morir; (fig: fade) desvanecerse,
desaparecer; **to be dying for sth/to do sth**
morirse por algo/de ganas de hacer algo
▶ **die away** vi (sound, light) perderse ▶ **die
down** vi apagarse; (wind) amainar ▶ **die out**
vi desaparecer

diesel ['di:zəl] n vehículo con motor Diesel
□ **diesel engine** n motor m Diesel
□ **diesel (oil)** n gasoil m

diet ['daɪət] n dieta; (restricted food) régimen m
♦ vi (also: **be on a ~**) estar a dieta, hacer
régimen

differ ['dɪfər] vi: **to ~ (from)** (be different) ser
distinto (a), diferenciarse (de); (disagree)
discrepar (de) □ **difference** n diferencia;

(*disagreement*) desacuerdo ❑ **different** *adj*
diferente, distinto ❑ **differentiate**
[dɪfə'renʃieit] *vi*: **to differentiate (between)**
distinguir (entre) ❑ **differently** *adv* de otro
modo, en forma distinta

difficult ['dɪfɪkʌlt] *adj* difícil ❑ **difficulty** *n*
dificultad *f*

diffident ['dɪfɪdənt] *adj* tímido

dig [dɪg] (*pt, pp* **dug**) *vt* (*hole, ground*) cavar ♦ *n*
(*prod*) empujón *m*; (*archeological*) excavación
f; (*remark*) indirecta; **to ~ one's nails into**
clavar las uñas en ▶ **dig into** *vt fus* (*savings*)
consumir ▶ **dig up** *vt* (*information*)
desenterrar; (*plant*) desarraigar

digest [*vb* dai'dʒɛst, *n* 'daidʒɛst] *vt* (*food*)
digerir; (*facts*) asimilar ♦ *n* resumen *m*
❑ **digestion** *n* digestión *f*

digit ['dɪdʒɪt] *n* (*number*) dígito; (*finger*) dedo
❑ **digital** *adj* digital ❑ **digital camera** *n*
cámara digital ❑ **digital TV** *n* televisión *f*
digital

dignified ['dɪgnɪfaid] *adj* grave, solemne

dignity ['dɪgnɪti] *n* dignidad *f*

digress [dai'grɛs] *vi*: **to ~ from** apartarse de

digs [dɪgz] (*BRIT: inf*) *npl* pensión *f*, alojamiento

dike [daɪk] (*US*) *n* dique *m*

dilapidated [dɪ'læpɪdeitɪd] *adj*
desmoronado, ruinoso

dilemma [dɪ'lɛmə] *n* dilema *m*

diligent ['dɪlɪdʒənt] *adj* diligente

dilute [dai'lu:t] *vt* diluir

dim [dɪm] *adj* (*light*) débil; (*outline*) indistinto;
(*room*) oscuro; (*inf: stupid*) menso (*MEX*), lerdo
(*LAm exc MEX, SP*) ♦ *vt* (*light*) bajar; (*US AUT*): **to ~
one's lights** poner luces de cruce

dime [daɪm] (*US*) *n* moneda de diez centavos

dimension [dɪ'menʃən] *n* dimensión *f*

diminish [dɪ'mɪnɪʃ] *vt, vi* disminuir

diminutive [dɪ'mɪnjutɪv] *adj* diminuto ♦ *n*
(*LING*) diminutivo

dimmers ['dɪmərz] (*US*) *npl* (*AUT: dipped
headlights*) luces *fpl* cortas; (*: parking lights*)
luces *fpl* de posición

dimple ['dɪmpəl] *n* hoyuelo

din [dɪn] *n* estruendo, estrépito

dine [daɪn] *vi* cenar ❑ **diner** *n* (*person*)
comensal *mf*; (*US: place*) restaurante; (*RAIL*)
coche comedor

dinghy ['dɪŋi] *n* bote *m*; (*also*: **rubber ~**)
lancha (neumática)

dingy ['dɪndʒi] *adj* (*room*) sombrío; (*color*)
sucio

dining car ['daɪnɪŋ,kɑːr] *n* (*RAIL*) coche-
comedor *m*

dining room *n* comedor *m*

dinner ['dɪnər] *n* (*evening meal*) cena; (*lunch*)
comida; (*public*) cena, banquete *m* ❑ **dinner
jacket** (*BRIT*) *n* smoking *m* ❑ **dinner party** *n*
cena ❑ **dinner time** *n* (*evening*) hora de
cenar; (*midday*) hora de comer

dinosaur ['daɪnəsɔːr] *n* dinosaurio

dip [dɪp] *n* (*slope*) pendiente *m*; (*in sea*) baño;
(*CULIN*) salsa ♦ *vt* (*in water*) mojar; (*ladle etc*)
meter; (*BRIT AUT*): **to ~ one's lights** poner luces
de cruce ♦ *vi* (*road etc*) descender, bajar

diploma [dɪ'ploumə] *n* diploma *m*

diplomacy [dɪ'plouməsi] *n* diplomacia

diplomat ['dɪpləmæt] *n* diplomático(-a)
❑ **diplomatic** [dɪplə'mætɪk] *adj* diplomático

dipstick ['dɪp,stɪk] *n* (*AUT*) varilla de nivel (del
aceite)

dip switch ['dɪp,swɪtʃ] *n* (*AUT*) interruptor *m*

dire [daɪər] *adj* calamitoso

direct [dɪ'rɛkt] *adj* directo; (*challenge*) claro;
(*person*) franco ♦ *vt* dirigir; (*order*): **to ~ sb to
do sth** mandar a algn hacer algo ♦ *adv*
derecho; **can you ~ me to ...?** ¿puede
indicarme dónde está ...? ❑ **direct debit**
(*BRIT*) *n* débito bancario (*LAm*)

direction [dɪ'rɛkʃən] *n* dirección *f*; **~s** *npl*
(*instructions*) instrucciones *fpl*; **sense of ~**
sentido de la dirección; **~s for use** modo de
empleo

directly [dɪ'rɛktli] *adv* (*in straight line*)
directamente; (*at once*) en seguida

director [dɪ'rɛktər] *n* director(a) *m/f*

directory [dɪ'rɛktəri] *n* (*TEL*) guía (telefónica);
(*COMPUT*) directorio ❑ **directory
assistance** (*US*) *n* (servicio de) información *f*
❑ **directory enquiries** (*BRIT*) *n*
= **directory assistance**

dirt [dɜːrt] *n* suciedad *f*; (*earth*) tierra ❑ **dirt-
cheap** *adj* baratísimo ❑ **dirty** *adj* sucio;
(*joke*) colorado (*MEX*), verde (*LAm exc MEX, SP*)
♦ *vt* ensuciar; (*stain*) manchar ❑ **dirty trick**
n juego sucio

disability [dɪsə'bɪlɪti] *n* incapacidad *f*

disabled [dɪs'eibəld] *adj*: **to be physically ~**
ser minusválido(-a); **to be mentally ~** ser
deficiente mental

disadvantage [dɪsəd'væntɪdʒ] *n*
desventaja, inconveniente *m*

disagree [dɪsə'griː] *vi* (*differ*) discrepar; **to ~
(with)** no estar de acuerdo (con)
❑ **disagreeable** *adj* desagradable; (*person*)
antipático ❑ **disagreement** *n* desacuerdo

disallow [dɪsə'lau] *vt* (*goal*) anular; (*claim*)
rechazar

disappear [dɪsə'pɪər] vi desaparecer
❑ **disappearance** n desaparición f

disappoint [dɪsə'pɔɪnt] vt decepcionar,
defraudar ❑ **disappointed** adj
decepcionado ❑ **disappointing** adj
decepcionante ❑ **disappointment** n
decepción f

disapproval [dɪsə'pruːvəl] n desaprobación
f

disapprove [dɪsə'pruːv] vi: **to ~ of** ver mal

disarmament [dɪs'ɑːrməmənt] n desarme
m

disarray [dɪsə'reɪ] n: **in ~** (army, organization)
desorganizado; (hair, clothes) desarreglado

disaster [dɪ'zæstər] n desastre m

disband [dɪs'bænd] vt disolver ♦ vi
desbandarse

disbelief [dɪsbə'liːf] n incredulidad f

disc [dɪsk] n disco; (COMPUT) = **disk**

discard [dɪ'skɑːrd] vt (old things) tirar; (fig)
descartar

discern [dɪ'sɜːrn] vt percibir, discernir;
(understand) comprender ❑ **discerning** adj
perspicaz

discharge [vb dɪs'tʃɑːrdʒ, n 'dɪstʃɑːrdʒ] vt
(task, duty) cumplir; (waste) verter; (patient)
dar de alta; (employee) despedir; (soldier)
licenciar; (defendant) poner en libertad ♦ n
(ELEC) descarga; (MED) supuración f; (dismissal)
despedida; (of duty) desempeño; (of debt)
pago, descargo

discipline ['dɪsɪplɪn] n disciplina ♦ vt
disciplinar; (punish) castigar

disc jockey n disc(-)jockey mf

disclaim [dɪs'kleɪm] vt negar

disclose [dɪs'kləʊz] vt revelar ❑ **disclosure**
[dɪs'kləʊʒər] n revelación f

disco ['dɪskəʊ] n abbr = **discotheque**

discomfort [dɪs'kʌmfərt] n incomodidad f;
(unease) inquietud f; (physical) malestar m

disconcert [dɪskən'sɜːrt] vt desconcertar

disconnect [dɪskə'nekt] vt separar; (ELEC etc)
desconectar

discontent [dɪskən'tent] n descontento
❑ **discontented** adj descontento

discontinue [dɪskən'tɪnjuː] vt interrumpir;
(payments) suspender; **"~d"** (COMM) "ya no se
fabrica"

discord ['dɪskɔːrd] n discordia; (MUS)
disonancia

discotheque ['dɪskətek] n discoteca

discount [n 'dɪskaʊnt, vb dɪs'kaʊnt] n
descuento ♦ vt descontar

discourage [dɪ'skɜːrɪdʒ] vt desalentar;
(advise against): **to ~ sb from doing** disuadir a
algn de hacer

discover [dɪ'skʌvər] vt descubrir; (error) darse
cuenta de ❑ **discovery** n descubrimiento

discredit [dɪs'kredɪt] vt desacreditar

discreet [dɪ'skriːt] adj (tactful) discreto;
(careful) circunspecto, prudente

discrepancy [dɪ'skrepənsɪ] n diferencia

discretion [dɪ'skreʃən] n (tact) discreción f; **at
the ~ of** a criterio de

discriminate [dɪ'skrɪmɪneɪt] vi: **to ~
between** distinguir entre; **to ~ against**
discriminar contra ❑ **discriminating** adj
entendido ❑ **discrimination**
[dɪskrɪmɪ'neɪʃən] n (discernment) perspicacia;
(prejudice) discriminación f

discuss [dɪ'skʌs] vt discutir; (a theme) tratar
❑ **discussion** n discusión f

disdain [dɪs'deɪn] n desdén m

disease [dɪ'ziːz] n enfermedad f

disembark [dɪsɪm'bɑːrk] vt, vi desembarcar

disentangle [dɪsɪn'tæŋgəl] vt soltar; (wire,
thread) desenredar

disfigure [dɪs'fɪgjər] vt (person) desfigurar;
(object) afear

disgrace [dɪs'greɪs] n ignominia; (shame)
vergüenza, escándalo ♦ vt deshonrar
❑ **disgraceful** adj vergonzoso

disgruntled [dɪs'grʌntld] adj disgustado,
descontento

disguise [dɪs'gaɪz] n disfraz m ♦ vt disfrazar;
in ~ disfrazado

disgust [dɪs'gʌst] n repugnancia ♦ vt
repugnar, dar asco a ❑ **disgusting** adj
repugnante, asqueroso; (behavior etc)
vergonzoso

⚠ Be careful not to translate **disgust** by the
Spanish word **disgustar**.

dish [dɪʃ] n (gen) plato; **to do** or **wash the ~es**
fregar los platos ▶ **dish out** vt repartir
▶ **dish up** (BRIT) vt servir ❑ **dishcloth** (BRIT)
n = **dishrag**

dishearten [dɪs'hɑːrtn] vt desalentar

disheveled (US) [dɪ'ʃevəld] (BRIT
dishevelled) adj (hair) despeinado;
(appearance) desarreglado

dishonest [dɪs'ɑːnɪst] adj (person) poco
honrado, tramposo; (means) fraudulento
❑ **dishonesty** n falta de honradez

dishonor (US) [dɪs'ɑːnər] (BRIT **dishonour**) n
deshonra ❑ **dishonorable** (US) (BRIT
dishonourable) adj deshonroso

dishrag ['dɪʃræg] (US) n estropajo

dishtowel ['dɪʃ,tauəl] (US) n paño de cocina, repasador m (RPl)

dishwasher ['dɪʃ,wɑːʃər] n lavaplatos m inv ❑ **dishwashing liquid** (US) n líquido m lavavajillas

disillusion [dɪsɪ'luːʒən] vt desilusionar

disinfect [dɪsɪn'fekt] vt desinfectar ❑ **disinfectant** n desinfectante m

disintegrate [dɪs'ɪntɪgreɪt] vi disgregarse, desintegrarse

disinterested [dɪs'ɪntrəstɪd] adj desinteresado

disjointed [dɪs'dʒɔɪntɪd] adj inconexo

disk [dɪsk] n (US: gen, also ANAT) disco; (COMPUT) disco, disquete m; **single-/double-sided ~** disco de una cara/dos caras ❑ **disk drive** n disc drive m ❑ **disk jockey** n = **disc jockey** ❑ **diskette** n = **disk**

dislike [dɪs'laɪk] n antipatía, aversión f ♦ vt tener antipatía a

dislocate ['dɪslˌʊkeɪt] vt dislocar

dislodge [dɪs'lɑːdʒ] vt sacar

disloyal [dɪs'lɔɪəl] adj desleal

dismal ['dɪzməl] adj (gloomy) deprimente, triste; (very bad) malísimo, fatal

dismantle [dɪs'mæntl] vt desmontar, desarmar

dismay [dɪs'meɪ] n consternación f ♦ vt consternar

dismiss [dɪs'mɪs] vt (worker) despedir; (pupils) dejar marchar; (soldiers) dar permiso para irse; (idea, LAW) rechazar; (possibility) descartar ❑ **dismissal** n despido

dismount [dɪs'maunt] vi apearse

disobedient [dɪsə'biːdɪənt] adj desobediente

disobey [dɪsə'beɪ] vt desobedecer

disorder [dɪs'ɔːrdər] n desorden m; (rioting) disturbios mpl; (MED) trastorno f ❑ **disorderly** adj desordenado; (meeting) alborotado; (conduct) escandaloso

disorganize [dɪs'ɔːrgənaɪz] vt desorganizar

disorient [dɪs'ɔːrɪənt] vt desorientar

disorientated [dɪs'ɔːrɪenteɪtɪd] adj desorientado

disown [dɪs'oun] vt (action) renegar de; (person) negar cualquier tipo de relación con

disparaging [dɪs'pærɪdʒɪŋ] adj despreciativo

dispassionate [dɪs'pæʃənɪt] adj (unbiased) imparcial

dispatch [dɪ'spætʃ] vt enviar ♦ n (sending) envío; (PRESS) informe m; (MIL) parte m

dispel [dɪ'spel] vt disipar

dispense [dɪ'spens] vt (medicines) preparar ▶ **dispense with** vt fus prescindir de ❑ **dispenser** n (container) distribuidor m automático ❑ **dispensing chemist** (BRIT) n farmacia

disperse [dɪ'spɜːrs] vt dispersar ♦ vi dispersarse

dispirited [dɪ'spɪrɪtɪd] adj desanimado, desalentado

displace [dɪs'pleɪs] vt desplazar, reemplazar ❑ **displaced person** n (POL) desplazado(-a)

display [dɪ'spleɪ] n (in store window) vidriera (LAm), escaparate m (SP); (exhibition) exposición f; (COMPUT) visualización f; (of feeling) manifestación f ♦ vt exponer; manifestar; (ostentatiously) lucir

displease [dɪs'pliːz] vt (offend) ofender; (annoy) fastidiar ❑ **displeased** adj: **displeased with** disgustado con ❑ **displeasure** [dɪs'pleʒər] n disgusto

disposable [dɪ'spouzəbəl] adj desechable; (income) disponible ❑ **disposable diaper** (US) (BRIT **disposable nappy**) n pañal m desechable

disposal [dɪ'spouzəl] n (of garbage) destrucción f; **at one's ~** a su disposición

dispose [dɪ'spouz] vi: **to ~ of** (unwanted goods) deshacerse de; (problem etc) resolver ❑ **disposed** adj: **disposed to do** dispuesto a hacer; **to be well-disposed towards sb** estar bien dispuesto hacia algn ❑ **disposition** [dɪspə'zɪʃən] n (nature) temperamento; (inclination) propensión f

disprove [dɪs'pruːv] vt refutar

dispute [dɪs'pjuːt] n disputa; (also: **industrial** or **labor ~**) conflicto (laboral) ♦ vt (argue) disputar, discutir; (question) cuestionar

disqualify [dɪs'kwɑːlɪfaɪ] vt (SPORT) descalificar; **to ~ sb for sth/from doing sth** incapacitar a algn para algo/hacer algo

disquiet [dɪs'kwaɪət] n preocupación f, inquietud f

disregard [dɪsrɪ'gɑːrd] vt (ignore) no hacer caso de

disrepair [dɪsrɪ'peər] n: **to fall into ~** (building) desmoronarse

disreputable [dɪs'repjutəbəl] adj (person) de mala fama; (behavior) vergonzoso

disrespect [dɪsrɪ'spekt] n falta de respeto ❑ **disrespectful** adj irrespetuoso

disrupt [dɪs'rʌpt] vt (plans) desbaratar, trastornar; (conversation) interrumpir

dissatisfaction [dɪssætɪs'fækʃən] n disgusto, descontento

dissatisfied [dɪs'sætɪsfaɪd] adj descontento

dissect [dɪ'sekt] vt disecar

dissent [dɪ'sent] n disensión f

dissertation [dɪsər'teɪʃən] n tesina

disservice [dɪs'sɜːrvɪs] n: **to do sb a ~** perjudicar a algn

dissimilar [dɪs'sɪmɪlər] adj distinto

dissipate ['dɪsɪpeɪt] vt disipar; (waste) desperdiciar

dissolve [dɪ'zɑːlv] vt disolver ♦ vi disolverse; **to ~ in(to) tears** deshacerse en lágrimas

dissuade [dɪ'sweɪd] vt: **to ~ sb (from)** disuadir a algn (de)

distance ['dɪstəns] n distancia; **in the ~** a lo lejos

distant ['dɪstənt] adj lejano; (manner) reservado, frío

distaste [dɪs'teɪst] n repugnancia
□ **distasteful** adj repugnante, desagradable

distended [dɪs'tendɪd] adj (stomach) hinchado

distill (US) [dɪs'tɪl] (BRIT **distil**) vt destilar
□ **distillery** n destilería

distinct [dɪs'tɪŋkt] adj (different) distinto; (clear) claro; (unmistakeable) inequívoco; **as ~ from** a diferencia de □ **distinction** n distinción f; (honor) honor m; (in exam) sobresaliente m □ **distinctive** adj distintivo

distinguish [dɪs'tɪŋgwɪʃ] vt distinguir; **to ~ o.s.** destacarse □ **distinguished** adj (eminent) distinguido □ **distinguishing** adj (feature) distintivo

distort [dɪs'tɔːrt] vt distorsionar; (shape, image) deformar □ **distortion** n distorsión f; deformación f

distract [dɪs'trækt] vt distraer □ **distracted** adj distraído □ **distraction** n distracción f; (confusion) aturdimiento

distraught [dɪs'trɔːt] adj loco de inquietud

distress [dɪs'tres] n (anguish) angustia, aflicción f ♦ vt afligir □ **distressing** adj angustioso; doloroso □ **distress signal** n señal f de socorro

distribute [dɪs'trɪbjuːt] vt distribuir; (share out) repartir □ **distribution** [dɪstrɪ'bjuːʃən] n distribución f, reparto □ **distributor** n (AUT) distribuidor m; (COMM) distribuidora

district ['dɪstrɪkt] n (of country) zona, región f; (of town) barrio; (ADMIN) distrito □ **district attorney** (US) n fiscal mf □ **district nurse** (BRIT) n enfermera que atiende a pacientes a domicilio

distrust [dɪs'trʌst] n desconfianza ♦ vt desconfiar de

disturb [dɪs'tɜːrb] vt (person: bother, interrupt) molestar; (: upset) perturbar, inquietar; (disorganize) alterar □ **disturbance** n (upheaval) perturbación f; (political etc: gen pl) disturbio; (of mind) trastorno □ **disturbed** adj (worried, upset) preocupado, angustiado; **emotionally disturbed** trastornado; (childhood) inseguro □ **disturbing** adj inquietante, perturbador(a)

disuse [dɪs'juːs] n: **to fall into ~** caer en desuso

disused [dɪs'juːzd] adj abandonado

ditch [dɪtʃ] n zanja; (irrigation ditch) acequia ♦ vt (inf: partner) deshacerse de; (: plan, car etc) abandonar

dither ['dɪðər] (pej) vi vacilar

ditto ['dɪtou] adv ídem, lo mismo

divan [dɪ'væn] n diván m; (BRIT: also: ~ **bed**) cama turca

dive [daɪv] (pt, pp **~d** or **dove**) n (from board) salto; (underwater) buceo; (of submarine) sumersión f ♦ vi (swimmer: into water) saltar; (: under water) zambullirse, bucear; (fish, submarine) sumergirse; (bird) lanzarse en picado; **to ~ into** (bag etc) meter la mano en; (place) meterse de prisa en □ **diver** n (underwater) buzo

diverse [daɪ'vɜːrs] adj diversos(-as), varios(-as)

diversion [dɪ'vɜːrʃən] n (distraction, MIL) diversión f; (of funds) distracción f; (BRIT AUT) desviación f

divert [dɪ'vɜːrt] vt (turn aside) desviar

divide [dɪ'vaɪd] vt dividir; (separate) separar ♦ vi dividirse; (road) bifurcarse □ **divided highway** (US) n carretera de doble calzada

dividend ['dɪvɪdend] n dividendo; (fig): **to pay ~s** proporcionar beneficios

divine [dɪ'vaɪn] adj (also fig) divino

diving ['daɪvɪŋ] n (SPORT) salto; (underwater) buceo □ **diving board** n trampolín m

divinity [dɪ'vɪnɪti] n divinidad f; (SCOL) teología

division [dɪ'vɪʒən] n división f; (sharing out) reparto; (disagreement) diferencias fpl; (COMM) sección f

divorce [dɪ'vɔːrs] n divorcio ♦ vt divorciarse de □ **divorced** adj divorciado □ **divorcee** [dɪvɔːr'seɪ] n divorciado(-a)

divulge [daɪ'vʌldʒ] vt divulgar, revelar

D.I.Y. (BRIT) adj, n abbr = **do-it-yourself**

dizzy ['dɪzi] adj (spell) de mareo; **to feel ~** marearse

DJ n abbr = **disc** or **disk jockey**

do

KEYWORD

[du:] (pt **did**, pp **done**)

n (inf: party etc): **we're having a little do on Saturday** damos una fiestecita el sábado; **it was a grand do** fue un acontecimiento a lo grande

♦ aux vb

1 (in negative constructions: not translated) **I don't understand** no entiendo

2 (to form questions: not translated) **didn't you know?** ¿no lo sabías?; **what do you think?** ¿qué opinas?

3 (for emphasis, in polite expressions): **people do make mistakes sometimes** sí que se cometen errores a veces; **she does seem late** a mí también me parece que se ha retrasado; **do sit down/help yourself** siéntate/sírvete por favor; **do take care!** ¡ten cuidado(, te pido)!

4 (used to avoid repeating vb): **she sings better than I do** canta mejor que yo; **do you agree? -- yes, I do/no, I don't** ¿estás de acuerdo? -- sí (lo estoy)/no (lo estoy); **she lives in Chicago -- so do I** vivo en Chicago -- yo también; **he didn't like it and neither did we** no le gustó a nosotros tampoco; **who made this mess? -- I did** ¿quién hizo este desorden? -- yo; **he asked me to help him and I did** me pidió que le ayudara y lo hice

5 (in question tags): **you like him, don't you?** te gusta, ¿verdad? or ¿no?; **I don't know him, do I?** creo que no lo conozco

♦ vt

1 (gen, carry out, perform etc): **what are you doing tonight?** ¿qué haces esta noche?; **what can I do for you?** ¿en qué puedo servirle?; **to do the dishes/cooking** fregar los platos/cocinar; **to do one's teeth/hair/ nails** lavarse los dientes/arreglarse el pelo/ arreglarse las uñas

2 (AUT etc): **the car was doing 90** el carro iba a 90; **we've done 200 miles already** ya hemos hecho 200 millas; **he can do 100 in that car** puede ir a 100 en ese carro

♦ vi

1 (act, behave) hacer; **do as I do** haz como yo

2 (get on, fare): **he's doing well/badly at school** le va bien/mal en la escuela; **the firm is doing well** la empresa anda or va bien; **how do you do?** mucho gusto; (less formal) ¿qué tal?

3 (suit): **will it do?** ¿sirve?, ¿está or va bien?

4 (be sufficient) bastar; **will $20 do?** ¿será bastante con $20?; **that'll do** así está bien;

that'll do! (in annoyance) ¡ya está bien!, ¡basta ya!; **to make do (with)** arreglárselas (con)

▶ **do away with** vt fus (kill, disease) eliminar; (abolish law etc) abolir; (withdraw) retirar

▶ **do up** vt (laces) atar; (zip, dress, shirt) abrochar; (BRIT: renovate room, house) renovar

▶ **do with** vt fus (need): **I could do with a drink/some help** no me vendría mal un trago/un poco de ayuda; (be connected) tener que ver con; **what has it got to do with you?** ¿qué tiene que ver contigo?

▶ **do without** vi pasar sin; **if you're late for dinner then you'll do without** si llegas tarde tendrás que quedarte sin cenar

♦ vt arreglárselas sin; **I can do without a car** puedo arreglármelas sin carro (LAm) or coche (SP)

dock [dɑːk] n (NAUT) muelle m; (LAW) banquillo (de los acusados) ♦ vi (enter dock) atracar; (SPACE) acoplarse; **~s** npl (NAUT) muelles mpl, puerto sg ❏ **docker** (BRIT) n trabajador m portuario, estibador m ❏ **dockyard** n astillero

doctor ['dɑːktər] n médico(-a); (Ph.D. etc) doctor(a) m/f ♦ vt (drink etc) adulterar ❏ **Doctor of Philosophy** n Doctor en Filosofía y Letras ❏ **doctor's office** (US) n consultorio

document ['dɑːkjəmənt] n documento ❏ **documentary** [dɑːkjə'mentəri] adj documental ♦ n documental m

dodge [dɑːdʒ] n (fig) truco ♦ vt evadir; (blow) esquivar

Dodgem® ['dɑːdʒəm] (BRIT) n coche mpl de choque

doe [dou] n (deer) cierva, gama; (rabbit) coneja

does [dʌz] vb see **do**; **doesn't** = **does not**

dog [dɑːg] n perro ♦ vt seguir los pasos de; (bad luck) perseguir ❏ **dog collar** n collar m de perro; (of clergyman) alzacuellos m inv ❏ **dog-eared** adj sobado

dogged ['dɑːgɪd] adj tenaz, obstinado

doghouse ['dɑːghaus] (US) n caseta del perro

dogsbody ['dɑːgzbɑːdi] (BRIT: inf) n burro de carga

doings ['duːŋz] npl (activities) actividades fpl

do-it-yourself n hágalo usted mismo (MEX), bricolaje m (LAm exc MEX, SP)

doldrums ['douldrəmz] npl: **to be in the ~** (person) estar abatido; (business) estar estancado

dole [doul] (BRIT) n (payment) subsidio de desempleo; **on the ~** desempleado ▶ **dole out** vt repartir

doll [dɑːl] n muñeca; (US: inf: woman) muñeca, gachí f

dollar ['dɑːlər] n dólar m

dolled up (inf) adj arreglado

dolphin ['dɑːlfɪn] n delfín m

domain [dou'meɪn] n (fig) campo, competencia; (land) dominios mpl ❑ **domain name** n (INTERNET) nombre m de dominio

dome [doum] n (ARCH) cúpula

domestic [də'mestɪk] adj (animal, duty) doméstico; (flight, policy) nacional ❑ **domesticated** adj domesticado; (home-loving) casero, hogareño

dominate ['dɑːmɪneɪt] vt dominar

domineering [dɑːmɪ'nɪərɪŋ] adj dominante

dominion [də'mɪnjən] n dominio

domino ['dɑːmɪnou] (pl **-es**) n ficha de dominó ❑ **dominoes** n (game) dominó

don [dɑːn] (BRIT) n profesor(a) m/f universitario(-a)

donate ['douneɪt] vt donar ❑ **donation** [dou'neɪʃən] n donativo

done [dʌn] pp of **do**

donkey ['dɑːŋki] n burro

donor ['dounər] n donante mf ❑ **donor card** n tarjeta de donante

don't [dount] cont = **do not**

donut ['dounʌt] (US) n = **doughnut**

doodle ['duːdl] vi hacer dibujitos or garabatos

doom [duːm] n (fate) suerte f ♦ vt: **to be ~ed to failure** estar condenado al fracaso

door [dɔːr] n puerta ❑ **doorbell** n timbre m ❑ **door handle** n perilla (LAm), tirador m (SP); (of car) manija ❑ **doorman** n (in hotel) portero ❑ **doormat** n tapete m (MEX), felpudo (LAm exc MEX, SP) ❑ **doorstep** n peldaño ❑ **door-to-door** adj de puerta en puerta ❑ **doorway** n entrada, puerta

dope [doup] n (inf: illegal drug) droga; (: person) imbécil mf ♦ vt (horse etc) drogar

dork [dɔːrk] (US: inf) n pazguato(-a) (inf)

dorm [dɔːrm] (US: building) residencia de estudiantes; (BRIT: room) dormitorio (colectivo)

dormant ['dɔːrmənt] adj inactivo

dormitory ['dɔːrmɪtɔːri] n (building) residencia de estudiantes; (BRIT: room) dormitorio (colectivo)

dormouse ['dɔːrmaus] (pl **-mice**) n lirón m

DOS n abbr (= disk operating system) DOS m

dosage ['dousɪdʒ] n dosis f inv

dose [dous] n dosis f inv

doss house ['dɑːs‚haus] (BRIT: inf) n pensión f de mala muerte

dossier ['dɑːsɪeɪ] n expediente m, dosier m

dot [dɑːt] n punto ♦ vi: **~ted with** salpicado de; **on the ~** en punto

dotcom, dot.com ['dɑːt‚kɑːm] n puntocom f, punto.com f

double ['dʌbəl] adj doble ♦ adv (twice): **to cost ~** costar el doble ♦ n doble m ♦ vt doblar ♦ vi doblarse; **on the ~, at the ~** (BRIT) corriendo ❑ **double bass** n contrabajo ❑ **double bed** n cama de matrimonio ❑ **double bend** (BRIT) n (AUT) = **double curve** ❑ **double-breasted** adj cruzado ❑ **double-click** n (COMPUT) hacer doble clic ❑ **double-cross** vt (trick) engañar; (betray) traicionar ❑ **double curve** (US) n (AUT) curva en S ❑ **double-decker** (BRIT) n autobús m de dos pisos ❑ **double glazing** (BRIT) n doble acristalamiento ❑ **double room** n habitación f doble ❑ **doubles** n (TENNIS) juego de dobles ❑ **doubly** adv doblemente

doubt [daut] n duda ♦ vt dudar; (suspect) dudar de; **to ~ that** dudar que ❑ **doubtful** adj dudoso; (person): **to be doubtful about sth** tener dudas sobre algo ❑ **doubtless** adv sin duda

dough [dou] n masa, pasta ❑ **doughnut** (US **donut**) n dona (MEX), buñuelo (LAm exc MEX, SP), berlinesa (RPl)

dove¹ [dʌv] n paloma

dove² [douv] pt of **dive**

dovetail ['dʌvteɪl] vi (fig) encajar

dowdy ['daudi] adj (person) mal vestido; (clothes) pasado de moda

down [daun] n (feathers) plumón m, flojel m ♦ adv (downwards) abajo, hacia abajo; (on the ground) por o en tierra ♦ prep abajo ♦ vt (inf: drink) beberse; **~ with X!** ¡abajo X! ❑ **down-and-out** n vagabundo(-a) ❑ **down-at-heel** adj venido a menos; (appearance) desaliñado ❑ **downcast** adj abatido ❑ **downfall** n caída, ruina ❑ **downhearted** adj desanimado ❑ **downhill** adv: **to go downhill** (also fig) ir cuesta abajo ❑ **download** vt (COMPUT) bajar ❑ **down payment** n entrada, pago al contado ❑ **downpour** n aguacero ❑ **downright** adj (nonsense, lie) manifiesto; (refusal) terminante ❑ **downsize** vi (ECON: company) reducir la plantilla ❑ **downspout** (US) n tubo de desagüe

Down's syndrome ['daunz‚sɪndroum] n síndrome m de Down

down: ❑ **downstairs** adv (below) (en el piso de) abajo; (downwards) escaleras abajo

❑ **downstream** adv aguas or río abajo

❑ **down-to-earth** adj práctico

❑ **downtown** adv en el centro de la ciudad

❑ **down under** (BRIT) adv en Australia (or Nueva Zelanda) ❑ **downward** ['daʊnwəd] adj, adv hacia abajo ❑ **downwards** ['daʊnwədz] adv hacia abajo

dowry ['daʊrɪ] n dote f

doz. abbr = **dozen**

doze [dəʊz] vi dormitar ▶ **doze off** vi quedarse medio dormido

dozen ['dʌzən] n docena; **a ~ books** una docena de libros; **~s of** cantidad de

Dr. abbr = **doctor; drive**

drab [dræb] adj gris, monótono

draft [dræft] n (first copy) borrador m; (POL: of bill) anteproyecto; (US: call-up) quinta; (US: of air) corriente f de aire; (US NAUT) calado ♦ vt (plan) preparar; (write roughly) hacer un borrador de; (US MIL conscript) reclutar, llamar al servicio militar; **~ beer** cerveza de barril ❑ **draft dodger** n prófugo m

draftsman (US) ['dræftsmən] (BRIT **draughtsman**) n delineante mf

drag [dræg] vt arrastrar; (river) dragar, rastrear ♦ vi (time) pasar despacio; (play, movie etc) hacerse pesado ♦ n (inf) lata; (women's clothing): **in ~** vestido de travesti; **~ and drop** vt (COMPUT) arrastrar y soltar ▶ **drag on** vi ser interminable

dragonfly ['drægənflaɪ] n libélula

drain [dreɪn] n desaguadero; (in street) sumidero; (source of loss): **to be a ~ on** consumir, agotar ♦ vt (land, marshes) desaguar; (reservoir) desecar; (vegetables) escurrir ♦ vi escurrirse ❑ **drainage** n (act) desagüe m; (MED, AGR) drenaje m; (sewage) alcantarillado ❑ **drainboard** (US) (BRIT **draining board**) n escurridero (LAm), escurreplatos m inv (SP) ❑ **drainpipe** n tubo de desagüe

drama ['drɑːmə] n (art) teatro; (play) obra dramática; (excitement) emoción f ❑ **dramatic** [drə'mætɪk] adj dramático; (sudden, marked) espectacular ❑ **dramatist** n dramaturgo(-a) ❑ **dramatize** vt (events) dramatizar

drank [dræŋk] pt of **drink**

drape [dreɪp] vt (cloth) colocar; (flag) colgar; **~s** npl (US) cortinas fpl

drastic ['dræstɪk] adj (measure) severo; (change) radical, drástico

draught [drɑːft] (BRIT) n = **draft** ❑ **draughtboard** (BRIT) n tablero de damas ❑ **draughts** (BRIT) n (game) juego de damas

draughtsman ['drɑːftsmən] (BRIT: irreg) n = **draftsman**

draw [drɔː] (pt **drew**, pp **~n**) vt (picture) dibujar; (cart) tirar de; (curtain) correr; (take out) sacar; (attract) atraer; (money) retirar; (wages) cobrar ♦ vi (SPORT) empatar ♦ n (SPORT) empate m; (lottery) sorteo ▶ **draw near** vi acercarse ▶ **draw out** vi (lengthen) alargarse ♦ vt sacar ▶ **draw up** vi (stop) pararse ♦ vt (chair) acercar; (document) redactar ❑ **drawback** n inconveniente m, desventaja ❑ **drawbridge** n puente m levadizo

drawer [drɔː] n cajón m

drawing ['drɔːɪŋ] n dibujo ❑ **drawing board** n tablero (de dibujante) ❑ **drawing pin** (BRIT) n chinche f (LAm), chincheta (SP) ❑ **drawing room** n salón m

drawl [drɔːl] n habla lenta y cansina

drawn [drɔːn] pp of **draw**

dread [dred] n pavor m, terror m ♦ vt temer, tener miedo or pavor a ❑ **dreadful** adj horroroso

dream [driːm] (pt, pp **~ed** or **dreamt** [dremt]) n sueño ♦ vt, vi soñar ❑ **dreamy** adj (distracted) soñador(a), distraído; (music) suave

dreary ['drɪərɪ] adj monótono

dredge [dredʒ] vt dragar

dregs [dregz] npl posos mpl; (of humanity) hez f

drench [drentʃ] vt empapar

dress [dres] n vestido; (clothing) ropa ♦ vt vestir; (wound) vendar ♦ vi vestirse; **to get ~ed** vestirse ▶ **dress up** vi vestirse de etiqueta; (in costumes) disfrazarse ❑ **dress circle** (BRIT) n principal m ❑ **dresser** n (furniture) aparador m; (: US) cómoda (con espejo) ❑ **dressing** n (MED) vendaje m; (CULIN) aliño ❑ **dressing gown** (BRIT) n bata ❑ **dressing room** n (THEATER) camarín m; (US SPORT, in store) vestuario ❑ **dressing table** n tocador m ❑ **dressmaker** n modista, costurera ❑ **dress rehearsal** n ensayo general

drew [druː] pt of **draw**

dribble ['drɪbəl] vi (baby) babear ♦ vt (ball) regatear

dried [draɪd] adj (fruit) seco; (milk) en polvo

drier ['draɪər] n = **dryer**

drift [drɪft] n (of current etc) flujo; (of snow) ventisquero; (meaning) significado ♦ vi (boat) ir a la deriva; (sand, snow) amontonarse ❑ **driftwood** n madera de deriva

drill [drɪl] n (drill bit) broca; (for wood, metal) taladro; (of dentist) fresa; (for mining etc) perforadora, barrena; (MIL) instrucción f ♦ vt perforar, taladrar; (*troops*) enseñar la instrucción a ♦ *vi* (*for oil*) perforar

drink [drɪŋk] (*pt* **drank**, *pp* **drunk**) *n* bebida; (*sip*) trago ♦ *vt, vi* beber; **to have a ~** tomar algo; tomar una copa *or* un trago; **a ~ of water** un trago de agua ❑ **drinker** *n* bebedor(a) *m/f* ❑ **drinking water** *n* agua potable

drip [drɪp] *n* (*act*) goteo; (*one drip*) gota; (*MED*) gota a gota *m* ♦ *vi* gotear ❑ **drip-dry** *adj* (*shirt*) inarrugable ❑ **dripping** *n* (*animal fat*) pringue *m*

drive [draɪv] (*pt* **drove**, *pp* **~n**) *n* (*journey*) viaje *m* (en automóvil); (*also*: **~way**) entrada; (*energy*) energía, vigor *m*; (*COMPUT: also*: **disk ~**) drive *m* ♦ *vt* (*car*) manejar (*LAm*), conducir (*SP*); (*nail*) clavar; (*push*) empujar; (*TECH: motor*) impulsar ♦ *vi* (*AUT: at controls*) manejar (*LAm*), conducir (*SP*); (*: travel*) pasearse en carro (*LAm*) *or* coche (*SP*); **left-/right-hand ~** conducción *f* a la izquierda/derecha; **to ~ sb mad** volver loco a algn

drivel ['drɪvəl] (*inf*) *n* tonterías *fpl*

driven ['drɪvən] *pp of* **drive**

driver ['draɪvər] *n* chofer *mf* (*LAm*), conductor(a) *m/f* (*SP*); (*of taxi, bus*) chofer *mf* (*LAm*), chófer *mf* (*SP*) ❑ **driver's license** (*US*) *n* licencia de manejo (*LAm*), carnet *m* de conducir (*SP*)

driveway ['draɪvweɪ] *n* entrada

driving ['draɪvɪŋ] *n* el manejar (*LAm*), el conducir (*SP*) ❑ **driving instructor** *n* instructor(a) *m/f* de manejo (*LAm*), profesor(a) *m/f* de autoescuela (*SP*) ❑ **driving lesson** *n* clase *f* de manejar (*LAm*) *or* conducir (*SP*) ❑ **driving licence** (*BRIT*) *n* licencia de manejo (*LAm*), carnet *m* de conducir (*SP*) ❑ **driving school** *n* escuela de manejo (*MEX*) *or* choferes (*LAm*), autoescuela (*SP*) ❑ **driving test** *n* examen *m* de manejar (*LAm*) *or* conducir (*SP*)

drizzle ['drɪzəl] *n* llovizna

drool [dru:l] *vi* babear

droop [dru:p] *vi* (*flower*) marchitarse; (*shoulders*) encorvarse; (*head*) inclinarse

drop [drɑːp] *n* (*of water*) gota; (*lessening*) baja; (*fall*) caída ♦ *vt* dejar caer; (*voice, eyes, price*) bajar; (*passenger*) dejar; (*omit*) omitir ♦ *vi* (*object*) caer; (*wind*) amainar; **~s** *npl* (*MED*) gotas *fpl* ▶ **drop off** *vi* (*sleep*) dormirse ♦ *vt* (*passenger*) dejar ▶ **drop out** *vi* (*withdraw*) retirarse ❑ **drop-out** *n* marginado(-a); (*SCOL*) *estudiante que abandona los estudios* ❑ **dropper** *n* cuentagotas *m inv* ❑ **droppings** *npl* excremento

drought [draut] *n* sequía

drove [drouv] *pt of* **drive**

drown [draun] *vt* ahogar ♦ *vi* ahogarse

drowsy ['drauzi] *adj* soñoliento; **to be ~** tener sueño

drug [drʌg] *n* medicamento; (*narcotic*) droga ♦ *vt* drogar; **to be on ~s** drogarse ❑ **drug addict** *n* drogadicto(-a) ❑ **druggist** (*US*) *n* farmacéutico(-a) ❑ **drugstore** (*US*) *n* farmacia

drum [drʌm] *n* tambor *m*; (*for oil, petrol*) bidón *m*; **~s** *npl* batería ❑ **drummer** *n* baterista *mf* (*LAm*), batería *mf* (*SP*)

drunk [drʌŋk] *pp of* **drink** ♦ *adj* borracho ♦ *n* (*also*: **~ard**) borracho(-a) ❑ **drunken** *adj* borracho; (*laughter, party*) de borrachos

dry [draɪ] *adj* seco; (*day*) sin lluvia; (*climate*) árido, seco ♦ *vt* secar; (*tears*) enjugarse ♦ *vi* secarse ▶ **dry up** *vi* (*river*) secarse ❑ **dry-cleaner's** *n* tintorería ❑ **dry-cleaning** *n* lavado en seco ❑ **dryer** *n* (*for hair*) secador *m*; (*US: for clothes*) secadora ❑ **dry goods** (*US*) *npl* artículos *mpl* de confección ❑ **dry rot** (*BRIT*) *n* putrefacción *f* de la madera (*por un hongo*)

DSS (*BRIT*) *n abbr* = **Department of Social Security**

DTP *n abbr* (= *desk-top publishing*) autoedición *f*

dual ['duəl] *adj* doble ❑ **dual carriageway** (*BRIT*) *n* carretera de doble calzada ❑ **dual-purpose** *adj* de doble uso

dubbed [dʌbd] *adj* (*FILM*) doblado

dubious ['du:biəs] *adj* indeciso; (*reputation, company*) sospechoso

duchess ['dʌtʃɪs] *n* duquesa

duck [dʌk] *n* pato ♦ *vi* agacharse ❑ **duckling** *n* patito

duct [dʌkt] *n* conducto, canal *m*

dud [dʌd] *n* (*object, tool*) engaño, engañifa ♦ *adj* (*check*) sin fondos; (*merchandise*) de mala calidad, chafa (*MEX*); (*shell, bomb*) que no estalla

dude [du:d] (*US: inf*) *n* tipo (*inf*)

due [du:] *adj* (*owed*): **he is ~ $50** se le deben 50 dólares; (*expected: event*): **the meeting is ~ on Wednesday** la reunión tendrá lugar el miércoles; (*: arrival*): **the train is ~ at 8am** el tren tiene su llegada para las 8; (*proper*) debido ♦ *n*: **to give sb his** (*or* **her**) **~** ser justo con algn ♦ *adv*: **~ north** derecho al norte; **~s** *npl* (*for club, union*) cuota; (*in harbor*) derechos *mpl*; **in ~ course** a su debido tiempo; **~ to** debido a; **to be ~ to** deberse a

duet [du:ɛt] *n* dúo

duffel bag ['dʌfəl-] *n* bolsa de lona

duffel coat ['dʌfəl-] *n* trenca, abrigo de tres cuartos

dug [dʌg] *pt, pp of* **dig**

duke [duːk] *n* duque *m*

dull [dʌl] *adj (light)* débil; *(stupid)* torpe; *(boring)* pesado; *(sound, pain)* sordo; *(weather, day)* gris ♦ *vt (pain, grief)* aliviar; *(mind, senses)* entorpecer

duly ['duːli] *adv* debidamente; *(on time)* a su debido tiempo

dumb [dʌm] *adj* mudo; *(US: pej: stupid)* estúpido ❑ **dumbfounded** ['dʌm'faundɪd] *adj* pasmado

dummy ['dʌmi] *n (tailor's dummy)* maniquí *m*; *(mock-up)* maqueta; *(BRIT: for baby)* chupón *m (LAm)*, chupete *m (SC, SP)* ♦ *adj* falso, postizo

dump [dʌmp] *n (US: also:* **garbage ~**; *BRIT: also:* **rubbish ~**) basurero, vertedero; *(inf: place)* cuchitril *m* ♦ *vt (put down)* dejar; *(get rid of)* deshacerse de; *(COMPUT: data)* transferir

dumpling ['dʌmplɪŋ] *n* bola de masa hervida

dumpster ['dʌmpstər] *(US) n* contenedor *m* de basura

dumpy ['dʌmpi] *adj* regordete(-a)

dunce [dʌns] *n* zopenco

dung [dʌŋ] *n* estiércol *m*

dungarees [dʌŋgə'riːz] *npl (for work)* overol *m (LAm)*, mameluco *(SC)*, peto *(SP)*; *(casual wear)* pantalón *m* de peto; *(US: jeans)* bluejeans *m (LAm)*, vaqueros *mpl (SP)*

dungeon ['dʌndʒən] *n* calabozo

duplex ['duːplɛks] *(US) n* dúplex *m*

duplicate [*n* 'duːplɪkət, *vb* 'duːplɪkeɪt] *n* duplicado ♦ *vt* duplicar; *(photocopy)* fotocopiar; *(repeat)* repetir; **in ~** por duplicado

durable ['duərəbəl] *adj* duradero

duration [du'reɪʃən] *n* duración *f*

during ['duərɪŋ] *prep* durante

dusk [dʌsk] *n* crepúsculo, anochecer *m*

dust [dʌst] *n* polvo ♦ *vt* sacudir *(MEX)*, quitar el polvo a *(LAm exc MEX, SP)*; *(cake etc)*: **to ~ with** espolvorear de ❑ **dustbin** *(BRIT) n* cubo o bote *m (MEX)* or tacho *(SC)* de la basura ❑ **duster** *n* paño, trapo ❑ **dustman** *(BRIT) n* basurero ❑ **dusty** *adj* polvoriento

Dutch [dʌtʃ] *adj* holandés(-esa) ♦ *n (LING)* holandés *m*; **the ~** *npl* los holandeses; **to go ~** *(inf)* pagar a escote, pagar cada uno lo suyo ❑ **Dutchman/woman** *n* holandés(-esa) *m/f*

duty ['duːti] *n* deber *m*; *(tax)* derechos *mpl* de aduana; **on ~** de servicio; *(at night etc)* de guardia; **off ~** libre (de servicio) ❑ **duty-free** *adj* libre de impuestos

duvet [duː'veɪ] *(BRIT) n* edredón *m*

DVD *n abbr (= digital versatile or video disc)* DVD *m*

dwarf [dwɔːrf] *(pl* **dwarves**) *n* enano(-a) ♦ *vt* empequeñecer

dwell [dwɛl] *(pt, pp* **dwelt**) *vi* morar ▸ **dwell on** *vt fus* explayarse en

dwindle ['dwɪndl] *vi* disminuir

dye [daɪ] *n* tinte *m* ♦ *vt* teñir

dying ['daɪɪŋ] *adj* moribundo

dyke [daɪk] *(BRIT) n* = **dike**

dynamic [daɪ'næmɪk] *adj* dinámico

dynamite ['daɪnəmaɪt] *n* dinamita

dynamo ['daɪnəmou] *n* dínamo *(LAm)*, dínamo *f (SP)*

dynasty ['daɪnəsti] *n* dinastía

Ee

E [iː] *n (MUS)* mi *m*

each [iːtʃ] *adj* cada *inv* ♦ *pron* cada uno; **~ other** el uno al otro; **they hate ~ other** se odian (entre ellos o mutuamente); **they have 2 books ~** tienen 2 libros por persona

eager ['iːgər] *adj (enthusiastic)* entusiasmado; **to be ~ to do sth** tener muchas ganas de hacer algo, impacientarse por hacer algo; **to be ~ for** tener muchas ganas de

eagle ['iːgəl] *n* águila

ear [ɪər] *n* oreja; oído; *(of corn)* espiga ❑ **earache** *n* dolor *m* de oídos ❑ **eardrum** *n* tímpano

earl [ɜːrl] *n* conde *m*

earlier ['ɜːrliər] *adj* anterior ♦ *adv* antes

early ['ɜːrli] *adv* temprano; *(before time)* con tiempo, con anticipación ♦ *adj* temprano; *(settlers etc)* primitivo; *(death, departure)* prematuro; *(reply)* pronto; **to have an ~ night** acostarse temprano; **in the ~** *or* **~ in the spring/19th century** a principios de primavera/del siglo diecinueve ❑ **early retirement** *n* jubilación *f* anticipada

earmark ['ɪər‚mɑːrk] *vt*: **to ~ (for)** reservar (para), destinar (a)

earn [ɜːrn] *vt (salary)* percibir; *(interest)* devengar; *(praise)* merecerse

earnest ['ɜːrnɪst] *adj (wish)* fervoroso; *(person)* serio, formal; **in ~** en serio

earnings ['ɜːrnɪŋz] *npl (personal)* sueldo, ingresos *mpl*; *(company)* ganancias *fpl*

ear: ❑ **earphones** *npl* auriculares *mpl* ❑ **earring** *n* pendiente *m*, arete *m (MEX)*, aro

(SC) ❑ **earshot** n: **within earshot** al alcance del oído

earth [ɜ:rθ] n tierra; (BRIT ELEC) cable m de toma de tierra ♦ vt (BRIT ELEC) conectar a tierra
❑ **earthenware** n loza (de barro)
❑ **earthquake** n terremoto
❑ **earthworm** n lombriz f ❑ **earthy** adj (fig: vulgar) grosero

ease [i:z] n facilidad f; (comfort) comodidad f ♦ vt (lessen: problem) mitigar; (: pain) aliviar; (: tension) reducir; **to ~ sth in/out** meter/sacar algo con cuidado; **at ~!** (MIL) ¡descansen! ▸ **ease off** or **up** vi (wind, rain) amainar; (slow down) aflojar la marcha

easel ['i:zəl] n caballete m

easily ['i:zɪlɪ] adv fácilmente

east [i:st] n este m ♦ adj del este, oriental; (wind) del este ♦ adv al este, hacia el este; **the E~** el Oriente; (POL) los países del Este

Easter ['i:stər] n Pascua (de Resurrección)
❑ **Easter egg** n huevo de Pascua

east: ❑ **easterly** adj (to the east) al este; (from the east) del este ❑ **eastern** adj del este, oriental; (oriental) oriental
❑ **eastward(s)** ['i:stwərd(z)] adv hacia el este

easy ['i:zɪ] adj fácil; (simple) sencillo; (comfortable) holgado, cómodo; (relaxed) tranquilo ♦ adv: **to take it** or **things ~** (not worry) tomarlo con calma; (rest) descansar
❑ **easy chair** n sillón m ❑ **easy-going** adj acomodadizo

eat [i:t] (pt **ate**, pp **~en**) vt comer ▸ **eat away at** vt fus corroer; mermar ▸ **eat into** vt fus corroer; (savings) mermar ❑ **eatery** (US: inf) n restaurante m

eaves [i:vz] npl alero

eavesdrop ['i:vzdrɑːp] vi: **to ~ (on)** escuchar a escondidas

ebb [ɛb] n reflujo ♦ vi bajar; (fig: also: ~ **away**) decaer

ebony ['ɛbənɪ] n ébano

e-book ['i:buk] n libro electrónico

e-business ['i:ˌbɪznɪs] n (company) negocio electrónico; (commerce) comercio electrónico

EC n abbr (= European Community) CE f

ECB n abbr (= European Central Bank) BCE m

eccentric [ɪk'sɛntrɪk] adj, n excéntrico(-a)

echo ['ɛkoʊ] (pl **~es**) n eco m ♦ vt (sound) repetir ♦ vi resonar, hacer eco

éclair [er'klɛər] n pastelillo relleno de crema y con chocolate por encima

eclipse [ɪ'klɪps] n eclipse m

ecology [ɪ'kɑːlədʒɪ] n ecología

e-commerce ['i:'kɑːmərs] n comercio electrónico, comercio E

economic [ˌi:kə'nɑːmɪk] adj económico; (business etc) rentable ❑ **economical** adj económico ❑ **economics** n (SCOL) economía ♦ npl (of project etc) rentabilidad f

economize [ɪ'kɑːnəmaɪz] vi economizar, ahorrar

economy [ɪ'kɑːnəmɪ] n economía
❑ **economy class** n (AVIAT) clase f económica ❑ **economy size** n tamaño económico

ecstasy ['ɛkstəsɪ] n éxtasis m inv; (drug) éxtasis m inv ❑ **ecstatic** [ɛks'tætɪk] adj extático

ECU [er'ku:] n abbr (= European Currency Unit) ECU m

Ecuador ['ɛkwədɔːr] n Ecuador m
❑ **Ecuadorian** adj, n ecuatoriano(-a)

eczema ['ɛksɪmə] n eczema m

edge [ɛdʒ] n (of knife) filo; (of object) borde m; (of lake) orilla ♦ vt (SEWING) ribetear; **on ~** (fig) = **edgy**; **to ~ away from** alejarse poco a poco de ❑ **edgeways** adv: **he couldn't get a word in edgeways** no pudo meter baza

edgy ['ɛdʒɪ] adj nervioso, inquieto

edible ['ɛdɪbl] adj comestible

Edinburgh ['ɛdnbərə] n Edimburgo

edit ['ɛdɪt] vt (be editor of) dirigir; (text, report) corregir, preparar ❑ **edition** [ɪ'dɪʃən] n edición f ❑ **editor** n (of newspaper) director(a) m/f; (of column): **foreign/political editor** encargado de la sección de extranjero/política; (of book) redactor(a) m/f ❑ **editorial** [ɛdɪ'tɔːrɪəl] adj editorial ♦ n editorial m

educate ['ɛdʒəkeɪt] vt (gen) educar; (instruct) instruir

education [ɛdʒə'keɪʃən] n educación f; (schooling) enseñanza; (SCOL) pedagogía
❑ **educational** adj (policy etc) educacional; (experience) docente; (toy) educativo

EEC n abbr (= European Economic Community) CEE f

eel [i:l] n anguila

eerie ['ɪərɪ] adj misterioso

effect [ɪ'fɛkt] n efecto ♦ vt efectuar, llevar a cabo; **to take ~** (law) entrar en vigor or vigencia; (drug) surtir efecto; **in ~** en realidad ❑ **effective** adj eficaz; (actual) verdadero ❑ **effectively** adv eficazmente; (in reality) efectivamente ❑ **effectiveness** n eficacia

effeminate [ɪ'fɛmɪnɪt] adj afeminado

efficiency [ɪ'fɪʃənsɪ] n eficiencia; rendimiento

efficient [ɪ'fɪʃənt] adj eficiente; (machine) de buen rendimiento

effort ['ɛfərt] n esfuerzo ❑ **effortless** adj sin ningún esfuerzo; (style) natural

effusive [ɪ'fju:sɪv] adj efusivo

e.g. adv abbr (= exempli gratia) p. ej.

egg [ɛg] n huevo; **hard-boiled/soft-boiled ~** huevo duro/tibio (MEX) or pasado por agua (LAm exc MEX, SP) or a la copa (SC) ▶ **egg on** vt incitar ❑ **eggcup** n huevera ❑ **eggplant** (US) n berenjena ❑ **eggshell** n cáscara de huevo

ego ['i:gou] n ego ❑ **egotism** n egoísmo ❑ **egotist** n egoísta mf

Egypt ['i:dʒɪpt] n Egipto ❑ **Egyptian** [i'dʒɪpʃən] adj, n egipcio(-a)

eiderdown ['aɪdər‚daun] n edredón m

eight [eɪt] num ocho ❑ **eighteen** num dieciocho ❑ **eighth** [eɪtθ] num octavo ❑ **eighty** num ochenta

Eire ['ɛərə] n Eire m

either ['i:ðər] adj cualquiera de los dos; (both, each) cada ♦ pron: ~ **(of them)** cualquiera (de los dos) ♦ adv tampoco ♦ conj: ~ **yes or no** o sí o no; **on ~ side** en ambos lados; **I don't like ~** no me gusta ninguno(-a) de los (las) dos; **no, I don't ~** no, yo tampoco

eject [ɪ'dʒɛkt] vt echar, expulsar; (tenant) desahuciar ❑ **ejector seat** n asiento proyectable

elaborate [adj ɪ'læbərɪt, vb ɪ'læbəreɪt] adj (complex) complejo ♦ vt (expand) ampliar; (refine) refinar ♦ vi explicar con más detalles

elastic [ɪ'læstɪk] n elástico ♦ adj elástico; (fig) flexible ❑ **elastic band** (BRIT) n gomita

elated [ɪ'leɪtɪd] adj: **to be ~** regocijarse

elbow ['ɛlbou] n codo

elder ['ɛldər] adj mayor ♦ n (tree) saúco, sabuco; (person) mayor ❑ **elderly** adj de edad, mayor ♦ npl: **the elderly** los mayores

eldest ['ɛldɪst] adj, n el (la) mayor

elect [ɪ'lɛkt] vt elegir ♦ adj: **the president ~** el presidente electo; **to ~ to do** optar por hacer ❑ **election** n elección f ❑ **electioneering** [ɪlɛkʃə'nɪərɪŋ] n campaña electoral ❑ **elective** adj (course) optativo; (assembly) electivo ♦ n (US SCOL) (asignatura) optativa ❑ **elector** n elector(a) m/f ❑ **electoral** adj electoral ❑ **electoral college** n colegio electoral ❑ **electorate** n electorado

electric [ɪ'lɛktrɪk] adj eléctrico ❑ **electrical** adj eléctrico ❑ **electric blanket** n manta eléctrica ❑ **electric fire** n estufa eléctrica ❑ **electrician** [ɪlɛk'trɪʃən] n electricista mf ❑ **electricity** [ɪlɛk'trɪsəti] n electricidad f

electrify [ɪ'lɛktrɪfaɪ] vt (with electricity) electrificar; (fig: audience) electrizar

electronic [ɪlɛk'trɑːnɪk] adj electrónico ❑ **electronic mail** n correo electrónico ❑ **electronics** n electrónica

elegant ['ɛlɪgənt] adj elegante

element ['ɛlɪmənt] n elemento; (ELEC) resistencia ❑ **elementary** [ɛlɪ'mɛntəri] adj elemental; (primitive) rudimentario ❑ **elementary school** (US) n centro de (enseñanza) primaria

elephant ['ɛlɪfənt] n elefante m

elevation [ɛlɪ'veɪʃən] n elevación f; (height) altura

elevator ['ɛlɪveɪtər] n (US) ascensor m, elevador m (MEX); (in warehouse etc) montacargas m inv

eleven [ɪ'lɛvən] num once ❑ **elevenses** (BRIT) npl café m de las once ❑ **eleventh** num undécimo

elicit [ɪ'lɪsɪt] vt: **to ~ (from)** sacar (de)

eligible ['ɛlɪdʒəbəl] adj: **an ~ young man/ woman** un buen partido; **to be ~ for sth** llenar los requisitos para algo

elm [ɛlm] n olmo

elongated ['i:lɔːŋgeɪtɪd] adj alargado

elope [ɪ'loup] vi fugarse (para casarse)

eloquent ['ɛləkwənt] adj elocuente

else [ɛls] adv: **something ~** otra cosa; **somewhere ~** en otra parte; **everywhere ~** en todas partes menos aquí; **where ~?** ¿dónde más?, ¿en qué otra parte?; **there was little ~ to do** apenas quedaba otra cosa que hacer; **nobody ~ spoke** no habló nadie más ❑ **elsewhere** adv (be) en otra parte; (go) a otra parte

elude [ɪ'lu:d] vt (idea etc) escaparse a; (capture) esquivar

elusive [ɪ'lu:sɪv] adj esquivo; (quality) difícil de encontrar

emaciated [ɪ'meɪʃieɪtɪd] adj demacrado

email, e-mail ['i:meɪl] n abbr (= electronic mail) correo electrónico, e-mail m ❑ **email address** n dirección f electrónica, email m

emancipate [ɪ'mænsɪpeɪt] vt emancipar

embankment [ɪm'bæŋkmənt] n terraplén m

embark [ɛm'bɑːrk] vi embarcarse ♦ vt embarcar; **to ~ on** (journey) emprender; (course of action) lanzarse a ❑ **embarkation** [ɛmbɑːr'keɪʃən] n (of people) embarco; (of goods) embarque m

embarrass [ɛm'bærəs] vt avergonzar; (government etc) dejar en mal lugar ❑ **embarrassed** adj (laugh, silence) embarazoso ❑ **embarrassing** adj (situation) violento; (question) embarazoso

❑ **embarrassment** n (shame) vergüenza; (problem): **to be an embarrassment for sb** poner en un aprieto a algn

⚠ Be careful not to translate **embarrassed** by the Spanish word **embarazada**.

embassy ['ɛmbəsɪ] n embajada

embedded [ɛm'bɛdɪd] adj (object) empotrado; (thorn etc) clavado

embellish [ɛm'bɛlɪʃ] vt embellecer; (story) adornar

embers ['ɛmbərz] npl brasa, ascua

embezzle [ɛm'bɛzəl] vt desfalcar, malversar

embitter [ɛm'bɪtər] vt (fig: sour) amargar

embody [ɛm'bɑːdɪ] vt (spirit) encarnar; (include) incorporar

embossed [ɛm'bɑːst] adj realzado

embrace [ɛm'breɪs] vt abrazar, dar un abrazo a; (include) abarcar ♦ vi abrazarse ♦ n abrazo

embroider [ɛm'brɔɪdər] vt bordar ❑ **embroidery** n bordado

embryo ['ɛmbrɪəʊ] n embrión m

emcee ['ɛm'siː] (US) n presentador(a) m/f

emerald ['ɛmərəld] n esmeralda

emerge [ɪ'mɜːrdʒ] vi salir; (arise) surgir

emergency [ɪ'mɜːrdʒənsɪ] n crisis f inv; **in an ~** en caso de urgencia; **state of ~** estado de emergencia ❑ **emergency brake** (US) n freno de mano ❑ **emergency cord** (US) n alarma (en tren) ❑ **emergency exit** n salida de emergencia ❑ **emergency landing** n aterrizaje m forzoso ❑ **emergency room** (US) n sala de urgencias ❑ **emergency services** npl (fire, police, ambulance) servicios mpl de urgencia or emergencia

emery board ['ɛmərɪˌbɔːrd] n lima de uñas

emigrate ['ɛmɪɡreɪt] vi emigrar

emissions [ɪ'mɪʃənz] npl emisión f

emit [ɪ'mɪt] vt emitir; (smoke) arrojar; (smell) despedir; (sound) producir

emotion [ɪ'məʊʃən] n emoción f ❑ **emotional** adj (needs) emocional; (person) sentimental; (scene) conmovedor(a), emocionante; (speech) emocionado

emperor ['ɛmpərər] n emperador m

emphasis ['ɛmfəsɪs] (pl **-ses**) n énfasis m inv

emphasize ['ɛmfəsaɪz] vt (word, point) subrayar, recalcar; (feature) hacer resaltar

emphatic [ɛm'fætɪk] adj (reply) categórico; (person) insistente

empire ['ɛmpaɪər] n imperio

employ [ɪm'plɔɪ] vt emplear ❑ **employee** n empleado(-a) ❑ **employer** n patrón(-ona) m/f; empresario(-a) ❑ **employment** n

(work) trabajo ❑ **employment agency** n agencia de colocaciones

empower [ɛm'paʊər] vt: **to ~ sb to do sth** autorizar a algn para hacer algo

empress ['ɛmprɪs] n emperatriz f

emptiness ['ɛmptɪnɪs] n vacío m; (of life etc) vaciedad f

empty ['ɛmptɪ] adj vacío; (place) desierto; (house) desocupado; (threat) vano ♦ vt vaciar; (place) dejar vacío ♦ vi vaciarse; (house etc) quedar desocupado ❑ **empty-handed** adj con las manos vacías

EMU n abbr (= European Monetary Union) UME f

emulate ['ɛmjʊleɪt] vt emular

emulsion [ɪ'mʌlʃən] n emulsión f; (also: ~ **paint**) pintura emulsión

enable [ɛ'neɪbəl] vt: **to ~ sb to do sth** permitir a algn hacer algo

enamel [ɪ'næməl] n esmalte m; (also: ~ **paint**) pintura esmaltada

enchant [ɛn'tʃænt] vt encantar ❑ **enchanting** adj encantador(a)

encl. abbr (= enclosed) adj.

enclose [ɛn'kləʊz] vt (land) cercar; (letter etc) adjuntar; **please find ~d** le mandamos adjunto

enclosure [ɛn'kləʊʒər] n cercado, recinto

encompass [ɛn'kʌmpəs] vt abarcar

encore [ɑːŋ'kɔːr] excl ¡otra!, ¡bis! ♦ n bis m

encounter [ɛn'kaʊntər] n encuentro ♦ vt encontrar, encontrarse con; (difficulty) tropezar con

encourage [ɪn'kɜːrɪdʒ] vt alentar, animar; (activity) fomentar; (growth) estimular ❑ **encouragement** n estímulo; (of industry) fomento

encroach [ɛn'krəʊtʃ] vi: **to ~ (up)on** invadir; (rights) usurpar; (time) adueñarse de

encyclop(a)edia [ɛnsaɪklə'piːdɪə] n enciclopedia

end [ɛnd] n fin m; (of table) extremo; (of street) final m; (SPORT) lado ♦ vt terminar, acabar; (also: **bring to an ~, put an ~ to**) acabar con ♦ vi terminar, acabar; **in the ~** al fin; **on ~** (object) de punta, de cabeza; **to stand on ~** (hair) erizarse; **for hours on ~** hora tras hora ▶ **end up** vi: **to end up in** terminar en; (place) ir a parar en

endanger [ɛn'deɪndʒər] vt poner en peligro; **an ~ed species** una especie en peligro de extinción

endearing [ɛn'dɪərɪŋ] adj simpático, atractivo

endeavor (US) [ɛn'dɛvər] (BRIT **endeavour**) n esfuerzo; (attempt) tentativa ♦ vi: **to ~ to do** esforzarse por hacer; (try) procurar hacer

ending ['ɛndɪŋ] n (of book) desenlace m; (LING) terminación f

endive ['ɛndaɪv] n (curly) escarola; (US: compact) endibia

endless ['ɛndlɪs] adj interminable, inacabable

endorse [ɛn'dɔːrs] vt (check) endosar; (approve) aprobar ❑ **endorsement** n (BRIT: on driver's license) nota de inhabilitación

endure [ɛn'duər] vt (bear) aguantar, soportar ♦ vi (last) durar

enemy ['ɛnəmi] adj, n enemigo(-a)

energetic [ɛnər'dʒɛtɪk] adj enérgico

energy ['ɛnərdʒi] n energía

enforce [ɛn'fɔːrs] vt (LAW) hacer cumplir

engage [ɛn'geɪdʒ] vt (attention) llamar; (interest) ocupar; (in conversation) abordar; (worker) contratar; (AUT): **to ~ the clutch** embragar ♦ vi (TECH) engranar; **to ~ in** dedicarse a, ocuparse en ❑ **engaged** adj (betrothed) prometido; (BRIT: busy, in use) ocupado; **to get engaged** prometerse ❑ **engaged tone** (BRIT) n (TEL) señal f de ocupado or comunicando ❑ **engagement** n (appointment) compromiso, cita; (booking) contratación f; (to marry) compromiso; (period) noviazgo ❑ **engagement ring** n anillo de compromiso

engaging [ɛn'geɪdʒɪŋ] adj atractivo

engine ['ɛndʒɪn] n (AUT) motor m; (RAIL) locomotora ❑ **engine driver** (BRIT) n maquinista mf

engineer [ɛndʒə'nɪər] n ingeniero; (BRIT: for repairs) mecánico; (on ship, US RAIL) maquinista m ❑ **engineering** n ingeniería

England ['ɪŋɡlənd] n Inglaterra

English ['ɪŋɡlɪʃ] adj inglés(-esa) ♦ n (LING) inglés m; **the ~** npl los ingleses mpl ❑ **the English Channel** n (el Canal de) la Mancha ❑ **Englishman/woman** n inglés(-esa) m/f

engraving [ɛn'greɪvɪŋ] n grabado

engrossed [ɛn'groust] adj: **~ in** absorto en

engulf [ɛn'gʌlf] vt (water) sumergir, hundir; (fire) prender; (fear) apoderarse de

enhance [ɛn'hæns] vt (gen) aumentar; (beauty) realzar

enjoy [ɪn'dʒɔɪ] vt (health, fortune) disfrutar or gozar de; **I ~ reading** me gusta leer; **to ~ o.s.** divertirse ❑ **enjoyable** adj agradable; (amusing) divertido ❑ **enjoyment** n (joy) placer m; (activity) diversión f

enlarge [ɛn'lɑːrdʒ] vt aumentar; (broaden) extender; (PHOT) ampliar ♦ vi: **to ~ on** (subject) tratar con más detalles ❑ **enlargement** n (PHOT) ampliación f

enlighten [ɛn'laɪtn] vt (inform) informar ❑ **enlightened** adj comprensivo ❑ **the Enlightenment** n (HIST) ≈ la Ilustración, ≈ el Siglo de las Luces

enlist [ɛn'lɪst] vt alistar; (support) conseguir ♦ vi alistarse

enmity ['ɛnmɪti] n enemistad f

enormous [ɪ'nɔːrməs] adj enorme

enough [ɪ'nʌf] adj: **~ time/books** bastante tiempo/bastantes libros ♦ pron bastante(s) ♦ adv: **big ~** bastante grande; **he has not worked ~** no ha trabajado bastante; **have you got ~?** ¿tiene usted bastante(s)?; **~ to eat** (lo) suficiente or bastante para comer; **~!** ¡basta ya!; **that's ~, thanks** con eso basta, gracias; **I've had ~ of him** estoy harto de él; **... which, strangely ~ ... ...** lo que, por extraño que parezca ...

enquire [ɛn'kwaɪər] vt, vi = **inquire**

enquiry [ɛn'kwaɪri] n pregunta; (investigation) investigación f, pesquisa; **"Enquiries"** "Información"

enrage [ɛn'reɪdʒ] vt enfurecer

enroll (US) [ɛn'roul] (BRIT **enrol**) vt (members) inscribir; (SCOL) matricular ♦ vi inscribirse; matricularse ❑ **enrollment** (US) (BRIT **enrolment**) n inscripción f; matriculación f

en route [ɑːn'ruːt] adv durante el viaje

ensemble [ɑːn'sɑːmbəl] n (whole) conjunto; (MUS) conjunto (musical)

en suite [ɑːn'swiːt] (BRIT) adj: **with ~ bathroom** con baño

ensure [ɛn'ʃuər] vt asegurar

entail [ɛn'teɪl] vt suponer

entangled [ɛn'tæŋɡld] adj: **to become ~ (in)** quedarse enredado (en) or enmarañado (en)

enter ['ɛntər] vt (room) entrar en; (club) hacerse socio de; (army) alistarse en; (sb for a competition) inscribir; (write down) anotar, apuntar; (COMPUT) meter ♦ vi entrar ▶ **enter for** (BRIT) vt fus presentarse para ▶ **enter into** vt fus (discussion etc) entablar; (agreement) llegar a, firmar

enterprise ['ɛntərpraɪz] n empresa; (spirit) iniciativa; **free ~** la libre empresa; **private ~** la iniciativa privada ❑ **enterprising** adj emprendedor(a)

entertain [ɛntər'teɪn] vt (amuse) divertir; (invite: guest) invitar (a casa); (idea) abrigar ❑ **entertainer** n artista mf ❑ **entertaining**

adj divertido, entretenido ❑ **entertainment** *n* (*amusement*) diversión *f*; (*show*) espectáculo

enthralled [en'θrɔ:ld] *adj* encantado

enthusiasm [en'θu:ziæzəm] *n* entusiasmo

enthusiast [en'θu:ziæst] *n* entusiasta *mf* ❑ **enthusiastic** [enθu:zi'æstɪk] *adj* entusiasta; **to be enthusiastic about** entusiasmarse por

entire [en'taɪər] *adj* entero ❑ **entirely** *adv* totalmente ❑ **entirety** [en'taɪrəti] *n*: **in its entirety** en su totalidad

entitle [en'taɪtl] *vt*: **to ~ sb to sth** dar a algn derecho a algo ❑ **entitled** *adj* (*book*) titulado; **to be entitled to do** tener derecho a hacer

entrance [*n* 'entrəns, *vb* en'træns] *n* entrada ♦ *vt* encantar, hechizar; **to gain ~ to** (*university etc*) ingresar en ❑ **entrance examination** *n* examen *m* de ingreso ❑ **entrance fee** *n* cuota ❑ **entrance ramp** (*US*) *n* (*AUT*) rampa de acceso

entrant ['entrənt] *n* (*in race, competition*) participante *mf*; (*in examination*) candidato(-a)

entrenched [en'trentʃd] *adj* inamovible

entrepreneur [ɑ:ntrəprə'nɜ:r] *n* empresario(-a)

entrust [en'trʌst] *vt*: **to ~ sth to sb** confiar algo a algn

entry ['entri] *n* entrada; (*in competition*) participación *f*; (*in register*) apunte *m*; (*in account*) partida; (*in reference book*) artículo; **"no ~"** "prohibido el paso"; (*AUT*) "dirección prohibida" ❑ **entry form** *n* hoja de inscripción ❑ **entry phone** *n* interfón *m* (*MEX*), portero eléctrico (*LAm*) or automático (*SP*)

envelop [en'veləp] *vt* envolver

envelope ['envələʊp] *n* sobre *m*

envious ['enviəs] *adj* envidioso; (*look*) de envidia

environment [en'vaɪərənmənt] *n* (*surroundings*) entorno; (*natural world*): **the ~** el medio ambiente ❑ **environmental** [en,vaɪərən'mentl] *adj* ambiental; medioambiental; ❑ **environment-friendly** *adj* no perjudicial para el medio ambiente

envisage [en'vɪzɪdʒ] *vt* prever

envoy ['envɔɪ] *n* enviado(-a)

envy ['envi] *n* envidia ♦ *vt* tener envidia a; **to ~ sb sth** envidiar algo a algn

epic ['epɪk] *n* épica ♦ *adj* épico

epidemic [epr'demɪk] *n* epidemia

epilepsy ['epɪlepsi] *n* epilepsia

episode ['epɪsəʊd] *n* episodio

epitomize [r'pɪtəmaɪz] *vt* epitomar, resumir

equal ['i:kwəl] *adj* igual; (*treatment*) equitativo ♦ *n* igual *mf* ♦ *vt* ser igual a; (*fig*) igualar; **to be ~ to** (*task*) estar a la altura de ❑ **equality** [i:'kwɒlɪti] *n* igualdad *f* ❑ **equalize** *vi* (*SPORT*) empatar ❑ **equally** *adv* igualmente; (*share etc*) a partes iguales

equate [r'kweɪt] *vt*: **to ~ sth with** equiparar algo con ❑ **equation** [r'kweɪʒən] *n* (*MATH*) ecuación *f*

equator [r'kweɪtər] *n* ecuador *m*

equilibrium [i:kwr'lɪbriəm] *n* equilibrio

equip [r'kwɪp] *vt* equipar; (*person*) proveer; **to be well ~ped** estar bien equipado ❑ **equipment** *n* equipo; (*tools*) avíos *mpl*

equity ['ekwɪti] *n* (*fairness*) equidad *f*; **equities** *npl* acciones *fpl* ordinarias

equivalent [r'kwɪvələnt] *adj*: **~ (to)** equivalente (a) ♦ *n* equivalente *m*

ER (*US*) *n abbr* (= *emergency room*) sala de urgencias

era ['ɪərə] *n* era, época

eradicate [r'rædɪkeɪt] *vt* erradicar

erase [r'reɪs] *vt* borrar ❑ **eraser** *n* goma de borrar

erect [r'rekt] *adj* erguido ♦ *vt* erigir, levantar; (*assemble*) montar ❑ **erection** *n* construcción *f*; (*assembly*) montaje *m*; (*PHYSIOLOGY*) erección *f*

ERM *n abbr* (= *Exchange Rate Mechanism*) tipo de cambio europeo

erode [r'rəʊd] *vt* (*GEO*) erosionar; (*metal*) corroer, desgastar; (*fig*) desgastar

erotic [r'rɒtɪk] *adj* erótico

errand ['erənd] *n* mandado (*LAm*), recado (*SP*)

erratic [r'rætɪk] *adj* desigual, poco uniforme

error ['erər] *n* error *m*, equivocación *f*

erupt [r'rʌpt] *vi* entrar en erupción; (*fig*) estallar ❑ **eruption** [r'rʌpʃən] *n* erupción *f*; (*of war*) estallido

escalate ['eskəleɪt] *vi* extenderse, intensificarse

escalator ['eskəleɪtər] *n* escalera móvil

escapade [eskə'peɪd] *n* travesura

escape [r'skeɪp] *n* fuga ♦ *vi* escaparse; (*flee*) huir, evadirse; (*leak*) fugarse ♦ *vt* (*responsibility etc*) evitar, eludir; (*consequences*) escapar a; (*elude*): **his name ~s me** no me sale su nombre; **to ~ from** (*place*) escaparse de; (*person*) escaparse a

escort [*n* 'eskɔ:rt, *vb* r'skɔ:rt] *n* acompañante *mf*; (*MIL*) escolta ♦ *vt* acompañar

Eskimo ['eskɪməʊ] *n* esquimal *mf*

especially [ɪ'speʃəlɪ] adv (above all) sobre todo; (particularly) en particular, especialmente

espionage ['espɪɑnɑ:ʒ] n espionaje m

esplanade ['esplə,nɑ:d] n (by sea) malecón m (LAm), costanera (SC), paseo marítimo (SP)

Esquire ['eskwaɪər] (abbr **Esq.**) n: **J. Brown, ~ Sr. D. J. Brown**

essay ['eseɪ] n (LITERATURE) ensayo; (SCOL: short) redacción f; (: long) trabajo

essence ['esəns] n esencia

essential [ɪ'senʃəl] adj (necessary) imprescindible; (basic) esencial ❏ **essentially** adv esencialmente ❏ **essentials** npl lo imprescindible, lo esencial

establish [ɪ'stæblɪʃ] vt establecer; (prove) demostrar; (relations) entablar; (reputation) ganarse ❏ **established** adj (business) conocido; (practice) arraigado ❏ **establishment** n establecimiento; **the Establishment** la clase dirigente

estate [ɪ'steɪt] n (land) finca, hacienda; (inheritance) herencia; (BRIT: also: **housing ~**) urbanización f ❏ **estate agent** (BRIT) n agente mf inmobiliario(-a) ❏ **estate car** (BRIT) n camioneta (LAm), rural f (RPI), ranchera (SP)

esteem [e'sti:m] n: **to hold sb in high ~** estimar en mucho a algn

esthetic [es'θetɪk] (US) adj estético

estimate [n 'estɪmɪt, vb 'estɪmeɪt] n estimación f, apreciación f; (assessment) tasa, cálculo; (COMM) presupuesto ♦ vt estimar, tasar; calcular ❏ **estimation** [estɪ'meɪʃən] n opinión f, juicio; cálculo

estranged [ɪ'streɪndʒd] adj separado

estuary ['estjuərɪ] n estuario, ría

e-tailing ['i:teɪlɪŋ] n venta en línea, venta vía o por Internet

etc. abbr (= et cetera) etc

eternal [ɪ'tɜːrnl] adj eterno

eternity [ɪ'tɜːrnɪtɪ] n eternidad f

ethical ['eθɪkəl] adj ético ❏ **ethics** n ética ♦ npl moralidad f

Ethiopia [i:θɪ'əʊpɪə] n Etiopía

ethnic ['eθnɪk] adj étnico ❏ **ethnic minority** n minoría étnica

ethos ['i:θɑːs] n genio, carácter m

etiquette ['etɪkɪt] n protocolo

EU n abbr (= European Union) UE f

eulogy ['ju:lədʒɪ] n elogio

euro ['juərəu] n euro

Euroland ['juərəulænd] n zona (del) euro

Europe ['juərəp] n Europa ❏ **European** [juərə'pi:ən] adj, n europeo(-a) ❏ **European Community** n Comunidad f Europea ❏ **European Union** n Unión f Europea

Eurozone ['juərəuzəun] n eurozona, zona euro

evacuate [ɪ'vækjueɪt] vt (people) evacuar; (place) desocupar

evade [ɪ'veɪd] vt evadir, eludir

evaporate [ɪ'væpəreɪt] vi evaporarse; (fig) desvanecerse ❏ **evaporated milk** n leche f evaporada

evasion [ɪ'veɪʒən] n evasión f

eve [i:v] n: **on the ~ of** en vísperas de

even ['i:vən] adj (level) llano; (smooth) liso; (speed, temperature) uniforme; (number) par ♦ adv hasta, incluso; (introducing a comparison) aún, todavía; **~ if, ~ though** aunque +subjun; **~ more** aun más; **~ so** aun así; **not ~** ni siquiera; **~ he was there** hasta él estuvo allí; **~ on Sundays** incluso los domingos; **to get ~ with sb** ajustar cuentas con algn

evening ['i:vnɪŋ] n tarde f; (late) noche f; **in the ~** por la tarde ❏ **evening class** n clase f nocturna ❏ **evening dress** n (no pl: formal clothes) traje m de etiqueta; (woman's) traje m de noche

event [ɪ'vent] n suceso, acontecimiento; (SPORT) prueba; **in the ~ of** en caso de ❏ **eventful** adj (life) activo; (day) ajetreado

eventual [ɪ'ventʃuəl] adj final ❏ **eventuality** [ɪventʃu'ælɪtɪ] n eventualidad f ❏ **eventually** adv (finally) finalmente; (in time) con el tiempo

⚠ Be careful not to translate **eventual** by the Spanish word **eventual**.

ever ['evər] adv (at any time) nunca, jamás; (at all times) siempre; (BRIT: in question): **why ~ not?** ¿y por qué no?; **the best ~** lo nunca visto; **have you ~ seen it?** ¿lo ha visto usted alguna vez?; **better than ~** mejor que nunca; **~ since** (adv) desde entonces; (conj) después de que ❏ **evergreen** n árbol m de hoja perenne ❏ **everlasting** adj eterno, perpetuo

every

KEYWORD

['evrɪ] adj

1 (each) cada; **every one of them** (persons) todos ellos(-as); (objects) cada uno de ellos (-as); **every store in the town was closed** todas las tiendas de la ciudad estaban cerradas

2 (all possible) todo(-a); **I gave you every assistance** te di toda la ayuda posible; **I have every confidence in him** tiene toda mi confianza; **we wish you every success** te deseamos toda suerte de éxitos
3 (showing recurrence) todo(-a); **every day/week** todos los días/todas las semanas; **every other car had been broken into** habían forzado uno de cada dos coches; **she visits me every other/third day** me visita cada dos/tres días; **every now and then** de vez en cuando

every: ❑ **everybody** pron = **everyone**
❑ **everyday** adj (daily) cotidiano, de todos los días; (usual) acostumbrado ❑ **everyone** pron todos(-as), todo el mundo ❑ **everything** pron todo; **this store sells everything** esta tienda vende de todo ❑ **everywhere** adv: **I've been looking for you everywhere** te he estado buscando por todas partes; **everywhere you go you meet ...** en todas partes encuentra ...

evict [I'vɪkt] vt desahuciar ❑ **eviction** n desahucio

evidence ['evɪdəns] n (proof) prueba; (of witness) testimonio; (sign) indicios mpl; **to give ~** prestar declaración, dar testimonio

evident ['evɪdənt] adj evidente, manifiesto ❑ **evidently** adv por lo visto

evil ['i:vəl] adj malo; (influence) funesto ♦ n mal m

evoke [I'vouk] vt evocar

evolution [evə'lu:ʃən] n evolución f

evolve [I'vɒlv] vt desarrollar ♦ vi evolucionar, desarrollarse

ewe [ju:] n oveja

ex- [eks] prefix ex

exact [Ig'zækt] adj exacto; (person) meticuloso ♦ vt: **to ~ sth (from)** exigir algo (de) ❑ **exacting** adj exigente; (conditions) arduo ❑ **exactly** adv exactamente; (indicating agreement) exacto

exaggerate [Ig'zædʒəreɪt] vt, vi exagerar ❑ **exaggeration** [Ig,zædʒə'reɪʃən] n exageración f

exalted [Ig'zɔːltɪd] adj eminente

exam [Ig'zæm] n abbr (SCOL) = **examination**

examination [Igzæmɪ'neɪʃən] n examen m; (MED) reconocimiento

examine [Ig'zæmɪn] vt examinar; (inspect) inspeccionar, escudriñar; (MED) reconocer ❑ **examiner** n examinador(a) m/f

example [Ig'zæmpəl] n ejemplo; **for ~** por ejemplo

exasperate [Ig'zæspəreɪt] vt exasperar, irritar ❑ **exasperation** [Igzæspə'reɪʃən] n exasperación f, irritación f

excavate ['ekskəveɪt] vt excavar

exceed [Ik'si:d] vt (amount) exceder; (number) pasar de; (speed limit) sobrepasar; (powers) excederse en; (hopes) superar ❑ **exceedingly** adv sumamente, sobremanera

excellent ['eksələnt] adj excelente

except [Ik'sept] prep (also: ~ **for**, ~**ing**) excepto, salvo ♦ vt exceptuar, excluir; ~ **if/when** excepto si/cuando; ~ **that** salvo que ❑ **exception** n excepción f; **to take exception to** ofenderse por ❑ **exceptional** adj excepcional

excerpt ['eksɜːpt] n extracto

excess [Ik'ses] n exceso; ~**es** npl (of cruelty etc) atrocidades fpl ❑ **excess baggage** n exceso de equipaje ❑ **excess fare** n suplemento ❑ **excessive** adj excesivo

exchange [Iks'tʃeɪndʒ] n intercambio; (conversation) diálogo; (also: **telephone ~**) central f (telefónica) ♦ vt: **to ~ (for)** cambiar (por) ❑ **exchange rate** n tipo de cambio

exchequer [eks'tʃekər] (BRIT) n: **the E~** ≈ Hacienda, ≈ la Dirección General Impositiva (RPI)

excise ['eksaɪz] n impuestos mpl indirectos or sobre el alcohol y el tabaco

excite [Ik'saɪt] vt (stimulate) estimular; (arouse) excitar ❑ **excited** adj: **to get excited** emocionarse ❑ **excitement** n (agitation) excitación f; (exhilaration) emoción f ❑ **exciting** adj emocionante

exclaim [Iks'kleɪm] vi exclamar ❑ **exclamation** [eksklə'meɪʃən] n exclamación f ❑ **exclamation point** (US) (BRIT **exclamation mark**) n punto de admiración

exclude [Iks'klu:d] vt excluir; exceptuar

exclusive [Iks'klu:sɪv] adj exclusivo; (club, district) selecto; ~ **of tax** excluyendo impuestos ❑ **exclusively** adv únicamente

excruciating [Iks'kru:ʃieɪtɪŋ] adj (pain) agudísimo, atroz; (noise, embarrassment) horrible

excursion [Ik'skɜːrʒən] n (tourist excursion) excursión f

excuse [n Iks'kju:s, vb Ik'skju:z] n disculpa, excusa; (pretext) pretexto ♦ vt (justify) justificar; (forgive) disculpar, perdonar; **to ~ sb from doing sth** dispensar a algn de hacer algo; ~ **me!** (attracting attention) ¡por favor!; (apologizing) ¡perdón!; ~ **me?** (US: what?)

¿perdone?, ¿mande? (*MEX*); **if you will ~ me** con su permiso

ex-directory [ˈɛksdɪˈrɛktəri] (*BRIT*) *adj* que no consta en la guía

execute [ˈɛksɪkjuːt] *vt* (*plan*) realizar; (*order*) cumplir; (*person*) ajusticiar, ejecutar ❑ **execution** [ɛksɪˈkjuːʃən] *n* realización *f*; cumplimiento; ejecución *f*

executive [ɪgˈzɛkjətɪv] *n* (*person, committee*) ejecutivo; (*POL: committee*) poder *m* ejecutivo ♦ *adj* ejecutivo

exemplify [ɪgˈzɛmplɪfaɪ] *vt* ejemplificar; (*illustrate*) ilustrar

exempt [ɪgˈzɛmpt] *adj*: ~ **from** exento de ♦ *vt*: **to ~ sb from** eximir a algn de ❑ **exemption** *n* exención *f*

exercise [ˈɛksəsaɪz] *n* ejercicio ♦ *vt* (*patience*) usar de; (*right*) valerse de; (*dog*) llevar de paseo; (*mind*) preocupar ♦ *vi* (*also*: **to take ~**) hacer ejercicio(s) ❑ **exercise bike** *n* bicicleta estática ❑ **exercise book** (*BRIT*) *n* cuaderno

exert [ɪgˈzɜːrt] *vt* ejercer; **to ~ o.s.** esforzarse ❑ **exertion** *n* esfuerzo

exhale [ɛksˈheɪl] *vt* despedir ♦ *vi* exhalar

exhaust [ɪgˈzɔːst] *n* (*AUT: also*: ~ **pipe**) escape *m*; (: *fumes*) gases *mpl* de escape ♦ *vt* agotar ❑ **exhausted** *adj* agotado ❑ **exhaustion** *n* agotamiento; **nervous exhaustion** postración *f* nerviosa ❑ **exhaustive** *adj* exhaustivo

exhibit [ɪgˈzɪbɪt] *n* (*ART*) obra expuesta; (*LAW*) objeto expuesto ♦ *vt* (*show: emotions*) manifestar; (: *courage, skill*) demostrar; (*paintings*) exponer ❑ **exhibition** [ɛksɪˈbɪʃən] *n* exposición *f*; (*of talent etc*) demostración *f*

exhilarating [ɪgˈzɪləreɪtɪŋ] *adj* estimulante, tónico

exile [ˈɛgzaɪl] *n* exilio; (*person*) exiliado(-a) ♦ *vt* desterrar, exiliar

exist [ɪgˈzɪst] *vi* existir; (*live*) vivir ❑ **existence** *n* existencia ❑ **existing** *adj* existente, actual

exit [ˈɛgzɪt] *n* salida ♦ *vi* (*THEATER*) hacer mutis; (*COMPUT*) salir (del sistema) ❑ **exit poll** *n* encuesta a la salida de los colegios electorales ❑ **exit ramp** (*US*) *n* (*AUT*) vía de acceso

⚠ Be careful not to translate **exit** by the Spanish word *éxito*.

exodus [ˈɛksədəs] *n* éxodo

exonerate [ɪgˈzɑːnəreɪt] *vt*: **to ~ from** exculpar de

exotic [ɪgˈzɑːtɪk] *adj* exótico

expand [ɪkˈspænd] *vt* ampliar; (*number*) aumentar ♦ *vi* (*population*) aumentar; (*trade etc*) expandirse; (*gas, metal*) dilatarse

expanse [ɪkˈspæns] *n* extensión *f*

expansion [ɪkˈspænʃən] *n* (*of population*) aumento; (*of trade*) expansión *f*

expect [ɪkˈspɛkt] *vt* esperar; (*require*) contar con; (*suppose*) suponer ♦ *vi*: **to be ~ing** (*pregnant woman*) estar embarazada ❑ **expectancy** *n* (*anticipation*) esperanza *f*; **life expectancy** esperanza de vida ❑ **expectant mother** *n* futura madre *f* ❑ **expectation** [ɛkspɛkˈteɪʃən] *n* (*hope*) esperanza; (*belief*) expectativa

expedient [ɪkˈspiːdiənt] *adj* conveniente, oportuno ♦ *n* recurso, expediente *m*

expedition [ɛkspəˈdɪʃən] *n* expedición *f*

expel [ɪkˈspɛl] *vt* arrojar; (*from place*) expulsar

expend [ɪkˈspɛnd] *vt* (*money*) gastar; (*time, energy*) consumir ❑ **expenditure** *n* gastos *mpl*, desembolso; consumo

expense [ɪkˈspɛns] *n* gasto, gastos *mpl*; (*high cost*) costa; **~s** *npl* (*COMM*) gastos *mpl*; **at the ~ of** a costa de ❑ **expense account** *n* cuenta de gastos

expensive [ɪkˈspɛnsɪv] *adj* caro, costoso

experience [ɪkˈspɪriəns] *n* experiencia ♦ *vt* experimentar; (*suffer*) sufrir ❑ **experienced** *adj* experimentado

experiment [ɪkˈspɛrɪmənt] *n* experimento ♦ *vi* hacer experimentos

expert [ˈɛkspɜːt] *adj* experto, perito ♦ *n* experto(-a), perito(-a); (*specialist*) especialista *mf* ❑ **expertise** [ɛkspɜːˈtiːz] *n* pericia

expiration [ɛkspəˈreɪʃən] *n* = **expiry**

expire [ɪkˈspaɪər] *vi* caducar, vencer ❑ **expiry** *n* vencimiento ❑ **expiry date** *n* (*of medicine, food item*) fecha de caducidad

explain [ɪkˈspleɪn] *vt* explicar ❑ **explanation** [ɛkspləˈneɪʃən] *n* explicación *f* ❑ **explanatory** [ɪkˈsplænətɔːri] *adj* explicativo; aclaratorio

explicit [ɪkˈsplɪsɪt] *adj* explícito

explode [ɪksˈploʊd] *vi* estallar, explotar; (*population*) crecer rápidamente; (*with anger*) reventar

exploit [*n* ˈɛksplɔɪt, *vb* ɪkˈsplɔɪt] *n* hazaña ♦ *vt* explotar ❑ **exploitation** [ɛksplɔɪˈteɪʃən] *n* explotación *f*

exploratory [ɪkˈsplɔːrətɔːri] *adj* de exploración; (*fig: talks*) exploratorio, preliminar

explore [ɪkˈsplɔːr] *vt* explorar; (*fig*) examinar; investigar ❑ **explorer** *n* explorador(a) *m/f*

explosion [ɪk'spləʊʒən] n explosión f
❑ **explosive** adj, n explosivo

exponent [ɪk'spəʊnənt] n (of theory etc)
partidario(-a); (of skill etc) exponente mf

export [vb ɪk'spɔːrt, n 'ekspɔːrt] vt exportar ♦ n
(process) exportación f; (product) producto de
exportación ♦ cpd de exportación
❑ **exporter** n exportador m

expose [ɪk'spəʊz] vt exponer; (unmask)
desenmascarar ❑ **exposed** adj expuesto

exposure [ɪk'spəʊʒər] n exposición f;
(publicity) publicidad f; (PHOT: speed) velocidad
f de obturación; (: shot) fotografía; **to die
from ~** (MED) morir de frío ❑ **exposure
meter** n fotómetro

express [ɪk'spres] adj (definite) expreso,
explícito; (letter etc) urgente ♦ n (train) rápido
♦ vt expresar ❑ **expression** n expresión f;
(of actor etc) sentimiento ❑ **expressly** adv
expresamente ❑ **expressway** (US) n
autopista

exquisite [ek'skwɪzɪt] adj exquisito

extend [ɪk'stend] vt (visit, street) prolongar;
(building) ampliar; (invitation) ofrecer ♦ vi
(land) extenderse; (period of time) prolongarse

extension [ɪk'stenʃən] n extensión f;
(building) ampliación f; (of time) prolongación
f; (TEL: in private house) línea derivada; (: in
office) extensión f

extensive [ɪk'stensɪv] adj extenso; (damage)
importante; (knowledge) amplio
❑ **extensively** adv: **he's traveled
extensively** ha viajado por muchos países

extent [ɪk'stent] n (breadth) extensión f;
(scope) alcance m; **to some ~** hasta cierto
punto; **to the ~ of ...** hasta el punto de ...; **to
such an ~ that ...** hasta tal punto que ...; **to
what ~?** ¿hasta qué punto?

extenuating [ɪk'stenjueɪtɪŋ] adj: ~
circumstances circunstancias fpl atenuantes

exterior [eks'tɪriər] adj exterior, externo ♦ n
exterior m

external [eks'stɜːrnl] adj externo

extinct [ɪk'stɪŋkt] adj (volcano) extinguido;
(race) extinto

extinguish [ɪk'stɪŋgwɪʃ] vt extinguir, apagar
❑ **extinguisher** n extintor m

extort [ɪk'stɔːrt] vt obtener por fuerza
❑ **extortionate** adj excesivo, exorbitante

extra ['ekstrə] adj adicional ♦ adv (in addition)
de más ♦ n (luxury, addition) extra m; (MOVIE,
THEATER) extra mf, comparsa mf

extra... ['ekstrə] prefix extra...

extract [vb ɪk'strækt, n 'ekstrækt] vt sacar;
(tooth) extraer; (money, promise) obtener ♦ n
extracto

extracurricular [ˌekstrəkə'rɪkjʊlər] adj
extraescolar, extracurricular

extradite ['ekstrədaɪt] vt extraditar

extra: ❑ **extramarital** adj
extramatrimonial ❑ **extramural**
[ˌekstrə'mjʊərəl] adj extraescolar
❑ **extraordinary** [ɪk'strɔːrdn,eri] adj
extraordinario; (odd) raro

extravagance [ɪk'strævəgəns] n derroche
m, despilfarro; (thing bought) extravagancia

extravagant [ɪk'strævəgənt] adj (lavish:
person) pródigo; (: gift) (demasiado) caro;
(wasteful) despilfarrador,a

extreme [ɪk'striːm] adj extremo, extremado
♦ n extremo ❑ **extremely** adv sumamente,
extremadamente

extricate ['ekstrɪkeɪt] vt: **to ~ sth/sb from**
librar algo/a algn de

extrovert ['ekstrəvərt] n extrovertido(-a)

eye [aɪ] n ojo ♦ vt mirar de soslayo, ojear; **to
keep an ~ on** vigilar ❑ **eyebath** n ojera
❑ **eyebrow** n ceja ❑ **eye drops** npl gotas
fpl para los ojos, colirio ❑ **eyeglasses** (US)
npl lentes mpl (LAm), gafas fpl (SP) ❑ **eyelash**
n pestaña ❑ **eyelid** n párpado ❑ **eye-liner**
n delineador m (de ojos) ❑ **eye-opener** n
revelación f, gran sorpresa ❑ **eye shadow** n
sombreador m de ojos ❑ **eyesight** n vista
❑ **eyesore** n monstruosidad f ❑ **eye
witness** n testigo mf presencial

e-zine ['iːˌziːn] n (COMPUT) revista digital

Ff

F [ef] n (MUS) fa m

F abbr = **Fahrenheit**

fable ['feɪbəl] n fábula

fabric ['fæbrɪk] n tejido, tela

⚠ Be careful not to translate **fabric** by the
Spanish word *fábrica*.

fabulous ['fæbjələs] adj fabuloso

façade [fə'sɑːd] n fachada

face [feɪs] n (ANAT) cara, rostro; (of clock) cara
(LAm), esfera (SP); (of mountain) cara, ladera;
(of building) fachada ♦ vt (direction) estar de
cara a; (situation) hacer frente a; (facts)
aceptar; **~ down** (person, card) boca abajo; **to
lose ~** desprestigiarse; **to make** or **pull a ~**

hacer muecas; **in the ~ of** (*difficulties etc*) ante; **on the ~ of it** a primera vista; **~ to ~** cara a cara ► **face up to** *vt fus* hacer frente a, arrostrar ❑ **face cloth** (*BRIT*) *n* manopla ❑ **face cream** *n* crema (de belleza) ❑ **face lift** *n* estirado facial; (*of building*) renovación *f* ❑ **face powder** *n* polvos *mpl* ❑ **face-saving** *adj* para salvar las apariencias ❑ **face value** *n* (*of stamp*) valor *m* nominal; **to take sth at face value** (*fig*) tomar algo en sentido literal

facility [fəˈsɪlɪti] *n* (*talent, ease*) facilidad *f*; (*ability*) habilidad *f*, facultad *f*; **facilities** *npl* (*buildings*) instalaciones *fpl*; (*equipment*) servicios *mpl*; **credit facilities** facilidades *fpl* de crédito

facing [ˈfeɪsɪŋ] *prep* frente a

facsimile [fækˈsɪmɪli] *n* (*replica*) facsímil(e) *m*; (*machine*) telefax *m*; (*fax*) fax *m*

fact [fækt] *n* hecho; **in ~** en realidad

factor [ˈfæktər] *n* factor *m*

factory [ˈfæktəri] *n* fábrica

factual [ˈfæktjuəl] *adj* basado en los hechos

faculty [ˈfækəlti] *n* facultad *f*; (*US: teaching staff*) personal *m* docente

fad [fæd] *n* novedad *f*, moda

fade [feɪd] *vi* desteñirse; (*sound, smile*) desvanecerse; (*light*) apagarse; (*flower*) marchitarse; (*hope, memory*) perderse

fag [fæg] (*BRIT: inf*) *n* (*cigarette*) cigarrillo, pitillo, pucho (*SC*)

fail [feɪl] *vt* (*candidate, test*) reprobar (*LAm*), suspender (*SP*); (*memory etc*) fallar a ♦ *vi* reprobar (*LAm*), suspender (*SP*); (*be unsuccessful*) fracasar; (*strength, brakes*) fallar; (*light*) acabarse; **to ~ to do sth** (*neglect*) dejar de hacer algo; (*be unable*) no poder hacer algo; **without ~** sin falta ❑ **failing** *n* falta, defecto ♦ *prep* a falta de ❑ **failure** [ˈfeɪljər] *n* fracaso; (*person*) fracasado(-a); (*mechanical etc*) fallo

faint [feɪnt] *adj* débil; (*recollection*) vago; (*mark*) apenas visible ♦ *n* desmayo ♦ *vi* desmayarse; **to feel ~** estar mareado, marearse

fair [fɛər] *adj* justo; (*hair, person*) rubio; (*weather*) bueno; (*good enough*) regular; (*considerable*) considerable ♦ *adv* (*play*) limpio ♦ *n* feria; (*BRIT: funfair*) parque de atracciones ❑ **fairly** *adv* (*justly*) con justicia; (*quite*) bastante ❑ **fairness** *n* justicia, imparcialidad *f* ❑ **fair play** *n* juego limpio

fairy [ˈfɛri] *n* hada ❑ **fairy tale** *n* cuento de hadas

faith [feɪθ] *n* fe *f*; (*trust*) confianza; (*sect*) religión *f* ❑ **faithful** *adj* (*loyal: troops etc*) leal; (*spouse*) fiel; (*account*) exacto ❑ **faithfully** *adv* fielmente; **yours faithfully** (*BRIT: in letters*) le saluda atentamente

fake [feɪk] *n* (*painting etc*) falsificación *f*; (*person*) impostor(a) *m/f* ♦ *adj* falso ♦ *vt* fingir; (*painting etc*) falsificar

falcon [ˈfælkən] *n* halcón *m*

fall [fɔːl] (*pt* **fell**, *pp* **~en**) *n* caída; (*in price etc*) descenso; (*US*) otoño ♦ *vi* caer(se); (*price*) bajar, descender; **~s** *npl* (*waterfall*) cascada, salto de agua; **to ~ flat** (*on one's face*) caerse (boca abajo); (*plan*) fracasar; (*joke, story*) no hacer gracia ► **fall back** *vi* retroceder ► **fall back on** *vt fus* (*remedy etc*) recurrir a ► **fall behind** *vi* quedarse atrás ► **fall down** *vi* (*person*) caerse; (*building, hopes*) derrumbarse ► **fall for** *vt fus* (*trick*) dejarse engañar por; (*person*) enamorarse de ► **fall in** *vi* (*roof*) hundirse; (*MIL*) alinearse ► **fall off** *vi* caerse; (*diminish*) disminuir ► **fall out** *vi* (*friends etc*) reñir; (*hair, teeth*) caerse ► **fall through** *vi* (*plan, project*) fracasar

fallacy [ˈfæləsi] *n* error *m*

fallen [ˈfɔːlən] *pp of* **fall**

fallout [ˈfɔːlaut] *n* lluvia radioactiva

fallow [ˈfælou] *adj* en barbecho

false [fɔːls] *adj* falso; **under ~ pretenses** con engaños ❑ **false alarm** *n* falsa alarma ❑ **false teeth** *npl* dentadura postiza

falter [ˈfɔːltər] *vi* vacilar; (*engine*) fallar

fame [feɪm] *n* fama

familiar [fəˈmɪljər] *adj* conocido, familiar; (*tone*) de confianza; **to be ~ with** (*subject*) conocer (bien)

family [ˈfæməli] *n* familia ❑ **family business** *n* negocio familiar ❑ **family doctor** (*BRIT*) *n* médico(-a) de cabecera ❑ **family room** (*US*) *n* (*in hotel*) habitación *f* familiar

famine [ˈfæmɪn] *n* hambre *f*, hambruna

famished [ˈfæmɪʃt] *adj* hambriento

famous [ˈfeɪməs] *adj* famoso, célebre ❑ **famously** *adv* (*get on*) estupendamente

fan [fæn] *n* abanico; (*ELEC*) ventilador *m*; (*of rock star*) fan *mf*; (*SPORT*) hincha *mf* ♦ *vt* abanicar; (*fire, quarrel*) atizar

fanatic [fəˈnætɪk] *n* fanático(-a)

fan belt *n* correa del ventilador

fanciful [ˈfænsɪful] *adj* (*design, name*) fantástico

fancy [ˈfænsi] *n* (*whim*) capricho, antojo; (*imagination*) imaginación *f* ♦ *adj* (*luxury*) lujoso, de lujo ♦ *vt* (*imagine*) imaginarse;

(think) creer; *(BRIT: feel like, want)* tener ganas de; **what do you ~?** ¿qué quieres tomar?, ¿qué te apetece?; **he fancies her** *(BRIT: inf)* le gusta (ella) mucho; **to take a ~ to** *(person: amorously)* quedarse prendado de, prendarse de ❑ **fancy dress** *(BRIT)* n disfraz m ❑ **fancy-dress ball** *(BRIT)* n baile m de disfraces

fanfare ['fænfer] n fanfarria (de trompeta)

fang [fæŋ] n colmillo

fanny pack ['fæni,pæk] *(US)* n riñonera

fantastic [fæn'tæstɪk] adj *(enormous)* enorme; *(strange, wonderful)* fantástico

fantasy ['fæntəsi] n *(dream)* sueño; *(unreality)* fantasía

FAQs npl abbr *(= frequently asked questions)* preguntas fpl frecuentes

far [fɑːr] adj *(distant)* lejano ♦ adv lejos; *(much, greatly)* mucho; **~ away, ~ off** (a lo) lejos; **~ better** mucho mejor; **~ from** lejos de; **by ~** con mucho; **go as ~ as the farm** vaya hasta la granja; **as ~ as I know** que yo sepa; **how ~?** ¿hasta dónde?; *(fig)* ¿hasta qué punto? ❑ **faraway** adj remoto; *(look)* distraído

farce [fɑːrs] n farsa

fare [feər] n *(on trains, buses)* precio (del boleto *(LAm)* or billete *(SP))*; *(in taxi: cost)* tarifa; *(food)* comida; **half ~** medio pasaje m; **full ~** pasaje completo

Far East n: **the ~** el Extremo Oriente

farewell [,fer'wel] excl, n adiós m

farm [fɑːrm] n rancho *(MEX)*, hacienda *(LAm)*, estancia *(RPI)*, cortijo *(SP)* ♦ vt cultivar ❑ **farmer** n granjero, ranchero *(MEX)*, hacendado *(LAm)*, estanciero *(RPI)* ❑ **farmhand** n peón m ❑ **farmhouse** n granja, rancho *(MEX)*, casa del hacendado *(LAm)*, casco de la estancia *(RPI)* ❑ **farming** n agricultura; *(of crops)* cultivo; *(of animals)* cría ❑ **farmland** n tierra de cultivo ❑ **farm worker** n = **farmhand** ❑ **farmyard** n corral m

far-reaching [fɑːr'riːtʃɪŋ] adj *(reform, effect)* de gran alcance

far-sighted ['fɑːr,saɪtɪd] adj *(US MED)* hipermétrope; *(fig)* con visión de futuro

fart [fɑːrt] *(inf!)* vi tirarse un pedo *(!)*

farther ['fɑːrðər] adv más lejos, más allá ♦ adj más lejano

farthest ['fɑːrðɪst] superlative of **far**

fascinate ['fæsɪneɪt] vt fascinar ❑ **fascination** [,fæsɪ'neɪʃən] n fascinación f

fascism ['fæʃɪzəm] n fascismo

fashion ['fæʃən] n moda; *(fashion industry)* industria de la moda; *(manner)* manera ♦ vt formar; **in ~** a la moda; **out of ~** pasado de moda; **after a ~** así así, más o menos ❑ **fashionable** adj de moda ❑ **fashion show** n desfile m de modelos

fast [fæst] adj rápido; *(dye, color)* resistente; *(clock)*: **to be ~** estar adelantado ♦ adv rápidamente, de prisa; *(stuck, held)* firmemente ♦ n ayuno ♦ vi ayunar; **~ asleep** profundamente dormido

fasten ['fæsən] vt atar, sujetar; *(coat, belt)* abrochar ♦ vi atarse; abrocharse ❑ **fastener, fastening** n cierre m; *(of door etc)* cerrojo

fast food n comida rápida, platos mpl preparados

fastidious [fæ'stɪdiəs] adj *(fussy)* quisquilloso

fat [fæt] adj gordo; *(book)* grueso; *(profit)* grande, pingüe ♦ n grasa; *(on person)* carnes fpl; *(for cooking)* manteca

fatal ['feɪtl] adj *(mistake)* fatal; *(injury)* mortal ❑ **fatality** [fə'tælɪti] n *(casualty)* víctima ❑ **fatally** adv fatalmente; mortalmente

fate [feɪt] n destino; *(of person)* suerte f ❑ **fateful** adj fatídico

father ['fɑːðər] n padre m ❑ **father-in-law** n suegro ❑ **fatherly** adj paternal

fathom ['fæðəm] n braza ♦ vt *(mystery)* desentrañar; *(understand)* lograr comprender

fatigue [fə'tiːg] n fatiga, cansancio

fatten ['fætn] vt, vi engordar

fatty ['fæti] adj *(food)* graso ♦ n *(inf)* gordito(-a), gordinflón(-ona) m/f

fatuous ['fætʃuəs] adj fatuo, necio

faucet ['fɔːsɪt] *(US)* n llave f, canilla *(RPI)*

fault [fɔːlt] n *(blame)* culpa; *(defect: in person, machine)* defecto; *(GEO)* falla ♦ vt criticar; **it's my ~** es culpa mía; **to find ~ with** criticar, poner peros a; **at ~** culpable ❑ **faulty** adj defectuoso

fauna ['fɔːnə] n fauna

favor *(US)* ['feɪvər] *(BRIT* **favour***)* n favor m; *(approval)* aprobación f ♦ vt *(proposition)* estar a favor de, aprobar; *(assist)* ser propicio a; **to do sb a ~** hacer un favor a algn; **to find ~ with sb** caer en gracia a algn; **in ~ of** a favor de ❑ **favorable** adj favorable ❑ **favorite** adj, n favorito, preferido

fawn [fɔːn] n cervato ♦ adj *(also: ~-colored)* color de cervato, leonado ♦ vi: **to ~ (up)on** adular

fax [fæks] n *(document)* fax m; *(machine)* telefax m ♦ vt mandar por telefax

FBI *(US)* n abbr *(= Federal Bureau of Investigation)* FBI m

fear [fɪər] n miedo, temor m ♦ vt tener miedo de, temer; **for ~ of** por si ☐ **fearful** adj temeroso, miedoso; (awful) terrible ☐ **fearless** adj audaz

feasible ['fi:zəbəl] adj factible

feast [fi:st] n banquete m; (BRIT REL: also: ~ **day**) fiesta ♦ vi festejar

feat [fi:t] n hazaña

feather ['fɛðər] n pluma

feature ['fi:tʃər] n característica; (article) artículo de fondo ♦ vt (movie) presentar ♦ vi: **to ~ in** tener un papel destacado en; **~s** npl (of face) facciones fpl ☐ **feature movie** (US) (BRIT **feature film**) n largometraje m

February ['fɛbruəri] n febrero

fed [fɛd] pt, pp of **feed**

federal ['fɛdərəl] adj federal

federation [fɛdə'reɪʃən] n federación f

fed up [fɛd'ʌp] adj: **to be ~ (with)** estar harto (de)

fee [fi:] n pago; (professional) derechos mpl, honorarios mpl; (of club) cuota; **school ~s** (BRIT) matrícula

feeble ['fi:bəl] adj débil; (joke) flojo

feed [fi:d] (pt, pp **fed**) n comida; (of animal) pienso; (on printer) dispositivo de alimentación ♦ vt alimentar; (animal) dar de comer a; (data, information): **to ~ into** meter en; (baby: breastfeed) dar el pecho a ▶ **feed on** vt fus alimentarse de ☐ **feedback** n reacción f, feedback m

feel [fi:l] (pt, pp **felt**) n (sensation) sensación f; (sense of touch) tacto; (impression): **to have the ~ of** parecerse a ♦ vt tocar; (pain etc) sentir; (think, believe) creer; **to ~ hungry/cold** tener hambre/frío; **to ~ lonely/better** sentirse solo/mejor; **I don't ~ well** no me siento bien; **it ~s soft** es suave al tacto; **to ~ like** (want) tener ganas de ▶ **feel around** or (BRIT) **about** vi tantear ☐ **feeler** n (of insect) antena ☐ **feeling** n (physical) sensación f; (foreboding) presentimiento; (emotion) sentimiento

feet [fi:t] npl of **foot**

feign [feɪn] vt fingir

fell [fɛl] pt of **fall** ♦ vt (tree) talar

fellow ['fɛloʊ] n tipo; (comrade) compañero; (of organization) socio(-a) ♦ cpd: **~ citizen** n conciudadano(-a); **~ countryman** n compatriota m; **~ men** npl semejantes mpl ☐ **fellowship** n compañerismo; (grant) beca

felony ['fɛləni] n crimen m

felt [fɛlt] pt, pp of **feel** ♦ n fieltro ☐ **felt-tip pen** (BRIT) n rotulador m

female ['fi:meɪl] n (pej: woman) mujer f, tía; (ZOOL) hembra ♦ adj femenino; hembra

feminine ['fɛmɪnɪn] adj femenino

feminist ['fɛmɪnɪst] n feminista

fence [fɛns] n valla, cerca ♦ vt (also: ~ **in**) cercar ♦ vi (SPORT) hacer esgrima ☐ **fencing** n esgrima

fend [fɛnd] vi: **to ~ for o.s.** valerse por sí mismo ▶ **fend off** vt (attack) rechazar; (questions) evadir

fender ['fɛndər] n guardafuego; (US AUT) salpicadera (MEX), guardabarros m inv (LAm exc MEX, SP)

ferment [vb fər'mɛnt, n 'fɜ:rmɛnt] vi fermentar ♦ n (fig) agitación f

fern [fɜ:rn] n helecho

ferocious [fə'roʊʃəs] adj feroz

ferret ['fɛrɪt] n hurón m

Ferris wheel ['fɛrɪs,wi:l] (US) n rueda de la fortuna (MEX), rueda gigante (LAm), noria (SP)

ferry ['fɛri] n (small) barca (de pasaje), balsa; (large: also: ~**boat**) transbordador m, ferry m ♦ vt transportar

fertile ['fɜ:rtl] adj fértil; (BIOL) fecundo ☐ **fertilize** ['fɜ:rtlaɪz] vt (BIOL) fecundar; (AGR) abonar ☐ **fertilizer** n abono

fervor (US) ['fɜ:rvər] (BRIT **fervour**) n fervor m

fester ['fɛstər] vi ulcerarse

festival ['fɛstɪvəl] n (REL) fiesta; (ART, MUS) festival m

festive ['fɛstɪv] adj festivo; **the ~ season** (BRIT: Christmas) las Navidades ☐ **festivities** [fɛs'tɪvɪtɪz] npl fiestas fpl

festoon [fɛs'tu:n] vt: **to ~ with** engalanar de

fetch [fɛtʃ] vt ir a buscar; (sell for) venderse por

fête [feɪt] n fiesta

fetus (US) ['fi:təs] (BRIT **foetus**) n feto

feud [fju:d] n (hostility) enemistad f; (quarrel) disputa

fever ['fi:vər] n fiebre f ☐ **fever blister** (US) n herpes m inv labial ☐ **feverish** adj febril

few [fju:] adj (not many) pocos ♦ pron pocos; algunos; **a ~** adj unos pocos, algunos ☐ **fewer** adj menos ☐ **fewest** adj los (las) menos

fiancé [fi:ɑ:n'seɪ] n novio, prometido ☐ **fiancée** n novia, prometida

fiasco [fɪ'æskoʊ] n fiasco, desastre m

fib [fɪb] n mentirilla

fiber (US) ['faɪbər] (BRIT **fibre**) n fibra ☐ **Fiberglass®** (US) (BRIT **fibreglass**) n fibra de vidrio

fickle ['fɪkəl] adj inconstante

fiction ['fɪkʃən] n ficción f ▫ **fictional** adj novelesco ▫ **fictitious** [fɪk'tɪʃəs] adj ficticio

fiddle ['fɪdl] n (MUS) violín m; (BRIT: cheating) trampa ♦ vt (BRIT: accounts) falsificar ► **fiddle with** vt fus juguetear con

fidget ['fɪdʒɪt] vi enredar; **stop ~ing!** ¡estáte quieto!

field [fi:ld] n campo; (fig) campo, esfera; (SPORT) cancha (LAm), campo (SP) ▫ **field hockey** (US) n hockey m (sobre hierba) ▫ **field marshal** (BRIT) n mariscal m ▫ **fieldwork** n trabajo de campo

fiend [fi:nd] n demonio

fierce [fɪərs] adj feroz; (wind, heat) fuerte; (fighting, enemy) encarnizado

fiery ['faɪərɪ] adj (burning) ardiente; (temperament) apasionado

fifteen ['fɪf'ti:n] num quince

fifth [fɪfθ] num quinto

fifty ['fɪftɪ] num cincuenta ▫ **fifty-fifty** adj (deal, split) a medias ♦ adv a medias, mitad por mitad

fig [fɪg] n higo

fight [faɪt] (pt, pp **fought**) n (gen) pelea; (MIL) combate m; (struggle) lucha ♦ vt luchar contra; (cancer, alcoholism) combatir; (election) intentar ganar; (emotion) resistir ♦ vi pelear, luchar ▫ **fighter** n combatiente mf; (plane) caza m ▫ **fighting** n combate m, pelea

figment ['fɪgmənt] n: **a ~ of the imagination** una quimera

figurative ['fɪgjurətɪv] adj (meaning) figurado; (style) figurativo

figure ['fɪgjər] n (DRAWING, GEOM) figura, dibujo; (number, cipher) cifra; (body, outline) tipo; (personality) figura ♦ vt (US) imaginar ♦ vi (appear) figurar ► **figure out** vt (work out) resolver ▫ **figurehead** n (NAUT) mascarón m de proa; (pej: leader) figura decorativa ▫ **figure of speech** n figura retórica

file [faɪl] n (tool) lima; (dossier) expediente m; (folder) carpeta; (COMPUT) fichero; (row) fila ♦ vt limar; (LAW: claim) presentar; (store) archivar ► **file in/out** vi entrar/salir en fila ▫ **filing cabinet** n fichero, archivador m

fill [fɪl] vt (space): **to ~ (with)** llenar (de); (vacancy, need) cubrir ♦ n: **to eat one's ~** llenarse ► **fill in** (BRIT) vt = **fill out** ► **fill out** (US) vt (form, application) rellenar ► **fill up** vt llenar (hasta el borde) ♦ vi (AUT) poner gasolina

fillet ['fɪleɪ] (US **filet**) n filete m ▫ **fillet steak** n filete m de ternera

filling ['fɪlɪŋ] n (CULIN) relleno; (for tooth) empaste m ▫ **filling station** (BRIT) n estación f de servicio

film [fɪlm] n (gen) película ♦ vt (scene) filmar ♦ vi rodar (una película) ▫ **film star** (BRIT) n astro, estrella de cine

filter ['fɪltər] n filtro ♦ vt filtrar ▫ **filter lane** (BRIT) n carril de selección ▫ **filter-tipped** adj con filtro

filth [fɪlθ] n suciedad f ▫ **filthy** adj sucio; (language) obsceno

fin [fɪn] n (gen) aleta

final ['faɪnl] adj (last) final, último; (definitive) definitivo, terminante ♦ n (BRIT SPORT) final f; **~s** npl (SCOL) examen m final; (US SPORT) final f

finale [fɪ'nɑ:lɪ] n final m

final: ▫ **finalist** n (SPORT) finalista mf ▫ **finalize** vt concluir, completar ▫ **finally** adv (lastly) por último, finalmente; (eventually) por fin

finance [fa'næns] n (money) fondos mpl; (personal finances) situación f económica ♦ vt financiar; **~s** npl finanzas fpl ▫ **financial** adj financiero

find [faɪnd] (pt, pp **found**) vt encontrar, hallar; (come upon) descubrir ♦ n hallazgo; descubrimiento; **to ~ sb guilty** (LAW) declarar culpable a algn ► **find out** vt averiguar; (truth, secret) descubrir; **to find out about** (subject) informarse sobre; (by chance) enterarse de ▫ **findings** npl (LAW) veredicto, fallo; (of report) recomendaciones fpl

fine [faɪn] adj excelente; (thin) fino ♦ adv (well) bien ♦ n (LAW) multa ♦ vt (LAW) multar; **to be ~** (person) estar bien; (weather) hacer buen tiempo ▫ **fine arts** npl bellas artes fpl

finery ['faɪnərɪ] n adornos mpl

finger ['fɪŋgər] n dedo ♦ vt (touch) manosear; **little/index ~** (dedo) meñique m/índice m ▫ **fingernail** n uña ▫ **fingerprint** n huella dactilar ▫ **fingertip** n yema del dedo

finish ['fɪnɪʃ] n (end) fin m; (SPORT) meta; (polish etc) acabado ♦ vt, vi terminar; **to ~ doing sth** acabar de hacer algo; **to ~ third** llegar el tercero ► **finish off** vt acabar, terminar; (kill) acabar con ► **finish up** (BRIT) vt acabar, terminar ♦ vi ir a parar, terminar ▫ **finish line** (US) (BRIT **finishing line**) n línea de llegada or meta

finite ['faɪnaɪt] adj finito; (verb) conjugado

fink [fɪŋk] (US: inf) n (person) soplón(-ona) m/f

Finland ['fɪnlənd] n Finlandia

Finn [fɪn] n finlandés(-esa) m/f ▫ **Finnish** adj finlandés(-esa) ♦ n (LING) finlandés m

fir [fə:r] n abeto

fire ['faɪər] n fuego; (in hearth) lumbre f; (accidental) incendio; (heater) estufa ♦ vt (gun) disparar; (interest) despertar; (inf: dismiss) despedir ♦ vi (shoot) disparar; **on ~** ardiendo, en llamas □ **fire alarm** n alarma de incendios □ **firearm** n arma de fuego □ **fire brigade** (BRIT) n = **fire department** □ **fire department** (US) n (cuerpo de) bomberos mpl □ **fire engine** (BRIT) n = **firetruck** □ **fire escape** n escalera de incendios □ **fire extinguisher** n extintor m (de incendios) □ **fireguard** n rejilla de protección □ **fireman** n bombero □ **fireplace** n chimenea □ **fireside** n: **by the fireside** al lado de la chimenea □ **fire station** n estación f (LAm) or cuartel m (RPI) or parque m (SP) de bomberos □ **firetruck** (US) n carro (LAm) or coche m (SP) de bomberos, autobomba m (RPI) □ **firewall** n (INTERNET) firewall m □ **firewood** n leña □ **fireworks** npl fuegos mpl artificiales

firing squad n pelotón m de ejecución

firm [fɜːrm] adj firme; (look, voice) resuelto ♦ n firma, empresa □ **firmly** adv firmemente; resueltamente

first [fɜːrst] adj primero ♦ adv (before others) primero; (when listing reasons etc) en primer lugar, primeramente ♦ n (person: in race) primero(-a); (AUT) primera; (BRIT SCOL) título de licenciado con calificación de sobresaliente; **at ~** al principio; **~ of all** ante todo □ **first aid** n primera ayuda, primeros auxilios mpl □ **first-aid kit** n botiquín m □ **first-class** adj (excellent) de primera (categoría); (ticket) de primera clase □ **First Family** (US) n la familia del presidente de EE.UU. □ **firsthand** adj de primera mano □ **First Lady** (US) n primera dama □ **first lieutenant** (US) n (AER) teniente mf, teniente primero (SC) □ **firstly** adv en primer lugar □ **first name** n nombre m (de pila) □ **first-rate** adj estupendo

fish [fɪʃ] n inv pez m; (food) pescado ♦ vt, vi pescar; **to go ~ing** ir de pesca □ **fisherman** n pescador m □ **fish farm** n criadero de peces □ **fish fingers** (BRIT) npl = **fish sticks** □ **fish hook** n anzuelo □ **fishing boat** n barca de pesca □ **fishing line** n sedal m □ **fishing rod** n caña (de pescar) □ **fishmonger's (shop)** (BRIT) n pescadería □ **fish sticks** (US) npl croquetas fpl de pescado □ **fishy** (inf) adj sospechoso

fist [fɪst] n puño

fit [fɪt] adj (suitable) adecuado, apropiado; (healthy) en (buena) forma ♦ vt (clothes) estar or sentar bien a; (install) poner; (equip) proveer, dotar; (facts) cuadrar or corresponder con ♦ vi (clothes) sentar bien; (in space, gap) caber; (facts) coincidir ♦ n (MED) ataque m; **to ~ to** (ready) a punto de; **~ for** apropiado para; **a ~ of anger/pride** un arranque de cólera/orgullo; **this dress is a good ~** este vestido me sienta bien; **by ~s and starts** a rachas ▸ **fit in** vi (fig: person) llevarse bien (con todos) □ **fitful** adj espasmódico, intermitente (BRIT) □ **fitment** (BRIT) n accesorio de montaje □ **fitness** n (MED) salud f □ **fitted carpet** (BRIT) n moqueta □ **fitted kitchen** n cocina amueblada □ **fitter** n ajustador m □ **fitting** adj apropiado ♦ n (of dress) prueba; (of piece of equipment) instalación f □ **fitting room** n probador m □ **fittings** npl instalaciones fpl

five [faɪv] num cinco □ **fiver** (inf) n (US) billete m de cinco dólares; (BRIT) billete m de cinco libras

fix [fɪks] vt (secure) fijar, asegurar; (mend) arreglar; (prepare) preparar ♦ n: **to be in a ~** estar en un aprieto ▸ **fix up** vt (meeting) arreglar; **to fix sb up with sth** proveer a algn de algo □ **fixation** [fɪk'seɪʃən] n obsesión f □ **fixed** adj (prices etc) fijo □ **fixture** n (SPORT) encuentro; **fixtures** npl (closets etc) instalaciones fpl fijas

fizzy ['fɪzɪ] (BRIT) adj (drink) gaseoso

fjord [fjɔːrd] n fiordo

flabbergasted ['flæbərgæstɪd] adj pasmado, alucinado

flabby ['flæbɪ] adj gordo

flag [flæg] n bandera; (stone) losa ♦ vi decaer ♦ vt: **to ~ sb down** hacer señas a algn para que se pare □ **flagpole** n asta de bandera □ **flagship** n buque m insignia; (fig) bandera

flair [fleər] n aptitud f especial

flak [flæk] (US **flack**) n (MIL) fuego antiaéreo; (inf: criticism) lluvia de críticas

flake [fleɪk] n (of rust, paint) escama; (of snow, soap) copo ♦ vi (also: ~ **off**) desconcharse

flamboyant [flæm'bɔɪənt] adj (dress) vistoso; (person) extravagante

flame [fleɪm] n llama, flama (MEX); **old ~** (lover) antiguo amor

flamingo [flə'mɪŋɡoʊ] n flamingo (MEX), flamenco (LAm exc MEX, SP)

flammable ['flæməbəl] adj inflamable, flamable (MEX)

flan [flæn] (BRIT) n tarta

⚠ Be careful not to translate **flan** by the Spanish word **flan**.

flank [flæŋk] n (of animal) ijar m; (of army) flanco ♦ vt flanquear

flannel ['flænl] n (fabric) franela; (BRIT: also: face ~) manopla

flap [flæp] n (of pocket, envelope) solapa ♦ vt (wings, arms) agitar ♦ vi (sail, flag) ondear

flare [flɛər] n llamarada; (MIL) bengala; (in skirt etc) vuelo ▶ **flare up** vi encenderse; (fig: person) encolerizarse; (: revolt) estallar

flash [flæʃ] n relámpago; (also: **news ~**) noticias fpl de última hora; (PHOT) flash m ♦ vt (light, headlights) lanzar un destello con; (news, message) transmitir; (smile) lanzar ♦ vi brillar; (warning light etc) lanzar destellos; **in a ~** en un instante; **he ~ed by or past** pasó como un rayo □ **flashback** n (MOVIE) flashback m □ **flashbulb** n lámpara or bombilla de flash □ **flash cube** n cubo de flash □ **flashlight** (US) n linterna

flashy ['flæʃi] (pej) adj ostentoso

flask [flæsk] n frasco; (also: **vacuum ~**) termo

flat [flæt] adj llano; (smooth) liso; (tire) desinflado; (beer) muerto; (refusal etc) rotundo; (MUS) desafinado; (rate) fijo; (BRIT: battery) descargado ♦ n (AUT) pinchazo; (MUS) bemol m; (BRIT: apartment) apartamento, departamento (LAm); **to work ~ out** trabajar a toda mecha □ **flatly** adv terminantemente, de plano □ **flatten** vt (also: **flatten out**) allanar; (smooth out) alisar; (building, plants) arrasar

flatter ['flætər] vt adular, halagar □ **flattering** adj halagüeño; (dress) que favorece □ **flattery** n adulación f

flatware ['flætwɛər] (US) n cubertería

flaunt [flɔ:nt] vt ostentar, lucir

flavor (US) ['fleivər] (BRIT **flavour**) n sabor m, gusto ♦ vt sazonar, condimentar; **strawberry-~ed** con sabor a fresa □ **flavoring** (US) (BRIT **flavouring**) n (in product) aromatizante m

flavorsome ['fleivərsəm] (US) adj (food, dish) sabroso; (wine) con mucho sabor, sabroso

flavour ['fleivər] (BRIT) n, vt = **flavor**

flaw [flɔ:] n defecto □ **flawless** adj impecable

flax [flæks] n lino

flea [fli:] n pulga □ **flea market** n la pulga (MEX), mercado de chácharas (MEX) or pulgas (LAm), mercadillo (SP)

fleck [flɛk] n (mark) mota

flee [fli:] (pt, pp **fled** [flɛd]) vt huir de ♦ vi huir, fugarse

fleece [fli:s] n vellón m; (wool) lana ♦ vt (inf) desplumar

fleet [fli:t] n flota; (of cars, trucks etc) escuadra

fleeting ['fli:tiŋ] adj fugaz

Flemish ['flɛmiʃ] adj flamenco

flesh [flɛʃ] n carne f; (skin) piel f; (of fruit) pulpa □ **flesh wound** n herida superficial

flew [flu:] pt of **fly**

flex [flɛks] n (BRIT) cordón m ♦ vt (muscles) tensar □ **flexible** adj flexible

flick [flik] n capirotazo; chasquido ♦ vt (with hand) dar un capirotazo a; (whip etc) chasquear; (switch) accionar ▶ **flick through** vt fus hojear

flicker ['flikər] vi (light) parpadear; (flame) vacilar

flier ['flaiər] n aviador(a) m/f

flight [flait] n vuelo; (escape) huida, fuga; (also: ~ **of steps**) tramo (de escaleras) □ **flight attendant** (US) n auxiliar mf de vuelo □ **flight deck** n (AVIAT: on plane) cabina de mandos; (: on aircraft carrier) cubierta de aterrizaje □ **flighty** adj (idea, remark) frívolo, poco serio; (person) caprichoso, voluble

flimsy ['flimzi] adj (thin) muy ligero; (building) endeble; (excuse) flojo

flinch [flintʃ] vi encogerse; **to ~ from** retroceder ante

fling [fliŋ] (pt, pp **flung**) vt arrojar

flint [flint] n pedernal m; (in lighter) piedra

flip [flip] vt dar la vuelta a; (switch: turn on) encender; (turn) apagar; (coin) echar a pico o mona (MEX), echar a cara o cruz (LAm exc MEX, SP)

flippant ['flipənt] adj poco serio

flipper ['flipər] n aleta

flirt [flə:rt] vi coquetear, flirtear ♦ n coqueta

float [flout] n flotador m; (in procession) carroza; (BRIT: money) reserva ♦ vi flotar; (swimmer) hacer la plancha

flock [flɔ:k] n (of sheep) rebaño; (of birds) bandada ♦ vi: **to ~ to** acudir en tropel a

flog [flɔ:g] vt azotar

flood [flʌd] n inundación f; (of letters, imports etc) avalancha ♦ vi inundar ♦ vt (place) inundarse; (people): **to ~ into** inundar □ **flooding** n inundaciones fpl □ **floodlight** n foco

floor [flɔ:r] n suelo; (story) piso; (of sea) fondo ♦ vt (question) dejar sin respuesta; (blow) derribar; **first** (US) or **ground** (BRIT) ~ planta baja; **second** (US) or **first** (BRIT) ~ primer piso □ **floorboard** n tabla □ **floor lamp** (US) n lámpara de pie □ **floor show** n cabaret m

flop [flɔ:p] n fracaso ♦ vi (fail) fracasar; (fall) derrumbarse □ **floppy** adj flojo n (COMPUT: also: **floppy disk**) disquete m, floppy m

flora ['flɔ:rə] n flora

floral ['flɔːrəl] *adj* (*pattern*) floreado

florid ['flɔːrɪd] *adj* florido; (*complexion*) rubicundo

florist ['flɔːrɪst] *n* florista *mf* ❑ **florist's (shop)** (BRIT) *n* = **flower store**

flounder ['flaundər] *vi* (*swimmer*) patalear; (*fig: economy*) estar en dificultades ♦ *n* (ZOOL) platija

flour ['flauər] *n* harina

flourish ['flʌrɪʃ] *vi* florecer ♦ *n* ademán *m*, movimiento (ostentoso)

flout [flaut] *vt* burlarse de

flow [fləu] *n* (*movement*) flujo; (*of traffic*) circulación *f*; (*tide*) corriente *f* ♦ *vi* (*river, blood*) fluir; (*traffic*) circular ❑ **flow chart** *n* organigrama *m*

flower ['flauər] *n* flor *f* ♦ *vi* florecer ❑ **flower bed** *n* macizo ❑ **flowerpot** *n* tiesto ❑ **flower seller** *n* florista *mf* ❑ **flower store** (US) *n* florería (LAm), floristería (SP) ❑ **flowery** *adj* (*fragrance*) floral; (*pattern*) floreado; (*speech*) florido

flown [fləun] *pp* of **fly**

flu [fluː] *n*: **to have ~** tener gripe or (MEX) gripa

fluctuate ['flʌktʃueɪt] *vi* fluctuar

fluent ['fluːənt] *adj* (*linguist*) que habla perfectamente; (*speech*) elocuente; **he speaks ~ French, he's ~ in French** domina el francés ❑ **fluently** *adv* con fluidez

fluff [flʌf] *n* pelusa ❑ **fluffy** *adj* de pelo suave

fluid ['fluːɪd] *adj* (*movement*) fluido, líquido; (*situation*) inestable ♦ *n* fluido, líquido

fluke [fluːk] (*inf*) *n* chiripa

flung [flʌŋ] *pt, pp* of **fling**

flunk [flʌŋk] (US) *vt* reprobar (LAm), suspender (SP)

fluoride ['fluəraɪd] *n* fluoruro

flurry ['flʌri] *n* (*of snow*) temporal *m*; **~ of activity** frenesí *m* de actividad

flush [flʌʃ] *n* rubor *m*; (*fig: of youth etc*) resplandor *m* ♦ *vt* limpiar con agua ♦ *vi* ruborizarse ♦ *adj*: **~ with** a ras de; **to ~ the toilet** tirar de la cadena ❑ **flushed** *adj* ruborizado

flustered ['flʌstərd] *adj* aturdido

flute [fluːt] *n* flauta

flutter ['flʌtər] *n* (*of wings*) revoloteo, aleteo ♦ *vi* revolotear; **a ~ of panic/excitement** una oleada de pánico/excitación

flux [flʌks] *n*: **to be in a state of ~** estar continuamente cambiando

fly [flaɪ] (*pt* **flew**, *pp* **flown**) *n* mosca; (BRIT: on pants: also: **flies**) bragueta ♦ *vt* (*plane*)

pilot(e)ar; (*cargo*) transportar (en avión); (*distances*) recorrer (en avión) ♦ *vi* volar; (*passengers*) ir en avión; (*escape*) evadirse; (*flag*) ondear ▶ **fly away** or **off** *vi* emprender el vuelo ❑ **fly-drive** *n*: **fly-drive vacation** (US) or **holiday** (BRIT) vacaciones que incluyen vuelo y alquiler de coche ❑ **flying** *n* (*activity*) (el) volar; (*action*) vuelo ♦ *adj*: **flying visit** visita relámpago; **with flying colors** con lucimiento ❑ **flying saucer** *n* platillo volante ❑ **flying start** *n*: **to get off to a flying start** empezar con buen pie ❑ **flyover** (BRIT) *n* paso a nivel ❑ **fly sheet** (BRIT) *n* (for tent) doble techo

foal [fəul] *n* potro

foam [fəum] *n* espuma ♦ *vi* hacer espuma ❑ **foam rubber** *n* goma espuma

fob [fɑːb] *vt*: **to ~ sb off with sth** despachar a algn con algo

focal point ['fəukəl,pɔɪnt] *n* (*fig*) centro de atención

focus ['fəukəs] (*pl* **~es**) *n* foco; (*center*) centro ♦ *vt* (*field glasses etc*) enfocar ♦ *vi*: **to ~ (on)** enfocar (a); (*issue etc*) centrarse en; **in/out of ~** enfocado/desenfocado

fodder ['fɑːdər] *n* pienso

foetus ['fiːtəs] (BRIT) *n* = **fetus**

fog [fɑːg] *n* niebla ♦ *vi* (*also*: **to ~ up**: *mirror, glasses*) empañarse ❑ **foggy** *adj*: **it's foggy** hay niebla, está brumoso ❑ **fog lamp** (BRIT) *n* = **fog light** ❑ **fog light** (US) *n* (AUT) faro antiniebla or de niebla

foil [fɔɪl] *vt* frustrar ♦ *n* hoja; (*tinfoil*) papel *m* (de) aluminio; (*complement*) complemento; (FENCING) florete *m*

fold [fəuld] *n* (*bend, crease*) pliegue *m*; (AGR) redil *m* ♦ *vt* doblar; (*arms*) cruzar ▶ **fold up** *vi* plegarse, doblarse; (*business*) quebrar ♦ *vt* (*map etc*) plegar ❑ **folder** *n* (for papers) carpeta; (COMPUT) directorio ❑ **folding** *adj* (*chair, bed*) plegable

foliage ['fəuliɪdʒ] *n* follaje *m*

folk [fəuk] *npl* gente *f* ♦ *adj* popular, folklórico; **~s** *npl* (*family*) familia *sg*, parientes *mpl* ❑ **folklore** *n* folklore *m* ❑ **folk song** *n* canción *f* popular

follow ['fɑːlou] *vt* seguir ♦ *vi* seguir; (*result*) resultar; **to ~ suit** hacer lo mismo ▶ **follow up** *vt* (*letter, offer*) responder a; (*case*) investigar ❑ **follower** *n* (*of person, belief*) partidario(-a) ❑ **following** *adj* siguiente ♦ *n* afición *f*, partidarios *mpl*

folly ['fɑːli] *n* locura

fond [fɑːnd] *adj* (*memory, smile etc*) cariñoso; (*hopes*) ilusorio; **to be ~ of** tener cariño a; (*pastime, food*) ser aficionado a

fondle [ˈfɑːndl] *vt* acariciar

font [fɑːnt] *n* pila bautismal; (*TYP*) fundición *f*

food [fuːd] *n* comida ☐ **food mixer** (*BRIT*) *n* batidora ☐ **food poisoning** *n* intoxicación *f* alimenticia ☐ **food processor** *n* procesador *m* de alimentos ☐ **food stamp** (*US*) *n* cupón para canjear por comida que reciben las personas de pocos recursos ☐ **foodstuffs** *npl* comestibles *mpl*

fool [fuːl] *n* tonto(-a), zonzo(-a) (*LAm*); (*BRIT CULIN*) puré de frutas y crema ♦ *vt* engañar ♦ *vi* (*gen*: **fool around**) bromear ☐ **foolhardy** *adj* temerario ☐ **foolish** *adj* tonto; (*careless*) imprudente ☐ **foolproof** *adj* (*plan etc*) infalible

foot [fut] (*pl* **feet**) *n* pie *m*; (*measure*) pie *m* (= 304 *mm*); (*of animal*) pata ♦ *vt* (*bill*) pagar; **on ~** a pie ☐ **footage** *n* (*FILM*) imágenes *fpl* ☐ **football** *n* balón *m*; (*US*: *game*) futbol *m* (*MEX*) or fútbol *m* (*LAm exc MEX, SP*) americano; (*BRIT*: *soccer*) futbol *m* (*MEX*), fútbol *m* (*LAm exc MEX, SP*) ☐ **football player** *n* (*US*) jugador(a) *m/f* de futbol (*MEX*) or fútbol (*LAm exc MEX, SP*) americano; (*BRIT*: *also*: **footballer**) futbolista *mf* ☐ **foot brake** *n* freno de pie ☐ **footbridge** *n* puente *m* para peatones ☐ **foothills** *npl* estribaciones *fpl* ☐ **foothold** *n* pie *m* firme ☐ **footing** *n* (*fig*) posición *f*; **to lose one's footing** perder el pie ☐ **footlights** *npl* candilejas *fpl* ☐ **footnote** *n* nota a pie de página ☐ **footpath** *n* sendero ☐ **footprint** *n* huella, pisada ☐ **footstep** *n* paso ☐ **footwear** *n* calzado

---

for

KEYWORD

[fɔːr] *prep*

1 (*indicating destination, intention*) para; **the train for Seattle** el tren con destino a *or* de Seattle; **he left for Rome** marchó para Roma; **he went for the paper** fue por el periódico; **is this for me?** ¿es esto para mí?; **it's time for lunch** es la hora de comer

2 (*indicating purpose*) para; **what('s) it for?** ¿para qué (es)?; **to pray for peace** rezar por la paz

3 (*on behalf of, representing*): **the representative for Harlem** el diputado por Harlem; **he works for the government/a local firm** trabaja para el gobierno/en una empresa local; **I'll ask him for you** se lo pediré por ti; **G for George** G de Gerona

4 (*because of*) por esta razón; **for fear of being criticized** por temor a ser criticado

5 (*with regard to*) para; **it's cold for July** hace frío para julio; **he has a gift for languages** tiene don de lenguas

6 (*in exchange for*) por; **I sold it for $20** lo vendí por $20; **to pay 80 cents for a ticket** pagar 80 centavos por un billete

7 (*in favor of*): **are you for or against us?** ¿estás con nosotros o contra nosotros?; **I'm all for it** estoy totalmente a favor; **vote for X** vote (a) X

8 (*referring to distance*): **there are roadworks for 5 miles** hay obras en 5 millas; **we walked for miles** caminamos kilómetros y kilómetros

9 (*referring to time*): **he was away for 2 years** estuvo fuera (durante) dos años; **it hasn't rained for 3 weeks** no ha llovido durante *or* en 3 semanas; **I have known her for years** la conozco desde hace años; **can you do it for tomorrow?** ¿lo podrás hacer para mañana?

10 (*with infinitive clauses*): **it is not for me to decide** la decisión no es cosa mía; **it would be best for you to leave** sería mejor que te fueras; **there is still time for you to do it** todavía te queda tiempo para hacerlo; **for this to be possible ...** para que esto sea posible ...

11 (*in spite of*) a pesar de; **for all his complaints** a pesar de sus quejas

♦ *conj* (*since, as: rather formal*) puesto que

forage [ˈfɔːrɪdʒ] *vi* (*animal*) forrajear; (*person*): **to ~ for** hurgar en busca de

foray [ˈfɔːreɪ] *n* incursión *f*

forbid [fərˈbɪd] (*pt* **forbad(e)** [fərˈbæd], *pp* **~den**) *vt* prohibir; **to ~ sb to do sth** prohibir a algn hacer algo ☐ **forbidding** *adj* amenazador(a)

force [fɔːrs] *n* fuerza ♦ *vt* forzar; (*push*) meter a la fuerza; **the F~s** *npl* (*BRIT*) las Fuerzas Armadas; **to ~ o.s. to do** hacer un esfuerzo por hacer; **in ~** en vigor ☐ **forced** *adj* forzado ☐ **force-feed** *vt* alimentar a la fuerza ☐ **forceful** *adj* enérgico

forcibly [ˈfɔːrsɪbli] *adv* a la fuerza; (*speak*) enérgicamente

ford [fɔːrd] *n* vado

fore [fɔːr] *n*: **to come to the ~** empezar a destacar

fore: ☐ **forearm** *n* antebrazo ☐ **foreboding** *n* presentimiento ☐ **forecast** *n* pronóstico ♦ *vt* pronosticar ☐ **forecourt** (*BRIT*) *n* patio ☐ **forefather** *n* antepasado ❑ **forefinger** n (dedo) índice m ❑ **forefront** n: **in the forefront of** en la vanguardia de

forego [fɔːˈrɡou] vt = **forgo**

foregone [ˈfɔːrɡɑːn] pp of **forego** ♦ adj: **it's a ~ conclusion** es una conclusión evidente

foreground [ˈfɔːrɡraund] n primer plano

forehead [ˈfɔːrɑd] n frente f

foreign [ˈfɔːrɪn] adj extranjero; (trade) exterior; (object) extraño ❑ **foreigner** n extranjero(-a) ❑ **foreign exchange** n divisas fpl ❑ **Foreign Office** (BRIT) n Secretaría (MEX) or Ministerio (LAm exc MEX) de Relaciones Exteriores, Ministerio de Asuntos Exteriores (SP) ❑ **Foreign Secretary** (BRIT) n Secretario (MEX) or Ministro (LAm exc MEX) de Relaciones Exteriores, Ministro de Asuntos Exteriores (SP)

fore: ❑ **foreleg** n pata delantera ❑ **foreman** n capataz m; (in construction) maestro de obras ❑ **foremost** adj principal ♦ adv: **first and foremost** ante todo

forensic [fəˈrensɪk] adj forense

fore: ❑ **forerunner** n precursor(a) m/f ❑ **foresee** (pt **foresaw**, pp **foreseen**) vt prever ❑ **foreseeable** adj previsible ❑ **foreshadow** vt prefigurar, anunciar ❑ **foresight** n previsión f

forest [ˈfɔːrɪst] n bosque m

forestry [ˈfɔːrɪstri] n silvicultura

foretaste [ˈfɔːrteɪst] n muestra

foretell [fɔːrˈtel] (pt, pp **foretold**) vt predecir, pronosticar

forever [fərˈevər] adv para siempre; (endlessly) constantemente

foreword [ˈfɔːrwərd] n prefacio

forfeit [ˈfɔːrfɪt] vt perder

forgave [fərˈɡeɪv] pt of **forgive**

forge [fɔːrdʒ] n herrería ♦ vt (signature, money) falsificar; (metal) forjar ▶ **forge ahead** vi avanzar mucho ❑ **forgery** n falsificación f

forget [fərˈɡet] (pt **forgot**, pp **forgotten**) vt olvidar ♦ vi olvidarse ❑ **forgetful** adj despistado ❑ **forget-me-not** n nomeolvides f inv

forgive [fərˈɡɪv] (pt **forgave**, pp **~n**) vt perdonar; **to ~ sb for sth** perdonar algo a algn ❑ **forgiveness** n perdón m

forgo [fɔːrˈɡou] (pt **forwent**, pp **foregone**) vt (give up) renunciar a; (go without) privarse de

forgot [fərˈɡɑːt] pt of **forget**

forgotten [fərˈɡɑːtn] pp of **forget**

fork [fɔːrk] n (for eating) tenedor m; (for gardening) horca, horqueta; (of roads)

bifurcación f ♦ vi (road) bifurcarse ▶ **fork out** (inf) vt (pay) desembolsar ❑ **forklift truck** n máquina elevadora

forlorn [fərˈlɔːrn] adj (person) triste, melancólico; (place) abandonado; (attempt, hope) desesperado

form [fɔːrm] n forma; (document) formulario; (BRIT SCOL) clase f ♦ vt formar; (idea) concebir; (habit) adquirir; **to ~ a line** (US) or **queue** (BRIT) hacer cola; **in top ~** (BRIT) en plena forma

formal [ˈfɔːrməl] adj (offer, receipt) por escrito; (person etc) correcto; (occasion, dinner) de etiqueta; (dress) correcto; (garden) (de estilo) clásico ❑ **formality** [fɔːrˈmælɪti] n (procedure) trámite m; corrección f; etiqueta ❑ **formally** adv oficialmente

format [ˈfɔːrmæt] n formato ♦ vt (COMPUT) formatear

formative [ˈfɔːrmətɪv] adj (years) de formación; (influence) formativo

former [ˈfɔːrmər] adj anterior; (earlier) antiguo; (ex) ex; **the ~ ... the latter ...** aquél ... éste ... ❑ **formerly** adv antes

formula [ˈfɔːrmjulə] n fórmula

forsake [fərˈseɪk] (pt **forsook**, pp **~n**) vt (gen) abandonar; (plan) renunciar a

fort [fɔːrt] n fuerte m

forte [fɔːrt] n fuerte m

forth [fɔːrθ] adv: **back and ~** de acá para allá; **and so ~** y así sucesivamente ❑ **forthcoming** adj próximo, venidero; (help, information) disponible; (character) comunicativo ❑ **forthright** adj franco ❑ **forthwith** adv en el acto

fortify [ˈfɔːrtɪfaɪ] vt (city) fortificar; (person) fortalecer

fortitude [ˈfɔːrtɪtuːd] n fortaleza

fortnight [ˈfɔːrtnaɪt] (BRIT) n quince días mpl; quincena ❑ **fortnightly** (BRIT) adj de cada quince días, quincenal ♦ adv cada quince días, quincenalmente

fortress [ˈfɔːrtrɪs] n fortaleza

fortunate [ˈfɔːrtʃənɪt] adj afortunado; **it is ~ that ...** (es una) suerte que ... ❑ **fortunately** adv afortunadamente

fortune [ˈfɔːrtʃən] n suerte f; (wealth) fortuna ❑ **fortune-teller** n adivino(-a)

forty [ˈfɔːrti] num cuarenta

forum [ˈfɔːrəm] n foro

forward [ˈfɔːrwərd] adj (movement, position) avanzado; (front) delantero; (in time) adelantado; (not shy) atrevido ♦ n (SPORT) delantero ♦ vt (letter) remitir; (career) promocionar; **to move ~** avanzar

❑ **forward(s)** *adv* (hacia) adelante
❑ **forward slash** *n* (*TYP*) barra diagonal
fossil ['fɑːsəl] *n* fósil *m*
foster ['fɑːstər] *vt* (*child*) acoger en una familia; fomentar ❑ **foster child** *n* hijo(-a) adoptivo(-a)
fought [fɔːt] *pt, pp of* **fight**
foul [faul] *adj* sucio, puerco; (*weather, smell etc*) asqueroso; (*language*) grosero; (*temper*) malísimo ♦ *n* (*SPORT*) falta ♦ *vt* (*dirty*) ensuciar ❑ **foul play** *n* (*LAW*) muerte *f* violenta
found [faund] *pt, pp of* **find** ♦ *vt* fundar ❑ **foundation** [faun'deɪʃən] *n* (*act*) fundación *f*; (*basis*) base *f*; (*also:* **foundation cream**) crema base; **foundations** *npl* (*of building*) cimientos *mpl*
founder ['faundər] *n* fundador(a) *m/f* ♦ *vi* hundirse
foundry ['faundri] *n* fundición *f*
fountain ['fauntən] *n* fuente *f* ❑ **fountain pen** *n* pluma-fuente *f* (*LAm*), (pluma) estilográfica (*SP*)
four [fɔːr] *num* cuatro; **on all ~s** a gatas ❑ **four-poster (bed)** *n* cama de dosel ❑ **fourteen** *num* catorce ❑ **fourth** *num* cuarto
fowl [faul] *n* ave *f* (de corral)
fox [fɑːks] *n* zorro ♦ *vt* confundir
foyer ['fɔɪər] *n* vestíbulo
fraction ['frækʃən] *n* fracción *f*
fracture ['fræktʃər] *n* fractura
fragile ['frædʒəl] *adj* frágil
fragment ['frægmənt] *n* fragmento
fragrant ['freɪgrənt] *adj* fragante, oloroso
frail [freɪl] *adj* frágil; (*person*) débil
frame [freɪm] *n* (*TECH*) armazón *m*; (*of person*) cuerpo; (*of picture, door etc*) marco; (*of glasses: also:* **~s**) montura ♦ *vt* enmarcar ❑ **frame of mind** *n* estado de ánimo ❑ **framework** *n* marco
France [fræns] *n* Francia
franchise ['fræntʃaɪz] *n* (*COMM*) licencia, concesión *f*; (*POL*) derecho de votar, sufragio
frank [fræŋk] *adj* franco ♦ *vt* (*letter*) franquear
frankfurter ['fræŋkˌfɜːrtər] *n* salchicha de Frankfurt
frankly *adv* francamente
frantic ['fræntɪk] *adj* (*distraught*) desesperado; (*hectic*) frenético
fraternity [frə'tɜːrnɪti] *n* (*feeling*) fraternidad *f*; (*group of people*) círculos *mpl*; (*US UNIV*) círculo estudiantil
fraud [frɔːd] *n* fraude *m*; (*person*) impostor(a) *m/f*

fraught [frɔːt] *adj*: **~ with** lleno de
fray [freɪ] *vi* deshilacharse
freak [friːk] *n* (*person*) fenómeno; (*event*) suceso anormal
freckle ['frekəl] *n* peca
free [friː] *adj* libre; (*gratis*) gratuito ♦ *vt* (*prisoner etc*) poner en libertad; (*jammed object*) soltar; **~ (of charge), for ~** gratis ❑ **freedom** *n* libertad *f* ❑ **Freefone®** ['friːˌfoun] (*BRIT*) *n* teléfono gratuito ❑ **free-for-all** *n* riña general ❑ **free gift** *n* prima ❑ **freehold** *n* propiedad *f* vitalicia ❑ **free kick** *n* tiro libre ❑ **freelance** *adj* independiente ♦ *adv* por cuenta propia ❑ **freeloader** (*inf*) *n* gorrón(-ona) *m/f* (*MEX, SP*), gorrero(-a) (*LAm*) ❑ **freely** *adv* libremente; (*liberally*) generosamente ❑ **Freemason** *n* francmasón *m* ❑ **Freepost®** (*BRIT*) *n* franqueo pagado ❑ **free-range** *adj* (*hen, eggs*) de granja ❑ **free trade** *n* libre comercio ❑ **freeway** (*US*) *n* autopista ❑ **free will** *n* libre albedrío; **of one's own free will** por su propia voluntad
freeze [friːz] (*pt* **froze**, *pp* **frozen**) *vi* (*weather*) helar; (*liquid, pipe, person*) helarse, congelarse ♦ *vt* helar; (*food, prices, salaries*) congelar ♦ *n* helada; (*on arms, wages*) congelación *f* ❑ **freeze-dried** *adj* liofilizado ❑ **freezer** *n* congelador *m*, freezer *m* (*SC*)
freezing ['friːzɪŋ] *adj* helado; **3 degrees below ~** tres grados bajo cero ❑ **freezing point** *n* punto de congelación
freight [freɪt] *n* (*goods*) carga; (*money charged*) flete *m* ❑ **freight car** (*US*) *n* vagón *m* de mercancías ❑ **freight train** (*US*) *n* tren *m* de mercancías
French [frentʃ] *adj* francés(-esa) ♦ *n* (*LING*) francés *m*; **the ~** *npl* los franceses ❑ **French bean** (*BRIT*) *n* ejote *m* (*MEX*), frijol *m* (*LAm*), chaucha (*RPl*), judía verde (*SP*) ❑ **French fried potatoes** *npl* = **French fries** ❑ **French fries** *npl* papas *fpl* (*LAm*) or patatas *fpl* (*SP*) fritas ❑ **Frenchman/woman** *n* francés(-esa) *m/f* ❑ **French window** *n* puerta de cristal
frenzy ['frenzi] *n* frenesí *m*
frequent ['friːkwənt] *adj* frecuente ♦ *vt* frecuentar ❑ **frequently** *adv* frecuentemente, a menudo
fresh [freʃ] *adj* fresco; (*bread*) tierno; (*new*) nuevo ❑ **freshen** *vi* (*wind, air*) soplar más recio ▸ **freshen up** *vi* (*person*) arreglarse, lavarse ❑ **fresher** (*BRIT: inf*) *n* = **freshman** ❑ **freshly** *adv* (*made, painted etc*) recién ❑ **freshman** (*US: irreg*) *n* (*UNIV*) estudiante *mf*

de primer año ❑ **freshness** n frescura ❑ **freshwater** adj (fish) de agua dulce

fret [frɛt] vi inquietarse

friar ['fraɪər] n fraile m; (before name) fray m

friction ['frɪkʃən] n fricción f

Friday ['fraɪdɪ] n viernes m inv

fridge [frɪdʒ] n refrigerador m (LAm), heladera (RPl), frigorífico (SP)

fried [fraɪd] adj frito

friend [frɛnd] n amigo(-a) ❑ **friendly** adj simpático; (government) amigo; (place) acogedor(a); (game) amistoso ❑ **friendly fire** n fuego amigo, disparos mpl del propio bando ❑ **friendship** n amistad f

frieze [friːz] n friso

fright [fraɪt] n (terror) terror m; (scare) susto; **to take ~** asustarse ❑ **frighten** vt asustar ❑ **frightened** adj asustado ❑ **frightening** adj espantoso ❑ **frightful** adj espantoso, horrible

frill [frɪl] n volante m

fringe [frɪndʒ] n (on lampshade etc) flecos mpl; (of forest etc) borde m, margen m; (BRIT: of hair) flequillo, fleco (MEX), cerquillo (CAm, RPl) ❑ **fringe benefits** npl ventajas fpl adicionales

frisk [frɪsk] vt cachear, registrar

frisky ['frɪskɪ] adj juguetón(-ona)

fritter ['frɪtər] n buñuelo ▸ **fritter away** vt desperdiciar

frivolous ['frɪvələs] adj frívolo

frizzy ['frɪzɪ] adj rizado; (US: hair) muy rizado

fro [frəʊ] adv see **to**

frock [frɒk] n vestido

frog [frɒg] n rana ❑ **frogman** n hombre-rana m

frolic ['frɒlɪk] vi juguetear

from
KEYWORD
[frʌm] prep

1 (indicating starting place) de, desde; **where do you come from?** ¿de dónde eres?; **from New York to Washington** de Nueva York a Washington; **to escape from sth/sb** escaparse de algo/algn

2 (indicating origin etc) de; **a letter/ telephone call from my sister** una carta/ llamada de mi hermana; **tell him from me that …** dígale de mi parte que …

3 (indicating time): **from one o'clock to** or **until** or **till two** de(sde) la una a or hasta las dos; **from January (on)** a partir de enero

4 (indicating distance) de; **the hotel is 1 mile from the beach** el hotel está a 1 milla de la playa

5 (indicating price, number etc) de; **prices range from $50 to $100** los precios van desde $50 a or hasta $100; **the interest rate was increased from 9% to 10%** el tipo de interés fue incrementado de un 9% a un 10%

6 (indicating difference) de; **he can't tell red from green** no sabe distinguir el rojo del verde; **to be different from sb/sth** ser diferente a algn/algo

7 (because of, on the basis of): **from what he says** por lo que dice; **weak from hunger** debilitado por el hambre

front [frʌnt] n (foremost part) parte f delantera; (of house) fachada; (of dress) delantero; (BRIT: promenade: also: **sea ~**) malecón m (LAm), costanera (SC), paseo marítimo (SP); (MIL, POL, METEOROLOGY) frente m; (fig: appearances) apariencias fpl ♦ adj (wheel, leg) delantero; (row, line) primero; **in ~ (of)** delante (de) ❑ **front door** n puerta principal ❑ **frontier** [frʌn'tɪər] n frontera ❑ **front page** n primera plana ❑ **front room** (BRIT) n salón m, sala ❑ **front-wheel drive** n tracción f delantera

frost [frɒst] n (also: **hoar~**) escarcha ❑ **frostbite** n congelación f ❑ **frosted** adj (cake) escarchado; (glass) deslustrado ❑ **frosting** (US) n escarcha ❑ **frosty** adj (weather) de helada; (welcome etc) glacial

froth [frɒθ] n espuma

frown [fraʊn] vi fruncir el ceño

froze [frəʊz] pt of **freeze**

frozen ['frəʊzən] pp of **freeze**

fruit [fruːt] n inv fruta; fruto; (fig) fruto; resultados mpl ❑ **fruiterer** n frutero(-a) ❑ **fruiterer's** n frutería ❑ **fruitful** adj provechoso ❑ **fruition** [fruː'ɪʃən] n: **to come to fruition** realizarse ❑ **fruit juice** n jugo (LAm) or zumo (SP) de fruta ❑ **fruit machine** (BRIT) n (máquina) tragamonedas f inv (LAm) or tragaperras f inv (SP) ❑ **fruit salad** n ensalada (LAm) or macedonia (SP) de frutas ❑ **fruit seller** (US) n frutero(-a) ❑ **fruit store** (US) n frutería

frustrate ['frʌstreɪt] vt frustrar

fry [fraɪ] (pt, pp **fried**) vt freír ❑ **frying pan** n sartén f

ft. abbr = **foot; feet**

fudge [fʌdʒ] n (CULIN) caramelo blando

fuel ['fjuəl] n (for heating) combustible m; (coal) carbón m; (wood) leña; (for engine) carburante m ❏ **fuel oil** n fuel-oil m, mazut m ❏ **fuel tank** n depósito (de combustible)

fugitive ['fju:dʒɪtɪv] n fugitivo(-a)

fulfill (US) [ful'fɪl] (BRIT **fulfil**) vt (function) cumplir con; (condition) satisfacer; (wish, desire) realizar ❏ **fulfillment** (US) (BRIT **fulfilment**) n satisfacción f; (of promise, desire) realización f

full [ful] adj lleno; (fig) pleno; (complete) completo; (maximum) máximo; (information) detallado; (price) íntegro; (skirt) amplio ♦ adv: **to know ~ well that** saber perfectamente que; **I'm ~ (up)** no puedo más; **~ employment** pleno empleo; **a ~ two hours** dos horas completas; **at ~ speed** a máxima velocidad; **in ~** (reproduce, quote) íntegramente ❏ **full-length** adj (novel etc) entero; (coat) largo; (portrait) de cuerpo entero ❏ **full moon** n luna llena ❏ **full-scale** adj (attack, war) en gran escala; (model) de tamaño natural ❏ **full stop** (BRIT) n punto ❏ **full-time** adj (work) de tiempo completo ♦ adv: **to work full-time** trabajar a tiempo completo ❏ **fully** adv completamente; (at least) por lo menos ❏ **fully-fledged** adj (teacher, lawyer) diplomado

fumble ['fʌmbəl] vi: **to ~ with** manejar torpemente

fume [fju:m] vi (rage) estar furioso ❏ **fumes** npl humo, gases mpl

fun [fʌn] n (amusement) diversión f; **to have ~** divertirse; **for ~** en broma; **to make ~ of** burlarse de

function ['fʌŋkʃən] n función f ♦ vi funcionar ❏ **functional** adj (operational) en buen estado; (practical) funcional

fund [fʌnd] n fondo; (reserve) reserva; **~s** npl (money) fondos mpl

fundamental [fʌndə'mentl] adj fundamental

funeral ['fju:nərəl] n (burial) entierro; (ceremony) funerales mpl ❏ **funeral home** (US) (BRIT **funeral parlour**) n funeraria ❏ **funeral service** n misa de difuntos, funeral m

funfair ['fʌnfeər] (BRIT) n parque m de atracciones

fungus ['fʌŋgəs] (pl **fungi** ['fʌŋgiː]) n hongo; (mold) moho

funnel ['fʌnl] n embudo; (of ship) chimenea

funny ['fʌni] adj gracioso, divertido; (strange) curioso, raro

fur [fɜːr] n piel f; (BRIT: in kettle etc) sarro ❏ **fur coat** n abrigo de pieles

furious ['fjuəriəs] adj furioso; (effort) violento

furlong ['fɜːrlɔːŋ] n octava parte de una milla, = 201.17 m

furnace ['fɜːrnɪs] n horno

furnish ['fɜːrnɪʃ] vt amueblar; (supply) suministrar; (information) facilitar ❏ **furnishings** npl muebles mpl

furniture ['fɜːrnɪtʃər] n muebles mpl; **piece of ~** mueble m

furrow ['fɜːrou] n surco

furry ['fɜːri] adj peludo

further ['fɜːrðər] adj (new) nuevo, adicional ♦ adv más lejos; (more) más; (moreover) además ♦ vt promover, adelantar ❏ **further education** (BRIT) n educación f superior ❏ **furthermore** adv además

furthest ['fɜːrðɪst] superlative of **far**

fury ['fjuəri] n furia

fuse [fju:z] n (US **fuze**) fusible m; (for bomb etc) mecha ♦ vt (metal) fundir; (fig) fusionar ♦ vi fundirse; fusionarse; (BRIT ELEC): **to ~ the lights** fundir los fusibles ❏ **fuse box** n caja de fusibles

fuss [fʌs] n (excitement) conmoción f; (trouble) alboroto; **to make a ~** armar un lío; **to make a ~ over** (US) or **of** (BRIT) sb mimar a algn ❏ **fussy** adj (person) exigente; (too ornate) recargado

futile ['fju:tl] adj vano

future ['fju:tʃər] adj futuro; (coming) venidero ♦ n futuro; (prospects) porvenir m; **in ~** de ahora en adelante

fuze [fju:z] (US) n = **fuse**

fuzz ['fʌz] n (on chin) vello; (fluff) pelusa ❏ **fuzzy** adj (PHOT) borroso; (BRIT: hair) muy rizado

Gg

G [dʒiː] n (MUS) sol m

g abbr (= gram(s)) gr.

G7 abbr (= Group of Seven) el G7, el Grupo de los Siete

gabble ['gæbl] vi hablar atropelladamente

gable ['geibəl] n aguilón m

gadget ['gædʒɪt] n aparato

Gaelic ['geilɪk] adj, n (LING) gaélico

gag [gæg] n (on mouth) mordaza; (joke) chiste m ♦ vt amordazar

gage [geidʒ] (US) n = **gauge**

gaiety ['geiti] n alegría

gaily ['geɪlɪ] adv alegremente

gain [geɪn] n (profit) ganancia; (increase): ~ (in) aumento (de) ♦ vt ganar ♦ vi (watch) adelantarse; **to ~ from/by sth** sacar provecho de algo; **to ~ on sb** ganar terreno a algn; **to ~ 3 lbs (in weight)** engordar 3 libras

gal. abbr = **gallon**

gala ['geɪlə] n fiesta

gale [geɪl] n (wind) vendaval m

gallant ['gælənt] adj valiente; (towards ladies) atento

gall bladder ['gɔːl,blædər] n vesícula biliar

gallery ['gælərɪ] n (for spectators) tribuna; (also: **art ~: public**) pinacoteca; (: private) galería de arte

gallon ['gælən] n galón m (US = 3,785 litros, BRIT = 4,546 litros)

gallop ['gæləp] n galope m ♦ vi galopar

gallows ['gæləʊz] n horca

gallstone ['gɔːlstəʊn] n cálculo biliar

galore [gə'lɔːr] adv en cantidad, en abundancia

gambit ['gæmbɪt] n (fig): (opening) ~ estrategia (inicial)

gamble ['gæmbəl] n (risk) riesgo ♦ vt jugar, apostar ♦ vi (take a risk) jugársela; (bet) apostar; **to ~ on** apostar a; (success etc) contar con ❏ **gambler** n jugador(a) ❏ **gambling** n juego

game [geɪm] n juego; (match) partido; (of cards) partida; (HUNTING) caza ♦ adj (willing): **to be ~ for anything** atreverse a todo; **big ~** caza mayor ❏ **gamekeeper** n guardabosques m inv

gammon ['gæmən] (BRIT) n (bacon) tocino ahumado; (ham) jamón m ahumado

gamut ['gæmət] n gama

gang [gæŋ] n (of criminals) pandilla; (of friends etc) grupo; (of workmen) brigada ▶ **gang up** vi: **to gang up on sb** aliarse contra algn

gangster ['gæŋstər] n gángster m

gangway ['gæŋweɪ] n (on ship) pasarela; (BRIT: in theater, bus etc) pasillo

gaol [dʒeɪl] (BRIT) n, vt = **jail**

gap [gæp] n hueco (LAm), vacío (SP); (in trees, traffic) claro; (in time) intervalo; (difference): ~ (between) diferencia (entre)

gape [geɪp] vi mirar boquiabierto; (shirt etc) abrirse (completamente) ❏ **gaping** adj (completamente) abierto

gap year n año sabático

garage [gə'rɑːʒ] n garaje m; (for repairs) taller m ❏ **garage sale** (US) n venta de objetos usados (en el garaje de una casa particular)

GARAGE SALE

En Estados Unidos, se suelen hacer **garage sales** en los garajes de las casas, que es donde la gente vende las cosas de su casa que ya no necesita. En estas operaciones de compraventa, el vendedor coloca los objetos a la venta en su garaje e invita a la gente del barrio a que pase a verlos y los compre. Un **yard sale** es una actividad parecida, pero que se hace en el jardín o el patio de la casa, en lugar del garaje.

garbage ['gɑːrbɪdʒ] (US) n basura; (inf: nonsense) tonterías fpl ❏ **garbage can** (US) n cubo or bote m (MEX) or tacho (SC) de la basura ❏ **garbage disposal unit** (US) n triturador m de basura ❏ **garbage man** (US) n basurero m ❏ **garbage truck** (US) n camión m de la basura

garbled ['gɑːrbəld] adj (distorted) falsificado, amañado

garden ['gɑːrdn] n jardín m; ~**s** npl (park) parque m ❏ **gardener** n jardinero(-a) ❏ **gardening** n jardinería

gargle ['gɑːrgəl] vi hacer gárgaras, gargarear (LAm)

garish ['gɛrɪʃ] adj chillón(-ona)

garland ['gɑːrlənd] n guirnalda

garlic ['gɑːrlɪk] n ajo

garment ['gɑːrmənt] n prenda (de vestir)

garnish ['gɑːrnɪʃ] vt (CULIN) aderezar

garrison ['gɛrɪsən] n guarnición f

garter ['gɑːrtər] n (US) liguero; (for sock) liga

gas [gæs] n gas m; (US: gasoline) gasolina; (fuel) combustible m ♦ vt asfixiar con gas ❏ **gas cooker** (BRIT) n estufa (MEX) or cocina (LAm exc MEX, SP) de gas ❏ **gas cylinder** n tanque m (MEX) or bombona (LAm exc MEX, SP) de gas ❏ **gas fire** n calentador m (MEX) or estufa (LAm exc MEX, SP) de gas

gash [gæʃ] n rajada (MEX), tajo (LAm), raja (SP); (wound) cuchillada ♦ vt rajar; acuchillar

gasket ['gæskɪt] n (AUT) junta de culata

gas mask n máscara antigás

gas meter n medidor m (LAm) or contador m (SP) de gas

gasoline ['gæsəliːn] (US) n gasolina

gasp [gæsp] n boqueada; (of shock etc) grito sofocado ♦ vi (pant) jadear

gas pedal (US) n acelerador m

gas pump (US) n (in car) bomba de gasolina; (in gas station) surtidor m de gasolina

gas station (US) n gasolinera

gas tank (US) n (AUT) tanque m or depósito (de gasolina)

gastric ['gæstrɪk] adj gástrico

gate [geɪt] n puerta; (iron gate) verja
❏ **gatecrash** vt (party) colarse en
❏ **gateway** n puerta

gather ['gæðər] vt (flowers, fruit) recoger; (assemble) reunir; (pick up) recoger; (SEWING) fruncir; (understand) entender ♦ vi (assemble) reunirse; to ~ speed ganar velocidad
❏ **gathering** n reunión f, asamblea

gaudy ['gɔ:dɪ] adj chillón(-ona)

gauge [geɪdʒ] (US **gage**) n (instrument) indicador m ♦ vt medir; (fig) juzgar

gaunt [gɔ:nt] adj (haggard) demacrado; (stark) desolado

gauntlet ['gɔ:ntlɪt] n (fig): to run the ~ of exponerse a; to throw down the ~ arrojar el guante

gauze [gɔ:z] n gasa

gave [geɪv] pt of **give**

gay [geɪ] adj (homosexual) gay; (joyful) alegre; (color) vivo

gaze [geɪz] n mirada fija ♦ vi: to ~ at sth mirar algo fijamente

gazelle [gə'zɛl] n gacela

gazumping [gə'zʌmpɪŋ] (BRIT) n subida del precio de una casa tras haber sido apalabrado

GB abbr = **Great Britain**

GCSE (BRIT) n abbr (= General Certificate of Secondary Education) examen final que se hace a los 16 años

gear [gɪər] n equipo, herramientas fpl; (TECH) engranaje m; (AUT) velocidad f, marcha ♦ vt (fig: adapt): to ~ sth to adaptar or ajustar algo a; top or (US) high/low ~ cuarta/primera velocidad; in ~ en marcha ▶ **gear up** vt (fig): to gear o.s. up to do sth prepararse (psicológicamente) para hacer algo ❏ **gear box** n caja de cambios ❏ **gear lever** (BRIT) n = **gear shift** ❏ **gear shift** (US) n palanca de cambios

geese [gi:s] npl of **goose**

gel [dʒɛl] n gel m

gem [dʒɛm] n piedra preciosa

Gemini ['dʒɛmɪnaɪ] n Géminis m

gender ['dʒɛndər] n género

gene [dʒi:n] n gen(e) m

general ['dʒɛnərəl] n general m ♦ adj general; in ~ en general ❏ **general delivery** (US) n lista de correos ❏ **general election** n elecciones fpl generales ❏ **generally** adv generalmente, en general ❏ **general practitioner** n médico general ❏ **general**

store n tienda (que vende de todo), almacén m (SC, SP)

generate ['dʒɛnəreɪt] vt (ELEC) generar; (jobs, profits) producir

generation [dʒɛnə'reɪʃən] n generación f

generator ['dʒɛnəreɪtər] n generador m

generic [dʒɪ'nɛrɪk] adj genérico

generosity [dʒɛnə'rɑːsɪtɪ] n generosidad f

generous ['dʒɛnərəs] adj generoso

genetic [dʒɪ'nɛtɪk] adj: ~ **engineering** ingeniería genética; ~ **fingerprinting** identificación f genética

Geneva [dʒɪ'niːvə] n Ginebra

genial ['dʒiːnɪəl] adj afable, simpático

genitals ['dʒɛnɪtlz] npl (órganos mpl) genitales mpl

genius ['dʒiːnjəs] n genio

genteel [dʒɛn'tiːl] adj fino, elegante

gentle ['dʒɛntl] adj apacible, dulce; (animal) manso; (breeze, curve etc) suave

⚠ Be careful not to translate **gentle** by the Spanish word **gentil**.

gentleman ['dʒɛntlmən] n señor m; (well-bred man) caballero

gently ['dʒɛntlɪ] adv dulcemente; suavemente

gentry ['dʒɛntrɪ] (BRIT) n alta burguesía

gents [dʒɛnts] (BRIT) n aseos mpl (de caballeros)

genuine ['dʒɛnjuɪn] adj auténtico; (person) sincero

geography [dʒɪ'ɑːgrəfɪ] n geografía

geology [dʒɪ'ɑːlədʒɪ] n geología

geometric(al) [dʒɪə'mɛtrɪk(əl)] adj geométrico

geranium [dʒɪ'reɪnɪəm] n geranio

geriatric [dʒɛrɪ'ætrɪk] adj, n geriátrico(-a)

germ [dʒɜːrm] n (microbe) microbio, bacteria; (seed, fig) germen m

German ['dʒɜːrmən] adj alemán(-ana) ♦ n alemán(-ana) m/f; (LING) alemán m
❏ **German measles** n rubeola

Germany ['dʒɜːrmənɪ] n Alemania

gesture ['dʒɛstʃər] n gesto; (symbol) muestra

get

KEYWORD

[gɛt] (pt, pp **got**, pp **gotten** (US)) vi

1 (become, be) ponerse, volverse; **to get old/ tired** envejecer/cansarse; **to get drunk** emborracharse; **to get dirty** ensuciarse; **to**

get married casarse; **when do I get paid?** ¿cuándo me pagan or se me paga?; **it's getting late** se está haciendo tarde

2 (go): **to get to/from** llegar a/de; **to get home** llegar a casa

3 (begin) empezar a; **to get to know sb** (llegar a) conocer a algn; **I'm getting to like him** me está empezando a gustar; **let's get going** or **started** ¡vamos (a empezar)!

4 (modal aux vb): **you've got to do it** tienes que hacerlo

♦ vt

1: **to get sth done** (finish) terminar algo; (have done) mandar hacer algo; **to get one's hair cut** cortarse el pelo; **to get the car going** or **to go** arrancar el carro (LAm) or coche (SP); **to get sb to do sth** conseguir or hacer que algn haga algo; **to get sth/sb ready** preparar algo/a algn

2 (obtain: money, permission, results) conseguir; (find: job, apartment) encontrar; (fetch: person, doctor) buscar; (object) ir a buscar, traer; **to get sth for sb** conseguir algo para algn; **get me Mr. Jones, please** (TEL) comuníqueme (LAm) or póngame (SP) con el Sr. Jones, por favor; **can I get you a drink?** ¿quieres algo de beber?

3 (receive: present, letter) recibir; (acquire: reputation) alcanzar; (: prize) ganar; **what did you get for your birthday?** ¿qué te regalaron por tu cumpleaños?; **how much did you get for the painting?** ¿cuánto sacaste por el cuadro?

4 (catch) agarrar (LAm), coger (SP); (hit: target etc) dar en; **to get sb by the arm/throat** agarrar (LAm) or coger (SP) a algn por el brazo/cuello; **get him!** ¡atrápalo! (LAm), ¡cógelo! (SP); **the bullet got him in the leg** la bala le dio en la pierna

5 (take, move) llevar; **to get sth to sb** hacer llegar algo a algn; **do you think we'll get it through the door?** ¿crees que lo podremos meter por la puerta?

6 (catch, take: plane, bus etc) tomar (LAm), coger (SP); **where do I get the train for New Orleans?** ¿dónde se toma (LAm) or se coge (SP) el tren para Nueva Orleáns?

7 (understand) entender; (hear) oír; **I've got it!** ¡ya lo tengo!, ¡eureka!; **I don't get your meaning** no te entiendo; **I'm sorry, I didn't get your name** lo siento, no entendí (LAm) or cogí (SP) tu nombre

8 (have, possess): **to have got** tener

▶ **get about** vi salir mucho; (BRIT: news) divulgarse

▶ **get along** vi (agree) llevarse bien; (depart) marcharse; (manage) = **get by**

▶ **get around** vt fus rodear; (fig: person) engatusar a

▶ **get at** vt fus (reach) alcanzar; (attack) atacar

▶ **get away** vi marcharse; (escape) escaparse

▶ **get away with** vt fus hacer impunemente

▶ **get back** vi (return) volver

♦ vt recobrar

▶ **get by** vi (pass) (lograr) pasar; (manage) arreglárselas

▶ **get down** vi bajarse

♦ vt fus bajar

♦ vt bajar; (depress) deprimir

▶ **get down to** vt fus (work) ponerse a

▶ **get in** vi entrar; (train) llegar; (arrive home) volver a casa, regresar

▶ **get into** vt fus entrar en; (vehicle) subir a; **to get into a rage** enfadarse

▶ **get off** vi (from train etc) bajar; (depart person, car) marcharse

♦ vt (remove) quitar

♦ vt fus (train, bus) bajar de

▶ **get on** vi (at exam etc): **how are you getting on?** ¿cómo te va?; (agree): **to get on (with)** llevarse bien (con)

♦ vt fus subir a

▶ **get out** vi salir; (of vehicle) bajar

♦ vt sacar

▶ **get out of** vt fus salir de; (duty etc) escaparse de

▶ **get over** vt fus (illness) recobrarse de

▶ **get through** vi (TEL) (lograr) comunicarse

▶ **get through to** vt fus (TEL) comunicar con

▶ **get together** vi reunirse

♦ vt reunir, juntar

▶ **get up** vi (rise) levantarse

♦ vt fus subir

▶ **get up to** vt fus (reach) llegar a; (prank) hacer

getaway ['getəweɪ] n: **to make one's ~** escaparse ❑ **getaway car** n: **the thieves' getaway car** el coche en el que huyeron los ladrones

get-together ['getəɡeðər] n (meeting) reunión f; (party) fiesta

geyser ['ɡaɪzər] n (water heater) calentador m de agua; (GEO) géiser m

ghastly ['ɡæstlɪ] adj horrible

gherkin ['ɡɜːkɪn] n pepinillo

ghetto ['ɡetəʊ] n gueto

ghetto blaster ['ɡetəʊˌblæstər] n grabadora (LAm) o casete m (SP) portátil (de gran tamaño)

ghost [gəust] n fantasma m

giant ['dʒaɪənt] n gigante mf ♦ adj gigantesco, gigante

gibberish ['dʒɪbərɪʃ] n galimatías m

giblets ['dʒɪblɪts] npl menudillos mpl

Gibraltar [dʒɪ'brɔːltər] n Gibraltar m

giddy ['gɪdi] adj mareado

gift [gɪft] n regalo; (ability) talento ▫ **gift certificate** (US) n vale-obsequio m ▫ **gifted** adj dotado ▫ **gift voucher** (BRIT) n = **gift certificate**

gigantic [dʒaɪ'gæntɪk] adj gigantesco

giggle ['gɪgl] vi reírse tontamente

gill [dʒɪl] n (measure) cuarto de pinta (US = 0,118 litros, BRIT = 0,148 litros)

gills [gɪlz] npl (of fish) branquias fpl, agallas fpl

gilt [gɪlt] adj, n dorado ▫ **gilt-edged** (BRIT) adj (COMM) de máxima garantía

gimmick ['gɪmɪk] n truco

gin [dʒɪn] n ginebra

ginger ['dʒɪndʒər] n jengibre m ▫ **ginger ale** (US) n gaseosa de jengibre ▫ **ginger beer** (BRIT) n = **ginger ale** ▫ **gingerbread** n pan m or galleta de jengibre

gingerly ['dʒɪndʒərli] adv con cautela

gipsy ['dʒɪpsi] n = **gypsy**

giraffe [dʒə'ræf] n jirafa

girder ['gɜːrdər] n viga

girl [gɜːrl] n (small) niña; (young woman) chica, joven f, muchacha; (daughter) hija; **an American ~** una (chica) americana ▫ **girlfriend** n (of girl) amiga; (of boy) novia ▫ **girlish** adj de niña

giro ['dʒaɪrəu] (BRIT) n (bank giro) giro bancario; (post office giro) giro postal; (state benefit) cheque quincenal del subsidio de desempleo

gist [dʒɪst] n lo esencial

give [gɪv] (pt gave, pp ~n) vt dar; (deliver) entregar; (as gift) regalar ♦ vi (break) romperse; (stretch: fabric) dar de sí; **to ~ sb sth, ~ sth to sb** dar algo a algn ► **give away** vt (give free) regalar; (betray) traicionar; (disclose) revelar ► **give back** vt devolver ► **give in** vi ceder ♦ vt entregar ► **give off** vt despedir ► **give out** vt distribuir ► **give up** vi rendirse, darse por vencido ♦ vt renunciar a; **to give up smoking** dejar de fumar; **to give o.s. up** entregarse ► **give way** vi ceder; (BRIT AUT) ceder el paso

giveaway ['gɪvəweɪ] n (revelation) revelación f; (gift) regalo

given name ['gɪvən'neɪm] (US) n nombre m de pila

glacier ['glæsər] n glaciar m

glad [glæd] adj contento

gladly ['glædli] adv con mucho gusto

glamor (US) ['glæmər] (BRIT **glamour**) n encanto, atractivo ▫ **glamorous** adj encantador(a), atractivo

glance [glæns] n ojeada, mirada ♦ vi: **to ~ at** echar una ojeada a ▫ **glancing** adj (blow) oblicuo

gland [glænd] n glándula

glare [gleər] n (of anger) mirada feroz; (of light) deslumbramiento, brillo ♦ vi deslumbrar; **to be in the ~ of publicity** ser el foco de la atención pública; **to ~ at** mirar con odio a ▫ **glaring** adj (mistake) manifiesto

glass [glæs] n vidrio, cristal m; (for drinking) vaso; (: with stem) copa; **~es** npl (spectacles) lentes mpl (LAm), gafas fpl (SP) ▫ **glasshouse** (BRIT) n invernadero ▫ **glassware** n cristalería

glaze [gleɪz] vt (window) poner cristales a; (pottery) vidriar ♦ n vidriado ▫ **glazier** ['gleɪzər] (BRIT) n vidriero(-a)

gleam [gliːm] vi brillar

glean [gliːn] vt (information) recoger

glee [gliː] n alegría, regocijo

glen [glen] n cañada

glib [glɪb] adj de mucha labia; (promise, response) poco sincero

glide [glaɪd] vi deslizarse; (AVIAT, birds) planear ▫ **glider** n (AVIAT) planeador m ▫ **gliding** n (AVIAT) vuelo sin motor

glimmer ['glɪmər] n luz f tenue; (of interest) muestra; (of hope) rayo

glimpse [glɪmps] n vislumbre m ♦ vt vislumbrar, entrever

glint [glɪnt] vi centellear

glisten ['glɪsən] vi relucir, brillar

glitter ['glɪtər] vi relucir, brillar

gloat [gləut] vi: **to ~ over** recrearse en

global ['gləubəl] adj mundial; **~ warming** (re)calentamiento global

globe [gləub] n globo; (model) globo terráqueo

gloom [gluːm] n oscuridad f; (sadness) tristeza ▫ **gloomy** adj (dark) oscuro; (sad) triste; (pessimistic) pesimista

glorious ['glɔːriəs] adj glorioso; (weather etc) magnífico

glory ['glɔːri] n gloria

gloss [glɔs] n (shine) brillo; (paint) pintura de aceite ► **gloss over** vt fus disimular

glossary ['glɔsəri] n glosario

glossy ['glɔsi] adj lustroso; (magazine) de lujo

glove [glʌv] n guante m ❑ **glove compartment** n (AUT) guantera

glow [gləu] vi brillar

glower ['glauər] vi: **to ~ at** mirar con ceño

glue [glu:] n goma (de pegar), cemento ♦ vt pegar

glum [glʌm] adj (person, tone) melancólico

glut [glʌt] n superabundancia

glutton ['glʌtn] n glotón(-ona) m/f; **a ~ for work** un(a) trabajador(a) m/f incansable

GM adj abbr (= genetically modified) transgénico

GMO (BRIT) n abbr (= genetically-modified organism) organismo transgénico

gnat [næt] n mosquito

gnaw [nɔ:] vt roer

gnome [nəum] n gnomo

go [gəu] (pt went, pp gone, pl goes) vi ir; (travel) viajar; (depart) irse, marcharse; (work) funcionar, marchar; (be sold) venderse; (time) pasar; (fit, suit): **to go with** hacer juego con; (become) ponerse; (break etc) estropearse, romperse ♦ n: **to have a go (at)** probar suerte (con); **to be on the go** no parar; **whose go is it?** ¿a quién le toca?; **he's going to do it** va a hacerlo; **to go for a walk** ir de paseo; **to go dancing** ir a bailar; **how did it go?** ¿qué tal salió or resultó?, ¿cómo ha ido?; **to go around the back** pasar por detrás ▶ **go about** vi (rumor) propagarse ♦ vt fus: **how do I go about this?** ¿cómo me las arreglo para hacer esto? ▶ **go ahead** vi seguir adelante ▶ **go along** vi ir ♦ vt fus bordear; **to go along with** (agree) estar de acuerdo con ▶ **go away** vi irse, marcharse ▶ **go back** vi volver ▶ **go back on** vt fus (promise) faltar a ▶ **go by** vi (time) pasar ♦ vt fus guiarse por ▶ **go down** vi bajar; (ship) hundirse; (sun) ponerse ♦ vt fus bajar ▶ **go for** vt fus (fetch) ir por; (like) gustar; (attack) atacar ▶ **go in** vi entrar ▶ **go in for** vt fus (competition) presentarse a ▶ **go into** vt fus entrar en; (investigate) investigar; (embark on) dedicarse a ▶ **go off** vi irse, marcharse; (explode) estallar; (event) realizarse; (BRIT: food) pasarse ♦ vt fus (check) revisar; **I'm going off him/the idea** ya no me gusta tanto él/la idea ▶ **go on** vi (continue) seguir, continuar; (happen) pasar, ocurrir; **to go on doing sth** seguir haciendo algo ▶ **go out** vi salir; (fire, light) apagarse ▶ **go over** vi (ship) zozobrar ♦ vt fus (check) revisar ▶ **go through** vt fus (town etc) atravesar ▶ **go up** vi, vt fus subir ▶ **go without** vt fus pasarse sin

goad [gəud] vt aguijonear

go-ahead adj (person) dinámico; (firm) innovador(a) ♦ n luz f verde

goal [gəul] n meta; (score) gol m ❑ **goalkeeper** n portero ❑ **goal line** n línea (de la portería) ❑ **goalpost** n poste m (de la portería)

goat [gəut] n cabra

gobble ['gɑ:bəl] vt (also: ~ **down**, ~ **up**) tragarse, engullir

go-between n intermediario(-a)

god [gɑ:d] n dios m ❑ **God** n Dios m ❑ **godchild** n ahijado(-a) ❑ **goddaughter** n ahijada ❑ **goddess** n diosa ❑ **godfather** n padrino ❑ **god-forsaken** adj dejado de la mano de Dios ❑ **godmother** n madrina ❑ **godsend** n don m del cielo ❑ **godson** n ahijado

goggles ['gɑ:gəlz] npl anteojos mpl protectores (LAm), gafas fpl protectoras (SP)

going ['gəuŋ] n (conditions) estado del terreno ♦ adj: **the ~ rate** la tarifa corriente or en vigor

gold [gəuld] n oro ♦ adj de oro ❑ **golden** adj (made of gold) de oro; (gold in color) dorado ❑ **goldfish** n pez m de colores, pez dorado (MEX) ❑ **gold mine** n (also fig) mina de oro ❑ **gold-plated** adj chapado en oro ❑ **goldsmith** n orfebre mf

golf [gɑ:lf] n golf m ❑ **golf ball** n (for game) pelota de golf ❑ **golf club** n club m de golf; (stick) palo (de golf) ❑ **golf course** n campo de golf ❑ **golfer** n golfista mf

gone [gɑ:n] pp of **go**

good [gud] adj bueno; (pleasant) agradable; (kind) bueno, amable; (well-behaved) educado ♦ n bien m, provecho; **~s** npl (COMM) mercancías fpl; **~!** ¡qué bien!; **to be ~ at** tener aptitud para; **to be ~ for** servir para; **it's ~ for you** te hace bien; **would you be ~ enough to ...?** ¿podría hacerme el favor de ...?, ¿sería tan amable de ...?; **a ~ deal (of)** mucho; **a ~ many** muchos; **to make ~** reparar; **it's no ~ complaining** no vale la pena (de) quejarse; **for ~** para siempre, definitivamente; **~ morning/afternoon!** ¡buenos días/buenas tardes!; **~ evening!** ¡buenas noches!; **~ night!** ¡buenas noches!; **~bye!** ¡adiós!; **to say ~bye** despedirse ❑ **Good Friday** n Viernes m Santo ❑ **good-looking** adj guapo ❑ **good-natured** adj amable, simpático ❑ **goodness** n (of person) bondad f; **for goodness sake!** ¡por Dios!; **goodness gracious!** ¡Dios mío! ❑ **goods train** (BRIT) n tren m de mercancías ❑ **goodwill** n buena voluntad f

Google® ['gu:gəl] n Google® ♦ vi, vt googlear

goose [gu:s] (pl geese) n ganso, oca

gooseberry ['guːzˌbɛri] n grosella espinosa; **to play ~** hacer de chaperón (*MEX*) or chaperona (*LAm*) or carabina (*SP*)

gooseflesh ['guːzˌflɛʃ] n = **goose pimples**

goose pimples npl carne f de gallina

gore [gɔːr] vt cornear ♦ n sangre f

gorge [gɔːrdʒ] n barranco ♦ vr: **to ~ o.s. (on)** atracarse (de)

gorgeous ['gɔːrdʒəs] adj (*thing*) precioso; (*weather*) espléndido; (*person*) guapísimo

gorilla [gəˈrɪlə] n gorila m

gorse [gɔːrs] n tojo

gory ['gɔːri] adj sangriento

go-slow (*BRIT*) n huelga de brazos caídos

gospel ['gɑːspəl] n evangelio

gossip ['gɑːsɪp] n (*scandal*) chismorreo; (*chat*) charla; (*scandalmonger*) chismoso(-a) ♦ vi chismorrear

got [gɑːt] pt, pp of **get** ❑ **gotten** (*US*) pp of **get**

gout [gaut] n gota

govern ['gʌvərn] vt gobernar; (*influence*) dominar ❑ **governess** n institutriz f ❑ **government** n gobierno ❑ **governor** n (*of colony, state*) gobernador(a) m/f; (*BRIT: of school etc*) miembro del consejo; (*BRIT: of jail*) director(a) m/f

gown [gaun] n (*dress*) vestido largo; (*JUR, UNIV*) toga

G.P. n abbr = **general practitioner**

grab [ɡræb] vt agarrar (*LAm*), coger (*SP*) ♦ vi: **to ~ at** intentar agarrar (*LAm*) or coger (*SP*)

grace [ɡreɪs] n gracia ♦ vt honrar; (*adorn*) adornar; **5 days' ~** un plazo de 5 días ❑ **graceful** adj grácil, sutil; (*style, shape*) elegante, gracioso ❑ **gracious** ['ɡreɪʃəs] adj amable

grade [ɡreɪd] n (*quality*) clase f, calidad f; (*in hierarchy*) grado; (*SCOL: mark*) nota; (*US: school class*) curso; (*US: slope*) pendiente f ♦ vt clasificar ❑ **grade crossing** (*US*) n paso a nivel ❑ **grade school** (*US*) n escuela primaria

gradient ['ɡreɪdɪənt] (*BRIT*) n pendiente f

gradual ['ɡrædʒuəl] adj paulatino ❑ **gradually** adv paulatinamente

graduate [n 'ɡrædʒuɪt, vb 'ɡrædʒueɪt] n (*US: of high school*) bachiller m/f; (*of university*) licenciado(-a), egresado(-a) (*LAm*) ♦ vi (*from high school*) terminar el bachillerato, recibirse de bachiller (*LAm*); (*from university*) licenciarse, recibirse (*LAm*) ❑ **graduate school** (*US*) n curso de posgrado ❑ **graduation** ['ɡrædʒuˈeɪʃən] n graduación f; (*ceremony*)

entrega del título; (*US*) entrega del título de bachillerato

graffiti [ɡrəˈfiːti] n graffiti mpl, pintadas fpl

graft [ɡræft] n (*AGR, MED*) injerto; (*bribery*) corrupción f; (*BRIT: inf*) trabajo duro ♦ vt injertar

grain [ɡreɪn] n (*single particle*) grano; (*corn*) granos mpl, cereales mpl; (*of wood*) fibra

gram [ɡræm] n gramo

grammar ['ɡræmər] n gramática ❑ **grammar school** n (*US*) centro de (enseñanza) primaria; (*BRIT*) centro de (enseñanza) secundaria (*al que se accede a través de un examen de ingreso*)

grammatical [ɡrəˈmætɪkəl] adj gramatical

gramme [ɡræm] (*BRIT*) n = **gram**

grand [ɡrænd] adj magnífico, imponente; (*wonderful*) estupendo; (*gesture etc*) grandioso ❑ **grandchildren** npl nietos mpl ❑ **granddad** (*inf*) n abuelito, yayo ❑ **granddaughter** n nieta ❑ **grandeur** ['ɡrændʒər] n magnificencia, lo grandioso ❑ **grandfather** n abuelo ❑ **grandma** (*inf*) n abuelita, yaya ❑ **grandmother** n abuela ❑ **grandpa** (*inf*) n = **granddad** ❑ **grandparents** npl abuelos mpl ❑ **grand piano** n piano de cola ❑ **grandson** n nieto ❑ **grandstand** n (*SPORT*) tribuna

granite ['ɡrænɪt] n granito

granny ['ɡræni] (*inf*) n abuelita, yaya

grant [ɡrænt] vt (*concede*) conceder; (*admit*) reconocer ♦ n (*SCOL*) beca; (*ADMIN*) subvención f; **to take sth/sb for ~ed** dar algo por sentado/no hacer ningún caso a algn

granulated sugar ['ɡrænjuːleɪtɪdˈʃuɡər] (*BRIT*) n azúcar m blanquilla

grape [ɡreɪp] n uva

grapefruit ['ɡreɪpfruːt] n toronja (*LAm*), pomelo (*SC, SP*)

graph [ɡræf] n gráfica ❑ **graphic** adj gráfico ❑ **graphics** n artes fpl gráficas ♦ npl (*drawings*) dibujos mpl

grapple ['ɡræpəl] vi: **to ~ with sth/sb** agarrar a algo/algn

grasp [ɡræsp] vt agarrar, asir; (*understand*) comprender ♦ n (*grip*) asimiento; (*understanding*) comprensión f ❑ **grasping** adj (*mean*) avaro

grass [ɡræs] n hierba; (*lawn*) césped m ❑ **grasshopper** n saltamontes m inv, chapulín m (*MEX, CAm*) ❑ **grass-roots** adj (*fig*) popular

grate [ɡreɪt] n parrilla de chimenea ♦ vi: **to ~ (on)** chirriar (sobre) ♦ vt (*CULIN*) rallar

grateful ['ɡreɪtfəl] adj agradecido

grater ['greɪtər] n rallador m

gratifying ['grætɪfaɪŋ] adj grato

grating ['greɪtɪŋ] n (iron bars) reja ♦ adj (noise) áspero

gratitude ['grætɪtuːd] n agradecimiento

gratuity [grə'tuːɪti] n (tip) propina

grave [greɪv] n tumba ♦ adj serio, grave

gravel ['grævəl] n grava

gravestone ['greɪvstoun] n lápida

graveyard ['greɪvjɑːrd] n cementerio

gravity ['grævɪti] n gravedad f

gravy ['greɪvi] n salsa de carne

gray (US) [greɪ] (BRIT **grey**) adj gris; (weather) sombrío ❑ **gray-haired** (US) (BRIT **grey-haired**) adj canoso

graze [greɪz] vi pacer ♦ vt (touch lightly) rozar; (scrape) raspar ♦ n (MED) abrasión f

grease [griːs] n (fat) grasa; (lubricant) lubricante m ♦ vt engrasar; lubrificar ❑ **greaseproof paper** (BRIT) n papel m encerado ❑ **greasy** adj grasiento

great [greɪt] adj grande; (inf) estupendo, chévere (CAm) ❑ **Great Britain** n Gran Bretaña ❑ **great-grandfather** n bisabuelo ❑ **great-grandmother** n bisabuela ❑ **greatly** adv muy; (with verb) mucho ❑ **greatness** n grandeza

Greece [griːs] n Grecia

greed [griːd] n (also: **-iness**) codicia, avaricia; (for food) gula; (for power etc) avidez f ❑ **greedy** adj avaro; (for food) glotón(-ona)

Greek [griːk] adj griego ♦ n griego(-a); (LING) griego

green [griːn] adj (also POL) verde; (inexperienced) novato ♦ n verde m; (stretch of grass) césped m; (GOLF) green m; **-s** npl (vegetables) verduras fpl ❑ **greenbelt** n zona verde ❑ **green card** n (AUT) carta verde; (US: work permit) permiso de residencia y trabajo en EE.UU. ❑ **greenery** n verdura ❑ **greengrocer** (BRIT) n verdulero(-a) ❑ **greenhouse** n invernadero ❑ **greenhouse effect** n efecto invernadero ❑ **greenhouse gas** n gases mpl de invernadero ❑ **greenish** adj verdoso

Greenland ['griːnlənd] n Groenlandia

greet [griːt] vt (welcome) dar la bienvenida a; (receive: news) recibir ❑ **greeting** n (welcome) bienvenida ❑ **greeting(s) card** n tarjeta de felicitación

grenade [grə'neɪd] n granada

grew [gruː] pt of **grow**

grey [greɪ] (BRIT) adj = **gray** ❑ **greyhound** n galgo

grid [grɪd] n reja; (ELEC) red f ❑ **gridlock** n (traffic jam) embotellamiento, retención f

grief [griːf] n dolor m, pena

grievance ['griːvəns] n motivo de queja, agravio

grieve [griːv] vi afligirse, acongojarse ♦ vt dar pena a; **to ~ for** llorar por

grievous ['griːvəs] adj: **~ bodily harm** (LAW) daños mpl corporales graves

grill [grɪl] n (on stove) parrilla; (also: **mixed ~**) parrillada ♦ vt (inf: question) interrogar; (BRIT) asar a la parrilla

grille [grɪl] n reja; (AUT) rejilla

grim [grɪm] adj (place) sombrío; (situation) triste; (person) ceñudo

grimace ['grɪməs] n mueca ♦ vi hacer muecas

grime [graɪm] n mugre f, suciedad f ❑ **grimy** adj mugriento, sucio

grin [grɪn] n sonrisa abierta or amplia ♦ vi sonreír abiertamente or ampliamente

grind [graɪnd] (pt, pp **ground**) vt (US: meat) picar; (coffee, pepper etc) moler; (make sharp) afilar ♦ n (work) rutina ▸ **grind away** (US) vt, vi matarse (estudiando), machetear (MEX), tragar (RPl), empollar (SP)

grip [grɪp] n (hold) asimiento; (control) control m, dominio; (of tire etc): **to have a good/bad ~** agarrarse bien/mal; (handle) asidero; (BRIT: holdall) maletín m ♦ vt agarrar; (viewer, reader) fascinar; **to get to ~s with** enfrentarse con ❑ **gripping** adj absorbente

grisly ['grɪzli] adj horripilante, horrible

gristle ['grɪsəl] n cartílago

grit [grɪt] n gravilla; (courage) valor m ♦ vt (road) poner gravilla en; **~s** npl (US CULIN) sémola; **to ~ one's teeth** apretar los dientes

groan [groun] n gemido; quejido ♦ vi gemir; quejarse

grocer ['grousər] n tendero(-a), abarrotero(-a) (MEX), almacenero(-a) (SC) ❑ **groceries** npl comestibles mpl, abarrotes mpl (MEX) ❑ **grocer's (shop)** (BRIT) n = **grocery** ❑ **grocery** n (US: also: **grocery store**) tienda de comestibles or (MEX, CAm) abarrotes, almacén (SC)

groin [grɔɪn] n ingle f

groom [gruːm] n mozo de cuadra; (also: **bride~**) novio ♦ vt (horse) almohazar; (fig): **to ~ sb for** preparar a algn para; **well-~ed** de buena presencia

groove [gruːv] n ranura, surco

grope [group]: **to ~ for** vt fus buscar a tientas

gross [grous] adj (neglect, injustice) grave; (vulgar: behavior) grosero; (: appearance) de

mal gusto; (*COMM*) bruto ❏ **grossly** *adv*
(*greatly*) enormemente

grotto ['grɑːtəu] *n* gruta

grotty ['grɒti] (*BRIT: inf*) *adj* horrible

ground [graund] *pt, pp of* **grind** ♦ *n* suelo,
tierra; (*SPORT*) campo, terreno; (*reason: gen pl*)
causa, razón *f*; (*US: also:* **~ wire**) tierra ♦ *vt* (*US
ELEC*) conectar con tierra; (*plane*) mantener en
tierra; **~s** *npl* (*of coffee etc*) poso; (*gardens etc*)
jardines *mpl*, parque *m*; **on the ~** en el suelo;
to the ~ al suelo; **to gain/lose** ganar/perder
terreno ❏ **ground cloth** (*US*) *n* tela
impermeable; suelo ❏ **grounding** *n* (*in
education*) conocimientos *mpl* básicos
❏ **groundless** *adj* infundado
❏ **groundsheet** (*BRIT*) *n* = **ground cloth**
❏ **ground staff** *n* personal *m* de tierra
❏ **groundwork** *n* preparación *f* ❏ **Ground
Zero** *n* zona cero

group [gruːp] *n* grupo; (*musical*) conjunto ♦ *vt*
(*also:* **~ together**) agrupar ♦ *vi* (*also:* **~
together**) agruparse

grouse [graus] *n inv* (*bird*) pavo, urogallo ♦ *vi*
(*complain*) quejarse

grove [grəuv] *n* arboleda

grovel ['grɒvəl] *vi* (*fig*): **to ~ before**
humillarse ante

grow [grəu] (*pt* **grew**, *pp* **~n**) *vi* crecer;
(*increase*) aumentar; (*expand*) desarrollarse;
(*become*) volverse ♦ *vt* cultivar; (*hair, beard*)
dejar crecer; **to ~ rich/weak** enriquecerse/
debilitarse ▶ **grow up** *vi* crecer, hacerse
hombre/mujer ❏ **grower** *n* cultivador(a)
m/f, productor(a) *m/f* ❏ **growing** *adj*
creciente

growl [graul] *vi* gruñir

grown [grəun] *pp of* **grow** ❏ **grown-up** *n*
adulto(-a), (*persona*) mayor *mf*

growth [grəuθ] *n* crecimiento, desarrollo;
(*what has grown*) brote *m*; (*MED*) tumor *m*

grub [grʌb] *n* larva, gusano; (*inf: food*) comida

grubby ['grʌbi] *adj* sucio, mugriento

grudge [grʌdʒ] *n* (*motivo de*) rencor *m* ♦ *vt*:
to ~ sb sth dar algo a algn de mala gana; **to
bear sb a ~** guardar rencor a algn

grueling (*US*) ['gruːəliŋ] (*BRIT* **gruelling**) *adj*
penoso, duro

gruesome ['gruːsəm] *adj* horrible

gruff [grʌf] *adj* (*voice*) ronco; (*manner*) brusco

grumble ['grʌmbəl] *vi* refunfuñar, quejarse

grumpy ['grʌmpi] *adj* gruñón(-ona)

grunt [grʌnt] *vi* gruñir

G-string ['dʒiːstrɪŋ] *n* tanga

guarantee [gærən'tiː] *n* garantía ♦ *vt*
garantizar

guarantor [gærən'tɔːr] *n* garante *mf*,
fiador(a) *m/f*

guard [gɑːd] *n* (*squad*) guardia; (*soldier*)
guardia *mf*; (*US: prison guard*) carcelero(-a);
(*BRIT RAIL*) jefe *m* de tren; (*on machine*)
dispositivo de seguridad; (*also:* **fire~**) rejilla de
protección ♦ *vt* guardar; (*prisoner*) vigilar; **to
be on one's ~** estar alerta ▶ **guard against**
vt fus (*prevent*) protegerse de ❏ **guarded** *adj*
(*fig*) cauteloso ❏ **guardian** *n* guardián(-ana)
m/f; (*of minor*) tutor(a) *m/f* ❏ **guard's van** *n*
(*BRIT RAIL*) furgón *m*

Guatemala [gwɑːtɪ'mɑːlə] *n* Guatemala
❏ **Guatemalan** *adj, n* guatemalteco(-a)

guerrilla [gə'rɪlə] *n* guerrillero(-a)

guess [ges] *vi* (*US: think*) suponer; (*estimate*)
adivinar ♦ *vt* adivinar; suponer ♦ *n* suposición
f, conjetura; **to take** *or* **have a ~** tratar de
adivinar ❏ **guesswork** *n* conjeturas *fpl*

guest [gest] *n* invitado(-a); (*in hotel*) huésped
mf ❏ **guest house** *n* (*US*) casa de invitados;
(*BRIT*) pensión *f* ❏ **guest room** *n* cuarto de
huéspedes

guffaw [gə'fɔː] *vi* reírse a carcajadas

guidance ['gaɪdns] *n* (*counseling*) consejo;
(*leadership*) dirección *f*; **under the ~ of** bajo la
dirección de

guide [gaɪd] *n* (*person*) guía *mf*; (*book, fig*) guía
♦ *vt* (*around museum etc*) guiar; (*lead*)
conducir; (*direct*) orientar ❏ (**girl**) **guide**
(*BRIT*) *n* exploradora ❏ **guidebook** *n* guía
❏ **guide dog** *n* perro *m* lazarillo *or* guía
❏ **guidelines** *npl* (*advice*) directrices *fpl*

guild [gɪld] *n* gremio

guilt [gɪlt] *n* culpabilidad *f* ❏ **guilty** *adj*
culpable

guinea pig ['gɪnɪˌpɪg] *n* conejillo de Indias,
cobaya; (*fig*) conejillo de Indias

guise [gaɪz] *n*: **in** *or* **under the ~ of** bajo
apariencia de

guitar [gɪ'tɑːr] *n* guitarra

gulf [gʌlf] *n* golfo; (*abyss*) abismo

gull [gʌl] *n* gaviota

gullible ['gʌlɪbəl] *adj* crédulo

gully ['gʌli] *n* barranco

gulp [gʌlp] *vi* tragar saliva ♦ *vt* (*also:* **~ down**)
tragarse

gum [gʌm] *n* (*ANAT*) encía; (*candy*) caramelo de
goma; (*BRIT: glue*) goma, cemento; (*also:*
chewing~) chicle *m* ♦ *vt* pegar con goma
❏ **gumboots** (*BRIT*) *npl* botas *fpl* de goma

gun [gʌn] *n* (*small*) pistola, revólver *m*;
(*shotgun*) escopeta; (*rifle*) fusil *m*; (*cannon*)
cañón *m* ❏ **gunboat** *n* cañonero
❏ **gunfire** *n* disparos *mpl* ❏ **gunman** *n*

pistolero ❑ **gunpoint** n: **at gunpoint** a mano armada ❑ **gunpowder** n pólvora ❑ **gunshot** n escopetazo

gurgle ['gɜːrgəl] vi (baby) gorgotear; (water) borbotear

gurney ['gɜːrni] (US) n camilla f

gush [gʌʃ] vi salir a raudales; (person) deshacerse en efusiones

gust [gʌst] n (of wind) ráfaga

gusto ['gʌstəu] n entusiasmo

gut [gʌt] n intestino; ~**s** npl (ANAT) tripas fpl; (courage) valor m

gutter [gʌtər] n (of roof) cloaca (MEX), canaleta (LAm exc MEX), canalón m (SP); (in street) alcantarilla

guy [gaɪ] n (man) tipo, chavo (MEX); (figure) monigote m; (BRIT: also: ~**rope**) cuerda, viento

guzzle ['gʌzəl] vi tragar ♦ vt engullir

gym [dʒɪm] n (also: ~**nasium**) gimnasio; (also: ~**nastics**) gimnasia ❑ **gymnast** n gimnasta mf ❑ **gym shoes** npl zapatillas fpl (de deporte) ❑ **gym slip** (BRIT) n túnica de colegiala

gynecologist (US) [gaɪnɪ'kɑːlədʒɪst] (BRIT **gynaecologist**) n ginecólogo(-a)

gypsy ['dʒɪpsi] n gitano(-a)

Hh

haberdasher ['hæbər,dæʃər] n (US) camisero(-a); (BRIT) mercero(-a)

haberdashery ['hæbər,dæʃəri] n (US) tienda de ropa (de caballero); (BRIT) mercería

habit ['hæbɪt] n hábito, costumbre f; (drug habit) adicción f; (costume) hábito

habitual [hə'bɪtʃuəl] adj acostumbrado, habitual; (drinker, liar) empedernido

hack [hæk] vt (cut) cortar; (slice) tajar ♦ n (pej: writer) escritor(a) m/f a sueldo ❑ **hacker** n (COMPUT) pirata mf informático(-a)

hackneyed ['hæknɪd] adj trillado

had [hæd] pt, pp of **have**

haddock ['hædək] (pl ~ or ~**s**) n abadejo, especie de bacalao

hadn't ['hædnt] cont = **had not**

haemorrhage ['hɛmərɪdʒ] (BRIT) n = **hemorrhage**

haemorrhoids ['hɛmərɔɪdz] (BRIT) npl = **hemorrhoids**

haggle ['hægəl] vi regatear

Hague [heɪg] n: **The** ~ La Haya

hail [heɪl] n granizo; (fig) lluvia ♦ vt saludar; (taxi) llamar a; (acclaim) aclamar ♦ vi granizar ❑ **hailstone** n (piedra de) granizo

hair [hɛər] n pelo, cabellos mpl; (one hair) pelo, cabello; (on legs etc) vello; **to do one's** ~ arreglarse el pelo; **to have gray** ~ tener canas fpl ❑ **hairbrush** n cepillo (para el pelo) ❑ **haircut** n corte m (de pelo) ❑ **hairdo** n peinado ❑ **hairdresser** n peluquero(-a) ❑ **hairdresser's** n peluquería ❑ **hair dryer** n secador m or (MEX) secadora de pelo ❑ **hairgrip** (BRIT) n horquilla ❑ **hairnet** n redecilla ❑ **hairpiece** n postizo ❑ **hairpin** n horquilla ❑ **hairpin curve** (US) (BRIT **hairpin bend**) n curva de horquilla ❑ **hairraising** adj espeluznante ❑ **hair removing cream** n crema depilatoria ❑ **hair spray** n laca ❑ **hairstyle** n peinado ❑ **hairy** adj peludo; velludo; (BRIT: inf: frightening) espeluznante

hake [heɪk] (pl **hake** or ~**s**) n merluza

half [hæf] (pl **halves**) n mitad f; (BRIT RAIL, BUS) boleto (LAm) or billete m (SP) de niño; (of beer) media pinta, tarro (MEX) ♦ adj medio ♦ adv medio, a medias; **two and a** ~ dos y media; ~ **a dozen** media docena; ~ **a pound** media libra; **to cut sth in** ~ cortar algo por la mitad ❑ **half-caste** ['hæf,kæst] (BRIT) n mestizo(-a) ❑ **half-hearted** adj indiferente, poco entusiasta ❑ **half-hour** n media hora ❑ **half-mast** n: **at half-mast** (flag) a media asta ❑ **half-price** adj, adv a mitad de precio ❑ **half term** (BRIT) n (SCOL) vacaciones de mediados del trimestre ❑ **half-time** n descanso ❑ **halfway** adv a medio camino; (halfway through) a mitad de

hall [hɔːl] n (US: passage) pasillo; (for concerts) sala; (entrance way) hall m; vestíbulo ❑ **hall of residence** (BRIT) n residencia

hallmark ['hɔːl,mɑːrk] n sello

hallo [hə'ləu] (BRIT) excl = **hello**

Hallowe'en [hælə'wiːn], **Halloween** n víspera de Todos los Santos

HALLOWE'EN

La tradición anglosajona dice que en la noche del 31 de octubre, **Hallowe'en**, víspera de Todos los Santos, es posible ver a brujas y fantasmas. En este día los niños se disfrazan y van de puerta en puerta llevando un farol hecho con una calabaza en forma de cabeza humana. Cuando se les abre la puerta gritan **"trick or treat"**, amenazando con gastar una broma a quien no les dé golosinas o dinero.

hallucination [həluːsɪˈneɪʃən] n alucinación f

hallway [ˈhɔːlweɪ] n vestíbulo

halo [ˈheɪləʊ] n (of saint) halo, aureola

halt [hɔːlt] n (stop) alto, parada ♦ vt parar; interrumpir ♦ vi pararse

halve [hæv] vt partir por la mitad

halves [hævz] npl of **half**

ham [hæm] n jamón m (cocido)

hamburger [ˈhæm,bɜːrgər] n hamburguesa

hamlet [ˈhæmlɪt] n aldea

hammer [ˈhæmər] n martillo ♦ vt (nail) clavar; (force): **to ~ an idea into sb/a message home** meter una idea en la cabeza a algn/ machacar una idea ♦ vi dar golpes

hammock [ˈhæmək] n hamaca

hamper [ˈhæmpər] vt estorbar ♦ n cesto

hand [hænd] n mano f; (of clock) aguja; (writing) letra; (worker) obrero ♦ vt dar, pasar; **to give** or **lend sb a ~** echar una mano a algn, ayudar a algn; **at ~** a mano; **in ~** (time) libre; (job etc) entre manos; **on ~** (person, services) a mano, al alcance; **to ~** (information etc) a mano; **on the one ~ ..., on the other ~ ...** por una parte ... por otra (parte) ... ► **hand in** vt entregar ► **hand out** vt distribuir ► **hand over** vt (deliver) entregar ❏ **handbag** n bolsa (MEX), cartera (LAm exc MEX), bolso (SP) ❏ **handbook** n manual m ❏ **handbrake** (BRIT) n freno de mano ❏ **handcuffs** npl esposas fpl ❏ **handful** n puñado

handicap [ˈhændi,kæp] n minusvalía; (disadvantage) desventaja; (SPORT) handicap m ♦ vt estorbar; **mentally/physically ~ped person** deficiente mf (mental)/ minusválido(-a) (físico(-a))

handicraft [ˈhændi,kræft] n artesanía; (object) objeto de artesanía

handiwork [ˈhændi,wɜːrk] n obra

handkerchief [ˈhænkərtʃɪf] n pañuelo

handle [ˈhændl] n (of door) manija, manilla; (of drawer) tirador m, agarradera (MEX); (of cup etc) asa; (of knife etc) mango; (for winding) manivela ♦ vt (touch) tocar; (deal with) encargarse de; (treat: people) manejar; **"handle with care"** "(manéjese) con cuidado", "frágil"; **to fly off the ~** perder los estribos ❏ **handlebar(s)** n(pl) manillar m

hand: ❏ **hand luggage** n equipaje m de mano ❏ **handmade** adj hecho a mano ❏ **handout** n (money etc) limosna; (leaflet) folleto ❏ **handrail** n pasamanos m inv ❏ **hands-free** adj (telephone etc) manos libres ❏ **handshake** n apretón m de manos

handsome [ˈhænsəm] adj guapo, buenmozo (MEX); (building) bello; (fig: profit) considerable

handwriting [ˈhænd,raɪtɪŋ] n letra

handy [ˈhændi] adj (close at hand) a la mano; (tool etc) práctico; (skillful) hábil, diestro

hang [hæŋ] (pt, pp **hung**) vt colgar; (criminal: pt, pp **hanged**) ahorcar ♦ vi (painting, coat etc) colgar; (hair, drapery) caer; **to get the ~ of sth** (inf) lograr dominar algo ► **hang around** or (BRIT) **about** vi haraganear ► **hang on** vi (wait) esperar ► **hang up** vi (TEL) colgar ♦ vt colgar

hanger [ˈhæŋər] n gancho (LAm), percha (SP) ❏ **hanger-on** n parásito

hang: ❏ **hang-gliding** n vuelo libre ❏ **hangover** n (after drinking) cruda (MEX, CAm), resaca (LAm exc MEX, SP) ❏ **hang-up** n complejo

hanker [ˈhæŋkər] vi: **to ~ after** añorar

hankie [ˈhæŋki], **hanky** n abbr = **handkerchief**

haphazard [hæpˈhæzərd] adj fortuito

happen [ˈhæpən] vi suceder, ocurrir; (chance): **he ~ed to hear/see** dió la casualidad de que oyó/vió; **as it ~s** da la casualidad de que ❏ **happening** n suceso, acontecimiento

happily [ˈhæpəli] adv (luckily) afortunadamente; (cheerfully) alegremente

happiness [ˈhæpɪnɪs] n felicidad f; (cheerfulness) alegría

happy [ˈhæpi] adj feliz; (cheerful) alegre; **to be ~ (with)** estar contento (con); **to be ~ to do** estar encantado de hacer; **~ birthday!** ¡feliz cumpleaños! ❏ **happy-go-lucky** adj despreocupado ❏ **happy hour** n horas en las que la bebida es más barata, happy hour f

harass [ˈhærəs] vt acosar, hostigar ❏ **harassment** n acoso

harbor (US) [ˈhɑːrbər] (BRIT **harbour**) n puerto ♦ vt (fugitive) dar abrigo a; (hope etc) abrigar

hard [hɑːrd] adj duro; (difficult) difícil; (work) arduo; (person) severo; (fact) innegable ♦ adv (work) mucho, duro; (think) profundamente; **to look ~ at** clavar los ojos en; **to try ~** esforzarse; **no ~ feelings!** ¡sin rencor(es)!; **to be ~ of hearing** ser duro de oído; **to be ~ done by** ser tratado injustamente ❏ **hardback** (also: **hardcover**) n libro de tapa dura or en cartoné, libro en edición de lujo (MEX) ❏ **hardball** (US) n (baseball) beisbol m (MEX), béisbol m (LAm exc MEX, SP) ❏ **hard cash** n dinero contante ❏ **hard disk** n (COMPUT) disco duro ❏ **harden** vt endurecer; (fig) curtir ♦ vi endurecerse;

curtirse ❏ **hard-headed** adj realista
❏ **hard labor** n trabajos mpl forzados

hardly ['hɑːrdlɪ] adv apenas; ~ **ever** casi nunca

hard: ❏ **hardship** n privación f ❏ **hard shoulder** (BRIT) n (AUT) arcén m, acotamiento (MEX), banquina (RPI) ❏ **hard-up** (inf) adj pelado, sin un centavo (MEX), pato (SC) ❏ **hardware** n ferretería; (COMPUT) hardware m; (MIL) armamento ❏ **hardware store** (US) (BRIT **hardware shop**) n ferretería ❏ **hard-wearing** (BRIT) adj resistente, duradero ❏ **hard-working** adj trabajador(a)

hardy ['hɑːrdɪ] adj fuerte; (plant) resistente

hare [heər] n liebre f ❏ **hare-brained** adj descabellado

harm [hɑːrm] n daño, mal m ◆ vt (person) hacer daño a; (health, interests) perjudicar; (thing) dañar; **out of ~'s way** a salvo ❏ **harmful** adj dañino ❏ **harmless** (person) inofensivo; (joke etc) inocente

harmonica [hɑːrˈmɑːnɪkə] n armónica

harmony ['hɑːrmənɪ] n armonía

harness ['hɑːrnɪs] n arreos mpl; (for child) arnés m; (safety harness) arneses mpl ◆ vt (horse) enjaezar, poner los arreos a; (resources) aprovechar

harp [hɑːrp] n arpa ◆ vi: **to ~ on (about)** machacar (con)

harrowing ['hærouɪŋ] adj angustioso

harsh [hɑːrʃ] adj (cruel) duro, cruel; (severe) severo; (sound) áspero; (light) deslumbrador(a)

harvest ['hɑːrvɪst] n (harvest time) siega; (of cereals etc) cosecha; (of grapes) vendimia ◆ vt cosechar

has [hæz] vb see **have**

hash [hæʃ] n (CULIN) picadillo; (fig: mess) lío; (hashish) hachís m

hashish ['hæʃɪʃ] n hachís m

hasn't ['hæzənt] cont = **has not**

hassle ['hæsəl] (inf) n lata

haste [heɪst] n prisa ❏ **hasten** ['heɪsən] vt acelerar ◆ vi darse prisa ❏ **hastily** adv de prisa; precipitadamente ❏ **hasty** adj apresurado; (rash) precipitado

hat [hæt] n sombrero

hatch [hætʃ] n (NAUT: also: **~way**) escotilla; (BRIT: also: **service ~**) ventanilla ◆ vi (bird) salir del cascarón ◆ vt incubar; (plot) tramar; **5 eggs have ~ed** han salido 5 pollos

hatchback ['hætʃbæk] n (AUT) tres or cinco puertas m

hatchet ['hætʃɪt] n hacha; **to bury the ~** (fig) enterrar el hacha de guerra

hate [heɪt] vt odiar, aborrecer ◆ n odio ❏ **hateful** adj odioso ❏ **hatred** ['heɪtrɪd] n odio

haughty ['hɔːtɪ] adj altanero

haul [hɔːl] vt tirar ◆ n (of fish) redada; (of stolen goods etc) botín m ❏ **haulage** (BRIT) n transporte m; (costs) gastos mpl de transporte ❏ **hauler** (US) (BRIT **haulier**) n transportista mf

haunch [hɔːntʃ] n anca; (of meat) pierna

haunt [hɔːnt] vt (ghost) aparecerse en; (obsess) obsesionar ◆ n guarida

---

have

KEYWORD

[hæv] (pt, pp **had**) aux vb

1 (gen) haber; **to have arrived/eaten** haber llegado/comido; **having finished** or **when he had finished, he left** cuando hubo acabado, se fue

2 (in tag questions): **you've done it, haven't you?** lo has hecho, ¿verdad? or ¿no?

3 (in short answers and questions): **I haven't** no; **so I have** pues, es verdad; **we haven't paid - - yes we have!** no hemos pagado -- ¡sí que hemos pagado!; **I've been there before, have you?** he estado allí antes, ¿y tú?

◆ modal aux vb (be obliged): **to have (got) to do sth** tener que hacer algo; **you don't have to tell her** no hay que or no debes decírselo

◆ vt

1 (possess): **he has (got) blue eyes/dark hair** tiene los ojos azules/el pelo negro

2 (referring to meals etc): **to have breakfast/ lunch/dinner** desayunar/comer/cenar; **to have a drink/a cigarette** tomar algo/fumar un cigarrillo

3 (receive) recibir; (obtain) obtener; **may I have your address?** ¿puedes darme tu dirección?; **you can have it for $10** te lo puedes quedar por $10; **I must have it by tomorrow** lo necesito para mañana; **to have a baby** tener un niño or bebé

4 (maintain, allow): **I won't have it/this nonsense!** ¡no lo permitiré!/¡no permitiré estas tonterías!; **we can't have that** no podemos permitir eso

5: **to have sth done** hacer or mandar hacer algo; **to have one's hair cut** cortarse el pelo; **to have sb do sth** hacer que algn haga algo

6 (experience, suffer): **to have a cold/flu** tener un resfriado/la gripe or (MEX) gripa; **she had her bag stolen/her arm broken** le robaron la bolsa (MEX) or el bolso (LAm exc MEX, SP)/se rompió un brazo; **to have an operation** operarse

17 (+ noun): **to have a swim/walk/rest** nadar/dar un paseo/descansar; **let's have a look** vamos a ver; **to have a meeting/party** celebrar una reunión/una fiesta; **let me have a try** déjame intentarlo

▶ **have on** vt (wear dress, hat etc) llevar
▶ **have out** vt: **to have it out with sb** (settle a problem etc) dejar las cosas en claro con algn

haven ['heɪvən] n puerto; (fig) refugio
haven't ['hævənt] cont = **have not**
havoc ['hævək] n estragos mpl
hawk [hɔːk] n halcón m
hay [heɪ] n heno ❑ **hay fever** n fiebre f del heno ❑ **haystack** n almiar m
haywire ['heɪwaɪər] (inf) adj: **to go ~** (plan) embrollarse
hazard ['hæzərd] n peligro ◆ vt aventurar ❑ **hazardous** adj peligroso ❑ **hazard (warning) lights** npl (AUT) señales fpl de emergencia
haze [heɪz] n neblina
hazelnut ['heɪzəl,nʌt] n avellana
hazy ['heɪzɪ] adj brumoso; (idea) vago
he [hiː] pron él; **he who ...** él que ..., quien ...
head [hɛd] n cabeza; (leader) jefe(-a) m/f; (of school, institution) director(a) m/f ◆ vt (list) encabezar; (group) capitanear; (company) dirigir; **~s or tails?** ¿pico o mona? (MEX), ¿cara o cruz? (LAm exc MEX, SP); **~ first** de cabeza; **~ over heels** (in love) perdidamente; **to ~ the ball** cabecear (la pelota) ▶ **head for** vt fus dirigirse a; (disaster) ir camino de ❑ **headache** n dolor m de cabeza ❑ **headdress** n tocado ❑ **heading** n título ❑ **headlamp** (BRIT) n = **headlight** ❑ **headland** n promontorio ❑ **headlight** n faro ❑ **headline** n titular m ❑ **headlong** adv (fall) de cabeza; (rush) precipitadamente ❑ **headmaster/mistress** (BRIT) n director(a) m/f (de escuela) ❑ **head office** n oficina central, central f ❑ **head-on** adj (collision) de frente ❑ **headphones** npl auriculares mpl ❑ **headquarters** npl sede f central; (MIL) cuartel m general ❑ **headrest** n reposacabezas m inv ❑ **headroom** n (in car) altura interior; (under bridge) límite m de altura ❑ **headscarf** (BRIT) n pañuelo ❑ **headstrong** adj testarudo ❑ **head waiter** n capitán m de meseros (MEX), maître m (LAm exc MEX, SP) ❑ **headway** n: **to make headway** (fig) hacer progresos ❑ **headwind** n viento contrario ❑ **heady**

adj (experience, period) apasionante; (wine) cabezón; (atmosphere) embriagador(a)
heal [hiːl] vt curar ◆ vi cicatrizarse
health [hɛlθ] n salud f ❑ **health care** n asistencia sanitaria ❑ **health food** n alimentos mpl orgánicos ❑ **the Health Service** (BRIT) n el servicio de sanidad or salud pública ❑ **healthy** adj sano, saludable
heap [hiːp] n montón m ◆ vt: **to ~ (up)** amontonar; **to ~ sth with** llenar algo hasta arriba de; **~s of** un montón de
hear [hɪər] (pt, pp heard [hɜːrd]) vt (also LAW) oír; (news) saber ◆ vi oír; **to ~ about** oír hablar de; **to ~ from sb** tener noticias de algn ❑ **hearing** n (sense) oído; (LAW) vista ❑ **hearing aid** n audífono ❑ **hearsay** n rumores mpl, hablillas fpl
hearse [hɜːrs] n coche m fúnebre
heart [hɑːrt] n corazón m; (fig) valor m; (of lettuce) cogollo; **~s** npl (CARDS) corazones mpl; **to lose/take ~** descorazonarse/cobrar ánimo; **at ~** en el fondo; **by ~** (learn, know) de memoria ❑ **heart attack** n infarto (de miocardio) ❑ **heartbeat** n latido (del corazón) ❑ **heartbreaking** adj desgarrador(a) ❑ **heartbroken** adj: **she was heartbroken about it** esto le partió el corazón ❑ **heartburn** n acedía ❑ **heart failure** n fallo cardíaco ❑ **heartfelt** adj (deeply felt) más sentido
hearth [hɑːrθ] n (fireplace) chimenea
hearty ['hɑːrtɪ] adj (person) campechano; (laugh) sano; (dislike, support) absoluto
heat [hiːt] n calor m; (SPORT: also: **qualifying ~**) prueba eliminatoria ◆ vt calentar ▶ **heat up** vi calentarse ◆ vt calentar ❑ **heated** adj caliente; (fig) acalorado ❑ **heater** n estufa; (in car) calentador m (MEX), calefacción f (LAm exc MEX, SP)
heath [hiːθ] (BRIT) n brezal m
heather ['hɛðər] n brezo
heating ['hiːtɪŋ] n calefacción f
heatstroke ['hiːt,strəʊk] n insolación f
heat wave n ola de calor
heave [hiːv] vt (pull) jalar (LAm) or tirar (SC, SP) (fuerte); (push) empujar con esfuerzo; (lift) levantar (con esfuerzo) ◆ vi (chest) palpitar; (retch) tener náuseas ◆ n jalón m (LAm), tirón m (SC, SP); empujón m; **to ~ a sigh** suspirar
heaven ['hɛvən] n cielo; (fig) una maravilla ❑ **heavenly** adj celestial; (fig) maravilloso
heavily ['hɛvɪlɪ] adv pesadamente; (drink, smoke) con exceso; (sleep, sigh) profundamente; (depend) mucho

heavy ['hɛvi] adj pesado; (work, blow) duro; (sea, rain, meal) fuerte; (drinker, smoker) grande; (responsibility) grave; (schedule) ocupado; (weather) bochornoso ◻ **heavy goods vehicle** n vehículo pesado ◻ **heavy-set** adj fornido ◻ **heavyweight** n (SPORT, fig) peso pesado

Hebrew ['hi:bru:] adj, n (LING) hebreo

heckle ['hɛkəl] vt interrumpir

hectic ['hɛktɪk] adj agitado

he'd [hi:d] cont = **he would; he had**

hedge [hɛdʒ] n seto ◆ vi contestar con evasivas; **to ~ one's bets** (fig) cubrirse

hedgehog ['hɛdʒ,hɔ:g] n erizo

heed [hi:d] vt (also: **take ~**: pay attention to) hacer caso de ◻ **heedless** adj: **to be heedless (of)** no hacer caso de (de)

heel [hi:l] n talón m; (of shoe) tacón m ◆ vt (shoe) poner tacón a

hefty ['hɛfti] adj (person) fornido; (package, profit) gordo

heifer ['hɛfər] n novilla, ternera

height [haɪt] n (of person) estatura; (of building) altura; (high ground) cerro; (altitude) altitud f; (fig: of season): **at the ~ of summer** en los días más calurosos del verano; (: of power etc) cúspide f; (: of stupidity etc) colmo ◻ **heighten** vt elevar; (fig) aumentar

heir [ɛər] n heredero ◻ **heiress** n heredera ◻ **heirloom** n reliquia de familia

held [hɛld] pt, pp of **hold**

helicopter ['hɛlɪkɑ:ptər] n helicóptero

hell [hɛl] n infierno; **~!** (inf) ¡demonios!

he'll [hi:l] cont = **he will; he shall**

hello [hə'lou] excl ¡hola!; (to attract attention) ¡oiga!; (surprise) ¡caramba!

helm [hɛlm] n (NAUT) timón m

helmet ['hɛlmɪt] n casco

help [hɛlp] n ayuda; (cleaner etc) criada, asistenta ◆ vt ayudar; **~!** ¡socorro!; **~ yourself** sírvete; **he can't ~ it** no es culpa suya ◻ **helper** n ayudante mf ◻ **helpful** adj útil; (person) servicial; (advice) útil ◻ **helping** n ración f ◻ **helpless** adj (incapable) incapaz; (defenseless) indefenso

hem [hɛm] n dobladillo ◆ vt poner or coser el dobladillo de ▶ **hem in** vt cercar

hemorrhage (US) ['hɛmərɪdʒ] (BRIT **haemorrhage**) n hemorragia

hemorrhoids (US) ['hɛmərɔɪdz] (BRIT **haemorrhoids**) npl hemorroides fpl

hen [hɛn] n gallina; (female bird) hembra

hence [hɛns] adv (therefore) por lo tanto; **2 years ~** de aquí a 2 años ◻ **henceforth** adv de hoy en adelante

hepatitis [hɛpə'taɪtɪs] n hepatitis f

her [hɜ:r] pron (direct) la; (indirect) le; (stressed, after prep) ella ◆ adj su; see also **me; my**

herald ['hɛrəld] n heraldo ◆ vt anunciar ◻ **heraldry** n heráldica

herb [ɜ:rb] n hierba

herd [hɜ:rd] n rebaño

here [hɪər] adv aquí; (at this point) en este punto; **~!** (present) ¡presente!; **~ is/are** aquí está/están; **~ she is** aquí está ◻ **hereabouts** adv por aquí ◻ **hereafter** adv en el futuro ◻ **hereby** adv (in letter) por la presente

heritage ['hɛrɪtɪdʒ] n patrimonio

hermit ['hɜ:rmɪt] n ermitaño(-a)

hernia ['hɜ:rniə] n hernia

hero ['hɪrou] (pl **~es**) n héroe m; (in book, movie) protagonista m

heroin ['hɛrouɪn] n heroína

heroine ['hɛrouɪn] n heroína; (in book, movie) protagonista

heron ['hɛrən] n garza

herring ['hɛrɪŋ] n arenque m

hers [hɜ:rz] pron (el) suyo ((la) suya) etc; see also **mine¹**

herself [hɜ:r'sɛlf] pron (reflexive) se; (emphatic) ella misma; (after prep) sí (misma); see also **oneself**

he's [hi:z] = **he is; he has**

hesitant ['hɛzɪtənt] adj vacilante

hesitate ['hɛzɪteɪt] vi vacilar; (in speech) titubear; (be unwilling) resistirse a ◻ **hesitation** [hɛzɪ'teɪʃən] n indecisión f; titubeo; dudas fpl

heterosexual [hɛtərou'sɛkʃuəl] adj heterosexual

heyday ['heɪdeɪ] n: **the ~ of** el apogeo de

HGV n abbr = **heavy goods vehicle**

hi [haɪ] excl ¡hola!; (to attract attention) ¡oiga!

hiatus [haɪ'eɪtəs] n vacío

hibernate ['haɪbərneɪt] vi invernar

hiccough ['hɪkʌp] vi = **hiccup**

hiccup ['hɪkʌp] vi hipar; **~s** npl hipo

hick [hɪk] (US) n (pej) pueblerino(-a)

hickory ['hɪkəri] (US) n nogal m americano, nuez f dura

hide [haɪd] (pt **hid**, pp **hidden**) n (skin) piel f ◆ vt esconder, ocultar ◆ vi: **to ~ (from sb)** esconderse or ocultarse (de algn) ◻ **hide-and-seek** n escondidas fpl (LAm), escondite m (SP)

hideous ['hɪdiəs] adj horrible

hiding ['haɪdɪŋ] n (beating) paliza; **to be in ~** (concealed) estar escondido

hierarchy ['haɪərɑːrkɪ] n jerarquía

hi-fi ['haɪfaɪ] n estéreo, hifi m ♦ adj de alta fidelidad

high [haɪ] adj alto; (speed, number) grande; (price) elevado; (wind) fuerte; (voice) agudo ♦ adv alto, a gran altura; **it is 20 m ~** tiene 20 m de altura; **~ in the air** en las alturas □ **highbrow** adj intelectual □ **highchair** n silla alta □ **higher education** n educación f or enseñanza superior □ **high-handed** adj despótico □ **high-heeled** adj de tacón alto □ **high jump** n (SPORT) salto de altura □ **the Highlands** npl las tierras altas de Escocia □ **highlight** n (fig: of event) punto culminante; (in hair) reflejo ♦ vt subrayar □ **highly** adv (paid) muy bien; (critical, confidential) sumamente; (a lot): **to speak/ think highly of** hablar muy bien de/tener en mucho a □ **highly strung** adj muy nervioso □ **highness** n altura; **Her/His Highness** Su Alteza □ **high-pitched** adj agudo □ **high-rise** n torre f de pisos ♦ adj: **high-rise block** torre f de pisos; **high-rise office block** edificio de oficinas (de muchas plantas) □ **high school** n escuela de secundaria, ≈ (escuela) preparatoria (MEX) □ **high season** (BRIT) n temporada alta □ **high street** (BRIT) n calle f principal (LAm) or mayor (SP) □ **highway** n (US: main road) carretera; autopista □ **Highway Code** (BRIT) n Código de la Circulación

hijack ['haɪdʒæk] vt secuestrar □ **hijacker** n secuestrador(a) m/f

hike [haɪk] vi (go walking) ir de excursión (a pie) ♦ n caminata □ **hiker** n excursionista mf □ **hiking** n senderismo

hilarious [hɪ'lerɪəs] adj divertidísimo

hill [hɪl] n colina; (high) montaña; (slope) cuesta □ **hillbilly** ['hɪl'bɪlɪ] n (US: inf, pej) n rústico(-a) montañés(-esa) □ **hillside** n ladera □ **hill walking** (BRIT) n senderismo (de montaña) □ **hilly** adj montañoso

hilt [hɪlt] n (of sword) empuñadura; **to the ~** (fig: support) incondicionalmente

him [hɪm] pron (direct) le, lo; (indirect) le; (stressed, after prep) él; see also **me** □ **himself** pron (reflexive) se; (emphatic) él mismo; (after prep) sí (mismo); see also **oneself**

hinder ['hɪndər] vt estorbar, impedir □ **hindrance** ['hɪndrəns] n estorbo

hindsight ['haɪndˌsaɪt] n: **with ~** en retrospectiva

Hindu ['hɪnduː] n hindú mf

hinge [hɪndʒ] n bisagra, gozne m ♦ vi (fig): **to ~ on** depender de

hint [hɪnt] n indirecta; (advice) consejo; (sign) dejo ♦ vt: **to ~ that** insinuar que ♦ vi: **to ~ at** hacer alusión a

hinterland ['hɪntərlænd] n interior m, hinterland m

hip [hɪp] n cadera

hippie ['hɪpɪ] (inf) n = **hippy**

hippopotamus [hɪpə'pɑːtəməs] (pl **~es** or **hippopotami**) n hipopótamo

hippy ['hɪpɪ] (inf) n hippy mf, hippie mf

hire ['haɪər] vt (worker) contratar; (BRIT: car, equipment) alquilar ♦ n (BRIT) alquiler m; **for ~** (BRIT) se alquila; (taxi) libre □ **hire(d) car** (BRIT) n carro (LAm) or coche m (SP) de alquiler □ **hire purchase** (BRIT) n compra a plazos

his [hɪz] pron (el) suyo ((la) suya) etc ♦ adj su; see also **mine**[1]; **my**

Hispanic [hɪ'spænɪk] adj hispánico

hiss [hɪs] vi silbar

historian [hɪ'stɔːrɪən] n historiador(a) m/f

historic(al) [hɪ'stɔːrɪk(əl)] adj histórico

history ['hɪstərɪ] n historia

hit [hɪt] (pt, pp **~**) vt (strike) golpear, pegar; (reach: target) alcanzar; (collide with: car) chocar contra; (fig: affect) afectar ♦ n golpe m; (success) éxito; **to ~ it off with sb** llevarse bien con algn □ **hit-and-run driver** n conductor(a) que atropella y huye

hitch [hɪtʃ] vt (fasten) atar, amarrar; (also: **~ up**) remangar ♦ n (difficulty) dificultad f; **to ~ a lift** pedir aventón (MEX), hacer autostop (LAm exc MEX, SP) or dedo (SC)

hitch-hike vi pedir aventón (MEX), hacer autostop (LAm exc MEX, SP) or dedo (SC) □ **hitch-hiking** n aventón m (MEX), autostop m (LAm exc MEX, SP)

hi-tech ['haɪ'tek] adj de alta tecnología

hitherto ['hɪðər'tuː] adv hasta ahora

HIV n abbr (= human immunodeficiency virus) VIH m

hive [haɪv] n colmena

HIV: □ **HIV-negative** adj VIH negativo □ **HIV-positive** adj VIH positivo

HMS (BRIT) abbr = **Her/His Majesty's Ship**

hoard [hɔːrd] n (treasure) tesoro; (stockpile) provisión f ♦ vt acumular; (goods in short supply) acaparar □ **hoarding** (BRIT) n (for posters) cartelera

hoarse [hɔːrs] adj ronco

hoax [houks] n trampa

hob [hɑːb] (BRIT) n quemador m

hobble ['hɑːbəl] vi cojear

hobby ['hɒbɪ] n pasatiempo, afición f

hobo ['həʊbəʊ] (US) n vagabundo

hockey ['hɒkɪ] n hockey m; (US: ice hockey) hockey m sobre hielo; (BRIT: on grass) hockey m (sobre hierba)

hodgepodge ['hɒdʒpɒdʒ] (US) n mezcolanza

hog [hɒg] n (US) cerdo, puerco ♦ vt (fig) acaparar; **to go the whole ~** poner toda la carne en el asador

hoist [hɔɪst] n (crane) grúa ♦ vt levantar, alzar; (flag, sail) izar

hold [həʊld] (pt, pp **held**) vt sostener; (contain) contener; (have: power, qualification) tener; (keep back) retener; (believe) sostener; (consider) considerar; (keep in position): **to ~ one's head up** mantener la cabeza alta; (meeting) celebrar ♦ vi (withstand pressure) resistir; (be valid) valer ♦ n (grasp) asimiento; (fig) dominio; **~ the line!** (TEL) ¡no cuelgue!; **to ~ one's own** (fig) defenderse; **to catch** or **get (a) ~ of** agarrarse o asirse de ▶ **hold back** vt retener; (secret) ocultar ▶ **hold down** vt (person) sujetar; (job) mantener ▶ **hold off** vt (enemy) rechazar ▶ **hold on** vi agarrarse bien; (wait) esperar; **hold on!** (TEL) ¡(espere) un momento! ▶ **hold on to** vt fus agarrarse a; (keep) guardar ▶ **hold out** vt ofrecer ♦ vi (resist) resistir ▶ **hold up** vt (raise) levantar; (support) apoyar; (delay) retrasar; (rob) asaltar □ **holdall** (BRIT) n bolsa □ **holder** n (container) receptáculo; (of ticket, record) poseedor(a) m/f; (of office, title etc) titular mf □ **holding** n (share) interés m; (farmland) parcela □ **holdup** n (robbery) atraco; (delay) retraso; (BRIT: in traffic) embotellamiento

hole [həʊl] n agujero

holiday ['hɒlɪdeɪ] n (public holiday) día m) feriado (LAm), (día m de) fiesta (SP); (BRIT) vacaciones fpl; **on ~** de vacaciones □ **holiday camp** (BRIT) n (also: **holiday centre**) colonia or centro de vacaciones □ **holiday-maker** (BRIT) n turista mf □ **holiday resort** n centro turístico

holiness ['həʊlɪnɪs] n santidad f

Holland ['hɒlənd] n Holanda

holler ['hɒlər] (US) vi, vt gritar

hollow ['hɒləʊ] adj hueco; (claim) vacío; (eyes) hundido; (sound) sordo ♦ n hueco; (in ground) hoyo ♦ vt: **to ~ out** excavar

holly ['hɒlɪ] n acebo

Hollywood ['hɒlɪwʊd] n Hollywood m

HOLLYWOOD

Hollywood es una barriada de Los Ángeles, en California, muy cercana a las sedes de los más importantes estudios cinematográficos norteamericanos, y donde viven muchas de las estrellas del cine norteamericano. El término **Hollywood** se puede referir tanto a la barriada, como a la industria cinematográfica, o a las películas producidas en **Hollywood**.

holocaust ['hɒləkɔːst] n holocausto

holy ['həʊlɪ] adj santo, sagrado; (water) bendito

homage ['hɒmɪdʒ] n homenaje m

home [həʊm] n casa; (country) patria; (institution) asilo ♦ cpd (domestic) casero, de casa; (BRIT: ECON, POL) nacional ♦ adv (direction) a casa; (right in: nail etc) a fondo; **at ~** en casa; (in country) en el país; (fig) como pez en el agua; **to go/come ~** ir/volver a casa; **make yourself at ~** ¡estás en tu casa! □ **home address** n domicilio □ **homecoming** n regreso al hogar □ **homecoming queen** (US) n reina de la fiesta de antiguos alumnos □ **homeland** n tierra natal □ **homeless** adj sin hogar or casa □ **homely** adj (simple) sencillo □ **homemade** adj casero □ **Home Office** (BRIT) n Secretaría de Gobernación (MEX), Ministerio del Interior (LAm exc MEX, SP)

homeopathic (US) [ˌhəʊmɪə'pæθɪk] (BRIT **homoeopathic**) adj homeopático

home: □ **home page** n página de inicio □ **home rule** n autonomía □ **Home Secretary** (BRIT) n Secretario de Gobernación (MEX), Ministro del Interior (LAm exc MEX, SP) □ **homesick** adj: **I'm homesick** extraño mi casa (LAm), tengo morriña (SP) □ **home town** n ciudad f natal □ **homeward** ['həʊmwəd] adj (journey) hacia casa □ **homework** n tarea, deberes mpl

homicide ['hɒmɪsaɪd] (US) n (act) homicidio

homoeopathic [ˌhəʊmɪə'pæθɪk] (BRIT) adj = **homeopathic**

homosexual [hɒməʊ'sɛksjʊəl] adj, n homosexual mf

Honduran [hɒn'dʊərən] adj, n hondureño(-a)

Honduras [hɒn'dʊərəs] n Honduras f

honest ['ɒnɪst] adj honrado; (sincere) franco, sincero □ **honestly** adv honradamente; francamente □ **honesty** n honradez f

honey ['hʌnɪ] n miel f; (inf: form of address) cariño □ **honeycomb** n panal m □ **honeymoon** n luna de miel □ **honeysuckle** n madreselva

honk [hɑːŋk] vi (AUT) tocar el claxon or la bocina, pitar

honor (US) ['ɑːnər] (BRIT **honour**) vt honrar; (commitment, promise) cumplir con ♦ n honor m, honra; **to graduate with ~s** ≈ licenciarse con matrícula (de honor) □ **honorable** (US) (BRIT **honourable**) adj honorable

honorary ['ɑːnəreri] adj (member, president) de honor; (title) honorífico; **~ degree** doctorado honoris causa

honour ['ɑːnər] (BRIT) vt, n = **honor**

honours degree (BRIT) n (SCOL) ≈ licenciatura (con calificación alta)

hood [hud] n capucha; (US AUT) cofre m (MEX), capó m (LAm exc MEX, SP); (BRIT AUT) capota; (of stove) campana

hoof [huːf] (pl **hooves**) n pezuña

hook [huk] n gancho; (on dress) corchete m, broche m; (for fishing) anzuelo ♦ vt enganchar; (fish) pescar

hooligan ['huːlɪgən] n vándalo, patotero (SC)

hoop [huːp] n aro

hooray [huːˈreɪ] excl = **hurray**

hoot [huːt] vi (owl) ulular; (BRIT AUT) tocar el claxon or la bocina, pitar; (siren) (hacer) sonar □ **hooter** (BRIT) n (AUT) claxon m, bocina; (NAUT) sirena

Hoover® ['huːvər] (BRIT) n aspiradora ♦ vt: **hoover** pasar la aspiradora por

hooves [huːvz] npl of **hoof**

hop [hɑːp] vi saltar, brincar; (on one foot) brincar (MEX) or saltar (LAm exc MEX) en un pie

hope [houp] vt, vi esperar ♦ n esperanza; **I ~ so/not** espero que sí/no □ **hopeful** adj (person) optimista; (situation) prometedor(a) □ **hopefully** adv con esperanza; (one hopes): **hopefully he will recover** esperamos que se recupere □ **hopeless** adj desesperado; (person): **to be hopeless** ser un desastre

hops [hɑːps] npl lúpulo

horizon [həˈraɪzən] n horizonte m □ **horizontal** [hɔːrɪˈzɑːntl] adj horizontal

hormone ['hɔːrmoun] n hormona

horn [hɔːrn] n cuerno; (MUS: also: **French ~**) trompa; (AUT) claxon m, bocina

hornet ['hɔːrnɪt] n avispón m

horoscope ['hɔːrəskoup] n horóscopo

horrible ['hɔːrɪbəl] adj horrible

horrid ['hɔːrɪd] adj horrible, horroroso

horrify ['hɔːrɪfaɪ] vt horrorizar

horror ['hɔːrər] n horror m □ **horror movie** n película de horror

hors d'oeuvre [ɔːrˈdɜːrv] n entremeses mpl

horse [hɔːrs] n caballo □ **horseback** n: **on horseback** a caballo □ **horse chestnut** n (tree) castaño de Indias; (nut) castaña de Indias □ **horseman/woman** n jinete m/amazona □ **horsepower** n caballo (de fuerza) □ **horse-racing** n carreras fpl de caballos □ **horseradish** n rábano picante □ **horseshoe** n herradura

hose [houz] n (stockings) medias fpl; (also: **~pipe**) manguera

hospitable [hɑːsˈpɪtəbəl] adj hospitalario

hospital ['hɑːspɪtl] n hospital m

hospitality [hɑːspɪˈtælɪti] n hospitalidad f

host [houst] n anfitrión m; (TV, RADIO) presentador m; (REL) hostia; (large number): **a ~ of** multitud de

hostage ['hɑːstɪdʒ] n rehén m

hostel ['hɑːstl] n hostal m; (youth) **~** albergue m juvenil

hostess ['houstɪs] n anfitriona; (TV, RADIO) presentadora; (BRIT: air hostess) aeromoza (LAm), azafata (SP)

hostile ['hɑːstl] adj hostil

hot [hɑːt] adj caliente; (weather) caluroso, de calor; (as opposed to warm) muy caliente; (spicy) picante; **to be ~** (person) tener calor; (object) estar caliente; (weather) hacer calor □ **hotbed** n (fig) semillero

hotchpotch ['hɑːtʃpɑːtʃ] (BRIT) n mezcolanza

hot dog n hotdog m (LAm), perrito caliente (LAm exc MEX, SP), pancho (RPl)

hotel [houˈtel] n hotel m

hot: □ **hothouse** n invernadero □ **hot line** n (POL) teléfono rojo □ **hotly** adv con pasión, apasionadamente □ **hot-water bottle** n bolsa de agua caliente

hound [haund] vt acosar ♦ n perro (de caza)

hour ['auər] n hora □ **hourly** adj (de) cada hora

house [n haus, pl hauzɪz, vb hauz] n (gen, firm) casa; (POL) cámara; (THEATER) sala ♦ vt (person) alojar; (collection) albergar; **on the ~** (fig) la casa invita □ **house arrest** n arresto domiciliario □ **houseboat** n casa flotante □ **housebound** adj confinado en casa □ **housebreaking** n allanamiento de morada □ **house guest** n invitado(-a) □ **household** n familia; (home) casa □ **housekeeper** n ama de llaves □ **housekeeping** n (work) trabajos mpl domésticos □ **housekeeping (money)** (BRIT) n dinero para gastos domésticos □ **house-warming party** n fiesta de inauguración de una casa □ **housewife** n ama de casa □ **housework** n tareas fpl (domésticas)

housing ['hauzɪŋ] n (act) alojamiento; (houses) viviendas fpl ❑ **housing development** (US) (BRIT **housing estate**) n fraccionamiento (MEX), complejo residencial or (LAm) habitacional

hovel ['hɔvəl] n casucha

hover ['hɔvər] vi flotar (en el aire) ❑ **hovercraft** n aerodeslizador m

how [hau] adv (in what way) cómo; **~ are you?** ¿cómo estás?; **~ much milk/many people?** ¿cuánta leche/gente?; **~ much does it cost?** ¿cuánto cuesta?; **~ long have you been here?** ¿cuánto hace que estás aquí?; **~ old are you?** ¿cuántos años tienes?; **~ tall is he?** ¿cómo es de alto?; **~ is school?** ¿cómo (te) va (en) la escuela?; **~ was the movie?** ¿qué tal la película?; **~ lovely/awful!** ¡qué bonito/horror!

however [hau'ɛvər] conj sin embargo, no obstante ♦ adv: **~ I do it** lo haga como lo haga; **~ cold it is** por mucho frío que haga; **~ fast he runs** por muy rápido que corra; **~ did you do it?** ¿cómo lo hiciste?

howl [haul] n aullido ♦ vi aullar; (person) dar alaridos; (wind) ulular

H.P. (BRIT) n abbr = **hire purchase**

h.p. abbr = **horsepower**

HQ n abbr = **headquarters**

HTML n abbr HTML m; (= hypertext markup language) lenguaje m de hipertexto

hub [hʌb] n (of wheel) cubo; (fig) centro

hubcap ['hʌb,kæp] n tapacubos m inv

huddle ['hʌdl] vi: **to ~ together** acurrucarse

hue [hju:] n color m, matiz m

huff [hʌf] n: **in a ~** enojado

hug [hʌg] vt abrazar; (thing) apretar con los brazos

huge [hju:dʒ] adj enorme

hull [hʌl] n (of ship) casco

hullo [hə'lou] excl = **hello**

hum [hʌm] vt tararear, canturrear ♦ vi tararear, canturrear; (insect) zumbar

human ['hju:mən] adj, n humano ❑ **humane** [hju:'meɪn] adj humano, humanitario ❑ **humanitarian** [hju:,mænɪ'terɪən] adj humanitario ❑ **humanity** [hju:'mænɪti] n humanidad f

humble ['hʌmbəl] adj humilde

humdrum ['hʌmdrʌm] adj (boring) monótono, aburrido

humid ['hju:mɪd] adj húmedo

humiliate [hju:'mɪlieɪt] vt humillar

humor (US) ['hju:mər] (BRIT **humour**) n humorismo, sentido del humor; (mood) humor m ♦ vt (person) complacer

humorous ['hju:mərəs] adj gracioso, divertido

hump [hʌmp] n (in ground) montículo; (camel's) giba

hunch [hʌntʃ] n (premonition) presentimiento ❑ **hunchback** n jorobado(-a) ❑ **hunched** adj jorobado

hundred ['hʌndrəd] num ciento; (before n) cien; **~s of** centenares de ❑ **hundredweight** n (US) = 45,3 kg, 100 libras; (BRIT) = 50,8 kg, 112 libras

hung [hʌŋ] pt, pp of **hang**

Hungarian [hʌŋ'gerɪən] adj, n húngaro(-a)

Hungary ['hʌŋgəri] n Hungría

hunger ['hʌŋgər] n hambre f ♦ vi: **to ~ for** (fig) tener hambre de, anhelar ❑ **hunger strike** n huelga de hambre

hungry ['hʌŋgri] adj: **~ (for)** hambriento (de); **to be ~** tener hambre

hunk [hʌŋk] n (of bread etc) trozo, pedazo; (inf: man) monumento, tío bueno

hunt [hʌnt] vt (seek) buscar; (SPORT) cazar ♦ vi (search): **to ~ (for)** buscar; (SPORT) cazar ♦ n búsqueda; caza, cacería ❑ **hunter** n cazador(a) m/f ❑ **hunting** n caza

hurdle ['hɜrdl] n (SPORT) valla; (fig) obstáculo

hurl [hɜrl] vt lanzar, arrojar

hurrah [hu'ra:] excl = **hurray**

hurray [hu'reɪ] excl ¡viva!

hurricane ['hɜːrɪkeɪn] n huracán m

hurried ['hɜːrɪd] adj (rushed) hecho de prisa ❑ **hurriedly** adv con prisa, apresuradamente

hurry ['hɜːri] n prisa ♦ vi (also: **~ up**) apresurarse, darse prisa ♦ vt (also: **~ up:** person) dar prisa a; (: work) apresurar, hacer de prisa; **to be in a ~** tener prisa

hurt [hɜːrt] (pt, pp ~) vt hacer daño a ♦ vi doler ♦ adj lastimado ❑ **hurtful** adj (remark etc) hiriente

hurtle ['hɜːrtl] vi: **to ~ past** pasar como un rayo; **to ~ down** ir a toda velocidad

husband ['hʌzbənd] n marido

hush [hʌʃ] n silencio ♦ vt hacer callar; **~!** ¡chitón!, ¡cállate! ▶ **hush up** vt encubrir

husk [hʌsk] n (of wheat) cáscara

husky ['hʌski] adj ronco ♦ n husky mf, perro esquimal

hustle ['hʌsəl] vt (hurry) dar prisa a ♦ n: **~ and bustle** ajetreo

hut [hʌt] n cabaña; (shed) cobertizo

hutch [hʌtʃ] n conejera

hyacinth ['haɪəsɪnθ] n jacinto

hydrant ['haɪdrənt] n (also: **fire ~**) boca de incendios

hydraulic [haɪ'drɔːlɪk] adj hidráulico

hydroelectric [haɪdrouˈlektrɪk] *adj*
hidroeléctrico

hydrofoil [ˈhaɪdrəfɔɪl] *n* hidroala *m*,
hidrodeslizador *m*

hydrogen [ˈhaɪdrədʒən] *n* hidrógeno

hygiene [ˈhaɪdʒiːn] *n* higiene *f* ❑ **hygienic**
[haɪˈdʒenɪk] *adj* higiénico

hymn [hɪm] *n* himno

hype [haɪp] (*inf*) *n* bombardeo publicitario

hypermarket [ˈhaɪpərˌmɑːrkɪt] (*BRIT*) *n*
hipermercado

hyphen [ˈhaɪfən] *n* guión *m*

hypnotize [ˈhɪpnətaɪz] *vt* hipnotizar

hypocrisy [hɪˈpɑːkrɪsi] *n* hipocresía
❑ **hypocrite** [ˈhɪpəkrɪt] *n* hipócrita *mf*
❑ **hypocritical** [hɪpəˈkrɪtɪkəl] *adj* hipócrita

hypothesis [haɪˈpɑːθɪsɪs] (*pl* **hypotheses**) *n*
hipótesis *f inv*

hysteria [hɪˈstiəria] *n* histeria ❑ **hysterical**
adj histérico; (*funny*) para morirse de risa
❑ **hysterics** *npl* histeria; **to be in hysterics**
(*fig*) morirse de risa

Ii

I [aɪ] *pron* yo

ice [aɪs] *n* hielo; (*BRIT: ice cream*) helado ♦ *vt*
(*cake*) alcorzar ♦ *vi* (*also:* **~ over, ~ up**) helarse
❑ **iceberg** *n* iceberg *m* ❑ **icebox** *n* (*US*)
refrigerador *m* (*LAm*), heladera (*RPl*), frigorífico
(*SP*); (*BRIT: part of refrigerator*) congelador *m*
❑ **ice cream** *n* helado ❑ **ice cube** *n* cubito
de hielo ❑ **iced** *adj* (*cake*) escarchado; (*drink*)
helado ❑ **ice hockey** (*BRIT*) *n* hockey *m*
sobre hielo

Iceland [ˈaɪslənd] *n* Islandia

ice: ❑ **ice lolly** (*BRIT*) *n* paleta (helada) (*MEX,
CAm*), palito (helado) (*RPl*), polo (*SP*) ❑ **ice
rink** *n* pista de hielo ❑ **ice skating** *n*
patinaje *m* sobre hielo

icicle [ˈaɪsɪkəl] *n* carámbano

icing [ˈaɪsɪŋ] *n* (*CULIN*) glaseado ❑ **icing
sugar** (*BRIT*) *n* azúcar *m* glas(eado)

icon [ˈaɪkɑːn] *n* icono

ICT *n abbr* (= *Information and Communications
Technology*) TI *f*, tecnología de la información

icy [ˈaɪsi] *adj* helado

I'd [aɪd] *cont* = **I would; I had**

idea [aɪˈdiːə] *n* idea

ideal [aɪˈdiːəl] *n* ideal *m* ♦ *adj* ideal

identical [aɪˈdentɪkəl] *adj* idéntico

identification [aɪˌdentɪfɪˈkeɪʃən] *n*
identificación *f*; (**means of**) **~** documentos
mpl personales

identify [aɪˈdentɪfaɪ] *vt* identificar

Identikit® [aɪˈdentɪkɪt] *n*: **Identikit (picture)**
retrato hablado (*LAm*)

identity [aɪˈdentɪti] *n* identidad *f* ❑ **identity
card** *n* cédula (*LAm*) or carnet *m* (*SP*) (de
identidad)

ideology [aɪdiˈɑːlədʒi] *n* ideología

idiom [ˈɪdiəm] *n* modismo; (*style of speaking*)
lenguaje *m*

⚠ Be careful not to translate **idiom** by the
Spanish word *idioma*.

idiosyncrasy [ɪdiouˈsɪŋkrəsi] *n* idiosincrasia

idiot [ˈɪdiət] *n* idiota *mf* ❑ **idiotic** [ɪdɪˈɑːtɪk]
adj tonto

idle [ˈaɪdl] *adj* (*inactive*) ocioso; (*lazy*)
holgazán(-ana); (*unemployed*) parado,
desocupado; (*machinery etc*) parado; (*talk etc*)
frívolo ♦ *vi* (*machine*) marchar en vacío

idol [ˈaɪdl] *n* ídolo ❑ **idolize** *vt* idolatrar

i.e. *abbr* (= *that is*) esto es

if [ɪf] *conj* si; **if necessary** si fuera necesario, si
hiciese falta; **if I were you** yo en tu lugar; **if
so/not** de ser así/si no; **if only I could!** ¡ojalá
pudiera!; *see also* **as**; **even**

igloo [ˈɪgluː] *n* iglú *m*

ignite [ɪgˈnaɪt] *vt* (*set fire to*) encender ♦ *vi*
encenderse

ignition [ɪgˈnɪʃən] *n* (*AUT: process*) ignición *f*;
(*: mechanism*) encendido; **to switch on/off
the ~** arrancar/apagar el motor ❑ **ignition
key** *n* (*AUT*) llave *f* de encendido (*LAm*) or
contacto (*SP*)

ignorant [ˈɪgnərənt] *adj* ignorante; **to be ~ of**
ignorar

ignore [ɪgˈnɔːr] *vt* (*person, advice*) no hacer
caso de; (*fact*) pasar por alto

I'll [aɪl] *cont* = **I will; I shall**

ill [ɪl] *adj* enfermo, malo ♦ *n* mal *m* ♦ *adv* mal;
to be ~ ponerse enfermo ❑ **ill-advised** *adj*
(*decision*) imprudente ❑ **ill-at-ease** *adj*
incómodo

illegal [ɪˈliːgəl] *adj* ilegal

illegible [ɪˈledʒɪbəl] *adj* ilegible

illegitimate [ɪlɪˈdʒɪtɪmət] *adj* ilegítimo

ill-fated *adj* malogrado

ill feeling *n* rencor *m*

illiterate [ɪˈlɪtərət] *adj* analfabeto

ill: ❑ **ill-mannered** *adj* mal educado
❑ **illness** *n* enfermedad *f* ❑ **ill-treat** *vt*
maltratar

illuminate [ɪˈluːmɪneɪt] vt (room, street) iluminar, alumbrar ❑ **illumination** [ɪluːmɪˈneɪʃən] n alumbrado; **illuminations** npl (BRIT: decorative lights) iluminaciones fpl, luces fpl

illusion [ɪˈluːʒən] n ilusión f; (trick) truco

illustrate [ˈɪləstreɪt] vt ilustrar

illustration [ɪləˈstreɪʃən] n (act of illustrating) ilustración f; (example) ejemplo, ilustración f; (in book) lámina

illustrious [ɪˈlʌstriəs] adj ilustre

I'm [aɪm] cont = **I am**

image [ˈɪmɪdʒ] n imagen f ❑ **imagery** n imágenes fpl

imaginary [ɪˈmædʒɪnɛri] adj imaginario

imagination [ɪmædʒɪˈneɪʃən] n imaginación f; (inventiveness) inventiva

imaginative [ɪˈmædʒɪnətɪv] adj imaginativo

imagine [ɪˈmædʒɪn] vt imaginarse

imbalance [ɪmˈbæləns] n desequilibrio

imitate [ˈɪmɪteɪt] vt imitar ❑ **imitation** [ɪmɪˈteɪʃən] n imitación f; (copy) copia

immaculate [ɪˈmækjulət] adj inmaculado

immaterial [ɪməˈtɪriəl] adj (unimportant) sin importancia

immature [ɪməˈtjuər] adj (person) inmaduro

immediate [ɪˈmiːdɪət] adj inmediato; (pressing) urgente, apremiante; (nearest: family) próximo; (: neighborhood) inmediato ❑ **immediately** adv (at once) en seguida; (directly) inmediatamente; **immediately next to** muy junto a

immense [ɪˈmɛns] adj inmenso, enorme; (importance) enorme

immerse [ɪˈmɜːrs] vt (submerge) sumergir; **to be ~d in** (fig) estar absorto en

immersion heater [ɪˈmɜːrʒən,hiːtər] (BRIT) n calentador m de inmersión

immigrant [ˈɪmɪɡrənt] n inmigrante mf ❑ **immigration** [ɪmɪˈɡreɪʃən] n inmigración f

imminent [ˈɪmɪnənt] adj inminente

immobile [ɪˈmoubəl] adj inmóvil

immoral [ɪˈmɔːrəl] adj inmoral

immortal [ɪˈmɔːrtl] adj inmortal

immune [ɪˈmjuːn] adj: ~ **(to)** inmune (a) ❑ **immunity** n (MED, of diplomat) inmunidad f

immunize [ˈɪmjunaɪz] vt inmunizar

impact [ˈɪmpækt] n impacto

impair [ɪmˈpɛər] vt perjudicar

impart [ɪmˈpɑːrt] vt comunicar; (flavor) proporcionar

impartial [ɪmˈpɑːrʃəl] adj imparcial

impassable [ɪmˈpæsəbəl] adj (barrier) infranqueable; (river, road) intransitable

impasse [ˈɪmpæs] n punto muerto

impassive [ɪmˈpæsɪv] adj impasible

impatience [ɪmˈpeɪʃəns] n impaciencia

impatient [ɪmˈpeɪʃənt] adj impaciente; **to get** or **grow ~** impacientarse

impeach [ɪmˈpiːtʃ] (US) vt (president) someter a un proceso de destitución

impeccable [ɪmˈpɛkəbəl] adj impecable

impede [ɪmˈpiːd] vt estorbar

impediment [ɪmˈpɛdɪmənt] n obstáculo, estorbo; (also: **speech ~**) defecto (del habla)

impending [ɪmˈpɛndɪŋ] adj inminente

imperative [ɪmˈpɛrətɪv] adj (tone) imperioso; (need) imprescindible

imperfect [ɪmˈpɜːrfɪkt] adj (goods etc) defectuoso ♦ n (LING: also: ~ **tense**) imperfecto

imperial [ɪmˈpɪriəl] adj imperial

impersonal [ɪmˈpɜːrsənl] adj impersonal

impersonate [ɪmˈpɜːrsəneɪt] vt hacerse pasar por; (THEATER) imitar

impertinent [ɪmˈpɜːrtnənt] adj impertinente, insolente

impervious [ɪmˈpɜːrviəs] adj impermeable; (fig): ~ **to** insensible a

impetuous [ɪmˈpɛtʃuəs] adj impetuoso

impetus [ˈɪmpətəs] n ímpetu m; (fig) impulso

impinge [ɪmˈpɪndʒ]: **to ~ on** vt fus (affect) afectar a

implant [n ˈɪmplænt, vb ɪmˈplænt] n implante m ♦ vt (organ, tissue) injertar, implantar

implement [n ˈɪmplɪmənt, vb ˈɪmplɪment] n implemento (LAm), instrumento (SP); (for cooking) utensilio ♦ vt (regulation) hacer efectivo; (plan) realizar

implicit [ɪmˈplɪsɪt] adj implícito; (belief, trust) absoluto

imply [ɪmˈplaɪ] vt (involve) suponer; (hint) dar a entender que

impolite [ɪmpəˈlaɪt] adj mal educado

import [vb ɪmˈpɔːrt, n ˈɪmpɔːrt] vt importar ♦ n (COMM) importación f; (: article) producto importado; (meaning) significado, sentido

importance [ɪmˈpɔːrtns] n importancia

important [ɪmˈpɔːrtnt] adj importante; **it's not ~** no importa, no tiene importancia

importer [ˈɪmpɔːrtər] n importador(a) m/f

impose [ɪmˈpouz] vt imponer ♦ vi: **to ~ on sb** abusar de algn ❑ **imposing** adj imponente, impresionante

imposition [ɪmpəˈzɪʃn] n (of tax etc) imposición f; **to be an ~ on** (person) molestar a

impossible [ɪmˈpɑːsɪbəl] *adj* imposible; (*person*) insoportable

impotent [ˈɪmpətənt] *adj* impotente

impound [ɪmˈpaʊnd] *vt* embargar

impoverished [ɪmˈpɑːvərɪʃt] *adj* necesitado

impractical [ɪmˈpræktɪkəl] *adj* (*person, plan*) poco práctico

imprecise [ɪmprɪˈsaɪs] *adj* impreciso

impregnable [ɪmˈpregnəbəl] *adj* (*castle*) inexpugnable

impress [ɪmˈpres] *vt* impresionar; (*mark*) estampar; **to ~ sth on sb** hacer entender algo a algn

impression [ɪmˈpreʃən] *n* impresión *f*; (*imitation*) imitación *f*; **to be under the ~ that** tener la impresión de que ❑ **impressionist** *n* impresionista *mf*

impressive [ɪmˈpresɪv] *adj* impresionante

imprint [ˈɪmprɪnt] *n* (*outline*) huella; (*PUBLISHING*) pie *m* de imprenta

imprison [ɪmˈprɪzən] *vt* encarcelar ❑ **imprisonment** *n* encarcelamiento; (*term of imprisonment*) cárcel *f*

improbable [ɪmˈprɑːbəbəl] *adj* improbable, inverosímil

improper [ɪmˈprɑːpər] *adj* (*unsuitable: conduct etc*) incorrecto; (: *activities*) deshonesto

improve [ɪmˈpruːv] *vt* mejorar; (*foreign language*) perfeccionar ♦ *vi* mejorarse ❑ **improvement** *n* mejoramiento; perfección *f*; progreso

improvise [ˈɪmprəvaɪz] *vt, vi* improvisar

impulse [ˈɪmpʌls] *n* impulso; **to act on ~** obrar sin reflexión ❑ **impulsive** [ɪmˈpʌlsɪv] *adj* irreflexivo

impure [ɪmˈpjʊər] *adj* (*adulterated*) adulterado; (*morally*) impuro ❑ **impurity** *n* impureza

in

KEYWORD

[ɪn] *prep*

1 (*indicating place, position, with place names*) en; **in the house/garden** en (la) casa/el jardín; **in here/there** aquí/ahí *or* allí dentro; **in Dublin/Ireland** en Dublín/Irlanda

2 (*indicating time*) en; **in spring** en (la) primavera; **in the afternoon** en (*LAm*) *or* por (*SP*) la tarde; **at 4 o'clock in the afternoon** a las 4 de la tarde; **I did it in 3 hours/days** lo hice en 3 horas/días; **I'll see you in 2 weeks** *or* **in 2 weeks' time** te veré dentro de 2 semanas

3 (*indicating manner etc*) en; **in a loud/soft voice** en voz alta/baja; **in pencil/ink** a lápiz/bolígrafo; **the boy in the blue shirt** el chico de la camisa azul

4 (*indicating circumstances*): **in the sun/shade/rain** al sol/a la sombra/bajo la lluvia; **a change in policy** un cambio de política

5 (*indicating mood, state*): **in tears** en lágrimas, llorando; **in anger/despair** enfadado/desesperado; **to live in luxury** vivir lujosamente

6 (*with ratios, numbers*): **1 in 10 households, 1 household in 10** una de cada 10 familias; **50 cents in the dollar** 50 centavos por dólar; **they lined up in twos** se alinearon de dos en dos

7 (*referring to people, works*) en; entre; **the disease is common in children** la enfermedad es común entre los niños; **in (the works of) Miller** en (las obras de) Miller

8 (*indicating profession etc*): **to be in teaching** estar en la enseñanza

9 (*after superlative*) de; **the best pupil in the class** el/la mejor alumno/(-a) de la clase

10 (*with present participle*): **in saying this** al decir esto

♦ *adv*: **to be in** (*person: at home*) estar en casa; (*at work*) estar; (*train, ship, plane*) haber llegado; (*in fashion*) estar de moda; **she'll be in later today** llegará más tarde hoy; **to ask sb in** hacer pasar a algn; **to run/limp etc in** entrar corriendo/cojeando *etc*

♦ *n*: **the ins and outs** (*of proposal, situation etc*) los detalles

in. *abbr* = **inch**

inability [ɪnəˈbɪlɪti] *n*: **~ (to do)** incapacidad *f* (de hacer)

inaccurate [ɪnˈækjʊrət] *adj* inexacto, incorrecto

inadequate [ɪnˈædɪkwət] *adj* (*income, reply etc*) insuficiente; (*person*) incapaz

inadvertently [ɪnədˈvɜːrtntli] *adv* por descuido

inadvisable [ɪnədˈvaɪzəbəl] *adj* poco aconsejable

inane [ɪˈneɪn] *adj* necio, fatuo

inanimate [ɪnˈænɪmət] *adj* inanimado

inappropriate [ɪnəˈprəʊpriət] *adj* inadecuado; (*improper*) poco oportuno

inarticulate [ɪnɑːrˈtɪkjʊlət] *adj* (*person*) incapaz de expresarse; (*speech*) mal pronunciado

inasmuch as [ɪnəz'mʌtʃəz] *conj* puesto que, ya que

inauguration [ɪnɔːgjʊ'reɪʃən] *n* ceremonia de apertura

inborn ['ɪnbɔːrn] *adj* (*quality*) innato

inbred ['ɪn'bred] *adj* innato; (*family*) engendrado por endogamia

Inc. [ɪŋk] *abbr* (*US: incorporated*) S.A.

incapable [ɪn'keɪpəbəl] *adj* incapaz

incapacitate [ɪnkə'pæsɪteɪt] *vt*: **to ~ sb** incapacitar a algn

incense [*n* 'ɪnsens, *vb* ɪn'sens] *n* incienso ♦ *vt* (*anger*) indignar, encolerizar

incentive [ɪn'sentɪv] *n* incentivo, estímulo

incessant [ɪn'sesənt] *adj* incesante, continuo ❑ **incessantly** *adv* constantemente

incest ['ɪnsest] *n* incesto

inch [ɪntʃ] *n* pulgada; **to be within an ~ of** estar a dos dedos de; **he didn't give an ~** no dio concesión alguna

incident ['ɪnsɪdənt] *n* incidente *m*

incidental [ɪnsɪ'dentl] *adj* accesorio; **~ to** relacionado con ❑ **incidentally** *adv* (*by the way*) a propósito

incite [ɪn'saɪt] *vt* provocar

inclination [ɪnklɪ'neɪʃən] *n* (*tendency*) tendencia, inclinación *f*; (*desire*) deseo; (*disposition*) propensión *f*

incline [*n* 'ɪnklaɪn, *vb* ɪn'klaɪn] *n* pendiente *m*, cuesta ♦ *vt* (*head*) poner de lado ♦ *vi* inclinarse; **to be ~d to** (*tend*) ser propenso a

include [ɪn'kluːd] *vt* (*incorporate*) incluir; (*in letter*) adjuntar ❑ **including** *prep* incluso, inclusive

inclusion [ɪn'kluːʒən] *n* inclusión *f*

inclusive [ɪn'kluːsɪv] *adj* inclusivo; **~ of tax** incluidos los impuestos

income ['ɪnkʌm] *n* (*earned*) ingresos *mpl*; (*from property etc*) renta; (*from investment etc*) rédito ❑ **income tax** *n* impuesto sobre la renta

incoming ['ɪnkʌmɪŋ] *adj* (*flight, government etc*) entrante

incomparable [ɪn'kɑːmpərəbəl] *adj* incomparable, sin par

incompatible [ɪnkəm'pætɪbəl] *adj* incompatible

incompetent [ɪn'kɑːmpɪtnt] *adj* incompetente

incomplete [ɪnkəm'pliːt] *adj* (*partial: achievement etc*) incompleto; (*unfinished: painting etc*) inacabado

incongruous [ɪn'kɑːŋgruəs] *adj* (*strange*) discordante; (*inappropriate*) incongruente

inconsiderate [ɪnkən'sɪdərət] *adj* desconsiderado

inconsistent [ɪnkən'sɪstənt] *adj* inconsecuente; (*contradictory*) incongruente; **~ with** (que) no concuerda con

inconspicuous [ɪnkən'spɪkjuəs] *adj* (*color, building etc*) discreto; (*person*) que llama poco la atención

inconvenience [ɪnkən'viːnjəns] *n* inconvenientes *mpl*; (*trouble*) molestia, incomodidad *f* ♦ *vt* incomodar

inconvenient [ɪnkən'viːnjənt] *adj* incómodo, poco práctico; (*time, place, visitor*) inoportuno

incorporate [ɪn'kɔːrpəreɪt] *vt* incorporar; (*contain*) comprender; (*add*) agregar ❑ **incorporated** *adj*: **incorporated company** (*US*) ≈ sociedad *f* anónima

incorrect [ɪnkə'rekt] *adj* incorrecto

increase [*n* 'ɪnkriːs, *vb* ɪn'kriːs] *n* aumento ♦ *vi* aumentar; (*grow*) crecer; (*price*) subir ♦ *vt* aumentar; (*price*) subir ❑ **increasing** *adj* creciente ❑ **increasingly** *adv* cada vez más, más y más

incredible [ɪn'kredɪbəl] *adj* increíble

incubator ['ɪŋkjubeɪtər] *n* incubadora

incumbent [ɪn'kʌmbənt] *adj*: **it is ~ on him to ...** le incumbe ... ♦ *n* titular *mf* (*de un cargo o dignidad*)

incur [ɪn'kɜːr] *vt* (*expenditure*) incurrir; (*loss*) sufrir; (*anger, disapproval*) provocar

indebted [ɪn'detɪd] *adj*: **to be ~ to sb** estar agradecido a algn

indecent [ɪn'diːsənt] *adj* indecente ❑ **indecent assault** *n* abusos *mpl* deshonestos ❑ **indecent exposure** *n* exhibicionismo

indecisive [ɪndɪ'saɪsɪv] *adj* indeciso

indeed [ɪn'diːd] *adv* efectivamente, en realidad; (*in fact*) en efecto; (*furthermore*) es más; **yes ~!** ¡claro que sí!

indefinitely [ɪn'defɪnɪtli] *adv* (*wait*) indefinidamente

indemnity [ɪn'demnɪti] *n* (*insurance*) indemnidad *f*; (*compensation*) indemnización *f*

independence [ɪndɪ'pendəns] *n* independencia

Independence Day n Día m de la Independencia

INDEPENDENCE DAY

El cuatro de julio es **Independence Day**, la fiesta nacional de Estados Unidos, que se celebra en conmemoración de la Declaración de Independencia (**Declaration of Independence**), escrita por Thomas Jefferson y aprobada en 1776. En ella se proclamaba la independencia total de Gran Bretaña de las trece colonias americanas que serían el origen de los Estados Unidos de América.

independent [ˌɪndɪˈpendənt] adj independiente

index [ˈɪndeks] (pl **~es**) n (in book) índice m; (: in library etc) catálogo; (pl indices: ratio, sign) exponente m ❏ **index card** n ficha ❏ **index** (US) adj indexado ❏ **index finger** n índice m ❏ **index-linked** (BRIT) adj = **indexed**

India [ˈɪndɪə] n la India ❏ **Indian** adj, n (from India) indio(-a); (Native American) indígena mf ❏ **Indian Ocean** n: **the Indian Ocean** el Océano Índico

indicate [ˈɪndɪkeɪt] vt indicar ❏ **indication** [ˌɪndɪˈkeɪʃən] n indicio, señal f ❏ **indicative** [ɪnˈdɪkətɪv] adj: **to be ~ of** indicar ❏ **indicator** n indicador m; (BRIT AUT) direccional f (MEX), intermitente m (LAm exc MEX, SP)

indices [ˈɪndɪsiːz] npl of **index**

indictment [ɪnˈdaɪtmənt] n acusación f

indifferent [ɪnˈdɪfrənt] adj indiferente; (mediocre) regular

indigenous [ɪnˈdɪdʒɪnəs] adj indígena

indigestion [ˌɪndɪˈdʒestʃən] n indigestión f

indignant [ɪnˈdɪgnənt] adj: **to be ~ at sth/with sb** indignarse por algo/con algn

indigo [ˈɪndɪgoʊ] adj de color añil ♦ n añil m

indirect [ˌɪndɪˈrekt] adj indirecto

indiscreet [ˌɪndɪˈskriːt] adj indiscreto, imprudente

indiscriminate [ˌɪndɪˈskrɪmɪnət] adj indiscriminado

indisputable [ˌɪndɪˈspjuːtəbəl] adj incontestable

indistinct [ˌɪndɪˈstɪŋkt] adj (noise, memory etc) confuso

individual [ˌɪndɪˈvɪdʒuəl] n individuo ♦ adj individual; (personal) personal; (particular) particular ❏ **individually** adv (singly) individualmente

indoctrinate [ɪnˈdɒktrɪneɪt] vt adoctrinar

indoor [ˈɪndɔːr] adj (swimming pool) cubierto; (plant) de interior; (sport) bajo cubierta ❏ **indoors** [ɪnˈdɔːrz] adv dentro

induce [ɪnˈduːs] vt inducir, persuadir; (bring about) producir; (labor) provocar ❏ **inducement** n (incentive) incentivo; (pej: bribe) soborno

indulge [ɪnˈdʌldʒ] vt (whim) satisfacer; (person) complacer; (child) mimar ♦ vi: **to ~ in** darse el gusto de ❏ **indulgence** n vicio; (leniency) indulgencia ❏ **indulgent** adj indulgente

industrial [ɪnˈdʌstriəl] adj industrial ❏ **industrial action** (BRIT) n huelga ❏ **industrial estate** (BRIT) n = **industrial park** ❏ **industrialist** n industrial mf ❏ **industrialize** vt industrializar ❏ **industrial park** (US) n zona (LAm) or polígono (SP) industrial

industrious [ɪnˈdʌstriəs] adj trabajador(a); (student) aplicado

industry [ˈɪndəstri] n industria; (diligence) aplicación f

inebriated [ɪˈniːbrieɪtɪd] adj borracho

inedible [ɪnˈedɪbəl] adj incomible; (poisonous) no comestible

ineffective [ˌɪnɪˈfektɪv] adj ineficaz, inútil

ineffectual [ˌɪnɪˈfektʃuəl] adj = **ineffective**

inefficient [ˌɪnɪˈfɪʃənt] adj ineficaz, ineficiente

inept [ɪnˈept] adj incompetente

inequality [ˌɪnɪˈkwɒlɪti] n desigualdad f

inert [ɪˈnɜːrt] adj inerte, inactivo; (immobile) inmóvil

inescapable [ˌɪnɪˈskeɪpəbəl] adj ineludible

inevitable [ɪnˈevɪtəbəl] adj inevitable ❏ **inevitably** adv inevitablemente

inexcusable [ˌɪnɪkˈskjuːzəbəl] adj imperdonable

inexpensive [ˌɪnɪkˈspensɪv] adj económico

inexperienced [ˌɪnɪkˈspɪəriənst] adj inexperto

infallible [ɪnˈfælɪbəl] adj infalible

infamous [ˈɪnfəməs] adj infame

infancy [ˈɪnfənsi] n infancia

infant [ˈɪnfənt] n niño(-a); (baby) niño pequeño, bebé m; (pej) aniñado

infantry [ˈɪnfəntri] n infantería

infant school (BRIT) n parvulario

infatuated [ɪnˈfætʃueɪtɪd] adj: **~ with** (in love) loco por

infatuation [ɪnˌfætʃuˈeɪʃən] n enamoramiento, pasión f

infect [ɪnˈfekt] vt (wound) infectar; (food) contaminar; (person, animal) contagiar ❏ **infection** n infección f; (fig) contagio ❏ **infectious** adj (also fig) contagioso

infer [ɪnˈfɜːr] vt deducir, inferir

inferior [ɪnˈfɪrɪər] adj, n inferior mf
□ **inferiority** [ɪnfɪrɪˈɔːrətɪ] n inferioridad f

infertile [ɪnˈfɜːrtl] adj estéril; (person) infecundo

infested [ɪnˈfɛstɪd] adj: ~ with plagado de

in-fighting n (fig) lucha(s) f(pl) interna(s)

infinite [ˈɪnfɪnɪt] adj infinito

infinitive [ɪnˈfɪnɪtɪv] n infinitivo

infinity [ɪnˈfɪnɪtɪ] n infinito; (an infinity) infinidad f

infirmary [ɪnˈfɜːrmərɪ] n (in school, institution) enfermería; (BRIT) hospital m

inflamed [ɪnˈfleɪmd] adj: to become ~ inflamarse

inflammable [ɪnˈflæməbəl] adj inflamable

inflammation [ɪnfləˈmeɪʃən] n inflamación f

inflatable [ɪnˈfleɪtəbəl] adj (ball, boat) inflable

inflate [ɪnˈfleɪt] vt (tire, price etc) inflar; (fig) hinchar □ **inflation** n (ECON) inflación f

inflexible [ɪnˈfleksəbəl] adj (rule) rígido; (person) inflexible

inflict [ɪnˈflɪkt] vt: to ~ sth on sb infligir algo en algn

influence [ˈɪnfluəns] n influencia ♦ vt influir en, influenciar; **under the ~ of alcohol** en estado de embriaguez □ **influential** [ɪnfluˈenʃəl] adj influyente

influenza [ɪnfluˈenzə] n gripe f, gripa (MEX)

influx [ˈɪnflʌks] n afluencia

inform [ɪnˈfɔːrm] vt: to ~ sb of sth informar a algn sobre or de algo ♦ vi: to ~ on sb delatar a algn

informal [ɪnˈfɔːrməl] adj (manner, tone) familiar; (dress, interview, occasion) informal; (visit, meeting) extraoficial □ **informality** [ɪnfɔːrˈmælɪtɪ] n informalidad f; sencillez f

informant [ɪnˈfɔːrmənt] n informante mf

information [ɪnfərˈmeɪʃən] n información f; (knowledge) conocimientos mpl; (US TEL) información f (telefónica); **a piece of ~** un dato □ **information desk** n (mostrador m de) información f □ **information office** n información f

informative [ɪnˈfɔːrmətɪv] adj informativo

informer [ɪnˈfɔːrmər] n (also: police ~) soplón(-ona) m/f

infrared [ɪnfrəˈred] adj infrarrojo

infrastructure [ˈɪnfrəstrʌktʃər] n (of system etc) infraestructura

infrequent [ɪnˈfriːkwənt] adj poco frecuente, infrecuente

infringe [ɪnˈfrɪndʒ] vt infringir, violar ♦ vi: to ~ on abusar de □ **infringement** n infracción f; (of rights) usurpación f

infuriating [ɪnˈfjʊrɪeɪtɪŋ] adj (habit, noise) enloquecedor(a)

ingenious [ɪnˈdʒiːnjəs] adj ingenioso □ **ingenuity** [ɪndʒɪˈnuːɪtɪ] n ingeniosidad f

ingenuous [ɪnˈdʒenjuəs] adj ingenuo

ingot [ˈɪŋgət] n lingote m, barra

ingrained [ɪnˈgreɪnd] adj arraigado

ingratiate [ɪnˈgreɪʃɪeɪt] vt: to ~ o.s. with congraciarse con

ingredient [ɪnˈgriːdɪənt] n ingrediente m

inhabit [ɪnˈhæbɪt] vt vivir en □ **inhabitant** n habitante mf

inhale [ɪnˈheɪl] vt inhalar ♦ vi (breathe in) aspirar; (in smoking) tragar

inherent [ɪnˈhɪrənt] adj: ~ in or to inherente a

inherit [ɪnˈherɪt] vt heredar □ **inheritance** n herencia; (fig) patrimonio

inhibit [ɪnˈhɪbɪt] vt inhibir, impedir □ **inhibited** adj (PSYCH) cohibido □ **inhibition** [ɪnhɪˈbɪʃən] n cohibición f

inhospitable [ɪnhɑːsˈpɪtəbəl] adj (person) inhospitalario; (place) inhóspito

inhuman [ɪnˈhjuːmən] adj inhumano

initial [ɪˈnɪʃəl] adj primero ♦ n inicial f ♦ vt firmar con las iniciales; **~s** npl (as signature) iniciales fpl; (abbreviation) siglas fpl □ **initially** adv al principio

initiate [ɪˈnɪʃɪeɪt] vt iniciar; **to ~ proceedings against sb** (LAW) entablar proceso contra algn

initiative [ɪˈnɪʃətɪv] n iniciativa

inject [ɪnˈdʒekt] vt inyectar; **to ~ sb with sth** inyectar algo a algn □ **injection** n inyección f

injunction [ɪnˈdʒʌŋkʃən] n interdicto

injure [ˈɪndʒər] vt (hurt) herir, lastimar; (fig: reputation etc) perjudicar □ **injured** adj (person, arm) herido, lastimado □ **injury** n herida, lesión f; (wrong) perjuicio, daño □ **injury time** (BRIT) n (SPORT) (tiempo de) compensación f (LAm) or descuento (SP)

⚠ Be careful not to translate **injury** by the Spanish word **injuria**.

injustice [ɪnˈdʒʌstɪs] n injusticia

ink [ɪŋk] n tinta

inkling [ˈɪŋklɪŋ] n sospecha; (idea) idea

inlaid [ˈɪnleɪd] adj (with wood, gems etc) incrustado

inland [adj ˈɪnlənd, adv ɪnˈlænd] adj (waterway, port etc) interior ♦ adv tierra adentro

❏ **Inland Revenue** (BRIT) n ≈ Hacienda, ≈ la Dirección General Impositiva (RPI)

in-laws npl suegros mpl

inlet ['inlet] n (GEO) ensenada, cala; (TECH) admisión f, entrada

inmate ['inmeit] n (in prison) preso(-a), presidiario(-a); (in asylum) internado(-a)

inn [in] n posada, mesón m

innate [i'neit] adj innato

inner ['inər] adj (courtyard, calm) interior; (feelings) íntimo ❏ **inner city** n barrios deprimidos del centro de una ciudad ❏ **inner tube** n (of tire) llanta (LAm), cámara (SP)

innings ['ininz] n (BASEBALL) entrada, turno

innocent ['inəsənt] adj inocente

innocuous [i'nɒkjuəs] adj inocuo

innovation [,inou'veiʃən] n novedad f

innuendo [,inju'endou] (pl ~es) n indirecta

inoculation [i,nɒkju'leiʃən] n inoculación f

inpatient ['inpeiʃənt] n paciente mf interno(-a)

input ['input] n entrada; (of resources) inversión f; (COMPUT) entrada de datos

inquest ['inkwest] n (coroner's) encuesta judicial

inquire [in'kwaiər] vi preguntar ♦ vt: to ~ whether preguntar si; to ~ about (person) preguntar por; (fact) informarse de
▶ **inquire into** vt fus investigar, indagar
❏ **inquiry** n pregunta; (investigation) investigación f, pesquisa; (BRIT): "Inquiries" "Información" ❏ **inquiry office** (BRIT) n oficina de información

inquisitive [in'kwizitiv] adj (curious) curioso

ins. abbr = inches

insane [in'sein] adj loco; (MED) demente; ~ **asylum** (US) manicomio, psiquiátrico

insanity [in'sæniti] n demencia, locura

inscription [in'skripʃən] n inscripción f; (in book) dedicatoria

inscrutable [in'skru:təbəl] adj inescrutable, insondable

insect ['insekt] n insecto ❏ **insecticide** [in'sektisaid] n insecticida m ❏ **insect repellent** n loción f contra insectos

insecure [,insi'kjuər] adj inseguro

insemination [in,semi'neiʃən] n: **artificial** ~ inseminación f artificial

insensitive [in'sensitiv] adj insensible

insert [vb in'sɜ:rt, n 'insɜrt] vt (into sth) introducir ♦ n encarte m ❏ **insertion** n inserción f

in-service ['in,sɜ:rvis] adj (training, course) a cargo de la empresa

inshore [in'ʃɔ:r] adj de bajura ♦ adv (be) cerca de la orilla; (move) hacia la orilla

inside [in'said] n interior m ♦ adj interior, interno ♦ adv (be) (por) dentro; (go) hacia dentro ♦ prep dentro de; (of time): ~ **10 minutes** en menos de 10 minutos; ~**s** npl (inf: stomach) tripas fpl ❏ **inside information** n información f confidencial ❏ **inside lane** n (AUT: in US, Europe) carril m derecho; (: in Britain) carril m izquierdo ❏ **inside out** adv (turn) al revés; (know) a fondo

insider dealing, insider trading n (STOCK EXCHANGE) abuso de información privilegiada

insight ['insait] n perspicacia

insignificant [,insig'nifikənt] adj insignificante

insincere [,insin'siər] adj poco sincero

insinuate [in'sinjueit] vt insinuar

insipid [in'sipid] adj soso, insulso

insist [in'sist] vi insistir; to ~ **on** insistir en; to ~ **that** insistir en que; (claim) exigir que ❏ **insistent** adj insistente; (noise, action) persistente

insole ['insoul] n plantilla

insolent ['insələnt] adj insolente, descarado

insomnia [in'sɒmniə] n insomnio

inspect [in'spekt] vt inspeccionar, examinar; (troops) pasar revista a ❏ **inspection** n inspección f, examen m; (of troops) revista ❏ **inspector** n inspector(a) m/f; (BRIT: on buses, trains) revisor(a) m/f

inspiration [,inspə'reiʃən] n inspiración f ❏ **inspire** [in'spaiər] vt inspirar

instability [,instə'biliti] n inestabilidad f

install (US) [in'stɔ:l] (BRIT **instal**) vt instalar; (official) nombrar ❏ **installation** [,instə'leiʃən] n instalación f

installment (US) [in'stɔ:lmənt] (BRIT **instalment**) n plazo; (of story) entrega; (of TV serial etc) capítulo; **in ~s** (pay, receive) a plazos ❏ **installment plan** (US) n plan m de financiación

instance ['instəns] n ejemplo, caso; **for ~** por ejemplo; **in the first ~** en primer lugar

instant ['instənt] n instante m, momento ♦ adj inmediato; (coffee etc) instantáneo ❏ **instantly** adv en seguida ❏ **instant replay** (US) n (SPORT) repetición f de la jugada

instead [in'sted] adv en cambio; ~ **of** en lugar de, en vez de

instep ['instep] n empeine m

instill (US) [in'stil] (BRIT **instil**) vt: to ~ **sth into** inculcar algo a

instinct ['instinkt] n instinto

institute [ˈɪnstɪtuːt] n instituto; (*professional body*) colegio ♦ vt (*begin*) iniciar, empezar; (*proceedings*) entablar; (*system, rule*) establecer

institution [ɪnstɪˈtuːʃən] n institución f; (MED: *home*) asilo; (: *asylum*) manicomio; (*of system etc*) establecimiento; (*of custom*) iniciación f

instruct [ɪnˈstrʌkt] vt: **to ~ sb in sth** instruir a algn en or sobre algo; **to ~ sb to do sth** dar instrucciones a algn de hacer algo ❑ **instruction** n (*teaching*) instrucción f; **instructions** npl (*orders*) órdenes fpl; **instructions (for use)** modo de empleo ❑ **instructor** n instructor(a) m/f

instrument [ˈɪnstrəmənt] n instrumento ❑ **instrumental** [ɪnstrəˈmentl] adj (MUS) instrumental; **to be instrumental in** ser (el) artífice de ❑ **instrument panel** n tablero (de instrumentos)

insufficient [ɪnsəˈfɪʃənt] adj insuficiente

insular [ˈɪnsələr] adj insular; (*person*) estrecho de miras

insulate [ˈɪnsəleɪt] vt aislar ❑ **insulation** [ɪnsəˈleɪʃən] n aislamiento

insulin [ˈɪnsəlɪn] n insulina

insult [n ˈɪnsʌlt, vb ɪnˈsʌlt] n insulto ♦ vt insultar ❑ **insulting** adj insultante

insurance [ɪnˈʃʊrəns] n seguro; **fire/life ~** seguro contra incendios/de vida ❑ **insurance agent** n agente mf de seguros ❑ **insurance policy** n póliza (de seguros)

insure [ɪnˈʃʊər] vt asegurar

intact [ɪnˈtækt] adj íntegro; (*unharmed*) intacto

intake [ˈɪnteɪk] n (*of food*) ingestión f; (*of air*) consumo; (BRIT SCOL): **an ~ of 200 a year** 200 matriculados al año

integral [ˈɪntɪɡrəl] adj (*whole*) íntegro; (*part*) integrante

integrate [ˈɪntɪɡreɪt] vt integrar ♦ vi integrarse

integrity [ɪnˈtɛɡrɪti] n honradez f, rectitud f

intellect [ˈɪntəlɛkt] n intelecto ❑ **intellectual** [ɪntəˈlɛktʃuəl] adj, n intelectual mf

intelligence [ɪnˈtɛlɪdʒəns] n inteligencia

intelligent [ɪnˈtɛlɪdʒənt] adj inteligente

intelligible [ɪnˈtɛlɪdʒɪbəl] adj inteligible, comprensible

intend [ɪnˈtɛnd] vt (*gift etc*): **to ~ sth for** destinar algo a; **to ~ to do sth** tener intención de or pensar hacer algo

intense [ɪnˈtɛns] adj intenso ❑ **intensely** adv (*extremely*) sumamente

intensify [ɪnˈtɛnsɪfaɪ] vt intensificar; (*increase*) aumentar

intensive [ɪnˈtɛnsɪv] adj intensivo ❑ **intensive care unit** n unidad f de cuidados intensivos

intent [ɪnˈtɛnt] n propósito; (LAW) premeditación f ♦ adj (*absorbed*) absorto; (*attentive*) atento; **to all ~s and purposes** prácticamente; **to be ~ on doing sth** estar resuelto a hacer algo

intention [ɪnˈtɛnʃən] n intención f, propósito ❑ **intentional** adj deliberado ❑ **intentionally** adv a propósito

intently [ɪnˈtɛntli] adv atentamente, fijamente

interact [ɪntərˈækt] vi relacionarse, interactuar ❑ **interactive** adj (COMPUT) interactivo

interchange [ˈɪntərtʃeɪndʒ] n intercambio; (*on highway*) paso a desnivel (LAm), nudo de carreteras (SP) ❑ **interchangeable** adj intercambiable

intercom [ˈɪntərkɑːm] n interfono

intercourse [ˈɪntərkɔːrs] n (*sexual*) relaciones fpl sexuales

interest [ˈɪntrɪst] n (*also* COMM) interés m ♦ vt interesar; **to be ~ed in** interesarse por ❑ **interesting** adj interesante ❑ **interest rate** n tipo or tasa de interés

interface [ˈɪntərfeɪs] n (COMPUT) interface m or f

interfere [ɪntərˈfɪər] vi: **to ~ in** entrometerse en; **to ~ with** (*hinder*) estorbar; (*damage*) estropear

interference [ɪntərˈfɪrəns] n intromisión f; (RADIO, TV) interferencia

interim [ˈɪntərɪm] n: **in the ~** en el ínterin ♦ adj provisional

interior [ɪnˈtɪriər] n interior m ♦ adj interior ❑ **interior designer** n diseñador(a) m/f de interiores (LAm), interiorista mf (SP)

interjection [ɪntərˈdʒɛkʃən] n interposición f; (LING) interjección f

interlock [ɪntərˈlɑːk] vi entrelazarse

interlude [ˈɪntərluːd] n intervalo; (THEATER) intermedio

intermediate [ɪntərˈmiːdiət] adj intermedio

intermission [ɪntərˈmɪʃən] n intermisión f; (THEATER) descanso

intern [vb ɪnˈtɜːrn, n ˈɪntɜːrn] vt internar ♦ n (US MED) médico(-a) interno(-a) residente

internal [ɪnˈtɜːrnl] adj (*layout, pipes, security*) interior; (*injury, structure, memo*) interno ❑ **internally** adv: **"not to be taken internally"** "para uso externo or tópico"

❑ **Internal Revenue Service** (US) n ≈ Hacienda, ≈ la Dirección General Impositiva (RPI)

international [ˌɪntərˈnæʃənl] adj internacional ♦ n (BRIT: match) partido internacional

Internet [ˈɪntərnɛt] n: **the ~** Internet m or f ❑ **Internet café** n cibercafé m ❑ **Internet Service Provider** n proveedor m de (acceso a) Internet ❑ **Internet user** n internauta m/f

internship [ˈɪntɜːrnʃɪp] (US) n cargo o período de aprendizaje de los médicos internos residentes

interplay [ˈɪntərpleɪ] n interacción f

interpret [ɪnˈtɜːrprɪt] vt interpretar; (translate) traducir; (understand) entender ♦ vi hacer de intérprete ❑ **interpreter** n intérprete mf

interrogate [ɪnˈtɛrəgeɪt] vt interrogar ❑ **interrogation** [ɪnˌtɛrəˈgeɪʃən] n interrogatorio

interrupt [ˌɪntəˈrʌpt] vt, vi interrumpir ❑ **interruption** n interrupción f

intersect [ˌɪntərˈsɛkt] vi (roads) cruzarse ❑ **intersection** [ˈɪntərˌsɛkʃən] n (of roads) cruce m

intersperse [ˌɪntərˈspɜːrs] vt: **to ~ with** salpicar de

interstate [ˈɪntərˌsteɪt] (US) n carretera interestatal

intertwine [ˌɪntərˈtwaɪn] vt entrelazarse

interval [ˈɪntərvəl] n intervalo; (SCOL) recreo; (THEATER, SPORT) descanso; **at ~s** a ratos, de vez en cuando

intervene [ˌɪntərˈviːn] vi intervenir; (event) interponerse; (time) transcurrir ❑ **intervention** n intervención f

interview [ˈɪntərvjuː] n entrevista ♦ vt entrevistarse con ❑ **interviewer** n entrevistador(a) m/f

intestine [ɪnˈtɛstɪn] n intestino

intimacy [ˈɪntɪməsɪ] n intimidad f

intimate [adj ˈɪntɪmət, vb ˈɪntɪmeɪt] adj íntimo; (friendship) estrecho; (knowledge) profundo ♦ vt dar a entender

into [ˈɪntu] prep en; (towards) a; (inside) hacia el interior de; **~ 3 pieces/French** en 3 pedazos/al francés

intolerable [ɪnˈtɑːlərəbəl] adj intolerable, insoportable

intolerant [ɪnˈtɑːlərənt] adj: **~ (of)** intolerante (con or para)

intoxicated [ɪnˈtɑːksɪkeɪtɪd] adj embriagado

intractable [ɪnˈtræktəbəl] adj (person) intratable; (problem) espinoso

intranet [ˈɪntrənɛt] n intranet f

intransitive [ɪnˈtrænsɪtɪv] adj intransitivo

intravenous [ˌɪntrəˈviːnəs] adj intravenoso

in-tray n bandeja de entrada

intricate [ˈɪntrɪkət] adj (design, pattern) intrincado

intrigue [ˈɪntriːg] n intriga ♦ vt fascinar ❑ **intriguing** adj fascinante

intrinsic [ɪnˈtrɪnsɪk] adj intrínseco

introduce [ˌɪntrəˈduːs] vt introducir, meter; (speaker, TV show etc) presentar; **to ~ sb (to sb)** presentar a algn (a algn); **to ~ sb to** (hobby, technique) introducir a algn a ❑ **introduction** [ˌɪntrəˈdʌkʃən] n introducción f; (of person) presentación f ❑ **introductory** [ˌɪntrəˈdʌktəri] adj introductorio; (lesson) de introducción; (offer) de lanzamiento

introvert [ˈɪntrəvɜːrt] n introvertido(-a) ♦ adj (also: ~ed) introvertido

intrude [ɪnˈtruːd] vi (person) entrometerse; **to ~ on** estorbar ❑ **intruder** n intruso(-a) ❑ **intrusion** [ɪnˈtruːʒən] n invasión f

intuition [ˌɪntuˈɪʃən] n intuición f

inundate [ˈɪnʌndeɪt] vt: **to ~ with** inundar de

invade [ɪnˈveɪd] vt invadir

invalid [n ˈɪnvəlɪd, adj ɪnˈvælɪd] n (MED) minusválido(-a) ♦ adj (not valid) inválido, nulo

invaluable [ɪnˈvæljuəbəl] adj inestimable

invariable [ɪnˈvɛəriəbəl] adj invariable

invent [ɪnˈvɛnt] vt inventar ❑ **invention** n invento; (lie) ficción f, mentira ❑ **inventive** adj inventivo ❑ **inventor** n inventor(a) m/f

inventory [ˈɪnvəntɔːri] n inventario

invert [ɪnˈvɜːrt] vt invertir

inverted commas (BRIT) npl comillas fpl

invest [ɪnˈvɛst] vt invertir ♦ vi: **to ~ in** (company etc) invertir (dinero) en; (fig: sth useful) comprar

investigate [ɪnˈvɛstɪgeɪt] vt investigar ❑ **investigation** [ɪnvɛstɪˈgeɪʃən] n investigación f, pesquisa

investment [ɪnˈvɛstmənt] n inversión f

investor [ɪnˈvɛstər] n inversionista mf

invigilator [ɪnˈvɪdʒɪleɪtər] (BRIT) n vigilante mf (en un examen)

invigorating [ɪnˈvɪgəreɪtɪŋ] adj vigorizante

invisible [ɪnˈvɪzɪbəl] adj invisible

invitation [ɪnvɪˈteɪʃən] n invitación f

invite [ɪnˈvaɪt] vt invitar; (opinions etc) solicitar, pedir ❑ **inviting** adj atractivo; (food) apetitoso

invoice [ˈɪnvɔɪs] n factura ♦ vt facturar

involuntary [ɪnˈvɑːləntəri] adj involuntario

involve [ɪn'vɒlv] vt suponer, implicar; tener que ver con; (concern, affect) corresponder; **to ~ sb (in sth)** comprometer a algn (con algo) ❑ **involved** adj complicado; **to be involved in** (take part) tomar parte en; (be engrossed) estar muy metido en ❑ **involvement** n participación f; dedicación f

inward ['ɪnwəd] adj (movement) interior, interno; (thought, feeling) íntimo ❑ **inward(s)** adv hacia dentro

I/O abbr (COMPUT: input/output) entrada/salida

iodine ['aɪədiːn] n yodo

ion ['aɪən] n ion m ❑ **ionizer** (US) (BRIT **ioniser**) n ionizador m

iota [aɪ'əʊtə] n jota, ápice m

IOU n abbr (= I owe you) pagaré m

IQ n abbr (= intelligence quotient) cociente m intelectual

IRA n abbr (= Irish Republican Army) IRA m

Iran [ɪ'ræn] n Irán m ❑ **Iranian** [ɪ'reɪnɪən] adj, n irani mf

Iraq [ɪ'rɑːk] n Iraq m ❑ **Iraqi** adj, n iraquí mf

irate [aɪ'reɪt] adj enojado, airado

Ireland ['aɪələnd] n Irlanda

iris ['aɪrɪs] (pl ~es) n (ANAT) iris m; (BOT) lirio

Irish ['aɪrɪʃ] adj irlandés(-esa) ♦ npl: **the ~** los irlandeses ❑ **Irishman/woman** n irlandés(-esa) m/f ❑ **Irish Sea** n: **the Irish Sea** el mar de Irlanda

iron ['aɪən] n hierro; (for clothes) plancha ♦ cpd de hierro ♦ vt (clothes) planchar ▶ **iron out** vt (fig) allanar

ironic(al) [aɪ'rɒnɪk(əl)] adj irónico

ironing ['aɪənɪŋ] n (activity) planchado; (clothes: ironed) ropa planchada; (: to be ironed) ropa por planchar ❑ **ironing board** n burro (MEX) or tabla (LAm exc MEX, SP) de planchar

ironmonger's (shop) ['aɪən,mʌŋɡəz(ʃɒːp)] (BRIT) n ferretería, quincallería

irony ['aɪrənɪ] n ironía

irrational [ɪ'ræʃənl] adj irracional

irreconcilable [ɪ,rekən'saɪləbl] adj (ideas) incompatible; (enemies) irreconciliable

irregular [ɪ'regjulər] adj irregular; (surface) desigual; (action, event) anómalo; (behavior) poco ortodoxo

irrelevant [ɪ'reləvənt] adj fuera de lugar, inoportuno

irreplaceable [ɪrɪ'pleɪsəbl] adj irre(e)mplazable

irresistible [ɪrɪ'zɪstəbl] adj irresistible

irresolute [ɪ'rezəluːt] adj indeciso

irrespective [ɪrɪ'spektɪv]: **~ of** prep sin tener en cuenta, no importa

irresponsible [ɪrɪ'spɒnsɪbl] adj (act) irresponsable; (person) poco serio

irrigate ['ɪrɪɡeɪt] vt regar ❑ **irrigation** [ɪrɪ'ɡeɪʃən] n riego

irritable ['ɪrɪtəbl] adj (person) de mal humor

irritate ['ɪrɪteɪt] vt fastidiar; (MED) picar ❑ **irritating** adj fastidioso ❑ **irritation** [ɪrɪ'teɪʃən] n fastidio; enfado; picazón f

IRS (US) n abbr = **Internal Revenue Service**

is [ɪz] vb see **be**

Islam [ɪs'lɑːm] n Islam m ❑ **Islamic** adj islámico

island ['aɪlənd] n isla ❑ **islander** n isleño(-a)

isle [aɪl] n isla

isn't ['ɪznt] cont = **is not**

isolate ['aɪsəleɪt] vt aislar ❑ **isolated** adj aislado ❑ **isolation** [aɪsə'leɪʃən] n aislamiento

ISP n abbr = **Internet Service Provider**

Israel ['ɪzreɪl] n Israel m ❑ **Israeli** [ɪz'reɪlɪ] adj, n israelí mf

issue ['ɪʃuː] n (problem, subject) cuestión f; (outcome) resultado; (of money etc) emisión f; (of newspaper etc) edición f ♦ vt (rations, equipment) distribuir, repartir; (orders) dar; (certificate, passport) expedir; (decree) promulgar; (magazine) publicar; (checks) extender; (money, stamps) emitir; **at ~** en cuestión; **to take ~ with sb (over)** estar en desacuerdo con algn (sobre); **to make an ~ of sth** hacer una cuestión de algo

Istanbul [ɪstæn'buːl] n Estambul m

---

it

KEYWORD

[ɪt] pron

1 (specific: subject: not generally translated) él (ella); (: direct object) lo, la; (: indirect object) le; (after prep) él (ella); (abstract concept) ello; **it's on the table** está en la mesa; **I can't find it** no lo (or la) encuentro; **give it to me** dámelo (or dámela); **I spoke to him about it** le hablé del asunto; **what did you learn from it?** ¿qué aprendiste de él (or ella)?; **did you go to it?** (party, concert etc) ¿fuiste?

2 (impersonal): **it's raining** llueve, está lloviendo; **it's 6 o'clock** son las 6; **August 10th** (US), **the 10th of August** (BRIT) es el 10 de agosto; **how far is it? – it's 10 miles/2 hours on the train** ¿a qué distancia está? – a 10 millas/2 horas en tren; **who is it? – it's me** ¿quién es? – soy yo

Italian [ɪ'tæljən] *adj* italiano ♦ *n* italiano(-a); (*LING*) italiano

italics [ɪ'tælɪks] *npl* cursiva

Italy ['ɪtəlɪ] *n* Italia

itch [ɪtʃ] *n* picazón *f* ♦ *vi* (*part of body*) picar; **to ~ to do sth** rabiar por hacer algo ❑ **itchy** *adj*: **my hand is itchy** me pica la mano

it'd ['ɪtəd] *cont* = **it would; it had**

item ['aɪtəm] *n* artículo; (*on agenda*) asunto (a tratar); (*also*: **news ~**) noticia ❑ **itemize** *vt* detallar

itinerary [aɪ'tɪnərɛrɪ] *n* itinerario

it'll ['ɪtl] *cont* = **it will; it shall**

its [ɪts] *adj* su; sus *pl*

it's [ɪts] *cont* = **it is; it has**

itself [ɪt'sɛlf] *pron* (*reflexive*) sí mismo(-a); (*emphatic*) él mismo (ella misma)

ITV *n abbr* (*BRIT: Independent Television*) *cadena de televisión comercial independiente del Estado*

I.U.D. *n abbr* (= *intra-uterine device*) DIU *m*

I've [aɪv] *cont* = **I have**

ivory ['aɪvərɪ] *n* marfil *m*

ivy ['aɪvɪ] *n* (*BOT*) hiedra ❑ **Ivy League** (*US*) *grupo de ocho universidades privadas muy prestigiosas de Nueva Inglaterra*

Jj

jab [dʒæb] *vt*: **to ~ sth into sth** clavar algo en algo ♦ *n* (*BRIT: inf: MED*) pinchazo

jack [dʒæk] *n* (*AUT*) gato; (*CARDS*) sota ▸ **jack up** *vt* (*AUT*) levantar con gato

jackal ['dʒækəl] *n* (*ZOOL*) chacal *m*

jacket ['dʒækɪt] *n* chaqueta, saco (*LAm*); (*of book*) sobrecubierta; (*of record*) funda

jack: ❑ **jackknife** *vi* colear ❑ **jackpot** *n* premio gordo

jaded ['dʒeɪdɪd] *adj* (*tired*) cansado; (*fed-up*) hastiado

jagged ['dʒægɪd] *adj* dentado

jail [dʒeɪl] *n* cárcel *f* ♦ *vt* encarcelar

jam [dʒæm] *n* mermelada; (*also*: **traffic ~**) embotellamiento; (*inf: difficulty*) apuro ♦ *vt* (*passage etc*) obstruir; (*mechanism, drawer etc*) atascar; (*RADIO*) interferir ♦ *vi* atascarse, trabarse; **to ~ sth into sth** meter algo a la fuerza en algo

Jamaica [dʒə'meɪkə] *n* Jamaica

jangle ['dʒæŋgəl] *vi* entrechocar (ruidosamente)

janitor ['dʒænɪtər] *n* portero, conserje *m*

January ['dʒænjʊɛrɪ] *n* enero

Japan [dʒə'pæn] *n* (el) Japón ❑ **Japanese** [dʒæpə'niːz] *adj* japonés(-esa) ♦ *n inv* japonés(-esa) *m/f*; (*LING*) japonés *m*

jar [dʒɑːr] *n* tarro, bote *m* ♦ *vi* (*sound*) chirriar; (*colors*) desentonar

jargon ['dʒɑːrgən] *n* jerga

jasmine ['dʒæzmɪn] *n* jazmín *m*

jaundice ['dʒɔːndɪs] *n* icteria

jaunt [dʒɔːnt] *n* excursión *f*

javelin ['dʒævlɪn] *n* jabalina

jaw [dʒɔː] *n* mandíbula

jay [dʒeɪ] *n* (*ZOOL*) arrendajo

jaywalker ['dʒeɪˌwɔːkər] *n* peatón(-ona) *m/f* imprudente

jazz [dʒæz] *n* jazz *m* ▸ **jazz up** *vt* (*liven up*) animar, avivar

jealous ['dʒɛləs] *adj* celoso; (*envious*) envidioso ❑ **jealousy** *n* celos *mpl*; envidia

jeans [dʒiːnz] *npl* pantalones *pl* de mezclilla (*MEX*), jeans (*LAm exc MEX*), vaqueros *mpl* (*SP*)

Jeep® [dʒiːp] *n* jeep *m*

jeer [dʒɪər] *vi*: **to ~ (at)** (*mock*) mofarse (de)

Jell-O® ['dʒɛloʊ] (*US*) *n* gelatina

jelly ['dʒɛlɪ] *n* (*US*: **jam**) mermelada; (*BRIT: dessert etc*) gelatina ❑ **jellyfish** *n inv* medusa, aguaviva (*RPl*)

jeopardy ['dʒɛpərdɪ] *n*: **to be in ~** estar en peligro

jerk [dʒɜːrk] *n* (*jolt*) sacudida; (*wrench*) tirón *m*; (*inf*) imbécil *mf* ♦ *vt* tirar bruscamente de ♦ *vi* (*vehicle*) traquetear

jersey ['dʒɜːrzɪ] *n* suéter *m* (*LAm*), jersey *m* (*SP*); (*fabric*) (tejido de) punto

Jesus ['dʒiːzəs] *n* Jesús *m*

jet [dʒɛt] *n* (*of gas, liquid*) chorro; (*AVIAT*) reactor *m*, jet *m* ❑ **jet-black** *adj* negro como el azabache ❑ **jet engine** *n* motor *m* a reacción ❑ **jet lag** *n* jet lag *m*, *desorientación f después de un largo vuelo* ❑ **jet liner** (*US*) *n* avión *m* de pasajeros

jettison ['dʒɛtɪsən] *vt* desechar

jetty ['dʒɛtɪ] *n* muelle *m*, embarcadero

Jew [dʒuː] *n* judío(-a)

jewel ['dʒuːəl] *n* joya; (*in watch*) rubí *m* ❑ **jeweler** (*US*) (*BRIT* **jeweller**) *n* joyero(-a) ❑ **jewelry** (*US*) (*BRIT* **jewellery**) *n* joyas *fpl*, alhajas *fpl* ❑ **jewelry store** (*US*) (*BRIT* **jeweller's (shop)**) *n* joyería

Jewish ['dʒuːɪʃ] *adj* judío

jibe [dʒaɪb] *n* mofa

jiffy ['dʒɪfɪ] (*inf*) *n*: **in a ~** en un santiamén

jigsaw ['dʒɪgsɔː] *n* (*also*: **~ puzzle**) rompecabezas *m inv*, puzzle *m*

jilt [dʒɪlt] vt dejar plantado a

jingle ['dʒɪŋgəl] n musiquilla ♦ vi tintinear

jinx [dʒɪŋks] n: **there's a ~ on it** está salado (LAm), es yeta (RPl), está gafado (SP)

jitters ['dʒɪtərz] (inf) npl: **to get the ~** ponerse nervioso

job [dʒɑːb] n (task) tarea; (post) empleo; **it's not my ~** no me incumbe a mí; **it's a good ~ that ...** menos mal que ...; **just the ~!** ¡estupendo! ❏ **job centre** (BRIT) n oficina estatal de colocaciones ❏ **jobless** adj desempleado, sin trabajo

jock [dʒɑːk] (US) n deportista m

jockey ['dʒɑːki] n jockey mf ♦ vi: **to ~ for position** maniobrar para conseguir una posición

jog [dʒɑːg] vt empujar (ligeramente) ♦ vi (run) hacer jogging; **to ~ sb's memory** refrescar la memoria a algn ▸ **jog along** vi (fig) ir tirando ❏ **jogging** n jogging m, footing m (SP)

join [dʒɔɪn] vt (things) juntar, unir; (club) hacerse socio de; (POL: party) afiliarse a; (line) ponerse en; (meet: people) reunirse con ♦ vi (roads) juntarse; (rivers) confluir ♦ n juntura ▸ **join in** vi tomar parte, participar ♦ vt fus tomar parte or participar en ▸ **join up** vi reunirse; (BRIT MIL) alistarse

joiner ['dʒɔɪnər] (BRIT) n carpintero(-a) ❏ **joinery** (BRIT) n carpintería

joint [dʒɔɪnt] n (TECH) junta, unión f; (ANAT) articulación f; (inf: place) tugurio; (: of cannabis) toque m (MEX), porro (LAm exc MEX, SP), churro (CAm); (BRIT CULIN) pieza de carne (para asar) ♦ adj (common) común; (combined) combinado; **~ account** (with bank etc) cuenta común

joke [dʒouk] n chiste m; (also: **practical ~**) broma ♦ vi bromear; **to play a ~ on** gastar una broma a ❏ **joker** n (CARDS) comodín m

jolly ['dʒɑːli] adj (merry) alegre; (enjoyable) divertido ♦ adv (BRIT: inf) muy, terriblemente

jolt [dʒoult] n (jerk) sacudida; (shock) susto ♦ vt (physically) sacudir; (emotionally) asustar

jostle ['dʒɑːsəl] vt dar empellones a, codear

jot [dʒɑːt] n: **not one ~** ni jota, ni pizca ▸ **jot down** vt apuntar ❏ **jotter** (BRIT) n bloc m

journal ['dʒɜːrnl] n (magazine) revista; (diary) periódico, diario ❏ **journalism** n periodismo ❏ **journalist** n periodista mf, reportero(-a)

journey ['dʒɜːrni] n viaje m; (distance covered) trayecto

jovial ['dʒouviəl] adj risueño, jovial

joy [dʒɔɪ] n alegría ❏ **joyful** adj alegre ❏ **joyous** adj alegre ❏ **joy ride** n (illegal) paseo en coche robado ❏ **joyrider** n joven que roba un coche para dar una vuelta y luego abandonarlo ❏ **joystick** n (AVIAT) palanca de mando; (COMPUT) mando

JP (BRIT) n abbr = **Justice of the Peace**

Jr abbr = **junior**

jubilant ['dʒuːbɪlənt] adj jubiloso

judge [dʒʌdʒ] n juez mf; (fig: expert) perito ♦ vt juzgar; (consider) considerar ❏ **judg(e)ment** n juicio

judiciary [dʒuːˈdɪʃieri] n poder m judicial

judicious [dʒuːˈdɪʃəs] adj juicioso

judo ['dʒuːdou] n judo

jug [dʒʌg] n jarra

juggernaut ['dʒʌgərnɔːt] (BRIT) n (huge truck) trailer m

juggle ['dʒʌgəl] vi hacer juegos malabares ❏ **juggler** n malabarista mf

juice [dʒuːs] n jugo (LAm), zumo (SP) ❏ **juicy** adj jugoso

jukebox ['dʒuːkbɑːks] n rocola (LAm), máquina de discos (RPl, SP)

July [dʒuːˈlaɪ] n julio

jumble ['dʒʌmbəl] n revoltijo ♦ vt (also: **~ up**) revolver ❏ **jumble sale** (BRIT) n venta de objetos usados con fines benéficos

jumbo ['dʒʌmbou] n jumbo

jump [dʒʌmp] vi saltar, dar saltos; (with fear etc) pegar un bote; (increase) aumentar ♦ vt saltar ♦ n salto; aumento; **to ~ the line** (US) or **queue** (BRIT) colarse

jumper ['dʒʌmpər] n (US: dress) jumper m (LAm), pichi m (SP); (BRIT: pullover) suéter m (LAm), jersey m (SP) ❏ **jumper cables** (US) npl cables mpl de arranque

jump leads (BRIT) npl = **jumper cables**

jump rope ['dʒʌmp,roup] (US) n cuerda de saltar (LAm), comba (SP)

jump suit (US) n overol m (LAm), enterito (RPl), mono (SP)

jumpy ['dʒʌmpi] (inf) adj nervioso

Jun. abbr = **junior**

junction ['dʒʌŋkʃən] n (RAIL) empalme m; (BRIT: of roads) cruce m

juncture ['dʒʌŋktʃər] n: **at this ~** en este momento, en esta coyuntura

June [dʒuːn] n junio

jungle ['dʒʌŋgəl] n selva, jungla

junior ['dʒuːnjər] adj (in age) menor, más joven; (brother/sister etc): **7 years her ~** siete años menor que ella; (position) subalterno ♦ n menor mf, joven mf ❏ **junior high school**

(US) n centro de (enseñanza) secundaria
❏ **junior school** (BRIT) n centro de (enseñanza) primaria

junk [dʒʌŋk] n (cheap goods) baratijas fpl; (garbage) basura ❏ **junk food** n comida chatarra (MEX) or basura (LAm exc MEX, SP)

junkie ['dʒʌŋki] (inf) n drogadicto(-a), yonqui mf

junk mail n propaganda de buzón

junk shop (BRIT) n tienda de objetos usados

junkyard n deshuesadero (MEX), depósito de chatarra (LAm exc MEX), desguace m (SP)

juror ['dʒurər] n jurado

jury ['dʒuri] n jurado

just [dʒʌst] adj justo ♦ adv (exactly) exactamente; (only) sólo, solamente; **he's ~ done it/left** acaba de hacerlo/irse; **~ right** perfecto; **~ two o'clock** las dos en punto; **she's ~ as clever as you** (ella) es tan lista como tú; **~ as well that ...** menos mal que ...; **~ as he was leaving** en el momento en que se marchaba; **~ before/enough** justo antes/ lo suficiente; **~ here** aquí mismo; **he ~ missed** ha fallado por poco; **~ listen to this** escucha esto un momento

justice ['dʒʌstɪs] n justicia; (US: judge) juez m; **to do ~ to** (fig) hacer justicia a ❏ **Justice Department** (US) n Ministerio de Justicia ❏ **Justice of the Peace** (BRIT) n juez m de paz

justify ['dʒʌstɪfaɪ] vt justificar; (text) alinear

jut [dʒʌt] vi (also: ~ out) sobresalir

juvenile ['dʒuːvənaɪl] adj (court) de menores; (humor, mentality) infantil ♦ n menor m de edad

Kk

K abbr (= one thousand) mil; (= kilobyte) kilobyte m, kilooocteto; (inf: thousand) **he earns 10K** gana 10.000 dólares

kangaroo [ˌkæŋɡə'ruː] n canguro

karaoke [ˌkærə'ouki] n karaoke m

karate [kə'rɑːti] n karate m

kebab [kə'bɑːb] n brocheta, alambre m (MEX)

keel [kiːl] n quilla; **on an even ~** (fig) en equilibrio

keen [kiːn] adj (interest, desire) grande, vivo; (eye, intelligence) agudo; (competition) reñido; (edge) afilado; (eager) entusiasta; **to be ~ to do** or **on doing sth** tener muchas ganas de

hacer algo; **to be ~ on sth/sb** interesarse por algo/algn

keep [kiːp] (pt, pp kept) vt (preserve, store) guardar; (hold back) quedarse con; (maintain) mantener; (detain) detener; (store) ser propietario de; (feed: family etc) mantener; (promise) cumplir; (chickens, bees etc) criar; (accounts) llevar; (diary) escribir; (prevent): **to ~ sb from doing sth** impedir a algn hacer algo ♦ vi (food) conservarse; (remain) seguir, continuar ♦ n (of castle) torreón m; (food etc) comida, subsistencia; (inf): **for ~s** para siempre; **to ~ doing sth** seguir haciendo algo; **to ~ sb happy** tener a algn contento; **to ~ a place clean** mantener un lugar limpio; **to ~ sth to o.s.** guardar algo para sí mismo; **to ~ sth (back) from sb** ocultar algo a algn; **to ~ time** (clock) mantener la hora exacta ▶ **keep on** vi: **to keep on doing** seguir or continuar haciendo; **to keep on (about sth)** no parar de hablar (de algo) ▶ **keep out** vi (stay out) permanecer fuera; **"keep out"** "prohibida la entrada" ▶ **keep up** vt mantener, conservar ♦ vi no retrasarse; **to keep up with** (pace) ir al paso de; (level) mantenerse a la altura de ❏ **keeper** n guardián(-ana) m/f ❏ **keep-fit** (BRIT) n gimnasia (de mantenimiento) ❏ **keeping** n (care) cuidado; **in keeping with** de acuerdo con ❏ **keepsake** n recuerdo

kennel ['kɛnl] n perrera; **~s** npl residencia canina

Kenya ['kɛnjə] n Kenia

kept [kɛpt] pt, pp of **keep**

kerb [kɜːb] (BRIT) n bordillo, cordón m de la banqueta (MEX) or vereda (RPl)

kernel ['kɜːnl] n (nut) almendra; (fig) meollo

kerosene ['kɛrəsiːn] n queroseno, keroseno

ketchup ['kɛtʃəp] n salsa de tomate, catsup m

kettle ['kɛtl] n hervidor m, pava (RPl) ❏ **kettle drum** n (MUS) timbal m

key [kiː] n llave f; (MUS) tono; (of piano, typewriter) tecla ♦ adj (issue etc) clave inv ♦ vt (also: ~ in) teclear ❏ **keyboard** n teclado ❏ **keyed up** adj (person) nervioso ❏ **keyhole** n ojo (de la cerradura) ❏ **keyhole surgery** n cirugía endoscópica ❏ **keynote** n (MUS) tónica; (of speech) punto principal or clave ❏ **key ring** n llavero

khaki ['kæki] n caqui

kick [kɪk] vt dar una patada a or un puntapié a; (inf: habit) quitarse de ♦ vi (horse) dar coces ♦ n patada; puntapié m; (of animal) coz f; (thrill): **he does it for ~s** lo hace por pura diversión ▶ **kick off** vi (SPORT) hacer el saque inicial

kid [kɪd] n (inf: child) chiquillo(-a), escuincle(-a) m/f (MEX), pibe(-a) m/f (RPI); (animal) cabrito; (leather) cabritilla ♦ vi (inf) bromear

kidnap ['kɪdnæp] vt secuestrar ❑ **kidnapper** (US **kidnaper**) n secuestrador(a) m/f ❑ **kidnapping** (US **kidnaping**) n secuestro

kidney ['kɪdnɪ] n riñón m ❑ **kidney bean** n frijol m (LAm), poroto (SC), judía (SP)

kill [kɪl] vt matar; (murder) asesinar ♦ n matanza; **to ~ time** matar el tiempo ❑ **killer** n asesino(-a) ❑ **killer app** n abbr (inf: = killer application) aplicación f de excelente rendimiento ❑ **killing** n (one) asesinato; (several) matanza; **to make a killing** (fig) hacer el agosto ❑ **killjoy** n aguafiestas mf inv

kiln [kɪln] n horno

kilo ['kiːləu] n kilo ❑ **kilobyte** n (COMPUT) kilobyte m, kiloocteto ❑ **kilogram** (US) ['kɪlə,græm] (BRIT **kilogramme**) n kilo, kilogramo ❑ **kilometer** (US) [kɪ'lɑːmɪtər] (BRIT **kilometre**) n kilómetro ❑ **kilowatt** ['kɪlə,wɑːt] n kilovatio

kilt [kɪlt] n falda escocesa

kin [kɪn] n see **next**

kind [kaɪnd] adj amable, atento ♦ n clase f, especie f; (species) género m; **in ~** (COMM) en especie; **a ~ of** una especie de; **to be two of a ~** ser tal para cual

kindergarten ['kɪndər,gɑːrtn] n jardín m de niños (MEX), jardín infantil (LAm exc MEX) or de infantes (RPI), parvulario (SP)

kind-hearted adj bondadoso, de buen corazón

kindle ['kɪndl] vt encender; (arouse) despertar

kindly ['kaɪndlɪ] adj amable; cariñoso ♦ adv bondadosamente, amablemente; **will you ~ ...** sea usted tan amable de ...

kindness ['kaɪndnɪs] n (quality) bondad f, amabilidad f; (act) favor m

king [kɪŋ] n rey m ❑ **kingdom** n reino ❑ **kingfisher** n martín m pescador ❑ **king-size** adj de tamaño extra

kiosk ['kiːɑːsk] n quiosco, (BRIT TEL) cabina

kipper ['kɪpər] n arenque m ahumado

kiss [kɪs] n beso ♦ vt besar; **to ~ (each other)** besarse ❑ **kiss of life** (BRIT) n respiración f boca a boca

kit [kɪt] n (equipment) equipo, (tools etc) (caja de) herramientas fpl; (assembly kit) juego de armar

kitchen ['kɪtʃɪn] n cocina ❑ **kitchen sink** n fregadero, lavaplatos m inv (MEX), pileta (RPI)

kite [kaɪt] n (toy) cometa, papalote m (MEX, CAm), barrilete m (RPI)

kitten ['kɪtn] n gatito(-a)

kitty ['kɪtɪ] n (funds) fondo común

km abbr (= kilometer) km

knack [næk] n: **to have the ~ of doing sth** tener el don de hacer algo

knapsack ['næp,sæk] n mochila

knead [niːd] vt amasar

knee [niː] n rodilla ❑ **kneecap** n rótula

kneel [niːl] (pt, pp **knelt**) vi (also: ~ **down**) arrodillarse

knew [nuː] pt of **know**

knickers ['nɪkərz] (BRIT) npl calzones mpl (LAm), bombachas fpl (RPI), bragas fpl (SP)

knick-knack ['nɪk,næk] n baratija, chuchería

knife [naɪf] (pl **knives**) n cuchillo ♦ vt acuchillar

knight [naɪt] n caballero; (CHESS) caballo ❑ **knighthood** (BRIT) n (title): **to receive a knighthood** recibir el título de Sir

knit [nɪt] vt tejer ♦ vi tejer; (bones) soldarse; **to ~ one's brows** fruncir el ceño ❑ **knitting** n tejido ❑ **knitting machine** n máquina de tejer ❑ **knitting needle** n aguja de tejer ❑ **knitwear** n prendas fpl (de tejido) de punto

knives [naɪvz] npl of **knife**

knob [nɑːb] n (of door) perilla (LAm), tirador m (SP); (of stick) puño; (on radio, TV) botón m

knock [nɑːk] vt (strike) golpear; (bump into) chocar contra; (inf) criticar ♦ vi (at door etc): **to ~ at/on** llamar a ♦ n golpe m; (on door) llamada ▸ **knock down** vt atropellar ❑ **knock off** (inf) vi (finish) salir del trabajo ♦ vt (from price) descontar; (inf: steal) birlar ▸ **knock out** vt dejar sin sentido; (BOXING) noquear, dejar K.O.; (in competition) eliminar ▸ **knock over** vt (object) tirar; (person) atropellar ❑ **knocker** n (on door) aldabón m ❑ **knockout** n (BOXING) nocaut m, K.O. ♦ cpd (competition etc) eliminatorio

knot [nɑːt] n nudo ♦ vt anudar

know [nəu] (pt **knew**, pp **~n**) vt (facts) saber; (be acquainted with) conocer; (recognize) reconocer, conocer; **to ~ how to swim** saber nadar; **to ~ about** or **of sb/sth** saber de algn/algo ❑ **know-how** n conocimientos mpl ❑ **knowing** adj (look) de complicidad ❑ **knowingly** adv (purposely) adrede; (smile, look) con complicidad ❑ **know-it-all** n sabelotodo mf

knowledge ['nɑːlɪdʒ] n conocimiento; (learning) saber m, conocimientos mpl ❑ **knowledgeable** adj entendido

knuckle ['nʌkəl] n nudillo

Koran [kə'ræn] n Corán m

Korea [kə'riːə] *n* Corea
kosher ['kouʃər] *adj* kosher, autorizado por la ley judía
Kosovo ['kousəvou] *n* Kosovo *m*

LI

L (*BRIT*) *abbr* = **learner driver**
l. *abbr* (= *liter*) l
lab [læb] *n abbr* = **laboratory**
label ['leɪbəl] *n* etiqueta ♦ *vt* etiquetar, poner una etiqueta a
labor (*US*) ['leɪbər] (*BRIT* **labour**) *n* (*hard work*) trabajo; (*labor force*) mano *f* de obra; (*MED*): **to be in ~** estar de parto ♦ *vi*: **to ~ (at sth)** trabajar (en algo) ♦ *vt*: **to ~ a point** insistir en un punto ❏ **Labor Day** *n* Día *m* del Trabajo or de los Trabajadores ❏ **labored** (*US*) (*BRIT* **laboured**) *adj* (*breathing*) fatigoso ❏ **laborer** (*US*) (*BRIT* **labourer**) *n* peón *m*; **farm laborer** peón *m*; (*day laborer*) jornalero ❏ **labor union** (*US*) *n* sindicato

LABOR DAY

Labor Day es una fiesta nacional en Estados Unidos y se celebra el primer lunes de septiembre. Todos los trabajadores tienen el día libre y aprovechan para disfrutar de un largo fin de semana, en honor del trabajo de todo el año. El fin de semana de **Labor Day** se considera también el final del verano.

laboratory ['læbrətɔːri] *n* laboratorio
laborious [ləˈbɔːriəs] *adj* penoso
labour *etc* ['leɪbər] (*BRIT*) *n, vb* = **labor** ❏ **Labour party** (*BRIT*) *n* el partido laborista, los laboristas *mpl*
lace [leɪs] *n* encaje *m*; (*of shoe etc*) cordón *m*, agujeta (*MEX*), cinta (*MEX*) ♦ *vt* (*shoes: also: ~ up*) atarse (los zapatos)
lack [læk] *n* (*absence*) falta ♦ *vt* carecer de; **he ~s confidence** le falta confianza, carece de confianza; **through** *or* **for ~ of** por falta de; **to be ~ing** faltar, no haber; **he is ~ing in confidence** le falta confianza en sí mismo
lacquer ['lækər] *n* laca
lad [læd] *n* muchacho, chico
ladder ['lædər] *n* escalera (de mano); (*BRIT*: *in tights*) carrera
laden ['leɪdn] *adj*: **~ (with)** cargado (de)
ladle ['leɪdl] *n* cucharón *m*
lady ['leɪdi] *n* señora; (*dignified, graceful*) dama; **"ladies and gentlemen ..."** "damas y

caballeros ...**"; young ~** señorita; **ladies' room** los servicios de señoras ❏ **ladybug** (*US*) (*BRIT* **ladybird**) *n* mariquita ❏ **ladylike** *adj* fino ❏ **Ladyship** *n*: **your Ladyship** su Señoría
lag [læg] *n* retraso ♦ *vi* (*also: ~ behind*) retrasarse, quedarse atrás ♦ *vt* (*BRIT*: *pipes*) revestir
lager ['lɑːgər] *n* cerveza (rubia)
lagoon [ləˈguːn] *n* laguna
laid [leɪd] *pt, pp* of **lay** ❏ **laid back** (*inf*) *adj* relajado ❏ **laid up** *adj*: **to be laid up (with)** tener que guardar cama (a causa de)
lain [leɪn] *pp* of **lie**
lake [leɪk] *n* lago
lamb [læm] *n* cordero; (*meat*) (carne *f* de) cordero ❏ **lamb chop** *n* chuleta de cordero ❏ **lambswool** *n* lana de cordero
lame [leɪm] *adj* cojo; (*excuse*) poco convincente
lament [ləˈment] *n* quejo ♦ *vt* lamentarse de
laminated ['læmɪneɪtɪd] *adj* (*metal*) laminado; (*wood*) contrachapado; (*surface*) plastificado
lamp [læmp] *n* lámpara ❏ **lamppost** *n* farol (*LAm*), farola (*SP*) ❏ **lampshade** *n* pantalla
lance [læns] *vt* (*MED*) abrir con lanceta
land [lænd] *n* tierra; (*country*) país *m*; (*piece of land*) terreno; (*estate*) tierras *fpl*, finca ♦ *vi* (*from ship*) desembarcar; (*AVIAT*) aterrizar; (*fig*: *fall*) caer, terminar ♦ *vt* (*passengers, goods*) desembarcar; **to ~ sb with sth** (*inf*) hacer cargar a algn con algo ► **land up** (*BRIT*) *vi*: **to land up in/at** ir a parar a/en ❏ **landfill site** *n* vertedero ❏ **landing** *n* aterrizaje *m*; (*of staircase*) rellano ❏ **landing gear** *n* (*AVIAT*) tren *m* de aterrizaje ❏ **landlady** *n* (*of rented apartment etc*) casera, dueña ❏ **landlord** *n* propietario; (*of rented apartment etc*) casero, dueño ❏ **landmark** *n* lugar *m* conocido; **to be a landmark** (*fig*) marcar un hito histórico ❏ **landowner** *n* terrateniente *mf* ❏ **landscape** *n* paisaje *m* ❏ **landscape gardener** *n* arquitecto de jardines ❏ **landslide** *n* (*GEO*) corrimiento de tierras; (*fig*: *POL*) victoria arrolladora
lane [leɪn] *n* (*in country*) camino; (*AUT*) carril *m*; (*in race*) calle *f*
language ['læŋgwɪdʒ] *n* lenguaje *m*; (*national tongue*) idioma *m*, lengua; **bad ~** palabrotas *fpl* ❏ **language laboratory** *n* laboratorio de idiomas
lank [læŋk] *adj* (*hair*) lacio
lanky ['læŋki] *adj* larguirucho
lantern ['læntərn] *n* linterna, farol *m*

lap [læp] n (of track) vuelta; (of body) regazo ♦ vt (also: ~ **up**) beber a lengüetadas ♦ vi (waves) chapotear; **to sit on sb's ~** sentarse en las rodillas de algn ▶ **lap up** vt (fig) tragarse

lapel [lə'pɛl] n solapa

Lapland ['læplænd] n Laponia

lapse [læps] n fallo; (moral) desliz m; (of time) intervalo ♦ vi (expire) caducar; (time) pasar, transcurrir; **to ~ into bad habits** caer en malos hábitos

laptop (computer) ['læptɒp-(kəm'pjuːtər)] n (ordenador m) portátil m

larch [lɑːrtʃ] n alerce m

lard [lɑːrd] n manteca (de cerdo)

larder ['lɑːrdər] n (BRIT) n despensa

large [lɑːrdʒ] adj grande; **at ~** (free) en libertad; (generally) en general ❑ **largely** adv (mostly) en su mayor parte; (introducing reason) en gran parte ❑ **large-scale** adj (map) en gran escala; (fig) importante

⚠ Be careful not to translate **large** by the Spanish word **largo**.

lark [lɑːrk] n (bird) alondra; (joke) broma

laryngitis [ˌlærɪn'dʒaɪtɪs] n laringitis f

laser ['leɪzər] n láser m ❑ **laser printer** n impresora (por) láser

lash [læʃ] n latigazo; (also: **eye~**) pestaña ♦ vt azotar; (tie): **to ~ to/together** atar a/atar ▶ **lash out** vi: **to lash out (at sb)** (hit) arremeter (contra algn); **to lash out against sb** lanzar invectivas contra algn

lass [læs] (BRIT) n chica

lasso ['læsəʊ] n lazo

last [læst] adj último; (end: of series etc) final ♦ adv (most recently) la última vez; (finally) por último ♦ vi durar; (continue) continuar, seguir; **~ night** anoche; **~ week** la semana pasada; **at ~** por fin; **~ but one** penúltimo ❑ **last-ditch** adj (attempt) último, desesperado ❑ **lasting** adj duradero ❑ **lastly** adv por último, finalmente ❑ **last-minute** adj de última hora

latch [lætʃ] n pestillo

late [leɪt] adj (far on: in time, process etc) al final de; (not on time) tarde, atrasado; (dead) fallecido ♦ adv tarde; (behind time, schedule) con retraso; **of ~** últimamente; **~ at night** a última hora de la noche; **in ~ May** hacia fines de mayo; **the ~ Mr. X** el difunto Sr X ❑ **latecomer** n rezagado(-a) ❑ **lately** adv últimamente ❑ **later** adj (date etc) posterior; (version etc) más reciente ♦ adv más tarde,

después ❑ **latest** adj último; **at the latest** a más tardar

lathe [leɪð] n torno

lather ['læðər] n espuma (de jabón) ♦ vt enjabonar

Latin ['lætɪn] n latín m ♦ adj latino ❑ **Latin America** n América latina ❑ **Latin-American** adj, n latinoamericano(-a)

latitude ['lætɪtuːd] n latitud f; (fig) libertad f

latter ['lætər] adj último; (of two) segundo ♦ n: **the ~** el último, éste ❑ **latterly** adv últimamente

laudable ['lɔːdəbəl] adj loable

laugh [læf] n risa ♦ vi reír(se); **(to do sth) for a ~** (hacer algo) en broma ▶ **laugh at** vt fus reírse de ▶ **laugh off** vt tomar a risa ❑ **laughable** adj ridículo ❑ **laughing stock** n: **the laughing stock of** el hazmerreír de ❑ **laughter** n risa

launch [lɔːntʃ] n lanzamiento; (boat) lancha ♦ vt (ship) botar; (rocket etc) lanzar; (fig) comenzar ▶ **launch into** vt fus lanzarse a ❑ **launch(ing) pad** n plataforma de lanzamiento

launder ['lɔːndər] vt lavar

Launderette® [lɔːn'drɛt] (BRIT) n = **Laundromat**

Laundromat® ['lɔːndrəmæt] (US) n lavandería (automática)

laundry ['lɔːndrɪ] n (dirty) ropa sucia; (clean) ropa lavada; (room) lavadero

lavatory ['lævətɔːrɪ] n wáter m

lavender ['lævəndər] n lavanda

lavish ['lævɪʃ] adj (amount) abundante; (person): **~ with** pródigo en ♦ vt: **to ~ sth on sb** colmar a algn de algo

law [lɔː] n ley f; (SCOL) derecho; (a rule) regla; (professions connected with law) jurisprudencia ❑ **law-abiding** adj respetuoso de la ley ❑ **law and order** n orden m público ❑ **law court** n tribunal m (de justicia) ❑ **lawful** adj legítimo, lícito ❑ **lawless** adj (action) criminal

lawmaker ['lɔːˌmeɪkər] (US) n legislador(a) m/f

lawn [lɔːn] n pasto (LAm), césped m (SP) ❑ **lawnmower** n máquina de cortar el pasto (LAm), cortacésped m (SP) ❑ **lawn tennis** (BRIT) n tenis m sobre hierba

law school (US) n (SCOL) facultad f de derecho

lawsuit ['lɔːsuːt] n pleito

lawyer ['lɔːjər] n abogado(-a); (for sales, wills etc) notario(-a)

lax [læks] adj laxo

laxative ['læksətɪv] n laxante m

lay [leɪ] (pt, pp **laid**) pt of **lie** ♦ adj laico; (not expert) lego ♦ vt (place) colocar; (eggs) poner; (cable) tender; (carpet) extender ► **lay aside** or **by** vt dejar a un lado ► **lay down** vt (pen etc) dejar; (rules etc) establecer; **to lay down the law** (pej) imponer las normas ► **lay off** vt (workers) despedir ► **lay on** (BRIT) vt (meal, facilities) proveer ► **lay out** vt (spread out) disponer, exponer ❑ **layabout** (BRIT: inf) n vago(-a) ❑ **lay-by** n (BRIT AUT) área de aparcamiento

layer ['leɪər] n capa

layman ['leɪmən] n lego

lay-off ['leɪˌɔːf] n despido

layout ['leɪˌaʊt] n (design) plan m, trazado; (PRESS) composición f

layover ['leɪˌoʊvər] n (US) parada f intermedia

laze [leɪz] vi (also: ~ **about**) holgazanear

lazy ['leɪzi] adj perezoso, vago; (movement) lento

lb. abbr libra; = **pound**

lead¹ [liːd] (pt, pp **led**) n (front position) delantera; (clue) pista; (ELEC) cable m; (THEATER) papel m principal; (BRIT: for dog) correa ♦ vt (walk etc in front) ir a la cabeza de; (guide): **to ~ sb somewhere** conducir a algn a algún sitio; (be leader) dirigir; (start, guide: activity) protagonizar ♦ vi (road, pipe etc) conducir a; (SPORT) ir primero; **to be in the ~** (SPORT) llevar la delantera; (fig) ir a la cabeza; **to ~ the way** llevar la delantera ► **lead away** vt llevar ► **lead back** vt (person, route) llevar de vuelta ► **lead on** vt (tease) engañar ► **lead to** vt fus producir, provocar ► **lead up to** vt fus (events) conducir a; (in conversation) preparar el terreno para

lead² [lɛd] n (metal) plomo; (in pencil) mina ❑ **leaded gas** (US) (BRIT **leaded petrol**) n gasolina con plomo

leader ['liːdər] n jefe(-a) m/f, líder mf; (SPORT) líder mf ❑ **leadership** n dirección f; (position) mando; (quality) iniciativa

leading ['liːdɪŋ] adj (main) principal; (first) primero; (front) delantero ❑ **leading lady** n (THEATER) primera actriz f ❑ **leading light** n (person) figura principal ❑ **leading man** n (THEATER) primer actor m

lead singer ['liːd'sɪŋər] n cantante mf

leaf [liːf] n (pl **leaves**) n hoja ♦ vi: **to ~ through** hojear; **to turn over a new ~** reformarse

leaflet ['liːflɪt] n folleto

league [liːg] n sociedad f; (SPORT) liga; **to be in ~ with** haberse confabulado con

leak [liːk] n (of liquid, gas) escape m, fuga; (in pipe) agujero; (in roof) gotera; (in security) filtración f ♦ vi (shoes, ship) hacer agua; (pipe) tener (un) escape; (roof) gotear; (liquid, gas) escaparse, fugarse; (fig) divulgarse ♦ vt (fig) filtrar

lean [liːn] (pt, pp ~**ed**, pt, pp **leant** [lɛnt] (BRIT)) adj (thin) flaco; (meat) magro ♦ vt: **to ~ sth on sth** apoyar algo en algo ♦ vi (slope) inclinarse; **to ~ against** apoyarse contra; **to ~ on** apoyarse en ► **lean back/forward** vi inclinarse hacia atrás/adelante ► **lean out** vi asomarse ► **lean over** vi inclinarse ❑ **leaning** n: leaning (toward) inclinación f (hacia) ❑ **leant** (BRIT) [lɛnt] pt, pp of **lean**

leap [liːp] (pt, pp ~**ed** or **leapt** [lɛpt]) n salto ♦ vi saltar ❑ **leapfrog** n pídola ❑ **leap year** n año bisiesto

learn [lɜːrn] (pt, pp ~**ed**, pt, pp ~**t** (BRIT)) vt aprender ♦ vi aprender; **to ~ about sth** enterarse de algo; **to ~ to do sth** aprender a hacer algo ❑ **learned** ['lɜːrnɪd] adj erudito ❑ **learner** n (BRIT: also: **learner driver**) principiante mf ❑ **learning** n el saber, conocimientos mpl

lease [liːs] n arriendo ♦ vt arrendar

leash [liːʃ] n correa

least [liːst] adj: **the ~** (slightest) el menor, el más pequeño; (smallest amount of) mínimo ♦ adv (+ vb) menos; (+ adj): **the ~ expensive** el (la) menos costoso(-a); **the ~ possible effort** el menor esfuerzo posible; **at ~** por lo menos, al menos; **you could at ~ have written** por lo menos podías haber escrito; **not in the ~** en absoluto

leather ['lɛðər] n cuero

leave [liːv] (pt, pp **left**) vt dejar; (go away from) abandonar; (place etc: permanently) salir de ♦ vi irse; (train etc) salir ♦ n permiso; **to ~ sth to sb** (money etc) legar algo a algn; (responsibility etc) encargar a algn de algo; **to be left** quedar, sobrar; **there's some milk left over** sobra o queda algo de leche; **on ~** de permiso ► **leave behind** vt (on purpose) dejar; (accidentally) olvidar, dejarse ► **leave out** vt omitir; excluir ❑ **leave of absence** n permiso de licencia (LAm) or excedencia (SP)

leaves [liːvz] npl of **leaf**

Lebanon ['lɛbənən] n: **the ~** el Líbano

lecherous ['lɛtʃərəs] (pej) adj lascivo

lecture ['lɛktʃər] n conferencia; (SCOL) clase f ♦ vi dar clase(s) ♦ vt (scold): **to ~ sb on or about sth** echar una reprimenda a algn por algo; **to give a ~ on** dar una conferencia sobre ❑ **lecturer** n conferencista mf (LAm), conferenciante mf (SP); (BRIT UNIV) profesor(a) m/f (universitario(-a))

led [lɛd] pt, pp of **lead**

ledge [lɛdʒ] n repisa; (of window) alféizar m; (of mountain) saliente m

ledger ['lɛdʒər] n libro mayor

leech [li:tʃ] n sanguijuela

leek [li:k] n puerro

leer [lɪər] vi: **to ~ at sb** mirar de manera lasciva a algn

leeway ['li:weɪ] n (fig): **to have some ~** tener cierta libertad de acción

left [lɛft] pt, pp of **leave** ♦ adj izquierdo; (remaining): **there are 2 ~** quedan dos ♦ n izquierda ♦ adv a la izquierda; **on** or **to the ~** a la izquierda; **the L~** (POL) la izquierda ☐ **left-handed** adj zurdo ☐ **the left-hand side** n la izquierda ☐ **left-luggage (office)** (BRIT) n consigna ☐ **leftovers** npl sobras fpl ☐ **left-wing** adj (POL) de izquierdas, izquierdista

leg [lɛg] n pierna; (of animal, chair) pata; (of pants) pernera; (CULIN: of lamb) pierna; (: of chicken) pata, pierna (MEX); (of journey) etapa

legacy ['lɛgəsɪ] n herencia

legal ['li:gəl] adj (permitted by law) lícito; (of law) legal ☐ **legal holiday** (US) n fiesta oficial ☐ **legalize** vt legalizar ☐ **legally** adv legalmente ☐ **legal tender** n moneda de curso legal

legend ['lɛdʒənd] n (also fig: person) leyenda

legislation [lɛdʒɪs'leɪʃən] n legislación f

legislature ['lɛdʒɪslətʃər] n cuerpo legislativo

legitimate [lɪ'dʒɪtɪmət] adj legítimo

leg-room n espacio para las piernas

leisure ['li:ʒər] n ocio, tiempo libre; **at ~** con tranquilidad ☐ **leisure centre** (BRIT) n centro de recreo ☐ **leisurely** adj sin prisa, lento

lemon ['lɛmən] n limón m ☐ **lemonade** n limonada ☐ **lemon tea** n té m con limón

lend [lɛnd] (pt, pp lent) vt: **to ~ sth to sb** prestar algo a algn ☐ **lending library** n biblioteca de préstamo

length [lɛŋθ] n (size) largo, longitud f; (distance): **the ~ of** todo a lo largo de; (of swimming pool, cloth) largo; (of wood, string) trozo; (amount of time) duración f; **at ~** (at last) por fin, finalmente; (lengthily) largamente ☐ **lengthen** vt alargar ♦ vi alargarse ☐ **lengthways** adv a lo largo ☐ **lengthy** adj largo, extenso

lenient ['li:nɪənt] adj indulgente

lens [lɛnz] n (of spectacles) cristal m, lente f; (of camera) objetivo

Lent [lɛnt] n Cuaresma

lent [lɛnt] pt, pp of **lend**

lentil ['lɛntɪl] n lenteja

Leo ['li:oʊ] n Leo

leotard ['li:ətɑ:rd] n mallas fpl

leprosy ['lɛprəsɪ] n lepra

lesbian ['lɛzbɪən] n lesbiana

less [lɛs] adj (in size, degree etc) menor; (in quality) menos ♦ pron, adv menos ♦ prep: ~ **tax/10% discount** menos impuestos/el 10 por ciento de descuento; ~ **than half** menos de la mitad; ~ **than ever** menos que nunca; ~ **and** ~ cada vez menos; **the ~ he works ...** cuanto menos trabaja ... ☐ **lessen** vi disminuir, reducirse ♦ vt disminuir, reducir ☐ **lesser** adj menor; **to a lesser extent** en menor grado

lesson ['lɛsən] n clase f; (warning) lección f

let [lɛt] (pt, pp ~) vt (allow) dejar, permitir; (BRIT: lease) alquilar; **to ~ sb do sth** dejar que algn haga algo; **to ~ sb know sth** comunicar algo a algn; ~**'s go!** ¡vamos!; ~ **him come** que venga; **"to ~"** "se alquila" ▶ **let down** vt (disappoint) defraudar; (BRIT: tire) desinflar ▶ **let go** vi, vt soltar ▶ **let in** vt dejar entrar; (visitor etc) hacer pasar ▶ **let off** vt (culprit) dejar escapar; (BRIT: gun) disparar; (bomb) accionar; (firework) hacer estallar ☐ **let on** (inf) vi divulgar ▶ **let out** vt dejar salir; (sound) soltar ▶ **let up** vi amainar, disminuir

lethal ['li:θəl] adj (weapon) mortífero; (poison, wound) mortal

letter ['lɛtər] n (of alphabet) letra; (correspondence) carta ☐ **letter bomb** n carta-bomba ☐ **letter box** (BRIT) n buzón m ☐ **lettering** n letras fpl

lettuce ['lɛtɪs] n lechuga

let-up n disminución f

leukemia (US) [lu:'ki:mɪə] (BRIT **leukaemia**) n leucemia

level ['lɛvəl] adj (flat) llano ♦ adv a nivel ♦ n nivel m; (height) altura ♦ vt nivelar; allanar; (destroy: building) derribar; (: forest) arrasar; **to be ~ with** estar a nivel de; **on the ~** (fig: honest) serio; **"A" ~s** (BRIT) ≈ examen m or calificación f en bachillerato ▶ **level off** or **out** vi (prices etc) estabilizarse ☐ **level crossing** (BRIT) n paso a nivel ☐ **level-headed** adj sensato

lever ['lɛvər] n (also fig) palanca ♦ vt: **to ~ sth up/off** levantar/quitar algo con palanca ☐ **leverage** n (using bar etc) apalancamiento; (fig: influence) influencia

levy ['lɛvɪ] n impuesto ♦ vt exigir, recaudar

lewd [lu:d] adj lascivo; (joke) colorado (MEX), verde (LAm exc MEX, SP)

liability [ˌlaɪəˈbɪləti] n (pej: person, thing) estorbo, lastre m; (JUR: responsibility) responsabilidad f; **liabilities** npl (COMM) pasivo

liable [ˈlaɪəbəl] adj (subject): ~ **to** sujeto a; (responsible): ~ **for** responsable de; (likely): ~ **to do** propenso a hacer

liaise [liˈeɪz] vi: **to ~ with** enlazar con □ **liaison** n (coordination) enlace m; (affair) relaciones fpl amorosas

liar [ˈlaɪər] n mentiroso(-a)

libel [ˈlaɪbəl] n calumnia ♦ vt calumniar

liberal [ˈlɪbərəl] adj liberal; (offer, amount etc) generoso

liberate [ˈlɪbəreɪt] vt (people: from poverty etc) librar; (prisoner) libertar; (country) liberar

liberty [ˈlɪbərti] n libertad f; **to be at ~** (criminal) estar en libertad; **to be at ~ to do** estar libre para hacer; **to take the ~ of doing sth** tomarse la libertad de hacer algo

Libra [ˈliːbrə] n Libra

librarian [laɪˈbreərɪən] n bibliotecario(-a)

library [ˈlaɪbrerɪ] n biblioteca

⚠ Be careful not to translate **library** by the Spanish word **librería**.

libretto [lɪˈbretou] n libreto

Libya [ˈlɪbɪə] n Libia □ **Libyan** adj, n libio(-a)

lice [laɪs] npl of **louse**

licence [ˈlaɪsəns] (BRIT) n = **license**

license [ˈlaɪsəns] n (US) licencia; (permit) permiso; (also: **driver's ~**) licencia de manejo (LAm), carnet m de conducir (SP) ♦ vt autorizar, dar permiso a □ **licensed** adj (car) matriculado; (BRIT: for alcohol) autorizado para vender bebidas alcohólicas □ **license plate** (US) n placa (LAm), chapa (RPl), matrícula (SP)

lick [lɪk] vt lamer; (inf: defeat) dar una paliza a; **to ~ one's lips** relamerse

licorice (US) [ˈlɪkərɪs] (BRIT **liquorice**) n regaliz m

lid [lɪd] n (of box, case) tapa; (of pan) tapadera

lido [ˈliːdou] n (BRIT) alberca (MEX), piscina (LAm exc MEX, SP), pileta (RPl)

lie [laɪ] (pt **lay**, pp **lain**) vi (rest) estar echado, estar acostado; (of object: be situated) estar, encontrarse; (tell lies: pt, pp **lied**) mentir ♦ n mentira; **to ~ low** (fig) mantenerse a escondidas ▶ **lie around** or (BRIT) **about** vi (things) estar tirado; (people) estar tumbado □ **lie-down** n (BRIT): **to have a lie-down** echarse (una siesta) □ **lie-in** (BRIT) n: **to have a lie-in** quedarse en la cama

lieu [luː]: **in ~ of** prep en lugar de

lieutenant [luːˈtenənt] n (MIL) teniente mf

life [laɪf] (pl **lives**) n vida; **to come to ~** animarse □ **life assurance** (BRIT) n = **life insurance** □ **life belt** (BRIT) n salvavidas m inv □ **lifeboat** n lancha de socorro □ **life coach** n profesional encargado de mejorar la situación laboral y personal de sus clientes □ **lifeguard** n socorrista mf, vigilante mf □ **life insurance** n seguro de vida □ **life jacket** n chaleco salvavidas □ **lifeless** adj sin vida; (dull) soso □ **lifelike** adj (model etc) que parece vivo; (realistic) realista □ **lifelong** adj de toda la vida □ **life preserver** (US) n chaleco salvavidas □ **life sentence** n cadena perpetua □ **life-size** adj de tamaño natural □ **life span** n vida □ **lifestyle** n estilo de vida □ **life support system** n (MED) sistema m de respiración asistida □ **lifetime** n (of person) vida; (of thing) período de vida

lift [lɪft] vt levantar; (end: ban, rule) levantar, suprimir ♦ vi (fog) disiparse ♦ n (BRIT: machine) ascensor m; **to give sb a ~** (BRIT) llevar a algn en el carro (LAm) or coche (SP) □ **lift-off** n despegue m

light [laɪt] (pt, pp ~**ed** or **lit**) n luz f; (lamp) luz f, lámpara; (AUT) faro; (for cigarette etc): **have you got a ~?** ¿tienes fuego? ♦ vt (candle, cigarette, fire) prender (LAm), encender (SP); (room) alumbrar ♦ adj (color) claro; (not heavy, also fig) ligero; (room) con mucha luz; (gentle, graceful) ágil; ~**s** npl (traffic lights) semáforo; **to come to ~** salir a luz; **in the ~ of** (new evidence etc) a la luz de ▶ **light up** vi (smoke) encender un cigarrillo; (face) iluminarse ♦ vt (illuminate) iluminar, alumbrar; (set fire to) encender □ **light bulb** n foco (MEX), bombilla (LAm exc MEX, SP), bujía (CAm), bombita (RPl) □ **lighten** vt (make less heavy) aligerar □ **lighter** n (also: **cigarette lighter**) encendedor m □ **light-headed** adj (dizzy) mareado; (excited) exaltado □ **light-hearted** adj (person) alegre; (remark etc) divertido □ **lighthouse** n faro □ **lighting** n (system) alumbrado □ **lightly** adv ligeramente; (not seriously) con poca seriedad; **to get off lightly** ser castigado con poca severidad □ **lightness** n (in weight) ligereza

lightning [ˈlaɪtnɪŋ] n relámpago, rayo □ **lightning rod** (US) (BRIT **lightning conductor**) n pararrayos m inv

light: □ **light pen** n lápiz m óptico □ **lightweight** adj (suit) ligero ♦ n (BOXING) peso ligero □ **light year** n año luz

like [laɪk] vt (thing): **I ~ swimming/apples** me gusta nadar/me gustan las manzanas ♦ prep como ♦ adj parecido, semejante ♦ n: **and the ~** y otros por el estilo; **his ~s and dislikes** sus gustos y aversiones; **I would ~, I'd ~** me gustaría; (for purchase) quisiera; **would you ~ a coffee?** ¿te apetece un café?; **to be** or **look ~ sb/sth** parecerse a algn/algo; **what does it look/taste/sound ~?** ¿cómo es/a qué sabe/cómo suena?; **that's just ~ him** es muy de él, es característico de él; **do it ~ this** hazlo así; **it is nothing ~ ...** no tiene parecido alguno con ... ☐ **likeable** adj simpático, agradable

likelihood ['laɪklihud] n probabilidad f

likely ['laɪkli] adj probable; **he's ~ to leave** es probable que se vaya; **not ~!** ¡ni hablar!

likeness ['laɪknɪs] n semejanza, parecido; **that's a good ~** se parece mucho

likewise ['laɪkwaɪz] adv igualmente; **to do ~** hacer lo mismo

liking ['laɪkɪŋ] n: **~ (for)** (person) cariño (a); (thing) afición (a); **to be to sb's ~** ser del gusto de algn

lilac ['laɪlæk] n (tree) lilo; (flower) lila

lily ['lɪli] n lirio, azucena; **~ of the valley** n lirio de los valles

limb [lɪm] n miembro

limber ['lɪmbər]: **to ~ up** vi (SPORT) hacer ejercicios de calentamiento

limbo ['lɪmbou] n: **to be in ~** (fig) quedar a la expectativa

lime [laɪm] n (tree) limero; (fruit) limón m verde (MEX), lima (LAm exc MEX, SP); (GEO) cal f

limelight ['laɪm,laɪt] n: **to be in the ~** (fig) ser el centro de atención

limerick ['lɪmərɪk] n tipo de poema humorístico de cinco versos

limestone ['laɪm,stoun] n piedra caliza

limit ['lɪmɪt] n límite m ♦ vt limitar ☐ **limited** adj limitado; **to be limited to** limitarse a ☐ **limited (liability) company** (BRIT) n sociedad f anónima

limousine ['lɪməzi:n] n limusina

limp [lɪmp] n: **to have a ~** tener cojera ♦ vi cojear ♦ adj flojo; (material) fláccido

limpet ['lɪmpɪt] n lapa

line [laɪn] n línea; (of people) cola; (rope) cuerda; (for fishing) sedal m; (wire) hilo; (row, series) fila, hilera; (of writing) renglón m, línea; (of song) verso; (on face) arruga; (RAIL) vía ♦ vt (road etc) llenar; (SEWING) forrar; **to ~ the streets** llenar las aceras; **in ~ with** alineado con; (according to) de acuerdo con ▶ **line up**

vi hacer cola ♦ vt alinear; (prepare) preparar; organizar

lined [laɪnd] adj (face) arrugado; (paper) rayado

linen ['lɪnɪn] n ropa blanca; (cloth) lino

liner ['laɪnər] n transatlántico m; (for bin) bolsa (de basura)

linesman ['laɪnzmən] n (SPORT) juez m de línea

line-up n (US: line) cola; (SPORT) alineación f

linger ['lɪŋgər] vi retrasarse, tardar en marcharse; (smell, tradition) persistir

lingerie ['lɑ:nʒə'reɪ] n lencería

linguist ['lɪŋgwɪst] n lingüista mf ☐ **linguistics** n lingüística

lining ['laɪnɪŋ] n forro; (ANAT) (membrana) mucosa

link [lɪŋk] n (of a chain) eslabón m; (relationship) relación f, vínculo; (INTERNET) enlace m ♦ vt vincular, unir; (associate): **to ~ with** or **to** relacionar con; **~s** npl (GOLF) campo de golf ▶ **link up** vt acoplar ♦ vi unirse

lino ['laɪnou] (BRIT) n = **linoleum**

linoleum [lɪ'nouliəm] n linóleo

lion ['laɪən] n león m ☐ **lioness** n leona

lip [lɪp] n labio ☐ **lip balm** n protector m labial

liposuction ['lɪpou,sʌkʃən] n liposucción f

lip: ☐ **lipread** vi leer los labios ☐ **lip salve** n = **lip balm** ☐ **lip service** n: **to pay lip service to sth** (pej) prometer algo de dientes para afuera ☐ **lipstick** n lápiz m de labios, lápiz labial (LAm)

liqueur [lɪ'kɜ:r] n licor m

liquid ['lɪkwɪd] adj, n líquido ☐ **liquidize** vt (CULIN) licuar ☐ **liquidizer** n licuadora

liquor ['lɪkər] n (US) alcohol m, bebidas fpl alcohólicas; (BRIT) licores mpl

liquorice ['lɪkərɪs] (BRIT) n = **licorice**

liquor store (US) n tienda de bebidas alcohólicas

Lisbon ['lɪzbən] n Lisboa

lisp [lɪsp] n ceceo ♦ vi cecear

list [lɪst] n lista ♦ vt (mention) enumerar; (put on a list) poner en una lista ☐ **listed building** (BRIT) n edificio de interés histórico-artístico

listen ['lɪsən] vi escuchar, oír; **to ~ to sth/sb** escuchar algo/a algn ☐ **listener** n oyente mf; (RADIO) radioyente mf

listless ['lɪstlɪs] adj apático, indiferente

lit [lɪt] pt, pp of **light**

liter (US) ['li:tər] (BRIT **litre**) n litro

literacy ['lɪtərəsi] n alfabetismo, capacidad f de leer y escribir

literal ['lɪtərəl] adj literal

literary ['lɪtərəri] adj literario

literate ['lɪtərət] adj alfabetizado, que sabe leer y escribir; (educated) culto

literature ['lɪtərətʃər] n literatura; (brochures etc) folletos mpl

lithe [laɪð] adj ágil

litigation [lɪtɪ'geɪʃən] n litigio

litre ['liːtər] (BRIT) n = **liter**

litter ['lɪtər] n (garbage) basura; (young animals) camada, cría ▫ **litter bin** (BRIT) n papelera ▫ **littered** adj: **littered with** (scattered) lleno de

little ['lɪtl] adj (small) pequeño; (not much) poco ♦ adv poco; **a ~** un poco (de); **~ house/ bird** casita/pajarito; **a ~ bit** un poquito; **~ by ~** poco a poco ▫ **little finger** n dedo meñique

live[1] [laɪv] adj (animal) vivo; (wire) conectado; (broadcast) en directo; (shell) cargado

live[2] [lɪv] vi vivir ▸ **live down** vt hacer olvidar ▸ **live on** vt fus (food, salary) vivir de ▸ **live together** vi vivir juntos ▸ **live up to** vt fus (fulfill) cumplir con

livelihood ['laɪvlihud] n sustento

lively ['laɪvli] adj vivo; (interesting: place, book etc) animado

liven up ['laɪvən'ʌp] vt animar ♦ vi animarse

liver ['lɪvər] n hígado

lives [laɪvz] npl of **life**

livestock ['laɪvˌstɑːk] n ganado

livid ['lɪvɪd] adj lívido; (furious) furioso

living ['lɪvɪŋ] adj (alive) vivo ♦ n: **to earn** or **make a ~** ganarse la vida ▫ **living conditions** npl condiciones fpl de vida ▫ **living room** n sala (de estar) ▫ **living standards** npl nivel m de vida ▫ **living wage** n jornal m suficiente para vivir

lizard ['lɪzərd] n lagarto; (small) lagartija

load [loud] n carga; (weight) peso ♦ vt (COMPUT) cargar; (also: **~ up**): **to ~ (with)** cargar (con or de); **a ~ of nonsense** (inf) tonterías fpl; **a ~ of**, **~s of** (fig) (gran) cantidad de, montones de ▫ **loaded** adj (vehicle): **to be loaded with** estar cargado de; (question) intencionado; (inf: rich) forrado (de dinero)

loaf [louf] (pl **loaves**) n (barra de) pan m

loan [loun] n préstamo ♦ vt prestar; **on ~** prestado

loath [louθ] adj: **to be ~ to do sth** estar poco dispuesto a hacer algo

loathe [louð] vt aborrecer; (person) odiar, detestar ▫ **loathing** n aversión f; odio

loaves [louvz] npl of **loaf**

lobby ['lɑːbi] n vestíbulo, sala de espera; (POL: pressure group) grupo de presión ♦ vt presionar

lobster ['lɑːbstər] n langosta

local ['loukəl] adj local ♦ n (BRIT: pub) bar m; **the ~s** los vecinos, los del lugar ▫ **local anesthetic** n (MED) anestesia local ▫ **local authority** (BRIT) n = **local government** ▫ **local call** n (TEL) llamada local (LAm) or metropolitana (SP) ▫ **local government** (US) n gobierno municipal ▫ **locality** [lou'kælɪti] n localidad f ▫ **locally** adv en la vecindad; por aquí

locate [lou'keɪt] vt (find) localizar; (situate): **to be ~d in** estar situado en

location [lou'keɪʃən] n situación f; **on ~** (FILM) en exteriores

loch [lɑːx] n lago

lock [lɑːk] n (of door, box) cerradura; (of canal) esclusa; (of hair) mechón m ♦ vt (with key) cerrar (con llave) ♦ vi (door etc) cerrarse (con llave); (wheels) trabarse ▸ **lock in** vt encerrar ▸ **lock out** vt (person) cerrar la puerta a ▸ **lock up** vt (criminal) meter en la cárcel; (mental patient) encerrar; (house) cerrar (con llave) ♦ vi echar la llave

locker ['lɑːkər] n lóker m (LAm), taquilla (SP)

locket ['lɑːkɪt] n relicario

locksmith ['lɑːkˌsmɪθ] n cerrajero(-a)

lockup ['lɑːkˌʌp] n (jail, cell) cárcel f

locum ['loukəm] n (BRIT MED) interino(-a)

locust ['loukəst] n langosta

lodge [lɑːdʒ] n casita (del guarda) ♦ vi (person): **to ~ (with)** alojarse (en casa de); (bullet, bone) incrustarse ♦ vt presentar ▫ **lodger** n huésped mf

lodgings ['lɑːdʒɪŋz] npl alojamiento

loft [lɑːft] n desván m

lofty ['lɑːfti] adj (noble) sublime; (haughty) altanero

log [lɑːg] n (of wood) leño, tronco; (written account) diario ♦ vt anotar ▸ **log in** or **on** vi (COMPUT) entrar en el sistema ▫ **log off**, **log out** vi (COMPUT) salir del sistema

logbook ['lɑːgˌbuk] n (NAUT) diario de a bordo; (AVIAT) libro de vuelo; (of car) documentación f

loggerheads ['lɑːgərˌhedz] npl: **to be at ~ (with)** estar en desacuerdo (con)

logic ['lɑːdʒɪk] n lógica ▫ **logical** adj lógico

login ['lɔːgɪn] n login m

logo ['lougou] n logotipo

loin [lɔɪn] n (CULIN) lomo, solomillo

loiter ['lɔɪtər] vi (linger) entretenerse

loll [lɔl] vi (also: **~ about**) repantigarse

lollipop ['lɔlipɔp] n chupaleta (MEX), pirulí m (LAm exc MEX), chupetín m (RPl), piruleta (SP) ❑ **lollipop man/lady** (BRIT) n persona encargada de ayudar a los niños a cruzar la calle

London ['lʌndən] n Londres ❑ **Londoner** n londinense mf

lone [loun] adj solitario

loneliness ['lounlinis] n soledad f; aislamiento

lonely ['lounli] adj (situation) solitario; (person) solo; (place) aislado

loner ['lounər] n solitario(-a)

lonesome ['lounsəm] (US) adj (person) solo

long [lɔːŋ] adj largo ♦ adv mucho tiempo, largamente ♦ vi: **to ~ for sth** anhelar algo; **so or as ~ as** mientras, con tal que; **don't be ~!** ¡no tardes!, ¡vuelve pronto!; **how ~ is the street?** ¿cuánto tiene la calle de largo?; **how ~ is the lesson?** ¿cuánto dura la clase?; **6 feet ~** que mide 6 pies, de 6 pies de largo; **6 months ~** que dura 6 meses, de 6 meses de duración; **all night ~** toda la noche; **he no ~er comes** ya no viene; **~ before** mucho antes; **before ~** (+ future) dentro de poco; (+ past) poco tiempo después; **at ~ last** al fin, por fin ❑ **long-distance** adj (race) de larga distancia; **a long-distance call** una llamada de larga distancia (LAm), una conferencia (SP) ❑ **long-haired** adj de pelo largo ❑ **longhand** n escritura sin abreviaturas ❑ **longing** n anhelo, ansia; (nostalgia) nostalgia ♦ adj anhelante

longitude ['lɔːŋdʒitjuːd] n longitud f

long: ❑ **long jump** n salto de longitud ❑ **long-life** adj (batteries) de larga duración; (BRIT: milk) uperizado ❑ **long-lost** adj desaparecido hace mucho tiempo ❑ **long-range** adj (plan) de gran alcance; (missile) de largo alcance ❑ **longshoreman** (US) n trabajador m portuario, estibador m (LAm) ❑ **long-sighted** (BRIT) adj hipermétrope ❑ **long-standing** adj de mucho tiempo ❑ **long-suffering** adj sufrido ❑ **long-term** adj a largo plazo ❑ **long wave** n onda larga ❑ **long-wearing** (US) adj resistente ❑ **long-winded** adj prolijo

loo [luː] n (BRIT: inf) n baño

look [luk] vi mirar; (seem) parecer; (building etc): **to ~ south/on to the sea** dar al sur/al mar ♦ n (gen): **to have a ~** mirar; (glance) mirada; (appearance) aire m, aspecto; **~s** npl (good looks) belleza; **~ (here)!** (expressing annoyance etc) ¡oye!; **~!** (expressing surprise) ¡mira! ► **look after** vt fus (care for) cuidar a; (deal with) encargarse de ► **look around** or (BRIT) **round** vi volver la cabeza ► **look at** vt fus mirar; (read quickly) echar un vistazo a ► **look back** vi mirar hacia atrás ► **look down on** vt fus (fig) despreciar, mirar con desprecio ► **look for** vt fus buscar ► **look forward to** vt fus esperar con ilusión; (in letters): **we look forward to hearing from you** quedamos a la espera de sus gratas noticias ► **look into** vt investigar ► **look on** vi mirar (como espectador) ► **look out** vi (beware): **to look out (for)** tener cuidado (de) ► **look out for** vt fus (seek) buscar; (await) esperar ► **look through** vt fus (examine) examinar ► **look to** vt fus (rely on) contar con ► **look up** vi mirar hacia arriba; (improve) mejorar ♦ vt (word) buscar ► **look up to** vt fus admirar ❑ **lookout** n (tower etc) puesto de observación; (person) vigía mf; **to be on the lookout for sth** estar al acecho de algo

loom [luːm] vi: **~ (up)** (threaten) surgir, amenazar; (event: approach) aproximarse

loony ['luːni] (inf) n, adj loco(-a)

loop [luːp] n lazo ♦ vt: **to ~ sth around sth** pasar algo alrededor de algo ❑ **loophole** n escapatoria

loose [luːs] adj suelto; (clothes) ancho; (morals, discipline) relajado; **to be on the ~** estar en libertad; **to be at a ~ end** or **~ ends** no saber qué hacer ❑ **loose change** (BRIT) n feria (MEX), morralla (MEX), sencillo (LAm exc MEX), suelto (SP) ❑ **loose chippings** npl (on road) gravilla suelta ❑ **loosely** adv libremente, aproximadamente ❑ **loosen** vt aflojar

loot [luːt] n botín m ♦ vt saquear

lop off [lɔp'ɔːf] vt (branches) podar

lop-sided adj torcido

lord [lɔːrd] n señor m; **L~ Smith** Lord Smith; **the L~** el Señor; **my ~** (to bishop) Ilustrísima; (to noble etc) Señor; **good L~!** ¡Dios mío!; **the (House of) L~s** (BRIT) la Cámara de los Lores ❑ **lordship** n: **your Lordship** su Señoría

lore [lɔːr] n tradiciones fpl

lorry ['lɔri] (BRIT) n camión m ❑ **lorry driver** (BRIT) n trailero(-a) (MEX), camionero(-a) (LAm exc MEX, SP)

lose [luːz] (pt, pp lost) vt perder ♦ vi perder, ser vencido; **to ~ (time)** (clock) atrasarse ❑ **loser** n perdedor(a) m/f

loss [lɔːs] n pérdida; **heavy ~es** (MIL) grandes pérdidas; **to be at a ~** no saber qué hacer; **to make a ~** sufrir pérdidas

lost [lɔst] *pt, pp of* **lose ♦** *adj* perdido ❏ **lost and found** (*US*) (*BRIT* **lost property**) *n* objetos *mpl* perdidos

lot [lɑːt] *n* (*group: of things*) grupo; (*at auctions*) lote *m*; (*plot*) terreno *m*; **the ~** el todo, todos; **a ~** (*large number: of books etc*) muchos; (*a great deal*) mucho, bastante; **a ~ of, ~s of** mucho(s) (*pl*); **I read a ~** leo bastante; **to draw ~s (for sth)** echar suertes (para decidir algo)

lotion [ˈloʊʃən] *n* loción *f*

lottery [ˈlɑːtəri] *n* lotería

loud [laʊd] *adj* (*voice, sound*) fuerte; (*laugh, shout*) estrepitoso; (*condemnation etc*) enérgico; (*gaudy*) chillón(-ona) **♦** *adv* (*speak etc*) fuerte; **out ~** en voz alta ❏ **loud-hailer** (*BRIT*) *n* megáfono ❏ **loudly** *adv* (*noisily*) fuerte; (*aloud*) en voz alta ❏ **loudspeaker** *n* altavoz *m*

lounge [laʊndʒ] *n* (*at airport etc*) sala; (*BRIT: in house*) salón *m*, sala (de estar); (*BRIT: also: ~bar*) salón-bar *m* **♦** *vi* (*also: ~ around*) reposar, holgazanear

louse [laʊs] (*pl* **lice**) *n* piojo

lousy [ˈlaʊzi] (*inf*) *adj* (*bad quality*) asqueroso, malísimo; (*ill*) pésimo (*LAm*), fatal (*SP*)

lout [laʊt] *n* vándalo, patotero (*SC*)

lovable [ˈlʌvəbəl] *adj* amable, simpático

love [lʌv] *n* (*romantic, sexual*) amor *m*; (*kind, caring*) cariño **♦** *vt* amar, querer; (*thing, activity*): **I ~ paella** me encanta la paella; "**~ from Anne**" (*on letter*) "un abrazo (de) Anne"; **I'd ~ to go** me encantaría ir; (*person in love*) **with** estar enamorado/enamorarse de; **to make ~** hacer el amor; **for the ~ of** por amor de; "**15 ~**" (*TENNIS*) "15 a cero" ❏ **love affair** *n* aventura (sentimental) ❏ **love letter** *n* carta de amor ❏ **love life** *n* vida sentimental

lovely [ˈlʌvli] (*BRIT*) *adj* (*delightful*) encantador(a); (*beautiful*) precioso

lover [ˈlʌvər] *n* amante *mf*; (*person in love*) enamorado; (*amateur*): **a ~ of** un(a) aficionado(-a) *or* un(a) amante de

loving [ˈlʌvɪŋ] *adj* amoroso, cariñoso; (*action*) tierno

low [loʊ] *adj, adv* bajo **♦** *n* (*METEOROLOGY*) área de baja presión; **to be ~ on** (*supplies etc*) andar mal de; **to feel ~** sentirse deprimido; **to turn (down) ~** bajar ❏ **low-alcohol** *adj* de bajo contenido en alcohol ❏ **low-calorie** *adj* bajo en calorías ❏ **low-cut** *adj* (*dress*) escotado

lower [ˈloʊər] *adj* más bajo; (*less important*) menos importante **♦** *vt* bajar; (*reduce*) reducir **♦** *vr*: **to ~ o.s. to** (*fig*) rebajarse a

low: ❏ **low-fat** *adj* (*milk, yogurt*) descremado (*LAm*), desnatado (*SP*); (*diet*) bajo en calorías ❏ **lowlands** *npl* (*GEO*) tierras *fpl* bajas ❏ **lowly** *adj* inferior ❏ **low season** (*BRIT*) *n* la temporada baja

loyal [ˈlɔɪəl] *adj* leal ❏ **loyalty** *n* lealtad *f* ❏ **loyalty card** (*BRIT*) *n* tarjeta de cliente

lozenge [ˈlɑːzɪndʒ] *n* (*MED*) pastilla

L.P. *n abbr* LP *m*; (= *long-playing record*) elepé *m*

L-plates [ˈelˌpleɪts] (*BRIT*) *npl* Letra L que deben llevar en los vehículos los aprendices de conductor

Ltd (*BRIT*) *abbr* (= *limited company*) S.A.

lubricate [ˈluːbrɪkeɪt] *vt* lubricar

luck [lʌk] *n* suerte *f*; **bad ~** mala suerte; **good ~!** ¡que tengas suerte!, ¡suerte!; **bad** *or* **hard** *or* **tough ~!** ¡qué pena! ❏ **luckily** *adv* afortunadamente ❏ **lucky** *adj* afortunado; (*at cards etc*) con suerte; (*object*) que trae suerte

ludicrous [ˈluːdɪkrəs] *adj* absurdo

lug [lʌg] *vt* (*drag*) arrastrar

luggage [ˈlʌgɪdʒ] *n* equipaje *m* ❏ **luggage rack** *n* (*on car*) baca, portaequipajes *m inv*

lukewarm [ˈluːkˈwɔːrm] *adj* tibio

lull [lʌl] *n* tregua **♦** *vt*: **to ~ sb to sleep** arrullar a algn; **to ~ sb into a false sense of security** dar a algn una falsa sensación de seguridad

lullaby [ˈlʌləbaɪ] *n* canción *f* de cuna

lumbago [lʌmˈbeɪgoʊ] *n* lumbago

lumber [ˈlʌmbər] *n* (*junk*) trastos *mpl* viejos; (*wood*) maderos *mpl* ▸ **lumber with** (*BRIT*) *vt*: **to be lumbered with sth** tener que cargar con algo ❏ **lumberjack** *n* maderero

luminous [ˈluːmɪnəs] *adj* luminoso

lump [lʌmp] *n* terrón *m*; (*fragment*) trozo; (*swelling*) bulto **♦** *vt* (*also: ~ together*) juntar ❏ **lump sum** *n* suma global ❏ **lumpy** *adj* (*sauce*) lleno de grumos; (*mattress*) lleno de bultos

lunatic [ˈluːnətɪk] *adj* loco

lunch [lʌntʃ] *n* comida (*MEX*), almuerzo (*LAm exc MEX, SP*) **♦** *vi* comer (*MEX*), almorzar (*LAm exc MEX, SP*) ❏ **lunch meat** (*US*) *n* fiambre *m* en conserva

luncheon [ˈlʌntʃən] *n* comida (*MEX*), almuerzo (*LAm exc MEX, SP*) ❏ **luncheon voucher** (*BRIT*) *n* vale *m* de comida

lunch time *n* hora de comer (*MEX*) *or* almorzar (*LAm exc MEX, SP*)

lung [lʌŋ] *n* pulmón *m*

lunge [lʌndʒ] *vi* (*also: ~ forward*) abalanzarse; **to ~ at** arremeter contra

lurch [lɜːrtʃ] *vi* dar sacudidas **♦** *n* sacudida; **to leave sb in the ~** dejar a algn plantado

lure [luər] n (*attraction*) atracción f ♦ vt tentar

lurid ['lurɪd] adj (*color*) chillón(-ona); (*account*) espeluznante

lurk [lɜːrk] vi (*person, animal*) estar al acecho; (*fig*) acechar

luscious ['lʌʃəs] adj (*attractive: person, thing*) precioso; (*food*) exquisito, delicioso

lush [lʌʃ] adj exuberante

lust [lʌst] n lujuria; (*greed*) codicia

luster (*US*) ['lʌstər] (*BRIT* **lustre**) n lustre m, brillo

lusty ['lʌsti] adj robusto, fuerte

Luxembourg ['lʌksəmbɜːrg] n Luxemburgo

luxuriant [lʌg'ʒuriənt] adj exuberante

luxurious [lʌg'ʒuriəs] adj lujoso

luxury ['lʌgʒəri] n lujo ♦ cpd de lujo

lying ['laɪɪŋ] n mentiras fpl ♦ adj mentiroso

lyrical ['lɪrɪkəl] adj lírico

lyrics ['lɪrɪks] npl (*of song*) letra

Mm

m. abbr = **meter**; **mile**; **million**

M.A. abbr = **Master of Arts**

mac [mæk] (*BRIT*) n impermeable m

macaroni [mækə'rouni] n macarrones mpl

machine [mə'ʃiːn] n máquina ♦ vt (*dress etc*) coser a máquina; (*TECH*) hacer a máquina ❏ **machine gun** n ametralladora ❏ **machine language** n (*COMPUT*) lenguaje m máquina ❏ **machinery** n maquinaria; (*fig*) mecanismo

macho ['mɑːtʃou] adj machista

mackerel ['mækərəl] n inv caballa

mackintosh ['mækɪntɒʃ] (*BRIT*) n impermeable m

mad [mæd] adj loco; (*idea*) disparatado; (*angry*) furioso; (*keen*): **he's ~ about tennis** el tenis le vuelve loco

madam ['mædəm] n señora

madden ['mædn] vt enloquecer

made [meɪd] pt, pp of **make**

Madeira [mə'dɪrə] n (*GEO*) Madera; (*wine*) vino de Madera

made-to-measure (*BRIT*) adj hecho a la medida

made-to-order (*US*) adj hecho a la medida

madly ['mædli] adv locamente

madman ['mædmən] n loco

madness ['mædnɪs] n locura

Madrid [mə'drɪd] n Madrid

magazine [mægə'ziːn] n revista; (*RADIO, TV*) programa m de entrevistas (y variedades)

maggot ['mægət] n gusano

magic ['mædʒɪk] n magia ♦ adj mágico ❏ **magician** [mə'dʒɪʃən] n mago(-a); (*conjurer*) prestidigitador(a) m/f

magistrate ['mædʒɪstreɪt] n juez mf de primera instancia

magnet ['mægnɪt] n imán m ❏ **magnetic** [mæg'netɪk] adj magnético; (*personality*) atrayente

magnificent [mæg'nɪfɪsənt] adj magnífico

magnify ['mægnɪfaɪ] vt (*object*) ampliar; (*sound*) aumentar ❏ **magnifying glass** n lupa

magpie ['mægpaɪ] n urraca

mahogany [mə'hɑːgəni] n caoba

maid [meɪd] n sirvienta, mucama (*RPI*); **old ~** (*pej*) solterona

maiden ['meɪdn] n doncella ♦ adj (*aunt etc: pej*) solterona; (*speech, voyage*) inaugural ❏ **maiden name** n apellido de soltera

mail [meɪl] n correo; (*letters*) correspondencia ♦ vt (*US*) echar al correo ❏ **mailbox** (*US*) n buzón m ❏ **mailing list** n lista de direcciones ❏ **mailman** (*US*) n cartero ❏ **mail order** n (*order*) pedido por correo

maim [meɪm] vt mutilar, lisiar

main [meɪn] adj principal, mayor ♦ n (*pipe*) cañería principal; (*US*) red f de suministro; **the ~s** npl (*BRIT*) la red de suministro; **in the ~** en general ❏ **mainframe** n (*COMPUT*) computadora (*LAm*) or ordenador m (*SP*) central ❏ **mainland** n tierra firme ❏ **mainly** adv principalmente ❏ **main road** n carretera general ❏ **mainstay** n (*fig*) pilar m ❏ **mainstream** n corriente f principal

maintain [meɪn'teɪn] vt mantener ❏ **maintenance** ['meɪntənəns] n mantenimiento; (*LAW*) pensión f alimenticia

maize [meɪz] (*BRIT*) n maíz m, choclo (*SC*)

majestic [mə'dʒestɪk] adj majestuoso

majesty ['mædʒɪsti] n majestad f; (*title*): **Your M~** Su Majestad

major ['meɪdʒər] n (*MIL*) mayor mf (*LAm*), comandante mf (*SP*) ♦ adj principal; (*MUS*) mayor

Majorca [mə'jɔːrkə] n Mallorca

majority [mə'dʒɔːrɪti] n mayoría

make [meɪk] (*pt, pp made*) vt hacer; (*manufacture*) fabricar; (*mistake*) cometer; (*speech*) pronunciar; (*cause to be*): **to ~ sb sad** poner triste a algn; (*force*): **to ~ sb do sth** obligar a algn a hacer algo; (*earn*) ganar;

(equal): **2 and 2 ~ 4** 2 y 2 son 4 ♦ *n* marca; **to ~ the bed** hacer la cama; **to ~ a fool of sb** poner a algn en ridículo; **to ~ a profit/loss** obtener ganancias/sufrir pérdidas; **to ~ it** (arrive) llegar; (achieve sth) tener éxito; **what time do you ~ it?** ¿qué hora tienes?; **to ~ do with** contentarse con ▸ **make for** *vt fus* (place) dirigirse a ▸ **make out** *vt* (decipher) descifrar; (understand) entender; (see) distinguir; (check) extender ▸ **make up** *vt* (invent) inventar; (prepare) hacer; (constitute) constituir ♦ *vi* reconciliarse; (with cosmetics) maquillarse ▸ **make up for** *vt fus* compensar □ **make-believe** *n* ficción *f*, invención *f* □ **maker** *n* fabricante *mf*; (of movie, program) autor(a) *m/f* □ **makeshift** *adj* improvisado □ **make-up** *n* maquillaje *m* □ **make-up remover** *n* desmaquillador *m*

making ['meɪkɪŋ] *n* (fig): **in the ~** en vías de formación; **to have the ~s of** (person) tener madera de

Malaysia [mə'leɪʒə] *n* Malasia, Malaisia

male [meɪl] *n* (BIOL) macho ♦ *adj* (sex, attitude) masculino; (child etc) varón

malfunction [mæl'fʌŋkʃən] *n* mal funcionamiento

malice ['mælɪs] *n* malicia □ **malicious** [mə'lɪʃəs] *adj* malicioso; rencoroso

malignant [mə'lɪgnənt] *adj* (MED) maligno

mall [mɔːl] (US) *n* (also: **shopping ~**) centro comercial

mallet ['mælɪt] *n* mazo

malnutrition [,mælnuː'trɪʃən] *n* desnutrición *f*

malpractice [mæl'præktɪs] *n* negligencia profesional

malt [mɔːlt] *n* malta; (BRIT: whiskey) whisky *m* de malta

Malta ['mɔːltə] *n* Malta □ **Maltese** [mɔːl'tiːz] *adj, n inv* maltés(-esa) *m/f*

mammal ['mæməl] *n* mamífero

mammoth ['mæməθ] *n* mamut *m* ♦ *adj* gigantesco

man [mæn] (pl **men**) *n* hombre *m*; (mankind) el hombre ♦ *vt* (NAUT) tripular; (MIL) guarnecer; (operate: machine) manejar; **an old ~** un viejo; **~ and wife** marido y mujer

manage ['mænɪdʒ] *vi* arreglárselas, ir tirando ♦ *vt* (be in charge of) dirigir; (control: person) manejar; (: ship) gobernar □ **manageable** *adj* (vehicle) manejable; (task) factible □ **management** *n* dirección *f* □ **manager** *n* director(a) *m/f*; (of pop star) manager *mf*; (SPORT) entrenador(a) *m/f* □ **manageress** *n* directora; entrenadora □ **managerial**

[,mænə'dʒɪriəl] *adj* directivo □ **managing director** (BRIT) *n* director(a) *m/f* general

mandarin ['mændərɪn] *n* (also: **~ orange**) mandarina; (person) mandarín *m*

mandatory ['mændətɔːri] *adj* obligatorio

mane [meɪn] *n* (of horse) crin *f*; (of lion) melena

maneuver (US) [mə'nuːvər] (BRIT **manoeuvre**) *vt, vi* maniobrar ♦ *n* maniobra

manfully ['mænfəlɪ] *adv* valientemente

mangle ['mæŋgəl] *vt* mutilar, destrozar

man: □ **manhandle** *vt* maltratar □ **manhole** *n* agujero de acceso □ **manhood** *n* madurez *f*; (state) virilidad *f* □ **man-hour** *n* hora-hombre *f* □ **manhunt** *n* (POLICE) búsqueda y captura

mania ['meɪnɪə] *n* manía □ **maniac** *n* maníaco(-a); (fig) maniático

manic ['mænɪk] *adj* frenético □ **manic-depressive** *n* maníaco(-a) depresivo(-a)

manicure ['mænɪkjʊr] *n* manicura

manifest ['mænɪfest] *vt* manifestar, mostrar ♦ *adj* manifiesto

manifesto [,mænɪ'festou] *n* manifiesto

manipulate [mə'nɪpjəleɪt] *vt* manipular

man: □ **mankind** *n* humanidad *f*, género humano □ **manly** *adj* varonil □ **man-made** *adj* artificial; (fibre) sintético

manner ['mænər] *n* manera, modo; (behavior) conducta, manera de ser; (type): **all ~ of things** toda clase de cosas; **~s** *npl* (behavior) modales *mpl*; **bad ~s** mala educación □ **mannerism** *n* peculiaridad *f*; (gesture) gesto

manoeuvre [mə'nuːvər] (BRIT) *n, vb* = **maneuver**

manor ['mænər] *n* (modern) finca; (BRIT: also: **~ house**) casa solariega

manpower ['mæn,paʊər] *n* mano *f* de obra

mansion ['mænʃən] *n* mansión *f*

manslaughter ['mæn,slɔːtər] *n* homicidio sin premeditación

mantelpiece ['mæntl,piːs] *n* repisa (de la chimenea)

manual ['mænjuəl] *adj* manual ♦ *n* manual *m*

manufacture [,mænju'fæktʃər] *vt* fabricar ♦ *n* fabricación *f* □ **manufacturer** *n* fabricante *mf*

manure [mə'nuər] *n* estiércol *m*

manuscript ['mænjuskrɪpt] *n* manuscrito

many ['meni] *adj, pron* muchos(-as); **a great ~** muchísimos, un buen número de; **~ a time** muchas veces

map [mæp] *n* mapa *m*; **to ~ out** *vt* proyectar

maple ['meɪpəl] *n* arce *m*, maple *m* (LAm)

mar [mɑːr] vt estropear

marathon ['mærəθəːn] n maratón m

marble ['mɑːrbəl] n mármol m; (toy) canica, bolita (SC)

March [mɑːrtʃ] n marzo

march [mɑːrtʃ] vi (MIL) marchar; (demonstrators) manifestarse ♦ n marcha; (demonstration) manifestación f

mare [meər] n yegua

margarine ['mɑːrdʒərən] n margarina

margin ['mɑːrdʒɪn] n margen m; (COMM: profit margin) margen (de beneficio) ❑ **marginal** adj marginal ❑ **marginal seat** (BRIT) n (POL) escaño obtenido por escasa mayoría

marigold ['mærɪgould] n caléndula

marijuana [mærɪ'wɑːnə] n mariguana (LAm), marihuana (SP)

marina [mə'riːnə] n puerto deportivo

marinate ['mærɪneɪt] vt marinar

marine [mə'riːn] adj marino ♦ n infante m de marina

marital ['mærɪtl] adj matrimonial; **~ status** estado civil

marjoram ['mɑːrdʒərəm] n mejorana

mark [mɑːrk] n marca, señal f; (in snow, mud etc) huella; (stain) mancha; (currency) marco; (BRIT SCOL) nota ♦ vt marcar; manchar; (damage: furniture) rayar; (indicate: place etc) señalar; (BRIT SCOL) calificar, corregir; **to ~ time** marcar el paso; (fig) marcar(se) un ritmo ❑ **marked** adj (obvious) marcado, acusado ❑ **marker** n (sign) marcador m; (bookmark) señal f

market ['mɑːrkɪt] n mercado ♦ vt (COMM) comercializar ❑ **market garden** (BRIT) n huerto ❑ **marketing** n marketing m ❑ **marketplace** n mercado ❑ **market research** n estudio de mercado

marksman ['mɑːrksmən] n tirador m

marmalade ['mɑːrməleɪd] n mermelada de naranja

maroon [mə'ruːn] vt: **to be ~ed** quedar aislado; (fig) quedar abandonado

marquee [mɑːr'kiː] n entoldado

marriage ['mærɪdʒ] n (relationship, institution) matrimonio; (wedding) boda; (act) casamiento ❑ **marriage certificate** n acta (MEX) or certificado (LAm exc MEX, SP) de matrimonio

married ['mærid] adj casado; (life, love) conyugal

marrow ['mærou] n médula; (BRIT: vegetable) calabacín m

marry ['mæri] vt casarse con; (father, priest etc) casar ♦ vi (also: **get married**) casarse

Mars [mɑːrz] n Marte m

marsh [mɑːrʃ] n pantano; (salt marsh) marisma

marshal ['mɑːrʃəl] n (MIL) mariscal m; (at sports meeting etc) oficial m; (US: of police, fire department) jefe(-a) m/f ♦ vt (thoughts etc) ordenar; (soldiers) formar

marshy ['mɑːrʃi] adj pantanoso

martial law ['mɑːrʃəl'lɔː] n ley f marcial

martyr ['mɑːrtər] n mártir mf ❑ **martyrdom** n martirio

marvel ['mɑːrvəl] n maravilla, prodigio ♦ vi: **to ~ (at)** maravillarse (de) ❑ **marvelous** (US) (BRIT **marvellous**) adj maravilloso

Marxist ['mɑːrksɪst] adj, n marxista mf

marzipan ['mɑːrzɪpæn] n mazapán m

mascara [mæ'skærə] n rímel m

masculine ['mæskjulɪn] adj masculino

mash [mæʃ] vt machacar ❑ **mashed potatoes** npl puré m de papas (LAm) or patatas (SP)

mask [mæsk] n máscara ♦ vt (cover): **to ~ one's face** ocultarse la cara; (hide: feelings) esconder

mason ['meɪsən] n (also: stone~) mampostero; (also: free~) masón m ❑ **masonry** n (building trade) albañilería; (stonework) mampostería

masquerade [mæskə'reɪd] vi: **to ~ as** disfrazarse de, hacerse pasar por

mass [mæs] n (people) muchedumbre f; (of air, liquid etc) masa; (of detail, hair etc) gran cantidad f; (REL) misa ♦ cpd masivo ♦ vi reunirse; concentrarse; **the ~es** npl las masas; **~es of** (inf) montones de

massacre ['mæsəkər] n masacre f

massage [mə'sɑːʒ] n masaje m ♦ vt dar masaje en

masseur [mæ'sɜːr] n masajista m

masseuse [mæ'suːz] n masajista f

massive ['mæsɪv] adj enorme; (support, changes) masivo

mass media npl medios mpl de comunicación

mass production n fabricación f en serie

mast [mæst] n (NAUT) mástil m; (RADIO, TV) torre f

master ['mæstər] n (of servant) amo; (of situation, house) dueño; (BRIT: in primary school) maestro; (BRIT: in secondary school) profesor m; (title for boys): **M~ X** Señorito X ♦ vt dominar ❑ **Master of Arts/Science** n maestría (LAm) or máster m (SP) en Letras/Ciencias ❑ **masterly** adj magistral ❑ **mastermind** n cerebro ♦ vt dirigir, planear

◻ **masterpiece** n obra maestra

◻ **mastery** n maestría

mat [mæt] n estera; (also: **door~**) tapete m (MEX), felpudo (LAm exc MEX, SP); (also: **table ~**) salvamanteles m inv ♦ adj = **mat(t)**

match [mætʃ] n fósforo, cerillo (MEX); (game) partido ♦ vt (go well with) hacer juego con; (equal) igualar; (correspond to) corresponderse con; (colours: also: ~ **up**) combinar ♦ vi hacer juego; **to be a good ~** hacer juego ◻ **matchbox** n caja de fósforos or (MEX) cerillos ◻ **matching** adj haciendo juego

mate [meɪt] n (workmate) colega mf; (animal: male) macho; (: female) hembra; (in navy) segundo de a bordo; (BRIT: inf: friend) amigo(-a) ♦ vi acoplarse, aparearse ♦ vt aparear

material [mə'tɪriəl] n (substance) materia; (information) material m; (cloth) tela, tejido ♦ adj material; (important) esencial; **~s** npl materiales mpl

maternal [mə'tɜːrnl] adj maternal

maternity [mə'tɜːrnɪti] n maternidad f ◻ **maternity dress** n vestido de embarazada

math [mæθ] (US) n = **mathematics**

mathematical [ˌmæθə'mætɪkəl] adj matemático

mathematician [ˌmæθəmə'tɪʃən] n matemático(-a)

mathematics [ˌmæθə'mætɪks] n matemáticas fpl

maths [mæθs] (BRIT) n = **mathematics**

matinée [ˌmæt'neɪ] n sesión f de tarde

matrices ['meɪtrisiːz] npl of **matrix**

matriculation [məˌtrɪkjuˈleɪʃən] n (formalización f de) matrícula

matrimony ['mætrɪmouni] n matrimonio

matrix ['meɪtrɪks] (pl **matrices**) n matriz f

matron ['meɪtrən] n (married woman) matrona; (BRIT) enfermera f jefe; (in school) enfermera

mat(t) [mæt] adj mate

matted ['mætɪd] adj enmarañado

matter ['mætər] n cuestión f, asunto; (PHYSICS) sustancia, materia; (reading matter) material m; (MED) pus m ♦ vi importar; **~s** npl (affairs) asuntos mpl, temas mpl; **it doesn't ~** no importa; **what's the ~?** ¿qué pasa?; **no ~ what** pase lo que pase; **as a ~ of course** por rutina; **as a ~ of fact** de hecho ◻ **matter-of-fact** adj pragmático, práctico

mattress ['mætrɪs] n colchón m

mature [mə'tʃuər] adj maduro ♦ vi madurar ◻ **maturity** n madurez f

maul [mɔːl] vt magullar

mauve [mouv] adj de color guinda (LAm) or malva (SP)

maximum ['mæksɪməm] (pl **maxima**) adj máximo ♦ n máximo

May [meɪ] n mayo

may [meɪ] (conditional **might**) vi (indicating possibility): **he ~ come** puede que venga; (be allowed to): **~ I smoke?** ¿puedo fumar?; (wishes): **~ you have a happy life together!** ¡que seáis felices!; **you ~ as well go** bien puedes irte

maybe ['meɪbiː] adv quizá(s)

May Day n el Primero de Mayo

mayhem ['meɪhəm] n caos m (total)

mayonnaise ['meɪəneɪz] n mayonesa

mayor ['meɪər] n alcalde m ◻ **mayoress** (BRIT) n alcaldesa

maze [meɪz] n laberinto

M.D. n abbr (= Doctor of Medicine) título universitario

me [miː] pron (direct) me; (stressed, after pron) mí; **can you hear me?** ¿me oyes?; **he heard ME** ¡me oyó a mí!; **it's me** soy yo; **give them to me** dámelos/las; **with/without me** conmigo/sin mí

meadow ['medou] n prado, pradera

meager (US) ['miːgər] (BRIT **meagre**) adj escaso, pobre

meal [miːl] n comida; (flour) harina ◻ **mealtime** n hora de comer

mean [miːn] (pt, pp **~t**) adj (unkind) mezquino, malo; (humble) humilde; (average) medio; (BRIT: with money) tacaño ♦ vt (signify) querer decir, significar; (refer to) referirse a; (intend): **to ~ to do sth** pensar or pretender hacer algo ♦ n medio, término medio; **~s** npl (way) medio, manera; (money) recursos mpl, medios mpl; **by ~s of** mediante, por medio de; **by all ~s!** ¡naturalmente!, ¡claro que sí!; **do you ~ it?** ¿lo dices en serio?; **what do you ~?** ¿qué quiere decir?; **to be ~t for sb/sth** ser para algn/algo

meander [mi'ændər] vi (river) serpentear

meaning ['miːnɪŋ] n significado, sentido; (purpose) sentido, propósito ◻ **meaningful** adj significativo ◻ **meaningless** adj sin sentido

meanness ['miːnnɪs] n (with money) tacañería; (unkindness) maldad f, mezquindad f; (humility) humildad f

meant [ment] pt, pp of **mean**

meantime ['miːntaɪm] *adv* (*also:* **in the ~**) mientras tanto

meanwhile ['miːnwaɪl] *adv* = **meantime**

measles ['miːzəlz] *n* sarampión *m*

measure ['mɛʒər] *vt, vi* medir ♦ *n* medida; (*ruler*) regla ☐ **measurements** *npl* medidas *fpl*

meat [miːt] *n* carne *f*; **cold ~** fiambre *m* ☐ **meatball** *n* albóndiga ☐ **meat grinder** (*US*) *n* picadora de carne ☐ **meat pie** *n* pastel *m* de carne

Mecca ['mɛkə] *n* La Meca

mechanic [mɪ'kænɪk] *n* mecánico(-a) ☐ **mechanical** *adj* mecánico ☐ **mechanics** *n* mecánica ♦ *npl* mecanismo

mechanism ['mɛkənɪzəm] *n* mecanismo

medal ['mɛdl] *n* medalla ☐ **medalist** (*US*) (*BRIT* **medallist**) *n* (*SPORT*) medallista *mf* ☐ **medallion** [mɪ'dæljən] *n* medallón *m*

meddle ['mɛdl] *vi*: **to ~ in** entrometerse en; **to ~ with sth** manosear algo

media ['miːdɪə] *npl* medios *mpl* de comunicación ♦ *npl of* **medium**

mediaeval [ˌmiːdɪ'iːvəl] (*BRIT*) *adj* = **medieval**

mediate ['miːdɪeɪt] *vi* mediar ☐ **mediator** *n* intermediario(-a), mediador(a) *m/f*

medic ['mɛdɪk] *n* (*doctor*) médico(-a); (*student*) estudiante *mf* de medicina

Medicaid ['mɛdɪkeɪd] (*US*) *n* programa de ayuda médica para los pobres

medical ['mɛdɪkəl] *adj* médico ♦ *n* reconocimiento médico

Medicare ['mɛdɪkɛr] (*US*) *n* programa de ayuda médica para los ancianos

medication [ˌmɛdɪ'keɪʃən] *n* medicación *f*

medicine ['mɛdɪsɪn] *n* medicina; (*drug*) medicamento, remedio (*LAm*)

medieval [ˌmiːdɪ'iːvəl] (*US*) *adj* medieval

mediocre [ˌmiːdɪ'oukər] *adj* mediocre

meditate ['mɛdɪteɪt] *vi* meditar

Mediterranean [ˌmɛdɪtə'reɪnɪən] *adj* mediterráneo; **the ~ (Sea)** el (Mar) Mediterráneo

medium ['miːdɪəm] (*pl* **media**) *adj* mediano, regular ♦ *n* (*means*) medio; (*pl* **mediums**: *person*) médium *mf* ☐ **medium wave** (*BRIT*) *n* onda media

meek [miːk] *adj* manso, sumiso

meet [miːt] (*pt, pp* **met**) *vt* encontrar; (*accidentally*) encontrarse con, tropezar con; (*by arrangement*) conocer; (*for the first time*) conocer; (*go and fetch*) ir a buscar; (*opponent*) enfrentarse con; (*obligations*) cumplir; (*encounter: problem*) hacer frente a; (*need*) satisfacer ♦ *vi* encontrarse; (*in session*) reunirse; (*join: objects*) unirse; (*for the first time*) conocerse ▶ **meet with** *vt fus* (*difficulty*) tropezar con; **to meet with success** tener éxito ☐ **meeting** *n* encuentro; (*arranged*) cita, compromiso; (*business meeting*) reunión *f*; (*POL*) mitin *m*

megabyte ['mɛgəˌbaɪt] *n* (*COMPUT*) megabyte *m*, megaocteto

megaphone ['mɛgəˌfoun] *n* megáfono

melancholy ['mɛlənkɑːli] *n* melancolía ♦ *adj* melancólico

mellow ['mɛlou] *adj* (*wine*) añejo; (*sound, color*) suave ♦ *vi* (*person*) ablandar

melody ['mɛlədi] *n* melodía

melon ['mɛlən] *n* melón *m*

melt [mɛlt] *vi* (*metal*) fundirse; (*snow*) derretirse ♦ *vt* fundir ☐ **meltdown** *n* (*in nuclear reactor*) fusión *f* de un reactor (nuclear) ☐ **melting pot** *n* (*fig*) crisol *m*

member ['mɛmbər] *n* (*gen, ANAT*) miembro; (*of club*) socio(-a); **M~ of Parliament** (*BRIT*) diputado(-a); **M~ of the European Parliament** (*BRIT*) eurodiputado(-a) ☐ **Member of the Scottish Parliament** (*BRIT*) *n* diputado(-a) del Parlamento escocés ☐ **membership** *n* (*members*) socios *mpl*; (*state*) afiliación *f* ☐ **membership card** *n* credencial *f* (*LAm*) or carnet *m* (*SP*) de socio

memento [mə'mɛntou] *n* recuerdo

memo ['mɛmou] *n* apunte *m*, nota

memoirs ['mɛmwɑːrz] *npl* memorias *fpl*

memorandum [ˌmɛmə'rændəm] (*pl* **memoranda**) *n* apunte *m*, nota; (*official note*) acta

memorial [mɪ'mɔːrɪəl] *n* monumento conmemorativo ♦ *adj* conmemorativo

memorize ['mɛməraɪz] *vt* aprender de memoria

memory ['mɛməri] *n* (*also: COMPUT*) memoria; (*instance*) recuerdo; (*of dead person*): **in ~ of** a la memoria de

men [mɛn] *npl of* **man**

menace ['mɛnɪs] *n* amenaza ♦ *vt* amenazar ☐ **menacing** *adj* amenazador(a)

mend [mɛnd] *vt* reparar, arreglar; (*darn*) zurcir ♦ *vi* reponerse ♦ *n* arreglo, reparación *f* zurcido ♦ *n*: **to be on the ~** ir mejorando; **to ~ one's ways** enmendarse ☐ **mending** *n* reparación *f*; (*of clothes*) arreglo

meningitis [ˌmɛnɪn'dʒaɪtɪs] *n* meningitis *f*

menopause ['mɛnəpɔːz] *n* menopausia

men's room (*US*) *n* baño de caballeros

menstruation [mɛnstru'eɪʃən] n menstruación f

mental ['mɛntl] adj mental □ **mentality** [mɛn'tælɪti] n mentalidad f

mention ['mɛnʃən] n mención f ♦ vt mencionar; (speak) hablar de; **don't ~ it!** ¡de nada!

menu ['mɛnjuː] n (set menu) menú m; (printed) carta; (COMPUT) menú m

MEP (BRIT) n abbr = **Member of the European Parliament**

merchandise ['mɜːrtʃəndaɪs] n mercancías fpl

merchant ['mɜːrtʃənt] n comerciante mf □ **merchant bank** (BRIT) n banco comercial □ **merchant marine** (US) (BRIT **merchant navy**) n marina mercante

merciful ['mɜːrsɪful] adj compasivo; (fortunate) afortunado

merciless ['mɜːrsɪlɪs] adj despiadado

mercury ['mɜːrkjuri] n mercurio

mercy ['mɜːrsi] n compasión f, (REL) misericordia; **at the ~ of** a la merced de

merely ['mɪrli] adv simplemente, sólo

merge [mɜːrdʒ] vt (join) unir ♦ vi unirse; (COMM) fusionarse; (colors etc) fundirse □ **merger** n (COMM) fusión f

meringue [məˈræŋ] n merengue m

merit ['mɛrɪt] n mérito ♦ vt merecer

mermaid ['mɜːrˌmeɪd] n sirena

merry ['mɛri] adj alegre; **M~ Christmas!** ¡Felices Pascuas! □ **merry-go-round** n carrusel m (LAm), calesita (RPl), tiovivo (SP)

mesh [mɛʃ] n malla

mesmerize ['mɛzməraɪz] vt hipnotizar

mess [mɛs] n (of situation) confusión f; (of room) revoltijo; (dirt) porquería; (MIL) comedor m ▶ **mess around** or (BRIT) **about** (inf) vi perder el tiempo; (pass the time) entretenerse ▶ **mess around** or (BRIT) **about with** (inf) vt fus divertirse con ▶ **mess up** vt (spoil) estropear; (dirty) ensuciar

message ['mɛsɪdʒ] n recado, mensaje m

messenger ['mɛsɪndʒər] n mensajero(-a)

Messrs (BRIT) abbr (on letters: = Messieurs) Sres

messy ['mɛsi] adj (dirty) sucio; (untidy) desordenado

met [mɛt] pt, pp of **meet**

metal ['mɛtl] n metal m □ **metallic** [məˈtælɪk] adj metálico

metaphor ['mɛtəfər] n metáfora

meteor ['miːtɪər] n meteoro □ **meteorite** n meteorito

meteorology [miːtɪə'rɑːlədʒi] n meteorología

meter ['miːtər] n (instrument) medidor m (LAm), contador m (SP); (US: unit) metro

method ['mɛθəd] n método

meths [mɛθs], **methylated spirit(s)** ['mɛθəleɪtɪd'spɪrɪt(s)] n (BRIT) alcohol m metilado or desnaturalizado

metre ['miːtər] (BRIT) n = **meter**

metric ['mɛtrɪk] adj métrico

metropolitan [mɛtrə'pɑːlɪtn] adj metropolitano; **the M~ Police** (BRIT) la policía londinense

mettle ['mɛtl] n: **to be on one's ~** estar dispuesto a mostrar todo lo que uno vale

mew [mjuː] vi (cat) maullar

mews [mjuːz] (BRIT) n: **~ flat** departamento or piso acondicionado en antiguos establos o cocheras

Mexican ['mɛksɪkən] adj, n mexicano(-a), mejicano(-a)

Mexico ['mɛksɪkou] n México (LAm), Méjico (SP) □ **Mexico City** n Ciudad f de México or Méjico

mezzanine ['mɛzəniːn] n (in store) entresuelo; (US: in theater) anfiteatro

miaow [miː'au] vi maullar

mice [maɪs] npl of **mouse**

micro... [maɪkrou] prefix micro...
□ **microchip** n microchip m
□ **micro(computer)** n microcomputadora (LAm), microordenador m (SP)
□ **microphone** n micrófono
□ **microprocessor** n microprocesador m
□ **microscope** n microscopio
□ **microwave** n (also: **microwave oven**) (horno de) microondas m inv

mid [mɪd] adj: **in ~ May** a mediados de mayo; **in ~ afternoon** a media tarde; **in ~ air** en el aire □ **midday** n mediodía m

middle ['mɪdl] n centro; (half-way point) medio; (waist) cintura ♦ adj de en medio; (course, way) intermedio; **in the ~ of the night** en plena noche □ **middle-aged** adj de mediana edad □ **the Middle Ages** npl la Edad Media □ **middle-class** adj de clase media □ **the middle class(es)** n(pl) la clase media □ **Middle East** n Oriente m Medio □ **middleman** n intermediario □ **middle name** n segundo nombre □ **middle-of-the-road** adj moderado □ **middle school** n (US) colegio para niños de doce a catorce años; (BRIT) colegio para niños de ocho o nueve a doce o trece años □ **middleweight** n (BOXING) peso medio

middling ['mɪdlɪŋ] adj mediano

midge [mɪdʒ] (BRIT) n mosquito

midget ['mɪdʒɪt] n enano(-a)

Midlands ['mɪdləndz] (BRIT) npl: **the ~** la región central de Inglaterra

midnight ['mɪdnaɪt] n medianoche f

midst [mɪdst] n: **in the ~ of** (crowd) en medio de; (situation, action) en mitad de

midsummer ['mɪd'sʌmər] n: **in ~** en pleno verano

midterm ['mɪd'tɜːrm] n vacaciones fpl de mitad de trimestre; **~ elections** npl (US) elecciones fpl a mitad del mandato (presidencial)

midway ['mɪd,weɪ] adj, adv: **~ (between)** a medio camino (entre); **~ through** a la mitad (de)

midweek ['mɪd'wiːk] adv entre semana

Midwest ['mɪd'west] (US) n medioooeste m (llanura central de EE.UU.)

MIDWEST

El **Midwest** es un área geográfica de la Norteamérica Central comprendida entre la frontera de Ohio por el este, las fronteras de Kansas y Missouri por el sur, las Montañas Rocosas por el oeste y Canadá por el norte. Culturalmente, el medioooeste es visto como la zona central de Estados Unidos y abundan los cultivos de trigo, maíz y otros alimentos básicos y la gente vive todavía, en la mayoría de los casos, en estructura de grupos familiares tradicionales.

midwife ['mɪd,waɪf] (pl **midwives**) n comadrona, partera

might [maɪt] vb see **may** ♦ n fuerza, poder m
□ **mighty** adj fuerte, poderoso

migraine ['maɪɡreɪn] n jaqueca, migraña

migrant ['maɪɡrənt] n, adj (bird) migratorio; (worker) emigrante

migrate ['maɪɡreɪt] vi emigrar

mike [maɪk] n abbr (= microphone) micro

mild [maɪld] adj (person) apacible; (climate) templado; (slight) ligero; (taste) suave; (illness) leve □ **mildly** adv ligeramente; suavemente; **to put it mildly** por no decir más

mile [maɪl] n milla □ **mileage** n número de millas, ≈ kilometraje m □ **mileometer** [maɪ'lɑːmɪtər] (BRIT) n = **milometer**
□ **milestone** n (on road) mojonera, mojón m

militant ['mɪlɪtnt] adj, n militante mf

military ['mɪlɪteri] adj militar

militia [mɪ'lɪʃə] n milicia

milk [mɪlk] n leche f ♦ vt (cow) ordeñar; (fig) chupar □ **milk chocolate** n chocolate m con leche □ **milkman** n lechero
□ **milkshake** n (leche f) malteada (LAm), batido (SP) □ **milky** adj lechoso □ **Milky Way** n Vía Láctea

mill [mɪl] n (windmill etc) molino; (coffee mill) molinillo; (factory) fábrica ♦ vt moler ♦ vi (also: **~ around**) arremolinarse

millennium [mə'leniəm] (pl **~s** or **millennia**) n milenio, milenario

miller ['mɪlər] n molinero

milli... ['mɪli] prefix: □ **milligram(me)** n miligramo □ **millimeter** (US) (BRIT **millimetre**) n milímetro

million ['mɪljən] n millón m; **a ~ times** un millón de veces □ **millionaire** [,mɪljə'neər] n millonario(-a)

milometer [maɪ'lɑːmɪtər] n ≈ cuentakilómetros m inv

mime [maɪm] n mímica; (actor) mimo mf ♦ vt remedar ♦ vi actuar de mimo

mimic ['mɪmɪk] n imitador(a) m/f ♦ adj mímico ♦ vt remedar, imitar

min. abbr = **minimum**; **minute(s)**

mince [mɪns] vt picar ♦ n (BRIT CULIN) carne f picada □ **mincemeat** n conserva de fruta picada; (BRIT) carne f picada □ **mince pie** n empanadilla rellena de fruta picada □ **mincer** (BRIT) n = **meat grinder**

mind [maɪnd] n mente f; (intellect) intelecto; (contrasted with matter) espíritu m ♦ vt (attend to, look after) ocuparse de, cuidar; (BRIT: be careful) tener cuidado con; (object to): **I don't ~ the noise** no me molesta el ruido; **it is on my ~** me preocupa; **to bear sth in ~** tomar or tener algo en cuenta; **to make up one's ~** decidirse; **I don't ~** me es igual; **~ you ...** te advierto que ...; **never ~!** ¡es igual!, ¡no importa!; (don't worry) ¡no te preocupes!; **"~ the step"** (BRIT) "cuidado con el escalón" □ **minder** (BRIT) n guardaespaldas m inv; (child minder) ≈ niñera □ **mindful** adj: **mindful of** consciente de □ **mindless** adj (work) de autómata; (BRIT: crime) sin motivo

mine¹ [maɪn] pron el mío/la mía etc ♦ adj: **this book is ~** este libro es mío; **a friend of ~** un(a) amigo(-a) mío/mía

mine² [maɪn] n mina ♦ vt (coal) extraer; (bomb: beach etc) minar □ **minefield** n campo de minas □ **miner** n minero(-a)

mineral ['mɪnərəl] adj mineral ♦ n mineral m; **~s** npl (BRIT: soft drinks) refrescos mpl □ **mineral water** n agua mineral

mingle ['mɪŋɡəl] vi: **to ~ with** mezclarse con

miniature ['mɪniətfər] adj (en) miniatura ♦ n miniatura

minibus ['mɪnɪ,bʌs] n microbús m

Minidisc® ['mɪnɪ,dɪsk] n minidisco ❑ **Minidisc® player** n minidisc m

minimal ['mɪnɪməl] adj mínimo

minimize ['mɪnɪmaɪz] vt minimizar; (play down) empequeñecer

minimum ['mɪnɪməm] (pl **minima**) n, adj mínimo

mining ['maɪnɪŋ] n explotación f minera

miniskirt ['mɪnɪ,skɜːrt] n minifalda

minister ['mɪnɪstər] n (REL) pastor m; (BRIT POL) secretario(-a) (LAm), ministro(-a) (SP) ♦ vi: **to ~ to** atender a

ministry ['mɪnɪstrɪ] n (REL) sacerdocio; (BRIT POL) secretaría (MEX), ministerio (LAm exc MEX, SP)

mink [mɪŋk] n visón m

minnow ['mɪnoʊ] n pececillo (de agua dulce)

minor ['maɪnər] adj (repairs, injuries) leve; (poet, planet) menor; (MUS) menor ♦ n (LAW) menor m de edad

Minorca [mɪ'nɔːrkə] n Menorca

minority [maɪ'nɔːrɪtɪ] n minoría

mint [mɪnt] n (plant) menta, hierbabuena; (candy) caramelo de menta ♦ vt (coins) acuñar; **the (US) M~** la Casa de la Moneda; **in ~ condition** en perfecto estado

minus ['maɪnəs] n (also: ~ **sign**) signo de menos ♦ prep menos; **12 ~ 6 equals 6** 12 menos 6 son 6; **~ two degrees** dos grados bajo cero

minute¹ ['mɪnɪt] n minuto; (fig) momento; **~s** npl (of meeting) actas fpl; **at the last ~** a última hora

minute² [maɪ'nuːt] adj minúsculo, diminuto; (search) minucioso

miracle ['mɪrəkəl] n milagro

mirage [mɪ'rɑːʒ] n espejismo

mirror ['mɪrər] n espejo; (in car) retrovisor m

mirth [mɜːrθ] n alegría

misadventure [,mɪsəd'ventfər] n desgracia

misapprehension [,mɪsæprɪ'henʃən] n equivocación f

misappropriate [,mɪsə'proʊprɪeɪt] vt malversar

misbehave [,mɪsbɪ'heɪv] vi portarse mal

miscalculate [,mɪs'kælkjuleɪt] vt calcular mal

miscarriage ['mɪskærɪdʒ] n (MED) aborto; **~ of justice** error m judicial

miscellaneous [,mɪsɪ'leɪnɪəs] adj varios(-as), diversos(-as)

mischief ['mɪstʃɪf] n travesuras fpl, diabluras fpl; (maliciousness) malicia ❑ **mischievous** ['mɪstʃɪvəs] adj travieso

misconception [,mɪskən'sepʃən] n idea equivocada; equivocación f

misconduct [mɪs'kɑːndʌkt] n mala conducta; **professional ~** falta profesional

misdemeanor (US) ['mɪsdɪmiːnər] (BRIT **misdemeanour**) n delito, ofensa

miser ['maɪzər] n avaro(-a)

miserable ['mɪzərəbəl] adj (unhappy) triste, desgraciado; (unpleasant, contemptible) miserable

miserly ['maɪzərlɪ] adj avariento, tacaño

misery ['mɪzərɪ] n tristeza; (wretchedness) miseria, desdicha

misfire [mɪs'faɪər] vi fallar

misfit ['mɪsfɪt] n inadaptado(-a)

misfortune [mɪs'fɔːrtʃən] n desgracia

misgiving [mɪs'gɪvɪŋ] n (apprehension) presentimiento; **to have ~s about sth** tener dudas acerca de algo

misguided [mɪs'gaɪdɪd] adj equivocado

mishandle [mɪs'hændl] vt (mismanage) manejar mal

mishap ['mɪshæp] n percance m, contratiempo

misinform [,mɪsɪn'fɔːrm] vt informar mal

misinterpret [,mɪsɪn'tɜːrprɪt] vt interpretar mal

misjudge [mɪs'dʒʌdʒ] vt juzgar mal

mislay [mɪs'leɪ] vt extraviar, perder

mislead [mɪs'liːd] vt llevar a conclusiones erróneas ❑ **misleading** adj engañoso

mismanage [mɪs'mænɪdʒ] vt administrar mal

misplace [mɪs'pleɪs] vt extraviar

misprint ['mɪsprɪnt] n errata, error m de imprenta

Miss [mɪs] n Señorita

miss [mɪs] vt (train etc) perder; (fail to hit: target) errar; (regret the absence of): **I ~ him** (yo) le echo de menos or a faltar; (fail to see): **you can't ~ it** no tiene pérdida ♦ vi fallar ♦ n (shot) tiro fallido or perdido ► **miss out** vt omitir

misshapen [mɪs'ʃeɪpən] adj deforme

missile ['mɪsəl] n (AVIAT) misil m; (object thrown) proyectil m

missing ['mɪsɪŋ] adj (pupil) ausente; (thing) perdido; (MIL): **~ in action** desaparecido en combate

mission ['mɪʃən] n misión f; (official representation) delegación f ❑ **missionary** n misionero(-a)

mist [mɪst] n (light) neblina; (heavy) niebla; (at sea) bruma ♦ vi (eyes: also: ~ **over**, ~ **up**) llenarse de lágrimas; (BRIT: windows: also: ~ **over**, ~ **up**) empañarse

mistake [mɪ'steɪk] n error m ♦ vt entender mal; **by** ~ por equivocación; **to make a** ~ equivocarse; **to ~ A for B** confundir A con B ❑ **mistaken** pp of **mistake** ♦ adj equivocado; **to be mistaken** equivocarse, engañarse

mister ['mɪstər] (inf) n señor m; see **Mr.**

mistletoe ['mɪsltou] n muérdago

mistook [mɪ'stuk] pt of **mistake**

mistress ['mɪstrɪs] n (lover) amante f; (of house) señora (de la casa); (of situation) dueña; (BRIT: in primary school) maestra; (: in secondary school) profesora

mistrust [mɪs'trʌst] vt desconfiar de

misty ['mɪsti] adj (day) neblinoso; (glasses etc) empañado

misunderstand [mɪsʌndər'stænd] vt, vi entender mal ❑ **misunderstanding** n malentendido

misuse [n mɪs'juːs, vb mɪs'juːz] n mal uso; (of power) abuso; (of funds) malversación f ♦ vt abusar de; malversar

mitt(en) ['mɪt(n)] n manopla

mix [mɪks] vt mezclar; (combine) unir ♦ vi mezclarse; (people) llevarse bien ♦ n mezcla
▶ **mix up** vt mezclar; (confuse) confundir ❑ **mixed** adj mixto; (feelings etc) encontrado ❑ **mixed-up** adj (confused) confuso, revuelto ❑ **mixer** n (for food) batidora; (for drinks) coctelera; (person): **he's a good mixer** tiene don de gentes ❑ **mixture** n mezcla; (also: **cough mixture**) jarabe m ❑ **mix-up** n confusión f

mm abbr (= millimeter) mm

moan [moun] n gemido ♦ vi gemir; (inf: complain): **to ~ (about)** (BRIT) quejarse (de)

moat [mout] n foso

mob [mɑːb] n multitud f ♦ vt acosar

mobile ['moubəl] adj móvil ♦ n móvil m ❑ **mobile home** n cámper m or f (LAm), casa rodante (SC), caravana (SP) ❑ **mobile phone** n teléfono celular (LAm) or móvil (SP)

mock [mɑːk] vt (ridicule) ridiculizar; (laugh at) burlarse de ♦ adj fingido; ~ **exam** (BRIT) examen de prueba ❑ **mockery** n burla ❑ **mock-up** n maqueta

mod [mɑːd] (BRIT) adj see **convenience**

mode [moud] n modo

model ['mɑːdl] n modelo; (fashion model, artist's model) modelo mf ♦ adj modelo ♦ vt (with clay etc) modelar; (copy): **to ~ o.s. on** tomar como modelo a ♦ vi ser modelo; **to ~ clothes** pasar modelos, ser modelo ❑ **model railroad** n ferrocarril m en miniatura

modem ['moudəm] n módem m

moderate [adj 'mɑːdərɪt, vb 'mɑːdəreɪt] adj moderado(-a) ♦ vi moderarse, calmarse ♦ vt moderar

modern ['mɑːdərn] adj moderno ❑ **modernize** vt modernizar

modest ['mɑːdɪst] adj modesto; (small) módico ❑ **modesty** n modestia

modify ['mɑːdɪfaɪ] vt modificar

mogul ['mougəl] n (fig) magnate m

mohair ['mouhɛər] n mohair m

moist [mɔɪst] adj húmedo ❑ **moisten** ['mɔɪsən] vt humedecer ❑ **moisture** n humedad f ❑ **moisturizer** n crema hidratante

molar ['moulər] n muela

molasses [mə'læsɪz] (US) n melaza

mold (US) ['mould] (BRIT **mould**) n molde m; (mildew) moho ♦ vt moldear; (fig) formar ❑ **moldy** (US) (BRIT **mouldy**) adj enmohecido

mole [moul] n (animal, spy) topo; (spot) lunar m

molest [mə'lɛst] vt importunar; (assault sexually) abusar sexualmente de

> ⚠ Be careful not to translate **molest** by the Spanish word **molestar**.

mollycoddle ['mɑːlɪkɑːdl] vt mimar

molt (US) [moult] (BRIT **moult**) vi (snake) mudar la piel; (bird) mudar las plumas

molten ['moultən] adj fundido; (lava) líquido

mom [mɑːm] (US) n mamá

moment ['moumənt] n momento; **at the** ~ de momento, por ahora ❑ **momentary** adj momentáneo ❑ **momentous** [mou'mɛntəs] adj trascendental, importante

momentum [mou'mɛntəm] n momento; (fig) ímpetu m; **to gather** ~ cobrar velocidad; (fig) ganar fuerza

mommy ['mɑːmi] (US) n mamá

Monaco ['mɑːnəkou] n Mónaco

monarch ['mɑːnərk] n monarca mf ❑ **monarchy** n monarquía

monastery ['mɑːnəstɛri] n monasterio

Monday ['mʌndi] n lunes m inv

monetary ['mʌnɪtɛri] adj monetario

money ['mʌni] n dinero; (currency) moneda; **to make ~** ganar dinero ❑ **money order** n giro ❑ **moneymaker** n fuente f de ganancias, negocio rentable ❑ **money-spinner** (BRIT: inf) n: **to be a money-spinner** dar mucho dinero

mongrel ['mʌŋgrəl] n (dog) perro mestizo

monitor ['mɑ:nitər] n (SCOL) monitor m; (also: **television** (BRIT: inf)) receptor m de control; (of computer) monitor m ♦ vt controlar

monk [mʌŋk] n monje m

monkey ['mʌŋki] n mono ❑ **monkey nut** (BRIT) n cacahuate m (MEX), maní m (LAm exc MEX), cacahuete m (SP) ❑ **monkey wrench** n llave f inglesa

monopoly [mə'nɑ:pəli] n monopolio

monotone ['mɑ:ətoun] n voz f (or tono) monocorde

monotonous [mə'nɑ:tnəs] adj monótono

monsoon [mɑ:n'su:n] n monzón m

monster ['mɑ:nstər] n monstruo

monstrous ['mɑ:nstrəs] adj (huge) enorme; (atrocious, ugly) monstruoso

month [mʌnθ] n mes m ❑ **monthly** adj mensual ♦ adv mensualmente

monument ['mɑ:njəmənt] n monumento

moo [mu:] vi mugir

mood [mu:d] n humor m; (of crowd, group) clima m; **to be in a good/bad ~** estar de buen/mal humor ❑ **moody** adj (changeable) de humor variable; (sullen) malhumorado

moon [mu:n] n luna ❑ **moonlight** n luz f de la luna ❑ **moonlighting** n pluriempleo ❑ **moonlit** adj: **a moonlit night** una noche de luna

Moor [muər] n moro(-a)

moor [muər] n páramo ♦ vt (ship) amarrar ♦ vi echar las amarras

Moorish ['muəriʃ] adj moro; (architecture) árabe, morisco

moorland ['muərlənd] (BRIT) n páramo, brezal m

moose [mu:s] n inv alce m

mop [mɑ:p] n trapeador m (LAm), fregona (SP); (of hair) mata, melena ♦ vt trapear (LAm), fregar (SP) ► **mop up** vt limpiar

mope [moup] vi estar or andar deprimido

moped ['mouped] n ciclomotor m

moral ['mɔ:rəl] adj moral ♦ n moraleja; **~s** npl moralidad f, moral f

morale [mə'ræl] n moral f

morality [mə'ræliti] n moralidad f

morass [mə'ræs] n pantano

---

more

KEYWORD

[mɔ:r] adj

1 (greater in number etc) más; **more people/work than before** más gente/trabajo que antes

2 (additional) más; **do you want (some) more tea?** ¿quieres más té?; **is there any more wine?** ¿queda vino?; **it'll take a few more weeks** tardará unas semanas más; **it's 2 miles more to the house** faltan 2 millas para la casa; **more time/letters than we expected** más tiempo del que/más cartas de las que esperábamos

♦ pron (greater amount, additional amount) más; **more than 10** más de 10; **it cost more than the other one/than we expected** costó más que el otro/más de lo que esperábamos; **is there any more?** ¿hay más?; **many/much more** muchos(as)/mucho más

♦ adv más; **more dangerous/easily (than)** más peligroso/fácilmente (que); **more and more expensive** cada vez más caro; **more or less** más o menos; **more than ever** más que nunca

---

moreover [mɔ:r'ouvər] adv además, por otra parte

morning ['mɔ:rniŋ] n mañana; (early morning) madrugada ♦ cpd matutino, de la mañana; **in the ~** por la mañana; **7 o'clock in the ~** las 7 de la mañana ❑ **morning sickness** n náuseas fpl matutinas

Morocco [mə'rɑ:kou] n Marruecos m

moron ['mɔ:rɑ:n] (inf) n imbécil mf

morphine ['mɔ:rfi:n] n morfina

Morse [mɔ:rs] n (also: **~ code**) (código) morse

morsel ['mɔ:rsəl] n (of food) bocado

mortar ['mɔ:rtər] n argamasa

mortgage ['mɔ:rgidʒ] n hipoteca ♦ vt hipotecar ❑ **mortgage company** (US) n ≈ banco hipotecario

mortuary ['mɔ:rtʃuɛri] n depósito de cadáveres

Moscow ['mɑ:skau] n Moscú

Moslem ['mɑ:zləm] adj, n = **Muslim**

mosque [mɑ:sk] n mezquita

mosquito [mə'ski:tou] (pl **~es**) n zancudo (LAm), mosquito (SP)

moss [mɔ:s] n musgo

most [moust] adj la mayor parte de, la mayoría de ♦ pron la mayor parte, la mayoría ♦ adv el más; (very) muy; **the ~** (also: + adj) el más; **~ of them** la mayor parte de ellos; **I saw the ~** yo vi el que más; **at the (very) ~** a lo sumo, todo lo más; **to make the ~ of** aprovechar (al máximo); **a ~ interesting book** un libro interesantísimo ❑ **mostly** adv en su mayor parte, principalmente

MOT (BRIT) n abbr (= Ministry of Transport); **the ~ (test)** revisión técnica de vehículos

motel [mou'tɛl] n motel m

moth [mɔːθ] n mariposa nocturna; (clothes moth) polilla

mother ['mʌðər] n madre f ♦ adj materno ♦ vt (care for) cuidar (como una madre) ❑ **motherhood** n maternidad f ❑ **mother-in-law** n suegra ❑ **motherly** adj maternal ❑ **mother-of-pearl** n nácar m ❑ **mother-to-be** n futura madre f ❑ **mother tongue** n lengua materna

motion ['mouʃən] n movimiento; (gesture) ademán m, señal f; (at meeting) moción f ♦ vt, vi: **to ~ (to) sb to do sth** hacer señas a algn para que haga algo ❑ **motionless** adj inmóvil ❑ **motion picture** n película

motivated ['moutiveitid] adj motivado

motive ['moutiv] n motivo

motley ['mɒtli] adj variado

motor ['moutər] n motor m; (BRIT: inf: vehicle) carro (LAm), coche m (SP) ♦ adj motor (f: motora or motriz) ❑ **motorbike** (BRIT) n = **motorcycle** ❑ **motorboat** n lancha motora ❑ **motorcar** (BRIT) n automóvil m ❑ **motorcycle** n motocicleta ❑ **motorcycle racing** n motociclismo ❑ **motorcyclist** n motociclista mf ❑ **motoring** (BRIT) n automovilismo ❑ **motorist** (BRIT) n conductor(a) m/f, automovilista mf ❑ **motor racing** n automovilismo ❑ **motor vehicle** n automóvil m ❑ **motorway** (BRIT) n autopista

mottled ['mɒtld] adj abigarrado

motto ['mɒtou] (pl ~es) n lema m; (watchword) consigna

mould [mould] (BRIT) n, vt = **mold**

moult [moult] (BRIT) vi = **molt**

mound [maund] n montón m, montículo

mount [maunt] n monte m ♦ vt montar, subir a; (jewel) engarzar; (picture) enmarcar; (exhibition etc) organizar ♦ vi (increase) aumentar ▸ **mount up** vi aumentar

mountain ['mauntən] n montaña ♦ cpd de montaña ❑ **mountain bike** n bicicleta de montaña ❑ **mountaineer** [,mauntə'niər] n alpinista mf (MEX, SP), andinista mf (LAm) ❑ **mountaineering** [,mauntə'nɪrɪŋ] n alpinismo (MEX, SP), andinismo (LAm) ❑ **mountainous** adj montañoso ❑ **mountain rescue team** n equipo de

rescate de montaña ❑ **mountainside** n ladera de la montaña

mourn [mɔːrn] vt llorar, lamentar ♦ vi: **to ~ for** llorar la muerte de ❑ **mourner** n doliente mf; dolorido(-a) ❑ **mourning** n luto; **in mourning** de luto

mouse [maus] (pl **mice**) n (ZOOL, COMPUT) ratón m ❑ **mouse pad, mouse mat** n (COMPUT) alfombrilla (del ratón) ❑ **mousetrap** n ratonera

mousse [muːs] n (CULIN) mousse f; (for hair) espuma (moldeadora)

moustache [məˈstɑːʃ] (BRIT) n = **mustache**

mousy ['mausi] adj (hair) pardusco

mouth [mauθ, pl mauðz] n boca; (of river) desembocadura ❑ **mouthful** n bocado ❑ **mouth organ** (BRIT) n armónica ❑ **mouthpiece** n (of musical instrument) boquilla; (spokesman) portavoz mf ❑ **mouthwash** n enjuague m bucal ❑ **mouth-watering** adj apetitoso

movable ['muːvəbəl] adj movible

move [muːv] n (movement) movimiento; (in game) jugada; (: turn to play) turno; (change: of house) mudanza; (: of job) cambio de trabajo ♦ vt mover; (emotionally) conmover; (POL: resolution etc) proponer ♦ vi moverse; (traffic) circular; (also: ~ house) trasladarse, mudarse; **to ~ sb to do sth** mover a algn a hacer algo; **to get a ~ on** darse prisa, apurarse (LAm) ▸ **move around** or (BRIT) **about** vi moverse; (travel) viajar ▸ **move along** vi avanzar, adelantarse ▸ **move away** vi alejarse ▸ **move back** vi retroceder ▸ **move forward** vi avanzar ▸ **move in** vi (to a house) instalarse; (police, soldiers) intervenir ▸ **move on** vi ponerse en camino ▸ **move out** vi (of house) mudarse ▸ **move over** vi apartarse, hacer sitio ▸ **move up** vi (employee) ser ascendido

moveable ['muːvəbəl] adj = **movable**

movement ['muːvmənt] n movimiento

movie ['muːvi] (US) n película; **to go to the ~s** ir al cine ❑ **movie theater** (US) n cine m

moving ['muːvɪŋ] adj (emotional) conmovedor(a); (that moves) móvil ❑ **moving van** (US) n camión m de mudanzas

mow [mou] (pt ~**ed**, pp ~**ed** or ~**n**) vt (grass, corn) cortar, segar ▸ **mow down** vt (shoot) acribillar ❑ **mower** n (also: lawnmower) máquina de cortar el pasto (LAm), cortacésped m (SP)

MP (BRIT) n abbr = **Member of Parliament**

MP3 ['empiː'θriː] n MP3 m ◻ **MP3 player** n
reproductor m MP3

m.p.h. abbr = **miles per hour** (60 m.p.h. =
96 k.p.h.)

Mr. (US) ['mɪstər] (BRIT **Mr**) n: ~ **Smith** (el) Sr.
Smith

Mrs. (US) ['mɪsɪz] (BRIT **Mrs**) n: ~ **Smith** (la) Sra.
Smith

Ms. (US) [mɪz] (BRIT **Ms**) n (= Miss or Mrs): ~
Smith (la) Sr(t)a. Smith

M.Sc. abbr = **Master of Science**

MSP (BRIT) n abbr = **Member of the
Scottish Parliament**

MTV n abbr = **music television**

much [mʌtʃ] adj mucho ◆ adv mucho; (before
pp) muy ◆ n or pron mucho; **how ~ is it?**
¿cuánto es?, ¿cuánto cuesta?; **too ~**
demasiado; **it's not ~** no es mucho; **as ~ as**
tanto como; **however ~ he tries** por mucho
que se esfuerce

muck [mʌk] n suciedad f ▸ **muck around** or
about (BRIT: inf) vi perder el tiempo; (enjoy
o.s.) entretenerse ▸ **muck up** (inf) vt arruinar,
estropear

mud [mʌd] n barro, lodo

muddle ['mʌdl] n desorden m, confusión f;
(mix-up) lío, embrollo ◆ vt (also: ~ **up**)
confundir, embrollar ▸ **muddle through** vi
salir del paso

muddy ['mʌdɪ] adj fangoso, cubierto de lodo

mudguard ['mʌdɡɑːrd] (BRIT) n salpicadera
(MEX), guardabarros m inv (LAm exc MEX, SP)

muffin ['mʌfɪn] n especie de pan dulce

muffle ['mʌfl] vt (sound) amortiguar;
(against cold) embozar ◻ **muffled** adj (noise
etc) amortiguado, apagado ◻ **muffler** (US) n
(AUT) silenciador m, mofle m (MEX, CAm)

mug [mʌg] n taza grande (sin platillo); (for
beer) tarro (MEX), jarra (LAm exc MEX, SP); (inf:
face) jeta ◆ vt (assault) atracar ◻ **mugging** n
atraco

muggy ['mʌgɪ] adj bochornoso

mule [mjuːl] n mula

multi... [mʌltɪ] prefix multi...

multi-level ['mʌltɪ'levəl] (US) adj de varios
pisos

multiple ['mʌltɪpəl] adj múltiple ◆ n
múltiplo ◻ **multiple sclerosis** n esclerosis
f múltiple

multiplex theater ['mʌltɪpleks'θiətər] (BRIT
multiplex cinema) n multicine(s) m(pl)

multiplication [ˌmʌltɪplɪ'keɪʃən] n
multiplicación f

multiply ['mʌltɪplaɪ] vt multiplicar ◆ vi
multiplicarse

multistorey [ˌmʌltɪ'stɔːri] (BRIT) adj = **multi-
level**

multitude ['mʌltɪtuːd] n multitud f

mum [mʌm] (BRIT: inf) n mamá ◆ adj: **to keep
~** mantener la boca cerrada

mumble ['mʌmbəl] vt, vi hablar entre
dientes, refunfuñar

mummy ['mʌmi] n (embalmed) momia; (BRIT:
mother) mamá

mumps [mʌmps] n paperas fpl

munch [mʌntʃ] vt, vi mascar

mundane [mʌn'deɪn] adj trivial

municipal [mjuː'nɪsɪpəl] adj municipal

murder ['mɜːrdər] n asesinato; (in law)
homicidio ◆ vt asesinar, matar ◻ **murderer/
ess** n asesino(-a) ◻ **murderous** adj
homicida

murky ['mɜːrki] adj (water) turbio; (street,
night) lóbrego

murmur ['mɜːrmər] n murmullo ◆ vt, vi
murmurar

muscle ['mʌsəl] n músculo; (fig: strength)
garra, fuerza ▸ **muscle in** vi entrometerse
◻ **muscular** ['mʌskjələr] adj muscular;
(person) musculoso

muse [mjuːz] vi meditar ◆ n musa

museum [mjuː'ziːəm] n museo

mushroom ['mʌʃruːm] n seta, hongo; (CULIN)
champiñón m ◆ vi crecer de la noche a la
mañana

music ['mjuːzɪk] n música ◻ **musical** adj
musical; (sound) melodioso; (person) con
talento musical ◆ n (show) comedia musical
◻ **musical instrument** n instrumento
musical ◻ **music hall** (BRIT) n teatro de
variedades ◻ **musician** [mjuː'zɪʃən] n
músico(-a)

Muslim ['mʌzləm] adj, n musulmán(-ana) m/f

muslin ['mʌzlɪn] n muselina

mussel ['mʌsəl] n mejillón m

must [mʌst] aux vb (obligation): **I ~ do it** tengo que
hacerlo, tengo que hacerlo; (probability): **he ~
be there by now** ya debe (de) estar allí ◆ n:
it's a ~ es imprescindible

mustache (US) ['mʌstæʃ] (BRIT **moustache**)
n bigote m

mustard ['mʌstərd] n mostaza

muster ['mʌstər] vt juntar, reunir

mustn't ['mʌsənt] cont = **must not**

mute [mjuːt] adj, n mudo(-a)

muted ['mjuːtɪd] adj callado; (color) apagado

mutiny ['mjuːtni] n motín m ◆ vi amotinarse

mutter ['mʌtər] vt, vi mascullar

mutton ['mʌtn] n carne f de cordero

mutual ['mjuːtʃuəl] adj mutuo; (interest) común □ **mutual fund** (US) n fondo de inversión mobiliaria □ **mutually** adv mutuamente

muzzle ['mʌzəl] n hocico; (for dog) bozal m; (of gun) boca ♦ vt (dog) poner un bozal a

my [maɪ] adj mi(s); **my house/brother/sisters** mi casa/mi hermano/mis hermanas; **I've washed my hair/cut my finger** me he lavado el pelo/cortado un dedo; **is this my pencil or yours?** ¿es este lápiz mío o tuyo?

myself [maɪˈself] pron (reflexive) me; (emphatic) yo mismo; (after prep) mí (mismo); see also **oneself**

mysterious [mɪˈstɪərɪəs] adj misterioso

mystery ['mɪstərɪ] n misterio

mystify ['mɪstɪfaɪ] vt (perplex) dejar perplejo

myth [mɪθ] n mito

Nn

n/a abbr (= not applicable) no interesa

nag [næg] vt (scold) regañar □ **nagging** adj (doubt) persistente; (pain) continuo

nail [neɪl] n (human) uña; (metal) clavo ♦ vt clavar; **to ~ sth to sth** clavar algo en algo; **to ~ sb down to doing sth** comprometer a algn a que haga algo □ **nailbrush** n cepillo de uñas □ **nail clippers** npl cortaúñas m inv □ **nailfile** n lima de uñas □ **nail polish** n esmalte m de uñas □ **nail polish remover** n quitaesmalte m □ **nail scissors** npl tijeras fpl para las uñas □ **nail varnish** (BRIT) n = **nail polish**

naïve [naɪˈiːv] adj ingenuo

naked ['neɪkɪd] adj (nude) desnudo; (flame) expuesto al aire

name [neɪm] n nombre m; (surname) apellido; (reputation) fama, renombre m ♦ vt (child) poner nombre a; (criminal) identificar; (price, date etc) fijar; **what's your ~?** ¿cómo se llama?; **by ~** de nombre; **in the ~ of** en nombre de; **to give one's ~ and address** dar las señas de algn □ **namely** adv a saber □ **namesake** n tocayo(-a)

nanny ['nænɪ] n niñera

nap [næp] n (sleep) sueñito (LAm), cabezada (SP); (in the afternoon) siesta

nape [neɪp] n: **~ of the neck** nuca, cogote m

napkin ['næpkɪn] n (also: **table ~**) servilleta

nappy ['næpɪ] (BRIT) n pañal m

narcotic [nɑːˈkɒtɪk] adj, n narcótico

narrow ['nærəʊ] adj estrecho, angosto; (fig: majority etc) corto; (: ideas etc) estrecho ♦ vi (road) estrecharse; (diminish) reducirse; **to have a ~ escape** escaparse por los pelos; **to ~ sth down** reducir algo □ **narrowly** adv (miss) por poco □ **narrow-minded** adj de miras estrechas

nasty ['nɑːstɪ] adj (remark) feo; (person) antipático; (revolting: taste, smell) asqueroso; (wound, disease etc) peligroso, grave

nation ['neɪʃən] n nación f

national ['næʃənl] adj nacional ♦ n ciudadano(-a) □ **national dress** n traje típico nacional □ **National Health Service** (BRIT) n servicio nacional de salud pública □ **national holiday** (US) n (día m) feriado (LAm), (día m de) fiesta (SP) □ **National Insurance** (BRIT) n Seguridad f Social □ **nationalism** n nacionalismo □ **nationalist** adj, n nacionalista mf □ **nationality** [ˌnæʃəˈnælɪtɪ] n nacionalidad f □ **nationalize** vt nacionalizar □ **nationally** adv (nationwide) a escala nacional; (as a nation) como nación □ **national park** n parque m nacional

nationwide ['neɪʃənˌwaɪd] adj a escala or nivel nacional

native ['neɪtɪv] n (local inhabitant) nativo(-a) ♦ adj (indigenous) indígena; (country) natal; (innate) natural, innato; **a ~ of Russia** un(a) natural mf de Rusia; **a ~ speaker of French** un hablante nativo de francés □ **Native American** adj, n americano(-a) nativo(-a) □ **native language** n lengua materna

NATIVE AMERICAN

El término **Native American** hace referencia a los pueblos indígenas de Norteamérica y a sus descendientes. En la actualidad, éste es el término considerado más correcto para referirse a este pueblo, ya que el término **Indian** (indio), que tenía el mismo uso, ya no se considera adecuado por venir del momento en que Cristóbal Colón, en sus primeras incursiones en la zona, llamó así a los nativos americanos, ya que pensaba equivocadamente que había llegado a Asia.

Nativity [nəˈtɪvɪtɪ] n: **the ~** Navidad f

NATO ['neɪtəʊ] n abbr (= North Atlantic Treaty Organization) OTAN f

natural ['nætʃərəl] adj natural □ **naturally** adv (speak etc) naturalmente; (of course) desde luego, por supuesto

nature ['neɪtʃər] n (also: **N~**) naturaleza; (group, sort) género, clase f; (character) carácter m, genio; **by ~** por or de naturaleza

naught [nɔːt] (US) n (MATH) cero

naughty ['nɔːti] adj (child) travieso

nausea ['nɔːziə] n náuseas fpl

nautical ['nɔːtɪkəl] adj náutico, marítimo; (mile) marino

naval ['neɪvəl] adj naval, de marina □ **naval officer** n oficial mf de marina

nave [neɪv] n nave f

navel ['neɪvəl] n ombligo

navigate ['nævɪgeɪt] vt gobernar ♦ vi navegar; (AUT) ir de copiloto □ **navigation** [nævɪ'geɪʃən] n (action) navegación f; (science) náutica □ **navigator** n navegador(a) m/f, navegante mf; (AUT) copiloto mf

navvy ['nævi] (BRIT) n peón m

navy ['neɪvi] n marina; (ships) armada, flota □ **navy(-blue)** adj azul marino

Nazi ['nɑːtsi] n nazi mf

NB, n.b. abbr (= nota bene) nótese

NBC (US) n abbr = **National Broadcasting Company**

near [nɪər] adj (place, relation) cercano; (time) próximo ♦ adv cerca ♦ prep (also: ~ to: space) cerca de, junto a; (: time) cerca de ♦ vt acercarse a, aproximarse a □ **nearby** adj cercano, próximo ♦ adv cerca □ **nearly** adv casi, por poco; **I nearly fell** por poco me caigo □ **near miss** n tiro cercano □ **nearside** (BRIT: AUT) n (in Europe etc) lado derecho; (in Britain) lado izquierdo □ **nearsighted** adj miope, corto de vista

neat [niːt] adj (place) ordenado, bien cuidado; (person) pulcro; (plan) ingenioso; (inf: wonderful) estupendo ♦ adv (whisky) con esmero; (skillfully) ingeniosamente

necessarily [nesɪ'serɪli] adv necesariamente

necessary ['nesɪseri] adj necesario, preciso

necessitate [nɪ'sesɪteɪt] vt hacer necesario

necessity [nɪ'sesɪti] n necesidad f; **necessities** npl artículos mpl de primera necesidad

neck [nek] n (of person, garment, bottle) cuello; (of animal) pescuezo ♦ vi (inf) besuquearse; **~ and ~** parejos □ **necklace** ['neklɪs] n collar m □ **neckline** n escote m □ **necktie** (US) n corbata

née [neɪ] adj: **~ Scott** de soltera Scott

need [niːd] n (lack) escasez f, falta; (necessity) necesidad f ♦ vt (require) necesitar; **I ~ to do it** tengo que o debo hacerlo; **you don't ~ to go** no hace falta que (te) vayas

needle ['niːdl] n aguja ♦ vt (fig: inf) picar, fastidiar

needless ['niːdlɪs] adj innecesario; **~ to say** huelga decir que

needlework ['niːdl,wɜːrk] n (activity) costura, labor f de aguja

needn't ['niːdnt] cont = **need not**

needy ['niːdi] adj necesitado

negative ['negətɪv] n (PHOT) negativo; (LING) negación f ♦ adj negativo □ **negative equity** (BRIT) n cantidad hipotecada que sobrepasa el valor de la vivienda

neglect [nɪ'glekt] vt (one's duty) faltar a, no cumplir con; (child) descuidar, desatender ♦ n (of house, garden etc) abandono; (of child) desatención f; (of duty) incumplimiento

negligee ['neglɪʒeɪ] n (nightgown) salto de cama, negligé m

negotiate [nɪ'gəuʃieɪt] vt (treaty, loan) negociar; (obstacle) franquear; (bend in road) tomar ♦ vi: **to ~ (with)** negociar (con) □ **negotiation** [nɪgəuʃi'eɪʃən] n negociación f, gestión f

neigh [neɪ] vi relinchar

neighbor (US) ['neɪbər] (BRIT **neighbour**) n vecino(-a) □ **neighborhood** (US) (BRIT **neighbourhood**) n (place) vecindad f, barrio; (people) vecindario □ **neighboring** (US) (BRIT **neighbouring**) adj vecino □ **neighborly** (US) (BRIT **neighbourly**) adj (person) amable; (attitude) de buen vecino

neither ['niːðər] adj ni ♦ conj: **I didn't move and ~ did John** no me he movido, ni Juan tampoco ♦ pron ninguno ♦ adv: **~ good nor bad** ni bueno ni malo; **~ is true** ninguno(-a) de los (las) dos es cierto(-a)

neon ['niːɑːn] n neón m □ **neon light** n lámpara de neón

nephew ['nefjuː] n sobrino

nerve [nɜːrv] n (ANAT) nervio; (courage) valor m; (impudence) descaro, frescura; **a fit of ~s** un ataque de nervios □ **nerve-racking** adj desquiciante

nervous ['nɜːrvəs] adj (anxious, ANAT) nervioso; (timid) tímido, miedoso □ **nervous breakdown** n crisis f nerviosa

nest [nest] n (of bird) nido; (wasps' nest) avispero ♦ vi anidar □ **nest egg** n (fig) ahorros mpl

nestle ['nesəl] vi: **to ~ down** acurrucarse

net [net] n (gen) red f; (fabric) tul m ♦ adj (COMM) neto, líquido ♦ vt agarrar (LAm) o coger (SP) con red; (SPORT) marcar □ **the Net** n (Internet) la Red □ **netball** n netball m, variedad de baloncesto jugado especialmente por mujeres

Netherlands ['neðərləndz] npl: **the ~** los Países Bajos

nett [net] adj = **net**

netting ['netɪŋ] n red f, redes fpl

nettle ['nɛtl] n ortiga

network ['nɛt,wɜːrk] n red f

neurotic [nu'rɑːtɪk] adj neurótico

neuter ['nuːtər] adj (LING) neutro ♦ vt castrar, capar

neutral ['nuːtrəl] adj (person) neutral; (color etc, ELEC) neutro ♦ n (AUT) punto muerto ❑ **neutralize** vt neutralizar

never ['nɛvər] adv nunca, jamás; **I ~ went** no fui nunca; **~ in my life** jamás en la vida; see also **mind** ❑ **never-ending** adj interminable, sin fin ❑ **nevertheless** adv sin embargo, no obstante

new [nuː] adj nuevo; (brand new) a estrenar; (recent) reciente ❑ **New Age** n Nueva Era, New Age m ❑ **newborn** adj recién nacido ❑ **newcomer** n recién llegado(-a) ❑ **New England** n Nueva Inglaterra ❑ **newfangled** (pej) adj modernísimo ❑ **new-found** adj (friend) nuevo; (enthusiasm) recién adquirido ❑ **newly** adv nuevamente, recién ❑ **newlyweds** npl recién casados mpl

NEW ENGLAND

Los estados de Nueva Inglaterra son los seis estados del noreste de EE.UU.: Maine, Vermont, New Hampshire, Massachusetts, Rhode Island y Connecticut. La región de Nueva Inglaterra fue colonizada por primera vez por Inglaterra décadas antes de la Revolución Americana y su sobrenombre como región ha resistido al paso del tiempo.

news [nuːz] n noticias fpl; **a piece of ~** una noticia; **the ~** (RADIO, TV) las noticias fpl ❑ **news agency** n agencia de noticias ❑ **newsagent** (BRIT) n vendedor(a) m/f de periódicos ❑ **newscaster** n (TV) presentador(a) m/f; (RADIO) locutor(a) m/f ❑ **newsdealer** (US) n vendedor(a) m/f de periódicos ❑ **news flash** n noticia de última hora ❑ **newsletter** n hoja informativa, boletín m ❑ **newspaper** n periódico, diario ❑ **newsprint** n papel m de periódico ❑ **newsreader** (BRIT) n = **newscaster** ❑ **newsreel** n noticiario ❑ **news stand** n quiosco o puesto de periódicos

newt [nuːt] n tritón m

New Year n Año Nuevo ❑ **New Year's** = **New Year's Day; New Year's Eve** ❑ **New Year's Day** n Día m de Año Nuevo ❑ **New Year's Eve** n noche de Fin de Año

New York ['nuː'jɔːrk] n Nueva York

New Zealand [nuː'ziːlənd] n Nueva Zelanda ❑ **New Zealander** n neozelandés(-esa) m/f

next [nɛkst] adj (house, room) vecino; (bus stop, meeting) próximo; (following: page etc) siguiente ♦ adv después; **the ~ day** el día siguiente; **~ time** la próxima vez; **~ year** el año próximo o que viene; **~ to** junto a, al lado de; **~ to nothing** casi nada; **~ please!** ¡el siguiente! ❑ **next door** adv en la casa de al lado ♦ adj vecino, de al lado ❑ **next-of-kin** n pariente m más cercano

NHS (BRIT) n abbr = **National Health Service**

nib [nɪb] n plumilla

nibble ['nɪbəl] vt mordisquear, mordiscar

Nicaragua [nɪkəˈrɑːgwə] n Nicaragua ❑ **Nicaraguan** adj, n nicaragüense mf

nice [naɪs] adj (likeable) simpático; (kind) amable; (pleasant) agradable; (attractive) bonito, lindo (LAm) ❑ **nicely** adv amablemente; bien

nick [nɪk] n (wound) rasguño; (cut, indentation) mella, muesca ♦ vt (BRIT: inf) birlar, robar; **in the ~ of time** justo a tiempo

nickel ['nɪkəl] n (metal) níquel m; (US: coin) moneda de 5 centavos

nickname ['nɪkneɪm] n apodo, mote m ♦ vt apodar

nicotine ['nɪkətiːn] n nicotina

niece [niːs] n sobrina

Nigeria [naɪˈdʒɪriə] n Nigeria ❑ **Nigerian** adj, n nigeriano(-a)

niggling ['nɪglɪŋ] adj (trifling) nimio, insignificante; (annoying) molesto

night [naɪt] n noche f; (evening) tarde f; **the ~ before last** anteanoche; **at ~, by ~** de noche, por la noche ❑ **nightcap** n (drink) bebida que se toma antes de acostarse ❑ **night club** n club m nocturno ❑ **nightdress** (BRIT) n = **nightgown** ❑ **nightfall** n anochecer m ❑ **nightgown** (US) n camisón m de noche ❑ **nightie** n = **nightdress**

nightingale ['naɪtɪŋgeɪl] n ruiseñor m

night: ❑ **nightlife** n vida nocturna ❑ **nightly** adj de todas las noches ♦ adv todas las noches, cada noche ❑ **nightmare** n pesadilla ❑ **night porter** (BRIT) n portero de noche ❑ **night school** n clase(s) f(pl) nocturna(s) ❑ **night shift** n turno nocturno ❑ **night-time** n noche f ❑ **night watchman** n vigilante m nocturno

nil [nɪl] (BRIT) n (SPORT) cero

Nile [naɪl] n: **the ~** el Nilo

nimble ['nɪmbəl] *adj* (*agile*) ágil, ligero; (*skillful*) diestro

nine [naɪn] *num* nueve

9-11, nine-eleven [naɪnɪ'lɛvn] *n* 11-S *m*

nineteen ['naɪntiːn] *num* diecinueve

ninety ['naɪntɪ] *num* noventa

ninth [naɪnθ] *adj* noveno

nip [nɪp] *vt* (*pinch*) pellizcar; (*bite*) morder

nipple ['nɪpəl] *n* (ANAT) pezón *m*; (US: *on baby's bottle*) tetina

nitrogen ['naɪtrədʒən] *n* nitrógeno

no

KEYWORD

[nou] (*pl* **noes**)
adv (*opposite of "yes"*) no; **are you coming? -- no (I'm not)** ¿vienes? -- no; **would you like some more? -- no thank you** ¿quieres más? -- no gracias

♦ *adj* (*not any*): **I have no money/time/books** no tengo dinero/tiempo/libros; **no other man would have done it** ningún otro lo hubiera hecho; **"no entry"** "prohibido el paso"; **"no smoking"** "prohibido fumar"
♦ *n* no *m*

nobility [nou'bɪlɪtɪ] *n* nobleza

noble ['noubəl] *adj* noble

nobody ['noubaːdɪ] *pron* nadie

nod [naːd] *vi* saludar con la cabeza; (*in agreement*) asentir con la cabeza; (*doze*) dar cabezadas ♦ *vt*: **to ~ one's head** inclinar la cabeza ♦ *n* saludo con la cabeza ► **nod off** *vi* dar cabezadas

noise [nɔɪz] *n* ruido; (*din*) escándalo, estrépito ❑ **noisy** *adj* ruidoso; (*child*) escandaloso

nominate ['naːmɪneɪt] *vt* (*propose*) proponer; (*appoint*) nombrar ❑ **nominee** [naːmɪ'niː] *n* candidato(-a)

non... [naːn] *prefix* no, des..., in... ❑ **non-alcoholic** *adj* no alcohólico ❑ **nonchalant** *adj* indiferente ❑ **non-committal** *adj* evasivo ❑ **nondescript** *adj* soso

none [nʌn] *pron* ninguno(-a) ♦ *adv* de ninguna manera; **~ of you** ninguno de vosotros; **I've ~ left** no me queda ninguno(-a); **he's ~ the worse for it** no le ha hecho ningún mal

nonentity [naː'nɛntɪtɪ] *n* cero a la izquierda, nulidad *f*

nonetheless [nʌnðə'lɛs] *adv* sin embargo, no obstante

non-existent *adj* inexistente

non-fiction *n* literatura no novelesca

nonplussed [naːn'plʌst] (US **nonplused**) *adj* perplejo

nonsense ['naːnsɛns] *n* tonterías *fpl*, disparates *fpl*; **~!** ¡tonterías!

non: ❑ **non-smoker** *n* no fumador(a) *m/f*
❑ **non-smoking** *adj* (de) no fumador
❑ **non-stick** *adj* (*pan, surface*) antiadherente
❑ **non-stop** *adj* continuo; (RAIL) directo ♦ *adv* sin parar

noodles ['nuːdlz] *npl* fideos *mpl* (*chinos*)

nook [nuk] *n*: **~s and crannies** escondrijos *mpl*

noon [nuːn] *n* mediodía *m*

no one, no-one *pron* = **nobody**

noose [nuːs] *n* (*of hangman*) soga, dogal *m*

nor [nɔːr] *conj* = **neither** ♦ *adv see* **neither**

norm [nɔːrm] *n* norma

normal ['nɔːrməl] *adj* normal ❑ **normally** *adv* normalmente

north [nɔːrθ] *n* norte *m* ♦ *adj* del norte, norteño ♦ *adv* al *or* hacia el norte; **the N~** (US) el Norte; *see also* **the South** ❑ **North Africa** *n* África del Norte ❑ **North America** *n* América del Norte ❑ **northeast** *n* nor(d)este *m* ❑ **northerly** ['nɔːrðərlɪ] *adj* (*point, direction*) norteño ❑ **northern** ['nɔːrðərn] *adj* norteño, del norte ❑ **Northern Ireland** *n* Irlanda del Norte ❑ **North Pole** *n* Polo Norte ❑ **North Sea** *n* Mar *m* del Norte ❑ **northward(s)** ['nɔːrθwərd(z)] *adv* hacia el norte ❑ **northwest** *n* nor(d)oeste *m*

THE NORTH

La Guerra Civil Americana (1861-1865) dividió al país en dos facciones opuestas: el norte industrial, que luchaba por abolir el ejercicio de la esclavitud y el sur, agrícola, que luchaba por mantenerla. La línea Mason-Dixon, que discurría por la frontera entre Pensilvania y Maryland, marcaba la división geográfica entre las dos y, aunque ya ha desaparecido el enfrentamiento entre el norte y el sur, la mayoría de los norteamericanos percibe que subsisten importantes diferencias culturales entre ambas regiones.

Norway ['nɔːrweɪ] *n* Noruega ❑ **Norwegian** [nɔːr'wiːdʒən] *adj, n* noruego(-a); (LING) noruego

nose [nouz] *n* (ANAT) nariz *f*; (ZOOL) hocico; (*sense of smell*) olfato ♦ *vi* (*also:* **~ around**) curiosear ❑ **nosebleed** *n* hemorragia nasal ❑ **nose dive** *n* (*of plane: deliberate*) picado

vertical; (: *involuntary*) caída en picado
❏ **nosey** [*inf*] *adj* curioso, fisgón(-ona)
nostalgia [nɑː'stældʒə] *n* nostalgia
nostril ['nɑːstrəl] *n* ventana de la nariz
nosy ['nouzi] (*inf*) *adj* = **nosey**
not [nɑːt] *adv* no; ~ **that** ... no es que ...; **it's
too late, isn't it?** es demasiado tarde,
¿verdad *or* no?; ~ **yet/now** todavía/ahora no;
why ~? ¿por qué no?; *see also* **all; only**
notably ['noutəbli] *adv* especialmente
notary ['noutəri] *n* notario(-a)
notch [nɑːtʃ] *n* muesca, corte *m*
note [nout] *n* (*MUS, record, letter*) nota; (*tone*)
tono; (*BRIT: banknote*) billete *m* ♦ *vt* (*observe*)
notar, observar; (*write down*) apuntar, anotar
❏ **notebook** *n* libreta, cuaderno ❏ **noted**
adj célebre, conocido ❏ **notepad** *n* bloc *m*
(de notas) ❏ **notepaper** *n* papel *m* de cartas
nothing ['nʌθɪŋ] *n* nada; (*zero*) cero; **he does
~** no hace nada; ~ **new** nada nuevo; ~ **much**
no mucho; **for ~** (*free*) gratis, sin pago; (*in
vain*) en balde
notice ['noutɪs] *n* (*announcement*) anuncio;
(*warning*) aviso; (*dismissal*) despido;
(*resignation*) dimisión *f*; (*period of time*) plazo
♦ *vt* (*observe*) notar, observar; **to bring sth to
sb's ~** (*attention*) llamar la atención de algn
sobre algo; **to take ~ of** tomar nota de,
prestar atención a; **at short ~** con poca
anticipación; **until further ~** hasta nuevo
aviso; **to hand in one's ~** dimitir
❏ **noticeable** *adj* evidente, obvio ❏ **notice
board** (*BRIT*) *n* tablón *m* de anuncios

⚠ Be careful not to translate **notice** by the
Spanish word *noticia*.

notify ['noutɪfaɪ] *vt*: **to ~ sb (of sth)**
comunicar (algo) a algn
notion ['noʊʃən] *n* idea; (*opinion*) opinión *f*
❏ **notions** *npl* (*SEWING*) artículos *mpl* de
mercería
notorious [nouˈtɔːriəs] *adj* notorio
nougat ['nuːgət] *n* turrón *m*
nought [nɔːt] (*BRIT*) *n* = **naught**
noun [naun] *n* nombre *m*, sustantivo
nourish ['nʌrɪʃ] *vt* nutrir; (*fig*) alimentar
❏ **nourishing** *adj* nutritivo
❏ **nourishment** *n* alimento, sustento
novel ['nɑːvəl] *n* novela ♦ *adj* (*new*) nuevo,
original; (*unexpected*) insólito ❏ **novelist** *n*
novelista *mf* ❏ **novelty** *n* novedad *f*
November [nouˈvembər] *n* noviembre *m*
novice ['nɑːvɪs] *n* (*REL*) novicio(-a)
now [nau] *adv* (*at the present time*) ahora;
(*these days*) actualmente, hoy día ♦ *conj*: ~

(*that*) ya que, ahora que; **right ~** ahora
mismo; **by ~** ya; **just ~** ahora mismo; ~ **and
then,** ~ **and again** de vez en cuando; **from ~
on** de ahora en adelante ❏ **nowadays**
['nauədeɪz] *adv* hoy (en) día, actualmente
nowhere ['nouwer] *adv* (*direction*) a ninguna
parte; (*location*) en ninguna parte
nozzle ['nɑːzəl] *n* boquilla
nuance ['nuːɑːns] *n* matiz *m*
nuclear ['nuːkliər] *adj* nuclear
nucleus ['nuːkliəs] (*pl* **nuclei**) *n* núcleo
nude [nuːd] *adj, n* desnudo(-a); **in the ~**
desnudo
nudge [nʌdʒ] *vt* dar un codazo a
nudist ['nuːdɪst] *n* nudista *mf*
nuisance ['nuːsəns] *n* molestia, fastidio;
(*person*) pesado, latoso; **what a ~!** ¡qué lata!
null [nʌl] *adj*: ~ **and void** nulo y sin efecto
numb [nʌm] *adj*: ~ **with cold/fear**
entumecido de frío/paralizado de miedo
number ['nʌmbər] *n* número; (*quantity*)
cantidad *f* ♦ *vt* (*pages etc*) numerar, poner
número a; (*amount to*) sumar, ascender a; **to
be ~ed among** figurar entre; **a ~ of** varios,
algunos; **they were ten in ~** eran diez
❏ **number plate** (*BRIT*) *n* placa (*LAm*), chapa
(*RPI*), matrícula (*SP*)
numeral ['nuːmərəl] *n* número, cifra
numerate ['nuːmərɪt] *adj* competente en
aritmética
numerous ['nuːmərəs] *adj* numeroso
nun [nʌn] *n* monja, religiosa
nurse [nɜːrs] *n* enfermero(-a); (*US: also:* ~**maid**)
niñera ♦ *vt* (*patient*) cuidar, atender
nursery ['nɜːrsəri] *n* (*institution*) guardería
infantil; (*room*) cuarto de los niños; (*for plants*)
vivero ❏ **nursery rhyme** *n* canción *f*
infantil ❏ **nursery school** *n* jardín *m* de
niños (*MEX*), jardín infantil (*LAm exc MEX*) or de
infantes (*RPI*), parvulario (*SP*) ❏ **nursery
slope** (*BRIT*) *n* (*SKI*) pista para principiantes
nursing ['nɜːrsɪŋ] *n* (*profession*) enfermería;
(*care*) asistencia, cuidado ❏ **nursing home**
n clínica de reposo
nut [nʌt] *n* (*TECH*) tuerca; (*BOT*) nuez *f*
❏ **nutcrackers** *npl* cascanueces *m inv*
nutmeg ['nʌtmeg] *n* nuez *f* moscada
nutritious [nuːˈtrɪʃəs] *adj* nutritivo,
alimenticio
nuts [nʌts] (*inf*) *adj* loco
nutshell ['nʌtʃel] *n*: **in a ~** en resumidas
cuentas
nylon ['naɪlɑːn] *n* nylon *m* ♦ *adj* de nylon; ~**s**
npl (*US*) medias de nylon

Oo

oak [ouk] n roble m ♦ adj de roble

O.A.P. (BRIT) n abbr = **old-age pensioner**

oar [ɔːr] n remo

oasis [ou'eisis] (pl **oases** [ou'eisiːz]) n oasis m inv

oath [ouθ] n juramento; (swear word) palabrota; **under ~, on ~** (BRIT) bajo juramento

oatmeal ['outmiːl] n harina de avena

oats [outs] n avena

obedience [ou'biːdiəns] n obediencia

obedient [ou'biːdiənt] adj obediente

obey [ou'bei] vt obedecer; (instructions, regulations) cumplir

obituary [ou'bitʃuəri] n obituario (LAm), necrología (SP)

object [n 'ɑːbdʒɪkt, vb əb'dʒɛkt] n objeto; (purpose) objeto, propósito; (LING) complemento ♦ vi: **to ~ to** estar en contra de; (proposal) oponerse a; **to ~ that** objetar que; **expense is no ~** no importa cuánto cuesta; **I ~!** ¡protesto! ❑ **objection** [əb'dʒɛkʃən] n protesta; **I have no objection to ...** no tengo inconveniente en que ... ❑ **objectionable** [əb'dʒɛkʃənəbəl] adj desagradable; (conduct) censurable ❑ **objective** [əb'dʒɛktiv] adj, n objetivo

obligation [ɑːblɪ'geiʃən] n obligación f; (debt) deber m; **without ~** sin compromiso

oblige [ə'blaidʒ] vt (do a favor for) complacer, hacer un favor a; **to ~ sb to do sth** forzar or obligar a algn a hacer algo; **I am ~d to you for your help** le agradezco mucho su ayuda ❑ **obliging** adj servicial, atento

oblique [ə'bliːk] adj oblicuo; (allusion) indirecto

obliterate [ə'blitəreit] vt borrar

oblivion [ə'bliviən] n olvido ❑ **oblivious** adj: **oblivious of** inconsciente de

oblong ['ɑːblɑːŋ] adj rectangular ♦ n rectángulo

obnoxious [əb'nɑːkʃəs] adj odioso, detestable; (smell) nauseabundo

oboe ['oubou] n oboe m

obscene [əb'siːn] adj obsceno

obscure [əb'skjuər] adj oscuro ♦ vt oscurecer; (hide: sun) esconder

observant [əb'zɜːrvənt] adj observador(a)

observation [ɑːbzər'veiʃən] n observación f; (MED) examen m

observe [əb'zɜːrv] vt observar; (rule) cumplir ❑ **observer** n observador(a) m/f

obsess [əb'sɛs] vt obsesionar ❑ **obsessive** adj obsesivo; obsesionante

obsolete [ɑːbsə'liːt] adj: **to be ~** estar en desuso

obstacle ['ɑːbstəkəl] n obstáculo; (nuisance) estorbo ❑ **obstacle race** n carrera de obstáculos

obstinate ['ɑːbstənit] adj terco, porfiado; (determined) obstinado

obstruct [əb'strʌkt] vt obstruir; (hinder) estorbar, obstaculizar ❑ **obstruction** n (action) obstrucción f; (object) estorbo, obstáculo

obtain [əb'tein] vt obtener; (achieve) conseguir

obvious ['ɑːbviəs] adj obvio, evidente ❑ **obviously** adv evidentemente, naturalmente; **obviously not** por supuesto que no

occasion [ə'keiʒən] n oportunidad f, ocasión f; (event) acontecimiento ❑ **occasional** adj poco frecuente, ocasional ❑ **occasionally** adv de vez en cuando

occupant ['ɑːkjupənt] n (of house) inquilino(-a); (of car) ocupante mf

occupation [ɑːkjə'peiʃən] n ocupación f; (job) trabajo; (pastime) ocupaciones fpl ❑ **occupational hazard** n riesgo profesional

occupier ['ɑːkjupaiər] n inquilino(-a)

occupy ['ɑːkjəpai] vt (seat, post, time) ocupar; (house) habitar; **to ~ o.s. in doing** pasar el tiempo haciendo

occur [ə'kɜːr] vi pasar, suceder; **it ~s to me that ...** se me ocurre que ... ❑ **occurrence** n acontecimiento; (existence) existencia

ocean ['ouʃən] n océano

o'clock [ə'klɑːk] adv: **it is 5 ~** son las 5

OCR n abbr = **optical character recognition/reader**

October [ɑːk'toubər] n octubre m

octopus ['ɑːktəpəs] n pulpo

odd [ɑːd] adj extraño, raro; (number) impar; (sock, shoe etc) suelto; **60-~** 60 y pico; **at ~ times** de vez en cuando; **to be the ~ one out** estar de más ❑ **oddity** n rareza; (person) excéntrico ❑ **odd-job man** n hombre que se dedica a hacer pequeños trabajos o arreglos, milusos m inv (MEX) ❑ **odd jobs** npl trabajillos mpl ❑ **oddly** adv curiosamente, extrañamente; see also **enough** ❑ **oddments** npl (COMM) restos mpl, retales mpl ❑ **odds** npl (in betting) apuestas fpl; **it**

makes no odds da lo mismo; **at odds** reñidos(-as); **odds and ends** minucias *fpl*, cosillas *fpl*

odometer [ou'dɑːmɪtər] (*US*) *n* cuentakilómetros *m inv*

odor (*US*) ['oudər] (*BRIT* **odour**) *n* olor *m*; (*unpleasant*) hedor *m*

of

KEYWORD

[ʌv] *prep*

1 (*gen*) de; **a friend of ours** un amigo nuestro; **a boy of 10** un chico de 10 años; **that was kind of you** eso fue muy amable por *or* de tu parte

2 (*expressing quantity, amount, time etc*) de; **a pound of flour** una libra de harina; **there were 3 of them** había tres; **3 of us went** tres de nosotros fuimos; **it's a quarter of six** (*US*) son las seis menos cuarto

3 (*from, out of*) de; **made of wood** (hecho) de madera

off [ɔːf] *adj, adv* (*engine*) desconectado; (*light*) apagado; (*faucet*) cerrado; (*milk*) cortado; (*canceled*) cancelado; (*BRIT: food: bad*) pasado, malo ♦ *prep* de; **to be ~** (*to leave*) irse, marcharse; **to be ~ sick** estar enfermo *or* de baja; **a day ~** un día libre *or* sin trabajar; **to have an ~ day** tener un día malo; **he had his coat ~** se había quitado el abrigo; **10% ~** (*COMM*) (con el) 10% de descuento; **5 miles ~ (the road)** a 5 millas (de la carretera); **~ the coast** frente a la costa; **I'm ~ meat** (*no longer eat/like it*) paso de la carne; **on the ~ chance** por si acaso; **~ and on** de vez en cuando

offal ['ɑːfəl] (*BRIT*) *n* (*CULIN*) menudencias *fpl* (*LAm*), achuras *fpl* (*RPl*), asaduras *fpl* (*SP*)

off-color (*US*) *adj* (*joke*) de mal gusto

off-colour (*BRIT*) *adj* (*ill*) indispuesto

offence [ə'fens] (*BRIT*) *n* = **offense**

offend [ə'fend] *vt* (*person*) ofender □ **offender** *n* delincuente *mf*

offense (*US*) [ə'fens] (*BRIT* **offence**) *n* (*crime*) delito; **to take ~ at** ofenderse por

offensive [ə'fensɪv] *adj* ofensivo; (*smell etc*) repugnante ♦ *n* (*MIL*) ofensiva

offer ['ɔːfər] *n* oferta, ofrecimiento; (*proposal*) propuesta ♦ *vt* ofrecer; (*opportunity*) facilitar; **"on ~"** (*COMM*) "en oferta" □ **offering** *n* ofrenda

offhand [ɔːf'hænd] *adj* informal ♦ *adv* de improviso

office ['ɔːfɪs] *n* (*place*) oficina; (*room*) despacho; (*position*) carga, oficio; **doctor's ~** (*US*) consultorio; **to take ~** entrar en

funciones □ **office automation** *n* ofimática, buromática □ **office building** (*US*) (*BRIT* **office block**) *n* bloque *m* de oficinas □ **office hours** *npl* horas *fpl* de oficina; (*US MED*) horas *fpl* de consulta

officer ['ɔːfɪsər] *n* (*MIL etc*) oficial *mf*; (*also:* **police ~**) agente *mf* de policía; (*of organization*) director(a) *m/f*

office worker *n* oficinista *mf*

official [ə'fɪʃəl] *adj* oficial ♦ *n* funcionario(-a), oficial *mf*

offing ['ɔːfɪŋ] *n*: **in the ~** (*fig*) en perspectiva

off: □ **off-licence** (*BRIT*) *n* (*shop*) tienda de bebidas alcohólicas □ **off-line** *adj, adv* (*COMPUT*) fuera de línea □ **off-peak** *adj* (*electricity*) de banda económica; (*ticket*) de precio reducido (*por viajar fuera de las horas pico*) □ **off-putting** (*BRIT*) *adj* (*person*) asqueroso; (*remark*) desalentador(a) □ **off-season** *adj, adv* fuera de temporada

offset ['ɔːfset] *vt* contrarrestar, compensar

offshoot ['ɔːfʃuːt] *n* (*fig*) ramificación *f*

offshore ['ɔːfʃɔːr] *adj* (*breeze, island*) costero; (*fishing*) de bajura

offside ['ɔːfsaɪd] *adj* (*SPORT*) fuera de juego; (*AUT: in US, Europe etc*) del lado izquierdo; (*in UK*) del lado derecho

offspring ['ɔːfsprɪŋ] *n inv* descendencia

off: □ **offstage** *adv* entre bastidores □ **off-the-rack** (*US*) (*BRIT* **off-the-peg**) *adv* confeccionado □ **off-white** *adj* crudo

often ['ɔːfən] *adv* a menudo, con frecuencia; **how ~ do you go?** ¿cada cuánto vas?

oftentimes ['ɔːfəntaɪmz] (*US*) *adv* muchas veces, frecuentemente

oh [ou] *excl* ¡ah!

oil [ɔɪl] *n* aceite *m*; (*petroleum*) petróleo; (*ART*) óleo ♦ *vt* engrasar □ **oilcan** *n* (*container*) lata de aceite □ **oilfield** *n* campo petrolífero □ **oil filter** *n* (*AUT*) filtro de aceite □ **oil painting** *n* pintura al óleo □ **oil rig** *n* plataforma petrolífera □ **oil tanker** *n* petrolero; (*truck*) camión *m* cisterna □ **oil well** *n* pozo de petróleo □ **oily** *adj* aceitoso; (*food*) grasiento

ointment ['ɔɪntmənt] *n* pomada, ungüento

O.K., okay ['ou'keɪ] *excl* ¡okey! (*LAm*), ¡vale! (*SP*) ♦ *adj* bien ♦ *vt* dar el visto bueno a

old [ould] *adj* viejo; (*former*) antiguo; **how ~ are you?** ¿cuántos años tienes?, ¿qué edad tienes?; **he's 10 years ~** tiene 10 años; **~er brother** hermano mayor □ **old age** *n* vejez *f* □ **old-age pensioner** (*BRIT*) *n* pensionista *mf* (de la tercera edad) □ **old-fashioned** *adj* anticuado, pasado de moda

olive ['ɑːlɪv] n (fruit) aceituna; (tree) olivo ♦ adj (also: **~-green**) verde oliva ❑ **olive oil** n aceite m de oliva

Olympic [ouˈlɪmpɪk] adj olímpico; **the ~ Games, the ~s** las Olimpíadas

omelet(te) ['ɑːmlɪt] n omelette f (LAm), tortilla francesa (SP)

omen ['oumən] n presagio

ominous ['ɑːmɪnəs] adj de mal agüero, amenazador(a)

omit [ouˈmɪt] vt omitir

---

on
KEYWORD

[ɑːn] prep

1 (indicating position) en; sobre; **on the wall** en la pared; **it's on the table** está sobre or en la mesa; **on the left** a la izquierda

2 (indicating means, method, condition etc): **on foot** a pie; **on the train/plane** (go) en tren/avión; (be) en el tren/el avión; **on the radio/television/telephone** por or en la radio/televisión/al teléfono; **to be on drugs** drogarse; (MED) estar en tratamiento; **to be on vacation/business** estar de vacaciones/en viaje de negocios

3 (referring to time): **on Friday** el viernes; **on Fridays** los viernes; **on June 20th** el 20 de junio; **a week on Friday** del viernes en una semana; **on arrival** al llegar; **on seeing this** al ver esto

4 (about, concerning) sobre, acerca de; **a book on physics** un libro de or sobre física
♦ adv

1 (referring to dress): **to have one's coat on** tener or llevar el abrigo puesto; **she put her gloves on** se puso los guantes

2 (referring to covering): **"screw the lid on tightly"** "cerrar bien la tapa"

3 (further, continuously): **to walk etc on** seguir caminando etc
♦ adj

1 (functioning, in operation: machine, radio, TV, light) prendido(-a) (LAm), encendido(-a) (SP); (: faucet) abierto(-a); (: brakes) echado(-a), puesto(-a); **is the meeting still on?** (in progress) ¿todavía continúa la reunión?; (not canceled) ¿va a haber reunión al fin?; **there's a good movie on at the movie theater** ponen una buena película en el cine

2: **that's not on!** (inf: not possible) ¡eso ni hablar!; (: not acceptable) ¡eso no se hace!

---

once [wʌns] adv una vez; (formerly) antiguamente ♦ conj una vez que; **~ he had left/it was done** una vez que se había marchado/se hizo; **at ~** en seguida, inmediatamente; (simultaneously) a la vez; **~ a week** una vez por semana; **~ more** otra vez; **~ and for all** de una vez por todas; **~ upon a time** érase una vez

oncoming ['ɑːnˌkʌmɪŋ] adj (traffic) (que viene) en dirección contraria

---

one
KEYWORD

[wʌn] num

un(o)/una; **one hundred and fifty** ciento cincuenta; **one by one** uno a uno
♦ adj

1 (sole) único; **the one book which** el único libro que; **the one man who** el único que

2 (same) mismo(-a); **they came in the one car** vinieron en un solo coche
♦ pron

1: **this one** éste (ésta); **that one** ése (ésa); (more remote) aquél (aquella); **I've already got (a red) one** ya tengo uno(-a) rojo(-a); **one by one** uno(-a) por uno(-a)

2: **one another** se (LAm), os (SP) {+ el uno al otro, unos a otros etc}; **do you two ever see one another?** ¿se ven ustedes dos alguna vez? (LAm), ¿vosotros dos os veis alguna vez? (SP); **the boys didn't dare look at one another** los chicos no se atrevieron a mirarse (el uno al otro); **they all kissed one another** se besaron unos a otros

3 (impers): **one never knows** nunca se sabe; **to cut one's finger** cortarse el dedo

---

one: ❑ **one-day excursion** (US) n excursión f de un día ❑ **one-man** adj (business) individual ❑ **one-man band** n hombre-orquesta m ❑ **one-off** (BRIT: inf) n (event) acontecimiento único

oneself [wʌnˈsɛlf] pron (reflexive) se; (after prep) sí; (emphatic) uno(-a) mismo(-a); **to hurt ~** hacerse daño; **to keep sth for ~** guardarse algo; **to talk to ~** hablar solo

one: ❑ **one-sided** adj (argument) parcial ❑ **one-to-one** adj (relationship) de dos ❑ **one-way** adj (street) de sentido único

ongoing ['ɑːnˌgouɪŋ] adj continuo

onion ['ʌnjən] n cebolla

online ['ɑːnˈlaɪn] adj, adv (COMPUT) en línea

onlooker ['ɑːnˌlukər] n espectador(a) m/f

only ['ounlɪ] adv solamente, sólo ♦ adj único, solo ♦ conj solamente que, pero; **an ~ child** un hijo único; **not ~ ... but also ...** no sólo ... sino también ...

onset ['ɑːnsɛt] n comienzo

onshore ['ɑːnˈʃɔːr] adj (wind) del mar

onslaught ['ɒnslɔːt] n ataque m, embestida

onto ['ɒntu] prep = **on to**

onward(s) ['ɒnwəd(z)] adv (move) (hacia) adelante; **from that time onward(s)** de ahora en adelante

onyx ['ɒnɪks] n ónice m, ónix m

ooze [uːz] vi rezumar

opaque [ou'peɪk] adj opaco

OPEC ['oupek] n abbr (= Organization of Petroleum-Exporting Countries) OPEP f

open ['oupən] adj abierto; (car) descubierto; (road, view) despejado; (meeting) público; (admiration) manifiesto ♦ vt abrir ♦ vi abrirse; (book etc: commence) comenzar; **in the ~ (air)** al aire libre ► **open on to** vt fus (room, door) dar a ► **open up** vt abrir; (blocked road) despejar ♦ vi abrirse, empezar ❏ **opening** n abertura; (start) comienzo; (opportunity) oportunidad f ❏ **opening hours** npl horario de apertura ❏ **open learning** n enseñanza flexible a tiempo parcial ❏ **openly** adv abiertamente ❏ **open-minded** adj imparcial ❏ **open-necked** adj (shirt) desabrochado; sin corbata ❏ **open-plan** adj: **open-plan office** gran oficina sin particiones

opera ['ɒpərə] n ópera ❏ **opera house** n teatro de la ópera

operate ['ɒpəreɪt] vt (machine) hacer funcionar; (company) dirigir ♦ vi funcionar; **to ~ on sb** (MED) operar a algn

operatic [ɒpə'rætɪk] adj de ópera

operating room ['ɒpəreɪtɪŋ,ruːm] (US) n sala de operaciones

operating table n mesa de operaciones

operation [ɒpə'reɪʃən] n operación f; (of machine) funcionamiento; **to be in ~** estar funcionando or en funcionamiento; **to have an ~** (MED) ser operado ❏ **operational** adj operacional, en servicio or funcionamiento

operative ['ɒpərətɪv] adj en vigor

operator ['ɒpəreɪtər] n (of machine) maquinista mf, operario(-a); (TEL) operador(a) m/f, telefonista mf

opinion [ə'pɪnjən] n opinión f; **in my ~** en mi opinión, a mi juicio ❏ **opinionated** adj testarudo ❏ **opinion poll** n encuesta, sondeo

opponent [ə'pounənt] n adversario(-a), contrincante mf

opportunity [ɒpə'tuːnɪti] n oportunidad f; **to take the ~ of doing** aprovechar la ocasión para hacer

oppose [ə'pouz] vt oponerse a; **to be ~d to sth** oponerse a algo; **as ~d to** a diferencia de ❏ **opposing** adj opuesto, contrario

opposite ['ɒpəzɪt] adj opuesto, contrario a; (house etc) de enfrente ♦ adv en frente ♦ prep en frente de, frente a ♦ n lo contrario

opposition [ɒpə'zɪʃən] n oposición f

oppressive [ə'presɪv] adj opresivo; (weather) agobiante

opt [ɒpt] vi: **to ~ for** optar por; **to ~ to do** optar por hacer ► **opt out** vi: **to opt out of** optar por no hacer

optical ['ɒptɪkəl] adj óptico

optician [ɒp'tɪʃən] n óptico(-a)

optimist ['ɒptəmɪst] n optimista mf ❏ **optimistic** [ɒptə'mɪstɪk] adj optimista

option ['ɒpʃən] n opción f ❏ **optional** adj facultativo, discrecional

or [ɔːr] conj o; (before o, ho) u; (with negative): **he hasn't seen or heard anything** no ha visto ni oído nada; **or else** si no

oral ['ɔːrəl] adj oral ♦ n examen m oral

orange ['ɒrɪndʒ] n (fruit) naranja ♦ adj naranja inv

orbit ['ɔːrbɪt] n órbita ♦ vt, vi orbitar

orchard ['ɔːrtʃərd] n huerto

orchestra ['ɔːrkɪstrə] n orquesta; (US: seating) platea

orchid ['ɔːrkɪd] n orquídea

ordain [ɔːr'deɪn] vt (REL) ordenar, decretar

ordeal [ɔːr'diːl] n calvario

order ['ɔːrdər] n orden m; (command) orden f; (good order) buen estado; (COMM) pedido ♦ vt (also: **put in ~**) arreglar, poner en orden; (COMM) pedir; (command) mandar, ordenar; **in ~ en** orden; (of document) en regla; **in (working) ~** en funcionamiento; **in ~ to do/ that** para hacer/que; **on ~** (COMM) pedido; **to be out of ~** estar desordenado; (not working) no funcionar; **to ~ sb to do sth** mandar a algn hacer algo ❏ **order form** n hoja de pedido ❏ **orderly** n (MIL) ordenanza m; (MED) camillero(-a), celador(a) m/f ♦ adj ordenado

ordinary ['ɔːrdneri] adj corriente, normal; (pej) común y corriente; **out of the ~** fuera de lo común

Ordnance Survey ['ɔːrdnəns,sɜːrveɪ] (BRIT) n servicio oficial de cartografía

ore [ɔːr] n mineral m

organ ['ɔːrgən] n órgano ❏ **organic** [ɔːr'gænɪk] adj orgánico ❏ **organism** n organismo

organization [ɔːrgənɪ'zeɪʃən] n organización f

organize ['ɔːrgənaɪz] vt organizar
❏ **organizer** n organizador(a) m/f

orgasm ['ɔːrgæzəm] n orgasmo

orgy ['ɔːrdʒi] n orgía

Orient ['ɔːriənt] n Oriente m ❏ **oriental**
[ɔːri'entl] adj oriental

orientate ['ɔːrienteit] vt: **to ~ o.s.** orientarse

origin ['ɔːrɪdʒɪn] n origen m

original [ə'rɪdʒɪnl] adj original; (first) primero;
(earlier) primitivo ♦ n original m
❏ **originally** adv al principio

originate [ə'rɪdʒɪneɪt] vi: **to ~ from, ~ in**
surgir de, tener su origen en

Orkneys ['ɔːrknɪz] npl: **the ~** (also: **the
Orkney Islands**) las Orcadas

ornament ['ɔːrnəmənt] n adorno; (trinket)
chuchería ❏ **ornamental** [ɔːrnə'mentl] adj
decorativo, de adorno

ornate [ɔːr'neɪt] adj muy ornado, vistoso

orphan ['ɔːrfən] n huérfano(-a)

orthopedic (US) [ɔːrθə'piːdɪk] (BRIT
orthopaedic) adj ortopédico

ostensibly [ɑː'stensɪbli] adv aparentemente

ostentatious [ɑːsten'teɪʃəs] adj ostentoso

osteopath ['ɑːstiəpæθ] n osteópata mf

ostracize ['ɑːstrəsaɪz] vt condenar al
ostracismo a

ostrich ['ɑːstrɪtʃ] n avestruz m

other ['ʌðər] adj otro ♦ pron: **the ~** (one) el (la)
otro(-a) ♦ adv: **~ than** aparte de; **~s** npl (other
people) otros; **the ~ day** el otro día
❏ **otherwise** adv de otra manera ♦ conj (if
not) si no

otter ['ɑːtər] n nutria

ouch [autʃ] excl ¡ay!

ought [ɔːt] (pt ~) aux vb: **I ~ to do it** debería
hacerlo; **this ~ to have been corrected** esto
debiera haberse corregido; **he ~ to win**
(probability) debe or debiera ganar

ounce [auns] n onza (28.35g)

our [auər] adj nuestro; see also **my** ❏ **ours**
pron (el) nuestro/(la) nuestra etc; see also
mine¹ ❏ **ourselves** pron pl (reflexive, after
prep) nosotros; (emphatic) nosotros mismos;
see also **oneself**

oust [aust] vt desbancar

out [aut] adv afuera, fuera; (not at home) fuera
(de casa); (light, fire) apagado; **~ there** allí
(fuera); **he's ~** (absent) no está, ha salido; **to
run ~** salir corriendo; **~ loud** en alta voz; **~ of**
(outside) fuera de; (because of: anger etc) por; **~
of gas** sin gasolina; **"~ of order"** "no
funciona"; **to be ~ in one's calculations** (BRIT)
equivocarse (en sus cálculos) ❏ **outage**

['autɪdʒ] (US) n (also: **power outage**) corte m
de luz, apagón m ❏ **out-and-out** adj (liar)
empedernido; (thief) redomado ❏ **outback**
n interior m ❏ **outboard** adj: **outboard
motor** (motor m) fueraborda m ❏ **outbreak**
n (of war) comienzo; (of disease) brote m; (of
violence etc) ola ❏ **outburst** n explosión f,
arranque m ❏ **outcast** n paria mf
❏ **outcome** n resultado ❏ **outcrop** n (of
rock) afloramiento ❏ **outcry** n protesta
❏ **outdated** adj anticuado, fuera de moda
❏ **outdo** vt superar ❏ **outdoor** adj exterior,
de aire libre; (clothes) de calle ❏ **outdoors**
adv al aire libre

outer ['autər] adj exterior, externo ❏ **outer
space** n espacio exterior

outfit ['autfɪt] n (clothes) conjunto

out: ❏ **outgoing** adj (character)
extrovertido; (retiring: president etc) saliente
❏ **outgoings** (BRIT) npl gastos mpl
❏ **outgrow** vt: **he has outgrown his
clothes** su ropa le queda pequeña ya
❏ **outhouse** n dependencia ❏ **outing** n
excursión f, paseo

out: ❏ **outlaw** n proscrito ♦ vt proscribir
❏ **outlay** n inversión f ❏ **outlet** n salida; (of
pipe) desagüe m; (US ELEC) tomacorriente m
(LAm), toma de corriente (SP); (also: **retail
outlet**) punto de venta ❏ **outline** n (shape)
contorno, perfil m; (sketch, plan) esbozo ♦ vt
(plan etc) esbozar; **in outline** (fig) a grandes
rasgos ❏ **outlive** vt sobrevivir a ❏ **outlook**
n (fig: prospects) perspectivas fpl; (: for weather)
pronóstico ❏ **outlying** adj remoto, aislado
❏ **outmoded** adj anticuado, pasado de
moda ❏ **outnumber** vt superar en número
❏ **out-of-date** adj (passport) caducado;
(clothes) pasado de moda ❏ **out-of-the-
way** adj apartado ❏ **outpatient** n paciente
mf externo(-a) ❏ **outpost** n puesto de
avanzada ❏ **output** n (volumen m de)
producción f, rendimiento; (COMPUT) salida

outrage ['autreɪdʒ] n escándalo; (atrocity)
atrocidad f ♦ vt ultrajar ❏ **outrageous**
[aut'reɪdʒəs] adj monstruoso

outright [adv ,aut'raɪt, adj 'aut,raɪt] adv (ask,
deny) francamente; (refuse) rotundamente;
(win) de manera absoluta; (be killed) en el acto
♦ adj franco; rotundo

outset ['autset] n principio

outside [aut'saɪd] n exterior m ♦ adj exterior,
externo ♦ adv fuera ♦ prep fuera de; (beyond)
más allá de; **at the ~** (fig) a lo sumo
❏ **outside lane** n (AUT: in US, Europe etc) carril
m de la izquierda; (in Britain) carril m de la
derecha ❏ **outside line** n (TEL) línea

(exterior) ❑ **outsider** n (*stranger*) extraño, forastero

out: ❑ **outsize** (*BRIT*) adj (*clothes*) de talla grande ❑ **outskirts** npl afueras fpl, alrededores mpl ❑ **outspoken** adj muy franco ❑ **outstanding** adj excepcional, destacado; (*remaining*) pendiente ❑ **outstay** vt: **to outstay one's welcome** quedarse más de la cuenta ❑ **outstretched** adj (*hand*) extendido ❑ **outstrip** vt (*competitors, demand*) dejar atrás, aventajar ❑ **out-tray** n bandeja de salida

outward ['autwərd] adj externo; (*journey*) de ida

outweigh [aut'weɪ] vt pesar más que

outwit [aut'wɪt] vt ser más listo que

oval ['ouvəl] adj ovalado ♦ n óvalo

ovary ['ouvəri] n ovario

oven ['ʌvn] n horno ❑ **ovenproof** adj resistente al horno

over ['ouvər] adv encima, por encima ♦ adj or adv (*finished*) terminado; (*surplus*) de sobra ♦ prep (por) encima de; (*above*) sobre; (*on the other side of*) al otro lado de; (*more than*) más de; (*during*) durante; ~ **here** (por) aquí; ~ **there** (por) allí or allá; **all** ~ (*everywhere*) por todas partes; ~ **and** ~ (*again*) una y otra vez; ~ **and above** además de; **to ask sb** ~ invitar a algn a casa; **to bend** ~ inclinarse

overall [adj, n 'ouvərɔːl, adv ,ouvər'ɔːl] adj (*length etc*) total; (*study*) de conjunto ♦ adv en conjunto ♦ n (*BRIT: protective coat*) guardapolvo; ~**s** npl (*US: dungarees*) overol m (*LAm*), mameluco (*SC*), peto (*SP*); (*BRIT: boiler suit*) overol m (*LAm*) or mono (*SP*) (de trabajo)

over: ❑ **overawe** vt: **to be overawed (by)** quedar impresionado (con) ❑ **overbalance** vi perder el equilibrio ❑ **overboard** adv (*NAUT*) por la borda ❑ **overbook** vt sobrereservar

overcast [ouvər'kæst] adj cubierto

overcharge [ouvər'tʃɑːrdʒ] vt: **to** ~ **sb** cobrar de más a algn

overcoat ['ouvərkout] n abrigo, sobretodo

overcome [ouvər'kʌm] vt vencer; (*difficulty*) superar

over: ❑ **overcrowded** adj atestado de gente; (*city, country*) superpoblado ❑ **overdo** vt exagerar; (*overcook*) cocer demasiado; **to overdo it** (*work etc*) pasarse ❑ **overdose** n sobredosis f inv ❑ **overdraft** n descubierto ❑ **overdraw** vt girar en descubierto ❑ **overdrawn** adj (*account*) en descubierto ❑ **overdue** adj retrasado ❑ **overestimate** vt sobreestimar

overflow [vb ,ouvər'flou, n 'ouvərflou] vi desbordarse ♦ n (*also*: ~ **pipe**) (cañería de) desagüe m

overgrown [,ouvər'groun] adj (*garden*) descuidado

overhaul [vb ,ouvər'hɔːl, n 'ouvərhɔːl] vt revisar, repasar ♦ n revisión f

overhead [adv ,ouvər'hed, adj, n 'ouvərhed] adv por arriba or encima ♦ adj (*cable*) aéreo ♦ n (*US*) = **overheads** ❑ **overheads** npl (*expenses*) gastos mpl generales

over: ❑ **overhear** vt oír por casualidad ❑ **overheat** vi (*engine*) recalentarse ❑ **overjoyed** adj encantado, lleno de alegría

overland ['ouvərlænd] adj, adv por tierra

overlap [ouvər'læp] vi traslaparse

over: ❑ **overleaf** adv al dorso ❑ **overload** vt sobrecargar ❑ **overlook** vt (*have view of*) dar a, tener vistas a; (*miss: by mistake*) pasar por alto; (*excuse*) perdonar

overnight [,ouvər'naɪt] adv durante la noche; (*fig*) de la noche a la mañana ♦ adj de noche; **to stay** ~ pasar la noche

overpass ['ouvərpæs] (*US*) n paso superior

overpower [,ouvər'pauər] vt dominar; (*fig*) embargar ❑ **overpowering** adj (*heat*) agobiante; (*smell*) penetrante

over: ❑ **overrate** vt sobreestimar ❑ **override** vt no hacer caso de ❑ **overriding** adj predominante ❑ **overrule** vt (*decision*) anular; (*claim*) denegar ❑ **overrun** vt (*country*) invadir; (*time limit*) rebasar, exceder

overseas [,ouvər'siːz] adv (*abroad: live*) en el extranjero; (: *travel*) al extranjero ♦ adj (*trade*) exterior; (*visitor*) extranjero

overshadow [,ouvər'ʃædou] vt: **to be ~ed by** estar a la sombra de

overshoot [,ouvər'ʃuːt] vt excederse

oversight ['ouvərsaɪt] n descuido

oversleep [,ouvər'sliːp] vi quedarse dormido

overstep [,ouvər'step] vt: **to** ~ **the mark** pasarse de la raya

overt [ou'vɜːrt] adj abierto

overtake [,ouvər'teɪk] vt sobrepasar; (*BRIT AUT*) adelantar

over: ❑ **overthrow** vt (*government*) derrocar ❑ **overtime** n horas fpl extras; (*US SPORT*) prórroga, tiempo suplementario ❑ **overtone** n (*fig*) tono

overture ['ouvərtʃuər] n (*MUS*) obertura; (*fig*) preludio

over: ❑ **overturn** vt volcar; (*fig: plan*) desbaratar; (: *government*) derrocar ♦ vi volcar ❑ **overweight** adj demasiado gordo or

pesado ❏ **overwhelm** [ouvər'wɛlm] vt aplastar; (emotion) sobrecoger
❏ **overwhelming** adj (victory, defeat) arrollador(a); (feeling) irresistible
❏ **overwork** vi trabajar demasiado
❏ **overwrought** [ouvər'rɔːt] adj sobreexcitado

owe [ou] vt: **to ~ sb sth, ~ sth to sb** deber algo a algn ❏ **owing to** prep debido a, por causa de

owl [aul] n búho, lechuza, tecolote m (MEX)

own [oun] vt: tener, poseer ♦ adj propio; **a room of my ~** una habitación propia; **on one's ~** solo, a solas; **to get one's ~ back** (BRIT) tomar revancha ▶ **own up** vi confesar
❏ **owner** n propietario(-a), dueño(-a)
❏ **ownership** n posesión f

ox [ɑːks] (pl **oxen**) n buey m ❏ **oxtail** n: **oxtail soup** sopa de rabo de buey

oxygen ['ɑːksɪdʒən] n oxígeno

oyster ['ɔɪstər] n ostión m (MEX), ostra (LAm exc MEX, SP)

oz. abbr = **ounce(s)**

ozone ['ouzoun]: ❏ **ozone friendly** adj que no daña la capa de ozono ❏ **ozone hole** n agujero m de/en la capa de ozono
❏ **ozone layer** n capa f de ozono

Pp

p (BRIT) abbr = **penny; pence**

P.A. n abbr = **personal assistant; public address system**

p.a. abbr = **per annum**

pa [pɑː] (inf) n papá m

pace [peɪs] n paso ♦ vi: **to ~ up and down** pasearse de un lado a otro; **to keep ~ with** llevar el mismo paso que ❏ **pacemaker** n (MED) marcapasos m inv, regulador m cardíaco; (SPORT: also: **pacesetter**) liebre f

Pacific [pə'sɪfɪk] n: **the ~ (Ocean)** el (Océano) Pacífico

pacifier ['pæsɪfaɪər] (US) n (for baby) chupón m (LAm), chupete m (SC, SP)

pack [pæk] n (packet) paquete m; (of dogs) jauría; (of people) manada, bando; (of cards) baraja; (bundle) fardo; (US: of cigarettes) paquete m; (backpack) mochila ♦ vt (fill) llenar; (in suitcase etc) meter, poner; (cram) llenar, atestar; **to ~ (one's bags)** hacerse la maleta; **to ~ sb off** despachar a algn; **~ it in!** (inf) ¡déjalo ya!

package ['pækɪdʒ] n paquete m; (bulky) bulto; (also: ~ **deal**) acuerdo global
❏ **package holiday** (BRIT) n vacaciones fpl organizadas ❏ **package tour** n viaje m organizado

packed lunch (BRIT) n almuerzo frío

packet ['pækɪt] n paquete m

packing ['pækɪŋ] n embalaje m ❏ **packing box** n caja de embalaje

pact [pækt] n pacto

pad [pæd] n (of paper) bloc m; (cushion) cojinete m; (inf: home) casa ♦ vt rellenar
❏ **padding** n (material) relleno

paddle ['pædl] n (oar) remo, canalete m; (US: for table tennis) pala, paleta ♦ vt remar en ♦ vi (with feet) chapotear ❏ **paddling pool** (BRIT) n alberca (MEX) or piscina (LAm exc MEX, SP) or pileta (RPl) para niños

paddock ['pædək] n corral m, potrero

padlock ['pædlɑːk] n candado

paediatrics etc [ˌpiːdɪ'ætrɪks] (BRIT) n = **pediatrics** etc

pagan ['peɪgən] adj, n pagano(-a)

page [peɪdʒ] n (of book) página; (of newspaper) plana ♦ vt (in hotel etc) llamar por altavoz a

pageant ['pædʒənt] n (procession) desfile m; (show) espectáculo ❏ **pageantry** n pompa

pager ['peɪdʒər] n (TEL) bíper m (LAm), busca m (SP)

paging device ['peɪdʒɪŋdɪˌvaɪs] n = **pager**

paid [peɪd] pt, pp of **pay** ♦ adj (work) remunerado; (vacation) pagado; (official etc) a sueldo; **to put ~ to** (BRIT) acabar con

pail [peɪl] n cubeta (MEX, SP), balde m (LAm)

pain [peɪn] n dolor m; **to be in ~** sufrir; **to take ~s to do sth** tomarse muchas molestias para hacer algo ❏ **pained** adj (expression) afligido ❏ **painful** adj doloroso; (difficult) penoso; (disagreeable) desagradable ❏ **painfully** adv (fig: very) terriblemente ❏ **painkiller** n analgésico ❏ **painless** adj indoloro, sin dolor ❏ **painstaking** adj (person) concienzudo, esmerado

paint [peɪnt] n pintura ♦ vt pintar; **to ~ the door blue** pintar la puerta de azul
❏ **paintbrush** n (of artist) pincel m; (of decorator) brocha ❏ **painter** n pintor(a) m/f
❏ **painting** n pintura ❏ **paintwork** n pintura

pair [pɛər] n (of shoes, gloves etc) par m; (of people) pareja; **a ~ of scissors** unas tijeras; **a ~ of pants** unos pantalones, un pantalón

pajamas [pə'dʒɑːməz] (US) npl piyama m (LAm), pijama m (SP)

Pakistan ['pækɪstæn] n Paquistán m
◻ **Pakistani** adj, n paquistaní mf

pal [pæl] (inf) n camarada mf (MEX), compinche mf (LAm), colega mf (SP)

palace ['pæləs] n palacio

palatable ['pælɪtəbəl] adj sabroso

palate ['pælɪt] n paladar m

pale [peɪl] adj (gen) pálido; (color) claro ♦ n: **to be beyond the ~** pasarse de la raya

Palestine ['pælɪstaɪn] n Palestina
◻ **Palestinian** [pælɪ'stɪniən] adj, n palestino(-a)

palette ['pælɪt] n paleta

pall [pɔːl] vi perder el interés

pallet ['pælɪt] n (for goods) palet m, palé m

pallid ['pælɪd] adj pálido

palm [pɑːm] n (ANAT) palma; (also: ~ tree) palmera, palma ♦ vt: **to ~ sth off on sb** (inf) encajar algo a algn ◻ **Palm Sunday** n Domingo de Ramos

paltry ['pɔːltri] adj irrisorio

pamper ['pæmpər] vt mimar

pamphlet ['pæmflɪt] n folleto

pan [pæn] n (also: sauce~) cacerola, cazuela, olla; (also: frying ~) sartén f; (for baking) molde m para el horno

Panama ['pænəmɑː] n Panamá m; **the ~ Canal** el Canal de Panamá

pancake ['pænkeɪk] n panqué m (MEX), panqueque m (LAm), crepe f (SP)

panda ['pændə] n panda m ◻ **panda car** (BRIT) n carro (LAm) or coche m (SP) patrulla

pandemonium [pændɪ'mouniəm] n pandemonio, jaleo

pander ['pændər] vi: **to ~ to** complacer a

pane [peɪn] n cristal m

panel ['pænl] n (of wood etc) panel m; (RADIO, TV) panel m de invitados ◻ **paneling** (US) (BRIT **panelling**) n paneles mpl

pang [pæŋ] n: **a ~ of regret** (una punzada de) remordimiento; **hunger ~s** retorcijones mpl (LAm) or retortijones mpl (SP) de hambre

panhandler ['pænhændlər] (US) n mendigo(-a)

panic ['pænɪk] n pánico ♦ vi aterrorizarse ◻ **panicky** adj (person) asustadizo ◻ **panic-stricken** adj aterrorizado, preso del pánico

pansy ['pænzi] n (BOT) pensamiento; (inf: pej) maricón m

pant [pænt] vi jadear

panther ['pænθər] n pantera

panties ['pæntiz] npl calzones mpl (LAm), bombachas fpl (RPl), bragas fpl (SP)

pantomime ['pæntəmaɪm] (BRIT) n obra musical representada en Navidad, basada en cuentos de hadas, ≈ pastorela (MEX); (mime) pantomima

pantry ['pæntri] n despensa

pants [pænts] n (US: clothing) pantalones mpl; (BRIT: underwear: woman's) calzones mpl (LAm), bombachas fpl (RPl), bragas fpl (SP); (: man's) calzoncillos mpl

pantyhose ['pæntihouz] (US) n pantis mpl, pantimedias fpl (MEX)

paper ['peɪpər] n papel m; (also: news~) periódico, diario; (academic essay) ensayo; (exam) examen m ♦ adj de papel ♦ vt tapizar (MEX), empapelar (LAm exc MEX, SP); ~**s** npl (also: identity ~s) papeles mpl, documentos mpl ◻ **paperback** n libro en rústica ◻ **paper bag** n bolsa de papel ◻ **paper clip** n clip m ◻ **paper hankie** (BRIT) n pañuelo desechable or de papel ◻ **paperweight** n pisapapeles m inv ◻ **paperwork** n papeleo

paprika [pæ'priːkə] n pimentón m, paprika

pap smear ['pæpsmɪər] (US) n Papanicolau m (LAm), citología (SP)

par [pɑːr] n par f; (GOLF) par m; **to be on a ~ with** estar a la par con

parachute ['pærəʃuːt] n paracaídas m inv

parade [pə'reɪd] n desfile m ♦ vt (show) hacer alarde de ♦ vi desfilar; (MIL) pasar revista

paradise ['pærədaɪs] n paraíso

paradox ['pærədɑːks] n paradoja ◻ **paradoxically** [pærə'dɑːksɪkli] adv paradójicamente

paraffin ['pærəfɪn] (BRIT) n (also: ~ oil) parafina

paragon ['pærəgɑːn] n modelo

paragraph ['pærəgræf] n párrafo

parallel ['pærəlel] adj en paralelo; (fig) semejante ♦ n (line) paralela; (fig, GEO) paralelo

paralyse ['pærəlaɪz] (BRIT) vt = **paralyze**

paralysis [pə'rælɪsɪs] n parálisis f inv

paralyze ['pærəlaɪz] (US) vt paralizar

paramedic [pærə'medɪk] n auxiliar mf sanitario(-a), paramédico(-a)

paramount ['pærəmaʊnt] adj: **of ~ importance** de suma importancia

paranoid ['pærənɔɪd] adj (person, feeling) paranoico

paraphernalia [pærəfər'neɪljə] n parafernalia; (gear) avíos mpl

parasite ['pærəsaɪt] n parásito(-a)

parasol ['pærəsɑːl] n parasol m, sombrilla

paratrooper ['pærətru:pər] n paracaidista mf

parcel ['pɑːrsəl] n paquete m ♦ vt (also: ~ up) empaquetar, embalar

parched [pɑːrtʃt] adj (person) muerto de sed

parchment ['pɑːrtʃmənt] n pergamino

pardon ['pɑːrdn] n (LAW) indulto ♦ vt perdonar; ~ me!, I beg your ~! (I'm sorry!) ¡perdone usted!; (I beg your) ~?, ~ me? (BRIT: what did you say?) ¿cómo?

parent ['pɛrənt] n (mother) madre f; (father) padre m; ~s npl padres mpl □ **parental** [pə'rɛntl] adj paternal/maternal

⚠ Be careful not to translate **parent** by the Spanish word **pariente**.

parenthesis [pə'rɛnθɪsɪs] (pl **parentheses** [pə'rɛnθɪsiːz]) n paréntesis m inv

Paris ['pærɪs] n París

parish ['pærɪʃ] n parroquia

Parisian [pə'riːʒən] adj, n parisino(-a), parisiense mf

park [pɑːrk] n parque m ♦ vt estacionar (LAm), aparcar (SP) ♦ vi estacionarse (LAm), aparcar (SP)

parking ['pɑːrkɪŋ] n estacionamiento (LAm), aparcamiento (SP); **"no ~"** "prohibido estacionarse (LAm) or aparcar (SP)" □ **parking lot** n (US) estacionamiento (LAm), aparcamiento (SP) □ **parking meter** n parquímetro □ **parking ticket** n multa por estacionamiento (indebido) (LAm) or de aparcamiento (SP)

parkway (US) ['pɑːrkweɪ] n avenida (ajardinada)

parliament ['pɑːrləmənt] n parlamento; (Spanish) Cortes fpl □ **parliamentary** [pɑːrlə'mɛntəri] adj parlamentario

parlor (US) ['pɑːrlər] (BRIT **parlour**) n sala (de estar)

parochial [pə'roukiəl] (pej) adj de miras estrechas

parole [pə'roul] n: **on ~** en libertad condicional

parquet [pɑːr'keɪ] n: **~ floor(ing)** parquet m, parqué m

parrot ['pærət] n loro, papagayo

parry ['pæri] vt parar

parsley ['pɑːrsli] n perejil m

parsnip ['pɑːrsnɪp] n chirivía, pastinaca

parson ['pɑːrsən] n cura m

part [pɑːrt] n (gen, MUS) parte f; (bit) trozo; (of machine) pieza; (THEATER etc) papel m; (of serial) entrega; (US: in hair) raya ♦ adv = **partly** ♦ vt separar ♦ vi (people) separarse; (crowd)

apartarse; **to take ~ in** tomar parte or participar en; **to take sb's ~** defender a algn; **for my ~** por mi parte; **for the most ~** en su mayor parte; **to ~ one's hair** hacerse la raya; **to take sth in good ~** (BRIT) tomar algo en buena parte ▸ **part with** vt fus desprenderse de; (money) pagar □ **part exchange** (BRIT) n: **in part exchange** como parte del pago

partial ['pɑːrʃəl] adj parcial; **to be ~ to** tener debilidad por

participant [pɑːr'tɪsɪpənt] n (in competition) concursante mf; (in campaign etc) participante mf

participate [pɑːr'tɪsɪpeɪt] vi: **to ~ in** participar en □ **participation** [pɑːr,tɪsɪ'peɪʃən] n participación f

participle ['pɑːrtɪsɪpəl] n participio

particle ['pɑːrtɪkəl] n partícula; (of dust) grano

particular [pər'tɪkjələr] adj (special) particular; (concrete) concreto; (given) determinado; (fussy) quisquilloso; (demanding) exigente; **in ~** en particular □ **particularly** adv (in particular) sobre todo; (difficult, good etc) especialmente □ **particulars** npl (information) datos mpl; (details) pormenores mpl

parting ['pɑːrtɪŋ] n (act) separación f; (farewell) despedida; (BRIT: in hair) raya ♦ adj de despedida

partisan ['pɑːrtɪzən] adj partidista ♦ n partidario(-a)

partition [pɑːr'tɪʃən] n (POL) división f; (wall) tabique m

partly ['pɑːrtli] adv en parte

partner ['pɑːrtnər] n (COMM) socio(-a); (SPORT, at dance) pareja; (spouse) cónyuge mf; (lover) pareja □ **partnership** n asociación f; (COMM) sociedad f

partridge ['pɑːrtrɪdʒ] n perdiz f

part-time adj, adv a tiempo parcial

party ['pɑːrti] n (POL) partido; (celebration) fiesta; (group) grupo; (LAW) parte f interesada ♦ cpd (POL) de partido □ **party dress** n vestido de fiesta

pass [pæs] vt (time, object) pasar; (place) pasar por; (overtake) adelantar, rebasar (MEX); (exam) aprobar; (approve) aprobar ♦ vi pasar; (SCOL) aprobar, ser aprobado ♦ n (permit) permiso; (membership card) credencial f (LAm), pase m (SP); (in mountains) puerto, desfiladero; (SPORT) pase m; (BRIT SCOL: also: ~ **mark**): **to get a ~ in** aprobar en; **to ~ sth through sth** pasar algo por algo; **to make a ~ at sb** (inf) hacer proposiciones a algn ▸ **pass**

away vi fallecer ▶ **pass by** vi pasar ♦ vt (ignore) pasar por alto ▶ **pass for** vt fus pasar por ▶ **pass on** vt transmitir ▶ **pass out** vi desmayarse ▶ **pass up** vt (opportunity) renunciar a ❑ **passable** adj (road) transitable; (tolerable) pasable

passage ['pæsɪdʒ] n (also: ~**way**) pasillo; (act of passing) tránsito; (fare, in book) pasaje m; (by boat) travesía; (ANAT) tubo

passbook ['pæsbʊk] n libreta or cartilla de ahorros

passenger ['pæsɪndʒər] n pasajero(-a), viajero(-a)

passer-by [,pæsər'baɪ] n transeúnte mf

passing ['pæsɪŋ] adj pasajero ♦ n (US AUT) adelantamiento m; **in ~** de paso ❑ **passing place** (BRIT) n (AUT) apartadero

passion ['pæʃən] n pasión f ❑ **passionate** adj apasionado

passive ['pæsɪv] adj (gen, also LING) pasivo ❑ **passive smoking** n el fumar pasivamente

Passover ['pæsouvər] n Pascua (judía)

passport ['pæspɔːrt] n pasaporte m ❑ **passport control** n control m de pasaportes ❑ **passport office** n oficina de pasaportes

password ['pæswɜːrd] n contraseña

past [pæst] prep (in front of) por delante de; (further than) más allá de; (later than) después de ♦ adj pasado; (president etc) antiguo ♦ n (time) pasado; (of person) antecedentes mpl; **he's ~ forty** tiene más de cuarenta años; **ten/quarter ~ eight** las ocho y diez/cuarto; **for the ~ few/3 days** durante los últimos días/últimos 3 días; **to run ~ sb** pasar a algn corriendo

pasta ['pɑːstə] n pasta

paste [peɪst] n pasta; (glue) engrudo ♦ vt pegar

pasteurized ['pæstʃəraɪzd] adj pasteurizado

pastille [,pæs'tiːl] n pastilla

pastime ['pæstaɪm] n pasatiempo

pastry ['peɪstri] n (dough) masa; (cake) pastel m

pasture ['pæstʃər] n pasto

pasty¹ ['pæsti] n empanada

pasty² ['peɪsti] adj (complexion) pálido

pat [pæt] vt dar una palmadita a; (dog etc) acariciar

patch [pætʃ] n (of material, eye patch) parche m; (mended part) remiendo; (of land) terreno ♦ vt remendar; **(to go through) a bad ~** (BRIT) (pasar por) una mala racha ▶ **patch up** vt reparar; **to patch things up (with sb)** hacer

las paces (con algn) ❑ **patchwork** n labor f de retazos, patchwork m ❑ **patchy** adj desigual

pâté ['pɑːteɪ] n paté m

patent ['pætnt] n patente f ♦ vt patentar ♦ adj patente, evidente ❑ **patent leather** n charol m

paternal [pə'tɜːrnl] adj paternal; (relation) paterno

path [pæθ] n camino, sendero; (trail, track) pista; (of missile) trayectoria

pathetic [pə'θetɪk] adj patético, penoso; (very bad) malísimo

pathological [pæθə'lɑːdʒɪkəl] adj patológico

pathway ['pæθweɪ] n sendero, vereda

patience ['peɪʃəns] n paciencia; (BRIT CARDS) solitario

patient ['peɪʃənt] n paciente mf ♦ adj paciente

patio ['pætiou] n patio

patriot ['peɪtriət] n patriota mf ❑ **patriotic** [peɪtri'ɑːtɪk] adj patriótico

patrol [pə'troul] n patrulla ♦ vt patrullar por ❑ **patrol car** n carro (LAm) or coche m (SP) patrulla ❑ **patrolman** (US) n policía m

patron ['peɪtrən] n (in store) cliente mf; (of charity) patrocinador(a) m/f; **~ of the arts** mecenas mf inv ❑ **patronize** vt (store) ser cliente de; (artist etc) proteger; (look down on) condescender con ❑ **patron saint** n santo(-a) patrón(-ona)

patter ['pætər] n golpeteo; (sales talk) labia ♦ vi (rain) tamborilear

pattern ['pætərn] n (SEWING) patrón m; (design) motivo, diseño

patty ['pæti] (US) n empanada

pauper ['pɔːpər] n pobre mf

pause [pɔːz] n pausa ♦ vi hacer una pausa

pave [peɪv] vt pavimentar; **to ~ the way for** preparar el terreno para

pavement ['peɪvmənt] n pavimento; (BRIT) banqueta (MEX), acera (LAm exc MEX, SP), andén m (CAm), vereda (SC)

pavilion [pə'vɪljən] n pabellón m

paving ['peɪvɪŋ] n pavimento, enlosado ❑ **paving stone** n losa

paw [pɔː] n pata

pawn [pɔːn] n (CHESS) peón m; (fig) instrumento ♦ vt empeñar ❑ **pawn broker** n prestamista mf, empeñero(-a) (MEX) ❑ **pawnshop** n monte m de piedad, casa de empeño(s)

pay [peɪ] (pt, pp **paid**) n (salary etc) sueldo, salario ♦ vt pagar ♦ vi (be profitable) rendir; **to ~ attention (to)** prestar atención (a); **to ~ sb a visit** hacer una visita a algn; **to ~ one's respects to sb** presentar sus respetos a algn ▶ **pay back** vt (money) reembolsar; (person) pagar ▶ **pay for** vt fus pagar ▶ **pay in** (BRIT) vt ingresar ▶ **pay off** vt saldar ♦ vi (scheme, decision) dar resultado ▶ **pay up** vt pagar (de mala gana) ❑ **payable** adj: **payable to** pagadero a ❑ **paycheck** (US) (BRIT **pay cheque**) n cheque m de sueldo ❑ **pay day** n día m de pago ❑ **payee** n portador(a) m/f ❑ **pay envelope** (US) n sobre m de pago ❑ **payment** n pago; **monthly payment** mensualidad f ❑ **pay packet** (BRIT) n = **pay envelope** ❑ **pay phone** n teléfono público ❑ **payroll** n nómina ❑ **pay slip** (BRIT) n recibo de sueldo ❑ **pay television** n televisión f de pago

PC n abbr = **personal computer**; (BRIT) = **police constable** ♦ adv abbr = **politically correct**

p.c. abbr = **per cent**

pea [piː] n chícharo (MEX, CAm), arveja (LAm), guisante m (SP)

peace [piːs] n paz f; (calm) paz f, tranquilidad f ❑ **peaceful** adj (gentle) pacífico; (calm) tranquilo, apacible

peach [piːtʃ] n durazno (LAm), melocotón m (SP)

peacock ['piːkɑːk] n pavo real

peak [piːk] n (of mountain) cumbre f, cima; (of cap) visera; (fig) apogeo, cumbre f ❑ **peak hours** npl horas fpl pico (LAm) or punta (SP) ❑ **peak period** n = **peak hours**

peal [piːl] n (of bells) repique m; **~ of laughter** carcajada

peanut ['piːnʌt] n cacahuate m (MEX), maní m (LAm exc MEX), cacahuete m (SP) ❑ **peanut butter** n mantequilla de cacahuate (MEX) or maní (LAm exc MEX) or cacahuete (SP)

pear [peər] n pera

pearl [pɜːrl] n perla

peasant ['pezənt] n campesino(-a)

peat [piːt] n turba

pebble ['pebəl] n guijarro

peck [pek] vt (also: **~ at**) picotear ♦ n picotazo; (kiss) besito ❑ **pecking order** n orden m de jerarquía ❑ **peckish** (BRIT: inf) adj: **I feel peckish** tengo un poco de hambre

peculiar [prˈkjuːlɪər] adj (odd) extraño, raro; (typical) propio, característico; **~ to** propio de

pedal ['pedl] n pedal m ♦ vi pedalear

pedantic [prˈdæntɪk] adj pedante

peddler ['pedlər] n: **drug ~** traficante mf; camello

pedestrian [prˈdestrɪən] n peatón(-ona) m/f ♦ adj pedestre ❑ **pedestrian crossing** (BRIT) n paso de peatones ❑ **pedestrian mall** (US) (BRIT **pedestrian precinct**) n zona peatonal

pediatrician (US) [ˌpiːdiəˈtrɪʃən] (BRIT **paediatrician**) n pediatra mf

pediatrics (US) [ˌpiːdiˈætrɪks] (BRIT **paediatrics**) n pediatría

pedigree ['pedɪɡriː] n (lineage) genealogía; (of animal) raza, pedigrí m ♦ cpd (animal) de raza

pee [piː] (inf) vi hacer pis or pipí

peek [piːk] vi (glance) echar una ojeada

peel [piːl] n piel f; (of orange, lemon) cáscara; (: removed) peladuras fpl ♦ vt pelar ♦ vi (paint etc) desconcharse; (wallpaper) despegarse; (skin) pelarse

peep [piːp] n (look) mirada furtiva; (of bird) pío ♦ vi (look) mirar furtivamente ▶ **peep out** vi salir (un poco) ❑ **peephole** n mirilla

peer [pɪər] vi: **to ~ at** escudriñar ♦ n (noble) par m; (equal) igual m; (contemporary) contemporáneo(-a) ❑ **peerage** n nobleza

peeved [piːvd] adj enojado

peg [peɡ] n (for coat etc) gancho, colgadero; (BRIT: also: **clothes ~**) pinza

Pekingese, Pekinese [ˌpiːkɪˈniːz] n (dog) pequinés(-esa) m/f

pelican ['pelɪkən] n pelícano ❑ **pelican crossing** (BRIT) n (AUT) paso de peatones (con semáforo)

pellet ['pelɪt] n bolita; (bullet) perdigón m

pelt [pelt] vt: **to ~ sb with sth** arrojar algo a algn ♦ vi (rain) llover a cántaros; (inf: run) correr ♦ n pellejo

pen [pen] n (fountain pen) pluma-fuente f (LAm), (pluma) estilográfica (SP); (ballpoint pen) bolígrafo, birome f (RPl); (for sheep) redil m

penal ['piːnl] adj penal ❑ **penalize** vt castigar

penalty ['penlti] n (gen) pena; (fine) multa ❑ **penalty (kick)** n (FOOTBALL) penalty m; (RUGBY) golpe m de castigo

penance ['penəns] n penitencia

pence [pens] (BRIT) npl of **penny**

pencil ['pensəl] n lápiz m ❑ **pencil case** n estuche m ❑ **pencil sharpener** n sacapuntas m inv

pendant ['pendənt] n colgante m

pending ['pendɪŋ] prep antes de ♦ adj pendiente

pendulum ['pendʒuləm] n péndulo

penetrate ['penitreit] vt penetrar

pen friend (BRIT) n amigo(-a) por correspondencia

penguin ['peŋgwin] n pingüino

penicillin [ˌpenɪ'sɪlɪn] n penicilina

peninsula [pə'nɪnsjulə] n península

penis ['piːnɪs] n pene m

penitentiary [ˌpenɪ'tenʃərɪ] (US) n cárcel f, prisión f

penknife ['pennaɪf] n navaja

pen name n seudónimo

penniless ['penɪlɪs] adj sin dinero

penny ['penɪ] (pl **pennies**, pl **pence** (BRIT)) n (US) centavo; (BRIT) penique m

pen pal n amigo(-a) por correspondencia

pension ['penʃən] n jubilación f
□ **pensioner** (BRIT) n jubilado(-a)
□ **pension fund** n fondo de pensiones

pentagon ['pentəgən] n: **the P~** (US POL) el Pentágono

> **PENTAGON**
>
> Se conoce como **Pentagon** al edificio de planta pentagonal que acoge las dependencias del Ministerio de Defensa estadounidense (**Department of Defense**) en Arlington, Virginia. En lenguaje periodístico se aplica también a la dirección militar del país.

Pentecost ['pentɪkɒst] n Pentecostés m

penthouse ['penthaus] n penthouse m, ático de lujo

pent-up ['pentʌp] adj reprimido

people ['piːpəl] npl gente f; (citizens) pueblo, ciudadanos mpl; (POL): **the ~** el pueblo ♦ n (nation, race) pueblo, nación f; **several ~ came** vinieron varias personas; **~ say that ...** dice la gente que ...

pep [pep] (inf): **~ up** vt animar

pepper ['pepər] n (spice) pimienta; (vegetable) pimiento ♦ vt: **to ~ with** (fig) salpicar de
□ **peppermint** n (sweet) caramelo de menta

pep talk n: **to give sb a ~** darle a algn unas palabras de ánimo

per [pɜːr] prep por; **~ person** por persona; **~ day/annum** al día/año □ **per capita** adj, adv per cápita

perceive [pər'siːv] vt percibir; (realize) darse cuenta de

per cent n por ciento

percentage [pər'sentɪdʒ] n porcentaje m

perception [pər'sepʃən] n percepción f; (insight) perspicacia; (opinion etc) opinión f
□ **perceptive** adj perspicaz

perch [pɜːtʃ] n (fish) perca; (for bird) percha ♦ vi: **to ~ (on)** (bird) posarse (en); (person) encaramarse (en)

percolator ['pɜːkəleɪtər] n (also: **coffee ~**) cafetera de filtro

perennial [pə'renɪəl] adj perenne

perfect [adj, n 'pɜːfɪkt, vb pər'fekt] adj perfecto ♦ n (also: **~ tense**) perfecto ♦ vt perfeccionar □ **perfectly** adv perfectamente

perforate ['pɜːfəreɪt] vt perforar

perform [pər'fɔːm] vt (carry out) realizar, llevar a cabo; (THEATER) representar; (piece of music) interpretar ♦ vi (well, badly) funcionar
□ **performance** n (of a play) representación f; (of actor, athlete etc) actuación f; (of car, engine, company) rendimiento; (of economy) resultados mpl □ **performer** n (actor) actor m, actriz f

perfume ['pɜːrfjuːm] n perfume m

perhaps [pər'hæps] adv quizá(s), tal vez

peril ['perɪl] n peligro, riesgo

perimeter [pə'rɪmɪtər] n perímetro

period ['pɪərɪəd] n período; (SCOL) clase f; (US: punctuation) punto; (MED) regla, período ♦ adj (costume, furniture) de época □ **periodic(al)** [pɪrɪ'ɑːdɪk(əl)] adj periódico □ **periodical** [pɪrɪ'ɑːdɪkəl] n periódico □ **periodically** adv de vez en cuando, cada cierto tiempo

peripheral [pə'rɪfərəl] adj periférico ♦ n (COMPUT) periférico, unidad f periférica

perish ['perɪʃ] vi perecer; (decay) echarse a perder □ **perishable** adj perecedero

perjury ['pɜːdʒərɪ] n (LAW) perjurio

perk [pɜːk] n extra m ▶ **perk up** vi (cheer up) animarse

perm [pɜːm] (BRIT) n permanente f

permanent ['pɜːrmənənt] adj permanente ♦ n (US) permanente f

permeate ['pɜːrmɪeɪt] vi penetrar, extenderse ♦ vt penetrar, impregnar

permissible [pər'mɪsɪbəl] adj permisible, lícito

permission [pər'mɪʃən] n permiso

permissive [pər'mɪsɪv] adj permisivo

permit [n 'pɜːrmɪt, vt pər'mɪt] n permiso; licencia ♦ vt permitir

pernickety [pər'nɪkɪtɪ] (BRIT) adj = **persnickety**

perplex [pər'pleks] vt dejar perplejo

persecute ['pɜːrsɪkjuːt] vt perseguir

persevere [ˌpɜːrsɪ'vɪər] vi persistir

Persian ['pɜːrʒən] adj, n persa mf; **the ~ Gulf** el Golfo Pérsico

persist [pər'sɪst] vi: **to ~ (in doing sth)** persistir (en hacer algo) ❑ **persistence** n persistencia ❑ **persistent** adj persistente; (determined) porfiado

persnickety [pər'snɪkɪti] (US: inf) adj quisquilloso

person ['pɜːrsən] n persona; **in ~** en persona ❑ **personal** adj personal; individual; (visit) en persona ❑ **personal assistant** n ayudante mf personal ❑ **personal column** (BRIT) n (sección f de) anuncios mpl personales ❑ **personal computer** n computadora (LAm) or ordenador m (SP) personal ❑ **personality** [ˌpɜːrsə'nælɪti] n personalidad f ❑ **personally** adv personalmente; (in person) en persona; **to take sth personally** tomarse algo a mal ❑ **personal organizer** n agenda ❑ **personals** n (sección f de) anuncios mpl personales ❑ **personal stereo** n Walkman® m ❑ **personify** [pər'sɑːnɪfaɪ] vt encarnar

personnel [ˌpɜːrsə'nel] n personal m

perspective [pər'spektɪv] n perspectiva

Perspex® ['pɜːrspeks] (BRIT) n Plexiglás® m

perspiration [ˌpɜːrspɪ'reɪʃən] n transpiración f

persuade [pər'sweɪd] vt: **to ~ sb to do sth** convencer or persuadir a algn para que haga algo

Peru [pə'ruː] n el Perú ❑ **Peruvian** adj, n peruano(-a)

perverse [pər'vɜːrs] adj perverso; (wayward) travieso

pervert [n 'pɜːrvərt, vb pər'vɜːrt] n pervertido(-a) ♦ vt pervertir; (truth, sb's words) tergiversar

pessimist ['pesɪmɪst] n pesimista mf ❑ **pessimistic** [ˌpesɪ'mɪstɪk] adj pesimista

pest [pest] n (insect) plaga; (fig) pesado(-a)

pester ['pestər] vt molestar, acosar

pesticide ['pestɪsaɪd] n pesticida m

pet [pet] n animal m (doméstico) ♦ cpd favorito ♦ vt acariciar; **teacher's ~** favorito(-a) (del profesor); **~ hate** manía

petal ['petl] n pétalo

peter ['piːtər] n: **to ~ out** vi agotarse, acabarse

petite [pə'tiːt] adj chiquita

petition [pə'tɪʃən] n petición f

petrified ['petrɪfaɪd] adj horrorizado

petrol ['petrəl] (BRIT) n gasolina ❑ **petrol can** (BRIT) n lata or bidón m de gasolina

petroleum [pə'trouliəm] n petróleo

petrol: ❑ **petrol pump** (BRIT) n (in garage) surtidor m de gasolina ❑ **petrol station** (BRIT) n gasolinera ❑ **petrol tank** (BRIT) n depósito or tanque m (de gasolina)

petticoat ['petikout] n enaguas fpl

petty ['peti] adj (mean) mezquino; (unimportant) insignificante ❑ **petty cash** n dinero para gastos menores ❑ **petty officer** n suboficial mf de marina

petulant ['petʃələnt] adj malhumorado

pew [pjuː] n banco

pewter ['pjuːtər] n peltre m

phantom ['fæntəm] n fantasma m

pharmacist ['fɑːrməsɪst] n farmacéutico(-a)

pharmacy ['fɑːrməsi] n farmacia

phase [feɪz] n fase f ♦ vt: **to ~ sth in/out** introducir/retirar algo por etapas

Ph.D. abbr = **Doctor of Philosophy**

pheasant ['fezənt] n faisán m

phenomenon [fə'nɑːmɪnɑːn] (pl **phenomena**) n fenómeno

philanthropist [fɪ'lænθrəpɪst] n filántropo(-a)

Philippines ['fɪlɪpiːnz] npl: **the ~** las Filipinas

philosopher [fɪ'lɑːsəfər] n filósofo(-a)

philosophy [fɪ'lɑːsəfi] n filosofía

phobia ['foubiə] n fobia

phone [foun] n teléfono ♦ vt telefonear, llamar por teléfono; **to be on the ~** (BRIT) tener teléfono; (be calling) estar hablando por teléfono ▸ **phone back** vt, vi volver a llamar ▸ **phone up** vt, vi llamar por teléfono ❑ **phone book** n directorio (telefónico) (MEX), guía telefónica (LAm exc MEX, SP) ❑ **phone booth** (US) n cabina telefónica ❑ **phone box** (BRIT) n = **phone booth** ❑ **phone call** n llamada telefónica ❑ **phonecard** n tarjeta telefónica ❑ **phone-in** (BRIT) n (RADIO, TV) programa m de participación (telefónica)

phonetics [fə'netɪks] n fonética

phoney ['founi] adj falso

photo ['foutou] n foto f ❑ **photocopier** n fotocopiadora ❑ **photocopy** n fotocopia ♦ vt fotocopiar

photograph ['foutəɡræf] n fotografía ♦ vt fotografiar ❑ **photographer** [fə'tɑːɡrəfər] n fotógrafo ❑ **photography** [fə'tɑːɡrəfi] n fotografía

phrase [freɪz] n frase f ♦ vt expresar ❑ **phrase book** n guía or manual m de conversación

physical ['fɪzɪkəl] adj físico ❑ **physical education** n educación f física ❑ **physically** adv físicamente

physician [fɪˈzɪʃən] n médico(-a)
physicist [ˈfɪzɪsɪst] n físico(-a)
physics [ˈfɪzɪks] n física
physiotherapy [ˌfɪziouˈθɛrəpi] n fisioterapia
physique [fɪˈziːk] n físico
pianist [ˈpiːənɪst] n pianista mf
piano [piˈænou] n piano
pick [pɪk] n (tool: also: **~-ax**) pico, piqueta; (US: plectrum) púa ♦ vt (select) elegir, escoger; (gather) recoger; (remove, take out) sacar, quitar; (lock) forzar; **take your ~** escoja lo que quiera; **the ~ of** lo mejor de; **to ~ one's nose/ teeth** hurgarse la nariz/limpiarse los dientes; **to ~ a quarrel with sb** meterse con algn ▶ **pick at** vt fus: **to pick at one's food** comer con poco apetito ▶ **pick on** vt fus (person) meterse con ▶ **pick out** vt escoger; (distinguish) identificar ▶ **pick up** vi (improve: sales) ir mejor; (: patient) reponerse ♦ vt recoger; (learn) aprender; (POLICE: arrest) detener; (person: for sex) ligar; (RADIO) captar; **to pick up speed** acelerarse; **to pick o.s. up** levantarse
pickax (US) [ˈpɪkæks] (BRIT **pickaxe**) n pico, piqueta
picket [ˈpɪkɪt] n piquete m ♦ vt piquetear (LAm)
pickle [ˈpɪkəl] n (also: **~s: as condiment**) escabeche m; (fig: mess) apuro ♦ vt encurtir
pickpocket [ˈpɪkpɔkɪt] n carterista mf
pickup [ˈpɪkʌp] n (small truck) furgoneta
picnic [ˈpɪknɪk] n picnic m ♦ vi ir de picnic
picture [ˈpɪktʃər] n cuadro; (painting) pintura; (photograph) fotografía; (TV) imagen f; (movie) película; (fig: description) descripción f; (: situation) situación f ♦ vt (imagine) imaginar; **the ~s** npl (BRIT) el cine □ **picture book** n libro ilustrado
picturesque [ˌpɪktʃəˈresk] adj pintoresco
pie [paɪ] n pastel m; (open) tarta; (small: of meat) empanada
piece [piːs] n pedazo, trozo; (of cake) trozo; (item): **a ~ of clothing/furniture/advice** una prenda (de vestir)/un mueble/un consejo ♦ vt: **to ~ together** juntar; (TECH) armar; **to take to ~s** desmontar □ **piecemeal** adv poco a poco □ **piecework** n trabajo a destajo
pie chart n gráfico de sectores or tarta
pier [pɪər] n muelle m, embarcadero
pierce [pɪərs] vt perforar
piercing [ˈpɪərsɪŋ] adj penetrante

pig [pɪg] n cerdo, chancho (LAm exc MEX); (pej: unkind person) asqueroso; (: greedy person) glotón(-ona) m/f
pigeon [ˈpɪdʒən] n paloma; (as food) pichón m □ **pigeonhole** n casilla
piggy bank [ˈpɪgibæŋk] n alcancía (LAm) or hucha (SP) (en forma de cerdito)
pig: □ **pigheaded** adj terco, testarudo □ **piglet** n cochinillo □ **pigpen** (US) n pocilga ▶ **pigskin** n piel f de cerdo □ **pigsty** (BRIT) n = **pigpen** □ **pigtail** n (girl's) trenza; (Chinese) coleta
pike [paɪk] n (fish) lucio
pilchard [ˈpɪltʃərd] n sardina
pile [paɪl] n montón m; (of carpet, cloth) pelo ♦ vt (also: **~ up**) amontonar; (fig) acumular ♦ vi (also: **~ up**) amontonarse; acumularse ▶ **pile into** vt fus (car) meterse en □ **piles** npl (MED) almorranas fpl, hemorroides mpl □ **pileup** n (AUT) accidente m múltiple or en cadena
pilfering [ˈpɪlfərɪŋ] n ratería
pilgrim [ˈpɪlgrɪm] n peregrino(-a) □ **pilgrimage** n peregrinación f, romería
pill [pɪl] n píldora; **the ~** la píldora
pillage [ˈpɪlɪdʒ] vt pillar, saquear
pillar [ˈpɪlər] n pilar m □ **pillar box** (BRIT) n buzón m
pillion [ˈpɪljən] n (of motorcycle) asiento trasero
pillow [ˈpɪlou] n almohada □ **pillowcase** n funda
pilot [ˈpaɪlət] n piloto ♦ cpd (scheme etc) piloto ♦ vt pilotar □ **pilot light** n piloto
pimp [pɪmp] n proxeneta m, padrote m (MEX), cafishio (SC)
pimple [ˈpɪmpəl] n grano
PIN [pɪn] n abbr (= personal identification number) PIN m, número de identificación personal
pin [pɪn] n alfiler m ♦ vt prender (con alfiler); **~s and needles** hormigueo; **to ~ sb down** (fig) hacer que algn concrete; **you can't ~ the blame on me** (fig) no podéis hacer que cargue con la culpa
pinafore [ˈpɪnəfɔːr] n (BRIT: also: **~ dress**) jumper m (LAm), pichi m (SP)
pinball [ˈpɪnbɔːl] n flipper m, pinball m
pincers [ˈpɪnsərz] npl pinzas fpl, tenazas fpl
pinch [pɪntʃ] n (of salt etc) pizca ♦ vt pellizcar; (inf: steal) birlar; **at a ~** en caso de apuro
pincushion [ˈpɪnkuʃən] n alfiletero, acerico
pine [paɪn] n (also: **~ tree, ~ wood**) pino ♦ vi: **to ~ for** suspirar por ▶ **pine away** vi morirse de pena

pineapple ['paɪnæpəl] n piña, ananá m (RPl)

ping [pɪŋ] n (noise) sonido metálico ❑ **ping-pong®** n ping-pong® m

pink [pɪŋk] adj rosado, (color de) rosa ♦ n (color) rosa; (BOT) clavel m, clavellina

pinpoint ['pɪn‚pɔɪnt] vt precisar

pint [paɪnt] n pinta (US = 0,47 litros, BRIT = 0,57 litros); (BRIT: inf: of beer) pinta

pin-up n póster m (de chicas eróticas)

pioneer [paɪə'nɪər] n pionero(-a)

pious ['paɪəs] adj piadoso, devoto

pip [pɪp] n (seed) pepita; **the ~s** (BRIT) la señal

pipe [paɪp] n tubo, caño; (for smoking) pipa ♦ vt conducir en cañerías; **~s** npl (gen) cañería; (also: **bagpipes**) gaita ❑ **pipe cleaner** n limpiapipas m inv ❑ **pipe dream** n sueño imposible ❑ **pipeline** n (for oil) oleoducto; (for gas) gasoducto ❑ **piper** n gaitero(-a)

piping ['paɪpɪŋ] adv: **to be ~ hot** estar que quema

piquant ['pi:kənt] adj picante; (fig) agudo

pique [pi:k] n pique m, resentimiento

pirate ['paɪrət] n pirata mf ♦ vt (cassette, book) piratear ❑ **pirate radio** (BRIT) n emisora pirata

Pisces ['paɪsi:z] n Piscis m

piss [pɪs] (inf!) vi mear ❑ **pissed** (inf!) adj (angry) cabreado; (BRIT: drunk) borracho

pistol ['pɪstl] n pistola

piston ['pɪstən] n pistón m, émbolo

pit [pɪt] n hoyo; (US: in fruit) pepita; (also: **coal ~**) mina; (in garage) foso de inspección; (BRIT: also: **orchestra ~**) platea ♦ vt: **to ~ one's wits against sb** medir fuerzas con algn; **~s** npl (AUT) box m

pitch [pɪtʃ] n (MUS) tono; (fig) punto; (tar) brea; (BRIT SPORT) campo, terreno ♦ vt (throw) arrojar, lanzar ♦ vi (fall) caer(se); **to ~ a tent** montar una tienda (de campaña) ❑ **pitch-black** adj oscuro or negro como boca de lobo ❑ **pitched battle** n batalla campal

pitcher ['pɪtʃər] n (US: jar) jarra; (BASEBALL) pítcher mf, lanzador(a) m/f

pitfall ['pɪtfɔ:l] n riesgo

pith [pɪθ] n (of orange) médula

pithy ['pɪθɪ] adj (fig) jugoso

pitiful ['pɪtɪfəl] adj (touching) lastimoso, conmovedor(a)

pitiless ['pɪtɪlɪs] adj despiadado

pittance ['pɪtns] n miseria

pity ['pɪtɪ] n compasión f, piedad f ♦ vt compadecer (se de); **what a ~!** ¡qué pena!

pizza ['pi:tsə] n pizza

placard ['plækərd] n letrero; (in march etc) pancarta

placate ['pleɪkeɪt] vt apaciguar

place [pleɪs] n lugar m, sitio; (seat) asiento; (position) puesto; (home): **at/to his ~** en/a su casa; (role: in society etc) papel m ♦ vt (object) poner, colocar; (identify) reconocer; (in race, exam) colocarse; **to take ~** tener lugar; **out of ~** (not suitable) fuera de lugar; **in the first ~** en primer lugar; **to change ~s with sb** cambiarse de sitio con algn; **~ of birth** lugar m de nacimiento ❑ **place mat** n mantel m individual

placid ['plæsɪd] adj apacible

plague [pleɪg] n plaga; (MED) peste f ♦ vt (fig) acosar, atormentar

plaice [pleɪs] n inv platija

plaid [plæd] n (material) tartán m

plain [pleɪn] adj (unpatterned) liso; (clear) claro, evidente; (simple) sencillo; (not handsome) poco atractivo ♦ adv claramente ♦ n llano, llanura ❑ **plain chocolate** (BRIT) n chocolate m amargo ❑ **plain-clothes** adj (police) vestido de paisano ❑ **plainly** adv claramente

plaintiff ['pleɪntɪf] n demandante mf

plait [plæt] (BRIT) n trenza

plan [plæn] n (drawing) plano; (scheme) plan m, proyecto ♦ vt proyectar, planificar ♦ vi hacer proyectos; **to ~ to do** pensar hacer

plane [pleɪn] n (AVIAT) avión m; (MATH, fig) plano; (also: **~ tree**) plátano; (tool) cepillo

planet ['plænɪt] n planeta m

plank [plæŋk] n tabla

planner ['plænər] n planificador(a) m/f

planning ['plænɪŋ] n planificación f; **family ~** planificación familiar ❑ **planning permission** n permiso de obras

plant [plænt] n planta; (machinery) maquinaria; (factory) fábrica ♦ vt plantar; (field) sembrar; (bomb) colocar

plaster ['plæstər] n (for walls) yeso; (also: **~ of Paris**) yeso (mate); (BRIT: also: **sticking ~**) curita (LAm), tirita (SP) ♦ vt enyesar; (cover): **to ~ with** llenar or cubrir de ❑ **plastered** (inf) adj borracho ❑ **plasterer** n yesero

plastic ['plæstɪk] n plástico ♦ adj de plástico ❑ **plastic bag** n bolsa de plástico

Plasticine® ['plæstɪsi:n] (BRIT) n plastilina®

plastic surgery n cirugía plástica

plate [pleɪt] n (dish) plato; (metal, in book) lámina; (dental plate) dentadura postiza

plateau ['plætou] (pl **~s** or **~x**) n meseta, altiplanicie f

plateaux [plæ'touz] npl of **plateau**

plate glass n vidrio cilindrado
platform ['plætfɔːrm] n (RAIL) andén m; (stage) estrado; (BRIT: on bus) plataforma; (at meeting) tribuna; (POL) programa m (electoral)
platinum ['plætnəm] adj, n platino
platoon [plə'tuːn] n pelotón m
platter ['plætər] n (dish) fuente f; (meal, course) plato
plausible ['plɔːzɪbəl] adj verosímil; (person) convincente
play [pleɪ] n (THEATER) obra, comedia ♦ vt (game) jugar; (compete against) jugar contra; (instrument) tocar; (part: in play etc) hacer el papel de; (tape, record) poner ♦ vi jugar; (band) tocar; (tape, record) sonar; **to ~ safe** ir a lo seguro ► **play down** vt quitar importancia a ► **play up** vi (cause trouble to) dar guerra ❑ **playboy** n playboy m ❑ **player** n jugador(a) m/f; (THEATER) actor (actriz) m/f; (MUS) músico(-a) ❑ **playful** adj juguetón(-ona) ❑ **playground** n (in school) patio de recreo; (in park) columpios mpl ❑ **playgroup** n jardín m de niños (MEX), jardín infantil (LAm exc MEX) or de infantes (RPl), guardería (infantil) (SP) ❑ **playing card** n naipe m, carta ❑ **playing field** n cancha (LAm) or campo (SP) de deportes ❑ **playmate** n compañero(-a) de juegos ❑ **play-off** n (SPORT) (partido de) desempate m ❑ **playpen** n corral m (LAm), parque m (SP) ❑ **plaything** n juguete m ❑ **playtime** n (SCOL) recreo ❑ **playwright** n dramaturgo(-a)
plc (BRIT) abbr (= public limited company) ≈ S.A.
plea [pliː] n súplica, petición f; (LAW) alegato, defensa ❑ **plea bargaining** n (LAW) acuerdo entre fiscal y defensor para agilizar los trámites judiciales
plead [pliːd] vt (LAW): **to ~ sb's case** defender a algn; (give as excuse) poner como pretexto ♦ vi (LAW) declararse; (beg): **to ~ with sb** suplicar or rogar a algn
pleasant ['plɛznt] adj agradable ❑ **pleasantries** npl cortesías fpl
please [pliːz] excl ¡por favor! ♦ vt (give pleasure to) dar gusto a, agradar ♦ vi (think fit): **do as you ~** haz lo que quieras; **~ yourself!** (inf) ¡haz lo que quieras!, ¡como quieras! ❑ **pleased** adj (happy) alegre, contento; **pleased (with)** satisfecho (de); **pleased to meet you** ¡encantado!, ¡tanto gusto! ❑ **pleasing** adj agradable, grato
pleasure ['plɛʒər] n placer m, gusto; **"it's a ~"** "el gusto es mío"
pleat [pliːt] n pliegue m
plectrum ['plɛktrəm] n púa, plectro

pledge [plɛdʒ] n (promise) promesa, voto ♦ vt prometer ❑ **Pledge of Allegiance** (US) n ≈ la jura de bandera

PLEDGE OF ALLEGIANCE

Los niños que asisten a la mayoría de los centros públicos norteamericanos tienen que realizar cada mañana el juramento de fidelidad o **Pledge of Allegiance**. Para ello se ponen en pie y con la mano derecha puesta sobre el pecho miran a la bandera estadounidense, mientras recitan: "Juro fidelidad a la bandera de Estados Unidos de América y a la república que representa, una nación, bajo el poder de Dios, indivisible, con libertad y justicia para todos."

plentiful ['plɛntɪful] adj copioso, abundante
plenty ['plɛntɪ] n: **~ of** mucho(s)/a(s)
pliable ['plaɪəbəl] adj flexible
pliers ['plaɪərz] npl alicates mpl, tenazas fpl
plight [plaɪt] n situación f difícil
plimsolls ['plɪmsəlz] (BRIT) npl zapatillas fpl de deporte
plinth [plɪnθ] n plinto
plod [plɒd] vi caminar con paso pesado; (fig) trabajar laboriosamente
plonk [plɒŋk] (inf) n (BRIT: wine) vino peleón ♦ vt: **to ~ sth down** dejar caer algo
plot [plɒt] n (scheme) complot m, conjura; (of story, play) argumento; (of land) terreno ♦ vt (mark out) trazar; (conspire) tramar, urdir ♦ vi conspirar
plough [plaʊ] (BRIT) n, vt = **plow** ❑ **ploughman's lunch** (BRIT) n comida de pub a base de pan, queso y encurtidos
plow (US) [plaʊ] (BRIT **plough**) n arado ♦ vt (earth) arar; **to ~ money into** invertir dinero en ► **plow through** vt fus (crowd) abrirse paso por la fuerza por
pluck [plʌk] vt (fruit) arrancar; (musical instrument) puntear; (bird) desplumar; (eyebrows) depilar; **to ~ up courage** hacer de tripas corazón
plug [plʌg] n tapón m; (ELEC) enchufe m, clavija; (AUT: also: **spark(ing) ~**) bujía ♦ vt (hole) tapar; (inf: advertise) dar publicidad a ► **plug in** vt (ELEC) enchufar
plum [plʌm] n (fruit) ciruela
plumb [plʌm] vt: **to ~ the depths of** sumergirse en las profundidades de
plumber ['plʌmər] n plomero(-a) (LAm), fontanero(-a) (CAm, SP)
plumbing ['plʌmɪŋ] n (trade) plomería (LAm), fontanería (CAm, SP); (piping) cañería

plummet ['plʌmɪt] vi: **to ~ (down)**
desplomarse

plump [plʌmp] adj rechoncho, rollizo ♦ vi: **to ~ for** (BRIT: inf: choose) optar por ▶ **plump up** vt mullir

plunder ['plʌndər] vt pillar, saquear

plunge [plʌndʒ] n zambullida ♦ vt sumergir, hundir ♦ vi (fall) caer; (dive) saltar; (person) arrojarse; **to take the ~** lanzarse
❏ **plunging** adj: **plunging neckline** escote m pronunciado

pluperfect [plu:'pɜ:rfɪkt] n pluscuamperfecto

plural ['plurəl] adj plural ♦ n plural m

plus [plʌs] n (also: **~ sign**) signo más ♦ prep más, y, además de; **ten/twenty ~** más de diez/veinte

plush [plʌʃ] adj lujoso

plutonium [plu:'touniəm] n plutonio

ply [plaɪ] vt (a trade) ejercer ♦ vi (ship) ir y venir ♦ n (of wool, rope) cabo; **to ~ sb with drink** no parar de ofrecer de beber a algn
❏ **plywood** n madera contrachapada

P.M. (BRIT) n abbr = **Prime Minister**

p.m. adv abbr (= post meridiem) de la tarde or noche

pneumatic [nu:'mætɪk] adj neumático
❏ **pneumatic drill** n martillo neumático

pneumonia [nu:'mounjə] n pulmonía

poach [poutʃ] vt (cook) escalfar; (steal) cazar (or pescar) furtivamente ♦ vi (hunt) cazar furtivamente; (fish) pescar furtivamente
❏ **poached** adj escalfado ❏ **poacher** n cazador(a) m/f furtivo(-a)

P.O. Box n abbr = **Post Office Box**

pocket ['pɑːkɪt] n bolsillo; (fig: small area) bolsa ♦ vt meter en el bolsillo; (steal) embolsar; **to be out of ~** (BRIT) salir perdiendo
❏ **pocketbook** (US) n bolsa (MEX), cartera (LAm exc MEX), bolso (SP) ❏ **pocket calculator** n calculadora de bolsillo
❏ **pocket knife** n navaja ❏ **pocket money** (BRIT) n dinero para gastos (personales); (children's) domingo (MEX), dinero de bolsillo (LAm exc MEX)

pod [pɑːd] n vaina

podgy ['pɑːdʒi] (BRIT) adj gordinflón(-ona)

podiatrist [pə'daɪətrɪst] (US) n pedicuro(-a), podólogo(-a)

poem ['pouəm] n poema m

poet ['pouɪt] n poeta (poetisa) m/f ❏ **poetic** [pou'etɪk] adj poético ❏ **poetry** n poesía

poignant ['pɔɪnjənt] adj conmovedor(a)

point [pɔɪnt] n punto; (tip) punta; (purpose) fin m, propósito; (use) utilidad f; (significant part)

lo significativo; (moment) momento; (also: **decimal ~**): **2 ~ 3 (2.3)** dos coma tres (2,3); (BRIT ELEC) toma (de corriente) ♦ vt señalar; (gun etc): **to ~ sth at sb** apuntar algo a algn ♦ vi: **to ~ at** señalar; **~s** npl (AUT) contactos mpl; (RAIL) agujas fpl; **to be on the ~ of doing sth** estar a punto de hacer algo; **to make a ~ of** poner empeño en; **to get/miss the ~** comprender/no comprender; **to come to the ~** ir al meollo; **there's no ~ (in doing)** no tiene sentido (hacer) ▶ **point out** vt señalar ▶ **point to** vt fus (fig) indicar, señalar
❏ **point-blank** adv (say, refuse) sin más hablar; (also: **at point-blank range**) a quemarropa ❏ **pointed** adj (shape) puntiagudo, afilado; (remark) intencionado
❏ **pointedly** adv intencionadamente
❏ **pointer** n (needle) aguja, indicador m
❏ **pointless** adj sin sentido ❏ **point of view** n punto de vista

poise [pɔɪz] n aplomo, elegancia

poison ['pɔɪzən] n veneno ♦ vt envenenar
❏ **poisoning** n envenenamiento
❏ **poisonous** adj venenoso; (fumes etc) tóxico

poke [pouk] vt (jab with finger, stick etc) empujar; (put): **to ~ sth in(to)** introducir algo en; **to ~ fun at sb** reírse de algn ▶ **poke around** or (BRIT) **about** vi fisgonear

poker ['poukər] n atizador m; (CARDS) póker m

poky ['pouki] adj estrecho

Poland ['poulənd] n Polonia

polar ['poulər] adj polar ❏ **polar bear** n oso polar

Pole [poul] n polaco(-a)

pole [poul] n palo; (fixed) poste m; (GEO) polo
❏ **pole bean** (US) n ejote m (MEX), frijol m (LAm), chaucha (RPl), judía verde (SP) ❏ **pole vault** n salto con garrocha (LAm) or pértiga (SP)

police [pə'li:s] n policía ♦ vt vigilar ❏ **police car** n carro (LAm) or coche m (SP) de policía
❏ **police chief** (US) n jefe(-a) m/f de policía (del distrito) ❏ **policeman** n policía m
❏ **police state** n estado policial ❏ **police station** n comisaría ❏ **policewoman** n mujer f policía

policy ['pɑːlisi] n política; (also: **insurance ~**) póliza

polio ['pouliou] n polio f

Polish ['pouliʃ] adj polaco ♦ n (LING) polaco

polish ['pɑːliʃ] n (for shoes) betún m, pomada (RPl); (for floor) cera (de lustrar); (shine) brillo, lustre m; (fig: refinement) educación f ♦ vt (shoes) bolear (MEX), lustrar (LAm exc MEX), limpiar (SP); (make shiny) pulir, sacar brillo a

▶ **polish off** vt (food) despachar

❏ **polished** adj (fig: person) elegante

polite [pə'laɪt] adj cortés, atento

❏ **politeness** n cortesía

political [pə'lɪtɪkəl] adj político

❏ **politically** adv políticamente; **politically correct** políticamente correcto

politician [pɒlɪ'tɪʃən] n político(-a)

politics ['pɒlɪtɪks] n política

poll [pəul] n (election) votación f; (also: **opinion ~**) sondeo, encuesta ♦ vt encuestar; (votes) obtener

pollen ['pɒlən] n polen m

polling day ['pəulɪŋdeɪ] (BRIT) n día m de elecciones

polling place (US) n centro electoral

polling station (BRIT) n = **polling place**

pollute [pə'luːt] vt contaminar

pollution [pə'luːʃən] n polución f, contaminación f del medio ambiente

polo ['pəuləu] n (sport) polo ❏ **polo-necked** (BRIT) adj de cuello vuelto ❏ **polo shirt** n polo

polyester [pɒli'estər] n poliéster m

polyethylene [pɒli'eθəliːn] n polietileno

polystyrene [pɒli'staɪriːn] n poliestireno

pomegranate ['pɒmɪgrænɪt] n granada

pomelo ['pɒmələu] (US) n toronja (LAm), pomelo (SC, SP)

pomp [pɒmp] n pompa

pompous ['pɒmpəs] adj pomposo

pond [pɒnd] n (natural) charca; (artificial) estanque m

ponder ['pɒndər] vt meditar

ponderous ['pɒndərəs] adj pesado

pong [pɒŋ] (BRIT: inf) n hedor m

pony ['pəuni] n poni m ❏ **ponytail** n coleta ❏ **pony trekking** (BRIT) n excursión f a caballo

poodle ['puːdl] n caniche m

pool [puːl] n (natural) charca; (also: **swimming ~**) alberca (MEX), piscina (LAm exc MEX, SP), pileta (RPI); (fig: of blood) charco; (: of light) foco; (game) billar m (americano) ♦ vt juntar; **~s** npl (BRIT) quinielas fpl; **typing ~** servicio de mecanografía

poop [puːp] n (sound) ruido seco; (MUS) (música) pop m; (drink) refresco; (US: inf: father) papá m ♦ vt (put quickly) meter (de prisa) ♦ vi reventar;

(cork) saltar ▶ **pop in/out** vi entrar/salir un momento ▶ **pop up** vi aparecer inesperadamente ❏ **popcorn** n palomitas fpl (de maíz), pororó (RPI)

pope [pəup] n papa m

poplar ['pɒplər] n álamo

popper ['pɒpər] (BRIT) n botón m de presión (LAm)

poppy ['pɒpi] n amapola

Popsicle® ['pɒpsɪkl] (US) n paleta (helada) (MEX, CAm), palito (helado) (RPI), polo (SP)

pop star n estrella del pop

populace ['pɒpjələs] n pueblo, plebe f

popular ['pɒpjələr] adj popular

population [pɒpjə'leɪʃən] n población f

pop-up menu ['pɒpʌp–] n (COMPUT) menú m emergente

porcelain ['pɔːrslɪn] n porcelana

porch [pɔːrtʃ] n (US: veranda) porche m, terraza; (of house) porche m, portal m; (of church) pórtico

porcupine ['pɔːrkjupaɪn] n puerco m espín

pore [pɔːr] n poro ♦ vi: **to ~ over** estudiar con detenimiento

pork [pɔːrk] n carne f de cerdo or (LAm exc MEX) chancho

pornography [pɔːr'nɑːgrəfi] n pornografía

porpoise ['pɔːrpəs] n marsopa

porridge ['pɔːrɪdʒ] n hojuelas fpl de avena (MEX), avena cocida (LAm), gachas fpl de avena (SP)

port [pɔːrt] n puerto; (NAUT: left side) babor m; (wine) vino de Oporto; **~ of call** puerto de escala

portable ['pɔːrtəbəl] adj portátil

porter ['pɔːrtər] n (for luggage) maletero(-a), mozo(-a) de equipajes; (doorkeeper) portero(-a)

portfolio [pɔːrt'fouliou] n cartera

porthole ['pɔːrthoul] n portilla, ventanilla

portion ['pɔːrʃən] n porción f; (of food) porción (LAm), ración f (SP)

portrait ['pɔːrtrɪt] n retrato

portray [pɔːr'treɪ] vt retratar; (actor) representar

Portugal ['pɔːrtʃəgəl] n Portugal m

Portuguese [pɔːrtʃə'giːz] adj portugués(-esa) ♦ n inv portugués(-esa) m/f; (LING) portugués m

pose [pouz] n postura, actitud f ♦ vi (pretend): **to ~ as** hacerse pasar por ♦ vt (question) plantear; **to ~ for** posar para

posh [pɒʃ] (BRIT: inf) adj elegante, de lujo

position [pə'zɪʃən] n posición f; (job) puesto; (situation) situación f ♦ vt colocar

positive ['pɑːzɪtɪv] adj positivo; (certain) seguro; (definite) definitivo

possess [pə'zɛs] vt poseer □ **possession** n posesión f; **possessions** npl (belongings) pertenencias fpl

possibility [ˌpɑːsɪ'bɪlɪti] n posibilidad f

possible ['pɑːsɪbəl] adj posible; **as big as ~** lo más grande posible □ **possibly** adv posiblemente; **I cannot possibly come** me es imposible venir

post [poust] n (job, situation) puesto; (pole) poste m; (BRIT: system, letters, delivery) correo ♦ vt (BRIT: send by post) echar al correo; (BRIT: appoint): **to ~ to** enviar a □ **postage** n franqueo, porte m □ **postage stamp** n timbre m (MEX), estampilla (LAm), sello (de correos) (SP) □ **postal** adj postal, de correos □ **postal order** (BRIT) n giro postal □ **postbox** (BRIT) n buzón m □ **postcard** n postal f □ **postcode** (BRIT) n código postal

postdate [ˌpoust'deɪt] vt (check) poner fecha posterior a

poster ['poustər] n cartel m

poste restante ['poustrɛ'stɑ̃nt] (BRIT) n lista de correos

postgraduate ['poust'grædʒuət] n posgraduado(-a)

posthumous ['pɑːstjuməs] adj póstumo

postman ['poustmən] n cartero

postmark ['poust,mɑːrk] n matasellos m inv

post-mortem [poust'mɔːrtəm] n autopsia

post office n (building) correo (LAm), (oficina de) correos m inv (SP); (organization): **the Post Office** Dirección f General de Correos (LAm), Correos m inv (SP) □ **Post Office Box** n apartado postal (LAm), casilla de correo (SC), apartado de correos (SP)

postpone [pous'poun] vt aplazar

postscript ['poustskrɪpt] n posdata

posture ['pɑːstʃər] n postura, actitud f

postwar ['poust'wɔːr] adj de la posguerra

posy ['pouzi] n ramillete m (de flores)

pot [pɑːt] n (for cooking) olla; (teapot) tetera; (coffeepot) cafetera; (for flowers) maceta; (for preserves) tarro; (inf: marijuana) mota (MEX), hierba (LAm exc MEX, SP) ♦ vt (plant) poner en tiesto; **to go to ~** (inf) irse al traste

potato [pə'teɪtou] n (pl ~es) papa (LAm), patata (SP) □ **potato chip** (US) n papa (LAm) or patata (SP) frita □ **potato peeler** n pelapapas m inv (LAm), pelapatatas m inv (SP)

potent ['poutnt] adj potente, poderoso; (drink) fuerte

potential [pə'tɛnʃəl] adj potencial, posible ♦ n potencial m □ **potentially** adv en potencia

pothole ['pɑːthoul] n (in road) bache m; (BRIT: underground) túnel m □ **potholing** (BRIT) n: **to go potholing** hacer espeleología

potluck [pɑːt'lʌk] n: **to take ~** conformarse con lo que haya

potted ['pɑːtɪd] adj (food) en conserva; (plant) en maceta or tiesto; (BRIT: shortened) resumido

potter ['pɑːtər] n alfarero(-a) ♦ vi: **to ~ around** or (BRIT) **about** hacer trabajitos □ **pottery** n cerámica; (factory) alfarería

potty ['pɑːti] n bacinica (LAm), pelela (SC), orinal m (SP)

pouch [pautʃ] n (ZOOL) bolsa; (for tobacco) petaca

poultry ['poultri] n aves fpl de corral; (meat) carne de ave

pounce [pauns] vi: **to ~ on** precipitarse sobre

pound [paund] n (weight) libra (= 453,6 gramos); (money) libra ♦ vt (beat) golpear; (crush) machacar ♦ vi (heart) latir □ **pound sterling** (BRIT) n libra esterlina

pour [pɔːr] vt echar; (tea etc) servir ♦ vi correr, fluir; **to ~ sb a drink** servir una bebida a algn ► **pour away** or **off** vt vaciar, verter ► **pour in** vi (people) entrar a raudales ► **pour out** vi salir en tropel ♦ vt (drink) echar, servir; (fig): **to pour out one's feelings** desahogarse □ **pouring** adj: **pouring rain** lluvia torrencial

pout [paut] vi hacer pucheros

poverty ['pɑːvərti] n pobreza, miseria □ **poverty-stricken** adj necesitado

powder ['paudər] n (also: **face ~**) polvos mpl ♦ vt polvorear; **to ~ one's face** empolvarse la cara □ **powder compact** n polvera □ **powdered milk** n leche f en polvo □ **powder room** n aseos mpl

power ['pauər] n poder m; (strength) fuerza; (nation, TECH) potencia; (energy) energía; (ELEC) corriente f ♦ vt impulsar; **to be in ~** (POL) estar en el poder □ **power cut** (BRIT) n = **power outage** □ **powered** adj: **powered by** impulsado por □ **power failure** n corte m del suministro eléctrico □ **powerful** adj poderoso; (engine) potente; (speech etc) convincente □ **powerless** adj: **powerless (to do)** incapaz de (hacer) □ **power outage** (US) n corte m de luz o de corriente □ **power point** (BRIT) n tomacorriente m (LAm), toma de corriente (SP) □ **power station** n central f eléctrica

p.p. abbr (= per procurationem): **~ J. Smith** p.p. (por poder de) J. Smith; (= pages) págs

PR *n abbr* = **public relations**

practical ['præktɪkəl] *adj* práctico
❏ **practicality** [ˌpræktɪ'kælɪtɪ] *n* factibilidad *f*
❏ **practical joke** *n* broma pesada
❏ **practically** *adv* (*almost*) casi

practice ['præktɪs] *n* (*habit*) costumbre *f*;
(*exercise, training*) práctica; (*SPORT*)
entrenamiento; (*MED: of profession*) práctica,
ejercicio; (*MED, LAW: business*) consulta ♦ *vt* (*US:
carry out*) practicar; (*: profession*) ejercer; (*: train
at*) practicar ♦ *vi* (*US*) ejercer; (*: train*) practicar; **in
~** (*in reality*) en la práctica; **out of ~**
desentrenado ❏ **practicing** *adj* (*Christian etc*)
practicante; (*lawyer*) en ejercicio

practise ['præktɪs] (*BRIT*) *vt, vi* = **practice**

practitioner [præk'tɪʃənər] *n* (*MED*)
médico(-a)

prairie ['prɛrɪ] *n* pampa

praise [preɪz] *n* alabanza(s) *f(pl)*, elogio(s)
m(pl) ♦ *vt* elogiar, alabar ❏ **praiseworthy**
adj loable

pram [præm] (*BRIT*) *n* cochecito

prank [præŋk] *n* travesura

prawn [prɔːn] *n* camarón *m* (*LAm*), gamba (*SP*)

pray [preɪ] *vi* rezar

prayer [prɛər] *n* oración *f*; (*entreaty*) ruego,
súplica

preach [priːtʃ] *vi* predicar ❏ **preacher** *n*
predicador(a) *m/f*

precaution [prɪ'kɔːʃən] *n* precaución *f*

precede [prɪ'siːd] *vt, vi* preceder

precedent ['presɪdənt] *n* precedente *m*

preceding [prɪ'siːdɪŋ] *adj* anterior

precinct ['priːsɪŋkt] *n* recinto; (*US POL*) distrito
electoral; (*US: of police*) distrito policial; **~s** *npl*
contornos *mpl*; **pedestrian ~** (*BRIT*) zona
peatonal; **shopping ~** (*BRIT*) centro comercial

precious ['prɛʃəs] *adj* precioso

precipitate [prɪ'sɪpɪteɪt] *vt* precipitar

precise [prɪ'saɪs] *adj* preciso, exacto
❏ **precisely** *adv* precisamente, exactamente

precocious [prɪ'kəʊʃəs] *adj* precoz

precondition [ˌpriːkən'dɪʃən] *n* condición *f*
previa

predecessor ['priːdɪsesər] *n* antecesor(a) *m/f*

predicament [prɪ'dɪkəmənt] *n* apuro

predict [prɪ'dɪkt] *vt* pronosticar
❏ **predictable** *adj* previsible ❏ **prediction**
[prɪ'dɪkʃən] *n* predicción *f*

predominantly [prɪ'dɔːmɪnəntlɪ] *adv* en su
mayoría

preempt (*US*) [priːˈemt] (*BRIT* **pre-empt**) *vt*
adelantarse a

preen [priːn] *vt*: **to ~ itself** (*bird*) limpiarse (las
plumas); **to ~ o.s.** pavonearse

preface ['prefəs] *n* prefacio

prefect ['priːfekt] (*BRIT*) *n* (*in school*)
monitor(a) *m/f*

prefer [prɪ'fɜːr] *vt* preferir; **to ~ doing** *or* **to do**
preferir hacer ❏ **preferable** ['prefərəbl] *adj*
preferible ❏ **preferably** ['prefərəblɪ] *adv* de
preferencia ❏ **preference** ['prefrəns] *n*
preferencia; (*priority*) prioridad *f*
❏ **preferential** [ˌprefə'renʃəl] *adj* preferente

prefix ['priːfɪks] *n* prefijo

pregnancy ['pregnənsɪ] *n* (*of woman*)
embarazo; (*of animal*) preñez *f*

pregnant ['pregnənt] *adj* (*woman*)
embarazada; (*animal*) preñada

prehistoric ['priːhɪs'tɔːrɪk] *adj* prehistórico

prejudice ['predʒʊdɪs] *n* prejuicio
❏ **prejudiced** *adj* (*person*) predispuesto

premarital [priː'mærɪtl] *adj* premarital

premature [prɪ'mətjʊər] *adj* prematuro

premier [prɪ'mɪər] *adj* primero, principal ♦ *n*
(*POL*) primer(a) *m/f* ministro(-a)

première [prɪ'mɪər] *n* estreno

premise ['premɪs] *n* premisa; **~s** *npl* (*of
business etc*) local *m*; **on the ~s** dentro del
local

premium ['priːmɪəm] *n* premio; (*insurance*)
prima; (*US: gasoline*) súper *f*; **to be at a ~** ser
muy solicitado ❏ **premium bond** (*BRIT*) *n*
*bono del estado que participa en una lotería
nacional*

premonition [ˌpreməˈnɪʃən] *n*
presentimiento

preoccupied [prɪ'ɑːkjəpaɪd] *adj* (*absorbed*)
ensimismado

prep [prep] *n* (*BRIT SCOL: study*) tarea, deberes
mpl

prepaid [ˌpriːˈpeɪd] *adj* franqueado

preparation [ˌprepəˈreɪʃən] *n* preparación *f*;
~s *npl* preparativos *mpl*

preparatory ['preparətɔːrɪ] *adj* preparatorio,
preliminar ❏ **preparatory school** *n* (*US*)
centro privado (*de enseñanza secundaria*);
(*BRIT*) centro privado (*de enseñanza primaria*)

prepare [prɪ'pɛər] *vt* preparar, disponer;
(*CULIN*) preparar ♦ *vi*: **to ~ for** (*action*)
prepararse *or* disponerse para; (*event*) hacer
preparativos para; **~d to** dispuesto a; **~d for**
listo para

preposition [ˌprepə'zɪʃən] *n* preposición *f*

preposterous [prɪ'pɑːstərəs] *adj* absurdo,
ridículo

prep school *n* = **preparatory school**

prerequisite [priːˈrekwɪzɪt] n requisito

Presbyterian [prezbɪˈtɪrɪən] adj, n presbiteriano(-a)

preschool [ˈpriːˌskuːl] adj preescolar ♦ n (US) jardín m de niños (MEX), jardín infantil (LAm exc MEX) or de infantes (RPl), parvulario (SP)

prescribe [prɪˈskraɪb] vt (MED) recetar

prescription [prɪˈskrɪpʃən] n (MED) receta

presence [ˈprezəns] n presencia; **in sb's ~** en presencia de algn; **~ of mind** aplomo

present [adj, n ˈprezənt, vb prɪˈzent] adj (in attendance) presente; (current) actual ♦ n (gift) regalo; (actuality): **the ~** la actualidad, el presente ♦ vt (introduce, describe) presentar; (expound) exponer; (give) presentar, dar, ofrecer; (THEATER) representar; **to give sb a ~** regalar algo a algn; **at ~** actualmente ❑ **presentable** [prɪˈzentəbl] adj: **to make o.s. presentable** arreglarse ❑ **presentation** [prezənˈteɪʃən] n presentación f; (of report etc) exposición f; (formal ceremony) entrega (de premios) ❑ **present-day** adj actual ❑ **presenter** (BRIT) n (TV) presentador(a) m/f; (RADIO) locutor(a) m/f ❑ **presently** adv (soon) dentro de poco; (US: now) ahora

preservative [prɪˈzɜːrvətɪv] n conservante m

preserve [prɪˈzɜːrv] vt (keep safe) preservar, proteger; (maintain) mantener; (food) conservar ♦ n (for game) coto, vedado; (often pl: jelly) mermelada

president [ˈprezɪdənt] n presidente(-a) m/f ❑ **presidential** [prezɪˈdenʃl] adj presidencial

press [pres] n (newspapers): **the P~** la prensa; (printer's) imprenta f; (of button) pulsación f ♦ vt empujar; (button etc) apretar; (clothes: iron) planchar; (put pressure on: person) presionar; (insist): **to ~ sth on sb** insistir en que algn acepte su (squeeze) apretar; (pressurize): **to ~ for** presionar por; **we are ~ed for time/money** andamos mal de tiempo/dinero ▶ **press on** vi avanzar; (hurry) apretar el paso ❑ **press agency** n agencia de prensa ❑ **press conference** n rueda de prensa ❑ **pressing** adj apremiante ❑ **press stud** (BRIT) n botón m de presión (LAm) ❑ **press-up** (BRIT) n plancha

pressure [ˈpreʃər] n presión f; **to put ~ on sb** presionar a algn ❑ **pressure cooker** n olla de (LAm) or a (SP) presión ❑ **pressure gage** (US) (BRIT **pressure gauge**) n manómetro ❑ **pressure group** n grupo de presión ❑ **pressurized** adj (container) a presión

prestige [preˈstiːʒ] n prestigio

presumably [prɪˈzuːməblɪ] adv es de suponer que

presume [prɪˈzuːm] vt: **to ~ (that)** suponer (que)

pretend [prɪˈtend] vt, vi (feign) fingir

⚠ Be careful not to translate **pretend** by the Spanish word **pretender**.

pretense (US) [ˈpriːtens] (BRIT **pretence**) n fingimiento; **under false ~s** con engaños

pretentious [prɪˈtenʃəs] adj presumido; (ostentatious) ostentoso, aparatoso

pretext [ˈpriːtekst] n pretexto

pretty [ˈprɪtɪ] adj bonito, lindo (LAm) ♦ adv bastante

prevail [prɪˈveɪl] vi (gain mastery) prevalecer; (be current) predominar ❑ **prevailing** adj (dominant) predominante

prevalent [ˈprevələnt] adj (widespread) extendido

prevent [prɪˈvent] vt: **to ~ sb from doing sth** impedir a algn hacer algo; **to ~ sth from happening** evitar que ocurra algo ❑ **preventative** adj = **preventive** ❑ **preventive** adj preventivo

preview [ˈpriːvjuː] n (of movie) preestreno

previous [ˈpriːvɪəs] adj previo, anterior ❑ **previously** adv antes

prewar [ˌpriːˈwɔːr] adj de antes de la guerra

prey [preɪ] n presa ♦ vi: **to ~ on** (feed on) alimentarse de; **it was ~ing on his mind** le atormentaba or obsesionaba

price [praɪs] n precio ♦ vt (goods) fijar el precio de ❑ **priceless** adj inestimable ❑ **price list** n lista de precios

prick [prɪk] n (sting) picadura, piquete m (MEX); (US MED inf) pinchazo ♦ vt picar (MEX), pinchar (LAm exc MEX, SP); **to ~ up one's ears** aguzar el oído

prickle [ˈprɪkl] n (sensation) picor m; (BOT) espina ❑ **prickly** adj espinoso; (fig: person) enojadizo ❑ **prickly heat** n fiebre f miliar, sarpullidos por el calor

pride [praɪd] n orgullo; (pej) soberbia ♦ vt: **to ~ o.s. on** enorgullecerse de

priest [priːst] n sacerdote m ❑ **priesthood** n sacerdocio

prim [prɪm] adj (demure) remilgado; (prudish) mojigato

primarily [praɪˈmerɪlɪ] adv ante todo

primary [ˈpraɪmerɪ] adj (first in importance) principal ♦ n (US POL) elección f primaria ❑ **primary school** n escuela primaria

prime [praɪm] adj primero, principal; (excellent) selecto, de primera clase ♦ n: **in the**

~ **of life** en la flor de la vida ♦ vt (wood: fig) preparar; ~ **example** ejemplo típico
❏ **Prime Minister** (BRIT) n primer(a) m/f ministro(-a)

primeval [praɪˈmiːvəl] adj primitivo

primitive [ˈprɪmɪtɪv] adj primitivo; (crude) rudimentario

primrose [ˈprɪmrəuz] n primavera, prímula

Primus (stove)® [ˈpraɪməs(ˌstouv)] (BRIT) n camping-gas m inv

prince [prɪns] n príncipe m

princess [prɪnˈses] n princesa

principal [ˈprɪnsɪpəl] adj principal, mayor ♦ n director(a) m/f ❏ **principality** [prɪnsɪˈpælɪti] n principado

principle [ˈprɪnsɪpəl] n principio; **in ~** en principio; **on ~** por principio

print [prɪnt] n (footprint) huella; (fingerprint) huella dactilar; (letters) letra de molde; (fabric) estampado; (ART) grabado; (PHOT) copia ♦ vt imprimir; (cloth) estampar; (write in capitals) escribir en letras de molde; **out of ~** agotado ❏ **printed matter** n impresos mpl ❏ **printer** n (person) impresor(a) m/f; (machine) impresora ❏ **printing** n (art) imprenta; (act) impresión f ❏ **printout** n (COMPUT) impresión f

prior [ˈpraɪər] adj anterior, previo; (more important) más importante; **~ to** antes de

priority [praɪˈɔːrɪti] n prioridad f; **to have ~ (over)** tener prioridad (sobre)

prison [ˈprɪzən] n cárcel f, prisión f ♦ cpd carcelario ❏ **prisoner** n (in prison) preso(-a); (captured person) prisionero ❏ **prisoner-of-war** n prisionero de guerra

privacy [ˈpraɪvəsi] n intimidad f

private [ˈpraɪvɪt] adj (personal) particular; (property, industry, discussion etc) privado; (person) reservado; (place) tranquilo ♦ n soldado raso; **"~"** (on envelope) "confidencial"; (on door) "prohibido el paso"; **in ~** en privado ❏ **private enterprise** n empresa privada ❏ **private eye** n detective mf privado(-a) ❏ **private property** n propiedad f privada ❏ **private school** n colegio privado or particular

privet [ˈprɪvɪt] n alheña, ligustro

privilege [ˈprɪvɪlɪdʒ] n privilegio; (prerogative) prerrogativa

privy [ˈprɪvɪ] adj: **to be ~ to** estar enterado de

prize [praɪz] n premio ♦ adj de primera clase ♦ vt apreciar, estimar ❏ **prize-giving** n distribución f de premios ❏ **prizewinner** n premiado(-a)

pro [prou] n (SPORT) profesional mf ♦ prep a favor de; **the ~s and cons** los pros y los contras

probability [prɒbəˈbɪlɪti] n probabilidad f; **in all ~** con toda probabilidad

probable [ˈprɒbəbl] adj probable

probably [ˈprɒbəbli] adv probablemente

probation [prouˈbeɪʃən] n: **on ~** (employee) a prueba; (LAW) en libertad condicional

probe [proub] n (MED, SPACE) sonda; (enquiry) encuesta, investigación f ♦ vt sondar; (investigate) investigar

problem [ˈprɒbləm] n problema m

procedure [prəˈsiːdʒər] n procedimiento; (bureaucratic) trámites mpl

proceed [prəˈsiːd] vi (do afterward): **to ~ to do sth** proceder a hacer algo; (continue): **to ~ (with)** continuar or seguir (con) ❏ **proceedings** npl acto(s) (pl); (LAW) proceso ❏ **proceeds** [ˈprousiːdz] npl (money) recaudación f, ganancias fpl

process [ˈprɒses] n proceso ♦ vt tratar, elaborar ❏ **processing** n tratamiento, elaboración f; (PHOT) revelado

procession [prəˈseʃən] n desfile m; **funeral ~** cortejo fúnebre

pro-choice [ˈprouˈtʃɔɪs] adj en favor del derecho a elegir de la madre

proclaim [prəˈkleɪm] vt (announce) anunciar

procrastinate [prəˈkræstɪneɪt] vi demorarse

procure [prouˈkjuər] vt conseguir

prod [prɒd] vt empujar ♦ n empujón m

prodigy [ˈprɒdɪdʒi] n prodigio

produce [n ˈprɒdjuːs, vt prəˈdjuːs] n (AGR) productos mpl agrícolas ♦ vt producir; (play, movie, program) presentar ❏ **producer** n productor(a) m/f; (of movie, program) director(a) m/f; (of record) productor(a) m/f

product [ˈprɒdʌkt] n producto

production [prəˈdʌkʃən] n producción f; (THEATER) montaje m ❏ **production line** n línea de producción

productivity [proudʌkˈtɪvɪti] n productividad f

profession [prəˈfeʃən] n profesión f ❏ **professional** adj profesional ♦ n profesional mf; (skilled person) experto(-a)

professor [prəˈfesər] n (US, CANADA) profesor(a) m/f universitario(-a); (BRIT) catedrático(-a)

proficient [prəˈfɪʃənt] adj experto, hábil

profile [ˈproufaɪl] n perfil m

profit [ˈprɒfɪt] n (COMM) beneficios mpl ♦ vi: **to ~ by** or **from** aprovechar or sacar provecho

de ❑ **profitability** [prɑ:fɪtə'bɪlti] n
rentabilidad f ❑ **profitable** adj (ECON)
rentable
profound [prə'faund] adj profundo
profusely [prə'fju:sli] adv profusamente
program (US) ['prougræm] (BRIT
programme) n programa m ♦ vt programar
❑ **programer** (US) (BRIT **programmer**) n
programador(a) m/f ❑ **programing** (US)
(BRIT **programming**) n programación f
progress [n 'prɑ:grɛs, vi prə'grɛs] n progreso;
(development) desarrollo ♦ vi progresar,
avanzar; **in ~** en curso ❑ **progressive**
[prə'grɛsɪv] adj progresivo; (person)
progresista
prohibit [prou'hɪbɪt] vt prohibir; **to ~ sb
from doing sth** prohibir a algn hacer algo
❑ **prohibition** [prouɪ'bɪʃən] n prohibición f;
(US): **Prohibition** Ley f Seca
project [n 'prɑ:dʒɛkt, vb prə'dʒɛkt] n proyecto
♦ vt proyectar ♦ vi (stick out) salir, sobresalir
❑ **projection** [prə'dʒɛkʃən] n proyección f;
(overhang) saliente m ❑ **projector**
[prə'dʒɛktər] n proyector m
pro-life ['prou'laɪf] adj pro-vida
prologue ['proulɑ:g] (US **prolog**) n prólogo
prolong [prə'lɑ:ŋ] vt prolongar, extender
prom [prɑ:m] n abbr = **promenade**; (US: ball)
baile m de gala
promenade [prɑ:mə'neɪd] n malecón m
(LAm), costanera (SC), paseo marítimo (SP)
❑ **promenade concert** (BRIT) n concierto
(en el que parte del público permanece de pie)
prominence ['prɑ:mɪnəns] n importancia
prominent ['prɑ:mɪnənt] adj (standing out)
saliente; (important) eminente, importante
promiscuous [prə'mɪskjuəs] adj (sexually)
promiscuo
promise ['prɑ:mɪs] n promesa ♦ vt, vi
prometer ❑ **promising** adj prometedor(a)
promote [prə'mout] vt (employee) ascender;
(product, pop star) hacer propaganda por;
(ideas) fomentar ❑ **promoter** n (of event)
promotor(a) m/f; (of cause etc) impulsor(a) m/f
❑ **promotion** n (advertising campaign)
campaña f de promoción; (in rank) ascenso
prompt [prɑ:mpt] adj rápido ♦ adv: **at 6
o'clock ~** a las seis en punto ♦ n (COMPUT)
aviso ♦ vt (urge) mover, incitar; (when talking)
instar; (THEATER) apuntar; **to ~ sb to do sth**
instar a algn a hacer algo ❑ **promptly** adv
rápidamente; (exactly) puntualmente
prone [proun] adj (lying) postrado; **~ to**
propenso a
prong [prɑ:ŋ] n diente m, punta

pronoun ['prounaun] n pronombre m
pronounce [prə'nauns] vt pronunciar
❑ **pronounced** adj (marked) marcado
pronunciation [prə,nʌnsi'eɪʃən] n
pronunciación f
proof [pru:f] n prueba ♦ adj: **~ against** a
prueba de
prop [prɑ:p] n apoyo, (fig) sostén m ♦ vt (also:
~ up) apoyar; (lean): **to ~ sth against** apoyar
algo contra
propaganda [prɑ:pə'gændə] n propaganda
propel [prə'pɛl] vt impulsar, propulsar
❑ **propeller** n hélice f
propensity [prə'pɛnsɪti] n propensión f
proper ['prɑ:pər] adj (suited, right) propio;
(exact) justo; (seemly) correcto, decente;
(authentic) verdadero; (referring to place): **the
village ~** (BRIT) el pueblo mismo ❑ **properly**
adv (adequately) correctamente; (decently)
decentemente ❑ **proper noun** n nombre m
propio
property ['prɑ:pərti] n propiedad f; (building)
propiedad, inmueble m ❑ **property
owner** n dueño(-a) de propiedades
prophecy ['prɑ:fɪsi] n profecía
prophesy ['prɑ:fɪsaɪ] vt (fig) predecir
prophet ['prɑ:fɪt] n profeta m
proportion [prə'pɔ:rʃən] n proporción f;
(share) parte f ❑ **proportional** adj:
proportional (to) en proporción (con)
❑ **proportional representation** n
representación f proporcional
❑ **proportionate** adj: **proportionate (to)**
en proporción (con)
proposal [prə'pouzəl] n (marriage) propuesta
de matrimonio; (plan) proyecto
propose [prə'pouz] vt proponer ♦ vi
declararse; **to ~ to do** tener intención de
hacer
proposition [prɑ:pə'zɪʃən] n propuesta
proprietor [prə'praɪətər] n propietario(-a),
dueño(-a)
propriety [prə'praɪəti] n decoro
pro rata [,prou'reɪtə] adv a prorrata
prose [prouz] n prosa
prosecute ['prɑ:sɪkju:t] vt (LAW) procesar
❑ **prosecution** [prɑ:sɪ'kju:ʃən] n proceso,
causa; (accusing side) acusación f
❑ **prosecutor** n acusador(a) m/f; (also:
public prosecutor) fiscal mf
prospect ['prɑ:spɛkt] n (possibility)
posibilidad f; (outlook) perspectiva ♦ vi: **to ~
for** buscar; **~s** npl (for work etc) perspectivas
fpl ❑ **prospecting** n prospección f
❑ **prospective** [prə'spɛktɪv] adj futuro

prospectus [prə'spɛktəs] n prospecto

prosper ['prɒspər] vi prosperar
❑ **prosperity** [prɒ'spɛrɪti] n prosperidad f
❑ **prosperous** adj próspero

prostitute ['prɒstɪtuːt] n prostituta; (male) prostituto

protect [prə'tɛkt] vt proteger ❑ **protection** n protección f ❑ **protective** adj protector(a)

protein ['prəʊtiːn] n proteína

protest [n 'prəʊtɛst, vb prə'tɛst] n protesta ♦ vi: **to ~ about** or **at/against** protestar por/contra ♦ vt (insist): **to ~ (that)** insistir en (que)

Protestant ['prɒtɪstənt] adj, n protestante mf

protester ['prəʊtɛstər] n manifestante mf

protracted [prə'træktɪd] adj prolongado

protrude [prə'truːd] vi salir, sobresalir

proud [praʊd] adj orgulloso; (pej) soberbio, altanero

prove [pruːv] vt probar; (show) demostrar ♦ vi: **to ~ (to be) correct** resultar correcto; **to ~ myself** demostrar mi valía

proverb ['prɒvɜːb] n proverbio, refrán m

provide [prə'vaɪd] vt proporcionar, dar; **to ~ sb with sth** proveer a algn de algo; **~d (that)** conj con tal de que, a condición de que
▶ **provide for** vt fus (person) mantener a; (problem etc) tener en cuenta ❑ **providing** conj: **providing (that)** a condición de que, con tal de que

province ['prɒvɪns] n provincia; (fig) esfera ❑ **provincial** [prə'vɪnʃəl] adj provincial; (pej) provinciano

provision [prə'vɪʒən] n (supplying) suministro, abastecimiento; (of contract etc) disposición f; **~s** npl (food) provisiones fpl ❑ **provisional** adj provisional

proviso [prə'vaɪzəʊ] n condición f, estipulación f

provocative [prə'vɒkətɪv] adj provocativo

provoke [prə'vəʊk] vt (cause) provocar, incitar; (anger) enojar

prowess ['praʊɪs] n destreza

prowl [praʊl] vi (also: ~ **around**) merodear ♦ n: **on the ~** de merodeo ❑ **prowler** n merodeador(a) m/f

proxy ['prɒksi] n: **by ~** por poderes

prudent ['pruːdənt] adj prudente

prune [pruːn] n ciruela seca or pasa ♦ vt podar

pry [praɪ] vi: **to ~ (into)** inmiscuirse or entrometerse (en)

P.S., PS n abbr (= postscript) P.D.

psalm [sɑːm] n salmo

pseudonym ['sjuːdnɪm] n seudónimo

psyche ['saɪki] n psique f

psychiatric [saɪki'ætrɪk] adj psiquiátrico

psychiatrist [saɪ'kaɪətrɪst] n psiquiatra mf

psychic ['saɪkɪk] adj (also: ~**al**) psíquico

psychoanalysis [saɪkəʊə'nælɪsɪs] n psicoanálisis m inv

psychoanalyze (US) [saɪkəʊ'ænəlaɪz] (BRIT **psychoanalyse**) vt psicoanalizar

psychological [saɪkə'lɒːdʒɪkəl] adj psicológico

psychologist [saɪ'kɒːlədʒɪst] n psicólogo(-a)

psychology [saɪ'kɒːlədʒi] n psicología

PTO abbr (= please turn over) sigue

pub [pʌb] (BRIT) n abbr (= public house) pub m, bar m

puberty ['pjuːbərti] n pubertad f

public ['pʌblɪk] adj público ♦ n: **the ~** el público; **in ~** en público; **to make ~** hacer público ❑ **public address system** n megafonía

publican ['pʌblɪkən] (BRIT) n dueño(-a) (de un pub or bar)

publication [pʌblɪ'keɪʃən] n publicación f

public: ❑ **public company** n sociedad f anónima ❑ **public convenience** (BRIT) n sanitarios mpl (LAm), aseos mpl públicos (SP) ❑ **public defender** (US) n (JUR) defensor(a) m/f de oficio ❑ **public holiday** n (día m) feriado (LAm), (día m de) fiesta (SP) ❑ **public house** (BRIT) n pub m, bar m

publicity [pʌb'lɪsɪti] n publicidad f

publicize ['pʌblɪsaɪz] vt publicitar

publicly ['pʌblɪkli] adv públicamente, en público

public: ❑ **public opinion** n opinión f pública ❑ **public relations** n relaciones fpl públicas ❑ **public school** n (US) colegio público; (BRIT) colegio privado ❑ **public-spirited** adj cívico ❑ **public transportation** n transporte m público

publish ['pʌblɪʃ] vt publicar ❑ **publisher** n (person) editor(a) m/f; (firm) editorial f ❑ **publishing** n (industry) industria editorial

pub lunch (BRIT) n almuerzo or comida (en un pub); **to go for a ~** almorzar or comer en un pub

pucker ['pʌkər] vt (pleat) arrugar; (brow etc) fruncir

pudding ['pʊdɪŋ] n pudín m; (BRIT: dessert) postre m; **black ~** morcilla

puddle ['pʌdl] n charco

pudgy ['pʌdʒi] (US) adj gordinflón(-ona)

puff [pʌf] n soplo; (of smoke, air) bocanada; (of breathing) resoplido ♦ vt: **to ~ one's pipe** dar pitadas (LAm) or caladas (SP) a la pipa ♦ vi (pant) jadear ▶ **puff out** vt hinchar ❏ **puff pastry** n hojaldre m ❏ **puffy** adj hinchado

pull [pul] n (tug): **to give sth a ~** dar un tirón a algo ♦ vt tirar de; (press: trigger) apretar; (haul) tirar, arrastrar; (close: curtain) echar ♦ vi tirar; **to ~ to pieces** hacer pedazos; **to not ~ one's punches** no andarse con bromas; **to ~ one's weight** hacer su parte; **to ~ o.s. together** sobreponerse; **to ~ sb's leg** tomar el pelo a algn ▶ **pull apart** vt (break) romper ▶ **pull down** vt (building) derribar ▶ **pull in** vi (car etc) pararse (a un lado); (train) llegar (a la estación) ▶ **pull off** vt (deal etc) cerrar ▶ **pull out** vi (car, train etc) salir ♦ vt sacar, arrancar ▶ **pull over** vi (AUT) hacerse a un lado ▶ **pull through** vi (MED) recuperarse, reponerse ▶ **pull up** vi (stop) parar ♦ vt (raise) levantar; (uproot) arrancar, desarraigar

pulley ['puli] n polea

Pullman® ['pulmən] (US) n (also: **Pullman car**) coche m cama

pullover ['pul,ouvər] n suéter m (LAm), jersey m (SP)

pulp [pʌlp] n (of fruit) pulpa

pulpit ['pulpit] n púlpito

pulsate ['pʌlseit] vi pulsar, latir

pulse [pʌls] n (ANAT) pulso; (rhythm) pulsación f; (BOT) legumbre f

pump [pʌmp] n (for gas) surtidor m; (for air) bomba; (US: shoe) escarpín m; (BRIT: sports shoe) zapatilla ♦ vt sacar con una bomba ▶ **pump up** vt inflar

pumpkin ['pʌmpkin] n calabaza

pun [pʌn] n juego de palabras

punch [pʌntʃ] n (blow) golpe m, puñetazo; (tool) punzón m; (drink) ponche m ♦ vt (hit): **to ~ sth/sb** dar un puñetazo or golpear a algn/ algo ❏ **punch line** n final (del chiste) ❏ **punch-up** (BRIT: inf) n pelea

punctual ['pʌŋktʃuəl] adj puntual

punctuation [pʌŋktʃu'eiʃən] n puntuación f

puncture ['pʌŋktʃər] (BRIT) n ponchadura (MEX), pinchazo (LAm exc MEX, SP) ♦ vt ponchar (MEX), pinchar (LAm exc MEX, SP)

pungent ['pʌndʒənt] adj acre

punish ['pʌniʃ] vt castigar ❏ **punishment** n castigo

punk [pʌŋk] n (also: ~ **rocker**) punki mf; (also: ~ **rock**) música punk; (US: inf: hoodlum) rufián m, matón m

punt [pʌnt] n (boat) batea

punter ['pʌntər] (BRIT) n (gambler) jugador(a) m/f; (inf) cliente mf

puny ['pjuːni] adj débil

pup [pʌp] n cachorro

pupil ['pjuːpəl] n alumno(-a); (of eye) pupila

puppet ['pʌpit] n títere m

puppy ['pʌpi] n cachorro, perrito

purchase ['pɜːtʃis] n compra ♦ vt comprar ❏ **purchaser** n comprador(a) m/f

pure [pjuər] adj puro

purée [pju'rei] n puré m

purely ['pjurli] adv puramente

purge [pɜːrdʒ] n (MED, POL) purga ♦ vt purgar

purify ['pjurifai] vt purificar, depurar

purple ['pɜːrpəl] adj purpúreo; morado

purpose ['pɜːrpəs] n propósito; **on ~** a propósito, adrede ❏ **purposeful** adj resuelto, determinado

purr [pɜːr] vi ronronear

purse [pɜːrs] n (US: handbag) bolsa (MEX), cartera (LAm exc MEX), bolso (SP); (BRIT: money) monedero ♦ vt fruncir

pursue [pər'suː] vt seguir ❏ **pursuer** n perseguidor(a) m/f

pursuit [pər'suːt] n (chase) caza; (occupation) actividad f

push [puʃ] n empuje m, empujón m; (of button) presión f; (drive) empuje m ♦ vt empujar; (button) apretar; (promote) promover ♦ vt (demand): **to ~ for** luchar por ▶ **push aside** vt apartar con la mano ❏ **push off** (inf) vi largarse ▶ **push on** vi seguir adelante ▶ **push through** vi (crowd) abrirse paso a empujones ♦ vt (measure) despachar ▶ **push up** vt (total, prices) hacer subir ❏ **pushcart** n carretilla (de mano) ❏ **pushchair** (BRIT) n sillita de paseo ❏ **pusher** n (drug pusher) camello mf ❏ **pushover** (inf) n: **it's a pushover** es pan comido ❏ **push-up** (US) n flexión f ❏ **pushy** (pej) adj agresivo

puss [pus] (inf) n gatito, minino

pussy(-cat) ['pusi,kæt] (inf) n = **puss**

put [put] (pt, pp ~) vt (place) poner, colocar; (put into) meter; (say) expresar; (a question) hacer; (estimate) estimar ▶ **put across** vt (ideas etc) comunicar ▶ **put around** vt (rumor) diseminar ▶ **put away** vt (store) guardar ▶ **put back** vt (replace) poner en su sitio; (BRIT: postpone) aplazar ▶ **put by** vt (BRIT: money) guardar ▶ **put down** vt (on ground) soltar; (in writing) apuntar; (revolt etc) sofocar; (BRIT: animal) sacrificar; **to put sth down to** atribuir algo a ▶ **put forward** vt (ideas) presentar, proponer ▶ **put in** vt (complaint) presentar; (*time*) dedicar ▶ **put off** vt (*postpone*) aplazar; (*discourage*) desanimar ▶ **put on** vt ponerse; (*light etc*) encender; (*play etc*) presentar; (*brake*) echar; (*record, radio etc*) poner; (*assume*) adoptar; (*gain*): **to put on weight** engordar ▶ **put out** vt (*fire, light*) apagar; (*garbage etc*) echar; (*cat etc*) echar; (*one's hand*) alargar; (*inf: person*): **to be put out** alterarse ▶ **put through** vt (*TEL*) comunicar (*LAm*), poner (*SP*); (*plan etc*) hacer aprobar ▶ **put up** vt (*raise*) levantar, alzar; (*hang*) colgar; (*build*) construir; (*increase*) aumentar; (*accommodate*) alojar ▶ **put up with** vt fus aguantar

putt [pʌt] n putt m, golpe m corto ▢ **putting green** n green m; (*miniature golf*) minigolf m

putty ['pʌtɪ] n masilla

put-up ['pʌtʌp] adj: **~ job** (*BRIT*) chanchullo, matufia (*RPI*)

puzzle ['pʌzəl] n rompecabezas m inv; (*also: crossword ~*) crucigrama m; (*mystery*) misterio ♦ vt dejar perplejo, confundir ♦ vi: **to ~ over sth** dar vueltas a algo ▢ **puzzling** adj desconcertante

pyjamas [pə'dʒɑːməz] (*BRIT*) npl pijama m (*LAm*), pijama m (*SP*)

pylon ['paɪlɒn] n torre f de alta tensión

pyramid ['pɪrəmɪd] n pirámide f

Pyrenees [pɪrə'niːz] npl: **the ~** los Pirineos

python ['paɪθən] n pitón f

Qq

Q-tip® ['kjuːtɪp] (*US*) n bastoncillo (de algodón)

quack [kwæk] n graznido; (*pej: doctor*) curandero(-a)

quad [kwɒd] n abbr = **quadrangle**; **quadruplet**

quadrangle ['kwɒdræŋgəl] n patio (*interior*)

quadruple [kwɒ'druːpəl] vt, vi cuadruplicar

quadruplets [kwɒ'druːplɪts] npl cuatrillizos(-as)

quail [kweɪl] n codorniz f ♦ vi: **to ~ at** or **before** amedrentarse ante

quaint [kweɪnt] adj extraño; (*picturesque*) pintoresco

quake [kweɪk] vi temblar ♦ n abbr = **earthquake**

Quaker ['kweɪkər] n cuáquero(-a)

qualification [kwɒlɪfɪ'keɪʃən] n (*ability*) capacidad f; (*often pl: diploma etc*) título; (*reservation*) salvedad f

qualified ['kwɒlɪfaɪd] adj capacitado; (*professionally*) titulado; (*limited*) limitado

qualify ['kwɒlɪfaɪ] vt (*make competent*) capacitar; (*modify*) modificar ♦ vi (*in competition*): **to ~ (for)** calificarse (para); (*in studies*): **to ~ (as)** titularse (en), recibirse (de) (*LAm*); (*be eligible*): **to ~ (for)** reunir los requisitos (para)

quality ['kwɒlɪtɪ] n calidad f; (*of person*) cualidad f ▢ **quality time** n tiempo dedicado a la familia y a los amigos

qualm [kwɑːm] n escrúpulo

quandary ['kwɒndrɪ] n: **to be in a ~** estar en un dilema

quantity ['kwɒntɪtɪ] n cantidad f; **in ~** en grandes cantidades ▢ **quantity surveyor** (*BRIT*) n aparejador(a) m/f

quarantine ['kwɒrəntiːn] n cuarentena

quarrel ['kwɒrəl] n pelea, riña ♦ vi pelearse, reñir

quarry ['kwɒrɪ] n cantera

quart [kwɔːrt] n ≈ litro

quarter ['kwɔːrtər] n cuarto, cuarta parte f; (*US: coin*) moneda de 25 centavos; (*of year*) trimestre m; (*district*) barrio ♦ vt dividir en cuartos; (*MIL: lodge*) alojar; **~s** npl (*barracks*) cuartel m; (*living quarters*) alojamiento; **a ~ of an hour** un cuarto de hora ▢ **quarterback** (*US*) n (*FOOTBALL*) mariscal mf de campo ▢ **quarterfinal** n cuartos mpl (de final) ▢ **quarterly** adj trimestral ♦ adv trimestralmente, cada tres meses ▢ **quarter note** (*US*) n (*MUS*) negra

quartet(te) [kwɔːr'tet] n cuarteto

quartz [kwɔːrts] n cuarzo

quash [kwɒʃ] vt (*verdict*) anular

quaver ['kweɪvər] (*BRIT*) n (*MUS*) corchea ♦ vi temblar

quay [kiː] n (*also: ~side*) muelle m

queasy ['kwiːzɪ] adj: **to feel ~** tener náuseas

queen [kwiːn] n reina; (*CARDS etc*) dama ▢ **queen mother** n reina madre

queer [kwɪər] adj raro, extraño ♦ n (*inf: highly offensive*) maricón m

quell [kwel] vt (*feeling*) calmar; (*rebellion etc*) sofocar

quench [kwentʃ] vt: **to ~ one's thirst** apagar la sed

query ['kwɪrɪ] n (*question*) pregunta ♦ vt dudar de

quest [kwest] n busca, búsqueda

question ['kwɛstʃən] n pregunta; (doubt) duda; (matter) asunto, cuestión f ♦ vt (doubt) dudar de; (interrogate) interrogar, hacer preguntas a; **beyond ~** fuera de toda duda; **out of the ~** imposible; ni hablar □ **questionable** adj dudoso □ **question mark** n signo de interrogación □ **questionnaire** [kwɛstʃə'nɛər] n cuestionario

queue [kju:] (BRIT) n cola ♦ vi (also: ~ **up**) hacer cola

quibble ['kwɪbəl] vi discutir (por tonterías)

quick [kwɪk] adj rápido; (agile) ágil; (mind) listo ♦ n: **to cut sb to the ~** (fig) herir a algn en lo más profundo; **be ~!** ¡date prisa! □ **quicken** vt apresurar ♦ vi apresurarse, darse prisa □ **quickly** adv rápidamente, de prisa □ **quicksand** n arenas fpl movedizas □ **quick-witted** adj agudo

quid [kwɪd] (BRIT: inf) n inv libra

quiet ['kwaɪət] adj (voice, music etc) bajo; (person, place) tranquilo; (ceremony) íntimo ♦ n silencio; (calm) tranquilidad f ♦ vt (US: calm) calmar; hacer callar ♦ vi (US: calm down) calmarse; (: grow silent) callarse □ **quieten** (BRIT: also: **quieten down**) vi, vt = **quiet** □ **quietly** adv tranquilamente; (silently) silenciosamente □ **quietness** n tranquilidad f; silencio

⚠ Be careful not to translate **quiet** by the Spanish word *quieto*.

quilt [kwɪlt] n edredón m

quin [kwɪn] n abbr = **quintuplet**

quintet(te) [kwɪn'tɛt] n quinteto

quintuplets [kwɪn'tʌplɪts] npl quintillizos(-as)

quip [kwɪp] n pulla, broma

quirk [kwɜːrk] n peculiaridad f; (accident) capricho

quit [kwɪt] (pt, pp = or **~ted**) vt dejar, abandonar; (premises) desocupar ♦ vi (give up) renunciar; (resign) dimitir

quite [kwaɪt] adv (rather) bastante; (entirely) completamente; **that's not ~ big enough** no acaba de ser lo bastante grande; **~ a few of them** un buen número de ellos; **~ (so)!** ¡así es!, ¡exactamente!

quits [kwɪts] adj: **~ (with)** en paz (con); **let's call it ~** dejémoslo en tablas

quiver ['kwɪvər] vi estremecerse

quiz [kwɪz] n concurso ♦ vt interrogar □ **quizzical** adj burlón(-ona)

quota ['kwoʊtə] n cupo, cuota

quotation [kwoʊ'teɪʃən] n cita; (estimate) presupuesto □ **quotation marks** npl comillas fpl

quote [kwoʊt] n cita; (estimate) presupuesto ♦ vt citar; (price) cotizar ♦ vi: **to ~ from** citar de; **~s** npl (inverted commas) comillas fpl

Rr

rabbi ['ræbaɪ] n rabino(-a)

rabbit ['ræbɪt] n conejo □ **rabbit hutch** n conejera

rabble ['ræbəl] (pej) n muchedumbre f; chusma

rabies ['reɪbiːz] n rabia

RAC (BRIT) n abbr = **Royal Automobile Club**

rac(c)oon [ræ'kuːn] n mapache m

race [reɪs] n carrera; (species) raza ♦ vt (horse) hacer correr; (engine) acelerar ♦ vi (compete) competir; (run) correr; (pulse) latir a ritmo acelerado □ **race car** (US) n carro (LAm) o coche m (SP) de carreras □ **race car driver** (US) n piloto mf de carreras □ **racecourse** n hipódromo □ **racehorse** n caballo de carreras □ **racetrack** n pista; (for cars) circuito; (for horses) hipódromo

racial ['reɪʃəl] adj racial □ **racing car** (BRIT) n = **race car** □ **racing driver** (BRIT) n = **race car driver**

racing ['reɪsɪŋ] n carreras fpl □ **racing car** (BRIT) n = **race car** □ **racing driver** (BRIT) n = **race car driver**

racism ['reɪsɪzəm] n racismo □ **racist** adj, n racista mf

rack [ræk] n (also: **luggage ~**) rejilla; (shelf) estante m; (also: **roof ~**) baca, portaequipajes m inv; (dish rack) escurreplatos m inv; (clothes rack) gancho (LAm), percha (SP) ♦ vt atormentar; **to ~ one's brains** devanarse los sesos

racket ['rækɪt] n (for tennis) raqueta; (noise) jaleo, bulla; (swindle) estafa, timo

racquet ['rækɪt] n raqueta

racy ['reɪsi] adj picante, atrevido

radar ['reɪdɑːr] n radar m

radiant ['reɪdiənt] adj radiante (de felicidad)

radiate ['reɪdieɪt] vt (heat) radiar; (emotion) irradiar ♦ vi (lines) extenderse

radiation [reɪdi'eɪʃən] n radiación f

radiator ['reɪdieɪtər] n radiador m

radical ['rædɪkəl] adj radical

radii ['reɪdiaɪ] npl of **radius**

radio ['reɪdɪou] n radio m (LAm) or f (SC, SP); **on the ~** por radio

radio... ['reɪdɪou] prefix: ❑ **radioactive** adj radioactivo ❑ **radiography** [reɪdɪ'ɑːgrəfɪ] n radiografía ❑ **radiology** [ˌreɪdɪ'ɑːlədʒɪ] n radiología

radio station n emisora

radiotherapy [reɪdɪou'θerəpɪ] n radioterapia

radish ['rædɪʃ] n rábano

radius ['reɪdɪəs] (pl **radii**) n radio

RAF n abbr = **Royal Air Force**

raffle ['ræfəl] n rifa, sorteo

raft [ræft] n balsa; (also: **life ~**) balsa salvavidas

rafter ['ræftər] n viga

rag [ræg] n (piece of cloth) trapo; (torn cloth) harapo; (pej: newspaper) periodicucho; (BRIT: for charity) actividades estudiantiles benéficas; **~s** npl (torn clothes) harapos mpl ❑ **rag doll** n muñeca de trapo

rage [reɪdʒ] n rabia, furor m ♦ vi (person) rabiar, estar furioso; (storm) bramar; **it's all the ~** (very fashionable) es el último grito, está muy de moda

ragged ['rægɪd] adj (edge) desigual, irregular; (appearance) andrajoso, harapiento

raid [reɪd] n (MIL) incursión f; (criminal) asalto; (by police) redada ♦ vt invadir, atacar; asaltar

rail [reɪl] n (on stair, balcony) barandilla, pasamanos m inv; (on bridge) pretil m; (of ship) barandilla; (also: **towel ~**) toallero; **~s** npl (RAIL) vía; **by ~** por ferrocarril, en tren ❑ **railing(s)** n(pl) vallado ❑ **railroad** (US) n ferrocarril m, vía férrea ❑ **railroad crossing** (US) n crucero de ferrocarril (MEX), paso a nivel (LAm exc MEX, SP) ❑ **railroad line** (US) n línea ferroviaria or de ferrocarril ❑ **railroad station** (US) n estación f de ferrocarril ❑ **railway** (BRIT) n = **railroad** ❑ **railwayman** (BRIT) n ferroviario

rain [reɪn] n lluvia ♦ vi llover; **in the ~** bajo la lluvia; **it's ~ing** llueve, está lloviendo ❑ **rainbow** n arco iris ❑ **raincoat** n impermeable m ❑ **raindrop** n gota de lluvia ❑ **rainfall** n precipitaciones fpl ❑ **rainforest** n selva tropical ❑ **rainy** adj lluvioso

raise [reɪz] n (US: in salary) aumento; (: in taxes) subida ♦ vt levantar; (increase) aumentar; (improve: morale) subir; (: standards) mejorar; (doubts) suscitar; (a question) plantear; (cattle, family) criar; (crop) cultivar; (army) reclutar; (loan) obtener; **to ~ one's voice** alzar la voz

raisin ['reɪzɪn] n pasa

rake [reɪk] n (tool) rastrillo; (person) libertino ♦ vt (garden) rastrillar

rally ['rælɪ] n (mass meeting) concentración f; (POL) mitin m; (AUT) rally m; (TENNIS) peloteo ♦ vt reunir ♦ vi recuperarse ▶ **rally around** or (BRIT) **round** vt fus (fig) dar apoyo a

RAM [ræm] n abbr (= random access memory) RAM f

ram [ræm] n carnero; (also: **battering ~**) ariete m ♦ vt (crash into) embestir contra, chocar con; (push: fist etc) empujar con fuerza

ramble ['ræmbəl] n caminata or excursión f (por el campo) ♦ vi (pej: also: **~ on**) divagar ❑ **rambler** (BRIT) n excursionista mf; (BOT) trepadora ❑ **rambling** adj (speech) inconexo; (house) laberíntico; (BOT) trepador(a)

ramp [ræmp] n rampa; **on/off ~** (US AUT) vía de acceso/salida

rampage ['ræmpeɪdʒ] n: **to be on the ~** desmandarse ♦ vi: **they went rampaging through the town** recorrieron la ciudad armando alboroto

rampant ['ræmpənt] adj (disease): **to be ~** estar muy extendido

ram raid (BRIT) vt atracar (rompiendo la vidriera con un vehículo)

ramshackle ['ræmʃækəl] adj destartalado

ran [ræn] pt of **run**

ranch [ræntʃ] n rancho (MEX), hacienda (LAm) or estancia (RPl) or finca (SP) (ganadera) ❑ **rancher** n ranchero (MEX), hacendado (LAm), estanciero (RPl), ganadero (SP)

rancid ['rænsɪd] adj rancio

rancor (US) ['ræŋkər] (BRIT **rancour**) n rencor m

random ['rændəm] adj hecho al azar, fortuito; (COMPUT, MATH) aleatorio ♦ n: **at ~** al azar

randy ['rændɪ] (BRIT: inf) adj caliente, cachondo (MEX), calentón (RPl)

rang [ræŋ] pt of **ring**

range [reɪndʒ] n (of mountains) cordillera; (of missile) alcance m; (of voice) registro; (series) variedad f, serie f; (of products) surtido; (stove) estufa (MEX) or cocina (LAm exc MEX, SP) (de carbón); (AGR) pradera; (MIL: also: **shooting ~**) campo de tiro ♦ vt (place) colocar; (arrange) arreglar ♦ vi: **to ~ over** (extend) extenderse por; **to ~ from ... to ...** oscilar entre ... y ...

ranger ['reɪndʒər] n guardabosques mf inv

rank [ræŋk] n (in row) fila; (MIL) rango; (status) categoría; (BRIT: also: **taxi ~**) parada or (MEX) sitio de taxis ♦ vi: **to ~ among** figurar entre ♦ adj fétido; rancio; **the ~ and file** (fig) las bases

ransack ['rænsæk] vt (search) registrar; (plunder) saquear

ransom ['rænsəm] n rescate m; **to hold to ~** (fig) hacer chantaje a

rant [rænt] vi divagar, desvariar

rap [ræp] vt golpear, dar un golpecito en ♦ n (music) rap m

rape [reɪp] n violación f; (BOT) colza ♦ vt violar
□ **rape (seed) oil** n aceite m de colza

rapid ['ræpɪd] adj rápido □ **rapidity** [rə'pɪdɪtɪ] n rapidez f □ **rapids** npl (GEO) rápidos mpl

rapist ['reɪpɪst] n violador m

rapport [ræ'pɔːr] n simpatía

rapturous ['ræptʃərəs] adj extático

rare [reər] adj raro, poco común; (CULIN: steak) sancochado (MEX), poco cocido (LAm exc MEX) or hecho (SP)

rarely ['reərlɪ] adv pocas veces

raring ['reərɪŋ] adj: **to be ~ to go** (inf) tener muchas ganas de empezar

rascal ['ræskəl] n pillo, pícaro

rash [ræʃ] adj imprudente, precipitado ♦ n (MED) sarpullido f; (of events) serie f

rasher ['ræʃər] (BRIT) n (of bacon) loncha

raspberry ['ræzberɪ] n frambuesa

rasping ['ræspɪŋ] adj: **a ~ noise** un ruido áspero

rat [ræt] n rata

rate [reɪt] n (ratio) razón f; (price) precio; (: of hotel etc) tarifa; (of interest) tipo; (speed) velocidad f ♦ vt (value) tasar; (estimate) estimar; **~s** npl (fees) tarifa; (BRIT: property tax) impuesto municipal; **to ~ sth/sb as** considerar algo/a algn como □ **rateable value** (BRIT) n valor m impuesto □ **ratepayer** (BRIT) n contribuyente mf

rather ['ræðər] adv: **it's ~ expensive** es algo caro; (too much) es demasiado caro; (to some extent) más bien; **there's ~ a lot** hay bastante; **I would** or **I'd ~ go** preferiría ir; **or ~** mejor dicho

rating ['reɪtɪŋ] n tasación f; (score) índice m; (of ship) clase f; **~s** npl (RADIO, TV) niveles mpl de audiencia

ratio ['reɪʃou] n razón f; **in the ~ of 100 to 1** a razón de 100 a 1

ration ['ræʃən] n ración f ♦ vt racionar; **~s** npl víveres mpl

rational ['ræʃənl] adj (solution, reasoning) lógico, razonable; (person) cuerdo, sensato □ **rationale** [ræʃə'nɑːl] n razón f fundamental □ **rationalize** vt justificar

rat race n lucha por la supervivencia, competencia feroz

rattle ['rætl] n golpeteo; (of train etc) traqueteo; (for baby) sonajero, sonaja (MEX) ♦ vi castañetear; (car, bus): **to ~ along** traquetear ♦ vt hacer sonar (agitando)
□ **rattler** (US) n = **rattlesnake**
□ **rattlesnake** n serpiente f de cascabel

raucous ['rɔːkəs] adj estridente, ronco

ravage ['rævɪdʒ] vt hacer estragos en, destrozar □ **ravages** npl estragos mpl

rave [reɪv] vi (in anger) encolerizarse; (with enthusiasm) entusiasmarse; (MED) delirar, desvariar ♦ n (inf: party) fiesta tecno

raven ['reɪvən] n cuervo

ravenous ['rævənəs] adj hambriento

ravine [rə'viːn] n barranco

raving ['reɪvɪŋ] adj: **~ lunatic** loco(-a) de atar

ravishing ['rævɪʃɪŋ] adj encantador(a)

raw [rɔː] adj crudo; (not processed) bruto; (sore) vivo; (inexperienced) novato, inexperto
□ **raw deal** (inf) n injusticia □ **raw material** n materia prima

ray [reɪ] n rayo; **~ of hope** (rayo de) esperanza

raze [reɪz] vt arrasar

razor ['reɪzər] n (open) navaja; (safety razor) rastrillo (MEX), máquina (LAm) or maquinilla (SP) de afeitar; (electric razor) rasuradora (MEX), máquina (LAm) or maquinilla (SP) (eléctrica) de afeitar □ **razor blade** n hoja de rasurar (MEX) or afeitar (LAm), cuchilla (de afeitar) (SP)

Rd. abbr = **road**

re [riː] prep con referencia a

reach [riːtʃ] n alcance m; (of river) cuenca ♦ vt alcanzar, llegar a; (achieve) lograr ♦ vi extenderse; within ~ al alcance (de la mano); out of ~ fuera del alcance ► **reach out** vt (hand) alargar ♦ vi: **to reach out for sth** alargar la mano para tomar algo

react [rɪ'ækt] vi reaccionar □ **reaction** n reacción f

reactor [rɪ'æktər] n (also: **nuclear ~**) reactor m (nuclear)

read [riːd, pt, pp red] (pt, pp ~) vi leer ♦ vt leer; (understand) entender; (BRIT: study) estudiar ► **read out** vt leer (en alta voz) □ **readable** adj (writing) legible; (book) leíble □ **reader** n lector(a) m/f; (BRIT: at university) profesor(a) m/f adjunto(-a) □ **readership** n (of paper etc) (número de) lectores mpl

readily ['redɪlɪ] adv (willingly) de buena gana; (easily) fácilmente; (quickly) en seguida

readiness ['redɪnɪs] n buena voluntad f; (preparedness) preparación f; **in ~** (prepared) listo, preparado

reading ['riːdɪŋ] n lectura; (on instrument) indicación f

ready ['redɪ] adj listo, preparado; (willing) dispuesto; (available) disponible ♦ adv: ~-cooked listo para comer; at the ~ (MIL) listo para tirar; to get ~ vi prepararse; vt preparar ❑ **ready-made** adj confeccionado ❑ **ready-to-wear** adj confeccionado

real [rɪəl] adj verdadero, auténtico; in ~ terms en términos reales ❑ **real estate** (US) n bienes mpl raíces ❑ **real estate agent** (US) n agente mf inmobiliario(-a) ❑ **realistic** [ˌrɪəˈlɪstɪk] adj realista

reality [rɪˈælətɪ] n realidad f

realization [ˌrɪəlaɪˈzeɪʃən] n comprensión f; (fulfillment, COMM) realización f

realize ['rɪəlaɪz] vt (understand) darse cuenta de

really ['rɪəlɪ] adv realmente; (for emphasis) verdaderamente; (actually): **what ~ happened** lo que pasó en realidad; ~? ¿de veras?; ~! (annoyance) ¡vamos!, ¡por favor!

realm [relm] n reino; (fig) esfera

Realtor® ['rɪəltər] (US) n agente mf inmobiliario(-a)

reap [rɪːp] vt segar; (fig) cosechar, recoger

reappear [ˌrɪːəˈpɪər] vi reaparecer

rear [rɪər] adj trasero ♦ n parte f trasera ♦ vt (cattle, family) criar ♦ vi (also: ~ up: horse) encabritarse ❑ **rearguard** n retaguardia

rearmament [ˌrɪːˈɑːrməmənt] n rearme m

rearrange [ˌrɪːəˈreɪndʒ] vt ordenar or arreglar de nuevo

rear-view mirror n (AUT) (espejo) retrovisor m

reason ['rɪːzən] n razón f ♦ vi: to ~ with sb tratar de que algn entre en razón; it stands to ~ that es lógico que ❑ **reasonable** adj razonable; (sensible) sensato ❑ **reasonably** adv razonablemente ❑ **reasoning** n razonamiento, argumentos mpl

reassurance [ˌrɪːəˈʃʊrəns] n consuelo

reassure [ˌrɪːəˈʃʊər] vt tranquilizar, alentar; to ~ sb that asegurar a algn que

rebate ['rɪːbeɪt] n (on tax etc) devolución f, reembolso

rebel [n 'rebəl, vi rɪ'bel] n rebelde mf ♦ vi rebelarse, sublevarse ❑ **rebellious** [rɪ'beljəs] adj rebelde; (child) revoltoso

rebirth [rɪːˈbɜːrθ] n renacimiento

rebound [vi rɪˈbaʊnd, n ˈrɪːbaʊnd] vi (ball) rebotar ♦ n rebote m; on the ~ de rebote

rebuff [rɪˈbʌf] n desaire m, rechazo

rebuild [rɪːˈbɪld] vt reconstruir

rebuke [rɪˈbjuːk] n reprimenda ♦ vt reprender

rebut [rɪˈbʌt] vt rebatir

recall [vb rɪˈkɔːl, n ˈrɪːkɔːl] vt (remember) recordar; (ambassador etc) retirar ♦ n recuerdo; retirada

recap ['rɪːkæp], **recapitulate** [ˌrɪːkəˈpɪtʃʊleɪt] vt, vi recapitular

rec'd abbr (= received) rbdo.

recede [rɪˈsiːd] vi (memory) ir borrándose; (hair) retroceder ❑ **receding** adj (forehead, chin) huidizo; **to have a receding hairline** tener entradas

receipt [rɪˈsiːt] n (document) recibo; (for package etc) acuse m de recibo; (act of receiving) recepción f; ~s npl (COMM) ingresos mpl

> ⚠ Be careful not to translate **receipt** by the Spanish word **receta**.

receive [rɪˈsiːv] vt recibir; (guest) acoger; (wound) sufrir ❑ **receiver** n (TEL) auricular m; (RADIO) receptor m; (of stolen goods) perista mf, recibidor(a) m/f (SC); (COMM) síndico(-a), administrador(a) m/f (jurídico(-a))

recent ['rɪːsənt] adj reciente ❑ **recently** adv recientemente; **recently arrived** recién llegado

receptacle [rɪˈseptɪkəl] n receptáculo

reception [rɪˈsepʃən] n recepción f; (welcome) acogida ❑ **reception desk** n recepción f ❑ **receptionist** n recepcionista mf

recess [rɪˈses] n (in room) hueco; (for bed) nicho; (secret place) escondrijo; (POL etc: cessation of business) clausura; (US JUR: short break) descanso; (US SCOL) recreo

recession [rɪˈseʃən] n recesión f

recipe ['resəpɪ] n receta; (for disaster, success) fórmula

recipient [rɪˈsɪpɪənt] n receptor(a) m/f; (of letter) destinatario(-a)

recital [rɪˈsaɪtl] n recital m

recite [rɪˈsaɪt] vt (poem) recitar

reckless ['rekləs] adj temerario, imprudente; (driving, driver) peligroso ❑ **recklessly** adv imprudentemente; de modo peligroso

reckon ['rekən] vt calcular; (consider) considerar; (think): **I ~ that ...** me parece que ... ▸ **reckon on** vt fus contar con ❑ **reckoning** n cálculo

reclaim [rɪˈkleɪm] vt (land, waste) recuperar; (land: from sea) rescatar; (demand back) reclamar

reclamation [ˌrekləˈmeɪʃən] n (of land) acondicionamiento

recline [rɪˈklaɪn] vi reclinarse ❑ **reclining** adj (seat) reclinable

recluse ['rekluːs] n recluso(-a)

recognition [ˌrekəgˈnɪʃən] n reconocimiento; **transformed beyond ~** irreconocible

recognizable [ˈrekəgnaɪzəbəl] adj: **~ (by)** reconocible (por)

recognize [ˈrekəgnaɪz] vt: **to ~ (by/as)** reconocer (por/como)

recoil [vi rɪˈkɔɪl, n ˈriːkɔɪl] vi (person): **to ~ from doing sth** retraerse de hacer algo ♦ n (of gun) retroceso

recollect [ˌrekəˈlekt] vt recordar, acordarse de ▢ **recollection** n recuerdo

recommend [ˌrekəˈmend] vt recomendar

reconcile [ˈrekənsaɪl] vt (two people) reconciliar; (two facts) compaginar; **to ~ o.s. to sth** resignarse a algo

recondition [ˌriːkənˈdɪʃən] vt (machine) reacondicionar

reconnoiter (US) [ˌriːkəˈnɔɪtər] (BRIT **reconnoitre**) vt, vi (MIL) reconocer

reconsider [ˌriːkənˈsɪdər] vt repensar

reconstruct [ˌriːkənˈstrʌkt] vt reconstruir

record [n ˈrekərd, vt rɪˈkɔːrd] n (MUS) disco; (of meeting etc) acta; (register) registro, partida; (file) archivo; (also: **criminal ~**) antecedentes mpl; (written) expediente m; (SPORT, COMPUT) récord m ♦ vt registrar; (MUS: song etc) grabar; **in ~ time** en un tiempo récord; **off the ~** (adj) no oficial; (adv) confidencialmente ▢ **record card** n (in file) ficha ▢ **recorded delivery** (BRIT) n entrega con acuse de recibo ▢ **recorder** n (MUS) flauta dulce or de pico ▢ **record holder** n (SPORT) plusmarquista mf ▢ **recording** n (MUS) grabación f ▢ **record player** n tocadiscos m inv

⚠ Be careful not to translate **record** by the Spanish word **recordar**.

recount [rɪˈkaunt] vt contar

re-count [ˈriːkaunt] n (POL: of votes) segundo recuento or escrutinio

recoup [rɪˈkuːp] vt: **to ~ one's losses** recuperar las pérdidas

recourse [ˈriːkɔːrs] n: **to have ~ to** recurrir a

recover [rɪˈkʌvər] vt recuperar ♦ vi (from illness, shock) recuperarse ▢ **recovery** n recuperación f

recreation [ˌrekriˈeɪʃən] n recreo ▢ **recreational** adj de recreo; **recreational drug** droga recreativa

recruit [rɪˈkruːt] n recluta mf ♦ vt reclutar; (staff) contratar

rectangle [ˈrektæŋgəl] n rectángulo ▢ **rectangular** [rekˈtæŋgjələr] adj rectangular

rectify [ˈrektɪfaɪ] vt rectificar

rector [ˈrektər] n (REL) párroco ▢ **rectory** n rectoría, casa del párroco

recuperate [rɪˈkuːpəreɪt] vi reponerse, restablecerse

recur [rɪˈkɜːr] vi repetirse; (pain, illness) reaparecer, producirse de nuevo ▢ **recurrence** n repetición f ▢ **recurrent** adj repetido

recycle [ˌriːˈsaɪkəl] vt reciclar

red [red] n rojo ♦ adj rojo; (hair) pelirrojo, (wine) tinto; **to be in the ~** (account) estar en números rojos; (business) tener un saldo negativo; **to give sb the ~ carpet treatment** recibir a algn con todos los honores ▢ **Red Cross** n Cruz f Roja ▢ **redcurrant** (BRIT) n grosella (roja) ▢ **redden** vt enrojecer ♦ vi enrojecerse

redeem [rɪˈdiːm] vt redimir; (promises) cumplir; (sth in pawn store) desempeñar; (fig, also REL) rescatar ▢ **redeeming** adj: **redeeming feature** rasgo or punto positivo

redeploy [ˌriːdɪˈplɔɪ] vt (resources) reorganizar

red: ▢ **red-haired** adj pelirrojo ▢ **red-handed** adj: **to catch sb red-handed** agarrar (LAm) or coger (SP) a algn con las manos en la masa ▢ **redhead** n pelirrojo(-a) ▢ **red herring** n (fig) pista falsa ▢ **red-hot** adj candente

redirect [ˌriːdɪˈrekt] vt (mail) reexpedir

red light n: **to go through a ~** (AUT) pasarse un alto (MEX, CAm) or una luz roja (LAm), saltarse un semáforo en rojo (SP) ▢ **red-light district** n zona roja (LAm), barrio chino (SP)

redo [ˌriːˈduː] vt rehacer

redress [rɪˈdres] vt reparar

Red Sea n: **the ~** el mar Rojo

red tape n (fig) trámites mpl, papeleo

reduce [rɪˈduːs] vt reducir; **to ~ sb to tears** hacer llorar a algn; **to be ~d to begging** no tener más remedio que mendigar; **"~ speed now"** (AUT) "reduzca or disminuya la velocidad"; **at a ~d price** (of goods) a precio reducido ▢ **reduction** [rɪˈdʌkʃən] n reducción f; (of price) rebaja; (discount) descuento; (smaller-scale copy) copia reducida

redundancy [rɪˈdʌndənsi] (BRIT) n (dismissal) despido; (unemployment) desempleo

redundant [rɪˈdʌndənt] adj (detail, object) superfluo; (BRIT: worker) sin trabajo; **to be made ~** quedar(se) sin trabajo

reed [riːd] n (BOT) junco, caña; (MUS) lengüeta

reef [ri:f] n (at sea) arrecife m

reek [ri:k] vi: **to ~ (of)** apestar (a)

reel [ri:l] n carrete m; (of film) rollo; (dance) baile escocés ♦ vt (also: **~ up**) devanar; (also: **~ in**) sacar ♦ vi (sway) tambalear(se)

ref [ref] (inf) n abbr = **referee**

refectory [rɪˈfektərɪ] n comedor m

refer [rɪˈfɜ:r] vt (send: patient) mandar; (: matter) remitir ♦ vi: **to ~ to** (allude to) referirse a, aludir a; (apply to) relacionarse con; (consult) consultar

referee [refəˈri:] n árbitro(-a), réferi mf (LAm); (BRIT: for job application): **to be a ~ for sb** proporcionar referencias a algn ♦ vt (game) arbitrar en

reference [ˈrefrəns] n referencia; (for job application: letter) carta de recomendación; **with ~ to** (COMM: in letter) con referencia or relación a ◻ **reference book** n libro de consulta ◻ **reference number** n número de referencia

refill [vt ˌri:ˈfɪl, n ˈri:fɪl] vt volver a llenar ♦ n repuesto, recambio

refine [rɪˈfaɪn] vt refinar ◻ **refined** adj (person) fino ◻ **refinement** n cultura, educación f; (of system) refinamiento

reflect [rɪˈflekt] vt reflejar ♦ vi (think) reflexionar, pensar; **it ~s badly/well on him** le perjudica/le hace honor ◻ **reflection** n (act) reflexión f; (image) reflejo; (criticism) crítica; **on reflection** pensándolo bien ◻ **reflector** n (AUT) captafaros m inv, reflectante m; (of light, heat) reflector m

reflex [ˈri:fleks] adj, n reflejo ◻ **reflexive** [rɪˈfleksɪv] adj (LING) reflexivo

reform [rɪˈfɔ:rm] n reforma ♦ vt reformar ◻ **reformatory** (US) n reformatorio

refrain [rɪˈfreɪn] vi: **to ~ from doing** abstenerse de hacer ♦ n estribillo

refresh [rɪˈfreʃ] vt refrescar ◻ **refresher course** (BRIT) n curso de reciclaje or actualización ◻ **refreshing** adj refrescante ◻ **refreshments** npl refrigerio

refrigerator [rɪˈfrɪdʒəreɪtər] n refrigerador m (LAm), heladera (RPl), frigorífico (SP)

refuel [ˌri:ˈfjuəl] vi repostar (combustible)

refuge [ˈrefju:dʒ] n refugio, asilo; **to take ~ in** refugiarse en

refugee [refjuˈdʒi:] n refugiado(-a)

refund [n ˈri:fʌnd, vb rɪˈfʌnd] n reembolso ♦ vt reembolsar, devolver

refurbish [ˌri:ˈfɜ:rbɪʃ] vt restaurar, renovar

refusal [rɪˈfju:zəl] n negativa; **to have first ~ on** tener opción de compra sobre

refuse¹ [rɪˈfju:z] vt rechazar; (invitation) declinar; (permission) denegar ♦ vi negarse; (horse) rehusar; **to ~ to do sth** negarse a hacer algo

refuse² [ˈrefju:s] n basura ◻ **refuse collection** n recogida de basuras

regain [rɪˈgeɪn] vt recobrar, recuperar

regal [ˈri:gəl] adj regio, real

regard [rɪˈgɑ:rd] n mirada; (esteem) respeto; (attention) consideración f ♦ vt (consider) considerar; **give my ~s to Alice** dale recuerdos a or saluda de mi parte a Alice; **"with kind ~s"** "un cordial saludo"; **~ing, as ~s, with ~ to** con respecto a, en cuanto a ◻ **regardless** adv a pesar de todo; **regardless of** sin reparar en

régime [reɪˈʒi:m] n régimen m

regiment [ˈredʒəmənt] n regimiento ◻ **regimental** [redʒɪˈmentl] adj militar

region [ˈri:dʒən] n región f; **in the ~ of** (fig) alrededor de ◻ **regional** adj regional

register [ˈredʒɪstər] n registro ♦ vt registrar; (birth) declarar; (car) matricular; (letter) certificar; (instrument) marcar, indicar ♦ vi (at hotel) registrarse; (as student) matricularse; (make impression) producir impresión ◻ **registered** adj (letter, package) certificado; (student, car) matriculado ◻ **registered mail** (US) n correo certificado ◻ **registered trademark** n marca registrada

registrar [ˈredʒɪstrɑ:r] n secretario(-a) (del registro civil)

registration [redʒɪˈstreɪʃən] n (for course etc) inscripción f; (BRIT AUT: = registration number) (número de) placa (LAm) or matrícula (SP) or chapa (RPl)

registry [ˈredʒɪstrɪ] n registro ◻ **registry office** (BRIT) n registro civil; **to get married in a registry office** casarse por lo civil

regret [rɪˈgret] n sentimiento, pesar m ♦ vt sentir, lamentar ◻ **regretfully** adv con pesar ◻ **regrettable** adj lamentable

regular [ˈregjələr] adj regular; (soldier) profesional; (usual) habitual; (: doctor) de cabecera ♦ n (client etc) cliente(-a) m/f habitual ◻ **regularly** adv con regularidad; (often) a menudo

regulate [ˈregjuleɪt] vt controlar ◻ **regulation** [regjuˈleɪʃən] n (rule) regla, reglamento; **safety regulations** normas de seguridad

rehearsal [rɪˈhɜ:rsəl] n ensayo

rehearse [rɪˈhɜ:rs] vt ensayar

reign [reɪn] n reinado; (fig) predominio ♦ vi reinar; (fig) imperar

reiki ['reɪkɪ] n reiki m

reimburse [,riːɪm'bɜːrs] vt reembolsar

rein [reɪn] n (for horse) rienda

reindeer ['reɪndɪr] n inv reno

reinforce [,riːɪn'fɔːrs] vt reforzar ❑ **reinforced concrete** n hormigón m armado ❑ **reinforcements** npl (MIL) refuerzos mpl

reinstate [,riːɪn'steɪt] vt reintegrar; (tax, law) reinstaurar

reiterate [riː'ɪtəreɪt] vt reiterar, repetir

reject [n 'riːdʒɛkt, vb rɪ'dʒɛkt] n (thing) desecho ♦ vt rechazar; (suggestion) desechar, descartar; (coin) expulsar ❑ **rejection** [rɪ'dʒɛkʃən] n rechazo

rejoice [rɪ'dʒɔɪs] vi: **to ~ at** or **over** alegrarse or regocijarse de

rejuvenate [rɪ'dʒuːvəneɪt] vt rejuvenecer

relapse ['riːlæps] n recaída

relate [rɪ'leɪt] vt (tell) contar, relatar; (connect) relacionar ♦ vi relacionarse ❑ **related** adj afín; (person) emparentado; **related to** (subject) relacionado con ❑ **relating to** prep referente a

relation [rɪ'leɪʃən] n (person) familiar mf, pariente mf; (link) relación f; **~s** npl (relatives) familiares mpl ❑ **relationship** n relación f; (personal) relaciones fpl; (also: **family relationship**) parentesco

relative ['relatɪv] n pariente mf, familiar mf ♦ adj relativo ❑ **relatively** adv (comparatively) relativamente

relax [rɪ'læks] vi descansar; (unwind) relajarse ♦ vt (one's grip) soltar, aflojar; (control) relajar; (mind, person) descansar ❑ **relaxation** [,riːlæk'seɪʃən] n descanso; (of rule, control) relajamiento; (entertainment) diversión f ❑ **relaxed** adj relajado; (tranquil) tranquilo ❑ **relaxing** adj relajante

relay ['riːleɪ] n (race) carrera de relevos ♦ vt (RADIO, TV) retransmitir

release [rɪ'liːs] n (liberation) liberación f; (from prison) puesta en libertad; (of gas etc) escape m; (of movie etc) estreno; (of record) lanzamiento ♦ vt (prisoner) poner en libertad; (gas) despedir, arrojar; (from wreckage) soltar; (catch, spring etc) desenganchar; (movie) estrenar; (book) publicar; (news) hacer público

relegate ['reləgeɪt] vt relegar; (BRIT SPORT): **to be ~d to** bajar a

relent [rɪ'lent] vi ablandarse ❑ **relentless** adj implacable

relevant ['relavant] adj (fact) pertinente; **~ to** relacionado con

reliable [rɪ'laɪəbəl] adj (person, firm) de confianza, de fiar; (method, machine) seguro, fiable; (source) fidedigno ❑ **reliably** adv: **to be reliably informed that ...** saber de fuente fidedigna que ...

reliance [rɪ'laɪəns] n: **~ (on)** dependencia (de)

relic ['relɪk] n (REL) reliquia; (of the past) vestigio

relief [rɪ'liːf] n (from pain, anxiety) alivio; (help, supplies) socorro, ayuda; (ART, GEO) relieve m

relieve [rɪ'liːv] vt (pain) aliviar; (bring help to) ayudar, socorrer; (take over from) sustituir; (: guard) relevar; **to ~ sb of sth** quitar algo a algn; **to ~ o.s.** ir al baño

religion [rɪ'lɪdʒən] n religión f ❑ **religious** adj religioso

relinquish [rɪ'lɪŋkwɪʃ] vt abandonar; (plan, habit) renunciar a

relish ['relɪʃ] n (CULIN) salsa; (enjoyment) entusiasmo ♦ vt (food etc) saborear; (enjoy): **to ~ sth** hacerle mucha ilusión a algn algo

relocate [,riːlou'keɪt] vt cambiar de lugar, mudar ♦ vi mudarse

reluctance [rɪ'lʌktəns] n reticencia

reluctant [rɪ'lʌktənt] adj reacio ❑ **reluctantly** adv de mala gana

rely on [rɪ'laɪ,ɑːn] vt fus depender de; (trust) contar con

remain [rɪ'meɪn] vi (survive) quedar; (be left) sobrar; (continue) quedar(se), permanecer ❑ **remainder** n resto ❑ **remaining** adj que queda(n); (surviving) restante(s) ❑ **remains** npl restos mpl

remand [rɪ'mænd] n: **on ~** en prisión preventiva ♦ vt: **to be ~ed in custody** quedar en libertad bajo fianza ❑ **remand home** (BRIT) n correccional f (LAm) or m (SP) (de menores)

remark [rɪ'mɑːrk] n comentario ♦ vt comentar ❑ **remarkable** adj (outstanding) extraordinario

remarry [,riː'mæri] vi volver a casarse

remedial [rɪ'miːdiəl] adj de recuperación

remedy ['remədi] n remedio ♦ vt remediar, curar

remember [rɪ'membər] vt recordar, acordarse de; (bear in mind) tener presente; (send greetings to): **~ me to him** dale recuerdos de mi parte ❑ **remembrance** n recuerdo ❑ **Remembrance Day** (BRIT) n día en el que se recuerda a los caídos en las dos guerras mundiales

remind [rɪ'maɪnd] vt: **to ~ sb to do sth** recordar a algn que haga algo; **to ~ sb of sth** (of fact) recordar algo a algn; **she ~s me of her**

mother me recuerda a mi madre
❏ **reminder** n (memento) recuerdo; (BRIT: letter etc) notificación f

reminisce [ˌrɛmɪˈnɪs] vi rememorar, recordar ❏ **reminiscent** adj: **to be ~ of sth** recordar algo

remiss [rɪˈmɪs] adj descuidado; **it was ~ of him** fue un descuido de su parte

remission [rɪˈmɪʃən] n remisión f; (REL) perdón m; (BRIT: reduction of prison sentence) disminución f de la pena

remit [rɪˈmɪt] vt (send money) remitir, enviar ❏ **remittance** n remesa, envío

remnant [ˈrɛmnənt] n resto; (of cloth) retal m; **~s** npl (COMM) restos mpl (de serie)

remorse [rɪˈmɔːrs] n remordimiento ❏ **remorseful** adj arrepentido ❏ **remorseless** adj (fig) implacable, inexorable

remote [rɪˈmout] adj (distant) remoto; (person) distante ❏ **remote control** n mando a distancia, control m remoto ❏ **remotely** adv remotamente; (slightly) levemente

remould [ˈriːmould] (BRIT) n = **retread**

removable [rɪˈmuːvəbəl] adj (detachable) separable

removal [rɪˈmuːvəl] n (taking away) traslado; (from office: dismissal) destitución f; (MED) extirpación f; (BRIT: from house) mudanza ❏ **removal van** (BRIT) n camión m de mudanzas

remove [rɪˈmuːv] vt quitar; (employee) destituir; (name: from list) tachar, borrar; (doubt) disipar; (abuse) suprimir, acabar con; (MED) extirpar

Renaissance [ˈrɛnɪsɑːns] n: **the ~** el Renacimiento

render [ˈrɛndər] vt (thanks) dar; (aid) proporcionar, prestar; (make): **to ~ sth useless** hacer algo inútil ❏ **rendering** n (MUS etc) interpretación f

rendezvous [ˈrɑːndeɪvuː] n cita

renew [rɪˈnuː] vt renovar; (resume) reanudar; (loan etc) prorrogar ❏ **renewable** adj renovable ❏ **renewal** n reanudación f; prórroga

renounce [rɪˈnauns] vt renunciar a; (right, inheritance) renunciar

renovate [ˈrɛnəveɪt] vt renovar

renown [rɪˈnaun] n renombre m ❏ **renowned** adj renombrado

rent [rɛnt] n (for house, apartment) alquiler m, renta (MEX) ♦ vt alquilar, rentar (MEX); **"for ~"**

(US) "se alquila or (MEX) renta" ❏ **rental** n (for television, car) alquiler m, renta (MEX)

rep [rɛp] n abbr = **representative**; **repertory**

repair [rɪˈpɛər] n reparación f, compostura ♦ vt reparar, componer; (shoes) remendar; **in good/bad ~** en buen/mal estado ❏ **repair kit** n caja de herramientas

repatriate [ˌriːˈpeɪtrieɪt] vt repatriar

repay [riːˈpeɪ] vt (money) devolver, reembolsar; (person) pagar; (debt) liquidar; (sb's efforts) devolver, corresponder a ❏ **repayment** n reembolso, devolución f; (sum of money) recompensa

repeal [rɪˈpiːl] n revocación f ♦ vt revocar

repeat [rɪˈpiːt] n (reposición f ♦ vt repetir ♦ vi repetirse ❏ **repeatedly** adv repetidas veces

repel [rɪˈpɛl] vt (drive away) rechazar; (disgust) repugnar ❏ **repellent** adj repugnante ♦ n: **insect repellent** repelente m de insectos

repent [rɪˈpɛnt] vi: **to ~ (of)** arrepentirse (de) ❏ **repentance** n arrepentimiento

repercussions [ˌriːpərˈkʌʃənz] npl consecuencias fpl

repertory [ˈrɛpərtɔːri] n (also: **~ theater**) teatro de repertorio

repetition [ˌrɛpɪˈtɪʃən] n repetición f

repetitive [rɪˈpɛtɪtɪv] adj repetitivo

replace [rɪˈpleɪs] vt (put back) volver a poner, devolver; (take the place) sustituir, reemplazar ❏ **replacement** n (act) reposición f; (thing) recambio; (person) suplente mf

replay [ˈriːpleɪ] n (SPORT) desempate m; (of tape, movie) repetición f

replenish [rɪˈplɛnɪʃ] vt rellenar; (stock etc) reponer

replica [ˈrɛplɪkə] n réplica

reply [rɪˈplaɪ] n respuesta, contestación f ♦ vi responder, contestar

report [rɪˈpɔːrt] n informe m; (PRESS etc) reportaje m; (of gun) estallido; (BRIT: also: **school ~**) boleta (MEX) or libreta (LAm) or boletín m (SP) de calificaciones ♦ vt informar de; (PRESS etc) hacer un reportaje sobre; (notify: accident, culprit) denunciar ♦ vi (make a report) presentar un informe; (present o.s.): **to ~ (to sb)** presentarse (ante algn) ❏ **report card** (US, SCOTLAND) n boleta (MEX) or libreta (LAm) or boletín m (SP) de calificaciones ❏ **reportedly** adv según se dice ❏ **reporter** n periodista mf

repose [rɪˈpouz] n: **in ~** (face, mouth) en reposo

reprehensible [ˌrɛprɪˈhɛnsɪbəl] adj reprensible, censurable

represent [ˌreprɪˈzent] vt representar; (COMM) ser agente de; (describe): **to ~ sth as** describir algo como ❏ **representation** [ˌreprɪzenˈteɪʃən] n representación f; **representations** npl (protest) quejas fpl ❏ **representative** n representante mf; (US POL) diputado(-a) ♦ adj representativo

repress [rɪˈpres] vt reprimir ❏ **repression** n represión f

reprieve [rɪˈpriːv] n (LAW) indulto; (fig) alivio

reprisals [rɪˈpraɪzəlz] npl represalias fpl

reproach [rɪˈprəʊtʃ] n reproche m ♦ vt: **to ~ sb for sth** reprochar algo a algn ❏ **reproachful** adj de reproche, de acusación

reproduce [ˌriːprəˈdjuːs] vt reproducir ♦ vi reproducirse ❏ **reproduction** [ˌriːprəˈdʌkʃən] n reproducción f

reprove [rɪˈpruːv] vt: **to ~ sb for sth** reprochar algo a algn

reptile [ˈreptaɪl] n reptil m

republic [rɪˈpʌblɪk] n república ❏ **republican** adj, n republicano(-a)

repudiate [rɪˈpjuːdɪeɪt] vt rechazar; (violence etc) repudiar

repulsive [rɪˈpʌlsɪv] adj repugnante

reputable [ˈrepjətəbəl] adj acreditado

reputation [ˌrepjəˈteɪʃən] n reputación f

reputed [rɪˈpjuːtɪd] adj supuesto ❏ **reputedly** adv según dicen or se dice

request [rɪˈkwest] n petición f; (formal) solicitud f ♦ vt: **to ~ sth of or from sb** solicitar algo a algn ❏ **request stop** (BRIT) n parada discrecional

require [rɪˈkwaɪər] vt (need: person) necesitar, tener necesidad de; (: thing, situation) requerir, exigir; (want) pedir; **to ~ sb to do sth** pedir a algn que haga algo ❏ **requirement** n requisito; (need) necesidad f

requisition [ˌrekwɪˈzɪʃən] n: **~ (for)** solicitud f (de) ♦ vt (MIL) requisar

rerun [ˈriːrʌn] n reposición f, repetición f

rescue [ˈreskjuː] n rescate m ♦ vt rescatar ❏ **rescue party** n expedición f de salvamento ❏ **rescuer** n salvador(a) m/f

research [rɪˈsɜːtʃ] n investigación f ♦ vt investigar ❏ **researcher** n investigador(a) m/f

resemblance [rɪˈzembləns] n parecido

resemble [rɪˈzembəl] vt parecerse a

resent [rɪˈzent] vt tomar a mal ❏ **resentful** adj resentido ❏ **resentment** n resentimiento

reservation [ˌrezərˈveɪʃən] n reserva; see also **Native American**

reserve [rɪˈzɜːrv] n reserva; (BRIT SPORT) suplente mf ♦ vt (seats etc) reservar; **~s** npl (MIL) reserva; **in ~** de reserva ❏ **reserved** adj reservado

reshuffle [ˈriːˈʃʌfəl] (BRIT) n: **Cabinet ~** (POL) remodelación f del gabinete

residence [ˈrezɪdəns] n (formal: home) domicilio; (length of stay) permanencia ❏ **residence permit** (BRIT) n permiso de permanencia

resident [ˈrezɪdənt] n (of area) vecino(-a); (in hotel) huésped mf ♦ adj (population) permanente; (doctor) residente ❏ **residential** [ˌrezɪˈdenʃəl] adj residencial

residue [ˈrezɪdjuː] n resto

resign [rɪˈzaɪn] vt renunciar a ♦ vi dimitir; **to ~ o.s. to** (situation) resignarse a ❏ **resignation** [ˌrezɪgˈneɪʃən] n dimisión f; (state of mind) resignación f ❏ **resigned** adj resignado

resilient [rɪˈzɪlɪənt] adj (material) elástico; (person) resistente

resist [rɪˈzɪst] vt resistir, oponerse a ❏ **resistance** n resistencia

resolute [ˈrezəluːt] adj resuelto; (refusal) tajante

resolution [ˌrezəˈluːʃən] n resolución f; (goal) propósito

resolve [rɪˈzɒlv] n resolución f ♦ vt resolver ♦ vi: **to ~ to do** resolver hacer ❏ **resolved** adj resuelto

resort [rɪˈzɔːrt] n (town) centro turístico; (recourse) recurso ♦ vi: **to ~ to** recurrir a; **in the last ~** como último recurso

resounding [rɪˈzaʊndɪŋ] adj sonoro; (fig) clamoroso

resource [ˈriːsɔːrs] n recurso; **~s** npl recursos mpl ❏ **resourceful** adj despabilado, ingenioso

respect [rɪˈspekt] n respeto ♦ vt respetar; **~s** npl recuerdos mpl, saludos mpl; **with ~ to** con respecto a; **in this ~** en cuanto a eso ❏ **respectable** adj respetable; (large: amount) apreciable; (passable) tolerable ❏ **respectful** adj respetuoso

respective [rɪˈspektɪv] adj respectivo ❏ **respectively** adv respectivamente

respite [ˈrespɪt] n respiro

respond [rɪˈspɒnd] vi responder; (react) reaccionar ❏ **response** n respuesta; reacción f

responsibility [rɪˌspɒnsəˈbɪlətɪ] n responsabilidad f

responsible [rɪ'spɑːnsəbəl] *adj* (*character*) serio, formal; (*job*) de confianza; (*liable*): ~ **(for)** responsable (de)

responsive [rɪ'spɑːnsɪv] *adj* sensible

rest [rest] *n* descanso, reposo; (*MUS, pause*) pausa, silencio; (*support*) apoyo; (*remainder*) resto ♦ *vi* descansar; (*be supported*): **to ~ on** descansar sobre *vt* (*lean*): **to ~ sth on/against** apoyar algo en or sobre/contra; **the ~ of them** (*people, objects*) los demás; **it ~s with him to ...** depende de él el que ... ❑ **rest area** (*US*) *n* (*AUT*) área de servicios

restaurant ['restərɑːnt] *n* restaurante *m* ❑ **restaurant car** (*BRIT*) *n* (*RAIL*) coche-comedor *m*

restful ['restfʊl] *adj* descansado, tranquilo

rest home *n* residencia de ancianos

restive ['restɪv] *adj* inquieto; (*horse*) rebelón(-ona)

restless ['restlɪs] *adj* inquieto

rest stop (*US*) *n* = **rest area**

restoration [restə'reɪʃən] *n* restauración *f*; devolución *f*

restore [rɪ'stɔːr] *vt* (*building, monarch*) restaurar; (*sth stolen*) devolver; (*peace, health*) restablecer

restrain [rɪ'streɪn] *vt* (*feeling*) contener, refrenar; (*person*): **to ~ (from doing)** disuadir (de hacer) ❑ **restrained** *adj* reservado ❑ **restraint** *n* (*restriction*) restricción *f*; (*moderation*) moderación *f*; (*of manner*) reserva

restrict [rɪ'strɪkt] *vt* restringir, limitar ❑ **restriction** *n* restricción *f*, limitación *f* ❑ **restrictive** *adj* restrictivo

rest room (*US*) *n* baño, servicios *mpl*

restructure [riː'strʌktʃər] *vt* reconvertir

result [rɪ'zʌlt] *n* resultado ♦ *vi*: **to ~ in** terminar en, tener por resultado; **as a ~ of** a consecuencia de

resume [rɪ'zuːm] *vt* reanudar ♦ *vi* comenzar de nuevo

⚠ Be careful not to translate **resume** by the Spanish word **resumir**.

résumé ['reɪzəmeɪ] *n* (*US: of work experience*) currículum *m* (vitae); (*summary*) resumen *m*

resumption [rɪ'zʌmpʃən] *n* reanudación *f*

resurgence [rɪ'sɜːrdʒəns] *n* resurgimiento

resurrection [rezə'rekʃən] *n* resurrección *f*

resuscitate [rɪ'sʌsɪteɪt] *vt* (*MED*) resucitar

retail ['riːteɪl] *adj, adv* al por menor ❑ **retailer** *n* minorista *mf* ❑ **retail price** *n* precio de venta al público

retain [rɪ'teɪn] *vt* (*keep*) retener, conservar ❑ **retainer** *n* (*fee*) anticipo; (*US*) frenos *mpl* (*LAm*), aparato(s) *m(pl)* (*SP*)

retaliate [rɪ'tælieɪt] *vi*: **to ~ (against)** tomar represalias (contra) ❑ **retaliation** [rɪˌtæli'eɪʃən] *n* represalias *fpl*

retarded [rɪ'tɑːrdɪd] *adj* retrasado

retch [retʃ] *vi* tener arcadas

retentive [rɪ'tentɪv] *adj* (*memory*) retentivo

retire [rɪ'taɪər] *vi* (*give up work*) jubilarse; (*withdraw*) retirarse; (*go to bed*) acostarse ❑ **retired** *adj* (*person*) jubilado ❑ **retiree** [rɪˌtaɪə'riː] (*US*) *n* jubilado(-a) ❑ **retirement** *n* (*giving up work: state*) retiro; (: *act*) jubilación *f* ❑ **retiring** *adj* (*leaving*) saliente; (*shy*) retraído

retort [rɪ'tɔːrt] *vi* contestar

retrace [ˌriː'treɪs] *vt*: **I ~d my steps** volví sobre mis pasos

retract [rɪ'trækt] *vt* (*statement*) retirar; (*claws*) retraer; (*undercarriage, antenna*) replegar

retrain [ˌriː'treɪn] *vt* reciclar ❑ **retraining** *n* readaptación *f* profesional

retread ['riːtred] *n* (*tire*) llanta (*LAm*) or neumático (*SP*) recauchutada(-o)

retreat [rɪ'triːt] *n* (*place*) retiro; (*MIL*) retirada ♦ *vi* retirarse

retribution [retrɪ'bjuːʃən] *n* desquite *m*

retrieval [rɪ'triːvəl] *n* recuperación *f*

retrieve [rɪ'triːv] *vt* recobrar; (*situation, honor*) salvar; (*COMPUT*) recuperar; (*error*) reparar ❑ **retriever** *n* perro cobrador (de caza)

retrospect ['retrəspekt] *n*: **in ~** retrospectivamente ❑ **retrospective** [retrə'spektɪv] *adj* retrospectivo; (*law*) retroactivo

return [rɪ'tɜːrn] *n* (*going or coming back*) vuelta, regreso; (*of sth stolen etc*) devolución *f*; (*FINANCE: from land, shares*) ganancia, ingresos *mpl* ♦ *cpd* (*journey*) de regreso; (*BRIT: ticket*) de ida y vuelta; (*BRIT: match*) de vuelta ♦ *vi* (*person etc: come or go back*) volver, regresar; (*symptoms etc*) reaparecer; (*regain*): **to ~ to** recuperar ♦ *vt* devolver; (*favor, love etc*) corresponder a; (*verdict*) pronunciar; (*POL: candidate*) elegir; **~s** *npl* (*COMM*) ingresos *mpl*; **in ~ (for)** a cambio (de); **by ~ mail** a vuelta de correo; **many happy ~s (of the day)!** ¡feliz cumpleaños!

reunion [riː'juːnjən] *n* (*of family*) reunión *f*; (*of two people, school*) reencuentro

reunite [ˌriːjuː'naɪt] *vt* reunir; (*reconcile*) reconciliar

rev [rev] n abbr (AUT: revolution) revolución f
♦ vt (AUT: also: ~ up) acelerar

reveal [rɪ'viːl] vt revelar ☐ **revealing** adj
revelador(a)

revel ['revəl] vi: **to ~ in sth/in doing sth** gozar
de algo/con hacer algo

revenge [rɪ'vɛndʒ] n venganza; **to take ~ on**
vengarse de

revenue ['revənuː] n ingresos mpl, rentas fpl

reverberate [rɪ'vɜːrbəreɪt] vi (sound)
resonar, retumbar; (fig: shock) repercutir

reverence ['revərəns] n reverencia

Reverend ['revərənd] adj (in titles): **the ~**
John Smith (Anglican) el Reverendo John
Smith; (Catholic) el Padre John Smith;
(Protestant) el Pastor John Smith

reversal [rɪ'vɜːrsəl] n (of order) inversión f; (of
direction, policy) cambio; (of decision)
revocación f

reverse [rɪ'vɜːrs] n (opposite) contrario; (back:
of cloth) revés m; (: of coin) reverso; (: of paper)
dorso; (AUT: also: ~ gear) reversa (MEX, CAm),
marcha atrás (LAm exc MEX, SP) ♦ adj (order)
inverso; (direction) contrario; (process)
opuesto ♦ vt (decision, AUT) meter reversa a
(MEX, CAm), dar marcha atrás a (LAm exc MEX,
SP); (position, function) invertir ♦ vi (AUT) meter
reversa (MEX, CAm), dar marcha atrás (LAm exc
MEX, SP) ☐ **reverse-charge call** (BRIT) n
llamada por cobrar (MEX) or a cobro revertido
(LAm exc MEX, SP) ☐ **reversing lights** (BRIT)
npl (AUT) luces fpl de reversa (MEX) or marcha
atrás (LAm exc MEX, SP)

revert [rɪ'vɜːrt] vi: **to ~ to** volver a

review [rɪ'vjuː] n (magazine, MIL) revista; (of
book, movie) reseña; (US SCOL) repaso ♦ vt
(assess) examinar, analizar; (MIL) pasar revista
a; (book, movie) reseñar; (US SCOL) repasar
☐ **reviewer** n crítico(-a)

revise [rɪ'vaɪz] vt (manuscript) corregir;
(opinion) modificar; (price, procedure) revisar;
(BRIT: subject, notes) repasar ♦ vi (BRIT: study)
repasar ☐ **revision** [rɪ'vɪʒən] n (of text)
revisión f; (of estimate, figures) corrección f; (of
offer) reconsideración f; (BRIT: for exam) repaso

revival [rɪ'vaɪvəl] n (recovery) reanimación f;
(of interest) renacimiento; (THEATER) reestreno;
(of faith) despertar m

revive [rɪ'vaɪv] vt resucitar; (custom)
restablecer; (hope) despertar; (play)
reestrenar ♦ vi (person) volver en sí; (business)
reactivarse

revolt [rɪ'voʊlt] n rebelión f ♦ vi rebelarse,
sublevarse ♦ vt dar asco a, repugnar
☐ **revolting** adj asqueroso, repugnante

revolution [revə'luːʃən] n revolución f
☐ **revolutionary** adj, n revolucionario(-a)
☐ **revolutionize** vt revolucionar

revolve [rɪ'vɑːlv] vi dar vueltas, girar; (life,
discussion): **to ~ around** or (BRIT) **round** girar
en torno a

revolver [rɪ'vɑːlvər] n revólver m

revolving [rɪ'vɑːlvɪŋ] adj (chair, door etc)
giratorio

revue [rɪ'vjuː] n (THEATER) revista

revulsion [rɪ'vʌlʃən] n asco, repugnancia

reward [rɪ'wɔːrd] n recompensa, premio ♦ vt:
to ~ (for) recompensar or premiar (por)
☐ **rewarding** adj gratificante

rewind [riː'waɪnd] vt rebobinar

rewire [riː'waɪər] vt (house) renovar la
instalación eléctrica de

rewritable [riː'raɪtəbl] adj reescribible

rheumatism ['ruːmətɪzəm] n reumatismo,
reúma m

Rhine [raɪn] n: **the ~** el (río) Rin

rhinoceros [raɪ'nɑːsərəs] n rinoceronte m

rhododendron [roʊdə'dɛndrən] n
rododendro

Rhone [roʊn] n: **the ~** el (río) Ródano

rhubarb ['ruːbɑːrb] n ruibarbo

rhyme [raɪm] n rima; (verse) poesía

rhythm ['rɪðəm] n ritmo

rib [rɪb] n (ANAT) costilla ♦ vt (mock) tomar el
pelo a

ribbon ['rɪbən] n cinta; **in ~s** (torn) hecho trizas

rice [raɪs] n arroz m ☐ **rice pudding** n arroz
m con leche

rich [rɪtʃ] adj rico; (soil) fértil; (food) pesado;
(: sweet) empalagoso; (abundant): **~ in**
(minerals etc) rico en ♦ npl: **the ~** los ricos
☐ **riches** npl riqueza ☐ **richly** adv
ricamente; (deserved, earned) bien

rickets ['rɪkɪts] n raquitismo

rid [rɪd] (pt, pp ~) vt: **to ~ sb of sth** librar a algn
de algo; **to get ~ of** deshacerse or
desembarazarse de

ridden ['rɪdn] pp of **ride**

riddle ['rɪdl] n (puzzle) acertijo; (mystery)
enigma m, misterio ♦ vt: **to be ~d with** estar
lleno or plagado de

ride [raɪd] (pt rode, pp ridden) n paseo;
(distance covered) viaje m, recorrido; (US: free
ride) viaje m gratuito ♦ vi (as sport) montar; (go
somewhere: on horse, bicycle) dar un paseo,
pasearse; (travel: on bicycle, motorcycle, bus)
viajar ♦ vt (a horse) montar a; (a bicycle,
motorcycle) ir en; (distance) recorrer; **to give**
sb a ~ (US) dar a algn un aventón (MEX), llevar

a algn en carro (*LAm*) or coche (*SP*); **to take sb for a ~** (*fig*) engañar a algn ❑ **rider** *n* (*on horse*) jinete *mf*; (*on bicycle*) ciclista *mf*; (*on motorcycle*) motociclista *mf*

ridge [rɪdʒ] *n* (*of hill*) cresta; (*of roof*) caballete *m*; (*wrinkle*) arruga

ridicule ['rɪdɪkjuːl] *n* burlas *fpl* ♦ *vt* poner en ridículo, burlarse de ❑ **ridiculous** [rɪ'dɪkjələs] *adj* ridículo

riding ['raɪdɪŋ] *n* equitación *f*; **I like ~** me gusta montar a caballo ❑ **riding school** *n* escuela de equitación

rife [raɪf] *adj*: **to be ~** ser muy común; **to be ~ with** abundar en

riffraff ['rɪf͜ræf] *n* gentuza

rifle ['raɪfəl] *n* rifle *m*, fusil *m* ♦ *vt* saquear ▶ **rifle through** *vt* (*papers*) registrar ❑ **rifle range** *n* campo de tiro; (*at fair*) tiro al blanco

rift [rɪft] *n* (*in clouds*) claro; (*fig*: *disagreement*) desavenencia

rig [rɪg] *n* (*truck*) vehículo articulado; (*also*: **oil ~**: *at sea*) plataforma petrolera ♦ *vt* (*election etc*) amañar ▶ **rig out** (*BRIT*) *vt* disfrazar ▶ **rig up** *vt* improvisar ❑ **rigging** (*NAUT*) aparejo

right [raɪt] *adj* (*correct*) correcto, exacto; (*suitable*) indicado, debido; (*proper*) apropiado; (*just*) justo; (*morally good*) bueno; (*not left*) derecho ♦ *n* bueno; (*title, claim*) derecho; (*not left*) derecha ♦ *adv* bien, correctamente; (*not left*) a la derecha; (*exactly*): **~ now** ahora mismo ♦ *vt* enderezar; (*correct*) corregir ♦ *excl* ¡bueno!, ¡está bien!; **to be ~** (*person*) tener razón; (*answer*) ser correcto; **is that the ~ time?** (*of clock*) ¿es esa la hora exacta or correcta?; **by ~s** en justicia; **on the ~** a la derecha; **to be in the ~** tener razón; **~ away** en seguida; **~ in the middle** justo en medio ❑ **right angle** *n* ángulo recto ❑ **righteous** ['raɪtʃəs] *adj* honrado; (*anger*) justificado ❑ **rightful** *adj* legítimo ❑ **right-handed** *adj* diestro ❑ **right-hand man** *n* brazo derecho ❑ **right-hand side** *n* derecha ❑ **rightly** *adv* correctamente, debidamente; (*with reason*) con razón ❑ **right of way** *n* (*on path etc*) derecho de paso; (*AUT*) prioridad *f* ❑ **right-wing** *adj* (*POL*) derechista

rigid ['rɪdʒɪd] *adj* rígido; (*person, ideas*) inflexible

rigmarole ['rɪgməroʊl] *n* galimatías *m inv*

rigor (*US*) ['rɪgər] (*BRIT* **rigour**) *n* rigor *m*

rigorous ['rɪgərəs] *adj* riguroso

rigour ['rɪgər] (*BRIT*) *n* = **rigor**

rile [raɪl] *vt* irritar

rim [rɪm] *n* borde *m*; (*of spectacles*) montura; (*of wheel*) rin *m* (*LAm*), llanta (*SP*)

rind [raɪnd] *n* (*of bacon*) corteza; (*of lemon etc*) cáscara; (*of cheese*) costra

ring [rɪŋ] (*pt* **rang**, *pp* **rung**) *n* (*of metal*) aro; (*on finger*) anillo; (*of people*) corro; (*of objects*) círculo; (*gang*) banda; (*for boxing*) cuadrilátero; (*of circus*) pista; (*bull ring*) ruedo, plaza; (*sound of bell*) timbrazo ♦ *vi* (*on telephone*) llamar (por teléfono); (*bell*) repicar; (*doorbell, phone*) sonar; (*also*: **~ out**) sonar; (*ears*) zumbar ♦ *vt* hacer sonar; (*doorbell*) tocar; (*BRIT TEL*) llamar (por teléfono); **to give sb a ~** (*BRIT TEL*) llamar a algn (por teléfono) ▶ **ring back** (*BRIT*) *vt*, *vi* (*TEL*) volver a llamar ▶ **ring off** (*BRIT*) *vi* (*TEL*) colgar, cortar la comunicación ▶ **ring up** (*BRIT*) *vt* (*TEL*) llamar (por teléfono) ❑ **ringing** *n* (*of bell*) repique *m*; (*of phone*) el sonar; (*in ears*) zumbido ❑ **ringing tone** (*BRIT*) *n* (*TEL*) tono (de llamada) ❑ **ringleader** *n* (*of gang*) cabecilla *m* ❑ **ringlets** *npl* rizos *mpl*, bucles *mpl* ❑ **ring road** (*BRIT*) *n* libramiento (*MEX*), carretera de circunvalación (*LAm exc MEX, SP*)

rink [rɪŋk] *n* (*also*: **ice ~**) pista de hielo

rinse [rɪns] *n* aclarado; (*dye*) tinte *m* ♦ *vt* aclarar; (*mouth*) enjuagar

riot ['raɪət] *n* motín *m*, disturbio ♦ *vi* amotinarse; **to run ~** desmandarse ❑ **riotous** *adj* alborotado; (*party*) bullicioso

rip [rɪp] *n* rasgón *m*, rasgadura ♦ *vt* rasgar, desgarrar ♦ *vi* rasgarse, desgarrarse ❑ **ripcord** *n* cable *m* de apertura

ripe [raɪp] *adj* maduro ❑ **ripen** *vt* madurar; (*cheese*) curar ♦ *vi* madurar

ripple ['rɪpəl] *n* onda, rizo; (*sound*) murmullo ♦ *vi* rizarse

rise [raɪz] (*pt* **rose**, *pp* **~n**) *n* (*slope*) cuesta, pendiente *f*; (*hill*) altura; (*in prices, temperature*) subida; (*fig*: *to power etc*) ascenso; (*BRIT*: *in wages*) aumento ♦ *vi* subir; (*waters*) crecer; (*sun, moon*) salir; (*person: from bed etc*) levantarse; (*also*: **~ up**: *rebel*) sublevarse; (*in rank*) ascender; **to give ~ to** dar lugar or origen a; **to ~ to the occasion** estar a la altura de las circunstancias ❑ **risen** ['rɪzən] *pp of* **rise** ❑ **rising** *adj* (*increasing*: *number*) creciente; (: *prices*) en aumento or alza; (*tide*) creciente; (*sun, moon*) naciente

risk [rɪsk] *n* riesgo, peligro ♦ *vt* arriesgar; (*run the risk of*) exponerse a; **to take** or **run the ~ of doing** correr el riesgo de hacer; **at ~** en peligro; **at one's own ~** bajo su propia responsabilidad ❑ **risky** *adj* arriesgado, peligroso

rissole ['rɪsoʊl] (*BRIT*) *n* croqueta

rite [raɪt] n rito; **last ~s** extremaunción f

ritual ['rɪtjʊəl] adj ritual ♦ n ritual m, rito

rival ['raɪvəl] n rival mf; (in business) competidor(a) m/f ♦ adj rival, opuesto ♦ vt competir con ❑ **rivalry** n competencia

river ['rɪvər] n río ♦ cpd (port) de río; (traffic) fluvial; **up/down ~** río arriba/abajo ❑ **riverbank** n orilla (del río) ❑ **riverbed** n lecho, cauce m

rivet ['rɪvɪt] n roblón m, remache m ♦ vt (fig) captar

Riviera [rɪvɪ'ɛrə] n: **the (French) ~** la Riviera or Costa Azul (francesa)

roach [rəʊtʃ] (US) n (cockroach) cucaracha

road [rəʊd] n camino; (highway etc) carretera; (in town) calle f ♦ cpd (accident) de tráfico; **major/minor ~** carretera principal/ secundaria ❑ **road accident** n accidente m de tráfico ❑ **roadblock** n barricada ❑ **road hog** n loco(-a) del volante ❑ **road map** n mapa m de carreteras ❑ **road rage** n conducta agresiva al volante ❑ **road safety** n seguridad f vial ❑ **roadside** n borde m (del camino) ❑ **roadsign** n señal f de tráfico ❑ **road user** n usuario(-a) de la vía pública ❑ **roadway** n calzada ❑ **roadworks** npl obras fpl ❑ **roadworthy** adj (car) en buen estado para circular

roam [rəʊm] vi vagar

roar [rɔːr] n rugido; (of vehicle, storm) estruendo; (of laughter) carcajada ♦ vi rugir; hacer estruendo; **to ~ with laughter** reírse a carcajadas; **to do a ~ing trade** hacer buen negocio

roast [rəʊst] n carne f asada, asado ♦ vt asar; (coffee) tostar ❑ **roast beef** n rosbif m

rob [rɒb] vt robar; **to ~ sb of sth** robar algo a algn; (fig: deprive) quitar algo a algn ❑ **robber** n ladrón(-ona) m/f ❑ **robbery** n robo

robe [rəʊb] n (for ceremony etc) toga; (bathrobe) bata de baño, albornoz m, salida de baño (RPl)

robin ['rɒbɪn] n petirrojo

robot ['rəʊbɒt] n robot m

robust [rəʊ'bʌst] adj robusto, fuerte

rock [rɒk] n roca; (boulder) peña, peñasco; (US: small stone) piedrecita; (BRIT: sweet) ≈ pirulí m ♦ vt (swing gently: cradle) balancear, mecer; (: child) arrullar; (shake) sacudir ♦ vi mecerse, balancearse; sacudirse; **on the ~s** (drink) con hielo; (marriage etc) en ruinas ❑ **rock and roll** n rocanrol m ❑ **rock-bottom** n (fig) punto más bajo

❑ **rocker** (US) n (chair) mecedora ❑ **rockery** n cuadro alpino

rocket ['rɒkɪt] n cohete m

rocking ♦ **rocking chair** n mecedora ❑ **rocking horse** n caballo de balancín

rocky ['rɒki] adj rocoso

rod [rɒd] n vara, varilla; (also: **fishing ~**) caña (de pescar)

rode [rəʊd] pt of **ride**

rodent ['rəʊdnt] n roedor m

roe [rəʊ] n (roe deer) corzo; (of fish): **hard/soft ~** hueva/lecha

rogue [rəʊg] n pícaro, pillo

role [rəʊl] n papel m

roll [rəʊl] n rollo; (of bank notes) fajo; (also: **bread ~**) bolillo (MEX), pancito (LAm exc MEX), panecillo (SP); (register, list) lista, nómina; (sound: of drums etc) redoble m ♦ vt hacer rodar; (also: **~ up:** string) enrollar; (: sleeves) remangar; (cigarette) liar, enrollar; (also: **~ out:** pastry) estirar, aplanar; (flatten: road, lawn) apisonar ♦ vi rodar; (drum) redoblar; (ship) balancearse ▶ **roll around** or **~ about** about vi (person) revolcarse; (object) rodar (por) ▶ **roll by** vi (time) pasar ▶ **roll over** vi dar una vuelta ▶ **roll up** vi (inf: arrive) aparecer ♦ vt (carpet) arrollar ❑ **roll call:** to take a **roll call** pasar lista ❑ **roller** n rodillo; (wheel) rueda; (for road) apisonadora; (for hair) rulo, tubo (MEX), rulero (RPl) ❑ **Rollerblade®** n patín m (en línea) ❑ **roller coaster** n montaña rusa ❑ **roller skates** npl patines mpl de rueda

rolling ['rəʊlɪŋ] adj (landscape) ondulado ❑ **rolling pin** n rodillo (de cocina) ❑ **rolling stock** n (RAIL) material m rodante

ROM [rɒm] n abbr (COMPUT: = read only memory) ROM f

Roman ['rəʊmən] adj romano(-a) ❑ **Roman Catholic** adj, n católico(-a) (romano(-a))

romance [rəʊ'mæns] n (love affair) romance m; (charm) romanticismo; (novel) novela romántica

Romania [rəʊ'meɪnɪə] (US) n Rumanía ❑ **Romanian** adj rumano ♦ n rumano(-a); (LING) rumano

Roman numeral n número romano

romantic [rəʊ'mæntɪk] adj romántico

Rome [rəʊm] n Roma

romp [rɒmp] n retozo, juego ♦ vi (also: **~ about**) jugar, brincar

rompers ['rɒmpəz] npl pelele m

roof [ruːf] (pl **~s**) n techo; (of house) techo, tejado ♦ vt techar, poner techo a; **the ~ of the mouth** el paladar ❑ **roofing** n techumbre f

❏ **roof rack** n (AUT) baca, portaequipajes m inv

rook [ruk] n (bird) graja; (CHESS) torre f

room [ruːm] n habitación f, cuarto; (also: bed~) dormitorio, recámara (MEX), pieza (SC); (in school etc) sala; (space, scope) sitio, cabida; ~s npl (lodging) alojamiento; "~s to let", "~s for rent" (US) "se alquilan cuartos", (MEX) rentan habitaciones"; single/double ~ habitación individual/doble ❏ **rooming house** (US) n pensión f ❏ **roommate** n compañero(-a) de cuarto ❏ **room service** n servicio de habitaciones ❏ **roomy** adj espacioso; (garment) amplio

roost [ruːst] vi posarse (para descansar or dormir)

rooster ['ruːstər] n gallo

root [ruːt] n raíz f ♦ vi arraigarse ▶ **root around** or (BRIT) **about** vi (fig) rebuscar ▶ **root for** vt fus (support) apoyar a ▶ **root out** vt desarraigar

rope [rəup] n cuerda; (NAUT) cable m ♦ vt (tie) atar or amarrar con (una) cuerda; (climbers: also: ~ **together**) encordarse; (an area: also: ~ **off**) acordonar; **to know the ~s** (fig) conocer los trucos (del oficio) ▶ **rope in** vt (fig): **to rope sb in** persuadir a algn a tomar parte

rosary ['rəuzəri] n rosario

rose [rəuz] pt of **rise** ♦ n rosa; (shrub) rosal m; (on watering can) roseta

rosé [rəuˈzeɪ] n vino rosado

rosebud ['rəuzbʌd] n capullo de rosa

rosebush ['rəuzbuʃ] n rosal m

rosemary ['rəuzmɛrɪ] n romero

roster ['rɒstər] n: **duty ~** lista de turnos

rostrum ['rɒstrəm] n tribuna

rosy ['rəuzi] adj rosado, sonrosado; **a ~ future** un futuro prometedor

rot [rɒt] n podredumbre f; (fig: pej) tonterías fpl ♦ vt pudrir ♦ vi pudrirse

rota ['rəutə] n (sistema m de) turnos mpl

rotary ['rəutəri] adj rotativo

rotate [rəuˈteɪt] vt (revolve) hacer girar, dar vueltas a; (jobs) alternar ♦ vi girar, dar vueltas ❏ **rotating** adj rotativo ❏ **rotation** [rəuˈteɪʃən] n rotación f

rotten ['rɒtn] adj podrido; (dishonest) corrompido; (inf: bad) asqueroso; **to feel ~** (sick) sentirse pésimo (LAm) or fatal (SP)

rotund [rəuˈtʌnd] adj regordete

rouble ['ruːbəl] (BRIT) n = **ruble**

rough [rʌf] adj (skin, surface) áspero; (terrain) quebrado; (road) desigual; (voice) bronco; (person, manner) tosco, grosero; (weather) borrascoso; (treatment) brutal; (sea) picado;

(town, area) peligroso; (cloth) basto; (plan) preliminar; (guess) aproximado ♦ n (GOLF): **in the ~** en rough or hierba alta; **to ~ it** vivir sin comodidades; **to sleep ~** (BRIT) dormir a la intemperie ❏ **roughage** n fibra(s) f(pl) ❏ **rough-and-ready** adj improvisado ❏ **rough copy** n = **rough draft** ❏ **rough draft** n borrador m ❏ **roughly** adv (handle) torpemente; (make) toscamente; (speak) groseramente; (approximately) aproximadamente ❏ **roughness** n (of surface) aspereza; (of person) rudeza

roulette [ruːˈlɛt] n ruleta

Roumania [ruːˈmeɪnɪə] (BRIT) n = **Romania**

round [raund] adj redondo ♦ n círculo; (of policeman) ronda; (of milkman) recorrido; (of doctor) visitas fpl; (game: of cards, in competition) partida; (of ammunition) cartucho; (BOXING) round m, asalto; (of talks, drinks) ronda; (BRIT: of toast) rebanada ♦ vt (corner) doblar ♦ prep (BRIT) alrededor de; (surrounding): ~ **his neck/the table** en su cuello/alrededor de la mesa; (in a circular movement): **to move ~ the room/sail ~ the world** dar una vuelta a la habitación/navegar por el mundo; (in various directions): **to move ~ a room/house** moverse por toda la habitación/casa; (approximately) alrededor de ♦ adv: **all ~** por todos lados; **the long way ~** por el camino menos directo; **all the year ~** durante todo el año; **it's just ~ the corner** (fig) está a la vuelta de la esquina; ~ **the clock** adv las 24 horas; **to go ~ to sb's (house)** ir a casa de algn; **to go ~ the back** pasar por atrás; **enough to go ~** bastante (para todos); **a ~ of applause** una ovación; **a ~ of drinks/sandwiches** una ronda de bebidas/bocadillos ▶ **round off** vt (speech etc) acabar, poner término a ▶ **round up** vt (cattle) acorralar; (people) reunir; (price) redondear ❏ **roundabout** (BRIT) n (AUT) rotonda, glorieta; (at fair) carrusel m (LAm), calesita (RPl), tiovivo (SP) ♦ adj (route, means) indirecto ❏ **rounders** (BRIT) n (game) juego similar al beisbol ❏ **roundly** adv (fig) rotundamente ❏ **round trip** (US) n viaje m de ida y vuelta, viaje redondo (MEX) ❏ **round trip ticket** (US) n boleto redondo (MEX), boleto (LAm) or billete m (SP) de ida y vuelta ❏ **roundup** n rodeo; (of criminals) redada; (of news) resumen m

rouse [rauz] vt (wake up) despertar; (stir up) suscitar ❏ **rousing** adj (cheer, welcome) caluroso

route [ruːt] n ruta, itinerario; (of bus) recorrido; (of shipping) derrota

routine [ruː'tiːn] *adj* rutinario ♦ *n* rutina; (THEATER) número

rove [rouv] *vt* vagar *or* errar por

row¹ [rou] *n* (line) fila, hilera; (KNITTING) pasada ♦ *vi* (in boat) remar ♦ *vt* conducir remando; **4 days in a ~** 4 días seguidos

row² [rau] (BRIT) *n* (racket) escándalo; (dispute) bronca, pelea; (scolding) regaño ♦ *vi* pelear(se)

rowboat ['rou,bout] (US) *n* barca de remos

rowdy ['raudi] *adj* (person: noisy) ruidoso; (occasion) alborotado

row house (US) *n* casa adosada

rowing ['rouiŋ] *n* remo ❑ **rowing boat** (BRIT) *n* bote *m* de remos

royal ['rɔiəl] *adj* real ❑ **Royal Air Force** (BRIT) *n* Fuerzas *fpl* Aéreas Británicas ❑ **royalty** *n* (royal persons) familia real; (payment to author) derechos *mpl* de autor

rpm *abbr* (= revs per minute) r.p.m.

R.S.V.P. *abbr* (= répondez s'il vous plaît) SRC

Rt. Hon. *abbr* (BRIT: Right Honourable) título honorífico de diputado

rub [rʌb] *vt* frotar; (scrub) restregar ♦ *n*: **to give sth a ~** frotar algo; **to ~ sb the wrong way** caer mal a algn ▶ **rub off** *vi* borrarse ▶ **rub off on** *vt fus* influir en ▶ **rub out** *vt* borrar

rubber ['rʌbər] *n* goma, hule *m* (MEX); (BRIT: eraser) goma de borrar ❑ **rubber band** *n* goma (elástica), gomita (RPl) ❑ **rubber boots** (US) *npl* botas *fpl* de agua ❑ **rubber plant** *n* ficus *m*

rubbing alcohol (US) *n* alcohol *m* de 90˚

rubbish ['rʌbiʃ] (BRIT) *n* basura; (waste) desperdicios *mpl*; (fig: pej) tonterías *fpl*; (junk) pacotilla ❑ **rubbish bin** (BRIT) *n* cubo *or* bote *m* (MEX) *or* tacho (SC) de la basura ❑ **rubbish dump** (BRIT) *n* vertedero, basurero

rubble ['rʌbəl] *n* escombros *mpl*

ruble (US) ['ruːbəl] (BRIT **rouble**) *n* rublo

ruby ['ruːbi] *n* rubí *m*

rucksack ['rʌkˌsæk] (BRIT) *n* mochila

rudder ['rʌdər] *n* timón *m*

ruddy ['rʌdi] *adj* (face) rubicundo; (BRIT: inf: damned) condenado

rude [ruːd] *adj* (impolite: person) mal educado; (: word, manners) grosero; (crude) crudo; (BRIT: indecent) indecente ❑ **rudeness** *n* mala educación

ruffle ['rʌfəl] *vt* (hair) despeinar; (clothes) arrugar; **to get ~d** (fig: person) alterarse

rug [rʌg] *n* alfombra, tapete *m* (MEX); (BRIT: blanket) manta

rugby ['rʌgbi] *n* rugby *m*

rugged ['rʌgid] *adj* (landscape) accidentado; (features) robusto

ruin ['ruːin] *n* ruina ♦ *vt* arruinar; (spoil) estropear; **~s** *npl* ruinas *fpl*, restos *mpl*

rule [ruːl] *n* (norm) norma, costumbre *f*; (regulation, ruler) regla; (government) dominio ♦ *vt* (country, person) gobernar ♦ *vi* gobernar; (LAW) fallar; **as a ~** por regla general ▶ **rule out** *vt* descartar, excluir ❑ **ruled** *adj* (paper) rayado ❑ **ruler** *n* (sovereign) soberano; (for measuring) regla ❑ **ruling** *adj* (party) gobernante; (class) dirigente ♦ *n* (LAW) fallo, decisión *f*

rum [rʌm] *n* ron *m*

Rumania [ruːˈmeiniə] (BRIT) *n* = **Romania**

rumble ['rʌmbəl] *n* (noise) ruido sordo ♦ *vi* retumbar, hacer un ruido sordo; (stomach, pipe) sonar

rummage ['rʌmidʒ] *vi* (search) hurgar ❑ **rummage sale** (US) *n* venta de objetos usados (con fines benéficos)

rumor (US) ['ruːmər] (BRIT **rumour**) *n* rumor *m* ♦ *vt*: **it is ~ed that ...** se rumorea que ...

rump [rʌmp] *n* (of animal) ancas *fpl*, grupa ❑ **rump steak** *n* filete *m* de lomo

rumpus ['rʌmpəs] *n* lío, jaleo

run [rʌn] (*pt* **ran**, *pp* **~**) *n* (fast pace): **at a ~** corriendo; (SPORT, in pantyhose) carrera; (outing) paseo, excursión *f*; (distance traveled) trayecto; (series) serie *f*; (THEATER) temporada; (SKI) pista; (POL) carrera ♦ *vt* correr; (operate: business) dirigir; (: competition, course) organizar; (: hotel, house) administrar, llevar; (COMPUT) ejecutar; (pass: hand) pasar; (PRESS: feature) publicar ♦ *vi* correr; (work: machine) funcionar, marchar; (bus, train: operate) circular, ir; (: travel) ir; (continue: play) seguir; (contract) ser válido; (flow: river) fluir; (colors, washing) desteñirse; (in election) ser candidato; **there was a ~ on** (meat, tickets) hubo mucha demanda de; **in the long ~** a la larga; **on the ~** en fuga; **I'll ~ you to the station** te llevaré a la estación (en coche); **to ~ a risk** correr un riesgo; **to ~ a bath** llenar la bañera ▶ **run around** *vi* (children) correr (por todos lados) ▶ **run across** *vt fus* (find) dar *or* topar con ▶ **run away** *vi* huir ▶ **run down** *vt* (car) atropellar; (criticize) criticar; (production) reducir; (factory) reducir la producción en; **to be run down** (per... estar debilitado ▶ **run in** (BRIT... ▶ **run into** *vt fus* (meet: per... tropezar con; (collide w... off** *vt* (water) dei... huir corrien... corrien...

(money etc) acabarse ▶ **run out of** vt fus
quedar sin ▶ **run over** vt (AUT) atropellar ♦ vt
fus (revise) repasar ▶ **run through** vt fus
(instructions) repasar ▶ **run up** vt (debt)
contraer; **to run up against** (difficulties)
tropezar con ❑ **runaway** adj (horse)
desbocado; (truck) sin frenos; (child) escapado
de casa

rung [rʌŋ] pp of **ring** ♦ n (of ladder) escalón m,
peldaño

runner ['rʌnər] n (in race: person) corredor(a)
m/f; (: horse) caballo; (on sled) patín m
❑ **runner bean** (BRIT) n ejote m (MEX), frijol m
(LAm), chaucha (RPl), judía verde (SP)
❑ **runner-up** n subcampeón(-ona) m/f

running ['rʌnɪŋ] n (sport) atletismo; (of
business) administración f ♦ adj (water, costs)
corriente; (commentary) continuo; **to be in/
out of the ~** tener/no tener
posibilidades de ganar algo; **6 days ~** 6 días
seguidos ❑ **running commentary** n (TV,
RADIO) comentario en directo; (on guided tour
etc) comentario detallado ❑ **running costs**
npl gastos mpl corrientes

runny ['rʌnɪ] adj fluido; (eyes) lloroso; **I've got
a ~ nose** no paro de moquear

run-of-the-mill adj común y corriente

runt [rʌnt] n (pej: animal) cría (más pequeña de
la camada); (person) redrojo, enano

run-up n: ~ **to** (BRIT: election etc) período
previo a

runway ['rʌnweɪ] n (AVIAT) pista de aterrizaje

rural ['rʊrəl] adj rural

rush [rʌʃ] n ímpetu m; (hurry) prisa; (COMM)
demanda; (current) corriente f fuerte; (of
feeling) torrente m; (BOT) junco ♦ vt apresurar;
(work) hacer de prisa ♦ vi correr, precipitarse
❑ **rush hour** n hora pico (LAm) or punta (SP)

rusk [rʌsk] (BRIT) n galleta (para bebés)

Russia ['rʌʃə] n Rusia ❑ **Russian** adj, n
ruso(-a); (LING) ruso

rust [rʌst] n herrumbre f, moho ♦ vi oxidarse

rustic ['rʌstɪk] adj rústico

rustle ['rʌsəl] vi susurrar ♦ vt (paper) hacer
crujir

rustproof ['rʌst,pruːf] adj inoxidable

rusty ['rʌstɪ] adj oxidado

rut [rʌt] n surco; (ZOOL) celo; **to be in a ~** ser
esclavo de la rutina

rutabaga [,ruːtə'beɪgə] (US) n nabo sueco

ruthless ['ruːθlɪs] adj despiadado

[r ̶ ̶ **aɪ]** n centeno ❑ **rye bread** n pan m de

Ss

Sabbath ['sæbəθ] n domingo; (Jewish)
sábado

sabotage ['sæbətɑːʒ] n sabotaje m ♦ vt
sabotear

saccharin (US) ['sækərɪn] (BRIT **saccharine**) n
sacarina

sachet [sæ'ʃeɪ] n sobrecito

sack [sæk] n (bag) saco ♦ vt (dismiss) despedir;
(plunder) saquear; **to get the ~** ser despedido
❑ **sacking** n despido; (material) arpillera

sacred ['seɪkrɪd] adj sagrado, santo

sacrifice ['sækrɪfaɪs] n sacrificio ♦ vt sacrificar

sad [sæd] adj (unhappy) triste; (deplorable)
lamentable

saddle ['sædl] n silla (de montar); (of cycle)
sillín m, asiento ♦ vt (horse) ensillar; **to be ~d
with sth** (inf) tener que cargar con algo
❑ **saddlebag** n alforja

sadistic [sə'dɪstɪk] adj sádico

sadly ['sædlɪ] adv lamentablemente; **to be ~
lacking in** ser muy deficiente en

sadness ['sædnɪs] n tristeza

s.a.e. abbr (= stamped addressed envelope)
sobre franqueado con las señas del remitente

safari [sə'fɑːrɪ] n safari m

safe [seɪf] adj (out of danger) fuera de peligro;
(not dangerous, sure) seguro; (unharmed) ileso
♦ n caja fuerte or de caudales; **~ and sound**
sano y salvo; **(just) to be on the ~ side** para
mayor seguridad ❑ **safe-conduct** n
salvoconducto ❑ **safe-deposit** n (vault)
cámara acorazada; (box) caja de seguridad
❑ **safeguard** n protección f, garantía ♦ vt
proteger, defender ❑ **safekeeping** n
custodia ❑ **safely** adv seguramente, con
seguridad; **to arrive safely** llegar bien
❑ **safe sex** n sexo seguro or sin riesgo

safety ['seɪftɪ] n seguridad f ❑ **safety belt** n
cinturón m (de seguridad) ❑ **safety pin** n
seguro (MEX), imperdible m (LAm exc MEX, SP),
alfiler m de gancho (SC) ❑ **safety valve** n
válvula de seguridad

saffron ['sæfrən] n azafrán m

sag [sæg] vi aflojarse

sage [seɪdʒ] n (herb) salvia; (man) sabio

Sagittarius [,sædʒɪ'terɪəs] n Sagitario

Sahara [sə'hærə] n: **the ~ (Desert)** el (desierto
del) Sáhara

said [sɛd] pt, pp of **say**

sail [seɪl] n (on boat) vela; (trip): **to go for a ~**
dar un paseo en barco ♦ vt (boat) gobernar

♦ vi (travel: ship) navegar; (SPORT) hacer vela; (begin voyage) salir; **they ~ed into Copenhagen** arribaron a Copenhague
▶ **sail through** vt fus (test) aprobar sin ningún problema; (life, situation) pasar sin esfuerzo por ❑ **sailboat** (US) n velero, barco de vela ❑ **sailing** n (SPORT) vela; **to go sailing** hacer vela ❑ **sailing boat** (BRIT) n barco de vela ❑ **sailing ship** n velero ❑ **sailor** n marinero, marino

saint [seint] n santo ❑ **saintly** adj santo

sake [seik] n: **for the ~ of** por (el bien de)

salad ['sæləd] n ensalada ❑ **salad bowl** n ensaladera ❑ **salad cream** (BRIT) n (especie f de) mayonesa ❑ **salad dressing** n aliño or (MEX) aderezo (para ensaladas)

salary ['sæləri] n sueldo

sale [seil] n venta; (at reduced prices) rebajas fpl, liquidación f; (auction) subasta; **~s** npl (total amount sold) ventas fpl, facturación f; **"for ~"** "se vende"; **to be on ~** (US) estar rebajado; (BRIT) estar a la venta; **on ~ or return** (BRIT: goods) venta por reposición ❑ **sales clerk** (US) (BRIT **sales assistant**) n vendedor(a) m/f (LAm), dependiente(-a) m/f (SP) ❑ **salesman/woman** n (in store) vendedor(a) m/f; (representative) representante mf ❑ **salesroom** n sala de subastas ❑ **sales slip** (US) n (for goods bought) recibo

salmon ['sæmən] n inv salmón m

salon [sə'lɒn] n (hairdressing salon) peluquería; (beauty salon) salón m de belleza

saloon [sə'luːn] n (US) bar m, taberna; (ship's lounge) cámara, salón m; (BRIT AUT) sedán m (LAm), turismo (SP)

salt [sɔːlt] n sal f ♦ vt salar; (put salt on) poner sal en ❑ **salt shaker** n (US) n salero ❑ **saltwater** adj de agua salada ❑ **salty** adj salado

salute [sə'luːt] n saludo; (of guns) salva ♦ vt saludar

salvage ['sælvɪdʒ] n (saving) salvamento, recuperación f; (things saved) objetos mpl salvados ♦ vt salvar

salvation [sæl'veɪʃən] n salvación f ❑ **Salvation Army** n Ejército de Salvación

same [seim] adj mismo ♦ pron: **the ~** el (la) mismo(-a), los (las) mismos(-as); **the ~ book as** el mismo libro que; **at the ~ time** (at the same moment) al mismo tiempo; (yet) sin embargo; **all** or **just the ~** sin embargo, aun así; **to do the ~ (as sb)** hacer lo mismo (que algn); **the ~ to you!** ¡igualmente!

sample ['sæmpəl] n muestra ♦ vt (food) probar; (wine) catar

sanatorium [sænə'tɔːriəm] (BRIT) n = **sanitarium**

sanction ['sæŋkʃən] n aprobación f ♦ vt sancionar; aprobar; **~s** npl (POL) sanciones fpl

sanctity ['sæŋktɪti] n santidad f; (inviolability) inviolabilidad f

sanctuary ['sæŋktʃuəri] n santuario; (refuge) asilo, refugio; (for wildlife) reserva

sand [sænd] n arena; (beach) playa ♦ vt (also: ~ down) lijar

sandal ['sændl] n sandalia

sand: ❑ **sandbox** (US) n (for children) cajón m de arena ❑ **sand castle** n castillo de arena ❑ **sand dune** n duna ❑ **sandpaper** n papel m de lija ❑ **sandpit** (BRIT) n = **sandbox** ❑ **sandstone** n piedra arenisca

sandwich ['sændwɪtʃ] n sandwich m ♦ vt intercalar; **~ed between** apretujado entre; **cheese/ham ~** sandwich de queso/jamón ❑ **sandwich course** (BRIT) n curso teórico-práctico

sandy ['sændi] adj arenoso; (color) rojizo

sane [sein] adj cuerdo; (sensible) sensato

⚠ Be careful not to translate **sane** by the Spanish word **sano**.

sang [sæŋ] pt of **sing**

sanitarium [sænɪ'teriəm] (US) n sanatorio

sanitary ['sænɪteri] adj sanitario; (clean) higiénico ❑ **sanitary napkin** (US) (BRIT **sanitary towel**) n toalla higiénica (LAm), compresa (SP)

sanitation [sænɪ'teɪʃən] n (in house) servicios mpl higiénicos; (in town) servicio de desinfección ❑ **sanitation department** (US) n departamento de limpieza y recogida de basuras

sanity ['sænɪti] n cordura; (of judgment) sensatez f

sank [sæŋk] pt of **sink**

Santa Claus ['sæntə'klɔːz] n Papá Noel, Santa Clos (MEX)

sap [sæp] n (of plants) savia ♦ vt (strength) minar, agotar

sapling ['sæplɪŋ] n árbol joven

sapphire ['sæfaɪər] n zafiro

Saran wrap® [sə'ræn,ræp] (US) n film m adherente (para envolver alimentos)

sarcasm ['sɑːrkæzəm] n sarcasmo

sardine [sɑːr'diːn] n sardina

Sardinia [sɑːr'dɪnɪə] n Cerdeña

SASE (US) n abbr (= self-addressed stamped envelope) sobre franqueado con las señas remitente

sash [sæʃ] n faja

sassy ['sæsɪ] (US) adj descarado

SAT (US) n abbr = **scholastic aptitude test**

sat [sæt] pt, pp of **sit**

Satan ['seɪtn] n Satanás m

satchel ['sætʃəl] n (child's) mochila

satellite ['sætəlaɪt] n satélite m ❑ **satellite dish** n antena parabólica ❑ **satellite television** n televisión f vía satélite

satin ['sætɪn] n raso ♦ adj de raso

satire ['sætaɪər] n sátira

satisfaction [,sætɪs'fækʃən] n satisfacción f

satisfactory [,sætɪs'fæktərɪ] adj satisfactorio

satisfy ['sætɪsfaɪ] vt satisfacer; (convince) convencer ❑ **satisfying** adj satisfactorio

Saturday ['sætərdɪ] n sábado

sauce [sɔːs] n salsa; (sweet) crema; jarabe m ❑ **saucepan** n cacerola, olla

saucer ['sɔːsər] n platillo

Saudi ['saudɪ]: ❑ **Saudi Arabia** n Arabia Saudí or Saudita ❑ **Saudi (Arabian)** adj, n saudí mf, saudita mf

sauna ['sɔːnə] n sauna

saunter ['sɔːntər] vi: to ~ **in/out** entrar/salir sin prisa

sausage ['sɑːsɪdʒ] n salchicha ❑ **sausage roll** (BRIT) n salchicha envuelta en hojaldre

sauté [sɑː'teɪ] adj salteado

savage ['sævɪdʒ] adj (cruel, fierce) feroz, furioso; (primitive) salvaje ♦ n salvaje mf ♦ vt (attack) embestir

save [seɪv] vt (rescue) salvar, rescatar; (money, time) ahorrar; (put away, keep: seat) guardar; (COMPUT) guardar; (avoid: trouble) evitar; (SPORT) parar ♦ vi (also: ~ **up**) ahorrar ♦ n (SPORT) parada ♦ prep salvo, excepto

saving ['seɪvɪŋ] n (on price etc) economía ♦ adj: **the ~ grace of** el único mérito de; **~s** npl ahorros mpl ❑ **savings account** n cuenta de ahorros ❑ **savings and loan association** (US) n sociedad f de ahorro y préstamo ❑ **savings bank** n caja de ahorros

savior (US) ['seɪvjər] (BRIT **saviour**) n salvador(a) m/f

savor (US) ['seɪvər] (BRIT **savour**) vt saborear ❑ **savory** (US) (BRIT **savoury**) adj sabroso; (dish: not sweet) salado

saw [sɔː] (pt ~**ed**, pp ~**ed** or ~**n**) pt of **see** ♦ n (tool) sierra ♦ vt serrar ❑ **sawdust** n (a)serrín m ❑ **sawed-off shotgun** n escopeta recortada or de cañones recortados ❑ **sawmill** n aserradero

xophone ['sæksəfoun] n saxófono

say [seɪ] (pt, pp **said**) n: to have one's ~ expresar su opinión ♦ vt decir; to have a or some ~ **in sth** tener voz or tener que ver en algo; to ~ **yes/no** decir que sí/no; **could you ~ that again?** ¿podría repetir eso?; **that is to ~** es decir; **that goes without ~ing** ni que decir tiene ❑ **saying** n dicho, refrán m

scab [skæb] n costra; (pej) rompehuelgas m inv (LAm), carnero (RPl)

scaffold ['skæfəld] n cadalso ❑ **scaffolding** n andamio, andamiaje m

scald [skɔːld] n escaldadura ♦ vt escaldar

scale [skeɪl] n (gen, MUS) escala; (of fish) escama; (of salaries, fees etc) escalafón m ♦ vi (mountain) escalar; (tree) trepar; **~s** npl (for weighing: small) balanza; (: large) báscula; **on a large ~** en gran escala; **~ of charges** tarifa, lista de precios ▶ **scale back** or **down** vt reducir a escala

scallion ['skæljən] (US) n cebolleta

scallop ['skæləp] n (ZOOL) venera; (SEWING) festón m

scalp [skælp] n cabellera ♦ vt escalpar; (US: inf: tickets) revender

scampi ['skæmpɪ] (BRIT) npl camarones mpl rebozados (LAm), gambas fpl rebozadas (SP)

scan [skæn] vt (examine) escudriñar; (glance at quickly) ojear; (TV, RADAR) explorar, registrar ♦ n (MED): to get (US) or have (BRIT) a ~ hacerse un escáner

scandal ['skændl] n escándalo; (gossip) habladurías fpl, chismes mpl

Scandinavia [,skændɪ'neɪvɪə] n Escandinavia ❑ **Scandinavian** adj, n escandinavo(-a)

scant [skænt] adj escaso ❑ **scanty** adj (meal) insuficiente; (clothes) ligero

scapegoat ['skeɪpgout] n chivo expiatorio, cabeza de turco

scar [skɑːr] n cicatriz f; (fig) señal f ♦ vt dejar señales en

scarce [skɛərs] adj escaso; to make o.s. ~ (inf) esfumarse ❑ **scarcely** adv apenas ❑ **scarcity** n escasez f

scare [skɛər] n susto, sobresalto; (panic) pánico ♦ vt asustar, espantar; to ~ **sb stiff** dar a algn un susto de muerte; **bomb ~** amenaza de bomba ▶ **scare away** or **off** vt ahuyentar ❑ **scarecrow** n espantapájaros m inv ❑ **scared** adj: to be scared estar asustado

scarf [skɑːrf] (pl ~**s** or **scarves**) n (long) bufanda; (square) pañuelo

scarlet ['skɑːrlɪt] adj escarlata ❑ **scarlet fever** n escarlatina

scarves [skɑːrvz] *npl of* **scarf**

scary ['skɛri] (*inf*) *adj* espeluznante, de miedo

scathing ['skeɪðɪŋ] *adj* mordaz

scatter ['skætər] *vt* (*spread*) esparcir, desparramar; (*disperse: clouds, crowd*) dispersar ♦ *vi* desparramarse; dispersarse ❏ **scatterbrained** *adj* ligero de cascos

scavenger ['skævəndʒər] *n* (*person*) basurero(-a)

scenario [sɪ'nɛriou] *n* (THEATER) argumento; (FILM) guión *m*; (*fig*) escenario

scene [siːn] *n* (THEATER, *fig etc*) escena; (*of crime etc*) escenario; (*view*) panorama *m*; (*fuss*) escándalo ❏ **scenery** *n* (THEATER) decorado; (*landscape*) paisaje *m* ❏ **scenic** *adj* pintoresco

⚠ Be careful not to translate **scenery** by the Spanish word *escenario*.

scent [sɛnt] *n* perfume *m*; olor *m*; (*fig: track*) rastro, pista

scepter (US) ['sɛptər] (BRIT **sceptre**) *n* cetro

sceptic *etc* ['skɛptɪk] (BRIT) *n* = **skeptic**

schedule ['skɛdʒuːl] *n* (*timetable of events*) programa *m*; (*trains, buses*) horario; (*list*) lista ♦ *vt* (*visit*) fijar la hora de; **to arrive on ~** llegar a la hora debida; **to be ahead of/behind ~** estar adelantado/en retraso ❏ **scheduled flight** *n* vuelo regular

scheme [skiːm] *n* (*plan*) plan *m*, proyecto; (*plot*) intriga; (*arrangement*) disposición *f*; (BRIT: *pension scheme etc*) sistema *m* ♦ *vi* (*intrigue*) intrigar ❏ **scheming** *adj* intrigante ♦ *n* intrigas *fpl*

schizophrenic [skɪtsə'frɛnɪk] *adj* esquizofrénico

scholar ['skɑːlər] *n* (*pupil*) alumno(-a); (*learned person*) sabio(-a), erudito(-a) ❏ **scholarship** *n* erudición *f*; (*grant*) beca

school [skuːl] *n* escuela, colegio; (*in university*) facultad *f* ♦ *cpd* escolar ❏ **school age** *n* edad *f* escolar ❏ **school board** *n* consejo escolar ❏ **schoolbook** *n* libro de texto ❏ **schoolboy** *n* colegial *m*, alumno ❏ **school children** *npl* colegiales *mpl*, alumnos *mpl* ❏ **schoolgirl** *n* colegiala, alumna ❏ **schoolhouse** (US) *n* escuela, colegio ❏ **schooling** *n* enseñanza ❏ **schoolmaster/mistress** *n* (*elementary*) maestro(-a); (*high school*) profesor(a) *m/f* ❏ **schoolroom** *n* aula, clase *f* ❏ **schoolteacher** *n* (*elementary*) maestro(-a); (*high school*) profesor(a) *m/f* ❏ **schoolwork** *n* trabajo de clase ❏ **schoolyard** (US) *n* patio de recreo

schooner ['skuːnər] *n* (*ship*) goleta

sciatica [saɪ'ætɪkə] *n* ciática

science ['saɪəns] *n* ciencia ❏ **science fiction** *n* ciencia ficción ❏ **scientific** [ˌsaɪən'tɪfɪk] *adj* científico ❏ **scientist** *n* científico(-a)

scissors ['sɪzərz] *npl* tijeras *fpl*; **a pair of ~** unas tijeras

scoff [skɑːf] *vt* (BRIT: *inf: eat*) engullir ♦ *vi*: **to ~ (at)** (*mock*) mofarse (de)

scold [skould] *vt* regañar

scone [skoun] (BRIT) *n* pan dulce con pasas, ≈ bísquet *m* (MEX), escón *m* (SC)

scoop [skuːp] *n* (*for flour etc*) pala; (PRESS) exclusiva ▶ **scoop out** *vt* excavar ▶ **scoop up** *vt* recoger

scooter ['skuːtər] *n* Vespa®, moneta (SC), scooter *m* (SP); (*toy*) patineta (MEX), patinete *m* (LAm exc MEX, SP), monopatín *m* (SC)

scope [skoup] *n* (*of plan*) ámbito; (*of person*) competencia; (*opportunity*) libertad *f* (de acción)

scorch [skɔːrtʃ] *vt* (*clothes*) chamuscar; (*earth, grass*) quemar, secar

score [skɔːr] *n* (*points etc*) puntuación *f*; (MUS) partitura; (*twenty*) veintena ♦ *vt* (*goal, point*) ganar; (*mark*) rayar; (*achieve: success*) conseguir ♦ *vi* marcar un tanto; (SPORT) marcar; (*keep score*) llevar el tanteo; **~s of** (*lots of*) decenas de; **on that ~** en lo que se refiere a eso; **to ~ 6 out of 10** obtener una puntuación de 6 sobre 10 ▶ **score out** (BRIT) *vt* tachar ❏ **scoreboard** *n* marcador *m*

scorn [skɔːrn] *n* desprecio ❏ **scornful** *adj* desdeñoso, despreciativo

Scorpio ['skɔːrpiou] *n* Escorpio

scorpion ['skɔːrpiən] *n* alacrán *m*, escorpión *m*

Scot [skɑːt] *n* escocés(-esa) *m/f*

Scotch [skɑːtʃ] *n* whisky *m* escocés ❏ **Scotch tape®** (US) *n* cinta Dúrex® (MEX), cinta Scotch® (LAm), celo (SP)

Scotland ['skɑːtlənd] *n* Escocia

Scots [skɑːts] *adj* escocés(-esa) ❏ **Scotsman/woman** *n* escocés(-esa) *m/f* ❏ **Scottish** *adj* escocés(-esa) ❏ **Scottish Parliament** *n* Parlamento escocés

scoundrel ['skaundrəl] *n* canalla *mf*, sinvergüenza *mf*

scout [skaut] *n* (MIL) explorador(a) *m/f*; (*also:* **boy ~**) boy(-)scout *m*; **girl ~** (US) (girl-)scout *f* ▶ **scout around** *vi* buscar

scowl [skaul] *vi* fruncir el ceño; **to ~ at sb** mirar con ceño a algn

scrabble ['skræbəl] vi (claw): **to ~ (at)** escarbar; (also: **to ~ around**: search) buscar a tientas ♦ n: **S-®** Scrabble® m

scraggly ['skrægli] (US) adj deforme

scraggy ['skrægi] (BRIT) adj descarnado

scram [skræm] (inf) vi largarse

scramble ['skræmbəl] n (climb) subida (difícil); (struggle) pelea ♦ vi: **to ~ through/ out** abrirse paso/salir con dificultad; **to ~ for** pelear por ▸ **scrambled eggs** npl huevos mpl revueltos

scrap [skræp] n (bit) trocito; (fig) pizca; (fight) riña, bronca; (also: **~ iron**) chatarra ♦ vt (discard) desechar, descartar ♦ vi reñir, armar una bronca; **~s** npl (waste) sobras fpl, desperdicios mpl □ **scrapbook** n álbum m de recortes □ **scrap dealer** n chatarrero(-a)

scrape [skreip] n: **to get into a ~** meterse en un lío ♦ vt raspar; (skin etc) rasguñar; (scrape against) rozar ♦ vi: **to ~ through** (test) aprobar por los pelos ▸ **scrape together** vt (money) arañar, juntar

scrap: □ **scrap heap** n (fig): **to be on the scrap heap** estar acabado □ **scrap merchant** (BRIT) n chatarrero(-a) □ **scrap paper** n papel m usado or de borrador

scratch [skrætʃ] n rasguño; (from claw) arañazo ♦ cpd: **~ team** equipo improvisado ♦ vt (paint, car) rayar; (with claw, nail) rasguñar, arañar; (rub: nose etc) rascarse ♦ vi rascarse; **to start from ~** partir de cero; **to be up to ~** cumplir con los requisitos

scrawl [skrɔːl] n garabatos mpl ♦ vi hacer garabatos

scrawny ['skrɔːni] adj flaco

scream [skriːm] n grito, chillido ♦ vi gritar, chillar

screech [skriːtʃ] vi chirriar

screen [skriːn] n (MOVIE, TV) pantalla; (movable barrier) biombo ♦ vt (conceal) tapar; (from the wind etc) proteger; (movie) proyectar; (candidates etc) investigar a □ **screening** n (MED) investigación f médica □ **screenplay** n guión m □ **screen saver** n (COMPUT) protector m de pantalla

screw [skruː] n tornillo ♦ vt (also: **~ in**) atornillar ▸ **screw up** vt (inf: ruin) chingar (MEX: inf), fregar (LAm: inf), joder (SP: inf); (BRIT: paper etc) arrugar; **to screw up one's eyes** arrugar el entrecejo □ **screwdriver** n desarmador m (MEX), destornillador m (MEX, CAm), destornillador m (LAm exc MEX, SP)

scribble ['skrɪbəl] n garabatos mpl ♦ vt, vi garabatear, hacer garabatos

script [skrɪpt] n (FILM etc) guión m; (writing) escritura, letra

Scripture(s) ['skrɪptʃər(z)] n(pl) Sagrada Escritura

scroll [skroul] n rollo ♦ vt (COMPUT) desplazar

scrounge [skraundʒ] (inf) vt: **to ~ sth off or from sb** obtener algo de algn de gorra ♦ n: **on the ~** de gorra □ **scrounger** n gorrón(-ona) m/f

scrub [skrʌb] n (land) maleza ♦ vt fregar, restregar; (inf: reject) cancelar, anular

scruff [skrʌf] n: **by the ~ of the neck** por el pescuezo

scruffy ['skrʌfi] adj desaliñado, piojoso

scrum(mage) ['skrʌm(ɪdʒ)] n (RUGBY) melé f

scruple ['skruːpəl] n (gen pl) escrúpulo

scrutinize ['skruːtɪnaɪz] vt escudriñar; (votes) escrutar □ **scrutiny** n examen m; escrutinio

scuff [skʌf] vt (shoes, floor) rayar

scuffle ['skʌfəl] n refriega

sculptor ['skʌlptər] n escultor(a) m/f

sculpture ['skʌlptʃər] n escultura

scum [skʌm] n (on liquid) espuma; (pej: people) escoria

scurry ['skɜːri] vi correr; **to ~ off** escabullirse

scuttle ['skʌtl] n carbonera ♦ vt (ship) barrenar ♦ vi: **to ~ away, ~ off** escabullirse

scythe [saɪð] n guadaña

sea [siː] n mar m ♦ cpd de mar, marítimo; **by ~** (travel) en barco; **on the ~** (boat) en el mar; (town) junto al mar; **to be all at ~** (fig) estar despistado; **out to ~** at **~** en alta mar □ **seaboard** n litoral m □ **seafood** n mariscos mpl (LAm), marisco (SP) □ **sea front** n malecón m (LAm), costanera (SC), paseo marítimo (SP) □ **sea-going** adj de altura □ **seagull** n gaviota

seal [siːl] n (animal) foca; (stamp) sello ♦ vt (close) cerrar ▸ **seal off** vt (area) acordonar

sea level n nivel m del mar

sea lion n león m marino

seam [siːm] n costura; (of metal) juntura; (of coal) veta, filón m

seaman ['siːmən] n marinero

seance ['seɪɑːns] n sesión f de espiritismo

seaplane ['siːpleɪn] n hidroavión m

seaport ['siːpɔːrt] n puerto de mar

search [sɜːrtʃ] n (for person, thing) busca, búsqueda; (COMPUT) búsqueda; (inspection: of sb's home) registro ♦ vt (look in) buscar en; (examine) examinar; (person, place) registrar ♦ vi: **to ~ for** buscar; **in ~ of** en busca de ▸ **search through** vt fus registrar □ **search engine** n (INTERNET) buscador m

❏ **searching** adj penetrante
❏ **searchlight** n reflector m ❏ **search party** n equipo de búsqueda ❏ **search warrant** n mandamiento (judicial)

sea: ❏ **seashore** n orilla del mar ❏ **seasick** adj mareado ❏ **seaside** n playa ❏ **seaside resort** n centro turístico costero, balneario (SC)

season ['siːzən] n (of year) estación f; (sporting etc) temporada; (of movies etc) ciclo ♦ vt (food) sazonar; **in/out of ~** en sazón/fuera de temporada ❏ **seasonal** adj estacional ❏ **seasoned** adj (fig) experimentado ❏ **seasoning** n condimento, aderezo ❏ **season ticket** n abono

seat [siːt] n (in bus, train) asiento; (chair) silla; (buttocks) culo, trasero; (of cycle) sillín m, asiento; (BRIT PARLIAMENT) escaño, curul m (MEX), banca (SC) ♦ vt sentar; (have room for) tener cabida para; **to be ~ed** sentarse ❏ **seat belt** n cinturón m de seguridad

sea: ❏ **sea water** n agua de mar ❏ **seaweed** n alga marina ❏ **seaworthy** adj en condiciones de navegar

sec. abbr = **second(s)**

secluded [sɪ'kluːdɪd] adj retirado

seclusion [sɪ'kluːʒən] n reclusión f

second ['sɛkənd] adj segundo ♦ adv en segundo lugar ♦ n segundo; (AUT: also: ~ **gear**) segunda; (COMM) artículo defectuoso; (BRIT SCOL degree) título de licenciado con calificación de notable ♦ vt (motion) apoyar ❏ **secondary** adj secundario ❏ **secondary school** n escuela secundaria ❏ **second-class** adj de segunda clase ♦ adv (RAIL) en segunda ❏ **second hand** n (on clock) segundero ❏ **secondhand** adj de segunda mano, usado ❏ **secondly** adv en segundo lugar ❏ **secondment** [sɪ'kɒndmənt] (BRIT) n traslado temporal ❏ **second-rate** adj de segunda categoría ❏ **second thoughts** npl: **to have second thoughts** cambiar de opinión; **on second thought** (US) or **thoughts** (BRIT) pensándolo bien

secrecy ['siːkrəsɪ] n secreto

secret ['siːkrɪt] adj, n secreto; **in ~** en secreto

secretarial [sɛkrɪ'tɛərɪəl] adj de secretario; (training, staff) de secretariado

secretary ['sɛkrətɛrɪ] n secretario(-a); **S~ of State** (US POL) Secretario (MEX) or Ministro (LAm exc MEX) de Relaciones Exteriores, Ministro de Asuntos Exteriores (SP); (BRIT POL) secretario(-a) (MEX), ministro(-a) (LAm exc MEX, SP)

secretive ['siːkrətɪv] adj reservado, sigiloso

secretly ['siːkrɪtlɪ] adv en secreto

sect [sɛkt] n secta ❏ **sectarian** [sɛk'tɛərɪən] adj sectario

section ['sɛkʃən] n sección f; (part) parte f; (of document) artículo; (of opinion) sector m; (cross-section) corte m transversal

sector ['sɛktər] n sector m

secular ['sɛkjulər] adj secular, seglar

secure [sɪ'kjuər] adj seguro; (firmly fixed) firme, fijo ♦ vt (fix) asegurar, afianzar; (get) conseguir

security [sɪ'kjurɪtɪ] n seguridad f; (for loan) fianza; (: object) prenda

sedan [sə'dæn] (US) n (AUT) sedán m (LAm), turismo (SP)

sedate [sɪ'deɪt] adj tranquilo ♦ vt tratar con sedantes

sedation [sɪ'deɪʃən] n (MED) sedación f

sedative ['sɛdɪtɪv] n sedante m, sedativo

seduce [sɪ'djuːs] vt seducir ❏ **seduction** [sɪ'dʌkʃən] n seducción f ❏ **seductive** [sɪ'dʌktɪv] adj seductor(a)

see [siː] (pt **saw**, pp ~**n**) vt ver; (accompany): **to ~ sb to the door** acompañar a algn a la puerta; (understand) ver, comprender ♦ vi ver ♦ n (arz)obispado; **to ~ that** (ensure) asegurar que; ~ **you soon!** ¡hasta pronto! ▸ **see around** or (BRIT) **about** vt fus atender a, encargarse de ▸ **see off** vt despedir ▸ **see through** vt fus (fig) calar ♦ vt (plan) llevar a cabo ▸ **see to** vt fus atender a, encargarse de

seed [siːd] n semilla; (in fruit) pepita; (fig: gen pl) germen m; (SPORT) cabeza mf de serie; **to go to ~** (plant) granar; (fig) descuidarse ❏ **seedling** n planta de semillero ❏ **seedy** adj (shabby) desaseado, raído

seeing ['siːɪŋ] conj: ~ **(that)** visto que, en vista de que ❏ **seeing-eye dog** (US) n perro guía

seek [siːk] (pt, pp **sought**) vt buscar; (post) solicitar

seem [siːm] vi parecer; **there ~s to be ...** parece que hay ... ❏ **seemingly** adv aparentemente, según parece

seen [siːn] pp of **see**

seep [siːp] vi filtrarse

seesaw ['siːsɔː] n balancín m

seethe [siːð] vi hervir; **to ~ with anger** estar furioso

see-through adj transparente

segment ['sɛgmənt] n (part) sección f; (of orange) gajo

segregate ['sɛgrɪgeɪt] vt segregar

seize [siːz] vt (grasp) agarrar, asir; (take possession of) secuestrar; (: territory) apoderarse de; (opportunity) aprovecharse de

▶ **seize (up)on** vt fus aprovechar ▶ **seize up** vi (TECH) agarrotarse

seizure ['siːʒər] n (MED) ataque m; (LAW, of power) incautación f

seldom ['seldəm] adv rara vez

select [sɪ'lekt] adj selecto, escogido ♦ vt escoger, elegir; (SPORT) seleccionar ❏ **selection** n selección f, elección f; (COMM) surtido

self [self] (pl **selves**) n uno mismo ♦ prefix auto...; **the ~** el yo ❏ **self-assured** adj seguro de sí mismo ❏ **self-catering** (BRIT) adj (apartment etc) con cocina ❏ **self-centered** (US) (BRIT **self-centred**) adj egocéntrico ❏ **self-confidence** n confianza en sí mismo ❏ **self-conscious** adj cohibido ❏ **self-contained** (BRIT) adj (apartment) independiente ❏ **self-control** n autocontrol ❏ **self-defense** (US) (BRIT **self-defence**) n defensa propia ❏ **self-discipline** n autodisciplina ❏ **self-employed** adj autónomo ❏ **self-evident** adj patente ❏ **self-governing** adj autónomo ❏ **self-indulgent** adj autocomplaciente ❏ **self-interest** n egoísmo ❏ **selfish** adj egoísta ❏ **selfishness** n egoísmo ❏ **selfless** adj desinteresado ❏ **self-made** adj: **self-made man** hombre m hecho a sí mismo ❏ **self-pity** n autocompasión ❏ **self-portrait** n autorretrato ❏ **self-possessed** adj sereno, dueño de sí mismo ❏ **self-preservation** n propia conservación f ❏ **self-respect** n amor m propio ❏ **self-righteous** adj santurrón(-ona) ❏ **self-sacrifice** n abnegación f ❏ **self-satisfied** adj satisfecho de sí mismo ❏ **self-service** (US **self-serve**) adj de autoservicio ❏ **self-sufficient** adj autosuficiente ❏ **self-taught** adj autodidacta

sell [sel] (pt, pp **sold**) vt vender ♦ vi venderse; **to ~ at or for $20** venderse a 20 dólares ▶ **sell off** vt liquidar ▶ **sell out** vi: **the tickets sold out in three hours** las entradas se agotaron en tres horas ❏ **sell-by date** (BRIT) n fecha de caducidad ❏ **seller** n vendedor(a) m/f ❏ **selling price** n precio de venta

Sellotape® ['seləʊˌteɪp] (BRIT) n cinta Dúrex® (MEX), cinta Scotch® (LAm), celo (SP)

selves [selvz] npl of **self**

semblance ['sembləns] n apariencia

semen ['siːmən] n semen m

semester [sə̩'mestər] n semestre m

semi... [semi] prefix semi..., medio... ❏ **semi-annual** (US) adj semestral ❏ **semicircle** n

semicírculo ❏ **semicolon** n punto y coma ❏ **semiconductor** n semiconductor m ❏ **semidetached (house)** (BRIT) n (casa) pareada or semiadosada (LAm), semicualificado (SP) ❏ **semi-final** n semifinal f

seminar ['semɪnɑːr] n seminario

seminary ['semɪnəri] n (REL) seminario

semiskilled ['semi̩skɪld] adj (work, worker) semicalificado (LAm), semicualificado (SP)

semi-skimmed (milk) (BRIT) n leche f semidescremada (LAm) or semidesnatada (SP)

senate ['senɪt] n senado; **the S~** (US) el Senado ❏ **senator** n senador(a) m/f

send [send] (pt, pp **sent**) vt mandar, enviar; (signal) transmitir ▶ **send away** vt despachar ▶ **send away for** vt fus pedir ▶ **send back** vt devolver ▶ **send for** vt fus mandar traer ▶ **send off** vt (goods) despachar; (BRIT SPORT: player) expulsar ▶ **send out** vt (invitation) mandar; (signal) emitir ▶ **send up** vt (person, price) hacer subir; (BRIT: parody) parodiar ❏ **sender** n remitente mf ❏ **send-off** n: **a good send-off** una buena despedida

senior ['siːnjər] adj (older) mayor, más viejo; (: on staff) de más antigüedad; (of higher rank) superior; (SCOL) estudiante mf del último año ❏ **senior citizen** n persona de la tercera edad ❏ **senior high school** (US) n escuela secundaria (superior), preparatoria (MEX) ❏ **seniority** [siːnɪ'jɔːrɪti] n antigüedad f

sensation [sen'seɪʃən] n sensación f ❏ **sensational** adj sensacional

sense [sens] n (faculty, meaning) sentido; (feeling) sensación f; (good sense) sentido común, juicio ♦ vt sentir, percibir; **it makes ~** tiene sentido ❏ **senseless** adj estúpido, insensato; (unconscious) sin conocimiento ❏ **sense of humor** n sentido del humor

sensible ['sensɪbəl] adj sensato; (reasonable) razonable, lógico

⚠ Be careful not to translate **sensible** by the Spanish word **sensible**.

sensitive ['sensɪtɪv] adj sensible; (touchy) susceptible

sensual ['senʃuəl] adj sensual

sensuous ['senʃuəs] adj sensual

sent [sent] pt, pp of **send**

sentence ['sentns] n (LING) oración f; (LAW) sentencia, fallo ♦ vt: **to ~ sb to death/to 5 years (in prison)** condenar a algn a muerte/a 5 años de cárcel

sentiment ['sɛntɪmənt] n sentimiento; (opinion) opinión f ❑ **sentimental** [sɛntɪˈmɛntl] adj sentimental

sentry ['sɛntrɪ] n centinela m

separate [adj 'sɛprɪt, vb 'sɛpəreɪt] adj separado; (distinct) distinto ♦ vt separar; (part) dividir ♦ vi separarse ❑ **separately** adv por separado ❑ **separates** npl (clothes) coordinados mpl ❑ **separation** [sɛpəˈreɪʃən] n separación f

September [sɛpˈtɛmbər] n septiembre m

septic ['sɛptɪk] adj séptico ❑ **septic tank** n fosa séptica

sequel ['siːkwəl] n consecuencia, resultado; (of story) continuación f

sequence ['siːkwəns] n sucesión f, serie f; (FILM) secuencia

sequin ['siːkwɪn] n lentejuela

serene [səˈriːn] adj sereno, tranquilo

sergeant ['sɑːrdʒənt] n sargento

serial ['sɪrɪəl] n (TV) serial m (LAm), serie f (SP); (book) novela por entregas ❑ **serialize** vt televisar or publicar por entregas ❑ **serial killer** n asesino(-a) múltiple ❑ **serial number** n número de serie

series ['sɪriːz] n inv serie f

serious ['sɪrɪəs] adj serio; (grave) grave ❑ **seriously** adv en serio; (ill, wounded etc) gravemente

sermon ['sɜːrmən] n sermón m

serrated [səˈreɪtɪd] adj serrado, dentellado

serum ['sɪrəm] n suero

servant ['sɜːrvənt] n servidor(a) m/f; (house servant) criado(-a)

serve [sɜːrv] vt servir; (customer) atender; (subj: train) pasar por; (apprenticeship) hacer; (prison term) cumplir ♦ vi (at table) servir; (TENNIS) sacar, servir ♦ n (TENNIS) saque m, servicio; **it ~s him right** se lo tiene merecido; **to ~ as/for/to do** servir de/para/para hacer ▶ **serve out** vt (food) servir ▶ **serve up** vt = serve out

service ['sɜːrvɪs] n servicio; (REL) oficio (religioso); (AUT) servicio (LAm), service m (RPI), revisión f (SP); (dishes etc) juego ♦ vt (car etc) hacer un servicio (LAm) or service (RPI) a, revisar (SP); (: repair) reparar; **the S~s** npl las fuerzas armadas; **to be of ~ to sb** ser útil a algn; **~ included/not included** servicio incluido/no incluido ❑ **serviceable** adj servible, utilizable ♦ **service area** (BRIT) n (on highway) área de servicios ❑ **service charge** (BRIT) n servicio ❑ **serviceman** n militar m ❑ **service provider** n (INTERNET)

proveedor m de servicios ❑ **service station** n estación f de servicio

serviette [sɜːrvɪˈɛt] (BRIT) n servilleta

session ['sɛʃən] n sesión f; **to be in ~** estar en sesión

set [sɛt] (pt, pp ~) n juego; (RADIO) aparato; (TV) televisor m; (of utensils) batería; (of cutlery) cubierto; (of books) colección f; (TENNIS) set m; (group of people) grupo; (MOVIE) plató m; (THEATER) decorado; (HAIRDRESSING) marcado ♦ adj (fixed) fijo; (ready) listo ♦ vt (place) poner, colocar; (fix) fijar; (adjust) ajustar, arreglar; (decide: rules etc) establecer, decidir ♦ vi (sun) ponerse; (jam, jelly) cuajarse; (concrete) fraguar; (bone) componerse; **to be ~ on doing sth** estar empeñado en hacer algo; **to ~ to music** poner música a; **to ~ on fire** prender fuego a; **to ~ free** poner en libertad; **to ~ sth going** poner algo en marcha; **to ~ sail** zarpar, hacerse a la vela; **to ~ the table** poner la mesa ▶ **set about** vt fus ponerse a ▶ **set aside** vt poner aparte, dejar de lado; (money, time) reservar ▶ **set back** vt (cost): **to set sb back $10** costar a algn diez dólares; **to set back (by)** (in time) retrasar (por) ▶ **set down** vt (record) poner por escrito ▶ **set off** vi partir ♦ vt (bomb) hacer estallar; (events) poner en marcha; (show up well) hacer resaltar ▶ **set out** vi salir ♦ vt (arrange) disponer; (state) exponer; **to set out to do sth** proponerse hacer algo ▶ **set up** vt establecer ❑ **setback** n revés m, contratiempo ❑ **set menu** n menú m

settee [sɛˈtiː] n sofá m

setting ['sɛtɪŋ] n (scenery) marco; (position) disposición f; (of sun) puesta; (of jewel) engaste m, montadura

settle ['sɛtl] vt (argument) resolver; (accounts) ajustar, liquidar; (MED: calm) calmar, sosegar ♦ vi (dust etc) depositarse; (weather) serenarse; (also: ~ down) instalarse; calmarse; **to ~ for sth** convenir en aceptar algo; **to ~ on sth** decidirse por algo ▶ **settle in** vi adaptarse ▶ **settle up** vi: **to settle up with sb** ajustar cuentas con algn ❑ **settlement** n (payment) liquidación f; (agreement) acuerdo, convenio; (village etc) pueblo ❑ **settler** n colono(-a), colonizador(a) m/f

setup ['sɛtʌp] n sistema m; (situation) situación f

seven ['sɛvən] num siete ❑ **seventeen** num diecisiete ❑ **seventh** num séptimo ❑ **seventy** num setenta

sever ['sɛvər] vt cortar; (relations) romper

several ['sɛvrəl] adj, pron varios(-as), algunos(-as); **~ of us** varios de nosotros

severance [ˈsevərəns] n (of relations) ruptura ❑ **severance pay** (BRIT) n indemnización f por despido

severe [sɪˈvɪər] adj severo; (serious) grave; (hard) duro; (pain) intenso ❑ **severity** [sɪˈverɪtɪ] n severidad f; gravedad f; intensidad f

sew [səu] (pt ~ed, pp ~n) vt, vi coser ▸ **sew up** vt coser, zurcir

sewage [ˈsuːɪdʒ] n aguas fpl residuales

sewer [ˈsuːər] n alcantarilla, cloaca

sewing [ˈsəuɪŋ] n costura ❑ **sewing machine** n máquina de coser

sewn [səun] pp of **sew**

sex [seks] n sexo; (lovemaking): **to have ~** tener relaciones sexuales ❑ **sexist** adj, n sexista mf ❑ **sexual** adj sexual ❑ **sexy** adj sexy

shabby [ˈʃæbɪ] adj (person) desaliñado; (clothes) raído, gastado; (behavior) ruin

shack [ʃæk] n choza, jacal m (MEX), rancho (LAm), bohío (CAm)

shackles [ˈʃækəlz] npl grilletes mpl

shade [ʃeɪd] n sombra; (for lamp) pantalla; (for eyes) visera; (of color) tono, tonalidad f; (small quantity): **a ~ (too big/more)** un poquitín (grande/más); (US: on window) persiana ♦ vt dar sombra a; (eyes) proteger del sol; **~s** npl (US: sunglasses) lentes mpl (LAm) or anteojos mpl (LAm) or gafas fpl (SP) de sol; **in the ~** en la sombra

shadow [ˈʃædou] n sombra ♦ vt (follow) seguir y vigilar ❑ **shadow cabinet** (BRIT) n (POL) gabinete m en la sombra, gabinete paralelo formado por el partido de oposición ❑ **shadowy** adj oscuro; (dim) indistinto

shady [ˈʃeɪdɪ] adj sombreado; (fig: dishonest) sospechoso; (: deal) turbio

shaft [ʃæft] n (of arrow, spear) astil m; (AUT, TECH) eje m; (of mine) pozo; (of lift) hueco, caja; (of light) rayo

shaggy [ˈʃægɪ] adj peludo

shake [ʃeɪk] (pt **shook**, pp ~n) vt sacudir; (building) hacer temblar; (bottle, cocktail) agitar ♦ vi (tremble) temblar; **to ~ one's head** (in refusal) negar con la cabeza; (in dismay) mover or menear la cabeza incrédulo; **to ~ hands with sb** dar or estrechar la mano a algn ▸ **shake off** vt sacudirse; (fig) deshacerse de ▸ **shake up** vt agitar; (fig) reorganizar ❑ **shaky** adj (hand, voice) trémulo; (building) inestable

shall [ʃæl] aux vb: **~ I help you?** ¿quieres que te ayude?; **I'll buy three, ~ I?** compro tres, ¿no te parece?

shallow [ˈʃæləu] adj poco profundo; (fig) superficial

sham [ʃæm] n fraude m, engaño ♦ vt fingir, simular

shambles [ˈʃæmbəlz] n desastre m

shame [ʃeɪm] n vergüenza ♦ vt avergonzar; **it is a ~ that/to do** es una lástima que/hacer; **what a ~!** ¡qué lástima! ❑ **shameful** adj vergonzoso ❑ **shameless** adj desvergonzado

shampoo [ʃæmˈpuː] n champú m ♦ vt lavar con champú ❑ **shampoo and dry** (US) n lavado y marcado ❑ **shampoo and set** (BRIT) n = **shampoo and dry**

shamrock [ˈʃæmrɒk] n trébol m (de Irlanda)

shandy [ˈʃændɪ] (BRIT) n cerveza con gaseosa

shan't [ʃænt] cont = **shall not**

shantytown [ˈʃæntɪˌtaun] n colonia proletaria (MEX), barriada (LAm), barrio de chabolas (SP)

shape [ʃeɪp] n forma ♦ vt formar, dar forma a; (sb's ideas) formar; (sb's life) determinar; **to take ~** tomar forma ▸ **shape up** vi (events) desarrollarse; (person) formarse ❑ **-shaped** suffix: **heart-shaped** en forma de corazón ❑ **shapeless** adj informe, sin forma definida ❑ **shapely** adj (body etc) esbelto

share [ʃeər] n (part) parte f, porción f; (contribution) cuota; (COMM) acción f ♦ vt dividir; (have in common) compartir; **to ~ out (among or between)** repartir (entre) ❑ **shareholder** n accionista mf

shark [ʃɑːrk] n tiburón m

sharp [ʃɑːrp] adj (blade, nose) afilado; (point) puntiagudo; (outline) definido; (pain) intenso; (MUS) desafinado; (contrast) marcado; (voice) agudo; (person: quick-witted) astuto, listo; (: dishonest) poco escrupuloso ♦ n (MUS) sostenido ♦ adv: **at 2 o'clock ~** a las 2 en punto ❑ **sharpen** vt afilar; (pencil) sacar punta a; (fig) agudizar ❑ **sharpener** n (also: **pencil sharpener**) sacapuntas m inv ❑ **sharp-eyed** adj de vista aguda ❑ **sharply** adv (turn, stop) bruscamente; (stand out, contrast) claramente; (criticize, retort) severamente

shatter [ˈʃætər] vt hacer añicos or pedazos; (fig: ruin) destruir, acabar con ♦ vi hacerse añicos

shave [ʃeɪv] vt afeitar, rasurar (MEX) ♦ vi afeitarse, rasurarse (MEX) ♦ n: **to have a ~** afeitarse, rasurarse (MEX) ❑ **shaver** n (also: **electric shaver**) rasuradora (MEX), máquina (LAm) or maquinilla (SP) (eléctrica) de afeitar

shaving [ˈʃeɪvɪŋ] n (action) afeitado, rasurado (MEX); **~s** npl (of wood etc) virutas fpl ❑ **shaving brush** n brocha de afeitar ❑ **shaving cream** n crema de afeitar or

(MEX) rasurar ❏ **shaving foam** n espuma de afeitar or (MEX) rasurar ❏ **shaving gel** n gel m de afeitar or (MEX) rasurar

shawl [ʃɔːl] n chal m

she [ʃiː] pron ella

sheaf [ʃiːf] (pl **sheaves**) n (of corn) gavilla; (of papers) fajo

shear [ʃɪər] (pt ~**ed**, pp ~**ed** or **shorn**) vt esquilar, trasquilar ❏ **shears** npl (for hedge) tijeras fpl de jardín

sheath [ʃiːθ] n vaina; (contraceptive) preservativo

sheaves [ʃiːvz] npl of **sheaf**

shed [ʃed] (pt, pp ~) n cobertizo ♦ vt (skin) mudar; (tears, blood) derramar; (load) derramar; (workers) despedir

she'd [ʃiːd] cont = **she had; she would**

sheen [ʃiːn] n brillo, lustre m

sheep [ʃiːp] n inv oveja ❏ **sheepdog** n perro pastor ❏ **sheepskin** n piel f de carnero

sheer [ʃɪər] adj (utter) puro, completo; (steep) escarpado; (material) diáfano ♦ adv verticalmente

sheet [ʃiːt] n (on bed) sábana; (of paper) hoja; (of glass, metal) lámina; (of ice) capa

sheik(h) [ʃeɪk] n jeque m

shelf [ʃelf] (pl **shelves**) n estante m

shell [ʃel] n (on beach) concha; (of egg, nut etc) cáscara; (explosive) proyectil m, obús m; (of building) armazón f ♦ vt (peas) desenvainar; (MIL) bombardear

she'll [ʃiːl] cont = **she will; she shall**

shellfish [ʃelfɪʃ] n inv crustáceo; (as food) mariscos mpl (LAm), marisco (SP)

shell suit n (BRIT) pants mpl y sudadera (MEX), equipo de deportes (LAm), jogging m (RPl), chándal m (SP)

shelter [ʃeltər] n abrigo, refugio ♦ vt (aid) amparar, proteger; (give lodging to) abrigar ♦ vi abrigarse, refugiarse ❏ **sheltered** adj (life) protegido; (spot) abrigado ❏ **sheltered housing** (BRIT) n viviendas vigiladas para ancianos y minusválidos

shelve [ʃelv] vt (fig) aplazar ❏ **shelves** npl of **shelf**

shepherd [ʃepərd] n pastor m ♦ vt (guide) guiar, conducir ❏ **shepherd's pie** (BRIT) n pastel de carne y puré de papas

sherbet [ʃɜːrbət] n (US: water ice) sorbete m; (BRIT: powder) polvos mpl azucarados

sheriff [ʃerɪf] n (in US) sheriff m; (in England) gobernador m civil; (in Scotland) juez mf

sherry [ʃeri] n jerez m

she's [ʃiːz] cont = **she is; she has**

Shetland [ʃetlənd] n (also: **the ~s, the ~ Isles**) las (Islas) Shetland

shield [ʃiːld] n escudo; (protection) blindaje m ♦ vt: **to ~ (from)** proteger (de)

shift [ʃɪft] n (change) cambio; (at work) turno; (also: **gear ~**) palanca de cambios ♦ vt trasladar; (remove) quitar ♦ vi moverse; **to ~ gear** (AUT) cambiar de marcha ❏ **shift work** n trabajo por turnos ❏ **shifty** adj sospechoso; (eyes) furtivo

shimmer [ʃɪmər] n brillo or reflejo trémulo

shin [ʃɪn] n espinilla

shine [ʃaɪn] (pt, pp **shone**) n brillo, lustre m ♦ vi brillar, relucir ♦ vt (shoes) lustrar, sacar brillo a; **to ~ a torch on sth** enfocar una linterna hacia algo

shingle [ʃɪŋɡəl] n (on beach) guijarros mpl; ~**s** n (MED) herpes m inv

shiny [ʃaɪni] adj brillante, lustroso

ship [ʃɪp] n barco, buque m ♦ vt (goods) embarcar; (send) transportar or enviar por barco ❏ **shipbuilding** n construcción f naval ❏ **shipment** n (goods) envío ❏ **shipping** n (act) transporte m; (ships) barcos mpl ❏ **shipwreck** n naufragio ♦ vt: **to be shipwrecked** naufragar ❏ **shipyard** n astillero

shire [ʃaɪər] (BRIT) n condado

shirt [ʃɜːrt] n camisa; **in (one's) ~ sleeves** en mangas de camisa

shiver [ʃɪvər] n escalofrío ♦ vi temblar, estremecerse; (with cold) tiritar

shoal [ʃoul] n (of fish) banco; (fig: also: ~**s**) tropel m

shock [ʃɑːk] n (impact) choque m; (ELEC) descarga (eléctrica); toque m (MEX), golpe m de corriente (LAm), calambre m (SP); (emotional) conmoción f; (start) sobresalto, susto; (MED) shock m ♦ vt dar un susto a; (offend) escandalizar ❏ **shock absorber** n amortiguador m ❏ **shocking** adj (awful) espantoso; (outrageous) escandaloso

shoddy [ʃɑːdi] adj de pacotilla

shoe [ʃuː] (pt, pp **shod**) n zapato; (for horse) herradura ♦ vt (horse) herrar ❏ **shoe brush** n cepillo para zapatos ❏ **shoelace** n cordón m, agujeta (MEX), cinta (MEX) ❏ **shoe polish** n betún m, pomada (RPl) ❏ **shoe store** (US) (BRIT **shoe shop**) n zapatería ❏ **shoestring** n cordón m, agujeta (MEX), cinta (MEX); (fig): **on a shoestring** con muy poco dinero

shone [ʃoun] pt, pp of **shine**

shook [ʃuk] pt of **shake**

shoot [ʃuːt] (pt, pp **shot**) n (on branch, seedling) retoño, vástago ♦ vt disparar; (kill) matar a tiros; (wound) pegar un tiro; (execute) fusilar; (movie) rodar, filmar ♦ vi (SOCCER) chutar
► **shoot down** vt (plane) derribar ► **shoot in/out** vi entrar corriendo/salir disparado
► **shoot up** vi (prices) dispararse
□ **shooting** n (shots) disparos mpl; (of movie) rodaje m; (BRIT HUNTING) caza con escopeta
□ **shooting star** n estrella fugaz

shop [ʃɔp] n (BRIT) tienda; (workshop) taller m
♦ vi (also: **go ~ping**) ir de compras □ **shop assistant** (BRIT) n vendedor(a) m/f (LAm), dependiente(-a) m/f (SP) □ **shop floor** (BRIT) n (fig) taller m, fábrica □ **shopkeeper** (BRIT) n comerciante mf □ **shoplifting** n hurto (en tiendas) □ **shopper** n comprador(a) m/f
□ **shopping** n (goods) compras fpl
□ **shopping bag** n bolsa de la compra
□ **shopping cart** (US) n carrito de la compra
□ **shopping center** (US) (BRIT **shopping centre**) n centro comercial □ **shopping channel** n canal m de televenta □ **shop-soiled** (BRIT) adj deteriorado □ **shop steward** (BRIT) n (INDUSTRY) representante mf sindical □ **shop window** n vidriera (LAm), escaparate m (SP)

shore [ʃɔːr] n orilla ♦ vt: **to ~ (up)** reforzar; **on ~** en tierra

shorn [ʃɔːrn] pp of **shear**

short [ʃɔːrt] adj corto; (in time) breve, de corta duración; (person) bajo; (curt) brusco, seco; (insufficient) insuficiente; **to be ~ of sth** estar falto de algo; **in ~** en pocas palabras; **~ of doing ...** fuera de hacer ...; **it is ~ for** es la forma abreviada de; **to cut ~** (speech, visit) interrumpir, terminar inesperadamente; **everything ~ of ...** todo menos ...; **to fall ~ of** no alcanzar; **to run ~ of sth** andar escaso de algo; **to stop ~** parar en seco; **to stop ~ of** detenerse antes de □ **shortage** n: **a shortage of** una falta de □ **shortbread** n galleta de mantequilla □ **short-change** vt devolver de menos a □ **short-circuit** n cortocircuito □ **shortcoming** n defecto, deficiencia □ **short(crust) pastry** (BRIT) n pasta quebrada □ **shortcut** n atajo
□ **shorten** vt acortar; (visit) interrumpir
□ **shortfall** n déficit m □ **shorthand** n taquigrafía □ **short-handed** adj falto de personal or mano de obra □ **shorthand typist** n taquimecanógrafo(-a) □ **short list** (BRIT) n (for job) lista de candidatos seleccionados □ **short-lived** adj efímero
□ **shortly** adv en breve, dentro de poco

shorts [ʃɔːts] npl pantalones mpl cortos; (US) calzoncillos mpl

short: □ **shortsighted** (BRIT) adj miope; (fig) imprudente □ **short-staffed** (BRIT) adj: **to be short-staffed** estar falto de personal
□ **short story** n cuento □ **short-tempered** adj enojadizo □ **short-term** adj (effect) a corto plazo □ **shortwave** n (RADIO) onda corta

shot [ʃɔt] pt, pp of **shoot** ♦ n (sound) tiro, disparo; (try) tentativa; (of alcohol) trago; (injection) inyección f; (PHOT) foto; **to be a good/poor ~** (person) tener buena/mala puntería; **like a ~** (without any delay) como un rayo □ **shotgun** n escopeta

should [ʃud] aux vb: **I ~ go now** debo irme ahora; **he ~ be there now** debe de haber llegado (ya); **I ~ like to** me gustaría; **I ~ go if I were you** (BRIT) yo en tu lugar me iría

shoulder [ˈʃouldər] n hombro; (US: on road) arcén m, acotamiento (MEX), banquina (RPI)
♦ vt (fig) cargar con □ **shoulder bag** n bolsa (MEX) or cartera (LAm exc MEX) (para colgar del hombro), (bolso de) bandolera (SP)
□ **shoulder blade** n omóplato

shouldn't [ˈʃudnt] cont = **should not**

shout [ʃaut] n grito ♦ vt gritar ♦ vi gritar, dar voces ► **shout down** vt acallar a gritos
□ **shouting** n griterío

shove [ʃʌv] n empujón m ♦ vt empujar; (inf: put): **to ~ sth in** meter algo a empujones
► **shove off** (inf) vi largarse

shovel [ˈʃʌvəl] n pala; (mechanical) excavadora ♦ vt mover con pala

show [ʃou] (pt **~ed**, pp **~n**) n (of emotion) demostración f; (semblance) apariencia; (exhibition) exposición f; (THEATER) función f, espectáculo; (TV) show m ♦ vt mostrar, enseñar; (courage etc) mostrar, manifestar; (exhibit) exponer; (movie) proyectar ♦ vi mostrarse; (appear) aparecer; **for ~** para impresionar; **on ~** (exhibits etc) expuesto
► **show in** vt (person) hacer pasar ► **show off** (pej) vi presumir ♦ vt (display) lucir
► **show out** vt: **to show sb out** acompañar a algn a la puerta ► **show up** vi (stand out) destacar; (inf: turn up) aparecer ♦ vt (unmask) desenmascarar □ **show business** n mundo del espectáculo □ **showdown** n enfrentamiento (final)

shower [ˈʃauər] n (rain) chubasco, chaparrón m; (of stones etc) lluvia; (for bathing) ducha, regadera (MEX); (party) fiesta con regalos ♦ vi llover ♦ vt (fig): **to ~ sb with sth** colmar a algn de algo; **to take a ~** ducharse □ **shower gel** n gel m de ducha □ **showerproof** adj impermeable

showing [ˈʃouɪŋ] n (of movie) proyección f

show jumping n hípica

shown [ʃəʊn] pp of **show**

show: ❑ **show-off** (inf) n (person)
fanfarrón(-ona) m/f ♦ ❑ **showpiece** n (of
exhibition) joya, pieza principal
❑ **showroom** n sala de muestras

shrank [ʃræŋk] pt of **shrink**

shrapnel [ˈʃræpnəl] n metralla

shred [ʃrɛd] n (gen pl) triza, jirón m ♦ vt hacer
trizas; (CULIN) desmenuzar ❑ **shredder** n
(vegetable shredder) picadora; (document
shredder) trituradora (de papel)

shrewd [ʃruːd] adj astuto

shriek [ʃriːk] n chillido ♦ vi chillar

shrill [ʃrɪl] adj agudo, estridente

shrimp [ʃrɪmp] n camarón m (LAm), gamba
(SP)

shrine [ʃraɪn] n santuario, sepulcro

shrink [ʃrɪŋk] (pt **shrank**, pp **shrunk**) vi
encogerse; (be reduced) reducirse; (also: ~
away) retroceder ♦ vt encoger ♦ n (inf: pej)
loquero(-a); **to ~ from (doing) sth** no
atreverse a hacer algo ❑ **shrink-wrap** vt
envolver en plástico

shrivel [ˈʃrɪvəl] (also: ~ **up**) vt (dry) secar ♦ vi
secarse

shroud [ʃraʊd] n mortaja, sudario ♦ vt: **~ed in
mystery** envuelto en el misterio

Shrove Tuesday [ˈʃrəʊvˈtuːzdɪ] n martes m
de carnaval

shrub [ʃrʌb] n arbusto ❑ **shrubbery** n
arbustos mpl

shrug [ʃrʌg] n encogimiento de hombros
♦ vt, vi: **to ~ (one's shoulders)** encogerse de
hombros ▸ **shrug off** vt negar importancia
a

shrunk [ʃrʌŋk] pp of **shrink**

shudder [ˈʃʌdər] n estremecimiento,
escalofrío ♦ vi estremecerse

shuffle [ˈʃʌfəl] vt (cards) barajar ♦ vi: **to ~
(one's feet)** arrastrar los pies

shun [ʃʌn] vt rehuir, esquivar

shunt [ʃʌnt] vt (train) maniobrar; (object)
empujar

shut [ʃʌt] (pt, pp ~) vt cerrar ♦ vi cerrarse
▸ **shut down** vt, vi cerrar ▸ **shut off** vt
(supply etc) cortar ▸ **shut up** vi (inf: keep
quiet) callarse ♦ vt (close) cerrar; (silence) hacer
callar ❑ **shutter** n contraventana; (PHOT)
obturador m

shuttle [ˈʃʌtl] n (for weaving, sewing)
lanzadera; (AVIAT) puente m aéreo; (train, bus)
servicio (regular) de enlace ❑ **shuttlecock**
n volante m ❑ **shuttle diplomacy** n viajes

mpl diplomáticos ❑ **shuttle service** n
servicio rápido y continuo entre dos puntos

shy [ʃaɪ] adj tímido ❑ **shyness** n timidez f

shyster [ˈʃaɪstər] (US: inf) n tramposo(-a) m/f,
estafador(a) m/f

Sicily [ˈsɪsɪlɪ] n Sicilia

sick [sɪk] adj (ill) enfermo; (nauseated)
mareado; (humor) de mal gusto; (vomiting): **to
be ~** (BRIT) vomitar; **to feel ~** tener náuseas; **to
be ~ of** (fig) estar harto de ❑ **sick bay** n
enfermería ❑ **sicken** vt dar asco a
❑ **sickening** adj (fig) repugnante, asqueroso

sickle [ˈsɪkəl] n hoz f

sick: ❑ **sick leave** n licencia (MEX, RPl) or
permiso (LAm) or baja (SP) por enfermedad
❑ **sickly** adj enfermizo; (smell) nauseabundo
❑ **sickness** n enfermedad f; (vomiting)
náuseas fpl ❑ **sick pay** n prestación f por
enfermedad

side [saɪd] n (gen) lado; (of body) costado; (of
lake) orilla; (of hill) ladera; (BRIT: team) equipo
♦ adj (door, entrance) lateral ♦ vi: **to ~ with sb**
tomar el partido de algn; **by the ~ of** al lado
de; **~ by ~** juntos(-as); **from ~ to ~** de un lado
para otro; **from all ~s** de todos lados; **to take
~s (with)** tomar partido (con) ❑ **sideboard**
n aparador m ❑ **sideboards** (BRIT) npl
= **sideburns** ❑ **sideburns** npl patillas fpl
❑ **side dish** n acompañamiento, guarnición
f ❑ **side drum** n tambor m ❑ **side effect** n
efecto secundario ❑ **sidekick** (inf) n secuaz
(inf) mf ❑ **sidelight** n (AUT: on side of car) luz f
lateral ❑ **sideline** n (SPORT) línea de banda;
(fig) segundo empleo ❑ **sidelong** adj de
reojo ❑ **side order** n plato de
acompañamiento ❑ **sideshow** n (stall) caseta
❑ **sidestep** vt (fig) esquivar ❑ **side street** n
calle f lateral ❑ **sidetrack** vt (fig) desviar
❑ **sidewalk** (US) n acera, banqueta (MEX),
andén m (CAm), vereda (SC) ❑ **sideways** adv
de lado

siding [ˈsaɪdɪŋ] n (RAIL) apartadero, vía muerta

siege [siːdʒ] n cerco, sitio

sieve [sɪv] n colador m ♦ vt cribar

sift [sɪft] vt cribar; (fig: information) escudriñar

sigh [saɪ] n suspiro ♦ vi suspirar

sight [saɪt] n (faculty) vista; (spectacle)
espectáculo; (on gun) mira, alza ♦ vt divisar; **in
~** a la vista; **out of ~** fuera de (la) vista; **on ~**
(shoot) sin previo aviso ❑ **sightseeing** n
turismo; **to go sightseeing** hacer turismo

sign [saɪn] n (with hand) señal f, seña; (trace)
huella, rastro; (notice) letrero; (written) signo
♦ vt firmar; (SPORT) fichar; **to ~ sth over to sb**
firmar el traspaso de algo a algn ▸ **sign on** vi
(BRIT: for course) inscribirse; (BRIT: as

unemployed) inscribirse como desempleado (*LAm*), apuntarse al paro (*SP*) ♦ *vt* (*employee*) contratar ▶ **sign up** *vi* (*MIL*) alistarse; (*for course*) inscribirse ♦ *vt* (*player*) fichar

signal ['sɪgnəl] *n* señal *f* ♦ *vi* señalizar ♦ *vt* (*person*) hacer señas a; (*message*) comunicar por señales ❑ **signalman** *n* (*RAIL*) guardavía *m*

signature ['sɪgnətʃər] *n* firma ❑ **signature tune** (*BRIT*) *n* sintonía (*de apertura de un programa*)

signet ring ['sɪgnət,rɪŋ] *n* anillo de sello

significance [sɪg'nɪfɪkəns] *n* (*importance*) trascendencia

significant [sɪg'nɪfɪkənt] *adj* significativo; (*important*) trascendente

signify ['sɪgnɪfaɪ] *vt* significar

sign language *n* lenguaje *m* por señas

signpost ['saɪnpoʊst] *n* señal *f*, indicador *m*

silence ['saɪləns] *n* silencio ♦ *vt* acallar; silenciar ❑ **silencer** *n* (*on gun*) silenciador *m*; (*BRIT AUT*) silenciador *m*, mofle *m* (*MEX, CAm*)

silent ['saɪlənt] *adj* silencioso; (*not speaking*) callado; (*movie*) mudo; **to remain ~** guardar silencio ❑ **silent partner** (*US*) *n* (*COMM*) socio(-a) capitalista

silhouette [sɪlu:'et] *n* silueta

silicon chip ['sɪlɪkən'tʃɪp] *n* chip *m* de silicio

silk [sɪlk] *n* seda ♦ *adj* de seda ❑ **silky** *adj* sedoso

silly ['sɪlɪ] *adj* (*person*) tonto; (*idea*) absurdo

silt [sɪlt] *n* sedimento

silver ['sɪlvər] *n* plata; (*money*) moneda suelta ♦ *adj* de plata; (*color*) plateado ❑ **silver paper** (*BRIT*) *n* papel *m* de plata ❑ **silver-plated** *adj* plateado ❑ **silversmith** *n* platero(-a) ❑ **silverware** *n* (vajilla de) plata ❑ **silvery** *adj* argentino

similar ['sɪmɪlər] *adj*: **~ (to)** parecido *or* semejante (a) ❑ **similarity** [sɪmɪ'lærɪtɪ] *n* semejanza ❑ **similarly** *adv* del mismo modo

simmer ['sɪmər] *vi* cocer *or* hervir a fuego lento

simple ['sɪmpəl] *adj* (*easy*) sencillo; (*foolish, COMM, interest*) simple ❑ **simplicity** [sɪm'plɪsɪtɪ] *n* sencillez *f* ❑ **simplify** ['sɪmplɪfaɪ] *vt* simplificar

simply ['sɪmplɪ] *adv* (*live, talk*) sencillamente; (*just, merely*) sólo

simulate ['sɪmjəleɪt] *vt* fingir, simular ❑ **simulated** *adj* simulado; (*fur*) de imitación

simultaneous [saɪməl'teɪnɪəs] *adj* simultáneo ❑ **simultaneously** *adv* simultáneamente

sin [sɪn] *n* pecado ♦ *vi* pecar

since [sɪns] *adv* desde entonces, después ♦ *prep* desde ♦ *conj* (*time*) desde que; (*because*) ya que, puesto que; **~ then, ever ~** desde entonces

sincere [sɪn'stər] *adj* sincero ❑ **sincerely** *adv*: **Sincerely yours** (*in letters*) (le saluda) atentamente ❑ **sincerity** [sɪn'serɪtɪ] *n* sinceridad *f*

sinew ['sɪnju:] *n* tendón *m*

sing [sɪŋ] (*pt* **sang**, *pp* **sung**) *vt, vi* cantar

Singapore [sɪŋə'pɔ:r] *n* Singapur *m*

singe [sɪndʒ] *vt* chamuscar

singer ['sɪŋər] *n* cantante *mf*

singing ['sɪŋɪŋ] *n* canto

single ['sɪŋgəl] *adj* único, solo; (*unmarried*) soltero; (*not double*) simple, sencillo ♦ *n* (*record*) sencillo, single *m*; (*BRIT: also:* **~ ticket**) boleto (*LAm*) *or* billete *m* (*SP*) sencillo; **~s** *npl* (*TENNIS*) individuales *mpl*; **~ bed** cama individual ▶ **single out** *vt* (*choose*) escoger ❑ **single-breasted** *adj* recto ❑ **single file** *n*: **in single file** en fila de uno ❑ **single-handed** *adv* sin ayuda ❑ **single-minded** *adj* resuelto, firme ❑ **single parent** *n* (*man*) padre *m* soltero; (*woman*) madre *f* soltera; **single parent family** familia monoparental ❑ **single room** *n* habitación *f* individual

singly ['sɪŋglɪ] *adv* uno por uno

singular ['sɪŋgjələr] *adj* (*odd*) raro, extraño; (*outstanding*) excepcional ♦ *n* (*LING*) singular *m*

sinister ['sɪnɪstər] *adj* siniestro

sink [sɪŋk] (*pt* **sank**, *pp* **sunk**) *n* fregadero, lavaplatos *m inv* (*MEX*), pileta (*RPl*) ♦ *vt* (*ship*) hundir; (*foundations*) excavar ♦ *vi* hundirse; **to ~ sth into** hundir algo en ▶ **sink in** *vi* (*fig*) penetrar, calar

sinner ['sɪnər] *n* pecador(a) *m/f*

sinus ['saɪnəs] *n* (*ANAT*) seno

sip [sɪp] *n* sorbo ♦ *vt* sorber, beber a sorbos

siphon ['saɪfən] *n* sifón *m* ▶ **siphon off** *vt* desviar

sir [sɜ:r] *n* señor *m*; **S~ John Smith** Sir John Smith; **yes ~** sí, señor

siren ['saɪərən] *n* sirena

sirloin ['sɜ:rlɔɪn] *n* (*also:* **~ steak**) solomillo

sister ['sɪstər] *n* hermana; (*BRIT: nurse*) enfermera jefe ❑ **sister-in-law** *n* cuñada

sit [sɪt] (*pt, pp* **sat**) *vi* sentarse; (*be sitting*) estar sentado; (*assembly*) reunirse; (*for painter*) posar ♦ *vt* (*BRIT: exam*) presentarse a ▶ **sit down** *vi* sentarse ▶ **sit in on** *vt fus* asistir a ▶ **sit up** *vi* incorporarse; (*BRIT: not go to bed*) velar

sitcom ['sɪt,kɒːm] *n abbr* (= *situation comedy*) telecomedia (de situación)

site [saɪt] *n* sitio; (*also:* **building ~**) obra ♦ *vt* situar

sit-in *n* (*demonstration*) sentada

sitting ['sɪtɪŋ] *n* (*of assembly etc*) sesión *f*; (*in canteen*) turno ❑ **sitting room** (*BRIT*) *n* sala de estar

situated ['sɪtʃʊeɪtɪd] *adj* situado

situation [sɪtʃʊ'eɪʃən] *n* situación *f*; "**~s vacant**" (*BRIT*) "ofertas de empleo"

six [sɪks] *num* seis ❑ **sixteen** *num* dieciséis ❑ **sixth** *num* sexto ❑ **sixty** *num* sesenta

size [saɪz] *n* tamaño; (*extent*) extensión *f*; (*of clothing*) talla, talle *m* (*RPl*); (*of shoes*) número ▶ **size up** *vt* formarse una idea de ❑ **sizeable** *adj* importante, considerable

sizzle ['sɪzəl] *vi* crepitar

skate [skeɪt] *n* patín *m*; (*fish: pl inv*) raya ♦ *vi* patinar ❑ **skateboard** *n* monopatín *m*, patineta (*SC*) ❑ **skateboarding** *n* monopatín *m*, patineta (*SC*) ❑ **skater** *n* patinador(a) *m/f* ❑ **skating** *n* patinaje *m* ❑ **skating rink** *n* pista de patinaje

skeleton ['skelɪtn] *n* esqueleto; (*TECH*) armazón *f*; (*outline*) esquema *m* ❑ **skeleton staff** *n* personal *m* reducido

skeptic (*US*) ['skeptɪk] (*BRIT* **sceptic**) *n* escéptico(-a) ❑ **skeptical** (*US*) (*BRIT* **sceptical**) *adj* escéptico

sketch [sketʃ] *n* (*drawing*) boceto; (*outline*) esbozo, bosquejo; (*THEATER*) sketch *m* ♦ *vt* dibujar; (*plan etc: also:* **~ out**) esbozar ❑ **sketchbook** *n* cuaderno de dibujo ❑ **sketchy** *adj* incompleto

skewer ['skjuːər] *n* pincho

ski [skiː] *n* esquí *m* ♦ *vi* esquiar ❑ **ski boot** *n* bota de esquí

skid [skɪd] *n* patinazo ♦ *vi* patinar

ski: ❑ **skier** *n* esquiador(a) *m/f* ❑ **skiing** *n* esquí *m* ❑ **ski jump** *n* salto de esquí

skilful ['skɪlfəl] (*BRIT*) *adj* = **skillful**

ski lift *n* telesilla *m*, telesquí *m*

skill [skɪl] *n* destreza, pericia; técnica ❑ **skilled** *adj* hábil, diestro; (*worker*) calificado (*LAm*), cualificado (*SP*) ❑ **skillful** (*US*) (*BRIT* **skilful**) *adj* diestro, experto

skim [skɪm] *vt* (*milk*) descremar (*LAm*); (*glide over*) rozar, rasar ♦ *vi*: **to ~ through** (*book*) hojear ❑ **skim milk** (*US*) (*BRIT* **skimmed milk**) *n* leche *f* descremada (*LAm*) or desnatada (*SP*)

skimp [skɪmp] *vt* (*also:* **~ on**: *work*) chapucear; (*cloth etc*) escatimar ❑ **skimpy** *adj* escaso; (*skirt*) muy corto

skin [skɪn] *n* piel *f*; (*complexion*) cutis *m* ♦ *vt* (*fruit etc*) pelar; (*animal*) despellejar ❑ **skin cancer** *n* cáncer *m* de piel ❑ **skin-deep** *adj* superficial ❑ **skin diving** *n* buceo ❑ **skinny** *adj* flaco ❑ **skintight** *adj* (*dress etc*) muy ajustado

skip [skɪp] *n* brinco, salto; (*BRIT: container*) contenedor *m* de basura ♦ *vi* brincar; (*BRIT: with rope*) saltar a la cuerda (*LAm*) or comba (*SP*) ♦ *vt* saltarse

ski: ❑ **ski pass** *n* forfait *m* (de esquí) ❑ **ski pole** *n* bastón *m* de esquí

skipper ['skɪpər] *n* (*NAUT, SPORT*) capitán *m*

skipping rope ['skɪpɪŋˌroup] (*BRIT*) *n* cuerda de saltar (*LAm*), comba (*SP*)

skirmish ['skɜːmɪʃ] *n* escaramuza

skirt [skɜːrt] *n* falda, pollera (*SC*) ♦ *vt* (*go around*) ladear ❑ **skirting board** (*BRIT*) *n* zoclo (*MEX*), zócalo (*LAm exc MEX, SP*)

ski slope *n* pista de esquí

ski suit *n* traje *m* de esquí

ski tow *n* remonte *m*

skittle ['skɪtl] (*BRIT*) *n* bolo; **~s** *n* (*game*) boliche *m*

skive [skaɪv] (*BRIT: inf*) *vi* haraganear, holgazanear

skull [skʌl] *n* calavera; (*ANAT*) cráneo

skunk [skʌŋk] *n* mofeta

sky [skaɪ] *n* cielo ❑ **skylight** *n* tragaluz *m*, claraboya ❑ **skyscraper** *n* rascacielos *m inv*

slab [slæb] *n* (*stone*) bloque *m*; (*flat*) losa; (*of cake*) trozo

slack [slæk] *adj* (*loose*) flojo; (*slow*) de poca actividad; (*careless*) descuidado ❑ **slacken** (*also:* **slacken off**) *vi* aflojarse ♦ *vt* aflojar; (*speed*) disminuir ❑ **slacks** *npl* pantalones *mpl*

slag heap ['slæg,hiːp] (*BRIT*) *n* escorial *m*, escombrera

slag off (*BRIT: inf*) *vt* poner como un trapo

slam [slæm] *vt* (*throw*) arrojar (violentamente); (*criticize*) criticar duramente ♦ *vi* (*door*) cerrarse de golpe; **to ~ the door** dar un portazo

slander ['slændər] *n* calumnia, difamación *f*

slang [slæŋ] *n* argot *m*; (*jargon*) jerga

slant [slænt] *n* sesgo, inclinación *f*; (*fig*) interpretación *f* ❑ **slanted** *adj* (*fig*) parcial ❑ **slanting** *adj* inclinado; (*eyes*) rasgado

slap [slæp] *n* palmada; (*in face*) bofetada ♦ *vt* dar una palmada or bofetada a; (*paint etc*): **to ~ sth on sth** embadurnar algo con algo ♦ *adv* (*directly*) exactamente, directamente ❑ **slapdash** *adj* descuidado ❑ **slapstick** *n* astracanada, bufonada ❑ **slap-up** *adj*: **a**

slap-up meal (*BRIT*) un banquetazo, una comilona

slash [slæʃ] *vt* acuchillar; (*fig: prices*) fulminar

slat [slæt] *n* tablilla, listón *m*

slate [sleɪt] *n* pizarra ♦ *vt* (*BRIT: fig: criticize*) criticar duramente

slaughter [ˈslɔːtər] *n* (*of animals*) matanza; (*of people*) carnicería ♦ *vt* matar □ **slaughterhouse** *n* rastro (*MEX*), matadero (*LAm exc MEX*)

Slav [slɑːv] *adj* eslavo

slave [sleɪv] *n* esclavo(-a) ♦ *vi* (*also: ~ away*) sudar tinta □ **slavery** *n* esclavitud *f*

slay [sleɪ] (*pt* slew, *pp* slain) *vt* matar

sleazy [ˈsliːzi] *adj* de mala fama

sled [sled] (*US*) *n* trineo

sledge [sledʒ] (*BRIT*) *n* = **sled**

sledgehammer *n* mazo

sleek [sliːk] *adj* (*shiny*) lustroso; (*car etc*) elegante

sleep [sliːp] (*pt*, *pp* slept) *n* sueño ♦ *vi* dormir; **to go to ~** quedarse dormido ► **sleep around** *vi* acostarse con cualquiera ► **sleep in** *vi* (*oversleep*) quedarse dormido □ **sleeper** *n* (*person*) durmiente *mf*; (*train*) coche-cama *m*, coche *m* dormitorio (*SC*); (*BRIT RAIL: on track*) durmiente *m* (*LAm*), traviesa (*SP*) □ **sleeping bag** *n* bolsa (*MEX*, *RPl*) or saco (*LAm exc MEX*, *SP*) de dormir □ **sleeping car** *n* coche-cama *m*, coche *m* dormitorio (*SC*) □ **sleeping partner** (*BRIT*) *n* (*COMM*) socio(-a) capitalista ♦ *m* □ **sleeping pill** *n* somnífero □ **sleepless** *adj*: **a sleepless night** una noche en blanco □ **sleepover** *n*: **we're having a sleepover at Paige's** pasamos la noche en casa de Paige □ **sleepwalker** *n* sonámbulo(-a) □ **sleepy** *adj* soñoliento; (*place*) tranquilo

sleet [sliːt] *n* aguanieve *f*

sleeve [sliːv] *n* manga; (*TECH*) manguito; (*BRIT: of record*) portada □ **sleeveless** *adj* sin mangas

sleigh [sleɪ] *n* trineo

sleight [slaɪt] *n*: **~ of hand** escamoteo

slender [ˈslendər] *adj* delgado; (*means*) escaso

slept [slept] *pt*, *pp* of **sleep**

slew [sluː] *pt* of **slay** ♦ *n* (*US: inf: range*) montón *m* ♦ *vi* (*BRIT: veer*) torcerse

slice [slaɪs] *n* (*of meat*) tajada; (*of bread*) rebanada; (*of lemon*) rodaja; (*BRIT: utensil*) pala ♦ *vt* cortar (en tajos), rebanar

slick [slɪk] *adj* (*skillful*) hábil, diestro; (*clever*) astuto ♦ *n* (*also: oil ~*) marea negra

slide [slaɪd] (*pt*, *pp* slid) *n* (*movement*) descenso, desprendimiento; (*in playground*) tobogán *m*, resbaladero (*MEX*); (*PHOT*) diapositiva; (*BRIT: also: hair ~*) pasador *m*, broche *m* (*MEX*) ♦ *vt* correr, deslizar ♦ *vi* (*slip*) resbalarse; (*glide*) deslizarse □ **sliding** *adj* (*door*) corredizo □ **sliding scale** *n* escala móvil

slight [slaɪt] *adj* (*slim*) delgado; (*frail*) delicado; (*pain etc*) leve; (*trivial*) insignificante; (*small*) pequeño ♦ *n* desaire *m* ♦ *vt* (*insult*) ofender, desairar; **not in the ~est** en absoluto □ **slightly** *adv* ligeramente, un poco

slim [slɪm] *adj* delgado, esbelto; (*fig: chance*) remoto ♦ *vi* adelgazar

slime [slaɪm] *n* limo, cieno

slimming [ˈslɪmɪŋ] *n* adelgazamiento

slimy [ˈslaɪmi] *adj* cenagoso

sling [slɪŋ] (*pt*, *pp* slung) *n* (*MED*) cabestrillo; (*weapon*) honda ♦ *vt* tirar, arrojar □ **slingshot** (*US*) *n* hulera (*MEX*), resortera (*MEX*), tirachinas *m inv* (*LAm exc MEX*, *SP*), honda (*SC*)

slip [slɪp] *n* (*slide*) resbalón *m*; (*mistake*) descuido; (*undergarment*) combinación *f*, fondo (*MEX*), viso (*RPl*); (*of paper*) papelito ♦ *vt* (*slide*) deslizar ♦ *vi* deslizarse; (*stumble*) resbalar(se); (*decline*) decaer; (*move smoothly*): **to ~ into/out of** (*room etc*) introducirse en/ salirse de; **to give sb the ~** eludir a algn; **a ~ of the tongue** un lapsus; **to ~ sth on/off** ponerse/quitarse algo ► **slip away** *vi* escabullirse ► **slip in** *vt* meter ♦ *vi* meterse ► **slip out** *vi* (*go out*) salir (un momento) ► **slip up** *vi* (*make mistake*) equivocarse; meter la pata □ **slipped disc** *n* vértebra dislocada

slipper [ˈslɪpər] *n* zapatilla, pantufla

slippery [ˈslɪpəri] *adj* resbaladizo

slip: □ **slip road** (*BRIT*) *n* (*to join motorway*) vía de acceso; (*to exit motorway*) vía de salida □ **slip-up** *n* (*error*) desliz *m* □ **slipway** *n* grada, gradas *fpl*

slit [slɪt] (*pt*, *pp* ~) *n* rajada (*MEX*), tajo (*LAm*), raja (*SP*); (*cut*) corte *m* ♦ *vt* rajar; cortar

slither [ˈslɪðər] *vi* deslizarse

sliver [ˈslɪvər] *n* (*of glass, wood*) astilla; (*of cheese etc*) raja

slob [slɑːb] (*inf*) *n* vago(-a), dejado(-a)

slog [slɑːg] (*BRIT*) *vi* sudar tinta; **it was a ~** costó trabajo (hacerlo)

slogan [ˈsləʊgən] *n* eslogan *m*, lema *m*

slope [sləʊp] *n* (*up*) cuesta, pendiente *f*; (*down*) declive *m*; (*side of mountain*) falda, vertiente m ♦ vi: **to ~ down** estar en declive; **to ~ up** inclinarse ❑ **sloping** adj en pendiente; en declive; (writing) inclinado

sloppy ['slɑːpi] adj (work) descuidado; (appearance) desaliñado

slot [slɑːt] n ranura ♦ vt: **to ~ into** encajar en

slot machine n (for gambling) (máquina) tragamonedas f inv (LAm) or tragaperras f inv (SP); (BRIT: vending machine) máquina expendedora

slouch [slautʃ] vi andar etc con los hombros caídos

Slovenia [sləu'viːnɪə] n Eslovenia

slovenly ['slʌvənli] adj desaliñado, desaseado; (careless) descuidado

slow [sləu] adj lento; (not clever) lento, corto; (watch): **to be ~** atrasar ♦ adv lentamente, despacio ♦ vt, vi (also: ~ down, ~ up) retardar; "~" (road sign) "reduzca or disminuya la velocidad" ❑ **slowdown** (US) n huelga de manos caídas ❑ **slowly** adv lentamente, despacio ❑ **slow motion** n: **in slow motion** a cámara lenta ❑ **slowpoke** (US) n tortuga f

sludge [slʌdʒ] n lodo, fango

slug [slʌg] n babosa; (bullet) bala, posta ❑ **sluggish** adj lento; (person) perezoso

sluice [sluːs] n (gate) esclusa; (channel) canal m

slum [slʌm] n barrio bajo

slump [slʌmp] n (economic) depresión f ♦ vi hundirse; (prices) caer en picado

slung [slʌŋ] pt, pp of **sling**

slur [slɜːr] n: **to cast a ~ on** insultar ♦ vt (speech) pronunciar mal

slush [slʌʃ] n nieve f sucia or fangosa

slut [slʌt] n putona

sly [slai] adj astuto; (smile) taimado

smack [smæk] n bofetada ♦ vt dar un azote a; (child, on face) abofetear ♦ vi: **to ~ of** saber a, oler a

small [smɔːl] adj pequeño ❑ **small ads** (BRIT) npl anuncios mpl por palabras ❑ **small change** n feria (MEX), morralla (MEX), sencillo (LAm exc MEX), suelto (SP) ❑ **smallholder** (BRIT) n granjero(-a), minifundista mf ❑ **small hours** npl: **in the small hours** a altas horas (de la noche) ❑ **smallpox** n viruela ❑ **small talk** n cháchara

smart [smɑːrt] adj elegante; (clever) listo, inteligente; (quick) rápido, vivo ♦ vi escocer, picar ► **smarten up** vi arreglarse ♦ vt arreglar

smash [smæʃ] n (also: ~~up) choque m; (MUS) exitazo ♦ vt (break) hacer pedazos; (car etc)

estrellar; (SPORT: record) batir ♦ vi hacerse pedazos; (against wall etc) estrellarse ❑ **smashing** (BRIT: inf) adj estupendo

smattering ['smætərɪŋ] n: **a ~ of** algo de

smear [smɪər] n mancha; (BRIT MED) Papanicolau m (LAm), citología (SP) ♦ vt untar ❑ **smear campaign** n campaña de desprestigio

smell [smel] (pt, pp **smelt** or **~ed**) n olor m; (sense) olfato ♦ vt, vi oler ❑ **smelly** adj maloliente

smile [smail] n sonrisa ♦ vi sonreír

smirk [smɜːrk] n sonrisa falsa or afectada

smith [smɪθ] n herrero ❑ **smithy** ['smɪði] n herrería

smog [smɑːg] n esmog m

smoke [sməuk] n humo ♦ vi fumar; (chimney) echar humo ♦ vt (cigarettes) fumar ❑ **smoked** adj (bacon) ahumado ❑ **smoke detector** n detector m de humo ❑ **smoker** n fumador(a) m/f; (BRIT RAIL) vagón m de fumadores ❑ **smoke screen** n cortina de humo ❑ **smoke shop** (US) n tabaquería (LAm), estanco (SP) ❑ **smoking** n: "**no smoking**" "prohibido fumar" ❑ **smoky** adj (room) lleno de humo; (taste) ahumado

⚠ Be careful not to translate **smoking** by the Spanish word **smoking**.

smolder (US) ['sməuldər] (BRIT **smoulder**) vi arder sin llama

smooth [smuːð] adj liso; (sea) tranquilo; (flavor, movement) suave; (sauce) fino; (person: pej) meloso ♦ vt (also: ~ out) alisar; (creases, difficulties) allanar

smother ['smʌðər] vt sofocar; (repress) contener

SMS n abbr (= short message service) SMS m

smudge [smʌdʒ] n mancha; borrón m ♦ vt manchar; emborronar

smug [smʌg] adj engreído, presumido

smuggle ['smʌgəl] vt pasar de contrabando ❑ **smuggler** n contrabandista mf ❑ **smuggling** n contrabando

smutty ['smʌti] adj (fig) colorado (MEX), verde (LAm exc MEX, SP)

snack [snæk] n bocado ❑ **snack bar** n cafetería

snag [snæg] n problema m

snail [sneil] n caracol m

snake [sneik] n serpiente f

snap [snæp] n (sound) chasquido; (BRIT: photograph) foto f ♦ adj (decision) instantáneo ♦ vt (break) quebrar; (fingers) castañetear ♦ vi quebrarse; (fig: speak sharply) contestar

bruscamente; **to ~ shut** cerrarse de golpe
▶ **snap at** vt fus (dog) intentar morder
▶ **snap off** vi partirse ▶ **snap up** vt agarrar
❏ **snap fastener** (US) n botón m de presión
(LAm) ❏ **snappy** (inf) adj (answer)
instantáneo; (slogan) conciso; **make it
snappy!** (hurry up) ¡date prisa! ❏ **snapshot**
n foto f (instantánea)

snare [snɛər] n trampa

snarl [snɑːrl] vi gruñir

snatch [snætʃ] n (small piece) fragmento ♦ vt
(snatch away) arrebatar; (fig) agarrar; **to ~
some sleep** encontrar tiempo para dormir

sneak [sniːk] (pt snuck) vi (US): **to ~ in/out**
entrar/salir a hurtadillas ♦ n (inf) soplón(-ona)
m/f; **to ~ up on sb** acercarse sigilosamente a
algn ❏ **sneakers** npl zapatillas fpl (de
deporte) ❏ **sneaky** adj furtivo

sneer [snɪər] vi reír con sarcasmo; (mock): **to ~
at** burlarse de

sneeze [sniːz] vi estornudar

sniff [snɪf] vi sollozar ♦ vt husmear, oler;
(drugs) esnifar

snigger [ˈsnɪgər] vi reírse con disimulo

snip [snɪp] n tijeretazo; (BRIT: inf: bargain)
ganga ♦ vt tijeretear

sniper [ˈsnaɪpər] n francotirador(a) m/f

snippet [ˈsnɪpɪt] n retazo

snob [snɑːb] n (e)snob mf ❏ **snobbery** n
(e)snobismo ❏ **snobbish** adj (e)snob

snooker [ˈsnuːkər] (BRIT) n snooker m

snoop [snuːp] vi: **to ~ about** fisgonear

snooze [snuːz] n cabezadita ♦ vi echar una
cabezadita

snore [snɔːr] n ronquido ♦ vi roncar

snorkel [ˈsnɔːrkəl] n (tubo) respirador m

snort [snɔːrt] n bufido ♦ vi bufar

snout [snaut] n hocico, morro

snow [snou] n nieve f ♦ vi nevar ❏ **snowball**
n bola de nieve ♦ vi (fig) multiplicarse,
aumentar ❏ **snowbound** adj bloqueado
por la nieve ❏ **snowdrift** n ventisquero
❏ **snowdrop** n campanilla ❏ **snowfall** n
nevada ❏ **snowflake** n copo de nieve
❏ **snowman** n muñeco de nieve
❏ **snowplow** (US) (BRIT **snowplough**) n
quitanieves m inv ❏ **snowshoe** n raqueta or
bota (de nieve) ❏ **snowstorm** n nevada,
nevasca

snub [snʌb] vt (person) desairar ♦ n desaire m,
repulsa ❏ **snub-nosed** adj chato

snuff [snʌf] n rapé m

snug [snʌg] adj (cozy) cómodo; (fitted)
ajustado

snuggle [ˈsnʌgəl] vi: **to ~ up to sb** arrimarse
a algn

so

KEYWORD

[sou] adv

1 (thus, likewise) así, de este modo; **if so** de
ser así; **I like swimming -- so do I** a mí me
gusta nadar -- a mí también; **I've got work to
do -- so has Paul** tengo trabajo que hacer --
Paul también; **it's 5 o'clock -- so it is!** son las
cinco -- ¡pues es verdad!; **I hope/think so**
espero/creo que sí; **so far** hasta ahora; (in
past) hasta este momento

2 (in comparisons etc: to such a degree) tan; **so
quickly (that)** tan rápido (que); **so big (that)**
tan grande (que); **he's like his sister but not
so clever** es como su hermana pero no tan
listo; **we were so worried** estábamos
preocupadísimos

3: **so much** adj, adv tanto; **so many** tantos
(-as)

4 (phrases): **10 or so** unos 10 (más o menos);
so long! (inf: goodbye) ¡hasta luego!
♦ conj

1 (expressing purpose): **so as to do** para hacer;
so (that) para que + subjun

2 (expressing result) así que; **so you see, I
could have gone** así que ya ves, (yo) podría
haber ido

soak [souk] vt (drench) empapar; (steep in
water) remojar ♦ vi remojarse, estar a remojo
▶ **soak in** vi penetrar ▶ **soak up** vt absorber

soap [soup] n jabón m ❏ **soap flakes** npl
escamas fpl de jabón ❏ **soap opera** n
telenovela, culebrón m ❏ **soap powder** n
detergente m en polvo ❏ **soapy** adj
jabonoso

soar [sɔːr] vi (on wings) remontarse; (rocket:
prices) dispararse; (building etc) elevarse

sob [sɑːb] n sollozo ♦ vi sollozar

sober [ˈsoubər] adj (serious) serio; (not drunk)
sobrio; (color, style) discreto ▶ **sober up** vt
quitar la borrachera

so-called adj (así) llamado

soccer [ˈsɑːkər] (US) n futbol m (MEX), fútbol m
(LAm exc MEX, SP) ❏ **soccer player** (US) n
futbolista mf

social [ˈsouʃəl] adj social ♦ n velada, fiesta
❏ **social club** n club m ❏ **socialism** n
socialismo ❏ **socialist** adj, n socialista mf
❏ **socialize** vi: **to ~ (with)** alternar
(con) ❏ **socially** adv socialmente ❏ **social
security** n seguridad f social ❏ **social**

work n asistencia social ❏ **social worker** n asistente(-a) m/f social

society [sə'saɪətɪ] n sociedad f; (club) asociación f; (also: **high ~**) alta sociedad

sociology [sousɪ'ɑ:lədʒɪ] n sociología

sock [sɑ:k] n calcetín m

socket ['sɑ:kɪt] n cavidad f; (ELEC) enchufe m

sod [sɑ:d] n (of earth) césped m; (BRIT: inf!) cabrón(-ona) m/f (!)

soda ['soudə] n (CHEM) sosa; (also: **~ water**) soda; (US: also: **~ pop**) gaseosa

sodium bicarbonate ['soudɪəm-baɪ'kɑ:rbənt] n bicarbonato sódico or de sodio

sofa ['soufə] n sofá m

soft [sɑ:ft] adj (lenient, not hard) blando; (gentle, not bright) suave ❏ **soft drink** n refresco ❏ **soften** ['sɑ:fən] vt ablandar; suavizar; (effect) amortiguar ♦ vi ablandarse; suavizarse ❏ **softly** adv suavemente; (gently) delicadamente, con delicadeza ❏ **softness** n blandura; suavidad f ❏ **software** n (COMPUT) software m

soggy ['sɑ:gɪ] adj empapado, revenido

soil [sɔɪl] n (earth) tierra, suelo ♦ vt ensuciar ❏ **soiled** adj sucio

solar ['soulər] adj: ❏ **solar energy** n energía solar ❏ **solar panel** n panel m solar

sold [sould] pt, pp of **sell** ❏ **sold out** adj (COMM) agotado

solder ['sɑ:dər] vt soldar ♦ n soldadura

soldier ['souldʒər] n soldado; (army man) militar m

sole [soul] n (of foot) planta; (of shoe) suela; (fish: pl inv) lenguado ♦ adj único

solemn ['sɑ:ləm] adj solemne

sole trader n (COMM) comerciante m exclusivo

solicit [sə'lɪsɪt] vt (request) solicitar ♦ vi (prostitute) importunar

solicitor [sə'lɪsɪtər] n (BRIT: for wills etc) ≈ notario(-a); (in court) ≈ abogado(-a); (US: officer) representante mf

solid ['sɑ:lɪd] adj sólido; (gold etc) macizo ♦ n sólido; **~s** npl (food) alimentos mpl sólidos

solidarity [sɑ:lɪ'dærɪtɪ] n solidaridad f

solitaire [sɑ:lɪ'teər] (US) n (game) solitario

solitary ['sɑ:lɪterɪ] adj solitario, solo ❏ **solitary confinement** n incomunicación f

solo ['soulou] n solo ♦ adv (fly) en solitario ❏ **soloist** n solista mf

soluble ['sɑ:ljəbəl] adj soluble

solution [sə'lu:ʃən] n solución f

solve [sɑ:lv] vt resolver, solucionar

solvent ['sɑ:lvənt] adj (COMM) solvente ♦ n (CHEM) (di)solvente m

somber (US) ['sɑ:mbər] (BRIT **sombre**) adj sombrío

---

some

KEYWORD

[sʌm] adj

1 (a certain amount or number): **some tea/water/cookies** té/agua/(unas) galletas; **there's some milk in the icebox** hay leche en el refri (LAm) or frigo (SP); **there were some people outside** había algunas personas fuera; **I've got some money, but not much** tengo algo de dinero, pero no mucho

2 (certain: in contrasts) algunos(-as); **some people say that ...** hay quien dice que ...; **some movies were excellent, but most were mediocre** hubo películas excelentes, pero la mayoría fueron mediocres

3 (unspecified): **some woman was asking for you** una mujer estuvo preguntando por ti; **he was asking for some book (or other)** pedía un libro; **some day** algún día; **some day next week** un día de la semana que viene

♦ pron

1 (a certain number): **I've got some** (books etc) tengo algunos(-as)

2 (a certain amount) algo; **I've got some** (money, milk) tengo algo; **could I have some of that cheese?** ¿me puede dar un poco de ese queso?; **I've read some of the book** he leído parte del libro

♦ adv: **some 10 people** unas 10 personas, una decena de personas

---

some: ❏ **somebody** pron = **someone** ❏ **someday** adv algún día ❏ **somehow** adv de alguna manera; (for some reason) por una u otra razón ❏ **someone** pron alguien ❏ **someplace** (US) adv = **somewhere**

somersault ['sʌmərsɔ:lt] n (deliberate) salto mortal; (accidental) vuelco ♦ vi dar un salto mortal; dar vuelcos

some: ❏ **something** pron algo; **would you like something to eat/drink?** ¿te gustaría cenar/tomar algo? ❏ **sometime** adv (in future) algún día, en algún momento; (in past): **sometime last month** durante el mes pasado ❏ **sometimes** adv a veces ❏ **somewhat** adv algo ❏ **somewhere** adv (be) en alguna parte; (go) a alguna parte; **somewhere else** (be) en otra parte; (go) a otra parte

son [sʌn] n hijo

song [sɑ:ŋ] n canción f

son-in-law n yerno

soon [su:n] adv pronto, dentro de poco; ~ **afterward** poco después; see also **as** ❏ **sooner** adv (time) antes, más temprano; (preference: rather): **I would sooner do that** preferiría hacer eso; **sooner or later** tarde o temprano

soot [sut] n hollín m

soothe [su:ð] vt tranquilizar; (pain) aliviar

sophisticated [sə'fɪstɪkeɪtɪd] adj sofisticado

sophomore ['sɑ:fmɔ:r] (US) n estudiante mf de segundo año

sopping ['sɑ:pɪŋ] adj: ~ **(wet)** empapado

soppy ['sɑ:pi] (pej) adj tonto

soprano [sə'prænou] n soprano f

sorcerer ['sɔ:rsərər] n hechicero

sore [sɔ:r] adj (painful) doloroso, que duele ♦ n llaga ❏ **sorely** adv: **I am sorely tempted to** estoy muy tentado a

sorrow ['sɑ:rou] n pena, dolor m; ~**s** npl pesares mpl ❏ **sorrowful** adj triste

sorry ['sɑ:ri] adj (regretful) arrepentido; (condition, excuse) lastimoso; ~! ¡perdón!, ¡perdone!; ~? ¿cómo?; **to feel ~ for sb** sentir pena por algn; **I feel ~ for him** me da lástima

sort [sɔ:rt] n clase f, género, tipo ♦ vt (also: ~ **out**: papers) clasificar; (: problems) arreglar, solucionar ❏ **sorting office** (BRIT) n oficina de clasificación postal

SOS n SOS m

so-so adv regular, así así

soufflé [su:'fleɪ] n suflé m

sought [sɔ:t] pt, pp of **seek**

soul [soul] n alma f ❏ **soulful** adj lleno de sentimiento

sound [saund] n (noise) sonido, ruido; (volume: on TV etc) volumen m; (GEO) estrecho ♦ adj (healthy) sano; (safe, not damaged) en buen estado; (reliable: person) digno de confianza; (sensible) sensato, razonable; (secure: investment) seguro ♦ adv: ~ **asleep** profundamente dormido ♦ vt (alarm) sonar ♦ vi sonar, resonar; (fig: seem) parecer; **to ~ like** sonar a ▶ **sound out** vt sondear ❏ **sound barrier** n barrera del sonido ❏ **sound bite** n frase f lapidaria ❏ **sound effects** npl efectos mpl sonoros ❏ **soundly** adv (sleep) profundamente; (defeated) completamente ❏ **soundproof** adj insonorizado ❏ **soundtrack** n (of movie) banda sonora

soup [su:p] n (thick) sopa; (thin) caldo ❏ **soup plate** n plato hondo or sopero ❏ **soupspoon** n cuchara sopera

sour ['sauər] adj agrio; (milk) cortado; **it's ~ grapes** (fig) es envidia

source [sɔ:rs] n fuente f

south [sauθ] n sur m ♦ adj del sur, sureño ♦ adv al sur, hacia el sur; **the S~** (US) los estados sureños, el Sur; see also **the North** ❏ **South Africa** n África del Sur ❏ **South African** adj, n sudafricano(-a) ❏ **South America** n Sudamérica, América del Sur ❏ **South American** adj, n sudamericano(-a) ❏ **south-east** n sudeste m ❏ **southerly** ['sʌðərli] adj sur; (from the south) del sur ❏ **southern** ['sʌðərn] adj del sur, meridional ❏ **South Pole** n Polo Sur ❏ **southward(s)** ['sauθwərd(z)] adv hacia el sur ❏ **south-west** n suroeste m

---

THE SOUTH

La Guerra Civil Americana (1861-1865) dividió al país en dos facciones opuestas: el norte industrial, que luchaba por abolir el ejercicio de la esclavitud y el sur, agrícola, que luchaba por mantenerla. La línea Mason-Dixon, que discurría por la frontera entre Pensilvania y Maryland, marcaba la división geográfica entre las dos y, aunque ya ha desaparecido el enfrentamiento entre el norte y el sur, la mayoría de los norteamericanos percibe que subsisten importantes diferencias culturales entre ambas regiones.

---

souvenir [,su:və'nɪər] n recuerdo

sovereign ['sɑ:vrɪn] adj, n soberano(-a) ❏ **sovereignty** n soberanía

soviet ['souvɪət] adj soviético; **the S~ Union** (HIST) la Unión Soviética

sow¹ [sou] (pt ~**ed**, pp ~**n**) vt sembrar

sow² [sau] n cerda, puerca

soy (US) ['sɔɪ] (BRIT **soya** ['sɔɪə]) n soya (LAm), soja (SP) ❏ **soy bean** n semilla de soya (LAm) or soja (SP) ❏ **soy sauce** n salsa de soya (LAm) or soja (SP)

spa [spɑ:] n balneario

space [speɪs] n espacio; (room) sitio ♦ cpd espacial ♦ vt (also: ~ **out**) espaciar ❏ **spacecraft** n = **spaceship** ❏ **spaceman/woman** n astronauta mf, cosmonauta mf ❏ **spaceship** n nave f espacial ❏ **spacing** n espaciado

spacious ['speɪʃəs] adj amplio

spade [speɪd] n (tool) pala, laya; ~**s** npl (CARDS) picas fpl; (: Spanish) espadas fpl

spaghetti [spə'geti] n espaguetis mpl

Spain [speɪn] n España

spam [spæm] n spam m, correo basura

span [spæn] n (of bird, plane) envergadura; (of arch) luz f; (in time) lapso ♦ vt extenderse sobre, cruzar; (fig) abarcar

Spaniard ['spænjərd] n español(a) m/f

spaniel ['spænjəl] n spaniel m, perro de aguas

Spanish ['spænɪʃ] adj español(a) ♦ n (LING) español m, castellano; **the ~** npl los españoles

spank [spæŋk] vt zurrar, nalguear (MEX, CAm)

spanner ['spænər] (BRIT) n llave f (inglesa)

spare [speər] adj de reserva; (surplus) sobrante, de más ♦ n = **spare part** ♦ vt (do without) pasarse sin; (refrain from hurting) perdonar; **to ~** (surplus) sobrante, de sobra ❏ **spare change** n cambio ❏ **spare part** n repuesto, refacción f (MEX) ❏ **spare time** n tiempo libre ❏ **spare tire** n (AUT) rueda de repuesto, llanta de refacción (MEX) or repuesto (LAm), rueda de auxilio (RPI)

sparingly adv con moderación

spark [spɑːrk] n chispa; (fig) chispazo ❏ **spark plug** n bujía

sparkle ['spɑːrkəl] n centelleo, destello ♦ vi (shine) relucir, brillar ❏ **sparkling** adj (eyes, conversation) brillante; (wine) espumoso; (mineral water) con gas

sparrow ['spærou] n gorrión m

sparse [spɑːrs] adj esparcido, escaso

spartan ['spɑːrtn] adj (fig) espartano

spasm ['spæzəm] n (MED) espasmo

spat [spæt] pt, pp of **spit**

spate [speɪt] n (fig): **a ~ of** un torrente de

spawn [spɔːn] vi desovar, frezar ♦ n huevas fpl

speak [spiːk] (pt **spoke**, pp **spoken**) vt (language) hablar; (truth) decir ♦ vi hablar; (make a speech) intervenir; **to ~ to sb/of or about sth** hablar con algn/de or sobre algo; **~ up!** ¡habla más alto! ❏ **speaker** n (in public) orador(a) m/f; (also: **loudspeaker**) altavoz m; (for stereo etc) bafle m; (POL): **the Speaker** (US) el Presidente del Congreso; (BRIT) el Presidente de la Cámara de los Comunes

spear [spɪər] n lanza ♦ vt alancear ❏ **spearhead** vt (attack etc) encabezar

spec [spek] (inf) n: **on ~** como especulación

special ['speʃəl] adj especial; (edition etc) extraordinario; (delivery) urgente ❏ **specialist** n especialista mf ❏ **speciality** [ˌspeʃiˈælɪti] (BRIT) n = **specialty** ❏ **specialize** vi: **to specialize (in)** especializarse (en) ❏ **specially** adv sobre todo, en particular ❏ **specialty** (US) (BRIT **speciality**) n especialidad f

species ['spiːʃiːz] n inv especie f

specific [spəˈsɪfɪk] adj específico ❏ **specifically** adv específicamente

specify ['spesɪfaɪ] vt, vi especificar, precisar

specimen ['spesɪmən] n ejemplar m; (MED: of urine, blood) muestra

speck [spek] n grano, mota

speckled ['spekəld] adj moteado

specs [speks] (inf) npl anteojos mpl (LAm), gafas fpl (SP)

spectacle ['spektəkəl] n espectáculo; **~s** npl (glasses) anteojos mpl (LAm), gafas fpl (SP) ❏ **spectacular** [spekˈtækjələr] adj espectacular; (success) impresionante

spectator [spekˈteɪtər] n espectador(a) m/f

specter ['spektər] (US) (BRIT **spectre**) n espectro

spectrum ['spektrəm] (pl **spectra**) n espectro

speculate ['spekjuleɪt] vi: **to ~ (on)** especular (en) ❏ **speculation** [spekjuˈleɪʃən] n especulación f

speech [spiːtʃ] n (faculty) habla; (formal talk) discurso; (spoken language) lenguaje m ❏ **speechless** adj mudo, estupefacto ❏ **speech therapist** n logopeda mf

speed [spiːd] n velocidad f; (haste) prisa; (promptness) rapidez f; **at full** or **top ~** a máxima velocidad ▶ **speed up** vi acelerarse ♦ vt acelerar ❏ **speedboat** n lancha motora ❏ **speedily** adv rápido, rápidamente ❏ **speeding** n (AUT) exceso de velocidad ❏ **speed limit** n límite m de velocidad, velocidad f máxima ❏ **speedometer** [spɪˈdɑːmɪtər] n velocímetro ❏ **speedway** n (sport) carreras fpl de motos ❏ **speedy** adj (fast) veloz, rápido; (prompt) pronto

spell [spel] (pt, pp **spelt** or **~ed**) n (also: **magic ~**) encanto, hechizo; (period of time) rato, período ♦ vt deletrear; (fig) anunciar, presagiar; **to cast a ~ on sb** hechizar a algn; **he can't ~** tiene faltas de ortografía ❏ **spellbound** adj embelesado, hechizado ❏ **spelling** n ortografía

spelunking ['spɪˌlʌŋkɪŋ] (US) n espeleología

spend [spend] (pt, pp **spent**) vt (money) gastar; (time) pasar; (life) dedicar ❏ **spendthrift** n despilfarrador(a) m/f, derrochador(a) m/f

sperm [spɜːrm] n esperma

sphere [sfɪər] n esfera

sphinx [sfɪŋks] n esfinge f

spice [spaɪs] n especia ♦ vt condimentar

spicy ['spaɪsi] adj picante

spider ['spaɪdər] n araña

spigot ['spɪgət] (US) n llave f, canilla (RPI)

spike [spaɪk] n (point) punta; (BOT) espiga

spill [spɪl] (*pt, pp* **spilt** *or* **~ed**) *vt* derramar, verter ♦ *vi* derramarse; **to ~ over** desbordarse

spin [spɪn] (*pt, pp* **spun**) *n* (AVIAT) barrena; (*trip in car*) paseo (en carro (LAm) *or* coche (SP)); (*on ball*) efecto ♦ *vt* (*wool etc*) hilar; (*ball etc*) hacer girar ♦ *vi* girar, dar vueltas

spinach ['spɪnɪtʃ] *n* espinaca; (*as food*) espinacas *fpl*

spinal ['spaɪnl] *adj* espinal ❑ **spinal cord** *n* columna vertebral

spin doctor *n* (POL) asesor(a) *m/f* político(-a)

spin-dryer (BRIT) *n* centrifugadora

spine [spaɪn] *n* columna vertebral; (*thorn*) espina ❑ **spineless** *adj* (*fig*) débil, pusilánime

spinning ['spɪnɪŋ] *n* hilandería; (SPORT) spinning *m* ❑ **spinning top** *n* peonza, trompo

spin-off *n* (*producto*) derivado

spinster ['spɪnstər] *n* solterona

spiral ['spaɪrəl] *n* espiral *f* ♦ *vi* (*fig: prices*) subir desorbitadamente ❑ **spiral staircase** *n* escalera de caracol

spire ['spaɪər] *n* aguja, chapitel *m*

spirit ['spɪrɪt] *n* (*soul*) alma *f*; (*ghost*) fantasma *m*; (*attitude, sense*) espíritu *m*; (*courage*) valor *m*, ánimo; **~s** *npl* (*drink*) licor(es) *m(pl)*; **in good ~s** alegre, de buen ánimo ❑ **spirited** *adj* enérgico, vigoroso

spiritual ['spɪrɪtʃuəl] *adj* espiritual ♦ *n* espiritual *m*

spit [spɪt] (*pt, pp* **spat**) *n* (*for roasting*) asador *m*, espetón *m*; (*saliva*) saliva ♦ *vi* escupir; (*sound*) chisporrotear; (BRIT: *rain*) lloviznar

spite [spaɪt] *n* rencor *m*, ojeriza ♦ *vt* causar pena a, mortificar; **in ~ of** a pesar de, pese a ❑ **spiteful** *adj* rencoroso, malévolo

spittle ['spɪtl] *n* saliva, baba

splash [splæʃ] *n* (*sound*) chapoteo; (*of color*) mancha ♦ *vt* salpicar ♦ *vi* (US: *also:* **~ around**) chapotear

spleen [spliːn] *n* (ANAT) bazo

splendid ['splendɪd] *adj* espléndido

splendor (US) ['splendər] (BRIT **splendour**) *n* esplendor *m*

splint [splɪnt] *n* tablilla

splinter ['splɪntər] *n* (*of wood etc*) astilla; (*in finger*) espigón *m* ♦ *vi* astillarse, hacer astillas

split [splɪt] (*pt, pp* **~**) *n* grieta; raja; (*fig*) división *f*; (POL) escisión *f* ♦ *vt* partir, rajar; (*party*) dividir; (*share*) repartir ♦ *vi* dividirse, escindirse ▶ **split up** *vi* (*couple*) separarse; (*meeting*) acabarse

spoil [spɔɪl] (*pt, pp* **~t** *or* **~ed**) *vt* (*damage*) dañar; (*mar*) estropear; (*child*) mimar,

consentir ♦ *vi* (*food*) estropearse, echarse a perder ❑ **spoils** *npl* botín *m* ❑ **spoilsport** *n* aguafiestas *m inv*

spoke [spəuk] *pt of* **speak** ♦ *n* rayo, radio

spoken ['spəukən] *pp of* **speak**

spokesman ['spəuksmən] *n* portavoz *m* ❑ **spokeswoman** ['spəuks,wumən] *n* portavoz *f*

sponge [spʌndʒ] *n* esponja; (*also:* **~ cake**) bizcocho ♦ *vt* (*wash*) lavar con esponja ♦ *vi*: **to ~ off** *or* **on sb** vivir a costa de algn ❑ **sponge bag** (BRIT) *n* bolsa de aseo

sponsor ['spɒnsər] *n* patrocinador(a) *m/f* ♦ *vt* (*applicant, proposal etc*) proponer ❑ **sponsorship** *n* patrocinio

spontaneous [spɒn'teɪnɪəs] *adj* espontáneo

spooky ['spuːki] (*inf*) *adj* espeluznante, horripilante

spool [spuːl] *n* carrete *m*

spoon [spuːn] *n* cuchara ❑ **spoon-feed** *vt* dar de comer (con cuchara) a; (*fig*) dar todo hecho a ❑ **spoonful** *n* cucharada

sport [spɔːrt] *n* deporte *m*; (*person*): **to be a good ~** ser muy buena gente *or* persona ♦ *vt* (*wear*) lucir, ostentar ❑ **sport coat** (US) *n* chaqueta deportiva *or* de sport ❑ **sporting** *adj* deportivo; (*generous*) caballeroso; **to give sb a sporting chance** dar a algn una (buena) oportunidad ❑ **sports car** *n* carro (LAm) *or* coche *m* (SP) deportivo ❑ **sports jacket** (BRIT) *n* = **sport coat** ❑ **sportsman** *n* deportista *m* ❑ **sportsmanship** *n* deportividad *f* ❑ **sportswear** *n* ropa de deporte *or* sport ❑ **sportswoman** *n* deportista ❑ **sporty** *adj* deportista

spot [spɒt] *n* sitio, lugar *m*; (*dot: on pattern*) punto, lunar *m*; (RADIO) espacio publicitario; (TV) espacio publicitario; (BRIT: *pimple*) grano; (BRIT: *small amount*): **a ~ of** un poquito de ♦ *vt* (*notice*) notar, observar; **on the ~** allí mismo ❑ **spot check** *n* reconocimiento rápido ❑ **spotless** *adj* inmaculado ❑ **spotlight** *n* foco, reflector *m* ❑ **spotted** *adj* (*pattern*) de puntos ❑ **spotty** (BRIT) *adj* (*face*) con granos

spouse [spaus] *n* cónyuge *mf*

spout [spaut] *n* (*of jug*) pico; (*of pipe*) caño ♦ *vi* salir en chorro

sprain [spreɪn] *n* torcedura ♦ *vt*: **to ~ one's ankle/wrist** torcerse el tobillo/la muñeca

sprang [spræŋ] *pt of* **spring**

sprawl [sprɔːl] *vi* tumbarse

spray [spreɪ] *n* rociada; (*of sea*) espuma; (*container*) spray *m*, aerosol *m*; (*for paint etc*) pistola rociadora; (of flowers) ramita ♦ vt rociar; (crops) regar

spread [sprɛd] (pt, pp ~) n extensión f; (for bread etc) pasta para untar; (inf: food) comilona ♦ vt extender; (butter) untar; (wings, sails) desplegar; (work, wealth) repartir; (scatter) esparcir ♦ vi (also: ~ out: stain) extenderse; (news) propagarse ▶ **spread out** vi (move apart) separarse ❑ **spread-eagled** adj abierto de piernas y brazos ❑ **spreadsheet** n hoja electrónica or de cálculo

spree [spri:] n: **to go on a ~** ir de juerga

sprightly ['spraɪtlɪ] adj vivo, enérgico

spring [sprɪŋ] (pt **sprang**, pp **sprung**) n (season) primavera; (leap) salto, brinco; (coiled metal) muelle m, resorte m; (of water) manantial m, fuente f ♦ vi saltar, brincar ▶ **spring up** vi (thing: appear) aparecer; (problem) surgir ❑ **springboard** n trampolín m ❑ **spring-clean(ing)** n limpieza general ❑ **springtime** n primavera

sprinkle ['sprɪŋkəl] vt (pour: liquid) rociar; (: salt, sugar) salpicar; **to ~ water etc on, ~ with water** etc rociar or salpicar de agua etc ❑ **sprinkler** n (for lawn) aspersor m; (to put out fire) rociador m contra incendios

sprint [sprɪnt] n (e)sprint m, carrera ♦ vi (e)sprintar

sprout [spraʊt] vi brotar, retoñar; **(Brussels) ~s** npl coles fpl or (SC) repollitos mpl de Bruselas

spruce [spru:s] n inv (BOT) pícea ♦ adj aseado, pulcro

sprung [sprʌŋ] pp of **spring**

spun [spʌn] pt, pp of **spin**

spur [spɜ:r] n espuela; (fig) estímulo, aguijón m ♦ vt (also: ~ on) estimular, incitar; **on the ~ of the moment** de improviso

spurious ['spjʊriəs] adj falso

spurn [spɜ:rn] vt desdeñar, rechazar

spurt [spɜ:rt] n chorro; (of energy) arrebato ♦ vi chorrear

spy [spaɪ] n espía mf ♦ vi: **to ~ on** espiar a ♦ vt (see) divisar, lograr ver ❑ **spying** n espionaje m

sq. abbr = **square**

squabble ['skwɑ:bəl] vi reñir, pelear

squad [skwɑ:d] n (MIL) pelotón m; (POLICE) brigada; (SPORT) equipo

squadron ['skwɑ:drən] n (MIL) escuadrón m; (AVIAT, NAUT) escuadra

squalid ['skwɑ:lɪd] adj vil; (fig: sordid) sórdido

squall [skwɔ:l] n (storm) chubasco; (wind) ráfaga

squalor ['skwɑ:lər] n miseria

squander ['skwɑ:ndər] vt (money) derrochar, despilfarrar; (chances) desperdiciar

square [skwɛər] n cuadro; (in town) plaza; (inf: person) anticuado(-a) ♦ adj cuadrado; (inf: ideas, tastes) trasnochado ♦ vt (arrange) arreglar; (MATH) cuadrar; (reconcile) compaginar; **all ~** igual(es); **to have a ~ meal** comer caliente; **2 meters ~** 2 metros en cuadro; **2 ~ meters** 2 metros cuadrados

square dance n cuadrilla

SQUARE DANCE

Un **square dance** es un tipo de baile típico de Norteamérica en el que las parejas realizan varios pasos de baile hasta ir formando una figura, como un cuadrado o dos círculos que se entrecruzan, aunque el término **square dance** también se puede referir a la fiesta en la que se hacen. **Hoedown** es también otro término que hace referencia a otro tipo de fiesta parecida. Normalmente se asocia este tipo de baile con el ambiente rural de EE.UU. y con la música country.

squarely adv de lleno

squash [skwɑ:ʃ] n (US BOT) calabaza; (SPORT) squash m; (BRIT: drink): **lemon/orange ~** jugo (LAm) or zumo (SP) de limón/naranja ♦ vt aplastar

squat [skwɑ:t] adj achaparrado ♦ vi (also: ~ down) agacharse, sentarse en cuclillas ❑ **squatter** n paracaidista mf (MEX), ocupante mf ilegal (LAm), okupa mf (SP)

squeak [skwi:k] vi (hinge) chirriar, rechinar; (mouse) chillar

squeal [skwi:l] vi chillar

squeamish ['skwi:mɪʃ] adj delicado, remilgado

squeeze [skwi:z] n presión f; (of hand) apretón m; (COMM) restricción f ♦ vt (hand, arm) apretar ▶ **squeeze out** vt exprimir

squelch [skwɛltʃ] vi chapotear

squid [skwɪd] n inv calamar m; (CULIN) calamares mpl

squiggle ['skwɪgəl] n garabato

squint [skwɪnt] vi bizquear, ser bizco ♦ n (MED) estrabismo

squirm [skwɜ:rm] vi retorcerse, revolverse

squirrel ['skwɜ:rəl] n ardilla

squirt [skwɜ:rt] vi salir a chorros ♦ vt chiscar

Sr. (US) (BRIT **Sr**) abbr = **senior**

St. (US) (BRIT **St**) abbr = **saint**; **street**

stab [stæb] n (with knife) puñalada; (of pain) pinchazo; (inf: try): **to have a ~ at (doing) sth** intentar (hacer) algo ♦ vt apuñalar

stable ['steibəl] adj estable ♦ n cuadra, caballeriza

stack [stæk] n montón m, pila ♦ vt amontonar, apilar

stadium ['steidiəm] n estadio

staff [stæf] n (work force) personal m, plantilla; (BRIT SCOL) cuerpo docente, profesorado ♦ vt proveer de personal

stag [stæg] n ciervo, venado

stage [steidʒ] n escena; (point) etapa; (platform) plataforma; (profession): **the ~** el teatro ♦ vt (play) poner en escena, representar; (organize) montar, organizar; **in ~s** por etapas ❏ **stagecoach** n diligencia ❏ **stage manager** n director(a) m/f de escena

stagger ['stægər] vi tambalearse ♦ vt (amaze) asombrar; (hours, vacation) escalonar ❏ **staggering** adj asombroso

stagnant ['stægnənt] adj estancado

stag party n despedida de soltero

staid [steid] adj serio, formal

stain [stein] n mancha; (coloring) tintura ♦ vt manchar; (wood) teñir ❏ **stained glass window** n vidriera (de colores) ❏ **stainless steel** n acero inoxidable ❏ **stain remover** n quitamanchas m inv

stair [steər] n (step) peldaño, escalón m; **~s** npl escaleras fpl ❏ **staircase** n = **stairway** ❏ **stairway** n escalera

stake [steik] n estaca, poste m; (COMM) interés m; (BETTING) apuesta ♦ vt (money) apostar; (life) arriesgar; (reputation) poner en juego; (claim) presentar una reclamación; **to be at ~** estar en juego

stale [steil] adj (bread) duro; (food) pasado; (smell) rancio; (beer) agrio

stalemate ['steil,meit] n tablas fpl; (fig) estancamiento

stalk [stɔːk] n tallo, caña ♦ vt acechar ▶ **stalk off** vi irse airado

stall [stɔːl] n (in market) puesto; (in stable) casilla (de establo) ♦ vt (AUT) calar; (fig) dar largas a ♦ vi (AUT) calarse; (fig) andarse con rodeos; **~s** npl (BRIT: in movie house, theater) butacas fpl

stallion ['stæljən] n semental m

stamina ['stæminə] n resistencia

stammer ['stæmər] n tartamudeo ♦ vi tartamudear

stamp [stæmp] n timbre m (MEX), estampilla (LAm), sello (SP); (mark) marca, huella; (on document) timbre m ♦ vi (also: ~ one's foot) patear ♦ vt (mark) marcar; (letter) franquear; (with rubber stamp) sellar ❏ **stamp album** n álbum m de timbres (MEX) or estampillas (LAm) or sellos (SP) ❏ **stamp collecting** n filatelia

stampede [stæm'piːd] n estampida

stance [stæns] n postura

stand [stænd] n (pt, pp **stood**) n (position) posición f, postura; (hall stand) perchero; (music stand) atril m; (SPORT) tribuna; (at exhibition) stand m; (BRIT: for taxis) parada, sitio (MEX) ♦ vi (be) estar, encontrarse; (be on foot) estar de pie; (rise) levantarse; (remain) quedar en pie; (BRIT: in election) presentar candidatura ♦ vt (place) poner, colocar; (withstand) aguantar, soportar; (invite to) invitar; **to make a ~** (fig) mantener una postura firme; **to ~ for parliament** (BRIT) presentarse (como candidato) a las elecciones ▶ **stand by** vi (be ready) estar listo ♦ vt fus (opinion) aferrarse a; (person) apoyar ▶ **stand down** vi (withdraw) ceder el puesto ▶ **stand for** vt fus (signify) significar; (tolerate) aguantar, permitir ▶ **stand in for** vt fus sustituir, suplir a ▶ **stand out** vi destacar ▶ **stand up** vi levantarse, ponerse de pie ▶ **stand up for** vt fus defender ▶ **stand up to** vt fus hacer frente a

standard ['stændərd] n patrón m, norma; (level) nivel m; (flag) estandarte m ♦ adj (size etc) normal, corriente; (text) básico; **~s** npl (morals) valores mpl morales ❏ **standard lamp** (BRIT) n lámpara de pie ❏ **standard of living** n nivel m de vida

stand-by ['stændbai] n (reserve) reserva; **to be on ~** estar sobre aviso ❏ **stand-by ticket** n (AVIAT) pasaje m (LAm) or billete m (SP) en lista de espera

stand-in ['stændin] n suplente mf

standing ['stændiŋ] adj (on foot) de pie, en pie; (permanent) permanente ♦ n reputación f; **of many years' ~** que lleva muchos años ❏ **standing joke** n bromas fpl de siempre ❏ **standing order** (BRIT) n (at bank) domiciliación f bancaria, orden f de pago permanente ❏ **standing room** n sitio (para estar) de pie

stand: ❏ **standpoint** n punto de vista ❏ **standstill** n: **at a standstill** (industry, traffic) paralizado; (car) parado; **to come to a standstill** quedar paralizado; pararse

stank [stæŋk] pt of **stink**

staple ['steipəl] n (for papers) grapa ♦ adj (food etc) básico ♦ vt grapar ❏ **stapler** n grapadora

star [stɑːr] n estrella; (celebrity) estrella, astro
♦ vt (THEATER, FILM) ser el/la protagonista de;
the ~s npl (ASTROLOGY) el horóscopo; **the S~s
and Stripes** la bandera de los Estados Unidos
starboard ['stɑːrbərd] n estribor m
starch [stɑːrtʃ] n almidón m
stardom ['stɑːrdəm] n estrellato
stare [steər] n mirada fija ♦ vi: **to ~ at** mirar fijo
starfish ['stɑːrˌfɪʃ] n estrella de mar
stark [stɑːrk] adj (bleak) severo, escueto ♦ adv:
~ naked en cueros, encuerado (MEX)
starling ['stɑːrlɪŋ] n estornino
starry ['stɑːri] adj estrellado ❏ **starry-eyed**
adj (innocent) ingenuo, iluso
start [stɑːrt] n principio, comienzo;
(departure) salida; (sudden movement) salto,
sobresalto; (advantage) ventaja ♦ vt empezar,
comenzar; (cause) causar; (found) fundar;
(engine) poner en marcha ♦ vi comenzar,
empezar; (with fright) asustarse,
sobresaltarse; (train etc) salir; **to ~ doing** or **to
do sth** empezar a hacer algo ▶ **start off** vi
empezar, comenzar; (leave) salir, ponerse en
camino ▶ **start up** vi comenzar; (car)
ponerse en marcha ♦ vt comenzar; poner en
marcha ❏ **starter** n (AUT) motor m de
arranque; (SPORT: official) juez mf de salida;
(BRIT CULIN) entrada (LAm), entrante m (SP)
❏ **starting point** n punto de partida
startle ['stɑːrtl] vt asustar, sobrecoger
❏ **startling** adj alarmante
starvation [stɑːrˈveɪʃən] n hambre f
starve [stɑːrv] vi tener mucha hambre; (to
death) morir de hambre ♦ vt hacer pasar
hambre
state [steɪt] n estado ♦ vt (say, declare) afirmar;
the S~s los Estados Unidos; **to be in a ~** estar
agitado ❏ **State Department** (US) n
Secretaría (MEX) or Ministerio (LAm exc MEX) de
Relaciones Exteriores, Ministerio de Asuntos
Exteriores (SP) ❏ **stately** adj majestuoso,
imponente ❏ **stately home** (BRIT) n casa
señorial or solariega ❏ **statement** n
afirmación f ❏ **statesman** n estadista m
static ['stætɪk] n (RADIO) estática, interferencias
fpl ♦ adj estático ❏ **static electricity** n
estática
station ['steɪʃən] n estación f; (RADIO) emisora,
estación f (LAm); (rank) posición f social ♦ vt
colocar, situar; (MIL) apostar
stationary ['steɪʃənerɪ] adj estacionario, fijo
stationer ['steɪʃənər] n dueño(-a) de una
papelería ❏ **stationer's (shop)** (BRIT) n
papelería ❏ **stationery** n papel m de
escribir, artículos mpl de escritorio

station master n (RAIL) jefe m de estación
station wagon (US) n camioneta (LAm),
rural f (RPl), ranchera (SP)
statistic [stəˈtɪstɪk] n estadística
❏ **statistics** n (science) estadística
statue ['stætʃuː] n estatua; **S~ of Liberty**
estatua f de la libertad
status ['steɪtəs] n estado; (reputation) estatus
m ❏ **status symbol** n símbolo de prestigio
statute ['stætʃuːt] n estatuto, ley f
❏ **statutory** adj estatutario
staunch [stɔːntʃ] adj leal, incondicional
stay [steɪ] n estancia (MEX, SP), estadía (LAm exc
MEX) ♦ vi quedar(se); (as guest) hospedarse; **to
~ put** seguir en el mismo sitio; **to ~ the night/
5 days** pasar la noche/estar 5 días ▶ **stay
behind** vi quedar atrás ▶ **stay in** vi
quedarse en casa ▶ **stay on** vi quedarse
▶ **stay out** vi (of house) no volver a casa; (BRIT:
on strike) permanecer en huelga ▶ **stay up** vi
(at night) velar, quedarse levantado
❏ **staying power** n aguante m
stead [sted] n: **in sb's ~** en lugar de algn; **to
stand sb in good ~** ser muy útil a algn
steadfast ['stedˌfæst] adj firme, resuelto
steadily ['stedli] adv constantemente;
(firmly) firmemente; (work, walk) sin parar;
(gaze) fijamente
steady ['stedi] adj (firm) firme; (regular)
regular; (person, character) sensato, juicioso;
(boyfriend) formal; (look, voice) tranquilo ♦ vt
(stabilize) estabilizar; (nerves) calmar
steak [steɪk] n filete m; (beef) bistec m
steal [stiːl] (pt **stole**, pp **stolen**) vt robar ♦ vi
robar; (move secretly) andar a hurtadillas
stealth [stelθ] n: **by ~** a escondidas,
sigilosamente ❏ **stealthy** adj cauteloso,
sigiloso
steam [stiːm] n vapor m; (mist) vaho, humo
♦ vt (CULIN) cocer al vapor ♦ vi echar vapor
❏ **steam engine** n máquina de vapor
❏ **steamer** n (buque m de) vapor m
❏ **steamroller** n apisonadora
❏ **steamship** n = **steamer** ❏ **steamy** adj
(room) lleno de vapor; (window) empañado;
(heat, atmosphere) bochornoso
steel [stiːl] n acero ♦ adj de acero
❏ **steelworks** n acería
steep [stiːp] adj escarpado, abrupto; (stair)
empinado; (price) exorbitante, excesivo ♦ vt
empapar, remojar
steeple ['stiːpəl] n aguja ❏ **steeplechase** n
carrera de obstáculos
steer [stɪər] vt (car) manejar (LAm), conducir
(SP); (person) dirigir ♦ vi manejar, conducir

❏ **steering** n (AUT) dirección f ❏ **steering wheel** n volante m

stem [stɛm] n (of plant) tallo; (of glass) pie m ♦ vt detener; (blood) restañar ► **stem from** vt fus ser consecuencia de

stench [stɛntʃ] n hedor m

stencil ['stɛnsəl] n (pattern) plantilla ♦ vt estarcir

stenographer [stə'nɑːɡrəfər] (US) n taquígrafo(-a)

step [stɛp] n paso; (on stair) peldaño, escalón m ♦ vi: **to ~ forward/back** dar un paso adelante/hacia atrás; **~s** npl (BRIT) = **stepladder; in/out of ~ (with)** acorde/en disonancia (con) ► **step down** vi (fig) retirarse ► **step on** vt fus pisar ► **step up** vt (increase) aumentar ❏ **stepbrother** n hermanastro ❏ **stepdaughter** n hijastra ❏ **stepfather** n padrastro ❏ **stepladder** n escalera de tijera, burro (MEX) ❏ **stepmother** n madrastra ❏ **stepping stone** n pasadera ❏ **stepsister** n hermanastra ❏ **stepson** n hijastro

stereo ['stɛrɪəu] n equipo de música, estéreo ♦ adj (also: **~phonic**) estéreo, estereofónico

sterile ['stɛraɪl] adj estéril ❏ **sterilize** vt esterilizar

sterling ['stɜːlɪŋ] adj (silver) de ley ♦ n (ECON) libras fpl esterlinas fpl; **one pound ~** (BRIT) una libra esterlina

stern [stɜːn] adj severo, austero ♦ n (NAUT) popa

stew [stuː] n estofado, guiso ♦ vt estofar, guisar; (fruit) cocer

steward ['stuːərd] n (on plane) aeromozo (LAm), auxiliar m de vuelo (SP); (on train) camarero ❏ **stewardess** n (on plane) aeromoza (LAm), azafata (SP); (on train) camarera

stick [stɪk] (pt, pp **stuck**) n palo; (of dynamite) barreno; (as weapon) macana (MEX), cachiporra (LAm), porra (SP); (walking stick) bastón m ♦ vt (glue) pegar; (inf: put) meter; (: tolerate) aguantar, soportar; (thrust): **to ~ sth into** clavar or hincar algo en ♦ vi pegarse; (be unmoveable) quedarse parado; (in mind) quedarse grabado ► **stick out** vi sobresalir ► **stick up** vi sobresalir ► **stick up for** vt fus defender ❏ **sticker** n (label) etiqueta engomada (with slogan) adhesivo ❏ **sticking plaster** (BRIT) n curita (LAm), tirita (SP) ❏ **stick shift** (US) n palanca de cambios

stick-up ['stɪkʌp] (inf) n asalto, atraco

sticky ['stɪki] adj pegajoso; (label) adhesivo; (fig) difícil

stiff [stɪf] adj rígido, tieso; (hard) duro; (manner) estirado; (difficult) difícil; (person) inflexible; (price) exorbitante ♦ adv: **scared/bored ~** muerto de miedo/aburrido como una ostra ❏ **stiffen** vi (muscles etc) agarrotarse ❏ **stiff neck** n tortícolis m inv ❏ **stiffness** n rigidez f, tiesura

stifle ['staɪfl] vt ahogar, sofocar ❏ **stifling** adj (heat) sofocante, bochornoso

stigma ['stɪɡmə] n (fig) estigma m

stile [staɪl] n portillo, portilla

stiletto [stɪ'lɛtəu] (BRIT) n (also: **~ heel**) tacón m de aguja

still [stɪl] adj quieto, inmóvil ♦ adv todavía; (even) aún; (nonetheless) sin embargo, aun así ❏ **stillborn** adj nacido muerto ❏ **still life** n naturaleza muerta, bodegón m

stilt [stɪlt] n zanco; (pile) pilar m, soporte m

stilted ['stɪltɪd] adj afectado

stimulate ['stɪmjəleɪt] vt estimular

stimulus ['stɪmjələs] (pl **stimuli** ['stɪmjəlaɪ]) n estímulo, incentivo

sting [stɪŋ] (pt, pp **stung**) n picadura, piquete m (MEX); (pain) escozor m; (organ) aguijón m ♦ vt, vi picar

stingy ['stɪndʒi] adj tacaño

stink [stɪŋk] (pt **stank**, pp **stunk**) n hedor m, tufo ♦ vi heder, apestar ❏ **stinking** adj hediondo, fétido; (BRIT: fig: inf) horrible

stint [stɪnt] n tarea, trabajo ♦ vi: **to ~ on** escatimar

stir [stɜːr] n (fig: agitation) conmoción f ♦ vt (tea etc) remover; (fig: emotions) provocar ♦ vi moverse ► **stir up** vt (trouble) fomentar

stirrup ['stɪrəp] n estribo

stitch [stɪtʃ] n (SEWING) puntada; (KNITTING) punto; (MED) punto (de sutura); (pain) punzada ♦ vt coser; (MED) suturar

stoat [stəut] n armiño

stock [stɑːk] n (COMM: reserves) existencias fpl, stock m; (: selection) surtido; (AGR) ganado, ganadería; (CULIN) caldo; (descent) raza, estirpe f; (FINANCE) capital m ♦ adj (fig: reply etc) clásico ♦ vt (have in stock) tener (existencias de), vender; **~s and shares** acciones y valores; **in ~** en existencias or almacén; **out of ~** agotado; **to take ~ of** (fig) asesorar, examinar ► **stock up with** vt fus abastecerse de ❏ **stockbroker** n agente mf or corredor(a) m/f de bolsa ❏ **stock cube** n pastilla de caldo ❏ **stock exchange** n bolsa ❏ **stockholder** (US) n accionista mf

stocking ['stɑːkɪŋ] n media

stock: ❏ **stock market** n bolsa (de valores) ❏ **stockpile** n reserva ♦ vt acumular,

almacenar ❑ **stocktaking** (BRIT) n (COMM)
inventario

stocky ['stɑːki] adj (strong) robusto; (short)
achaparrado

stodgy ['stɑːdʒi] adj indigesto, pesado

stoke [stouk] vt atizar

stole [stoul] pt of **steal** ♦ n estola

stolen ['stoulən] pp of **steal**

stomach ['stʌmək] n (ANAT) estómago; (belly)
vientre m ♦ vt tragar, aguantar
❑ **stomachache** n dolor m de estómago

stone [stoun] n piedra; (BRIT: in fruit) hueso;
(: weight) 6.348 kg ♦ adj de piedra ♦ vt
apedrear; (BRIT: fruit) deshuesar ❑ **stone-
cold** adj helado ❑ **stone-deaf** adj sordo
como una tapia ❑ **stonework** n (art)
cantería ❑ **stony** adj pedregoso; (fig) frío

stood [stud] pt, pp of **stand**

stool [stuːl] n taburete m

stoop [stuːp] vi (also: ~ **down**) doblarse,
agacharse; (also: **have a ~**) ser cargado de
espaldas

stop [stɑːp] n parada; (BRIT: in punctuation)
punto ♦ vt parar, detener; (break) suspender;
(block: pay) suspender; (: check) invalidar; (also:
put a ~ to) poner término a ♦ vi pararse,
detenerse; (end) acabarse; **to ~ doing sth**
dejar de hacer algo ▶ **stop dead** vi pararse
en seco ▶ **stop off** vi interrumpir el viaje
▶ **stop up** vt (hole) tapar ❑ **stopgap** n
(person) interino(-a); (thing) recurso
(provisional) ❑ **stoplights** (US) npl (traffic
lights) semáforo; (brake lights) luces fpl de
freno ❑ **stopover** n parada; (AVIAT) escala

stoppage ['stɑːpɪdʒ] n (strike) huelga;
(blockage) obstrucción f

stopper ['stɑːpər] n tapón m

stop press (BRIT) n noticias fpl de última hora

stopwatch ['stɑːpwɒtʃ] n cronómetro

storage ['stɔːrɪdʒ] n almacenaje m
❑ **storage heater** n acumulador m

store [stɔːr] n (US) tienda; (BRIT: depot) almacén
m; (stock) provisión f; (reserve) reserva,
repuesto ♦ vt almacenar; **~s** npl víveres mpl; **in
~: to be in ~ for sb** (fig) esperar a algn
▶ **store up** vt acumular ❑ **storekeeper**
(US) n comerciante mf ❑ **storeroom** n
despensa

storey ['stɔːri] (BRIT) n piso

stork [stɔːrk] n cigüeña

storm [stɔːrm] n tormenta; (fig: of applause)
salva; (: of criticism) nube f ♦ vi (fig) rabiar ♦ vt
tomar por asalto ❑ **stormy** adj tempestuoso

story ['stɔːri] n historia; (lie) mentira; (US: in
building) piso ❑ **storybook** n libro de
cuentos

stout [staut] adj (strong) sólido; (fat) gordo,
corpulento; (resolute) resuelto ♦ n cerveza
negra

stove [stouv] n (for cooking) estufa (MEX),
cocina (LAm exc MEX, SP); (for heating)
calentador m (MEX), estufa (LAm exc MEX, SP)

stow [stou] vt (also: ~ **away**) meter, poner;
(NAUT) estibar ❑ **stowaway** n polizón(-ona)
m/f

straggle ['strægəl] vi (houses etc) extenderse;
(lag behind) rezagarse

straight [streɪt] adj (not bent) recto, derecho; (frank)
franco, directo; (simple) sencillo ♦ adv
derecho, directamente; (drink) solo; **to put** or
get sth ~ dejar algo en claro; **~ away, ~ off** en
seguida ❑ **straighten** vt (also: **straighten
out**) enderezar, poner derecho ❑ **straight-
faced** adj serio ❑ **straightforward** adj
(simple) sencillo; (honest) honrado, franco

strain [streɪn] n tensión f; (TECH) presión f;
(MED) torcedura; (breed) tipo, variedad f ♦ vt
(back etc) hacerse daño en; (resources) agotar;
(stretch) estirar; (food, tea) colar; **~s** npl (MUS)
son m ❑ **strained** adj (laugh) forzado;
(relations) tenso; **a strained muscle** un
esguince ❑ **strainer** n colador m

strait [streɪt] n (GEO) estrecho; **to be in dire ~s**
pasar grandes apuros ❑ **strait-jacket** n
camisa de fuerza ❑ **strait-laced** adj
mojigato

strand [strænd] n (of thread) hebra; (of hair)
trenza; (of rope) ramal m

stranded adj (person: without money)
desamparado; (: without transport) tirado,
botado (LAm)

strange [streɪndʒ] adj (not known)
desconocido; (odd) raro, extraño
❑ **strangely** adv de un modo raro; see also
enough ❑ **stranger** n desconocido(-a);
(from another area) forastero(-a)

⚠ Be careful not to translate **stranger** by the
Spanish word **extranjero**.

strangle ['stræŋgəl] vt estrangular
❑ **stranglehold** n (fig) control m absoluto

strap [stræp] n correa; (of slip, dress) tirante m

strategic [strə'tiːdʒɪk] adj estratégico

strategy ['strætɪdʒi] n estrategia

straw [strɔː] n paja; (drinking straw) pajita,
popote m (MEX); **that's the last ~!** ¡es la gota
que colma el vaso!, ¡esto ya es el colmo!

strawberry ['strɔːbəri] n fresa, frutilla (SC)

stray [streɪ] adj (animal) extraviado; (bullet) perdido; (scattered) disperso ♦ vi extraviarse, perderse

streak [striːk] n raya; (in hair) raya ♦ vt rayar ♦ vi: **to ~ past** pasar como un rayo

stream [striːm] n riachuelo, arroyo; (of people, vehicles) riada, caravana; (of smoke, insults etc) chorro ♦ vt (BRIT SCOL) dividir en grupos por habilidad ♦ vi correr, fluir; **to ~ in/out** (people) entrar/salir en tropel

streamer ['striːmər] n serpentina

streamlined ['striːmˌlaɪnd] adj aerodinámico

street [striːt] n calle f □ **streetcar** (US) n tranvía m □ **street lamp** n farol m □ **street light** n farol m (LAm), farola (SP) □ **street plan** n plano de la ciudad □ **streetwise** (inf) adj espabilado; **to be streetwise** sabérselas todas

strength [streŋθ] n fuerza; (of girder, knot etc) resistencia; (fig: power) poder m □ **strengthen** vt fortalecer, reforzar

strenuous ['strenjuəs] adj (energetic, determined) enérgico

stress [stres] n presión f; (mental strain) estrés m; (accent) acento ♦ vt subrayar, recalcar; (syllable) acentuar

stretch [stretʃ] n (of sand etc) trecho ♦ vi estirarse; (extend): **to ~ to** or **as far as** extenderse hasta ♦ vt extender, estirar; (make demands) exigir el máximo esfuerzo a ▶ **stretch out** vi tenderse ♦ vt (arm etc) extender; (spread) estirar

stretcher ['stretʃər] n camilla

strewn [struːn] adj: **~ with** cubierto or sembrado de

stricken ['strɪkən] adj (person) herido; (city, industry etc) condenado; **~ with** (disease) afectado por

strict [strɪkt] adj severo; (exact) estricto □ **strictly** adv severamente, estrictamente

stride [straɪd] (pt **strode**, pp **stridden**) n zancada, tranco ♦ vi dar zancadas, andar a trancos

strife [straɪf] n lucha

strike [straɪk] (pt, pp **struck**) n huelga; (of oil etc) descubrimiento; (attack) ataque m ♦ vt golpear, pegar; (oil etc) descubrir; (bargain, deal) cerrar ♦ vi declarar la huelga; (attack) atacar; (clock) dar la hora; **on ~** (workers) en huelga; **to ~ a match** encender un fósforo or (MEX) cerillo ▶ **strike down** vt derribar ▶ **strike up** vt (MUS) empezar a tocar; (conversation) entablar; (friendship) trabar □ **strikebreaker** n rompehuelgas m inv

(LAm), carnero (RPl) □ **striker** n huelguista mf; (SPORT) delantero □ **striking** adj asombroso

string [strɪŋ] (pt, pp **strung**) n cuerda; (row) hilera ♦ vt: **to ~ together** ensartar; **the ~s** npl (MUS) las cuerdas; **to ~ out** extenderse; **to pull ~s** (fig) mover palancas □ **string bean** n ejote m (MEX), frijol m (LAm), chaucha (RPl), judía verde (SP) □ **string(ed) instrument** n (MUS) instrumento de cuerda

stringent ['strɪndʒənt] adj riguroso, severo

strip [strɪp] n tira; (of land) franja; (of metal) cinta, lámina; (cartoon) tira cómica ♦ vt desnudar; (paint) quitar; (also: ~ **down**: machine) desmontar ♦ vi desnudarse □ **strip cartoon** (BRIT) n tira cómica

stripe [straɪp] n raya; (MIL) galón m □ **striped** adj a rayas, rayado

strip lighting (BRIT) n alumbrado fluorescente

stripper ['strɪpər] n artista mf de striptease

strive [straɪv] (pt **strove**, pp **~n** ['strɪvn]) vi: **to ~ for sth/to do sth** luchar por conseguir/hacer algo

strode [strəud] pt of **stride**

stroke [strəuk] n (blow) golpe m; (SWIMMING) brazada; (MED) derrame m cerebral, apoplejía; (of paintbrush) toque m ♦ vt acariciar; **at a ~** de un solo golpe

stroll [strəul] n paseo, vuelta ♦ vi dar un paseo or una vuelta □ **stroller** (US) n (for child) sillita de paseo

strong [strɔːŋ] adj fuerte; **they are 50 ~** son 50 □ **stronghold** n fortaleza; (fig) baluarte m □ **strongly** adv fuertemente, con fuerza; (believe) firmemente □ **strongroom** n cámara acorazada

strove [strəuv] pt of **strive**

struck [strʌk] pt, pp of **strike**

structure ['strʌktʃər] n estructura; (building) construcción f

struggle ['strʌgəl] n lucha ♦ vi luchar

strum [strʌm] vt (guitar) rasguear

strung [strʌŋ] pt, pp of **string**

strut [strʌt] n puntal m ♦ vi pavonearse

stub [stʌb] n (of ticket etc) talón m; (of cigarette) colilla; **to ~ one's toe on sth** dar con el dedo (del pie) contra algo ▶ **stub out** vt apagar

stubble ['stʌbəl] n rastrojo; (on chin) barba (incipiente)

stubborn ['stʌbərn] adj terco, testarudo

stuck [stʌk] pt, pp of **stick** ♦ adj (jammed) atascado □ **stuck-up** adj creído, engreído

stud [stʌd] n (shirt stud) corchete m; (earring) pendiente m, arete m (MEX), aro (SC); (also: ~

farm) caballeriza; (*also:* ~ **horse**) caballo semental; (*BRIT: of boot*) taco; (*inf*) semental *m* ♦ *vt* (*fig*): **~ded with** salpicado de

student ['stu:dnt] *n* estudiante *mf* ♦ *adj* estudiantil ❑ **student driver** (*US*) *n* conductor(a) *mf* en prácticas

studio ['stu:diəu] *n* estudio; (*artist's*) ʇaller *m* ❑ **studio apartment** (*US*) (*BRIT* **studio flat**) *n* estudio

studious ['stu:diəs] *adj* estudioso; (*studied*) calculado ❑ **studiously** *adv* (*carefully*) con esmero

study ['stʌdi] *n* estudio ♦ *vt* estudiar; (*examine*) examinar, investigar ♦ *vi* estudiar

stuff [stʌf] *n* materia; (*substance*) material *m*, sustancia; (*things*) cosas *fpl* ♦ *vt* llenar; (*animals*) disecar; (*inf: push*) meter ❑ **stuffing** *n* relleno ❑ **stuffy** *adj* (*room*) mal ventilado; (*person*) anticuado

stumble ['stʌmbəl] *vi* tropezar, dar un traspié; **to ~ across, ~ on** (*fig*) tropezar con ❑ **stumbling block** *n* tropiezo, obstáculo

stump [stʌmp] *n* (*of tree*) tocón *m*; (*of limb*) muñón *m* ♦ *vt*: **to be ~ed for an answer** no saber qué contestar

stun [stʌn] *vt* dejar sin sentido

stung [stʌŋ] *pt, pp* of **sting**

stunk [stʌŋk] *pp* of **stink**

stunning ['stʌnɪŋ] *adj* (*fig: news*) pasmoso; (*: outfit etc*) sensacional

stunt [stʌnt] *n* (*in movie*) escena peligrosa; (*publicity stunt*) truco publicitario ❑ **stuntman** *n* especialista *m*, doble *m*

stupid ['stu:pɪd] *adj* estúpido, tonto ❑ **stupidity** [stu:'pɪdɪti] *n* estupidez *f*

sturdy ['stɜ:rdi] *adj* robusto, fuerte

stutter ['stʌtər] *n* tartamudeo ♦ *vi* tartamudear

sty [staɪ] *n* (*for pigs*) pocilga

stye [staɪ] *n* (*MED*) orzuelo

style [staɪl] *n* estilo ❑ **stylish** *adj* elegante, a la moda

stylus ['staɪləs] *n* aguja

suave [swɑ:v] *adj* cortés

sub... [sʌb] *prefix* sub... ❑ **subconscious** *adj* subconsciente ❑ **subcontract** *vt* subcontratar ❑ **subdivide** *vt* subdividir ❑ **subdivision** *n* subdivisión *f*

subdue [səb'du:] *vt* sojuzgar; (*passions*) dominar ❑ **subdued** *adj* (*light*) tenue; (*person*) sumiso, manso

subject [*n* 'sʌbdʒɪkt, *vb* səb'dʒɛkt] *n* súbdito; (*SCOL*) asignatura; (*matter*) tema *m*; (*LING*) sujeto ♦ *vt*: **to ~ sb to sth** someter a algn a algo; **to be ~ to** (*law*) estar sujeto a; (*person*)

ser propenso a ❑ **subjective** [səb'dʒɛktɪv] *adj* subjetivo ❑ **subject matter** *n* (*content*) contenido

sublet [sʌb'lɛt] *vt* subarrendar

submarine ['sʌbmə,ri:n] *n* submarino

submerge [səb'mɜ:rdʒ] *vt* sumergir ♦ *vi* sumergirse

submissive [səb'mɪsɪv] *adj* sumiso

submit [səb'mɪt] *vt* someter ♦ *vi*: **to ~ to sth** someterse a algo

subnormal [,sʌb'nɔ:rməl] *adj* anormal

subordinate [sə'bɔ:rdɪnɪt] *adj, n* subordinado(-a)

subpoena [səb'pi:nə] *n* (*LAW*) citación *f*

subscribe [səb'skraɪb] *vi* suscribir; **to ~ to** (*opinion, fund*) suscribir, aprobar; (*newspaper*) suscribirse a ❑ **subscriber** *n* (*to periodical*) subscriptor(a) *m/f*; (*to telephone*) abonado(-a)

subscription [səb'skrɪpʃən] *n* abono; (*to magazine*) subscripción *f*

subsequent ['sʌbsɪkwənt] *adj* subsiguiente, posterior ❑ **subsequently** *adv* posteriormente, más tarde

subside [səb'saɪd] *vi* hundirse; (*flood*) bajar; (*wind*) amainar ❑ **subsidence** [səb'saɪdns] *n* hundimiento; (*in road*) socavón *m*

subsidiary [səb'sɪdieri] *adj* secundario ♦ *n* filial *f*

subsidize ['sʌbsɪdaɪz] *vt* subvencionar

subsidy ['sʌbsɪdi] *n* subvención *f*

subsistence [səb'sɪstəns] *n* subsistencia

substance ['sʌbstəns] *n* sustancia

substantial [səb'stænʃl] *adj* sustancial, sustancioso; (*fig*) importante

substantiate [səb'stænʃɪeɪt] *vt* comprobar

substitute ['sʌbstɪtu:t] *n* (*person*) suplente *mf*; (*thing*) sustituto ♦ *vt*: **to ~ A for B** sustituir A por B, reemplazar B por A ❑ **substitute teacher** (*US*) *n* profesor(a) *m/f* suplente

subtitle ['sʌb,taɪtl] *n* subtítulo

subtle ['sʌtl] *adj* sutil ❑ **subtlety** *n* sutileza

subtotal ['sʌb,toutl] *n* subtotal *m*, total *m* parcial

subtract [səb'trækt] *vt* restar, sustraer ❑ **subtraction** *n* resta, sustracción *f*

suburb ['sʌbɜrb] *n* barrio residencial; **the ~s** las afueras (de la ciudad) ❑ **suburban** [sə'bɜ:rbən] *adj* suburbano; (*train etc*) de cercanías, local ❑ **suburbia** [sə'bɜ:rbiə] *n* barrios *mpl* residenciales

subway ['sʌbweɪ] *n* (*US*) metro, subte *m* (*RPl*); (*BRIT*) paso subterráneo

succeed [sək'si:d] *vi* (*person*) tener éxito; (*plan*) salir bien ♦ *vt* suceder a; **to ~ in doing**

lograr hacer ❑ **succeeding** adj (following) sucesivo

success [sək'sɛs] n éxito ❑ **successful** adj exitoso; (business) próspero; **to be successful (in doing)** lograr (hacer) ❑ **successfully** adv con éxito

⚠ Be careful not to translate **success** by the Spanish word *suceso*.

succession [sək'sɛʃən] n sucesión f, serie f

successive [sək'sɛsɪv] adj sucesivo, consecutivo

succinct [sək'sɪŋkt] adj sucinto

such [sʌtʃ] adj tal, semejante; (of that kind): **~ a book** tal libro; (so much): **~ courage** tanto valor ♦ adv tan; **~ a long trip** un viaje tan largo; **~ a lot of** tanto(s)/a(s); **~ as** (like) tal como; **as ~** como tal ❑ **such-and-such** adj tal o cual

suck [sʌk] vt chupar; (bottle) sorber; (breast) mamar ❑ **sucker** n (ZOOL) ventosa; (inf) bobo, primo

suction ['sʌkʃən] n succión f

Sudan [su'dæn] n Sudán m

sudden ['sʌdn] adj (rapid) repentino, súbito; (unexpected) imprevisto; **all of a ~** de repente ❑ **suddenly** adv de repente

suds [sʌdz] npl espuma de jabón

sue [su:] vt demandar

suede [sweid] n ante m, gamuza

suet ['su:it] n sebo

Suez [su:'ɛz] n: **the ~ Canal** el Canal de Suez

suffer ['sʌfər] vt sufrir, padecer; (tolerate) aguantar, soportar ♦ vi sufrir; **to ~ from** (illness etc) padecer ❑ **sufferer** n víctima, (MED) enfermo(-a) ❑ **suffering** n sufrimiento

sufficient [sə'fɪʃənt] adj suficiente, bastante ❑ **sufficiently** adv suficientemente, bastante

suffocate ['sʌfəkeit] vi ahogarse, asfixiarse ❑ **suffocation** [ˌsʌfə'keɪʃən] n asfixia

sugar ['ʃugər] n azúcar m ♦ vt echar azúcar a, azucarar ❑ **sugar beet** n betabel m (MEX), remolacha (azucarera) (LAm exc MEX, SP) ❑ **sugar cane** n caña de azúcar

suggest [səg'dʒɛst] vt sugerir ❑ **suggestion** n sugerencia ❑ **suggestive** (pej) adj indecente

suicide ['su:isaid] n suicidio; (person) suicida mf; see also **commit** ❑ **suicide bomber** n terrorista mf suicida ❑ **suicide bombing** n atentado suicida

suit [su:t] n (man's) traje m; (woman's) conjunto; (LAW) pleito; (CARDS) palo ♦ vt

convenir; (clothes) sentar a, ir bien a; (adapt): **to ~ sth to** adaptar or ajustar algo a; **well ~ed** (well matched: couple) hecho el uno para el otro ❑ **suitable** adj conveniente; (apt) indicado ❑ **suitably** adv convenientemente; (impressed) apropiadamente

suitcase ['su:tkeis] n maleta, valija (RPl)

suite [swi:t] n (of rooms, MUS) suite f; (furniture): **bedroom/dining room ~** (juego de) dormitorio/comedor

suitor ['su:tər] n pretendiente m

sulfur (US) ['sʌlfər] (BRIT **sulphur**) n azufre m

sulk [sʌlk] vi estar de mal humor ❑ **sulky** adj malhumorado

sullen ['sʌlən] adj hosco, huraño

sulphur ['sʌlfər] (BRIT) n = **sulfur**

sultana [sʌl'tænə] n (fruit) pasa (sultana or de Esmirna)

sultry ['sʌltri] adj (weather) bochornoso

sum [sʌm] n suma; (total) total m ▶ **sum up** vt resumir ♦ vi hacer un resumen

summarize ['sʌməraiz] vt resumir

summary ['sʌməri] n resumen m ♦ adj (justice) sumario

summer ['sʌmər] n verano ♦ cpd de verano; **in ~** en verano ❑ **summerhouse** n (in garden) cenador m, glorieta ❑ **summertime** n (season) verano ❑ **summer vacation** n vacaciones fpl de verano

summit ['sʌmit] n cima, cumbre f; (also: **~ conference, ~ meeting**) (conferencia) cumbre f

summon ['sʌmən] vt (person) llamar; (meeting) convocar; (LAW) citar ▶ **summon up** vt (courage) armarse de ❑ **summons** n llamamiento, llamada ♦ vt (LAW) citar

sump [sʌmp] (BRIT) n (AUT) cárter m

sumptuous ['sʌmptjuəs] adj suntuoso

sun [sʌn] n sol m ❑ **sunbathe** vi tomar el sol ❑ **sunblock** n crema or filtro solar (de protección total) ❑ **sunburn** n (painful) quemadura; (tan) bronceado ❑ **sunburnt** adj quemado por el sol

Sunday ['sʌndi] n domingo ❑ **Sunday school** n catequesis f (dominical)

sundial ['sʌndaɪəl] n reloj m de sol

sundown ['sʌndaun] n anochecer m

sundries npl artículos mpl varios

sundry ['sʌndri] adj varios(-as), diversos(-as); **all and ~** todos sin excepción

sunflower ['sʌnflauər] n girasol m

sung [sʌŋ] pp of **sing**

sunglasses ['sʌn,glæsɪz] npl lentes mpl (LAm) or anteojos mpl (LAm) or gafas fpl (SP) de sol

sunk [sʌŋk] pp of **sink**

sun: ☐ **sunlight** n luz f del sol ☐ **sunlit** adj soleado ☐ **sunny** adj soleado; (day) de sol; (fig) alegre ☐ **sunrise** n salida del sol ☐ **sun roof** n (AUT) techo corredizo ☐ **sunscreen** n protector m solar ☐ **sunset** n puesta del sol ☐ **sunshade** n (over table) sombrilla; (awning) toldo ☐ **sunshine** n sol m ☐ **sunstroke** n insolación f ☐ **suntan** n bronceado ☐ **suntan oil** n aceite m bronceador ☐ **sun-up** (US) n amanecer m, salida del sol

super ['suːpər] (inf) adj genial

superannuation ['suːpərænjuˈeɪʃən] n jubilación f, pensión f

superb [suːˈpɜːrb] adj magnífico, espléndido

Super Bowl (US) n el Super Tazón (LAm), el (LAm) la (SP) Super Bowl

supercilious [ˌsuːpərˈsɪliəs] adj altanero

superficial [ˌsuːpərˈfɪʃəl] adj (person, damage, cut) superficial

superfluous [suˈpɜːrfluəs] adj superfluo, de sobra

superhuman [ˌsuːpərˈhjuːmən] adj sobrehumano

superimpose [ˌsuːpərɪmˈpouz] vt sobreponer

superintendent [ˌsuːpərɪnˈtendənt] n (of institution) director(a) m/f; (of building) conserje m; (POLICE) inspector(a) m/f jefe

superior [suˈpɪriər] adj superior; (smug) desdeñoso ♦ n superior m ☐ **superiority** [suˌpɪriˈɔːrɪti] n superioridad f

superlative [suˈpɜːrlətɪv] n superlativo

superman ['suːpər,mæn] n superhombre m

supermarket ['suːpər,mɑːrkɪt] n supermercado

supernatural [ˌsuːpərˈnætʃərəl] adj sobrenatural ♦ n: **the** ~ lo sobrenatural

superpower ['suːpər,pauər] n (POL) superpotencia

supersede [ˌsuːpərˈsiːd] vt suplantar

superstar ['suːpər,stɑːr] n superestrella, gran estrella

superstitious [ˌsuːpərˈstɪʃəs] adj supersticioso

supertanker ['suːpər,tæŋkər] n superpetrolero

supervise ['suːpərvaɪz] vt supervisar ☐ **supervision** [ˌsuːpərˈvɪʒən] n supervisión f ☐ **supervisor** n supervisor(a) m/f

supper ['sʌpər] n cena

supple ['sʌpəl] adj flexible

supplement [n 'sʌplɪmənt, vb 'sʌplɪmənt] n suplemento ♦ vt suplir ☐ **supplemental** [ˌsʌplɪˈmentl], **supplementary** [ˌsʌplɪˈmentəri] adj suplementario ☐ **supplementary benefit** (BRIT) n subsidio suplementario de la seguridad social

supplier [səˈplaɪər] n (COMM) distribuidor(a) m/f

supply [səˈplaɪ] vt (provide) suministrar; (equip): **to ~ (with)** proveer (de) ♦ n provisión f; (of gas, water etc) suministro; **supplies** npl (food) víveres mpl; (MIL) pertrechos mpl ☐ **supply teacher** (BRIT) n profesor(a) m/f suplente

support [səˈpɔːrt] n apoyo; (TECH) soporte m ♦ vt apoyar; (financially) mantener; (uphold, TECH) sostener ☐ **supporter** n (POL etc) partidario(-a); (SPORT) aficionado(-a)

⚠ Be careful not to translate **support** by the Spanish word **soportar**.

suppose [səˈpouz] vt suponer; (imagine) imaginarse; (duty): **to be ~d to do sth** deber hacer algo ☐ **supposedly** [səˈpouzɪdli] adv según cabe suponer ☐ **supposing** conj en caso de que

suppress [səˈpres] vt suprimir; (yawn) ahogar

supreme [suˈpriːm] adj supremo ☐ **Supreme Court** (US) n Tribunal m Supremo, Corte f Suprema (LAm)

surcharge ['sɜːrtʃɑːrdʒ] n recargo

sure [ʃuər] adj seguro; (definite, convinced) cierto; **to make ~ of sth/that** asegurarse de algo/asegurar que; **~!** (of course) ¡claro!, ¡por supuesto!; **~ enough** efectivamente ☐ **surely** adv (certainly) seguramente

surf [sɜːrf] n olas fpl ♦ vi hacer surf ♦ vt (INTERNET): **to ~ the Net** navegar por Internet

surface ['sɜːrfɪs] n superficie f ♦ vt (road) revestir ♦ vi salir a la superficie; **by ~ mail** por vía terrestre

surfboard ['sɜːrf,bɔːrd] n tabla de surf

surfeit ['sɜːrfɪt] n: **a ~ of** un exceso de

surfing ['sɜːrfɪŋ] n surf m

surge [sɜːrdʒ] n oleada, oleaje m ♦ vi (wave) romper; (people) avanzar en tropel

surgeon ['sɜːrdʒən] n cirujano(-a)

surgery ['sɜːrdʒəri] n cirugía; (BRIT: room) consultorio ☐ **surgery hours** (BRIT) npl horas fpl de consulta

surgical ['sɜːrdʒɪkəl] adj quirúrgico ☐ **surgical spirit** (BRIT) n alcohol m de 90°

surname ['sɜːrneɪm] n apellido

surpass [sər'pæs] vt superar, exceder

surplus ['sɜːrpləs] n excedente m; (COMM) superávit m ◆ adj excedente, sobrante

surprise [sər'praɪz] n sorpresa ◆ vt sorprender ❑ **surprising** adj sorprendente ❑ **surprisingly** adv: **it was surprisingly easy** me etc sorprendió lo fácil que fue

surrender [sə'rendər] n rendición f, entrega ◆ vi rendirse, entregarse

surreptitious [ˌsʌrəp'tɪʃəs] adj subrepticio

surrogate ['sʌrəgɪt] n sucedáneo ❑ **surrogate mother** n madre f de alquiler

surround [sə'raund] vt rodear, circundar; (MIL etc) cercar ❑ **surrounding** adj circundante ❑ **surroundings** npl alrededores mpl, cercanías fpl

surveillance [sər'veɪləns] n vigilancia

survey [n sə'rveɪ, vb sər'veɪ] n inspección f, reconocimiento; (inquiry) encuesta ◆ vt examinar, inspeccionar; (look at) mirar, contemplar ❑ **surveyor** n (of land) agrimensor(a) m/f

survival [sər'vaɪvəl] n supervivencia

survive [sər'vaɪv] vi sobrevivir; (custom etc) perdurar ◆ vt sobrevivir a ❑ **survivor** n superviviente mf

susceptible [sə'septəbəl] adj: ~ **(to)** (disease) susceptible (a); (flattery) sensible (a)

sushi ['suːʃi] n sushi m

suspect [adj, n 'sʌspekt, vb sə'spekt] adj, n sospechoso(-a) ◆ vt (person) sospechar de; (think) sospechar

suspend [sə'spend] vt suspender ❑ **suspended sentence** n (LAW) libertad f condicional ❑ **suspender belt** (BRIT) n liguero ❑ **suspenders** npl (US) tirantes mpl, tiradores mpl (RPl); (BRIT) ligas fpl

suspense [sə'spens] n incertidumbre f, duda; (in movie etc) suspenso (LAm), suspense m (SP); **to keep sb in ~** mantener a algn en suspenso or suspense

suspension [sə'spenʃən] n (gen, AUT) suspensión f; (from team) exclusión f ❑ **suspension bridge** n puente m colgante

suspicion [sə'spɪʃən] n sospecha; (distrust) recelo ❑ **suspicious** adj receloso; (causing suspicion) sospechoso

sustain [sə'steɪn] vt sostener, apoyar; (suffer) sufrir, padecer ❑ **sustainable** adj sostenible ❑ **sustained** adj (effort) sostenido

sustenance ['sʌstɪnəns] n sustento

SUV n todoterreno inv, SUV m

swab [swɑːb] n (MED) algodón m

swagger ['swægər] vi pavonearse

swallow ['swɑːloʊ] n (bird) golondrina ◆ vt tragar; (fig, pride) tragarse ▶ **swallow up** vt (savings etc) consumir

swam [swæm] pt of **swim**

swamp [swɑːmp] n pantano, ciénaga ◆ vt (with water etc) inundar; (fig) abrumar, agobiar ❑ **swampy** adj pantanoso

swan [swɑːn] n cisne m

swap [swɑːp] n canje m, intercambio ◆ vt: **to ~ (for)** cambiar (por)

swarm [swɔːrm] n (of bees) enjambre m; (fig) multitud f ◆ vi (bees) formar un enjambre; (people) pulular; **to be ~ing with** ser un hervidero de

swastika ['swɑːstɪkə] n esvástica

swat [swɑːt] vt aplastar

sway [sweɪ] vi mecerse, balancearse ◆ vt (influence) mover, influir en

swear [swɛər] (pt **swore**, pp **sworn**) vi (curse) maldecir; (promise) jurar ◆ vt jurar ❑ **swearword** n palabrota

sweat [swet] n sudor m ◆ vi sudar

sweater ['swetər] n suéter m (LAm), jersey m (SP)

sweatshirt ['swetʃɜːrt] n sudadera

sweat suit (US) n pants mpl y sudadera (MEX), equipo de deportes (LAm), jogging m (RPl), chándal m (SP)

sweaty ['sweti] adj sudoroso

Swede [swiːd] n sueco(-a)

swede [swiːd] (BRIT) n nabo (sueco)

Sweden ['swiːdn] n Suecia ❑ **Swedish** adj sueco ◆ n (LING) sueco

sweep [swiːp] (pt, pp **swept**) n (act) barrido; (also: **chimney ~**) deshollinador(a) m/f ◆ vt barrer; (with arm) empujar; (current) arrastrar ◆ vi barrer; (arm etc) moverse rápidamente; (wind) soplar con violencia ▶ **sweep away** vt barrer ▶ **sweep past** vi pasar majestuosamente ▶ **sweep up** vi barrer ❑ **sweeping** adj (gesture) dramático; (generalized: statement) generalizado

sweet [swiːt] n, adj dulce; (fig: kind) dulce, amable; (: attractive) mono; (BRIT: candy) dulce m, caramelo; (BRIT: pudding) postre m ❑ **sweet corn** n maíz m (dulce), choclo (SC) ❑ **sweeten** vt (add sugar to) poner azúcar a; (person) endulzar ❑ **sweetheart** n novio(-a) ❑ **sweetness** n dulzura ❑ **sweet pea** n chícharo (MEX, CAm) or guisante m (SP) de olor, arveja (LAm)

swell [swel] (pt **~ed**, pp **swollen** or **~ed**) n (of sea) marejada, oleaje m ◆ adj (US: inf: excellent) estupendo, fenomenal ◆ vt hinchar, inflar ◆ vi (also: ~ **up**) hincharse; (numbers) aumentar;

(sound, feeling) ir aumentando ❑ **swelling** n *(MED)* hinchazón f

sweltering ['sweltərɪŋ] *adj* sofocante, de mucho calor

swept [swept] *pt, pp of* **sweep**

swerve [swɜːrv] *vi* girar bruscamente

swift [swɪft] n *(bird)* vencejo ♦ *adj* rápido, veloz ❑ **swiftly** *adv* rápidamente

swig [swɪg] *(inf)* n *(drink)* trago

swill [swɪl] *vt (also: ~ out, ~ down)* lavar, limpiar con agua

swim [swɪm] *(pt* **swam***, pp* **swum***)* n: **to go for a ~** ir a nadar *or* a bañarse ♦ *vi* nadar; *(head, room)* dar vueltas ♦ *vt* nadar; *(river etc)* cruzar a nado ❑ **swimmer** n nadador(a) m/f ❑ **swimming** n natación f ❑ **swimming cap** n gorra *(LAm)* or gorro *(SP)* de baño ❑ **swimming costume** *(BRIT)* n = **swimsuit** ❑ **swimming pool** n alberca *(MEX)*, piscina *(LAm exc MEX, SP)*, pileta *(RPl)* ❑ **swimming trunks** *(BRIT)* n traje m de baño *(de hombre) (LAm)*, malla *(RPl)* or bañador m *(SP)* (de hombre) ❑ **swimsuit** n traje m de baño *(de mujer) (LAm)*, malla *(RPl)* or bañador m *(SP)* (de mujer)

swindle ['swɪndl] n estafa ♦ *vt* estafar

swine [swaɪn] *(inf!)* n canalla *mf* (!)

swing [swɪŋ] *(pt, pp* **swung***)* n *(in playground)* columpio; *(movement)* balanceo, vaivén m; *(change of direction)* viraje m; *(rhythm)* ritmo ♦ *vt* balancear; *(also: ~ around)* voltear, girar ♦ *vi* balancearse, columpiarse; *(also: ~ around)* dar media vuelta; **to be in full ~** estar en plena marcha ❑ **swing bridge** n puente m giratorio

swingeing ['swɪndʒɪŋ] *(BRIT)* adj *(cuts)* atroz

swinging door *(US)* *(BRIT* **swing door***)* n puerta giratoria

swipe [swaɪp] *vt (hit)* golpear fuerte; *(inf: steal)* birlar

swirl [swɜːrl] *vi* arremolinarse

Swiss [swɪs] *adj, n inv* suizo(-a)

switch [swɪtʃ] n *(for light etc)* interruptor m; *(change)* cambio ♦ *vt (change)* cambiar de ▶ **switch off** *vt* apagar; *(engine)* parar ▶ **switch on** *vt* prender *(LAm)*, encender *(SP)* ❑ **switchboard** n *(TEL)* conmutador m *(LAm)*, centralita *(SP)*

Switzerland ['swɪtsərlənd] n Suiza

swivel ['swɪvl] *vi (also: ~ around)* girar

swollen ['swoʊlən] *pp of* **swell**

swoon [swuːn] *vi* desmayarse

swoop [swuːp] n *(by police etc)* redada ♦ *vi (also: ~ down)* calarse

swop [swɒp] *n, vt =* **swap**

sword [sɔːrd] n espada ❑ **swordfish** n pez m espada

swore [swɔːr] *pt of* **swear**

sworn [swɔːrn] *pp of* **swear** ♦ *adj (statement)* bajo juramento; *(enemy)* implacable

swot [swɒt] *(BRIT)* vt, vi matarse *(estudiando)*, machetear *(MEX)*, tragar *(RPl)*

swum [swʌm] *pp of* **swim**

swung [swʌŋ] *pt, pp of* **swing**

sycamore ['sɪkəmɔːr] n sicomoro

syllable ['sɪləbl] n sílaba

syllabus ['sɪləbəs] n programa m de estudios

symbol ['sɪmbl] n símbolo

symmetry ['sɪmɪtri] n simetría

sympathetic [ˌsɪmpə'θetɪk] *adj (understanding)* comprensivo; *(showing pity)* compasivo; **to be ~ to a cause** apoyar una causa

> ⚠ Be careful not to translate **sympathetic** by the Spanish word *simpático*.

sympathize ['sɪmpəθaɪz] *vi*: **to ~ with** *(person)* compadecerse de; *(feelings)* comprender; *(cause)* apoyar ❑ **sympathizer** n *(POL)* simpatizante *mf*

sympathy ['sɪmpəθi] n *(pity)* compasión f; **sympathies** *npl (tendencies)* tendencias *fpl*; **with our deepest ~** nuestro más sentido pésame; **in ~** en solidaridad

symphony ['sɪmfəni] n sinfonía

symptom ['sɪmptəm] n síntoma m, indicio

synagogue ['sɪnəgɔːg] n sinagoga

syndicate ['sɪndɪkɪt] n sindicato; *(of newspapers)* agencia *(de noticias)*

syndrome ['sɪndroʊm] n síndrome m

synopsis [sɪ'nɑːpsɪs] *(pl* **synopses** [sɪ'nɑːpsiːz]*)* n sinopsis *f inv*

synthesis ['sɪnθəsɪs] *(pl* **syntheses** ['sɪnθəsiːz]*)* n síntesis *f inv*

synthetic [sɪn'θetɪk] *adj* sintético

syphilis ['sɪfɪlɪs] n sífilis f

syphon ['saɪfən] *n =* **siphon**

Syria ['sɪriə] n Siria ❑ **Syrian** *adj, n* sirio(-a)

syringe [sə'rɪndʒ] n jeringuilla, jeringa

syrup ['sɪrəp] n jarabe m; *(also:* **golden ~***)* almíbar m

system ['sɪstəm] n sistema m; *(ANAT)* organismo ❑ **systematic** [ˌsɪstə'mætɪk] *adj* sistemático, metódico ❑ **system disk** n *(COMPUT)* disco del sistema ❑ **systems analyst** n analista *mf* de sistemas

Tt

ta [tɑ:] (BRIT: inf) excl ¡gracias!

tab [tæb] n lengüeta; (label) etiqueta; (check) cuenta; **to keep ~s on** (fig) vigilar

tabby ['tæbɪ] n (also: ~ cat) gato atigrado

table ['teɪbəl] n mesa; (of statistics etc) cuadro, tabla ♦ vt (BRIT: motion etc) presentar; **to set the ~** poner la mesa □ **tablecloth** n mantel m □ **table d'hôte** [tɑ:bəl'dout] adj del día □ **table lamp** n lámpara de mesa □ **table of contents** n índice m de materias □ **tablespoon** n cuchara de servir; (also: **tablespoonful**: as measurement) cucharada

tablet ['tæblɪt] n (MED) pastilla, comprimido; (of stone) lápida

table tennis n ping-pong m, tenis m de mesa

table wine n vino de mesa

tabloid ['tæblɔɪd] n prensa amarilla or sensacionalista

tack [tæk] n (nail) tachuela; (fig) rumbo ♦ vt (nail) clavar con tachuelas; (BRIT: stitch) hilvanar ♦ vi virar

tackle ['tækəl] n (fishing tackle) equipo de pesca; (for lifting) aparejo ♦ vt (difficulty) enfrentarse con; (challenge: person) hacer frente a; (grapple with) agarrar; (SOCCER) entrar; (FOOTBALL) placar

tacky ['tækɪ] adj pegajoso; (pej) ordinario, chabacano

tact [tækt] n tacto, discreción f □ **tactful** adj discreto, diplomático

tactics ['tæktɪks] n, npl táctica

tactless ['tæktlɪs] adj indiscreto

tadpole ['tædpoul] n renacuajo

taffy ['tæfɪ] (US) n toffee m, caramelo masticable

tag [tæg] n (label) etiqueta ► **tag along** vi ir (or venir) también

tail [teɪl] n cola; (of shirt, coat) faldón m ♦ vt (follow) vigilar a; **~s** npl (formal suit) frac m ► **tail away** vi (in size, quality etc) ir disminuyendo ► **tail off** vi = **tail away** □ **tailback** (BRIT) n (AUT) cola □ **tail end** n cola, parte f final □ **tailgate** n (AUT) puerta trasera

tailor ['teɪlər] n sastre m □ **tailoring** n (cut) corte m; (craft) sastrería □ **tailor-made** adj hecho a la medida

tailpipe (US) n tubo de escape

tailwind ['teɪl,wɪnd] n viento de cola

tainted ['teɪntɪd] adj (food) pasado; (water, air) contaminado; (fig) manchado

take [teɪk] (pt took, pp ~n) vt tomar; (grab) agarrar (LAm), coger (SP); (gain: prize) ganar; (require: effort, courage) exigir; (tolerate: pain etc) aguantar; (hold: passengers etc) tener cabida para; (accompany, bring, carry) llevar; (exam) presentarse a ♦ n (US COMM) caja, recaudación f; **to ~ sth from** (drawer etc) sacar algo de; (person) quitar algo a; **I ~ it that ...** supongo que ...; **to ~ a bath/shower** bañarse/ducharse ► **take after** vt fus parecerse a ► **take apart** vt desmontar ► **take away** vt (remove) quitar; (carry) llevar; (MATH) restar ► **take back** vt (return) devolver; (one's words) retractarse de ► **take down** vt (building) derribar; (letter etc) apuntar ► **take in** vt (deceive) engañar; (understand) entender; (include) abarcar; (lodger) acoger, recibir ► **take off** vi (AVIAT) despegar ♦ vt (remove) quitar ► **take on** vt (work) aceptar; (employee) contratar; (opponent) desafiar ► **take out** vt sacar ► **take over** vt (business) tomar posesión de; (country) tomar el poder ♦ vi: **to take over from sb** reemplazar a algn ► **take to** vt fus (person) coger cariño a, encariñarse con; (activity) aficionarse a ► **take up** vt (a dress) acortar; (occupy: time, space) ocupar; (engage in: hobby etc) dedicarse a; (accept): **to take sb up on sth** aceptar algo de algn □ **takeaway** (BRIT) adj, n = **takeout** □ **takeoff** n (AVIAT) despegue m □ **takeout** (US) adj (food) para llevar ♦ n establecimiento de comida para llevar □ **takeover** n (COMM) absorción f

takings ['teɪkɪŋz] (BRIT) npl (COMM) ingresos mpl

talc [tælk] n (also: **~um powder**) (polvos mpl de) talco

tale [teɪl] n (story) cuento; (account) relación f; **to tell ~s** (fig) contar chismes

talent ['tælənt] n talento □ **talented** adj de talento, talentoso

talk [tɔ:k] n charla; (conversation) conversación f; (gossip) habladurías fpl, chismes mpl ♦ vi hablar; **~s** npl (POL etc) conversaciones fpl; **to ~ about** hablar de; **to ~ sb into doing sth** convencer a algn para que haga algo; **to ~ sb out of doing sth** disuadir a algn de que haga algo; **to ~ shop** hablar del trabajo ► **talk over** vt discutir □ **talkative** adj hablador(a) □ **talk show** n programa m de entrevistas

tall [tɔ:l] adj alto; (object) grande; **to be 6 feet ~** (person) ≈ medir 1 metro 80

tally ['tælɪ] n cuenta ♦ vi: **to ~ (with)** corresponder (con)

talon ['tælən] n garra

tambourine [ˌtæmbə'riːn] n pandereta

tame [teɪm] adj domesticado; (fig) mediocre

tamper ['tæmpər] vi: **to ~ with** tocar, andar con

tampon ['tæmpɑːn] n tampón m

tan [tæn] n (also: **sun~**) bronceado ♦ vi ponerse moreno ♦ adj (color) café (MEX), marrón (LAm exc MEX, SP)

tang [tæŋ] n sabor m fuerte

tangent ['tændʒənt] n (MATH) tangente f; **to go off at a ~** (fig) salirse por la tangente

tangerine [ˌtændʒə'riːn] n tangerina (LAm), mandarina (SP)

tangle ['tæŋɡəl] n enredo; **to get in(to) a ~** enredarse

tank [tæŋk] n (water tank) depósito, tanque m; (for fish) acuario; (MIL) tanque m

tanker ['tæŋkər] n (ship) buque m, petrolero; (truck) camión m cisterna

tanned [tænd] adj (skin) moreno

tantalizing ['tæntəlaɪzɪŋ] adj tentador(a)

tantamount ['tæntəmaunt] adj: **~ to** equivalente a

tantrum ['tæntrəm] n rabieta

tap [tæp] n (gas tap) llave f; (gentle blow) golpecito; (on sink etc) llave f, canilla (RPI) ♦ vt (hit gently) dar golpecitos en; (resources) utilizar, explotar; (telephone) intervenir; **on ~** (fig: resources) a mano ☐ **tap dancing** n tap m (MEX), claqué m (LAm exc MEX)

tape [teɪp] n (also: **magnetic ~**) cinta magnética; (cassette) cinta; (adhesive tape) cinta adhesiva; (for tying) cinta ♦ vt (record) grabar (en cinta); (stick with tape) pegar con cinta adhesiva ☐ **tape deck** n pletina, platina ☐ **tape measure** n cinta métrica, metro

taper ['teɪpər] n cirio ♦ vi afilarse

tape recorder n grabadora

tapestry ['tæpɪstrɪ] n (object) tapiz m; (art) tapicería

tar [tɑːr] n (for roads) alquitrán m, chapopote m (MEX); (in cigarettes) alquitrán

target ['tɑːrɡɪt] n blanco

tariff ['tærɪf] n (on goods) arancel m; (BRIT: in hotels etc) tarifa

tarmac ['tɑːræk] n (AVIAT) pista (de aterrizaje); (BRIT: on road) asfaltado

tarnish ['tɑːrnɪʃ] vt deslustrar

tarp [tɑːrp] (US) n = **tarpaulin**

tarpaulin [tɑːr'pɔːlɪn] n lona impermeable

tarragon ['tærəɡən] n estragón m

tart [tɑːrt] n (CULIN) tarta; (BRIT: inf: prostitute) puta ♦ adj agrio, ácido ▸ **tart up** (BRIT: inf) vt (building) remozar; **to tart o.s. up** acicalarse

tartan ['tɑːrtn] n tela escocesa

tartar ['tɑːrtər] n (on teeth) sarro ☐ **tartar(e) sauce** n salsa tártara

task [tæsk] n tarea; **to take to ~** reprender ☐ **task force** n (MIL, POLICE) grupo de operaciones

taste [teɪst] n (sense) gusto; (flavor) sabor m; (also: **after~**) sabor m, dejo; (sample): **have a ~!** ¡prueba un poquito!; (fig) muestra, idea ♦ vt probar ♦ vi: **to ~ of** or **like** (fish, garlic etc) saber a; **you can ~ the garlic (in it)** se nota el sabor a ajo; **in good/bad ~** de buen/mal gusto ☐ **tasteful** adj de buen gusto ☐ **tasteless** adj (food) soso; (remark etc) de mal gusto ☐ **tasty** adj sabroso, rico

tatters ['tætərz] npl: **in ~** hecho jirones

tattoo [tæ'tuː] n tatuaje m; (BRIT: spectacle) espectáculo militar ♦ vt tatuar

tatty ['tætɪ] (BRIT: inf) adj cochambroso

taught [tɔːt] pt, pp of **teach**

taunt [tɔːnt] n burla ♦ vt burlarse de

Taurus ['tɔːrəs] n Tauro

taut [tɔːt] adj tirante, tenso

tax [tæks] n impuesto ♦ vt gravar (con un impuesto); (fig: memory) poner a prueba; (: patience) agotar ☐ **taxable** adj (income) gravable ☐ **taxation** [tæk'seɪʃən] n impuestos mpl ☐ **tax avoidance** n evasión f de impuestos ☐ **tax disc** (BRIT) n (AUT) adhesivo del impuesto de circulación ☐ **tax evasion** n evasión f fiscal ☐ **tax-free** adj libre de impuestos

taxi ['tæksɪ] n taxi m ♦ vi (AVIAT) rodar (por la pista) ☐ **taxi driver** n taxista mf ☐ **taxi rank** (BRIT) n = **taxi stand** ☐ **taxi stand** (US) n parada or (MEX) sitio de taxis

tax: ☐ **tax payer** n contribuyente mf ☐ **tax relief** n desgravación f fiscal ☐ **tax return** n declaración f de la renta

TB n abbr = **tuberculosis**

tea [tiː] n té m; (BRIT: meal) ≈ merienda; cena ☐ **tea bag** n bolsita de té ☐ **tea break** (BRIT) n descanso para el té

teach [tiːtʃ] (pt, pp **taught**) vt: **to ~ sb sth, ~ sth to sb** enseñar algo a algn ♦ vi (be a teacher) ser profesor-a, enseñar ☐ **teacher** n (in high school) profesor(a) m/f; (in elementary school) maestro(-a) ☐ **teaching** n enseñanza

teacup ['tiːkʌp] n taza de té

tea kettle ['tiːkɛtl] (US) n hervidor m, pava (RPI)

teak [tiːk] n (madera de) teca

team [tiːm] n equipo; (of horses) tiro

teamster ['tiːmstər] (US) n camionero(-a)

teamwork n trabajo en or de equipo

teapot ['tiːpɒt] n tetera

tear¹ [tɪər] n lágrima; **in ~s** llorando

tear² [tɛər] (pt **tore**, pp **torn**) n rasgón m, desgarrón m ♦ vt romper, rasgar ♦ vi rasgarse
▶ **tear along** vi (rush) precipitarse ▶ **tear up** vt (sheet of paper etc) romper

tearful ['tɪərfəl] adj lloroso

tear gas ['tɪərˌɡæs] n gas m lacrimógeno

tearoom ['tiːˌruːm] n salón m de té

tease [tiːz] vt tomar el pelo a

tea set n servicio de té

teaspoon n cucharita; (also: **~ful**: as measurement) cucharadita

teat [tiːt] n (of animal) teta; (BRIT: of bottle) tetina

teatime ['tiːˌtaɪm] (BRIT) n hora del té

tea towel (BRIT) n paño de cocina

technical ['tɛknɪkəl] adj técnico
❑ **technical college** (BRIT) n = escuela politécnica ❑ **technicality** [ˌtɛknɪˈkælɪtɪ] n (point of law) formalismo; (detail) detalle m técnico ❑ **technically** adv en teoría; (regarding technique) técnicamente

technician [tɛkˈnɪʃən] n técnico(-a)

technique [tɛkˈniːk] n técnica

technological [ˌtɛknəˈlɒdʒɪkəl] adj tecnológico

technology [tɛkˈnɒlədʒɪ] n tecnología

teddy (bear) ['tɛdɪ(ˌbɛr)] n osito de peluche

tedious ['tiːdɪəs] adj pesado, aburrido

teem [tiːm] vi: **to ~ with** rebosar de; **it is ~ing (with rain)** llueve a cántaros

teen [tiːn] adj = **teenage** ♦ n (US) = **teenager**

teenage ['tiːneɪdʒ] adj (fashions etc) juvenil; (children) adolescente ❑ **teenager** n adolescente mf

teens [tiːnz] npl: **to be in one's ~** ser adolescente

tee-shirt ['tiːˌʃɜːrt] n = **T-shirt**

teeter ['tiːtər] vi balancearse; (fig): **to ~ on the edge of** estar al borde de

teeth [tiːθ] npl of **tooth**

teethe [tiːð] vi: **he's teething** le están saliendo dientes (LAm)

teething ['tiːðɪŋ] n dentición f ❑ **teething ring** n mordedor m ❑ **teething troubles** (BRIT) npl (fig) problemas mpl iniciales

teetotal ['tiːˈtəʊtl] adj abstemio

telegram ['tɛlɪɡræm] n telegrama m

telegraph ['tɛlɪɡræf] n telégrafo

telepathy [təˈlɛpəθɪ] n telepatía

telephone ['tɛləfəʊn] n teléfono ♦ vt llamar por teléfono, telefonear; (message) dar por teléfono; **to be on the ~** (talking) hablar por teléfono; (BRIT: possessing telephone) tener teléfono ❑ **telephone booth** (US) n cabina telefónica ❑ **telephone box** (BRIT) n = **telephone booth** ❑ **telephone call** n llamada telefónica ❑ **telephone directory** n directorio (telefónico) (MEX), guía telefónica (LAm exc MEX, SP) ❑ **telephone number** n número de teléfono ❑ **telephone pole** (US) n poste m telegráfico ❑ **telephonist** [təˈlɛfəʊnɪst] (BRIT) n telefonista mf

telesales ['tɛlɪˌseɪlz] npl televentas fpl

telescope ['tɛlɪskəʊp] n telescopio

television ['tɛlɪvɪʒən] n televisión f; **on ~** por televisión ❑ **television set** n televisor m

teleworking ['tɛlɪˌwɜːrkɪŋ] n teletrabajo

tell [tɛl] (pt, pp **told**) vt decir; (relate: story) contar; (distinguish): **to ~ sth from** distinguir algo de ♦ vi (talk): **to ~ (of)** contar; (have effect) tener efecto; **to ~ sb to do sth** mandar a algn hacer algo ▶ **tell off** vt: **to tell sb off** regañar a algn ❑ **teller** (US) n (in bank) cajero(-a) ❑ **telling** adj (remark, detail) revelador(a) ❑ **telltale** adj (sign) indicador(a)

telly ['tɛlɪ] (BRIT: inf) n abbr (= **television**) tele f

temp [tɛmp] n abbr (= **temporary**) trabajador(a) m/f temporal

temper ['tɛmpər] n (nature) carácter m; (mood) humor m; (bad temper) (mal) genio; (fit of anger) acceso de ira ♦ vt (moderate) moderar; **to be in a ~** estar furioso; **to lose one's ~** enfadarse, enojarse

temperament ['tɛmprəmənt] n (nature) temperamento

temperate ['tɛmpərət] adj (climate etc) templado

temperature ['tɛmpərətʃər] n temperatura; **to have** or **run a ~** tener fiebre

temple ['tɛmpəl] n (building) templo; (ANAT) sien f

tempo ['tɛmpəʊ] (pl **~s** or **tempi** ['tɛmpiː]) n (MUS) tempo, tiempo; (fig) ritmo

temporarily [ˌtɛmpəˈrɛrɪlɪ] adv temporalmente

temporary ['tɛmpərərɪ] adj provisional; (passing) transitorio; (worker, job) temporal

tempt [tɛmpt] vt tentar; **to ~ sb into doing sth** tentar a algn a hacer algo ❑ **temptation** [tɛmpˈteɪʃən] n tentación f ❑ **tempting** adj tentador(a); (food) apetitoso

ten [tɛn] *num* diez

tenacity [tə'næsɪtɪ] *n* tenacidad *f*

tenancy ['tɛnənsɪ] *n* arrendamiento, alquiler *m*

tenant ['tɛnənt] *n* inquilino(-a)

tend [tɛnd] *vt* cuidar ♦ *vi*: **to ~ to do sth** tener tendencia a hacer algo

tendency ['tɛndənsɪ] *n* tendencia

tender ['tɛndər] *adj* (*person, care*) tierno, cariñoso; (*meat*) tierno; (*sore*) sensible ♦ *n* (*comm: offer*) oferta; (*money*): **legal ~** moneda de curso legal ♦ *vt* ofrecer ❑ **tenderness** *n* ternura; (*of meat*) blandura

tenement ['tɛnəmənt] *n* bloque *m* de departamentos (*LAm*) or pisos (*SP*)

tennis ['tɛnɪs] *n* tenis *m* ❑ **tennis ball** *n* pelota de tenis ❑ **tennis court** *n* cancha (*LAm*) or pista (*SP*) de tenis ❑ **tennis player** *n* tenista *mf* ❑ **tennis racket** *n* raqueta de tenis

tenor ['tɛnər] *n* (*MUS*) tenor *m*

tenpin bowling ['tɛnpɪn,boulɪŋ] (*BRIT*) *n* boliche *m* (*MEX*), (juego de) bolos *mpl* (*LAm exc MEX, SP*)

tense [tɛns] *adj* (*person*) nervioso; (*moment, atmosphere*) tenso; (*muscle*) tenso, en tensión ♦ *n* (*LING*) tiempo

tension ['tɛnʃən] *n* tensión *f*

tent [tɛnt] *n* carpa (*LAm*), tienda (de campaña) (*SP*)

tentative ['tɛntətɪv] *adj* (*person, smile*) indeciso; (*conclusion, plans*) provisional

tenterhooks ['tɛntər,huks] *npl*: **on ~** sobre ascuas

tenth [tɛnθ] *num* décimo

tent peg (*BRIT*) *n* estaca

tent pole *n* palo (de carpa) (*LAm*), mástil *m* (de tienda) (*SP*)

tenuous ['tɛnjuəs] *adj* tenue

tenure ['tɛnjuər] *n* (*of land etc*) tenencia; (*of office*) ejercicio

tepid ['tɛpɪd] *adj* tibio

term [tɜːrm] *n* (*word*) término; (*period*) período; (*scol*) trimestre *m* ♦ *vt* llamar; **~s** *npl* (*conditions, comm*) condiciones *fpl*; **in the short/long ~** a corto/largo plazo; **to be on good ~s with sb** llevarse bien con algn; **to come to ~s with** (*problem*) aceptar

terminal ['tɜːrmɪnl] *adj* (*disease*) mortal; (*patient*) terminal ♦ *n* (*ELEC*) polo; (*COMPUT*) terminal *f* (*MEX*) or *m* (*LAm exc MEX, SP*); (*also:* **air ~**) terminal *f* (del aeropuerto); (*BRIT: also:* **coach ~**) terminal *f* (de autobuses)

terminate ['tɜːrmɪneɪt] *vt* terminar

terminus ['tɜːrmɪnəs] (*pl* **termini** ['tɜːrmɪnaɪ]) *n* (*last station: of bus route*) última parada

term paper (*US*) *n* trabajo (escrito) trimestral

terrace ['tɛrəs] *n* terraza; (*BRIT: row of houses*) hilera de casas adosadas; **the ~s** (*BRIT SPORT*) las gradas *fpl* ❑ **terraced** *adj* (*garden*) en terrazas; (*BRIT: house*) adosado

terrain [tɛ'reɪn] *n* terreno

terrible ['tɛrɪbl] *adj* terrible, horrible; (*inf*) atroz ❑ **terribly** *adv* terriblemente; (*very badly*) malísimamente

terrier ['tɛrɪər] *n* terrier *m*

terrific [tə'rɪfɪk] *adj* (*very great*) tremendo; (*wonderful*) fantástico, fenomenal

terrify ['tɛrɪfaɪ] *vt* aterrorizar

territory ['tɛrɪtɔːrɪ] *n* territorio

terror ['tɛrər] *n* terror *m* ❑ **terrorism** *n* terrorismo ❑ **terrorist** *n* terrorista *mf*

test [tɛst] *n* (*gen, CHEM*) prueba; (*MED*) análisis *m*; (*SCOL*) prueba, test *m*; (*also:* **driving ~**) examen *m* de manejar (*LAm*) or conducir (*SP*) ♦ *vt* probar, poner a prueba; (*MED, SCOL*) examinar

testament ['tɛstəmənt] *n* testamento; **the Old/New T~** el Antiguo/Nuevo Testamento

testicle ['tɛstɪkəl] *n* testículo

testify ['tɛstɪfaɪ] *vi* (*LAW*) prestar declaración; **to ~ to sth** atestiguar algo

testimony ['tɛstɪmounɪ] *n* (*LAW*) testimonio

test: ❑ **test match** (*BRIT*) *n* (*CRICKET, RUGBY*) partido internacional ❑ **test tube** *n* probeta

tetanus ['tɛtnəs] *n* tétano

tether ['tɛðər] *vt* atar (con una cuerda) ♦ *n*: **to be at the end of one's ~** no aguantar más

TexMex ['tɛks'mɛks] *adj* típico de México al estilo norteamericano

TEXMEX

El término **TexMex** se usa para describir un tipo de comida cuya base son algunos platos de origen mexicano que han sido adaptados a los gustos y los ingredientes de los norteamericanos. El nombre se deriva de la frontera geográfica entre Texas y México, ya que éste fue el punto en que se produjo el paso de la frontera y donde surgió este tipo de comida, mezcla de la gastronomía de los dos países. Entre los platos más típicos están los burritos, los tacos, los nachos y las fajitas, servidos al estilo norteamericano, con queso y crema de leche amarga añadidos.

text [tɛkst] *n* texto ♦ *vt*: **to ~ sb** enviar un mensaje (de texto) a algn ❑ **textbook** *n* libro de texto

textiles ['tɛkstaɪlz] npl tejidos mpl; (textile industry) industria textil

text: ❏ **text message** n mensaje m de texto ❏ **text messaging** n (envío de) mensajes mpl de texto

texture ['tɛkstʃər] n textura

Thailand ['taɪlænd] n Tailandia

Thames [tɛmz] n: **the ~** el (río) Támesis

than [ðæn] conj (in comparisons): **more ~ 10/ once** más de 10/una vez; **I have more/less ~ you/Paul** tengo más/menos que tú/Paul; **she is older ~ you think** es mayor de lo que piensas

thank [θæŋk] vt dar las gracias a, agradecer; **~ you (very much)** (muchas) gracias; **~ God!** ¡gracias a Dios! ❏ **thankful** adj: **thankful (for)** agradecido (por) ❏ **thankless** adj ingrato ❏ **thanks** npl gracias fpl ♦ excl (also: **many thanks, thanks a lot**) ¡gracias!; **thanks to** prep gracias a ❏ **Thanksgiving (Day)** n día m de Acción de Gracias

THANKSGIVING (DAY)

En Estados Unidos el cuarto jueves de noviembre es **Thanksgiving Day**, fiesta oficial en la que se recuerda la celebración que hicieron los primeros colonos norteamericanos (**Pilgrims** o **Pilgrim Fathers**) tras la estupenda cosecha de 1621, por la que se dan gracias a Dios. En Canadá se celebra una fiesta semejante el segundo lunes de octubre, aunque no está relacionada con dicha fecha histórica.

that
KEYWORD

[ðæt] (pl those) adj
(demonstrative) ese(-a), (pl) esos(-as); (more remote) aquel (aquella), (pl) aquellos(-as); **leave those books on the table** deja esos libros sobre la mesa; **that one day** ese (ésa); (more remote) aquel (aquélla); **that one over there** ése(-a) de ahí; aquél (aquélla) de allí
♦ pron
1 (demonstrative) ése(-a), (pl) ésos(-as); (neuter) eso; (more remote) aquél (aquélla), (pl) aquéllos(-as); (neuter) aquello; **what's that?** ¿qué es eso (or aquello)?; **who's that?** ¿quién es ése(-a) or aquél (aquélla); **is that you?** ¿eres tú?; **will you eat all that?** ¿vas a comer todo eso?; **that's my house** ésa es mi casa; **that's what he said** eso es lo que dijo; **that is (to say)** es decir

2 (relative: subject, object) que; (with preposition) (el (la)) que etc, el (la) cual etc; **the book (that) I read** el libro que leí; **the books that are in the library** los libros que están en la biblioteca; **all (that) I have** todo lo que tengo; **the box (that) I put it in** la caja en la que or donde lo puse; **the people (that) I spoke to** la gente con la que hablé

3 (relative: of time) que; **the day (that) he came** el día (en) que vino
♦ conj que; **he thought that I was sick** creyó que yo estaba enfermo
♦ adv (demonstrative): **I can't work that much** no puedo trabajar tanto; **I didn't realize it was that bad** no creí que fuera tan malo; **that high** así de alto

thatched [θætʃt] adj (roof) de paja; (cottage) con techo de paja

thaw [θɔ:] n deshielo ♦ vi (ice) derretirse; (food) descongelarse ♦ vt (food) descongelar

the
KEYWORD

[ðə, ði:] def art
1 (gen) el (la), (pl) los (las) (NB 'el' immediately before f n beginning with stressed (h)a; a + el = al; de+ el = del); **the boy/girl** el chico/la chica; **the books/flowers** los libros/las flores; **to the mailman/from the drawer** al cartero/del cajón; **I haven't the time/money** no tengo tiempo/dinero
2 (+ adj to form n) los; lo; **the rich and the poor** los ricos y los pobres; **to attempt the impossible** intentar lo imposible
3 (in titles): **Elizabeth the First** Isabel primera; **Peter the Great** Pedro el Grande
4 (in comparisons): **the more he works the more he earns** cuanto más trabaja más gana

theater (US) ['θɪətər] (BRIT **theatre**) n teatro; (US: also: **movie ~**) cine m; (also: **lecture ~**) aula; (BRIT MED: also: **operating theatre**) quirófano ❏ **theater-goer** (US) (BRIT **theatre-goer**) n aficionado(-a) al teatro

theatrical [θɪ'ætrɪkl] adj teatral

theft [θɛft] n robo

their [ðɛər] adj su ❏ **theirs** pron (el) suyo ((la) suya etc); see also **my; mine**[1]

them [ðɛm] pron (direct) los/las; (indirect) les; (stressed, after prep) ellos (ellas); see also **me**

theme [θi:m] n tema m ❏ **theme park** n parque m temático ❏ **theme song** n tema m musical

themselves [ðəm'sɛlvz] *pl pron* (*subject*) ellos mismos (ellas mismas); (*complement*) se; (*after prep*) sí (mismos (as)); *see also* **oneself**

then [ðɛn] *adv* (*at that time*) entonces; (*next*) después; (*later*) luego, después; (*and also*) además ♦ *conj* (*therefore*) en ese caso, entonces ♦ *adj*: **the ~ president** el entonces presidente; **by ~** para entonces; **from ~ on** desde entonces

theology [θɪ'ɑːlədʒi] *n* teología

theory [θɪri] *n* teoría

therapist [θɛrəpɪst] *n* terapeuta *mf*

therapy [θɛrəpi] *n* terapia

there
KEYWORD

[ðɛər] *adv*

1: **there is, there are** hay; **there is no one here/no bread left** no hay nadie aquí/no queda pan; **there has been an accident** ha habido un accidente

2 (*referring to place*) ahí; (*distant*) allí; **it's there** está ahí; **put it in/on/up/down there** ponlo ahí dentro/encima/arriba/abajo; **I want that book there** quiero ese libro de ahí; **there he is!** ¡ahí está!

3: **there, there** (*esp to child*) vamos, ea, ea

there: □ **thereabouts** *adv* por ahí □ **thereafter** *adv* después □ **thereby** *adv* así, de ese modo □ **therefore** *adv* por lo tanto □ **there's** *cont* = **there is**; **there has**

thermal [θɜːrməl] *adj* termal; (*paper*) térmico

thermometer [θər'mɑːmɪtər] *n* termómetro

Thermos® [θɜːrməs] *n* (*US: also*: **Thermos bottle**; *BRIT: also*: **Thermos flask**) termo

thermostat [θɜːrməstæt] *n* termostato

thesaurus [θɪ'sɔːrəs] *n* tesauro, diccionario ideológico

these [ðiːz] *pl adj* estos(-as) ♦ *pl pron* éstos(-as)

thesis [θiːsɪs] (*pl* **theses** [θiːsiːz]) *n* tesis *f inv*

they [ðeɪ] *pl pron* ellos (ellas); (*stressed*) ellos (mismos) (ellas (mismas)); **~ say that ...** (*it is said that*) se dice que ... □ **they'd** *cont* = **they had; they would** □ **they'll** *cont* = **they shall; they will** □ **they're** *cont* = **they are** □ **they've** *cont* = **they have**

thick [θɪk] *adj* (*in consistency*) espeso; (*in size*) grueso; (*stupid*) torpe ♦ *n*: **in the ~ of the battle** en lo más reñido de la batalla; **it's 20 cm ~** tiene 20 cm de grosor □ **thicken** *vi* espesarse ♦ *vt* (*sauce etc*) espesar □ **thickness** *n* espesor *m*; grueso □ **thickset** *adj* fornido

thief [θiːf] (*pl* **thieves** [θiːvz]) *n* ladrón(-ona) *m/f*

thigh [θaɪ] *n* muslo

thimble [θɪmbəl] *n* dedal *m*

thin [θɪn] *adj* (*person, animal*) flaco; (*in size*) delgado; (*in consistency*) poco espeso; (*hair, crowd*) escaso ♦ *vt*: **to ~ (down)** diluir

thing [θɪŋ] *n* cosa; (*object*) objeto, artículo; (*matter*) asunto; (*mania*): **to have a ~ about sb/sth** estar obsesionado con algn/algo; **~s** *npl* (*belongings*) efectos *mpl* (personales); **the best ~ would be to ...** lo mejor sería ...; **how are ~s?** ¿qué tal?

think [θɪŋk] (*pt, pp* **thought**) *vi* pensar ♦ *vt* pensar, creer; **what did you ~ of them?** ¿qué te parecieron?; **to ~ about sth/sb** pensar en algo/algn; **I'll ~ about it** lo pensaré; **to ~ of doing sth** pensar en hacer algo; **I ~ so/not** creo que sí/no; **to ~ well of sb** tener buen concepto de algn ► **think over** *vt* reflexionar sobre, meditar ► **think up** *vt* (*plan etc*) idear □ **think tank** *n* grupo de expertos, gabinete *m* estratégico

thinly [θɪnli] *adv* (*cut*) fino; (*spread*) ligeramente

third [θɜːrd] *adj* (*before n*) tercer(a); (*following n*) tercero(-a) ♦ *n* tercero(-a); (*fraction*) tercio; (*BRIT SCOL: degree*) título de licenciado con calificación de aprobado □ **thirdly** *adv* en tercer lugar □ **third party insurance** (*BRIT*) *n* seguro contra terceros □ **third-rate** *adj* (*de calidad*) mediocre □ **Third World** *n* Tercer Mundo

thirst [θɜːrst] *n* sed *f* □ **thirsty** *adj* (*person, animal*) sediento; (*work*) que da sed; **to be thirsty** tener sed

thirteen [θɜːr'tiːn] *num* trece

thirty [θɜːrti] *num* treinta

this
KEYWORD

[ðɪs] (*pl* **these**) *adj*

(*demonstrative*) este(-a); (*pl*) estos(-as); (*neuter*) esto; **this man/woman** este hombre (esta mujer); **these children/flowers** estos chicos/ estas flores; **this one (here)** éste(-a), esto (de aquí)

♦ *pron* (*demonstrative*) éste(-a); (*pl*) éstos(-as); (*neuter*) esto; **who is this?** ¿quién es éste/ ésta?; **what is this?** ¿qué es esto?; **this is where I live** aquí vivo; **this is what he said** esto es lo que dijo; **this is Mr. Brown** (*in introductions*) le presento al Sr. Brown; (*photo*) éste es el Sr. Brown; (*on telephone*) habla (*LAm*) or soy (*SP*) el Sr. Brown

♦ *adv* (*demonstrative*): **this high/long** *etc* así de alto/largo *etc*; **this far** hasta aquí

thistle [θɪsəl] *n* cardo

thong [θɑ:ŋ] n (strap) correa; ~s npl (US: sandals) chanclas fpl

thorn [θɔ:rn] n espina

thorough ['θɜ:rou] adj (search) minucioso; (wash) a fondo; (knowledge, research) profundo; (person) meticuloso
❑ **thoroughbred** adj (horse) de pura sangre
❑ **thoroughfare** n calle f; **"no thoroughfare"** "prohibido el paso"
❑ **thoroughly** adv (search) minuciosamente; (study) profundamente; (wash) a fondo; (utterly: bad, wet etc) completamente, totalmente

those [ðouz] pl adj esos (esas); (more remote) aquellos(-as)

though [ðou] conj aunque ♦ adv sin embargo

thought [θɔ:t] pt, pp of **think** ♦ n pensamiento; (opinion) opinión f
❑ **thoughtful** adj pensativo; (serious) serio; (considerate) atento ❑ **thoughtless** adj desconsiderado

thousand ['θauzənd] num mil; **two ~** dos mil; **~s of ...** miles de ... ❑ **thousandth** num milésimo

thrash [θræʃ] vt azotar; (defeat) derrotar
▶ **thrash around** or (BRIT) **about** vi debatirse ▶ **thrash out** vt discutir a fondo

thread [θrɛd] n hilo; (of screw) rosca ♦ vt (needle) enhebrar ❑ **threadbare** adj raído

threat [θrɛt] n amenaza ❑ **threaten** vi amenazar ♦ vt: **to threaten sb with/to do** amenazar a algn con/con hacer

three [θri:] num tres ❑ **three-dimensional** adj tridimensional ❑ **three-piece** adj de tres piezas ❑ **three-piece suite** (BRIT) n (juego de) sofá m y dos sillones (LAm), tresillo (SP) ❑ **three-ply** adj (wool) de tres cabos

threshold ['θrɛʃhould] n umbral m

threw [θru:] pt of **throw**

thrift store ['θrɪft,stɔ:r] (US) n tienda de artículos de segunda mano que dedica su recaudación a causas benéficas

thrifty ['θrɪfti] adj económico

thrill [θrɪl] n (excitement) emoción f; (shudder) estremecimiento ♦ vt emocionar; **to be ~ed** (with gift etc) estar encantado ❑ **thriller** n novela (or obra or película) de suspenso (LAm) or suspense (SP) ❑ **thrilling** adj emocionante

thrive [θraɪv] (pt, pp ~d) vi (grow) crecer; (do well): **she seems to ~ on adversity** parece que se crece ante la adversidad ❑ **thriving** adj próspero

throat [θrout] n garganta; **to have a sore ~** tener dolor de garganta

throb [θrɑ:b] vi (heart) latir; (wound) dar punzadas; (engine) vibrar

throes [θrouz] npl: **in the ~ of** en medio de

throne [θroun] n trono

throng [θrɑ:ŋ] n multitud f, muchedumbre f ♦ vt agolparse en

throttle ['θrɑ:ti] n (AUT) acelerador m ♦ vt estrangular

through [θru:] prep por, a través de; (time) durante; (by means of) por medio de, mediante; (owing to) gracias a ♦ adj (ticket, train) directo ♦ adv completamente, de parte a parte; de principio a fin; **(from) Monday ~ Friday** (US) de lunes a viernes; **to put sb ~ to sb** (TEL) poner or pasar a algn con algn; **to be ~** (TEL) tener comunicación; (have finished) haber terminado; **"no ~ road"** (BRIT) "calle sin salida" ❑ **throughout** prep (place) por todas partes de, por todo; (time) durante todo ♦ adv por or en todas partes

throw [θrou] (pt **threw**, pp **~n**) n tiro; (SPORT) lanzamiento; (cover: for sofa) cubresofá ♦ vt tirar, echar; (SPORT) lanzar; (rider) derribar; (fig) desconcertar; **to ~ a party** dar una fiesta
▶ **throw away** vt tirar; (money) derrochar
▶ **throw off** vt deshacerse de ▶ **throw out** vt tirar; (person) echar; expulsar ▶ **throw up** vi devolver, vomitar ❑ **throwaway** adj desechable, de usar y tirar; (remark) hecho de paso ❑ **throw-in** n (SPORT) saque m

thru [θru:] (US) prep, adj, adv = **through**

thrush [θrʌʃ] n tordo, zorzal m

thrust [θrʌst] (pt, pp ~) vt empujar con fuerza

thud [θʌd] n golpe m sordo

thug [θʌɡ] n matón m

thumb [θʌm] n (ANAT) pulgar m ♦ vt: **to ~ a ride** (US) or **lift** (BRIT) pedir aventón (MEX), hacer autostop (LAm exc MEX, SP) or dedo (SC)
▶ **thumb through** vt fus (book) hojear
❑ **thumbtack** (US) n chinche f (LAm), chincheta (SP)

thump [θʌmp] n golpe m; (sound) ruido seco or sordo ♦ vt golpear ♦ vi (heart etc) palpitar

thunder ['θʌndər] n trueno ♦ vi tronar; (train etc): **to ~ past** pasar con gran estruendo ❑ **thunderbolt** n rayo ❑ **thunderclap** n trueno ❑ **thunderstorm** n tormenta ❑ **thundery** adj tormentoso

Thursday ['θɜ:rzdi] n jueves m inv

thus [ðʌs] adv así, de este modo

thyme [taɪm] n tomillo

thyroid ['θaɪrɔɪd] n (also: ~ **gland**) tiroides m inv

tic [tɪk] n tic m

tick [tɪk] n (sound: of clock) tictac m; (ZOOL) garrapata; (mark) visto (bueno), palomita (MEX) ♦ vi hacer tictac ♦ vt (BRIT) marcar; **in a ~** (BRIT: inf) en un instante ▶ **tick off** vt (US: inf) fastidiar, dar la lata a (inf); (BRIT) marcar; (: person) reñir ▶ **tick over** (BRIT) vi (engine) girar en marcha lenta; (fig) ir tirando

ticket ['tɪkɪt] n boleto (LAm), billete m (SP); (for movies etc) entrada; (in store: on goods) etiqueta; (for raffle) papeleta; (for library) tarjeta; (parking ticket) multa por estacionamiento (indebido) (LAm) or de aparcamiento (SP) ❑ **ticket collector** n revisor(a) m/f ❑ **ticket office** n (THEATER) boletería (LAm), taquilla (SP); (RAIL) mostrador m de boletos (LAm) or billetes (SP)

tickle ['tɪkəl] vt hacer cosquillas a ♦ vi hacer cosquillas ❑ **ticklish** adj (person) cosquilloso; (problem) delicado

tidal ['taɪdl] adj de marea ❑ **tidal wave** n maremoto

tidbit ['tɪdbɪt] (US) n (food) bocado, aperitivo; (news) noticia jugosa

tiddlywinks ['tɪdli,wɪŋks] n (juego de) la pulga

tide [taɪd] n marea; (fig: of events etc) curso, marcha ▶ **tide over** vt (help out) ayudar a salir del apuro

tidy ['taɪdi] adj (room etc) ordenado; (dress, work) limpio; (person) (bien) arreglado ♦ vt (also: **~ up**) recoger, ordenar

tie [taɪ] n (string etc) atadura; (US: also: **neck~**) corbata; (fig: link) vínculo, lazo; (SPORT etc: draw) empate m ♦ vt atar ♦ vi (SPORT etc) empatar; **to ~ in a bow** atar con un lazo; **to ~ a knot in sth** hacer un nudo en algo ▶ **tie down** vt (fig: person: restrict) atar; (: to price, date etc) obligar a ▶ **tie up** vt (package) envolver; (dog, person) atar; (arrangements) concluir; **to be tied up** (busy) estar ocupado

tier [tɪər] n grada; (of cake) piso

tiger ['taɪgər] n tigre m

tight [taɪt] adj (rope) tirante; (money) escaso; (clothes) ajustado; (bend) cerrado; (shoes, schedule) apretado; (budget) ajustado; (security) estricto; (inf: drunk) borracho ♦ adv (squeeze) muy fuerte; (shut) bien ❑ **tighten** vt (rope) estirar; (screw, grip) apretar; (security) reforzar ♦ vi estirarse; apretarse ❑ **tight-fisted** adj tacaño ❑ **tightly** adv (grasp) muy fuerte ❑ **tightrope** n cuerda floja ❑ **tights** npl (for sport, ballet) leotardos mpl; (BRIT: everyday clothes) pantis mpl, pantimedias fpl (MEX)

tile [taɪl] n (on roof) teja; (on floor) baldosa; (on wall) azulejo ❑ **tiled** adj de tejas; de baldosas; (wall) revestido de azulejos

till [tɪl] n (US: drawer) cajón m; (BRIT: machine) caja (registradora) ♦ vt (land) cultivar ♦ prep, conj = **until**

tilt [tɪlt] vt inclinar ♦ vi inclinarse

timber ['tɪmbər] n (material) madera

time [taɪm] n tiempo; (epoch: often pl) época; (by clock) hora; (moment) momento; (occasion) vez f; (MUS) compás m ♦ vt calcular or medir el tiempo de; (race) cronometrar; (remark, visit etc) elegir el momento para; **a long ~** mucho tiempo; **4 at a ~** de 4 en 4; 4 a la vez; **for the ~ being** de momento, por ahora; **from ~ to ~** de vez en cuando; **at ~s** a veces; **in ~** (soon enough) a tiempo; (after some time) con el tiempo; (MUS) al compás; **in a week's ~** dentro de una semana; **in no ~** en un abrir y cerrar de ojos; **any ~** cuando sea; **on ~** a la hora; **5 ~s 5** 5 por 5; **what ~ is it?** ¿qué hora es?; **to have a good ~** pasarlo bien, divertirse ❑ **time bomb** n bomba de tiempo or relojería ❑ **timeless** adj eterno ❑ **time limit** n plazo ❑ **timely** adj oportuno ❑ **time off** n tiempo libre ❑ **timer** n (in kitchen etc) reloj m automático ❑ **time scale** (BRIT) n escala de tiempo ❑ **time-share** n multipropiedad f ❑ **time switch** (BRIT) n temporizador m ❑ **timetable** n (program of events) programa m; (BRIT: for trains, buses; at school) horario ❑ **time zone** n huso horario

timid ['tɪmɪd] adj tímido

timing ['taɪmɪŋ] n (SPORT) cronometraje m; **the ~ of his resignation** el momento que eligió para dimitir

tin [tɪn] n estaño; (also: **~ plate**) hojalata; (BRIT: can) lata ❑ **tinfoil** n papel m de aluminio

tinge [tɪndʒ] n matiz m ♦ vt: **~d with** teñido de

tingle ['tɪŋgəl] vi (person): **to ~ (with)** estremecerse (de); (hands etc) hormiguear

tinker ['tɪŋkər] n: **~ with** vt fus jugar con, tocar

tinned [tɪnd] (BRIT) adj (food) en lata, en conserva

tin opener ['tɪn,oupənər] (BRIT) n abrelatas m inv

tinsel ['tɪnsəl] n oropel m (LAm), espumillón m (SP)

tint [tɪnt] n matiz m; (for hair) tinte m ❑ **tinted** adj (hair) teñido; (glass, glasses) ahumado

tiny ['taɪni] adj minúsculo, pequeñito

tip [tɪp] n (end) punta; (gratuity) propina; (advice) consejo; (BRIT: for rubbish) vertedero ♦ vt (waiter) dar una propina a; (tilt) inclinar; (empty: also: ~ out) vaciar, echar; (overturn: also: ~ over) volcar ❑ **tip-off** n (hint) advertencia ❑ **tipped** (BRIT) adj (cigarette) con filtro

Tipp-Ex® ['tɪp,ɛks] n Tipp-Ex® m

tipsy ['tɪpsi] (inf) adj alegre, mareado

tiptoe ['tɪptəu] n: **on ~** de puntillas

tire (US) ['taɪər] n (BRIT **tyre**) neumático, llanta (LAm) ♦ vt cansar ♦ vi cansarse; (become bored) aburrirse ❑ **tire pressure** n presión f de los neumáticos ❑ **tired** adj cansado; **to be tired of sth** estar harto de algo ❑ **tireless** adj incansable ❑ **tiresome** adj aburrido ❑ **tiring** adj cansado

tissue ['tɪʃuː] n tejido; (paper handkerchief) kleenex® m, pañuelo de papel ❑ **tissue paper** n papel m de seda

tit [tɪt] n (bird) herrerillo (común); **~ for tat** ojo por ojo

titbit ['tɪtbɪt] (BRIT) n = **tidbit**

title ['taɪtl] n título ❑ **title deed** n (LAW) título de propiedad, escritura ❑ **title role** n papel m principal

TM abbr = **trademark**

to
KEYWORD

[tuː] prep

1 (direction) a; **to go to France/Chicago/ school/the station** ir a Francia/Chicago/al colegio/a la estación; **to go to Claude's/the doctor's** ir a casa de Claude/al médico; **the road to San Francisco** la carretera de San Francisco

2 (as far as) hasta, a; **from here to Seattle** de aquí a or hasta Seattle; **to count to 10** contar hasta 10; **from 40 to 50 people** entre 40 y 50 personas

3 (with expressions of time): **ten to nine** diez para las nueve (LAm), las nueve menos diez (RPI, SP)

4 (for, of): **the key to the front door** la llave de la puerta principal; **she is secretary to the director** es la secretaria del director; **a letter to his wife** una carta a or para su esposa

5 (expressing indirect object) a; **to give sth to sb** dar algo a algn; **to talk to sb** hablar con algn; **to be a danger to sb** ser un peligro para algn; **to carry out repairs to sth** hacer reparaciones en algo

6 (in relation to): **3 goals to 2** 3 goles a 2; **30 miles to the gallon** ≈ 94 litros a los cien (kms)

7 (purpose, result): **to come to sb's aid** venir en auxilio or ayuda de algn; **to sentence sb to death** condenar a algn a muerte; **to my great surprise** con gran sorpresa mía ♦ with vb

1 (simple infin): **to go/eat** ir/comer

2 (following another vb): **to want/try/start to do** querer/intentar/empezar a hacer

3 (with vb omitted): **I don't want to** no quiero

4 (purpose, result) para; **I did it to help you** lo hice para ayudarte; **he came to see you** vino a verte

5 (equivalent to relative clause): **I have things to do** tengo cosas que hacer; **the main thing is to try** lo principal es intentarlo

6 (after adj etc): **ready to go** listo para irse; **too old to ...** demasiado viejo (como) para ... ♦ adv: **pull/push the door to** tirar de/ empujar la puerta

toad [təud] n sapo ❑ **toadstool** n hongo venenoso (LAm), seta venenosa (SP)

toast [təust] n (CULIN) pan m tostado (MEX), tostada (LAm exc MEX, SP); (drink, speech) brindis m ♦ vt (CULIN) tostar; (drink to) brindar por ❑ **toaster** n tostadora (LAm), tostador m (SP)

tobacco [tə'bækəu] n tabaco ❑ **tobacconist** n tabaquero(-a) (LAm), estanquero(-a) (SP) ❑ **tobacconist's (shop)** (BRIT) n tabaquería (LAm), estanco (SP)

toboggan [tə'bɔːgən] n trineo

today [tə'deɪ] adv, n (also fig) hoy m

toddler ['tɔːdlər] n niño(-a) pequeño(-a) (que empieza a caminar)

toe [təu] n dedo (del pie); (of shoe) punta; **to ~ the line** (fig) conformarse ❑ **toenail** n uña del pie

toffee ['tɔːfiː] (BRIT) n toffee m, caramelo masticable ❑ **toffee apple** n manzana acaramelada

together [tə'gɛðər] adv juntos; (at same time) al mismo tiempo, a la vez; **~ with** junto con

toil [tɔɪl] n trabajo duro, labor f ♦ vi trabajar duramente

toilet ['tɔɪlət] n inodoro; (BRIT: room) (cuarto de) baño, servicio ♦ cpd (soap etc) de aseo ❑ **toilet paper** n papel m higiénico ❑ **toiletries** npl artículos mpl de perfumería or tocador ❑ **toilet roll** (BRIT) n rollo de papel higiénico

token ['təukən] n (sign) señal f, muestra; (souvenir) recuerdo; (disk) ficha ♦ adj (strike, payment etc) simbólico; **book/record ~** (BRIT) vale m para comprar libros/discos; **gift ~** (BRIT) vale-regalo

Tokyo ['toukiou] n Tokio

told [tould] pt, pp of **tell**

tolerable ['tɑːlərəbəl] adj (bearable) soportable; (fairly good) pasable

tolerant ['tɑːlərənt] adj: **~ of** tolerante con

tolerate ['tɑːləreit] vt tolerar

toll [toul] n (of casualties) número de víctimas; (tax, charge) peaje m, cuota (MEX) ♦ vi (bell) doblar ❑ **toll-free** (US) adv: **to call toll-free** llamar gratuitamente

tomato [tə'meitou] (pl **~es**) n tomate m

tomb [tuːm] n tumba

tomboy ['tɑːm,bɔi] n marimacho m or f

tombstone ['tuːm,stoun] n lápida

tomcat ['tɑːmkæt] n gato (macho)

tomorrow [tə'mɔːrou] adv, n (also: fig) mañana; **the day after ~** pasado mañana; **~ morning** mañana por la mañana

ton [tʌn] n tonelada (US = 907 kg, BRIT = 1016 kg); (metric ton) tonelada métrica; **~s of ...** (inf) montones de ...

tone [toun] n tono ♦ vi (also: **~ in**) armonizar ▶ **tone down** vt (criticism) suavizar; (color) atenuar ▶ **tone up** vt (muscles) tonificar ❑ **tone-deaf** adj con mal oído

tongs [tɑːnz] npl (for coal) tenazas fpl; (curling tongs) tenacillas fpl

tongue [tʌŋ] n lengua; **~ in cheek** irónico ❑ **tongue-tied** adj (fig) mudo ❑ **tongue-twister** n trabalenguas m inv

tonic ['tɑːnik] n (MED) tónico; (also: **~ water**) (agua) tónica

tonight [tə'nait] adv, n esta noche

tonsil ['tɑːnsəl] n amígdala ❑ **tonsillitis** [,tɑːnsɪ'laitis] n amigdalitis f

too [tuː] adv (excessively) demasiado; (also) también; **~ much** demasiado; **~ many** demasiados(-as)

took [tuk] pt of **take**

tool [tuːl] n herramienta ❑ **toolbar** n barra de herramientas ❑ **tool box** n caja de herramientas

toot [tuːt] n pitido ♦ vi tocar el claxon or la bocina, pitar

tooth [tuːθ] (pl **teeth**) n (ANAT, TECH) diente m; (molar) muela ❑ **toothache** n dolor m de muelas ❑ **toothbrush** n cepillo de dientes ❑ **toothpaste** n dentífrico, pasta de dientes ❑ **toothpick** n palillo (de dientes), mondadientes m inv

top [tɑːp] n (of mountain) cumbre f, cima; (of tree) copa; (of head) coronilla; (of ladder, page) lo alto; (of table) superficie f; (of cupboard) parte f de arriba; (lid: of box) tapa; (: of bottle, jar) tapón m; (of list etc) cabeza; (toy) peonza; (garment) blusa; camiseta; (US AUT) capota ♦ adj de arriba; (in rank) principal, primero; (best) top, de primera ♦ vt (exceed) exceder; (be first in) encabezar; **on ~ of** (above) sobre, encima de; (in addition to) además de; **from ~ to bottom** de arriba abajo ▶ **top off** (US) vt llenar ▶ **top up** (BRIT) vt = **top off** ❑ **top floor** n último piso ❑ **top hat** n sombrero de copa ❑ **top-heavy** adj (object) mal equilibrado

topic ['tɑːpik] n tema m ❑ **topical** adj actual

top: ❑ **topless** adj (bather, bikini) topless inv ❑ **top-level** adj (talks) al más alto nivel ❑ **topmost** adj más alto

topple ['tɑːpəl] vt derribar ♦ vi caerse

top-secret adj de alto secreto

topsy-turvy [,tɑːpsi'tɜːrvi] adj al revés ♦ adv patas arriba

torch [tɔːrtʃ] n antorcha; (BRIT: electric) linterna

tore [tɔːr] pt of **tear²**

torment [n 'tɔːrmɛnt, vt tɔːr'mɛnt] n tormento ♦ vt atormentar; (fig: annoy) fastidiar

torn [tɔːrn] pp of **tear²**

torrent ['tɔːrənt] n torrente m

tortoise ['tɔːrtəs] n tortuga ❑ **tortoiseshell** adj de carey

torture ['tɔːrtʃər] n tortura ♦ vt torturar; (fig) atormentar

Tory ['tɔːri] (BRIT) adj, n (POL) conservador(a) m/f

toss [tɑːs] vt tirar, echar; (one's head) sacudir; **to ~ a coin** echar a pico o mona (MEX), echar a cara o cruz (LAm exc MEX, SP); **to ~ up for sth** jugar a pico o mona or a cara o cruz algo; **to ~ and turn** (in bed) dar vueltas

tot [tɑːt] n (child) nene(-a) m/f; (BRIT: drink) copita

total ['toutl] adj total, entero; (emphatic: failure etc) completo, total ♦ n total m, suma ♦ vt (add up) sumar; (amount to) ascender a ❑ **totally** adv totalmente

touch [tʌtʃ] n tacto; (contact) contacto ♦ vt tocar; (emotionally) conmover; **a ~ of** (fig) un poquito de; **to get in ~ with sb** ponerse en contacto con algn; **to lose ~** (friends) perder contacto ▶ **touch on** vt fus (topic) aludir (brevemente) a ▶ **touch up** vt (paint) retocar ❑ **touch-and-go** adj arriesgado ❑ **touchdown** n aterrizaje m; (on sea) amerizaje m; (US FOOTBALL) touchdown m, anotación f ❑ **touched** adj (moved) emocionado ❑ **touching** adj (moving) conmovedor(a) ❏ **touchline** n (SPORT) línea de banda ❏ **touchy** adj (person) susceptible

tough [tʌf] adj (material) resistente; (meat) duro; (problem etc) difícil; (policy, stance) inflexible; (person) fuerte ❏ **toughen** vt endurecer

toupee [tuːˈpeɪ] n peluca

tour ['tuər] n viaje m, vuelta; (also: **package ~**) viaje m organizado; (of town, museum) visita; (by band etc) gira ◆ vt recorrer, visitar ❏ **tour guide** n guía mf turístico(-a)

tourism ['tuərɪzəm] n turismo

tourist ['tuərɪst] n turista mf ◆ cpd turístico ❏ **tourist office** n oficina de turismo

tousled ['tauzəld] adj (hair) despeinado

tout [taut] vt (wares) ofrecer, pregonar; (BRIT: tickets) revender ◆ vi (BRIT): **to ~ for business** tratar de captar clientes ◆ n (BRIT: also: **ticket ~**) revendedor(a) m/f

tow [tou] vt remolcar; **"in ~"** (US AUT) "a remolque"

toward(s) [tɔːrd(z)] prep hacia; (attitude) respecto a, con; (purpose) para

towel ['tauəl] n toalla ❏ **toweling** (US) (BRIT **towelling**) n (fabric) felpa ❏ **towel rack** (US) (BRIT **towel rail**) n toallero

tower ['tauər] n torre f ❏ **tower block** (BRIT) n bloque m (de apartamentos) ❏ **towering** adj muy alto, imponente

town [taun] n ciudad f; **to go to ~** ir a la ciudad; (fig) echar la casa por la ventana ❏ **town center** (US) (BRIT **town centre**) n centro de la ciudad ❏ **town council** (BRIT) n ayuntamiento, municipio ❏ **town hall** n ayuntamiento ❏ **town plan** n plano de la ciudad ❏ **town planning** (BRIT) n urbanismo

towrope ['tou,roup] n cable m de remolque

tow truck (US) n grúa

toy [tɔɪ] n juguete m ▶ **toy with** vt fus jugar con; (idea) acariciar ❏ **toystore** (US) (BRIT **toyshop**) n juguetería

trace [treɪs] n rastro ◆ vt (draw) trazar, delinear; (locate) encontrar; (follow) seguir la pista de ❏ **tracing paper** n papel m de calco

track [træk] n (mark) huella, pista; (path: gen) camino, senda; (: of bullet etc) trayectoria; (: of suspect, animal) pista, rastro; (RAIL) vía; (SPORT) pista; (on tape, record) canción f; (US SCOL) agrupamiento de alumnos según su capacidad ◆ vt seguir la pista de; **to keep ~ of** mantenerse al tanto de, seguir ▶ **track down** vt (prey) seguir el rastro de; (sth lost) encontrar ❏ **track and field** n (SPORT)

atletismo ❏ **tracksuit** (BRIT) n pants mpl y sudadera (LAm), equipo de deportes (LAm), jogging m (RPl), chándal m (SP)

tract [trækt] n (GEO) región f

traction ['trækʃən] n (power) tracción f; **in ~** (MED) en tracción

tractor ['træktər] n tractor m

trade [treɪd] n comercio; (skill, job) oficio; (US: exchange) cambio ◆ vi negociar, comerciar ◆ vt (exchange): **to ~ sth (for sth)** cambiar algo (por algo) ▶ **trade in** vt (old car etc) entregar como parte del pago ❏ **trade fair** n feria comercial or de muestras ❏ **trademark** n marca (de fábrica) ❏ **trade name** n marca registrada ❏ **trader** n comerciante mf ❏ **tradesman** n (storekeeper) comerciante mf ❏ **trade union** (BRIT) n sindicato ❏ **trade unionist** (BRIT) n sindicalista mf

tradition [trəˈdɪʃən] n tradición f ❏ **traditional** adj tradicional

traffic ['træfɪk] n (gen, AUT) tráfico, circulación f ◆ vi: **to ~ in** (pej: liquor, drugs) traficar con or en ❏ **traffic circle** (US) n rotonda, glorieta ❏ **traffic cop** n agente mf de tránsito (MEX), guardia mf de tráfico (LAm exc MEX, SP) ❏ **traffic jam** n atasco ❏ **traffic lights** npl semáforo ❏ **traffic warden** (BRIT) n agente mf de tránsito (MEX), guardia mf de tráfico (LAm exc MEX, SP)

tragedy ['trædʒɪdi] n tragedia

tragic ['trædʒɪk] adj trágico

trail [treɪl] n (tracks) rastro, pista; (path) camino, sendero; (dust, smoke) estela ◆ vt (drag) arrastrar; (follow) seguir la pista de ◆ vi arrastrar; (in contest etc) ir perdiendo ▶ **trail behind** vi quedar a la zaga ❏ **trailer** n (AUT) remolque m; (US: caravan) cámper m or f (LAm), casa rodante (SC), caravana (SP); (FILM) avance m ❏ **trailer park** (US) n camping m para cámpers (LAm) or caravanas (SP) ❏ **trailer truck** (US) n tráiler m

train [treɪn] n tren m; (of dress) cola; (series) serie f ◆ vt (educate, teach skills to) formar; (sportsman) entrenar; (dog) adiestrar; (point: gun etc): **to ~ on** apuntar a ◆ vi (SPORT) entrenarse; (learn a skill): **to ~ as a teacher** estudiar magisterio or para profesor; **one's ~ of thought** el razonamiento de uno ❏ **trained** adj (worker) calificado (LAm), cualificado (SP); (animal) amaestrado ❏ **trainee** [treɪˈniː] n aprendiz(a) m/f ❏ **trainer** n (SPORT: coach) entrenador(a) m/f; (of animals) domador(a) m/f; (BRIT: shoe): **trainers** zapatillas fpl (de deporte) ❏ **training** n formación f; entrenamiento; **to**

be in training (SPORT) estar entrenando
❑ **training shoes** npl zapatillas fpl (de deporte)

trait [treɪt] n rasgo

traitor ['treɪtər] n traidor(a) m/f

tram [træm] (BRIT) n (also: ~car) tranvía m

tramp [træmp] n (person) vagabundo(-a); (US: inf: pej: woman) puta

trample ['træmpəl] vt: **to ~ (underfoot)** pisotear

trampoline ['træmpəliːn] n cama elástica

tranquil ['træŋkwɪl] adj tranquilo
❑ **tranquilizer** (US) (BRIT **tranquillizer**) n (MED) sedante m, tranquilizante m

transact [træn'zækt] vt (business) despachar
❑ **transaction** n transacción f, operación f

transfer [n 'trænsfər, vb træns'fɜːr] n (of employees) traslado; (of money, power) transferencia; (BRIT: picture, design) calcomanía; (: SPORT) traspaso ♦ vt trasladar; transferir; **to ~ the charges** (BRIT TEL) llamar por cobrar (MEX) or a cobro revertido (LAm exc MEX, SP)

transform [træns'fɔːrm] vt transformar

transfusion [træns'fjuːʒən] n transfusión f

transient ['trænʃənt] adj transitorio

transistor [træn'zɪstər] n (ELEC) transistor m
❑ **transistor radio** n transistor m

transit ['trænzɪt] n: **in ~** en tránsito

transitive ['trænzɪtɪv] adj (LING) transitivo

transit lounge (BRIT) n sala de tránsito

translate [trænz'leɪt] vt traducir
❑ **translation** n traducción f ❑ **translator** n traductor(a) m/f

transmit [trænz'mɪt] vt transmitir
❑ **transmitter** n transmisor m

transparency [træns'pɜːrnsɪ] n transparencia; (BRIT PHOT) diapositiva

transparent [træns'pɜːrənt] adj transparente

transpire [træns'paɪər] vi (turn out) resultar; (happen) ocurrir, suceder; **it ~d that ...** se supo que ...

transplant ['trænsplænt] n (MED) transplante m

transport [n 'trænspɔːrt, vt træns'pɔːrt] n (BRIT) transporte m; (car) carro (LAm), coche m (SP) ♦ vt transportar ❑ **transportation** [trænspər'teɪʃən] (US) n transporte m; **mass transportation** transporte m público ❑ **transport café** (BRIT) n bar m de carretera

transvestite [trænz'vestaɪt] n travesti mf

trap [træp] n (snare, trick) trampa; (carriage) carruaje m ♦ vt agarrar (LAm), coger (SP); (trick)

engañar; (confine) atrapar ❑ **trap door** n escotilla

trapeze [træ'piːz] n trapecio

trappings ['træpɪŋz] npl adornos mpl

trash [træʃ] n (US: garbage) basura; (nonsense) tonterías fpl; (pej): **the book/movie is ~** el libro/la película no vale nada ❑ **trash can** (US) n cubo or bote m (MEX) or tacho (SC) de la basura

travel ['trævəl] n el viajar ♦ vi viajar ♦ vt (distance) recorrer; **~s** npl (journeys) viajes mpl
❑ **travel agent** n agente mf de viajes
❑ **traveler** (US) (BRIT **traveller**) n viajero(-a)
❑ **traveler's check** (US) (BRIT **traveller's cheque**) n cheque m de viaje ❑ **traveling** (US) (BRIT **travelling**) n: **I love traveling** me encanta viajar ❑ **travel sickness** n mareo

trawler ['trɔːlər] n pesquero (de arrastre)

tray [treɪ] n bandeja, charola (MEX); (on desk) cajón m

treacherous ['tretʃərəs] adj traidor, traicionero; (dangerous) peligroso

treacle ['triːkəl] (BRIT) n melaza

tread [tred] (pt **trod**, pp **trodden**) n (step) paso, pisada; (sound) ruido de pasos; (of stair) escalón m; (of tire) banda de rodadura ♦ vi pisar ▸ **tread on** vt fus pisar

treason ['triːzən] n traición f

treasure ['treʒər] n tesoro ♦ vt (value: object, friendship) apreciar; (: memory) guardar

treasurer ['treʒərər] n tesorero(-a)

treasury ['treʒərɪ] n: **the T~** (US: also: **the T~ Department**) ≈ Hacienda, ≈ la Dirección General Impositiva (RPl)

treat [triːt] n (present) regalo ♦ vt tratar; **to ~ sb to sth** invitar a algn a algo

treatment ['triːtmənt] n tratamiento

treaty ['triːtɪ] n tratado

treble ['trebəl] adj triple ♦ vt triplicar ♦ vi triplicarse ❑ **treble clef** n (MUS) clave f de sol

tree [triː] n árbol m; **~ trunk** tronco (de árbol)

trek [trek] n (long journey) largo viaje m; (tiring walk) caminata

trellis ['trelɪs] n enrejado

tremble ['trembəl] vi temblar

tremendous [trɪ'mendəs] adj tremendo, enorme; (excellent) estupendo

tremor ['tremər] n temblor m; (also: **earth ~**) temblor m de tierra

trench [trentʃ] n zanja

trend [trend] n (tendency) tendencia; (of events) curso; (fashion) moda ❑ **trendy** adj de moda

trespass ['trespæs] *vi*: **to ~ on** entrar sin permiso en; **"no ~ing"** "prohibido el paso"

trestle ['tresəl] *n* caballete *m*

trial ['traɪəl] *n* (LAW) juicio, proceso; (*test: of machine etc*) prueba; **~s** *npl* (*hardships*) dificultades *fpl*; **by ~ and error** por ensayo y error

triangle ['traɪæŋgəl] *n* (MATH, MUS) triángulo

tribe [traɪb] *n* tribu *f*

tribunal [traɪˈbjuːnl] *n* tribunal *m*

tributary ['trɪbjuteri] *n* (*river*) afluente *m*

tribute ['trɪbjuːt] *n* homenaje *m*, tributo; **to pay ~** to rendir homenaje a

trick [trɪk] *n* (*skill, knack*) tino, truco; (*conjuring trick*) truco; (*joke*) broma; (CARDS) baza ♦ *vt* engañar; **to play a ~ on sb** gastar una broma a algn; **that should do the ~** a ver si funciona así ❑ **trickery** *n* engaño

trickle ['trɪkl] *n* (*of water etc*) goteo ♦ *vi* gotear

tricky ['trɪki] *adj* difícil; delicado

tricycle ['traɪsɪkəl] *n* triciclo

trifle ['traɪfəl] *n* bagatela; (BRIT CULIN) dulce de bizcocho borracho, gelatina, fruta y natillas, sopa inglesa (RPl) ♦ *adv*: **a ~ long** un poquito largo ❑ **trifling** *adj* insignificante

trigger ['trɪgər] *n* (*of gun*) gatillo ▶ **trigger off** *vt* desencadenar

trim [trɪm] *adj* (*house, garden*) en buen estado; (*person, figure*) esbelto ♦ *n* (*haircut etc*) recorte *m*; (*on car*) guarnición *f* ♦ *vt* (*neaten*) arreglar; (*cut*) recortar; (*decorate*) adornar; (NAUT: *a sail*) orientar ❑ **trimmings** *npl* (CULIN) guarnición *f*

trip [trɪp] *n* viaje *m*; (*excursion*) excursión *f*; (*stumble*) traspié *m* ♦ *vi* (*stumble*) tropezar; (*go lightly*) andar a paso ligero; **on a ~** de viaje ▶ **trip up** *vi* tropezar, caerse ♦ *vt* hacer tropezar or caer

tripe [traɪp] *n* (CULIN) panza (MEX), mondongo (*LAm exc MEX*), callos *mpl* (SP)

triple ['trɪpl] *adj* triple ❑ **triplets** ['trɪplɪts] *npl* trillizos(-as) *mpl/fpl* ❑ **triplicate** ['trɪplɪkɪt] *n*: **in triplicate** por triplicado

trite [traɪt] *adj* trillado

triumph ['traɪʌmf] *n* triunfo ♦ *vi*: **to ~ (over)** vencer ❑ **triumphant** [traɪˈʌmfənt] *adj* (*team etc*) vencedor(a); (*wave, return*) triunfal

trivia ['trɪviə] *npl* trivialidades *fpl*

trivial ['trɪviəl] *adj* insignificante; (*commonplace*) banal

trod [trɒd] *pt of* **tread**

trodden ['trɒdn] *pp of* **tread**

trolley ['trɒli] *n* (US: *also:* **~ car**) tranvía; (BRIT) carrito ❑ **trolley bus** *n* trolebús *m*

trombone [trɒmˈboun] *n* trombón *m*

troop [truːp] *n* grupo, banda; **~s** *npl* (MIL) tropas *fpl* ▶ **troop in/out** *vi* entrar/salir en tropel ❑ **trooping the color** (BRIT) *n* (*ceremony*) desfile *m* (*con la bandera*)

trophy ['troufi] *n* trofeo

tropical ['trɒpɪkəl] *adj* tropical

trot [trɒt] *n* trote *m* ♦ *vi* trotar; **on the ~** (BRIT: *fig*) seguidos(-as)

trouble ['trʌbəl] *n* problema *m*, dificultad *f*; (*worry*) preocupación *f*; (*bother, effort*) molestia, esfuerzo; (*unrest*) inquietud *f*; (MED): **stomach** *etc* **~** problemas *mpl* de estómago *etc* ♦ *vt* (*disturb*) molestar; (*worry*) preocupar, inquietar ♦ *vi*: **to ~ to do sth** molestarse en hacer algo; **~s** *npl* (POL etc) conflictos *mpl*; (*personal*) problemas *mpl*; **to be in ~** estar en un apuro; **it's no ~!** ¡no es molestia (ninguna)!; **what's the ~?** (*with broken* TV *etc*) ¿cuál es el problema?; (*doctor to patient*) ¿qué pasa? ❑ **troubled** *adj* (*person*) preocupado; (*country, epoch, life*) agitado ❑ **troublemaker** *n* alborotador(a) *m/f* ❑ **troubleshooter** *n* (*in conflict*) apagafuegos *mf inv*, experto(-a) (*en conflictos*) ❑ **troublesome** *adj* molesto

trough [trɒf] *n* (*also:* **drinking ~**) abrevadero; (*also:* **feeding ~**) comedero; (*depression*) depresión *f*

troupe [truːp] *n* grupo

trousers ['trauzərz] (BRIT) *npl* pantalones *mpl*; **short ~** pantalones *mpl* cortos

trousseau ['truːsou] (*pl* **~x** or **~s** ['truːsouz]) *n* ajuar *m*

trout [traut] *n inv* trucha

trowel ['trauəl] *n* (*of gardener*) desplantador *m*; (*of builder*) paleta

truant ['truːənt] *n*: **to play ~** (BRIT) hacer novillos, irse de pinta (MEX)

truce [truːs] *n* tregua

truck [trʌk] *n* (US: *vehicle*) camión *m*; (BRIT RAIL) vagón *m* ❑ **truck driver** (US) *n* camionero(-a) ❑ **trucker** (US) *n* camionero(-a) ❑ **truck farm** (US) *n* huerto

true [truː] *adj* verdadero; (*accurate*) exacto; (*genuine*) auténtico; (*faithful*) fiel; **to come ~** realizarse

truffle ['trʌfəl] *n* trufa

truly ['truːli] *adv* (*really*) realmente; (*truthfully*) verdaderamente; (*faithfully*): **yours ~** (*in letter*) le saluda atentamente

trump [trʌmp] *n* triunfo

trumpet ['trʌmpɪt] *n* trompeta

truncheon ['trʌntʃən] (BRIT) *n* macana (MEX), cachiporra (*LAm*), porra (SP)

trundle ['trʌndl] *vi*: **to ~ along** ir sin prisas

trunk [trʌŋk] *n* (*of tree, person*) tronco; (*of elephant*) trompa; (*case*) baúl *m*; (*US AUT*) cajuela (*MEX*), maletero (*LAm exc MEX, SP*), baúl (*RPl*); **~s** *npl* (*also*: **swimming ~s**) traje *m* de baño (*de hombre*) (*LAm*), malla (*RPl*) or bañador *m* (*SP*) (de hombre)

truss [trʌs] *vt*: **~ (up)** atar

trust [trʌst] *n* confianza; (*responsibility*) responsabilidad *f*; (*LAW*) fideicomiso ♦ *vt* (*rely on*) tener confianza en; (*hope*) esperar; (*entrust*): **to ~ sth to sb** confiar algo a algn; **to take sth on ~** fiarse de algo ❏ **trusted** *adj* de confianza ❏ **trustee** [trʌs'ti:] *n* (*LAW*) fideicomisario; (*of school*) administrador *m* ❏ **trustful** *adj* confiado ❏ **trusting** *adj* confiado ❏ **trustworthy** *adj* digno de confianza

truth [tru:θ, *pl* tru:ðz] *n* verdad *f* ❏ **truthful** *adj* veraz

try [traɪ] *n* tentativa, intento; (*RUGBY*) ensayo ♦ *vt* intentar; (*test: also*: **~ out**) probar, someter a prueba; (*LAW*) juzgar, procesar; (*strain: patience*) hacer perder ♦ *vi* probar; **to have a ~** probar suerte; **to ~ to do sth** intentar hacer algo; **~ again!** ¡vuelve a probar!; **~ harder!** ¡esfuérzate más!; **well, I tried** al menos lo intenté ▶ **try on** *vt* (*clothes*) probarse ▶ **try out** *vt* (*US*) (*team, role etc*) poner a prueba ❏ **trying** *adj* (*experience*) cansado; (*person*) pesado

tsar [zɑ:r] *n* zar *m*

T-shirt ['ti:ʃɜ:rt] *n* camiseta

T-square *n* regla T

tub [tʌb] *n* cubeta (*MEX, SP*), balde *m* (*LAm*); (*US: bath*) tina (*LAm*), bañadera (*RPl*), bañera (*SP*)

tube [tu:b] *n* tubo; (*for tire*) cámara de aire; **the ~** (*US: inf: television*) la tele (*inf*); (*BRIT: underground*) metro, subte *m* (*RPl*)

tuberculosis [tu,bɜ:rkjə'lousɪs] *n* tuberculosis *f inv*

tube station (*BRIT*) *n* estación *f* de metro or (*RPl*) subte

tubular ['tu:bjulər] *adj* tubular

TUC (*BRIT*) *n abbr* (= Trades Union Congress) federación nacional de sindicatos

tuck [tʌk] *vt* (*put*) poner ▶ **tuck away** *vt* (*money*) guardar; (*building*): **to be tucked away** esconderse, ocultarse ▶ **tuck in** *vt* (*shirt, blouse*) meter dentro; (*child*) arropar ♦ *vi* (*BRIT: eat*) comer con apetito ▶ **tuck up** *vt* (*skirt, sleeves*) remangar; (*BRIT: child*) arropar ❏ **tuck shop** *n* (*BRIT SCOL*) puesto de chucherías

Tuesday ['tu:zdɪ] *n* martes *m inv*

tuft [tʌft] *n* mechón *m*; (*of grass etc*) manojo

tug [tʌg] *n* (*ship*) remolcador *m* ♦ *vt* tirar de ❏ **tug-of-war** *n* juego del tira y afloja (*con una cuerda*); (*fig*) estira (*MEX*) or tira (*LAm exc MEX, SP*) y afloja *m*

tuition [tu'ɪʃən] *n* (*US: school fees*) matrícula; (*BRIT*) enseñanza; (*: private tuition*) clases *fpl* particulares

tulip ['tu:lɪp] *n* tulipán *m*

tumble ['tʌmbəl] *n* (*fall*) caída ♦ *vi* caer; **to ~ to sth** (*inf*) caer en la cuenta de algo ❏ **tumbledown** *adj* destartalado ❏ **tumble dryer** (*BRIT*) *n* secadora

tumbler ['tʌmblər] *n* (*glass*) vaso

tummy ['tʌmi] (*inf*) *n* barriga

tumor (*US*) ['tu:mər] (*BRIT* **tumour**) *n* tumor *m*

tuna ['tu:nə] *n inv* (*also*: **~ fish**) atún *m*

tune [tu:n] *n* melodía ♦ *vt* (*MUS*) afinar; (*RADIO, TV, AUT*) sintonizar; **to be in/out of ~** (*instrument*) estar afinado/desafinado; (*singer*) cantar afinadamente/desafinar; **to be in/out of ~ with** (*fig*) estar de acuerdo en/ desacuerdo con ▶ **tune in** *vi*: **to tune in (to)** (*RADIO, TV*) sintonizar (con) ▶ **tune up** *vi* (*musician*) afinar (su instrumento) ❏ **tuneful** *adj* melodioso ❏ **tuner** *n*: **piano tuner** afinador(a) *m/f* de pianos

tunic ['tu:nɪk] *n* túnica

Tunisia [tu:'ni:zə] *n* Túnez *m*

tunnel ['tʌnl] *n* túnel *m*; (*in mine*) galería ♦ *vi* abrir un túnel/una galería

turban ['tɜ:rbən] *n* turbante *m*

turbulent ['tɜ:rbjulənt] *adj* turbulento

tureen [tu'ri:n] *n* sopera

turf [tɜ:rf] *n* césped *m*; (*BRIT: clod*) tepe *m* ♦ *vt* cubrir de césped ❏ **turf out** (*BRIT: inf*) *vt* echar a la calle

Turk [tɜ:rk] *n* turco(-a)

Turkey ['tɜ:rki] *n* Turquía

turkey ['tɜ:rki] *n* pavo, guajolote *m* (*MEX*)

Turkish ['tɜ:rkɪʃ] *adj*, *n* turco

turmoil ['tɜ:rmɔɪl] *n*: **in ~** revuelto

turn [tɜ:rn] *n* turno; (*in road*) curva; (*of mind, events*) rumbo; (*THEATER*) número; (*BRIT MED*) ataque *m* ♦ *vt* girar, volver; (*collar, steak*) dar la vuelta a; (*page*) pasar; (*change*): **to ~ sth into** convertir algo en ♦ *vi* volver; (*person: look back*) volverse; (*reverse direction*) dar la vuelta; (*milk*) cortarse; (*become*): **to ~ nasty/forty** ponerse feo/cumplir los cuarenta; **a good ~** un favor; **it gave me quite a ~** me dio un susto; **"no left ~"** (*AUT*) "prohibido girar a la izquierda"; **it's your ~** te toca a ti; **in ~** por turnos; **to take ~s (at)** turnarse (en) ▶ **turn around** or (*BRIT*) **round** *vi* volverse; (*rotate*)

girar ► **turn away** vi apartar la vista ♦ vi
rechazar ► **turn back** vi volverse atrás ♦ vt
hacer retroceder; (clock) retrasar ► **turn
down** vt (refuse) rechazar; (reduce) bajar;
(fold) doblar ► **turn in** vi (inf: go to bed)
acostarse ♦ vt (fold) doblar hacia dentro
► **turn off** vi (from road) desviarse ♦ vt (light,
radio etc) apagar; (faucet) cerrar; (engine)
parar ► **turn on** vt (light, radio etc) prender
(LAm), encender (SP); (faucet) abrir; (engine)
poner en marcha ► **turn out** vt (light, gas)
apagar; (produce) producir ♦ vi (voters)
concurrir; **to turn out to be ...** resultar ser ...
► **turn over** vi (person) volverse ♦ vt (object)
dar la vuelta a; (page) volver ► **turn up** vi
(person) llegar, presentarse; (lost object)
aparecer ♦ vt (gen) subir □ **turning** n (in
road) vuelta □ **turning point** n (fig)
momento decisivo

turnip ['tɜːrnɪp] n nabo

turn: □ **turnout** n concurrencia
□ **turnover** n (COMM: amount of money)
volumen m de ventas; (: of goods)
movimiento □ **turnpike** (US) n autopista de
peaje □ **turn signal** (US) n direccional f
(MEX), intermitente m (LAm exc MEX, SP)
□ **turnstile** n torniquete m □ **turntable** n
plato □ **turn-up** (BRIT) n (on pants) vuelta

turpentine ['tɜːrpəntaɪn] n (also: **turps**)
trementina

turquoise ['tɜːrkwɔɪz] n (stone) turquesa
♦ adj turquesa

turret ['tʌrɪt] n torreón m

turtle ['tɜːrtl] n tortuga □ **turtleneck
(sweater)** n (US) suéter m (LAm) or jersey m
(SP) de cuello alto; (BRIT) suéter m or jersey m
de cuello vuelto or de tortuga

tusk [tʌsk] n colmillo

tutor ['tuːtər] n profesor(a) m/f (particular)
□ **tutorial** [tuːˈtɔːriəl] n (SCOL) seminario

tuxedo [tʌkˈsiːdou] (US) n esmoquin m

TV [ˌtiːˈviː] n abbr (= television) tele f

twang [twæŋ] n (of instrument) punteado; (of
voice) timbre m nasal

tweezers ['twiːzərz] npl pinzas fpl

twelfth [twelfθ] num duodécimo

twelve [twelv] num doce; **at ~ o'clock**
(midday) a mediodía; (midnight) a
medianoche

twentieth ['twentiθ] adj vigésimo

twenty ['twenti] num veinte

24/7 [ˌtwentiˌfɔːrˈsevən] adv abbr (= 24 hours a
day, 7 days a week) 24 horas al día, 7 días a la
semana

twice [twaɪs] adv dos veces; **~ as much** dos
veces más

twiddle ['twɪdl] vi: **to ~ (with) sth** dar vueltas
a algo; **to ~ one's thumbs** (fig) estar de
brazos cruzados

twig [twɪg] n ramita

twilight ['twaɪlaɪt] n crepúsculo

twin [twɪn] adj, n gemelo(-a) ♦ vt hermanar
□ **twin-bedded room** (BRIT) n habitación f
con camas gemelas

twine [twaɪn] n bramante m ♦ vi (plant)
enroscarse

twinge [twɪndʒ] n (of pain) punzada; (of
conscience) remordimiento

twinkle ['twɪŋkəl] vi centellear; (eyes)
brillar

twirl [twɜːrl] vt dar vueltas a ♦ vi dar
vueltas

twist [twɪst] n (action) torsión f; (in road, coil)
vuelta; (in wire, flex) doblez f; (in story) giro ♦ vt
torcer; (weave) trenzar; (roll around) enrollar;
(fig) deformar ♦ vi serpentear

twister ['twɪstər] (US) n (tornado) huracán
m

twit [twɪt] (BRIT: inf) n imbécil

twitch [twɪtʃ] n (pull) tirón m; (nervous) tic m
♦ vi crisparse

two [tuː] num dos; **to put ~ and ~ together**
(fig) atar cabos □ **two-bit** (US) adj de poca
monta □ **two-door** adj (AUT) de dos puertas
□ **two-faced** adj (pej: person) falso
□ **twofold** adv: **to increase twofold**
doblarse □ **two-piece (suit)** n traje m de
dos piezas □ **two-piece (swimsuit)** n
bikini m, dos piezas m inv □ **twosome** n
(people) pareja □ **two-way** adj: **two-way
traffic** circulación f de doble sentido

tycoon [taɪˈkuːn] n: **(business) ~** magnate
m

type [taɪp] n (category) tipo, género; (model)
tipo; (TYP) tipo, letra ♦ vt (letter etc) escribir a
máquina □ **type-cast** adj (actor) encasillado
□ **typeface** n letra □ **typescript** n texto
mecanografiado □ **typewriter** n máquina
de escribir □ **typewritten** adj
mecanografiado

typhoid ['taɪfɔɪd] n tifoidea

typical ['tɪpɪkəl] adj típico

typing ['taɪpɪŋ] n mecanografía

typist ['taɪpɪst] n mecanógrafo(-a)

tyrant ['taɪərənt] n tirano(-a)

tyre ['taɪər] (BRIT) n neumático, llanta (LAm)

Uu

U-bend ['ju:,bend] (BRIT) n (AUT, in pipe) sifón m

udder ['ʌdər] n ubre f

UFO [ju:ɛf'ou] n abbr (= unidentified flying object) OVNI m

ugh [ɜːh] excl ¡uf!

ugly ['ʌgli] adj feo; (dangerous) peligroso

UHT (BRIT) abbr (= UHT milk) leche f UHT or uperizada

UK n abbr = **United Kingdom**

ulcer ['ʌlsər] n úlcera; (mouth ulcer) llaga

Ulster ['ʌlstər] n Ulster m

ulterior [ʌl'tɪriər] adj: ~ **motive** segundas intenciones fpl

ultimate ['ʌltɪmət] adj último, final; (greatest) máximo ❑ **ultimately** adv (in the end) por último, al final; (fundamentally) a fin de cuentas

ultra- ['ʌltrə] prefix ultra-

umbilical cord [ʌm'bɪlɪkəl,kɔːrd] n cordón m umbilical

umbrella [ʌm'brelə] n paraguas m inv; (for sun) sombrilla

umpire ['ʌmpaɪər] n árbitro(-a)

umpteen ['ʌmpti:n] adj enésimos(-as) ❑ **umpteenth** adj: **for the umpteenth time** por enésima vez

UN n abbr (= United Nations) ONU f

unable [ʌn'eɪbəl] adj: **to be ~ to do sth** no poder hacer algo

unaccompanied [ʌnə'kʌmpənid] adj no acompañado; (song) sin acompañamiento

unaccustomed [ʌnə'kʌstəmd] adj: **to be ~ to** no estar acostumbrado a

unanimous [ju:'nænəməs] adj unánime

unarmed [ʌn'ɑːrmd] adj (defenseless) inerme; (without weapon) desarmado

unattached [ʌnə'tætʃt] adj (person) soltero y sin compromiso; (part etc) suelto

unattended [ʌnə'tendid] adj desatendido

unattractive [ʌnə'træktɪv] adj poco atractivo

unauthorized [ʌn'ɔːθəraɪzd] adj no autorizado

unavoidable [ʌnə'vɔɪdəbəl] adj inevitable

unaware [ʌnə'weər] adj: **to be ~ of** ignorar ❑ **unawares** adv de improviso

unbalanced [ʌn'bælənst] adj (report) poco objetivo; (mentally) trastornado

unbearable [ʌn'berəbəl] adj insoportable

unbeatable [ʌn'bi:təbəl] adj (team) invencible; (price) inmejorable; (quality) insuperable

unbelievable [ʌnbɪ'li:vəbəl] adj increíble

unbend [ʌn'bend] vi (relax) relajarse ♦ vt (wire) enderezar

unbiased [ʌn'baɪəst] adj imparcial

unborn [ʌn'bɔːrn] adj no nacido

unbroken [ʌn'broukən] adj (seal) intacto; (series) continuo; (record) no batido; (spirit) indómito

unbutton [ʌn'bʌtn] vt desabrochar

uncalled-for [ʌn'kɔːldfɔːr] adj gratuito, inmerecido

uncanny [ʌn'kæni] adj extraño

unceremonious [ʌnserɪ'mouniəs] adj (abrupt, rude) brusco, hosco

uncertain [ʌn'sɜːrtn] adj incierto; (indecisive) indeciso

unchanged [ʌn'tʃeɪndʒd] adj igual, sin cambios

uncivilized [ʌn'sɪvɪlaɪzd] adj inculto; (fig: behavior etc) bárbaro; (hour) inoportuno

uncle ['ʌŋkəl] n tío

uncomfortable [ʌn'kʌmfərtəbəl] adj incómodo; (uneasy) inquieto

uncommon [ʌn'kɑːmən] adj poco común, raro

uncompromising [ʌn'kɑːmprəmaɪzɪŋ] adj intransigente

unconcerned [ʌnkən'sɜːrnd] adj indiferente, despreocupado

unconditional [ʌnkən'dɪʃənl] adj incondicional

unconscious [ʌn'kɑːnʃəs] adj inconsciente, sin sentido; (unaware): **to be ~ of** no darse cuenta de ♦ n: **the ~** el inconsciente

uncontrollable [ʌnkən'troubəbəl] adj (child etc) incontrolable; (temper) indomable; (laughter) incontenible

unconventional [ʌnkən'venʃənl] adj poco convencional

uncouth [ʌn'ku:θ] adj grosero, inculto

uncover [ʌn'kʌvər] vt descubrir; (take lid off) destapar

undecided [ʌndɪ'saɪdɪd] adj (character) indeciso; (question) no resuelto

under ['ʌndər] prep debajo de; (less than) menos de; (according to) según, de acuerdo con; (sb's leadership) bajo ♦ adv debajo, abajo; **~ there** allí abajo; **~ repair** en reparación

under... ['ʌndər] prefix sub □ **underage** adj menor de edad; (drinking etc) por menores (de edad) □ **underbrush** (US) n maleza

❑ **undercarriage** (BRIT) n (AVIAT) tren m de aterrizaje ❑ **undercharge** vt cobrar de menos ❑ **underclothes** npl ropa interior ❑ **undercoat** n (paint) primera mano ❑ **undercover** adj secreto ❑ **undercurrent** n (fig) trasfondo ❑ **undercut** vt irreg vender más barato que ❑ **underdeveloped** adj subdesarrollado ❑ **underdog** n desvalido(-a) ❑ **underdone** adj (CULIN) sancochado (MEX), poco cocido (LAm exc MEX) or hecho (SP) ❑ **underestimate** vt subestimar ❑ **underexposed** adj (PHOT) subexpuesto ❑ **underfed** adj desnutrido ❑ **underfoot** adv debajo de los pies ❑ **undergo** vt irreg sufrir; (treatment) recibir ❑ **undergraduate** n estudiante mf (universitario) ❑ **underground** n (POL) movimiento clandestino; (BRIT: railroad) metro, subte m (RPI) ♦ adj (parking lot) subterráneo ♦ adv (work) en la clandestinidad ❑ **underhand(ed)** adj (fig) socarrón, turbio ❑ **underlie** vt irreg (fig) subyacer tras or bajo ❑ **underline** vt subrayar ❑ **undermine** vt socavar, minar ❑ **underneath** [ʌndərˈniːθ] adv debajo ♦ prep debajo de, bajo ❑ **underpaid** adj mal pagado ❑ **underpants** npl (for men) calzoncillos mpl; (US: for women) calzones mpl (LAm), bombachas fpl (RPI), bragas fpl (SP) ❑ **underpass** n (for cars) paso a desnivel; (for pedestrians) paso subterráneo ❑ **underprivileged** adj desfavorecido ❑ **underrate** vt menospreciar, subestimar ❑ **undershirt** (US) n camiseta ❑ **undershorts** (US) npl calzoncillos mpl ❑ **underside** n parte f inferior ❑ **underskirt** (BRIT) n enaguas fpl

understand [ʌndərˈstænd] vt, vi entender, comprender; (assume) tener entendido ❑ **understandable** adj comprensible ❑ **understanding** adj comprensivo ♦ n comprensión f, entendimiento; (agreement) acuerdo

understatement [ˈʌndərˌsteɪtmənt] n modestia (excesiva); **that's an ~!** ¡eso es decir poco!

understood [ʌndərˈstʊd] pt, pp of **understand** ♦ adj (agreed) acordado; (implied): **it is ~ that** se sobreentiende que

understudy [ˈʌndərˌstʌdi] n suplente mf

undertake [ʌndərˈteɪk] vt emprender; **to ~ to do sth** comprometerse a hacer algo

undertaker [ˈʌndərˌteɪkər] n (employee) empleado(-a) de una funeraria

undertaking [ˈʌndərˌteɪkɪŋ] n empresa; (promise) promesa

under: ❑ **undertone** n: **in an undertone** en voz baja ❑ **underwater** adv bajo el agua ♦ adj submarino ❑ **underwear** n ropa interior ❑ **underworld** n (of crime) hampa ❑ **underwriter** n (INSURANCE) asegurador(a) m/f

undesirable [ʌndɪˈzaɪrəbəl] adj (person) indeseable; (thing) poco aconsejable

undo [ʌnˈduː] vt (laces) desatar; (button etc) desabrochar; (spoil) deshacer ❑ **undoing** n ruina, perdición f

undoubted [ʌnˈdaʊtɪd] adj indudable

undress [ʌnˈdrɛs] vi desnudarse

undulating [ˈʌndʒuleɪtɪŋ] adj ondulante

unduly [ʌnˈduːli] adv excesivamente, demasiado

unearth [ʌnˈɜːrθ] vt desenterrar

unearthly [ʌnˈɜːrθli] adj (hour) inverosímil

uneasy [ʌnˈiːzi] adj intranquilo, preocupado; (feeling) desagradable; (peace) inseguro

uneducated [ʌnˈedʒukeɪtɪd] adj ignorante, inculto

unemployed [ʌnɪmˈplɔɪd] adj desempleado ♦ npl: **the ~** los desempleados

unemployment [ʌnɪmˈplɔɪmənt] n desempleo ❑ **unemployment line** (US) n cola de desempleados (LAm) or del paro (SP)

unending [ʌnˈendɪŋ] adj interminable

unerring [ʌnˈɜːrɪŋ] adj infalible

uneven [ʌnˈiːvn] adj desigual; (road etc) lleno de baches

unexpected [ʌnɪksˈpektɪd] adj inesperado ❑ **unexpectedly** adv inesperadamente

unfailing [ʌnˈfeɪlɪŋ] adj (support) indefectible; (energy) inagotable

unfair [ʌnˈfeər] adj: **~ (to sb)** injusto (con algn)

unfaithful [ʌnˈfeɪθfəl] adj infiel

unfamiliar [ʌnfəˈmɪljər] adj extraño, desconocido; **to be ~ with** desconocer

unfashionable [ʌnˈfæʃənəbəl] adj pasado or fuera de moda

unfasten [ʌnˈfæsən] vt (knot) desatar; (dress) desabrochar; (open) abrir

unfavorable (US) adj **unfavourable** (BRIT) adj desfavorable

unfeeling [ʌnˈfiːlɪŋ] adj insensible

unfinished [ʌnˈfɪnɪʃt] adj inacabado, sin terminar

unfit [ʌnˈfɪt] adj bajo de forma; (incompetent): **~ (for)** incapaz (de); **~ for work** no apto para trabajar

unfold [ʌnˈfəʊld] vt desdoblar ♦ vi abrirse

unforeseen [ʌnfɔːˈsiːn] adj imprevisto

unforgettable [ʌnfərˈgetəbəl] adj inolvidable

unfortunate [ʌnˈfɔːrtʃənət] adj desgraciado; (event, remark) inoportuno ❑ **unfortunately** adv desgraciadamente

unfounded [ʌnˈfaʊndɪd] adj infundado

unfriendly [ʌnˈfrendli] adj antipático; (behavior, remark) hostil, poco amigable

ungainly [ʌnˈgeɪnli] adj desgarbado

unglued [ʌnˈgluːd] adj: **to come ~** despegarse; (US: fig) fracasar

ungodly [ʌnˈgɑːdli] adj: **at an ~ hour** a una hora inverosímil

ungrateful [ʌnˈgreɪtfəl] adj desagradecido, ingrato

unhappiness [ʌnˈhæpɪnɪs] n tristeza, desdicha

unhappy [ʌnˈhæpi] adj (sad) triste; (unfortunate) desgraciado; (childhood) infeliz; **~ about/with** (arrangements etc) poco contento con, descontento de

unharmed [ʌnˈhɑːrmd] adj ileso

unhealthy [ʌnˈhelθi] adj (place) malsano; (person) enfermizo; (fig: interest) morboso

unheard-of adj inaudito, sin precedente

unhurt [ʌnˈhɜːrt] adj ileso

unidentified [ʌnaɪˈdentɪfaɪd] adj no identificado, sin identificar; see also **UFO**

uniform [ˈjuːnɪfɔːrm] n uniforme m ♦ adj uniforme

unify [ˈjuːnɪfaɪ] vt unificar, unir

uninhabited [ʌnɪnˈhæbɪtɪd] adj desierto

unintentional [ʌnɪnˈtenʃənl] adj involuntario

union [ˈjuːnjən] n unión f; (BRIT: also: **trade ~**) sindicato ♦ cpd (BRIT) sindical ❑ **Union Jack** n bandera del Reino Unido

unique [juːˈniːk] adj único

unison [ˈjuːnɪsən] n: **in ~** (speak, reply, sing) al unísono

unit [ˈjuːnɪt] n unidad f; (section: of furniture etc) elemento; (team) grupo; **kitchen ~** módulo de cocina

unite [juːˈnaɪt] vt unir ♦ vi unirse ❑ **united** adj unido; (effort) conjunto ❑ **United Kingdom** n Reino Unido ❑ **United Nations (Organization)** n Naciones fpl Unidas ❑ **United States (of America)** n Estados mpl Unidos

unit trust (BRIT) n bono fiduciario

unity [ˈjuːnɪti] n unidad f

universe [ˈjuːnɪvɜːrs] n universo

university [juːnɪˈvɜːrsɪti] n universidad f

unjust [ʌnˈdʒʌst] adj injusto

unkempt [ʌnˈkempt] adj (appearance) descuidado; (hair) despeinado

unkind [ʌnˈkaɪnd] adj poco amable; (behavior, comment) cruel

unknown [ʌnˈnəʊn] adj desconocido

unlawful [ʌnˈlɔːfəl] adj ilegal, ilícito

unleaded [ʌnˈledɪd] adj (gas, fuel) sin plomo

unless [ʌnˈles] conj a menos que; **~ he comes** a menos que venga; **~ otherwise stated** salvo indicación contraria

unlike [ʌnˈlaɪk] adj (not alike) distinto de or a; (not like) poco propio de ♦ prep a diferencia de

unlikely [ʌnˈlaɪkli] adj improbable; (unexpected) inverosímil

unlimited [ʌnˈlɪmɪtɪd] adj ilimitado

unlisted [ʌnˈlɪstɪd] (US) adj (TEL) que no figura en la guía

unload [ʌnˈləʊd] vt descargar

unlock [ʌnˈlɑːk] vt abrir (con llave)

unlucky [ʌnˈlʌki] adj desgraciado; (object, number) que da mala suerte; **to be ~** tener mala suerte

unmarried [ʌnˈmærɪd] adj soltero

unmistak(e)able [ʌnmɪsˈteɪkəbəl] adj inconfundible

unnatural [ʌnˈnætʃərəl] adj (gen) antinatural; (manner) afectado; (habit) perverso

unnecessary [ʌnˈnesəseri] adj innecesario, inútil

unnoticed [ʌnˈnəʊtɪst] adj: **to go** or **pass ~** pasar desapercibido

UNO [ˈjuːnəʊ] n abbr (= United Nations Organization) ONU f

unobtainable [ʌnəbˈteɪnəbəl] adj imposible de conseguir; (TEL) desconectado

unobtrusive [ʌnəbˈtruːsɪv] adj discreto

unofficial [ʌnəˈfɪʃəl] adj no oficial; (news) sin confirmar

unorthodox [ʌnˈɔːrθədɑːks] adj poco ortodoxo or convencional

unpack [ʌnˈpæk] vi deshacer el equipaje ♦ vt deshacer

unpalatable [ʌnˈpælətəbəl] adj incomible; (truth) desagradable

unparalleled [ʌnˈpærəleld] adj (unequalled) incomparable

unpleasant [ʌnˈplezənt] adj (disagreeable) desagradable; (person, manner) antipático

unplug [ʌnˈplʌg] vt desenchufar, desconectar

unpopular [ʌnˈpɑːpjələr] *adj* impopular, poco popular

unprecedented [ʌnˈprɛsɪdɛntɪd] *adj* sin precedentes

unpredictable [ʌnprɪˈdɪktəbəl] *adj* imprevisible

unprofessional [ʌnprəˈfɛʃənl] *adj* (*attitude, conduct*) poco ético

unqualified [ʌnˈkwɑːlɪfaɪd] *adj* sin título, no calificado (*LAm*); (*success*) total

unquestionably [ʌnˈkwɛstʃənəbli] *adv* indiscutiblemente

unreal [ʌnˈriːəl] *adj* irreal; (*extraordinary*) increíble

unrealistic [ʌnriːəˈlɪstɪk] *adj* poco realista

unreasonable [ʌnˈriːzənəbəl] *adj* irrazonable; (*demand*) excesivo

unrelated [ʌnrɪˈleɪtɪd] *adj* sin relación; (*family*) no emparentado

unreliable [ʌnrɪˈlaɪəbəl] *adj* (*person*) informal; (*machine*) poco fiable

unremitting [ʌnrɪˈmɪtɪŋ] *adj* constante

unreservedly [ʌnrɪˈzɜːrvɪdli] *adv* sin reserva

unrest [ʌnˈrɛst] *n* inquietud *f*, malestar *m*; (*POL*) disturbios *mpl*

unroll [ʌnˈroʊl] *vt* desenrollar

unruly [ʌnˈruːli] *adj* indisciplinado

unsafe [ʌnˈseɪf] *adj* peligroso

unsaid [ʌnˈsɛd] *adj*: **to leave sth ~** dejar algo sin decir

unsatisfactory [ʌnsætɪsˈfæktəri] *adj* poco satisfactorio

unsavory (*US*) [ʌnˈseɪvəri] (*BRIT* **unsavoury**) *adj* (*fig*) repugnante

unscrew [ʌnˈskruː] *vt* destornillar; (*lid*) desenroscar

unscrupulous [ʌnˈskruːpjʊləs] *adj* sin escrúpulos

unsettled [ʌnˈsɛtld] *adj* inquieto, intranquilo; (*weather*) variable

unshaven [ʌnˈʃeɪvən] *adj* sin afeitar or (*MEX*) rasurar

unsightly [ʌnˈsaɪtli] *adj* feo

unskilled [ʌnˈskɪld] *adj* (*work*) no especializado; (*worker*) no calificado (*LAm*) or cualificado (*SP*)

unspeakable [ʌnˈspiːkəbəl] *adj* indecible; (*awful*) incalificable

unstable [ʌnˈsteɪbəl] *adj* inestable

unsteady [ʌnˈstɛdi] *adj* inestable

unstuck [ʌnˈstʌk] *adj*: **to come ~** despegarse; (*BRIT: fig*) fracasar

unsuccessful [ʌnsəkˈsɛsfəl] *adj* (*attempt*) infructuoso; (*writer, proposal*) sin éxito; **to be ~** (*in attempting sth*) no tener éxito, fracasar
❏ **unsuccessfully** *adv* en vano, sin éxito

unsuitable [ʌnˈsuːtəbəl] *adj* inapropiado; (*time*) inoportuno

unsure [ʌnˈʃʊər] *adj* inseguro, poco seguro

unsuspecting [ʌnsəsˈpɛktɪŋ] *adj* desprevenido, confiado

unsympathetic [ʌnsɪmpəˈθɛtɪk] *adj* poco comprensivo; (*unlikeable*) antipático

unthinkable [ʌnˈθɪŋkəbəl] *adj* inconcebible, impensable

untidy [ʌnˈtaɪdi] *adj* (*room*) desordenado; (*appearance*) desaliñado

untie [ʌnˈtaɪ] *vt* desatar

until [ənˈtɪl] *prep* hasta ♦ *conj* hasta que; **~ he comes** hasta que venga; **~ now** hasta ahora; **~ then** hasta entonces

untimely [ʌnˈtaɪmli] *adj* inoportuno; (*death*) prematuro

untold [ʌnˈtoʊld] *adj* (*story*) nunca contado; (*suffering*) indecible; (*wealth*) incalculable

untoward [ʌnˈtɔːrd] *adj* adverso

unused [ʌnˈjuːzd] *adj* sin usar

unusual [ʌnˈjuːʒəl] *adj* insólito, poco común; (*exceptional*) inusitado

unveil [ʌnˈveɪl] *vt* (*statue*) descubrir

unwanted [ʌnˈwɑːntɪd] *adj* (*clothing*) viejo; (*pregnancy*) no deseado

unwelcome [ʌnˈwɛlkəm] *adj* inoportuno; (*news*) desagradable

unwell [ʌnˈwɛl] *adj*: **to be/feel ~** estar indispuesto/sentirse mal

unwieldy [ʌnˈwiːldi] *adj* difícil de manejar

unwilling [ʌnˈwɪlɪŋ] *adj*: **to be ~ to do sth** estar poco dispuesto a hacer algo
❏ **unwillingly** *adv* de mala gana

unwind [ʌnˈwaɪnd] *irreg vt* desenvolver ♦ *vi* (*relax*) relajarse

unwise [ʌnˈwaɪz] *adj* imprudente

unwitting [ʌnˈwɪtɪŋ] *adj* inconsciente

unworthy [ʌnˈwɜːrði] *adj* indigno

unwrap [ʌnˈræp] *vt* abrir, desenvolver

unwritten [ʌnˈrɪtn] *adj* (*agreement*) tácito, verbal; (*rules, law*) no escrito

---

up
KEYWORD

[ʌp] *prep*: **to go/be up sth** subir/estar subido en algo; **he went up the stairs/the hill** subió las escaleras/la colina; **we walked/climbed**

up the hill subimos la colina; **they live further up the street** viven más arriba en la calle; **go up that road and turn left** sigue por esa calle y gira a la izquierda
♦ *adv*

1 (*upwards, higher*) más arriba; **up in the mountains** en lo alto (de la montaña); **put it a bit higher up** ponlo un poco más arriba *or* alto; **up there** ahí *or* allí arriba; **up above** en lo alto, por encima, arriba

2: **to be up** (*out of bed*) estar levantado; (*prices, level*) haber subido

3: **up to** (*as far as*) hasta; **up to now** hasta ahora *or* la fecha

4: **to be up to** (*depending on*): **it's up to you** depende de ti; **he's not up to it** (*job, task etc*) no es capaz de hacerlo; **his work is not up to the required standard** su trabajo no da la talla; (*inf: be doing*): **what is he up to?** ¿que estará tramando?
♦ *n*: **ups and downs** altibajos *mpl*

upbringing [ˈʌpbrɪŋɪŋ] *n* educación *f*

update [ʌpˈdeɪt] *vt* poner al día

upgrade [ʌpˈɡreɪd] *vt* (*house*) modernizar; (*employee*) ascender

upheaval [ʌpˈhiːvəl] *n* trastornos *mpl*; (*POL*) agitación *f*

uphill [ˈʌpˈhɪl] *adj* cuesta arriba; (*fig: task*) duro, difícil ♦ *adv*: **to go ~** ir cuesta arriba

uphold [ʌpˈhould] *vt* defender

upholstery [ʌpˈhoulstəri] *n* tapicería

upkeep [ˈʌpˌkiːp] *n* mantenimiento

upon [əˈpɑːn] *prep* sobre

upper [ˈʌpər] *adj* superior, de arriba ♦ *n* (*of shoe: also:* **~s**) empeine *m* ❑ **upper-class** *adj* de clase alta ❑ **upper hand** *n*: **to have the upper hand** tener la sartén por el mango ❑ **uppermost** *adj* el más alto; **what was uppermost in my mind** lo que me preocupaba más

upright [ˈʌpraɪt] *adj* derecho; (*vertical*) vertical; (*fig*) honrado

uprising [ˈʌpraɪzɪŋ] *n* sublevación *f*

uproar [ˈʌprɔːr] *n* escándalo

uproot [ʌpˈruːt] *vt* desarraigar

upset [*n* ˈʌpˌset, *vb, adj* ʌpˈset] *n* (*to plan etc*) revés *m*, contratiempo; (*MED*) trastorno ♦ *vt* (*glass etc*) volcar; (*plan*) alterar; (*person*) molestar, disgustar ♦ *adj* molesto, disgustado; (*stomach*) revuelto

upshot [ˈʌpˌʃɑːt] *n* resultado

upside-down *adv* al revés; **to turn sth ~** (*fig*) poner algo patas arriba

upstairs [ʌpˈsteərz] *adv* arriba ♦ *adj* (*room*) de arriba ♦ *n* el piso superior

upstart [ˈʌpˌstɑːrt] *n* advenedizo(-a)

upstream [ʌpˈstriːm] *adv* río arriba

uptake [ˈʌpteɪk] *n*: **to be quick/slow on the ~** ser muy listo/torpe

uptight [ʌpˈtaɪt] *adj* tenso, nervioso

up-to-date *adj* al día

uptown [ˈʌpˌtaun] (*US*) *adv* hacia las afueras ♦ *adj* exterior, de las afueras

upturn [ˈʌpˌtɜːrn] *n* (*in luck*) mejora; (*COMM: in market*) resurgimiento

upward [ˈʌpwərd] *adj* ascendente ❑ **upward(s)** *adv* hacia arriba; (*more than*): **upward(s) of** más de

urban [ˈɜːrbən] *adj* urbano

urchin [ˈɜːrtʃɪn] *n* pilluelo, golfillo

urge [ɜːrdʒ] *n* (*desire*) deseo ♦ *vt*: **to ~ sb to do sth** animar a algn a hacer algo

urgent [ˈɜːrdʒənt] *adj* urgente; (*voice*) apremiante

urinate [ˈjuːrɪneɪt] *vi* orinar

urine [ˈjuːrɪn] *n* orina

urn [ɜːrn] *n* urna; (*also:* **tea ~**) recipiente metálico grande para hacer té

Uruguay [ˈjuːrəɡwaɪ] *n* Uruguay *m* ❑ **Uruguayan** [juːrəˈɡwaɪən] *adj, n* uruguayo(-a)

U.S., US *n abbr* (= *United States*) EE.UU.

us [ʌs] *pron* nos; (*after prep*) nosotros(-as); *see also* **me**

U.S.A., USA *n abbr* (= *United States of America*) EE.UU.

USAF *n abbr* = **United States Air Force**

usage [ˈjuːsɪdʒ] *n* (*LING*) uso

use [*n* juːs, *vb* juːz] *n* uso, empleo; (*usefulness*) utilidad *f* ♦ *vt* usar, emplear; **she ~d to do it** (*ella*) solía *or* acostumbraba hacerlo; **in ~** en uso; **out of ~** en desuso; **to be of ~** servir; **it's no ~** (*pointless*) es inútil; (*not useful*) no sirve; **to be ~d to** estar acostumbrado a, acostumbrar ▶ **use up** *vt* (*food*) consumir; (*money*) gastar ❑ **used** *adj* (*car*) usado, de segunda mano ❑ **useful** *adj* útil ❑ **usefulness** *n* utilidad *f* ❑ **useless** *adj* (*unusable*) inservible; (*pointless*) inútil; (*person*) inepto ❑ **user** *n* usuario(-a) ❑ **user-friendly** *adj* (*computer*) de fácil manejo

usher [ˈʌʃər] *n* (*in court*) ujier *mf*; (*in theater, cinema etc*) acomodador(a) *m/f* ❑ **usherette** [ʌʃəˈret] *n* (*in movie theater*) acomodadora

U.S.S.R., USSR *n* (*HIST*): **the ~** la URSS

usual ['juːʒuəl] *adj* normal, corriente; **as ~** como de costumbre □ **usually** *adv* normalmente

utensil [juːˈtensɪl] *n* utensilio; **kitchen ~s** utensilios *mpl or* batería de cocina

uterus ['juːtərəs] *n* útero

utility [juːˈtɪlɪti] *n* utilidad *f*; *(public utility)* (empresa de) servicio público □ **utility room** *n* lavadero, cuarto de triques *(MEX)*

utilize ['juːtɪlaɪz] *vt* utilizar

utmost ['ʌtmoust] *adj* mayor ♦ *n*: **to do one's ~** hacer todo lo posible

utter ['ʌtər] *adj* total, completo ♦ *vt* pronunciar, proferir □ **utterly** *adv* completamente, totalmente

U-turn ['juːˈtɜːrn] *n* cambio de sentido

Vv

v. *abbr* = **verse**; **versus**; **verb**; (= *volt*) v; (= *vide*) véase

vacancy ['veɪkənsi] *n* (*room*) habitación *f* libre; (*BRIT: job*) vacante *f*; **"no vacancies"** "completo"

vacant ['veɪkənt] *adj* desocupado, libre; (*expression*) distraído

vacate [veɪˈkeɪt] *vt* (*house, room*) desocupar; (*job*) dejar (vacante)

vacation [veɪˈkeɪʃən] (*US*) *n* vacaciones *fpl*

vaccinate ['væksɪneɪt] *vt* vacunar

vaccine [væk'siːn] *n* vacuna

vacuum ['vækjuːm] *n* vacío □ **vacuum bottle** (*US*) *n* termo □ **vacuum cleaner** *n* aspiradora □ **vacuum flask** (*BRIT*) *n* termo □ **vacuum-packed** *adj* envasado al vacío

vagina [vəˈdʒaɪnə] *n* vagina

vagrant ['veɪɡrənt] *n* vagabundo(-a)

vague [veɪɡ] *adj* vago; (*memory*) borroso; (*ambiguous*) impreciso; (*person: absent-minded*) distraído; (: *evasive*): **to be ~** no decir las cosas claramente □ **vaguely** *adv* vagamente; distraídamente; con evasivas

vain [veɪn] *adj* (*conceited*) presumido; (*useless*) vano, inútil; **in ~** en vano

valentine ['væləntaɪn] *n* (*also*: ~ **card**) tarjeta para el día de los enamorados, tarjeta para el Día del Amor y la Amistad (*MEX*)

valet ['væleɪ] *n* valet *m*, ayuda *m* de cámara

valid ['vælɪd] *adj* válido; (*law*) vigente

valley ['væli] *n* valle *m*

valor (*US*) ['vælər] (*BRIT* **valour**) *n* valor *m*

valuable ['væljəbəl] *adj* (*jewel*) de valor; (*time*) valioso □ **valuables** *npl* objetos *mpl* de valor

valuation [vælju'eɪʃən] *n* tasación *f*, valuación *f*; (*judgement of quality*) valoración *f*

value ['væljuː] *n* valor *m*; (*importance*) importancia ♦ *vt* (*fix price of*) tasar, valorar; (*esteem*) apreciar; **~s** *npl* (*principles*) principios *mpl* □ **value added tax** (*BRIT*) *n* impuesto al valor agregado (*LAm*) or sobre el valor añadido (*SP*) □ **valued** *adj* (*appreciated*) apreciado

valve [vælv] *n* válvula

van [væn] *n* (*AUT*) camioneta, furgoneta

vandal ['vændl] *n* vándalo(-a) □ **vandalism** *n* vandalismo □ **vandalize** *vt* dañar, destruir

vanilla [vəˈnɪlə] *n* vainilla

vanish ['vænɪʃ] *vi* desaparecer

vanity ['vænɪti] *n* vanidad *f*

vantage point ['væntɪdʒ,pɔɪnt] *n* (*for views*) punto panorámico, mirador *m*

vapor (*US*) ['veɪpər] (*BRIT* **vapour**) *n* vapor *m*; (*on breath, window*) vaho

variable ['vεəriəbəl] *adj* variable

variation [vεri'eɪʃən] *n* variación *f*

varicose ['værɪkous] *adj*: **~ veins** varices *fpl*, várices *fpl* (*LAm*)

varied ['vεrid] *adj* variado

variety [vəˈraɪəti] *n* (*diversity*) diversidad *f*; (*type*) variedad *f* □ **variety show** *n* espectáculo de variedades

various ['vεriəs] *adj* (*several: people*) varios(-as); (*reasons*) diversos(-as)

varnish ['vɑːrnɪʃ] *n* barniz *m*; (*BRIT: nail varnish*) esmalte *m* ♦ *vt* barnizar; (*nails*) pintar (con esmalte)

vary ['vεri] *vt* variar; (*change*) cambiar ♦ *vi* variar

vase [veɪs] *n* jarrón *m*

> ⚠ Be careful not to translate **vase** by the Spanish word *vaso*.

Vaseline® ['væsiliːn] *n* vaselina®

vast [væst] *adj* enorme

VAT (*BRIT*) *n abbr* (= *value added tax*) IVA *m*

vat [væt] *n* cuba

Vatican ['vætɪkən] *n*: **the ~** el Vaticano

vaudeville ['vɔːdvɪl] (*US*) *n* vodevil *m*

vault [vɔːlt] *n* (*of roof*) bóveda; (*tomb*) panteón *m*; (*in bank*) cámara acorazada ♦ *vt* (*also*: ~ **over**) saltar (por encima de)

vaunted ['vɔːntɪd] *adj*: **much ~** cacareado, alardeado

VCR *n abbr* = **video cassette recorder**

VD *n abbr* = **venereal disease**

VDT (*US*) *n abbr* (= *visual display terminal*) monitor *m*

VDU (*BRIT*) *n abbr* (= *visual display unit*) monitor *m*

veal [vi:l] *n* (carne *f* de) ternera

veer [vɪər] *vi* (*vehicle*) virar, torcer; (*wind*) girar

vegan ['vi:gən] *n* vegetariano(-a) estricto(-a)

vegeburger, **veggie burger** ['vedʒi,bɜːrgər] *n* hamburguesa vegetariana *or* vegetal

vegetable ['vedʒtəbəl] *n* (*BOT*) vegetal *m*; (*edible plant*) hortaliza ♦ *adj* vegetal; **~s** *npl* (*cooked*) verduras *fpl*

vegetarian [vedʒɪ'terɪən] *adj, n* vegetariano(-a)

vehement ['vi:ɪmənt] *adj* vehemente, apasionado

vehicle ['vi:ɪkəl] *n* vehículo; (*fig*) medio

veil [veɪl] *n* velo ♦ *vt* velar ☐ **veiled** *adj* (*fig*) velado

vein [veɪn] *n* vena; (*of ore etc*) veta

velocity [vɪ'lɑːsɪti] *n* velocidad *f*

velvet ['velvɪt] *n* terciopelo

vending machine ['vendɪŋməʃi:n] *n* máquina expendedora

veneer [və'nɪər] *n* chapa, enchapado; (*fig*) barniz *m*

venereal disease [vɪ'nɪrɪəldɪ,zi:z] *n* enfermedad *f* venérea

Venetian blind [vɪ'ni:ʃən'blaɪnd] *n* persiana veneciana

Venezuela [venɪ'zweɪlə] *n* Venezuela ☐ **Venezuelan** *adj, n* venezolano(-a)

vengeance ['vendʒəns] *n* venganza; **with a ~** (*fig*) con creces

venison ['venɪsən] *n* (carne *f* de) venado

venom ['venəm] *n* veneno; (*bitterness*) odio ☐ **venomous** *adj* (*snake*) venenoso; (*look*) lleno de odio

vent [vent] *n* (*in jacket*) respiradero; (*in wall*) rejilla (de ventilación) ♦ *vt* (*fig: feelings*) desahogar

ventilator ['ventɪleɪtər] *n* ventilador *m*

venture ['ventʃər] *n* empresa ♦ *vt* (*opinion*) ofrecer ♦ *vi* arriesgarse, lanzarse; **business ~** empresa (comercial)

venue ['venju:] *n* lugar *m*

veranda(h) [və'rændə] *n* terraza, porche *m*

verb [vɜːrb] *n* verbo ☐ **verbal** *adj* verbal

verbatim [vɜːr'beɪtɪm] *adj, adv* palabra por palabra

verdict ['vɜːrdɪkt] *n* veredicto, fallo; (*fig*) opinión *f*, juicio

verge [vɜːrdʒ] *n* (*fig*) borde *m*, margen *m*; (*BRIT: of road*) borde *m*; **to be on the ~ of doing sth** estar a punto de hacer algo ▶ **verge on** *vt fus* rayar en

verify ['verɪfaɪ] *vt* comprobar, verificar

vermin ['vɜːrmɪn] *npl* (*animals*) alimañas *fpl*; (*insects, fig*) parásitos *mpl*

vermouth [vɜːr'mu:θ] *n* vermut *m*

versatile ['vɜːrsətaɪl] *adj* (*person*) polifacético; (*machine, tool etc*) versátil

verse [vɜːrs] *n* poesía, verso; (*stanza*) estrofa; (*in bible*) versículo

version ['vɜːrʒən] *n* versión *f*

versus ['vɜːrsəs] *prep* contra

vertebra ['vɜːrtɪbrə] (*pl* **~e**) *n* vértebra

vertical ['vɜːrtɪkəl] *adj* vertical

verve [vɜːrv] *n* brío

very ['veri] *adv* muy ♦ *adj*: **the ~ book which** el mismo libro que; **the ~ last** el último de todos; **at the ~ least** al menos; **~ much** muchísimo

vessel ['vesəl] *n* (*ship*) barco; (*container*) vasija, recipiente *m*; *see* **blood**

vest [vest] *n* (*US*) chaleco; (*BRIT*) camiseta ☐ **vested interests** *npl* (*COMM*) intereses *mpl* creados

vet [vet] *vt* (*candidate*) investigar ♦ *n abbr* (*BRIT*) = **veterinarian**

veteran ['vetərən] *n* excombatiente *mf*, veterano(-a)

veterinarian [vetərə'nerɪən] (*US*) *n* veterinario(-a)

veterinary surgeon ['vetərəneri'sɜːrdʒən] (*BRIT*) *n* = **veterinarian**

veto ['vi:tou] (*pl* **~es**) *n* veto ♦ *vt* vetar, prohibir

vex [veks] *vt* fastidiar ☐ **vexed** *adj* (*question*) controvertido

VHF *abbr* (= *very high frequency*) VHF *f*

VHS *abbr* = **video home system**

via ['vaɪə] *prep* por; (*by plane*) vía

vibrant ['vaɪbrənt] *adj* (*lively*) animado; (*bright*) vivo; (*voice*) vibrante

vibrate [vaɪ'breɪt] *vi* vibrar

vicar ['vɪkər] *n* párroco ☐ **vicarage** (*BRIT*) *n* parroquia

vice [vaɪs] *n* (*evil*) vicio; (*BRIT TECH*) tornillo de banco

vice- [vaɪs] *prefix* vice- ☐ **vice-chairman** *n* vicepresidente *m*

Vice President *n* vicepresidente(-a) *m/f*

vice squad *n* brigada antivicio

vice versa [vaɪsə'vɜːrsə] *adv* viceversa

vicinity [vɪ'sɪnɪti] *n*: **in the ~ (of)** cercano (a)

vicious ['vɪʃəs] adj (attack) violento; (words) cruel; (horse, dog) resabido ❑ **vicious circle** n círculo vicioso

victim ['vɪktɪm] n víctima

victor ['vɪktər] n vencedor(a) m/f

victory ['vɪktərɪ] n victoria

video ['vɪdɪou] cpd video (LAm), vídeo (SP) ♦ n (video movie) película de video (LAm) or vídeo (SP); (also: ~ **cassette**) cinta de video or vídeo; (BRIT: also: ~ **cassette recorder**) (aparato de) video or vídeo ❑ **video game** n videojuego ❑ **video tape** n cinta de video (LAm) or vídeo (SP)

vie [vaɪ] vi: **to ~ (with sb for sth)** competir (con algn por algo)

Vienna [vɪ'ɛnə] n Viena

Vietnam [ˌviːɛt'nɑːm] n Vietnam m ❑ **Vietnamese** [ˌviˌɛtnə'miːz] n inv, adj vietnamita mf

view [vjuː] n vista; (outlook) perspectiva; (opinion) opinión f, criterio ♦ vt (look at) mirar; (fig) considerar; **on ~** (in museum etc) expuesto; **in full ~ (of)** en plena vista (de); **in ~ of the weather/the fact that** en vista del tiempo/del hecho de que; **in my ~** en mi opinión ❑ **viewer** n espectador(a) m/f; (TV) telespectador(a) m/f ❑ **viewfinder** n visor m de imagen ❑ **viewpoint** n (attitude) punto de vista; (place) mirador m

vigor (US) ['vɪgər] (BRIT **vigour**) n energía, vigor m

vile [vaɪl] adj vil, infame; (smell) asqueroso; (temper) endemoniado

villa ['vɪlə] n (country house) casa de campo; (suburban house) chalet m

village ['vɪlɪdʒ] n aldea; (large) pueblo ❑ **villager** n aldeano(-a)

villain ['vɪlən] n (scoundrel) malvado(-a); (in novel) malo(-a); (BRIT: criminal) maleante mf

vindicate ['vɪndɪkeɪt] vt vindicar, justificar

vindictive [vɪn'dɪktɪv] adj vengativo

vine [vaɪn] n vid f

vinegar ['vɪnɪgər] n vinagre m

vineyard ['vɪnjərd] n viña, viñedo

vintage ['vɪntɪdʒ] n (year) vendimia, cosecha ♦ cpd de época ❑ **vintage wine** n vino añejo

vinyl ['vaɪnl] n vinilo

viola [vɪ'oulə] n (MUS) viola

violate ['vaɪəleɪt] vt violar

violence ['vaɪələns] n violencia

violent ['vaɪələnt] adj violento; (intense) intenso

violet ['vaɪələt] adj violeta ♦ n (plant) violeta

violin [vaɪə'lɪn] n violín m ❑ **violinist** n violinista mf

VIP n abbr (= very important person) VIP m

virgin ['vɜːrdʒɪn] n virgen f

Virgo ['vɜːrgou] n Virgo

virtually ['vɜːrtʃuəlɪ] adv prácticamente

virtual reality [ˌvɜːrtʃuəlrɪ'ælɪtɪ] n (COMPUT) realidad f virtual

virtue ['vɜːrtʃuː] n virtud f; (advantage) ventaja; **by ~ of** en virtud de

virtuous ['vɜːrtʃuəs] adj virtuoso

virus ['vaɪrəs] n (also COMPUT) virus m inv

visa ['viːzə] n visa (LAm), visado (SP)

vise [vaɪs] (US) n (TECH) tornillo de banco

visible ['vɪzəbəl] adj visible

vision ['vɪʒən] n (sight) vista; (foresight, in dream) visión f

visit ['vɪzɪt] n visita ♦ vt (US: person: also: ~ **with**) visitar, hacer una visita a; (place) ir a, (ir a) conocer ❑ **visiting hours** npl (in hospital etc) horas fpl de visita ❑ **visitor** n (in museum) visitante mf; (invited to house) visita; (tourist) turista mf

visor ['vaɪzər] n visera

vista ['vɪstə] n (lit) vista, panorama m; (fig) perspectiva, horizonte m

visual ['vɪʒuəl] adj visual ❑ **visual aid** n medio visual ❑ **visual display unit** n monitor m ❑ **visualize** vt imaginarse

vital ['vaɪtl] adj (essential) esencial, imprescindible; (dynamic) dinámico; (organ) vital ❑ **vitally** adv: **vitally important** de vital importancia ❑ **vital statistics** npl datos mpl demográficos; (of woman's body) medidas fpl

vitamin ['vaɪtəmɪn] n vitamina

vivacious [vɪ'veɪʃəs] adj vivaz, alegre

vivid ['vɪvɪd] adj (account) gráfico; (light) intenso; (imagination, memory) vivo ❑ **vividly** adv gráficamente; (remember) vívidamente

V-neck ['viːˌnɛk] n suéter m (LAm) or jersey m (SP) (de cuello) de pico

vocabulary [vou'kæbjuləri] n vocabulario

vocal ['voukəl] adj vocal; (articulate) elocuente ❑ **vocal cords** npl cuerdas fpl vocales

vocation [vou'keɪʃən] n vocación f ❑ **vocational** adj profesional

vodka ['vɑːdkə] n vodka m

vogue [voug] n: **in ~** en boga

voice [vɔɪs] n voz f ♦ vt expresar ❑ **voice mail** n buzón m de voz

void [vɔɪd] n vacío; (hole) hueco ♦ adj (invalid) nulo, inválido; (empty): ~ of carente or desprovisto de

volatile ['vɒlətl] adj (situation) inestable; (person) voluble; (liquid) volátil

volcano [vɒl'keɪnəʊ] (pl ~es) n volcán m

volition [və'lɪʃən] n: of one's own ~ por propia voluntad

volley ['vɒlɪ] n (of gunfire) ráfaga; (of stones etc) lluvia; (fig) torrente m; (TENNIS etc) volea ❑ **volleyball** n voleibol m

volt [vəʊlt] n voltio ❑ **voltage** n voltaje m

volume ['vɒljuːm] n (gen) volumen m; (book) tomo

voluntary ['vɒləntərɪ] adj voluntario

volunteer [vɒlən'tɪər] n voluntario(-a) ♦ vt (information) ofrecer ♦ vi ofrecerse (de voluntario); to ~ to do ofrecerse a hacer

vomit ['vɒmɪt] n vómito ♦ vt, vi vomitar

vote [vəʊt] n voto; (votes cast) votación f; (right to vote) derecho de votar; (franchise) sufragio ♦ vt (propose): to ~ that proponer que ♦ vi votar, ir a votar; ~ of thanks agradecimiento ❑ **voter** n votante mf ❑ **voting** n votación f

vouch [vaʊtʃ]: to ~ for vt fus garantizar, responder de

voucher ['vaʊtʃər] n (for meal, gas) vale m

vow [vaʊ] n voto ♦ vt: to ~ to do/that jurar hacer/que

vowel ['vaʊəl] n vocal f

voyage ['vɔɪdʒ] n viaje m

vulgar ['vʌlɡər] adj (rude) ordinario, grosero; (in bad taste) de mal gusto ❑ **vulgarity** [vʌl'ɡærɪtɪ] n grosería; mal gusto

vulnerable ['vʌlnərəbəl] adj vulnerable

vulture ['vʌltʃər] n buitre m

Ww

wad [wɒd] n bolita; (of banknotes etc) fajo

waddle ['wɒdl] vi andar como un pato, anadear

wade [weɪd] vi: to ~ through (water) vadear; (fig: book) leer con dificultad ❑ **wading pool** (US) n piscina para niños

wafer ['weɪfər] n barquillo

waffle ['wɒfəl] n (CULIN) gofre m ♦ vi (BRIT: inf) enrollarse

waft [wɒft] vt llevar por el aire ♦ vi flotar

wag [wæɡ] vt menear, agitar ♦ vi moverse, menearse

wage [weɪdʒ] n (also: ~s) sueldo, salario ♦ vt: to ~ war hacer la guerra ❑ **wage earner** n asalariado(-a) ❑ **wage packet** (BRIT) n (sobre m de la) paga

wager ['weɪdʒər] n apuesta

wagon ['wæɡən] (BRIT: also: **waggon**) n (horse-drawn) carro; (BRIT RAIL) vagón m

wail [weɪl] n gemido ♦ vi gemir

waist [weɪst] n cintura ❑ **waistcoat** (BRIT) n chaleco ❑ **waistline** n talle m

wait [weɪt] n (interval) pausa ♦ vi esperar; to lie in ~ for acechar a; I can't ~ to (fig) me muero de ganas de; to ~ for esperar (a) ▸ **wait behind** vi quedarse ▸ **wait on** vt fus servir a ❑ **waiter** n mesero (LAm), mozo (SC), camarero (SP) ❑ **waiting** n: "no waiting" (BRIT AUT) "prohibido detenerse" ❑ **waiting list** n lista de espera ❑ **waiting room** n sala de espera ❑ **waitress** n mesera (LAm), moza (SC), camarera (SP)

waive [weɪv] vt suspender

wake [weɪk] (pt woke or (US) ~d, pp woken or (US) ~d) vt (also: ~ up) despertar ♦ vi (also: ~ up) despertarse ♦ n (for dead person) velatorio, velorio (LAm); (NAUT) estela ❑ **waken** vt, vi = **wake**

Wales [weɪlz] n País m de Gales; **the Prince of ~** el príncipe de Gales

walk [wɔːk] n (stroll) paseo; (hike) excursión f a pie, caminata; (gait) paso, andar m; (in park etc) paseo ♦ vi andar, caminar; (for pleasure, exercise) pasear ♦ vt (distance) recorrer a pie, andar; (dog) pasear; **10 minutes' ~ from here** a 10 minutos de aquí andando; **people from all ~s of life** gente de todas las esferas ▸ **walk out** vi (audience) salir; (workers) declararse en huelga ▸ **walk out on** (inf) vt fus abandonar ❑ **walker** n (person) transeúnte mf, caminante mf ❑ **walkie-talkie** n walkie-talkie m ❑ **walking** n (el) andar or caminar ❑ **walking shoes** npl zapatos mpl para caminar ❑ **walking stick** n bastón m ❑ **Walkman®** n Walkman® m ❑ **walkout** n huelga ❑ **walkover** (inf) n: **it was a walkover** fue pan comido ❑ **walk-up** (US) n (building) edificio sin ascensor ❑ **walkway** n paseo

wall [wɔːl] n pared f; (exterior) muro; (city wall etc) muralla ❑ **walled** adj amurallado; (garden) con tapia

wallet ['wɒlɪt] n cartera, billetera

wallflower ['wɔːlflaʊər] n alhelí m; **to be a ~** (fig) no tener con quien bailar

wallow ['wɒləʊ] vi revolcarse

wallpaper ['wɔːlˌpeɪpər] n (for walls) papel m pintado or tapiz; (COMPUT) fondo de escritorio ♦ vt empapelar

Wall Street (US) n Wall Street m

WALL STREET

Wall Street es una calle situada en el extremo sur de la isla de Manhattan en Nueva York, considerada como el centro financiero de EE.UU. La primera Bolsa de Estados Unidos se fundó en el número 68 de Wall Street en 1792 y la nueva Bolsa de Nueva York, la más importante de Estados Unidos, aún está situada en Wall Street. Cuando los norteamericanos hablan del estado de su economía se suelen referir a la "situación de Wall Street", como sinónimo del nivel de negocio del momento en la Bolsa de Nueva York.

walnut ['wɔːlnʌt] n nuez f; (tree) nogal m

walrus ['wɔːlrəs] (pl ~ or ~es) n morsa

waltz [wɔːlts] n vals m ♦ vi bailar el vals

wand [wɑːnd] n (also: **magic** ~) varita (mágica)

wander ['wɑːndər] vi (person) vagar; deambular; (thoughts) divagar ♦ vt recorrer, vagar por

wane [weɪn] vi menguar

wangle ['wæŋgəl] vt agenciarse

want [wɑːnt] vt querer, desear; (need) necesitar ♦ n: **for ~ of** por falta de; **~s** npl (needs) necesidades fpl; **to ~ to do** querer hacer; **to ~ sb to do sth** querer que algn haga algo ❏ **wanted** adj (criminal) buscado; **"wanted"** (in advertisements) "se busca" ❏ **wanting** adj: **to be found wanting** no estar a la altura de las circunstancias, no dar la talla

WAP [wæp] n abbr (COMPUT: = wireless application protocol) WAP f

war [wɔːr] n guerra; **to make ~ (on)** declarar la guerra (a)

ward [wɔːrd] n (in hospital) sala; (POL) distrito electoral; (LAW: child: also: ~ **of court**) pupilo(-a) ♦ **ward off** vt (blow) desviar, parar; (attack) rechazar

warden ['wɔːrdn] n (of park, game reserve) guardián(-ana) m/f; (US: governor) director(a) m/f; (BRIT: also: **traffic** ~) guardia mf

warder ['wɔːrdər] (BRIT) n guardián(-ana) m/f carcelero(-a)

wardrobe ['wɔːrdroʊb] n armario, ropero; (clothes) vestuario

warehouse ['wɛrˌhaʊs] n almacén m, bodega (MEX)

wares [wɛərz] npl mercancías fpl

warfare ['wɔːrfɛr] n guerra

warhead ['wɔːrhɛd] n cabeza armada

warily ['wɛrɪli] adv con cautela, cautelosamente

warm [wɔːrm] adj caliente; (thanks) efusivo; (clothes etc) abrigado; (welcome, day) caluroso; **it's ~** hace calor; **I'm ~** tengo calor ▶ **warm up** vi (room) calentarse; (person) entrar en calor; (athlete) hacer ejercicios de calentamiento ♦ vt calentar ❏ **warm-hearted** adj afectuoso ❏ **warmly** adv afectuosamente ❏ **warmth** n calor m

warn [wɔːrn] vt avisar, advertir ❏ **warning** n aviso, advertencia ❏ **warning light** n luz f de advertencia ❏ **warning triangle** n (AUT) triángulo de peligro or advertencia

warp [wɔːrp] vi (wood) combarse ♦ vt combar; (mind) pervertir

warrant ['wɔːrənt] n autorización f; (LAW: to arrest) orden f de detención; (: to search) mandamiento de registro

warranty ['wɔːrənti] n garantía

warren ['wɔːrən] n (of rabbits) madriguera; (fig) laberinto

warrior ['wɔːriər] n guerrero(-a)

Warsaw ['wɔːrsɔː] n Varsovia

warship ['wɔːrʃɪp] n buque m or barco de guerra

wart [wɔːrt] n verruga

wartime ['wɔːrˌtaɪm] n: **in ~** en tiempos de guerra, en la guerra

wary ['wɛri] adj cauteloso

was [wʌz] pt of **be**

wash [wɑːʃ] vt lavar; (sweep, carry: sea etc) llevar ♦ vi lavarse ♦ n (clothes etc) lavado; (of ship) estela; **to ~ the dishes** lavar or fregar (los platos); **to ~ against/over sth** llegar hasta/ cubrir algo; **to have a ~** (BRIT) lavarse ▶ **wash away** vt (stain) quitar lavando; (river etc) llevarse ▶ **wash off** vi quitarse (al lavar) ▶ **wash up** vi (US) lavarse; (BRIT) lavar or fregar los platos ❏ **washable** adj lavable ❏ **washbowl** (US) (BRIT **washbasin**) n lavabo ❏ **washcloth** (US) n toallita (para lavarse) ❏ **washer** n (TECH) arandela ❏ **washing** n (dirty) ropa sucia or para lavar; (clean) ropa lavada ❏ **washing machine** n lavadora ❏ **washing powder** (BRIT) n detergente m (en polvo)

Washington ['wɑːʃɪŋtən] n Washington m

wash: ❏ **washing-up** n platos mpl (para fregar) ❏ **washing-up liquid** (BRIT) n líquido lavavajillas ❏ **wash-out** n (inf) n fracaso ❏ **washroom** (US) n baño

wasn't ['wʌzənt] cont = **was not**

wasp [wɔːsp] n avispa

wastage ['weɪstɪdʒ] n desgaste m; (loss) pérdida

waste [weɪst] n derroche m, despilfarro; (of time) pérdida; (food) sobras fpl; (garbage) basura, desperdicios mpl ♦ adj (material) de desecho; (left over) sobrante; (land) baldío, descampado ♦ vt malgastar, derrochar; (time) perder; (opportunity) desperdiciar; **~s** npl (area of land) tierras fpl baldías ► **waste away** vi consumirse ❑ **wastebasket** (US) n papelera, (COMPUT) papelera de reciclaje ❑ **waste disposal unit** (BRIT) n triturador m de basura ❑ **wasteful** adj derrochador(a); (process) antieconómico ❑ **waste ground** (BRIT) n terreno baldío ❑ **wastepaper basket** n papelera ❑ **waste pipe** n tubo de desagüe

watch [wɔːtʃ] n (also: **wrist~**) reloj m; (MIL: group of guards) centinela m; (act) vigilancia; (NAUT: spell of duty) guardia ♦ vt (look at) mirar, observar; (: game, program) ver; (spy on, guard) vigilar; (be careful of) cuidarse de, tener cuidado de ♦ vi ver, mirar; (keep guard) montar guardia; "**~ the step**" (US) "cuidado con el escalón" ► **watch out** vi cuidarse, tener cuidado ❑ **watchdog** n perro guardián; (fig) organismo regulador or de control ❑ **watchful** adj vigilante, sobre aviso ❑ **watchmaker** n relojero(-a) ❑ **watchman** n see **night watchman** ❑ **watch strap** n correa (de reloj)

water ['wɔːtər] n agua ♦ vt (plant) regar ♦ vi (eyes) llorar; **her mouth ~ed** se le hizo la boca agua ► **water down** vt (milk etc) aguar; (fig: story) dulcificar, diluir ❑ **water closet** n wáter m (LAm), váter m (SP) ❑ **watercolor** (US) (BRIT **watercolour**) n acuarela ❑ **watercress** n berro ❑ **waterfall** n cascada ❑ **water heater** n calentador m de agua ❑ **watering can** n regadera ❑ **water lily** n nenúfar m ❑ **waterline** n (NAUT) línea de flotación ❑ **waterlogged** adj (ground) inundado ❑ **water main** n cañería del agua ❑ **watermelon** n sandía ❑ **waterproof** adj impermeable ❑ **watershed** n (GEO) cuenca; (fig) momento crítico ❑ **water-skiing** n esquí m acuático ❑ **watertight** adj hermético ❑ **waterway** n vía fluvial or navegable ❑ **waterworks** n central f depuradora ❑ **watery** adj (coffee etc) aguado; (eyes) lloroso

watt [wɔːt] n vatio

wave [weɪv] n (of hand) señal f con la mano; (on water) ola; (RADIO, in hair) onda; (fig) oleada ♦ vi agitar la mano; (flag etc) ondear ♦ vt (handkerchief, gun) agitar ❑ **wavelength** n longitud f de onda

waver ['weɪvər] vi (voice, love etc) flaquear; (person) vacilar

wavy ['weɪvɪ] adj ondulado

wax [wæks] n cera ♦ vt encerar ♦ vi (moon) crecer ❑ **wax paper** (US) n papel m de cera ❑ **waxworks** n museo de cera ♦ npl figuras fpl de cera

way [weɪ] n camino; (distance) trayecto, recorrido; (direction) dirección f, sentido; (manner) modo, manera; (habit) costumbre f; **which ~? -- this ~** ¿por dónde?, ¿en qué dirección? -- por aquí; **on the ~** (en route) en (el) camino; **to be on one's ~** estar en camino; **to be in the ~** bloquear el camino; (fig) estorbar; **to go out of one's ~ to do sth** desvivirse por hacer algo; **under ~** en marcha; **to lose one's ~** extraviarse; **in a ~** en cierto modo or sentido; **no ~!** (inf) ¡de eso nada!; **by the ~ ...** a propósito ...; **the ~ back** el camino de vuelta; "**~ in**" (BRIT) "entrada"; "**~ out**" (BRIT) "salida"; "**give ~**" (BRIT AUT) "ceda el paso"

waylay [weɪ'leɪ] vt detener

wayward ['weɪwəd] adj díscolo

W.C. n (BRIT) wáter m (LAm), váter m (SP)

we [wiː] pl pron nosotros(-as)

weak [wiːk] adj débil, flojo; (tea etc) poco cargado, claro ❑ **weaken** vi debilitarse; (give way) ceder ♦ vt debilitar ❑ **weakling** n debilucho(-a); (morally) pelele m ❑ **weakness** n debilidad f; (fault) punto débil; **to have a weakness for** tener debilidad por

wealth [welθ] n riqueza; (of details) abundancia ❑ **wealthy** adj rico

wean [wiːn] vt destetar

weapon ['wepən] n arma

wear [weər] (pt **wore**, pp **worn**) n (use) uso; (deterioration through use) desgaste m; (clothing): **sports/baby~** ropa de deporte/ bebé ♦ vt (clothes) llevar; (shoes) calzar; (damage: through use) gastar, usar ♦ vi (last) durar; (rub through etc) desgastarse; **evening ~** ropa de etiqueta ► **wear away** vt gastar ♦ vi desgastarse ► **wear down** vt gastar; (strength) agotar ► **wear off** vi (pain etc) pasar, desaparecer ► **wear out** vt desgastar; (person, strength) agotar ❑ **wear and tear** n desgaste m

weary ['wɪrɪ] adj cansado; (dispirited) abatido ♦ vi: **to ~ of** cansarse de

weasel ['wiːzəl] n (ZOOL) comadreja

weather ['weðər] n tiempo ♦ vt (storm, crisis) hacer frente a; **under the ~** (fig: sick) indispuesto, pachucho ❑ **weatherbeaten** adj (skin) curtido; (building) deteriorado (por la intemperie) ❑ **weathercock** n veleta ❑ **weather forecast** n pronóstico del tiempo, parte m meteorológico ❑ **weatherman** n hombre m del tiempo ❑ **weather vane** n = **weathercock** ❑ **weatherwoman** n mujer f del tiempo

weave [wi:v] (pt **wove**, pp **woven**) vt (cloth) tejer; (fig) entretejer ❑ **weaver** n tejedor(a) m/f ❑ **weaving** n tejeduría

web [web] n (of spider) telaraña; (on duck's foot) membrana; (network) red f; **the (World Wide) W~** el or la Web

webcam ['web,kæm] n webcam f

webcast ['web,kæst] n transmisión por Internet

web page n página web

website ['web,saɪt] n sitio Web

wed [wed] (pt, pp **-ded**) vt casar ♦ vi casarse

we'd [wi:d] cont = **we had**; **we would**

wedding ['wedɪŋ] n boda; **silver/golden ~ (anniversary)** bodas fpl de plata/de oro ❑ **wedding day** n día m de la boda ❑ **wedding dress** n traje m de novia ❑ **wedding present** n regalo de boda(s) ❑ **wedding ring** n alianza

wedge [wedʒ] n (of wood etc) cuña; (of cake) trozo ♦ vt acuñar; (push) apretar

Wednesday ['wenzdɪ] n miércoles m inv

wee [wi:] (SCOTLAND) adj pequeñito

weed [wi:d] n maleza (LAm), yuyo (RPl) ♦ vt escardar, desherbar ❑ **weedkiller** n herbicida m ❑ **weedy** adj (BRIT: person) enclenque

week [wi:k] n semana; **a ~ today/on Friday** de hoy/del viernes en ocho días ❑ **weekday** n día m laborable or entre semana ❑ **weekend** n fin m de semana ❑ **weekly** adv semanalmente, cada semana ♦ adj semanal ♦ n semanario

weep [wi:p] (pt, pp **wept**) vi, vt llorar ❑ **weeping willow** n sauce m llorón

weigh [weɪ] vt, vi pesar; **to ~ anchor** levar anclas ▶ **weigh down** vt sobrecargar; (fig) agobiar ▶ **weigh up** (BRIT) vt sopesar

weight [weɪt] n peso; (metal weight) pesa; **to lose/put on ~** adelgazar/engordar ❑ **weightlifter** n levantador(a) m/f de pesas ❑ **weighty** adj pesado; (matters) de relevancia or importancia

weir [wɪər] n presa

weird [wɪərd] adj raro, extraño

welcome ['welkəm] adj bienvenido ♦ n bienvenida ♦ vt dar la bienvenida a; (be glad of) alegrarse de; **thank you -- you're ~** gracias -- de nada

weld [weld] n soldadura ♦ vt soldar

welfare ['welfɛr] n bienestar m; (US: social aid) asistencia social; **to be on ~** recibir asistencia social ❑ **welfare state** n estado del bienestar

well [wel] n pozo ♦ adv bien ♦ adj: **to be ~** estar bien (de salud) ♦ excl ¡vaya!, ¡bueno!; **as ~** también; **as ~ as** además de; **~ done!** ¡bien hecho!; **get ~ soon!** ¡que te mejores pronto!; **to do ~** (business) ir bien; (person) tener éxito ▶ **well up** vi (tears) saltar

we'll [wi:l] cont = **we will**; **we shall**

well: ❑ **well-behaved** adj bueno ❑ **wellbeing** n bienestar m ❑ **well-built** adj (person) fornido ❑ **well-deserved** adj merecido ❑ **well-dressed** adj bien vestido ❑ **well-groomed** adj de buena presencia ❑ **well-heeled** (inf) adj (wealthy) rico

wellingtons ['welɪntənz] (BRIT) npl (also: **wellington boots**) botas fpl de goma

well: ❑ **well-known** adj (person) conocido ❑ **well-mannered** adj educado ❑ **wellmeaning** adj bienintencionado ❑ **well-off** adj adinerado, acomodado ❑ **well-read** adj leído ❑ **well-to-do** adj acomodado ❑ **well-wisher** n admirador(a) m/f

Welsh [welʃ] adj galés(-esa) ♦ n (LING) galés m; **the ~** npl los galeses; **the ~ Assembly** el Parlamento galés ❑ **Welshman** n galés m ❑ **Welsh rarebit, Welsh rabbit** n pan m con queso fundido ❑ **Welshwoman** n galesa

went [went] pt of **go**

wept [wept] pt, pp of **weep**

were [wɜːr] pt of **be**

we're [wɪər] cont = **we are**

weren't [wɜːrənt] cont = **were not**

west [west] n oeste m ♦ adj occidental, del oeste ♦ adv al or hacia el oeste; **the W~** el Oeste, el Occidente ❑ **westerly** adj occidental; (wind) del oeste ❑ **western** adj occidental ♦ n (FILM) western m, película del oeste ❑ **West Germany** n Alemania Occidental ❑ **West Indian** adj, n antillano(-a) ❑ **West Indies** npl Antillas fpl ❑ **westward(s)** adv hacia el oeste

wet [wet] adj (damp) húmedo; (wet through) mojado; (rainy) lluvioso ❑ **well** conservador(a) m/f moderado(-a); **to get ~** mojarse; "**~ paint**" "recién pintado" ❑ **wet suit** n traje m de buzo

we've [wi:v] cont = **we have**

whack [wæk] vt golpear

whale [weɪl] n (ZOOL) ballena

wharf [wɔːrf] (pl **wharves**) n muelle m

what

KEYWORD

[wɑːt] adj

1 (in direct/indirect questions) qué; **what size is he?** ¿qué talla usa?; **what color/shape is it?** ¿de qué color/forma es?

2 (in exclamations): **what a mess!** ¡qué desastre!; **what a fool I am!** ¡qué tonto soy!

♦ pron

1 (interrogative) qué; **what are you doing?** ¿qué haces or estás haciendo?; **what is happening?** ¿qué pasa or está pasando?; **what is it called?** ¿cómo se llama?; **what about me?** ¿y yo qué?; **what about doing ...?** ¿qué tal si hacemos ...?

2 (relative) lo que; **I saw what you did/was on the table** vi lo que hiciste/había en la mesa

♦ excl (disbelieving) ¡cómo!; **what, no coffee!** ¡que no hay café!

whatever [wɑːtˈevər] adj: **~ book you choose** cualquier libro que elijas ♦ pron: **do ~ is necessary** haga lo que sea necesario; **~ happens** pase lo que pase; **no reason ~ or whatsoever** ninguna razón sea la que sea; **nothing ~** nada en absoluto

whatsoever [wɑːtsouˈevər] adj see **whatever**

wheat [wi:t] n trigo

wheedle [ˈwiːdl] vt: **to ~ sb into doing sth** engatusar a algn para que haga algo; **to ~ sth out of sb** sonsacar algo a algn

wheel [wi:l] n rueda; (AUT: also: **steering ~**) volante m; (NAUT) timón m ♦ vt (baby carriage etc) empujar ♦ vi (also: **~ around**) dar la vuelta, girar ❑ **wheelbarrow** n carretilla ❑ **wheelchair** n silla de ruedas ❑ **wheel clamp** n (AUT) cepo

wheeze [wi:z] vi resollar

when

KEYWORD

[wɛn] adv

cuando; **when did it happen?** ¿cuándo ocurrió?; **I know when it happened** sé cuándo ocurrió

♦ conj

1 (at, during, after the time that) cuando; **be careful when you cross the road** ten cuidado al cruzar la calle; **that was when I needed you** fue entonces que te necesité

2 (on, at which): **on the day when I met him** el día en qué le conocí

3 (whereas) cuando

whenever [wɛnˈevər] conj cuando; (every time that) cada vez que ♦ adv cuando sea

where [wɛər] adv dónde ♦ conj donde; **this is ~** aquí es donde ❑ **whereabouts** adv dónde ♦ n: **nobody knows his whereabouts** nadie conoce su paradero ❑ **whereas** conj visto que, mientras ❑ **whereby** pron por lo cual ❑ **wherever** conj dondequiera que; (interrogative) dónde ❑ **wherewithal** n recursos mpl

whether [ˈwɛðər] conj si; **I don't know ~ to accept or not** no sé si aceptar o no; **~ you go or not** vayas o no vayas

which

KEYWORD

[wɪtʃ] adj

1 (interrogative: direct, indirect) qué; **which picture(s) do you want?** ¿qué cuadro(s) quieres?; **which one?** ¿cuál?

2: **in which case** en cuyo caso; **we arrived at 8 pm, by which time the theater was full** llegamos allí a las 8, cuando el teatro estaba lleno

♦ pron

1 (interrogative) cual; **I don't mind which** el/la que sea

2 (relative: replacing noun) que; (: replacing clause) lo que; (: after preposition) (el (la)) que etc, el/la cual etc; **the apple which you ate/which is on the table** la manzana que comiste/que está en la mesa; **the chair on which you are sitting** la silla en la que estás sentado; **he said he knew, which is true/I feared** dijo que lo sabía, lo cual or lo que es cierto/me temía

whichever [wɪtʃˈevər] adj: **take ~ book you prefer** tome (LAm) or coja (SP) el libro que prefiera; **~ book you want** cualquier libro que quiera

while [waɪl] n rato, momento ♦ conj mientras; (although) aunque; **for a ~** durante algún tiempo ► **while away** vt pasar

whim [wɪm] n capricho

whimper [ˈwɪmpər] n sollozo ♦ vi lloriquear

whimsical [ˈwɪmzɪkəl] adj (person) caprichoso; (look) juguetón(-ona)

whine [waɪn] n (of pain) gemido; (of engine) zumbido; (of siren) aullido ♦ vi gemir; zumbar; (fig: complain) gimotear

whip [wɪp] n (for training animals) látigo; (POL: person) encargado de la disciplina partidaria en el parlamento ♦ vt azotar; (CULIN) batir; (move quickly): **to ~ sth out/off** sacar/quitar algo de un tirón ❏ **whipped cream** n crema batida (LAm), nata montada (SP) ❏ **whip-round** (BRIT) n colecta

whirl [wɜːrl] vt hacer girar, dar vueltas a ♦ vi girar, dar vueltas; (leaves etc) arremolinarse ❏ **whirlpool** n remolino ❏ **whirlwind** n torbellino

whirr [wɜːr] vi zumbar

whisk [wɪsk] n (CULIN) batidor m ♦ vt (CULIN) batir; **to ~ sb away** or **off** llevar volando a algn

whiskers ['wɪskərz] npl (of animal) bigotes mpl; (of man) patillas fpl

whiskey ['wɪski] (US, IRELAND) n whisky m

whisky ['wɪski] (BRIT, CANADA) n = **whiskey**

whisper ['wɪspər] n susurro ♦ vi, vt susurrar

whistle ['wɪsəl] n (sound) silbido; (object) silbato ♦ vi silbar

white [waɪt] adj blanco; (pale) pálido ♦ n blanco; (of egg) clara; **the W~ House** (in US) la Casa Blanca ❏ **white coffee** n café m con leche ❏ **white-collar worker** n oficinista mf ❏ **white elephant** n (fig) elefante m blanco ❏ **white lie** n mentirilla ❏ **whiteness** n blancura ❏ **white noise** n ruido blanco ❏ **White Pages** (US) npl (TEL) Páginas fpl Blancas ❏ **white paper** n (POL) libro blanco ❏ **whitewash** n (paint) cal f ♦ vt blanquear

whiting ['waɪtɪŋ] n inv (fish) pescadilla

Whitsun ['wɪtsən] (BRIT) n Pentecostés m

whizz [wɪz] vi: **to ~ past** or **by** pasar a toda velocidad ❏ **whizz kid** (inf) n prodigio

who [huː] pron
KEYWORD

1 (interrogative) quién; **who is it?, who's there?** ¿quién es?; **who are you looking for?** ¿a quién buscas?; **I told her who I was** le dije quién era yo

2 (relative) que; **the man/woman who spoke to me** el hombre/la mujer que habló conmigo; **those who can swim** los que saben or sepan nadar

whodun(n)it [huː'dʌnɪt] (inf) n novela policíaca

whoever [huː'evər] pron: **~ finds it** cualquiera or quienquiera que lo encuentre;

ask ~ you like pregunta a quien quieras; **~ he marries** no importa con quién se case

whole [houl] adj (entire) todo, entero; (not broken) intacto ♦ n todo; (all): **the ~ of the town** toda la ciudad, la ciudad entera ♦ n (total) total m; (sum) conjunto; **on the ~, as a ~** en general ❏ **wholefood(s)** (BRIT) n(pl) alimento(s) m(pl) integral(es) ❏ **wholehearted** adj sincero, cordial ❏ **wholemeal** (BRIT) adj = **whole wheat** ❏ **wholesale** n venta al por mayor ♦ adj al por mayor; (fig: destruction) sistemático ❏ **wholesaler** n mayorista mf ❏ **wholesome** adj sano ❏ **whole wheat** (US) adj integral ❏ **wholly** adv totalmente, enteramente

whom [huːm] pron
KEYWORD

1 (interrogative): **whom did you see?** ¿a quién viste?; **to whom did you give it?** ¿a quién se lo diste?; **tell me from whom you received it** dígame de quién lo recibió

2 (relative) que; **to whom** a quien(es); **of whom** de quien(es), del/de la que etc; **the man whom I saw/to whom I wrote** el hombre que vi/a quien escribí; **the lady about/with whom I was talking** la señora de (la) que/con quien or (la) que hablaba

whooping cough ['huːpɪŋ,kɔːf] n tos f ferina

whore [hɔːr] (inf: pej) n puta

whose [huːz] adj
KEYWORD

1 (possessive: interrogative): **whose book is this?, whose is this book?** ¿de quién es este libro?; **whose pencil have you taken?** ¿de quién es el lápiz que has cogido?; **whose daughter are you?** ¿de quién eres hija?

2 (possessive: relative) cuyo(-a), (pl) cuyos(-as); **the man whose son you rescued** el hombre cuyo hijo rescataste; **those whose passports I have** aquellas personas cuyos pasaportes tengo; **the woman whose luggage was stolen** la mujer a quien le robaron el equipaje ♦ pron de quién; **whose is this?** ¿de quién es esto?; **I know whose it is** sé de quién es

why [waɪ] adv
KEYWORD

por qué; **why not?** ¿por qué no?; **why not do it now?** ¿por qué no lo haces (or hacemos etc) ahora?

♦ *conj*: **I wonder why he said that** me pregunto por qué dijo eso; **that's not why I'm here** no es por eso (por lo) que estoy aquí; **the reason why** la razón por la que
♦ *excl* (*expressing surprise, shock, annoyance*) ¡hombre!, ¡vaya! (*explaining*): **why, it's you!** ¡hombre, eres tú!; **why, that's impossible!** ¡pero sí eso es imposible!

wicked ['wɪkɪd] *adj* malvado, cruel

wicket ['wɪkɪt] *n* (CRICKET: *stumps*) palos *mpl* (: *grass area*) terreno de juego

wide [waɪd] *adj* ancho; (*area, knowledge*) vasto, grande; (*choice*) amplio ♦ *adv*: **to open ~** abrir de par en par; **to shoot ~** errar el tiro ❏ **wide-angle lens** *n* objetivo gran angular ❏ **wide-awake** *adj* bien despierto ❏ **widely** *adv* (*traveled*) mucho; (*spaced*) muy; **it is widely believed/known that ...** mucha gente piensa/sabe que ... ❏ **widen** *vt* ensanchar; (*experience*) ampliar ♦ *vi* ensancharse ❏ **wide open** *adj* abierto de par en par ❏ **widespread** *adj* extendido, general

widow ['wɪdou] *n* viuda ❏ **widowed** *adj* viudo ❏ **widower** *n* viudo

width [wɪdθ] *n* anchura; (*of cloth*) ancho

wield [wiːld] *vt* (*sword*) blandir; (*power*) ejercer

wife [waɪf] (*pl* **wives**) *n* esposa, mujer *f*

wig [wɪg] *n* peluca

wiggle ['wɪgl] *vt* menear

wild [waɪld] *adj* (*animal*) salvaje; (*plant*) silvestre; (*person*) furioso, violento; (*idea*) descabellado; (*rough: sea*) bravo; (: *land*) agreste; (: *weather*) muy revuelto ❏ **wilderness** ['wɪldənɪs] *n* desierto ❏ **wildlife** *n* flora y fauna ❏ **wildly** *adv* (*behave*) locamente; (*lash out*) a diestro y siniestro; (*guess*) a lo loco; (*happy*) a más no poder ❏ **wilds** *npl* regiones *fpl* salvajes, tierras *fpl* vírgenes ❏ **the Wild West** *n* el oeste americano

THE WILD WEST

La expresión **the Wild West** hace referencia al área oeste de EE.UU. durante el período inicial de la colonización de los americanos a mitad del siglo XIX, tras el descubrimiento del oro en California en 1848. En esta época, muchos norteamericanos del este se trasladaron al lejano oeste en busca de fortuna, lo que dio lugar a un importante movimiento migratorio conocido como la fiebre del oro (**the golden rush**).

wilful ['wɪlful] (BRIT) *adj* = **willful**

will
KEYWORD
[wɪl] *aux vb*

1 (*forming future tense*): **I will finish it tomorrow** lo terminaré *or* voy a terminar mañana; **I will have finished it by tomorrow** lo habré terminado para mañana; **will you do it? -- yes I will/no I won't** ¿lo harás? -- sí/no

2 (*in conjectures, predictions*): **he will** *or* **he'll be there by now** ya habrá *or* debe (de) haber llegado; **that will be the mailman** será *or* debe ser el cartero

3 (*in commands, requests, offers*): **will you be quiet!** ¿quieres callarte?; **will you help me?** ¿quieres ayudarme?; **will you have a cup of tea?** ¿te apetece un té?; **I will not put up with it!** ¡no lo soporto!
♦ *vt* (*pt, pp* **willed**): **to will sb to do sth** desear que algn haga algo; **he willed himself to go on** con gran fuerza de voluntad, continuó
♦ *n* voluntad *f*; (*testament*) testamento

willful (US) ['wɪlful] (BRIT **wilful**) *adj* (*action*) deliberado; (*obstinate*) testarudo

willing ['wɪlɪŋ] *adj* (*with goodwill*) de buena voluntad; (*enthusiastic*) entusiasta; **he's ~ to do it** está dispuesto a hacerlo ❏ **willingly** *adv* con mucho gusto ❏ **willingness** *n* buena voluntad

willow ['wɪlou] *n* sauce *m*

willpower ['wɪl‚pauər] *n* fuerza de voluntad

willy-nilly [‚wɪli'nɪli] *adv* a la fuerza, quieras o no

wilt [wɪlt] *vi* marchitarse

wimp [wɪmp] (*inf*) *n* pelele *m*

win [wɪn] (*pt, pp* **won**) *n* victoria, triunfo ♦ *vt* ganar; (*obtain*) conseguir, lograr ♦ *vi* ganar ▶ **win over** *vt* convencer a ▶ **win round** (BRIT) *vt* = **win over**

wince [wɪns] *vi* encogerse

winch [wɪntʃ] *n* torno

wind¹ [wɪnd] *n* viento; (MED) gases *mpl* ♦ *vt* (*take breath away from*) dejar sin aliento a

wind² [waɪnd] (*pt, pp* **wound**) *vt* enrollar; (*wrap*) envolver; (*clock, toy*) dar cuerda a ♦ *vi* (*road, river*) serpentear ▶ **wind up** *vt* (*clock*) dar cuerda a; (*debate, meeting*) concluir, terminar

windfall ['wɪnd‚fɔːl] *n* golpe *m* de suerte

winding ['waɪndɪŋ] *adj* (*road*) tortuoso; (*staircase*) de caracol

wind instrument ['wɪnd‚ɪnstrəmənt] *n* (MUS) instrumento de viento

windmill ['wɪndmɪl] *n* molino de viento

window ['wɪndəu] n ventana; (in car, train) ventanilla; (in store etc) vidriera (LAm), escaparate m (SP) ❑ **window box** n jardinera ❑ **window cleaner** n (person) limpiacristales mf inv ❑ **window ledge** n alféizar m, repisa ❑ **windowpane** n cristal m ❑ **window seat** n asiento junto a la ventana ❑ **window shade** (US) n persiana ❑ **window-shopping** n: **to go window-shopping** ir a ver escaparates ❑ **windowsill** n alféizar m, repisa

windpipe ['wɪnd,paɪp] n tráquea

wind power n energía eólica

windscreen ['wɪndskriːn] (BRIT) n = **windshield**

windshield ['wɪndʃiːld] (US) n parabrisas m inv ❑ **windshield washer** n lavaparabrisas m inv ❑ **windshield wiper** n limpiaparabrisas m inv, limpiador m (MEX)

windswept ['wɪnd,swept] adj azotado por el viento

windy ['wɪndɪ] adj de mucho viento; **it's ~** hace viento

wine [waɪn] n vino ❑ **wine bar** n bar m (especializado en vinos) ❑ **wine cellar** n bodega ❑ **wine glass** n copa de vino ❑ **wine list** n carta de vinos ❑ **wine waiter** n escanciador m

wing [wɪŋ] n ala; (BRIT AUT) aleta; ~**s** npl (THEATER) bastidores mpl ❑ **winger** n (SPORT) extremo

wink [wɪŋk] n guiño, pestañeo ♦ vi guiñar, pestañear

winner ['wɪnər] n ganador(a) m/f

winning ['wɪnɪŋ] adj (team) ganador(a); (goal) decisivo; (smile) encantador(a) ❑ **winnings** npl ganancias fpl

winter ['wɪntər] n invierno ♦ vi invernar ❑ **wintry** adj invernal

wipe [waɪp] n: **to give sth a ~** pasar un trapo sobre algo ♦ vt limpiar; (tape) borrar ▶ **wipe off** vt limpiar con un trapo; (remove) quitar ▶ **wipe out** vt (debt) liquidar; (memory) borrar; (destroy) destruir ▶ **wipe up** vt limpiar

wire ['waɪər] n alambre m; (ELEC) cable m (eléctrico); (US TEL) telegrama m ♦ vt (house) poner la instalación eléctrica en; (also: ~ up) conectar; (US: person: telegram) telegrafiar

wiring ['waɪərɪŋ] n instalación f eléctrica

wiry ['waɪərɪ] adj (person) enjuto y fuerte; (hair) crespo

wisdom ['wɪzdəm] n sabiduría, saber m; (good sense) cordura ❑ **wisdom tooth** n muela del juicio

wise [waɪz] adj sabio; (sensible) juicioso

...wise [waɪz] suffix: **time~** en cuanto a or respecto al tiempo

wish [wɪʃ] n deseo ♦ vt querer; **best ~es** (on birthday etc) felicidades fpl; **with best ~es** (in letter) saludos mpl, recuerdos mpl; **to ~ sb goodbye** despedirse de algn; **he ~ed me well** me deseó mucha suerte; **to ~ to do/sb to do sth** querer hacer/que algn haga algo; **to ~ for** desear ❑ **wishful** adj: **that's just wishful thinking** no son más que ilusiones

wisp [wɪsp] n mechón m; (of smoke) voluta

wistful ['wɪstfəl] adj pensativo

wit [wɪt] n ingenio, gracia; (also: ~**s**) inteligencia; (person) chistoso(-a)

witch [wɪtʃ] n bruja ❑ **witchcraft** n brujería ❑ **witch hunt** n (fig) caza de brujas

with

KEYWORD

[wɪð, wɪθ] prep

1 (accompanying, in the company of) con (con + mi, ti, sí = conmigo, contigo, consigo); **I was with him** estaba con él; **we stayed with friends** nos quedamos en casa de unos amigos; **I'm (not) with you** (don't understand) (no) te entiendo; **to be with it** (inf: person: up-to-date) estar al tanto; (: alert) ser despabilado

2 (descriptive, indicating manner etc) con; de; **a room with a view** una habitación con vistas; **the man with the brown hat/blue eyes** el hombre del sombrero marrón/de ojos azules; **red with anger** rojo de ira; **to shake with fear** temblar de miedo; **to fill sth with water** llenar algo de agua

withdraw [wɪθ'drɔː] vt retirar, sacar ♦ vi retirarse; **to ~ money (from the bank)** retirar fondos (del banco) ❑ **withdrawal** n retirada; (of money) reintegro ❑ **withdrawal symptoms** npl (MED) síndrome m de abstinencia ❑ **withdrawn** adj (person) reservado, introvertido

wither ['wɪðər] vi marchitarse

withhold [wɪθ'həuld] vt (money) retener; (decision) aplazar; (permission) negar; (information) ocultar

within [wɪð'ɪn] prep dentro de ♦ adv dentro; ~ **reach (of)** al alcance (de); ~ **sight (of)** a la vista (de); ~ **the week** antes de acabar la semana; ~ **a mile (of)** a menos de una milla (de)

without [wɪð'aut] prep sin; **to go ~ sth** pasar sin algo

withstand [wɪθ'stænd] vt resistir a

witness ['wɪtnɪs] n testigo mf ♦ vt (event) presenciar; (document) atestiguar la veracidad de to (fig) ser testimonio de □ **witness box** (BRIT) n = **witness stand** □ **witness stand** (US) n tribuna de los testigos

witty ['wɪti] adj ingenioso

wives [waɪvz] npl of **wife**

wk. abbr = **week**

wobble ['wɒbəl] vi temblar; (chair) cojear

woe [wəʊ] n desgracia

woke [wəʊk] pt of **wake**

woken ['wəʊkən] pp of **wake**

wolf [wʊlf] n lobo □ **wolves** [wʊlvz] npl of **wolf**

woman ['wʊmən] (pl women) n mujer f □ **woman doctor** n doctora □ **womanly** adj femenino

womb [wuːm] n matriz f, útero

women ['wɪmɪn] npl of **woman**

women's lib (inf: pej) n liberación f de la mujer

women's rights n derechos de la mujer

women's room (US) n baño (LAm) or servicio (SP) de señoras

won [wʌn] pt, pp of **win**

wonder ['wʌndər] n maravilla, prodigio; (feeling) asombro ♦ vi: **to ~ whether/why** preguntarse si/por qué; **to ~ at** asombrarse de; **to ~ about** pensar sobre or en; **it's no ~ (that)** no es de extrañarse (que +subjun) □ **wonderful** adj maravilloso

won't [wəʊnt] cont = **will not**

wood [wʊd] n (timber) madera; (forest) bosque m □ **wood carving** n (act) tallado en madera; (object) talla en madera □ **wooded** adj arbolado □ **wooden** adj de madera; (fig) inexpresivo □ **woodpecker** n pájaro carpintero □ **woodwind** n (MUS) instrumentos mpl de viento de madera □ **woodwork** n carpintería □ **woodworm** n carcoma

wool [wʊl] n lana; **to pull the ~ over sb's eyes** (fig) engatusar a algn □ **woolen** (US) (BRIT **woollen**) adj de lana □ **woolens** (US) (BRIT **woollens**) npl géneros mpl de lana □ **wooly** (US) (BRIT **woolly**) adj lanudo, de lana; (fig: ideas) confuso

word [wɜːd] n palabra; (news) noticia; (promise) palabra (de honor) ♦ vt redactar; **in other ~s** en otras palabras; **to break/keep one's ~** faltar a la palabra/cumplir la promesa; **to have ~s with sb** reñir con algn □ **wording** n redacción f □ **word processing** n procesamiento or tratamiento

de textos □ **word processor** n procesador m de textos

wore [wɔːr] pt of **wear**

work [wɜːk] n trabajo; (job) empleo, trabajo; (ART, LITERATURE) obra ♦ vi trabajar; (mechanism) funcionar, marchar; (medicine) ser eficaz, surtir efecto ♦ vt (shape) trabajar; (stone etc) tallar; (mine etc) explotar; (machine) manejar, hacer funcionar; **to be out of ~** no tener trabajo; **to ~ loose** (part) desprenderse; (knot) aflojarse ► **work on** vt fus trabajar en, dedicarse a; (principle) basarse en ► **work out** vi (plans etc) salir bien, funcionar ♦ vt (problem) resolver; (plan) elaborar; **it works out at $200** suma 200 dólares ► **work up** vt: **to get worked up** excitarse □ **workable** adj (solution) práctico, factible □ **workaholic** [wɜːrkəˈhɑːlɪk] n adicto(-a) al trabajo □ **workbook** n libro de ejercicios □ **worker** n trabajador(a) m/f, obrero(-a) □ **workforce** n mano f de obra □ **working class** n clase f obrera □ **working-class** adj obrero □ **working order** n: **in working order** en funcionamiento □ **workman** n obrero □ **workmanship** n habilidad f, trabajo □ **works** n (BRIT: factory) fábrica ♦ npl (of clock, machine) mecanismo □ **worksheet** n hoja de trabajo □ **workshop** n taller m □ **workstation** n terminal f de trabajo □ **work-to-rule** (BRIT) n huelga de brazos caídos

world [wɜːld] n mundo ♦ cpd (champion) del mundo; (power, war) mundial; **to think the ~ of sb** (fig) tener a algn en gran estima □ **worldly** adj mundano □ **worldwide** adj mundial, universal □ **Worldwide Web** n: **the World-Wide Web** el WWW

worm [wɜːrm] n (also: earth~) lombriz f

worn [wɔːrn] pp of **wear** ♦ adj usado □ **worn-out** adj (object) gastado; (person) rendido, agotado

worried ['wɜːrid] adj preocupado

worrisome ['wɜːrisəm] (US) adj preocupante, inquietante

worry ['wɜːri] n preocupación f ♦ vt preocupar, inquietar ♦ vi preocuparse □ **worrying** (BRIT) adj = **worrisome**

worse [wɜːrs] adj, adv peor ♦ n lo peor; **a change for the ~** un empeoramiento □ **worse off** adj (financially): **to be worse off** tener menos dinero; (fig): **you'll be worse off this way** de esta forma estarás peor que nunca □ **worsen** vt, vi empeorar

worship ['wɜːrʃip] n adoración f ♦ vt adorar; (BRIT: in titles): **Your W~** (to mayor) señor alcalde; (to judge) Su Señoría

worst [wɜːrst] adj, adv peor ♦ n lo peor; **at ~** en el peor de los casos

worth [wɜːrθ] n valor m ♦ adj: **to be ~** valer; **it's ~ it** vale or merece la pena; **to be ~ one's while (to do)** valer or merecer la pena (hacer) ❏ **worthless** adj sin valor; (useless) inútil ❏ **worthwhile** adj (activity) que vale or merece la pena; (cause) loable

worthy ['wɜːrðɪ] adj respetable; (motive) honesto; **~ of** digno de

---

would

KEYWORD

[wʊd] aux vb

1 (conditional tense): **if you asked him he would do it** si se lo pidieras, lo haría; **if you had asked him he would have done it** si se lo hubieras pedido, lo habría or hubiera hecho

2 (in offers, invitations, requests): **would you like a cookie?** ¿quieres una galleta?; (formal) ¿querría una galleta?; **would you ask him to come in?** ¿quiere hacerle pasar?; **would you open the window please?** ¿quiere or podría abrir la ventana, por favor?

3 (in indirect speech): **I said I would do it** dije que lo haría

4 (emphatic): **it would have to snow today!** ¡tenía que nevar precisamente hoy!

5 (insistence): **she wouldn't behave** no quiso comportarse bien

6 (conjecture): **it would have been midnight** sería medianoche; **it would seem so** parece ser que sí

7 (indicating habit): **he would go there on Mondays** iba allí los lunes

---

would-be (pej) adj presunto

wouldn't ['wʊdnt] cont = **would not**

wound[1] [wuːnd] n herida ♦ vt herir

wound[2] [waʊnd] pt, pp of **wind**[2]

wove [wəʊv] pt of **weave**

woven ['wəʊvən] pp of **weave**

wow [waʊ] (inf) excl ¡vaya!, ¡hala!

wrap [ræp] vt (also: **~ up**) envolver ❏ **wrapper** n (on chocolate) papel m; (BRIT: of book) sobrecubierta ❏ **wrapping paper** n papel m de envolver; (gift-wrap) papel m de regalo

wreak [riːk] vt: **to ~ havoc (on)** hacer estragos (en); **to ~ vengeance (on)** vengarse (de)

wreath [riːθ, pl riːðz] n (funeral wreath) corona

wreck [rɛk] n (ship: destruction) naufragio; (: remains) restos mpl del barco; (US: accident) accidente m; (pej: person) ruina ♦ vt (car etc) destrozar; (chances) arruinar ❏ **wreckage** n restos mpl; (of building) escombros mpl

wren [rɛn] n (ZOOL) chochín m, carrizo

wrench [rɛntʃ] n (tug) tirón m; (US: non-adjustable) llave f fija (de tuercas); (BRIT: adjustable) llave f inglesa; (fig) dolor m ♦ vt arrancar; **to ~ sth from sb** arrebatar algo violentamente a algn

wrestle ['rɛsəl] vi: **to ~ (with sb)** luchar (con or contra algn) ❏ **wrestler** n luchador(a) m/f (de lucha libre) ❏ **wrestling** n lucha libre

wretched ['rɛtʃɪd] adj miserable

wriggle ['rɪgəl] vi (also: **~ around**) menearse, retorcerse

wring [rɪŋ] (pt, pp wrung) vt retorcer; (wet clothes) escurrir; (fig): **to ~ sth out of sb** sacar algo por la fuerza a algn

wrinkle ['rɪŋkəl] n arruga ♦ vt arrugar ♦ vi arrugarse

wrist [rɪst] n muñeca ❏ **wristwatch** n reloj m de pulsera

writ [rɪt] n mandato judicial

writable ['raɪtəbl] adj escribible

write [raɪt] (pt wrote, pp written) vt escribir; (check) extender ♦ vi escribir ► **write down** vt escribir; (note) apuntar ► **write off** vt (debt) cancelar (por incobrable); (fig) desechar por inútil ► **write out** vt escribir ► **write up** vt redactar ❏ **write-off** (BRIT) n siniestro total ❏ **writer** n escritor(a) m/f

writhe [raɪð] vi retorcerse

writing ['raɪtɪŋ] n escritura; (handwriting) letra; (of author) obras fpl; **in ~** por escrito ❏ **writing paper** n papel m de escribir

written ['rɪtn] pp of **write**

wrong [rɔːŋ] adj (wicked) malo; (unfair) injusto; (incorrect) equivocado, incorrecto; (not suitable) inoportuno, inconveniente; (reverse) del revés ♦ adv equivocadamente ♦ n injusticia ♦ vt ser injusto con; **you are ~ to do it** haces mal en hacerlo; **you are ~ about that, you've got it ~** en eso estás equivocado; **to be in the ~** no tener razón, tener la culpa; **what's ~?** ¿qué pasa?; **to go ~** (person) equivocarse; (plan) salir mal; (machine) estropearse ❏ **wrongful** adj injusto ❏ **wrongly** adv mal, incorrectamente; (by mistake) por error ❏ **wrong number** n (TEL): **you've got the wrong number** se ha equivocado de número

wrote [rəʊt] pt of **write**

wrought iron ['rɔːt,aɪərn] n hierro forjado

wrung [rʌŋ] pt, pp of **wring**
wt. abbr = **weight**
WWW n abbr (= World Wide Web) WWW m

Xx

Xmas ['eksməs] n abbr = **Christmas**
X-ray ['eks,rei] n radiografía ♦ vt radiografiar, sacar radiografías de
xylophone ['zailəfoun] n xilófono

Yy

yacht [jɑːt] n yate m ☐ **yachting** n (sport) (navegación f a) vela ☐ **yachtsman/ woman** n navegante mf
yam [jæm] n ñame m; (US: sweet potato) batata, camote m (MEX, SC)
Yank [jæŋk] (pej) n yanqui mf
Yankee ['jæŋki] (pej) n = **Yank**
yap [jæp] vi (dog) aullar
yard [jɑːrd] n (courtyard, farmyard) patio; (US: garden) jardín m; (measure) yarda (91,44 cm) ☐ **yard sale** (US) n venta de objetos usados (en el jardín de una casa particular); see also **garage sale** ☐ **yardstick** n (fig) criterio, norma
yarn [jɑːrn] n hilo; (tale) cuento, historia
yawn [jɔːn] n bostezo ♦ vi bostezar ☐ **yawning** adj (gap) muy abierto
yd(s). abbr = **yard(s)**
yeah [jeə] (inf) adv sí
year [jiər] n año; **to be 8 ~s old** tener 8 años; **an eight-~-old child** un niño de ocho años (de edad) ☐ **yearly** adj anual ♦ adv anualmente, cada año
yearn [jɜːrn] vi: **to ~ for sth** añorar algo, suspirar por algo
yeast [jiːst] n levadura
yell [jel] n grito, alarido ♦ vi gritar
yellow ['jelou] adj amarillo
yelp [jelp] n aullido ♦ vi aullar
yes [jes] adv sí ♦ n sí m; **to say/answer ~** decir/ contestar que sí
yesterday ['jestərdei] adv ayer ♦ n ayer m; **~ morning/evening** ayer por la mañana/tarde; **all day ~** todo el día de ayer
yet [jet] adv ya; (negative) todavía ♦ conj sin embargo, a pesar de todo; **it is not finished** **~** todavía no está acabado; **the best ~** el/la mejor hasta ahora; **as ~** hasta ahora, todavía
yew [juː] n tejo
yield [jiːld] n (AGR) cosecha; (COMM) rendimiento ♦ vt ceder; (results) producir, dar; (profit) rendir ♦ vi rendirse, ceder; (US AUT) ceder el paso
YMCA n abbr (= Young Men's Christian Association) Asociación f de Jóvenes Cristianos
yog(h)urt ['jougərt] n yogur m
yoke [jouk] n yugo
yokel ['joukəl] n palurdo(-a)
yolk [jouk] n yema (de huevo)

you

KEYWORD

[juː] pron

1 (subject: familiar) tú, (pl) ustedes (LAm), vosotros(-as) (SP); (polite) usted, (pl) ustedes; **you are very kind** eres/es etc muy amable; **you Mexicans enjoy your food** a ustedes (or vosotros) los mexicanos les (or os) gusta la; **you and I will go** iremos tú y yo

2 (object: direct: familiar) te, (pl) les (LAm), os (SP); (polite) le, (pl) les, (f) la, (pl) las; **I know you** te/lo etc conozco

3 (object: indirect: familiar) te, (pl) les (LAm), os (SP); (polite) le, (pl) les; **I gave the letter to you yesterday** te/os etc di la carta ayer

4 (stressed): **I told you to do it** te dije a ti que lo hicieras, es a ti a quien dije que lo hicieras see also **3, 5**

5 (after prep: NB: con + ti = contigo: familiar) ti, (pl) ustedes (LAm), vosotros(-as) (SP); (: polite) usted, (pl) ustedes; **it's for you** es para ti/ vosotros etc

6 (comparisons: familiar) tú, (pl) ustedes (LAm), vosotros(-as) (SP); (: polite) usted, (pl) ustedes; **she's younger than you** es más joven que tú/vosotros etc

7 (impersonal: one): **fresh air does you good** el aire puro (te) hace bien; **you never know** nunca se sabe; **you can't do that!** ¡eso no se hace!

you'd [juːd] cont = **you had**; **you would**
you'll [juːl] cont = **you will**; **you shall**
young [jʌŋ] adj joven ♦ npl (of animal) cría; (people): **the ~** los jóvenes, la juventud ☐ **younger** adj (brother etc) menor ☐ **youngster** n joven mf

your [jɔːr] *adj* tu; *(pl)* vuestro; *(formal)* su; *see also* **my**

you're [juər] *cont* = **you are**

yours [jɔːrz] *pron* tuyo *(pl)*, vuestro; *(formal)* suyo; *see also* **faithfully**; **mine¹**; **sincerely**

yourself [jɔːrˈself] *pron* tú mismo; *(complement)* te; *(after prep)* ti (mismo); *(formal)* usted mismo; (: *complement)* se; (: *after prep)* sí (mismo) ❑ **yourselves** *pl pron* vosotros mismos; *(after prep)* vosotros (mismos); *(formal)* ustedes (mismos); (: *complement)* se; (: *after prep)* sí mismos; *see also* **oneself**

youth [juːθ, *pl* juːðz] *n* juventud *f*; *(young man)* joven *m* ❑ **youth club** *n* club *m* juvenil ❑ **youthful** *adj* juvenil ❑ **youth hostel** *n* albergue *m* juvenil

you've [juːv] *cont* = **you have**

Yugoslav [juːɡouˈslɑːv] *adj, n* (HIST) yugoslavo(-a)

Yugoslavia [juːɡouˈslɑːviə] *n* (HIST) Yugoslavia

yuppie [ˈjʌpi] *(inf) adj, n* yupi *mf*

YWCA *n abbr* (= *Young Women's Christian Association*) Asociación *f* de Jóvenes Cristianas

zany [ˈzeini] *adj* estrafalario

zap [zæp] *vt* (COMPUT) borrar

zeal [ziːl] *n* celo, entusiasmo ❑ **zealous** [ˈzeləs] *adj* celoso, entusiasta

zebra [ˈziːbrə] *n* cebra ❑ **zebra crossing** (BRIT) *n* paso de peatones

zero [ˈzɪrou] *n* cero

zest [zest] *n* ánimo, vivacidad *f*; *(of orange)* piel *f*

zigzag [ˈzɪɡzæɡ] *n* zigzag *m* ♦ *vi* zigzaguear, hacer eses

zinc [zɪŋk] *n* cinc *m*, zinc *m*

zip [zɪp] *n* (BRIT: *also:* ~ **fastener**) zíper *m* (MEX, CAm), cierre *m* (LAm), cremallera (SP) ♦ *vt* (*also:* ~ **up**) cerrar el cierre *or* la cremallera de ❑ **zip code** (US) *n* código postal

zipper [ˈzɪpər] (US) *n* zíper *m* (MEX, CAm), cierre *m* (LAm), cremallera (SP)

zodiac [ˈzoudiæk] *n* zodíaco

zone [zoun] *n* zona

zoo [zuː] *n* (jardín *m*) zoo *m*

zoology [zouˈɑːlədʒi] *n* zoología

zoom [zuːm] *vi*: to ~ **past** pasar zumbando ❑ **zoom lens** *n* zoom *m*

zucchini [zuˈkiːni] (US) *n(pl)* calabacín(ines) *m(pl)*, calabacita(s) *f(pl)* (MEX)